ENCYCLOPEDIA
OF THE
SECOND
WORLD
WAR

ENCYCLOPEDIA
OF THE
SECOND
WORLD
WAR

BRYAN PERRETT & IAN HOGG

★

Presidio

ACKNOWLEDGEMENTS

The majority of the photographs in this book have been supplied by the Robert Hunt Library, whose staff we thank for their help and co-operation. We also thank the following for permission to reproduce copyright photographs:
Barnaby's Picture Library 2
The Imperial War Museum 112
Novosti Press Agency 10
RAC Tank Museum, Bovingdon 7

Published in the United States by Presidio Press, 31 Pamaron Way, Novato, CA 94949

Published in the United Kingdom by Longman Group UK Limited

Library of Congress Cataloging-in-Publication Division
    Hogg, Ian V., 1926–
        Encyclopedia of the Second World War.
        1. World War, 1939–1945—Dictionaries.
    I. Perrett, Bryan. II. Title.
    D740.H64 1989   940.53'03   89–8533

    ISBN 0–89141–362–6

This book was designed and produced by JOHN CALMANN AND KING LTD, LONDON

Design: Karen Stafford
Picture Research: Sara Waterson
Maps: Richard Natkiel
Drawings: Leslie Trebrinski
Typeset by Wyvern Typesetting Ltd, Bristol
Origination by Estil Crom SA, Barcelona
Printed in Spain by Cayfosa.

Title page:
Alerted US troops watch dogfights between Allied and enemy planes, Germany 1944.

Page 6:
Aftermath of bombing, Saarbrucken 1945.

PREFACE

After spending a lifetime studying the subject, the eminent historian Sir Basil Liddell Hart commented that the more he studied military history, the more conscious he became of how little he really knew. Likewise, the Duke of Wellington once remarked that one might as well strive to write the history of a ball as of a battle. While something of an over-simplification, the latter contains a germ of truth. Every military historian knows that if he interviews two survivors from the same platoon, let alone company or battalion, the probability is that he will receive two widely differing versions of the same event, heavily influenced by personal perspective and memory. From the outset, therefore, we were aware that our endeavours would fall short of the formal definition of encyclopedia, given that World War II was global in its nature and was fought on land, at sea and in the air at the political, grand strategic, strategic, operative, tactical, scientific and economic levels with a greater intensity than any conflict in history, coupled with the fact that the archives still contain numerous secrets, many of which will remain under lock and key until they are no longer relevant. To some questions, no answers exist other than eternal silence.

Despite this, we have retained the word *encyclopedia* in our title because we believe that we have included the essential information on World War II for the majority of readers, including entries on the important personalities, campaigns, battles, events, warships, aircraft, land warfare weapons, electronic warfare, intelligence, abbreviations and operational codenames. In preparing these we were aware that many books on World War II topics are written by military historians for the benefit of other military historians and those with a service background, and that these sometimes make demands on the general reader which detract from the value of the work. Our purpose, therefore, has been two-fold. First, we have sought to produce a volume which will meet the general reader's needs by providing relevant entries which give insight into the vast body of published work covering every aspect of World War II. Secondly, extensive cross-referencing, either by direct reference or the use of small capitals within the text, provides the means to go beyond the bounds of a specific entry. We have also cited additional works of reference where appropriate, and provided an extensive bibliography.

Ian Hogg

Bryan Perrett

An A-4 rocket ready for firing, standing on the wagon of a special train, January 1945.

A-4 Rocket

The A-4 (Aggregat 4) rocket was the German ballistic missile, known also as the V-2 (Vergeltungswaffen 2 – Vengeance Weapon 2), used to bombard England and various Continental targets in 1944–45. Design began at PEENEMUNDE in 1936 as a rocket to supplant heavy artillery. It was a long-range fin-stabilized rocket weighing about 13.6 tons at launch and carrying a warhead loaded with one ton of Amatol high explosive. The motor was a bi-fuel type using liquid oxygen and alcohol and could burn for 70 seconds. Control of the flight was achieved by turning the rocket on to a pre-set trajectory immediately after launch, using programmed controls, and then shutting off the rocket motor at a point

calculated to allow the missile to continue on a ballistic trajectory to reach its selected target. The warhead was fuzed with a simple electrical contact system which closed on impact and which had a slight delay sufficient to allow the warhead to bury itself about one metre in the ground before detonating.

The accuracy of the A-4 was such that rockets fired at London, at a mean range of 183 miles (295km), could be expected to fall anywhere within a rectangle 16 miles (26km) long by 13 miles (21km) wide. Production began in early 1944 and by 8 September, when the attack on England began, some 1800 had been stockpiled. In all about 10,000 were produced of which 1115 were launched against England, 1341 against ANTWERP, 65 against Brussels, 98 against Liège, 15 against Paris, 5 into Luxembourg and 11 against the REMAGEN BRIDGE.

A9 – Cruiser Tank Mark I (UK)
The A9 was designed during the mid-1930s as a replacement for the old Vickers Medium and

A9 cruiser tank.

was the first British tank to be equipped with a powered turret traverse. Approximately 100 were built, serving with the 1st Armoured Division in France in 1940 and with the 2nd and 7th Armoured Divisions in the Western Desert until the end of 1941. *Weight* 12 tons; *speed* 25mph (40kph); *armour* 14mm; *armament* 1 2-pdr or 1 3.7in howitzer in close support models; 3 Vickers .303in machine guns; *engine* AEC petrol 150hp; *crew* 6.

A10 – Cruiser Tank Marks II and IIA (UK)
The A10 was developed in parallel with the A9 as an infantry support vehicle but it was insufficiently armoured for this role and, despite its low speed, was re-classified as a cruiser tank. 175 were built, serving with the 1st Armoured Division in France in 1940 and with the 2nd and 7th Armoured Divisions in the Western Desert until late 1941. *Weight* 13.75 tons; *speed* 16mph (25.75kph); *armour* 30mm; *armament Cruiser Mark II* – 1 2-pdr gun; 1 Vickers machine gun; *Cruiser Mark IIA*

A10 cruiser tank.

– 1 2-pdr gun or 1 3.7in howitzer in close support models; 2 Besa machine guns; *engine* AEC petrol 150hp; *crew Cruiser Mark II* 4; *Cruiser Mark IIA* 5.

A13 – Cruiser Tank Marks III, IV and IVA (UK)

The A13 was the first of a long line of British Cruiser tanks to employ the Christie "big-wheel" suspension. In September 1936 Lieutenant-Colonel G. le Q. MARTEL, then Assistant Director of Mechanization, attended the Red Army manoeuvres and was impressed by the performance of the Russian BT SERIES of fast tanks. On his return home he arranged for a Christie tank to be purchased privately by the Morris organization, who then carried out the design work. The result was the Cruiser Tank Mark III, which mounted a similar turret to the A10. The Cruiser Tank Mark IV followed the same layout but protection was increased and a new turret designed incorporating spaced armour; the Cruiser Tank Mark IVA benefited from an improved transmission and mantlet. 65 Mark III and 655 Mark IV Series cruiser tanks were built, serving in France during 1940, in the Western Desert until the end of 1941, and in training. *Weight* 14–14.75 tons; *speed* 30mph (48kph); *armour Cruiser Tank Mark III* 14mm; *Cruiser Tank Marks IV and IVA* 30mm; *armament* 1 2-pdr gun; 1 Vickers machine gun, replaced by a Besa machine gun on the Cruiser Tank Mark IVA; *engine* Nuffield Liberty petrol 340hp; *crew* 4.

"A" Class Destroyers (UK)

Displacement 1350 tons; *dimensions* 323ft×32ft 3in (98.4×9.8m); mean draught 8ft 6in (2.6m); *machinery* 2-shaft geared turbines producing shp 34,000; *speed* 35 knots; *armament* 4×4.7in (4×1); 2×2-pdr AA (2×1); 8×21in torpedo tubes (2×4), various 20mm and 40mm added during war; *complement* 138; *number in class* 11, launched 1929–30.

AA Anti-aircraft (UK).

AAA Anti-Aircraft Artillery (USA).

Aa River, France, 1940

A canalized river south of Gravelines reached by 1st Panzer Division during the evening of 23 May. Bridgeheads across the river were seized but the following morning further drives by the Panzer corps on the DUNKIRK pocket were halted on this line by HITLER's personal order.

Aachen, Germany, 1944

Encirclement commenced by US 1st Army in September 1944 and fell after a week's fierce fighting, 13–20 October, in which both sides sustained heavy casualties. Aachen was the first German city to be captured by the Allies and its fall coincidentally effected the first breach in the SIEGFRIED LINE.

AA&QMG Assistant Adjutant and Quartermaster General (UK). The Senior administrative staff officer in a British Army division.

AASF Advanced Air Striking Force. An element of the RAF in France, 1939–40, consisting of ten squadrons of FAIREY BATTLE aircraft under French command.

Abadite

Smoke generators installed to protect the Abadan oil refineries, operating on fuel oil pumped from the refineries themselves.

ABCA Army Bureau of Current Affairs (UK). An organization for the education of troops in current affairs designed to keep them informed of world events.

ABDA American-British-Dutch-Australian Command. Organization set up early in 1942 to co-ordinate the defence of the Dutch East Indies. Disbanded after the collapse of Java.

Abdiel Class Cruiser Minelayers (UK)

Displacement 2650 tons; *dimensions* 418ft×40ft (127.4×12.2m); mean draught 11ft 3in (3.43m); *machinery* 2-shaft geared turbines producing shp 72,000; *speed* 40 knots; *armament* 6×4in (3×2); 4×2-pdr AA (1×4); 8×0.5in AA (2×4) or 4×4in AA (2×2); 4×40mm AA (2×2); 12×20mm AA (6×2); 156 mines; *complement* 246; *number in class* 6, launched 1940–43.

Aberdeen

British 8th Army attack on THE CAULDRON during the Battle of GAZALA-KNIGHTSBRIDGE, 1942.

"Aberdeen", Burma, 1944

The codename for Chindit base north-west of INDAW.

Abrasive Grease

A sabotage material manufactured in Britain and supplied to resistance groups in France and other occupied countries by the SOE (SPECIAL OPERATIONS EXECUTIVE). Resembling common machine grease, it in fact contained various elements which made it destructive to any moving surfaces to which it was applied. A much favoured application was in the bearing journals of railway wagons, which caused damage and overheating during journeys.

Abwehr

The information-gathering and counter-espionage service of the German High Command. Formed in 1933, it was commanded by Admiral CANARIS from 1935 and was an efficient service, though it later suffered considerably from interference by the SD. Eventually, under HIMMLER, the RHSA (see GESTAPO) took over the Abwehr's functions and Canaris was dismissed in February 1944.

ACC Allied Control Commission. An authority set up by the British, US, French and Soviet governments to govern Germany in the immediate postwar period until control could be handed back to the German authorities. Replaced AMGOT.

ACC Army Catering Corps (UK). A corps set up during the war to provide cooks and catering specialists and to set a consistent standard of cookery throughout the British Army.

Acciaio Class Submarines (Italy)

Displacement 643 tons (714/871 tons normal); *dimensions* 197ft 6in×21ft (60.19×6.4m); *machinery* 2-shaft diesel/electric motors hp 1400/800; *speed* 14/7.5 knots; *armament* 1×3.9in; 1–2×20mm AA; 2–4×13.2mm AA; 6×21in torpedo tubes and 8 torpedoes; *complement* 50; *number in class* 13, launched 1941–42.

Accolade

British attack on DODECANESE Islands, 1943.

Achilles, HMNZS – Leander Class Cruiser

Achilles took part in the Battle of the RIVER PLATE. She was based in New Zealand 1940–43 and then joined the Home Fleet for a year. She joined the British Pacific Fleet in 1945.

Achilles – Tank Destroyer (UK)

Name given to the American GUN MOTOR CARRIAGE M10 when re-armed with the British 17-pdr gun. This very successful conversion began entering service with British troops early in 1945.

Achse (Axis)

German disarmament of Italian army and fleet following the Allied invasion of Italy, September 1943. Also known as Alarich and Konstantin.

Acoustic Torpedoes and Acoustic Mines

Acoustic torpedoes were fitted with a sonic sensor which picked up the propellor noise of the target vessel and directed the torpedo towards it. The device was introduced by the German Navy in 1943 but produced less satisfactory results than the standard torpedo, only 10 per cent of the 700 launched sinking their targets. The majority tended to explode short of the target and there was a tendency for rogue torpedoes to home in on their launch vessel; the submarine *U-377* is believed to have been lost in this way. Acoustic mines operated on a similar principle and were intended to explode when the enemy vessel was overhead, but these too suffered from malfunctions and premature detonation. The Allied counter-measure consisted of a noise-producing towed sledge known as the Foxer. This produced a greater level of sound than the ship's machinery and served to decoy and confuse acoustic devices.

Acrobat

Planned British advance in Libya, 1941.

Adachi, Lt Gen Hatazo (1890–1947)

Adachi commanded Japanese troops in New Guinea. Appointed commander of 18th Army in November 1942, he assumed command and fought desperately to stem the Allied attacks which drove him back down the KOKODA TRAIL and from Buna, Salamaua and Madang to his base in Rabaul. Forced to abandon NEW GUINEA, he decided to make a stand in HOLLANDIA, where his army was trapped around Wewak by Australian and US troops under General Hall. He held out until the end of the war, not surrendering until 13 September 1945. He was subsequently tried for war crimes and sentenced to life imprisonment, but died shortly thereafter.

Adder

British add-on flamethrower for use with SHERMAN tank; official description Flamethrower, Transportable No. 6.

Addis Ababa, Ethiopia, 1941

Liberated on 6 April 1941 by British forces under Lieutenant-General Sir Alan CUNNINGHAM following their successful advance from Kenya through Italian Somaliland and eastern Ethiopia, during which Jijiga was taken on 17 March and Harar on 29 March. Emperor HAILE SELASSIE returned to his capital in May.

ADGB Air Defence of Great Britain. The command organization which included AA guns and fighter aircraft, devoted to the protection of the United Kingdom against air attack.

Adlergerät

A German infra-red telescope used to detect aircraft at night by the heat emitted from their exhausts and also to direct searchlights on to aircraft before exposing the light. Manufactured by Zeiss and Leitz, it was used in some numbers in the early part of the war before RADAR became common.

Adlertag (Eagle Day)

Full-scale Luftwaffe attack on British air defences during the Battle of BRITAIN, 13 August 1940.

Admin Box, Battle of the, Burma, 1944

The successful defence of 7th Indian Division's administrative area at Sinzewa, east of the NGAKYEDAUK PASS, against repeated attacks by the Japanese 55th Division, which incurred crippling casualties. The siege, which lasted from 5 to 23 February, was broken by 5th Indian Division advancing through the Ngakyedauk Pass. The battle provided British and Indian troops with their first clear-cut victory over the Japanese and was notable for the use of tanks both during the defence and the relief operation. It was also notable for the adoption of an uncompromising attitude towards the Japanese who, at one stage in the fighting, overran the Main Dressing Station, butchering the wounded and the medical staff.

Admiral Graf Spee, KMS – Deutschland Class Pocket Battleship

Commanded by Captain Hans LANGSDORFF, the *Admiral Graf Spee* sailed from Germany several days before the outbreak of war. She cruised in the South Atlantic and briefly in the Indian Ocean, sinking nine British merchant

KMS Admiral Graf Spee, *scuttled off Montevideo, December 1939.*

KMS Admiral Hipper *in dry dock.*

ships totalling 50,000 tons. On 13 December 1939 she sustained damage during the Battle of the RIVER PLATE and entered Montevideo for repairs. Fearing that his ship would be sunk by British reinforcements converging on the area, Langsdorff scuttled her on 17 December. See also the ALTMARK INCIDENT.

Admiral Hipper, KMS – Heavy Cruiser

The name ship of her class. On 8 April 1940, while taking part in the German invasion of NORWAY, the *Admiral Hipper* was rammed and damaged by the British destroyer GLOWWORM, which did not survive the action. During a cruise in the North Atlantic 1940–41, the *Hipper* sank seven ships with a total tonnage of 32,806. In July 1942 her presence in northern Norwegian waters contributed to the disaster which befell the British CONVOY PQ-17.

However, on 31 December 1942 a joint attack by the *Hipper*, LÜTZOW and escorting destroyers on Convoy JW-51B resulted in the disastrous Battle of THE BARENTS SEA. This failure so enraged HITLER that *Hipper* and the majority of the German Navy's heavy surface units were de-commissioned shortly afterwards. *Hipper* sustained bomb damage at KIEL in April 1945.

Admiral Hipper Class Heavy Cruisers (Ger)

Displacement 12,500 tons; *dimensions* 690ft 4in×71ft 10in (210.4×21.8m); mean draught 25ft 10in (7.9m); *machinery* geared turbines delivering 132,000 shp to three shafts; *speed* 33.4 knots; *protection* main belt 2.75in–3.1in; deck 0.5in–2in; turrets 2.75in–4.1in; *armament* 8×8in (4×2); 12×4.1in DP; 12×37mm AA; 24×20mm AA; 12×21in torpedo tubes; *aircraft* 2 floatplanes; *complement* 1450; *number in class* 3, launched 1937–38.

Admiral Scheer, KMS – Deutschland Class Pocket Battleship

The *Admiral Scheer* left Germany for the Atlantic on 23 October 1940 and returned on 1 April 1941, having sunk or captured 17 ships totalling 113,233 tons. On 5 November 1940 she attacked the large Convoy HX-84, but a suicidal counter-attack by the JERVIS BAY enabled all but six of the ships to escape. *Scheer* was based for a while in Norwegian waters but in the summer of 1944 moved to the Baltic where she supported the retreating German army with naval gunfire. On the night of 9/10 April 1945 she sustained serious bomb damage at KIEL and capsized.

Admiralty Islands, Bismarck Sea, 1944

A group of islands lying approximately 200 miles (320km) north of NEW GUINEA, captured by the US 1st Cavalry Division 29 February–23 March. Some 3000 Japanese were killed and 89 taken prisoner. American casualties were

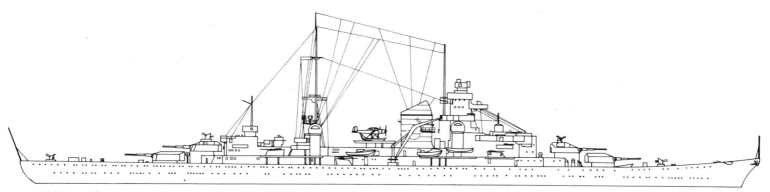

Admiral Hipper class cruiser.

290 killed and 1976 wounded. The capture of the Admiralty Islands completed the encirclement of the main Japanese bases at RABAUL and Kavieng which remained isolated for the remainder of the war.

Adolf Hitler Line, Italy, 1944

A heavily-fortified lay-back to the GUSTAV LINE, more accurately known as the Dora or Senger Line, lying on the western sector of the front some 50 miles (80km) south of ROME and stretching from Terracina on the coast to a point four miles (6km) north of CASSINO. When the line was broken by I Canadian Corps on 23 May the Allied 5th Army was able to effect a junction with the troops in the ANZIO beach-head, from which the US VI Corps was already breaking out in the direction of Rome.

Adua Class Submarines (Italy)

Displacement 623 tons (698/866 tons normal); *dimensions* 197ft 6in×21ft (60.2×6.45m); *machinery* 2-shaft diesel electric motors hp 1200/800; *speed* 14/7.5 knots; *armament* 1×3.9in; 2–4×13.2mm AA; 6×21in torpedo tubes and 12 torpedoes; *complement* 45; *number in class* 17, launched 1936–38.

AEAF Allied Expeditionary Air Force.

AEC Armoured Cars (UK)

	Mark I	Mark II	Mark III
Weight	11 tons	12.7 tons	12.7 tons
Speed	36mph (60kph)	41mph (66kph)	41mph (66kph)
Armour	30mm	30mm	30mm
Armament	1 2-pdr 1 Besa mg	1 6-pdr 1 Besa mg	1 75mm 1 Besa mg
Engine	AEC Diesel 105bhp	AEC Diesel 158bhp	AEC Diesel 158bhp
Crew	3	4	4

Originally designed by the Associated Equipment Company as a private venture incorporating many of the components of the Matador artillery tractor. The Mark I served in the Middle East and was equipped with the same turret as the 2-pdr marks of the VALENTINE infantry tank, although some were adapted to carry a 6-pdr turret. The later Marks were driven by a more powerful engine and were fitted with specially designed turrets incorporating heavier armament; they saw active service in North-West Europe and a number were supplied to TITO's Partisans in 1944. A notable feature of the AEC Series of armoured cars was their protection factor, which was almost twice that of the DAIMLER ARMOURED CAR. A total of 629 were built, of which 122 were Mark Is.

AEF Allied Expeditionary Force.

Aegean Theatre, Mediterranean

Following the withdrawal of Italy from the Axis alliance, the British attempted to establish their presence in the Aegean by effecting landings on KOS, Samos and Leros, off the Turkish coast, on 12 September 1943. Unfortunately, commitments elsewhere left them with inadequate resources to meet the heavy German response, which enjoyed the benefit of almost total air superiority. The Germans made amphibious landings on Kos (3 October) and Leros (12 November), backed in each case with limited airborne drops, and after brief but fierce fighting both islands fell. Samos was evacuated during the night of 19/20 November. British and Greek naval losses included six destroyers, two submarines and ten coastal craft sunk; the RAF lost 115 aircraft; and army casualties amounted to 4800, most of whom were captured. German losses included 12 merchant ships and 20 landing craft sunk, plus 4000 personnel casu-

alties, including a large proportion drowned. Subsequent British activity in the Aegean consisted of clandestine operations and raiding carried out by special forces and, until the general German withdrawal from Greece the following year, this policy succeeded in tying down large numbers of troops who were badly needed elsewhere.

Aeronca L3 Grasshopper (USA)

Originally developed as a two-seat trainer, the YO-58 Defender, this was then developed into an observation and liaison machine and about 1500 were built. There were a number of minor variations in equipment from time to time, and a variety of engines were fitted as supply dictated, but in general the aircraft remained much the same throughout the war. *Span* 35ft (10.68m); *engine* 65hp in-line; *speed* 80mph (129kph).

Afmadu, Italian Somaliland, 1941

Bombed by the South African Air Force on 10 February and abandoned by its Italian garrison when threatened by the advance of 12th African Division from Kenya.

AFN American Forces Network. Radio service set up in Britain, and later in Europe, to provide radio entertainment for US forces.

Afrika Korps

The first German troops to arrive in Africa landed at Tripoli on 14 February 1941 and belonged to the 5th Light Division, a formation based on units drawn from the 3rd Panzer Division and which itself became 21st Panzer Division that October. This was followed in April 1941 by the 15th Panzer Division, and together these two formed the Deutsches Afrika Korps (DAK). A motorized infantry formation known as the Afrika Division was raised locally from independent units in

August 1941 and on 27 November was renamed the 90th Light Division, despite the fact that it lacked an armoured element. These formations were known collectively as Panzer Group Afrika from 15 August, being elevated to the status of Panzer Army Afrika on 30 January 1942 by the addition of six Italian divisions, one of which was armoured. The only other German formations to serve in the desert phase of the North African War were the 164th Light Division, consisting of infantry drawn from the garrison of CRETE, and the Ramcke Parachute Demonstration Brigade, which arrived in the summer of 1942. This represented about two per cent of the German Army's overall strength, and five to ten per cent of that of the Panzerwaffe.

AFV Armoured Fighting Vehicle (UK).

AG Adjutant-General (US).

Agano Class Cruisers (Jap)

Displacement 6652 tons; *dimensions* 594ft×49ft 9in (181×15.2m); mean draught 18ft 6in (5.6m); *machinery* 4-shaft geared turbines producing shp 100,000; *speed* 35 knots; *protection* deck .75in; turrets 1in; magazine 2in; machinery 2.25in; *armament* 6×5.9in (3×2); 4×3.1in AA (2×2); 6×25mm AA; 8×24in torpedo tubes (2×4); 16 depth charges; *aircraft* 2 (1 catapult); *number in class* 4, launched 1941–44.

AGF Army Ground Forces (US). US military command which replaced the pre-war Boards of Infantry, Cavalry, Artillery etc, in order to co-ordinate the provision of weapons, munitions and equipment to the army and also to standardize training and organization.

A-Go

Japanese plan for counteroffensive in the MARIANAS, 1944.

Agordat, Eritrea, 1941

Captured by 4th Indian Division on 31 January after a three-day battle. The Italian garrison, partially surrounded, managed to break out to the east but was forced to abandon much of its artillery and heavy equipment.

AGRA Army Group, Royal Artillery (UK). A group of non-divisional British Artillery units under the control of an Army commander, to

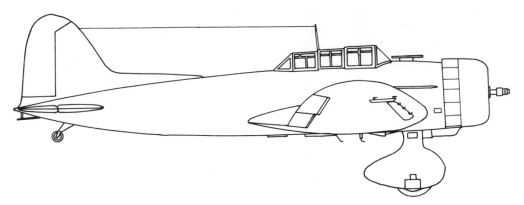

Aichi D3A1 dive bomber.

be allotted as determined by operational requirements. In effect, an artillery reserve.

AI Airborne Intercept. Type of RADAR used in fighters to detect enemy bombers.

Aichi Aircraft (Jap)

Aichi B7A (Grace) A two-seater monoplane torpedo bomber, first flown in May 1942 and in production March 1944, though few ever reached service. It carried one torpedo or 2200lb of bombs and was armed with two 20mm cannon and one .50in (12.7mm) machine gun. *Span* 47.25ft (14.4m); *engine* 1 1875hp radial; *speed* 337mph (542kph).

Aichi D3A (Val) Placed in production in 1937, this was one of Japan's principal warplanes. A two-seater, it was the first all-metal, low-wing monoplane dive-bomber to enter Japanese service and it was used at PEARL HARBOR and in the other attacks which accompanied Japan's entry into the war. Strongly built and highly manoeuvrable, it was one of the few dive-bombers also capable of performing well as a fighter. A variant was the D3A2, built 1942–44, with a more powerful engine. *Span* 47ft (14.3m); *engine* 1 1300hp radial; *armament* 2 7.7mm machine guns, 830lb (375kg) of bombs; *speed* 266mph (428kph).

Aichi E13A (Jake) Designed in 1938, this naval floatplane was used to reconnoitre the raid on PEARL HARBOR in 1941. A single-float low-wing monoplane, about 1200 were built before it was superseded by the E16A. Carried by most Japanese warships, it was widely used in the Pacific and saw action in most of the naval battles. *Span* 47.5ft (14.49m); *engine* 1 1080hp radial; *armament* 3 machine guns; *speed* 234mph (376.5kph).

Aichi E16A1 (Paul) Named Zuiun ("Auspicious Cloud") by the Japanese, this was a

three-seat low-wing monoplane single-float seaplane developed for reconnaissance, though it was also used as a dive-bomber. Though effective, it did not go into production until half-way through the war and less than 300 were built. *Span* 42ft (12.81m); *engine* 1 1300hp radial; *armament* 2 20mm cannon, 3 machine guns, 1100lb (500kg) of bombs; *speed* 280mph (450.52kph).

Aichi H9A1 Originally designed as a training machine, this was a large twin-engined monoplane flying boat with a maximum speed of 202mph (325kph). 31 were built in 1942–43 and some were used in anti-submarine patrol duties towards the end of the war, carrying two 550lb (250kg) of bombs or depth charges.

Aichi M6A1 Japanese name Seiran ("Mountain Haze"). This was designed as a single-float seaplane bomber to be carried by fleet submarines, but only 28 were made of which only nine entered service.

Aida

Axis plan for a drive on the Nile Delta, 1942.

AIF Australian Imperial Force.

Ainsworth, R Adm Walden (1886–1960)

An American naval officer who held various commands in the Pacific theatre. He is principally known for his part in the Battles of KULA GULF and KOLOMBANGARA in 1943, when his force repulsed Japanese attempts to reinforce their troops in the Solomon Islands.

Airborne Cigar

A British electronic jamming device carried in certain Lancaster bombers for the purpose of jamming German night-fighter controller communications. The device required a special operator who watched a cathode-ray tube on his receiver. This indicated any signal appearing and the operator then tuned his jammer to the same frequency. The use of the cathode-ray tube display enabled the operator to see if the German transmitter changed its frequency and allowed him to follow it with constant jamming. Airborne Cigar aircraft of 101 Squadron, RAF accompanied all major bombing raids from October 1943 onwards.

Airborne Radar

A term which applies to any radar equipment mounted in aircraft but which is usually applied to RADAR mounted in night fighters for the detection and attack of bombers. Developed and put to use by the Royal Air Force in 1941 for this role and later adapted to anti-submarine search; the system was also adopted by the Luftwaffe with considerable success.

Air Observation Posts

A British term for light aircraft used for the visual control of artillery fire. First used in North Africa, 1942, they became an extremely valuable adjunct to the normal ground forward observers. The aircraft were BRITISH TAYLORCRAFT "AUSTER" monoplanes, unarmed, and in spite of their slow speed they were surprisingly manoeuvrable and rarely fell victim to enemy aircraft. They were not intended to fly over enemy territory, but merely to gain the advantage of a high viewpoint from within their own lines.

Air Raid Precautions

A general term covering methods of passive defence against air attack. These included an organization of Air Raid Wardens, who supervised shelters, organized rescue work, extinguished incendiary bombs and looked after the welfare of air raid victims. A Heavy Rescue Service was responsible for searching for victims beneath wrecked buildings. Under various titles these services were provided in all combatant countries, and the ARP services worked closely with civil police and fire brigades.

Airspeed Oxford (UK)

This trainer had its origins in the 1934 Envoy airline feeder and appeared in RAF service in 1938. A twin-engined monoplane, it was used as an aircrew trainer and also in communications, ambulance and army co-operation tasks. Models differed principally in engines, though the Oxford I was a bombing and gunnery trainer and carried a power-operated gun turret. Over 8700 were built and a number remained in service after 1945. *Span* 53.3ft (16.25m); *engines* 2 355hp radial; *crew* 3; *speed* 182mph (293kph).

Ajax, HMS – Leander Class Cruiser

Ajax took part in the Battle of the RIVER PLATE. She joined the Mediterranean Fleet in 1940 and served with FORCE H. After refitting in the USA during 1943, she returned to the Mediterranean for the rest of the war.

AKA   Cargo ship, Attack (US).

Akagi, IJN – Aircraft Carrier

Akagi was based on a battlecruiser hull and was completed in 1927, being extensively refitted in 1937–38. She served as Vice-

ARP men at the end of a night of rescue work in south-west London.

IJN Akagi, *under attack by US B-17 bombers, takes evasive action during the Battle of Midway, 1942.*

Admiral NAGUMO's flagship during the attack on PEARL HARBOR and subsequent operations, later penetrating the Indian Ocean, where her aircraft took part in the sinking of the British carrier HMS HERMES and other warships. During the Battle of MIDWAY she raided Midway Island itself but was twice hit by 1×1000lb and 1×500lb bombs dropped by dive bombers from the USS ENTERPRISE. These started uncontrollable fires and Nagumo was compelled to shift his flag to a light cruiser. After nine hours, *Akagi* was torpedoed and sunk by one of her escorting destroyers. *Displacement* 36,500 tons; *dimensions* 855ft×102ft 8in (260.7x31m); mean draught 28ft 3in (8.61m); *machinery* 4-shaft geared steam turbines producing 133,000 shp; *speed* 31.2 knots; *armament* 6×7.9in in casemates; 12×4.7in AA (6×2); 28×25mm AA (14×2); *aircraft* 63; *complement* 1340.

Akitsuki Class Destroyers (Jap)

Displacement 2701 tons; *dimensions* 440ft 4in×38ft (134×11.6m); mean draught 13ft 6in (4.1m); *machinery* 2-shaft geared turbines producing shp 52,000; *speed* 33 knots; *armament* 8×3.9in AA (4×2); 4×25mm AA (2×2); 4×24in torpedo tubes; 6 depth charge throwers and 72 depth charges; *complement* 250; *number in class* 13, launched 1941–44.

Akyab Island, Burma, 1945

Lying off the ARAKAN coast, Akyab possessed several airfields which made it of great strategic importance. Assault landings were to have been made by 25th Indian Division and No. 3 Commando on 3 January 1945 but the previous day an artillery air observation officer failed to see any Japanese and, landing, was told by local inhabitants that they had gone. The island was promptly occupied and its airfields were returned to operational condition by 5 January.

Alabama, USS – South Dakota Class Battleship

Served with the British Home Fleet during 1943 before being transferred to the Pacific, where she saw action at the GILBERT ISLANDS, KWAJALEIN, TRUK, the MARIANAS, Palau, LEYTE GULF and OKINAWA.

Alamein, First Battle of, Egypt, 1942

A series of engagements lasting from 1 to 27 July in which the British 8th Army under the personal command of General Sir Claude AUCHINLECK, the Commander-in-Chief Middle East, halted the drive of Field-Marshal Erwin ROMMEL's Axis army into Egypt. Although both sides received reinforcements during the battle, neither was strong enough to impose its will on the other. Thus, while the Axis advance was effectively checked, 8th Army was unable to break out to the west, despite heavy and costly fighting at RUWEISAT RIDGE and Tel el

First Battle of Alamein: Rommel's advance is halted.

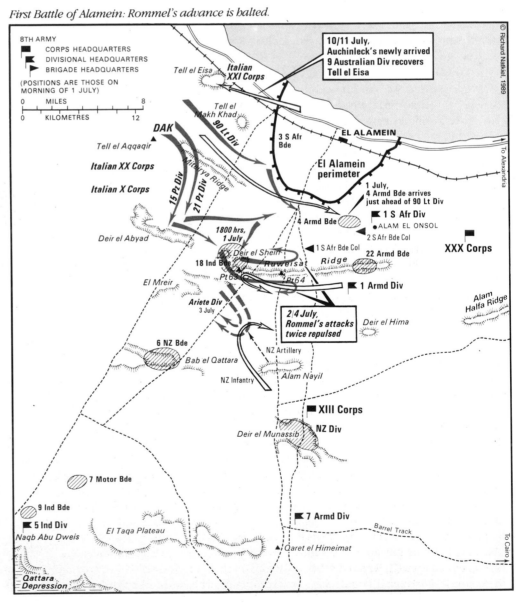

Eisa. By 27 July both armies were exhausted and the battle had resulted in an apparent stalemate, with both sides digging in with minefields and preparing to regroup. However, the British held the strategic advantage since they were operating close to their base and were being reinforced at a rate which the Axis forces, with their over-extended supply lines, could not match. Furthermore, Rommel was contained by a 40-mile static front stretching from the sea to the Qattara Depression, and as a withdrawal would gain him nothing it could be confidently predicted that he would renew his attack as soon as he felt strong enough to do so. It remained only for the British to prepare accordingly. See ALAM HALFA. See also *The Unknown Alamein* by Charles Messenger (Ian Allan).

Alamein, Second Battle of, Egypt, 1942

Fought between the British 8th Army, commanded by Lieutenant-General Bernard MONTGOMERY, and the Axis army under Field-Marshal Erwin ROMMEL (who was absent on sick leave during its early stages) and lasting from 2140 on 23 October until 4 November. The 8th Army's strength was 195,000 men; 1029 tanks plus an immediate reserve of 200 and a further 1000 in workshops; 2311 artillery weapons, including 908 medium and field guns; and 750 aircraft, of which 530 were serviceable. The Axis army numbered 104,000 (50,000 German and 54,000 Italian); 520 tanks, including 31 light PzKw IIs and 278 Italian M-13/40s; 1219 artillery weapons, including 475 medium and field guns; and 675 aircraft of which 150 German and 200 Italian were serviceable. A major British offensive had long been regarded as inevitable and the Axis defences were laid out in depth behind deep minebelts with German and Italian formations alternating along the front. The four armoured divisions (15th and 21st Panzer, *Ariete* and *Littorio*) were deployed behind the front in positions from which they could contain any breakthrough, although they were critically short of fuel. The first phase of the British offensive involved a diversionary attack by XIII Corps on the southern sector while further north the infantry of XXX Corps fought to secure two major corridors through the minebelts in the area of Miteiriya and KIDNEY RIDGES through which the 1st and 10th Armoured Divisions could be passed.

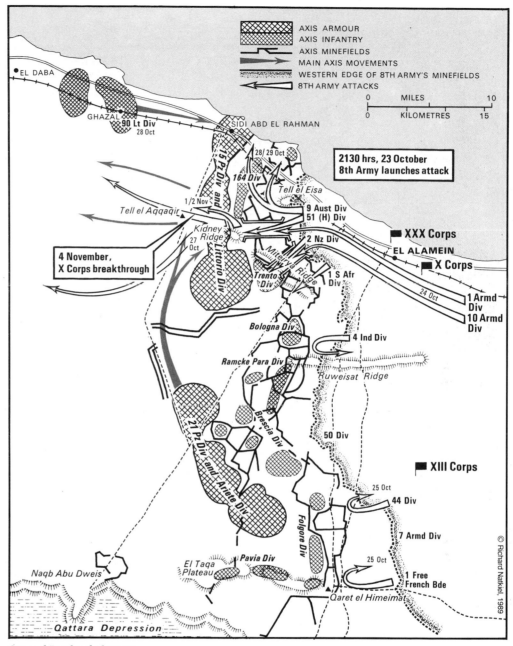

Second Battle of Alamein.

However, progress was slow and Montgomery, fully aware of his opponents' fuel shortage, decided to fight what he described as a "crumbling" battle, switching the emphasis of his attack from point to point, thereby compelling the Axis armour to react. On 26 October the 9th Australian Division attacked on the coastal sector, all but isolating part of the German 164th Light Division and an Italian Bersaglieri Battalion, and succeeded in attracting a major armoured counter-attack. Montgomery promptly shifted the emphasis back to the Kidney Ridge area and a major tank battle took place at Tel el Aqqaqir on 2 November. In this the British sustained the greater loss but Axis also suffered severely and could not support the rate of attrition. By nightfall on 3 November there were only 30 serviceable German tanks. In obedience to HITLER's directives, Rommel hung on a little while longer but began extracting the remains of his army on 4 November. The British pursuit was slow to develop and was hindered by heavy rain and fuel shortage, enabling Rommel to disengage. The Axis losses amounted to 10,000 killed, 15,000 wounded, 30,000 captured, most of their tanks and heavy weapons, and 84 aircraft. General Georg Stumme, com-

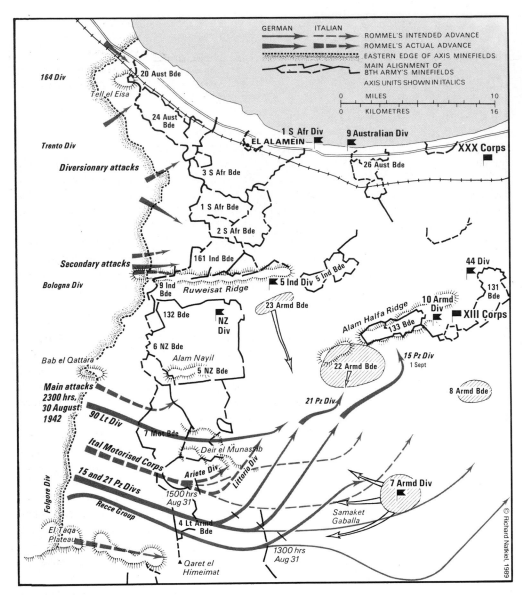

Battle of Alam Halfa, 1942.

Map legend:

GERMAN	ITALIAN	
→	→	ROMMEL'S INTENDED ADVANCE
⇒	⇒	ROMMEL'S ACTUAL ADVANCE
·····		EASTERN EDGE OF AXIS MINEFIELDS
⊣⊢⊣⊢		MAIN ALIGNMENT OF 8TH ARMY'S MINEFIELDS
		AXIS UNITS SHOWN IN ITALICS

MILES 0 — 10
KILOMETRES 0 — 16

© Richard Natkiel, 1989

Alam Halfa, Battle of, Egypt, 1942

His advance into Egypt having been checked during the First Battle of ALAMEIN, ROMMEL built up the strength of his Axis army until he had amassed 203 German and 243 Italian tanks. With these he hoped to break through the southern sector of the Alamein Line and then swing north to the coast, throwing the British 8th Army off balance and compelling it to withdraw. His plan was predictable and a defence scheme prepared by General AUCHINLECK was adopted by Lieutenant-General Bernard MONTGOMERY, the new commander of 8th Army, which had 700 tanks available to meet the attack.

Rommel began his attack during the night of 30/31 August but was halted south of Alam Halfa Ridge by a co-ordinated defence in which tanks, artillery, anti-tank guns and ground-attack aircraft all played a part. On 2 September he cancelled the operation and retired through the minebelts, having sustained 3000 casualties (including Major-General von Bismarck, commanding 21st Panzer Division, killed during the first night), 49 tanks, 60 artillery weapons and 400 lorries. British losses amounted to 1640 killed and wounded, 68 tanks and 18 anti-tank guns. The victory did much to restore 8th Army's morale but its importance lies in the fact that in its aftermath Rommel found himself in a strategic straitjacket in which he could neither advance nor retreat while his opponents prepared methodically for the decisive Second Battle of ALAMEIN.

Alamo Force

Codename for headquarters US 6th Army while operating as ground task force headquarters under GHQ South-West Pacific Area.

New Zealand troops round up prisoners after the second Battle of Alamein, 1942.

manding Panzerarmee Afrika during Rommel's absence, sustained a fatal heart attack on 24 October, his place being taken by the commander of the Afrika Korps, General von THOMA, pending Rommel's return the following evening. Von Thoma was himself captured during the final stages of the battle. The 8th Army's losses were 2350 killed, 8950 wounded and 2260 missing, 111 artillery weapons and 97 aircraft; 500 tanks were disabled, but most were repairable. Second Alamein was the decisive battle of the Desert War and, coupled with Operation TORCH, the Anglo-American landings in Algeria and Morocco on 8 November, it spelled the end of Axis hopes in the North African theatre of war. See also *Alamein* by C. E. Lucas Phillips (Heinemann); *El Alamein* by Michael Carver (Batsford); and *Desert Warfare* by Bryan Perrett (Patrick Stephens).

Alarich See ACHSE.

Alaska Class Battlecruisers (USA)

The two ships in this class, *Alaska* and *Guam*, were not completed until 1945 but both saw active service at OKINAWA. *Displacement* 27,500 tons; *dimensions* 808ft 6in×91ft (246.4×27.7m); mean draught 31ft 6in (9.6m); *machinery* 4-shaft geared turbines producing shp 150,000; *speed* 33 knots; *protection* main belt 9in; turrets 12.75in; *armament* 9×12in (3×3); 12×5in (6×2); 56×40mm AA; 30–34×20mm AA *aircraft* 4; *complement* 2200; *number in class* 2.

Alban Hills, Italy, 1944

A range of hills lying inland from the ANZIO beach-head. When the Allied landing took place on 22 January 1944 under the command of Major-General John P. LUCAS, no attempt was made to secure these although they were vital ground which provided a view across the beach-head area. It has been argued that the capture of the Alban Hills during the early stages of the Anzio operation would have resulted in the collapse of the GUSTAV LINE and the early capture of ROME. As it was, the beach-head was quickly contained by KESSELRING'S rapid response and the hills remained untaken until the general break-out in May.

Japanese troops land in the Aleutians, 1942.

Albania, 1939–45

Balkan kingdom on the Adriatic invaded and annexed by Italy in April 1939. Served as a springboard for the abortive Italian invasion of Greece in October 1940, which was thrown back across the frontier by a Greek counteroffensive during November and December. In April 1941 the Axis invasion of Greece through Bulgaria and Yugoslavia compelled the Greeks to withdraw from Albania. By the end of the year Communist-organized partisan activity had commenced and this increased in intensity as the war progressed. Following the Italian capitulation in 1943, the partisans inherited large quantities of arms and were joined by many former Italian soldiers. Repeated German drives against the partisans met with little success. Faced with a deteriorating situation on the Eastern Front, the Germans themselves withdrew from Albania in the autumn of 1944. See also ZOG, KING OF ALBANIA.

Albert Canal, Belgium, 1940

Together with the Meuse, the Albert Canal was intended by the Belgian General Staff to serve as a defensible line in the event of a German invasion. The plan collapsed when Fort EBEN EMAEL, covering the junction of the canal with the Meuse, was captured on 10 May.

Albert Line, Italy, 1944

An interim defence line on either side of Lake Trasimeno held briefly in June by KESSELRING's Army Group C as it withdrew to the prepared defences of the GOTHIC LINE following the fall of ROME.

Alecto

A British assault gun developed in response to a 1942 General Staff requirement for a light self-propelled gun to support infantry operations, the Alecto employed the chassis of the HARRY HOPKINS light tank and was armed with a 95mm Howitzer Mark III, mounted well forward in a lightly armoured open-topped superstructure. It was eventually decided that the vehicle was more suited to the reconnaissance role, but none of the few built ever saw active service.

Aleutian Islands, Northern Pacific, 1942–43

A chain of US-owned, sparsely inhabited islands stretching from Alaska towards the Asian mainland. In June 1942 the Japanese occupied the two most westerly islands, Attu and Kiska, as part of the diversionary manoeuvres during their MIDWAY campaign. American efforts to dislodge them originated at the Dutch Harbour base on Umnak in the central Aleutians. On 11 May 1943 an amphibious task force under Rear-Admiral Francis W. Rockwell put the US 7th Infantry Division ashore on Attu and during the next 18 days all but 29 of the 2500-strong Japanese garrison were killed; American losses were 561 killed and 1136 wounded. On 15 August a joint Canadian-American force of some 34,000 men landed on Kiska to find it deserted, the Japanese having withdrawn their garrison under cover of fog and darkness on 29 July. See also Battle of the KOMANDORSKI ISLANDS.

Alexander, FM Sir Harold Rupert, 1st Earl of Tunis (1891–1969)

One of the British Army's outstanding commanders in World War II, Alexander had served in France in 1914–18 and later on the North-West Frontier. In 1937, at the age of 45, he became the youngest general in the Army, commanding 1st Division, one of the only four regular divisions in England. In September 1939 1st Division formed part of the BRITISH EXPEDITIONARY FORCE (BEF) to France, and at DUNKIRK Alexander was chosen to command the last corps to remain on the beaches.

General Harold Alexander, while second-in-command to Eisenhower, March 1943.

He was the last British soldier to leave. In February 1942 he was given command of the army in BURMA and conducted the withdrawal from RANGOON. Emerging from an unmitigated disaster with heightened prestige, he replaced AUCHINLECK as Commander-in-Chief Middle East, directing the campaigns in which MONTGOMERY's 8TH ARMY defeated ROMMEL at the Second Battle of ALAMEIN and thereafter. After US and British troops joined forces in Tunisia, Alexander was appointed Deputy Allied Commander-in-Chief in North Africa, under EISENHOWER, and as commander of 18th Army Group (1st and 8th Armies) he co-ordinated the capture of Tunis in May 1943. Alexander was a strong supporter of the invasion of Sicily and Italy but his handling of the campaign on the Italian mainland was handicapped by the greater priority accorded to OVERLORD, prompting him to make frequent complaints about lack of landing craft and other vital equipment. In December 1944 he was appointed Supreme Allied Commander in the Mediterranean, and received the surrender of German troops in Italy on 29 April 1945.

Alexandria, Egypt, 1940–43

The base of the British Mediterranean Fleet and departure point for west-bound MALTA relief convoys. On 19 December 1941 Italian HUMAN TORPEDOES penetrated the harbour and severely damaged the battleships *Queen Elizabeth* and *Valiant*. The air defence of Alexandria, while successful, absorbed considerable resources, notably large numbers of 3.7-in anti-aircraft guns, which had a slightly better performance than the dreaded German 88mm and might otherwise have been similarly employed in the anti-tank role.

Algeciras, Spain, 1941

Used as a base by the Italian 10th Flotilla, whose frogmen and HUMAN TORPEDOES, operating with the connivance of the Spanish authorities from a merchant ship in the harbour, launched attacks on British shipping in nearby Gibraltar.

Algerine Class Minesweeping Sloops (UK)

Displacement 850 tons; *dimensions* 225ft×35ft 6in (68.5×10.82m); mean draught 8ft 6in (2.6m); *machinery* 2-shaft geared turbines or reciprocating, shp or ihp 2000; *speed* 16.5 knots; *armament* 1×4in; 8×20mm AA (4×2); machine guns (variable); *complement* 85; *number in class* 118, launched 1941–45.

Algiers, North Africa, 1942

The objective of Major-General Charles RYDER's Eastern Task Force during Operation TORCH. The landings took place on 8 November and were met with sporadic resistance, two British destroyers flying the US flag being damaged when they penetrated the harbour to disembark American troops. However, discussions between General Mark CLARK and Admiral Jean DARLAN resulted in a general ceasefire.

Aliakmon Line, Greece, 1941

A 60-mile defence line running north-west from a point on the coast north of Mount Olympus to Mount Kaymakchalan on the Yugoslav border. The line, into which a British and Commonwealth Corps was moving, was abandoned after it was outflanked in April by the German thrust into Greece from Yugoslavia which penetrated the yawning gap between these positions and the main body of the Greek Army in ALBANIA.

Alkemade, F/Sgt N. S.

Alkemade was rear-gunner in an AVRO LANCASTER bomber of RAF BOMBER COMMAND on a raid over BERLIN on 24/25 March 1944. Over the RUHR the aircraft was hit by gunfire and set on fire. Alkemade, unable to reach his parachute, jumped clear of the aircraft and fell an estimated 18,000ft, landing in the branches of pine-trees and falling from there into a deep snowdrift. He survived the fall with relatively slight injuries. His feat was attested to by the Luftwaffe (his charred parachute having been found in the remains of his aircraft) and was confirmed by the RAF after the war.

Allen M. Sumner Class Destroyers (USA)

Displacement 2200 tons; *dimensions* 376ft 6in×41ft (115×12.5m); mean draught 19ft (5.8m); *machinery* 2-shaft geared turbines producing shp 60,000; *speed* 36.5 knots; *armament* 6×5in (3×2); 12×40mm AA; 10×21in torpedo tubes; *complement* 350; *number in class* 58, launched 1943–45.

Allways Fuze

A type of fuze used with hand grenades, designed to detonate on impact at the target. It used a heavy ball held between conical surfaces, so that whichever way the grenade and fuze landed, the ball would move under its own inertia, forcing the cones apart and so drive a needle into a detonator. Examples triggered by this type of fuze include British Grenade Hand No. 69 and Italian Grenade Model 35.

ALO Air Liaison Officer. British army officer attached to an RAF unit, or RAF officer attached to an Army unit, to act as a channel for calling down tactical air support for ground troops.

Alpenveilchen (Alpine Violet)

Axis invasion of ALBANIA, 11 January 1940.

Altenfjord, Norway, 1942–44

German naval base on the northern coast from which heavy surface units were able to mount sorties against the Arctic convoys to the Soviet Union. See also TIRPITZ and X-CRAFT.

Altmark Incident, the, 1940

The *Altmark* had served as the ADMIRAL GRAF SPEE's supply ship and was trying to reach home with 299 captured British merchant

The German support vessel Altmark *in Norwegian waters.*

seamen aboard when she was detected off the Norwegian coast. On 16 February 1940 she was boarded and captured in Jössing Fjord by the destroyer HMS *Cossack*, commanded by Captain Philip VIAN, the captives' release being signalled by the now historic cry of "The Navy's here!" Protests from the Norwegian government regarding violation of neutral territorial waters ceased when it transpired that the *Altmark* was armed. HITLER, however, was becoming increasingly concerned about the safety of his sea-borne iron ore traffic from NARVIK and the incident was a major factor in his decision to invade Norway.

Amba Alagi, Battle of, Ethiopia, 1941

A mountain in north-eastern Ethiopia selected by the Italian Viceroy, the Duke of AOSTA, for his last stand. The final battle was fought among peaks 10–12,000ft (3–3600m) high, defended by 7000 Italians with 40 guns. Between 3 and 19 May these positions were successfully assaulted by part of the 5th Indian Division, a South African brigade group and an Ethiopian contingent. The harsh treatment accorded their prisoners by the Ethiopians encouraged the Italians to surrender to regular troops and the Viceroy capitulated on 19 May, being granted the honours of war.

Ambon Island, Dutch East Indies, 1942

Its small garrison of Dutch and Australian troops was overrun by the Japanese between 31 January and 3 February. Over half the 809 Australians captured were either killed on the spot or died from the combined effects of torture and starvation.

Ambrosio, Gen Vittorio (1897–1958)

Ambrosio commanded the 2nd Italian Army in YUGOSLAVIA in 1941 and was promoted to Chief of Staff Italian Army in January 1942 and Chief of the General Staff in February 1943. He was involved in the fall of MUSSOLINI and the renunciation of the alliance with Germany. In November 1943 he was demoted by Marshal BADOGLIO to Inspector-General of the Army.

AMC (Auto-Mitrailleuse de Combat) Renault M1935 – Light Tank (Fr)

Developed for use by French mechanized cavalry units. A later version was armed with a 25mm anti-tank gun and co-axial machine gun. *Weight* 14.5 tons; *speed* 25mph (40kph); *armour* 40mm; *armament* 1 47mm gun; 1 7.5mm machine gun; *engine* Renault 180hp 6-cylinder; *crew* 3.

AMGOT Allied Military Government of Occupied Territories. US-British organization charged with the reorganization and administration of liberated or conquered territory whilst hostilities were still in force. The principal tasks were to maintain order and security, feed the population, and reorganize such social functions as health, police, public works, communications, transport and industry. In the case of liberated friendly countries, military and civilian personnel from these countries were utilized and the civil functionaries on the spot were usually retained in their posts; moreover, much of the civil powers' authority was confirmed and intervention by AMGOT was minimal. In conquered areas AMGOT retained all the requisite powers and exercised full authority until replaced by the ACC (Allied Control Commission).

Amiot 143 (Fr)

Developed to a 1928 demand for a reconnaissance bomber, the French Amiot 143 entered service in 1935. An all-metal twin-engined midwing monoplane, the wings were so thick that mechanics could pass through them and attend to the engines in flight. Slow and with poor manoeuvrability, the Amiot performed valiantly in 1940 but was easy prey for German fighters. The remainder served out their time as transports until 1944. *Span* 80.5ft (24.55m); *engines* 2 900hp radial; *crew* 5; *armament* 4 7.5mm machine guns, 1760lb (800kg) of bombs; *speed* 193mph (310kph).

AMMISCA American Military Mission to China.

AMR (Auto-Mitrailleuse de Reconnaissance) – Light Tank (Fr)

Used by the reconnaissance units of infantry divisions and by the infantry elements of mechanized cavalry and light mechanized divisions. Later versions were armed with either a 25mm anti-tank gun or coaxially mounted 13.2mm and 7.5mm machine guns. The vehicle bore some superficial similarity to the VICKERS LIGHT TANK Series. *Weight* 6 tons; *speed* 31.25mph (50kph); *armour* 13mm; *armament* 1 7.5mm machine gun; *engine* Renault 80hp; *crew* 2.

Amtracs (USA)

See LANDING VEHICLES TRACKED.

Anakim

Allied plan for the re-conquest of BURMA, 1942–43.

Anami, Gen Korechika (1887–1945)

Anami was the commander of various Japanese armies in CHINA, from 1938 to 1943. He then directed operations in NEW GUINEA in 1943–44. In December 1944 he became

Director-General of Japanese Army Aviation, and was appointed Minister of War in April 1945. He committed suicide on 15 August 1945.

Anders, Gen Wladyslav (1892–1970)

A Polish officer in command of the Nowogrodek Cavalry Brigade, Anders was captured by the Russians in September 1939 and imprisoned in Lubianka jail. He was released in July 1941 and allowed to go to Palestine where he formed an army of some 70,000 Poles, most of whom had also been released from Soviet captivity. This force, Polish II Corps, fought at TOBRUK and in the Western Desert, captured CASSINO in Italy in May 1944, and liberated Bologna in April 1945. After the death of General SIKORSKI, Anders became the Polish leader-in-exile, but he ignored the political problems facing Poland and concentrated on the military tasks, as a result of which the Communists were able to outmanoeuvre him politically. He remained in Britain after the war, becoming the leader of the expatriate Polish community there.

Anderson, Sir John (1882–1958)

Anderson was Home Secretary 1939–40, and became famous for his espousal of the "Anderson Shelter", a simple air-raid shelter which was erected in gardens by tens of thousands and which saved many lives during air raids on Britain. He was Lord President of the Council, 1940–43, and sat on the Manpower Committee. He held the post of Chancellor of the Exchequer 1943–45 and was also in charge of the "Tube Alloys" project, the British part of the atomic bomb development programme.

Animoso Class Destroyer Escorts (Italy)

Displacement 1204–1709 tons; *dimensions* 292ft 9in×32ft 3in (89.2×9.82m); mean draught 11ft 6in (3.5m); *machinery* 2-shaft geared turbines producing shp 15,500; *speed* 26 knots; *armament* 2 or 3×3.9in; 10–12×20mm AA; 4×17.7in torpedo tubes; 4–6 depth charge throwers; equipped for minelaying; *complement* 180; *number in class* 16, launched 1942–43.

Anklet

Commando raid on the LOFOTEN ISLANDS, 26 December 1941.

Anschluss

Meaning a bonding together, the term was used by the Nazi leadership to imply a home-coming, to justify the incorporation of external ethnic German populations within the Third Reich. It was used principally in connection with the annexation of Austria in March 1938 following a protracted period of Nazi-inspired unrest and political instability. The German invasion was followed by a reign of terror in which the Nazis ruthlessly eliminated their opponents.

Anti-aircraft Artillery

Artillery specifically designed for the attack of aircraft and characterized by the ability to elevate to high angles and a high rate of fire. Divided into three types, Light, Medium and Heavy. Light AA guns were of 20–40mm calibre and were basically enlarged machine guns, used against low-flying aircraft. Medium guns were of 50–90mm calibre and equipped all mobile and the bulk of static defences. Heavy guns were of 105–150mm calibre, for static defences of large cities and essential targets. Medium and heavy guns were for the attack of high-flying bombers.

The anti-aircraft problem, viewed purely as a gunnery problem, meant the attack of a fast-moving target capable of moving in three planes, and it demanded sophisticated fire control methods. It was necessary to know the course, speed and height of the target and then to forecast where it would be by the time the shell reached that altitude. This calculation was performed by predictors, the basic data being furnished by optical height and range finders or by RADAR, and it was predicated on the assumption that the target would continue to fly at its indicated course and speed. Anti-aircraft gunnery improved immensely during the war, largely due to electronic innovations in fire control, and by 1945 AA guns averaged one target destroyed for about 1500 rounds fired.

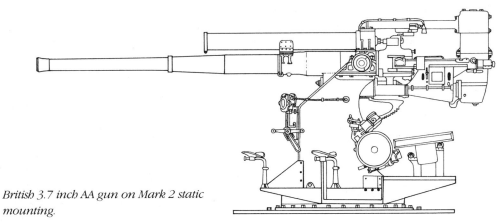

British 3.7 inch AA gun on Mark 2 static mounting.

German self-propelled quadruple 20mm light AA gun on a three-quarter tracked carriage.

Soviet 37mm gun in Königsberg, 1945.

Anti-aircraft Rockets

Anti-aircraft rockets were developed as a cheaper solution to the problems of air defence, since the construction of rockets and their associated launching devices was much quicker and demanded less advanced engineering than the manufacture of guns of similar performance. Unguided rockets were developed in Britain in the mid-1930s in order to supplement the slow production of guns, but they were not used much until 1942 due to technical and operational difficulties. They were eventually used in large Z BATTERIES protecting certain vital ports and cities. Unguided rockets were employed less by other countries; however Germany put a great deal of effort into developing guided missiles of various types, though none completed their development before the war ended.

Anti-Comintern Pact

A treaty signed by Germany and Japan in November 1936, and which was later extended to include Italy, Hungary and Spain. The purpose was to block Soviet expansion and limit the extent of its interference in the affairs of countries outside the USSR. Secret clauses also bound the signatories not to make political agreements with the Soviet Union. Should any signatory become involved in war with the Soviet Union, discussions would follow on joint action. The Pact was renounced by Japan when Germany and Russia signed the Non-Aggression Pact in August

Rockets stream towards Okinawa from an LSM(R), March 1945.

British 2pr anti-tank gun, Western Desert 1941.

1939, but they rejoined when, in November 1941, the Anti-Comintern was renewed for a further five years. New signatories at this time were Bulgaria, Croatia, Denmark, Finland, Romania, Slovakia, Manchukuo and the Chinese government in Nanking.

Anti-personnel Mines

Mines deployed for the purpose of incapacitating the enemy's foot soldiers, as opposed to ANTI-TANK MINES, used against armoured vehicles. They fell into two broad categories: the first, and simplest, was a small canister with a charge of a few ounces of explosive, buried in the ground with a sensor of some type exposed above the ground. This sensor might react when stepped on, or it might be attached to a trip-wire which the man's foot would catch in passing. In either case the result would fire the charge of explosive, and the result was usually that the man lost his foot or lower leg, if he was not killed. The second, more complex, type was the "bounding" or "bouncing" mine, in which an explosive mine containing metal fragments was buried inside a steel mortar tube beneath the ground. On being fired by the sensor unit, the mortar would blow the mine into the air, where it would detonate at about waist height, spreading fragments and blast around the point of burst. This type of mine was usually fatal.

Anti-tank Grenades

Anti-tank grenades were developed by most of the belligerent armies in order to provide infantrymen with some easily-portable form of attacking tanks. They took two methods of approach: either to overcome the tank's armour by the blast force of a charge of explosive, or to penetrate the armour by utilizing the SHAPED CHARGE principle. The former method was exemplified by the British No. 73 grenade, a metal canister containing a powerful charge of explosive. The latter was exemplified by the British No. 68 rifle grenade, a fin-stabilized bomb, or by the German Hohladungsgranat, a stick grenade with magnets which enabled the bomb to attach itself to the armour before detonating. All these grenades were moderately successful in the first half of the war, but became overmatched by the thicker armour of later tanks, and they were generally replaced by shoulder-fired weapons such as the BAZOOKA, PIAT and PANZERFAUST.

Anti-tank Guns

Artillery weapons designed primarily for the attack of armoured vehicles. As a result they had limited elevation but wide traversing ability to enable the tracking of moving targets. They were usually of low profile so as to be easily concealed, and generally had semi-automatic breech mechanisms which ejected the empty cartridge case during the recoil movement and automatically closed the breech as soon as they were re-loaded.

At the outbreak of war most countries were using weapons of 37–40mm calibre, firing steel projectiles of about 2.2lb (1kg) weight which could defeat 45mm of homogeneous armour plate at a range of 1640ft (500m). The 1940 campaigns soon showed that these guns were marginal against the contemporary armour, and a fresh generation appeared in 1940–41, around 50–57mm calibre, firing a 6.6lb (3kg) shot to defeat 80mm at a range of 1640ft (500m). The adoption of thicker, and also face-hardened, armour made the second generation obsolescent by mid-1942, which led to the general adoption of weapons in the 75–90mm calibre group firing projectiles weighing 13–20lb (6–9kg) to defeat 150mm at 1640ft (500m). In addition to steel shot and shell, tungsten-cored high-velocity ammunition was developed and this increased the penetration possibilities by a considerable factor. The British 76mm 17-pounder, for

British 6pr anti-tank gun, also adopted by the US Army as their 57mm Gun M1.

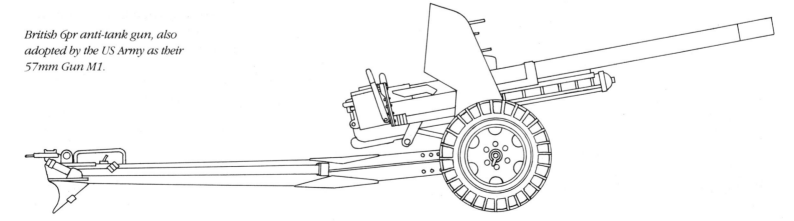

Royal Engineers prepare a string of 8 Mark V anti-tank mines ready to be pulled across the road, 1943.

example, could defeat 230mm of face-hardened plate at a range of 3280ft (1000m), striking at an angle of 60 degrees from the surface of the plate; the German 8.8cm PAK 43 could pierce 192mm of armour under the same conditions.

At the end of the war a fourth generation of "super" anti-tank guns was under development, the British 94mm 32-pounder, the German 12.8cm PAK 44 and the American 105mm T5. The PAK 44 could defeat 230mm of armour at 1000m/60° with ordinary steel shot; the other two never reached production and their performance is unknown. However, their weight (8–10 tonnes) was so great that they had become too cumbersome to man-handle in the field, and they were replaced in postwar years by recoilless guns and, later, by missiles.

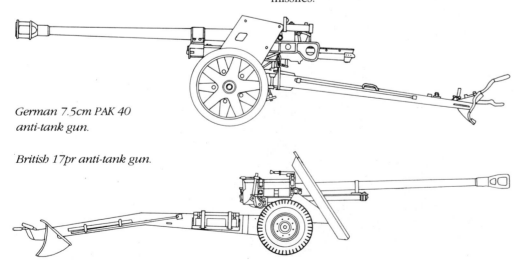

German 7.5cm PAK 40 anti-tank gun.

British 17pr anti-tank gun.

Anti-tank Mines

Anti-tank mines could be buried in the ground and detonated by the pressure of a tank passing over them. Such mines were produced and employed by all belligerents, though the German Army was perhaps the principal exponent. The anti-tank mine was a fairly simple piece of equipment, usually no more than a steel casing with 6.6–11lb (3–5kg) of high explosive and a pressure plate on top, supported by a spring which would not be affected by a man's foot, but would be easily compressed by the weight of a tank. This would detonate the charge and so damage the track and immobilize the tank, in some cases rupturing the thin floor armour and incapacitating the crew.

Anti-tank Rifles

Anti-tank rifles were issued to infantry from about 1935 onwards for the purpose of attacking armoured vehicles. As the name implies they were no more than extremely powerful rifles, delivering armour-piercing bullets at velocities sufficient to allow them to penetrate up to 12-15mm of armour at ranges of up to about 656ft (200m). In general, the calibre was greater than a conventional rifle; the British Boys rifle was of .55in (14mm) and several armies adopted 20mm weapons. The German Army used a different approach, retaining the standard 7.92mm rifle calibre but propelling the bullet with a greatly over-sized cartridge to produce high velocity. By 1942 these weapons were no longer effective against tanks except at suicidally short ranges and they were rapidly superseded by SHAPED-CHARGE weapons.

Anton

German occupation of southern France, November 1942. Initially known as *Attila*.

Antonescu, Marshal Ion (1886–1946)

Romanian Minister of War from 1932 to 1940, he went on to become Premier. As Premier, he seized power, forcing the abdication of King Carol, restoring Carol's son Michael to the throne, and in 1941 allying Romania with Germany against the Soviet Union. Arrested in August 1944 on King MICHAEL's orders, he was subsequently executed in BUCHAREST.

Antonov A7 (USSR)

A high-wing monoplane glider, the Antonov was designed to win a contest for a "partisan transport glider" in 1940. Some 400 were built but there is little record of their use. *Span* 62.25ft (18.99m); towed by TUPOLEV SB-2 or ILYUSHIN DB-3.

Antwerp, Belgium, 1944

Liberated by the British 11th Armoured Division on 4 September 1944. It was essential that its largely undamaged port facilities should be brought into use as quickly as possible to ease the logistic burden of hauling supplies all the way from northern France to the front line. Unfortunately, this proved impossible while General von Zangen's German 15th Army held both banks of the SCHELDT estuary from Antwerp to the sea and a series of major operations had to be mounted by Canadian 1st Army to clear them of the enemy. By early November these had been brought to a successful conclusion and minesweeping commenced. On 28 November the first heavy cargoes reached Antwerp and by mid-December the port was handling 19,000 tons a day. See also BEVELAND PENINSULA, BRESKENS POCKET, SCHELDT and WALCHEREN.

Anvil

Allied plan for the invasion of southern France. Executed as DRAGOON.

ANZAC Australian and New Zealand Army Corps.

Anzio, Italy, 1944

The amphibious operation at Anzio, codenamed SHINGLE, was an imaginative attempt to outflank the GUSTAV LINE and the deadlocked fighting at CASSINO by landing a force on the west coast of Italy behind German lines. The idea was proposed by CHURCHILL. The assault force, commanded by Major-General John P. LUCAS and consisting initially of the British 1st and US 3rd Infantry Divisions, landed on 22 January and achieved complete surprise. Instead of exploiting this success and capturing the ALBAN HILLS inland, thereby severing German communications between Rome and Cassino, Lucas chose to consolidate his beach-head, which was 15 miles wide and seven deep. The time lost enabled KESSELRING to concentrate his forces, and between 3 and 10 February a series of ferocious counter-attacks were launched against the British 1st Infantry Division by

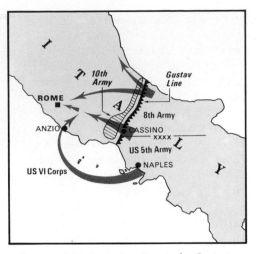

Relation of the Anzio landing to the Gustav Line.

General MACKENSEN's 14th Army, forcing it back from Campoleone to CARROCETO and the APRILIA FACTORY. Reinforcement divisions began reaching the beach-head, but between 16 and 20 February the Germans renewed their counter-attacks and were only halted after bitter fighting. On 23 February Lucas was

The Anzio Beach-head: Operation Shingle *and the German counter-attack, January–February 1944.*

German prisoners and collaborators confined in a cage at the Antwerp zoo, September 1944.

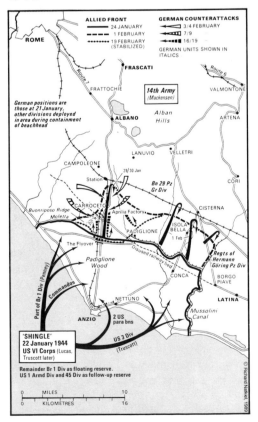

replaced as commander of US VI Corps by Major-General Lucien K. TRUSCOTT. Further German attacks were mounted between 29 February and 2 March but were contained by concentrated artillery fire and massive air attacks. During the next three months the Anzio beach-head came to resemble a World War I battlefield. On 23 May, VI Corps commenced break-out operations as part of the Allied drive which culminated in the capture of ROME. At Anzio each side sustained approximately 30,000 casualties.

Anzio Annie

The name given by Allied troops to a German 21cm K5(E) railway gun which shelled the ANZIO beach-head from long range. It is reputed to have been kept inside a tunnel when not firing, to protect it from Allied air attack. It was later captured at Civitavecchia and is now an exhibit at Aberdeen Proving Ground, Maryland.

Aoba Class Cruisers (Jap)

Displacement 8300 tons; *dimensions* 602ft 6in×51ft 9in (183.6×15.8m); mean draught 18ft 6in (5.7m); *machinery* 4-shaft geared turbines producing shp 108,456; *speed* 34.5 knots; *protection* deck 2in; turrets 5in; *armament* 6×8in (3×2); 4×4.7in AA (4×1); 8×25mm AA (4×2); 4×13mm AA (2×2); 8×24in torpedo tubes (2×4); *aircraft* 1 (1 catapult); *complement* 773; *number in class* 2, launched 1926.

AOC Air Officer Commanding (UK).

AOP Air Observation Post (UK).

Aosta, Duke Amadeo of (1898–1942)

A cousin of KING VICTOR EMMANUEL, a General of the Italian Air Force and Viceroy of ETHIOPIA. On 3 August 1940 he invaded British Somaliland, but was comprehensively defeated in the British counter offensive launched in January 1941. Aosta surrendered with 18,000 troops at Amba Alagi on 16 May 1941. He died in captivity in Kenya in 1942.

Apamama Atoll, Gilbert Islands, Central Pacific, 1943

Lying approximately 100 miles south-east of TARAWA, Apamama was known to be lightly held by the Japanese and had a potential as an air base. The USMC Reconnaissance Company of Major-General Holland M. SMITH's V

Arab Legion cavalry, Transjordan, July 1940.

Amphibious Corps was landed by submarine on 21 November. The majority of the 22-strong garrison committed suicide rather than surrender.

Aphrodite

German electronic countermeasure intended to foil Allied anti-submarine aircraft. It consisted of a buoy to which was attached a gas-filled balloon on about 99ft (30m) of wire, and with a number of metal foil reflectors. When released by a U-boat these would reflect RADAR signals and thus attract attention while the submarine submerged and slipped away. In practice the device was never seen by AIRBORNE RADAR, only by surface ships, and in consequence was of little use.

APO Army Post Office.

Apostle I

Allied occupation of NORWAY, 10 May 1945.

Aprilia Factory, Anzio, 1944

Model farming community established by Mussolini near CARROCETO and the scene of bitter fighting during German counter-attacks on the ANZIO beach-head.

Aquila – Aircraft Carrier (Italy)

Originally the passenger liner *Roma*. Conversion began at Genoa in July 1941, and when Italy surrendered in September 1943 *Aquila* was almost ready for sea trials. She fell into German hands but was damaged by bombs on 16 June 1944 and by a joint British/Italian human torpedo attack on 19 April 1945, after which she was scuttled. *Aquila* displaced

23,500 tons and had a maximum speed of 30 knots. Had she become operational she would have carried 36 aircraft. Armament would have consisted of 8×5.3in low angle, 12×2.56in AA, 22×20m AA; complement would have been 1430.

Arab Legion

Raised in 1920 for internal security duties in the British mandated territory then known as Transjordan, the Arab Legion was commanded by British officers. In 1931 its strength of 750 was supplemented by the addition of a camel-mounted Desert Patrol, commanded by the then Major (later Lieutenant-General Sir John) Glubb. In 1939 Glubb was appointed the Legion's commanding officer, setting the high standards which are maintained today by the Royal Jordanian Army. The Legion saw active service in IRAQ and SYRIA 1941–42. Despite its nickname of "Glubb's Girls", awarded because of the long hair worn by its members, the Legion was highly respected for its efficiency.

Arado Aircraft (Ger)

Arado Ar 96B A two-seat low-wing monoplane used as an advanced trainer, it was adopted by the Luftwaffe as the standard training aircraft in 1940. Two versions were built, one for primary and one for advanced work, which differed only in the instrumentation and equipment. *Span* 36ft (10.98m); *engine* 450hp in-line; *speed* 210mph (338kph).
Arado Ar 196 A twin-float low-wing monoplane used for reconnaissance and anti-submarine work by the German Navy and normally carried by German warships for

catapult launching. It was also used for coastal patrolling and light bombing and saw action in almost all Western sea areas. A variant was the Ar 196V which used a single float. *Span* 41ft (12.5m); *engine* 900hp radial; *crew* 2; *armament* 2 20mm cannon, 2 7.92mm machine guns, 220lb (100kg) of bombs; *speed* 193mph (310kph).

Arado Ar 232 The Ar 232 was a high-wing monoplane transport aircraft; though a sound design only 40 were built, since there were ample numbers of smaller transport aircraft and the large capacity of the Ar 232 was rarely needed. There were two distinct models, the Ar 232 with twin engines and the Ar 232B with four engines and a larger wing span. *Span* (Ar 232) 104.3ft (31.8m), (Ar 232B) 110ft (33.55m); *engines* (Ar 232) 2 2000hp radial, (Ar 232B) 4 690hp radial; *crew* 4; *payload* 11,020lb (5000kg); *speed* 211mph (339.5kph).

Arado Ar 234 Known as the Blitz (Lightning), this was the world's first jet-engined bomber, a high-wing monoplane with two engines and tricycle undercarriage. It first flew in June 1943 and went into production in June 1944. The single-seat cockpit was pressurized, and an autopilot and ejection seat were fitted. The Ar 234 was extensively used on the Western Front in 1944–45, notably in the Battle of the BULGE and against the REMAGEN bridge over the Rhine. A late variant model was the Ar 234C which had four jet engines, though few of these were built. *Span* 46.25ft (14.1m); *engines* 2 1980lb (898kg)/st turbojet; *armament* 2 20mm cannon; *speed* 461mph (742kph).

Arado Ar 240 A twin-engined midwing monoplane intended as a high-altitude reconnaissance, fighter and dive-bomber, the Ar 240 first flew in 1940 but subsequent development was hampered by changes in policy and specification so that only 15 were ever built. A variant was the Ar 440 which used different engines. *Span* 54.5ft (16.6m); *crew* 2; *engines* 2 1750hp in-line; *speed* 454mph (730kph).

Arakan, Burma, 1943–45

A coastal region of great strategic significance from which it was possible to gain access to central Burma. Three British offensives were mounted in the area, the first of which began in December 1942 with an advance down the Mayu Peninsula, the intention being to restore confidence after the defeats of the previous year by securing limited objectives. After halting the advance at DONBAIK the Japanese

counter-attacked in March and, infiltrating through the jungle, induced the British into a hasty withdrawal by threatening their communications. The second offensive, mounted by XV Corps (Lieutenant-General A. F. P. Christison) in December 1943, also involved an advance down the Mayu Peninsula towards AKYAB but was halted by determined resistance shortly after MAUNGDAW had been taken on 9 January 1944. The Japanese again reacted by attempting to sever British communications but were themselves surrounded in February when General SLIM committed fresh formations to the offensive, and sustained a severe defeat during the Battle of the ADMIN BOX. During this period the arrival of Spitfire fighters also deprived the Japanese of the air superiority they had hitherto enjoyed in this theatre. It was now the turn of the Japanese to rush reinforcements into the area and heavy fighting continued until the monsoon broke in May. The British not only retained their gains but were also able to release the 5th and 7th Indian Divisions for use on the Central Front, where the Japanese offensive against IMPHAL and KOHIMA had begun. The third Arakan offensive began in December 1944 and was again mounted by XV Corps, consisting of a renewed advance down the Mayu Peninsula, accompanied by amphibious landings at AKYAB, Kangaw, Myebon, RAMREE ISLAND (January 1945), Cheduba Island and Ruywa (February 1945). General Christison's corps crowned this series of achievements by taking RANGOON on 3 May, following an amphibious landing the previous day.

Araki, Gen Sadao (1877–1966)

Araki served as Japanese War Minister from 1931 to 1934, and as Minister of Education 1938–39. He was a supporter of larger military appropriations and a member of the "Strike North" school which advocated expansion northward in conflict with the USSR. He was sentenced to life imprisonment by the International Military Tribunal in 1948 but released on grounds of ill-health in 1955.

Arcadia Conference

A meeting between CHURCHILL and ROOSEVELT in Washington DC, 22 December 1941 to 7 January 1942. The principal conclusions from this conference were first to confirm the primacy of Germany as the main opponent, and secondly to establish the Combined

Chiefs of Staff as the directing authority for the entire Allied military effort.

Archangel, Soviet Union, 1941–45

A major port on the White Sea and one of the termini of the Allied ARCTIC CONVOYS to Russia. The principal disadvantage of this destination was that it was closed by ice for up to five months of the year, whereas MURMANSK was not.

Archer Class Escort Carriers (UK)

All based on mercantile hulls. *Archer* was driven by four diesel motors instead of the usual two and was a knot faster. *Avenger* formed part of the escort of the important CONVOY PQ-18; she was torpedoed and sunk by *U-155* west of Gibraltar on 15 November 1942. *Displacement* 8200 tons; *dimensions* 492ft 3in × 66ft 3in (150 × 20m); mean draught 23ft 3in (7m); *machinery* 1-shaft diesel motor producing bhp 8500; *speed* 16.5 knots; *armament* 3 × 4in AA (3 × 1); 15 × 20mm AA (4 × 2 and 7 × 1); *aircraft* 15 (max); *complement* 555; *number in class* 5, launched 1939–41.

Archer – Tank Destroyer (UK)

The Archer consisted of the hull and chassis of the VALENTINE tank on which a 17-pdr gun was mounted in a fixed, open-topped superstructure, pointing over the vehicle's rear. One problem associated with this arrangement was that the vehicle had to be reversed into its firing position; a second was the limited degree of traverse available, amounting to only 11 degrees either side of the centreline; and a third was that the weapon recoiled directly over the driver's seat. Nevertheless, following its introduction in the autumn of

Archer tank destroyer.

Corvette HMS Honeysuckle *moored alongside HMS* Trumpeter, *Murmansk 1945.*

1944, the vehicle was popular with its crews and rendered good service in Italy and North-West Europe. The Archer was manned by a crew of four. It remained in service with the British Army for some years after the war and saw further action with the Egyptian Army during its 1956 war with Israel. A total of 665 were built by Vickers.

Archimede Class Submarines (Italy)

Both members of this class were lost as a result of surface gun actions. *Galileo Galilei* surrendered after being damaged in a duel with the trawler HMS *Moonstone* in the Red Sea on 19 June 1940 and was taken into British service as *X.2. Ferraris* was scuttled to prevent capture after an engagement with the escort destroyer HMS *Lamerton* and aircraft in the North Atlantic on 25 October 1941. *Displacement* 880 tons (985/1259 tons normal); *dimensions* 231ft 3in×22ft 6in (70.5×6.8m); *machinery* 2-shaft diesel/electric motors hp 3000/1300; *speed* 17/8.5 knots; *armament* 2×3ft 9in; 2×13.2mm AA; 8×21in torpedo tubes and 16 torpedoes; *complement* 55; *number in class* 2, launched 1934.

Arctic Convoys

Following HITLER's invasion of Russia in June 1941, the UK, followed by the USA after its entry into the war, made every effort not only to make good the horrendous loss of equip-ment sustained during the German onslaught, but also to keep Russia supplied with weapons and raw materials throughout the war. This meant despatching convoys around North Cape to Murmansk and Archangel, negotiating some of the worst sea and weather conditions in the world. In winter, the Polar pack-ice line advanced south, forcing convoys to pass south of Bear Island and close to the Luftwaffe's northern bases. In summer the pack ice retreated, enabling convoys to pass north of Bear Island, but the perpetual daylight exposed ships to attack.

The convoys commenced in August 1941, initially without serious opposition, but early in 1942 attacks by U-boats and Luftwaffe anti-shipping squadrons began to increase, while the threat from heavy surface warships based in Norway was always present. Allied resources were stretched by the Battle of the ATLANTIC and in the Mediterranean, and had German inter-service co-operation been greater it is probable that the combined efforts of their surface units, the U-boat arm and the Luftwaffe could have severed this lifeline. In July 1942, assisted by a faulty British appreciation of the situation, the Germans did succeed in destroying two-thirds of CONVOY PQ-17. Further co-operation to destroy con-voys was inhibited by Hitler's concern for the safety of his heavy surface ships. When aircraft carriers began providing air cover for convoys

in September 1942 the Luftwaffe began to sustain serious losses and in November that year many of its anti-shipping squadrons were transferred south to counter the Allied inva-sion of French North Africa. A foray by Ger-man surface units against Convoy JW-51B the following month ended in failure and led to the withdrawal of most of them into the Baltic. Following the loss of the *Scharnhorst* a year later, the *Tirpitz* alone remained in northern Norwegian waters, until she was finally sunk in November 1944. The U-boat threat con-tinued unabated but was contained by improved Allied techniques. Even so, the Arc-tic Convoys remained the most demanding of all Allied naval operations in World War II. By this means the Soviet armies received thousands of tanks and aircraft as well as the 356,000 motor trucks, 50,000 jeeps, 1500 loco-motives and 9800 freight cars which provided the logistic back-up essential for their Eastern Front victories of 1943–45. See also BARENTS SEA, CONVOY PQ-17, CONVOY PQ-18, NORTH CAPE, and TIRPITZ.

Ardeer Aggie

The Ardeer Aggie was a British experimental 10in (254mm) calibre recoilless gun devel-oped by Imperial Chemical Industries at their Ardeer factory. It fired a 10in shell and dis-charged an equivalent weight of sand rearwards to obtain recoillessness. Intended to arm tanks for the attack of fortifications in the Atlantic Wall, the design was abandoned in 1944 for reasons of impracticality.

Ardennes, Europe, 1940 and 1944

A range of rolling, heavily wooded hills and steep-sided valleys in eastern Belgium and Luxembourg, mistakenly believed to be tank-proof by the French General Staff during the interwar years, a view which was not shared by senior German officers. The area was used as a springboard for the SICHELSCHNITT drive of May 1940 and again for the abortive German thrust towards ANTWERP in December 1944. See also FRANCE, BELGIUM and HOLLAND 1940 and Battle of the BULGE.

Area Bombing

Area bombing was a system of aerial bom-bardment resorted to by the Allies, particu-larly the British, in 1942. It simply meant that bombers would drop bombs on designated areas rather than on specific targets within those areas. The tactic was based on the assumption that by drenching a given area with bombs any war production plant or military installations within it would be damaged and at the same time civilian morale would suffer. The policy was adopted because the bomb-aiming techniques of the time could not guarantee hitting precise targets.

It is questionable whether the area bombing campaign achieved results in any way commensurate with the effort and investment involved; German industry proved more resilient than anticipated. After initial setbacks and production losses, decentralization programmes soon allowed output to be resumed and even increased. Whilst civilian suffering, hardship and loss of life were considerable, the morale effect proved to be miscalculated.

Arethusa Class Cruisers (UK)

Displacement 5270 tons; *dimensions* 506×51ft (154×15.5m); mean draught 13ft (3.96m); *machinery* 4-shaft geared turbines producing shp 64,000; *speed* 32.25 knots; *protection* main belt 2in; deck 2in; turrets 1in; DCT 1in; *armament* 6×6in (3×2); 8×4in AA (4×2); 8×2-pdr AA (2×4); 8×0.5in (2×4); 6×21in (2×3) torpedo tubes; *aircraft* 1; *complement* 450; *number in class* 4, launched 1934–36.

Argenta Gap, Italy, 1945

A neck of land lying between Lake Comacchio and the marshes of the Massa Lombarda, carrying a road and railway north to Ferrara along the only strip of firm ground in the area. Despite having been strengthened during the winter months the German defences were overwhelmed in April by Lieutenant-General Charles Keightley's British V Corps using specialized armour, including LVTs which lifted the 56th Division and No. 9 Commando across the lake to carry out assault landings in the enemy's rear, these amphibious operations being codenamed IMPACT PLAIN (11 April) and IMPACT ROYAL (13 April). The 6th Armoured Division passed through and out into open country in what was to be the final advance of the war in Italy.

Argentan, France, 1944

A town on the upper reaches of the Orne River which marked the southern shoulder of the FALAISE GAP in August 1944. MONTGOMERY ordered General Henry CRERAR's Canadian 1st Army to advance south and capture first

Falaise then Argentan, thus closing the exit from the gap through which the remnants of the German armies in western France were streaming. However, the Canadians were held up by determined opposition and had not taken Falaise when Major-General Wade E. Haislip's US XV Corps from PATTON's 3rd Army arrived in the vicinity of Argentan on 13 August, having driven north from Le Mans specifically to close the trap. Haislip received orders from BRADLEY via Patton to hold his ground rather than take Argentan and the gap remained open until 19 August. Bradley wished to avoid a head-on clash between the leading elements of the two Allied army groups and was waiting for Montgomery to authorize the entry of American troops into 21st Army Group's area. For his part, Montgomery believed that the Canadians should close the gap but underestimated the desperate nature of the German resistance they were facing.

Argonaut, USS – Minelaying Submarine

Argonaut was the largest submarine to serve with the US Navy until the nuclear-powered *Triton* was launched in 1958. She was also its only minelaying submarine but was converted to a submarine transport immediately after PEARL HARBOR. She was sunk by Japanese destroyers off RABAUL on 10 January 1943. *Displacement* 2710/4080 tons; *dimensions* 381×34ft (116×10.3m); *machinery* 2-shaft diesels producing shp 3175/2400; *speed* 15/8 knots; *armament* 2×6in; 4×21in torpedo tubes (bow); 80 mines; *complement* 89; *launched* 1927.

Argonauta Class Submarines (Italy)

Displacement 611 tons (650/810 tons normal); *dimensions* 210ft 9in×18ft 9in (64×5.7m); *machinery* 2-shaft diesel/electric motors hp 1200/800; *speed* 14/8 knots; *armament* 1×4in; 2×13.2mm AA; 6×21in torpedo tubes and 12 torpedoes; *complement* 44; *number in class* 7, launched 1931–32.

Argument

Allied air offensive aimed at destroying Germany's war industry, 1944.

Argus, HMS – Aircraft Carrier

Argus was based on the hull of the merchant vessel *Conte Rosso*, launched in 1917. She served with the Mediterranean Fleet 1939–40,

the Home Fleet 1940–41, Force H during 1942, and again with the Home Fleet 1943–44. In 1944 she was placed in reserve as an accommodation ship. *Displacement* 22,600 tons; *dimensions* 667ft×92ft 9in (203.3×28.2m); mean draught 24ft (7.3m); *machinery* 4-shaft geared turbines producing shp 50,000; *speed* 24 knots; *protection* main belt 4–7in; deck 1–4in; *armament* 9×6in; 4×4in AA; 8×2-pdr AA; *aircraft* 21; *complement* 748.

Arisaka Rifle

The standard rifle of the Japanese forces, the Arisaka rifle was originally developed in 1897 by a commission under Colonel Arisaka. It was basically a MAUSER design with a unique bolt-action. The first weapons were the Meiji 30th Year rifle and 30th Year carbine. In 1905 the design was improved by adopting a bolt closer to Mauser's pattern and the 38th Year rifle and carbine were introduced. In 1911 came the 44th Year carbine for artillery and cavalry. All these weapons were in 6.5mm calibre, but experience in the Sino-Japanese actions in Manchuria in the 1930s led to the adoption of a 7.7mm bullet in 1939. The Type 99 rifle of that year was little more than a 38th Year rifle in 7.7mm calibre, though somewhat shorter than the earlier weapon.

Arizona, USS – Pennsylvania Class Battleship

Sunk at her berth during the Japanese attack on PEARL HARBOR, the *Arizona* was never salvaged and remains a memorial to all American servicemen who died on 7 December 1941.

Ark – Armoured Ramp Carrier (UK)

The Ark was conceived as a tracked armoured vehicle, fitted with quick-release folding ramps fore and aft, which could be driven bodily into an anti-tank ditch or against a sea wall, thereby enabling other vehicles to drive over it; in the case of particularly deep anti-tank ditches the causeway could be constructed by driving one Ark on top of another. Turretless SHERMAN and CHURCHILL tanks were both evaluated in this role and the latter was found to be the more suitable. The Churchill Ark I could span 28 feet (8.5m) and was fitted with trackways, a total of 50 being built. The Churchill Ark II (UK Pattern) had longer ramps and could span 47.5 feet (14.5m), the Churchill Ark II (Italian Pattern) was very similar but lacked trackways. The Churchill

Ark, based on Churchill chassis.

Ark Royal, HMS – Aircraft Carrier

In 1939 *Ark Royal* was despatched to the South Atlantic during the hunt for the ADMIRAL GRAF SPEE. She then served with the Home and Mediterranean Fleets during 1940–41 and took part in the destruction of the BISMARCK. In the Mediterranean she provided air cover for convoys and reinforced the fighter strength of MALTA with deliveries of aircraft. *Ark Royal* became a particular target of the Axis propaganda apparatus, which prematurely claimed her destruction on several occasions. She was torpedoed by *U-81* off GIBRALTAR on 13 November 1941 and sank under tow the following day. *Launched* 13 April 1937; *displacement* 22,000 tons; *dimensions* 800ft×94ft 9in (243.8×28.8m); mean draught 22ft 9in (6.9m); *machinery* 3-shaft geared turbines with shp 80,000, *speed* 30.75 knots; protection main belt 4.5in; deck 2.5–3in; *armament* 16×4.5in AA (8×2); 48×2-pdr AA (6×8); 32×0.5in mg (8×4); *aircraft* 72; *complement* 1575.

Great Eastern was a super-Ark capable of spanning 60 feet (18.3m), the forward ramp being propelled across the obstruction by batteries of 3-inch rockets, but this version was never used operationally. The Arks entered service in 1944 and were extensively employed in France, North-West Europe and Italy.

belt 11in; turrets 12in; *armament* 12×12in (6×2); 16×5in; 8×3in AA; *aircraft* 3; *complement* 1650.

A destroyer takes off survivors from the sinking Ark Royal, *November 1941.*

Arkansas, USS – Battleship

Arkansas was launched in 1911 and served with the Grand Fleet 1917–18. She was modernised 1925–27. During World War II she served in the Atlantic 1941–44 and formed part of the bombardment force for the Allied invasion of NORMANDY. She then supported the invasion of southern France before transferring to the Pacific, where she was engaged at IWO JIMA and OKINAWA in 1945. *Displacement* 26,100 tons; *dimensions* 562ft×106ft 3in (171.3×32.3m); mean draught 26ft (7.9m); *machinery* 4-shaft geared turbines producing shp 28,000; *speed* 21 knots; *protection* main

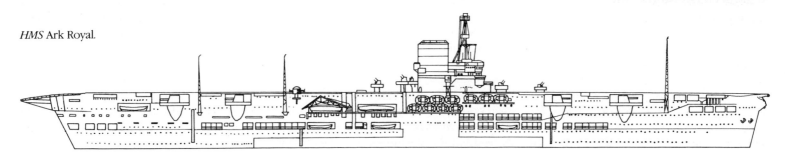

HMS Ark Royal.

Armed Merchant Cruisers

Ocean going merchant vessels requisitioned for war service and armed offensively. The Royal Navy employed a total of 60 ships of this type, all former passenger liners with twin screws and a minimum speed of 15 knots, typical armament being six or eight 6-inch guns, two 3-inch anti-aircraft guns and a number of lighter automatic AA weapons. In British service armed merchant cruisers generally served as convoy escorts but were too vulnerable and their losses were heavy. By the spring of 1944 their use had been discontinued and many were converted to other roles. The German Navy used a variety of specially converted, fast and heavily armed vessels which could alter their appearance. These were employed as commerce raiders and often produced valuable results, but five of the nine active German armed merchant cruisers were sunk and after March 1943 no further operations of this type were mounted. The Imperial Japanese Navy also employed a small number of armed merchant cruisers as commerce raiders in the Indian Ocean, with disappointing results. See also ATLANTIS, BENGAL, JERVIS BAY, KORMORAN and RAWALPINDI.

Armoured Divisions

The usual order of battle consisted of divisional headquarters, an armoured brigade, an armoured reconnaissance battalion, a motorized infantry brigade, a motorized artillery regiment, an anti-tank battalion, an anti-aircraft battalion, an engineer battalion and divisional service units. Organization varied slightly between armies but by 1942 it was generally accepted that the tank element should be reduced to provide a better balance with the divisional infantry and artillery assets. The American armoured divisions also contained three COMBAT COMMAND headquarters which were capable of controlling detached BATTLE GROUPS and were thus extremely flexible organizations.

Armoured Division, 79th

Formed as a conventional armoured division under Major-General P. C. S. HOBART in October 1942. In April 1943 Hobart was ordered to convert the division to a specialist assault formation and to develop the appropriate armoured vehicles and techniques necessary for this task, with particular reference for the forthcoming invasion of Western Europe, for which the DIEPPE raid provided many lessons. The composition of the division varied but included several armoured brigades each of which specialized in the use of AVRES, CANAL DEFENCE LIGHTS, CRABS, CROCODILES, DD SHERMANS, KANGAROOS or LVTS, these vehicles being known collectively to the rest of the British Army as "Hobo's Funnies". The division was unique and functioned in the manner of a plant-hire corporation, assessing the operational requirements of other formations and then attaching the appropriate specialist teams from its various brigades; once an operation had been completed the teams returned to divisional control. The 79th Armoured Division played a major role in the D-DAY landings on the British sector, the capture of the Channel ports, the clearance of the Scheldt and the crossing of the Rhine, but its teams also took part in many more actions in NORMANDY and North-West Europe.

Armour Piercing Ammunition

A general term for ammunition designed to defeat armoured vehicles or ships or armour carried in aircraft. In the case of small arms (machine guns) it usually consisted of a hard steel core inside a softer metal jacket, capable of penetrating 12–15mm of homogeneous steel armour at a range of 3280ft (100m). In artillery calibres the design became more involved as the war progressed. The initial pattern was a hardened steel shot or shell, the latter having a very small amount of explosive in a base cavity, fuzed so as to detonate after the shell had passed through the armour. In general, shot was used by British artillery, shell by other countries. Plain steel shot was found to disintegrate on impact when the striking velocity was greater than about 2700ft per second (825m per second), and a soft steel "penetrating cap" was added; this distributed the impact stress more evenly, and, at the velocity involved, the cap acted as a lubricant to facilitate penetration. Capped shot was found to be of particular value when attacking face-hardened armour, which was introduced in about 1941.

In order to allow even greater striking velocities, the use of tungsten carbide was adopted; this, being heavier than steel, had to be made in the form of a core held within a lightweight body so as to produce a projectile sufficiently light in weight to allow the desired high velocity to be reached. Using cored shot and high velocities (3280ft (1000m) per second and above) virtually doubled the penetrative power of artillery. There were ballistic drawbacks to this design, which led to the adoption of squeeze-bore and discarding sabot projectiles. In the former the surrounding light metal sheath was squeezed down in calibre by firing through a tapered gun barrel; in the latter the light sheath was separated from the core and discarded during flight. In both cases the kinetic energy was concentrated into a small diameter which gave a further increase in performance.

Alternative methods of defeating armour were achieved by using high explosives in special forms; the shaped charge used an explosive mass with its face hollowed out so as to "focus" the explosive blast effect into a small area and thus penetrate armour, while the "squash-head" (known during the war years as "Wall-buster") deposited a poultice of plastic explosive which set up destructive vibrations in the target material. Armour-piercing aerial bombs and naval shells relied entirely upon kinetic energy and hard-pointed bodies to achieve penetration, since at the velocities and ranges involved there was no point in adopting the more elaborate solutions.

Armstrong-Whitworth Aircraft (UK)

Armstrong-Whitworth Albemarle Produced from 1941 to 1944, this was originally intended as a bomber and carefully designed to use the minimum of scarce light alloys. It was not a success in the bombing role, but became a general transport and glider tug, and was employed in the airborne landings in Sicily, Normandy and Arnhem. It was the first British military aircraft to use a tricycle undercarriage. *Span* 77ft (23.5m); *crew* 4; *engines* 2 1590hp radial; *armament* (in bomber version only) 6 machine guns; *speed* 265mph (426kph).

Armstrong-Whitworth Whitley This all-metal monoplane was the first British bomber to fly over Berlin and the first to bomb both Germany and Italy. Designed in 1934 and in production from 1937 to 1943, it was used as a night bomber, leaflet dropper, trainer, and anti-submarine and reconnaissance aircraft, as well as being employed as a glider tug and paratroop transport in training roles. There were several variant models, differing in engines and equipment. *Span* 84ft (25.6m); *engines* (typically) 2 1075hp in-line; *crew* 5; *armament* 5 machine guns, 7000lb (3175kg) of bombs; *speed* 228mph (367kph).

Army

A major formation consisting of army head-quarters, army troops at the personal disposal of the army commander, and one or more CORPS.

The German Army grouped its Panzer corps into Panzer armies and the Soviet Army formed tank armies from its tank and mechanized corps, but the British and American armies did not favour such groupings. An army was normally, but by no means invariably, the command of a full General.

Army, British 1st

An Allied army containing American and French elements which served in Algeria and Tunisia 1942–43.

Army, British 2nd

Served NORMANDY and North-West Europe 1944–45.

Army, British 8th

Formed in 1941 and fought throughout the North African, Sicilian and Italian campaigns.

Army, British 14th

Formed in October 1943, serving in north-eastern India and BURMA.

Army, Canadian 1st

Served in NORMANDY and North-West Europe 1944–45.

Army, French 1st

Fought on the right flank of the BRITISH EXPEDITIONARY FORCE during the 1940 campaign in the West and was trapped in Belgium by the German thrust to the Channel coast. Reformed in 1944 and served on the southern flank of the Western Front, participating in the final Allied advance into Germany.

Army, German 1st

Fought in France in 1940 and remained there on occupation duties until 1944, when it withdrew to Germany. It surrendered in Bavaria, May 1945.

Army, German 4th

Served in POLAND 1939 and in the West 1940. From 1941 onwards it fought on the Eastern Front. The Army was severely mauled during the Soviet summer offensive of 1944 and its remnants were destroyed in East Prussia the following year.

Army, German 6th

Originally raised as the 10th Army and as such fought in POLAND in 1939. It was redesignated 6th Army early in 1940 and in May of that year served in Belgium. It then fought on the Eastern Front from 1941 until forced to surrender at STALINGRAD in February 1943. A new 6th Army was formed shortly after and served on the Eastern Front for the rest of the war.

Army, German 7th

Took part in the 1940 campaign in the West and performed occupation duties in France until 1944. It fought in NORMANDY and the Battle of the BULGE before surrendering to US troops in Czechoslovakia in May 1945.

Army, German 8th

Formed in Poland 1939 but disbanded the following year. Reformed July 1943 and served on the southern sector of the Eastern Front for the remainder of the war.

Army, German 9th

Formed in 1940 and took part in the campaign in the West. Served on the central sector of the Eastern Front from 1941 onwards and in 1945 was destroyed during the Soviet drive on BERLIN.

Army, German 10th

Formed in Poland 1939 but redesignated 6TH Army early 1940. Reformed in August 1943 and served in Italy for the remainder of the war.

Army, German 11th

Formed in late 1940 and served on the southern sector of the Eastern Front 1941–42, including the siege of SEVASTOPOL. In December 1942 the army was redesignated Army Group Don and took part in the abortive STALINGRAD relief operations. An 11th Army was reformed in April 1945 following the encirclement of the RUHR but was soon overwhelmed by the advance of the Western Allies.

Army, German 12th

Formed in the spring of 1940 and participated in the campaign in the West. In 1941 it saw further active service in the Balkans where it remained on occupation duties, being expanded to Army Group E during the winter of 1942–43. A 12th Army was reformed in the HARZ MOUNTAINS in April 1945 but surrendered the following month.

Army, German 14th

Existed briefly in 1939. Reformed in northern Italy autumn 1943 and committed at ANZIO February 1944. Remained in Italy for the remainder of the war.

Army, German 15th

Formed in late 1940 as an occupation force, northern France and Belgium. Retreated into Holland September 1944 and was then transferred to the AACHEN sector. The Army was destroyed in the RUHR Pocket April 1945. See also ARMY, GERMAN 25TH.

Army, German 16th

Formed in 1940 and took part in the campaign in the West. Served on the northern sector of the Eastern Front 1941–45.

Army, German 17th

Formed in late 1940 and served on the southern sector of the Eastern Front 1941–45, including the CAUCASUS and CRIMEA.

Army, German 18th

Formed in the spring of 1940 and took part in the campaign in the West, capturing PARIS. Served on the Eastern Front 1941–45, including the siege of LENINGRAD.

Army, German 19th

Formed in February 1943 as occupation troops in former Vichy France. Withdrew northwards into Germany August 1944 and was largely destroyed in the Black Forest region the following year.

Army, German 20th Mountain

Formed as the Army of Lapland during the winter of 1941–42 and redesignated 20th Mountain Army in 1942. Served on the MURMANSK sector 1941–44 and withdrew into northern Norway in autumn 1944.

Army, German 21st

Raised in the summer of 1941 from XXI Corps as the Army of Norway and was responsible for German operations on the MURMANSK sector and in Finland until absorbed by the new 20TH MOUNTAIN ARMY in late 1944. A new 21st Army was raised north of BERLIN in April 1945 but surrendered on 2 May.

Army, German 24th
Raised in the Tyrol in April 1945 in an abortive attempt to prevent an Allied drive from Italy into Austria.

Army, German 25th
Formed in Holland in late 1944 following the departure of 15TH ARMY HQ to the AACHEN sector of the Western Front. Fought in Holland and north-west Germany 1944–45.

Army, German 1st Panzer
Formed from Panzer Group I in late 1941 and served for the remainder of the war on the Eastern Front.

Army, German 2nd Panzer
Formed from Panzer Group II in December 1941 and served on the Eastern Front until late 1943, when it was transferred to Croatia. A year later the Army returned to the Eastern Front, where it fought against the Russians in Hungary.

Army, German 3rd Panzer
Formed in late 1941 from Panzer Group III and served for the remainder of the war on the Eastern Front.

Army, German 4th Panzer
Formed in late 1941 from Panzer Group IV and served on the Eastern Front.

Army, German 5th Panzer
Formed in Tunisia December 1942 and destroyed the following May. Reformed August 1944 in NORMANDY and subsequently fought in the Battle of the BULGE. The army's remnants were destroyed in the RUHR pocket.

Army, German 6th Panzer
Formed in the autumn of 1944 and fought in the Battle of the BULGE, after which it was awarded the honorific title of SS. In 1945 the army was posted to the Eastern Front and took part in the Lake BALATON counteroffensive. It finished the war in Austria.

Army, Italian 10th
Destroyed in a series of battles December 1940–February 1941 by the British Western Desert Force (later XIII Corps). See BARDIA, BEDA FOMM, SIDI BARRANI, TOBRUK.

Army, Japanese 14th
Overran PHILIPPINE ISLANDS in 1942.

Army, Japanese 15th
Overran Thailand and BURMA in 1942, but sustained serious defeats at IMPHAL and KOHIMA in 1944 and was destroyed during the British offensive the following year.

Army, Japanese 16th
Overran the Netherlands East Indies and adjacent British possessions in 1942.

Army, Japanese 17th
Established on GUADALCANAL September 1942 but was unable to dislodge the Americans and, having itself sustained critical loss, was finally evacuated in February 1943. The army maintained garrisons elsewhere in the SOLOMON ISLANDS but these were overwhelmed one by one.

Army, Japanese 18th
Failed in its attempt to capture PORT MORESBY, Papua, in 1942 and was defeated at Buna after it had been forced to retreat across the Owen Stanley range. The army's strength was further weakened by a series of Allied amphibious operations along the northern coast of NEW GUINEA and its remnants were isolated by the HOLLANDIA operation.

Army, Japanese 23rd
Based in southern China. Elements captured HONG KONG in December 1941.

Army, Japanese 25th
Overran MALAYA and captured SINGAPORE, 1942.

Army, Japanese 28th
Tasked with the defence of the ARAKAN and southern BURMA. The Army was destroyed by a series of amphibious operations mounted by the British XV Corps, 1944–45, and most of its survivors died or were killed trying to escape across Burma to Thailand.

Army, Japanese 31st
Formed the garrison of the MARIANAS ISLANDS. See SAIPAN.

Army, Japanese 32nd
Destroyed defending OKINAWA, 1 April–22 June 1945.

Army, Japanese 33rd
Responsible for the defence of northern BURMA against the Allied armies. Virtually destroyed by the joint offensives of 1945.

Army, Japanese 35th
Responsible for the defence of the central and southern PHILIPPINE ISLANDS but subordinate to YAMASHITA's 14th Area Army. See LEYTE.

Army, Japanese Kwantung
Army group based in MANCHURIA consisting of seven armies, overwhelmed by the Soviet onslaught in August 1945.

Army, US 1st
US 1st Army was activated on 1 October 1933 and held its first field exercises in 1935. On the outbreak of war in 1939 it became involved in training and preparing for field operations, and was combined with the Eastern Defense Command in June 1941. The Army embarked for England in October 1943, where it began training for the invasion of Europe. Under the command of Lieutenant-General BRADLEY 1st Army landed on OMAHA and UTAH beaches on 6 June 1944, after which it was involved in clearing the Cherbourg peninsula and Operation COBRA. Lieutenant-General Courtney HODGES took over command in August 1944, and under his command 1st Army advanced through Belgium and Luxembourg and took AACHEN on 21 October. In November it launched an offensive, in conjunction with US 9th Army, against the RUHR River Dams. It then defended the northern sector during the Battle of the BULGE, captured Cologne and seized the REMAGEN BRIDGE across the Rhine. On 25 April 1945 scout elements of 1st Army made contact with Soviet troops at TORGAU, on the Elbe, which ended 1st Army's combat operations in Europe. Headquarters 1st Army then redeployed to the USA in preparation for operations in Japan, but the Japanese surrender cancelled these plans.

Army, US 2nd
US 2nd Army was activated in Chicago on 1 October 1933 but remained virtually a paper organization until October 1940 when it became active as a training army. It continued in this function throughout the rest of the war years, providing a constant flow of trained personnel and units.

Army, US 3rd
US 3rd Army was activated in 1933 in Fort Sam Houston, Texas, but remained as a headquarters cadre until 1939. Thereafter it became a training formation until it was sent

A toast is drunk in vodka after the historic link-up between the Red Army and US 1st Army at Torgau-on-the-Elbe.

to England early in 1944 and came under the command of Lieutenant-General PATTON. The army remained in England until early July 1944 when it moved to the COTENTIN peninsula in NORMANDY. After action in Normandy 3rd Army advanced across Northern France, Rhineland, Alsace-Lorraine, the Ardennes and into Czechoslovakia. It was also involved in the Battle of the BULGE, where it relieved BASTOGNE, afterwards resuming its attacks on the SIEGFRIED LINE. On the night of 22 March 1945, 3rd Army made the first assault crossing of the Rhine near Oppenheim, after which it pivoted south, crossed the Danube and entered Austria and Czechoslovakia, where it was when the war ended in Europe.

Army, US 4th

US 4th Army was activated at Omaha, Nebraska, in August 1932. On the outbreak of war in Europe it took on the role of training troops and formations. In March 1941 it became responsible for the defence of the US Pacific coast, including Alaska. In 1943 elements of 4th Army landed in the ALEUTIAN ISLANDS to evict the Japanese who had seized them in the spring of 1942, and the islands were secured by the end of the year. 4th Army

was then reorganized and spent the remainder of the war in a training role.

Army, US 5th

US 5th Army was organized on 5 January 1943 at Oujda, French Morocco, under the command of Lieutenant-General Mark W. CLARK. After training in North Africa, it initiated the first American assault on the mainland of Europe when it landed at SALERNO on 9 September 1943. Thereafter 5th Army fought steadily up the Italian peninsula, participating in the Naples-Foggia, ANZIO, Rome-Arno, North Apennines and Po Valley campaigns. On 16 December 1944 Lieutenant-General Lucien J. TRUSCOTT replaced General Clark as commander. On 2 May 1945 the German Army in Italy surrendered, and after a short period of occupation duty US 5th Army returned to the USA where it was inactivated at Camp Myles Standish, Massachusetts, on 2 October 1945.

Army, US 6th

US 6th Army was activated at Fort Sam Houston, Texas, on 25 January 1943, and was immediately sent to Australia where Lieutenant-General Walter KRUEGER took com-

mand. After a period of training, 6th Army entered combat in June 1943, assaulting Kiriwina and Woodlark Islands off NEW GUINEA. Thereafter the Army acted as the spearhead of MACARTHUR's "island-hopping" advance through the Southern Pacific, taking part in operations at Arawe, CAPE GLOUCESTER, the ADMIRALTY ISLANDS, Aitape, Wakde, BIAK, and Morotai among many others. Their advance ended with their capture of the PHILIPPINE ISLANDS. On 1 July 6th Army handed over control of tactical operations in the Philippines to 8th Army and began preparing for the invasion of Japan. After a short period of occupation duty in Japan, 6th Army was inactivated at Kyoto on 26 January 1946.

Army, US 7th

US 7th Army was activated on 10 July 1943, at sea aboard the Allied invasion convoy sailing for SICILY. Commanded by Lieutenant-General George S. PATTON, 7th Army took part in the Sicily assault, overran western Sicily and captured Palermo on 22 July. The conquest of the island was completed with the occupation of MESSINA on 16 August. Following this campaign 7th Army was stripped of its operational units to feed other armies, and the Headquarters returned to ALGIERS. It was fleshed out with fresh troops early in 1944 when planning for the invasion of southern France began, an operation which took place under the command of Lieutenant-General Alexander PATCH. After the landings, 7th Army drove northwards up the Rhone Valley to Montelimar, Lyon and Besançon to join the Allied forces advancing west from NORMANDY. During the winter, 7th Army crossed the Moselle and fought through the Vosges, took Strasbourg and reached the Rhine near Worms, eventually taking Heidelberg. Continuing into Bavaria, the 7th took NUREMBERG, Augsburg, DACHAU and MUNICH, moving southwards to Austria to take Innsbruck and Salzburg and BERCHTESGADEN. They eventually arrived at the Brenner Pass to make contact with the US 5th Army advancing from Italy on 4 May 1945. After the German surrender 7th Army served in the occupation forces, with headquarters at Heidelberg, where it was eventually inactivated in June 1946.

Army, US 8th

US 8th Army was activated at Memphis, Tennessee, on 10 June 1944, with its staff drawn mainly from 2nd Army. It was immediately ordered to the Pacific and arrived at HOL-LANDIA, NEW GUINEA on 4 September. Placed under the command of Lieutenant-General Robert L. EICHELBERGER, it conducted some minor operations in the Mapis-Asia islands before taking control of operations in LEYTE on 26 December 1944 as well as responsibility for operations in the islands south of LUZON. In the course of over 60 individual assaults on islands in the Pacific, the army gained the nickname of the "Amphibious Eighth". Enemy resistance ended on 15 August and 8th Army began preparing for the invasion of Japan. After the Japanese surrender it served as an occupation force in Japan until called into combat by the Korean War.

Army Group

Consisted of army group headquarters, formations at the personal disposal of the army group commander, and one or more armies. Known as Fronts in the Soviet Army.

Arnhem, Holland, 1944

City on the Neder Rijn (Lower Rhine) selected by MONTGOMERY as the final objective of Operation MARKET GARDEN, the Allied plan to secure a crossing of the Rhine in the immediate aftermath of the German collapse in NORMANDY and so shorten the war by several months. Arnhem and its vital bridge were to be taken by Major-General Roy URQUHART's British 1st Airborne Division. Simultaneously, bridges to the south (over the Rhine, Maas and the Waal) were to be seized by the US 101st Airborne Division at EINDHOVEN and Veghel, and by the US 82nd Airborne Division at Grave. The British XXX Corps, under Lieutenant-General Brian HORROCKS, was then to execute a lightning 64-mile advance along this "airborne corridor", relieving each division in turn.

On the afternoon of 17 September, 1st Airborne Division was para-dropped or airlanded west of Arnhem. Unfortunately, the two armoured divisions of the II SS Panzer Corps were refitting in the Arnhem area after their ordeal in Normandy. Under the direction of Field-Marshal Walter MODEL, they were able to contain the British in the suburb of OOSTERBEEK and establish blocking positions to the south of Arnhem, although the 2nd Battalion The Parachute Regiment, commanded by Lieutenant-Colonel (later Major-General Sir John) Frost, managed to penetrate the town and secure the northern end of the

Arnhem bridge, holding it against impossible odds for several days. Elsewhere, XXX Corps relieved the American divisions and captured the bridge at NIJMEGEN but was unable to break through the strong defensive front at Elst, some miles beyond. On 21 September Major-General Stanislaw SOSABOWSKI's Polish 1st Parachute Brigade was dropped at Driel on the south bank of the Neder Rijn, almost opposite Oosterbeek, where they were joined the following day by part of the 43rd (Wessex) Division, which had fought its way past the flank of the main German defences. On the 25th Montgomery decided to withdraw the remnants of 1st Airborne Division and that night 2163 men were ferried from Oosterbeek to the south bank. The Arnhem operation had been a very gallant failure, the reasons for which included landing too far from the objective, a communications failure at the critical moment and poor flying weather which restricted the amount of support the division could be given. 1st Airborne

Division's casualties amounted to 1130 killed and 6000 captured, of whom approximately half were wounded. German losses at Arnhem were 3300 killed and wounded.

Arnim, Col Gen von (1889–1971)

A divisional commander in 1941, von Arnim later commanded a corps during the invasion of Russia. At the end of 1942 he was appointed commander of the 5th Panzer ARMY in Africa, and in March 1943 was appointed Commander Army Group Afrika and Commander-in-Chief Tunisia. By that time the AFRIKA KORPS in Tunisia was in a hopeless position, and von Arnim and his force surrendered on 12 May 1942. He remained a prisoner for the rest of the war.

Arnold, Gen H. "Hap" (1886–1950)

As Chief of US Army Air Forces, 1941–46, and a member of the US Joint Chiefs of Staff throughout the war, Arnold was instrumental

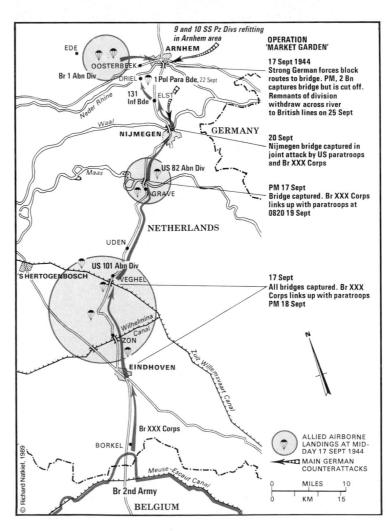

Arnhem: Operation Market Garden, September 1944.

in preparing US industry for the mass-production of military aircraft. He was also responsible for the immense training programmes which produced over two million airmen by 1944. He strongly favoured precision strategic bombing and frequently argued against the British policy of AREA BOMBING. When the USAAF was disbanded and the US Air Force formed in September 1947, Arnold became its first five-star Commanding General.

Arras, France, 1940

A counter-attack mounted under the overall command of Major-General H. E. Franklyn on 21 May, using the 1st Army Tank Brigade, 8th and 6th Battalions Durham Light Infantry and part of the French 3rd *Division Légère Mécanique*, the last covering the right flank of the advance. The attack struck the right flank of ROMMEL's 7th Panzer Division, advancing westwards south of Arras, and cut it in two, overrunning two motor rifle regiments when the German 37mm anti-tank guns proved useless against the thick armour of the British MATILDAS. Part of the neighbouring 3rd SS Division *Totenkopf* also bolted. Rommel eventually rallied his division, principally by using the 88mm guns of his anti-aircraft regiment in an anti-tank role, but his report that he was being attacked by "hundreds" of tanks resulted in the German higher command halting the drive of the Panzer divisions to the coast for 24 hours. This delay contributed materially to the success of the DUNKIRK evacuation.

Arromanches-les-Bains, France, 1944

Coastal town at the western end of GOLD BEACH, captured on D-DAY by 50th (Northumbrian) Division.

ARV Armoured Recovery Vehicle (UK).

Asashio Class Destroyers (Jap)

Displacement 1961 tons; *dimensions* 388×34ft (118×10.4m); mean draught 12ft (3.65m); *machinery* 2-shaft geared turbines producing shp 50,000; *speed* 35 knots; *armament* 5×6in DP (3×2); 4×25mm AA (2×2); 8×24in torpedo tubes (2×4); *complement* 200; *number in class* 10, launched 1936–37.

Asdic

Developed by and named after the Anglo-French Allied *S*ubmarine *D*etection *I*nvestigation *C*ommittee during World War I, although it was never used operationally in that war. Asdic was capable of locating submerged submarines by bouncing a sound signal from their hulls, the echo indicating the range and bearing of the target from the transmitting vessel, which would close in until a DEPTH CHARGE or HEDGEHOG attack could be launched. The system's principal drawback was that false or distorted readings could be given by wrecks, shoals of fish and changes in water temperature. Also, it was not effective against surfaced targets, and submarine commanders took advantage of this defect to attack on the surface at night until the development of improved radar made this practice increasingly dangerous. Asdic nonetheless remained a major weapon, and the improved sets were matched by increasing skill in their use. Also referred to as SONAR.

ASF Army Service Force (US). American military command responsible for supply and maintenance to the field armies.

ASSU Air Support Signals Unit (UK). A communications network between front-line troops and a Royal Air Force airfield designed to speed up calls for tactical air support.

A-Stoff

Liquid oxygen used in German rocket motors.

Astoria Class Heavy Cruisers (USA)

Displacement 9950 tons; *dimensions* 588ft×61ft 9in (179×18.8m); mean draught 19ft 6in (5.9m); *machinery* 4-shaft geared turbines producing shp 107,000; *speed* 32.5 knots; *armament* 9×8in (3×3); 8×5in AA (8×1); *aircraft* 4; *complement* 1050; *number in class* 7, launched 1933–36.

ASV Air to Surface Vessel (UK). Airborne RADAR used to detect ships.

AT Anti-tank (US).

ATC Air Transport Command.

Athens, Greece, 1941, 1944–45

Athens was occupied 27 April during the BALKAN CAMPAIGN of 1941. As the Germans withdrew from Greece in the autumn of 1944, hostility between the country's Royalist and Communist factions threatened to erupt into civil war. Having obtained STALIN's agreement that Greece should remain within the British

Luftwaffe auxiliaries on the Acropolis.

sphere of influence, CHURCHILL then offered the Greek government British troops as a means of preserving order. The offer was accepted and Operation MANNA began on 4 October with a landing at Patrai in the Peloponnese. Following the departure from Athens of the 10,000-strong German garrison on 12 October, their place was taken by the British two days later and on the 16th the Greek government returned to the capital. Street fighting between the rival factions broke out on 3 December and lasted six weeks, during which the British were themselves frequently under fire and compelled to use force. Both sides then agreed to a British-sponsored truce. Full-scale civil war broke out again in May 1946, ending with the defeat of the Communists in 1949.

A/Tk Anti-tank (UK).

Atlanta Class Light Cruisers (USA)

Displacement 6000 tons; *dimensions* 541ft 6in×53ft 3in (165×16.2m); mean draught 16ft 6in (4.98m); *machinery* 2-shaft geared turbines producing shp 75,000; *speed* 32 knots; *armament* 12–16×5in DP; 10–24×40mm AA; 8×21in torpedo tubes; *complement* 800; *number in class* 11, launched 1941–46.

USS Atlanta, *lost at the First Battle of Guadalcanal.*

Atlanta, USS – Atlanta Class Light Cruiser

Present at the Battles of MIDWAY and the EASTERN SOLOMONS. On 13 November 1942 *Atlanta* was sunk during the First Battle of GUADALCANAL.

Atlantic

Holding operations mounted by British and Canadian troops, NORMANDY 1944.

Atlantic, Battle of the, 1939–45

The Battle of the Atlantic was the longest campaign of World War II, lasting from 3 September 1939, when the liner *Athenia* was sunk by *U-30*, until the German surrender on 7 May 1945. The German Navy's objective was to starve the UK into submission, and to this end employed not only its expanding U-boat arm but also heavy units of its surface fleet and commerce raiders, while the Luftwaffe's FOCKE-WULF FW 200 CONDOR squadrons attacked Allied shipping from the air. The acquisition of bases on the Norwegian and French Atlantic coasts in 1940 enabled the Germans to broaden the scope of their operations and gave them immediate access to the disputed waters. The British, despite adopting the convoy system almost immediately (see ARCTIC CONVOY), suffered from a lack of escorts, many of which were retained in home waters until

the fear of invasion had passed, and many merchantmen sailed unescorted during this period. Taking advantage of the situation, the U-boats began operating in packs, shadowing convoys during the day and attacking at night on the surface, where the escorts' ASDIC was less effective. For the German submarine crews this was remembered as the "Happy Time", for between July and October 1940 they sank 217 ships for the loss of only two U-boats. However, as the prospect of invasion receded, more escorts became available and

the British response became more co-ordinated with the establishment of Western Approaches Command at Liverpool and the Newfoundland Escort Force at St John's. The Condor menace was reduced by the development of CAM Ships (CATAPULT-AIRCRAFT MERCHANT SHIPS), and later escort carriers which gave convoys their own organic air cover, while the RAF's COASTAL COMMAND began operating against U-boats off the west coast of Europe. In September 1941 the United States Navy, while technically still non-belligerent, commenced escorting convoys from a point 400 miles (650km) west of Iceland. Admiral DÖNITZ, increasingly frustrated, transferred his attention to the coast of West Africa, but when the United States entered the war he concentrated his efforts in the Western Atlantic, the Caribbean and the Gulf of Mexico, the result being a second "Happy Time" for the U-boats during which they sank 65 ships in February 1942, 86 in March, 69 in April, and 111 in May. In June the US Navy's introduction of convoys and air escorts in home waters went some way to curbing this but 1942, like the previous year, undoubtedly ended in a German victory. Science, however, was beginning to work in favour of the Allies. It became possible to fix the position of a transmitting U-boat by means of High Frequency Direction Finding; escorts fitted with the Type 271 centimetric radar could pick up objects as small as a U-boat's conning tower, making the surfaced attack at night extremely hazardous; the forward-firing HEDGEHOG, entering service in the spring of 1943, permitted escorts to maintain Asdic contact throughout an engagement;

USCGS Spencer *dropping depth charges while on North Atlantic convoy duty.*

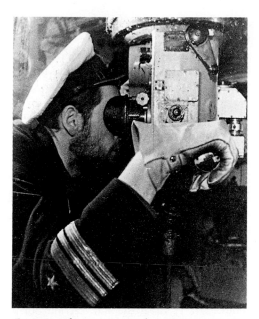
German U-boat commander using a periscope.

Air-to-Surface Vessel (ASV) airborne radar and LEIGH LIGHTS enabled Coastal Command aircraft to detect and kill surfaced U-boats during the hours of darkness and the arrival of the CONSOLIDATED B-24 LIBERATOR long-range bomber closed the air cover gap which had existed in mid-Atlantic. In addition, the number of escorts available had now increased appreciably, allowing the Allied navies to commit hunter-killer support groups, often containing an escort carrier, the sole purpose of which was submarine destruction. Even so, 1943 opened disastrously for the Allies, with the U-boats sinking 203,000 tons of shipping in January, 359,000 tons in February and 627,000 tons in March. This was twice the rate of merchant ship construction, and for every U-boat sunk two more were launched. The battle had reached its crisis, but in May 41 U-boats were lost, making a total of 114 for the first five months of the year. By July the number of U-boats had begun to fall, and the tonnage of Allied merchant ships launched exceeded that lost for the first time in the war. Dönitz conceded that he had lost but refused to give up the struggle. U-boats were fitted with the SCHNORKEL, which enabled them to run submerged while charging their batteries, and their anti-aircraft armament was augmented. However, their losses continued to mount while their monthly sinkings were often trivial and only once exceeded 100,000 tons for the rest of the war. The German defeat in France in 1944 deprived Dönitz of his best operational bases, and thereafter the bulk of

U-boat activity was confined to the approaches and coastal waters of the British Isles. Ironically, had the war continued the fortunes of the U-boat arm would have taken an up-turn as boats driven by the WALTER TURBINE, capable of out-running Allied escorts and long submerged endurance, began entering service. In comparison to the U-boats, the contribution made by the German surface fleet and commerce raiders was small and had effectively ended by 1942. For the Allies, the Battle of the Atlantic was possibly the most important campaign of the war; had they lost it the British capacity to wage war would have been irreparably damaged, no invasion of Europe would have been possible, and Hitler would have been free to concentrate his energies against the Soviet Union.

Atlantic Charter
A policy statement drawn up and signed by ROOSEVELT and CHURCHILL on 12 August 1941. In essence, its eight points were: that the US and UK did not seek new territories; no territorial changes could be made without the agreement of the people involved; the right of self-determination; free trade; joint economic development; freedom from fear and want; freedom of the seas; and the abandonment of the use of force.

Atlantic Wall, 1942–44
The grandiose name given to German coastal defence scheme stretching 1700 miles (2735km) from the North Cape to the Spanish frontier. In fact, only the most sensitive sectors were fortified, leaving long stretches of lightly defended coast between. Even so, the scale of construction was immense. Under the supervision of the Organization TODT, millions of tons of concrete went into the building of gun emplacements, command, observation and signal posts, bunkers and anti-tank walls, much of the unskilled physical work being undertaken by slave labour, including Russian prisoners of war. In addition to these impressive structures, most of which still survive, there were extensive beach defences including mines, barbed wire, anti-tank ditches, steel tetrahedra and hedgehogs, metal stakes and girder constructions, the last two being intentionally submerged at high water so as to disable landing craft. These elements were all closely studied by the Allies, as was the experience of the DIEPPE raid. As a result, solutions to many of the problems posed by the defences

were provided by the specialized AFVs developed for Major-General P. C. S. HOBART's 79th Armoured Division. These ensured that casualties incurred during the D-DAY and other assault landings on the west coast of Europe were remarkably light, given the nature of such undertakings. In the final analysis, the Atlantic Wall did not justify the effort and treasure which had been poured into it. Once the Allies had established themselves ashore the garrisons of some coastal zones which HITLER had declared fortresses, including the Channel Islands and Dunkirk, were left to rot until the war ended.

Atlantis – Surface Raider (Ger)
Also known as Ship 16 and Raider C. Commanded by Captain Bernhard Rogge, *Atlantis* sailed on 11 March 1940 and cruised in the Atlantic, Indian and Pacific Oceans, sinking 22 ships of 145,697 tons. She was sunk in the South Atlantic on 22 November 1941 by the cruiser HMS *Devonshire*. Her survivors were picked up by the raider supply ship *Python*, which was herself sunk by the cruiser HMS *Dorsetshire* on 1 December 1941. The survivors of both vessels were picked up by German and Italian submarines. See also SS AUTOMEDON. *Displacement* 7862 tons; *speed* 16 knots; *armament* 6×5.9in; 1×3in; 2×37mm AA; 2×20mm AA; 4×21in torpedo tubes; equipped for minelaying; *aircraft* 2; *complement* 350.

Atomic Bomb
An aerial bomb relying upon the explosive power of a nuclear reaction, used to destroy HIROSHIMA and NAGASAKI in August 1945 and, *inter alia*, end the war with Japan. The potential power of a nuclear reaction – "splitting the atom" – had been contemplated by various physicists in pre-war years and several of these scientists fled from Germany with the rise of Nazi power. In January 1939 a conference in Washington assembled such scientists as Niels Bohr, Enrico Fermi and Leo Szilard and the question of an atomic explosive was discussed, leading to a proposal being put forward to President ROOSEVELT in March 1939. Similar conclusions had been reached in Britain, where a committee known as "Tube Alloys" had been formed to carry out research. In 1942 the two countries combined their knowledge, and the USA set about building the necessary plant to produce an atomic munition. Known as the "Manhattan Engineer

General Auchinleck with NCO instructors in the Punjab, 1944.

District" for security, this project built a 78 square mile (125.5sq km) plant at Oak Ridge, Tennessee and a 39 square mile (62.75sq km) plant in Washington state. In December 1942 Fermi set the first self-sustaining atomic pile in operation, and on 16 July 1945 the first bomb was successfully detonated at Alamagordo, New Mexico. German scientists had also seen the potential of a nuclear explosive but instead of using uranium as their raw material decided to use heavy water. This was a false trail which was made more difficult by the Allied attacks on the only heavy water supply in Norway. The German research into atomic devices was called to a halt in 1943.

ATS Auxiliary Territorial Service (UK). Female component of the British Army.

Attacker Class Escort Carriers (UK)

Displacement 11,420 tons; *dimensions* 492ft×69ft 6in (150×21.2m); mean draught 23ft 3in (7m); *machinery* 1-shaft geared turbines producing shp 9350; *speed* 17 knots; *armament* 2×4in AA (2×1); 8×40mm AA (4×2); 15×20mm AA (15×1); *aircraft* 18; *complement* 646; *number in class* 8, launched 1941–42.

Attila

See ANTON.

Attlee, Clement Richard (1883–1967)

Leader of the Labour Party from 1935 to 1955, Leader of the Opposition and Deputy Prime Minister in the coalition War Cabinet from 1940 to 1945. He replaced CHURCHILL as Prime Minister in July 1945, and remained in office until October 1951. Although politically and temperamentally Winston Churchill's opposite, the two respected each other and worked well together.

Attu Island, Northern Pacific, 1942–43

See ALEUTIAN ISLANDS.

Auchinleck, Sir Claude John Eyre (1884–1981)

Auchinleck was a great Indian Army officer, rising to Commander-in-Chief India by 1939. He was brought home to command IV Corps, serving as GOC commanding Northern NORWAY in 1940 followed by a spell as GOC Southern Command. He returned to India in January 1941 before being chosen by CHURCHILL to replace WAVELL as Commander-in-Chief Middle East. Auchinleck immediately set about planning a counteroffensive CRUSADER, which opened on 18 November 1941 after he had successfully resisted intense pressure from Churchill to launch it prematurely. The AFRIKA KORPS captured TOBRUK on 21 June 1942. Auchinleck took personal command of 8th Army, and in July inflicted a crucial defeat on ROMMEL in the First Battle of ALAMEIN. However, Churchill never forgave Auchinleck for the loss of Tobruk, and on 15 August he was replaced by ALEXANDER. He returned to India as Commander-in-Chief in June 1943. He was appointed Field-Marshal in 1946 and in the following year Supreme Commander India and Pakistan.

Audacity, HMS – Escort Aircraft Carrier

Audacity was the Royal Navy's first escort carrier, converted by adding a flight deck to the hull of the captured German liner *Hannover*. Displacing 5537 tons, she had a maximum speed of 15 knots. Her armament consisted of one 4-inch and six 20mm anti-aircraft guns. As neither hangar nor lift were fitted, her six aircraft were permanently parked on the flight deck. She entered service in June 1941 and demonstrated the value of the escort carrier concept before she was torpedoed and sunk by *U-751* west of Portugal on 21 December 1941.

Augsburg, Germany, 1942

Aircraft production and heavy engineering centre. On 17 April the RAF carried out a daylight precision bombing raid on the MAN diesel engine factory, causing some damage but not enough to seriously disrupt production. Of the 12 Lancasters employed seven were lost and the remainder damaged. Not for the first time the raid revealed the impracticality of daylight precision attacks by heavy bombers and reinforced the RAF's belief in a night bomber offensive.

Auschwitz (Oswiecim), Poland

German extermination camp in southern Poland, close to Kattowice. Originally set up as a minor concentration, screening and transit

Selection for the gas chambers at Auschwitz.

camp, in March 1941 orders were given for its expansion to take 130,000 prisoners, some 10,000 of whom were to be employed by the IG Farben synthetics factory set up nearby. In the late summer the equipment for mass gassing was installed and the first such executions took place in September 1941. Major operations against the Jews began in March 1942 with the arrival of Slovakian Jews, followed by shipments from Eastern and Western Europe, Norway, Croatia and Greece. It is estimated that about two million people were killed before the camp was closed in 1944.

Austen Gun
An Australian submachine gun developed in 1941. The name is derived from "Australian Sten". The design adopted features of the British Sten and German MP38. About 20,000 were manufactured but it was never popular and was superseded by the Owen gun.

Autoblinda AB40/41 Series
The layout of these seven-ton Italian armoured cars was very similar to that of the British DAIMLER. The early pattern of turret, mounting twin 8mm Breda machine guns, was later replaced by the L6 light tank turret containing a 20mm cannon and a coaxial 8mm machine gun. A further machine gun was mounted in the hull. Maximum armour thickness was 15mm. Manned by a crew of three, the ABs were powered by an 80hp Fiat engine which enabled them to achieve 48mph (77kph) on roads as well as a good cross-country performance.

Automedon, SS – Blue Funnel Liner (UK)
7528-ton Blue Funnel liner intercepted and sunk by the German surface raider ATLANTIS in the Indian Ocean on 11 November 1940 while on passage to SINGAPORE. Unknown to the ship's master the papers in his safe included the British War Cabinet's top secret appreciation of the inherent strategic weakness of Malaya and Singapore. These documents were seized by the German boarding party and passed to the Japanese, who later used them in planning their invasion.

Avalanche
Allied landing at SALERNO, September 1943.

AVGAS Aviation gasoline (US).

Avia Aircraft (Czech)
Avia Av-135 A single-seat fighter which was under development when the Germans occupied Czechoslovakia in 1939. Work was permitted to continue and 12 machines were eventually built, which were delivered to the Bulgarian Air Force in 1941. *Span* 35.5ft (10.8m); *engine* 890hp in-line; *armament* 1 20mm cannon, 2 machine guns; *speed* 330mph (530kph).
Avia B-534 A single-seat biplane fighter produced from 1934 to 1938, this was considered to be probably the best of its type in existence at that time. Some 445 were built and most were used by the Luftwaffe as training machines. Three squadrons with Czech pilots were formed to fight against the Russians in 1941 but they achieved little and most of the pilots deserted to the Soviets with their aircraft. *Span* 31ft (9.5m); *engine* 850hp in-line; *armament* 4 machine guns; *speed* 245mph (394kph).

Avonmouth
Allied expedition to NARVIK, May 1940.

Avranches, France, 1944
Situated at the base of the COTENTIN PENINSULA, Avranches was captured by Lieutenant-General Courtney HODGES' US 1st Army on 30 July, five days after the start of Operation COBRA, the American break-out from the NORMANDY beach-head. Lieutenant-General George S. PATTON's recently activated US 3rd Army passed through the gap and, detaching one corps into Brittany, swung east to form the beginnings of the FALAISE pocket. HITLER promptly ordered von KLUGE to counter-attack at MORTAIN and drive through to the coast at Avranches, so closing the gap and trapping Patton's Army, but this attempt to restore the situation was defeated on 7 August.

AVRE (Assault Vehicle Royal Engineers)
The experience provided by the DIEPPE raid confirmed the need for a multipurpose armoured vehicle for British assault engineers. The hull of the CHURCHILL infantry tank was selected as the basis for this because of its heavy armour, roomy interior and obvious adaptability. The vehicle was fitted with a specially designed turret mounting a 290mm muzzle-loading spigot mortar which threw a 40-lb (18kg) bomb known as "General Wade's Flying Dustbin" and was used to crack open concrete fortifications. This had a maximum range of 230 yards (210m) but its accuracy declined sharply beyond 80 yards (73m). Reloading was carried out through a sliding hatch above the co-driver's seat. An experimental version of the AVRE was armed with the ARDEER AGGIE weapon system but this was found to be impractical. Standardized external fittings enabled the AVRE to be used in a variety of ways. It could carry a fascine eight feet (2.4m) in diameter and up to 14 feet (4.3m) wide which could be dropped into ditches or anti-tank trenches, forming a causeway; it could lay a Small Box Girder (SBG) bridge with a 40-ton capacity across gaps of up to 30 feet (9.15m); it

Avres with Fascine tank.

could be fitted with a Bobbin which unrolled a carpet of hessian and metal tubing ahead of the vehicle, so producing a firm track across soft going; it could place "Onion" or "Goat" demolition charges against an obstacle, firing these by remote control after it had reversed away; and it could be used to push Mobile Bailey or Skid Bailey bridges into position. The AVRE first saw action during the invasion of NORMANDY on 6 June 1944 and was employed throughout the campaign in North-West Europe. It equipped the 79th Armoured Division's three Assault Regiments Royal Engineers, each of which had an establishment of 60. It also played an important part in the final stages of the Italian campaign, where each of the two Armoured Engineer regiments had 18 plus other specialized armoured vehicles.

Avro Aircraft (UK)

Avro Anson This aircraft began life as a small airliner for Imperial Airways and was then evolved in 1934 to meet an RAF demand for a reconnaissance machine. It entered service in March 1936 and remained in use until after the war. Originally used for coastal reconnaissance, it was later relegated to training, while others were employed as ambulances and light transports. Over 10,000 were built in Britain and Canada, and there were a number of minor variants which differed in engines and equipment. *Span* 56.5ft (17.2m); *engines* 2 350hp radial; *crew* 6; *armament* 2 machine guns, 364lb (165kg) of bombs; *speed* 188mph (302kph).

Avro Lancaster Developed from the unsuccessful MANCHESTER by replacing the two Rolls-Royce Vulture engines with four Merlins, the Lancaster first flew on 27 June 1941, and was rapidly developed into the RAF's best heavy bomber of the war. Designed originally to carry 4000lb (1814kg) bombs, it was soon adapted to carry an 8000lb (3628kg) bomb, then the ballistic 12,000lb (5443kg) Tallboy bomb, the BOUNCING BOMB which breached the RUHR DAMS, and finally, the vast 22,000lb (9980kg) Grand Slam or "earthquake" bomb. The aircraft made its first operational sorties on 3 March 1942, and on 17 April 12 Lancasters carried out a daring low-level daylight raid on Augsburg, during which seven were lost and two Victoria Crosses were won.

On 11 September 1944 Lancasters of 617 Squadron sank the German battleship TIRPITZ in a Norwegian fjord with Tallboy bombs, and on 14 March 1945 demolished the Bielefeld Viaduct with Grand Slams. In late 1944/early 1945 huge formations of these aircraft undertook daylight operations in the face of reduced Luftwaffe opposition. By February 1946, 7374 had been built. A late model, the Mark VII, armed with .50 machine guns, was intended for employment in "Tiger Force" in the Far East in 1945, but the Pacific War ended before the force could be deployed.

Mark III. *Span* 102ft (31m); *engines* 4 1460hp in-line Merlin; *speed* 287mph (462km/hr); *service ceiling* 24,500ft (7468m); *range* with 14,000lbs (6350kg) of bombs, 1660 miles (2670km); *armament* 8×.303 or 6×.303 and 2×.50in machine guns.

The Avro Lancaster, Mark I version, being loaded with bombs.

Avro Manchester Produced to meet the RAF 1936 demand for a heavy bomber, the Manchester was a twin-engined monoplane designed to use the new Rolls-Royce Vulture engines. It had a good performance when the engines allowed and 200 were built, which were operational from 1940 to June 1942. However, the unreliability of the engines argued against the machine's success, and eventually it was withdrawn. By abandoning the engines and enlarging the design to take four proven engines, it became the LANCASTER. *Span* 90ft (27.5m); *engines* 2 1760hp in-line; *crew* 7; *armament* 8 machine guns, 10,360lb (4700kg) of bombs; *speed* 265mph (426kph).

Avro York The York was a transport aircraft requested by the RAF in 1942 and produced by taking the wings and engines of the successful Lancaster bomber and attaching a new fuselage and tail unit. However, since the USA was producing an ample supply of transport machines, few Yorks were built during the war, the majority of the 257 finally produced being delivered afterwards. During the war years they were principally used as VIP transport; subsequently they were employed on more mundane duties and played an important part in the Berlin Airlift of 1949. *Span* 102ft (31.1m); *engines* 4 1280hp in-line; *speed* 300mph (483kph).

AWL Absent without leave (UK).

AWOL Absent without leave (US).

Axis

A term describing the alliance between Germany and Italy, which arose from a newspaper phrase "the Berlin-Rome Axis". Later including Japan in the phrase "the Axis powers".

Axthelm, Lt Gen Walther von

Luftwaffe officer appointed Inspector-General of Anti-Aircraft Artillery in 1942. Later he assumed responsibility for the V-1 flying bomb campaign against Britain.

Azeville Fort, France, 1944

Situated on the east coast of the COTENTIN PENINSULA, the guns of this heavily fortified complex continued to harass unloading operations on UTAH beach after the initial landings on D-DAY. The fort was stormed in a dashing attack by the 3rd Battalion US 22nd Infantry Regiment on 9 June.

B

German troops inspect Soviet BA armoured cars, Poland 1939.

"B" Class Destroyers (UK)
Displacement 1360 tons; *dimensions* 323ft×32ft 3in (98.4×9.8m); mean draught 8ft 6in (2.6m); *machinery* 2-shaft geared turbines producing shp 34,000; *speed* 35 knots; *armament* 4×4.7in (4×1); 2×2-pdr AA (2×1); 8×21in torpedo tubes (2×4); machine guns added during war; *complement* 138; *number in class* 9, launched 1930.

BA Series Armoured Cars (USSR)
The Soviet Army entered World War II with both heavy and light armoured cars. The six-ton BA-10 heavy armoured car was based on a six-wheeled commercial chassis and first appeared in 1932, armed with a 37mm gun and coaxial 7.62mm machine gun, a second machine gun being mounted in the hull. Improved models were produced in 1935 and 1937, mounting a 45mm main armament. These vehicles were manned by a crew of

four, had a maximum speed of 34mph (55kph) and were protected by 15mm armour. The 2.5-ton BA-20 light armoured car was based on a four-wheeled private car chassis and entered service in 1937. It was armed with a single turret-mounted 7.62mm machine gun. The BA-20 had a two-man crew, a maximum speed of 50mph (80kph) and was protected by 10mm armour. The majority of these vehicles were destroyed or abandoned during the German invasion of the Soviet Union but a number of BA-10s were taken into German service. The BA-64 scout car appeared in 1942, based on a four-wheeled light truck chassis. It retained the essential characteristics of the BA-20 but had a much improved cross-country performance and well angled armour. The BA-64 was armed with a single turret-mounted 7.62mm or 14.5mm machine gun. The vehicle remained in service for some years after the war.

Bachstelze
A towed rotor-kite (similar to an unpowered helicopter) made by the Focke-Achgelis company for the German Navy and used as a reconnaissance machine by U-boats. The theory was that the U-boat could tow the kite at an altitude of about 330ft (150m) some 1320ft (600m) astern whilst surfaced for cruising and battery charging. The additional height gained by the observer piloting the kite would allow him to search both for convoys to attack and for approaching enemy warships or aircraft. Although much used in 1941–42, it was later abandoned due to the delays entailed in recovering and stowing the machine in the face of increasing Allied air activity.

Bach-Zelewski, General Erich von dem
Bach-Zelewski was the SS officer in charge of all anti-PARTISAN and anti-guerrilla operations from 1942. He commanded the troops which suppressed the WARSAW UPRISING, 1 August–3 October 1944.

Bader, Sqn Ldr Douglas R. S. (1910–82)
An officer in the Royal Air Force, Bader lost both legs as the result of a crash in 1931. He re-entered the RAF in June 1940 and became a highly successful fighter pilot, prominent in the Battle of BRITAIN. Captured after a mid-air collision in 1941 over France, he escaped but was re-captured and imprisoned in COLDITZ for the remainder of the war.

Badger
Canadian RAM III medium tank fitted with British WASP flame projector.

Badoglio, Marshal Pietro (1871–1950)
Badoglio fought in the Italo-Ethiopian War of 1895–97, the Italo-Turkish War of 1911–12, and was a general during World War I, playing a part in the planning of the battles of the Isonzo. He was Chief of Staff 1919–21, Ambas-

Left to right: General Eboze Muti, Benito Mussolini and Marshal Pietro Badoglio, Rome 1939.

Baedecker Raids

A series of German air raids on Britain in the period April–October 1942, so-called because the targets were towns of historical and cultural interest taken from the Baedecker Guide to Britain. The raids began on 25 April with an attack on Exeter. In the following seven months there were 38 further raids directed at such non-military targets as Bath, Norwich and Canterbury. The impact of the raids was small as the number of aircraft committed to them dwindled, both through losses in action (some 80 aircraft) or transfers to other fronts. Over half the total tonnage dropped in the campaign, 2979 tons, was delivered in the first two months. The heaviest attack was on Bath on 25/26 April.

Bagration, Operation, Soviet Union, 1944

Major Soviet offensive by Bagramyan's 1st Baltic Front, CHERNYAKHOVSKY's 3rd Belorussian Front, Zhakarov's 2nd Belorussian Front and Rokossovsky's 1st Belorussian Front against Field-Marshal Ernst BUSCH's Army Group Centre on 22 June 1944, the third anniversary of Operation BARBAROSSA. In terms of manpower the two sides were evenly matched with about 1,200,000 men each, but the Russians possessed a superiority of 4000 tanks to 900 German, 28,600 artillery weapons against 10,000, and 5300 aircraft against 1300. Busch was aware of Soviet preparations and requested permission to withdraw his command behind the River Berezina so that the Russian blow would strike empty space, dislocating the offensive's timetable and creating conditions suitable for a counterstroke. HITLER rejected the suggestion out of hand and ordered Busch to stand and fight. The result was that large numbers of German troops were cut off at VITEBSK on 27 June, at Mogilev on the 28th, at Bobruysk on the 29th and east of MINSK on 3 July as no fewer than 40 Soviet tank brigades and numerous mechanized cavalry groups swept across what had once been eastern Poland, reaching Wilno on 13 July, LUBLIN on the 23rd and BREST-Litovsk on the 28th. When the offensive finally ran down as it approached the VISTULA, it had torn a 250-

sador to Brazil 1924–25, was promoted Field-Marshal in 1925, and was Chief of the General Staff until 1928 when he became Governor-General of Libya. He commanded the Italian forces in the invasion of Ethiopia in 1935 and for a short time became Viceroy. Appointed Chief of Staff once more in June 1940, he resigned in December in protest at MUSSOLINI's invasion of Greece.

After the arrest of Mussolini on 25 June 1943, Badoglio was appointed Prime Minister by KING VICTOR EMMANUEL III. He foresaw that in the event of Italy making a separate peace with the Allies, the Germans would continue to fight in Italy, and his aim thus became one of limiting the damage that the warring armies were liable to inflict on the country. He tried, unsuccessfully, to persuade the Allies to invade in the north, so as to avoid the long and costly process of campaigning up the peninsula. After negotiations in Lisbon between Badoglio's emissaries and Allied representatives, Italy signed a secret act of surrender on 3 September 1943. On the same day Allied forces crossed the Straits of Messina and landed on mainland Italy. The news of the surrender was broadcast on 8 September, and the Germans immediately occupied Rome to forestall a possible Allied airborne attack. Badoglio resigned in June 1944.

Operation Bagration, June–August 1944.

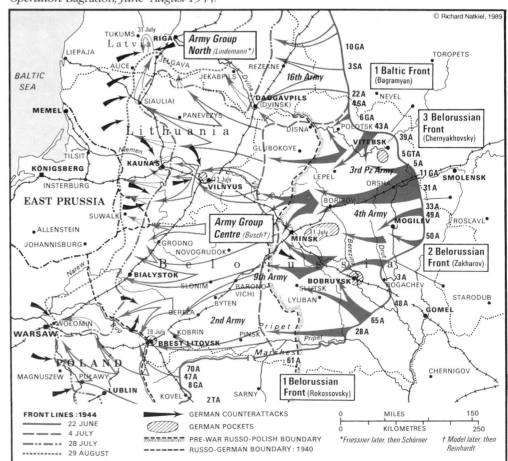

Operation Bagration: *Soviet tanks and infantry with artillery support, 1944.*

mile gap in the German line, advanced 450 miles (724km) in four weeks and eliminated the equivalent of 25 enemy divisions. Army Group Centre had been virtually destroyed where it stood and as a direct consequence of this Army Group North was isolated. Whether, at the end, the Soviets still possessed the means or the will to assist the concurrent rising of the Polish Home Army in WARSAW remains the subject of debate. Operation *Bagration* dealt the Wehrmacht a blow from which it never fully recovered and is regarded by Soviet historians as being the decisive battle of the Great Patriotic War. See *The Road to Berlin* by John Erickson (Weidenfeld and Nicolson) and *World War II – Decisive Battles of the Soviet Army* by V. Larionov and others (Progress Publishers, Moscow).

Bailey Bridge

A British prefabricated bridge, comprising a set of components which could be assembled in a number of ways so as to give various load-carrying capacities and spans. Named for its inventor, it became a standard engineer device and was widely used for bridging in every theatre of war. Many Bailey bridges remained in place as substitutes for demolished bridges until well after the war.

Balaton, Lake, Hungary, 1945

The area of the last German offensive on the Eastern Front, codenamed *Frühlings-erwachen* (Spring Awakening) but sometimes referred to as the "Ardennes of the East", the intention being to mount a spoiling attack on TOLBUKHIN's 3rd Ukrainian Front with two German armies (2nd and 6th SS Panzer) and preserve the Hungarian oilfield at Nagykanizsa. The offensive began on 5 March and succeeded in establishing a 20-mile deep salient in the Russian line. On 16 March a counter-attack by the Soviet 9th Guards Army routed the Hungarian 3rd Army, which was covering the left flank of the operation, and the offensive was hastily abandoned. *Frühlingserwachen* had absorbed most of Germany's remaining armour and resulted in the loss of over 500 tanks and assault guns, 300 artillery weapons and 40,000 men.

Balbo, Marshal Italo (1896–1940)

Balbo was a well-known figure in Italian aviation and had served as Minister of Aviation in the 1930s. A prominent and colourful member of the Fascist party, his popularity with the people incurred the jealousy of MUSSOLINI. Balbo, for his part, cared little for Mussolini and frequently spoke of him in belittling terms. In order to remove him from the public eye, he was appointed Governor of Libya in 1936, but he voiced his objections to Mussolini's friendship with HITLER, having no liking for the Germans, and tried to persuade Mussolini to remain aloof from the war. Shortly after Italy's entrance into the war Balbo was killed when the aircraft in which he was returning from Italy to Libya was shot down over Tobruk by the Italian air defences.

Balck, Gen Hermann (1893–)

Balck joined the German Army in 1913 and was commissioned in 1914 in the light infantry. A good wartime soldier, his peacetime career was uneventful and he did not reach the rank of Lieutenant-Colonel until

1938. In 1939 he was given command of 1st Rifle Regiment, 1st Panzer Division and showed considerable ability in both Poland and France. Promoted to Colonel in December 1940, he commanded 3rd Panzer Regiment, in May 1941 2nd Panzer Brigade, in May 1942 11 Panzer Division, and in August 1942 received promotion to Major-General. In January 1943 as a Lieutenant-General he was given command of the "Grossdeutschland" Division. In 1944 he was General commanding Army Group G in France and then 6th Army in Hungary.

Bali Island, Dutch East Indies, 1942

Captured by the Japanese on 19 February. See also LOMBOK STRAIT.

Balikpapan, Borneo, 1942 and 1945

Coastal town at the heart of an oil producing area of south-east Borneo, captured by the Japanese on 24 January 1942, it was recaptured by the Australian 7th Division on 3 July 1945.

Balkan Campaigns, Yugoslavia and Greece, 1941

Alarmed by Italian reverses in North Africa and Albania, HITLER had already decided to assist MUSSOLINI by invading Greece through Bulgaria (Operation *Margarita*) when on 27 March an anti-Nazi coup took place in Yugoslavia. Concerned that his projected invasion of the Soviet Union should have a secure southern flank, he therefore decided that Yugoslavia should be invaded as well (Operation *Punishment*). The conquest of Yugoslavia

Italian troops advance to the front, Greece 1941.

The Balkan Campaigns of 1941.

German casualties in Yugoslavia amounted to a mere 558, while 345,000 Yugoslav soldiers were taken prisoner. The campaign in Creece cost Germany 4500 casualties; Greek losses amounted to 70,000 killed or wounded and 270,000 captured while Wilson's corps sustained nearly 12,000 casualties and lost all its heavy equipment, although 80 per cent of its personnel were lifted out. The Balkan Campaigns of 1941 were brilliant demonstrations of the BLITZKRIEG technique but in the wider sphere they delayed the start of the German invasion of the Soviet Union and this in itself contributed to the eventual failure of Operation BARBAROSSA.

Balkon

A German sound-locating device used by U-boats, enabling them to detect the screw noises of either targets or enemy warships. It took its name from the balcony-like housing built on to the bow of the submarine to house the acoustic detectors.

Balloons, Barrage

Captive balloons flown above target areas and ships as a deterrent to dive-bombers and to keep attacking aircraft at a certain height where they were more vulnerable to anti-aircraft gun fire. Now and again plans were put forward for attaching "aprons" of wire between balloons, fixing mines to the balloon cables, and making various other refinements, but few of these proved to be of any value. Barrage balloons were used by all combatants at one time or another.

Balloons, Japanese

After two years of research and experiment, in November 1944 the Japanese Army began launching free balloons from Honshu. About 9000 were released, which crossed the Pacific Ocean at a height of about 35,000 feet (10,675m), the stratospheric airstream carrying them to the United States and Canada in three to five days. The balloons were hydrogen-filled and carried a regulating mechanism which periodically released gas or ballast to maintain height. When the last pack of ballast was released, the mechanism released two incendiary or high explosive bombs weighing about 10lb (4.5kg) each, after which an explosive charge would destroy the balloon. Some balloons carried, instead of bombs, a radio transmitter which could be monitored by position-finding equipment

began on 6 April and was carried out by Field-Marshal LIST's 12th Army in the south and General von WEICHS' 2nd Army and Field-Marshal von KLEIST's 1st Panzer Army in the north. Simultaneously, smaller operations were mounted on the coast by the Italian 2nd Army and in the Banat by the Hungarian 3rd Army. The Yugoslav armed forces, poorly armed and split by racial, religious and political differences, offered little resistance and on 17 April surrendered unconditionally. Greece was also invaded on 6 April. The defenders of the METAXAS LINE were engaged frontally by 12th Army's XXX Corps but were outflanked by an armoured thrust which reached Thes-

saloniki and forced a surrender on 9 April. Driving south from Yugoslavia, General Stumme's XL Motorized Corps penetrated the lightly held gap between the ALIAKMON LINE and the main body of the Greek Army in ALBANIA. Recognizing the inevitability of defeat, General Alexander PAPAGOS, the Greek Commander-in-Chief, indicated to General WILSON, the commander of the British Corps in Greece, that the Greeks would continue fighting until the British had re-embarked, and his troops held out until 23 April. Wilson conducted a fighting retreat through the Pass of Thermopylae to the Peloponnesus, where his troops continued embarking until 27 April.

and thus track the balloon stream across the ocean and confirm the general direction of drift.

It had been estimated that about 10 per cent of the balloons would reach the American continent; about 150 were actually reported as having landed, from the Aleutian islands to Mexico, and from California to as far inland as Michigan. Probably many more dropped their bombs and self-destroyed without witnesses in the mountainous regions. The only casualties caused were on 5 May 1945 when a picnic party near Bly, Oregon, USA, discovered a bomb and, disturbing it, caused it to detonate and kill six members of the group. Nevertheless, the bombs could have been a threat had the caprices of wind and weather brought them down over populated centres. Due to a rigid news blackout in the USA and Canada on the subject, no reports of balloon bombs were ever made public and the Japanese, who had been relying on picking up public announcements to give an indication of the success of the campaign, concluded that no balloons were reaching America and therefore abandoned the project.

Baltic Campaign, 1944–45

Following the destruction of the German Army Group Centre in June–July 1944, the Soviet Army mounted a series of major offensives on the Baltic sector of the Eastern Front. Bagramyan's 1st Baltic Front advanced across Latvia to reach the coast near MEMEL (Klaipeda) while 2nd and 3rd Baltic Fronts, commanded respectively by YEREMENKO and Maslennikov, drove through Lithuania and invested Riga. Simultaneously, Govorov's Leningrad Front swept through Estonia. The combined effect of these advances was to isolate Field-Marshal SCHÖRNER's Army Group North, containing the remnants of 33 divisions, in the Kurland Peninsula. In February 1945 KÖNIGSBERG (Kaliningrad) was invested, followed by DANZIG (Gdansk) and Gdynia. The German Navy, however, retained command of the sea and was able to evacuate 1,500,000 refugees and a substantial number of military personnel from KURLAND. Danzig and Gdynia were similarly evacuated in March 1945, as were Königsberg, Kolberg and Pillau the following month, although shipping losses were heavy. German attempts to withdraw along the coast into Schleswig-Holstein were frustrated by the British capture of LÜBECK on 2 May.

Baltimore Class Heavy Cruisers (USA)

Displacement 13,600–13,700 tons; *dimensions* 675ft×70ft 9in (205×21.5m); mean draught 20ft 6in (6.15m); *machinery* 4-shaft geared turbines producing shp 120,000; *speed* 33 knots; *armament* 9×8in (3×3); 12×5in DP (6×2); 48×40mm AA; 22–28×20mm (single); *aircraft* 4 (2 catapults); *complement* 1700; *number in class* 18, launched 1942–45.

Bandar Pahlevi, Iran, 1941

Port on the south-western shore of the Caspian Sea, occupied by Russian troops during the Anglo-Soviet intervention of August 1941.

Bandar Shah, Iran, 1941

Port on the south-eastern shore of the Caspian Sea, occupied by Russian troops during the Anglo-Soviet intervention of August 1941. The town was also the terminus of the Trans-Iranian Railway, along which some five million tons of Allied military aid was subsequently passed to the Soviet Union.

Bangor Class Minesweeping Sloops (UK)

Displacement 590–672 tons; *dimensions* 162–180ft×28ft–28ft 6in (49.4–54.8m×8.5–8.7m); mean draught 8ft 3in (2.48m); *machinery* 2-shaft diesel bhp 2000, or 2-shaft reciprocating ihp 2400, or 2-shaft geared turbines shp 2400; *speed* 16 knots; *armament* various. Typical 1×3in AA; 4×0.5in or .303in AA mg (2×2); *complement* 60–87; *number in class* 113, launched 1940–43.

Barbarossa, Operation, Soviet Union, 1941

The codename for the German invasion of the Soviet Union on 22 June 1941. Three army groups were employed: von RUNDSTEDT's Army Group South, consisting of 52 infantry divisions, including the Romanian 3rd and 4th Armies with a total of 15 divisions, a Hungarian motorized corps of two divisions and an Italian corps, spearheaded by the five Panzer divisions of 1st Panzer Group under von KLEIST; von BOCK's Army Group Centre, containing 42 infantry divisions and nine Panzer divisions, the latter being divided between 2nd Panzer Group (GUDERIAN) and 3rd Panzer Group (HOTH); and von LEEB's Army Group North, containing seven infantry divisions and the three Panzer divisions of HÖPNER's 4th Panzer Group. A total of 3332 German tanks were available, in contrast with the Soviet Army's tank strength of approximately 24,000. The Luftwaffe's four Air Fleets quickly obtained air superiority, destroying 1489 Soviet aircraft on the ground and 322 more in the air during the first day's fighting, rising to 4990 during the next week. The most serious opposition was encountered by Army Group South and resulted in the Battle of BRODY-DUBNO, which imposed a temporary check, but elsewhere the Panzer groups penetrated deep into the Russian heartland. On 19 July HITLER interfered personally in the conduct of operations and although the result of this was the reduction of a huge Soviet pocket near KIEV in September, it meant that

Spanish fascist troops of the "Blue Division" fight for the Germans in Operation Barbarossa, *December 1941.*

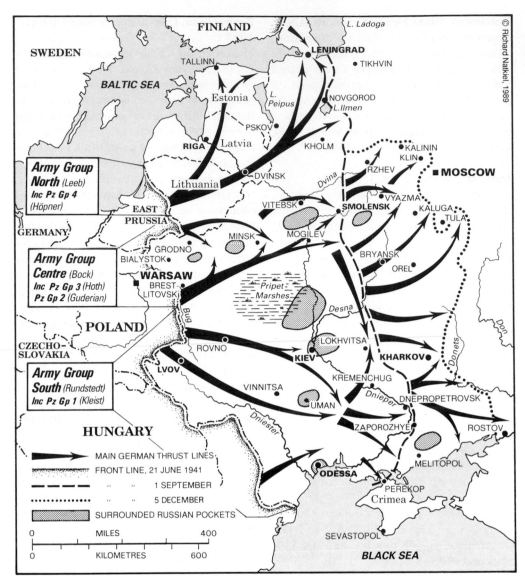

Operation Barbarossa, *1941.*

the drive on the vital strategic objective of MOSCOW had to be suspended. When it was resumed in October, the autumn rains seriously reduced mobility and these were followed by the first snows of winter. German infantry actually penetrated the capital's suburbs on 4 December but were driven out, while elsewhere Soviet reinforcements from Siberia were reaching the front and recovering some of the lost ground. Hitler reluctantly accepted that *Barbarossa* had run its course and ordered his troops to hold their present positions.

Despite the ultimate failure of the operation, the German Army had not only carved out nine major pockets at BIALYSTOK, MINSK, SMOLENSK, UMAN, Gomel, Kiev, BRYANSK, VYAZMA and against the Azov coast, yielding 2,250,000

prisoners, 9327 tanks and 16,179 guns, the equivalent of 150 divisions, but also 13 smaller pockets which resulted in the capture of a further 736,000 men, 4960 tanks and 9033 guns. Soviet casualties in killed and wounded have never been quantified. The Germans sustained approximately 800,000 personnel casualties during *Barbarossa* and 2300 tanks were lost; almost all their higher formation-commanders were relieved or replaced. The principal reasons for the operation's failure were the late start induced by the BALKAN CAMPAIGN; Hitler's interference; and underestimation of physical difficulties involved in maintaining and supplying armoured formations over the vast distances involved. The consequence was to embed the Wehrmacht in a large-scale protracted conflict in which vic-

tory was at best dubious. See *Operation Barbarossa* by Bryan Fugate (Presidio), *Barbarossa: Invasion of Russia 1941* by John Keegan (Macdonald), *The German Army 1933–1945* by Matthew Cooper (Macdonald and Jane's), *The Road to Stalingrad* by John Erickson (Weidenfeld and Nicolson).

Barbey, R Adm Daniel E. (1889–1969)

A graduate of Annapolis in 1912, Barbey saw mixed sea and shore service for many years, during which he commanded the battleship USS *New York*. In 1937–40 he was Captain, War Plans Section, of the Bureau of Navigation where he developed an interest in amphibious warfare. In 1941 he became Chief of Staff and Aide to the Amphibious Force, Atlantic Fleet, and established the Amphibious Warfare Section of the Navy Department. He was responsible for the development of the Landing Ship Dock (LSD), Landing Ship Tank (LST) and the DUKW amphibious truck. He was promoted Rear-Admiral in 1942, and in January 1943 assumed command of the VII Amphibious Force, 7th Fleet, responsible for all amphibious operations in MACARTHUR's South-West Pacific area, a post he retained until the end of the war. In late 1945 he assumed command of the 7th Fleet and in 1951 retired to become director of Civil Defence for Washington State.

Bardia, Libya, 1941 and 1942

A fortified port in eastern Cyrenaica stormed by 6th Australian Division on 3–5 January 1941, yielding 38,000 Italian prisoners, 120 tanks, 400 guns and 700 vehicles. Reoccupied by Axis troops during ROMMEL's 1941 advance. In the aftermath of Operation CRUSADER, 2nd South African Division successfully assaulted the defences 31 December 1941–2 January 1942, taking 8000 prisoners.

Barents Sea, Battle of the, 1942–43

At 1800 on 30 December 1942 a German squadron consisting of the pocket battleship *Lützow*, the cruiser *Admiral Hipper* (Flag) and six destroyers, commanded by Vice-Admiral Oscar Kummetz, left Alten Fjord in northern Norway to intercept the Murmansk-bound Convoy JW-51B, which was protected by six destroyers and five smaller escorts under Captain R. Sherbrooke. Kummetz intended launching converging attacks on the convoy with *Admiral Hipper* and three destroyers from the north and *Lützow* and three destroyers from the south. At 0725 on 31 December he had the convoy in sight and the *Admiral Hipper*'s group closed in, opening fire at 0915 in poor visibility. The British destroyers launched a series of vigorous counter-attacks which held him at bay while the convoy turned away to the south-east. This brought it into contact with the *Lützow*'s group and a major German success seemed inevitable. However, the *Lützow*'s commander, Captain Stänge, was unable to identify friend from foe in the poor light and hesitated. The delay enabled the British destroyers to lay a smoke screen so that *Lützow* did not open fire until 1140. In the meantime *Admiral Hipper* had damaged the destroyer *Obedient*, crippled the *Onslow*, sunk a third, *Achates*, and blown apart the minesweeper *Bramble*. At this point *Admiral Hipper* was hit by three 6-inch shells in rapid succession and her speed dropped to 28 knots. The shells came from the cruisers *Sheffield* and *Jamaica*, which, under Rear-Admiral Robert BURNETT, had just escorted Convoy JW-51A into Murmansk and turned back to cover JW-51B. Simultaneously, the German destroyer *Friedrich Eckholdt* was sunk. Kummetz, over-burdened with orders regarding the safety of his heavy ships, gave the order to break contact at 1149 and retired. The fiasco so enraged HITLER that the following month Grand Admiral Erich RAEDER was replaced as Commander-in-Chief of the German Navy by Grand Admiral Karl DÖNITZ and the majority of the fleet's surviving heavy ships were confined to training duties in the Baltic. Captain Sherbrooke's gallant defence of the convoy won him the Victoria Cross.

Barham, HMS – Queen Elizabeth Class Battleship

A veteran of Jutland, *Barham* served with the Home Fleet of 1939–40 and then with FORCE H. She transferred to the Mediterranean Fleet in 1941 and took part in the Battle of CAPE MATAPAN. She was torpedoed by *U-331* off Sollum on 25 November 1941 and sank with heavy loss of life.

Bari, Italy, 1943

Seaport, used by Allied forces as a port of supply after the invasion of Italy. Bari was the scene of an unusual accident in December 1943 when the ammunition ship *John Harvey*, carrying a cargo of mustard gas, was bombed and sunk during an air raid. The gas escaped and floated on the surface of the sea, affecting many survivors of the sinking. Their condition went unrecognized in the hospitals, and many died before adequate treatment was begun.

Barking Creek, Battle of, 1939

The unofficial name given to an erroneous engagement by the RAF over the outskirts of London on 6 September 1939. A report of German aircraft approaching across the North Sea caused fighters to be flown off to intercept. More raiders were reported, more fighters flown off. One hour later, after the RAF had lost three aircraft, it transpired that the initial sighting had been of an RAF training aircraft inland, but the bearing had been read 180° from its correct position. Subsequently the fighters were also plotted in the wrong area, apparently adding to the raiding force. In fact there were no German aircraft involved.

An ammunition ship explodes in the Barents Sea.

Baron Flail Tank (UK)

A mine-clearing device based on the MATILDA infantry tank, the Baron incorporated a revolving cylinder carried some ten feet (3m) ahead of the vehicle on arms attached to the hull sides. The cylinder was driven by an externally mounted engine and was fitted with chains which beat the ground in the manner of a flail, exploding mines in its path. The Baron Mark I prototype was completed towards the end of 1941, the cylinder being driven by a 60hp Chrysler engine. This was replaced on the Mark II by a 73hp Bedford engine but this still failed to provide sufficient power for the flail drive. The Mark III, therefore, was fitted with two 73hp Bedford engines mounted in armoured housings one each side of the hull, this model also dispensed with the tank turret, which was replaced by a fixed armoured cab for the flail operator. Some 60 Mark IIIs were built and used for training. The Baron could clear a lane ten feet (3m) wide at a speed of 0.25mph (0.4kph). See also SCORPION and CRAB.

Bartolomeo Colleoni – Condottieri Class Cruiser (Italy)

Launched in 1930, the *Bartolomeo Colleoni* maintained an average speed of 40.9 knots during her trials and had the reputation of being the fastest cruiser afloat. During an engagement north-west of Crete on 19 July 1940 she was crippled by the fire of the cruiser HMAS SYDNEY and sunk by the latter's escorting destroyers.

Baruch, Bernard Mannes (1870–1965)

Financial adviser to President ROOSEVELT, in 1941 Baruch became a special adviser to the Office of War Mobilization. He was instrumental in harnessing US industry to war production. In 1946 he was appointed by President TRUMAN as the US representative to the United Nations Atomic Energy Commission.

Bastia, Italy, 1945

Town in the ARGENTA GAP containing an important bridge over the River Reno, captured by the British 78th Division on 14 April 1945.

Bastogne, Belgium, 1944

A town and major road-rail junction lying on the centre-line of the German advance during the Battle of the BULGE, possession of which

US supply lines in Bastogne, January 1945.

was vital for both sides. Garrisoned by the recently arrived US 101st Airborne Division and Combat Command B 10th Armored Division under the overall command of Brigadier-General Anthony McAULIFFE, Bastogne was isolated by the 2nd Panzer, Panzer Lehr and 26th Volksgrenadier Divisions, 18–21 December, and then subjected to a series of heavy attacks. These reached their climax on Christmas Day, when the defences were breached in two places, the penetrations being contained by McAuliffe's skilfully deployed reserves. The following day Bastogne was relieved from the south by 4th Armored Division (US 3rd Army), although fierce fighting continued for several days.

Bataan, Philippines, 1942

A peninsula on the island of LUZON. Upon the invasion of Luzon by the Japanese on 10 December 1941, MACARTHUR, after the initial battles, withdrew his forces into the Bataan peninsula to fight a delaying action in the hope of relief. Relief was not forthcoming, and on 12 March MacArthur handed over command of the forces to General King and flew to Australia. After fighting further delaying actions, General King was forced to surrender to the Japanese on 9 April 1942.

About 78,000 US and Philippine troops went into captivity, a high proportion of whom died in the subsequent "Death March" out of Bataan.

Bat Guided Bomb

An American RADAR-homing bomb developed from 1941 onwards, through a number of different projects. Originally intended for use against surface ships, the specification was changed to make it an anti-submarine weapon; but before this could be completed the submarine threat receded and it was again specified for use against surface ships. The final design was based on a 1000lb (454kg) general-purpose bomb, to which was added radar homing, wings and steerable fins. Named because, like a bat, it sent out pulses and listened to the echoes. From May 1945 it was in use in the Pacific, being carried on CONSOLIDATED PBY-2 PRIVATEER aircraft and directed against Japanese shipping with considerable success. With modified radar, numbers were also used against bridges in Burma.

Bathurst Class Minesweeping Sloops (UK)

Displacement 650 tons; *dimensions* 186×31ft (55.8×9.3m); mean draught 8ft 3in (2.48m); *machinery* 2-shaft reciprocating ihp 1750–2000; *speed* 15–16 knots; *armament* 1×4in or 3in AA; 1×20mm AA; 4×.303in mg AA (2×2); *complement* 60–87; *number in class* 63, launched 1940–43.

Battalion

Consisted of battalion headquarters, headquarters company/battery/squadron and generally three or more companies/batteries/squadrons. In the British and Commonwealth armies the term was used synonymously with regiment and three or more battalions constituted a brigade. In other armies an armoured, infantry or artillery regiment consisted of up to three battalions.

Battery

A specific group of guns forming an administrative and tactical unit. Usually six or eight guns made up a battery but in the case of super-heavy or railway artillery a pair or even one gun could constitute a battery.

Battleaxe

British offensive, Western Desert, June 1941.

Battle Class Destroyers (UK)

These vessels were designed specifically for the Pacific theatre of war and possessed a wide operational radius as well as a heavy anti-aircraft armament. Only five were completed

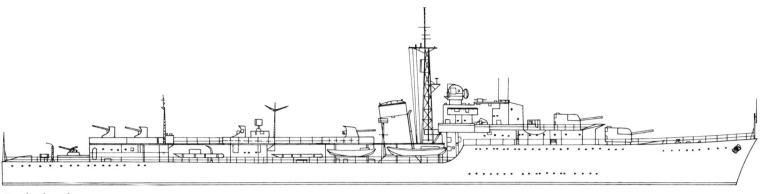

Battle class destroyer.

in time to see active service, with the Home Fleet and in the Pacific in 1945. A second group of Battle Class destroyers had been laid down and, although several were launched 1945–46, the majority were cancelled. *Displacement* 2315 tons; *dimensions* 379ft×40ft 3in (115.5×12.26m); *mean draught* 10ft 6in (3.2m); *machinery* 2-shaft geared turbines producing shp 50,000; *speed* 35.75 knots; *armament* 4×4.5in DP (2×2); 1×4in and 12×40mm AA (4×2 and 4×1) or 14×40mm AA (4×2 and 6×1); 8×21in torpedo tubes (2×4); *complement* 247; *number in class* 16, launched 1943–45.

Battle Group

Generally an all-arms force of armoured, infantry, artillery, engineer and support elements detached from its parent formation(s), usually for a specific mission.

Baytown

British 8th Army's crossing of the Strait of Messina to invade southern Italy, September 1943.

Bazna, Elyesa "Cicero" (d. 1970)

Bazna, a Turkish citizen of Albanian origin, was employed in pre-war days as a valet to the German Ambassador in Ankara. He left this post and obtained similar employment with the British Embassy, eventually becoming valet to the Ambassador, Knatchbull-Huguesson. In October 1943 he contacted his former employers and offered them a number of secret British documents for £20,000 each. He had copied the Ambassador's personal key and was able to remove documents from the Embassy safe and photograph them. Given the codename "Cicero" by the Abwehr, Bazna continued to supply them with over 400 valuable documents, covering such items as the

Teheran and Cairo Conferences and the forthcoming Allied invasion of Europe, for which he was paid about £300,000. The staff of the British embassy eventually became suspicious and Bazna vanished overnight. Little use was made of the information, since the Germans suspected the whole affair to be a British "plant". Bazna's ambition had been to make money to open an hotel in South America, which he eventually did; but shortly afterwards he was arrested for passing forged currency, when it was discovered that the Germans had paid him entirely in forged British banknotes.

Bazooka

American shoulder-fired anti-tank rocket launcher, properly known as the 2.36in (60mm) Rocket Launcher M1A1 or M9. It was a lightweight tube (in two pieces in the M9 model) which the firer placed on his shoulder and aimed by a simple sight. A fin-stabilized

Two US paratroopers demonstrate the loading of a bazooka, Oujda, North Africa, 1943.

rocket with shaped charge warhead was inserted into the rear end of the tube and fired electrically. The effective range was about 450ft (137m) and the warhead could penetrate about 8in (203mm) of armour. The name was derived from a burlesque musical instrument played by Bob Burns, an American comedian of the 1940s.

BCOS British Chiefs of Staff.

BD Base detonating (US). Refers to a type of shell fuze.

Bearn – Aircraft Carrier (Fr)

Laid down as a battleship in 1914 and launched in 1920, *Bearn* was converted to aircraft carrier in 1923–27. When France surrendered in June 1940 she was at Martinique and was disarmed by the Governor. However, on his resignation in June 1943 she was reactivated as part of the Free French Naval Force and after refitting in the USA was employed as an aircraft transport, her low speed making her unsuitable for use as an active carrier. *Displacement* 22,146 tons; *dimensions* 600×115ft (182×35m); mean draught 30ft 6in (9.3m); *machinery* 2-shaft turbines producing shp 22,200 (inner shafts only), plus two sets of reciprocating engines with hp 36,200 coupled to all four shafts, used when manoeuvring or cruising; *speed* 21.5 knots (trials); *protection* main belt 80mm; flight deck 25mm; *armament* 8×155mm (8×1); 6×75mm AA; 8×37mm AA; 4×550mm torpedo tubes; *aircraft* 40; *complement* 865.

Beaverbrook, Lord Maxwell Aitken (1879–1964)

A Canadian press baron, Beaverbrook ran the British information services during World War I and became a close friend of CHURCHILL.

In 1940 Churchill made him Minister of Aircraft Production, and by ruthless organizational overhauls he managed to keep production ahead of losses throughout the Battle of BRITAIN. He then became Minister of Supply (1941–42) and Lord Privy Seal (1943–45) and administered the British end of the Lend-Lease Scheme.

Beaverette (UK)

Named after Lord BEAVERBROOK, at whose instigation it was produced, the Beaverette was a lightly armoured patrol car based on the Standard Fourteen private car chassis. Marks I and II were open-topped, had a maximum speed of 40mph (64kph) and were armed with a BREN light machine gun or a BOYS anti-tank rifle. Marks III and IV were fitted with a turret, had a maximum speed of 24mph (39kph) and were armed with a Bren light machine gun or two Vickers "K" guns. All marks were manned by a crew of three. A total of 2800 Beaverettes were produced for Home Defence in the aftermath of the DUNKIRK evacuation. They were used by the RAF for airfield protection as well as by the Army.

Beck, Gen Ludwig (1880–1944)

General Beck was appointed Chief of Staff of the German Army in 1933, and later resigned in 1938 in protest against Hitler's war plans. He then became the centre of a group of officers disaffected with the Nazi Party, and in 1944 allied himself with STAUFFENBERG in the JULY BOMB PLOT. Promptly arrested, he was forced to commit suicide that evening.

Beda Fomm, Libya, 1941

On 5 February the Italian 10th Army, withdrawing from Cyrenaica to Tripolitania, was ambushed south of BENGHAZI by the outnumbered British 7th Armoured Division which had cut across the base of the Benghazi Bulge through MECHILI and Msus and established a road block at Beda Fomm. Repeated attempts to break through were beaten off and on 7 February 10th Army surrendered. More than 25,000 prisoners were taken, as well as over 100 tanks, 216 guns and 1500 wheeled vehicles; General Tellera, 10th Army's commander, was mortally wounded during the fighting. The strategy which led to this crushing victory, ending the first campaign in the Western Desert, was devised by Lieutenant-General Richard O'CONNOR, the commander of the British XIII Corps.

Bedell Smith, Lt Gen Walter (1895–1961)

Bedell Smith enlisted in the ranks of the US Army and rose to become a staff officer of considerable ability. In 1941 he was Secretary of the US Joint Chiefs of Staff, and thereafter Secretary of the Anglo-American Combined Chiefs of Staff. In September 1942 he was appointed General EISENHOWER's Chief of Staff, a post he retained until the end of the war. In this position he negotiated the Italian Armistice of 1943 and arranged the surrender of the German Forces in North-West Europe in 1945.

Beechcraft Aircraft (USA)

Beechcraft AT-10 Wichita Developed just before the war as a twin-engined cabin monoplane for civil transport purposes, the AT-10 was adopted by the USAAF as a transitional trainer for aircrew, over 2300 being produced before production ceased in 1944. Built of plywood, it had a span of 44ft (13.4m), two 295hp radial engines and a maximum speed of 190mph (306kph).

Beechcraft UO-43 Traveller This was another adapted civil cargo aircraft, a single-engined biplane with retractable undercarriage. About 400 were put to use by the USAAF and US Navy, and 105 were supplied to the British Royal Navy (RN) under Lend-Lease arrangements. Powered by a 450hp radial engine, it had a span of 32ft (9.76m) and a top speed of 195mph (314kph).

Beechcraft UO-45 Expediter This was first flown in 1936 as a civil airline feeder and numbers were built for the USAAF and US Navy, as well as being supplied to the RAF and RN. They were principally used for light transport duties, though some in naval hands were used for submarine reconnaissance. The Expediter was a twin-engined monoplane with a span of 47.6ft (14.5m), two 450hp radial engines, and a top speed of 206mph (331kph).

Beethoven Gerät

German guided missile carried beneath a fighter aircraft; the codename referred to the combination and not simply to the missile itself.

BEF British Expeditionary Force (UK). The British forces sent to France in 1939. During the "Phoney War" period, it was facetiously said to mean "Back Every Fortnight", a reference to frequent leaves of absence.

Beirut, Lebanon, 1941

The objective of 7th Australian Division during the campaign against the Vichy French forces in SYRIA, secured on 15 July.

Belaia, Ethiopia, 1941

A mountain fortress 80 miles south-west of Lake Tana, used by Emperor HAILE SELASSIE as his first headquarters during the 1941 campaign.

Belgium, 1940–45

See ANTWERP; BASTOGNE; BRUSSELS; BULGE, BATTLE OF THE; FRANCE, BELGIUM, HOLLAND, 1940; GEMBLOUX GAP; ST VITH.

Belgorod, Soviet Union, 1943

A city and important railway junction 50 miles (80km) north of KHARKOV captured by the Voronezh Front in February during the Soviet offensive which followed the fall of STALINGRAD. On 18 March it was recaptured by Panzergrenadier Division *Grossdeutschland* during von MANSTEIN's counteroffensive.

Bell P-39 Airacobra fighter in flight.

When the line stabilized, Belgorod lay just below the southern shoulder of the KURSK salient, the elimination of which was the object of Operation ZITADELLE, the last major German offensive on the Eastern Front. The failure of this and the subsequent Soviet advance resulted in the final liberation of the city by Voronezh and Steppe Fronts on 5 August.

Belgrade, Yugoslavia, 1941 and 1944

Although declared an open city, Belgrade was subjected to a series of devastating air attacks by the Luftwaffe on 6 April 1941 and was occupied by German troops six days later. On 14 October 1944 TITO's Partisans and the Soviet 3rd Ukrainian Front launched a joint attack which captured the city centre. German troops were finally withdrawn on 19 October. See also BALKAN CAMPAIGNS.

Bell Aircraft (USA)

Bell P-39 Airacobra A highly unconventional machine for its day, the Airacobra's Allison supercharged engine was placed behind the pilot, driving the propeller by a transfer shaft and gearbox. This allowed a cannon to be carried in the nose, firing through the propeller boss. The prototype flew in 1939 and a number were ordered by the French government. By the time these aircraft were ready, France had collapsed and the order was taken over by Britain. The first machines reached the RAF in July 1941 but after initial service tests were withdrawn. The US Air Force had better success with later models and over 9000 were eventually manufactured before production ended in mid-1944, large numbers of these serving with considerable success with the Red Air Force in the Soviet Union. *Span* 34ft (10.37m); *engine* 1200hp in-line; *armament* 1 37mm or 20mm cannon, 4 machine guns; *speed* 385mph (619kph).

Bell P-59 Airacomet The first American jet aircraft to fly, the Airacomet was developed in 1942 using two British Whittle engines. Subsequent development took some time and it was not until 1944 that production models were delivered to the US Army and Navy Air Forces. Only 66 were built, and they were used as advanced trainers. *Span* 45.5ft (13.9m); *engines* 2 2000lb (907kg)/st thrust turbo jets; *armament* 1 37mm cannon, 3 .50 machine guns; *speed* 413mph (665kph).

Bell P-63 Kingcobra An improved model of the AIRACOBRA, with longer wing and tail sur-

faces and more power. Some 3000 were built but relatively few were used by the US forces and then only in training roles. Most were supplied to the Soviet and Free French air forces in 1944, and in their hands they proved effective ground-support fighters. *Span* 38.3ft (11.7m); *engine* 1 1510hp in-line; *armament* 1 37mm cannon, 4 machine guns; *speed* 410mph (660kph).

Belorussia, Soviet Union, 1941 and 1944

Western area of the Soviet Union bordering on Poland, East Prussia and the Baltic States. During Operation BARBAROSSA the German invaders were actually welcomed by a large portion of the population which had suffered severely under STALIN. This goodwill soon vanished under the harsh conditions imposed by the Nazi civil administration and turned to hatred when SS *Einsatzgruppen* began committing atrocities in the rear areas. Belorussia was liberated during Operation BAGRATION, which lasted from 22 June to 29 August 1944 and was mounted by ROKOSSOVSKY's 1st Belorussian Front, Zhakarov's 2nd Belorussian Front, CHERNYAKHOVSKY's 3rd Belorussian Front and Bagramyan's 1st Baltic Front. This resulted in a 450-mile advance which eliminated the equivalent of 25 German divisions and virtually destroyed Army Group Centre as well as isolating Army Group North in the Baltic States.

Belsen: a furnace in which the Germans burned the bodies of their victims.

Belsen, Germany

A German concentration camp on the Lüneberg heath near Hanover. Commanded by Josef KRAMER, although not an extermination camp the conditions were harsh and typhus had broken out in 1945 resulting in thousands of deaths. When the camp was captured by British troops on 13 April 1945, several thousand bodies were strewn around the camp and the remaining inmates were barely alive. This was the first camp with such conditions to be discovered by the Allies, and the publication of films and accounts came as a major shock to the general public.

Murdered Russian prisoners in the concentration camp near Borisov, Minsk region.

Benes, President Edouard (1884–1948)

President of Czechoslovakia at the time of the MUNICH Agreement in 1938, Benes resigned in the face of political defeat and left for France. In 1939, after the German occupation of the whole of CZECHOSLOVAKIA, Benes formed the Czech National Committee in Paris and in 1940 moved it to London. He actively promoted the formation of Czech military and air force units within the British forces, and was involved in the decision to assassinate HEYDRICH. His Provisional Government was recognized by the British in July 1940 and all the Allies had given it full recognition by the end of 1942. In 1942 he was assured of Russian support by MOLOTOV, and a Czech brigade was formed in the Red Army. In the following year, in order to accommodate the Communist element in Czechoslovakia, he signed a Pact of Friendship and Mutual Assistance in Moscow which promised close postwar co-operation. He returned to Prague in May 1945 and was re-elected to the Presidency in 1946. After the Communist take-over in 1948 he resigned, and died shortly afterwards.

Bengal, HMIS – Bathurst Class Minesweeping Sloop

On 11 November 1942 the *Bengal*, commanded by Lieutenant-Commander William J. Wilson, was escorting the 6200-ton Dutch tanker *Ondina* across the Indian Ocean from Fremantle to Diego Suarez when they were intercepted by the Japanese armed merchant cruisers *Hokoko Maru* (10,493 tons) and *Kyosumi Maru* (8631 tons) each armed with five 5-inch guns. Although his ship was hopelessly outclassed, Wilson ordered the *Ondina* to head for safety while he engaged the enemy. Shells from the *Bengal* and the tanker's stern gun simultaneously struck the *Hokoko Maru*, causing a heavy explosion and starting fires which raged until the Japanese vessel blew up, leaving no trace. Although over 200 rounds were fired at the *Bengal*, she sustained only one direct hit, minor damage and no casualties. However, she was still engaged with the *Kyosumi Maru*, and when her ammunition was expended Wilson was forced to retire under cover of a smoke screen. The surviving raider pursued and torpedoed the *Ondina*, sustaining further damage in the process, and machine-gunned her crew in their boats before making off. The tanker did not sink and was re-boarded by her crew and brought safely into Fremantle.

Benghazi, Libya, 1941–42

A port in western Cyrenaica captured by the British XIII Corps on 6 February 1941, recaptured by the Axis on 4 April, captured again by the British in December and recovered by ROMMEL in January 1942. The port finally passed into British hands on 20 November 1942 during the general advance which followed the Second Battle of ALAMEIN. Benghazi was not defensible as it was immediately isolated by hostile movement across the base of the arc of coastline known as the "Benghazi Bulge". The Bulge itself contained several airfields, possession of which was reflected in the fortunes of MALTA. Benghazi itself was an important entry point for Axis supplies.

Bennett, AVM Donald (1910–1968)

Bennett was one of the most brilliant airmen produced by his native Australia. In the early months of the war he was one of the directors of the transatlantic ferry, flying aircraft from the USA to Britain. After rejoining the RAF he was given command of No. 10 Squadron BOMBER COMMAND and in 1941 was shot down over Norway while attacking the German battleship TIRPITZ. He escaped by parachute, and led his crew back to England via Sweden. On 15 August 1942 Bennett was appointed to command the PATHFINDER FORCE, which he led throughout the war. Early in 1944 Bennett established the Light Night Striking Force equipped with the de Havilland Mosquito. Bennett was a difficult and arrogant personality who forced respect rather than won affection but, nevertheless, he was one of the great operational air commanders of the war.

Benson-Livermore Class Destroyers (USA)

Displacement 1630 tons; *dimensions* 348ft 3in×36ft 3in (10.6×11m); mean draught 10ft 3in (3m); *machinery* 2-shaft geared turbines producing shp 50,000; *speed* 36 knots; *armament* 4×5in; 4 to 10×.50in AA; 5×21in torpedo tubes; or 5×5in; 10×21in torpedo tubes; *complement* 250; *number in class* 96, launched 1939–43.

Berchtesgaden, Germany, 1945

A town in southern Bavaria near which HITLER built the mountain retreat at which numerous pre-war and wartime conferences were held and decisions made. During the German collapse in 1945 Berchtesgaden was to have been the centre of a so-called National Redoubt from which resistance to the Allies would have continued, but the plan came to nothing. The town was captured on 4 May 1945 by the US 7th Army, all traces of Hitler's presence being destroyed to prevent the area becoming a Nazi shrine.

Bergen, Norway, 1940

Captured on 9 April by German troops landed from the light cruisers *Köln* and *Königsberg*, two naval auxiliaries and torpedo boats. During the engagement *Königsberg* and the auxi-

Benson-Livermore class destroyer.

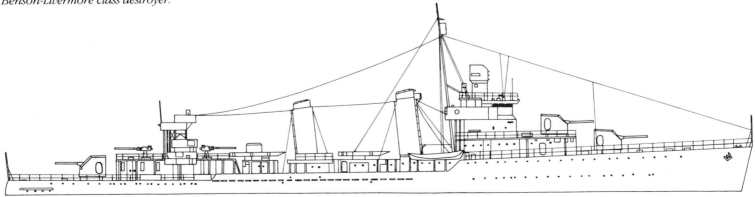

liary *Bremse* were damaged by the fire of shore batteries. The following day *Königsberg* was dive-bombed and sunk in the harbour by Fleet Air Arm Skuas flying from Scapa Flow.

Beria, Lavrenty P. (1899–1954)

Head of the NKVD, the Soviet intelligence and counter-espionage force, during the war years, Beria was also a member of the GKO and took an active part in the day-to-day conduct of the war. He was given command of the Partisan forces behind German lines, which were generally effective, though Beria used terror tactics to goad local civil populations into aiding the Partisans and opposing the Germans. After the war his control of the secret police and his intrigues made him very unpopular within the Communist hierarchy, and when his protector STALIN died in 1953, Beria did not long survive him.

Beriev Be-2 (USSR)

This was one of the few flying boats employed by the Soviet Air Force. Developed in 1931, it was a high-wing monoplane intended for short range coastal reconnaissance but was also used for general transport duties. In spite of its age it appears to have been used continuously throughout the war years. *Span* 44ft (13.4m); *engine* 680hp in-line; *speed* 136mph (219kph).

Beriev MDR-6 (BE-4) (USSR)

A flying boat developed in 1936 for reconnaissance purposes. Relatively few were built, and its sole wartime use was in the maritime reconnaissance, coastal patrol and mine-laying roles, principally protecting the northern approaches to Murmansk. A high-wing monoplane with a span of 65ft (19.8m); it had two 1100hp radial engines; giving it a top speed of 225mph (362kph); it was armed with two machine guns and 1100lb (500kg) of bombs or depth charges.

Berlin, Battle of

General term referring to a series of 16 heavy raids on Berlin which began on 18/19 November 1943 and ended in March 1944. Berlin was a difficult target for RAF BOMBER COMMAND, being at long range and well defended, and with the route lying across heavily defended areas. The attacks involved 9111 bomber sorties, and considerable damage was done, though it never approached the scale achieved against Hamburg or other cities. The

Russians celebrating the Fall of Berlin atop the Reichstag.

cost was high for the limited results achieved, 492 bombers failing to return, while nearly 100 more were destroyed in crashes on return, mainly due to damage suffered; this represented a loss rate of 6.5%.

Berlin, Germany, 1945

The Soviet offensive aimed at the capture of Berlin, already devastated by Allied air attack, began on 16 April with westward drives by ZHUKOV's 1st Belorussian Front and KONEV's 1st Ukrainian Front, the spearheads of which isolated the city in a pincer movement on 25 April. A series of concentric attacks followed, the Russians fighting their way through the suburbs and into the central area in the face of desperate resistance. The Reichstag building was captured on 1 May, although the Red Flag had actually been raised over the building while fighting was in progress the previous day. On 2 May General Karl Weidling, the recently appointed Commandant of the city, surrendered unconditionally, HITLER having committed suicide in the *Führerbunker* on 30 April. It seems probable that between 16 April and 2 May Zhukov and Konev sustained not

Fall of Germany, April–May 1945.

less than 100,000 killed in the taking of Berlin. German military casualties are unknown but must have been comparable. The number of prisoners taken is estimated at 136,000 and includes a high proportion of old men and boys drafted into the ranks for the battle. It is believed that about 100,000 civilians died as a result of the fighting.

Bernadotte, Count Folke (1895–1948)

Bernadotte was the nephew of the king of Sweden and Vice Chairman of the Swedish Red Cross, positions which enabled him to arrange for exchanges of prisoners between Britain and Germany. Whilst arranging a transfer of Scandinavian political prisoners in 1945 he came into contact with HIMMLER, who put forward various peace proposals for Bernadotte to communicate to the Allies. He did, but the Allies rejected them.

Bernhard

A German communications system for controlling night fighters. Devised in the closing months of the war in an endeavour to find a system proof against Allied jamming and interference, it used a special transmitter to send teleprinter-coded messages which were picked up by the fighter aircraft on a special receiver (known as "Bernhardine") and printed on tape. This gave the aircraft's direction from the control station and also information about its target, and the data was updated at one-minute intervals. The system was efficient and would have entered full service in mid-1945 had the war not ended.

Bernhard

German plan to drop counterfeit bank notes over the United Kingdom in an attempt to undermine the British economy.

Bernhard, Prince of the Netherlands (1911–)

Born in Germany, Bernhard was married to Princess Juliana, the heir to the Dutch throne. After the German invasion of the Netherlands in 1940, he fled to London and became a pilot in the Royal Air Force. He was later appointed Liaison Officer to the Dutch Resistance movement and reorganized the Dutch intelligence service. In 1944 he became Commander-in-Chief of the Dutch Armed Forces and secretly returned to the Netherlands to organize resistance groups.

Bernhard Line, Italy, 1943

The German defence line stretching from the GARIGLIANO River to Castel di Sangri in the Apennines, designed to impose delay on the Allies as they approached the main GUSTAV LINE positions. Penetrated in November 1943. Also known as the Reinhard Line and by the Allies as the Winter Line.

Berthier Rifle

André Berthier designed several rifles and carbines which were used by the French Army from 1890 to 1945. Fundamentally they were the earlier Lebel rifle adapted to a clip-loaded box magazine instead of a tubular magazine. The weapons were first developed in 8mm calibre and these remained in service until the late 1920s, when the 7.5mm cartridge was adopted as the French standard. At that time two or three rifle and carbine models were redesigned and rebuilt to accept the new cartridge. Although officially superseded in 1936 by the MAS36 rifle, in fact large numbers of Berthier rifles and carbines remained in the hands of troops during the war.

Bertram

British 8th Army deception plan prior to the Second Battle of ALAMEIN.

Besa Machine Guns

Two machine guns designed by the Czech company Zbrojowka Brno were adopted by the British Army, and both were manufactured by the Birmingham Small Arms (BSA) company, hence the name Besa. The first was the Czech ZB vz/53 in 7.92mm calibre, adopted for use as a coaxial gun in tanks in 1939. It was belt-fed, and the first models had two rates of fire; later models did away with this and had only the high rate of 800 rounds per minute. The second was the 15mm ZB vz/60, adopted in 1940, a heavy weapon which was principally used as turret armament in light armoured cars.

Bessarabia, Romania, 1940

Area of north-eastern Romania lying between the Pruth and Dniestr rivers, forcibly annexed by STALIN in June 1940.

Beveland Peninsula, Holland, 1944

Forming the northern shore of the West SCHELDT and dominating the approach to ANTWERP from the sea, the peninsula was held by the German 70th Division, which formed part of General von Zangen's 15th Army. During the last week of October the advance of the Canadian 2nd Infantry Division along the neck of land connecting the peninsula with the mainland was fiercely contested, but the defenders were outflanked by an amphibious landing on 28 October by a brigade of 52nd (Lowland) Division and part of 79th Armoured Division. The peninsula was secured on the following day.

Bevin, Ernest (1881–1951)

A British Labour party politician, Bevin was appointed Minister of Labour and National Service by CHURCHILL in 1940, with sweeping powers to give the government absolute authority over all industry and all labour. In 1941 he introduced conscription for women, and by a series of Essential Works Orders made it illegal for workers to leave their jobs or employers to dismiss workers without approval, suspended the 48-hour week, outlawed strikes, and directed workers into vital industries. He also assisted in drawing up plans for the postwar demobilization of the armed forces, which proved highly successful and more fair in their application than those of 1918–19. In the postwar Labour government he became a respected Foreign Secretary.

BGS   Brigadier, General Staff (UK).

Bhamo, Burma, 1944

Town in northern Burma, south of MYITKYINA, attacked on 10 November by the 38th Division of Lieutenant-General SUN LI-JEN's Chinese New 1st Army as part of the strategy to re-open road communications between Burma and China. The 1200-strong Japanese garrison resisted until the night of 14/15 December when the 900 survivors broke out.

Bhose, Subhas Chandra (1897–1945)

An Indian politician with strong anti-British views, in 1939 Bhose was president of the Congress Party. He left India in 1941 and visited Germany where he began recruiting Indian prisoners-of-war for his "Indian Nationalist Army". He did the same when visiting Japan in 1943 but the INA was never very effectual. It was during a further recruiting flight to Japan that Bhose's aircraft crashed on Formosa and he was killed.

Biak Island, New Guinea, 1944

Lying off the northern coast of NEW GUINEA, Biak was used by the Japanese as an air base. The US 41st Division and Australian troops landed on 27 May and met unexpectedly determined resistance which was not finally suppressed until 29 June. The Allies sustained over 2700 casualties and the Japanese over 9000.

Bialystok, Soviet Union, 1941 and 1944

A Polish city north-east of WARSAW, absorbed into the USSR following the Soviet invasion of Poland in 1939. During Operation BARBAROSSA the Panzer groups of GUDERIAN and HOTH encircled most of PAVLOV's troops in two major pockets at Bialystok and MINSK. When these surrendered on 3 July 1941, 290,000 Russian soldiers marched into captivity, abandoning

masses of equipment which included 2585 tanks and 1449 guns. Shaken by the scale of the disaster, STALIN summoned Pavlov to Moscow and had him shot. Bialystok was liberated by the 2nd Belorussian Front on 27 July 1944 during Operation BAGRATION. The Soviet advance was materially assisted by the Polish Secret Army in and around the city, although this group was promptly disarmed by the Russians when they arrived.

Biber

A one-man submarine operated by the German Navy. Displacing some three tons, with a length of about 29.5ft (9m), it carried two torpedoes beneath the hull. A small number were built and employed off the Scheldt estuary to harass Allied shipping in 1944–45 but with relatively little effect.

Bicycle Troops

Although some European armies still maintained bicycle units when war broke out, the idea had little practical application on the mechanized battlefield. In the Far East, however the Japanese commandeered thousands of civilian bicycles when they invaded MALAYA, BURMA and the PHILIPPINES and these not only enabled them to maintain the momentum of their advance but also provided a useful method of bringing supplies forward in difficult country.

Nazi bicycle troops, Paris 1940.

Biggin Hill, United Kingdom, 1940

A RAF fighter base and sector control station south-east of London which played a prominent part in the Battle of BRITAIN. During the phase of the battle in which the Luftwaffe threw the main weight of its attacks on Fighter Command airfields, Biggin Hill was attacked repeatedly and sustained such serious damage that the Operations Room was moved to a shop in the nearby village. However, while senior Luftwaffe officers believed that the base's three fighter squadrons had been eliminated, one continued to fly from Biggin Hill and the other two used alternative airfields. See *Full Circle – The Story of Air Fighting* by Air Vice-Marshal J. E. Johnson (Chatto and Windus) and *Fighter – The True Story of the Battle of Britain* by Len Deighton (Jonathan Cape).

Bigot

Security classification covering plans for the Allied invasion of NORMANDY.

Big Week

The week commencing 20 February 1944 when Operation ARGUMENT was launched as part of a directive, codename POINTBLANK, designed to attack the German aircraft industry. A series of heavily-escorted bombing raids were to be made on German aviation and associated factories in an effort to bring the Luftwaffe's fighter forces to battle.

Available to undertake the attacks were 30 four-squadron heavy bomber groups of the US 8th Air Force, supported by 17 three-squadron fighter groups, all these aircraft being based in England, and a further 12 heavy bomber groups and four fighter groups of the US 15th Air Force in Italy. This force was further supported by elements of RAF Fighter and Bomber Commands. In defence, the Luftwaffe mustered some 38 Gruppen of single-engined fighters and seven more of twin-engined "destroyers". The offensive opened on 20 February when the US 8th Air Force attacked various aircraft factories with over 1000 aircraft; on 21 February they attacked factories around Brunswick with 764 heavy bombers; the next day Halberstadt was bombed by 8th AF machines, while 15th AF bombers flew from their Italian bases to attack Regensburg. On the 24th, 266 US bombers attacked the ball-bearing factories at Schweinfurt by day, and 734 RAF bombers followed up by night. On the same day 15th AF units attacked an aircraft plant at Steyr, Austria, and

An RAF Hurricane pilot prepares to take off from Biggin Hill airfield.

oil refineries at Fiume. On 25 February Regensburg, Augsburg, Stuttgart and SCHWEINFURT were attacked. When the week ended, bad weather preventing further attacks, 8148 bombing sorties had been undertaken by the US air forces and BOMBER COMMAND, 19,177 tons of bombs being dropped; 8th AF had flown 3300 of these sorties and dropped 6000 tons. 224 bombers and 41 fighters were lost by the Americans, whose escort fighters claimed 166 German interceptors shot down in return, while bomber gunners – notorious for overclaiming – considered that they had added more than 400 others. While targets on the ground had been hard-hit, the effects had not been decisive as buildings, rather than the machine tools within them, had been the major sufferers. In the air the objectives of Argument had been more effectively met; during February 1944 the Luftwaffe air defences lost 355 fighters with 155 more damaged – the majority of these losses occurring during Big Week.

Billotte, Gen Gaston Herve Gustav (1875–1940)

Commander of the French 1st Army Group under GEORGES and GAMELIN in May 1940, and one of the few French commanders in whom

the British had any confidence. Following the German invasion of Belgium on 10 May he supervised the advance to the DYLE and the subsequent withdrawals to the Escaut and the Dendre. He was planning a counter-attack when, on 21 May, he was mortally injured in a road accident. He died two days later.

Biological Warfare

The use of disease as a weapon. Britain, the USA, Germany and Japan all conducted experiments and research to discover methods of disseminating certain infectious diseases among their enemies, though they never put any of them into use. Such diseases as anthrax, pneumonic plague and spotted fever were examined, together with various methods of releasing their bacillus in airborne form. The conclusion generally reached was that, whilst such distribution was possible, biological warfare was a two-edged weapon since the subsequent course of the disease could be neither foreseen nor controlled and it could well infect friendly troops and civilians. Except for some extended field trials said to have been conducted by the Japanese in North China against Chinese troops, without noticeable success, biological warfare was never attempted.

BIOS British Intelligence Objectives Sub-Committee (UK). An organization set up to obtain all possible information about German wartime technical and economic developments as these were uncovered in the wake of the advancing army.

Birdcage
Allied leaflet drop on Japanese prisoner-of-war camps announcing the surrender of Japan, 1945.

Bir el Gubi, Libya, 1941
A defended position 35 miles (56km) south of TOBRUK denied to the British by the Italian *Ariete* Armoured Division during the early stages of Operation CRUSADER.

Bir Hacheim, Libya, 1942
A fortified box at the southern end of the GAZALA Line held by Brigadier-General Marie Pierre KOENIG's 1st Free French Brigade. From 27 May until 10 June the Brigade repulsed repeated German and Italian attacks. It broke out successfully during the night of 10/11 June, some 2500 men of its original 3700 reaching safety. See *March or Die – France and the Foreign Legion* by Tony Geraghty (Grafton).

Birke (Birch)
German plan for the withdrawal from Finland, 1944.

Birkenau, Poland
A subsidiary camp of AUSCHWITZ, the German concentration camp in southern Poland, and used principally to house slave labour employed in various munitions factories in the area. As the labourers' health failed, they were retransferred to Auschwitz for execution.

KMS Bismarck.

Birmingham Class Cruiser
HMAS *Adelaide*, launched 1918. See also IMPROVED BIRMINGHAM CLASS. *Displacement* 5100 tons; *dimensions* 462ft 9in×49ft 9in (141×15.2m); *mean draught* 15ft 9in (4.5m); *machinery* 2-shaft geared turbines producing shp 25,000; *speed* 25.5 knots; *protection* main belt 3in; deck 2in; gun shields 1in; *armament* 8×6in (8×1); 3×4in AA (3×1); *complement* 470.

Bishop Self-propelled Gun (UK)
A stop-gap developed urgently in response to a June 1941 request from the Middle East for a self-propelled mounting for the 25-pdr gun. The weapon was installed on the hull of a VALENTINE infantry tank and protected by a tall superstructure of light armour plate. The arrangement was clumsy and cramped and the vehicle performed poorly across country. Ammunition stowage was limited to 32 rounds and a standard limber was generally towed to supplement this. Bishops took part in the Second Battle of ALAMEIN but were withdrawn after the campaign in SICILY.

Bishop self-propelled 25-pdr gun.

Bismarck, KMS – Battleship
Bismarck was launched on 14 February 1939 and commissioned in August 1940. On 20 May 1941, flying the flag of Vice-Admiral Günther LÜTJENS and accompanied by the heavy cruiser PRINZ EUGEN, she left the Baltic for the Atlantic, to prey on the British convoy routes. However, the Admiralty was aware of the ships' departure and on 23 May they were detected in the Denmark Strait and shadowed by the cruisers HMS SUFFOLK and NORFOLK. On 24 May they were intercepted by the battleship HMS PRINCE OF WALES and the battlecruiser HMS HOOD. Both German ships con-

Bismarck class battleship.

centrated their fire on the *Hood*, which blew up. They then shifted their fire to the *Prince of Wales*, which was damaged but managed to score several hits on the *Bismarck* before she obeyed orders to break contact; these resulted in the loss of one-third of the German battleship's fuel and the shipping of 200 tons of water. Later that day Lütjens detached *Prinz Eugen* and decided to make for BREST. During the evening the *Bismarck* was attacked by aircraft from HMS VICTORIOUS but sustained only minor damage. Contact with the German vessel was lost during the night but was regained when a long signal from Lütjens was intercepted by British radio direction-finding stations, her position being verified by a Catalina flying boat at 1030 on 26 May. Both the Home Fleet and Force H were now converging on *Bismarck*. That evening an attack by Swordfish torpedo bombers from HMS ARK ROYAL damaged her steering gear beyond repair. She was further harried throughout the night by destroyer attacks. On the morning of 27 May *Bismarck* was pounded into a wreck by the guns of the battleships HMS KING GEORGE V and *Rodney*, the *coup de grâce* being administered with torpedoes fired by the cruiser HMS *Dorsetshire*. Only 107 of her complement survived. *Displacement* 50,153 tons; *dimensions* 823ft 6in×118ft (251x36m); mean draught 30ft 7in (9.22m); *machinery* 3-shaft geared steam turbines producing 138,000shp; *speed* 29 knots; *protection* main belt 12.6in; deck 2–4.7in; turrets and barbettes 9–14in; *armament* 8×15in (4×2); 12×5.9in (6×2); 16×4.1in AA; 16×37mm AA; 12×20mm AA; *aircraft* 2 floatplanes; *complement* 2192.

Biting

British Combined Operations raid on the German RADAR station at BRUNEVAL, February 1942.

Bizerta, Tunisia, 1943

The capture of this northern port by US II Corps on 7 May, coupled with the capture of Tunis the same day by the British 7th Armoured Division, signalled the end of organized Axis resistance in North Africa. Some 40,000 prisoners were taken in the American sector.

Blackburn Aircraft (UK)

Blackburn Botha A high-wing twin-engined monoplane designed in 1938 to fill an RAF demand for a Coastal Command reconnais-sance and torpedo-bombing machine. It proved to be underpowered for its role and after a short service career was withdrawn and subsequently served out its time as a training machine. *Span* 59ft (18m); *engines* 2 880hp radial; *speed* 250mph (402kph).

Blackburn Roc A Fleet Air Arm fighter which was roughly the equivalent of the RAF's Defiant. A low-wing monoplane with radial engine, it carried a powered four-gun turret behind the pilot's position. It proved underpowered and saw virtually no active service, being relegated to training. *Span* 46ft (14m); *engine* 1 905hp radial; *crew* 2; *armament* 4 machine guns; *speed* 196mph (315kph).

Blackburn Skua The Skua was the predecessor of the Roc (above) and closely resembled it, though without the turret; the rear gunner had one hand-operated gun. Used as a fighter and dive-bomber it claimed the first German aircraft shot down by the Fleet Air Arm and on 10 April 1940 sank the German cruiser *Königsberg* in Bergen harbour. It was withdrawn from combat duties in 1941 and relegated to the training role. *Span* 46ft (14m); *engine* 1 830hp radial; *crew* 2; *armament* 5 machine guns; *speed* 225mph (362kph).

Blackcock

British offensive on the RUHR, January 1945.

Blacker Bombard

British anti-tank weapon invented by Lieutenant-Colonel Blacker RA, principally issued to Home Guard units, though a small number were used by the Army and Royal Air Force in defensive positions. The weapon operated on the spigot principle; a large bomb (20–29lb, 9–13kg) had a hollow tail tube containing a propelling cartridge. The bomb was loaded into a cradle, and, on firing the weapon, a heavy steel rod (the spigot) was propelled into the tail tube, firing the cartridge. The bomb was thus blown off the spigot and to the target about 200–400 yards (183–366m) away. The force of the explosion also blew the spigot back into its housing, so cocking it ready for the next shot. The spigot principle has the advantage that no conventional barrel is needed for the weapon, and in wartime this was a considerable saving in production time.

Blackett, Patrick M. S. (1897–1974)

A British physicist, Blackett was a member of the Tizard Committee for the scientific study of air defence from 1935, and was responsible for presenting the concept of RADAR to the services and gaining their co-operation. In 1941 he became scientific adviser to RAF Coastal Command, and in 1942 set up an Operational Research facility at the Admiralty and applied scientific methodology to the U-boat war. He was subsequently responsible for the growth of operational research in all arms of the British services.

Blacklist

American plan for the occupation of Japan.

"Blackpool", Burma, 1944

Chindit base south of MOGAUNG.

Black Prince – A43 Infantry Tank (UK)

An improved version of the CHURCHILL infantry tank developed by Vauxhall Motors Ltd from September 1943 onwards. The choice of the 17-pdr as main armament made a larger turret a necessity and this in turn required a wider hull to accommodate it, although the design incorporated as many mechanical components as possible from the Churchill Mark VII. By May 1945 six prototypes had been constructed but as the CENTURION main battle tank had commenced its production run the project was cancelled. *Weight* 50 tons; *speed* 11mph (18kph); *armour* 152mm; *armament* 1 17-pdr gun; 2 Besa machine guns; *engine*: *Bedford petrol 350hp; crew* 5.

Blackstone

Unit of the Western Task Force which landed at Safi, Morocco, during Operation TORCH.

Black Swan Class Escort Sloops (UK)

See also MODIFIED BLACK SWAN CLASS. *Displacement* 1250–1300 tons; *dimensions* 299ft 6in×37ft 6in (91.3×11.4m); mean draught 8ft 6in (2.56m); *machinery* 2-shaft geared turbines producing shp 3600; *speed* 19.25 knots; *armament* 6×4in AA (3×2); 4×2-pdr AA (1×4) and 4×0.5in AA (1×4) or 12×20mm AA (6×2); *complement* 180–195; *number in class* 13, launched 1939–43.

Blamey, Gen Sir Thomas (1884–1951)

An Australian, Blamey served as Chief of Staff to Monash during World War I, retiring after the war to become Commissioner of Police for the state of Victoria. In February 1940 he was recalled to take command of the Australian Independent Force in the Middle

East. He arrived in Greece in 1941 just in time to supervise the withdrawal of ANZAC forces from Greece and Crete, after which he became Deputy Commander-in-Chief Middle East. He returned to Australia in 1942 to become Commander-in-Chief of Allied Land Forces under General MACARTHUR, a post he retained until the end of the war. He then took personal command of Australian forces in NEW GUINEA, recaptured Buna, and remained in command of Australian troops in that theatre. A good fighting soldier and a sound administrator, he was popular with his troops but less so with MacArthur with whose strategic concepts he did not always agree.

Blaskowitz, Col Gen Johannes von (1883–1946)

Blaskowitz served as a general in France, afterwards commanding the Army of Occupation in Poland. Here he made several ineffectual protests against the activities of the SS against the Jews. Transferred to France in 1944, he commanded Army Group G in the south, but after the American landings in Operation DRAGOON was relieved of his command when the city of Nancy was given up without HITLER's permission. He later commanded Army Group H (known as *Festung Holland*) in the Netherlands with considerable skill and eventually surrendered to the Canadian Army in May 1945. Arrested by the Allies, he was to be tried for war crimes at NUREMBERG but committed suicide in prison.

Blau, Fall (Case Blue)

German plan for offensive by Army Groups A and B in southern Russia, 1942.

Bletchley Park, United Kingdom

A country house situated near Bletchley, Buckinghamshire, some 50 miles (80km) north of London, purchased by the British government before the war to house its Codes and Cyphers School. It became the home of the ULTRA interception and decoding service.

Blissful

American landing on Choiseul, Solomon Islands, October 1943.

The "Blitz"

British nickname for the campaign of night bombing launched against the UK by the LUFTWAFFE when losses by day during the Battle of BRITAIN became too costly. The first

attack was made on London on the night of 7/8 September 1940 and was followed by raids by 150–300 bombers on all but ten nights until 12/13 November. 13,000 tons of high explosive and almost one million incendiary bombs were dropped, which killed more than 13,000 people and injured 20,000 more. In mid-November, targets were changed to include other industrial cities and major ports. During the night of 14/15 November Coventry was attacked by 437 bombers which devastated the centre of the city, killing 380, injuring 800 and cutting British aircraft production by 20 per cent. Raids followed on Southampton, Birmingham, Cardiff, Portsmouth, Avonmouth and London again; bad weather reduced the scale of the attack from December 1940 until February 1941. When

the attacks increased during the spring, so the defences began to take a larger toll due to the increasing use of radar in night fighters and controlling anti-aircraft artillery. However, during March and April some German bomber units were moved to the Mediterranean area for operations against Malta and the Balkans, and in May more units were moved east to prepare for the invasion of Russia. From a peak strength of 44 "Gruppen", the Luftwaffe bombing force in the west fell to four "Gruppen" by June, thus effectively ending the "Blitz". It is estimated that about 40,000 civilians were killed and 46,000 injured, more than one million homes destroyed or damaged, and a considerable degree of damage was done to the manufacturing facilities of the country.

Civilians shelter from the Blitz in a London Underground station.

Blitzkrieg

Term coined by the Germans to describe their method of waging war by rapid armoured thrusts supported by tactical aircraft. Employed for the first time in the invasion of POLAND in 1939, the essence of Blitzkrieg was the taking of calculated risks in moving rapidly without flank protection so as to keep the enemy unbalanced and apprehensive, and the whole concept was based upon a shrewd assessment of the enemy's training and mental conditioning. The soldiers of 1939–40 were anticipating war in the same mould as that of 1914–18, with static fronts and ponderous manoeuvres, and the rapid movement of armoured columns, together with the sudden onslaught of dive-bombers and ground-attack aircraft, completely unnerved them. Such rapid movement also caused rumour to exaggerate results, so that the opposing commanders rarely had any sound idea of where the German forces had reached or in what direction they were moving.

Blizna, southern Poland

German test establishment in southern Poland, used for firing tests of the A-4 ROCKET in 1943–44. As a result of a rocket fired from here going off course, Polish underground forces managed to reach the missile before the Germans, removed several vital parts, and sent them to England, where they were of assistance in determining various technical features of the rocket and assessing its likely performance.

Bloch Aircraft (Fr)

Bloch MB-152 A low-wing monoplane fighter, the Bloch 152 officially went into service in 1938; at the outbreak of war 86 had been supplied but without propellers or gunsights. Almost 600 had been delivered by the time of the French collapse, and the Luftwaffe seized the 173 which remained in a serviceable condition. Development continued under the Vichy government and eventually a very good fighter (the MB-155) resulted, but it was never used. *Span* 34.5ft (10.5m); *engine* 1080hp radial; *armament* 2 20mm cannon, 2 machine guns; *speed* 325mph (523kph).

Bloch 174 A twin-engined low-wing monoplane intended for reconnaissance and light bombing duties. First produced in 1939, 50 were delivered by May 1940 and a few were used against the German invasion. It later saw service in North Africa, and a number were taken by the Luftwaffe. *Span* 58.75ft (18m); *engines* 2 1140hp radial; *crew* 3; *armament* 7 machine guns; *speed* 330mph (531kph).

Blockbuster

British offensive on the Lower Rhine, 1945.

Blohm & Voss Aircraft (Ger)

Blohm & Voss BV 138 This was an unusual aircraft, a flying boat comprising a short hull, a high monoplane wing, twin tail booms with engines on their front ends, and a third central nacelle with a front engine and a gunner's cockpit at the rear. Designed as a reconnais-

sance machine, the prototype flew in 1937 but there were delays in placing it in production, and the first machines were used as transports in Norway. Later designs, with more powerful engines, were successful in their designed role. *Span* 88ft (26.8m); *engines* 3 880hp in-line; *crew* 5; *armament* 2 20mm cannon, 2 machine guns, 4 depth charges or 1455lb (660kg) of bombs; *speed* 170mph (274kph).

Blohm & Voss BV 141 This was another unique design, a single-engined monoplane with the fuselage carrying only the engine and fuel, and with the pilot seated in a small nacelle mounted asymmetrically on the starboard wing. Only a handful were built and these were employed on reconnaissance duties in Russia. *Span* 57.25ft (17.5m); *engine* 1560hp radial; *crew* 3; *armament* 4 7.9mm machine guns and 440lb (200kg) of bombs; *speed* 272mph (438kph).

Blohm & Voss BV 222 "Wiking" This large flying boat had been designed before the war as a transatlantic airliner, but was not completed until 1940, and a total of 14 were built. A six-engined monoplane, it had a crew of 11 and could carry up to 110 fully-equipped infantry or 110,000lb (50,000kg) of cargo; it could stay in the air for 28 hours. With a wingspan of 151ft (46m) and six 1000hp in-line engines, it had a top speed of 242mph (389kph). It was widely used for transport work, notably in the Mediterranean theatre.

Blomberg, FM Werner von (1878–1943)

After a World War I career in which he won the Pour le Mérite, von Blomberg was appointed Reich Defence Minister on 29 January 1933, having been manoeuvred into this position by the German President, von Hindenburg, with the object of keeping the incoming Chancellor, Adolf HITLER, under control. Instead, von Blomberg became an admirer of Hitler, and in May 1935 he was appointed Commander-in-Chief of the three armed services in addition to his ministerial responsibilities, elevating him to a position of military authority surpassing that of any other peacetime general in German history. In 1936, on the occasion of his 57th birthday, he was promoted Field-Marshal. After an unwise marriage to a lady of dubious reputation, he was forced to resign on the grounds that he had brought the officer corps into disrepute, a move calculated by Hitler to undermine the confidence of the Army and enable him to

The uncommon Blohm and Voss Bv 141, used for reconnaissance tasks.

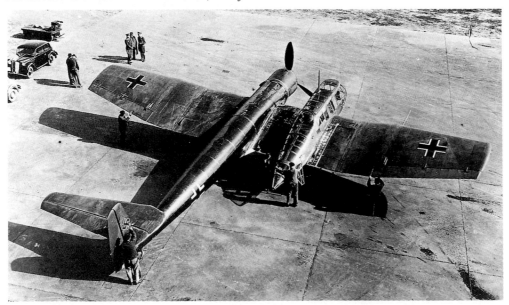

replace some of its leaders with his own appointees.

Blücher, KMS – Admiral Hipper Class Heavy Cruiser

Sunk on 9 April 1940 by torpedoes fired from Kaholm fortress while transporting troops up Oslo Fjord during the German invasion of NORWAY.

Bluecoat

British offensive at CAUMONT, NORMANDY, August 1944.

Blue Line, the, Soviet Union, 1943

The defensive line established by the German 17th Army on the Taman Peninsula between the Sea of Azov and the Black Sea. The defences included the city of Novorossiysk, which was stormed by the North Caucasus Front, 9–16 September, compelling the Germans to withdraw across the Kerch Straits into the CRIMEA.

Blume (Flower)

German codeword giving warning of Allied attack on the West Wall.

Blumentritt, Gen Günther von (1892–1967)

Von Blumentritt was an officer on the General Staff and acted as Operations Chief for von RUNDSTEDT during the Polish and French campaigns. In January 1942 he became Chief of Staff to von KLUGE and the 4th Army in Russia. He returned to von Rundstedt in France in September 1942 and assisted in planning counter-invasion measures. After a short period as Model's Chief of Staff, October 1944 saw him commanding XII SS Corps, in January 1945 25th Army, and in March 1945 1st Parachute Army. He surrendered to the British Army in Lübeck.

BMRA Brigade Major, Royal Artillery (UK).

Bobbin Carpet Layer

See AVRE.

Bock, FM Fedor von (1885–1945)

Von Bock commanded the Army Group North during the invasion of POLAND and Army Group B during the invasion of the Low Countries and France. For the invasion of Russia he commanded Army Group Centre, which advanced from Poland to MOSCOW and

was there held by the Red Army. Suffering from severe stomach cramps and unable to exercise command, he was removed by HITLER. He returned to the Eastern Front early in 1942 to replace von Reichenau in command of Army Group South, but during his advance into the Caucasus in July 1942 he was dismissed, following a dispute with Hitler. He later died in a British air raid.

Bodenplatte (Baseplate)

Luftwaffe attack on Allied airfields in Belgium and Holland, January 1945.

Bodyguard

Allied deception plans prior to OVERLORD.

Bodyline

British scientific committee set up to examine the threat posed by German V-WEAPONS, leading to CROSSBOW.

Boeing Aircraft (USA)

Boeing B-17 Flying Fortress One of the earliest four-engined bombers, the B-17 first flew in 1935. After the Munich Crisis of 1938 the YB-17A and B-17B, with turbo-supercharged radial engines and the new Norden bombsight were ordered. Following the outbreak of war in Europe the more powerful and better armed B-17C and D were ordered

in 1940, 20 being supplied to the RAF. These were employed for high altitude sorties over Northern Europe and North Africa, but proved to be underarmed, and after brief service were passed to COASTAL COMMAND for patrol bomber duties. The B-17E was then developed, incorporating considerable additional armament and armour, including a tail turret.

On the outbreak of the Pacific War B-17Cs and Ds in the Philippines and Dutch East Indies were replaced by E versions. Others were sent to England to begin formation of the US 8TH AIR FORCE for strategic bombing duties over Europe. After initial raids over Northern France, many were diverted to North Africa late in 1942 for the Tunisian campaign. The USAAF was convinced that close formations of these heavily-armed bombers could penetrate enemy air space by day without fighter cover. Once they began operating deep into Germany, however, German fighters began to inflict increasingly heavy losses. The E had been followed by the similar, but more numerous and more heavily-armed, B-17F, which was to form the bulk of US heavy bombing strength throughout 1943 and into 1944. To maintain supply to Europe the B-17 was withdrawn from the Pacific theatres during 1943 in favour of the longer-range CONSOLIDATED B-24 LIBERATOR.

Boeing B-17 on bombing sortie over Sizo, Solomon Islands, October 1942.

1944 brought the main production variant, the B-17G, which featured a "chin" turret for improved forward protection against head-on attacks. A heavily-armed "escort fighter" version of the B-17F proved unsuccessful, but from late 1943/early 1944 onwards, fighter escorts deeper into the target areas became possible. By August 1944 4574 B-17s were at the fronts in 33 bomber groups, and the aircraft remained the backbone of the USAAF strategic air effort in Europe until the end of the war. Losses were extremely heavy, particularly in 1943, and the life expectancy of USA B-17 crews was at times very low. It was, none the less, one of the outstanding bombers of the war and enjoyed a very long service life. *Span* 103.75ft (31.62m); engines 4 1200hp radial; *speed* (B-17F) 317mph (510km/hr); *service ceiling* 36,600ft (11,155m); *range* 3300 miles (5310km); *armament* 9×.50in, 1×.30in machine guns; bomb load 6000lb (2721kg) normal, 12,800lb (5800kg) maximum.

Boeing B-29 Superfortress Developed as a replacement for the B-17, the B-29 first flew on 21 September 1942 as the first production pressurized high-altitude heavy bomber. It weighed nearly twice as much as the B-17 and employed remotely-controlled machine gun turrets sighted through periscopes. The first service aircraft were sent to China in 1944 in order to raid Japan, but in July 1944 the capture of the MARIANAS ISLANDS allowed airfields to be built, and 180 B-24s were flown in to form the US 20th Air Force. Raiding began with an attack on TOKYO on 24 November 1944. The first attacks were made by day at high altitude, which restricted the bombloads, and results were poor. In March 1945 General LEMAY ordered low-level night incendiary raids, which allowed a greatly increased bombload. On 9 March a raid by 334 aircraft burned out 16 square miles (41km²) of Tokyo, killing 80,000 people, the most destructive raid of the entire war. On 6 August 1945 Colonel Paul W. Tibbets dropped the first atomic bomb on HIROSHIMA from a B-29, followed three days later by Major Charles W. Sweeney who released a similar weapon on NAGASAKI, leading to the Japanese surrender and the end of the war. *Span* 141.25ft (43m); *engines* 4 2200hp Wright Cyclone radial; *speed* 357mph (575km/hr); *service ceiling* 36,000ft (10,970m); *range* with 10,000lb (4536kg) of bombs, 3250 miles (5230km); *armament* 10×.50 machine guns, 1×20mm cannon, up to 20,000lb (9072kg) of bombs.

Boeing Stearman PT-13/17 Kaydet Designed by the Stearman Company, the design was taken over by Boeing after the war had begun and with the resources of the larger company it was possible to turn these training biplanes out in large numbers for USAAF and US Naval use. Over 10,000 were built in various forms, and many were also supplied to other countries including Britain and China. The Kaydet had a span of 32ft (9.75m), a single 220hp radial engine, and a top speed of 124mph (200kph).

Bofors Gun

The Bofors Company of Sweden have designed many weapons, but in the context of World War II Bofors Gun always means the 40mm anti-aircraft gun developed by that company in 1929 and subsequently adopted throughout the world. Of the major armies in 1939–45 only the Soviets did not adopt it, largely because they had already taken a 37mm Bofors design into use. The gun fired from four-round clips at a rate of 120rpm and had a maximum horizontal range of 10,800 yards (9882m) and an effective ceiling of 5000ft (1525m). It fired a 2lb (.9kg) high explosive shell fitted with an impact fuze and tracer and which destroyed itself after seven seconds of flight if it missed its target. The first guns used in the war were entirely manually operated and used open sights. Later models used power control and had predictors to improve the chance of hitting.

Bofors 40mm anti-aircraft gun, 1st US Army, Remagen, Germany, March 1945.

Bogue Class Escort Carriers (USA)

Displacement 9800 tons; *dimensions* 495ft 9in×69ft 6in (149×21m); mean draught 23ft 3in (6.9m); *machinery* 1-shaft geared turbine producing shp 8500; *speed* 18 knots; *armament* 2×5in (2×1); 20×40mm AA; *aircraft* 21; *complement* 890; *number in class* 11, launched 1941–42.

Bohr, Niels (1885–1962)

A Danish physicist, Bohr had won the Nobel Prize in 1922. He fled from Denmark to Sweden in 1942 and in the following year went to the USA where he became one of the principals in the atomic bomb programme.

Boise, USS – Brooklyn Class Light Cruiser

Boise sustained serious damage and heavy casualties during the Battle of CAPE ESPERANCE. She was repaired at Philadelphia and supported the Allied landings on SICILY and at SALERNO before returning to the Pacific, where she fought at HOLLANDIA, LEYTE, MINDORO and BORNEO.

Bold

An anti-detection device for German submarines, Bold (also known as *Pillenwerfer*) consisted of a perforated canister filled with a chemical compound based on calcium carbide. When ejected into the sea, reaction with the water caused a violent effervescence which set up a dense screen of bubbles in the surrounding water and formed a reflecting screen which sent back ASDIC or SONAR signals without revealing the U-boat behind the screen. It was frequently used to escape from Allied submarine hunters.

Bolero

1942 Allied plan for the build-up of American and Canadian forces in the United Kingdom.

Bologna, Italy, 1945

A city of Romagna captured on 21 April by II Polish Corps and US 34th Division during the final Allied offensive in Italy. See also ARGENTA GAP.

"Bomb Alley", 1941–42

The name given by the British to that part of the Mediterranean lying between CRETE and the North African coast during the period in which it was dominated by the Luftwaffe and the *Regia Aeronautica*.

Heavy clusters of incendiary bombs fall towards Dresden, 1945.

Bomb Disposal Squads

Units formed to defuze and render harmless unexploded bombs and other devices in the aftermath of air attack, generally in industrial and populated areas. This dangerous work was further complicated by the growing sophistication of the bombs themselves, which often incorporated time fuzes, anti-handling devices and booby traps.

Bomber Command

RAF Bomber Command was formed in 1936 and was wedded to the policy of strategic bombing propounded by TRENCHARD. On the outbreak of war it had neither the equipment nor the expertise to carry out a strategic offensive against Germany, its total strength being 349 aircraft, most of which were obsolescent. Heavy losses sustained in daylight raids in December 1939 forced the adoption of night bombing, which commenced in May 1940, though the navigational equipment and expertise were not sufficiently advanced to obtain the desired results. By 1941 the role of Bomber Command had become the subject of inter-service dispute, the Royal Navy pressing hard for the use of the

Command's resources in the Battle of the ATLANTIC, and strong support for this came from TIZARD, who argued that the strategic bombing offensive was consuming a disproportionate share of the available aircraft production and scientific resources which was not justified by the results achieved. Weight was added to this argument by the BUTT REPORT of August 1941, which revealed the inaccuracy of attacks against targets in Germany. In spite of these setbacks, Bomber Command remained the only British force capable of striking directly against Germany, and this simple fact ensured the continuation of the bombing offensive.

Operational efficiency improved greatly in 1942 with the arrival of the four-engined HANDLEY-PAGE HALIFAX, SHORT STIRLING and AVRO LANCASTER bombers, together with radar and other navigational aids. Although between late 1941 and early 1943 the front-line strength of the Command remained virtually unchanged, the new equipment considerably improved destructive ability; Bomber Command's Commander-in-Chief, Air Marshal Sir Arthur HARRIS was thus able to pursue his policy of AREA BOMBING. This was not accom-

plished without severe losses; between 1939 and 1945 55,573 aircrew were killed and 9784 made prisoner. As the war neared its end Bomber Command emerged as a powerful instrument of destruction, as demonstrated at DRESDEN in February 1945. However, it only achieved its aim of 1942 – the wholesale destruction of German cities – at a time when its purpose was gone and the enemy was on the verge of collapse.

The decisiveness of Bomber Command's contribution to victory will always remain a matter of controversy. The channelling of the cream of Britain's wartime technology and production facilities into Bomber Command may well have accounted for up to one-third of the country's war effort. As a result, the British had to rely upon America for all their transport aircraft, most of their landing craft and a high proportion of their tanks. The bombing campaign forced the Germans to divert to air defence considerable manpower and material resources which would otherwise have been used elsewhere, but it failed to impose a brake on German war production until late in 1944 and did not break civilian morale.

Bombersage

Bombersage was one of several designs for upward-firing gun assemblies to be fitted to German fighter aircraft. This one consisted of a bundle of 30mm recoilless gun barrels mounted vertically behind the cockpit of the aircraft so that the projectiles were fired upwards and the cartridge cases and gases were ejected downwards. The system demanded that the pilot fly beneath his target, and the battery of guns was automatically fired by an optical detector when the target was directly overhead.

BOMREP Bombing report. A report rendered to headquarters by field units after a bombing attack, indicating damage and also the direction of the attack.

Bone, Algeria, 1942

During Operation TORCH Bone airfield was the objective of Lieutenant-Colonel Geoffrey Pine-Coffin's 3rd Battalion The Parachute Regiment *and* a Luftwaffe parachute battalion. On 12 November the British won the race by a narrow margin, the German transport aircraft turning away when the British parachutes were sighted above the airfield. Bone then became the base for an attempt by the British 36th Brigade (78th Division) to seize BIZERTA, through which Axis reinforcements were pouring into Tunisia, by *coup de main*. The Germans, however, were present in greater strength and halted the drive in the hills west of Mateur.

Bonhöffer, Dietrich (1906–45)

A German Protestant theologian, Bonhöffer was opposed to HITLER and the Nazi ideology from the very beginning. In 1935 he was deprived of permission to preach, but on the outbreak of war obtained a post with the Abwehr. On a visit to Sweden in May 1942 he put forward suggestions for an armistice to the Bishop of Chichester. He was arrested in April 1943 and imprisoned in Flossenberg concentration camp, where he was executed on 9 April 1945.

Bon Homme Richard, USS – Essex Class Aircraft Carrier

Originally CV.10 but re-named YORKTOWN prior to launch on 21 January 1943. Name transferred to CV.31, launched 29 April 1944. Mounted raids against the Japanese mainland during the closing stages of the war.

Bonin Islands, Pacific, 1945

A chain of islands lying 700 miles (1126km) south-east of Japan containing airfields the acquisition of which was necessary for the Allied advance on the Japanese homeland. See IWO JIMA.

Bonus

First Allied plan for the capture of DIEGO SUAREZ, Madagascar.

Boozer

Boozer was the codename of a British passive RADAR receiver, tuned to the frequencies of the German air defence radar sets. If an aircraft was illuminated by a gun-laying radar, an orange light flashed on the pilot's panels; if illuminated by a night fighter radar, a red light flashed. Warning of imminent attack was thus conveyed.

Bordeaux, France, 1940 and 1942

A city and port on the River Garonne in south-west France, the seat of the government during the final days before the French collapse of June 1940. Occupied by the Germans, Bordeaux offered an apparently safe refuge for their blockade runners since it lay some 70 miles upstream from the Bay of Biscay. However, on the night of 7 December 1942 the submarine HMS *Tuna* launched canoeists of the Royal Marine Boom Patrol Detachment (RMBPD), under Major H. G. Hasler, off the river mouth and during the next 72 hours these made their way upstream, losing two canoes in the tide race and a third sunk after striking an underwater object. On the night of 10/11 December Hasler used the two surviving canoes to attack shipping in Bordeaux harbour, placing LIMPET MINES on four freighters, a tanker and a small warship. These exploded the following morning, wrecking one of the merchantmen and damaging the others so seriously that they required months in dry dock. Of the raiders only Hasler and his crewman, Marine Sparks, managed to return to England. Two men drowned on the first night of the raid, and the rest were captured and shot. The incident inspired the film *Cockleshell Heroes*.

Borghese, Prince Valerio (1912–   )

Prince Borghese was an Italian naval officer and was commanding a submarine in 1941 when Italy entered the war. In September 1940 he ferried a party of two-man "human torpedo" craft into Algeciras Bay to attack ships in Gibraltar, the start of a series of attacks which were highly successful. The following year he was placed in command of the underwater division of the assault craft force, and in December led the raid on Alexandria harbour which resulted in damage to two British battleships, *Valiant* and *Queen Elizabeth*. In 1943 he was given command of the entire assault craft flotilla and returned to Gibraltar where he audaciously set up a base in Algeciras inside an Italian merchant ship undergoing repairs. From the base he raided Gibraltar. When the Italian Armistice was signed he was planning an attack on New York harbour.

Boris III, King of Bulgaria (1894–1943)

Boris allied Bulgaria with Germany after considerable pressure from HITLER, and in March 1941 declared war on Britain. In December he declared war on the USA but steadfastly refused to do so against the USSR. He died in mysterious circumstances on 28 August 1943, shortly after a meeting with Hitler.

Bor Komorowski, Gen Tadeusz (1895–1956)

Bor Komorowski was the Polish underground army commander and leader of the WARSAW Uprising of August–September 1944. Born Komorowski, he adopted the pseudonym "Bor" as a cover name during his underground activity, and after release from German imprisonment adopted the compound name. He had joined the Polish Army (Malopolski Lancers) in 1918 and was Colonel in charge of the Cavalry Training School in 1939. After Poland's defeat he remained in the country and organized resistance and underground activities, eventually becoming the Commander-in-Chief of the POLISH HOME ARMY. After the Warsaw Uprising he was imprisoned by the Germans in COLDITZ but survived and was handed over to American troops in May 1945. He lived in Britain in retirement for the remainder of his life.

Bormann, Martin (1900–45?)

After serving in World War I, Bormann joined the same Freikorps as GÖRING in 1918. He was among the first to join the Nazi Party, and became its national organizer. After the defection of Hess to Britain in 1941, HITLER appointed him head of the Party Chancery and in 1943 made him his Secretary. In this post he had full control of access to Hitler, preventing any bad news from reaching the Führer. His strategic and tactical views were similar to those of Hitler, and it has often been suggested that some of Hitler's more stupid errors were the result of his adopting Bormann's ideas. Bormann tried to reach an accommodation with the Soviets in 1945, but this came to nothing, and he succeeded in concealing the negotiations from Hitler. He remained at Hitler's side until the latter's suicide on 30 April 1945, after which he vanished. He has frequently been reported as living in South America, equally frequently reported dead, the last time in 1985.

Borneo (Kalimantan), East Indies, 1942 and 1945

During February 1942 the key areas around the coast of Borneo were swiftly secured by the Japanese, who possessed overwhelming local superiority, particularly in the air. By the middle of 1945 the area had been bypassed by the Allied advance on the Japanese mainland, but Australian and Dutch troops made a series of landings to recapture the principal oilfields including Tarakan (1 May–22 June), Brunei Bay (10 June) and BALIKPAPAN (1–10 July).

Bornholm Island, Denmark, 1945

A Danish island in the Baltic. Its German garrison refused to surrender until 9 May, when Russian troops occupied the island, remaining there until the spring of 1946.

Bottomley, ACM Sir Norman Howard (1891–1970)

Commissioned into the East Yorkshire Regiment in 1914, Bottomley was seconded to the Royal Flying Corps in 1915. He served in Egypt in 1921–24, commanded No. 4 (Army Co-operation) Squadron in 1929 and instructed at the RAF Staff College 1931–33. After further service in India he became Senior Air Staff Officer BOMBER COMMAND 1938–40 and then commanded a bomber group in 1940–41. After a tour in Air Staff Operations, he became Deputy Chief of Air Staff in 1943–45, Air Officer Commanding-in-Chief BOMBER COMMAND 1945–47 and Inspector-General of the RAF in 1947–48, retiring in 1948. Among other duties, Bottomley took over the "CROSSBOW" investigation of the German flying bomb threat from Duncan Sandys and remained a member of the Crossbow Committee throughout its life.

US infantry and armour advance on Bougainville, March 1944.

Bougainville, Solomon Islands, 1942–44

Occupied by the Japanese 17th Army in March 1942. On 1 November 1943 the US 3rd Marine Division landed at EMPRESS AUGUSTA BAY (Operation CHERRYBLOSSOM) and secured a beach-head ten miles (16km) wide and five (8) deep in which it was reinforced by the US Army's 37th Division. The Japanese launched a series of savage but unco-ordinated counter-attacks, lasting until March 1944, in which they lost an estimated 9000 men. The Americans incurred approximately 2000 casualties. The Japanese Navy – debilitated by a series of crushing defeats – was unable to supply the remnants of the garrison, whose ranks were further depleted by starvation. The remnants were eventually hunted down by Australian troops.

Boulogne, France, 1940 and 1944

Attacked by 2nd Panzer Division on 22 May 1940. The garrison, consisting of 20th Guards Brigade and French troops, resisted fiercely but the town's Old Citadel was stormed on the 24th. The Allies surrendered the following day, 5000 prisoners being taken. Following the Allied victory in NORMANDY, Boulogne was assaulted on 17 September 1944 by the Canadian 3rd Infantry Division, supported by the specialized armour of the 79th Armoured Division. Targets within the perimeter were also subjected to air attack and engaged by the coastal battery on North Foreland, firing across the English Channel. The 10,000-strong German garrison surrendered on 22 September, but demolition in the harbour area was so thorough that the port could not be used for many months.

Boulton-Paul Defiant (UK)

The Defiant was introduced in 1937 and heralded a new tactical philosophy; instead of fixed forward-firing guns it carried a power-driven turret behind the pilot, armed with four .303in Browning machine guns. Entering service early in 1940, it was soon found to have a fatal flaw – enemy aircraft could attack from below with impunity, being out of reach of the turret guns. It was transferred to employment as a night fighter, later carrying early AIRBORNE RADAR, and in this role was more effective. About 1060 were built before production ended in early 1943. *Span* 39ft (11.9m); *engine* 1 1280hp in-line; *crew* 2; *speed* 313mph (504kph).

Bouncing Betty

The name loosely applied to any type of bouncing mine, i.e., a mine which consisted of a small mortar which, on being tripped, discharged a bomb into the air to burst and scatter fragments at approximately waist height. The first to see service was the German S-MINE and this was later followed by the British Shrapnel mine Mark 1 and the American anti-personnel mine M2. The American mine was called "Bouncing Betty" by US troops and the name then spread to cover other, similar, models.

Bouncing Bomb

The common name for a rotating bomb devised by Dr Barnes WALLIS for the attack on the RUHR Dams. The bomb was a large cylinder, slung beneath an adapted Lancaster bomber so that it could be given rotation in the direction of flight prior to being dropped. When dropped from a carefully specified height, the bomb struck the surface of the reservoir and bounced along the water for a considerable distance before sinking. If dropped at the correct distance from the dam, it would bounce up to the dam and then sink making contact with the dam wall, until an hydrostatic fuze detonated the explosive at the correct depth to breach the dam.

Bouncing Mortar Bomb

A German 81mm Wurfgranate 39 mortar bomb, this resembled a standard mortar bomb but the rounded nose was a separate component pinned to the remainder of the body and contained a small charge of smokeless powder and an impact fuze. On striking the ground the fuze ignited the powder which exploded, blowing off the nose and causing the body of the bomb to be thrown back into the air. At the same time a short delay fuze was ignited, and this detonated the explosive filling of the bomb when it was several feet in the air, so causing fragments to be distributed in all directions. On hard ground it was highly effective, giving an air-burst effect without the need to set fuzes; on softer ground it was less effective. The idea was copied by the British, in a 3-inch MORTAR bomb, but after trials it was not considered sufficiently reliable (due to variations in the ground) to be worth manufacturing.

Bourgebus Ridge, France, 1944

A gently sloping ridge south-east of CAEN attacked by three British armoured divisions (7th, 11th and Guards) on 18 July 1944 during Operation GOODWOOD. The attack was repulsed with serious loss by a particularly strong anti-tank defence which included 78 88mm guns, almost 500 artillery weapons, 30 TIGER tanks and armoured reserves. Although a tactical failure, the attack was a strategic success in that it led to the Germans concentrating the bulk of their strength against the British and Canadian sectors of the front instead of against the American sector, where the Allied breakout from the NORMANDY beach-head was planned.

Bourrasque Class Destroyers (Fr)

Three members of this class, *Bourrasque*, *Orage* and *Siroco*, were sunk during the DUNKIRK evacuation. *Displacement* 1800–2000 tons; *dimensions* 347ft×31ft 6in (105.7×9.6m); mean draught 14ft (4.2m); *machinery* 2-shaft geared turbines producing shp 31,000; *speed* 33 knots; *armament* 4×130mm; 1×75mm AA; 6×550mm torpedo tubes; 2 depth charge throwers; *complement* 138; *number in class* 12, launched 1924–25.

Boys Rifle

A British anti-tank rifle of .55 inch calibre, developed in the mid-1930s under the name "Stanchion". It received its final name in commemoration of Captain Boys, the leader of the design team, who died shortly before the rifle entered service. It was a manual bolt-action rifle of considerable power, and the bullet could penetrate 21mm of armour at a range of 984ft (300m). A tungsten-cored bullet was later developed, but by 1941 the rifle was ineffective against the newer types of tank and was superseded by the PIAT projector. A Mark 2 version with a short barrel was developed in 1942 for use by paratroops, but the requirement was abandoned and the design never produced in quantity.

BRA Brigadier, Royal Artillery (UK).

Bradley, Gen Omar (1894–1982)

Bradley was a General Instructor at West Point, 1934–38, and in 1941 was appointed Commandant of the Infantry School, Fort Ben-

Left to right: Generals Bradley, Eisenhower and Patton in Bastogne, December 1944.

ning. When the USA entered the war, Bradley was given command of the reactivated 82nd Infantry Division and then transferred to command 28th Infantry Division. Early in 1943 he was given the role of "trouble-shooter" with II Corps in North Africa. He recommended the sacking of the existing commander and his replacement by PATTON, under whom Bradley initially served as Deputy Commander. He was then chosen by EISENHOWER to lead the US landings in NORMANDY as commander of US 1st Army. Once ashore, Bradley handled the logistical build-up with great efficiency and, under the overall command of MONTGOMERY, captured CHERBOURG, cleared the COTENTIN PENINSULA and broke out from the bridge-head at St Lô on 25 July 1944. On 1 August Bradley assumed command of the newly-formed 12th Army Group, which broke through the SIEGFRIED LINE on 21 October, and he went on to command the US campaign until the end of the war. Bradley served as the US Army's Chief of Staff in 1948–49, and in August 1949 became Chairman of the Joint Chiefs of Staff, a post he held until his retirement in August 1953.

Brakemine

A British surface-to-air guided missile project, begun in 1943. The Cossor company carried out development, aided by Anti-Aircraft Command Workshops, and the first drawings were made in February 1944. After various changes the designers settled upon a tubular missile with wings and six rocket motors. The first firings took place in September 1944 and work continued until 1947, by which time the dispersion of the AA experimental staff and lack of official backing caused it to be abandoned.

Brandenburgers

The name given to the German Army's commando and special operations troops, responsible directly to the ABWEHR. Formed in October 1939, the first unit was redesignated Baulehrabteiling z.b.V. 800 (800th Special Construction Training Battalion) on 10 January 1940. As the war progressed the organization expanded first to regimental then to divisional strength. Brandenburg units served during the 1940 campaign in the West, in the Balkans, Russia, North Africa and Italy, but much of their potential was wasted by employment as conventional troops. HITLER'S distrust of the Army after the 1944 JULY BOMB

PLOT led to the division's conversion to the Panzergrenadier role and its special operations function was transferred to the newly raised SS *Jagdverbände* (Raiding Detachments). See also NACHTIGALL GRUPPE.

Brassard

Allied amphibious landing on Elba, 17 June 1944.

Brauchitsch, FM Walther von (1881–1948)

Von Brauchitsch was Commander-in-Chief of the German Army, 1938–41. In the 1920s he was active in work on mechanization and the employment of aircraft, became Director of Army Training and Inspector of Artillery, and then commanded Army Group IV. HITLER appointed him Commander-in-Chief to replace von FRITSCH, and subsequently von Brauchitsch was compliant to the Führer's directives. He thus bore a heavy measure of responsibility for the political subservience of the German Army and General Staff. Hitler had a considerable moral hold over von Brauchitsch, having personally secured his divorce and financed his marriage to the divorced wife of a fellow-officer, a lady with an extremely shady past. After the failure before MOSCOW in December 1941, Hitler dismissed von Brauchitsch, who had suffered a series of heart attacks, and assumed the post of Commander-in-Chief. Von Brauchitsch remained on the active list but was unemployed for the remainder of the war and died awaiting trial for war crimes.

General Field-Marshal von Brauchitsch returning home from a reconnaissance flight.

Eva Braun, in Hitler's "Eagle's Nest" at Berchtesgaden.

Braun, Eva (1912–45)

Eva Braun was HITLER's mistress from 1932 until their deaths in 1945. She had met Hitler when working as an assistant to Heinrich Hoffmann, Hitler's photographer, and she was thereafter kept discreetly in the background. It was not until late in the war that she made public appearances, and then only because her sister had married General Fegelein, the ex-jockey who was HIMMLER's representative with Hitler. Hitler finally married her during the early hours of 29 April 1945, in the *Führerbunker* in Berlin, and they committed suicide together on the following day.

Braun, Wernher von (1912–77)

Von Braun became interested in astronomy at preparatory school, and, while attending the Berlin Technical College in 1929–30, became a regular visitor to the rocket experiments carried out by the amateur German Rocket Society at Reinickendorf. He was convinced that rockets could provide the vehicle to outer space, and when the Society began to falter for lack of money in 1932 von Braun found employment with the Army Weapons Department as a technical assistant in the rocket development section, investigating liquid fuels. He eventually became technical director at the Army Rocket Research Centre at PEENEMUNDE and designed a number of rockets, notably the A-4, a ballistic missile. He surrendered to the US Army in 1945 with his research team, and they were removed to the USA to continue their work for the US govern-

ment in postwar years, when von Braun became a principal figure in the NASA space programme.

Braunschweig (Brunswick)

German offensives aimed at STALINGRAD and the CAUCASUS, 1942.

Brazilian Expeditionary Force

Token force despatched by Brazil to fight with the Allied armies in Italy. The first Brazilian units began entering the line under US IV Corps (US 5th Army) during the battle of the GOTHIC LINE.

Breda Ba 65 (Italy)

A single-engined low-wing monoplane used by the Italian air force as a ground-attack machine in the Western Desert. *Span* 40.5ft (12.35m); *engine* 1 900hp radial; *crew* 2; *armament* 2 12.7mm and 2 7.7mm machine guns, 2200lb (1000kg) of bombs; *speed* 255mph (410kph).

Breda Machine Guns

Italian machine guns manufactured by the SA Ernesto Breda of Brescia from 1924 to 1945. Both blowback and gas operating systems were used, but all lacked primary extraction and required their ammunition to be lubricated by a built-in oil pump. The Model 30 in 6.5mm calibre was used by the infantry and had the unusual feature of a side-mounted magazine hinged to the gun so that it had to be folded forward to be refilled from rifle clips.

Italian parachutist with Breda Model 30 machine gun.

The 8mm Model 37 was the standard battalion heavy machine gun and also was unusual for the fact that it fed its cartridges into the side by means of a tray; after firing, the empty cases were extracted and replaced in the tray as it was fed out of the other side of the gun. A tank machine gun and various aircraft machine guns were also manufactured.

Breguet 691/693 (Fr)

Developed from a prototype twin-engined fighter, the Breguet 690, the Bre 691 and 693 were built as light attack bombers. Some 224 of both versions had been delivered by 1940, and saw brief service before the French collapse. *Span* 60.3ft (18.4m); *engines* 2 700hp radial; *crew* 2; *armament* 1 20mm cannon and 4 machine guns, 880lb (400kg) of bombs; *speed* 300mph (483kph).

Bremen, Germany, 1945

A city and port on the River Weser captured by the British XXX Corps under Lieutenant-General B. G. HORROCKS, 20–26 April.

Bren Gun

A standard light machine gun used by British and Commonwealth troops from 1936 to the present day, the Bren was designed in Czechoslovakia by Zbrojowka Brno as the ZB26. After extensive trials in Britain it was adopted in .303in calibre, which necessitated

changing the magazine from a straight-sided box to the characteristic curved box mounted on top of the gun. There were several models, the changes being largely concerned with speeding up and simplifying production during the war. Most Bren guns were manufactured in Britain at the Royal Small Arms Factory, Enfield, and the name was constructed from *Br*no and *En*field. Large numbers were also manufactured in Canada by the John Inglis company of Toronto. The Bren proved extremely reliable, and is still used, in 7.62mm NATO calibre, as the Machine Gun L4.

Bren Gun Carrier (UK)

Popular but imprecise term for the UNIVERSAL CARRIER series of light general purpose tracked vehicles.

Brenner Pass, Austria–Italy, 1940

The scene of meetings between HITLER and MUSSOLINI to determine joint strategy. At the meeting held on 4 October 1940 Hitler deliberately concealed from his fellow dictator the fact that he was in process of occupying ROMANIA. Mussolini was furious when he discovered the truth and announced that for his part he would occupy GREECE, a decision which in the long term was to have serious consequences for the Axis alliance.

Brereton, Gen Lewis M. (1890–1967)

Brereton was a US Army officer during World War I and transferred to the Air Corps where he became a fighter pilot. In the interwar years he held various command and staff appointments and on the outbreak of war in 1941 was appointed Commander of the US Far East Air Force. After the fall of the PHILIPPINES, he was moved to India and became Commander US Middle East Air Force. In October 1942 he was appointed to command the 9th Air Force, which made a significant contribution to the success of the Tunisian campaign. He then took 9th Air Force to England, building it up as a tactical force which played an important role in the build-up to Operation OVERLORD and gave valuable support to US ground forces in the latter half of 1944. In August 1944 he was made Commander 1st Allied Airborne Army and took part in the planning and coordination of various airborne operations, including Operation MARKET GARDEN at NIJMEGEN, EINDHOVEN and ARNHEM.

Breskens Pocket, Holland, 1944

A large area on the south shore of the SCHELDT retained by the isolated German 64th Division when ANTWERP was liberated. The reduction of the pocket commenced on 6 October with an attack against its southern perimeter by one

An original Czech-manufactured Mark 1 Bren machine gun.

Hitler and Mussolini at the Brenner Pass, October 1940. On the right is Count Ciano, Italian Foreign Minister.

brigade of the Canadian 3rd Infantry Division. On 8 October the defenders were outflanked by a second brigade landing from LVTs west of the Braakman Inlet, joined by a third brigade two days later. German resistance was stubborn and troops from the Canadian 4th Armoured Division and 52nd (Lowland) Division were fed into the battle. The town of Breskens fell on 21 October, followed by Fort Fredrik-Hendrik, covering the southern entrance to the Scheldt, on the 21st, but in some areas resistance continued until 2 November. The Canadians sustained 2000 casualties; 12,700 prisoners were taken.

Breslau (Wroclaw), Germany (now Poland), 1945

The principal city of German Silesia, situated on the River Oder. Isolated on 15 February by 5th Guards and 6th Armies (1st Ukrainian Front) during the Soviet spring offensive. The 40,000-strong garrison did not surrender until 6 May.

Brest, France, 1944

A fortress and naval base in western Brittany held by a 38,000-strong German garrison, under General Hermann RAMCKE, which included the 2nd Parachute Division. When Major-General Troy MIDDLETON's US VIII Corps commenced its assault on 25 August, Ramcke's men fought tenaciously for every position and did not capitulate until 18 September. In the closing stages of the assault

British Crocodile flamethrowing tanks from 79th Armoured Division were used to suppress certain fortifications. The Americans sustained 10,000 casualties and 35,000 prisoners were taken. Demolition and the heavy fighting had so wrecked the harbour installations that they were useless.

Bretagne Class Battleships (Fr)

The two members of this class, *Bretagne* and *Provence*, were extensively refitted 1932–35. *Bretagne* blew up and capsized during the British attack on MERS-EL-KEBIR on 3 July 1940. *Provence* was badly damaged during the same attack and was moved to TOULON that November, and scuttled there in 1942. *Displacement* 21,300 tons; *dimensions* 544ft 6in×88ft 6in (166×26.9m); mean draught 30ft (9m); *machinery* 4-shaft geared turbines producing shp 43,000; *speed* 20 knots; *protection* main belt 9in; deck 1.5in; turrets 13/15.5in; *armament* 10×340mm (5×2); 14×138mm (14×1); 8×75mm AA; 12×13.2mm AA; *complement* 1133; *number in class* 2, both launched 1913.

Bretton Woods

The site, in New Hampshire, USA, of an International Monetary Conference convened 1 July 1944. This was the culminating conference of a series which set up the International Monetary Fund and the World Bank and established terms of reference which were to govern the world's monetary policies until the 1970s.

Brevity

British offensive in the Western Desert, May 1941.

Brewster F2A Buffalo (USA)

This was the US Navy's first monoplane fighter, entering service in 1939. Numbers were exported to Finland, Britain, Belgium and the Netherlands East Indies; they performed extremely well in combat in Finland,

RAAF Brewster F2A Buffalo aircraft of No 453 Squadron, Singapore 1941.

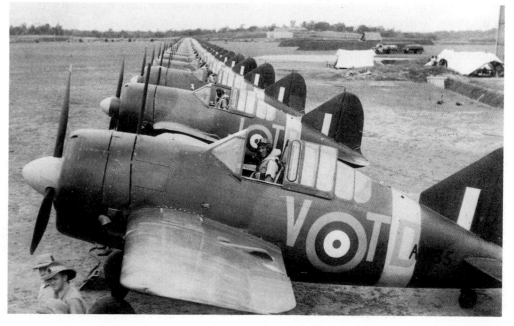

but disappointingly in Crete, Singapore and the East Indies. Flown by US Marine Corps pilots, a handful were wiped out in the defence of Midway Island. Production ended in 1942, by which time the F2A had been outclassed by its opposition. *Span* 35ft (10.6m); *engine* 1 1200hp radial; *armament* 4 machine guns; *speed* 321mph (516kph).

Brewster SB2A Buccaneer (USA)

A single-engined monoplane dive-bomber for naval use, the Buccaneer (also known as the Bermuda in RAF service) first flew in 1941 and was supplied to the US Navy, Britain and the Netherlands East Indies. Once in service the aircraft was found to fall far short of its requirements and most were relegated to training roles. *Span* 47ft (14m); *engine* 1 1700hp radial; *crew* 3; *armament* 4 machine guns, *speed* 275mph (442kph).

Brigade

An armoured or infantry formation consisting of brigade headquarters, three or more battalions and supporting units. A British or Commonwealth brigade had a strength approximately equivalent to that of a regiment in other armies. The formation was also used by the Soviet Army, although the size of the brigade's composite units tended to be smaller.

Brigade Group

A reinforced brigade supplemented by artillery, engineer and reconnaissance units, generally formed for a specific mission.

Brigs Peak, Eritrea, 1941

A mountain feature forming part of the KEREN defences which changed hands repeatedly during heavy fighting in February and March.

Brin Class Submarines (Italy)

Displacement 913 tons (1016–1266 tons normal); *dimensions* 237ft 9in×22ft (72.2×6.7m); *machinery* 2-shaft diesel/electric motors hp 3400/1300; *speed* 17.25/8 knots; *armament* 1×3.9in; 4×13.2mm AA; 8×21in torpedo tubes and 14 torpedoes; *complement* 59; *number in class* 5, launched 1938–39.

Bristol Aircraft (UK)

Bristol Beaufighter Based on the BEAUFORT, the Beaufighter went into service late in 1940 fitted with the first AIRBORNE RADAR for night

fighting. Later versions were adapted for a rocket-aimed ground-support role and as torpedo-bombers. Numbers were also used by the USAAF as night fighters. Described once as "two large engines followed closely by an aircraft" the speed, manoeuvrability and firepower of the Beaufighter made it one of the most valuable RAF aircraft of the war. It remained in service, latterly as a training aircraft, until 1959. *Span* 58ft (17.7m); *engines* 2 1770hp radial; *crew* 2; *armament* 4 20mm cannon, 6–7 machine guns, 1100lb (500kg) of bombs and rockets or 2127lb (965kg) of torpedoes; *speed* 330mph (531kph).

Bristol Beaufort The Beaufort torpedo-bomber was derived from the BLENHEIM but was considerably heavier. It first flew in 1938 and entered service in October 1939, but delays due to engine design problems meant that it was not operational until late 1940. Used extensively for minelaying and torpedo-bombing by RAF COASTAL COMMAND, numbers were also built in Australia and operated with great success in the Pacific. *Span* 58ft (17.7m); *engines* 2 1130hp radial; *crew* 4; *armament* 4 machine guns, 2200lb (1000kg) of bombs, mines or torpedoes; *speed* 265mph (426kph).

Bristol Blenheim This medium bomber began as a fast executive transport built to the order of Lord Rothermere. Carrying a pilot and six passengers at 240mph (386kph), it was considerably faster than any current RAF fighter when it appeared in 1934, and the design was modified into a bomber which went into service late in 1936. Eventually 1136 were built; many of these were used in bombing missions during the early part of the war

Bristol Blenheim I light bomber.

and a large quantity were exported to Finland, Yugoslavia, Greece, Romania and Turkey. Main production versions were the marks J, IV and V; many were converted as long-range or night fighters, suitably armed and equipped with RADAR. *Span* 56.3ft; *engines* 2 950hp radial; *crew* 3; *armament* (bomber) 2–4 machine guns, 1000lb (450kg) of bombs, (fighter) 5–6 machine guns; *speed* 250mph (402kph).

Bristol Bombay This high-wing monoplane first flew in 1935 but the RAF did not begin to take deliveries until early 1939, by which time it was almost obsolete. Designed as a transport vehicle with an auxiliary bomber role, only 50 were built and were used principally in the Middle East, where a few undertook some night bombing in North Africa. *Span* 95.75ft (29m); *engines* 2 1010hp radial; *crew* 3; *armament* 2 machine guns; *speed* 192mph (309kph).

Bristol Buckingham This aircraft was developed in 1941–42 as a day bomber version of the BEAUFIGHTER but was frustrated by changes in the specification which demanded conflicting features of heavy armament, heavy bomb load, long range and high speed. Eventually some 119 were built and employed as transports, couriers and trainers. *Span* 72ft (22m); *engines* 2 2500hp radial; *crew* 4; *armament* 10 machine guns, 3970lb (180kg) of bombs; *speed* 336mph (540kph).

Britain, Battle of

The Battle of Britain lasted from 10 July 1940 until late in 1940 and was caused by the German air attack on Britain which was intended as a necessary preliminary to Opera-

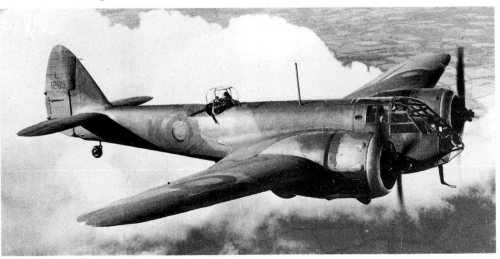

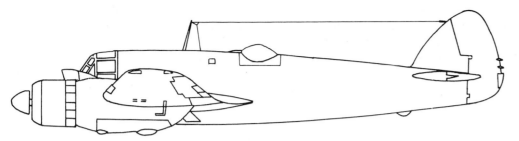

Bristol Beaufighter Mk IF.

tion SEALION, the invasion of Britain. The aim was to destroy the air defences of the country so that they would be unable to interfere with the seaborne invasion. The Luftwaffe strength was about 2800 aircraft, the RAF had about 700 fighters, but this imbalance was offset by the British deployment of early warning RADAR and their adept use of radio to control their fighter aircraft. The first stage of the Battle featured German attacks on ports and shipping in the English Channel, accompanied by some costly aerial fighting. In consequence the British were forced to stop all Channel convoys and on 10 August the Luftwaffe switched to attacking airfields on the south coast of England. Heavy attacks were made for ten days, during which the Luftwaffe lost 602 aircraft and the RAF 260, the RAF's greatest loss being in pilots, which were harder to replace than aircraft. However, at this point GÖRING lost his nerve and ordered that the attacks be switched again, this time to raids on London. These began on 7 September and were at their heaviest on 15 September, when 56 German aircraft were shot down. These severe losses, together with an apparent lack of effect against the RAF, led both to the withdrawal of the greater part of the German bomber force from day operations, and on 17 September to an indefinite postponement of Operation Sealion. This removed some of the urgency from the air battle, although daylight air raids continued until late in the year, coupled with a growing night offensive. From July to November 1940 the Luftwaffe lost some 1537 aircraft to British action, while in the same period the RAF lost a similar number (over 1000 of them fighters); nearly 500 pilots were killed or missing, and some 400 more were wounded or injured.

British Expeditionary Force (BEF)

The title of the British forces serving in France, 1939–40. In May 1940 the BEF consisted of 10 infantry divisions, one under-strength tank brigade and an RAF Air Component of 500 fighters and light bombers. See also FRANCE, BELGIUM, HOLLAND 1940 and DUNKIRK EVACUATION.

British Somaliland, Africa, 1940–41

On 3 August 1940 Italian troops under Lieutenant-General Nasi invaded British Somaliland from Ethiopia. The heavily outnumbered British under Major-General A. R. Godwin-Austen fought a delaying action at Tug Argan, then withdrew to Berbera, and were evacuated by sea. The British sustained 250 casualties and the Italians 2052. Following the British invasion of ITALIAN SOMALILAND in January 1941, the Italians withdrew from British Somaliland. On 16 March British troops from the Aden garrison landed at Berbera and reoccupied the territory.

British Taylorcraft Auster (UK)

This was originally an American light civil aircraft, of which over 1600 were built by the British subsidiary company during the war. It was principally employed as an artillery observation machine and on liaison and communications duties, and served in every theatre of war and for several years after 1945. Slow but highly manoeuvrable, it gave an excellent field of vision and had a high survivability rate in the face of enemy aircraft. *Span* 36ft (11m); *engine* 1 130hp in-line; *speed* 130mph (209kph).

Broadhurst, ACM Sir Harry (1905–)

Joining the RAF in 1926, Broadhurst served in bomber squadrons until 1928, thereafter serving in India until 1931. In 1932–36 he served in fighter squadrons and then became Chief Instructor of the Flying Training School in Egypt. After attending the RAF Staff College in 1938 he commanded a fighter squadron in 1939 and then 60th Fighter Wing in France in 1939–40. After this he commanded the Fighter Sector, Wittering, during the Battle of BRITAIN with distinction. He was appointed Senior Air Staff Officer and Air Officer Commanding Western Desert in 1942–43 and returned to Britain to command 83 Group in the European campaign of 1944–45.

Wreckage of a German aircraft at Victoria Station, September 1940.

"Broadway", Burma, 1944

A Chindit base east of Mohnyin incorporating a defended airfield established in March. Despite air and ground attacks, Broadway continued to function until 13 May.

Brody-Dubno, Battle of, Soviet Union, 1941

Major counter-attack mounted by Colonel-General Mikhail KIRPONOS' South West Front against General Ewald von KLEIST's 1st Panzer Group, the armoured spearhead of von RUND-STEDT's Army Group South during Operation BARBAROSSA. Kirponos was able to concentrate the IV, VIII, IX, XV, XIX and XXII Mechanized Corps, containing some of the best-equipped and most efficient tank divisions in the Soviet Army, and by 25 June these were converging on Kleist's four Panzer divisions (11th, 13th, 14th and 16th) in the area of Brody. A fierce but untidy tank battle, the largest of the war until KURSK, raged for the next four days. Much of the Russians' numerical superiority was written down when the Luftwaffe pounced on the tank columns during their approach march and the rest was squandered in piece-meal and unco-ordinated attacks. Inexperience, poor tactics, breakdowns and fuel shortage also contributed to the Soviet losses. Finally, Kirponos was forced to extract what remained of his corps and retreat on KIEV but he had inflicted substantial loss in return and imposed a check on Army Group South that was to contribute to the eventual failure of Operation Barbarossa.

Brooke, FM Alan Francis (1883–1963)

Brooke was born in France of an Irish family and was commissioned into the Royal Field Artillery in 1902. After serving in Ireland and India he went to France, eventually serving as Brigade Major in the 18 Division Artillery. Between the wars he held a number of staff appointments, including Commandant School of Artillery 1929–32 and Inspector of Artillery 1935–36. He then became Director of Military Training 1935–37 and later commanded the Anti-Aircraft Corps 1937–39 and Southern Command. In September 1939 he took command of the 2nd British Army Corps and was largely responsible for the successful extrication of British and French troops from DUNKIRK. In July 1940 Brooke was appointed Commander-in-Chief Home Forces and was responsible for preparations to repel the expected German invasion. In December

1941 he became Chief of the Imperial General Staff, remaining in this post until 1946, combining its functions with that of Chairman of the British Chiefs of Staff Committee from March 1942. In this position he was CHURCH-ILL's executive officer, and negotiated tactfully with the Americans, putting Churchill's views before them in a logical and persuasive manner. His strategic direction of British field commanders was a considerable factor in their successes.

Brooke-Popham, ACM Sir Robert (1878–1953)

Brooke-Popham was the Air Marshal in charge of Far Eastern Command in 1941, responsible for the RAF's operations in SINGAPORE and HONG KONG. On assuming his post in 1940 he pointed out the serious shortage of aircraft in his command but received little response; he also attempted to improve inter-service co-operation, with equally little success. As a result, when the Japanese attacks came, the air forces were able to do little to stop them. At the end of 1941 he was relieved of his command, a convenient scapegoat for pre-war parsimony.

Brooklyn Class Light Cruisers (USA)

Displacement 9475–10,000 tons; *dimensions* 608ft 6in×61ft 9in (185.4×18.8m); mean draught 19ft 6in (5.88m); *machinery* 4-shaft geared turbines producing shp 100,000; *armament* 15×6in (5×3); 8×5in; 6×533mm (2×3) torpedo tubes; *aircraft* 4; *complement* 1300; *number in class* 9, launched 1936–38.

Broome Airfield, W. Australia, 1942

On 4 March Japanese Zeros raided Broome airfield and harbour, destroying 16 flying boats and seven aircraft without loss to themselves.

Browning, Lt Gen Sir Frederick "Boy" (1896–1965)

Commissioned into the Grenadier Guards in 1915, by 1939 Browning was commanding the 2nd Battalion. In 1940 he was selected to command the first British airborne unit, which became the 1st Airborne Division. In May 1943 he became Major-General Airborne Forces, and in 1944 Lieutenant-General Commanding I Airborne Corps. A flamboyant and arrogant man, he was largely responsible for the poor planning which led to the fiasco at ARNHEM. In November 1944 he was sent to BURMA as Chief of Staff to Lord MOUNTBATTEN.

Brummbär (Grizzly Bear) (Ger)

A heavy assault gun developed as a result of the fierce street fighting in STALINGRAD. The Brummbär was based on the PANZERKAMPFWA-GEN IV tank chassis and was armed with the 150mm L/12 howitzer. The vehicle entered service in April 1943 and equipped the Heavy Infantry Gun Companies of Panzergrenadier Regiments as well as 45-strong Heavy Assault Battalions which were at the disposal of senior commanders. A total of 313 were built.

Brummbär heavy assault gun.

BT-7 cruiser tanks on parade pre-war.

Bruneval Raid, France, 1942

Commanded by Major Frost, C Company 2nd Battalion, The Parachute Regiment dropped close to the Bruneval RADAR installation, near Le Havre, during the night of 27/28 February and covered the removal of vital components by an RAF technician. The raiders were evacuated by the Royal Navy.

Bruno

A "family" name given to a series of 22 German railway guns built 1936–40. The family consisted of the 9.4in (24cm) Theodor Bruno, 11in (28cm) kurz Bruno, 11in (28cm) lange Bruno, 11in (28cm) schwere Bruno and 11in (28cm) Bruno neue. These guns were principally used on the Eastern Front.

Brussels, Belgium, 1940 and 1941

Occupied by the German 6th Army, 17 May 1940, Brussels was liberated 3 September 1944 by the Guards Armoured Division during the Allied advance through Belgium.

Bryansk, Soviet Union, 1941 and 1943

The centre of a pocket formed by German advance during Operation TAIFUN in 1941; see VYAZMA-BRYANSK, BATTLE OF. The city of Bryansk was liberated by Bryansk Front in September 1943 during the Soviet general advance which followed the German defeat at KURSK.

B-Stoff

Mixture of hydrazine hydrate and water used as German rocket motor fuel.

BT Series – Cruiser Tanks (USSR)

Having evaluated the Christie M1931 chassis, which was capable of running on either tracks or wheels, the Soviet Army decided that it would form the basis of its projected *Bystrochodyi* (Fast Tank) series. Throughout the series, the CHRISTIE SUSPENSION was faithfully reproduced in all seven marks and was to astonish foreign observers with its resilience and robustness. The final drive system also displayed typical Christie ingenuity. When the vehicle was travelling on tracks, rollers on the rear sprocket engaged alternate lugs on the track, while for running on wheels alone a chain drive passed from the drive sprocket to a second sprocket mounted behind the rearmost roadwheel. Wheels-only use was rare but on these occasions the tracks were stowed along their respective cat-walks. Another unusual feature for the time was the use of a steering wheel in conjunction with a clutch-and-brake system for directional control. The most important vehicles in the series were the BT-2 of 1931, which was armed with a 37mm gun; the BT-5 of 1933, armed with a 45mm gun; and the BT-7 of 1936 armed with a 76.2mm gun. The secondary armament of the BT-5 and BT-7 was respectively one and two 7.62mm machine guns. The majority of vehicles in the series were driven by 350hp petrol aero engines but the later models of the BT-7 were fitted with the famous V-2 12-cylinder 500hp diesel engine. The BTs saw active service in Spain, Manchuria, Finland and during the 1939 invasion of eastern Poland. Unfortunately their best features were largely wasted as a result of dogmatic confusion within the higher echelons of the Soviet Army. Few survived the German invasion of 1941. *Weight* 10.2–14.8 tons; *speed* 37mph (59.5kph) on tracks, 69mph (111kph) on wheels; *armour* 13–22mm; *crew* 3.

Bucharest, Romania, 1944

Following the invasion of Romania on 20 August by the Soviet 2nd and 3rd Ukrainian Fronts, King MICHAEL ordered the arrest of Marshal ANTONESCU on 23 August and announced that his country had accepted the Allied armistice terms. On 24 August German troops were fired on when they attempted to enter Bucharest and the following day the Luftwaffe made an air attack on the Royal Palace. The new Romanian government used these incidents as an excuse to declare war on Germany on 25 August. Soviet troops reached the capital on 31 August.

Buchenwald, Germany

Concentration camp established in July 1937 near Weimar. Used originally as a forced labour camp for political and criminal detainees, it later became a site for the concentration of Jews, from whence they were shipped to extermination camps.

Buckley Class Destroyer Escorts (USA)

Displacement 1400 tons; *dimensions* 306×37ft (93.2×11.1m); mean draught 9ft 6in (2.9m); *machinery* 2-shaft turbo-electric drive producing shp 12,000; *speed* 23.5 knots; *armament* 3×3in; 6×40mm AA; 3×21in torpedo tubes; *complement* 220; *number in class* 102, launched 1943–44. A further 46 vessels of this class were transferred to the Royal Navy.

Bucknall, Lt Gen Corfield (1894–1980)

Commissioned into the Middlesex Regiment, Bucknall was commanding the 1st Battalion on the outbreak of war in 1914 and served throughout in various regimental and staff posts. After the war he went to the Sudan with the Egyptian Army for some time, then returned to England for more staff jobs. At the outbreak of World War II he was commanding the 2nd Bn Middlesex Regiment but was appointed Colonel on the War Office staff. He subsequently commanded 5th Division in SICILY and Italy with distinction and took XXX

Russian infantry advance on Budapest.

Corps to Europe in June 1944. Here he proved insufficiently aggressive for MONTGOMERY's taste and was relieved of his command. He subsequently became General Officer Commanding Northern Ireland until his retirement in 1947.

Budapest, Hungary, 1944–45

On 15 October 1944 Admiral Miklos HORTHY, the Regent of Hungary, offered to conclude peace with the Allies. After the defection of Romania (SEE BUCHAREST) HITLER was unwilling to lose his last remaining ally in Europe. Budapest was occupied by German troops and Horthy was deposed in a coup led by Colonel Otto SKORZENY, who installed the pro-German puppet Szalasy as head of state. On 26 December the Soviet 2nd and 3rd Ukrainian Fronts, commanded respectively by MALINOVKSY and TOLBUKHIN, encircled Budapest. The garrison, consisting of IX SS Mountain Corps, with four German and two Hungarian divisions commanded by SS Oberstgruppenführer Karl von Pfeffer-Wildenbruch, was ordered to hold out until relieved. The situation was hopeless and on 11 February 1945 Pfeffer-Wildenbruch ordered his troops to break out, abandoning their 10,600 wounded. Of the 30,000 Germans and Hungarians who made the attempt, less than 700 succeeded in reaching the German lines to the west. See also BALATON, LAKE.

Budenny, Marshal Semyon Mikhaelovitch (1883–1973)

A conscript into the Tsar's army, Budenny rose to the rank of Company Sergeant-Major by 1917, joined the Revolutionaries and by 1920 was commanding a cavalry army, meeting defeat against the Poles in 1919–20. In 1934 he became a member of the Revolutionary Military Council and in 1935 was appointed Marshal of the Soviet Union. A strong supporter of Stalin, he survived the 1937–38 GREAT PURGE era, and after the German invasion in 1941 he was made Commander-in-Chief of armies in the Ukraine and Bessarabia. Stalin reinforced this group heavily in order to defend Kiev, but Budenny, a relatively untalented soldier with little experience of command in the field, was outgeneralled by the Germans and lost Kiev along with about half the active strength of the Red Army. He was forthwith awarded the title of Hero of the Soviet Union and made supervisor of recruit training, a post in which he could do little harm. He played no further part in active operations, but was appointed Commander of Cavalry in January 1943.

Buerat Line, Libya, 1943

A defensive position established by ROMMEL in Tripolitania during his withdrawal to Tunisia. On 15 January the 51st (Highland) Division mounted a frontal attack while the 7th Armoured Division attempted to outflank the defences to the south. Rommel disengaged and continued his retreat.

Buffalo

See LANDING VEHICLES TRACKED.

Büffelbewegung (Buffalo Stampede)

German operations on the central front, Russia, 1943.

Bukhovina, Romania, 1940

Northern province, part of which was occupied by and ceded to the Soviet Union in June.

Bukit Timah, Malaya, 1942

On 15 February Lieutenant-General Arthur PERCIVAL unconditionally surrendered SINGAPORE to Lieutenant-General Tomoyuki YAMASHITA, the formalities being concluded in a room at the Ford factory at Bukit Timah, two miles (3.2km) north-west of the city. Approximately 130,000 British, Australian and Indian troops marched into captivity.

Bulgaria, 1941–44

Although Bulgaria joined the Axis alliance on 1 March 1941 and permitted the invasion of GREECE and YUGOSLAVIA to be launched from her territory in the following month, her position for much of the war was anomalous in that she was technically engaged in hostilities against the United Kingdom and the United States but not against the Soviet Union. German troops were withdrawn when the Soviet Army overran ROMANIA in August 1944. The Soviet Union declared war on Bulgaria on 5 September but an armistice was granted the same day and on 8 September Bulgaria declared war on Germany.

Bulge, Battle of, Belgium and Luxembourg, 1944

Conceived by HITLER as a drive through the ARDENNES, across the Meuse and on to ANTWERP, the effect being to isolate those Allied armies north of the corridor so formed, this German counteroffensive was originally codenamed *Christrose*, later changed to WACHT AM RHEIN. Three armies were employed: DIETRICH's 6th Panzer; von MANTEUFFEL's 5th Panzer; and Brandenberger's 7th; in addition, a "Trojan Horse" force of English-speaking Germans in American uniforms, commanded by Colonel Otto SKORZENY, was inserted to cause confusion in the American rear areas. The offensive opened on 16 December along a 70-mile (113-km) sector of front from Monschau to Echternach, striking General Courtney HODGES' US 1st Army of General Omar BRADLEY's 12th Army Group and, despite the suspicions of some Allied officers, achieved both tactical and strategic surprise. Furthermore, because this sector had hitherto remained quiet it was known to the Americans as the Ghost Front and was held by six divi-

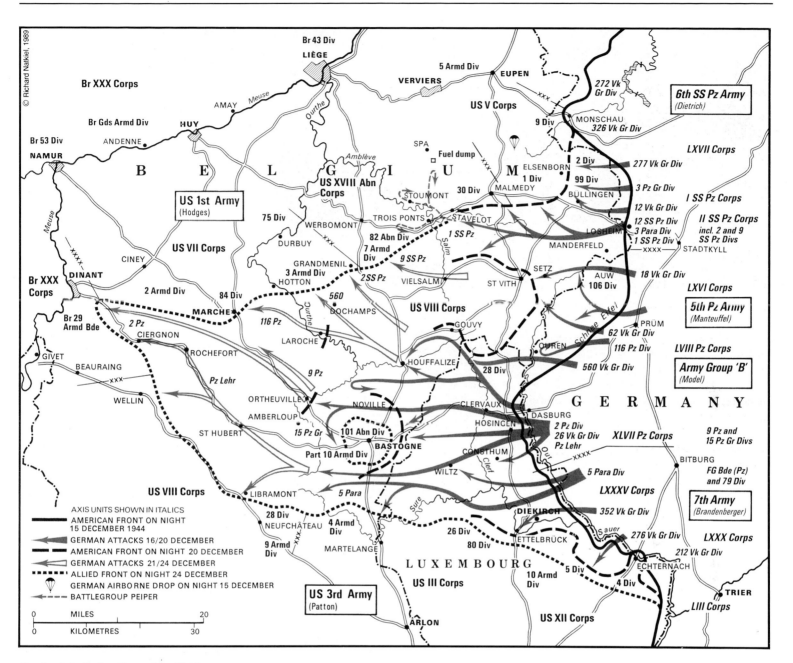

© Richard Natkiel, 1989

AXIS UNITS SHOWN IN ITALICS
▬▬▬ AMERICAN FRONT ON NIGHT 15 DECEMBER 1944
◄▬▬ GERMAN ATTACKS 16/20 DECEMBER
▬▬▬ AMERICAN FRONT ON NIGHT 20 DECEMBER
◄━━▷ GERMAN ATTACKS 21/24 DECEMBER
▪▪▪▪▪ ALLIED FRONT ON NIGHT 24 DECEMBER
▽ GERMAN AIRBORNE DROP ON NIGHT 15 DECEMBER
◄─ ─ ─ BATTLEGROUP PEIPER

MILES 20
KILOMETRES 30

Battle of the Bulge, December 1944.

sions, three of which were resting and three of which inexperienced. Poor flying weather kept the Allied air forces grounded and some 9000 Americans were captured on the Schnee EIFEL during the initial breakthrough. On the flanks the German advance was contained but in the centre 5th Panzer Army continued to make good progress for the next two days. However, the failure of the Germans to capture vital fuel dumps; the defence of ST VITH by Brigadier General Robert Hasbrouck's 7th Armoured Division; and BASTOGNE by Brigadier General Anthony McAULIFFE's 101st Airborne Division were all serious factors which

weighed heavily against the prospect of *Wacht am Rhein* succeeding. Once the first shock had passed, the Allied commanders acted quickly and decisively. EISENHOWER appointed MONTGOMERY commander of all forces north of the Bulge and the latter constructed a hard defensive shoulder with his American divisions while the British XXX Corps moved south to block the German advance at the Meuse. Bradley remained in command south of the Bulge, where PATTON's 3rd Army broke through to relieve Bastogne on 26 December. On 24 and 25 December the German spearhead, consisting of the 2nd Panzer and Panzer

Lehr Divisions, was defeated and forced to withdraw by the British 11th Armoured and the US 2nd Armored Divisions. The weather had now improved sufficiently for the Allied air forces to intervene in the battle, the crisis of which had passed. Heavy fighting continued, but on 3 January 1945 the Allies went over to the offensive and by 16 January the Bulge had been eliminated. The battle cost each side about 800 tanks. The Germans suffered 100,000 personnel casualties, the Americans 81,000 and the British 1400. The majority of senior German officers recognized that in view of the Wehrmacht's lack of resources,

Bund Deutscher Mädchen at summer camp.

notably fuel, *Wacht am Rhein* amounted to little more than a gamble, the net result of which was to delay Allied operations in the West by about six weeks, but at the cost of most of Germany's armoured reserve. See also MALMEDY. For detailed accounts see *The Battle of the Bulge* by Charles B. MacDonald.

Bund Deutscher Mädchen

The League of German Girls was the female counterpart of the HITLERJUGEND. It stressed the importance of the traditional female roles in German national life while simultaneously inculcating Nazi values at camps and rallies.

Bungo Strait, Japan, 1945

The waters separating the islands of Kyushu and Shikoku and providing the south-western exit from the Inland Sea. The departure of the giant battleship YAMATO on her suicide mission was spotted in the Strait by the submarine USS *Threadfin* during the evening of 6 April and duly reported.

Burcorps

Shortened form of I Burma Corps, formed to resist the Japanese invasion of BURMA in 1942. The corps consisted of the inexperienced 1st Burma and 17th Indian Divisions, reinforced by the veteran 7th Armoured Brigade.

Burke, R Adm Arleigh (1901–)

Burke joined the US Navy at the end of World War I and in 1943 was a Rear-Admiral in the South Pacific, where his skilful and aggressive handling of Destroyer Squadron 23 gained him the nickname of "31-knot Burke". His squadron covered the BOUGAINVILLE landings and fought over 20 successful engagements with Japanese naval forces. In 1944–45 he was Chief of Staff of Fast Carrier Task Force 58, and in 1945 was appointed Chief of the R & D Division of the Naval Bureau of Ordnance.

Burma (1942–1945)

Lower Burma was invaded on 12 January 1942 by Lieutenant-General Shojiro Iida's 15th

Army. The British forces, consisting of two understrength divisions commanded by Lieutenant-General Thomas Hutton, withdrew to the Rivers Salween and Sittang, but were forced to abandon these positions in February. Hutton was replaced by Lieutenant-General Sir Harold ALEXANDER on 5 March and the latter decided to abandon RANGOON and withdraw overland to India. This retreat, the longest in the British Army's history, continued until May and was assisted by the Chinese 5th and 6th Armies under Lieutenant-General Joseph STILWELL which had entered Burma to protect their land link with China, the BURMA ROAD, and by the tanks of the 7th Armoured Brigade, which had reached Rangoon shortly before it was evacuated. During the retreat, which ended with the British retiring across the CHINDWIN and the Chinese withdrawing to northern Burma, Major-General William SLIM commanded the British Burcorps from 19 March. British casualties amounted to 30,000 of the 42,000 men involved, but many of these were Burmese who simply gave up and went home. The 95,000 Chinese also sustained heavy losses and only the 38th Division, commanded by Major-General SUN LI-JEN, emerged as a fighting formation. The Japanese, who had enjoyed air superiority throughout, lost only 7000 men. In December a limited British counter-offensive was mounted in the ARAKAN, but in March 1943 the Japanese reacted so effectively that the result was counterproductive. Meanwhile, between February and April 1943, Brigadier Orde WINGATE's Chindits mounted their first operation behind Japanese lines, cutting the Mandalay–Myitkyina railway. Although their casualties were disproportionately heavy the incident proved that Allied troops were capable of engaging the Japanese in a jungle environment. On the northern sector Stilwell's Chinese-American army commenced offensive operations in the HUKAWNG VALLEY.

A second British counteroffensive in the Arakan was mounted by Lieutenant-General A. F. P. Christison's XV Corps in January 1944. Once more the Japanese reacted violently, but by now they had lost their air superiority and British self-confidence had been restored. Before the monsoon rains put an end to the fighting the Japanese had sustained a major defeat during the Battle of the ADMIN BOX. On the Central Front, however, Lieutenant-General Masakuzu KAWABE, the commander of

The Japanese capture of the Yenangyaung oilfields in Burma.

the Japanese Burma Area Army, mounted an offensive codenamed U-GO, the object of which was to secure easily defended positions along the crest of the Naga Hills. The 15th Army, now commanded by Lieutenant-General Renya MUTAGUCHI and consisting of three divisions, crossed the Chindwin and advanced on IMPHAL and KOHIMA. Imphal was besieged from 5 April until 22 June but Lieutenant-General G. A. P. SCOONES' IV Corps, supplied and reinforced by air, was able to resist the unco-ordinated attacks of two Japanese divisions. At Kohima Mutaguchi's third division was halted by heavy fighting and then thrown back by Lieutenant-General Montagu STOPFORD's XXXIII Corps, which broke through to relieve Imphal. The 15th Army, starving and lacking supplies of every kind, was forced into a disorderly withdrawal behind the Chindwin, leaving behind 53,000 dead and all its equipment. Simultaneously, the second Chindit expedition had disrupted Japanese communications and then marched north to assist Stilwell, who had been joined by an American long-range penetration group, MERRILL'S MARAUDERS, in his capture of MOGAUNG (26 June). MYITKYINA, however, did not fall to Stilwell's troops until 3 August.

The efforts of Stilwell and his successor, Lieutenant-General Dan SULTAN, to re-establish land communications with China finally succeeded in January 1945. Meanwhile General Slim, commanding the British 14th Army, planned the destruction of the Burma

Area Army, commanded since the U-Go disaster by General Hoyotaro Kimura. In January–February 1945, XXX Corps advanced beyond the Chindwin and established bridgeheads across the Irrawaddy on either side of MANDALAY, deliberately attracting repeated counter-attacks. In great secrecy IV Corps, commanded by Lieutenant-General F. W. MES-SERVY, moved through the KABAW and Gangaw Valleys and on 13 February crossed the Irrawaddy at Pakokku, 100 miles (160km)

downstream from Mandalay. The Japanese communications centre at MEIKTILA was then captured by a fast-moving armoured column, effectively isolating the 15th and 33rd Armies to the north in a move which the Japanese themselves described as the master stroke of the campaign. All attempts to recapture Meik-tila failed and the Japanese front collapsed, Mandalay falling on 21 March. Slim directed both corps to execute a parallel dash south to Rangoon before the monsoon broke. The city fell to XV Corps on 2 May, following the last of a series of amphibious landings which had been made along the Arakan coast. The last major act in the Burma campaign was the attempted escape across the Sittang of thousands of Japanese fugitives, the majority belonging to 28th Army, which had been stationed in the Arakan. Few of them survived. See *Defeat into Victory*, by Viscount Slim (Cassell); *Battle of Burma* by E. D. Smith (Batsford) and *Tank Tracks to Rangoon* by Bryan Perrett (Robert Hale).

Burma Area Army

Title of the Japanese army group responsible for the occupation and defence of BURMA.

Burma Road, Burma–China, 1942–45

Once the Japanese had sealed off China's coastline, the only means by which China could receive war material was along the overland route running from LASHIO in Burma

The construction of the Burma Road extension, 1943.

to KUNMING in China. The severing of this vital artery was, therefore, one of the reasons which led to the successful Japanese invasion of BURMA and resulted directly in the involvement of Chinese troops under General Joseph STILWELL in that theatre of war. While the Japanese controlled the road, supplies had to be flown from bases in north-eastern India over the eastern Himalayas, which became known as the "HUMP". Stilwell was anxious to reopen the road, but it was not until May 1944 that CHIANG KAI-SHEK agreed to support him with a joint offensive from the Chinese end of the road, using a 72,000-strong army known as Y-Force commanded by Marshal Wei Lihuang. Stilwell was recalled in October, but his strategy was maintained by his successor, Lieutenant-General Dan Sultan, and on 27 January 1945 the latter's New 1st Army effected a junction with Y-Force at Mong Yu on the Burma Road. The first road convoy left Namkham the following day and reached Kunming on 4 February.

Burnett, Adm Sir Robert Lindsay (1887–1959)

Burnett was trained in HMS *Britannia* and commissioned in 1910 as a Lieutenant Physical Training Instructor. Assigned to the fleet, he saw action at Heligoland Bight and the Dogger Bank and received his first command, a torpedo-boat, in 1915. He later commanded destroyers in the Grand Fleet until 1918. After the war he filled a number of physical training posts until 1939 when he became Captain of the RN Barracks, Chatham. Appointed Rear-Admiral in November 1940, he commanded the Home Fleet minelaying flotilla in northern waters, and in 1942 became Flag Officer Destroyers. In 1944 he became Commander-in-Chief, South Atlantic. During 1941–44 he was largely concerned with the ARCTIC CONVOYS to Russia, and in December 1943 successfully outmanoeuvred the German battleship SCHARNHORST, delivering it into the hands of the fleet for sinking. Appointed Admiral in 1946, he retired in 1951.

Burza (Tempest)

Polish Home Army plan for guerrilla operations in support of Allied offensives.

Busch, FM Ernst (1885–1945)

Busch served in a staff appointment during the campaign in France and was promoted Field-Marshal in 1940. In the invasion of Russia he commanded 16th Army, apparently satisfactorily, and in October 1943 replaced von KLUGE as commander of Army Group Centre. This appears to have been above his level of capability, and he was relieved of his command in June 1944. He was inactive until the following April when he was suddenly recalled by HITLER and appointed Commander-in-Chief North-West, stationed in Norway. After Hitler's death he became a member of DÖNITZ' short-lived government and died in captivity awaiting trial for war crimes.

Bushey Park, United Kingdom, 1943–45

The headquarters of the United States Strategic Air Forces, located west of London.

Butterblume

Butterblume was originally a German infra-red airborne intercept equipment, to direct fighters to their targets by detecting the exhaust or engine heat. It was later converted into a mapping device, being capable of locating objects by the heat radiated from chimneys, locomotives and so forth. In this role it would have performed in much the same manner as the British H2S RADAR as a target locator. The developmental model was approaching completion when the war ended.

Butterfly Bomb

The British name for the German anti-personnel bomb SD-1, given because of its appearance after landing. Weighing about 4.4lb (2kg), it was a cast-iron cylindrical container loaded with TNT and having a sheet-metal outer casing in two halves. After release these halves sprang open and acted as an air-brake to stabilize the bomb as it fell; they also acted on a screwed rod so as to arm the fuze during the fall. The fuze could be set to detonate the bomb on impact or, more often, after a set time interval. Where this exceeded the dropping time, the bomb lay on the ground for some time before detonating. It also frequently failed to operate at the set time, but detonated when disturbed. Painted bright yellow, these bombs were a common hazard in Britain in 1940–41.

Butt Report

A report drawn up by a member of the War Cabinet secretariat, D. M. Butt in late 1941, which analyzed the performance of RAF BOMBER COMMAND over a three month period. It drew attention to the inaccuracy of bombing at that time and threw grave doubts upon the value of the bombing programme. As a result, navigational training was improved and the provision of electronic navigation systems speeded up, leading to an improvement in bombing accuracy.

Buttress

Preliminary Allied plan for the invasion of southern Italy, 1943.

Bv246 Glide Bomb

A German weapon intended for the attack of Allied "Loran" navigational transmitters. With the ability to glide for almost 124 miles (200km), these bombs could be released while the carrying aircraft was well clear of the target, and the "Radieschen" RADAR homing device would then steer them to the transmitter. Ten bombs were tested in Germany in 1944–45 but almost all proved unstable in flight due to gyro-stabilizer faults. The bomb was never placed in service.

BWP British Way and Purpose (UK). A propaganda publication by ABCA to provide troops with information on current affairs and world events, from the point of view of British motivation for the war effort.

Bzura, Battle of the, Poland, 1939

Counter-attack along the line of the River Bzura mounted by elements of the Polish Pomorze and Poznan Armies against the northern flank of von RUNDSTEDT's Army Group A on 9 September in an attempt to break out of the ring of encircling German armies. Rundstedt was able to contain the threat by temporarily halting 10th Army's drive on WARSAW and redeploying his armour westwards. Simultaneously, infantry divisions from von BOCK's Army Group B began closing in on the Polish rear. Heavy fighting continued until the 15th but the fate of the two Polish armies was sealed and 170,000 of their men were captured.

C

"C" Class Cruisers (UK)

Displacement 4290 tons; *dimensions* 450ft×42ft 9in (137×13m); mean draught 14ft 3in (4.35m); *machinery* 2-shaft geared turbines producing shp 40,000; *speed* 29 knots; *protection* main belt 3in; deck 1in; gun shields 1in; *armament* 5×6in (5×1); 2×3in AA (2×1); 2×2-pdr AA (2×1), 8×21in torpedo tubes (4×2) (8/10×100mm, 2×76mm, 2×2-pdr in some); *complement* 400; *number in class* 3, launched 1916–17.

"C" Class (New) Destroyers (UK)

Only eight of these vessels were completed in time to see active service, serving with the Home Fleet until they went to the East Indies in 1945. *Displacement* 1710 tons; *dimensions* 362ft 9in×35ft 9in (110×10.5m); mean draught 10ft (3.1m); *machinery* 2-shaft geared turbines producing shp 40,000; *speed* 36.75 knots; *armament* 4×4.5in DP (4×1); 4×40mm AA (1×2 and 2×1); 4×20mm AA (2×2); 4/8×21in torpedo tubes (1 or 2×4); *complement* 186; *number in class* 32, launched 1943–45.

"C" and "D" Class Destroyers (UK)

Displacement 1375 tons; *dimensions* 329ft×33ft (100×10m); mean draught 8ft 6in (2.6m); *machinery* 2-shaft geared turbines producing shp 36,000; *speed* 35.5 knots; *armament* 4×4.7in (4×1); 2×2-pdr AA (2×1); 8×21in torpedo tubes (2×4); *complement* 145; *number in class* 14, launched 1931–32.

Caballo Island, Philippines, 1942

Situated in the entrance to MANILA Bay, south of CORREGIDOR, and defended by FORT HUGHES.

Caen, France, 1944

A city and communications centre in NORMANDY. Due in part to a counter-attack by 21st Panzer Division, the British 2nd Army failed to capture the city on D-DAY. However, MONTGOMERY succeeded in drawing most of the German armour on to this sector by mounting a series of offensive operations, notably EPSOM (26 June–1 July) and GOODWOOD (18–21 July), thereby ensuring that the planned break-out on the American sector, Operation COBRA, would meet the minimum possible opposition. During the evening of 7 July, 467 Lancasters of BOMBER COMMAND dropped 2560 tons of bombs on Caen, reducing much of it to rubble and inflicting heavy civilian casualties. That part of the city north of the Orne was captured by 2nd Army on the following day, but the suburb of Vaucelles remained in German hands until 20 July.

Caesar Line, Italy, 1944

The German defence line crossing the ALBAN HILLS and stretching through Valmontone into the Apennines above Avezzano. After a week's heavy fighting, the American 36th Division of Lieutenant-General Mark CLARK's US 5th Army broke through the defences near Valmontone during the night of 30 May, opening the road TO ROME.

Cagni Class Submarines (Italy)

The largest attack submarines built for the Royal Italian Navy. They were designed for protracted commerce raiding, and as the small 17.7-inch torpedo was considered adequate against merchant ships it was possible to carry a far larger number of re-loads than in other classes of submarine. *Displacement* 1504 tons (1680/2170 tons normal); *dimensions* 288ft 3in×25ft 6in (87.8×7.77m); *machinery* 2-shaft diesel/electric motors hp 4370/1800; *speed* 17/8.5 knots; *armament* 2×3.9in; 4×13.2mm AA; 14×17.7in torpedo tubes and 36 torpedoes; *complement* 85; *number in class* 4, all launched 1940.

Cairo, Egypt, 1940–43

The location of British General Headquarters Middle East. Because of widespread nationalist, anti-British and pro-Axis feelings among large sections of the population, Cairo was a natural centre for espionage and counter-espionage activity and a proportion of the British troops in Egypt was always held in reserve for counter-insurgency contingencies. As the war progressed, the British presence increased to the point at which a nationalist coup became impossible, but when ROMMEL advanced into Egypt in July 1942 it was clear that he would be sincerely welcomed by many Egyptians. During this period, subsequently known as "The Flap", something approaching a panic evacuation developed until the front was stabilized by the First Battle of ALAMEIN. So many confidential files were burned in one day that it became known as "Ash Wednesday". Those who were permanently stationed in and around Cairo were scathingly referred to by the fighting troops as the "Short Range Desert Group" or "Groppi's Light Horse", after the famous bar, although the stricture was only justified in a minority of cases. In November 1943 a conference was held in Cairo to co-ordinate the aims of the Western Allies. It was agreed that the main Anglo-American assault on HITLER's Europe, codenamed *Overlord*, should be made from the west through France, and that this should be accompanied by an Allied landing in southern France, Operation *Anvil*; it was also agreed that Korea would be granted independence once Japan had been defeated.

Calabria, Action off, 1940

On 9 July 1940 Admiral Sir Andrew CUNNINGHAM's Mediterranean Fleet, consisting of three battleships, one aircraft carrier and five cruisers, was escorting a convoy from Malta to Alexandria when it encountered an Italian force of two battleships and 16 cruisers under Admiral Campioni, covering the passage of a convoy from Italy to North Africa. The battleships of both sides opened fire and after WARSPITE had scored a hit on *Giulio Cesare* at a range of 26,000 yards (23,800m), starting fires, Campioni turned away under cover of a smoke screen. The British sustained only superficial damage during the exchange of gunfire. The engagement ended with indiscriminate but ineffective air attacks on both fleets by the Italian air force.

Calais, France, 1940 and 1944

Attacked by 10th Panzer Division on 24 May 1940. Brigadier C. N. Nicholson's garrison, consisting of the 30th Infantry Brigade, 3rd Royal Tank Regiment and French troops, resisted until its last remnants were overwhelmed in the citadel and port area during the evening of 26 May after a defence described by the Germans as heroic. On 24 September 1944 the Canadian 3rd Division, supported by teams of specialized armour from 79th Armoured Division, began fighting its way through the much stronger German defences and on 30 September the 7500-strong garrison surrendered, having rendered the harbour installations unusable. See also CAP GRIZ NEZ.

Caledon Class Cruisers (UK)

Displacement 4180 tons; *dimensions* 450ft×42ft 9in (137×13m); mean draught 14ft 3in (4.3m); *machinery* 2-shaft geared turbines producing shp 40,000; *speed* 29 knots; *protection* main belt 3in; deck 1in; gun shields 1in; *armament* 5×6in (5×1); 2×3in AA (2×1); 2×2-pdr AA (2×1) 8×21in torpedo tubes (4×2); *complement* 400; *number in class* 3, launched 1916–17.

California Class Battleships (USA)

Displacement 32,600 tons; *dimensions* 624×108ft (190×32.9m); mean draught 30ft 6in (9.3m); *machinery* 4-shaft turbo-electric drive producing shp 30,000; *speed* 21 knots; *protection* main belt 14in; turrets 18in; *armament* 12×14in (4×3); 12×5in (12×1); 12×5in AA; *aircraft* 3; *complement* 2200; *number in class* 2, both launched 1919.

California, USS – California Class Battleship

California was sunk during the Japanese attack ON PEARL HARBOR but was raised, re-built and recommissioned in May 1944. Her displacement was increased to 37,000 tons and modern secondary armament installed, including 16×5in DP (8×2) and 56×40mm AA. She served at GUAM, SAIPAN, LEYTE, the Battle of the SURIGAO STRAIT, IWO JIMA and OKINAWA.

Callaghan, R Adm Daniel J. (1890–1942)

Callaghan was Naval Aide to President ROOSEVELT in 1938–41, after which he was given command of the heavy cruiser *San Francisco*, which was undergoing repairs in PEARL HARBOR at the time of the Japanese attack.

He became Chief of Staff to the COMNAV-SOPAC (Commander US Naval Forces South Pacific), and returned to sea when his ship was repaired. Commanding a force of two heavy and three light cruisers and eight destroyers in the First Battle of GUADALCANAL, 12/13 November 1942, he sailed his ship straight through a Japanese flotilla, severely damaging an enemy battleship and two other warships and sinking one. Rear-Admiral Callaghan was killed in the action, which was an American victory as the Japanese fleet was prevented from landing at GUADALCANAL.

Camm, Sir Sydney (1893–1966)

Sydney Camm became interested in aviation at an early age, and by the time he was 19 had designed and built a successful man-carrying glider. Trained as a woodworker, in 1914 he joined the Martynside Aircraft Company and rapidly rose to carrying out major design work. In 1923 he joined Hawker Aircraft as senior draughtsman, and within two years was their chief designer. His first design for Hawker was the Cygnet biplane, which won numerous competitions in 1925–26, but from 1925 onwards Camm specialized in military designs. The first fully Camm design was the Hawker Hart light bomber of 1928; together with its variants the Hind, Osprey, Audax and Nimrod, over 3000 were sold around the world. He then redesigned the Hart into the Fury fighter, universally recognized as one of the most elegant biplanes ever made. In 1933 he began studies on a fighter to be built

around the Rolls-Royce Merlin engine. In 1934 the Air Ministry issued Specification F36/34, and his resulting modified design produced the HAWKER HURRICANE fighter, of which 14,500 were built. By 1939 he was working on the TYPHOON, the replacement for the Hurricane, which appeared in service in 1942, whereupon he turned to the jet engine and developed the Sea Hawk and the Hunter; the latter took the world air speed record in 1953. He then designed a number of supersonic military aircraft, all of which fell foul of changing government policies, and from 1958 worked on the problems of Vertical Take-Off aircraft. He received the CBE in 1941 and was knighted in 1953.

Campbell, Brig "Jock" (1894–1942)

Campbell was an officer in the Royal Horse Artillery who devised and commanded "Jock Columns", mobile columns of infantry and artillery, in the Western Desert 1941–42. He was awarded the Victoria Cross for his handling of the Support Group of 7th Armoured Division in the Battle of SIDI REZEGH (21–22 November 1941), during which he was wounded. He had just been appointed Commander 7th Armoured Division when he was killed in a road accident on 26 February 1942.

Campbeltown, HMS – Destroyer

Campbeltown was one of the fifty old "FLUSH DECK" destroyers transferred by the United States to the Royal Navy in September 1940. Under the command of Commander Robert

HMS Campbeltown *at St Nazaire.*

Ryder she played the major role in the attack on the dry dock at ST NAZAIRE during the night of 27/28 March 1942 when, disguised as a German warship and with her bows packed with explosives, she rammed the dock gates. The following morning the demolition charges exploded, completely wrecking the dock and killing a party of German senior officers who had boarded the abandoned destroyer.

Canal Defence Light (CDL) – Searchlight Tank (UK)

A tank turret designed by A. V. M. Mitzakis during the 1930s, housing a high intensity arc lamp and two reflectors, capable of projecting a beam 1000 yards (915m) with an illuminated width of 350 yards (320m). The beam passed through a vertical slit two feet high and two inches wide and a flickering effect, intended to dazzle the enemy, could be achieved by means of an oscillating steel shutter. The device was purchased by the War Office in 1937, being described as a Canal Defence Light for security purposes. The turret was originally fitted to the MATILDA infantry tank, power for the searchlight being supplied by the main engines. By 1942 two Matilda CDL regiments were present in the Middle East but had not completed their training in time to take part in the Second Battle of ALAMEIN. The CDL was also fitted experimentally to the CHURCHILL infantry tank but the GRANT medium tank was eventually standardized as the principal CDL mounting, the 75mm gun being retained in the sponson while the CDL turret replaced the upper 37mm gun turret. Power for the searchlight was provided by a generator installed in the Grant's roomier interior. The 79th Armoured Division contained a CDL brigade which landed in NORMANDY in August 1944. This was not employed and was equipped with other vehicles. However, 24 CDLs were used operationally by 49 RTR during the RHINE and ELBE crossings in 1945. In May of that year a CDL regiment was formed for service in the Far East but was not employed. In American service the Grant CDL was known by the codename of the T10 Shop Tractor.

Canaris, Adm Wilhelm (1887–1945)

Canaris was head of German Armed Forces Intelligence Service (Abwehr) from 1935. A U-boat commander in World War I, he remained in the Navy after the war and gradually came to specialize in intelligence. He was not a member of the Nazi party and appeared to have a love of intrigue which involved him in a number of anti-Nazi projects. There is a suspicion that his service was responsible for leaking information to the Allies, but his part in this is unlikely to be proved and there is some suggestion that this was devised by British intelligence to conceal their successful ULTRA code-breaking activities. Canaris flirted with various anti-Nazi plotters and was arrested after the JULY BOMB PLOT against Hitler. Even here, however, there is the suggestion that he was "framed" by HIMMLER so that the latter could gain control of the intelligence services. Canaris was executed at Flossenburg concentration camp on 9 April 1945.

Canberra, HMAS – Kent Class Cruiser

Served in the South Atlantic and East Indies before taking part in the SOLOMON ISLANDS campaign. She was so seriously damaged during the Battle of SAVO ISLAND that she was abandoned and sunk by torpedoes and gunfire from Allied destroyers. The decision aroused controversy, although the cruiser had undoubtedly sustained severe damage.

Canberra, USS – Baltimore Class Heavy Cruiser

Launched on 19 April 1943, *Canberra* served at ENIWETOK, HOLLANDIA, the MARIANAS, Palau, and LEYTE. She was seriously damaged by Japanese torpedo bombers off FORMOSA on 13 October 1944.

Canea, Crete, 1941

A city in western CRETE and the objective of the German Group Centre. The reinforced 3rd Parachute-Rifle Regiment dropped on 20 May but was pinned down by the Allied defenders. Canea did not fall until 27 May when events elsewhere dictated an Allied withdrawal.

Cannon Class Destroyer Escorts (USA)

Displacement 1240 tons; *dimensions* 306ft×36ft 6in (93.2×11.1m); mean draught 8ft 9in (2.67m); *machinery* 2-shaft diesel-electric drive producing shp 12,000; *speed* 21 knots; *armament* 3×3in; 6×40mm AA; 3×21in torpedo tubes; *complement* 200; *number in class* 66, launched 1943–44.

Cape Bon, Action off, 1941

Following the destruction of the DUISBERG CONVOY on 9 November 1941 the Royal Italian Navy attempted for a while to transport fuel to the Axis armies in North Africa by fast cruisers. One such run, made by the cruisers *Alberico da Barbiano* and *Alberto di Guissano*, accompanied by the torpedo boat *Cigno*, took place during the night of 12/13 December 1941, the intention being that the ships would make a landfall at Cape Bon and continue along the coast of Tripoli. They were, however, spotted by British reconnaissance aircraft and the 4th Destroyer Flotilla (*Sikh*, *Maori*, *Legion* and the Dutch *Isaac Sweers*) under Commander G. H. Stokes, eastward bound from Gibraltar to join Admiral CUNNINGHAM's fleet, was ordered to intercept them off Cape Bon. At first Stokes thought he had missed his prey but when the Italians retreated to avoid a suspected air attack the two groups began approaching each other rapidly, with the British flotilla inshore and concealed by the bulk of the headland. At 0223 the destroyers opened fire and launched their torpedoes. The Italians were taken completely by surprise and both cruisers were sunk, their deck cargo of cased petrol blazing fiercely. *Cigno* escaped but returned later with other Italian ships to pick up survivors.

Cape Engaño   See LEYTE GULF, Battle of.

Cape Esperance, Battle of, 1942

During the night of 11/12 October 1942 Rear-Admiral Aritomo Goto's cruiser squadron, consisting of the cruisers *Aoba* (Flag), *Furutaka*, *Kinugasa* and the destroyers *Hatsuyuki* and *Fubuki*, was detailed to cover the landing of reinforcements on GUADALCANAL and then bombard HENDERSON FIELD. Simultaneously, Rear-Admiral Norman Scott, commanding a force containing the cruisers *San Francisco* (Flag), *Boise, Salt Lake City* and *Helena* and the destroyers *Farenholt, Duncan, Laffey, Buchanan* and *McCalla*, was screening the approach of an American convoy with supplementary orders to destroy enemy shipping in the area. At 2330 the American squadron was west of Savo Island and steaming in line ahead when the Japanese ships were detected approaching in columns from the north. Scott would have been in position to cross Goto's T and deliver crushing broadsides had he not just issued a somewhat complex order to reverse course which forfeited much of the advantage. Even so, the Japanese were taken completely by surprise when at the point-blank range of 5000 yards (4570m) fire was opened at 2346.

Aoba, seriously damaged, ablaze and with Goto mortally wounded on her bridge, turned out of the fight followed by *Furutaka* which has sustained similar damage and been hit in the engine room by a torpedo from the destroyer *Duncan*. *Fubuki*, illuminated by *San Francisco*, was torn to pieces by concentrated gunfire and blew up. However, *Duncan* was concurrently engaged with *Kinugasa* and *Hatsuyuki* and, being unexpectedly out of position, was also hit repeatedly by her own side. At 0200, with fires raging from stem to stern, she was abandoned and sank the following day. *Farenholt*, too, was damaged by the fire of the American cruisers and forced to withdraw. The remainder of Scott's ships pursued the retreating Japanese, *Boise* being seriously damaged by *Kinugasa*, which was hit in turn by *Salt Lake City*. Scott broke off the action at 0020, and later the crippled *Furutaka* rolled over and sank. Next day two Japanese destroyers, *Murakumo* and *Natsugumo*, were sunk by air attack. If not a great victory, the action was a definite success which did much to restore American morale after the debacle at SAVO ISLAND two months earlier.

Cape Gloucester, New Britain, 1944

The US 1st Marine Division was put ashore on 26 December, securing a beach-head and two airfields in four days' fighting in which over 1000 Japanese were killed.

US Marines land at Cape Gloucester, December 1943.

Cape Matapan, Battle of, 1941

On 26 March 1941 Admiral Angelo Iachino, with the battleship *Vittorio Veneto*, eight cruisers and nine destroyers, left his Italian bases to execute sweeps north and south of Crete against the British convoy route between Alexandria and Greece. Aware of his opponent's intentions, Admiral Sir Andrew CUNNINGHAM began concentrating his own fleet, consisting of the battleships *Warspite*, *Barham* and *Valiant*, the aircraft carrier *Formidable*, four cruisers and thirteen destroyers. The Italians were detected by a British flying boat off Ionia on the 27th and by dawn next morning both fleets were converging on Gavdo Island, south of Crete. The British cruisers made contact with the enemy and withdrew under fire, hoping to lure the Italians towards their battleships. Iachino, however, already alarmed by an abortive air strike from *Formidable* at 1058, guessed their intentions and, not wishing to become involved in a general engagement, reversed course at 1127. Cunningham recognized that the only way of catching him was to damage *Vittorio Veneto* and at 1530 a second air strike scored a torpedo hit on her stern. Despite this, the battleship soon regained speed, and a third air strike was launched. This missed *Vittorio Veneto* but severely damaged the cruiser *Pola*, bringing her to a standstill. Iachino detached her sister ships *Zara* and *Fiume*, plus four destroyers, to stand by her while he continued his withdrawal. At 2200 Cunningham obtained radar contact with the Italian cruisers and at 2230 *Zara*, *Fiume* and two destroyers were suddenly illuminated at 3000 yards (2750m) and quickly blown apart by the 15-inch guns of the British battleships. *Pola* was similarly destroyed three hours later. Iachino succeeded in reaching home with the damaged *Vittorio Veneto* but with the loss of almost 2500 men.

Cape Spartivento, Battle of, Mediterranean Sea, 1940

On 27 November Admiral Inigo Campioni, with the battleships *Vittorio Veneto* and *Giulio Cesare*, six cruisers and 14 destroyers, attempted to intercept a convoy escorted by FORCE H, commanded by Vice-Admiral Sir James SOMERVILLE and consisting of the old battleship *Ramillies*, the battlecruiser *Renown*, the aircraft carrier *Ark Royal*, five cruisers and 10 destroyers. Somerville ordered his convoy to sail away to the south-

Vittorio Veneto *in action.*

east and turned to meet the enemy. There was an exchange of gunfire between the opposing cruiser squadrons in which the cruiser *Berwick* sustained damage, but then Campioni discovered the hitherto unsuspected presence of *Ark Royal*. Conscious that in the aftermath of TARANTO he was responsible for preserving Italy's two remaining serviceable battleships, he signalled his fleet to turn away for Naples. Subsequent strikes against their respective opponents by the Fleet Air Arm and the land-based *Regia Aeronautica* were ineffective. In material terms the engagement was inconclusive, although it provided an insight into the Italian Navy's state of mind. The British convoy reached MALTA safely.

Cape St George, Battle of, 1943

A squadron of five Japanese destroyers engaged on a re-supply mission to BOUGAINVILLE was intercepted south-east of New Ireland by five American destroyers under Captain Arleigh Burke on 25 November 1943. Three of the Japanese ships were sunk. The Americans sustained no loss.

Capetown Class Cruisers (UK)

Displacement 4290 tons; *dimensions* 451ft 6in×43ft 6in (137.6×13m); mean draught 14ft 3in (4.3m); *machinery* 2-shaft geared turbines producing shp 40,000; *speed* 29 knots; *protection* main belt 3in; deck 1in; *armament* 8×4in AA (4×2); 4×2-pdr AA (1×4); 8×0.5in AA (2×4); *complement* 400; *number in class* 5, launched 1918–19.

Cap Gris Nez, France, 1944

A heavily-defended coastal fortification between CALAIS and BOULOGNE containing two major battery positions, one at Framzelle with four 15-inch guns and one at Haringzelles

with four 11-inch guns, capable of engaging targets on the south coast of England. The defences were stormed on 29 September by the Canadian 3rd Division, supported by 79th Armoured Division's specialist armour.

Capital

Restoration of Allied land communictions between northern BURMA and CHINA, 1944. See also EXTENDED CAPITAL.

Capitani Romani Class Light Cruisers (Italy)

Displacement 5400 tons; *dimensions* 466ft 6in×47ft 3in (142×14.4m); mean draught 13ft 5in (4.1m); *machinery* 2-shaft geared turbines producing shp 110,000; *speed* 40+ knots; *armament* 8×5.3in; 8×37mm AA; 8×20mm AA; 8×21in torpedo tubes; *complement* 420; *number in class* 4, launched 1940–41; at the time of Italy's surrender a further four had been launched but not completed and four more were on the stocks; all laid down 1939–40.

Caproni Aircraft (Italy)

Caproni CA133 The CA133 was the last of three models developed as support machines for the Italian Army in Africa. Tri-motored, they were extremely versatile and performed in the bombing, troop carrying, reconnaissance, ground attack and forward supply roles with great success. *Span* 69.6ft (21.2m); *engines* 3 460hp radial; *armament* 1 or 2 machine guns, up to 2200lb (1000kg) of bombs; *speed* 175mph (282kph).

Caproni CA135 Although developed for the Italian Air Force this machine was purchased only in small numbers as three-engined designs were preferred. Some were bought

Captured Caproni CA133 bomber flown to an RAF station in the Sudan.

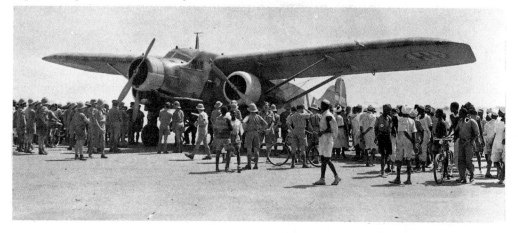

by Peru in pre-war days and about 100 by Hungary, who used them with the Luftwaffe on the Eastern Front. *Span* 61.6ft (18.8m); *engines* 2 1000hp radial; *crew* 5; *armament* 3 to 6 machine guns and up to 3525lb (1600kg) of bombs; *speed* 275mph (442kph).

Captain Class Frigates (UK)

Formerly American destroyer escorts. The majority were returned to the US Navy 1945–46.

Diesel Electric Group *Displacement* 1085 tons; *dimensions* 289ft 6in×35ft (88.2×10.6m); mean draught 9ft (2.7m); *machinery* 2-shaft diesel-electric motors with bhp 6000; *speed* 20 knots; *armament* 3×3in AA (3×1); 2×40mm AA (1×2); 10×20mm AA (10×1); *complement* 200; *number in group* 32, launched 1942–43.

Turbo-Electric Group *Displacement* 1300 tons; *dimensions* 306ft×36ft 9in (93.2×11m); mean draught 9ft (2.7m); *machinery* 2-shaft geared turbines-electric motors producing shp 12,000; *speed* 26 knots; *armament* 3×3in AA (3×1); 2×40mm AA (1×2); 8 or 10×20mm AA (8 or 10×1); *complement* 200; *number in group* 46, launched 1943.

Capuzzo, Fort, Libya, 1940 and 1941

An Italian frontier post south of BARDIA. The post had little defensive capacity and was quickly reduced to ruins when it changed hands several times. From December 1941 its importance declined.

Capuzzo, Trigh, 1940–43

A desert track running westwards from Fort CAPUZZO past SIDI REZEGH and EL ADEM to join the Trigh el Abd at the Rotonda Mteifel.

Carbine

The class name for any short rifle, habitually applied to weapons carried by artillery, cavalry, engineers etc, whose primary role was not the use of the rifle. During World War II it came to be applied principally to the American Carbine M1 and subsequent models. This was a light rifle firing a short .30 calibre cartridge, intended to arm drivers, mortar men and others who required a personal defence weapon of greater range than a pistol. Developed by the Winchester company, it was a gas-operated semi-automatic weapon with an effective range of about 150 yards (137m). Later versions permitted automatic fire.

Carentan, France, 1944

A town at the base of the COTENTIN PENINSULA the capture of which was necessary to effect a junction between the US VII Corps in the UTAH beach-head with US V Corps in the OMAHA beach-head as soon as possible after the D-DAY landings. On D-Day the US 101st Airborne Division (VII Corps) dropped north of the town but was badly scattered and unable to make much progress in this direction due to opposition from the German 6th Parachute-Rifle Regiment. On 12 June the American paratroopers captured Carentan, overcoming stiff resistance by the German 352nd Division, where they were joined on the same day by elements of the US 29th Division (V Corps).

Carlson, Lt Col Evans F.

Carlson commanded 2nd Marine Raider Battalion at GUADALCANAL where his employment of COMMANDO tactics earned his unit the nickname "Carlson's Raiders". Before the outbreak of war he had been an adviser to CHIANG KAI-SHEK and had observed guerrilla operations behind Japanese lines in CHINA, which gave him a considerable advantage in knowing both his enemy and the tactics appropriate to defeating him. Carlson was forced to retire in July 1946 as a result of wounds received on SAIPAN, where he won a second Purple Heart (his first having been awarded in World War I).

Carpathian Mountains, Central Europe, 1944–45

Running from north-west to south-east from southern Poland along the approximate line of the common frontier of Czechoslovakia, Hungary and northern Romania with the Soviet Union, the Carpathians posed a serious physical barrier to armies advancing from the east and also effectively divided the Eastern Front into northern and southern sectors. In September 1944 KONEV's 1st Ukrainian Front and Petrov's 4th Ukrainian Front commenced operations to open the passes, but the strategically important Dukla Pass was not secured until November and fighting in the mountains continued until 1945.

Carpet

A US Army Air Force electronic jamming device used by bombers of the 8th Air Force from late 1943 onwards. It was a jamming transmitter operating on the frequency used by the German WURZBURG Radar.

Carpet Bombing

Carpet Bombing was the name given to a method of bombing used by heavy bombers to assist operations by ground troops. It consisted of commencing bombing at a specified "start line" and dropping bombs along a defined corridor to a "finish line" so as to destroy all obstacles and defensive posts in the area and permit the ground troops to advance behind the bombing. It is analogous to an artillery barrage.

Carpiquet, France, 1944

A fortified village and airfield west of CAEN tenaciously defended by the 12th SS Panzer Division *Hitlerjugend*. After extremely bitter fighting the positions were captured by the Canadian 3rd Division on 9 July.

Carroceto, Italy, 1944

A town on the perimeter of the ANZIO beach-head and the scene of heavy German counter-attacks in February.

Carrot

Early mechanically-placed British explosive device tested with MATILDA and CHURCHILL infantry tanks. In addition to demolition tasks Carrot was also intended to detonate mines by its own explosion. Later, more sophisticated devices were GOAT and ONION; see AVRE.

Carton de Wiart, Gen Sir Adrian (1880–1963)

Carton de Wiart served as a trooper in the South African War and was afterwards commissioned into the 4th Dragoon Guards. He won the Victoria Cross leading the 8th Battalion, the Gloucestershire Regiment at the Battle of the Somme in 1916. After 1918 he led the British Military Mission to Poland and then resigned his commission and took up residence there. Recalled to England in June 1939 he was again given the leadership of the Military Mission to Poland. He escaped from the country via Romania during the German invasion, and in 1940 was given command of the Central Norway Force, which he managed to extricate from there with little loss. In 1941 he was sent on a mission to YUGOSLAVIA, but his aircraft crashed and he was captured by the Italians. After escaping and being recaptured, he was sent with General Zanussi to Lisbon in 1943 to discuss Armistice terms. On the failure of this mission, he was then sent back to London to negotiate the Italian surrender proposal. After this he became CHURCHILL's representative to CHIANG KAI-SHEK and remained in China until 1946. He was wounded innumerable times during his career, and lost one eye and one hand; his black eye-patch made him a well-known figure in British military circles, and reputedly provided Evelyn Waugh with the model for his formidable fictional creation, Colonel Ritchie-Hook.

Cartwheel

Allied plan to isolate the Japanese naval base at RABAUL.

Casablanca, Morocco, 1942

During Operation TORCH the major part of the Western Task Force, commanded by Major-General George S. PATTON, landed at Fedala, north of the city, meeting opposition from French troops and naval units. On 11 November the Americans were about to launch a major attack on Casablanca when Admiral DARLAN issued orders for a ceasefire.

Casablanca Class Escort Carriers (USA)

Displacement 7800 tons; *dimensions* 512ft 3in×65ft 3in (154×19.5m); mean draught 19ft 9in (6m); *machinery* 1-shaft reciprocating producing shp 9000; *speed* 19.25 knots; *armament* 1×5in; 16×40mm; *aircraft* 28; *complement* 860; *number in class* 50, launched 1943–44.

Casablanca Conference, Morocco, 1943

Codenamed Symbol, the conference was attended by CHURCHILL, ROOSEVELT and their Chiefs of Staff, commencing on 14 January. Four days of frank discussion and hard

Left to right: Admiral King, Winston Churchill, President Roosevelt. Standing: Major-General Ismay (second from left), Lord Mountbatten (third from left) and Field-Marshal Dill (right). Casablanca, January 1943.

bargaining produced agreement on the following: priority was to be given to winning the Battle of the ATLANTIC; the Soviet Union would continue to be supplied with war material; joint preparations would continue in the United Kingdom for a full-scale invasion of France in 1944; the bomber offensive against Germany was to be intensified; planning was to commence for the invasion of SICILY following the final defeat of the Axis forces in North Africa; operations in the Pacific would be extended to include the recapture of the ALEUTIANS and an offensive directed against Japanese bases in the Caroline and MARSHALL Islands; the British would prepare to take the offensive in BURMA. At the end of the conference Roosevelt announced that the only terms acceptable to the Allies would be the unconditional surrender of the Axis. This proved to be counterproductive in that it actually prolonged German and Japanese resistance.

Casablanca class escort carrier.

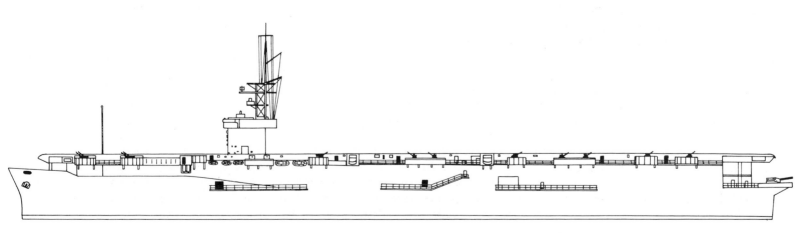

Caserta, Italy, 1944–45

A town 15 miles (24km) north-east of NAPLES which became Allied General Headquarters in Italy.

Cassino, Italy, 1944

The heavily fortified town of Cassino, overlooked by a 1700ft (518m) feature surmounted by a large Benedictine monastery, dominated the LIRI valley through which ran Route 6, the only practicable road by which the Allies could reach ROME, and was the lynchpin of the GUSTAV LINE. So strong were the defences that the Allies attempted to outflank them by effecting an amphibious landing behind the German lines at ANZIO. When this failed, it became clear that the Cassino position, held by General von VIETINGHOFF's German 10th Army, would have to be taken by the direct assault of the US 5th Army (Lieutenant-General Mark CLARK) and the British 8th Army (Lieutenant-General Sir Oliver LEESE). The first attempt, lasting from 17 January until 12 February, was made by the British X Corps, the US II Corps and the French Corps. Some gains were made but almost all were lost to counter-attacks. Unjustified suspicions that the Germans had incorporated the monastery in their defences led to its being heavily bombed on 15 February. Immediately afterwards the 4th Indian Division made some limited gains north of Monastery Hill and the 2nd New Zealand Division captured Cassino railway station, only to lose it again on 18 February. On 15 March the town was pulverized by 1000 tons of bombs and the fire of 600 guns, the station and Castle Hill falling to the New Zealanders after a further three days of ferocious fighting against the German 1st Parachute Division. The 4th Indian Division also succeeded in reaching Hangman's Hill, but this proved to be untenable and was abandoned on the 24th. There was now a lull, during which the Allies made preparation for a major offensive, including a deception plan to convince the Germans that a break-out was to be made from the Anzio beach-head. The last battle of Cassino commenced at 2300 on 11 May, when 2000 guns opened fire on the German positions. The Polish II Corps isolated Monastery Hill from the north while the British XIII Corps crossed the RAPIDO river to cut Route 6 west of the town. Simultaneously, the French and US II Corps attacked south of the Liri. Complete surprise was achieved and although the Germans

Shattered remains of Cassino after its seizure by the British and Polish, on 18 May 1944.

fought hard their defences were overwhelmed. By the morning of 18 May the town had been cleared and the Poles had captured the ruins of the monastery. The four-month struggle had cost the Allies 21,000 casualties, including 4100 killed; German losses were comparable. See *Cassino* by Dominick Graham (Pan/Ballantine).

Castle Class Corvettes (UK)

Five completed as rescue ships. *Displacement* 1010 tons; *dimensions* 252ft×36ft 9in (76.8×11.2m); mean draught 10ft (3m); *machinery* 1-shaft reciprocating engine with ihp 2880; *speed* 16.5 knots; *armament* 1×4in; 10×20mm AA (2×2 and 6×1); 1 Squid; *complement* 120; *number in class* 44, launched 1943–44.

Casualties

The total number of casualties arising from World War II is impossible to compute with any accuracy. The best overall figures which can be advanced are that military battle deaths totalled some 15 million, military wounded about 25 million, and civilian deaths about 38 million. Figures for the major combatants, from the best official sources, are as follows: Britain & Commonwealth (including Australia, Canada, India, South Africa, New Zealand & Colonies): *Military dead* 418,765; *Military wounded* 475,057; *Civilian dead* 90,843.

China: *Military dead* 1,324,516; *Military wounded* 1,762,000; *Civilian dead* Not available.

Finland: *Military dead* 79,047; *Military wounded* 50,000; *Civilian dead* Not available.

France: *Military dead* 205,707; *Military wounded* 390,000; *Civilian dead* 173,260.

Germany: *Military dead* 3,300,000; *Military wounded* Not available; *Civilian dead* 593,000.

Greece: *Military dead* 16,357; *Military wounded* 49,933; *Civilian dead* 155,300.

Italy: *Military dead* 262,420; *Military wounded* 120,000; *Civilian dead* 93,000.

Japan: *Military dead* 1,140,430; *Military wounded* 295,250; *Civilian dead* 953,000.

Poland: *Military dead* 320,000; *Military wounded* 530,000; *Civilian dead* (includes approximately 3 million murdered Jews) 6,028,000.

Soviet Union: *Military and civil dead* 6,115,000; *Military and civil wounded* 14,012,000. (The much-quoted figure of "twenty million Soviet dead" appears to have no basis in fact; the figures quoted here are derived from official Soviet figures quoted at Nuremberg. Adding dead and wounded gives some 20 million *casualties*, and the transition to "dead" is an easy step.)

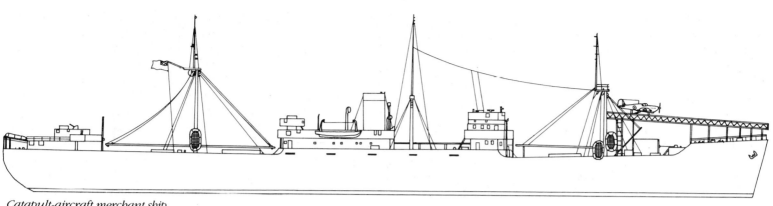

Catapult-aircraft merchant ship.

USA: *Military dead* 292,131; *Military wounded* 671,278; *Civilian dead* 5,662 (Merchant marine).

Jewish deaths: An estimated 5,993,000 Jews were murdered in extermination and labour camps, some 66% of European Jewry. The major sources were as follows: *Baltic States* 228,000; *Belgium* 40,000; *Bulgaria* 14,000; *Czechoslovakia* 155,000; *France* 90,000; *Germany/Austria* 210,000; *Greece* 54,000; *Hungary* 450,000; *Netherlands* 105,000; *Poland* 3,000,000; *Romania* 300,000; *Russia (German-held)* 1,252,000.

Catapult-Aircraft Merchant Ship (CAM Ship) (UK)

These vessels were introduced to combat German air attacks on convoys outside the range of friendly fighter cover in mid-Atlantic. Suitable merchant ships were fitted with a catapult which launched a fighter to intercept

A Hawker Hurricane being catapulted from a CAM ship.

the attacking aircraft, the first such action taking place on 11 January 1941. The fighters employed were the FAIREY FULMAR and, later, the HAWKER HURRICANE. The system's major disadvantage was that once the attackers had been shot down or driven off, the pilot was compelled to ditch his own aircraft and await rescue. The need for CAM Ships declined steadily after escort carriers entered service in the autumn of 1941. See also MERCHANT AIR-CRAFT CARRIERS.

Catchpole

American landing on ENIWETOK, MARSHALL ISLANDS, 1944.

Caterpillar Club

A club formed by the Irving Airchute Company, manufacturers of service parachutes, membership of which was confined to those whose lives were saved by an Irving

parachute. It was established as a civil club in pre-war days; its membership was rapidly expanded by RAF personnel during the war years.

Caucasus, Soviet Union, 1942–43

In June 1942 an invasion of the Caucasus was launched by Field-Marshal LIST's Army Group A, the principal objective being the capture of the oilfields at Maikop, Grozny and Baku. The Maikop oilfield was overrun in August but attempts to secure the passes through the main Caucasus range were defeated. HITLER had meanwhile become obsessed with the capture of STALINGRAD, and the success of the Soviet counteroffensive there in November placed Army Group A in serious danger of isolation. List had already warned Hitler that his troops were badly overextended and been dismissed for his pains in September. Thereafter the Führer exercised personal command of the Caucasus sector until 21 November, when he appointed von KLEIST army group commander. In December the Soviet Transcaucasus Front also went over to the offensive and throughout January and February 1943 Kleist was forced to execute a difficult withdrawal through ROSTOV to avoid encirclement by the Red Army's South Front, only the Taman Peninsula being retained. See also the BLUE LINE.

Caudron Aircraft (Fr)

Caudron 714 A lightweight fighter aircraft designed to a French Air Force specification in 1938. It went into production in 1939 and 100 were ordered, fifty of which were diverted for the Finnish Air Force, though few were in fact delivered. The remainder went into French service to be flown by Polish pilots, but saw relatively little combat before being either destroyed or captured in 1940.

Span 29.5ft (9m); *engine* 1 450hp in-line; *armament* 4 machine guns; *speed* 300mph (483kph).

Caudron Goeland A transport and training aircraft which first appeared in 1934 in both civil versions and as a French Air Force machine. A variant model was developed as an ambulance aircraft. In 1940 several were captured by the Germans and production continued during the war, the output being split between the French and German air forces and the Lufthansa airline. *Span* 57.6ft (17.6m); *engines* 2 220hp in-line; *speed* 200mph (322kph).

Cauldron, The, Libya, 1942

The name given to the area into which the AFRIKA KORPS and the Italian *Ariete* Armoured Division retired after the failure of the move with which ROMMEL opened the GAZALA battle. The approximate boundaries of The Cauldron were Sidra Ridge in the north, Aslagh Ridge to the east and the box held by the British 150th Brigade to the west. It took until 5 June for RITCHIE to mount a major attack on The Cauldron and by then Rommel had overwhelmed the 150 Brigade Box (1 June) and restored his communications. Ritchie's attack failed and Rommel broke out to inflict a severe defeat on 8th Army.

Caumont, France, 1944

A town in NORMANDY captured by the US 1st Division (V Corps) on 12 July. As the US 1st Army prepared to break out of its beach-head, the inter-army boundary was adjusted, transferring Caumont to the British 2nd Army sector. Determined to prevent VON KLUGE moving his Panzer Divisions against the Americans, MONTGOMERY ordered 2nd Army to strike south from Caumont with two corps, O'CONNOR's VIII (Guards Armoured, 11th Armoured, 15th [Scottish] Divisions and 6th [Guards] Tank Brigade) and BUCKNALL's XXX (7th Armoured, 43rd [Wessex], 50th [Northumbrian] Divisions and 8th Armoured Brigade), the object being to capture Hills 361 and 309 and exploit towards Vire in the hope of attracting a counter-attack by the German armour. The operation, codenamed *Bluecoat*, began at first light on 30 July. The 15th Division, spearheaded by 6th (Guards) Tank Brigade, smashed through the German 326th Division and secured Hill 309 after a six-mile advance. The following day good reconnaissance enabled the 11th Armoured Division to

exploit a gap in the enemy line and that night the division pushed across the River Souleuvre and established itself on the hills near Le Beny Bocage. On the XXX Corps sector progress was less satisfactory but in the overall context Operation *Bluecoat* achieved its purpose.

Cavalier – A24 Cruiser Tank Mark VII (UK)

An unsuccessful interim attempt to produce a better armed and armoured cruiser tank than the CRUSADER. Design work started early in 1941 and the pilot model was completed in January 1942. Several hundred were built but as their mechanical performance was actually inferior to that of the Crusader they were retained for training in the United Kingdom. In 1943 about half were converted to Artillery Observation Post tanks and saw active service in North West Europe. Originally designated Cromwell I. See also CENTAUR and CROMWELL. *Weight* 26.5 tons; *speed* 24mph (39kph); *armour* 76mm; *armament* 1 6-pdr gun; 1 or 2 Besa machine guns; *engine* Nuffield Liberty petrol 410hp; *crew* 5.

Cavallero, Marshal Ugo (1880–1943)

Cavallero served with the Italian Army during World War I but resigned after the Armistice and went into business. In 1925 he became Under-Secretary of War but went back to commerce as director of Ansaldo shipbuilding yard in 1928. He returned to the Army to take part in the Abyssinian War and in 1940, as a Marshal of Italy, was appointed Chief of the

General Staff in place of BADOGLIO. He imposed a much firmer leadership on the Army than hitherto and, with his pre-war commercial experience, was able to make improvements in Italian War production. However, constant Italian defeats weakened his political position, and he became convinced that there was a plot to unseat him and bring the Army under Fascist party control. He took various clandestine actions to counter this plot, which led to his being suspected of attempting to depose MUSSOLINI. He was replaced as Chief of Staff in January 1943, and in August 1943 was arrested for plotting to overthrow the Duce; the charge failed and he was released, but later committed suicide on 14 September 1943 when it appeared that the truth of his intriguing might be made public.

Cavalry, 1939–45

By 1939 it was generally accepted that cavalry had little place on the modern battlefield and in most armies the process of mechanization was already well advanced. The Polish Army, however, still retained 11 brigades of cavalry and on a number of occasions these were engaged in gallant but futile counter-attacks against German armoured formations. In 1940 the French Army employed five cavalry divisions, containing both mounted troops and light tanks, in the reconnaissance role, but these were no match for their fully mechanized opponents. The British 1st Cavalry Division was sent to Palestine where it was employed mainly on internal security duties; by the end of 1941 its regiments had

Cossacks of the 4th Cavalry Corps on the march near Tiraspol, May 1944.

lost their horses and were in process of converting to other arms. The German Army's 1st Cavalry Division saw active service in Poland, France and during the early part of the campaign in Russia but became 24th Panzer Division in 1942: the Waffen SS also formed the 8th SS Cavalry Division *Florian Geyer*, which performed the mounted reconnaissance role in brigade strength on the Eastern Front 1941–42 before being mechanized.

Because of its vastness and the fact that the line was never continuous, the Eastern Front provided the only arena in which cavalry was used to any appreciable extent. The Soviet Army possessed numerous cavalry corps, each consisting of two divisions containing three mounted regiments, an armoured element varying in size from battalion to regiment, and an artillery regiment. In addition to the traditional cavalry roles, these were used to prey on the German flanks and rear areas. As the war progressed, the cavalry corps were grouped together in pairs and given additional armour, this higher formation being known as a cavalry-mechanized group. By no means all Soviet cavalrymen wished to fight for STALIN and sufficient Cossacks deserted to enable the Germans to form their own Cossack Cavalry Corps of three divisions. In the Pacific theatre of war the US 26th Cavalry (Philippine Scouts) fought a number of mounted actions during the Japanese invasion of the PHILIPPINE ISLANDS in 1942, and the Japanese themselves made limited use of mounted troops in the less mechanized environment of CHINA.

Cavour Class Battleships (Italy)

Conte di Cavour was sunk by British aircraft at TARANTO on 12 November 1940. She was refloated and towed to Trieste for repairs, but the work had not been completed when Italy surrendered in August 1943. She was captured by the Germans and finally sunk on 15 February 1945. *Giulio Cesare*, the second ship of this class, survived the war and was transferred to the Soviet Union in 1948. *Displacement* 23,619 tons; *dimensions* 611ft 6in×92ft (186.4×28m); mean draught 30ft (9.1m); *machinery* 2-shaft geared turbines producing shp 93,300; *speed* 28 knots; *protection* main belt 9.8in; deck 5.4in; turrets 11in; *armament* 10×12.6in; 12×4.7in; 8×3.9in AA; 8×37mm AA; 12×20mm AA; *complement* 1236; *number in class* 2, both launched 1910 and rebuilt 1933–37.

Cebu, Philippines, 1945

An island held by 14,500 Japanese troops under the personal leadership of Lieutenant-General Sosaku SUZUKI. On 26 March the US Americal Division landed near Cebu City and, after the initial landings had been disrupted by minefields, advanced inland. The Japanese retired into prepared positions in the hills from which they were driven after three weeks' fighting. The survivors spent the rest of the war as fugitives in the mountains of northern Cebu. Suzuki was killed by air attack while trying to reach MINDANAO.

Centaur – A27L Cruiser Tank Mark VIII (UK)

A second interim attempt to produce a better armed and armoured cruiser tank than the CRUSADER, the first being the CAVALIER. The vehicle employed the same hull and turret as the Cavalier but was fitted with a Merritt-Brown gearbox and provision was made during the design stage for replacing the Liberty engine with the Rolls-Royce Meteor V-12 600hp engine when this became available. The pilot model was completed in June 1942 and although it was found to be underpowered some 950 were built. Of these 80 were Close Support models armed with a 95mm howitzer and these equipped the Royal Marines Armoured Support Group during the NORMANDY landings. The remainder were either used in their original form for training, or up-graded to CROMWELL standard by installing the Meteor engine, or converted to special purpose roles. These included two

versions of anti-aircraft tank armed with Oerlikon or Polsten cannon, an Artillery Observation Post tank, an armoured recovery vehicle and a dozer tank, the last two being turretless. The Centaur was originally designated Cromwell II. *Weight* 27.5 tons; *speed* 27mph (43kph); *armour* 76mm; *armament* 1 6-pdr gun; 1 or 2 Besa machine guns (Centaur I); 1 75mm gun; 1 or 2 Besa machine guns (Centaur III); 1 95mm howitzer; 1 or 2 Besa machine guns (Centaur IV); *engine* Nuffield Liberty petrol 395hp; *crew* 5.

Centurion – A41 Cruiser Tank (UK)

By mid-1943 it was apparent that the potential of the existing cruiser tank series had reached its limit and it was decided to design a new heavy cruiser tank with special emphasis on mechanical performance and reliability, ease of maintenance, adequate firepower to defeat the German TIGER and PANTHER, and armour proof against the enemy's formidable 88mm tank and anti-tank guns. Simultaneously it was agreed to incorporate components which had already proved their efficiency, including the 17-pdr gun, the Meteor engine and the Merritt-Brown gearbox. For increased protection the glacis plate was angled back and skirting plates were added to the sides as a defence against shaped charge ammunition. A Horstman bogie suspension system was employed as the configuration of the hull was unsuitable for the traditional Christie system, and an auxiliary generator was installed to charge the vehicle batteries while the main engine was not in use. A mock-up of the vehicle was ready

Centurion Mark I.

by May 1944 and 20 prototypes were ordered. A year later the first six of these were sent to Germany for combat evaluation with the Guards Armoured Division but arrived just too late to see action. It is interesting to note that while the General Staff's appreciation of 1943 stressed the continued need for both cruiser and infantry tanks, the Centurion came close to Field-Marshal MONTGOMERY's concept of a capital or main battle tank and further development of the two families virtually ceased when the war ended. The Centurion proved to be one of the finest tank designs ever conceived and subsequently evolved through 13 Marks, serving with distinction in Korea, the Middle East, India and Vietnam. It remains active in some armies today. *Weight* 42 tons; *speed* 23mph (37kph); *armour* 125mm; *armament* 1 17-pdr gun; 1 20mm Polsten cannon or 1 7.92mm Besa machine gun mounted coaxially; *engine* Rolls-Royce Meteor V-12 600hp petrol; *crew* 4.

Cerberus

Break-out from BREST of the German warships SCHARNHORST, GNEISENAU and PRINZ EUGEN and their subsequent passage up-Channel to home waters, February 1942. Also known as "The Channel Dash".

Ceres Class Cruisers (UK)

Displacement 4190 tons; *dimensions* 451ft 6in×43ft 6in (135.3×13.08m); mean draught 14ft 3in (4.2m); *machinery* 2-shaft geared turbines producing shp 40,000; *speed* 29 knots; *protection* main belt 3in; deck 1in; gun shields 1in; *armament* 5×6in (5×1); 2×3in AA (2×1); 2×2-pdr AA (2×1); 8×21in torpedo tubes (4×2); or 10×4in AA (10×1); 16×2-pdr AA (2×8); or 8×4in AA (4×2); 4×2-pdr AA (1×4); 8×0.5in AA (2×4); *complement* 400; *number in class* 5, launched 1917.

Cessna AT-17 Bobcat (USA)

The Cessna AT-17 was originally a commercial passenger aircraft and was taken into military use as an advanced trainer, becoming known as the Bobcat in US service and the Crane in Canadian use. Large numbers were employed under the Commonwealth Air Training Scheme, and it was also adapted as a light five-seat personnel transport. *Span* 42ft (12.8m); *engines* 2 225hp radial; *speed* 175mph (282kph).

Ceylon, Pacific, 1942   See COLOMBO.

CGS   Chief of the General Staff (US).

Chad, French Equatorial Africa, 1941–43

Colonial province in which the French garrison was sympathetic to DE GAULLE, joining the Long Range Desert Group to attack MURZUQ in January 1941 and ejecting the Italians from KUFRA OASIS in March 1941. In the autumn of 1942 General Philippe LECLERC assembled a force of 555 French and 2713 Colonial and African troops and embarked on a remarkable desert march northwards from Lake Chad to join the British 8th Army, clearing Fezzan of the Italians and reaching TRIPOLI on 26 January 1943. While serving with 8th Army Leclerc's group was known as L Force.

Chaffee – Light Tank M24 (USA)

By 1942 it was apparent that the 37mm gun of the STUART light tank series was no longer adequate and the following year the US Army took the decision to build a new light tank armed with a 75mm gun. The twin Cadillac engines and Hydra-matic transmission which had proved successful in the M5 Stuart were retained but a torsion bar suspension was adopted in place of vertical volute springing. The pilot model of the M24 was delivered in October 1943 and production commenced in March 1944. The tank began reaching American tank battalions later that year, serving in the European theatre of operations. A few were supplied to the British Army which named the tank Chaffee in honour of General Adna Chaffee, who had played so great a part in founding the American Armored Force, and the US Army followed suit. Altogether Cadillac and Massey-Harris built 4731 of these vehicles, including variants, the most notable of which were the HOWITZER MOTOR CARRIAGES M37 and M41 and an anti-aircraft vehicle, the Gun Motor Carriage M19, armed with twin 40mm cannon. The Chaffee remained in service for many years and took part in the

Chaffee light tank M24.

Korean War. *Weight* 18 tons; *speed* 35mph (56kph); *armour* 30mm; *armament* 1 75mm gun; 2 .30-cal Browning machine guns; 1 .50-cal Browning AA machine gun; *engines* Twin Cadillac 44T24 petrol 110hp each; *crew* 5.

Chain Home

Chain Home was the British early warning RADAR system established along the south and east coasts from 1938 onwards. It allowed location of aircraft flying at average altitudes, to a distance of about 60 miles (96km), and was later augmented by CHAIN HOME LOW which identified low-flying raiders.

Chain Home Low

Chain of RADAR stations established on the southern and eastern coasts of the United Kingdom to detect low-flying aircraft, signals being transmitted at 1.5-metre frequency.

Challenger – A30 Cruiser Tank (UK)

An unsuccessful attempt to develop a cruiser tank armed with a 17-pdr gun using an extended CROMWELL-type chassis. The prototype trials revealed that the chassis was overloaded and brought to light a variety of gunnery problems. The design was eventually overtaken by the SHERMAN Firefly, but 200 were built. In the autumn of 1944 a number were issued to Cromwell-equipped armoured reconnaissance regiments in North-West Europe to augment their firepower. *Weight* 31.5 tons; *speed* 32mph (51kph); *armour* 102mm; *armament* 1 17-pdr gun; 1 .30-cal Browning machine gun; *engine* Rolls-Royce Meteor 600hp petrol; *crew* 5.

Chamberlain, Neville (1869–1940)

British statesman and Prime Minister from 1937 to 1940. He became a Conservative Member of Parliament in 1918, was Minister of Health 1924–29 and Chancellor of the Exchequer in 1931. He succeeded Stanley Baldwin as Prime Minister in 1937 and took charge of foreign policy, which led to the resignation of his Foreign Secretary EDEN in 1938. Chamberlain's belief in appeasement led to concessions to HITLER over CZECHO-SLOVAKIA in 1938 (the MUNICH Agreement), but this belief was shaken when the remainder of Czechoslovakia was annexed by Germany in March 1939. Chamberlain was not at ease in directing the war, and after the failure of the Norway campaign he resigned on 10 May 1940 to be succeeded by Winston CHURCHILL. He

Chamberlain (centre) with von Ribbentrop (right) in Munich, September 1938.

Char B – Heavy Tank (Fr)

Developed during the interwar years, the Char B was the principal weapon of the *Divisions Cuirassées* in 1940. Well armed and heavily armoured for the period, it was a formidable opponent but suffered the defect of mounting a one-man turret. Fuel consumption was heavy and the tracks and side radiator louvres were vulnerable to enemy fire. The majority of the 320 available in May 1940 were destroyed in action or abandoned for lack of fuel. Some were taken over by the Germans and used in the Channel Islands. *Weight* 32 tons; *speed* 18mph (29kph); *armour* 60mm; *armament* 1 47mm gun in turret; 1 75mm howitzer in glacis; 2 7.5mm machine guns; *engine* Renault 270/300hp petrol; *crew* 4.

Char 2C – Breakthrough Tank (Fr)

Developed in the years immediately following World War I, the huge Char 2C belonged to the era of trench warfare. One of the four machine guns was housed in a sub-turret at

remained a member of the War Cabinet, but was now a broken and sick man, dying only a few months later.

Champion

Allied plan for offensive in BURMA 1943.

Changi, Malaya, 1942–45

A military cantonment at the eastern end of SINGAPORE Island used by the Japanese as a prison camp for white prisoners of war and a number of civilians.

Channel Islands, 1940–45

The Channel Islands were demilitarized and evacuated by British troops on 28 June 1940. Numbers of the civil population were also evacuated to the British mainland, but a high proportion remained behind. The islands were occupied by German troops on 30 June. The islands were fortified by the Germans, all the civil population being removed from Alderney for this purpose, and numbers of civilians were removed to Germany for labour purposes. Apart from an abortive Commando raid against GUERNSEY on 11 July 1940 the islands were left alone for the remainder of the war, though the constant possibility of attack led the Germans to maintain a substantial garrison. The German forces surrendered on 9 May 1945.

Char B1 heavy tank.

Char B tanks take part in a pre-war parade in Paris.

the rear of the vehicle, and the remainder in the hull sides and bow. Six of these vehicles were available in 1940 but were wrecked by air attack on their railway flats before they could see action. *Weight* 70 tons; *speed* 8mph (13kph); *armour* 45mm; *armament* 1 75mm gun or 1 155mm howitzer; 4 7.5mm machine guns; *engines* 2 Daimler 250hp petrol coupled to electric drive system; *crew* 13.

Char D Series – Medium Tanks (Fr)

The Char D1 was the French Army's first medium tank and entered service in 1931, the intention being that it should replace the ageing RENAULT FT. It was joined by the more heavily armoured D2 the following year. D1 and D2 production figures were respectively 180 and 150.

	D1	D2
Weight	14 tons	20 tons
Speed	12mph (19kph)	14mph (22kph)
Armour	30mm	40mm
Armament	1 37mm gun or 1 47mm gun	1 47mm gun;
	2 7.5mm m.g.	2 7.5mm m.g.
Engine	Renault 100hp petrol	Renault 150hp petrol
Crew	3	3

Chariot

British commando raid on ST NAZAIRE, 28 March 1942.

Chase, Maj Gen William C. (1895–1986)

Chase was commissioned into the US Cavalry in 1916 and served with a machine-gun battalion in the American Expeditionary Force in France in 1918. In 1921 he left the Army and took up teaching, but returned to soldiering in 1925, attending both the Cavalry School and the Infantry School. He was assigned to the Command and General Staff School 1929–31, then went to the PHILIPPINES. He subsequently held various staff posts until in February 1943 he took command of 1 Cavalry Brigade. In 1944 this unit led the assault on the ADMIRALTY ISLANDS, and later took part in the reoccupation of the Philippines. On 3 February 1945 he led the first columns to enter Manila and then commanded 38th Infantry Division against the Japanese holding out in BATAAN and also supervised the airborne assault to retake CORREGIDOR. In July 1945 he assumed command of 1 Cavalry Division and in September took the unit to Japan, where it was the first American

General Chennault inspecting maintenance of his "Flying Tigers".

unit to enter Tokyo. In 1949 he became Chief of Staff 3rd Army, and in 1951 went to Taiwan as Military Adviser to CHIANG KAI-SHEK. He retired in 1955.

Chatellerault Machine Gun

A French light machine gun, the Modèle 24/29, was used as the squad automatic weapon. It was a gas-operated, magazine-fed gun in 7.5mm calibre. The standard 24/29 version used a top-mounted box magazine and was fired from a bipod. A second version, the Modèle 31, used a large side-mounted drum magazine and was intended for use of fortifications of the MAGINOT LINE and also in tanks.

Chedlet

British 500lb (226kg) Smoke Bomb Mark 2, containing 24 segmental smoke generators.

Chelmno, western Poland, 1941–44

A German extermination camp, close to Kolo. Established in December 1941, it was the first of the death camps, initially employing mobile vans which killed the occupants by exhaust gas. In early 1942 escapees from Chelmno provided the first reports that Jews were being systematically exterminated, but the information was thought to be exaggerated and no credence was placed upon it for some time. An estimated 340,000 persons were killed before its closure in 1944.

Chennault, Maj Gen Claire L. (1890–1958)

Chennault was a pilot in the pre-war US Army Air Corps who was retired on medical grounds in 1937. He then took up a post as an adviser and trainer on aviation in China. In November 1940 he returned to the USA and organized a 200-man force of ex-service pilots and engineers to return to China as the "American Volunteer Group", less formally known as "Chennault's Flying Tigers". In 1941 this force operated with considerable success against Japanese aircraft over southern China and Burma, destroying nearly 300 Japanese aircraft in six months' fighting. In 1942 he returned to active duty with the USAAF and was immediately appointed commander of the 14th US (Voluntary) Air Force in China, which was simply a regularized version of the Flying Tigers. He came into conflict with STILWELL, CHIANG KAI-SHEK'S military adviser, over the allocation of supplies and strategy.

Having obtained a large share of the available aviation equipment, in 1943 Chennault mounted a strong offensive against the Japanese. The Japanese countered with a powerful counter-attack, Ichi-Go, which inflicted severe damage on the Chinese and American ground forces. Chennault resigned in a fit of pique in July 1945 when his advice on the reorganization of the Chinese Air Force was ignored.

Cherbourg, France, 1940 and 1944

A major port located at the tip of the COTENTIN PENINSULA used to evacuate British and Allied troops from France in June 1940, and captured by Major-General Erwin ROMMEL's 7th Panzer Division on 19 June. In June 1944 the capture of Cherbourg was an early priority for the Allies as it would enable the American armies to be supplied direct from the United States instead of via the United Kingdom, a task rendered the more urgent since the great gale of 19 June had seriously damaged the American MULBERRY harbour. The assault of Lieutenant-General J. Lawton COLLINS' US VII Corps commenced on 21 June, followed by air attacks which delivered 1100 tons of bombs. Although the defences were penetrated, many Germans continued to hold out in isolated fortifications, the fighting reaching a climax on 25 June when the American attacks were supported by the fire of three battleships, four cruisers and several destroyers. In spite of this battering, the last of the harbour forts did not surrender until 29 June. Some 39,000 Germans were captured but the harbour facilities had been wrecked by demolition and were not restored to working order for several months.

Chernyakhovsky, Gen Ivan (1906–45)

Little is known of Chernyakhovsky's background, but he was one of the few Jews to attain prominence in the Red Army and one of the youngest of its senior commanders. As Commander-in-Chief of 60th Army he took Voronezh in January 1943 and KURSK in the following December. Appointed to the command of the 3rd Belorussian Front, he led the right flank attack against MINSK in July 1944 and drove 3rd Panzer Army out of VITEBSK. He then retook LATVIA and swept on to East Prussia, defeating the considerable German defences outside KÖNIGSBERG. He was killed by artillery fire near Mehlsack in February 1945.

Cherryblossom

American landing on BOUGAINVILLE, SOLOMON ISLANDS, 1 November 1943.

Cherwell, Lord Frederick (1886–1957)

Cherwell, the erstwhile Professor Frederick Lindemann, had been CHURCHILL's scientific adviser during his wilderness years in the 1930s and had sat on the shortlived Committee for the Study of Aerial Defence. After the outbreak of war Churchill rewarded his loyalty with a peerage and, in 1942, a seat in the Cabinet as Paymaster-General. Cherwell was an extremely influential advocate of AREA BOMBING, crucially reinforcing the arguments of BOMBER COMMAND with a paper of February 1942 in which he urged the destruction of the built-up areas of 58 towns in Germany of over 100,000 inhabitants. At first he was sceptical about the practical application of nuclear fission to weapon systems, but later recognized its potential and persuaded Churchill to set up an organization to handle this work in co-operation with American scientists engaged on similar work. This project was given the codename TUBE ALLOYS. Cherwell also advised Churchill on the probable accuracy and effect of the German V-1 rocket.

Cheshire, Gp Capt Leonard (b 1917)

A leading bomber pilot of the RAF, Cheshire had learned to fly as a member of the Oxford University Volunteer Reserve Squadron. Mobilized on the outbreak of war, he soon demonstrated outstanding qualities of leadership, and was eventually appointed to command 617 Squadron which specialized in high precision target marking and set new standards in navigation and accuracy. In June 1944 he was appointed to HQ Eastern Air Command, South-east Asia, and in 1945 to the British Joint Staff Mission in Washington. From here he was appointed as the official British observer for the deployment of the atomic bomb and went to TINIAN with the special bombing force. On 9 August 1945 he was present at NAGASAKI, in the accompanying camera aircraft, watched the dropping of the bomb, and flew over the target area 10 minutes afterwards.

Chiang Kai-Shek, Gen (1897–1975)

Leader of the Kuomintang and head of state of Nationalist CHINA. He became involved in Kuomintang politics in the 1920s and, with the support of the Army, became its leader in 1925 and broke with the Communists in 1927. After Japan's attacks in 1937 he moved his government first to Hankow and then to CHUNGKING. Following the entry of the USA into the war, Chiang was confirmed by Allied leaders as an Allied supreme commander. Two Americans, STILWELL and CHENNAULT, were appointed his deputies, but Chiang tended to bypass them, causing considerable friction, particularly with Stilwell. Under Chennault's guidance Chiang pursued an air offensive against the

Trident conference: Chiang Kai-Shek, Madame Chiang and General Stilwell.

Japanese, but this merely provoked damaging retaliation. His land forces were ineffectual, although they kept over a million Japanese troops tied down in China. In postwar years he was ousted by the Communists and moved to Taiwan on 7 December 1949.

China, 1937–45

Although Japan had been pursuing an aggressive expansionist policy towards China since 1931, full-scale war did not begin until a contrived clash occurred at the Marco Polo Bridge near Lukouchiao on 7 July 1937. A Japanese invasion followed, resulting in the capture of Peking (28 July), Shanghai (8 November) and Nanking (13 December). During 1938 the Japanese extended their conquests and despite reverses at Taierchwang in April and Chengchow in July succeeded in capturing Canton (21 October) and HANKOW (25 October). The Chinese Nationalist leader CHIANG KAI-SHEK, who shared an uneasy alliance with MAO TSE-TUNG's Communists, moved his capital to CHUNGKING in Szechwan province. In 1939 the Japanese, unable to bring the war to a conclusion, embarked on a policy of attrition and captured most of China's remaining seaports. After this, the only supply routes available to the Chinese were a narrow-gauge railway running from KUNMING to Haiphong in French Indo-China and the BURMA ROAD, running from Kunming to Lashio in Burma. Following the fall of France in June 1940 Japanese pressure forced the French to close the rail route; the British closed the Burma Road on 18 July but reopened it on 18 October. In 1940 the Chinese Communists launched their successful "Hundred Regiments Offensive", which attacked Japanese outposts and communications. The Japanese response was to mount a series of punitive raids which continued for the next three years. In January 1941 the fragile truce between Nationalists and Communists was shattered when fighting broke out between the two factions at Anhwei, the effect being seriously to hinder the war effort

against Japan. Later that year, however, the American Volunteer Group, better known as the FLYING TIGERS, began flying with the Chinese Air Force. In December the Japanese captured the British colony of HONG KONG and, following their invasion of Burma in January 1942, cut the Burma Road in April despite the despatch of Chinese troops under STILWELL. This reduced the amount of aid reaching China to whatever could be flown over "THE HUMP", and for the rest of the year there was only limited military activity in China itself. The situation in 1943 was similar, although the Japanese mounted a series of local offensives to seize the rice crop, one of which was defeated by the Chinese at Changteh in

December. In May 1944 the Japanese, having established a tacit truce with the Communists, mounted a major offensive in East China, codenamed Ichi-Go, which succeeded in capturing seven of the US 14th Air Force's 12 airfields. The offensive was only halted in December by the arrival of two experienced Chinese divisions which had been fighting to reopen the Burma Road. The Japanese renewed their offensive in January 1945, capturing three more airfields, although the Burma Road was finally opened to traffic. Another airfield was lost in April but later that month Chinese counter-attacks finally stabilized the front. General Yasuji Okamura, commanding the China Expeditionary Army,

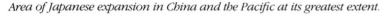

Area of Japanese expansion in China and the Pacific at its greatest extent.

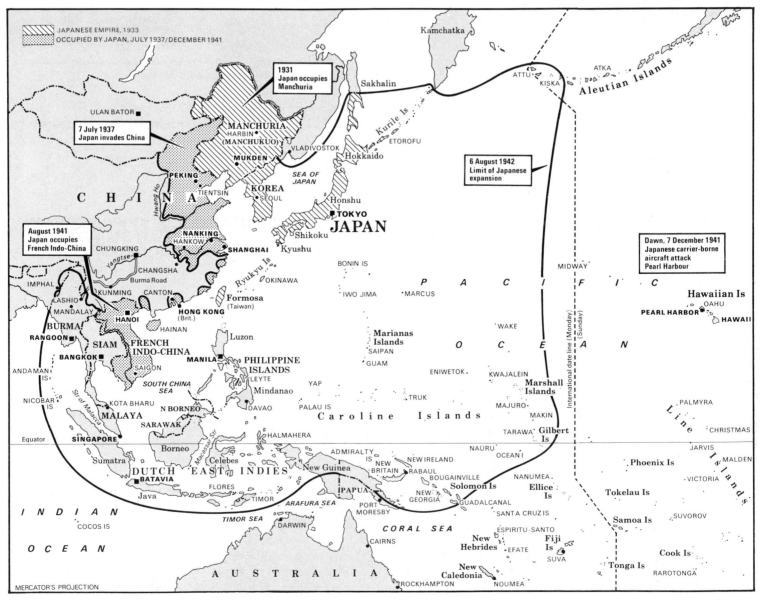

Chinese officer cadets carry out a sandtable exercise.

recognized that his troops were over-extended and commenced a general withdrawal the following month. On 15 August hostilities ceased. China is estimated to have mobilized up to 10 million men of whom 500,000 were killed and 1,700,000 wounded; civilian dead numbered approximately one million. See also MANCHURIA.

China–Burma–India Theater (CBI), 1942–44

Created in July 1942 for administrative reasons under the command of Lieutenant-General Joseph W. STILWELL, CBI was responsible for the American military support of CHINA and for the control, subject to British approval, of Chinese and American troops in BURMA and India. The organization was dissolved in October 1944 when Major-General Albert C. WEDEMEYER replaced Stilwell as Chief of Staff to CHIANG KAI-SHEK.

Chindits, 1943–45

Long-range penetration group formed by the then Brigadier Orde WINGATE in 1943 for air-supplied operations behind the Japanese lines in BURMA, the name being taken from their distinctive arm badge of a *chinthe* or stone lion which guarded the entrance to Burmese temples. The success of the small Chindit operation of 1943, conducted by troops of 77th Brigade, led to the group being expanded to six infantry brigades. In the field

the Chindits were divided into 300-strong "columns", each of which was a self-contained force with its own mule train, heavy weapons and a signals detachment drawn from the RAF. In 1944 the Chindits operated against the Japanese rear while the latter were conducting their U-GO offensive against IMPHAL and

KOHIMA, tying down the equivalent of two-and-a-half divisions, and were then directed north to assist Lieutenant-General Joseph STILWELL's Chinese-American army, the advance of which had been stalled by the stubborn Japanese defence of MYITKYINA. Following the death of Major-General Wingate on 24 March 1944, command of the Chindits passed to Major-General Walter LENTAIGNE. More was probably asked of the Chindits than of any other troops who fought in World War II, the health of many survivors being permanently broken by exhaustion and disease. When the Special Air Service Regiment was reformed during the postwar Malayan Emergency it used Chindit methods as its model. See *Chindits – Long Range Penetration* by Michael Calvert (Pan/Ballantine).

Chindwin River, Burma, 1942–44

The approximate front line of the Central Burma Front from mid-1942 until the Japanese U-GO offensive of 1944, aimed at IMPHAL and KOHIMA.

Chin Hills, Burma, 1944

Range of steep, jungle-clad hills approximately 100 miles (160km) across, located south of IMPHAL and protecting India against invasion from the east.

Chindits in enemy-occupied Burma.

Chittagong, India, 1942–45

Port, railhead and airbase on the north-eastern coast of the Bay of Bengal providing a base for operations in the ARAKAN.

Chiyoda Class Aircraft Carriers (Jap)

Both vessels of this class, *Chiyoda* and *Chitose*, were originally completed as seaplane tenders and in 1943 they were converted to light aircraft carriers. As the 3rd Carrier Division they fought at the Battle of the PHILIPPINE SEA. During the Battle of LEYTE GULF they formed part of Admiral OZAWA's Decoy Force and on 25 October 1944 both were sunk by air attack. *Displacement* 11,190 tons; *dimensions* 621ft 6in×68ft 3in (189.3×20.8m); mean draught 24ft 6in (7.5m); *machinery* 4-shaft geared turbines and diesels producing hp 56,800; *speed* 29 knots; *armament* 8×5in AA; 30×25mm AA (10×3); *aircraft* 30; *complement* 800 est; *number in class* 2.

Chowringhee, Burma, 1944

CHINDIT base located south of the confluence of the Shweli and IRRAWADDY Rivers.

Christie M1931 Suspension

The most significant of the inventions of the American engineer J. Walter Christie, who was fascinated by the concept of providing fighting vehicles with the ability to travel at speed across country. In essence the M1931 suspension consisted of large solid-rubber tyred roadwheels independently attached to pivoting lever arms in the hull side, cushioned by heavy coil springs, the latter being housed between the inner and outer walls of the vehicle hull. An objection to this arrangement is that it consumes vital space that could otherwise be put to good use within the vehicle, but as regards smooth cross-country performance and speed the M1931 did all that was asked of it. The US Army purchased three examples of the suspension and the Soviet Army two, the latter employing it as the basis for its BT SERIES and subsequent evolutionary developments which led to the renowned T-34 medium tank. The British Army also employed the suspension on the majority of its Cruiser tanks, commencing with the A13.

Chuikov, Gen Vasili (1900–1982)

Chuikov volunteered for the Red Army in 1918 and in 1920 fought against the White Russians and the Poles. He later attended the Frunze Military Academy and was then sent as adviser to CHIANG KAI-SHEK in 1926, remaining with the Chinese Nationalists until 1937. Returning to the Soviet Union, he was appointed to the Ministry of War in 1941–42. In the winter of 1942 he was given command of the 62nd Army at STALINGRAD, holding the right bank of the Volga throughout the siege. Redesignated the 8th Guards Army, the formation remained under his command for the remainder of the war and fought all the way to BERLIN. His account of the Stalingrad battle, *The Beginning of the Road*, is considered to be one of the most readable military memoirs. Chuikov held a number of higher command posts in the postwar period, culminating in Commander-in-Chief Soviet Land Forces in 1960.

Chungking, China, 1938–45

A city on the upper Yangtze Kiang to which CHIANG KAI-SHEK moved his wartime capital following the Japanese advances of 1938.

Churchill, Winston Leonard Spencer (1874–1965)

The elder son of Lord Randolph Churchill, in 1895 Churchill entered the 4th Hussars via Sandhurst and immediately obtained leave to go to Cuba, where he began his career as a war correspondent, which was to take him to India in 1897, Sudan in 1898, and South Africa in 1899, where he was captured by the Boers.

Churchill inspecting a Thompson sub machinegun.

After escaping, he fought at Spion Kop and Pretoria. Returning to England as a hero, in 1900 he became Conservative MP for Oldham, though in 1904 he changed to the Liberal party. Shortly afterwards the Liberals took office, and Churchill became Under-Secretary of State for the Colonies. Other posts followed; in 1908 he became President of the Board of Trade, in 1910 Home Secretary, and in 1911 First Lord of the Admiralty. His espousal of the disastrous Gallipoli campaign in 1915 led to his temporary political eclipse, and he re-entered the army. Later in the year Churchill returned to politics, and with the publication of the report of the Dardanelles Commission, which vindicated Churchill, he was made Minister of Munitions in July 1917 and in 1919 became Secretary for War. During the 1920s he held various posts, including Chancellor of the Exchequer from 1924 to 1929, but then remained out of office until 1939. In 1930 his opposition to the Labour government's Indian policy led to his resignation from the Conservative shadow cabinet, and he was once more relegated to the political sidelines. In 1932 he began pressing for preparation against the German threat.

On 3 September 1939 Churchill returned to office as First Lord of the Admiralty. After the failure of the Norwegian campaign he succeeded CHAMBERLAIN as Prime Minister on 10 May 1940, the day of the German invasion of the Low Countries, and formed a National Government, assuming the additional responsibility of Minister of Defence. After the fall of France his stubborn spirit and remarkable gift of oratory were vital in sustaining British morale. His friendship with ROOSEVELT was crucial to Britain's survival and was instrumental in producing the concept of Lend-Lease of war material at a critical time.

Churchill's strongly-held anti-Communist beliefs were sorely tried in 1941 when it became necessary to ally Britain with Russia against Germany, but he offered every possible aid to STALIN. However this stopped short of committing unprepared troops to a "Second Front" in north-west Europe simply to ease the pressure on the Eastern Front. His frequent meetings with Roosevelt were of value in agreeing overall strategy, and the major conferences at CASABLANCA, CAIRO, Teheran and YALTA, attended variously by Roosevelt, Stalin and Chiang Kai-Shek, held the Grand Alliance together and laid down the basic principles upon which the war was waged. As a war leader he was prone to wildcat schemes but was well served by Alanbrooke, his Chief of Staff, who was capable of deflecting him from less wise objectives.

After the German surrender the Coalition broke up, and Churchill formed a "caretaker" government. In June he went to his final wartime conference at POTSDAM, to settle various questions with Stalin and to join with President TRUMAN in a final warning to Japan. His attempts to obtain postwar freedom for Poland and Czechoslovakia were brushed aside, and before he could return to the subject a general election in Britain voted his government out of office.

Churchill – A22 Infantry Tank Mark IV (UK)

When war broke out in September 1939 many British senior officers felt that the fighting on the Western Front would take the form of the later battles of 1918 and the Superintendent of Tank Design was requested to produce pilot models of a Heavy Infantry Tank with a wide trench-crossing capacity and the ability to negotiate the worst shell-torn ground. The design was designated A20 and the first prototypes were evaluated in June 1940, in the immediate aftermath of the DUNKIRK evacuation. The Army was then desperately short of tanks and to accelerate production it was decided to build a scaled down version using the same Bedford Twin-Six 350hp engine employed in the A20. This project was officially known as the A22 but was called Churchill in the interests of national morale. Vauxhall Motors Ltd were instructed to have the vehicle in production within one year and actually achieved this. The first Churchills to enter service suffered from a series of teething troubles but constant modification and improvement succeeded in producing a vehicle which was mechanically reliable by the time it was committed to action in 1942.

The Churchill carried a wider variety of armament than any other British tank design. Marks I and II were armed with a 2-pdr gun and a 3-inch howitzer to give a balanced armour-piercing/high explosive capability, as the 2-pdr did not then fire an HE round. Subsequent development involved up-gunning to 6-pdr and then 75mm standard, Marks V and VIII being armed with a 95mm howitzer for close support. The lack of a high explosive round for the 6-pdr in North Africa led to the ingenious conversion known as the NA75

Churchill Mark III.

(North Africa 75mm), conceived by Major Percy Morrell, REME, and resulted in 200 Mark IVs being fitted with the SHERMAN's 75mm gun, which had a dual AP/HE capability. The 75mm gun, however, represented the limit of the design's potential, although the 17-pdr armed BLACK PRINCE is sometimes referred to as a Super-Churchill. A variety of turrets were employed, all of them cast with the exception of that of the Mark III, which was of welded construction. The hull was unusual for a British vehicle in that sponson escape hatches were provided for the crew, these being a legacy of the A20, one version of which was to have been armed with two 2-pdrs mounted in sponsons in the manner of World War I tanks. The Churchill was also unusual in that it was steered by a tiller-bar, while the four-speed Merritt-Brown gearbox provided controlled differential steering, thus permitting the

Churchill IV infantry tank.

vehicle to neutral-turn about its own axis.

As well as being heavily armoured, the Churchill possessed two further qualities which made it remarkable. First, it was capable of crossing the heaviest going and climbing hills so steep that the enemy considered them tank-proof. Secondly, its roomy hull permitted conversion to many other roles, including the ARK and the AVRE, the need for which had been established during the DIEPPE raid. There was also a turretless bridgelayer which launched a 30-foot (9.15m) 60-ton capacity bridge over the front of the vehicle by means of hydraulic arms; these vehicles were first issued at brigade level but most Churchill regiments had several on strength by the end of the war. Other developments included a gun carrier, of which 24 were built for Home Defence in 1941. This consisted of a fixed armoured superstructure mounted well

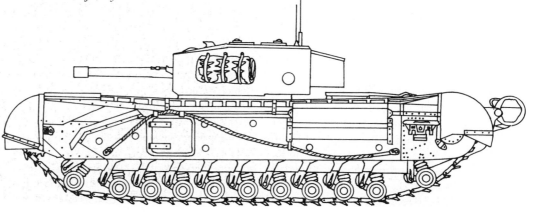

forward on the hull, housing a 3-inch gun in the front plate. The majority of these were converted to SNAKE carriers. The Churchill's most dramatic and feared conversion was, however, the CROCODILE flame-throwing tank. Churchills first went into action with the Canadian Calgary Regiment at Dieppe on 19 August 1942. Six took part in the Second Battle of ALAMEIN with a combat evaluation unit named "Kingforce". Two Churchill-equipped Tank Brigades served in Tunisia and, later, in Italy. Three such Tank Brigades saw action in NORMANDY and North-West Europe, one of which was converted to the Crocodile role. Churchills were also supplied to the Soviet Army in sufficient numbers to equip at least one heavy tank regiment. Total Churchill production was 5640 vehicles.

Weight	Marks I and II	38.5 tons
	Marks III to VI	39 tons
	Marks VII and VIII	40 tons
Speed	15.5mph (25kph) (Marks VII and VIII 12.5mph (20kph))	
Armour	Marks I to VI	102mm
	Marks VII and VIII	152mm
Armament	Mark I	1 2-pdr in turret; 1 3-inch howitzer in front plate; 1 Besa m.g.
	Mark II	1 3-inch howitzer in turret; 1 2-pdr in front plate; 1 Besa m.g.
	Marks III and IV	1 6-pdr gun; 2 Besa m.g.
	Mark IV (NA75)	1 75mm gun ex-Sherman; 1 .30-cal Browning m.g. in coaxial mounting; 1 Besa m.g. in hull
	Mark V	1 95mm howitzer; 2 Besa m.g.
	Mark VI	1 75mm gun; 2 Besa m.g.
	Mark VII	1 75mm gun; 2 Besa m.g.
	Mark VIII	1 95mm howitzer; 2 Besa m.g.
Engine	Bedford 350hp petrol	
Crew	5.	

Chu Teh, Gen (1886–1976)

Of peasant stock, Chu Teh attended the Yunnan Military Academy, graduating in 1911. He participated in the overthrow of the Manchus and later in the revolt against Yuan Shih-Kai. In 1922 he visited Europe where he joined the Communist Party. He was expelled from Germany in 1926 and returned to China, where he

General Chu Teh addressing his men.

took a significant part in the Army mutiny at Nanchang. This failed, and he fled into the mountains in 1927, where he assisted MAO TSE-TUNG to form the Kiangsi Soviet. Chu Teh led the "Long March" in 1934, and in 1937 reluctantly allied his forces with CHIANG KAI-SHEK against the Japanese, inflicting a severe defeat on the Japanese 5th Division at Pingsinkuan on 25 September 1937. After this he concentrated on political activity, but in 1945 resumed military command to fight the Nationalists, thereafter retaining command of the Chinese People's Liberation Army until 1954.

Ciano, Count Galeazzo (1903–44)

Ciano was the son-in-law of Benito MUSSOLINI, which assured him rapid advancement in the Italian diplomatic service in spite of his lack of experience. He became Foreign Minister in 1936 and, with some misgivings, signed the "Pact of Steel" with HITLER in May 1939. He resigned in February 1943 but remained a member of the Fascist Grand Council and voted for Mussolini's removal in July. Tricked

by the Germans into fleeing to the north of Italy, he was captured, imprisoned and shot on 11 January 1944. His *Diaries* are full of sharp observations on the upper levels of the Nazi hierarchy.

Cibik Ridge, Bougainville, 1943

A vital hill near the EMPRESS AUGUSTA BAY beach-head captured by a US Marine Corps patrol commanded by Lieutenant Steven J. Cibik on 18 November. A fierce nine-day struggle ensued as the Americans reinforced the position and the Japanese attempted to recapture it. The Japanese sustained 1200 killed and were driven off. The action is also referred to in operational histories as the Battle of Piva Forks, after the nearby Piva river.

CIC Counter-Intelligence Corps (US).

Cicero

See BAZNA.

CIGS Chief of the Imperial General Staff (UK).

C-in-C Commander-in-Chief.

CIOS Combined Intelligence Objectives Sub-Committee. Combined British-USA organization set up to uncover all possible information about German and Japanese technical and economic developments in the wake of the advancing armies.

Cisterna, Italy, 1944

A town on Route 7 (The Appian Way) lying 16 miles (26km) inland from ANZIO. On 30 January the US 3rd Division, spearheaded by the 1st, 3rd and 4th Ranger Battalions, attacked Cisterna, which was held by the Hermann Göring Division. The 1st and 3rd Ranger Battalions were counter-attacked, cut off and forced to surrender after an heroic fight against odds. On 29 February the Germans mounted a major counter-attack into the beach-head from Cisterna, which was contained after several days' heavy fighting. When the US VI Corps began its break-out from the beach-head on 23 May, Cisterna was defended by the German 362nd Division, which had all but ceased to exist when the town fell two days later, although it inflicted 950 casualties on the US 3rd Division and seriously reduced the tank strength of the US 1st Armored Division.

General Mark Clark, January 1944.

Clarion

Allied air offensive against German communications, February 1945.

Clark, Gen Mark (1896–1983)

Mark Clark graduated from West Point in 1917 and served in France in 1918, being seriously wounded while serving as an infantry battalion commander. In the interwar years he became a staff officer and came to prominence as assistant to General MacNair in expanding and training the US Army in 1941–42. As EISENHOWER's Chief of Staff for Ground Forces in July 1942, he assisted with the planning of the TORCH landings in North Africa, and in October 1942 carried out secret negotiations with French commanders in a fruitless attempt to persuade them not to oppose the

Allied landings. In 1943 he was appointed to the command of the US 5th Army in Italy and continued in this post for the remainder of the war, becoming Commander 15th Army Group and, after 1945, commander of the US Army Occupation Force in Austria. Clark was a brilliant staff officer, a brave soldier, and a highly ambitious man. However, in the field he displayed a poor tactical grasp, and his planning of operations was stereotyped. He was often jealous of rival generals and avid for publicity, which coloured his attitude to his Allies and distorted his operational planning.

Clark Field, Luzon, Philippines, 1941 and 1945

The centre of the American complex of air bases some 80 miles (128km) north of MANILA and the only airfield suitable for heavy bombers. The Japanese attacked Clark Field with 108 bombers and 84 fighters at 1215 on 8 December 1941, just as the American B-17s were lined up for take-off. This raid eliminated the American air threat to the Japanese invasion fleet which was already approaching the Philippines. In 1945 the Clark Field complex and the nearby hills were defended at YAMASHITA's specific order by the 30,000-strong Kembu Group, but this was overwhelmed by the US XIV Corps in a battle lasting from 23 to 31 January.

Clay, Gen Lucius (1897–1977)

A military engineer and logistics expert, Clay managed the US Army's procurement until sent to France as a Base Commander in 1944 shortly after the NORMANDY landings. He then became Deputy Director of the Office of War Mobilization until April 1945, when, under EISENHOWER, he became Deputy Military Governor of the US Zone of Occupation in Germany. He was an important voice in the setting up of the postwar Federal German Government.

Claymore

British commando raid on the LOFOTEN ISLANDS, March 1941.

Cleanslate

American landing on Russell Island, SOLOMON ISLANDS, 21 February 1943.

Cleve, Germany, 1945

A town captured by 15th (Scottish) Division and 6th (Guards) Tank Brigade on 11 February. See REICHSWALD, BATTLE OF THE.

Cleveland-Fargo Class Light Cruisers (USA)

Displacement 10,000 tons; *dimensions* 610ft 3in×66ft 6in (186×20m); mean draught 20ft (6m); *machinery* 4-shaft geared turbines producing shp 100,000; *speed* 33 knots; *armament* 12×6in (4×3); 12×5in (6×2); 28×40mm AA; *aircraft* 4; *complement* 1200; *number in class* 29, launched 1941–45.

"Club Route", Europe, 1944–45

The name given to the British XII Corps' route and line of communications during the campaign in North-West Europe, it was also adopted as the title of the Corps' history.

Coast Artillery

Artillery for the defence of harbours and naval bases from attack by warships was positioned in important strategic places on the coast and provided with the requisite means of fire control. The many gun batteries mounted on the coasts of Europe for anti-invasion defence did not qualify as coast artillery since they did not have the necessary fire control to engage moving warships.

Coast defence artillery fell into three classes: first, there was the light, quick-firing, artillery used to defend against raids by fast motorboats; second, medium guns for the immediate protection of ports; and third,

Cleveland-Fargo class cruiser.

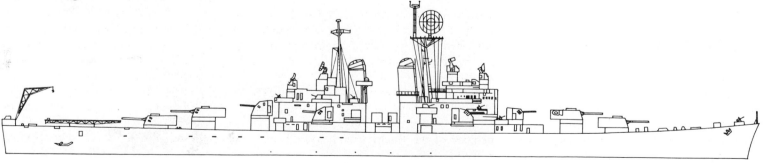

A Japanese 203mm coastal defence gun on Betio Island, Tarawa.

long-range heavy guns which could attack armoured capital ships at ranges beyond those at which the ship could open an effective fire against the shore. High-angle MORTARS were used by some countries, heavy guns which fired armour-piercing shells at a steep trajectory so as to drop on the lightly-armoured decks of warships. The fire control systems required for coast artillery of all types depended upon accurate range-finding allied with a prediction device which would determine the course and speed of the ship and predict its position at the time the shell arrived at that range. Light guns used sights incorporating range-finding and fired by eye; medium and heavy guns relied upon an external fire control system and usually fired on data supplied to them, without necessarily seeing the target.

Coast defence artillery was rarely engaged during the war but when it was, it was invariably successful. Notable engagements include the Norwegian defence of Oslo by the OSKARSBORG fortress, the defence of MALTA against Italian "human torpedo" raids and the defence of the LENINGRAD approaches in the Baltic by the Fortress of Kronstadt. The major fortresses of SINGAPORE, HONG KONG and COR-REGIDOR, whilst successful as sea defences, were overcome from the land side due to the failure of conventional land defence. In each of these defeats the coast artillery guns were used to fire landwards where their geographic location permitted, but this was of little avail without other forms of support.

Coastal Command

This command was formed by the RAF to undertake all over-sea air operations around the United Kingdom. At the outbreak of war it had 19 squadrons formed into one training and three operational groups. Their equipment was a variety of flying boats, some HUDSON and AVRO ANSON patrol-bombers, and some VICKERS VILDEBEESTE torpedo-bombers.

From the start of the war the Command was active against U-boats attacking supply ships and convoys in the Western Approaches and elsewhere, and played an important part in the campaign in NORWAY. Eventually, long range coastal fighter units, first with BRISTOL BLENHEIMS and later with BEAUFIGHTERS, were added to the Command's strength, together with light bombers and more modern BEAUFORT torpedo-bombers for anti-shipping work. By June 1941 the strength had increased to 33 squadrons and a Photographic Reconnaissance Unit.

From 1941 to 1944 the Command played a major role in the Battle of the ATLANTIC, establishing bases at Gibraltar, the Azores and Iceland. Strength had increased to 49 squadrons by early 1943, to which were added Fleet Air Arm, BOMBER COMMAND, USAAF and US Navy squadrons on attachment. By the end of the war the Command had claimed the destruction of 169 U-boats and four Italian submarines, and shared 22 more with naval forces, figures which subsequently proved to be optimistically high but which still indicate the vast amount of patrol work performed, in which aircraft were aided by ASV RADAR and the LEIGH LIGHT. The anti-shipping role had been steadily taken over by higher performance aircraft, including torpedo-carrying BEAUFIGHTERS and DE HAVILLAND MOSQUITOS with rocket weapons. In 39,305 sorties, 150 warships totalling 86,303 tons and 193 cargo and other ships totalling 427,501 tons were claimed sunk for the loss of 797 aircraft.

Before her last sortie, KMS Bismarck *was discovered in Dobric Fjord by this photograph taken by an aircraft of Coastal Command.*

Coastwatchers

A volunteer group of planters, traders, colonial officials and officers organized by Commander Eric Feldt, RAN, who chose to remain in or to return to the SOLOMON ISLANDS after they had been occupied by the Japanese. Assisted by loyal natives, the Coastwatchers remained in hiding in the jungle and reported Japanese naval and air movements by radio, the information thus provided being of inestimable value during the protracted fighting for possession of GUADALCANAL. Many of these courageous men, the majority of whom were Australians, were caught by the Japanese or succumbed to tropical diseases.

Cobra

American break-out from the NORMANDY beach-head, 1944.

Cockade

Element of Allied deception plan prior to OVERLORD.

Cockatrice

British flamethrower mounted on an armoured Bedford truck for home defence.

Colditz

A small town south-west of Leipzig, Colditz contains a castle fortress which was used during World War II as a prisoner-of-war camp for special categories of prisoner. Its fortified construction made it secure and nominally escape-proof, and it was used to house prisoners with important political connections and also prisoners of ordinary military categories who had a record of escapes from other prison camps. These men regarded Colditz as a challenge, and many ingenious escape attempts were made, 130 of which were sufficiently successful to get the escapees outside the castle. Most, however, were recaptured, and only 32 prisoners made successful escapes. The castle was finally liberated by Allied troops on 16 April 1945.

Collins, Gen J. Lawton (1886–1963)

Collins came to prominence leading the US 25th Infantry Division on GUADALCANAL in 1942, where he relieved the 1st Marine Division and completed the capture of the island. He later commanded part of XIV Corps in NEW GUINEA. In December 1943 he was sent to England to assume command of VII Corps which landed on UTAH beach on 6 June 1944. His forces

captured Cherbourg on 24 June, closed the FALAISE GAP, and crossed the Seine to move into Belgium and take Mons, Namur and Liège. Collins commanded counter-attack forces in the Battle of the BULGE and captured Houffalize. After crossing the Rhine at REMAGEN and (with the help of US 1st and 9th Armies) enveloping the Ruhr, his troops pushed on to meet the Soviet XXXVI Corps on the River Elbe at Torgau on 25 April 1945. Popular with his troops and a sound tactician, Collins' quickness of manoeuvre earned him the nickname "Lightning Joe".

Colmar Pocket, France, 1944–45

Formed by the advance of the French 1st Army to Mulhouse and the Upper Rhine (18 November) and the liberation of Strasbourg by the US 7th Army, the effect being to trap the remnants of the German 17th Army in the Vosges Mountains. The reduction of the pocket began in January 1945 and was completed by 9 February after HITLER had reluctantly given permission for the survivors to withdraw across the Rhine. The Allies sustained 18,000 casualties, the Germans approximately 36,000.

Cologne, Germany, 1945

Captured by Lieutenant-General J. Lawton COLLINS' US VII Corps on 5 March, the city had already been reduced to rubble by Allied air attacks and the Rhine bridges had been blown. See THOUSAND-BOMBER RAID.

Colombo, Ceylon, 1942

A British naval base attacked by aircraft from Vice-Admiral NAGUMO's 1st Air Fleet on 5 April, the old destroyer *Tenedos* and the armed merchant cruiser *Hector* being sunk and the submarine depot ship *Lucia* damaged. Later that day Japanese aircraft also sank the cruisers *Dorsetshire* and *Cornwall* south of Ceylon. On 9 April Nagumo mounted an air attack on the second British naval base in Ceylon, Trincomalee, but this was found to be empty. However, the elderly carrier *Hermes* was discovered at sea 65 miles to the south. She was promptly attacked and sunk, as were the destroyer *Vampire*, the corvette *Hollyhock*, the fleet auxiliary *Athelstane* and the tanker *British Sergeant*. Simultaneously, a squadron of RAF Blenheims delivered the first air attack experienced by Nagumo's carrier task force, narrowly missing the carrier *Akagi*. Elsewhere, a detached Japanese squadron in

the Bay of Bengal sank 18 unescorted merchant vessels (a total of 93,000 tons). Having sustained the loss of only 19 aircraft. Nagumo then withdrew from the area. His incursion had revealed the vulnerability of Admiral Sir James SOMERVILLE's largely obsolete Eastern Fleet, the older battleships of which were detached to Kilindini on the coast of Kenya while the remainder of the fleet retired to Bombay. The Japanese threat was not renewed and the Eastern Fleet returned to Ceylon in the middle of 1943.

Colony Class Frigates (UK)

Formerly American vessels; returned to the US Navy 1946. *Displacement* 1318 tons; *dimensions* 304ft×37ft 6in (92.6×11.3m); mean draught 12ft (3.6m); *machinery* 2-shaft reciprocating engines with ihp 5500; *speed* 18 knots; *armament* 3×3in AA (3×1); 4×40mm AA (2×2); 4×20mm AA (4×1); *complement* 120; *number in class* 21, launched 1943.

Colorado Class Battleships (USA)

The three members of this class (*Colorado*, *Maryland* and WEST VIRGINIA) provided fire support for numerous amphibious operations during the war in the Pacific. *Displacement* 32,500 tons; *dimensions* 624×97ft (190.3×29.6m); mean draught 30ft (9m); *machinery* 4-shaft turbo-electric drive producing shp 31,000; *speed* 21 knots; *protection* main belt 16in; turrets 18in; *armament* 8×16in (4×2); 10×5in (10×1); 8×5in AA (8×1); *aircraft* 3; *complement* 2375; *number in class* 3, launched 1920–21.

Colossus Class Aircraft Carriers (UK)

Only *Colossus*, *Glory*, *Venerable* and *Vengeance* became operational before the end of the war. They served with the Pacific Fleet, as did *Perseus* and *Pioneer*, which were completed as aircraft maintenance carriers. *Venerable* later served with the Royal Netherlands Navy as *Karel Doorman* and then with the Argentine Navy as *Veinticinco de Mayo*, playing a brief part in the Falklands War of 1982. *Displacement* 13,190 tons; *dimensions* 695ft×80ft 3in (211×24.5m); mean draught 18ft 3in (5.48m); *machinery* 2-shaft geared turbines producing shp 42,000; *speed* 23.5 knots; *armament* 12×2-pdr AA (6×4); 19×40mm AA (19×1), 6×4 2-pdr; *or* 12×2-pdr AA (3×4); 10×20mm AA (10×1), 6×4 2-pdr; *aircraft* 48; *complement* 1076; *number in class* 10, launched 1943–44.

Comacchio, Lake, Italy, 1945

See ARGENTA GAP.

Combat Command

The American equivalent of a British brigade headquarters. In 1942 each American armoured division contained two combat commands, increased to three the following year; these were designated CCA, CCB and CCR. Divisional commanders could allocate resources to a combat command for particular operations.

Combined Operations

A British term used to denote operations involving elements from all three services, particularly amphibious landings and assaults. The first Chief of Combined Operations, Admiral of the Fleet Sir Roger Keyes, was appointed in July 1940 and was succeeded by Vice-Admiral Lord Louis MOUNTBATTEN in October 1941. The Chief of Combined Operations had the equivalent status of a Chief of Staff and he and his headquarters were responsible for all aspects of training and inter-service co-ordination, the production of assault shipping and landing craft, and for the organization, training and employment of the COMMANDOS. From such small beginnings as the control of isolated raids on the enemy coast, Combined Operations Headquarters was eventually responsible for the Allied landings in NORMANDY on 6 June 1944, the largest amphibious assault in history.

Comet – A34 Cruiser Tank (UK)

A second and successful attempt to design a cruiser tank armed with a 17-pdr gun, using the basic CROMWELL hull, taking advantage of the lessons learned during the development of the CHALLENGER. The Comet was armed with a shorter version of the 76.2mm 17-pdr, officially classified QF 77mm. It was the last in the long series of British cruiser tanks to employ the CHRISTIE SUSPENSION and was capable of meeting the German PANTHER on more or less equal terms. The Comet saw active service with 11th Armoured Division after the crossing of the RHINE in March 1945. The vehicle remained in service for many years after the war. *Weight* 32.5 tons; *speed* 29mph (47kph); *armour* 101mm; *armament* 1 17-pdr gun; 2 Besa machine guns; *engine* Rolls-Royce Meteor 600hp petrol; *crew* 5.

Commandos

Conceived by Lieutenant-Colonel Dudley Clarke, Military Assistant to the Chief of Imperial General Staff, General Sir John DILL, in the immediate aftermath of DUNKIRK as a means of carrying the war to the enemy with a series of amphibious raids. On 5 June 1940 Clarke informed Dill of his idea, which was submitted to CHURCHILL the following day. On 8 June Clarke was told that the scheme had been approved and was ordered to mount a cross-Channel raid at the earliest possible moment; simultaneously, the appropriate administrative section was established at the War Office. Suitable volunteers were recruited from every branch of the Army, the units thus formed being named Commandos after the mobile, hard-hitting Boer groups which had tied down so many British troops during the South African War 1899–1902. Initially, ten Independent Companies were raised, each consisting of 20 officers and 270 men, but the basic unit soon became the full Commando, each of which contained a headquarters troop, five rifle troops and a heavy weapons troop equipped with medium machine guns and mortars. In 1942 the Royal Marines also began forming Commandos and an Inter-Allied Commando was formed from Polish, Belgian and French volunteers. The Commandos were trained to a far higher standard than the average infantryman. In addition to the normal military skills, they were instructed in rock climbing, boat craft, knife-fighting, unarmed combat and survival techniques. The training itself made heavy demands on the recruit's physical abilities, stamina and determination, but ensured that the hallmark of Commando operations became speed, aggression and ruthless execution of the mission demanded. When the United States Army began forming similar RANGER Battalions the initial training was carried out at the Commando Training Centre at Achnacarry in Scotland.

The first Commando raids, carried out in June and July 1940, were small, amateurish affairs, but these led to larger, more productive raids on the LOFOTEN ISLANDS, SPITZBERGEN, VAAGSO and ST NAZAIRE, and to participation in major amphibious operations such as DIEPPE, all of which confirmed their status as an élite. Commandos fought in every major theatre of war in which British troops were employed, including the Middle East, North Africa, SICILY, Italy, NORMANDY, North-West Europe, MADAGASCAR, and BURMA. No fewer than eight Victoria Crosses were awarded to Commando soldiers. See *The Commandos 1940–1946* by Charles Messenger.

Commencement Bay Class Escort Carriers (USA)

Improved SANGAMON CLASS. Of the 19 vessels launched, two were never commissioned and only three took part in the final stages of the war against Japan. *Displacement* 10,900 tons; *dimensions* 557×75ft (167×22.5m); mean draught 30ft 6in (9m); *machinery* 2-shaft geared turbines producing shp 16,000; *speed* 19 knots; *armament* 2×5in (2×1); 36×40mm AA; *aircraft* 34; *complement* 1066; *number in class* 19, launched 1944–45.

Commonwealth Aircraft (Australia)

Commonwealth CA6 Wackett Named after its designer, a Wing-Commander in the RAAF, this aircraft first flew in October 1939 and was

Comet cruiser tank at Schwarzenbeck, east of Hamburg, May 1945.

The Wirraway, the Australian-built version of the North American AT-6 Texan, known by the RAF as the "Harvard".

adopted as an intermediate training machine. *Span* 37ft (11.3m); *engine* 1 175hp radial; *speed* 110mph (177kph).

Commonwealth CA12 Boomerang The Boomerang was a single-seat fighter-bomber developed from the WIRRAWAY for emergency use in Australian service. 250 were built and they were all employed in the south-west Pacific theatre for bombing, ground-attack, reconnaissance and army co-operation tasks. *Span* 36.25ft (11m); *engine* 1 1200hp radial; *armament* 2 20mm cannon, 4 machine guns and 1 500lb (227kg) bomb; *speed* 300mph (483kph).

Commonwealth Wirraway This was an Australian-built version of the North American NA33 manufactured under licence. It first flew early in 1937 and went into service shortly before the outbreak of war, as a trainer and light reconnaissance bomber. *Span* 43ft (13m); *engine* 1 600hp radial; *armament* 2 fixed and one flexible .303 machine guns, up to 1500lb (680kg) of bombs; *speed* 220mph.

Company

Tactical and administrative unit consisting of company headquarters and three or more PLATOONS.

Compass

British offensive in the Western Desert, commencing December 1940.

Composition B

An American term, later adopted world-wide, for a high explosive compounded by mixing Hexogen into molten TNT. The proportion is usually 60 per cent TNT and 40 per cent Hexogen, although this can vary slightly. It was used principally as a shell filling to improve the blast and violence of the TNT, since Hexogen cannot be used alone in a shell filling due to its sensitivity.

Concentration Camps

The principle of "concentrating" refugees, prisoners, or other groups of people whose freedom was inimical to national security is not new; the British Army used "concentration camps" to gather in Boer families during the South African War, and whilst the conditions were harsh this was due more to administrative inefficiency than to deliberate policy. It was not until the rise of the dictatorships that the concentration camp acquired a new and more sinister meaning. On 21 March 1939 HIMMLER directed the construction of the first German *Konzentrationslager* at DACHAU on an experimental basis, the intention being to provide a rigorous labour regime for political prisoners and other enemies of the German state. This was followed by other camps at RAVENSBRUCK (1934), SACHSENHAUSEN (1936), BUCHENWALD (1937), Flossenburg (1938), and MAUTHAUSEN (1938). The camps were officially described as "State Camps for Rehabilitation and Labour", and between 1933 and 1944 an estimated million Germans were imprisoned. By 1938, however, the original intentions had been degraded and vivisection experiments and euthanasia were being practised, and

Concentration camps created by Himmler.

prisoners were routinely worked, starved or beaten to death.

During the course of the war the influx of deportees and prisoners required many new camps, and in 1942 the conversion to extermination centres began, due to the decision to liquidate Jews, gypsies and other "non-Aryan" elements of the European population. At the same time the prisoners were to be exploited as slave labour as far as possible, and this conflict between economic demands for labour and ideological demands for extermination led to administrative inefficiency to which many, unwittingly, were to owe their lives. In 1942 the administration of the camps was transferred to the Economic and Administration bureau of the ss to extract the maximum labour potential, and this has been estimated to have saved tens of thousands of Jewish lives due to the loss of documents during the transfer of control.

Condottieri Class Light Cruisers (Italy)

See also BARTOLOMEO COLLEONI. *Displacement* 11,250 tons; *dimensions* 612ft 5in×61ft 11in (186.6×18.3m); mean draught 17ft (5.1m); *machinery* 2-shaft geared turbines producing shp 102,000; *speed* 35 knots; *protection* main belt 5.1in; deck 1.6in; turrets 5.3in; *armament* 10×6in (*Groups 1–4* 8×6in); 8×3.9in AA (*Groups 1–4* 6×3.9in AA); 8×37mm AA (omitted on *Group 2*); 10×20mm AA (*Group 1* 8×13.2mm, *Group 2* 16×20mm, *Groups 3 and 4* 12×20mm); 6×21in torpedo tubes (*Groups 1–3* 4×21in torpedo tubes, *Group 4* 6×21in torpedo tubes); 2 depth charge throwers (*Group 5* only); all groups equipped for minelaying; *aircraft* 2; *complement* 521 (*Group 1*) – 892 (*Group 5*); *number in class*; *Group 1* 4, launched 1930; *Group 2* 2, launched 1931–32; *Group 3* 2, launched 1934; *Group 4* 2, launched 1934–35; *Group 5* 2, launched 1936.

Coningham, AM Sir Arthur (1895–1948)

Coningham served in World War I and was attached to the New Zealanders, from which time dates his service nickname of "Maori", often corrupted to "Mary". Having originally joined the Royal Flying Corps in 1916, he was granted a permanent commission in the RAF as a flight-lieutenant in 1919 and in 1939 was an Air Commodore, commanding No. 4 Group, BOMBER COMMAND. He was then sent to

North Africa where he commanded the Desert Air Force and developed that force's considerable ability in tactical support of ground forces. In 1943 he went to Algeria to command the 1st Allied TAF, and later commanded the air forces used in the capture of SICILY and the early part of the Italian campaign. In January 1944 he returned to England to take command of 2nd Tactical Air Force, which was responsible for support of the NORMANDY invasion. Here his force performed admirably, destroying German columns attempting to counter the invasion.

Conscientious objector

A person who objected to enlistment in the military forces on the grounds of religious or other objections to taking life.

Conscription

The raising of armies by compulsory induction of civilians. Conscription was normal in almost all European countries prior to 1938, when it was introduced into Britain, where it remained in force until 1963. In the USA it was introduced in 1940 as "Selective Service". In most countries there were exemptions for certain classes of students, skilled men in occupations connected with the production of war material, food or other essential services. Exemption on religious grounds was also recognized. In Britain the conscription of women was introduced in December 1941. Married women living with their husbands were exempt, as were women with children under 14. Of those not exempt, only women between the ages of 19 and 24 were called up.

Consolidated Aircraft (USA)

Consolidated PBY Catalina Developed to meet a naval specification for a cantilever monoplane flying boat, the Catalina was noteworthy for its extremely long operating range of some 2500 miles (4000km). The US Navy ordered 60 in 1935, and placed further contracts before the first was begun. With some modifications, the PBY remained in production throughout the war and served with distinction in all theatres in the hands of the American, British and Canadian forces. A small number were also supplied to Russia, and were there copied in large numbers as the GST. *Span* 104ft (31.7m); *engines* 2 1200hp radial; *crew* 8; *armament* 5 machine guns and up to 4000lb (1800kg) of bombs; *speed* 195mph (314kph).

Consolidated PB2Y Coronado Designed to a US Navy specification for a four-engined patrol bomber and flew in 1937. Entering service in 1941 it was used for patrol bombing and reconnaissance duties. A transport version was also developed, capable of carrying 44 passengers or 17,700lb (8000kg) of cargo, and there was an ambulance version for moving casualties. A high-wing monoplane flying boat, the Coronado had a *span* of 115ft (35m); *engines* 4 1200hp radial; *crew* 10 (as bomber) or 5 (as transport); *armament* 8 machine guns, up to 12,000lb (5500kg) of bombs,

A Consolidated PBY Catalina of 413 Squadron on the shores of Kaggola Lake, Ceylon 1942.

depth charges or torpedoes; *speed* 225mph (362kph).

Consolidated B-24 Liberator This four-engined bomber was designed to a USAAF specification in 1939. At the time of its inception it was the most complex and expensive aeroplane ever built, yet it was manufactured in greater numbers than any other American aircraft and in more variations to suit more roles than any previous design. Total production of all versions was 19,203. Due to the unusual Davis high-aspect-ratio wing the B-24 was exceptionally fuel-efficient when cruising and with a maximum range of 2200 miles (3540km) with a full bomb load was capable of cruising further than any other landplane of the period. It was widely employed as heavy bomber, passenger and cargo transport, tanker, maritime patrol, reconnaissance and anti-submarine aircraft with US, British and Commonwealth forces. *Span* 110ft (33.5m);

engines 4 1200hp radial; *crew* 12; *armament* 10 machine guns, up to 7950lb (3600kg) of bombs; *speed* 300mph (483kph).

Consolidated PB4Y-2 Privateer This was ordered by the US Navy in 1943 as a four-engined maritime patrol bomber based on the Liberator design. The B-24 airframe was lengthened and strengthened so as to withstand low-level missions. Over 700 were built but relatively few entered service before the war ended and it was used only in the Pacific theatre. After the war numbers were also operated by the French and Chinese. *Span* 110ft (33.5m); *engines* 4 1350hp radial; *crew* 11; *armament* 12 machine guns, 6000lb (2725kg) of bombs; *speed* 247mph (397kph).

Controlled Submarine Mining

A coastal defence measure adopted by every country requiring such defences. The mines were similar to standard naval mines but

instead of being activated by a passing ship, they were fired by electric impulses sent from a shore station. The mines were laid in carefully-plotted fields in the vicinity of naval bases and harbours, and overseen by concealed firing posts. When a ship passed into the minefield it was tracked by instruments which displayed its position on a chart in relation to the positions of the mines. When the ship's position coincided with that of a mine, the electrical circuit was closed and the mine detonated. Controlled minefields were used as an adjunct to coast defence guns, usually to cover an area which could not conveniently be commanded by artillery.

Convoy PQ-17, 1942

On 27 June 1942 Convoy PQ 17, consisting of 34 Allied merchantmen, sailed from Iceland for Russia. The convoy was protected by a close escort under Commander J. E. Broome

Convoy PQ-17, July 1942.

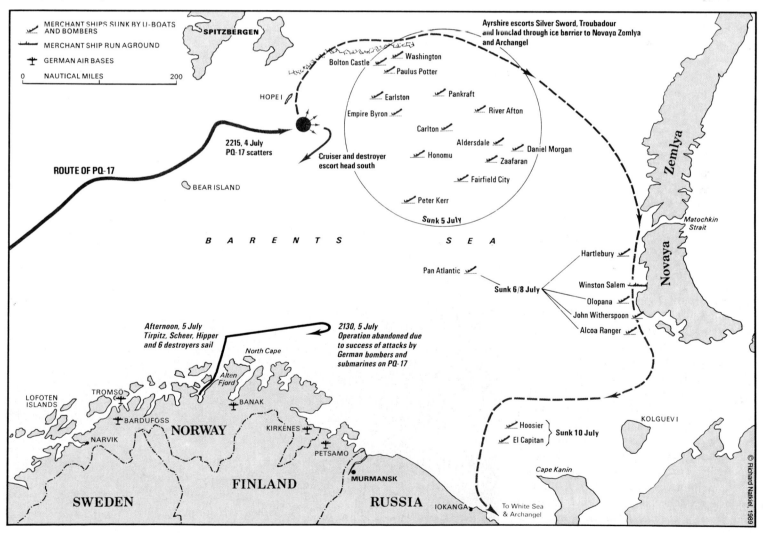

and a covering force which included four cruisers under the command of Rear-Admiral Louis Hamilton, while the Home Fleet under Admiral Sir John TOVEY provided distant back-up. The convoy was detected by German reconnaissance aircraft east of Jan Mayen Island on 1 July and the following day the battleship *Tirpitz*, the pocket battleships *Admiral Scheer* and *Lützow*, the cruiser *Admiral Hipper* and escorting destroyers left their Norwegian bases to intercept. During these movements *Lützow* and three destroyers ran aground and took no further part in the operation. The German commanders, however, were unaware of the precise location of the Home Fleet and, having been forbidden by HITLER to continue their mission unless it could be established beyond doubt that no British aircraft carrier was within range, dropped anchor in Altenfjord on 4 July. At the Admiralty in London all that was known was that the enemy's heavy surface units were at sea and that they were capable of over-whelming PQ-17's covering force and close escort before the Home Fleet could intervene. In the light of this, the First Sea Lord, Admiral Sir Dudley POUND, reached a controversial decision and at 2111 that night despatched a signal ordering the cruisers to withdraw to the west at high speed, followed at 2123 by the order for the convoy to disperse and proceed independently to Russian ports. The German surface fleet put to sea again on 5 July and returned after a brief and abortive cruise, but the scattered merchantmen were so savagely mauled by U-boats and the Luftwaffe that only 11 survived. The lost cargoes included 210 aircraft, 430 tanks and 3350 motor vehicles. The disaster was the worst ever to befall an ARCTIC CONVOY.

Convoy PQ-18, 1942

Because of the disaster which had befallen CONVOY PQ-17, the next ARCTIC CONVOY to Russia, PQ-18, did not leave the UK until 2 September 1942. The convoy, numbering 40 Allied merchantmen, was protected by a cruiser screening force and a heavy close escort which included the carrier HMS *Avenger*, with distant cover provided by the Home Fleet. On this occasion German surface units did not attempt to intervene but from 12 September onwards the convoy was subjected to air and submarine attacks until it reached its destination. Thirteen of the merchantmen were sunk, plus three from the homeward-

bound Convoy QP-4, but in return the Germans sustained the loss of four U-boats, two reconnaissance aircraft, six bombers and 33 torpedo bombers. PQ-18 marked the end of the Luftwaffe's massed torpedo attacks against the Arctic convoys, and following the Allied landings in French North Africa in November 1942, many of its Norwegian-based anti-shipping units were posted to the Mediterranean.

Copenhagen, Denmark, 1940

See DENMARK.

Coral Sea, Battle of, May 1942

A significant but confused battle, this took place between 4–8 May 1942 and was the first sea battle to be fought entirely by aircraft, no warship of either side ever seeing one of the other. The Japanese were moving to take PORT MORESBY in NEW GUINEA and TULAGI in the south SOLOMONS. Superior US intelligence discovered this plan and the force landing at Tulagi was attacked by aircraft from the US carrier YORKTOWN. Task Force 17, under Rear-Admiral FLETCHER, now began searching for the main Japanese carrier force, while the Japanese, under Rear-Admiral TAKAGI and aided by land-based aircraft from RABAUL, were searching for the US force. Both sides deployed a number of minor flotillas over a wide area, and these dispositions ultimately led to the Japanese defeat. One Japanese air attack, intended for the US carrier force on 7 May, actually found and sank the US destroyer SIMS and damaged the fleet oiler *Neosho*. While these aircraft were away, US aircraft attacked their parent carrier. On the same day a major US attack, heading for four minor

Japanese ships mistakenly reported as an enemy main force, accidentally found the Japanese carrier SHOHO and its escort, and sank the carrier. One Japanese strike actually flew over a US carrier force but failed to attack, thinking the ships were Japanese. On 8 May both sides finally located their opposing carrier forces and launched strikes; the Japanese *Shokaku* was disabled, while the USS LEXINGTON was so badly damaged that it had to be sunk several hours later by US torpedo fire. Tactically the battle was a victory for the Japanese: they had sunk one US carrier and two major warships, while the US attacks had only sunk one carrier and damaged another. Strategically, though, it was a US victory because the Japanese had been forced to abandon their attempt to seize Port Moresby and the threat to Australia had been averted.

Coriano Ridge, Italy, 1944

See GOTHIC LINE.

Corinth Canal, Greece, 1941

The canal separating mainland Greece from the Peloponnesus and running through a gorge 150ft (45m) deep, spanned by a road bridge. On 26 April the German 2nd Parachute Rifle Regiment dropped astride the defences of the bridge, which it attempted to seize by *coup de main*. However, following the explosion of the demolition charges the bridge collapsed into the canal. Some accounts suggest that the charges were detonated by the rifle fire of two British officers, others that they blew up as a result of the fire of a light anti-aircraft gun which was engaging the German engineers. As a result of

Convoy PQ-18 under air attack, September 1942.

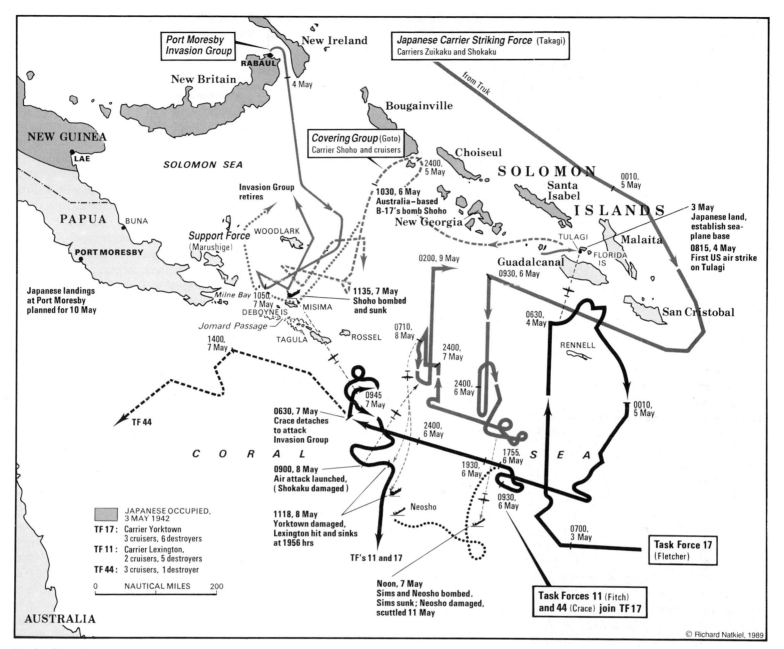

Battle of the Coral Sea, May 1942.

the incident the British evacuation from the Peloponnesus was extended by two days.

Corkscrew

Allied occupation of Pantellaria, June 1943.

Corona

Codename given to a British radio countermeasure intended to interfere with the German voice control of night fighters. A powerful transmitter in Britain, tuned to the German frequency, would interrupt the orders with recitations, reading from

newspapers, recordings of Hitler's speeches, confusing orders, anything which would interfere with the command functions being transmitted from Germany. The tactic was moderately successful.

Coronet

American plan for the invasion of Honshu, Japan, 1945.

Corps

1. Major formation consisting of corps headquarters, corps troops at the personal disposal

of the corps commander, and one or more DIVISIONS. The German Army grouped its Panzer divisions into Panzer corps and the Soviet Army also formed tank and mechanized corps, but the composition of British and American corps varied in accordance with the prevailing situation. Normally but not invariably a Lieutenant-General's command. 2. Administrative grouping of troops performing a specific support function within an army, for example the Royal Army Service Corps or the US Signal Corps.

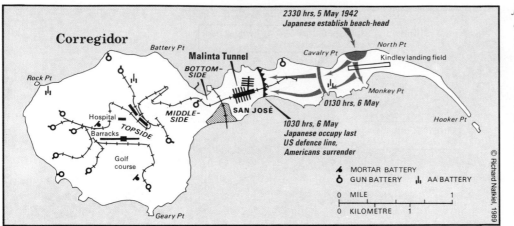

2330 hrs, 5 May 1942
Japanese establish beach-head

Corregidor

Battery Pt

North Pt
Kindley landing field
Cavalry Pt

Malinta Tunnel
BOTTOM-
SIDE
Rock Pt

Monkey Pt
0130 hrs, 6 May

Hospital
MIDDLE-
SIDE
SAN JOSÉ
Hooker Pt

Barracks
TOPSIDE
1030 hrs, 6 May
Japanese occupy last
US defence line,
Americans surrender

Golf
course

MORTAR BATTERY
GUN BATTERY   AA BATTERY

0   MILE   1
0   KILOMETRE   1

Geary Pt

© Richard Natkiel, 1989

*Japanese landings
on Corregidor,
5–6 May 1942.*

Corregidor, Philippines, 1942 and 1945

Island in Manila Bay, which was strongly fortified by the US Army in the aftermath of the Spanish-American War (1898) and became

American and Filipino soldiers surrender at Malinta tunnel, Corregidor.

Fort MILLS. It was besieged by the Japanese after the surrender of US forces on the BATAAN peninsula and suffered heavy artillery and aerial bombing. Most of the above-ground structures were destroyed and several of the gun and mortar batteries put out of action. Japanese infantry landed at night on 5 May 1942, and General WAINWRIGHT, the commander, surrendered on the following day. The island was recaptured in a combined seaborne and airborne attack by US forces on 16 February 1945.

Corsica, 1942–43

Occupied by the Italians following the Allied landings in French North Africa and briefly reinforced with a German division. The island was abandoned by the Axis when the Allies invaded the Italian mainland in September 1943, control being assumed by Free French troops and local Resistance groups.

COSSAC Chief of Staff to the Supreme Allied Commander (Designate). A post established in Britain to provide a commander for the planning of the D-DAY invasion before the actual military commander had been appointed.

Cossack, HMS – Tribal Class Destroyer

Commanded by the then Captain Philip VIAN, *Cossack* was responsible for the rescue of captured British merchant seamen during the ALTMARK INCIDENT. She subsequently took part in the Second Battle of NARVIK under Captain R. St V. Sherbrooke and executed successful torpedo attacks on BISMARCK during the early hours of 27 May 1941. *Cossack* was torpedoed in the Atlantic on 23 October 1941 and sank west of Gibraltar four days later.

Cotentin Peninsula, France, 1944

Having consolidated its beach-head after the D-DAY landings, Major-General J. Lawton COLLINS' US VII Corps fought its way across the base of the peninsula, which was defended by the German 709th Division and elements of the 77th, 91st and 243rd Divisions. On 19 June Collins swung north with three divisions (4th, 9th and 79th) to attack CHERBOURG while Major-General Troy MIDDLETON's US VIII Corps protected his rear. Cherbourg fell on 26 June, although some fortifications in the harbour continued to resist for a further three days. The last pocket of German resistance surrendered at the Cap de la Hague on 30 June. German losses in the Cotentin probably exceeded 50,000; American casualties amounted to 2811 killed, 13,546 wounded and 5744 missing. See *The Struggle for Europe* by Chester Wilmot (Collins).

Cotton Cake

Smoke generator developed locally by the British Army in the Middle Eastern theatre.

County Class (Dorsetshire Group) Cruisers (UK)

See KENT and LONDON Groups. *Displacement* 9975 tons; *dimensions* 630×66ft (187× 19.8m); mean draught 17ft (5.1m); *machinery* 4-shaft geared turbines producing shp 80,000; *speed* 32.25 knots; *protection* deck 4in; turrets 2in; DCT 3in; *armament* 8×8in (4×2); 8×4in AA (4×2); 16×2-pdr AA (2×8); 8×0.5in (2×4); 8×21in (2×4) torpedo tubes; *aircraft* 1; *complement* 650; *number in class* 2, launched 1928–29.

County Class (Kent Group) Cruisers (UK)

See DORSETSHIRE and LONDON Groups. *Displacement* 9830–10,570 tons; *dimensions* 630×61ft (192×18.6m); mean draught 16ft 3in (4.8m); *machinery* 4-shaft geared turbines producing shp 80,000; *speed* 31.5 knots; *protection* main belt 5in; deck 1.5in; turrets 2in; *armament* 8×8in (4×2); 8×4in AA (4×2); 8×2-pdr AA (2×4); 8×0.5in AA; 4 or 8×21in torpedo tubes (some); *aircraft* 3 (or 1), (1 catapult); *complement* 710; *number in class* 7, launched 1926–27.

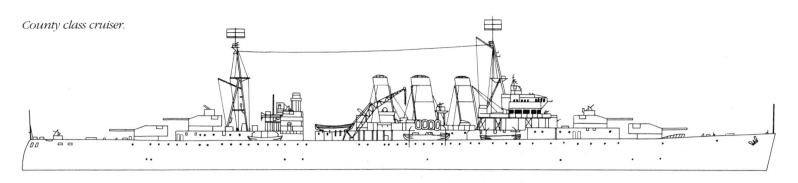

County class cruiser.

County Class (London Group) Cruisers (UK)

Later County class. See DORSETSHIRE and KENT Groups. *Displacement* 9830–9850 tons; *dimensions* 633×66ft (192×20m); mean draught 17ft (5.1m); *machinery* 4-shaft geared turbines producing shp 80,000; *speed* 32.25 knots; *protection* main belt 5in; deck 4in; turrets 2in; *armament* 8×8in (4×2); 8×4in AA (8×1, *London* 4×2); 8×2-pdr AA (2×4), *London* 16×2-pdr AA (2×8); 8×0.5in AA *London* only; 8×21in torpedo tubes (2×4); *aircraft* 1, *London* 3; *complement* 650; *number in class* 4, launched 1927–28.

Courageous Class Aircraft Carriers (UK)

Formerly battlecruisers, these ships were converted to aircraft carriers 1924–30. *Courageous* was torpedoed and sunk by *U-29* west of Ireland on 17 September 1939. Her well-protected aviation fuel tanks were almost full but did not catch fire. See also GLORIOUS. *Displacement* 22,500 tons; *dimensions* 786ft 3in×90ft 6in (239.7×27m); mean draught 24ft (7.2m); *machinery* 4-shaft geared turbines producing shp 90,000; *speed* 30.5 knots; *protection* main belt 2in; deck 3in; *armament* 16×4.7in AA (16×1); 4×8 2pdr, 15×20mm (*Furious*, 1945); *aircraft* 48; *complement* 1216; *number in class* 2, both launched 1916.

Courbet Class Battleships (Fr)

The two survivors of this class, *Courbet* and *Paris*, were launched respectively in 1911 and 1912, and were both in British ports when France surrendered in June 1940. By then their maximum speed had dropped to 16 knots and they were unsuitable for active operations. *Courbet* was handed over to the Free French Naval Force and was later sunk as a breakwater during the Allied invasion of NORMANDY. *Paris* was used as an accommodation ship for exiled Polish naval personnel, and was returned to France in 1945. The ships displaced 25,850 tons and their main armament consisted of twelve 305mm guns.

Covenanter – Cruiser Tank Mark V (A13 Mark III) (UK)

Essentially an up-armoured version of the A13, developed by the London, Midland and Scottish Railway Company just prior to the outbreak of war. A total of 1771 Convenanters were built, the majority being retained in the United Kingdom for training although a few were sent to the Middle East. A Close Support version was armed with a 3-inch howitzer. A number were converted to bridgelayers, mounting a 34-feet (10.37-m) 30-ton capacity scissors bridge. *Weight* 18 tons; *speed* 31mph (50kph); *armour* 40mm; *armament* 1×2-pdr gun; 1 Besa machine gun; *engine* Meadows 280hp petrol; *crew* 4.

Coventry, United Kingdom, 1940

In mid-November 1940 a new phase of the BLITZ began when the Luftwaffe switched the weight of its air offensive from the bombardment of London to a strategic attack on Britain's heavy industry and war production. The first attack in this offensive – codenamed MONDSCHEINSERENADE (Moonlight Serenade) – was launched on the night of 14/15 November against the city of Coventry, a key centre of aircraft production. At 1920 on the 14th the first pathfinding He111 of KGr 100 arrived over the city, dropping its bombs under X-GERAT guidance. During the next 45 minutes 13 He111s of KGr 100 – joined by bombers of Luftflotten 2 and 3 – dropped 10,224 incendiaries and 48 HE bombs on the east part of the city centre. 449 German bombers raided Coventry, dropping 503 tons of high explosive and 881 canisters of incendiaries in an attack which lasted 11 hours. Some 550 people were killed and over 1,200 injured. Approximately 60,000 buildings, including three-quarters of the city centre, were destroyed. The bombing of Coventry provided a clear indication of the results which could be achieved by AREA BOMBING, the swamping of civil defences, the dislocation of the city's utilities and the creation of uncontrollable fires in a compact conurbation proving far more effective than the precision bombing of specific industrial targets Subsequently, BOMBER COMMAND incorporated incendiary marking into its night bombing techniques. See also DRESDEN, Hamburg.

Coventry Armoured Car (UK)

Intended to replace the DAIMLER and HUMBER armoured cars, the prototypes were completed in 1944. The vehicle did not see active service in World War II but subsequently a number were employed by the French Army in Vietnam. A Mark II version was armed with a 75mm gun in place of the 2-pdr. *Weight* 11.5 tons; *speed* 41mph (66kph); *armour* 14mm; *armament* 1 2-pdr gun; 1 Besa machine gun; *engine* Hercules 175hp; *crew* 4.

Cowan, Maj Gen David Tennant (1896–1983)

"Punch" Cowan became a Second Lieutenant in the Argyll and Sutherland Highlanders in 1914, rising to the rank of captain during the war. In 1917 he joined the 6th Gurkha Rifles, remaining with them until 1940 and serving in Waziristan in 1919–20. He attended the Staff College, Quetta, in 1927–28 and was Chief Instructor at the Indian Military Academy in 1932–34. In 1941 he became Deputy Director Military Training, GHQ India, and in 1942 was appointed GOC 17th Indian Division which he subsequently led in BURMA until 1945.

CP Command post (US).

CRA Commander, Royal Artillery (UK).

Crab – Mineclearing Tank (UK)

The most successful flail tank design of the war, developed from the SCORPION series and

Crab flail tank.

employing the SHERMAN Mark V, power for the flail rotor being drawn from the tank's main engine. The Crab could clear a lane 9.75 feet (3m) wide at a speed of 1.25mph (2kph). When the flail was not in use the tank could employ its main armament. The 30th Armoured Brigade (79th Armoured Division) contained three Crab regiments which fought throughout the campaign in NORMANDY and North-West Europe and Crabs also took part in the final stages of the fighting in Italy.

Craven Class Destroyers (USA)

Displacement 1500 tons; *dimensions* 341ft 6in×36ft (104×10.8m); *mean draught* 10ft (3m); *machinery* 2-shaft geared turbines producing shp 49,000; *speed* 36.5 knots; *armament* 4×5in; 4×1.1in AA; 16×21in torpedo tubes; *complement* 250; *number in class* 22, launched 1936–39.

CRDA Aircraft (Italy)

CRDA Cant Z1007 Alcione CRDA stands for Cantieri Riuniti dell'Adriatico, and the name was invariably shortened to Cant. The Z1007 was developed in 1936–37 and after modification to suit the Italian Air Force several hundred were built. They were operated in the Mediterranean theatre with success. A low-wing monoplane with a span of 81.3ft (24.8m); the Z1007 was powered by three 1000hp Piaggio radial engines to reach a top speed of 280mph (450kph). With a crew of five, it carried six machine guns and up to 4400lb (2000kg) of bombs and torpedoes.

CRDA Cant Z506B Airone This aircraft originated as a civil passenger and cargo seaplane and was then adapted for torpedo-bombing and reconnaissance purposes. It was widely used in the Mediterranean on patrol and anti-shipping missions but was vulnerable unless heavily escorted. It survived until 1959 as an air-sea rescue machine. *Span* 87ft (26.5m); *engines* 3 750hp radial; *armament* 4 machine guns, up to 2755lb (1250kg) of bombs; *crew* 5; *top speed* 215mph (346kph).

CRDA Cant Z501 Gabbiano The Z501 was a parasol-wing flying boat of which about 200 were in Italian service at the outbreak of war. Used for fleet reconnaissance and light bombing they were an effective aircraft and continued in use after the Italian surrender. With a span of 74ft (22.5m), the single 900hp engine was mounted in a midwing nacelle, at the rear of which sat an observer/gunner. More machine guns were mounted in the bow and amidships, and some 1100lb (500kg) of bombs could be carried; the aircraft had a top speed of 170mph (274kph).

CRE Commander, Royal Engineers (UK).

Creagh, Maj Gen Sir Michael O'Moore (1892–1970)

Creagh was commissioned into the 7th Hussars in 1911, served for most of his Army life with cavalry regiments and in February 1940 was appointed to command 7th Armoured Division. He led this division with great success throughout 1940–41, but in Operation BATTLEAXE, against TOBRUK in June 1941, was less than successful, though the fault lay largely with higher command. Nevertheless, in the general housecleaning of higher commanders which took place in the wake of Battleaxe, Creagh was relieved of his command and thereafter held no position of importance, retiring in 1944.

Creasy, Adm George (1895–1972)

At the outbreak of war Creasy was commanding a destroyer flotilla in the Mediterranean. He later took part in the Norwegian campaign, and served as Chief of Staff to the First Sea Lord. In September 1940 he was appointed Director of Anti-Submarine Warfare and remained in this post until 1942, when he was given command of HMS *Duke of York*. After promotion to Rear-Admiral, he headed the naval section of the COSSAC staff, planning the invasion of Europe.

Crerar, Gen Henry (1888–1965)

Crerar was appointed Chief of the Canadian General Staff in 1940 and sent to London to organize the training of Canadian troops as they arrived in Britain. In 1941 he resigned his post and accepted a drop in rank in order to command in the field, becoming Commander of I Canadian Corps, leading them in Sicily and capturing Catania. In 1943 he returned to Britain and took command of 1st Canadian Army, taking part in the invasion in June 1944. His army was involved at CAEN and FALAISE in 1944, then took Le Havre, Boulogne, Calais and finally, with eight British divisions attached, cleared the mouth of the SCHELDT estuary. His forces later broke through the SIEGFRIED LINE in Operation VERITABLE and entered Germany.

Crete, 1941

Following the evacuation of mainland Greece, Crete was held by 32,000 British and Commonwealth troops and 10,000 Greek infantry, all short of artillery and transport, commanded by Major-General Bernard FREYBERG of the 2nd New Zealand Division. The Axis possessed complete air superiority and bombed the defences daily from 13 May as a prelude to launching Operation MERKUR, the airborne invasion of the island. In overall command of this was Colonel-General Alexander Lohr, whose plan was to seize the island's airfields with Lieutenant-General Kurt STUDENT's 7th Air Division and then air-land the 5th Mountain Division, commanded by Major-General Julius Ringel. The two formations would then clear the island, receiving further reinforcements and heavy weapons by sea.

German invasion of Crete, May 1941.

On 20 May German paratroops dropped at MALEME, CANEA, RETIMO, and HERAKLION. In the desperate fighting which followed the drops, the paratroopers suffered heavy casualties, and during the night the Royal Navy sank or dispersed the seaborne German reinforcement convoys with heavy loss of life. However, 36 hours after their initial drop, the Germans seized control of Maleme airfield and during the next four days their strength grew steadily while the Luftwaffe's ground-attack wings continued to hammer the defenders. By 28 May Freyberg had concluded that the island could not be held and most of his troops retired to Sfakia on the south coast, although some were taken off at Heraklion. British and Commonwealth casualties amounted to 3600 killed and wounded and 12,000 taken prisoner. The Royal Navy evacuated

German parachutists in the invasion of Crete, May 1941.

some 18,000 men to Egypt but at the heavy cost of three cruisers and six destroyers lost to air attack and many more warships badly damaged. German losses were 6000 killed and wounded and 220 aircraft destroyed. The 7th Air Division sustained over 50% casualties, and HITLER refused to sanction another large-scale airborne operation.

Crimea, Soviet Union, 1941–44
Invaded in October 1941 by General Erich von MANSTEIN's German 11th Army, which laid siege to SEVASTOPOL. On 26 December the Soviet 44th and 51st Armies began landing on the KERCH PENINSULA in an attempt to relieve the fortress. Manstein contained their advance and in May 1942 they were eliminated during Operation *Bustard*. The following month Manstein mounted a major assault on Sevastopol (Operation *Sturgeon*), which finally fell on 3 July. During the latter half of 1943, the Soviet general advance left the German 17th Army isolated in the Crimea. In April 1944 TOLBUKHIN's 4th Ukrainian Front broke through the defences on the Perekop Isthmus and the Soviet Independent Coastal Army under General I. E. Petrov landed on the Kerch Peninsula. The Germans retired within Sevastopol, which was taken on 9 May after a two-day assault, although by then much of 17th Army had been evacuated by sea.

Cripps, Sir Richard Stafford (1889–1952)
A Socialist politician who had a varied career before the war, swinging to and from pacifism at various times. Expelled from the Labour Party in 1939, from 1940 to 1942 he was British ambassador in Moscow, where he mistakenly believed that his left-wing background would give him greater influence than would be achieved by a career diplomat. He was then

sent to India to persuade Indian politicians to co-operate with the war effort in return for a promise of post war independence. In November 1942 he returned to Britain to become Minister of Aircraft Production.

Crocker, Gen Sir John Tredinnick (1895–1953)
Crocker served in the Artists' Rifles and the Machine Gun Corps in World War I and transferred to the Tank Corps in 1923. In 1940 he commanded an armoured brigade in France and in 1942 commanded IX Corps in TUNISIA where he was wounded. In 1944–45 he commanded I Corps in France and Germany with distinction. After the war he was C-in-C Middle East Forces from 1947 to 1950, later being appointed Adjutant-General of the Forces.

Crocodile – Flamethrowing Tank (UK)
WASP II flamethrowing equipment fitted to a CHURCHILL VII which was coupled to a two-wheeled armoured trailer containing 400 gallons (1818l) of inflammable liquid. From the coupling, a pipe led under the tank's belly to emerge into the driving compartment where it joined the flame gun, which occupied the space usually containing the hull machine gun. On leaving the flame gun the fluid was ignited electrically and threw a jet up to 120 yards (109m), the blazing liquid clinging to anything it touched. The propellant gas was pressurized nitrogen contained in cylinders which were also housed in the trailer, permitting flaming for 100 seconds in short bursts. The Crocodile was the most efficient flamethrowing tank of the war, hated and feared by its enemies. On some occasions its appearance alone was sufficient to induce surrender but on others the enemy's anti-tank gunners would attempt to disable the trailer before the vehicle could be brought within flaming range. There were, too, incidents in which captured Crocodile crews were shown no mercy. Once its flaming liquid had been expended the trailer could be dropped, leaving the parent vehicle to fight as a gun tank. Crocodiles served in NORMANDY and North-West Europe, where eventually all three regiments of 31st Tank Brigade (79th Armoured Division) were equipped with them. They were also present during the closing stages of the war in Italy. A squadron was later sent to Korea but fought as gun tanks as no opportunity for flaming presented itself.

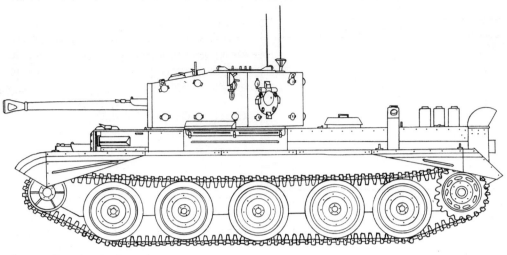

Cromwell cruiser tank.

Cromwell

Codeword to be used throughout British Home Forces in the event of a German invasion, 1940–41.

Cromwell – A27M Cruiser Tank Mark VIII (UK)

The Cromwell was the culmination of the second generation of cruiser tank development begun with the CAVALIER and CENTAUR. The pilot model was delivered in January 1942 and production commenced a year later. Almost immediately greater emphasis was placed on arming infantry and cruiser tanks with a weapon possessing dual armour piercing/high explosive capability. This led to the development of the British 75mm tank gun which was fitted to the Cromwell Marks IV, V and VII, the earlier Marks being up-gunned retrospectively. The Cromwell was one of the fastest tanks of the war, later models being governed down to 32mph (51kph) to restrict wear and tear. Orders for 3500 were placed although it is very doubtful whether these were fulfilled. A number were converted to Command and Artillery Observation Post roles by fitting extra radios and replacing the gun with a dummy. During the campaign in NORMANDY and North-West Europe Cromwells equipped the armoured reconnaissance regiments of British and Polish armoured divisions, as well as the three armoured regiments of 22nd Armoured Brigade (7th Armoured Division).

Weight	Marks I to VI 27.5 tons
	Marks VII and VIII 28 tons
Speed	Marks I to VI 40mph (64kph)
	Marks VII to VIII 32mph (51kph)
Armour	76mm (101mm on models with additional appliqué plates)
Armament	Marks I to III 1 6-pdr gun; 2 Besa m.g.
	Marks IV, V and VII 1 75mm gun; 2 Besa m.g.
	Marks VI and VIII 1 95mm howitzer; 2 Besa m.g.
Engine	Rolls-Royce Meteor 600hp petrol
Crew	5.

Crossbow

Allied operations against V-WEAPON sites, 1944.

Crow, Sir Alwyn Douglas (1894–1965)

Dr Alwyn Crow was commissioned into the East Surrey Regiment in 1914 and served on the Western Front until 1916. In 1917 he was appointed to the Proof and Experimental establishment at Woolwich Arsenal and became Director of Ballistic Research from 1919 to 1939. He was then appointed Chief Superintendent of Projectile Design, a somewhat evasive job-description which concealed his function as the leading figure in British rocket development from 1935 onwards.

Under his guidance the 2-inch and 3-inch anti-aircraft rockets were developed by 1938, though for reasons outside his control they were not employed in any number until 1941. He also supervised the adaptation of these rockets to the air-to-ground role, and was concerned with the development of the first workable proximity fuze, an electro-optical model used in 1941–42 with air defence rockets. From 1940 to 1945 he was Director of Projectile Design, and in 1945 became Director Guided Projectiles, Ministry of Supply,

until 1946. He then went to Washington as the Head of the Technical Section of the Joint Service Mission to the USA, a post he retained until his retirement in 1953.

Cruiser Tanks

See A9, A10, A13, CAVALIER, CENTAUR, CENTURION, CHALLENGER, COMET, COVENANTER, CROMWELL and CRUSADER; also BT SERIES and CHRISTIE SUSPENSION.

Crusader – A15 Cruiser Tank Mark VI (UK)

Designed as an improved version of the COVENANTER with better obstacle crossing capability. The pilot model was delivered in March 1940 and quantity production was authorized shortly after. A total of 5300 were built under the parentage of the Nuffield organization, including a proportion of Mark I and II Close Support models armed with a 3-inch howitzer in place of the 2-pdr gun. The vehicle had a disastrous baptism of fire during Operation BATTLEAXE (June 1941) when numbers had to be abandoned because of broken fan drives and clogged air filters. After these and other faults had been remedied the Crusader took part in all the Eighth Army's battles in the Western Desert and also served with the First Army in Tunisia. Despite being under-armoured, the Crusader was popular with its crews and the Germans found its speed unsettling. It was withdrawn from first line service in May 1943 and converted to a variety of roles. These included several anti-aircaft tanks, of which the most important were armed with either a single Bofors 40mm cannon in an open mounting or twin Oerlikon 20mm cannon in an enclosed turret; Command and Artillery Observation Post tanks; gun tractor for the 17-pdr anti-tank gun; and a tankdozer. The majority of these conversions were employed during the campaign in North-West Europe.

	Mark I	Mark II	Mark III
Weight	19 tons	19 tons	19.75 tons
Speed	27mph (43kph)	27mph (43kph)	27mph (43kph)
Armour	40mm	49mm	51mm
Armament	1 2-pdr gun; 2 Besa m.g.	1 2-pdr gun; 1 or 2 Besa m.g.	1 6-pdr gun; 1 Besa m.g.
Engine	Nuffield Liberty 340hp petrol		
Crew	5	4–5	3

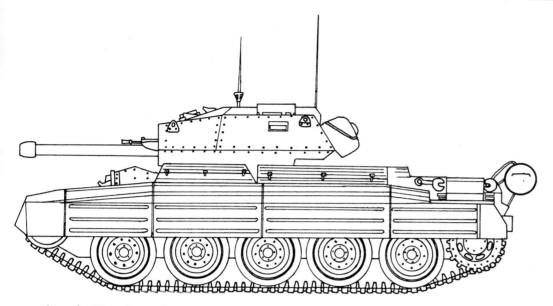

Crusader III cruiser tank.

Crusader, Operation, Libya, 1941

Mounted in November 1941 by the British 8th Army, commanded by Lieutenant-General Sir Alan CUNNINGHAM, the object was to relieve TOBRUK and destroy the Axis army in Cyrenaica. The plan required Lieutenant-General W. H. Godwin-Austen's XIII Corps (4th Indian Division, 2nd New Zealand Division and 1st Army Tank Brigade) to bypass the frontier defences to the south, containing some positions and assaulting others from the rear, and strike north to the Via Balbia along which it would advance, towards Tobruk. Fur-

Operation Crusader, *opening moves.*

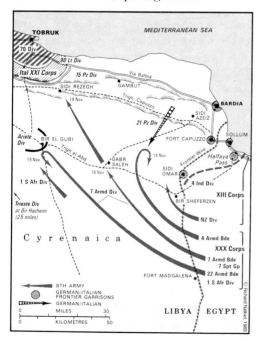

ther south, Major General Willoughby Norrie's XXX Corps (7th Armoured Division, 1st South African Division and 22nd Guards Brigade) was to strike north-westwards across the desert, destroy the enemy's armour and effect a junction with the Tobruk garrison (70th Division, Polish Carpathian Brigade and 32nd Army Tank Brigade), which would simultaneously break out in the area Belhamed/Ed Duda. The Axis forces consisted of Lieutenant-General Ludwig CRÜWELL's Afrika Korps with 15th and 21st Panzer Divisions and one motorized division; Lieutenant-General Gastone Gambara's Italian XX Mobile Corps (*Ariete* Armoured and *Trieste* Motorized Divisions); and Lieutenant-General Enea Navarini's Italian XXI Corps with five infantry divisions. In effective command was General Erwin ROMMEL, although technically the Italian XX Mobile Corps lay outside his immediate control. For *Crusader* 8th Army fielded 201 infantry tanks and 523 cruisers; Axis tank strength was 139 PzKw IIIs, 35 PzKw IVs and 146 M.13s. The 8th Army crossed the frontier on 18 November and did not encounter serious opposition until the following day. By 21 November, however, a confused and hard-fought series of actions had developed on and around SIDI REZEGH airfield, in which the Tobruk garrison had begun to break out against opposition from the Afrika Division (later known as the 90th Light), which was itself trying to defend the airfield against the 7th Armoured Brigade and the 7th Armoured Division Support Group, who were in turn under attack from the south-

east by the Afrika Korps, whose anti-tank gunners were holding off pursuit by the 4th and 22nd Armoured Brigades. This phase of the battle ended with the three armoured brigades of 7th Armoured Division in disarray and on 24 November Rommel decided to lead his armour eastwards in a lightning foray to the frontier, believing that this would unnerve Cunningham and induce him to withdraw. In Cairo AUCHINLECK held similar views and on 26 November replaced Cunningham with his own Deputy Chief of Staff, Major General Neil RITCHIE. For the Axis, Rommel's foray (often referred to as The Dash to the Wire) proved to be disastrous, for during his absence XIII Corps continued its advance and on the night of 26/27 November the 2nd New Zealand Division effected a junction with the Tobruk garrison. Rommel hastened back from the frontier and was briefly able to reimpose the siege, but he was now faced with a revitalized 7th Armoured Division and in a series of actions against both British corps his strength was steadily eroded. By 5 December 8th Army re-established contact with Tobruk. With great reluctance Rommel accepted that his army would be destroyed if he did not retreat and on 7 December he commenced an orderly withdrawal to EL AGHEILA, abandoning Cyrenaica and the isolated Axis garrisons at BARDIA, Halfaya Pass and SOLLUM, which were forced to surrender. During *Crusader* Axis casualties amounted to 38,000 killed, wounded and missing as against 18,000 British and Commonwealth; some 300 German and Italian tanks were destroyed compared with 278 British, although many of the latter were subsequently repaired. See *Tobruk* by Michael Carver (Batsford).

Crüwell, Gen Ludwig (1892–1953)

Crüwell was commissioned into a dragoon regiment in 1912, served through World War I and was a member of Germany's postwar army. In 1938 he was given command of 6 Panzer Regiment and in December 1939 was promoted Major-General. In 1940 he received command of 11 Panzer Division and in 1941 was appointed commander of the AFRIKA KORPS. He served well under General ROMMEL and during the latter's absence in 1942 commanded Panzer Armee Afrika. He was captured on 29 May 1942 in North Africa when his Storch observation aircraft was shot down, and spent the remainder of the war as a prisoner.

C-Stoff

Mixture of Hydrazine Hydrate and Methanol used as German rocket motor fuel.

Culin Hedgerow Device (USA)

Invented by an American NCO, Sergeant Curtis G. Culin, in response to the tactical limitations imposed by the NORMANDY *bocage*, where the fields were separated by earth banks topped by thick hedgerows. Tanks were unable to force their through these without exposing their vulnerable belly plates to the enemy's fire. Culin's solution was to weld steel tusks on to the bow of the tank. These would then dig into the bank, simultaneously loosening the earth and preventing the vehicle's nose from rising and in due course sustained pressure would enable the tank to push through into the field beyond, taking a section of hedgerow with it. Over 500 vehicles were fitted with the device, which was known as the Rhinoceros, and the idea was also adopted by the British Army; much of the steel used was obtained locally from dismantled German beach defence obstacles. Culin was rewarded with the Legion of Merit for his ingenuity.

Culverin

Projected British operations against the Japanese in Malaya and Sumatra, 1944.

Cunningham, Gen Sir Alan (1887–)

The younger brother of Admiral CUNNINGHAM, General Cunningham led the forces which drove the Italians from ETHIOPIA in 1940–41. In August 1941 he assumed command of the newly formed 8th Army in North Africa and one of his first tasks was to conduct Operation CRUSADER. Here he failed to exhibit his customary dash and, in the words of one critic, "lost the battle in his mind". Failing to press home his attack, he was relieved by AUCHINLECK on 26 November 1941 and for the rest of the war was employed in adminstrative roles. At the close of the war he became the last High Commissioner in Palestine.

Cunningham, Adm Sir Andrew Browne (1883–1963)

On 1 June 1939 Cunningham was appointed Admiral and Commander-in-Chief of the British Mediterranean Fleet. After Italy's entry into the war in 1940 his principal task was the defeat of the Italian Fleet and the maintenance of the supply routes to MALTA and Egypt. Seiz-ing the initiative, Cunningham directed the naval air attack against TARANTO, which put three Italian battleships out of action, and the night battle of CAPE MATAPAN, which ended Italy's hopes of controlling the Mediter-ranean. He was then involved in actions off CRETE, where his forces attempted to deny the island to German reinforcements and evacu-ated British and Commonwealth troops, los-ing three cruisers and six destroyers in these operations. In May 1942 he was sent to Washington as a British representative on the Joint Chiefs of Staff. He soon returned to active service as chief of Allied naval operations in the TORCH landings in French North Africa and the HUSKY landings in Sicily. In September 1943 he received the formal surrender of the Italian Fleet on board HMS *Warspite*, his orig-inal flagship in the Mediterranean. In October 1943 he was recalled to London and appoin-ted First Sea Lord and Chief of Naval Staff, succeeding POUND, until 1946.

Cunningham, Gp Capt John (1917–)

A pre-war test pilot for the De Havilland Aircraft company, Cunningham was an out-standing night fighter pilot, who gained the nickname "Cats-Eyes", dreamed up in a public relations endeavour to credit him with his victories without revealing that he was using airborne radar to detect his targets. Among his more remarkable feats was that of forcing a Heinkel bomber to crash by outmanoeuvring him and without firing a shot. In the first eight months of 1940 he downed 12 German aircraft.

Curtin, John (1885–1945)

An Australian politician, Curtin was leader of the Labour Party in opposition at the outbreak of war. He opposed conscription in 1939–40 and refused to join a coalition government. In October 1941 he brought about the fall of the Fadden government and took office as Prime Minister with a majority of one. When Japan entered the war Curtin immediately stepped up conscription and set about the task of reorienting Australian alliances so as to attach more firmly to the USA. This upset several Commonwealth politicians, including CHURCHILL and SMUTS, but his wisdom was proved later in the war when he backed British policies in the Pacific. In 1941–42 he also filled the posts of Minister of Defence Co-ordination and chairman of the War Advisory Council. He then became Minister of Defence and in 1943 achieved a Parliamentary majority when he successfully led the Labour Party to victory in a general election. After visiting the UK, USA and Canada in 1944 he fell ill, and died in July 1945. Curtin was a powerful leader and one who was well-suited to the position in which Australia found herself in 1941, keenly aware that the axis of power in the Pacific had shifted away from Britain towards the United States.

Curtiss Aircraft (USA)

Curtiss C-46 Commando Originally designed as a civil airliner in 1936, this aircraft first flew in 1940. It was then adopted by the USAAF as a transport machine and over 3300 were built. As a passenger aircraft it could carry up to 40 personnel, and it was also used in cargo, ambulance, glider towing and paratroop roles. Widely used in the Far Eastern theatres, its first appearance in Europe was not until March 1945 when it carried parachute troops for the RHINE CROSS-ING. *Span* 108ft (33m); *engines* 2 2000hp radial; *crew* 5; *payload* about 15,500lb (7000kg); *speed* 265mph (426kph).

Curtiss SBC Cleveland The SBC was a biplane dive-bomber which was in US Naval service at the outbreak of war. Fifty were ordered by the French but arrived too late to see service; five of these finished up in Britain where they were tested by the RAF. *Span* 34ft (10.4m); *crew* 2; *engine* 1 950hp radial; *arma-ment* 2 machine guns and 1 1100lb (500kg) bomb; *speed* 237mph (381kph).

Curtiss SC-1 Seahawk Design of this machine began in 1942 to replace the SEAMEW but it did not enter service until June 1945. A single-float monoplane, it was a seaborne scout aircraft for the US Navy and some 600 were built. *Span* 41ft (12.5m); *engine* 1 1350hp radial; *crew* 2; *armament* 2 .50 machine guns, 500lb (225kg) of bombs; *speed* 313mph (504kph).

Curtiss SO3C Seamew A single-float monoplane reconnaissance machine for ship-borne use by the US Navy, the Seamew was originally known as the seagull and first flew in 1940. Landplane versions were also devel-oped for carrier employment. Largely used by the US Navy, about 100 were supplied to the RAF who used them principally as trainers. *Span* 38ft (11.6m); *engine* 1 520hp in-line; *crew* 2; *armament* 2 .30 machine guns, 650lb (295kg) of bombs; *speed* 190mph (305kph).

Curtiss P-40 Warhawk This was the first

mass-produced American single-seat fighter and went into production in 1939. The early models were built for the USAAF, and the RAF (where they were called "Tomahawks"), and later for the Soviets. A later version, the P-40E was known to the RAF as the "Kittyhawk" and was the first model to go into large-scale production, over 2300 being made.

Numerous later versions were developed and total production of the P-40 series was over 14,000. Although outperformed in many respects by its contemporaries, the P-40 was a tough and versatile aircraft which was used on every front at some time or other. *Span* 37.3ft (11.4m); *engine* 1 1200hp in-line; *crew* 1; *armament* 6 .50 machine guns, 1650lb (750kg) of bombs; *speed* 350mph (563kph).

Curtiss SB2C Helldiver Designed as a US Navy dive-bomber, the Helldiver first flew in 1940 but did not enter service until 1943. This delay was due to the prototype crashing, which resulted in a long investigation, and to a US Navy reappraisal of the dive-bomber role in the wake of PEARL HARBOR. Consequently, by increasing armament and protection and making the entire machine stronger the original design was considerably modified. It played an important role in US operations in the Pacific and over 7000 were built. *Span* 49.75ft (15m); *engine* 1 1900hp radial; *crew* 2; *armament* 2 20mm cannon or 4 machine guns in wing, 1 or 2 machine guns, 990lb (450kg) of bombs; *speed* 290mph (467kph).

Cutter, Cdr Slade D., USN

Second highest-scoring American submarine commander of World War II. When the USA entered the war Cutter was serving as executive officer of the "P" CLASS submarine USS *Pompano* which made successful war patrols in the area of the Marshall Islands and in the East China Sea. In November 1942 he joined the GATO CLASS submarine USS *Seahorse* while she was fitting out, was appointed her executive officer when she was commissioned on 31 March 1943, and assumed command on 30 September 1943. Under Cutter's command *Seahorse* made four patrols, during which she was credited with sinking 21 ships totalling 142,300 tons. He was relieved in August 1944 and after a period on the staff of the Commander Submarines, US Atlantic Fleet, assumed command of the TENCH CLASS submarine USS *Requin* when she was commissioned on 28 April 1945, holding this appointment until 28 October 1946.

Curtiss P-40s of the 16th Fighter Flight Squadron, lined up for take-off at an air base in China, October 1942.

Curtiss Tomahawk IIA fighter.

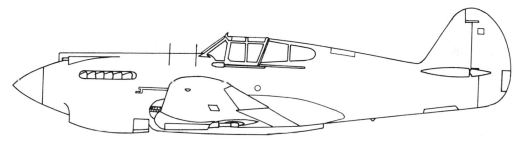

CV3/33 and CV3/35 – Tankettes (Italy)

Developed from the Carden Loyd Tankette Mark VI, the *Carro Veloce* (Fast Tank) series were little more than tracked machine gun carriers, although flamethrower and bridgelayer versions were also produced. They equipped infantry support battalions and cavalry groups, each with a strength of 43 vehicles. In 1938 their designation was changed to L3/33 and L3/35, the L standing for *Leggero* or Light. They saw active service during the Spanish Civil War and the Italian invasion of France in 1940, in East and North Africa, and in the Balkans and Russia, but despite attempts to up-gun the design with a 20mm cannon they were hopelessly outclassed by almost every other armoured vehicle in service. About 2500 were built. *Weight* 3.3 tons; *speed* 26mph (42kph); *armour* 13.5mm; *armament* 2 Breda 8mm machine guns; *engine* Fiat SPA 43hp petrol; *crew* 2.

CWAC   Canadian Women's Army Corps.

CWS   Chemical Warfare Service (US).

Cyrenaica, 1940–42

Eastern province of the Italian colony of Libya and the scene of much heavy fighting during the North African campaign. See BARDIA, BEDA FOMM, BENGHAZI, BIR EL GUBI, BIR HACHEIM, CAPUZZO, DERNA, EL AGHEILA, GAZALA, JEBEL AKHDAR, MECHILI, SIDI REZEGH, TOBRUK.

Czechoslovakia, 1939

Having annexed the Sudetenland in September 1938, HITLER blatantly ignored the provisions of the MUNICH Agreement and occupied the remainder of Czechoslovakia in March 1939. The acquisition of the Czech armaments industry and tank fleet enabled the German Army to take the field with less risk in 1939. Strategically, the possession of Czechoslovakia enabled the German armies to outflank the strongest Polish armies in September 1939.

Czestochowa, Poland, 1945

A city liberated by KONEV's 1st Ukrainian Front during the Soviet Vistula-Oder offensive of January 1945.

D

"D" Class Cruisers (UK)
Displacement 4,850 tons; *dimensions* 472ft 6in×46ft 6in (144×14.1m); mean draught 14ft 6in (4.4m); *machinery* 2-shaft geared turbines producing shp 40,000; *speed* 29 knots; *protection* main belt 3in; deck 1in; gun shields 1in; *armament* 6×6in (6×1); 3×4in AA (3×1); 2×2-pdr AA (2×1); 12×21in (4×3) torpedo tubes; *complement* 450; *number in class* 8, launched 1917–19.

"D" Class Destroyers (UK)
See "C" and "D" Class Destroyers.

Dachau, Germany, 1939–45
The first German concentration camp established by the Nazi government, early in 1933. Just north of Munich, it remained a detention and forced labour camp, operated by the SS, until 1945.

Daimler Armoured Car (UK)
Introduced in 1941, the Daimler Armoured Car saw active service in North Africa, Italy, North-West Europe and Burma. The design incorporated four-wheel drive with independent suspension and the provision of rear steering for the vehicle commander. During the later stages of the war the LITTLEJOHN ADAPTER was sometimes fitted to the 2-pdr to increase its armour-piercing capability. Total production amounted to 2694 vehicles. *Weight* 7.5 tons; *speed* 50mph (80kph); *armour* 16mm; *armament* 1 2-pdr gun; 1 Besa machine gun; *engine* Daimler 95hp petrol; *crew* 3.

Daimler Scout Car (UK)
Designed in 1938 by the BSA Company prior to its amalgamation with the Daimler organization. The vehicle possessed four-wheel drive with independent suspension and the early models had four-wheel steering although this was dispensed with when the car revealed a dangerous tendency to roll. An armoured roof was also fitted to the early models. The Daimler Scout Car served in the reconnaissance troops of armoured regiments, with armoured car regiments, and as a liaison vehicle on all major battlefronts where British and Commonwealth troops were engaged, and remained active long after the war. It was known universally as the Dingo, although the name actually belonged to a rival design submitted by Alvis. A total of 6626 were built. *Weight* 3.15 tons; *speed* 55mph (88kph); *armour* 30mm; *armament* 1 Bren light machine gun; *engine* Daimler 55hp; *crew* 2.

Dakar, British Attacks on, 1940
On 7 July 1940 a British force under Captain Onslow, consisting of the aircraft carrier HMS HERMES and two cruisers, arrived off the French West African naval base of Dakar and presented the authorities there with the same ultimatum which had been delivered at MERS-EL-KEBIR four days earlier, the object being to prevent the battleship RICHELIEU, then lying in

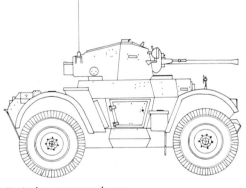

Daimler armoured car.

Dakar harbour, from falling into German hands. The ultimatum was rejected and at dawn the following day the *Richelieu* was seriously damaged by torpedo bombers.

It was then decided to mount a joint British/Free French operation aimed at the capture of Dakar. It was hoped this would result in France's African Empire joining DE GAULLE without the need for further hostilities. The operation, codenamed *Menace*, involved a naval force under Vice-Admiral CUNNINGHAM, consisting of two battleships, an aircraft carrier, five cruisers, sixteen destroyers and two sloops, plus several small Free French vessels; and a landing force, consisting of 4200 British and 2700 Free French troops, under the command of Major-General Irwin. Meanwhile Dakar, which remained loyal to the Vichy government, had been reinforced, and when the invasion fleet arrived off the base on 23 September 1940 Governor Boisson rejected all approaches from the Gaullist faction. The landings proved abortive and were cancelled. The British and French warships, the latter supported by coastal batteries, exchanged fire until the 25th. Several French submarines and a destroyer were sunk, but damage was also sustained by the British ships, notably the battleship *Resolution*, which was hit by a torpedo. Ironically, Cunningham, Irwin and De Gaulle decided that the operation should be abandoned, just as the Governor was preparing to surrender.

Daladier, Edouard (1884–1970)
A French Radical-Socialist politician, Daladier became Premier of France in April 1938. After signing the Munich Agreement in September 1938 he lost socialist support and relied more upon the right-wing element of his government. He declared war against Germany on 3 September 1939, proscribed the Communist Party shortly afterwards, and supported a madcap scheme to aid the Finns in the Winter War. His government fell in March 1940. He became Minister of War under his successor REYNAUD and continued to support General

GAMELIN. After the German invasion of France he fled to North Africa and attempted to organize resistance there but was arrested and returned to France. He was put on trial by the Vichy government charged with leading France into war while unprepared, but his forthright denials led to the abandonment of the trial. Imprisoned, he was deported to Germany in 1943 and interned in BUCHENWALD and DACHAU concentration camps, which he was fortunate to survive until released in April 1945.

Damascus, Syria, 1941

The objective of General Legentilhomme's Free French Division, Brigadier W. L. Lloyd's 5th Indian Brigade Group, including the Transjordan Frontier Force, joined by the 2/3rd Australian Infantry Battalion, during the campaign against the Vichy French forces in Syria. Bitter resistance was encountered during the Allied advance, particularly at Mezze, but on 21 June the city was evacuated by its garrison.

Danzig (Gdansk), Poland, 1939 and 1945

A free state and port on the Baltic lying within the POLISH CORRIDOR. The city, which contained a large German population dominated by the Nazi Party, was used by HITLER to generate tension between Germany and Poland during the immediate pre-war period, numerous incidents being deliberately provoked to demonstrate an alleged anti-German feeling among the Poles. Danzig was captured by ROKOSSOVSKY's 2nd Belorussian Front on 30 March 1945; 10,000 prisoners were taken and 45 submarines captured in the harbour.

DAR 10F (Bulgaria)

This light reconnaissance and dive-bomber was built by DAR, the Bulgarian State Aircraft Factory, in 1940–42. It was a low-wing monoplane with a 950hp Fiat radial engine and fixed undercarriage, and had a maximum speed of 295mph (475kph). Armament comprised two 20mm cannon and two machine guns in the wings and two flexible machine guns in the rear cockpit, plus 990lb (450kg) of bombs.

Dardo Class Destroyers (Italy)

Displacement 2100 tons; *dimensions* 315×32ft (96×9.7m); mean draught 10ft 3in (3.1m); *machinery* 2-shaft geared turbines producing shp 44,000; *speed* 38 knots; *armament* 4×4.7in; 8×20mm AA; 6×21in torpedo tubes; 2 depth charge throwers; equipped for minelaying; *complement* 185; *number in class* 4, launched 1930–32.

Darlan, Adm Jean François (1881–1942)

In 1939 Darlan was Commander-in-Chief of the French Navy. On the fall of France he assured CHURCHILL that the Fleet, the second most powerful in Europe, would not fall into German hands. However, he then accepted the post of Minister of the Navy in PÉTAIN's government and ordered the French Navy to North Africa, where it was subsequently bombarded by the British Navy at MERS-EL-KEBIR to ensure that it did not come under German control. In February 1941 he became Vice-Premier of France under Pétain and collaborated with the Germans in an endeavour to obtain better conditions for the French. These efforts met with no success. In early 1942 LAVAL returned to power and Darlan was sent as High Commissioner in North Africa. When the North African invasion took place, the US government recognized him as the head of the French Government, in direct conflict with the British recognition of DE GAULLE. This could have raised problems, but the matter was conveniently solved when Darlan was assassinated by a young French monarchist on Christmas Eve 1942.

Darnand, Adm Joseph (1897–1945)

After retiring from the navy in pre-war years, Darnand became an extreme right-wing politician, joining the Action Française party and the fascist *Cagoule*. After the 1940 armistice, he became one of PÉTAIN's most enthusiastic supporters and in 1941 founded the *Service d'Ordre Legionnaire*, a security police force operating in the Vichy zone. In 1942 this became the *Milice Française*, which, in cooperation with the German police and security forces, operated against the French resistance. He became an officer in the WAFFEN-SS, and was notorious as the first Vichy minister to take an oath of allegiance to HITLER and to wear a German uniform. After the liberation of France he fled to Germany and became a member of the Sigmaringen Government, a pseudo-government organized by the Germans in order to promote various ideas of using French ex-Milice against the Russians and as a pro-German "resistance" inside France. At the end of the war he was returned to France, tried, and executed by firing squad on 3 October 1945.

Dartboard

Dartboard was the codename given to a British radio countermeasure used to jam the German "Anne-Marie" forces radio station at Stuttgart in 1943. It had been discovered that this station broadcast music selected in accordance with a simple code – waltzes for Munich, jazz for Berlin and so on – to indicate to night fighters the areas under bomber attack in a manner which, it was hoped, would escape jamming. "Dartboard" dashed this hope.

Darwin, Northern Australia, 1942

The city and naval base sustained a major air attack by 135 Japanese aircraft on 19 February. The American destroyer *Peary* and five merchant vessels were sunk, extensive damage to the port facilities being aggravated by the explosion of a ship carrying depth charges. Casualties in the raid were 240 killed and 150 injured; the Japanese lost 15 aircraft. Further raids of lower intensity followed, but these declined after American fighter squadrons began arriving in the area on 17 March.

Daugavpils (Dvinsk), Latvia, 1941 and 1944

A city containing two important bridges across the Dvina, captured on 26 June 1941 by LVI Panzer Corps during the German Army Group North's advance on LENINGRAD. Liberated by 1st Baltic Front (Bagramyan) on 27 July 1944.

DD (Duplex Drive) Tanks

The concept of a swimming tank, kept afloat by a collapsible canvas screen attached to the hull and driven by a screw which drew its power from the vehicle's main engine, was pioneered by Mr Nicholas Straussler during the interwar years, the idea being that once the tank had reached dry land the screen would be lowered and the normal drive engaged, enabling it to perform as a normal gun tank. In June 1941 its feasibility was demonstrated using a TETRARCH light tank driven by a single screw. Following this three VALENTINE DDs were successfully evaluated and an order was placed for 625, the first batch being delivered in March 1943. These were used for training although a few were employed operationally during the final

American troops wade ashore from landing craft, Omaha Beach.

stages of the Italian campaign. DD trials were also carried out on the STUART but the ultimate choice devolved on the SHERMAN medium tank because of its superior firepower. The Sherman weighed almost twice as much as the Valentine and because of this twin screws were used in conjunction with a larger screen for extra buoyancy. An order for 573 Sherman DDs was placed, deliveries commencing early in 1944. At this point the US Army also became interested in the project and placed orders of its own so that by June 1944 there were sufficient Sherman DDs to equip five British, two Canadian and three American battalions. During the NORMANDY landings on 6 June 1944 sea conditions were worse than had ever been experienced in training. On some sectors the seas were so heavy that the DDs had to be landed directly from their beached LSTs, but elsewhere the tanks swam ashore to provide the assault infantry with immediate fire support, so fulfilling their purpose. The worst DD casualties occurred off OMAHA BEACH, where a battalion was launched 6000 yards out and 27 of its 31 tanks foundered. Sherman DDs were also used during the crossing of the RHINE in March 1945 and the final offensive in Italy. The war ended before they could be employed operationally in the Far East.

D-Day, France, 6 June 1944

The day on which Operation *Overlord*, the Allied invasion of NORMANDY, was launched. This was preceded by a month-long air offensive directed against road and rail communications in France, including the lower Seine

bridges, accompanied by a steady increase in Resistance activity. Simultaneously, an elaborate deception plan, codenamed FORTITUDE, succeeded in convincing HITLER that the Allied landings would be made in the Pas de Calais area, with the result that numerous reserves were retained under the Führer's personal control to meet this contingency. General

EISENHOWER, the Allied Supreme Commander, had appointed General Sir Bernard MONTGOMERY commander of the cross-Channel assault, which would be delivered by Lieutenant-General Omar BRADLEY's US 1st Army on the right and Lieutenant-General Sir Miles DEMPSEY's British 2nd Army on the left. In command of the naval aspects of this, the largest amphibious invasion in history, was Admiral Sir Bertram RAMSAY, who was responsible for co-ordinating a huge armada which included 1213 warships, including the bombardment force, 4126 landing ships and landing craft of various types, 736 ancillary vessels and 864 merchant vessels. In addition, there were two prefabricated MULBERRY harbours. The British and American tactical air forces were commanded by Air Marshal Sir Trafford LEIGH-MALLORY, these being joined by the heavy bombers of General Carl SPAATZ's Strategic Air Force for the period of the invasion. On the German side, the Commander-in-Chief West was Field-Marshal Gerd von RUNDSTEDT, a capable professional whose every decision required Hitler's approval. The invasion sector was manned on 6 June by three infantry divisions and one Panzer division of Colonel-General Friedrich Dollman's 7th

D-Day, June 1944. From left: Rear-Admiral Kirk, Lieutenant-General Bradley, Rear-Admiral Struble and Major-General Keen.

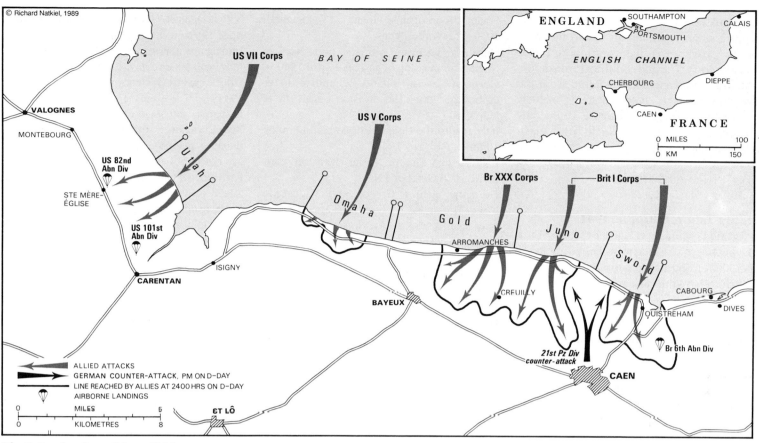

© Richard Natkiel, 1989

ALLIED ATTACKS
GERMAN COUNTER-ATTACK, PM ON D-DAY
LINE REACHED BY ALLIES AT 2400 HRS ON D-DAY
AIRBORNE LANDINGS

The D-Day landings, 6 June 1944.

Army, which formed part of Field-Marshal Erwin ROMMEL's Army Group B. The Luftwaffe's Luftflotte 3 had only 319 operational aircraft available on D-Day.

Shortly after midnight the US 82nd and 101st Airborne Divisions were dropped at the western flank of the selected beach-head areas to secure five causeways over flooded ground in the region of the Rivers Merderet and Douve; simultaneously, the British 6th Airborne Division dropped on the eastern flank and captured bridges over the Caen Canal and the River Orne. The seaborne landings commenced at half-tide, i.e. from 0630 onwards, when most of the German beach obstacles were visible. At UTAH BEACH, lying beyond the Vire estuary, the US 4th Division landed a mile south of its target beaches but advanced inland and by 1300 was in contact with the American paratroopers. At midnight the Utah beach-head was four miles wide and nine deep. Across the Vire the US 2nd Ranger Battalion captured the coast defence battery at Pointe du Hoe but at OMAHA BEACH, to the east, the US 1st and 29th Infantry Divisions were pinned down by unsubdued defences and by midnight had only penetrated 1.5 miles

(2.4km) inland, having sustained over 3000 casualties. Further east, the British Second Army's landings had the benefit of a more prolonged naval bombardment and the leading elements included 79th Armoured Division's teams of special purpose armoured vehicles, which had been designed specifically to overcome the defences of Hitler's so-called ATLANTIC WALL. The 50th (Northumbrian) Division landed on GOLD BEACH, capturing Arromanches, and by midnight had reached the outskirts of Bayeux, which fell the following day. The Canadian 3rd Division landed on JUNO BEACH and, despite congestion, struck inland to a depth of seven miles (11km). The British 3rd Division came ashore on SWORD BEACH and, with 6th Airborne Division, had advanced to within sight of CAEN by midnight. The German response to the landings was hindered by a complicated command structure, poor communications and the belief that they were only a feint designed to draw attention away from the Pas de Calais; consequently, Hitler declined to commit his reserve armoured divisions until it was too late. During the afternoon the 21st Panzer Division, which was already present in the

battle area, launched a counter-attack from Caen into the area between the Juno and Sword beach-heads but was halted and driven back. Other factors which limited the German reaction was the Allies' complete air superiority, which not only dominated the battlefield but also interdicted the movement of reinforcements into the area, and the tremendous weight of naval gunfire available to support the landings. By midnight 57,500 American and 75,000 British and Canadian troops and their equipment were ashore and the process of linking the beach-heads had begun. Allied casualties amounted to 2500 killed and approximately 8500 wounded and missing; given the strength of the defences and the adverse sea conditions prevailing, these figures were remarkably low. The Allied air forces had flown some 14,000 sorties in which 127 aircraft were lost and 63 damaged. The German loss is unknown. See *Victory in the West Vol 1 – The Battle of Normandy* by Major L. F. Ellis and others (HMSO); *The Struggle for Europe* by Chester Wilmot (Collins); *Victory in Normandy* by Major-General David Belchem (Chatto and Windus); and *Airborne Operations* (Salamander).

Deacon (UK)

6-pdr anti-tank gun and gunshield mounted on the back of a lightly armoured AEC Matador lorry. The gun could not be dismounted and the arrangement suffered from the principal faults of *portée* systems, namely vulnerability and the fact that it could only engage to the rear. The vehicle had a maximum speed of 19mph (30kph). 175 were sent to North Africa in 1942 and were withdrawn from service in May 1943.

Debra Tabor, Ethiopia, 1941

A fortified mountain village east of Lake Tana. Having been subjected to sustained air attack, the 5000-strong Italian garrison surrendered to British-led Ethiopian groups in June.

Declarations of War

Japan against China: None. The Sino-Japanese War began with the Marco Polo Bridge Incident, 7 July 1937.

Germany against Poland: None. Poland invaded 1 September 1939.

United Kingdom, France, Australia and New Zealand against Germany: 3 September 1939.

South Africa against Germany: 6 September 1939.

Canada against Germany: 10 September 1939.

Soviet Union against Poland: None. The occupation of eastern Poland by Soviet troops began on 17 September 1939.

Soviet Union against Finland: 13 November 1939 (The Winter War).

Germany against Denmark and Norway: None. The invasion began on 9 April 1940.

Germany against Holland, Belgium and Luxembourg: None. The invasion began on 10 May 1940.

Italy against the United Kingdom and France: 10 June 1940.

Italy against Greece: None. Invasion commenced 28 October 1940.

Germany against Greece and Yugoslavia: None. The invasion began on 6 April 1941.

Italy against Yugoslavia: None. The invasion began on 6 April 1941.

Germany against Soviet Union: None. The invasion began on 22 June 1941.

Italy and Romania against Soviet Union: 22 June 1941.

Hungary and Slovakia against Soviet Union: 23 June 1941.

Finland against Soviet Union: 26 June 1941.

United Kingdom and Soviet Union against Iran: None. The occupation began on 25 August 1941.

United Kingdom against Finland, Hungary and Romania: 5 December 1941.

Japan against the United Kingdom and the United States: 7 December 1941.

United States against Germany and Italy: 11 December 1941.

Brazil against Germany and Italy: 22 August 1942.

Bolivia against Germany, Italy and Japan: 7 April 1943.

Iran against Germany: 9 September 1943.

Italy against Germany: 13 October 1943.

Liberia against Germany and Japan: 25 January 1944.

Romania against Germany: 25 August 1944.

Bulgaria against Germany: 8 September 1944.

Ecuador against Germany and Japan: 2 February 1945.

Peru against Germany and Japan: 13 February 1945.

Chile against Japan: 14 February 1945.

Venezuela against Germany and Japan: 16 February 1945.

Turkey and Uruguay against Germany and Japan: 23 February 1945.

Egypt against Germany and Japan: 24 February 1945.

Syria against Germany and Japan: 26 February 1945.

Lebanon against Germany and Japan: 27 February 1945.

Saudi Arabia against Germany and Japan: 1 March 1945.

Iran against Japan: 1 March 1945.

Finland against Germany: 4 March 1945 but a state of war declared to have existed from 15 September 1944.

Argentina against Germany and Japan: 27 March 1945.

Brazil against Japan: 6 June 1945.

Soviet Union against Japan: 8 August 1945.

Mediterranean war zone.

General de Gaulle (right), 5th Army Front.

De Gaulle, Gen Charles André Joseph Marie (1890–1970)

A military theorist of limited attainments, De Gaulle assumed command of the Free French movement after the collapse of France in 1940. He became Prime Minister of France 1944–46 and President of the Fifth Republic 1958–68. De Gaulle was commissioned from St Cyr in 1913 into the 33rd Infantry Regiment, was wounded at Verdun in 1916, and became a prisoner of war until the Armistice. He then instructed at St Cyr, attended l'Ecole Supérieure de Guerre and graduated in 1924 to a staff post with Marshal PÉTAIN. Thereafter he held a number of staff positions and argued unsuccessfully for various theories of mobile warfare instead of reliance upon the MAGINOT LINE. Commanding a tank brigade in 1939, he was given command of the half-formed 4th Armoured Division in May 1940. Though this formation was made up of scattered elements and lacked both air support and fuel, by resolute leadership De Gaulle managed to make attacks at Laon and Abbeville which delayed the German advance for a short time. On 6 June he was summoned to Paris and appointed Under-Secretary of State for War and National Defence in Paul REYNAUD's short-lived government. In this capacity he visited London to confer with CHURCHILL, then returned to France where he proposed a retreat towards Brittany and a somewhat imaginative last-ditch stand. On 16 June Reynaud resigned, and De Gaulle, in danger of arrest by General Weygand for his political

views, flew to Britain. On 18 June he made his historic broadcast, calling on the people of France to continue the fight against Germany and join him, making himself head of the Free French movement. For this he was cashiered by Weygand, and in August he was condemned to death *in absentia* by a French military court. For the remainder of the war, though nominally the Commander-in-Chief of the Free French Army, he was more concerned with obtaining political advantages; a proud and exceedingly prickly man, he was obsessed with maintaining the position and prestige of France as a great power. He was always suspicious of British motives, being convinced that Britain was intent upon usurping power in SYRIA and the LEBANON. When North Africa was invaded he was incensed to find that the Americans refused to allow Free French troops to take part in the operation, and the American choice of General GIRAUD as their candidate for leadership of the French was productive of a long and bitter wrangle. He was also not informed of the date of the invasion of France, nor was he invited to the major conferences at YALTA and POTSDAM. He returned to France eight days after the Allied invasion, and on 10 September 1944 set up a provisional government, resigning in January 1946.

Degenkolb, Direktor Gerhard

Degenkolb was a director of the Demag Heavy Engineering Works before the war, and in 1940 was appointed to head the Locomotives Special Committee, charged with overhauling locomotive production and placing it on a war footing. This he did with ruthless energy and great success. In January 1943 he was made head of the A-4 Production Committee, to apply some drive to the then ill-conceived manufacturing programme for ballistic missiles. He made himself thoroughly disliked by the scientists but ensured that the weapon entered production as a viable military device.

Degtyarev Machine Guns

A series of machine guns developed for use by the Soviet Army by Vasilly Degtyarev (1880–1959) who left school at the age of 11, worked in Tula Arsenal, and eventually became a major-general, Director of Technical Sciences and Deputy of the Supreme Soviet. He began designing machine guns in 1921 and developed the DP (Degtyarova Pekhotny) light gun for infantry use and the DT (Degtyarova

Tankovii) for tank use. Introduced in 1928 these 7.62mm weapons became the standard guns of the army and were produced in huge quantities. They were simple, reliable and robust, being gas-operated and loaded from a drum magazine above the gun. Degtyarev then produced the PPD (Pistolet Pulemyot Degtyarova) submachine gun in 1934, a simple blowback weapon using a 71-round drum magazine, and this was produced in large numbers until 1941, when it was gradually replaced by simpler designs.

De Guingand, Maj Gen Sir Francis (1900–79)

De Guingand was appointed Military Assistant to the Secretary of State for War, Hore-Belisha. After the latter's resignation, he went into intelligence for a time and in 1942 was Director of Military Intelligence, Middle East. Here he caught the eye of MONTGOMERY who appointed him his Chief of Staff, a post which he held until the war's end. An excellent staff officer, he was not only good at the military planning aspects of his job but also had a gift for diplomacy which was invaluable in dealing with the various Allied headquarters and senior officers which impinged upon Montgomery's operations.

De Havilland Aircraft (UK)

De Havilland Dominie This was a militarized version of the pre-war Dragon Rapide biplane airliner, and numbers were in service with the RAF in 1939. It was used as a trainer for radio and navigation aircrew and also as a general passenger transport and communications machine. *Span* 48ft (14.6m); *engines* 2 200hp in-line; *speed* 157mph (252kph).

De Havilland Tiger Moth One of the most famous training aircraft in the world, the Tiger Moth entered RAF service in 1932, over 5000 being acquired before the war ended. Another 3000 were built overseas for the Commonwealth Air Training Scheme, and some were used by the USAAF as the PT-24. Over 400 were also built as radio-controlled target planes for anti-aircraft gunnery training, known as the Queen Bee. *Span* 29.3ft (8.9m); *crew* 2; *engine* 1 130hp in-line; *speed* 110mph (177kph).

De Havilland Mosquito The De Havilland company conceived this machine in 1938 as a high-speed unarmed day bomber, capable of out-running any fighter opposition, but it was

De Havilland Mosquitos of RAF Coastal Command attacking U-boats.

not until early 1940 that the RAF placed an order. The prototype flew late in 1940 and deliveries commenced in mid-1941. The design was varied so that photographic reconnaissance, bombing, fighter and ground attack machines were eventually produced. The principal novelty about the Mosquito was its wooden construction, aimed at evading the scarcity of light alloy. It was particularly successful as a light precision bomber and as a RADAR-equipped night fighter. Over 7700 were built, 6710 of them during the war. *Span* 54ft (16.5m); *engines* 2 1635hp in-line; *crew* 2; *armament* (fighter) 4 20mm cannon, (bomber) 4400lb (2000kg) of bombs; *speed* 408mph (656kph).

Deir el Shein, Egypt, 1942

A depression at the western end of RUWEISAT RIDGE held on 1 July 1942 by 18th Indian Infantry Brigade and an *ad hoc* artillery group, supported by nine patched-up Matilda tanks. This force succeeded in delaying the eastwards advance of 15th and 21st Panzer Divisions throughout the day, knocking out 18 of their 55 tanks, although the position was overrun during the evening. The engagement marked the beginning of the First Battle of ALAMEIN and blunted the spearhead of ROMMEL's drive into Egypt. See *Alamein* by C. E. Lucas Phillips (Heinemann).

De Lattre de Tassigny, Gen Jean (1889–1952)

De Lattre de Tassigny was commissioned into the French cavalry before World War I and in 1914 was severely wounded in a mounted duel with a German Lancer. He recovered and

remained in the Army, and by 1939 was a General and Chief of Staff of the French 5th Army. He relinquished this post to command the 14th Division during the German invasion of 1940. A non-political general, he declared his loyalty to the Army after the French capitulation and was sent by the Vichy government to Tunisia. Here he expressed some pro-Allied sympathies and was recalled to France and was later sentenced to ten years' imprisonment for his objection to the German occupation of Vichy France. He escaped in 1943 and reached England, where he placed himself under DE GAULLE's command and subsequently led the 1st French Army in North Africa and later during the liberation of France. He signed the German surrender on behalf of France in Berlin on 9 May 1945. After the war he became the first commander of NATO Land Forces, Europe, in 1948 and was Commander-in-Chief in Indo-China, 1950–52.

De Lisle Carbine

A British special forces weapon, the De Lisle CARBINE was basically a Lee-Enfield rifle action chambered for the .45 Colt Automatic Pistol cartridge with an integral silencer of high efficiency. The weapon was used only by Commando and similar forces, and was probably the most silent of all wartime silenced weapons. Due to its size it was effective at quite long ranges and was extremely accurate. Two versions were made, one with a conventional wooden stock, and one with a folding metal stock.

Demon

British evacuation from Greece, April 1941.

Dempsey, Lt Gen Sir Miles (1896–1969)

Dempsey was a General in the British Army in 1939 and commanded the 13th Infantry Brigade in France, leading them out through Dunkirk. In June 1941 he was given command of an Armoured Division, and in December 1942 became acting commander of XIII Corps under MONTGOMERY. A skilled and unassuming leader, Dempsey continued to command XIII Corps in SICILY and Italy and then returned to England to take command of 2nd British Army in the invasion of Europe. After the German surrender he was appointed Commander-in-Chief Allied Forces South-East Asia, a post he held until the Japanese surrender.

Demyansk, Soviet Union, 1942

During the Soviet counteroffensive of January–February 1942 the 100,000 men of the German II Corps (16th Army) were encircled by North-West Front in a pocket centred on Demyansk, south of Lake ILMEN. Until relieved by a counter-attack from Staraya Russya on 19 May they were supplied and reinforced by the Luftwaffe, which flew in 64,844 tons of supplies and 30,500 men, extensive use being made of cargo gliders. In addition, 25,400 casualties were flown out, the total cost of the operation being 265 aircraft. The first major airlift in history, this led GÖRING to overestimate the Luftwaffe's capacity to sustain similar operations in radically different circumstances, notably at STALINGRAD.

Denmark, 1940–45

Having been advised that it would be necessary for the Luftwaffe to use Danish airfields to support the invasion in NORWAY, HITLER decided that Denmark should be occupied simultaneously. The German plan involved two motorized brigade groups crossing the frontier on 9 April and driving up the Jutland peninsula to the Aalborg airfields, which had already been secured by parachute and airlanding operations, as had the vital bridges between the islands; at Copenhagen, the old battleship *Schleswig-Holstein* was to force the harbour entrance and land an infantry battalion to take over the capital. Some Danish troops near the border engaged the invaders but King Christian recognized that the position was hopeless and ordered resistance to cease. The king remained in Denmark, personally opposing the Germans' anti-Semitic pressure, and many Danish Jews escaped to

German troops march into Aalborg, Denmark, 1940.

Sweden. Opposition to the occupation grew into a Resistance movement which eventually numbered 20,000. The German surrender to Field-Marshal MONTGOMERY on 4 May 1945 included Denmark in its terms and the Resistance took over pending the arrival of British troops from north-west Germany and the Danish Brigade which had been training secretly in Sweden. Possible Soviet designs on Denmark were forestalled by the rapid despatch of British troops to Wismar and LÜBECK on the Baltic.

Denmark Strait, Battle of

See BISMARCK, KMS and HOOD, HMS.

Depth Charge

Developed during World War I and first used in July 1916, the depth charge was an anti-submarine warfare weapon consisting of a drum casing containing a heavy explosive charge which could be fuzed to detonate at a pre-determined depth. It was rolled in succession from racks at the stern of the hunting vessel, later supplemented by throwers which dropped a pattern around the target area. If close enough, the concussion waves generated by the multiple explosions were sufficient to damage the submarine's hull and force it to surface. The principal drawback of the stern-release system was that when passing over the target the hunting vessel lost ASDIC contact and was often unable to regain it because of disturbed water, but this difficulty was resolved by the development of the forward-firing HEDGEHOG and SQUID systems. Depth charges were also dropped by aircraft engaged on anti-submarine patrol, in a similar manner to dropping bombs.

Derna, Libya, 1941

A small port in Cyrenaica, captured by 6th Australian Division on 29 January following a stand by the Italian 60th Division. See BEDA FOMM.

Desert Rats

Term frequently and incorrectly applied to all members of the British 8th Army who fought in North Africa. The original Desert Rats were members of the 7th Armoured Division, which adopted the jerboa as its divisional symbol from May 1940 onwards.

Dessie, Ethiopia, 1941

A town 250 miles (402km) north of ADDIS ABABA protected by strong defensive positions in the mountains at Kombolchia, a few miles to the south. These were successfully outflanked and attacked by Brigadier Dan Pienaar's 1st South African Brigade Group on 22 April, 8000 prisoners being taken. The town was abandoned by the Italians.

Deutschland Class (Old) Pre-Dreadnought Battleships (Ger)

The two survivors of this class, *Schlesien* and *Schleswig-Holstein*, were both veterans of Jutland, converted to Cadet Training Ships in 1936. In 1939 they bombarded Polish shore installations, then served throughout the war in the Baltic with the Training Squadron, latterly supporting land operations with their gunfire. *Schlesien* was mined and sunk in shallow water off Swinemunde in May 1945; *Schleswig-Holstein* sustained bomb damage and was scuttled in shallow water at Gdynia on 21 March 1945. *Displacement* 12,100 tons; *dimensions* 418×73ft (127.6×22.2m); mean draught 27ft (8.2m); *machinery* 3-shaft triple expansion coal/oil fired engines ihp 17,000; *speed* 18 knots; *protection* main belt 9.75in; deck 3in; turrets 11in; *armament* (1944) 4×11in (2×2); 6×4.1in AA; 10×40mm AA; 22×20mm AA; *complement* 743; *number in class* 2 (originally 5), both launched 1906.

Deutschland Class Pocket Battleships

After the loss of the ADMIRAL GRAF SPEE the class was redesignated Heavy Cruisers and *Deutschland* was re-named LÜTZOW. Secondary armament varied during the war. *Displacement* 11,700 tons; *dimensions* 616ft×67ft 6in (187×20.6m); mean draught 19ft (5m); *machinery* 8 diesels delivering 54,000 shp to 2 shafts; *speed* 26 knots; *protection* main belt 3.1in; deck 1.8in; turrets 3.3–5.5in; barbettes 3.9in; *armament* 6×11in (2×3); 8×150mm (8×1) AA; 6×88mm (3×2) AA; 8×37mm (4×2) AA; 10×20mm (10×1) AA; 8×533mm (2×4) torpedo tubes; *aircraft* 2 floatplanes; *complement* 1150; *number in class* 3, launched 1931–34.

Deuxième Bureau

The principal French military intelligence agency. In 1935 the Bureau informed the French High Command (GQG) that the Ger-

Deutschland class pocket battleship.

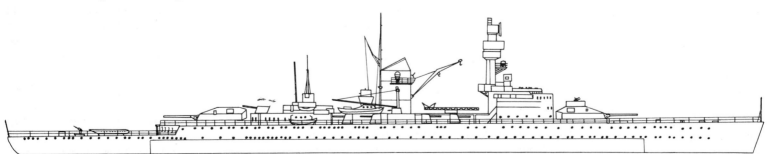

man Army had formed its first Panzer divisions and accurately forecast their likely role. Three years later it warned that the Wehrmacht possessed a technical superiority over the French armed forces and in 1939 suggested that any German offensive would be directed through Belgium, although it correctly interpreted the lessons of the campaign in Poland and the nature of the BLITZKRIEG technique. By May 1940 it was aware of the German order of battle in the West, although its estimate of the German tank strength as being in excess of 7000 was wildly inflated. The correct figure was 2439, against which the French Army alone was able to field some 3000 tanks; furthermore, the majority of the German tanks were in the light class and no match for the better-armed and armoured French vehicles. The Bureau's principal failure lay in its inability to identify the principal thrust line of the German offensive before 17 May, when an intercepted radio message confirmed that this was directed at the Channel coast rather than Paris. Even this piece of vital intelligence was not relayed promptly to GAMELIN at GQG. See FRANCE, BELGIUM, HOLLAND 1940.

Devers, Gen Jacob (1887–)

The Commander of US Armed Forces who in 1943 was appointed to command US Forces in Britain. In view of his lack of combat experience, he was made second-in-command to General Maitland WILSON of the British Army in the Mediterranean Theatre. Devers was given command of the DRAGOON landings in southern France on 15 August 1944. His force met with little resistance and by September had cut through France to join up with the other Allied armies, whereupon he was given command of 6th Army Group comprising the 7th US and 1st French Armies. This force performed well and finished the war in Bavaria.

Dewoitine Aircraft

Dewoitine D500 Designed in 1930 the D500 was the most modern-looking fighter of its day and was innovative in using light alloy with stressed skin wings in its construction. A low-wing monoplane with open cockpit, it was also notable for being the first fighter to fire a cannon through the hub of the propeller, the gun lying between the engine cylinder banks. As well as being adopted by the French Air Force the D500 was widely exported, but

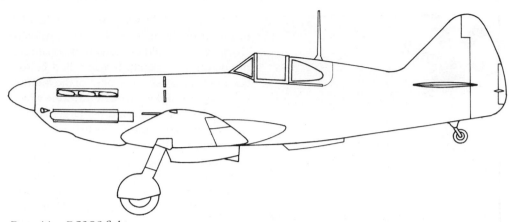

Dewoitine D520S fighter.

by the outbreak of war it was obsolescent. *Span* 39.6ft (12m); *engine* 1 860hp in-line; *armament* 1 20mm cannon, 4 machine guns; *speed* 250mph (402kph).

Dewoitine D520 The best French fighter in 1940, the D520 first flew in 1938 and production began just as war broke out; rather surprisingly, it reached ten aircraft per day by June 1940. It performed exceptionally well in the 1940 battles, and after 1940 was put back into production by the Vichy government. In 1942 the Germans seized over 400, supplying them to Italy, Romania and Bulgaria. *Span* 33.5ft (10.2m); *engine* 910hp in-line; *armament* 1 20mm cannon, 4 machine guns; *speed* 330mph (531kph).

DFS 230 Glider

This was the first glider used to transport airborne troops into action, and was first employed in Belgium in May 1940 during the attack on the fort of EBEN EMAEL. It could be towed by a variety of aircraft, though the Ju 52 and He 111 were usually used, and could carry 3086lb (1400kg) or eight fully-equipped soldiers. It was fitted with wheels for takeoff, which were then jettisoned, and landed on two skids beneath the forepart of the fuselage. It had a wingspan of 68.5ft (20.9m).

Dido Class Cruisers (UK)

Displacement Group 1 5600 tons; *Group 2* 5950 tons; *dimensions* 512ft×50ft 6in (156× 15.4m); *mean draught Group 1* 14ft (4.2m); *Group 2* 14ft 9in (4.47m); *machinery* 4-shaft geared turbines producing shp 62,000; *speed* 33 knots; *protection* main belt 3in; deck 2in; turrets 2in; *armament Group 1* 10×5.25in DP (5×2); 8×2-pdr AA (2×4); 8×0.5in AA (2×4); 6×21in torpedo tubes (2×3); *Group 2* 8×5.25in DP (4×2); 12×2-pdr AA (3×4);

12×20mm AA (6×2); 6×21in torpedo tubes; *complement Group 1* 530; *Group 2* 535; *number in class Group 1* 11, launched 1939–41; *Group 2* 5, launched 1942.

Diego Suarez, Madagascar, 1942

On 5 May the British Force 121, commanded by Major-General Robert Sturges and consisting of a commando unit and two infantry brigade groups, made amphibious landings and, after overcoming stiff resistance from the Vichy French garrison, captured the port and naval base. The British sustained 109 killed and 284 wounded, the French 200 killed and 500 wounded. This was the first major Allied amphibious operation of the war. See also MADAGASCAR and MIDGET SUBMARINES, JAPANESE.

Dieppe, Raid on, August 1942

Codenamed "JUBILEE", this raid on the German-held resort and seaport on a heavily defended sector of the French coast was mounted primarily to soothe Soviet complaints about the lack of a "Second Front" in Europe. It was also intended to provide battle experience for the troops involved, 5000 Canadians of the 2nd Canadian Division and 1000 men of Nos. 3 and 4 Commandos. The raiding force crossed the Channel on the night of 18/19 August. Landings had been planned on eight beaches with the aim of destroying heavy coastal batteries and other installations before withdrawal. The only success was achieved on the western flank, by No. 4 Commando, which silenced the "Hess" battery. On the left flank and in the centre the Germans, who were on full alert, directed heavy fire into the landing craft and the few tanks which struggled up the shingly beach. The decision to withdraw was made at 0900, but another three hours of fighting followed

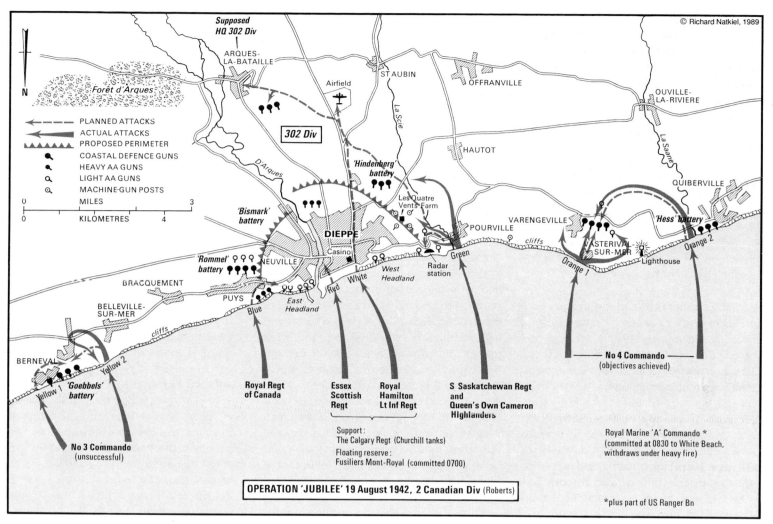

© Richard Natkiel, 1989

OPERATION 'JUBILEE' 19 August 1942, 2 Canadian Div (Roberts)

*plus part of US Ranger Bn

The Dieppe Raid, 19 August 1942.

Canadian POWs at Dieppe, 1942.

before the last survivors were taken off. The Canadians lost 215 officers and 3,164 men; the Commandos lost 24 officers and 223 men; German losses were 345 killed and 268 wounded. All the equipment and vehicles landed were lost, including 28 tanks. The Royal Navy lost 81 officers, 469 men and 34 ships, including the destroyer *Berkeley*, which was torpedoed to prevent her falling into enemy hands. In the battle for air superiority over the beach-head the RAF lost 107 aircraft and the Luftwaffe an approximately equal number. This "reconnaissance in force" had been a disastrous operation and a salutary warning of the dangers of a premature invasion of northern Europe. However, in spite of its failure it taught the Allies many valuable lessons in organization and tactics which were put to good use in Operation OVERLORD.

Dietl, Col Gen Eduard (1890–1944)

Dietl was an early supporter of HITLER, joining the fledgling Nazi Party in 1920 and taking part in the failed Munich putsch of November 1923. In 1939 he was a Major-General in command of 3rd Mountain Division, which he led in the attack on POLAND and in the NORWAY campaign. In the latter he played a crucial role in the capture of NARVIK. He was promoted Lieutenant-General, and in Operation BAR-

General "Sepp" Dietrich of the SS.

BAROSSA led a mountain corps in an unsuccessful attempt to seize the Russian port of MURMANSK. In January 1942 Dietl was promoted Colonel-General, commanding all German forces in Lapland. He died in an air crash in the summer of 1944.

Dietrich, Gen Sepp (1892–1976)

Dietrich enlisted in 1911 and rose to the rank of Sergeant-Major during World War I. By 1918 he was in a tank battalion, and in postwar years he became involved with the early Nazi party. He was given command of HITLER'S bodyguard in 1928 which, after the purge of the SA in June 1934, became the "Leibstandarte SS Adolf Hitler". He continued to command this formation until it became the foremost unit of the WAFFEN SS, fighting as a regiment in Poland, as a Combat Group in France in 1940, as a Brigade in August 1940 and as a Division for the invasion of Greece in 1941. It also fought in Russia in 1941–42, and again in 1943–44, and then returned to Belgium. Dietrich led the division against the British and US forces in NORMANDY in 1944 and was promoted to Colonel-General and awarded the Diamonds to the Knight's Cross. Appointed to command the 6th SS Panzer Army, he led them against the US Army in the Ardennes in December 1944. After being withdrawn, he then took this army to Hungary to recapture BUDAPEST in March 1945, but failed and retreated into Austria. After doing his best to ensure that his men would not fall into Russian hands, Dietrich surrendered to the US Army in May 1945. He was tried as a war criminal by the Americans and in 1946 sentenced to 25 years imprisonment for the murder of US prisoners-of-war at Malmédy. He was released in 1955. In 1957 he was sentenced to 18 months imprisonment by a German civil court for his part in the suppression of the SA in 1934.

Dietrich was no military theorist, and had little professional training to qualify him for his high rank, but he had an instinctive grasp of tactics and an excellent understanding of man-management and leadership which ensured a high state of efficiency and loyalty among his troops.

Dill, FM Sir John (1881–1944)

Dill served as Director of Military Operations and as Commandant of the Staff College prior to 1939. On the outbreak of war he commanded I Corps in France, and in April 1940 returned to England to become Vice-Chief of the Imperial General Staff (VCIGS), succeeding General IRONSIDE as CIGS in the following month. Dill adhered to a policy of caution, which did not endear him to CHURCHILL, and in December 1941, suffering from overwork and strain, he was replaced in his post by General BROOKE. He then accompanied Churchill to Washington and remained there as Head of the British Joint Services Mission. In this post he was a considerable asset, his tact and diplomacy ensuring the best possible co-operation between the two countries. On his death in 1944, the US Army arranged for his burial in Arlington National Cemetery.

Dimapur, India, 1944

A railhead and supply base in Manipur from which an all-weather road extended to KOHIMA and IMPHAL.

Dinant, Belgium, 1940 and 1944

A town in the area of which HOTH'S XV Panzer Corps secured crossings of the Meuse in May 1940. On 24 and 25 December 1944 the spearhead of the 5th Panzer Army was defeated by the British 11th Armoured and US 2nd Armored Divisions to the east of the town. See FRANCE, BELGIUM, HOLLAND, 1940 and BULGE, BATTLE OF THE.

Diredawa, Ethiopia, 1941

An administrative centre with a large Italian civilian population which suffered severely at the hands of the Ethiopians when the garrison withdrew. When the 1st South African Brigade Group reached the town on 29 March, it took 36 hours to restore order.

Displaced Persons

A term which, strictly interpreted, defined those persons who by virtue of territorial changes due to the war had become stateless; for example, those inhabitants of the area of Eastern Poland which had come under Soviet domination and who had no desire to become Soviet citizens. However, the term also came to embrace those people who had been forcibly uprooted from their homes by the Ger-

Ethnic Germans expelled from the Sudetenland by the Czechs, 1945.

mans, for slave labour and other purposes, and transported elsewhere and who, at the end of the war, had no homes to which to return. Many fended for themselves, established new identities and started new lives, but the majority had to be accommodated in special camps in Europe, under the control of various United Nations relief organizations, in which they could be fed and housed and from which they were eventually able to find new homes and occupations.

Diver
British countermeasures against V1 flying bomb attack, 1944.

Division
The organization of the infantry division varied slightly between armies and was subject to restructuring as the war progressed, but a representative order of battle might consist of divisional headquarters, three infantry regiments (brigades in British and Commonwealth armies), a reconnaissance battalion, three or more field artillery battalions, an anti-tank battalion, a light anti-aircraft battalion, an engineer battalion, a signals battalion and divisional service units. Airborne divisions had a smaller establishment which might consist of divisional headquarters, two parachute regiments (brigades), one air-landing regiment (brigade), a reconnaissance battalion, two or more air-landing anti-tank batteries, one or more air-landing light anti-aircraft batteries, two or more parachute engineer companies, one parachute signals company and divisional service units, although this varied considerably. A division was normally commanded by a Major-General. See also ARMOURED DIVISIONS.

DNC Director of Naval Construction (UK).

Dniepr River, 1943
In September 1943 Field-Marshal Erich von MANSTEIN obtained HITLER's reluctant permission for Army Group South to withdraw behind the Dniepr before its front collapsed under sustained Soviet pressure. The Dniepr, Europe's third longest river with a width varying between 400 yards and two miles, was promptly declared by Hitler to be Germany's Eastern Rampart, civilian labour being conscripted to construct defence lines along its length while the Germans converged on selected crossing points at KIEV, Kanev,

Soviet troops and captured German equipment, Battle of the Dniepr.

Cherkassy, Kremenchug and Dniepopetrovsk, leaving behind them a deliberately devastated zone in which it was hoped – vainly, in the event – that the Russians would be unable to operate for a period. At this period the approximate strengths of the contending armies in the Ukraine were: Germans – 1,240,000 men, 2100 tanks, 12,600 guns and 2000 aircraft; Soviets – 2,633,000 men, 2400 tanks, 51,200 guns and 2850 aircraft.

The German withdrawal was followed up energetically by ROKOSSOVSKY's Central Front, VATUTIN's Voronezh Front, KONEV's Steppe Front, MALINOVSKY's South-West Front and TOLBUKHIN's South Front, these being redesignated Belorussian Front and 1st, 2nd, 3rd and 4th Ukrainian Fronts respectively on 20 October. The Germans could not be strong everywhere and the Russians were soon able to seize and expand bridgeheads from which their advance continued, Kiev falling on 6 November and ZHITOMIR on the 12th. During the river-crossing operations a Soviet airborne drop was made by three parachute brigades near Kanev on 24 September; this ended disastrously with only 2300 of the 7000 paratroopers surviving to join local partisan groups. Elsewhere, however, although German tactical skill inflicted severe losses, the Russians had overrun the Eastern Rampart by the end of the year.

Dodecanese Islands, 1943, 1944
An Italian-owned group of islands lying off the south-western coast of Turkey. See AEGEAN THEATRE and KOS.

Dodge Vehicles (USA)
The half-ton 4×4 Dodge Weapons Carrier T207 was introduced in 1941 and remained in general use throughout the US Army for many years. An improved version, the T215, was developed as an ambulance, command and communications vehicle. The most notable derivative was the GUN MOTOR CARRIAGE M6, which was armed with a 37mm anti-tank gun mounted in the manner of the British *portées*. Some 82,000 half-ton vehicles were built, a number being supplied to the United Kingdom and the Soviet Union under the Lend-Lease programme. The T207 and T215 had Dodge six-cylinder petrol engines developing respectively 85 and 92bhp.

The three-quarter ton 4×4 Dodge Command and Reconnaissance Vehicle T214 was introduced in 1942 and also had a long service career. A number of versions were produced, including command, reconnaissance and communications vehicles, ambulance and light maintenance. The vehicle was powered by a Dodge six-cylinder petrol engine producing 92bhp. It was occasionally referred to as The Beep, i.e. Big Jeep.

Dologorodoc, Fort, Eritrea, 1941

Situated on a 2000ft (609m) peak of the same name dominating the road to KEREN, the fort was captured by 9th Indian Infantry Brigade (5th Indian Division) on 15/16 March and held against repeated counter-attacks.

Domino

British jamming device used against the German Y-GERÄT navigation beam. A receiver detected the ranging signal emitted by the bomber's receiver and this was then re-broadcast on the frequency of the German ground station, giving a spurious range value.

Don, River, Soviet Union, 1942

Crossed by the German Army Groups A and B during the offensive directed at the CAUCASUS and STALINGRAD. During Operation URANUS, the Soviet South-West Front, commanded by VATUTIN, attacked on 19 November from bridgeheads which had been retained on the west bank, routing the Romanian 3rd Army, and swung south to close in on the rear of the German 6th Army at Stalingrad, severing its communications by capturing the vital Don bridge at Kalach on 23 November. As the Soviet offensive extended along the front, both German army groups were compelled to withdraw well to the west of the Don.

Donau-60

The German infra-red system for controlling coastal gunfire. Four thermal sensors were deployed along the coastline at intervals of 2–3 miles (3–5km), each being a parabolic mirror with a bolometer at the focal point. Each could detect and give a bearing to a ship target, locating them by the heat from funnels or other parts of the superstructure. These bearings were transmitted to a central fire control station which determined the position of the target and deduced firing data for artillery. Made by Zeiss, between 20 and 30 per month were manufactured during 1939–40 and were installed at various points on the Channel coast.

Donbaik, Burma, 1943–44

Located ten miles (16km) north of Foul Point at the tip of the Mayu Peninsula and the scene of abortive and costly attacks January–March 1943 by 14th Indian Division during the first ARAKAN offensive. During the third Arakan offensive Donbaik fell to 25th Indian Division on 23 December 1944.

Donbass, Soviet Union, 1943

A coal-mining and industrial region of the south-eastern Ukraine the retention of which HITLER claimed was vital to Germany's interest. For sound military reasons von MANSTEIN wished to abandon the area and in mid-September convinced Hitler of the necessity of doing so, thus enabling his overstretched Army Group South to withdraw to the DNIEPR.

Dönitz, Adm Karl (1891–1984)

Commissioned into the German Navy in 1910, Dönitz was Flag Officer U-boats from 1939 to 30 January 1943, when he replaced Admiral RAEDER as Commander-in-Chief of the German Navy. At this point in the war the U-boats, operating in "wolf packs", were enjoying their greatest success; in January–March 1943, 108 Allied merchantmen were sunk at a cost of only 15 U-boats. New technology, improved escort vessels and increased air support turned the tide against the U-boats in the summer of 1943 and thereafter the German Navy, while remaining in being, was never a serious threat. Dönitz spent the remainder of the war seeking technical solutions to allied superiority. He retained the respect of HITLER, who had lost faith in the Army and the Luftwaffe, which in contrast to the Navy had suffered crippling losses during the last two years of the war. Convinced that he had been betrayed by his generals, the Führer chose Dönitz as his successor on 29 April 1945. After

Hitler's suicide, Dönitz negotiated the capitulation of the German forces in the West. He was arrested on 23 May, and at the NUREMBERG TRIALS sentenced to ten years' imprisonment.

Donnerschlag (Thunderclap)

Planned breakout of German 6th Army from STALINGRAD, 1942.

Donovan, Gen William (1883–1959)

"Wild Bill" Donovan was a lawyer who, acquainted with the US Secretary of the Navy Knox, was made the latter's unofficial observer in Britain in 1939–40. His reports came to the notice of President ROOSEVELT, and Donovan was then sent on a number of missions for the President, notably to observe and report on the various resistance movements in Europe and the Middle East. In June 1942 he was made Director of the Office of Strategic Services (OSS) and assumed responsibility for organizing American clandestine activities in all theatres of war.

Doolittle, Lt Col James Harold (1896–1958)

"Jimmy" Doolittle became an aviator in the US Army in 1917. In postwar years he attained considerable fame as an air racer and record-breaker, while at the same time working as an engineer with the US Army Air Corps on the development of flight instruments. In 1940 he

Admiral Karl Dönitz.

Mitchell B-25s on the deck of USS Hornet, *before the Doolittle Raid on Tokyo, April 1942.*

returned to the service as a Major, charged with organizing aircraft production in ex-automobile factories. He then moved into a more active role and in 1942 he led the famous raid on Tokyo on 18 April 1942, using a flight of B-25 bombers launched from the aircraft carrier *Hornet*. The aircraft bombed Tokyo and other targets and flew on to land at airfields in China. Doolittle received the Congressional Medal of Honor for leading this raid. He was then appointed commander of the 12th Air Force for Operation TORCH, the landings in North Africa, after which he commanded the North-West African Strategic Air Force. Returning to England in 1944, he assumed command of the 8th Air Force, carrying out strategic bombing against Germany. At the end of the war in Europe he led the 8th Air Force to the Pacific theatre to launch strategic bombing attacks against Japan.

Doolittle Raid

The name given to an air raid on Tokyo led by Lieutenant-Colonel James H. DOOLITTLE on 18 April 1942. Planned by General H. H. ARNOLD, the raid involved flying Army bombers off an aircraft carrier (USS *Hornet*), bombing Tokyo, and then flying on into China where they were to remain as support for the Chinese army. The aircraft were NORTH AMERICAN B-25 MITCHELL BOMBERS, stripped of extraneous equipment, including much of their armament, and given auxiliary fuel tanks. The 16 aircraft achieved complete surprise and bombed military targets in the Tokyo, Nagoya, Kobe and Yoko-hama areas. Due to having flown off at too great a range (having been seen by a Japanese patrol vessel), the aircraft had insufficient fuel to reach their destinations and all crashed, though many of their crews parachuted into CHINA. Three were captured and executed by the Japanese, 49 escaped safely to the Chinese forces, while others were imprisoned. Although the material damage was relatively slight, the effect on both US and Japanese morale was considerable.

Doomsday

Allied liberation of NORWAY, 1945.

Dora Line, Italy, 1944

See ADOLF HITLER LINE.

Dora Nordhausen

A German forced-labour camp and factory complex, primarily for the assembly of A4 ROCKETS, aero-engines and other munitions. Largely underground, it was in the Harz mountains some 50 miles (80km) north of Erfurt.

Doria Class Battleships (Italy)

Displacement 23,887 tons; *dimensions* 613ft×91ft 9in (186.9×28m); mean draught 34ft (10.4m); *machinery* 2-shaft geared turbines producing shp 87,000; *speed* 27 knots; *protection* main belt 9.8in; deck 5.4in; turrets 11in; *armament* 10×12.6in; 12×5.3in; 10×3.5in AA; 19×37mm AA; 12×20mm AA; *complement* 1495; *number in class* 2, both launched 1913 and rebuilt 1937–40.

Dorman-Smith, Maj Gen Eric (1895–1969)

Born in Ireland, Dorman-Smith was commissioned into the Northumberland Fusiliers in 1914 and served with distinction on the Western Front. Between the wars he was an instructor at Sandhurst and the Staff College, commanded the 1st Battalion Northumberland Fusiliers, and from 1938–40 was Director of Military Training, India. He then became Commandant of the Middle East Staff College at Haifa and in June 1942 was appointed Deputy Chief of General Staff Middle East. Later in the month he became Chief of Staff to General AUCHINLECK, but in August was removed from this post on the orders of Winston CHURCHILL. He later commanded infantry brigades in Britain and on the ANZIO beach-head, and finally retired in December 1944. In 1947 he resumed the family name of Dorman-O'Gowan. A man with a fertile brain and considerable imagination, it has been said that Dorman-Smith could produce five solutions to any tactical problem, one of which might be a winner. He appears to have been the author of the term "battle group" and certainly was constantly pressing the advantages of small mobile columns in the desert. He was fortunate to be chief of staff to two commanders who were receptive to some of his ideas, but he also made enemies, and he was eventually made the scapegoat for 8th Army's tactical shortcomings.

Dornberger, Maj Gen Walter

A qualified engineer and artillery captain in the German Army, in 1930 Dornberger was placed in charge of a small unit of the Army Weapons Office charged with development of military rocket weapons. He gradually assumed more responsibility until he eventually became a Major-General and Special Army Commissioner for V-WEAPONS. Under his control the entire German army rocket programme was worked out, and he was largely responsible for the setting up of the PEENEMUNDE research establishment. He tended to see political plots on all sides and frequently resisted well-meant plans to improve the production facilities for rocket weapons. He surrendered to US troops in Bavaria on 2 May 1945.

Dornier Do-172 medium bombers.

Dornier Aircraft (Ger)

Dornier Do 17 Known during the war as the "Flying Pencil" due to its slender fuselage, the Do 17 was a twin-engined high-wing monoplane bomber which had originally been designed under the guise of a fast mail-carrier. Production was under way by 1937 and some were used in Spain during the Civil War. There were several improved and variant models during its life, including reconnaissance versions. *Span* 59ft (18m); *engines* (late production versions) 2 1000hp radial; *crew* 4 or 5; *armament* 6 machine guns and up to 2200lb (1000kg) of bombs; *speed* 263mph (423kph).

Dornier Do 18 Originally designed as a transatlantic mail aircraft for Lufthansa, from which was developed a military version, the Do 18 was a flying boat with cantilever wing and with two engines mounted back-to-back in a central wing nacelle. It was widely used on maritime reconnaissance and air–sea rescue duties, and there was also a trainer version. *Span* 77.75ft (23.7m); *engines* 2 700hp in-line; *crew* 4; *armament* 1 13mm machine gun, 1 20mm cannon and 440lb (200kg) of bombs; *speed* 160mph (257kph).

Dornier Do 24 Although a German design, the Do 24 had been built under licence in

Dornier Do 17 medium bomber.

Holland for the Dutch East Indies Naval Air Force. A tri-motor high-wing monoplane flying boat, with a distinct Dornier family resemblance, it was used for reconnaissance, bombing and transport purposes and saw considerable action during the opening months of the Pacific War in 1942. In 1940 the Germans seized those still remaining in Holland and adopted them for air–sea rescue purposes, after which they put the design back into production in Germany and Holland and used it for reconnaissance duties. Some were also used by the French Navy from 1944. *Span* 88.5ft (27m); *engines* 3 1000hp radial; *crew* 5 or 6; *armament* 1 20mm cannon, 2 machine guns and 1300lb (600kg) of bombs; *speed* 211mph (339kph).

Dornier Do 217 This was a further development of the DO 17 which entered service in 1941 and was employed in bombing, torpedo-carrying, anti-shipping and reconnaissance roles and as a night fighter. There were a number of variations, including changes of engine due to wartime supply difficulties or the addition of RADAR or adaptation to carry guided bombs. About 1700 were built and a small number were supplied to Italy. *Span* 62.3ft (19m); *engines* 2 1600hp radial; *crew* 4; *armament* (bomber) 1 15mm and 5 7.92mm

machine guns, and up to 6600lb (3000kg) of bombs, (fighter) 4 20mm cannon and 4 machine guns in the nose and 2 flexible 13mm machine guns for rear defence; *speed* 325mph (523kph).

Dornier Do 335 This most unconventional machine, known unofficially as the Pfeil (Arrow) was a single-seat monoplane fighter with an engine at each end of the fuselage, one driving a front tractor propeller, and the other driving a rear pusher propeller. A two-seat version was also developed. Armed with one 30mm and two 15mm cannon, and with a top speed of 450mph (724kph), development of the Do 335 was not completed before the war ended.

Dortmund–Ems Canal, 1940 and 1944

An important inland waterway connecting the industrial areas of the RUHR with the north-west German ports via the Ems. On 13 August 1940 the bank was breached during an early precision bombing attack by the RAF and the canal was out of use for 12 days. The raid was carried out by 12 Hampden bombers despite the heavy anti-aircraft defences and its leader, Flight-Lieutenant Learoyd, was awarded the Victoria Cross. The canal remained a prime target throughout the war and on the night of 23/24 September 1944 was subjected to a night precision attack by 141 aircraft, 14 of which were lost. During this attack 11 12,000lb (5443kg) Tallboy bombs were dropped, breaching the banks and draining a six-mile section.

Douglas Aircraft (USA)

Douglas B-18 Bolo The B-18 was a twin-engined monoplane medium bomber developed from the highly successful Douglas DC-3 commercial airliner in 1936. 350 were built and went into service but they saw no combat as bombers, being converted for maritime reconnaissance, coastal patrolling and advanced training. Twenty were supplied to Canada, also for maritime work, where they were known as the Digby. *Span* 89.5ft (27.3m); *engines* 2 1000hp radial; *speed* 215mph (346kph).

Douglas A-20 Havoc/Boston This began life as a bomber for the French Air Force in 1939, and a few actually reached France before the collapse in 1940. The balance of the order was taken by the RAF as the Boston, and most were then converted into night fighters as the Havoc. The design was then adopted by the

USAAF as the A-20 bomber, but almost all were then converted into P-70 night fighters and the remainder to photographic machines. An improved version, the A-20C, could carry a 2000lb (900kg) torpedo and was supplied to Russia in large numbers. The principal production model was the A-20G of which over 1800 were built. *Span* 61.3ft (18.6m); *crew* 3; *engines* 2 1600hp radial; *armament* 9 machine guns or 5 machine guns and 4 20mm cannon, up to 4400lb (2000kg) of bombs; *speed* 315mph (507kph).

Douglas A-26 Invader A further development of the A-20 design which first flew in July 1942. Developed as a light bomber and ground attack machine, a night fighter variant was also developed, as was an attack version carrying a 75mm gun. About 2300 were built and had begun replacing the A-20 when the war ended. *Span* 70ft (21.3m); *engines* 2 2000hp radial; *armament* 10 machine guns, up to 2200lb (1000kg) of bombs; *speed* 375mph (603kph).

Douglas C-47 Skytrain/Dakota This immortal aircraft began life as a commercial airliner, the Douglas DC-3, in 1935. The military version was known as the C-47 Skytrain in US service, and was given the name Dakota by the RAF to whom over 1200 were supplied. It could be fitted with folding benches and used for troop transport, or with reinforced floor, landing gear and a large cargo-loading door and used as a cargo carrier. It was the mainstay of Allied air transport units in every theatre of war. Total military production reached 10,123 aircraft, and some are still flying today. *Span* 95ft (29m); *engines* 2 1200hp radial; *crew* 4; *speed* 230mph (370kph).

Douglas C53 Skytrooper This was another version of the Douglas DC-3 which was used solely as a troop transport. It differed from the C-47 in having the normal airliner floor and entry door but was otherwise of the same dimensions and performance.

Douglas C54 Skymaster This aircraft began life as the Douglas DC-4 52-seat airliner in 1938. In 1941 it was adapted for USAAF requirements as a transport with 26 seats and space for cargo. It was the principal transatlantic ferry machine and was used on transport duties all over the world and occasionally as a glider tug. *Span* 117.5ft (35.8m); *engines* 4 1350hp radial; *crew* 6; *speed* 275mph (442kph).

Douglas TBD-1 Devastator This was a single-engined monoplane torpedo-bomber which entered US service in 1937. Although poorly armed, it nevertheless performed well in the early stages of the Pacific war and did great damage to Japanese shipping, but was withdrawn after suffering crippling losses during the Battle of MIDWAY. *Span* 50ft (15.25m); *engine* 1 900hp radial; *crew* 2; *armament* 2 machine guns, 1 torpedo or 1 1000lb (450kg) bomb; *speed* 205mph (330kph).

Douglas SBD Dauntless This was originally a design by the Northrop company which was absorbed by Douglas in 1937; work continued on developing a light dive bombing and reconnaissance machine for the US Navy and the Dauntless was introduced into service with US Marine Corps squadrons in 1939, after which the US Navy and USAAF took numbers. Although obsolescent by 1941, these immensely rugged aircraft rendered excellent service in the Pacific War, sinking more Japanese shipping than any other Allied weapon, stopping the Japanese Imperial Fleet at the Battle of MIDWAY and playing a major role at CORAL SEA and in the SOLOMONS. Over 5900 were built before production ended in July 1944. *Span* 41.5ft (12.6m); *engine* 1 1200hp radial; *crew* 2; *armament* 4 machine guns, up to 1100lb (500kg) of bombs; *speed* 250mph (402kph).

Douglas, AM Sir William Sholto (1893–1969)

In 1939 Douglas was Assistant Chief of Air Staff and later became Deputy Chief. In November 1940 he succeeded DOWDING as Chief of Fighter Command, taking it on to the offensive with a policy of fighter sweeps over France. In January 1943 he was sent to command the RAF in the Middle East, and in the following year returned to England to take over COASTAL COMMAND. He was then made responsible for much of the air planning for the invasion of Europe and had special responsibility for keeping the English Channel clear of U-boats during that critical period.

Dowding, ACM Sir Hugh (1882–1970)

"Stuffy" Dowding first flew with the RFC in World War I, and in later years held the posts of Director of Training and Air Officer Commanding-in-Chief in Palestine and Transjordan. He was a member of the Air Council for Supply, 1930–36, and was responsible for the allocation of funds for the development of RADAR. In 1936 he assumed command of the newly formed FIGHTER COMMAND, which he organized into a highly effective fighting force. His awareness of scientific developments enabled him to build up an interlinked organization of radar and radio communication which enabled Fighter Command to deploy aircraft precisely where they were needed, rather than rely on inefficient standing patrols to intercept raiders. By the outbreak of war Dowding had expanded Fighter Command from a single group based in south-east England to an integrated defence

Douglas C-47 Skytrain/Dakota.

system covering the whole of the British Isles. His foresight was absolutely crucial in the summer of 1940 when the Battle of BRITAIN was successfully fought under his command. His sure grasp of operational realities brought him into conflict with the British War Cabinet during the Battle for France, when he resisted demands to throw vital fighter squadrons into what was clearly a doomed campaign. This undoubtedly saved Britain during the great daylight offensives mounted by the Luftwaffe in August–September 1940. Nevertheless, his aloof and intransigent manner offended CHURCHILL and other senior figures, and in November 1940 he was replaced by Sholto DOUGLAS. After undertaking a mission to the USA for the Ministry of Aircraft Production, he retired in 1942. A remote and austere figure, firmly believing that a divine hand was guiding his actions, Dowding never received the recognition that was his due.

Downfall

Overall American plan for the invasion of Japan, 1945.

DPD Director of Projectile Development (UK). The cover name devised to conceal the functions of the department developing air defence rockets and missiles.

Dracula

British airborne and amphibious assault on RANGOON, May 1945.

Dragoon

Allied invasion of southern France, August 1944.

Dresden, Germany, 1945

Attacked during the night of 13/14 February by 773 aircraft of the RAF's BOMBER COMMAND which dropped 2660 tons of high explosive and incendiary bombs on the city, creating the worst firestorm of the war. Some eight square miles (20 square km) were devastated and, since the city was crowded with refugees and virtually bereft of air defences, more people died than in any other city attacked from the air. Some sources place the numbers killed in excess of 100,000, but the real figure will never be known. During 14 and 15 February the destruction was completed by the US 8th Air Force. The necessity of the air offensive has always been questioned, and in the military context it yielded no strategic benefit.

Driant, Fort, France

One of the forts of METZ in north-eastern France. Defended by battle-hardened students from a nearby NCO School, in 1944 it repulsed several attacks by the US Third Army under General Walton H. Walker and held up the advance of the US XX Corps for almost three months. It was eventually encircled and its defenders starved into submission.

Drum, Fort, Philippines, 1941–42

An American coast-defence fort in Manila Bay, built of concrete on a small island and filling the gap between CORREGIDOR and the eastern side of the bay. Constructed in 1909–14 it was armed with four 14-inch guns in two turrets, with four 6-inch guns in casemates in the sides. Completely self-contained, it was virtually impervious to Japanese artillery and air attacks and was still in functioning order when the US forces surrendered in May 1942. In 1945 it had to be retaken by US troops, who pumped a gasoline mixture down into the fort interior through the ventilation shafts and then fired explosive charges on the deck. The resulting fire burned for several days and not one of the Japanese garrison survived.

DSR Director of Scientific Research (UK).

Dufferin, Fort, Burma, 1945

Citadel of Mandalay, second largest city of Burma. It proved a very difficult obstacle to the Allied troops capturing the city, resisting the point-blank fire of 5.5-inch (140mm) guns at 400 yards (365m) range. Low-level bombers were used to breach its ramparts, but before the assault went in the majority of the Japanese slipped away through drains, leaving some 350 civilian prisoners to surrender the fort to the British on 20 March 1945.

Duisberg Convoy, 1941

During the night of 8/9 November 1941 the Royal Italian Navy attempted to run a convoy of seven merchantmen, including two tankers, from Messina to Tripoli. The convoy, commonly named after the German ship *Duisberg* which formed part of it, had a close escort of seven destroyers under Captain Ugo Bisciani and a covering force consisting of the cruisers *Trieste* and *Trento* and four destroyers, the operation being under the overall command of Vice-Admiral Bruno Brivonesi. A Maryland reconnaissance aircraft reported its progress at 1640 on 8 November,

and an hour later Force K (the cruisers *Aurora* and *Penelope* and the destroyers *Lance* and *Lively*) under Captain William Agnew left Malta to intercept. At 0040 the convoy was sighted six miles (9.6km) distant, silhouetted against the moon. The luck of the subsequent engagement lay with the British. Brivonesi's covering force had been protecting its exposed flank but was now on the northern leg of its patrol line, leaving the way open for Agnew to attack. Fire was opened on the Italians at 0057. One of the close escorts, *Fulmine*, was sunk and another, *Graecale*, was crippled. Bisciani, under the impression that the convoy had been attacked by aircraft, ordered the close escort to make smoke; by the time he realized his error his radio antenna had been shot away. To the north, Brivonesi was unable to interpret the confused mêlée as Agnew's ships circled the convoy, damaging the destroyer *Euro* and sinking every one of the merchant vessels before turning for home at 0200. Finally, at dawn the submarine *Upholder* (Lieutenant-Commander Malcolm WANKLYN) torpedoed and sank the destroyer *Libeccio*. The destruction of the Duisberg Convoy was a high point in the British effort to strangle the Axis lifeline to North Africa and forced ROMMEL to cancel his planned assault on TOBRUK, and also to meet the CRUSADER offensive with inadequate fuel supplies.

Duka-88

A recoilless 88mm gun developed by Rheinmetall-Borsig of Germany as a heavy aircraft weapon. Development began in 1936, and the gun was intended to be suspended in a cowling beneath the fuselage and fitted with automatic loading gear. It was to fire a 19.8lb (9kg) shrapnel shell and piped gas from in front of the cartridge to a jet nozzle directed to the rear, so giving the necessary recoillessness. Although the gun was successfully test-fired, the project was abandoned in September 1939 due to the demands of more urgent projects.

Duke of York, HMS – King George V Class Battleship

Served with the Home Fleet throughout the war, sinking the battlecruiser SCHARNHORST during the Battle of the NORTH CAPE, 26 December 1943. In 1945 she joined the Pacific Fleet and was present at the Japanese surrender in Tokyo Bay.

Dukla Pass, Czechoslovakia–Poland, 1944 See CARPATHIAN MOUNTAINS.

DUKW Amphibious Cargo Carrier

Essentially the American 6×6 truck fitted with buoyancy tanks and driven by a screw when afloat. The vehicle had a cargo capacity of two and a half tons and was used to ferry stores from ships lying off-shore to dumps within a beach-head. DUKWs played an important part in the NORMANDY landings, the campaign in North-West Europe and in the Pacific war zone.

Dulles, Allen Welsh (1893–1969)

An American lawyer, appointed as President ROOSEVELT's special envoy in Switzerland in 1942, and also an agent of the OSS. From Switzerland he soon built up a network of informers and agents among the French resistance. Over a long period of time he held talks with various German figures attempting to bring about a German surrender. In 1945 his negotiations with SS General WOLFF were effective in bringing about the German capitulation of in Italy.

Dunkerque Class Battleships (Fr)

Dunkerque was launched in 1935. She was damaged during the British attack on MERS-EL-KEBIR on 3 July 1940 and sunk by torpedo aircraft from HMS ARK ROYAL three days later. Refloated, she was moved to TOULON in February 1942 and scuttled there on 27 November. Her sister ship *Strasbourg* was also present at Mers-el-Kebir during the British attack but escaped damage and reached Toulon on 4 July. She was scuttled there on 27 November 1942, refloated the following July and finally sunk by bombs on 18 August 1944. *Displacement* 26,500 tons; *dimensions* 702ft×101ft 9in (213.9×31m); mean draught 28ft (8.5m); *machinery* 4-shaft geared turbines producing shp 100,000; *speed* 29.5 knots; *protection* main belt 9in; deck 5in; turrets 14in; *armament* 8×330mm (2×4); 16×130mm DP (3×4 and 2×2); 8×37mm AA; 32×13.2mm AA; *aircraft* 2; *complement* 1431; *number in class* 2.

Dunkirk Evacuation, 1940

The evacuation of the Dunkirk pocket, containing 400,000 Allied soldiers including the bulk of the British Expeditionary Force, was planned by Vice-Admiral Bertram RAMSAY, then Flag Officer Dover, under the codename Operation *Dynamo*, and commenced at 1900

on 26 May 1940. Ramsay assembled over 1000 vessels, including destroyers and smaller warships, cross-channel ferries, pleasure steamers, coasters, trawlers and craft as small as cabin cruisers, manned by their civilian owners. Initially it had been thought that as few as 45,000 men could be picked up, yet when the evacuation ended at 0340 on 4 June no less than 338,000 had been taken to safety. Throughout, the evacuation area remained under heavy attack by the Luftwaffe and the contracting perimeter of the pocket was

under constant pressure. Six British and three French destroyers were sunk and 19 were damaged; 56 other ships and 161 small craft were sunk. The apparent absence of British aircraft above the embarkation zone resulted in unjustified criticism, for the RAF, flying from airfields in England, had broken up many of the German air attacks before they could reach the beaches, destroying over 100 aircraft and losing a similar number. The scale of the evacuation undoubtedly surprised and disappointed the German High Command,

France 1940: The Panzer corridor and the formation of the Dunkirk pocket.

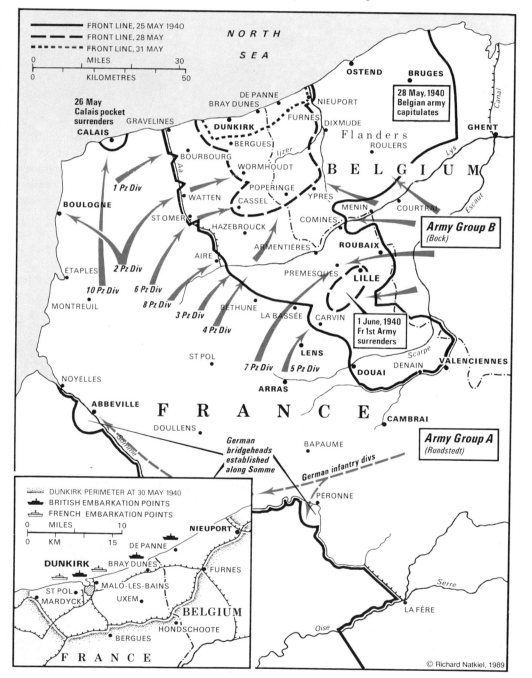

Troops on the beaches, Dunkirk, May 1940.

providing as it did an unsatisfactory ending to the otherwise perfect execution of its plan to destroy the Allies' northern armies. On the other hand, the Germans were justified in believing that the troops in the Dunkirk pocket no longer presented a threat, and therefore starting to re-deploy their armoured formations against the French armies to the south; had those armoured formations been used against the pocket it could hardly have survived as long as it did. Again, the German Navy, having been crippled during the recent campaign in NORWAY, was in no position to offer serious opposition. CHURCHILL himself was quick to point out that Dunkirk was an escape and not a victory, but nevertheless it had an inspiring effect on British morale.

Duppel

Duppel was the German name for what the Allies called WINDOW, metallized paper strips dropped from aircraft to blind RADAR sets. The Germans were aware of such a system well before it was ever used against them, but, like the Allies, refrained from using it since it might be copied and used against them. The German name came from the location (Duppel, in Denmark) of the original German trials of the idea, carried out in January 1943.

Dutch East Indies, Pacific, 1942, 1945

Included Java, Sumatra, Timor, Borneo, the Celebes and the western half of New Guinea and in January 1942 fell within the ABDA (American, British, Dutch and Australian) command areas under General Sir Archibald WAVELL. The Japanese possessed complete naval and air superiority and in a two-month campaign starting on 11 January were able to land at will throughout the islands, overcoming the frequently determined resistance of isolated Allied garrisons. On 8 March the Dutch civil administration surrendered unconditionally. See Battle of the JAVA SEA and

Japanese troops land on Borneo, 1942.

Battle of LOMBOK STRAIT. The area was by-passed during the Allied advance on the Japanese homeland but between May and August 1945 Australian and Dutch troops carried out a successful series of operations at Tarakan, Brunei Bay and BALIKPAPAN. Following the surrender of Japan the Dutch, with British assistance, attempted to re-establish control over the islands in September 1945. This was fiercely resisted by Indonesian nationalists and, despite a number of military successes against the rebels, the Dutch were forced to grant full sovereignty on 2 November 1949.

Dyle River, Belgium, 1940

A defensive line selected by the Allies in the event of a German invasion of Belgium. The plan required the British Expeditionary Force (BEF) to take up positions along the river, towards which the Belgian Army would withdraw from the frontier, while the French 1st and 7th Armies came into line on, respectively, the right and left flanks. Although the BEF successfully completed its advance into Belgium and was dug in along the Dyle by the evening of 11 May, the German breakthrough on the ARDENNES sector of the front rendered the position untenable. See FRANCE, BELGIUM, HOLLAND 1940.

Dynamo

DUNKIRK evacuation, May–June, 1940.

E

"E" Class Cruisers (UK)

Displacement 7550–7580 tons; *dimensions* 570ft×54ft 6in (173×16.6m); mean draught 16ft 3in (4.9m); *machinery* 4-shaft geared turbines producing shp 80,000; *speed* 33 knots; *protection* main belt 3in; deck 1in; gunshields 1in; *armament* 7×6in (7×1 *or* 1×2 and 5×1); 3×4in AA (3×1); 2×2-pdr AA; 16×21in torpedo tubes (4×4); *aircraft* 1; *complement* 572; *number in class* 2, launched 1919–20.

"E" and "F" Class Destroyers (UK)

Displacement 1375 tons; *dimensions* 329ft×33ft 3in (100×10.15m); mean draught 8ft 6in (2.58m); *machinery* 2-shaft geared turbines producing shp 36,000; *speed* 35.5 knots; *armament* 4×4.7in (4×1); 8×0.5in AA (2×4); 8×21in torpedo tubes (2×4); *complement* 145; *number in class* 18, launched 1934.

EAC European Advisory Commission.

Eagle, HMS – Aircraft Carrier

Originally laid down as a battleship for the Chilean Navy, *Eagle* was purchased in 1917 and launched the following year as an aircraft carrier, being completed in 1920. During World War II she served in the East Indies 1939–40, with the Mediterranean Fleet 1940–41, in the South Atlantic 1941–42 and with Force H in 1942. She was torpedoed and sunk by *U-73* north of Algiers on 11 August 1942 while escorting the PEDESTAL CONVOY to Malta. *Displacement* 22,600 tons; *dimensions* 667ft×105ft 3in (203×32m); mean draught 27ft (8.2m); *machinery* 4-shaft geared turbines producing shp 50,000; *speed* 24 knots; *protection* main belt 7in; deck 4in; gunshields 1in; *armament* 9×6in (9×1); 4×4in AA (4×1); 8×2-pdr AA (1×8); *aircraft* 21; *complement* 748.

Eaker, General Ira C. (1898–   )

Eaker was a peacetime US Army Air Force officer with a high reputation as a skilled pilot. In February 1942 he arrived in England as the commander of the US 8th Air Force's Bomber Command. On 17 August 1942 he flew on the first all-American bombing operation in Europe when 12 B-17s of 97th Bombardment Group, under the command of Colonel Frank A. Armstrong, Jr, raided the marshalling yards at Rouen, in France. At the end of 1942 Eaker succeeded SPAATZ as the commander of 8th Air Force. A vigorous advocate of precision daylight bombing, he nevertheless initially underestimated the difficulties of operations over Germany. Early in 1943 Eaker was given the task of transforming the decisions taken at the CASABLANCA CONFERENCE (January 1943) into practical orders for the prosecution of the Allied Combined Bomber Offensive, which accommodated the very different aims and methods of RAF BOMBER COMMAND and the US 8th Air Force. The plan which emerged, generally referred to as the "Eaker Plan", was subsequently to form the basis of the POINT-BLANK Directive, issued on 10 June 1943. Eaker commanded the Allied air support for Operation DRAGOON and, operating from French airfields, continued to support the Allied advance with strategic and tactical support attacks until the end of the war.

EAM National Liberation Front (Greece). The directing body which commanded EDES and ELAS forces.

East African Campaign, 1940–41

Italy's East African Empire, consisting of Eritrea, Ethiopia and Italian Somaliland, was held by 91,000 Italian and 199,000 Ethiopian troops under the command of the Viceroy, the Duke of AOSTA. When Italy declared war on the United Kingdom on 10 June 1940, very few British troops were available to meet the threat which these posed to the Sudan, Kenya and British Somaliland. However, beyond capturing the towns of Kassala in the Sudan and Moyale in Kenya in July and overrunning BRITISH SOMALILAND in August, the Italians were conscious of their strategic isolation and remained on the defensive. Under the direction of Lieutenant-General Sir Alan CUN-

NINGHAM, preparations were made for a counteroffensive from Kenya into Italian Somaliland. This began on 29 January 1941 and was led by Major-General A. R. Godwin-Austen's 12th African Division (1st South African Brigade Group, 22nd East African and 24th Gold Coast Brigades), joined the following month by 23rd Nigerian Brigade. The terrain presented greater difficulties than the negligible resistance offered by General de Simone's troops and MOGADISHU was captured on 25 February. Following this collapse, British Somaliland was abandoned by the Italians. The weakness of the enemy was now apparent to Cunningham and he decided to pursue them into southern Ethiopia with Major-General Wetherall's 11th African Division, reinforced by two brigades of 12th Division, including the South Africans. The pace of the campaign accelerated sharply, Jijiga being captured on 17 March, DIREDAWA on 29 March and ADDIS ABABA, the Ethiopian capital, on 6 April. Cunningham had advanced over 1000 miles (1600km), averaging 35 miles (50km) a day, and taken 50,000 prisoners at a cost of 135 killed, 310 wounded and 56 missing.

Meanwhile, what amounted to a separate campaign was being fought in the north. Kassala was abandoned on 18 January and Major-General William Platt, the GOC Sudan, followed up the Italian withdrawal into Eritrea with the 4th Indian Division (Major-General Noel Beresford-Peirse) and 5th Indian Division (Major-General Lewis Heath) while GIDEON FORCE under the then Major Orde WINGATE waged a guerrilla war and fomented insurrection in north-west Ethiopia. The Italians, commanded by General Frusci, made a three-day stand at AGORDAT and then withdrew to KEREN where, in a hard-fought series of actions in the mountains, they were able to stem the British advance until 27 March. The capture of Asmara, the Eritrean capital, was followed by that of the Red Sea port and naval base of MASSAWA on 9 April. Cunningham and Platt now converged on the remaining Italian armies in Ethiopia, the former capturing DES-

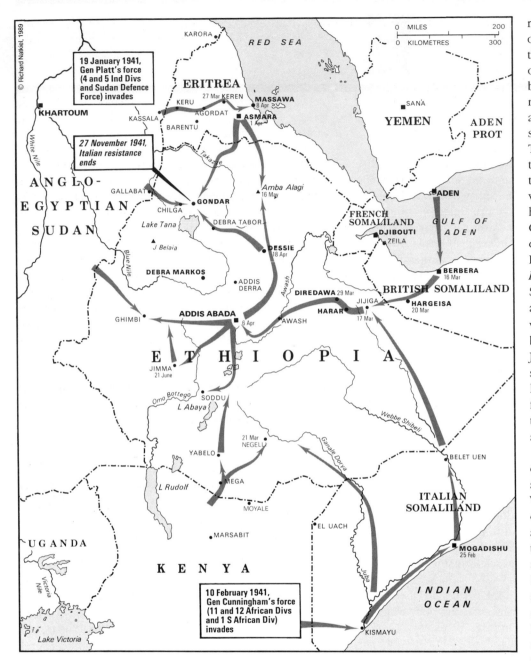

The East African Campaign.

Within the map:

19 January 1941, Gen Platt's force (4 and 5 Ind Divs and Sudan Defence Force) invades

27 November 1941, Italian resistance ends

10 February 1941, Gen Cunningham's force (11 and 12 African Divs and 1 S African Div) invades

SIE on 22 April. The Viceroy's army was trapped between the 1st South African Brigade Group and 5th Indian Division (now commanded by Major-General A. G. O. M. Mayne) and although it took up strong positions at AMBA ALAGI it was forced to surrender on 19 May. The final phase of the campaign involved mopping up isolated Italian pockets. The 11th African Division captured JIMMA on 21 June, forcing a group of two divisions under General Gazzera to retreat to the north-west, where it was trapped by a Belgian brigade from the Congo and forced to surrender on 3 July. In September the promoted Lieutenant-

General Sir William Platt was appointed commander of the new East African Command, Cunningham having left to command the 8th Army in Egypt. The last Italian force in Ethiopia, commanded by General Nasi, was surrounded in its heavily fortified mountain positions at GONDAR and surrendered after heavy fighting on 27 November. See also AFMADU and DEBRA TABOR.

Eastern Solomons, Battle of the, 1942

After the start of the campaign on GUADALCANAL, the Japanese made frequent sorties by the "TOKYO EXPRESS" to deliver

reinforcements to the island. The first group of troops was severely mauled in the battle of the TENARU (ILU) RIVER, and the Japanese ordered another reinforcement which was to be escorted by Admiral TANAKA, with his normal fleet enhanced by the addition of the aircraft carriers SHOKAKU and *Zuikaku* and several other warships from YAMAMOTO's fleet. This, it was hoped, would tempt the US fleet in the area into close action. Bait was provided in the form of the Japanese carrier RYUJO, which was sent on ahead of the main fleet to fly off her aircraft to make ground attacks on Guadalcanal. Alerted by intelligence, Admiral GHORMLEY ordered Admiral FLETCHER's Task Force 61, centred on the carriers SARATOGA, *Enterprise* and *Wasp* into the Eastern Solomons, and on 23 August 1942 scouting aircraft reported a sighting of some Japanese warships. A striking force of dive and torpedo bombers was flown from *Saratoga*, but the Japanese had seen the scout plane, had reversed course, and were concealed by rain and low cloud so that the American force failed to find its target. Fletcher, suspecting the whole thing to be an intelligence scare with no substance, now sent *Wasp* south to refuel.

Early the next morning a scout plane discovered the *Ryujo* and after some delay a strike force was launched from *Enterprise*. When this was airborne another scout discovered the *Shokaku* and *Zuikaku* and attempted to divert the strike force to these targets without success. The *Ryujo* was attacked and sunk, but the major force had been despatched to the minor target, and only a few aircraft reached *Shokaku* and did little damage. The Japanese, meanwhile, had launched major air forces against the US carriers. Despite Fletcher having prepared for this by having some 51 fighters airborne over his fleet, there were difficulties in control, coupled with the problem of US aircraft returning from their strikes mingling with Japanese attacks, and a force of Japanese bombers penetrated the American defences and hit the *Enterprise* several times. The damage was not fatal however, and within an hour the carrier was back in operation. Shortly afterwards her steering failed, just as a second Japanese strike came in search of her; this force failed, and the *Enterprise* was able to complete repairs and get under way once more. During this time, the *Saratoga* had been undiscovered and had been able to fly off strikes which found and severely damaged the

Japanese seaplane-carrier *Chitose*. With nightfall both sides withdrew and the indecisive battle came to an end. Meanwhile, land-based US aircraft from Guadalcanal had found the troop convoy, sunk one transport and a destroyer, and severely damaged a cruiser. The remaining two troop transports were ordered to retire to the Shortland Islands, where the troops would be reloaded into destroyers for another attempt. On balance, therefore, the Eastern Solomons can be counted as a US victory since the Japanese objectives – the reinforcement of the island and the destruction of the US fleet – had not been achieved.

East Prussia, Germany, 1939 and 1945

Although separated from the main body of Germany by the POLISH CORRIDOR, in 1939 East Prussia provided the route into Poland from the north, rendering the position of the Polish armies to the west untenable. In January 1945 the province was overrun by Bagramyan's 1st Baltic Front, CHERNYAKHOVSKY's 3rd Belorussian Front and ROKOSSOVSKY's 2nd Belorussian Front, which possessed a total of 1,670,000 men, 3300 tanks, 28,000 artillery weapons and 10,000 aircraft. The German Army Group Centre, with 596,000 men, 700 tanks, 8000 artillery weapons and 1300 aircraft, was forced back against the Baltic and isolated, thereby removing a threat to the northern flank of the Soviet advance into central Germany. Russian soldiers, on enemy soil for the first time, indulged in an orgy of wanton killing, rape and savage destruction in reprisal for German atrocities in their own homeland.

Eben Emael, Belgium, 1940

A fort guarding vital bridges at the confluence of the ALBERT CANAL and Maas River. Considered impregnable because of its position and construction, it was attacked by a specially trained force of German glider-borne troops on 10 May 1940. The gliders landed on top of the fort and the troops used shaped charge demolition bombs to put the gun turrets out of action; this was the first combat use of shaped charges. The airborne troops were unable to enter the fort, for artillery fire from neighbouring forts. On 11 May they were relieved by advance troops of REICHENAU's 6th Army, crossing the Albert Canal by boat, and the fort surrendered. Of the 85 airborne troops who had landed, only six were killed and 15 wounded.

Eberbach, Gen Heinrich (1895–   )

Commissioned into an infantry regiment in 1915, Eberbach served through World War I and then retired, becoming a police officer. He rejoined the German Army in 1935 and was appointed Commanding Officer of the 35th Panzer Regiment in 1938. He proved to be an exceptionally gifted commander of armour and was rapidly promoted, becoming a Major-General in 1942. In 1944 he was commander of Panzer Group West, from which was formed Panzer Group Eberbach, which fought with distinction against the British and Canadian forces outside CAEN. In August 1944 he took command of 7th Army, but was captured nine days later and remained a prisoner for the rest of the war.

Eclipse

Allied plan for the postwar division of Germany.

Edelweiss

Drive by German Army Group A through the CAUCASUS to the Baku oilfields.

Eden, Sir Anthony (1897–1977)

After serving with distinction in World War I, Eden entered politics. In 1933 he was Minister for League of Nations Affairs and in 1935 became Foreign Secretary in Baldwin's government. He resigned his post in 1938 over a disagreement with CHAMBERLAIN over the latter's policy of appeasement, but in 1940 was invited by CHURCHILL to become Dominions Secretary, then Secretary of State for War and finally Foreign Secretary. In this post he travelled extensively, notably on various missions to Russia. He had few illusions about STALIN's ambitions and attempted to dissuade Churchill from being too generous in his concessions, without avail. A man of immense charm, he also had immense stamina and undoubtedly did his best work during the war years.

Eder Dam, Germany, 1943

Regulated the level of the Weser, controlled flooding on the Eder and Fulda rivers and provided hydro-electric power for the RUHR industrial complex. Together with the MÖHNE DAM, the Eder Dam was destroyed by "bouncing bombs" dropped by Lancasters of the RAF's No. 617 Squadron during the night of 16/17 May. The raid was a landmark in precision bombing techniques and had a profound psychological effect, but the damage caused to the German war economy was slight. See also GIBSON, Wing-Commander Guy and WALLIS, Sir Barnes.

EDES National Democratic Greek Army. Greek resistance force which came into existence during the German occupation. Composed of royalists, republicans and other political moderates, EDES was, together with ELAS, of considerable assistance in driving the German forces from Greece in 1944. Once the Germans had left, EDES was disbanded.

Edsall Class Destroyer Escorts (USA)

Displacement 1200 tons; *dimensions* 306ft×36ft 9in (91.8×11.07m); *mean draught* 8ft 9in (2.66m); *machinery* 2-shaft geared diesels producing shp 6000; *speed* 21 knots; *armament* 3×3in; 8×40mm AA; 3×21in torpedo tubes; *complement* 200; *number in class* 85, launched 1942–43.

EFI Expeditionary Force Institutes (UK). Canteen and welfare organization attached to armies outside the United Kingdom.

The Eder Dam after the raid, showing a 180-ft breach in the dam.

Egerland

A German tactical and fire control RADAR set for the control and direction of anti-aircraft gun batteries, and the first German service equipment to operate on the 9cm wavelength. The first installation was made near Berlin in January 1945 and 1000 sets were ordered, though only two installations were ever completed. It consisted of two co-ordinated radar sets, *Kulmbach* for detecting targets, and *Marbach* for controlling gunfire.

Egypt, 1939–42

See ALAMEIN, First and Second Battles of; ALAM HALFA; ALEXANDRIA; CAIRO; NIBEIWA; RUWEISAT RIDGE; SIDI BARRANI; SOLLUM, etc.

Eiche (Oak)

German plan to rescue MUSSOLINI, 1943.

Eichelberger, Lt Gen Robert L. (1886–1961)

Eichelberger was the Commandant of West Point Military Academy on the outbreak of war and was rapidly posted to command the US I Corps in the Pacific. He fought a successful campaign in NEW GUINEA, defeating the Japanese at Buna in January 1943. In September 1944 he was given command of the 8th Army and led it in the recapture of the PHILIPPINES.

Eichmann, Col Adolf (1906–62)

Eichmann was an SS officer in charge of the Gestapo's Section IV BG, responsible for controlling the Jewish population of the German-occupied territories. In 1941 he organized mass deportations of Jews from Germany and Bohemia to concentration camps in Poland. After the Wannsee Conference (January 1942), he was charged with the "final solution of the Jewish Problem" and proceeded to organize the death camps and specified the design of gas chambers and crematoria. He appears to have had no particular animosity towards Jews in general, but merely looked upon his task as his duty to the wishes of Hitler. He vanished in 1945 but was discovered in 1960 in South America, from where he was abducted by an Israeli group and placed on trial in Tel Aviv, where he was sentenced to death and executed in 1962.

Eifel Mountains, Germany, 1944–45

A range of rolling, wooded hills contiguous to the ARDENNES.

German 8.8cm Pak 43 anti-tank gun.

Eighty-Eight Gun

German 88mm anti-aircraft gun developed by Krupp in the early 1930s and placed in service in 1933 as the 8.8cm Flak 18. It was employed in Spain during the Civil War and its capabilities as an emergency anti-tank gun were there appreciated and tested, leading to the general issue of armour-piercing ammunition. An improved version, the 8.8cm Flak 36, was introduced in 1936, but this was ballistically the same as the Flak 18, and both remained in service until 1945. A further model, the Flak 41, appeared in 1942; this had a better ballistic performance but only a few hundred were built.

The Flak 18 and 36 fired a 20.7lb (9.4kg) shell at 2688ft (820m) per second to an effective ceiling of 26,230ft (8000m). The Flak 41 fired the same shell at 3278ft (1000m) per second to an effective ceiling of 35,000ft (10,675m). Both could fire highly effective anti-tank ammunition, and were highly valued for their power when the standard anti-tank guns were relatively feeble. The 8.8cm calibre was adopted for a "pure" anti-tank gun in 1943, the weapon being known as the 88mm PAK 43. Firing a 22lb (10kg) tungsten-cored shot this could defeat 184mm of armour at 6557ft (2000m) range. This gun was also adapted as a tank gun, being used on various models of the TIGER and PANTHER tanks, as well as in self-propelled tank destroyers.

Eilbote (Express Messenger)

German counteroffensive in northern Tunisia, January 1943.

Eichmann (right) with Hitler and Himmler (centre) at Mauthausen extermination centre. Kaltenbrunner leads the parade.

Eindhoven, Holland, 1944

During Operation MARKET GARDEN Major-General Maxwell TAYLOR's US 101st Airborne Division dropped north of the city on 17 September, capturing bridges over the Zuid Willems Vaart and Veghel Canals; the bridge over the Wilhelmina Canal at Son was also captured in a damaged but repairable condition. The following morning the paratroopers penetrated Eindhoven and were relieved by the British XXX Corps that night.

Einhorn

German operations against Greek partisans, July 1944.

Einsatzgruppen (Operations Groups)

The German title for four SS formations which followed the invading army into Russia in 1941 tasked with the execution of Jews, Communists and other non-Aryan elements in the occupied territories. Three thousand men were detailed for these duties, undergoing training in Saxony in March–April 1941. Officers were recruited from the SS, SD, GESTAPO and Sicherheitspolizei. The men came from these organizations and also from the Kriminalpolizei, State Police, Ordnungspolizei and WAFFEN-SS. Einsatzgruppe A was attached to Army Group North and cleared the BALTIC States and north-east Russia; Gruppe B followed Army Group Centre through MINSK and SMOLENSK; Gruppe C followed Army Group South through the UKRAINE, and Gruppe D followed the 11th Army to the Crimea, clearing the southern Ukraine en route. Their techniques were simple and brutal, generally rounding up Jews and Communists and shooting them in some convenient ditch. A small number of gas trucks were used, largely as an experiment, but shooting was the primary method. Between 1941 and 1944 some 2,000,000 Jews and other anti-German elements were executed by the Einsatzgruppen.

Eire, 1939–45

Although Eire was still a member of the British Commonwealth, the government of Eamonn de Valera was determined to remain neutral. Friction arose with the United Kingdom over naval bases which had been handed over to Ireland in 1938 and which the Royal Navy wished to use, the lack of these contributing to the loss of Allied lives and shipping during the Battle of the ATLANTIC. Conversely, many Irish-

men did not agree with the anti-British stance of the de Valera administration and the proportion of the population joining the British armed services was comparable to that of any Commonwealth country.

Eisenhower, Gen Dwight David (1890–1969)

Eisenhower spent World War I training recruits and by 1920 had reached the rank of major. In 1929 he visited Europe to prepare a report on US operations in 1918 and became a leading expert on the subject. In 1941, now a Lieutenant-Colonel, he was appointed Chief of Staff US 3rd Army, and in 1942 he became Chief of the War Plans Division on the staff of General MARSHALL. He was then appointed as Chief of Operations Division. In June 1942 he was made commander of US troops in Europe and in November, as Lieutenant-General, commanded the TORCH landings in North Africa. Here he neglected his command role for local politics until the US defeat at KASSERINE abruptly reminded him of his responsibilities. In 1943 he was nominated Supreme Commander of the Allied Expeditionary Force for Operation OVERLORD, and was promoted General of the Army in December 1944.

After the war he served briefly as Commander of the US Occupation Forces in Germany, then returned to the USA to become Chief of

General Eisenhower (left) confers with Lieutenant-General Clark.

Staff until 1948 when he retired. In 1951 he returned to service to become Supreme Commander Allied Powers, resigning in 1952 to enter politics, becoming the 34th President of the USA in the following year.

Eisenhower was an excellent staff officer, organizer and administrator, a less effective field commander. Nevertheless, his appointment as Supreme Commander for the Allied invasion of Europe was certainly instrumental in ensuring victory, since he had an unrivalled ability to weld a number of temperamental subordinates into a working team.

El Adem, Libya, 1940–42

An airfield south of TOBRUK which changed hands with the ebb and flow of fighting in Cyrenaica, El Adem was successfully raided by RAF Blenheims on 10 June 1940, the date of Italy's declaration of war on Britain.

El Agheila, Libya, 1941–42

A defensive position situated on a neck of land between the sea and extensive salt marshes in western Cyrenaica. On 24 March 1941 a German reconnaissance unit drove in the British outpost here, this action marking the beginning of ROMMEL's first offensive in North Africa. Following the CRUSADER battles, Rommel withdrew behind the El Agheila bottleneck and, having been reinforced, counter-attacked his dispersed opponents on 21 January 1942 and forced them to abandon their recent gains in the BENGHAZI bulge. Following his defeat at the Second Battle of ALAMEIN, Rommel withdrew to El Agheila but on 13 December 1942 was levered out of the position when the 2nd New Zealand Division executed a wide turning movement through the desert to the south.

El Alamein, Egypt, 1942

See ALAMEIN, First and Second Battles of.

ELAS

Ellinikos Laikos Apelephthericon Stratos (Greek – Committee of the People's Army). Greek resistance group, Communist-led and dominated, which came into existence during the German occupation of the country and which, after the Germans had left, attempted to take control of Greece.

Elbe River, Germany, 1945

Together with its tributary the Mulde, the Elbe was designated as the natural meeting point of the Anglo-American and Soviet armies during their converging advance into central Germany. The US 9th Army reached the Elbe at Magdeburg on 11 April and secured crossings the following day. The question arose as to whether the advance should be continued to BERLIN, only 53 miles (85km) distant, but having been advised that this might result in as many as 100,000 casualties, EISENHOWER, worried by the possibility that the Nazi leaders would create their National Redoubt in the south, refused to sanction the attempt. Further north, the British 2nd Army crossed the Elbe on 29 April and advanced to the Baltic coast, where contact was made with the leading Soviet elements at Wismar on 2 May.

Elbing (Elblag), Germany, 1945

A city in EAST PRUSSIA. During the evening of 23 January the leading unit of the Soviet 5th Guards Tank Army (2nd Belorussian Front) surprised the garrison and drove straight through to the Baltic coast. By dawn the defences had been closed but the withdrawal of the German Second Army behind the VISTULA left Elbing isolated and on 10 February the pocket was eliminated.

Electric Gun

Two German proposals for electric guns were considered during the war. The first was by Engineer Muck who proposed a multi-barrel weapon buried in a hillside and launching shells by a solenoid effect; this was critically examined and found impractical. The second was proposed by Engineer Hansler and was based on a French idea from 1918; this used two bus-bars carrying electricity and a winged missile which spanned the two to create a magnetic field – the principle which later became the linear motor. This was proposed as an anti-aircraft weapon to fire a 1.1lb (500g) shell and work on a prototype began in February 1945 but was overtaken by the end of the war. In subsequent years the idea was examined by the Allies, who came to the conclusion that a single six-"barrel" gun would require a power station sufficient to provide for a small city. The idea has recently been revived as part of the American SDI "Star Wars" project.

Electronic Warfare

The term coined to describe the various techniques for counteracting the RADAR and radio devices employed by the opposing forces. Radio signals, the dropping of WINDOW by small groups of aircraft and emissions of jam-

ming were employed to dupe defending radar operators into identifying flights which were only feints as the main attacking formations and to divert defending fighters to intercept these, thus allowing the real bombing force then to approach and attack their chosen target in the face of only limited opposition. Defenders developed systems for their fighters and anti-aircraft guns which "homed" onto the navigational aids, IFF and other equipment fitted to the incoming bombers, while the attackers were subsequently able in their turn to jam such devices, or to use them for their own escorting fighters to home onto. This electronic countermeasures war thus became a game of check and counter check played by each side's scientists which resulted in extremely rapid developments in radar and radio technology, the setting up of specialist countermeasures units, and played an increasingly important part in the success or failure of the opposing side's air forces when operating by night.

Elefant – Heavy Tank Destroyer (Ger)

Based on the unsuccessful Porsche contender of the TIGER E tank design, the vehicle was also known variously as Ferdinand, after Dr Ferdinand Porsche, and as the Tiger (P). The Elefant's gun was housed in a fixed superstructure mounted on the rear of the hull. A total of 90 were built and of these 76 entered service in July 1943 with two heavy tank destroyer battalions, taking part in the attack on the northern shoulder of the KURSK salient. Once within the Soviet defences many fell victim to tank-hunting parties as they

Elefant heavy tank destroyer.

lacked a machine gun for local defence. The survivors of the battle were fitted with a hull machine gun and sent to Italy, where they performed well in the semi-static conditions prevailing, their thick armour proving all but impervious to Allied anti-tank guns. *Weight* 67 tons; *speed* 12mph (19kph); *armour* 200mm; *armament* 1 88mm gun Pak 43/2; *engines* 2 Maybach 320hp petrol; *crew* 6.

Elephant Point, Burma, 1945

The peninsula dominating the entrance to Rangoon River. On 1 May the 2/3rd Gurkha Parachute Battalion dropped to the west of Elephant Point and eliminated the Japanese defences prior to the amphibious landing of 26th Indian Division (Major-General H. M. Chambers) in Rangoon River the following day. RANGOON itself was entered unopposed on 3 May. The Elephant Point drop was the only occasion during the Burma campaign when a parachute unit was employed in the role for which it had been trained.

El Hamma, Tunisia, 1943

A small town and coastal plain inland from Gabes, penetrated on 26 March by 2nd New Zealand Division and 1st Armoured Division, which had outflanked the defences of the MARETH LINE by moving south of the MATMATA HILLS and then through the TEBAGA GAP. The Axis forces holding the Mareth Line were forced to withdraw to avoid encirclement.

Elkton

Overall American strategy for the elimination of the Japanese naval base at RABAUL, 1943.

USS Denver, *took part in the Battle of Empress Augusta Bay, November 1943.*

Elsenborn Ridge, Belgium 1944

Feature lying on the northern shoulder of the German penetration during the Battle of the BULGE, stubbornly defended by Major-General Leonard GEROW's US V Corps, consisting of the 1st Infantry Division, 2nd Infantry Division, 9th Infantry Division and 99th Infantry Division, against repeated attacks by the 12th and 227th Volksgrenadier, 12th SS Panzer HITLER-JUGEND and 3rd Panzergrenadier Divisions, the effect being to stall the advance of DIETRICH's 6th Panzer Army.

Embry, AVM Sir Basil (1902–77)

On the outbreak of war Embry was a Wing Commander and CO of No. 107 Squadron, RAF BOMBER COMMAND. After operations over Norway and France, for which he was decorated, he was shot down in May 1940 and taken prisoner by the Germans. He escaped and, in spite of being recaptured twice, eventually made his way to England in time to serve in FIGHTER COMMAND during the Battle of BRITAIN. In 1943 he became acting Air Vice-Marshal given command of No. 2 Bomber Group, and in this position he personally led three particularly daring precision attacks on the Gestapo headquarters in Aarhus, Copenhagen and Odense in Denmark, which enabled imprisoned Danish resistance members to escape.

Emden, KMS – Light Cruiser

Emden took part in the Norwegian Campaign of 1940, then became a mine training ship. She served in the Baltic and in 1944 supported army operations with gunfire. In January 1945 she was used to evacuate the coffin of Field-Marshal von Hindenburg from Königsberg (Kalinin) following its removal from the Tannenberg Memorial, which was about to be overrun by the Soviet Army. She was scuttled at Kiel in April 1945 after sustaining bomb damage. *Displacement* 5600 tons; *dimensions* 508×47ft (154.8×14.3m); mean draught 17ft 6in (5.33m); *machinery* 2-shaft geared turbines producing shp 46,000; *speed* 29 knots; *protection* main belt 3–4in; turrets 2in; *armament* 8×5.9in (8×1); 3×3.5in AA (3×1); 4×37mm AA; 4×21in torpedo tubes; *complement* 630; *launched* 1925.

Emile Bertin – Light Cruiser (Fr)

Disarmed at Martinique when France surrendered in 1940. Reactivated in 1943 and joined the Free French Naval Force. Supported the Allied landings on the south coast of France in 1944. *Displacement* 5886 tons; *dimensions* 580×52ft (177×15.6m); mean draught 18ft (5.4m); *machinery* 4-shaft geared turbines producing shp 102,000; *speed* 34 knots; *armament* 9×152mm (3×3); 4×90mm AA (2×2); 8×37mm AA; 8×13.2mm AA; 6×550mm torpedo tubes; equipped for minelaying; *aircraft* 2 (1 catapult); *complement* 711; *launched* 1933.

Emmerich, Germany, 1945

An industrial town on the lower Rhine devastated by bombing and captured by the Canadian II Corps on 1 April after a fierce three-day battle.

Empress Augusta Bay, Battle of, 1943

Following the landing of the 3rd Marine Division on BOUGAINVILLE on 1 November 1943, a Japanese naval squadron commanded by Rear-Admiral Sentaro Omori and consisting of the cruisers *Myoko*, *Maguro*, *Sendai* and *Agano*, escorted by six destroyers, was detailed to attack the American transports in Empress Augusta Bay. These were protected by the cruisers *Montpelier*, *Cleveland*, *Columbia* and *Denver*, plus eight destroyers, under the overall command of Rear-Admiral A. S. Merrill, who deployed his ships in a long arc across the mouth of the bay. At 0230 on 2 November the American radar revealed Omori's squadron approaching in three columns. At 0246 a flare dropped by a Japanese floatplane warned Omori of his danger and he began to swing his columns into line ahead. Merrill promptly gave the order to open fire and within minutes *Sendai* had been reduced to a blazing, sinking wreck. During the ensuing confusion two Japanese destroyers, *Samidare* and *Shiratsuyu*, collided heavily and a third, *Matsukaze*, was rammed by *Myoko* with fatal consequences. At 0337 Omori broke contact and withdrew. Only one American destroyer sustained serious damage in the engagement.

Enfidaville, Tunisia, 1943

Captured 21 April by 50th (Northumbrian) Division during the holding attacks carried out by the British 8th Army while the Allied 1st Army launched its final offensive against the Axis in the Tunisian mountains.

Engebi Island, Marshall Islands, 1944

See ENIWETOK ATOLL.

England, USS – Buckley Class Destroyer Escort

Named after a naval reserve ensign killed during the attack on PEARL HARBOR. *England*, commanded by Lieutenant-Commander W. B. Pendleton, was awaiting convoy duty at Purvis Bay when, on 18 May 1944, she was detailed to operate against the Japanese submarine supply line to BOUGAINVILLE in company with the destroyer escorts *George* and *Raby*, under the overall command of Commander Hamilton Hains. At 1355 on 19 May *England* obtained a sound contact and launched a HEDGEHOG attack which resulted in the immediate destruction of the submarine *I-16*. During the early hours of 22 May all three ships hunted down the *RO-106*, which blew up after being hit by a salvo from *England*'s hedgehog. The following day *RO-104* was destroyed by *England* in a very similar engagement. Shortly before dawn on 24 May *George*'s radar picked up *RO-116* on the surface. The submarine dived but *England* established sound contact and tore her apart with a full hedgehog salvo. On 25 May Hains received orders to proceed to Seeadler Harbour, and while on passage picked up a radar contact shortly before midnight. *Raby* launched an attack and lost contact but *England* quickly picked up the scent and destroyed her fifth victim, the *RO-108*, at a depth of 250 feet (76.2m). At Seeadler Harbour the group was joined by the destroyer

escort *Spangler* with additional supplies of hedgehog ammunition and then returned to its patrol area, cooperating with a larger hunter-killer group based on the escort carrier *Hoggatt Bay*. Late on 30 May the destroyer *Hazelwood* established a sound contact and Hains' group was detailed to deal with it. *George* and *Raby* hunted unsuccessfully for some hours before the enemy submarine, *RO-105*, unwisely surfaced and switched on her searchlight before diving again. *England* and *Spangler* joined the hunt but Hains confined the action to maintaining sound contact until daylight. At dawn *George*, *Raby* and *Spangler* attacked in succession but missed; *England*, however, did not and the *RO-105* disintegrated in a tremendous underwater explosion. The *England*'s destruction of six enemy submarines in twelve days is unparalleled in the history of anti-submarine warfare but with the exception of a congratulatory signal from Admiral KING this extraordinary feat went largely unrecognized.

Enigma

The trade name for the electrical coding machine used by the German forces for high-level communications. In principle it relied upon a typewriter keyboard coupled to three or more rotors, the starting positions of which could be varied and which "stepped" at each keystroke to ensure that pressing the same key did not produce the same enciphered letter. Thus the coded message was proof against elementary decoding. See ULTRA.

USS England *underway, off San Francisco.*

Eniwetok Atoll, Marshall Islands, 1944

After the unexpectedly rapid capture of KWAJALEIN ATOLL it was decided that the American assault on Eniwetok Atoll, lying 325 miles (523km) distant at the western edge of the Marshalls group and defended by Major-General Yoshima Nishida's 2500-strong 1st Amphibious Brigade, should follow immediately. The islands were subjected to preliminary air attack and Admiral Hill's task force, which included Tactical Group 1 (22nd Marine and 106th Infantry Regiments) commanded by Brigadier-General Thomas Watson, penetrated the 17- by 21-mile (27- by 33-km) lagoon on 17 February. Following further air attacks and a heavy naval bombardment, LVTs put two battalions of 22nd Marines ashore on Engebi Island at 0842 on 18 February, these being followed by supporting armour. By 1450 the island and its airstrip had been overrun, although mopping-up continued until the following morning. On 19 February two battalions of 106th Infantry, reinforced with a battalion of 22nd Marines, mounted a similar assault on Eniwetok Island, which was cleared by 1630 on 21 February. The third major objective, Parry Island, was successfully assaulted by 22nd Marines on 22 February. Almost all of Nishida's men chose to die fighting. Marine casualties amounted to 254 killed and 555 wounded; Army elements lost 94 killed and 311 wounded.

Enogai Inlet, New Georgia (Solomon Islands), 1943

The location of a Japanese battery of four 140mm naval guns commanding the Kula Gulf. During Operation TOENAILS, the American invasion of NEW GEORGIA, the three battalions of Colonel Harry B. Liversedge's Northern Landing Group came ashore at Rice Anchorage on 5 July and, with the assistance of Coastwatchers and native scouts, cut its way through the jungle and succeeded in capturing the battery from the rear on 10 July. The Americans sustained the loss of 48 killed, 77 wounded and four missing; the 350-strong garrison of Enogai was wiped out. See also KULA GULF, Battle of.

Enterprise, USS – Yorktown Class Aircraft Carrier

Enterprise took part in the Battle of MIDWAY and provided air cover for the GUADALCANAL landings. She sustained damage during the Battle of the EASTERN SOLOMONS and again at the

Battle of SANTA CRUZ and also participated in the Battles of GUADALCANAL. Her subsequent service included the GILBERT ISLANDS, KWAJALEIN, TRUK, HOLLANDIA, SAIPAN, the Battle of the PHILIPPINE SEA, Palau, LEYTE and IWO JIMA. She was damaged by Kamikaze air attack off OKINAWA on 11 and 13 April 1945.

Enzian

A German subsonic ground-to-air missile which carried a 1100lb (500kg) warhead. Launched by four solid-fuel rockets, it was sustained in flight by a liquid-fuel rocket and was guided in flight by radio signals. Once in the area of a target, it would detect it by infra-red, acoustic or radar homing heads – the final design was never settled – which would steer the missile to the target. Development began in 1943 as "Flak Rakete 1", and it was named Enzian in early 1944. Altogether 60 development models were built and 38 were launched in test flights, about 16 of which used radio control. The project was stopped in January 1945.

Epsom

Offensive by British 2nd Army south-west of CAEN, June–July 1944.

Eritrea, 1940–41

See EAST AFRICAN CAMPAIGN, KEREN, MASSAWA.

Enzian air defence missile on launching ramp converted from an 88mm AA gun mounting.

Escaut River, Belgium, 1940

The line to which the Allied armies in Belgium completed their withdrawal from the DYLE on 19 May. German advances to the south made this equally untenable.

Espiritu Santo, New Hebrides, 1942–43

An American naval and air base which played a critical part in the SOLOMON ISLANDS campaign. See *Guadalcanal* by Adrian Stewart (William Kimber).

Essen, Germany, 1939–45

An industrial city in the RUHR and home of the Krupp armaments works, Essen was raided by the RAF's Bomber Command, and later the 8th USAAF, throughout the war. Essen was heavily defended and, because it was shrouded by perpetual industrial haze, a difficult target to hit. However, the latter problem was overcome by the OBOE blind-bombing device and on the night of 5/6 March 1943 the Krupp works were heavily damaged and 160 acres of the city devastated; RAF BOMBER COMMAND

American troops ride through the ruins of Essen, April 1945.

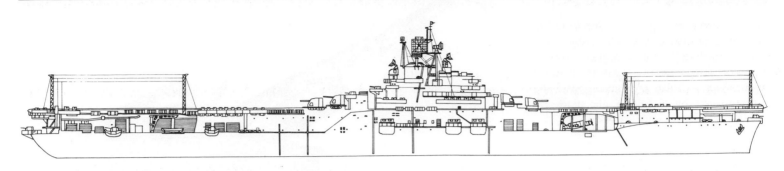

Essex class aircraft carrier.

employed 442 aircraft on this raid, of which 14 were lost and 38 damaged. In 1945 Essen formed part of the Ruhr Pocket and was captured by the US 9th Army in April.

Essex Class Aircraft Carriers (USA)

Displacement CV9 27,100 tons, *CV14 long hulled* 36,000; *dimensions* 872ft (265m) or 888ft (270m)×93ft (28.4m); mean draught 28ft 6in (8.58m); *machinery* 4-shaft geared turbines producing shp 150,000; *speed* 33 knots; *armament* 8×5in (4×2) and 4×5in (4×1); 17×4 40mm AA, 35×2 40mm AA; *aircraft* 100; *complement* 3500; *number in class* 24, launched 1942–45.

Estonia, 1940

Formerly an independent Baltic republic, Estonia was occupied by the Soviet Union on 15/16 June under the pretext of mutual security.

ETA Estimated time of arrival.

Ethiopia, 1940–41

See EAST AFRICAN CAMPAIGN; ADDIS ABABA; AMBA ALAGI; DEBRA TABOR; DESSIE; DIREDAWA; GONDAR; JIMMA.

ETO European Theater of Operations (US).

Etorofu Class Escorts (Jap)

Displacement 870 tons; *dimensions* 255ft×32ft 6in (77.7×9.9m); mean draught 10ft (3m); *machinery* 2-shaft geared diesels producing shp 4200; *speed* 19.75 knots; *armament* 3×4.7in (3×1); 4×25mm AA (2×2); 36 depth charges and 6 throwers; *complement* 147; *number in class* 14, all launched 1943.

ETOUSA European Theater of Operations, US Army (US).

Evacuation

A system of removing women and children from major cities in danger from air attack and relocating them in rural areas or towns thought less likely to be targets. A large-scale evacuation of London began in September 1939. About 1.5 million people made use of the government's evacuation scheme. The anticipated air raids failed to materialize, and by January 1940 more than half of the official evacuees had returned home. Meanwhile, in the period preceding and following the outbreak of war at least two million more people had carried out their own private evacuation. The onset of the BLITZ prompted a fresh wave of evacuation, in which some 1.3 million people were evacuated by the government. By 1942 almost half of them had drifted home. Some evacuation took place from LONDON in 1944–45 during the V-1 and V-2 campaigns. Evacuation schemes were also operated in

Child evacuees leave Liverpool.

Germany, increasing in scale as the Allied bombing offensive was stepped up. After the raids on HAMBURG in July–August 1943, nearly two-thirds of its civilian population of 1.2 million were evacuated through the length and breadth of Germany and into German communities in Poland and Czechoslovakia. In spite of the ferocity of the area bombing campaign, many evacuees drifted back to their parent communities, just like their British counterparts.

Evarts Class Destroyer Escorts (USA)

Displacement 1140 tons; *dimensions* 283ft 6in×35ft (86×10.5m); mean draught 8ft 3in (2.5m); *machinery* 2-shaft diesel-electric motors producing shp 6000; *speed* 21 knots; *armament* 3×3in; 4×40mm; 5×20mm; *complement* 170; *number in class* 68, launched 1942–44.

Excess

Naval supply of MALTA, 1941–43.

Exeter, HMS – York Class Cruiser (UK)

Exeter played a major part in the Battle of the RIVER PLATE, during which she received severe damage. After refitting she served with the Home Fleet 1940–41 and was transferred to the Eastern Fleet the following year. She fought in the Battle of the JAVA SEA, being again seriously damaged, and was sunk by Japanese surface units in the aftermath of the engagement.

Exporter

British-Australian operations against Vichy French forces in SYRIA, June–July 1941.

Extended Capital

British offensive resulting in the capture of MANDALAY, MEIKTILA and RANGOON, 1945. See also CAPITAL.

F

"F" Class Destroyers
See "E" and "F" Class Destroyers.

Fabius
Allied rehearsal for the NORMANDY landings, 1944.

FAC
Forward Air Controller (UK). A pilot attached to the forward infantry for the purpose of directing tactical fighter aircraft on to ground targets. A pilot was selected for this task since he was in direct radio communication with the aircraft and could speak to the aircraft pilot in his own technical terms.

Factory, the, Anzio, Italy, 1944
See APRILIA FACTORY.

Fairchild Aircraft (USA)
Fairchild AT-21 Gunner This was a highly specialized twin-engined monoplane, equipped for the training of aerial gunners. It had midships and nose turret gun positions and sufficient room inside to carry students who could change places on the guns during a training flight. 175 were built from 1942 onwards and were used exclusively by the USAAF. *Span* 52.6ft (16m); *engines* 2 520hp in-line; *crew* 2; *speed* 225mph (362kph).

Fairchild P-T19/23/26 These three aircraft were basically the same, differing only in internal equipment and engines. Single-engined low-wing monoplanes, they were produced in large numbers by several factories and used as a basic flying trainer by the US services and in Canada. *Span* 36ft (11m); *engine* 1 200hp in-line; *speed* 135mph (217kph).

Fairchild UC-61 Forwarder This was a high-wing monoplane adapted from the commercial Fairchild Model 24, and was originally adapted for service with the RAF as the Argus. The USAAF then took it into service as the UC-61. Several hundred were built and they were used for light transport and communications duties. *Span* 36.3ft (11m); *engine* 1 165 or 200hp radial; *speed* 130mph (209kph).

Fairey Aircraft (UK)

Fairey Albacore In most respects the Albacore was an updated SWORDFISH having an enclosed cabin, more power and a generally more modern appearance. A single-engined biplane torpedo bomber, it was intended to replace the Swordfish, though it never did so completely.

Employed for mine-laying, anti-shipping patrols and night bombing from shore bases, it was first used from aircraft carriers in 1941, dropping torpedos at the Battle of CAPE MATAPAN. Some 800 were built, but by the end of 1943 very few remained in service. *Span* 50ft (15.25m); *engine* 1 1130hp radial; *crew* 2 or 3; *armament* 3 machine guns, up to 2200lb (1000kg) of bombs or 1 18inch torpedo; *speed* 160mph (257kph).

Fairey Barracuda The Royal Navy's first monoplane torpedo bomber, designed to replace the ALBACORE. Unfortunate delays occurred in its development, but it eventually reached service in 1943 and proved to be moderately successful.

One of the most important missions performed by Barracudas was the bombing of the German battleship TIRPITZ in Kaafjord, Norway in April 1944. *Span* 49ft (14.9m); *engine* 1 1640hp in-line; *crew* 3; *armament* 2 machine guns, up to 2000lb (900kg) of bombs or 1 18inch torpedo; *speed* 225mph (362kph).

Fairey Battle This monoplane light day bomber was developed in response to a 1932 specification and was obsolescent by 1939, though it continued in service until late 1940. Combat showed that it was underpowered and underarmed, leaving it highly vulnerable to modern fighters, and after severe losses with the Advanced Air Striking Force in France in May 1940 it was withdrawn from first-line service, being relegated to a training role. *Span* 54ft (16.5m); *engine* 1 1030hp in-line; *crew* 2; *armament* 2 machine guns, up to 1000lb (450kg) of bombs; *speed* 240mph (386kph).

Fairey Firefly This was designed to replace the FULMAR and went into service with the Royal Navy in 1942. A carrier-borne fighter and reconnaissance machine, it had a reasonable performance and was easy to handle. It saw some action in the Pacific theatre, and was to remain in service until the middle 1950s. *Span* 44.5ft (13.5m); *engine* 1 1730hp in-line; *crew* 2; *armament* 4 20mm cannon, up to 1100lb (500kg) of bombs or 8 rocket launchers; *speed* 316mph (508kph).

Fairey Fulmar This low-wing eight-gun monoplane two-seat fighter went into service as a carrier-borne machine with the Royal Navy in 1940 and performed a wide range of duties including reconnaissance, escort, convoy protection and night bombing. Despite being rather slow, it performed well and enjoyed considerable success in the Mediterranean theatre. *Span* 46.5ft (14.2m); *engine* 1 1080hp in-line; *crew* 2; *armament* 8 machine guns; *speed* 280mph (450kph).

Fairey Seafox This was a catapult-launched floatplane carried by warships for patrol and reconnaissance duties. In fact this type of aircraft was little used by the Royal Navy, and only 64 were ever built. Due to the peculiar demands of catapult launching, the Seafox was unusual in having an open cockpit for the pilot and a covered one for the observer. A biplane with twin floats, the *wingspan* was 40ft (12.2m); *engine* 1 395hp in-line; *crew* 2; *armament* 1 machine gun; *speed* 125mph (201kph).

Fairey Swordfish One of the most famous British aircraft of the war, affectionately known as the "Stringbag" since it could carry a wide variety of loads, the Swordfish was a slow, open-cockpit biplane which by any sane reckoning was obsolete long before the war began. In spite of this it was in service throughout the war and played its part in many major actions, such as the Battle of CAPE MATAPAN, the sinking of the BISMARCK and the Siege of MALTA. Nominally a torpedo-bomber, it was also used as a convoy escort, for anti-submarine patrol and as a reconnaissance

Final adjustments made to the torpedo carried by a Mark I Fairey Swordfish aboard HMS Battler.

machine. *Span* 45.5ft (13.9m); *engine* 1 690hp radial; *crew* 2 or 3; *armament* 2 machine guns, 1 torpedo or mine, or up to 1100lb (500kg) of bombs, or 8 rocket launchers; *speed* 138mph (222kph).

Falaise Gap, France, 1944

The area through which the German 7th Army, 5th Panzer Army and Panzer Group EBERBACH attempted to escape from the pocket formed by the southwards advance of the Canadian 1st and British 2nd Armies and the northwards advance of the US 1st and 3rd Armies following the latter's breakout from

The Falaise pocket.

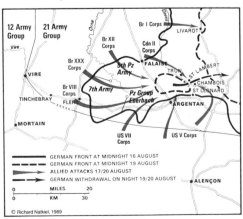

the NORMANDY beach-head. The pocket, which began forming on 13 August, was subjected to incessant artillery fire and air attack as it contracted; the gap was finally closed on 19 August, although fighting continued until the 21st. It is estimated that only 20,000 of the 80,000 Germans in the pocket escaped; of the remainder, 10,000 were killed and 50,000 surrendered. Amid the wreckage in the pocket the Americans found 380 tanks and self-propelled guns, over 700 artillery weapons and 5000 assorted vehicles; on the British and Canadian sectors the figures were 187 tanks and self-propelled guns, 157 armoured cars and armoured personnel carriers, 252 artillery weapons and 2500 motor vehicles of various types. No count was made of the thousands of horse-drawn vehicles or dead draught animals. See ARGENTAN. See also *The Killing Ground – The Battle of the Falaise Gap August 1944* by James Lucas and James Barker (Batsford).

Falkenhausen, General Alexander von (1878–1966)

Von Falkenhausen was German military governor of Belgium and northern France from 1940 to 1944. A regular soldier, he deliberately evaded many GESTAPO and SS instructions and attempted to mitigate the conditions of the occupation for the local population, though he was punctilious in maintaining German control and did not neglect German interests in such matters as the direction of industry and production of warlike equipment for the German economy. He was implicated, by others, in the JULY BOMB PLOT and was recalled to Berlin where he was imprisoned by the Gestapo, who failed to uncover any evidence against him. At the end of the war he was again imprisoned, this time by the Allies, and in 1951 was sentenced by a Belgian court to 12 years' imprisonment, of which he served only two days.

Falkenhorst, Col-Gen Niklaus von (1885–1968)

After commanding the XXI Corps during the invasion of Poland in 1939, von Falkenhorst commanded the German invasion of Norway in 1940 and, in spite of short notice and a force of only five divisions, succeeded in placing the country under German control. He remained as military commander until 1944, keeping the population under control by repressive measures. Put on trial at the end of the war, he was sentenced to death, but his sentence was commuted to 20 years' imprisonment and he was released in 1953.

Falkland Islands, South Atlantic, 1939

Because of the need to safeguard the sea route round Cape Horn, a 2000-strong British garrison consisting of infantry and anti-aircraft units was despatched to the islands on the outbreak of war to prevent their possible seizure by Argentina, where German influence was strong. The islands assumed even greater importance during the hunt for the German pocket battleship ADMIRAL GRAF SPEE and the damaged cruiser HMS *Exeter* retired there after the Battle of the RIVER PLATE.

Fallujah, Iraq, 1941

A town on the Euphrates captured by a flying column known as Habforce (Major-General J. G. W. Clark) on 18 May and held against three days of Iraqi counter-attacks before the advance to Baghdad was resumed.

Fantail   See LANDING VEHICLES TRACKED.

FANY   First Aid Nursing Yeomanry (UK). An all-female nursing organization operating in British military hospitals.

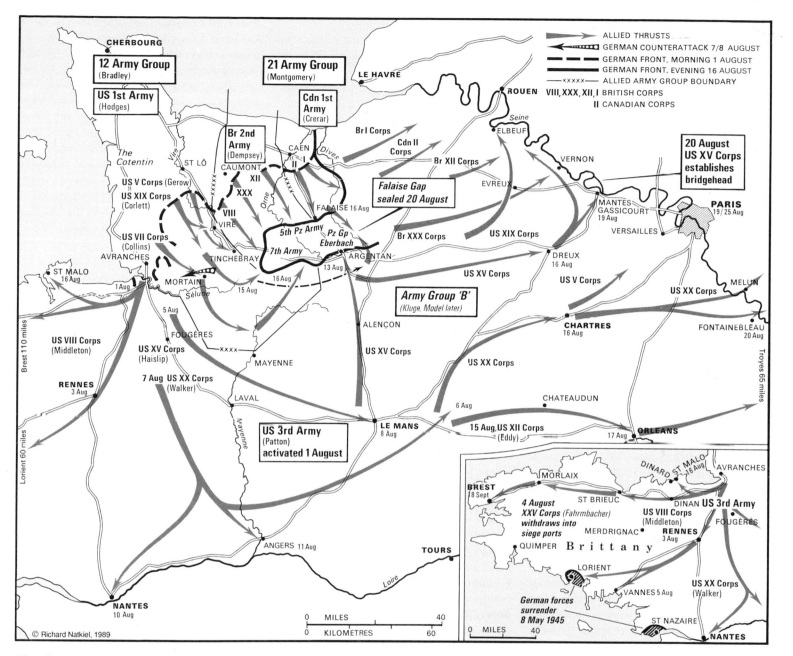

The Allied Breakout from Normandy, August 1944.

Farman F-222 (Fr)

This high-wing bomber was designed in 1930 and served as the principal heavy bomber of the French Air Force for many years. By the outbreak of war it was obsolete, but numbers were used for bombing and leaflet raids into Germany and Czechoslovakia in 1939–40. After the collapse of France they were used by the Luftwaffe as general transports. *Span* 118ft (36m); *engines* 4 950hp radial; *crew* 5; *armament* 3 machine guns, up to 5510lb (2500kg) of bombs; *speed* 185mph (298kph).

Farouk, King of Egypt (1920–65)

Farouk succeeded to the throne in 1936, but had little talent for governing and no particular love for the British who were occupying his country. He supported the growing Egyptian Nationalist Movement, allied himself with various dubious political parties, appointed a pro-Nazi prime minister, and flirted with neo-Nazi groups, sympathies which gave rise to considerable Anglo-Egyptian political tension throughout the war years.

Farragut Class Destroyers (USA)

Displacement 1395 tons; *dimensions* 341ft 6in×34ft 3in (104×10.4m); *mean draught* 9ft (2.7m); *machinery* 2-shaft geared turbines producing shp 42,800; *speed* 36.5 knots; *armament* 5×5in (5×1); 8×21in torpedo tubes (2×4); *complement* 250; *number in class* 8, launched 1934–35.

Fat Boy

Code name for the plutonium nuclear bomb dropped on NAGASAKI on 9 August 1945, the name being derived from the bomb's shape. "Fat Boy" used an implosion method of operation which required a much greater diameter than LITTLE BOY.

FCM 36 – Infantry Tank (Fr)

100 of these vehicles were built 1936/37 by the *Société des Forges et Chantiers de la Méditer-ranée* (FCM). *Weight* 12.8 tons; *speed* 16mph (26kph); *armour* 40mm; *armament* 1 37mm gun; 1 7.5mm machine gun; *engine* Berliet 100hp diesel; *crew* 2.

FCNL French Committee for National Liberation.

Félix

German plan to capture Gibraltar, the Canary and Cape Verde Islands.

Felsennest, Germany, 1940

The name given by HITLER to his field head-quarters during the 1940 campaign in the West. This was located in bunkers of the West Wall at Munstereifel, in the foothills of the EIFEL MOUNTAINS, close to Bonn. An approx-imate translation is Nest in the Crags.

Ferdinand (Ger) See ELEFANT.

Fergusson, Brig Sir Bernard Edward, Lord Ballantrae (1911–)

Bernard Fergusson was aide-de-camp to General WAVELL in 1935–37, and after the out-break of war was Wavell's intelligence officer in Palestine. He later acted as an observer in the short Syrian campaign, and on the staff of GHQ India. In 1942 he joined WINGATE's first CHINDIT Brigade and commanded No. 5 Col-umn in the 1943 expedition into BURMA. He then commanded 16th Infantry Division, which acted as a column in Wingate's 1944 expedition. In postwar years he was Gov-ernor-General of New Zealand from 1962–67.

FFI FRENCH FORCES OF THE INTERIOR.

FG 42 Rifle

A German parachutist's rifle (Fallschirm Gewehr 42) firing the standard 7.92mm MAUSER cartridge. When the Sturmgewehr 43 was under development, the German air-borne troops were offered the weapon, but they refused it since it used a reduced-power cartridge. Instead, they pushed for the development of the FG 42, a rifle capable of single shots or automatic fire. Gas-operated, it pioneered the "straight-line" design which reduced muzzle climb during automatic fire. About 7000 were made, and it was first used during the rescue of Mussolini.

Fiat Aircraft (Italy)

Fiat BR20 Cicogna A low-wing monoplane bomber, the Cicogna appeared in 1936 and was used in the Spanish Civil War; a small number were also sold to Japan. In 1940 a few were flown to Belgium from where they made sporadic raids over England, but they were then withdrawn to be used in Greece and over MALTA. Some 600 were built but few remained at the time of Italy's surrender. *Span* 70.6ft (21.5m); *engines* 2 1000hp radial; *crew* 4; *armament* 4 machine guns, up to 3500lb (1600kg) of bombs; *speed* 255mph (410kph).

Fiat CR32 An open-cockpit biplane fighter, the CR32 appeared in 1933 and was a modern-looking all-metal machine which formed the major fighter strength of the Italian Air Force in the late 1930s. Numbers went to Spain, forming a useful part of Franco's air strength. By 1939 they were being replaced, but some were still used in North and East Africa, and Greece during 1940–41. *Span* 31ft (9.5m); *engine* 1 600hp in-line; *armament* 4 machine guns, 220lb (100kg) of bombs; *speed* 235mph (378kph).

Fiat CR42 Falco In many ways a continuation of the CR32 line, this was another open-cockpit biplane fighter which was adopted by the Italian, Belgian, Hungarian and Swedish air forces in 1939–40. Over 1700 were built and, apart from 50 which were operated by the Italians against Britain from Belgian bases in 1940–41, most were employed in the Mediter-ranean and North African theatres. *Span* 32ft (9.8m); *engine* 1 840hp radial; *armament* 2 12.7mm machine guns, 440lb (200kg) of bombs; *speed* 267mph (430kph).

Fiat G12 The G12 was a tri-motor monoplane troop or cargo transport which went into service in 1941. Relatively few were built. *Span* 94ft (28.7m); *engines* 3 770hp radial; *speed* 240mph (386kph).

Fiat G50 Freccia One of the first modern low-wing monoplane fighters to appear in Italian service, the G50 appeared in 1937 and some were used in Spain in 1938–39. A basi-cally sound design, but was underpowered by contemporary standards and was no match for Allied aircraft. A number operated with some success in Finland until 1944. *Span* 35ft (10.7m); *engine* 1 840hp radial; *armament* 2 12.7mm machine guns; *speed* 290mph (467kph).

Fiat G55 The G55 was an improved version of the G50 and probably the best fighter the Italians developed during the war. It did not appear until 1943 and few had been delivered before the Italian surrender. Production con-tinued, and about 100 were used by the Italian Fascist air arm supporting the German forces in Italy in 1944. *Span* 38.75ft (11.8m); *engine* 1 1475hp in-line; *armament* 1 20mm cannon, 2 12.7mm machine guns; *speed* 385mph (619kph).

Fiat RS14 A twin-engined mid-wing monoplane floatplane reconnaissance-bom-ber, the RS14 was an excellent machine, but was only built in small numbers. *Span* 64ft (19.5m); *engines* 2 840hp radial; *crew* five; *armament* 1 12.7mm and 2 7mm machine guns, up to 880lb (400kg) of bombs or depth charges; *speed* 242mph (389kph).

Field Artillery

Field artillery is artillery mobile enough to accompany a field army. Employed as the immediate support of the division, it encompasses guns and howitzers in the 75mm to 120mm range of calibres.

British: The British field artillery piece was the 25-pounder (87mm) gun-howitzer. This fired a 25lb (11.3kg) shell to a maximum range of 13,400yds (12,256m), was towed behind a special tractor and manned by six men. It also fired a 20lb (9.07kg) steel armour-piercing shot which could defeat any wartime

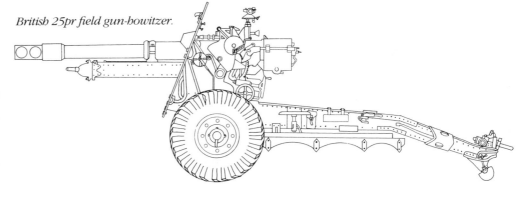

British 25pr field gun-howitzer.

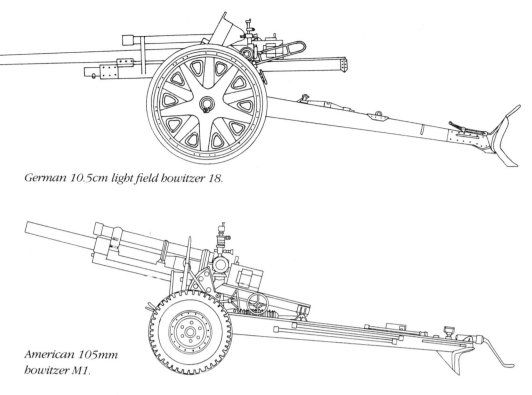

German 10.5cm light field howitzer 18.

American 105mm howitzer M1.

tank. The 25pr did not appear until the Norwegian campaign in 1940; the campaign in France was fought using the 18/25pr, an earlier 18pr (84mm) gun refitted with the 87mm barrel. Due to technical problems this weapon could not fire to the full range of the 25pr gun, but it was entirely replaced by 1941.

USA: The US Army standard divisional piece was the 105mm howitzer M1, firing a 33lb (15kg) shell to 12,196yds (11,160m) range. The US also used a number of 75mm guns and howitzers, though these were almost all supplanted by the 105mm howitzer by 1942.

Germany: The standard German weapon was the 105mm light field howitzer Model 18, firing a 32.6lb (14.8kg) shell to a range of 11,666yds (10,675m). This weapon was gradually improved during the war, by the addition of a muzzle brake and a more powerful cartridge, until it attained a range of 13,470yds (12,325m). A replacement, the 105mm howitzer Model 43, was under development as the war ended; this would have achieved a range of 16,393yds (15,000m).

USSR: The Soviet field artillery had a diversity of different weapons of 76mm and 85mm calibre. The 76mm Model 1939 gun was a representative example, firing a 13.45lb (6.1kg) shell to 13,317yds (12,185m) range. The 85mm Divisional Gun Model 1944 fired a 20.9lb (9.5kg) shell to 16,940yds (15,500m) range.

Japan: The Japanese employment of artillery was somewhat different to that of other armies, but their most common field gun was the 75mm Meiji 38 Improved which fired a 14.55lb (6.6kg) shell to 13,115yds (12,000m).

Italy: The standard Italian field gun was the 75mm howitzer Model 935 which fired a 14lb (6.35kg) shell to a range of 10,273yds (9,400m). This was accompanied by the 105mm howitzer Model 28, firing a 34lb (15.5kg) shell to 14,426yds (13,200m) range.

Fieseler, Gerhard

Fieseler was a German aircraft designer with a factory in Kassel which produced the FIESELER "STORCH" reconnaissance aircraft. He was responsible for the original design and for some of the production of the FZG-76 or V-1 Flying Bomb.

Fieseler Fi 156 Storch (Ger)

Designed in 1935, this high-wing monoplane was taken into service by the Luftwaffe as a general reconnaissance and communications aircraft. It was later adapted for staff transport, ambulance and army co-operation roles. Over 2500 were built and it was employed in all theatres of war. *Span* 46.75ft (14.2m); *engine* 1 240hp in-line; *crew* 2; *armament* 1 machine gun; *speed* 110mph (177kph).

Fighter Command

RAF Fighter Command was formed in 1936, under Air Marshal DOWDING, for the air defence of south-east England. Initially it comprised two Groups, Nos. 11 and 12, with their fighter squadrons and the chain of south and east COAST RADAR stations. After the outbreak of war No. 10 Group was formed to defend the south-west, while No. 12 Group's duties were extended to include northern England, Scotland and the Northern Isles.

In this form the Command undertook the defence of the UK during the German attacks of 1940–41, known as the Battle of BRITAIN and the BLITZ. In 1941 three more Groups were formed to cover the West Midlands, the north of England, Scotland, the Orkneys and Shetlands. By summer 1941 the Command had 79 squadrons and organized and controlled the daylight air offensive over western France and the Low Countries as well as maintaining the defence of Britain. The most active day of the war for Fighter Command occurred on 19 August 1942 when 2339 sorties were flown in support of the DIEPPE landings; air supremacy was achieved, for a loss of over 100 fighters.

In November 1943 many squadrons were transferred to 2 Tactical Air Force for support of the Normandy landings. The Command continued to control these units until the invasion took place, after which it was renamed "Air Defence of Great Britain", retaining only 43 squadrons. Thereafter the role of the Command was relatively minor until the war ended, though it played a notable part in the defence against the V-1 attacks in the summer of 1944. In October 1944 the title "Fighter Command" was resumed.

Fiji Class Cruisers (UK)

Displacement 8000 tons; *dimensions* 555ft 6in×62ft (169×18.9m); mean draught 16ft 6in (5m); *machinery* 4-shaft geared turbines producing shp 72,500; *speed* 33 knots; *protection* main belt 3.25in; deck 2in; turrets 2in; *armament* 12×6in (4×3); 8×4in AA (4×2); 9×2-pdr AA (2×4 and 1×1); 8×0.5in (2×4); 6×21in (2×3) torpedo tubes; *aircraft* 3; *complement* 730; *number in class* 11, launched 1939–42.

Filbert

A British electronic decoy consisting of a naval barrage balloon with a metallic RADAR reflector inside it. Towed by a light craft, it gave a radar echo similar to that from a major war-

Einsatzgruppen firing squad, Poland.

ship and numbers were used in the "Moonshine" flotillas, which produced a spurious fleet attacking the Pas de Calais, drawing German attention away from the genuine invasion fleet attacking Normandy in June 1944.

Final Solution, the

A German euphemism for the extermination of European Jewry (*die Endlösung*). Hitler's anti-Semitism can be traced from his earliest writings, but the phrase arises from a statement by HIMMLER to Rudolf HOESS, commandant of AUSCHWITZ, in May or June 1941, that Hitler had given orders "for the final solution of the Jewish question". Extermination squads (EINSATZGRUPPEN) were formed to follow the armies into Russia and murder all Jews and non-Aryans, Communist officials and ranking Soviet prisoners. Extermination camps were set up in Poland to which Jews were shipped from concentration camps and ghettos throughout Europe to be killed by gassing and shooting. Accounting was not strict, and there is no absolute record of how many Jews were killed, but the best estimate is that a total of 5,570,000 died. In addition it is probable that another million people, including gypsies, Communists, Soviet prisoners-of-war, incurable invalids and other non-Aryan and unwanted categories, were also murdered.

Finland, 1939–45

Despite her gallant resistance during the Winter War of 1939–40, Finland was forced to accede to Soviet demands, the most important of which was the cessation of the southern portion of the KARELIAN Isthmus. In 1941 she allied herself with Germany and, when Operation BARBAROSSA began, declared war on the Soviet Union on 26 June 1941. In the Karelian Isthmus, Marshal MANNERHEIM's army group advanced as far as the former national boundary but refused to go further, a factor which contributed to the survival of LENINGRAD. Elsewhere, however, Finnish troops and Colonel-General von FALKENHORST's German Norway Army (later re-designated 20th Mountain Army) attempted unsuccessfully to cut the Leningrad–MURMANSK railway, although Kirkenes and PETSAMO in the far north were captured. A Soviet counteroffensive in January–February 1942 was defeated and subsequently the front remained relatively quiet. In June 1944, with the German armies everywhere in retreat, a fresh Soviet offensive broke through the Karelian defence lines and on 4 September an armistice was concluded between Finland and Russia. Clashes between Finnish and German troops followed, and on 4 March 1945 Finland formally declared war on Germany.

Finschhafen, New Guinea, 1943

Settlement and old German fort at the tip of the HUON PENINSULA, captured on 2 October after the Australian 9th Division's 20th Brigade had made a landing six miles (10km) north of the town on 22 September while the 4th Brigade's 22nd Battalion advanced along the coast from the west. The Japanese were found to be present in the area in greater strength than had been anticipated and their 20th Division mounted a series of counter-attacks throughout October and November. The Australians, however, were reinforced with HQ 9th Division, 24th and 26th Brigades and a

German troops on the Arctic Front, Finland.

Results of firestorm bombing of Hamburg, July 1943.

squadron of MATILDA tanks, and continued to push the enemy back into the hinterland until his potential was exhausted. See SATTELBERG.

Firebrand

Projected Allied invasion of Corsica, 1944.

Firefly – Sherman Conversion (UK)

Name given to SHERMAN medium tank re-armed with British 17-pdr gun. This had been suggested as early as January 1943 as a safeguard against the failure of the CHALLENGER project. The feasibility of the idea was demonstrated in November 1943 and quantity conversion was authorized in February 1944. The conversion dispensed with the hull gunner, the additional space available being used for ammunition stowage. The Firefly was initially issued on the scale of one per troop until early 1945 when greater numbers became available. Until the COMET appeared it was the only tank in British service capable of engaging the TIGER and PANTHER on anything like equal terms. The Sherman Marks converted were M4A1, M4A3 and M4A4, known respectively in British service as Sherman IIC, Sherman IVC and Sherman VC.

Firestorm

The firestorm was a phenomenon unknown prior to the RAF air raid on Hamburg in July 1943. During the course of this raid a large number of incendiary bombs were dropped into a congested urban area, leading to a considerable number of fires. The heated air, due to these fires, rose into the atmosphere, and this displacement drew in cold, fresh air from the surrounding districts. The introduction of this current of air into the fire area led to the fires burning more fiercely, giving off more heat, causing more hot air to rise faster, drawing in more cool air, and thus forming a cycle which was self-accelerating. Eventually the incoming air was moving at very high speeds, sufficient to knock people over, or even carry them along, and the fires became an inferno incapable of being controlled. The same phenomenon was later observed in other German and Japanese cities which were heavily bombed by incendiaries.

Fitch, R Adm Aubrey (1883–1978)

A career naval officer, Fitch was a Task Force Commander under NIMITZ. During the Battle of the CORAL SEA his Task Force 11 included the carrier USS *Lexington*, from which Fitch launched the air attacks which sank two Japanese carriers. The *Lexington* was severely bombed and sank soon afterwards. In 1944 Fitch was promoted to Deputy Chief of Naval Operations.

Flail Tanks (Allied)

See BARON, CRAB and SCORPION.

Flak

A German abbreviation for "Flugzeug Abwehr Kanone" – aircraft attack gun, i.e. anti-aircraft gun. Widely adopted by Allied aviators as a slang term to describe hostile fire and is still so used. A "Flak Jacket" was the American term for body armour issued to aircrews.

Flash Spotting

Technique of detecting enemy artillery by visual observation of the muzzle flash given off on firing. It relied upon observers spread across the front and connected by radio or wire, who reported the bearing and exact time of the flash to a central plotting room. Here flashes seen by different observers at the same time could be plotted and a position for the enemy gun consequently deduced. In good conditions an accuracy of about 220ft (100m) could be achieved, but the general adoption of flashless propellants in the latter part of the war made the system less valuable.

Flensburg, Germany, 1945

A town near the Danish border which housed the last headquarters of Grand Admiral Karl DÖNITZ, who had succeeded HITLER as Head of State and Supreme Commander of the Wehrmacht.

Fletcher, V Adm Frank J. (1885–1973)

Fletcher was in tactical command of US naval forces at the Battle of the CORAL SEA. In the Battle of MIDWAY, Fletcher's flagship, *Yorktown*, was crippled but not before the crucial sinking of three of the four carriers in NAGUMO's First Carrier Strike Force. The latter part of the battle was fought by Admiral SPRUANCE. In August 1942, during the opening phases of the US invasion of GUADALCANAL, Fletcher withdrew the three carriers which were providing air cover for the landings, leaving the ground troops in an exposed position. He later argued against providing Navy aircraft to assist in the defence of Guadalcanal, but was overruled by NIMITZ. Shortly afterwards he was transferred to command the North Pacific Fleet and remained there until the war ended. He retired in 1947.

Fletcher Class Destroyers (USA)

Displacement 2050 tons; *dimensions* 376ft 6in×39ft 6in (114×12m); mean draught 17ft 9in (5.3m); *machinery* 2-shaft geared turbines producing shp 60,000; *speed* 37 knots; *armament* 5×5in; 6 to 10×40mm or 20mm AA; 10×21in torpedo tubes; *complement* 300; *number in class* 175, launched 1942–44.

Fliegerfaust

A German nine-barrelled rocket launcher designed to be fired from a man's shoulder at low-flying aircraft. The barrels were 20mm calibre and the projectile was a standard 20mm cannon shell with a rocket motor attached. The effective range against aircraft was about 1640ft (500m), the maximum range about 6560ft (2000m). The design had been perfected by March 1945 and several thousand were ordered, but mass-production never began and only a few were found after the war.

F-Lighters – German Coastal Craft

Shallow draught vessels of barge-like construction which could be used as coastal escorts, anti-aircraft ships, supply carriers or troop transports, heavily armed with one 88mm dual-purpose gun, one 40mm AA and numerous 37mm and 20mm mountings. First encountered in 1941, they operated in the Mediterranean, Adriatic and Tyrrhenian Seas, in the Gulf of Genoa and off the southern coast of France. Their firepower outmatched that of Allied MTBs and PT boats, and so they could only be sunk by these by means of torpedoes launched at short range.

Flintlock

American invasion of the MARSHALL ISLANDS, 1944.

Florence, Italy, 1944

The 6th South African Armoured Division (British XIII Corps, and US 5th Army) entered Florence 4 August 1944 during the German withdrawal from ROME to the GOTHIC LINE. Because of its immense store of cultural treasures Field Marshal KESSELRING had declared Florence an open city, but all the bridges across the Arno had been blown with the exception of the ancient Ponte Vecchio, the approaches to which were heavily mined and blocked with the rubble of demolished buildings.

Flower Class Corvettes (UK)

See also MODIFIED FLOWER CLASS. *Displacement* 925 tons; *dimensions* 205×33ft (62.5×9.9m); mean draught 11ft 6in (3.48m); *machinery* 1-shaft reciprocating engine with ihp 2750; *speed* 16 knots; *armament* 1×4in; 1×2-pdr AA or 4×0.5in AA (1×4); 4×.303in AA (2×2); *complement* 85; *number in class* 215, launched 1940–42.

USS Heermann *(Fletcher class) laying smoke, early in the Action off Samar, October 1944.*

Fletcher class destroyer.

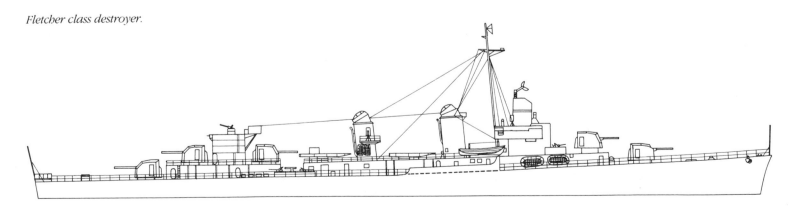

"Flush-Deck" Class Destroyers (USA)

Also known as "four-stackers" in American service because of the number of funnels. Prior to the war many had been converted to light minelayers, fast minesweepers and seaplane tenders. A further 50 were transferred to the UK in 1940 in exchange for bases in the West Indies. See also TOWN CLASS. *Displacement* 1090–1190 tons; *dimensions* 314ft 6in×31ft 9in (95.8×9.6m); mean draught 8ft 9in (2.69m); *machinery* 2-shaft geared turbines producing shp 26,000; *speed* 35 knots; *armament* 4×4in; 1×3in; 12×21in torpedo tubes; *complement* 150; *number in class* 81, launched 1917–21.

Flushing, Holland, 1944

A heavily-defended port on the south coast of WALCHEREN. On 1 November No. 4 Commando crossed the SCHELDT from BRESKENS and effected an assault landing at 0630, followed by 155 Brigade (52nd (Lowland) Division) at 0800. During the day the sea front and central area of the town were captured. No. 47 Commando, which had come ashore further west, also converged on Flushing. By the evening of 3 November organized resistance had ended.

Flutto Class Submarines (Italy)

Sparide, *Murena*, *Nautilo* and *Grongo* were all scuttled at La Spezia when Italy surrendered; refloated, they were taken into service by the German Navy as, respectively, *UIT 15*, *UIT 16*, *UIT 19* and *UIT 20*. *Displacement* 750 tons (905/1068 tons normal); *dimensions* 207×23ft (63.1×6.98m); *machinery* 2-shaft diesel/electric motors hp 2400/800; *speed* 16/8.5 knots; *armament* 1×3.9in; 2×20mm AA; 2–4×13.2mm AA; 6×21in torpedo tubes (4 bow, 2 stern); and 12 torpedoes; *complement* 54; *number in class* 8, launched 1942–43.

Flying Dustbin

The nickname for the projectile fired by the British recoiling spigot MORTAR, mounted on the Assault Vehicle Royal Engineers (AVRE). The weapon was a spigot mortar, in which a steel rod was driven into the hollow tail of the projectile, held on a cradle. The rod exploded a cartridge inside the tail, so that the bomb was blown forward and the rod was blown back to re-cock it for the next shot. The Flying Dustbin was a 40lb (18kg) demolition bomb consisting of a cylinder about one ft (305mm) in diameter and one ft (305mm) long, with a tail tube and fins attached at the rear end. It had a range of about 100yds (91.5m) and was a devastating munition when fired at concrete obstacles or field fortifications.

Focke-Wulf FW190, the best of the German fighters.

Flying Tigers

The "Flying Tigers" was the nickname given to the American Volunteer Group (AVG), an organization of American aviators recruited in the USA by Major-General Claire CHENNAULT for service in CHINA, fighting for the Nationalist Army. Chennault had retired in 1937 and went to China to establish flying schools. He then set up a series of airfields and in 1940–41 went to the USA and recruited ex-US Air Force, Navy, Marine, and commercial pilots and aviation engineers for the AVG. Three squadrons were formed, which fought against the Japanese over China and BURMA, claiming some 300 Japanese aircraft destroyed. In 1942 Chennault was reclaimed by the US Army and made Major-General, commanding the 14th US Army Air Force, which was developed from the nucleus provided by the AVG.

Flyover, the, Anzio, Italy, 1944

A road bridge 1.5 miles (2.5km) south of CARROCETO where German counter-attacks on the beach-head were finally halted in February.

Focke-Wulf Aircraft (Ger)

Focke-Wulf FW189 Ubu The FW189 was a twin-boom, central crew nacelle monoplane designed as a reconnaissance, liaison and training machine, which was principally employed on reconnaissance over the Eastern Front. An exceptionally manoeuvrable and tough machine, it later became outclassed by its opposition and ended as a general communications and ambulance aircraft. *Span* 60.6ft (18.4m); *engines* 2 450hp in-line; *crew* 3; *armament* 4 machine guns, 220lb (100kg) of bombs; *speed* 220mph (354kph).

Focke-Wulf FW190 Probably the best German fighter of the war, and among the best fighters used by any combatant, the FW190 appeared in 1941. Most production aircraft were powered by radial engines, but in 1944 a much-developed version, the FW190D-9, was introduced with an in-line engine as an air-superiority machine of high performance. The basic radial-engined version proved readily adaptable as a fighter-bomber and several heavily-armoured ground-attack versions were developed, capable of carrying up to 1100lb (500kg) of bombs. *Span* 34.5ft (10.5m); *engine* (FW190A), 1 1700hp radial, (FW190D) 1 1770hp in-line; *armament* (FW190A) 4 20mm cannon, 2 machine guns, (FW190D) 2 20mm cannon, 2 13mm machine guns; *speed* (FW190A) 408mph (656kph), (FW190D) 426mph (685kph).

Focke-Wulf FW200 Condor Designed as a long-distance airliner, the pre-war aircraft made several record flights around the world and was exported in some numbers. In 1938 the Japanese asked for a conversion to the

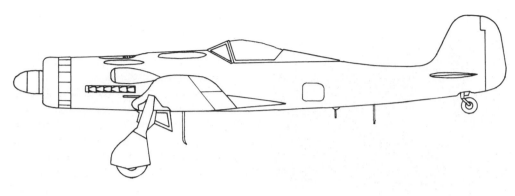

Focke-Wulf Ta152 fighter.

maritime reconnaissance role, and this led to the Luftwaffe adopting it in similar form. The Condor became a formidable enemy to Allied shipping, sinking tens of thousands of tons in the Atlantic until 1942, when Allied countermeasures gained supremacy. The Condor then became a transport machine in various land theatres. *Span* 108.25ft (33m); *engines* 4 1200hp radial; *crew* 8; *armament* 1 20mm cannon, 5 machine guns, up to 4630lb (2100kg) of bombs; *speed* 224mph (360kph).

Focke-Wulf Ta152 The Ta152 was an improved FW190D, the new nomenclature referring to the designer, Kurt Tank. It was fitted with a more powerful engine and a 30mm cannon firing through the airscrew boss, had a ceiling of 40,000ft (12,200m) and could outrun most Allied fighters. The design did not appear until early in 1944 and less than 70 were built, so it had little overall effect on the Luftwaffe's fortunes. *Span* 36ft (11m); *engine* 1 2100hp in-line; *armament* 4 20mm, 1 30mm cannon; *speed* 465mph (748kph).

Föhn

A multiple anti-aircraft free rocket launcher, the only one of its kind used by Germany. It was intended to fire large numbers of rockets as barrages against low-flying bombers; it was also deployed as a ground-to-ground bombardment weapon during the closing weeks of the war, and the rockets were proposed as the air-to-air armament for the NATTER fighter. The launcher was a simple framework carrying racks for 35 rockets and was carried on a trailer. The rocket was the 7.3cm R. Spreng-granate, a spin-stabilized rocket with a warhead of .62lb (280g) of Cyclonite high explosive and a simple impact fuze. No reli-

able figures for range or velocity were ever found for this weapon, and it seems that very few were actually deployed before the war ended.

Fokker Aircraft (Netherlands)

Fokker CX The CX was a typical two-seater reconnaissance-bomber biplane of the mid-1930s. As well as being used by the Netherlands it was built under licence in Finland, and both nations used them in combat in 1939–40. *Span* 39.3ft (12m); *engine* 1 650hp in-line (Netherlands) or 1 835hp radial (Finland); *armament* 2 machine guns, 880lb (400kg) of bombs; *speed* 199/210mph (320/338kph).

Fokker DXX1 This marked Fokker's transition from biplane to low-wing modern monoplane and was originally designed for the Netherlands East Indies Army. It attracted export orders and became the principal fighter in Holland, Finland and Denmark. Anachronistic in retaining a fixed undercarriage, it was otherwise an effective machine and those in Holland gave good service before being overrun by the Luftwaffe in 1940. *Span* 36ft (11m); *engine* 1 830hp radial; *armament* 4 machine guns, except Danish which had 2 20mm cannon and 2 machine guns; *speed* 285mph (458kph).

Folgore Class Destroyers (Italy)

Displacement 2090 tons; *dimensions* 315×30ft (96×9m); mean draught 10ft 9in (3.27m); *machinery* 2-shaft geared turbines producing shp 44,000; *speed* 38 knots; *armament* 4×4.7in; 2×37mm AA; 8×20mm AA; 6×21in torpedo tubes; 2 depth charge throwers; equipped for minelaying; *complement* 183; *number in class* 4, all launched 1931.

Fondouk Pass, Tunisia, 1943

Early in April an opportunity existed for the Allies to intercept the withdrawal of the Italian 1st Army from the WADI AKARIT by striking through the Fondouk Pass with Lieutenant-General Crocker's British IX Corps and capturing Kairouan, deep in the Axis rear. Pichon and the hills on the left of the pass were to be captured by 128 Brigade (46th Division) with tank support, while the high ground on the right would be taken by the US 34th Division and 751 Tank Battalion; the British 6th Armoured Division was then to break through the pass and out into open country. The pass and the surrounding hills were defended by the 999th Light African Division, a German penal formation the members of which had been promised remission if they fought well. The battle began on 8 April and, while Pichon and most of the hills on the left were taken, the attack of the US 34th Division broke down under heavy fire. Shortly after dawn on 9 April the 6th Armoured Division was committed prematurely; the leading regiment of 26th Armoured Brigade, 17th/21st Lancers, sustained serious casualties and the division's advance was temporarily halted. Later in the day the last remaining feature on the left, Djebel Rhorab, was captured and the Americans also made some progress. During the evening 26th Armoured Brigade renewed its advance, using the dry bed of the River Marguellil, and broke out of the pass the following morning. By then, however, the chance of trapping the Italian 1st Army had gone. Anglo-American friction in the aftermath of the battle ultimately resulted in a better mutual understanding of each other's methods. See *From the Desert to the Baltic* by Major-General G. P. B. Roberts (William Kimber) and *Through Mud and Blood* by Bryan Perrett (Robert Hale).

FOO Forward Observing Officer. An artillery officer attached to forward elements of the infantry and able to call down artillery fire at their request.

Forager

American assault on the MARIANAS islands, 1944.

Forced Labour

A system used by the German government to provide sufficient unskilled labour for war industries, construction, clearing of air raid

Force H in the Mediterranean, HMS Ark Royal *(centre) with HMS* Renown *and HMS* Sheffield *near Gibraltar.*

damage and other tasks. Foreign workers – many of them little more than slaves – played an important part in raising German war production between 1941 and 1944 by 230 per cent. They fell into four categories: the concentration camp *Aussenkommandos*; *Ostarbeiter*, from the Eastern territories; prisoners-of-war; and *Fremdarbeiter*, workers recruited from the occupied Western countries. The *Fremdarbeiter* workers formed a separate society, with their own camps, canteens and newspapers, with which German civilians had little contact. By 1943 there were 12 million foreign workers in Germany.

Force H

Formed at Gibraltar in June 1940 under Vice-Admiral Sir James SOMERVILLE as a powerful squadron capable of operating in either the Western Mediterranean or the Atlantic as the situation demanded. The composition of the Force varied in proportion to the resources available and, depending upon the importance of the missions undertaken, could include one or more capital ships and/or aircraft carriers. Force H took part in the bombardment of the French Fleet at MERS-EL-KEBIR and the hunt for the German battleship BISMARCK, but its most critical role was the protection of convoys through the Western Mediterranean to Malta, notably the PEDESTAL CONVOY.

Ford Island, Hawaii, 1941

An island in PEARL HARBOR to the east of which was "Battleship Row", where most of the US Pacific Fleet's battleships were moored during the Japanese attack on 7 December.

Ford Scout Car (Canada)

Very similar in layout and appearance to the DAIMLER SCOUT CAR. Also known as the Lynx. 3255 were built by the Ford Motor Company of Canada. *Weight* 4 tons; *speed* 57mph (92kph); *armour* 30mm; *armament* 1 Bren light machine gun; *engine* Ford 95hp petrol; *crew* 2.

Fordson Armoured Car (UK)

Fordson truck chassis fitted with the armoured hulls and turrets of obsolete ROLLS-ROYCE armoured cars during 1940. The vehicle was armed with a Boys anti-tank rifle mounted coaxially in the turret with a water-cooled Vickers machine gun, plus two air-cooled Vickers "K" or Browning machine guns on a ring mounting above the turret. Twenty of these conversions were made in

Cairo, equipping the RAF's No. 2 Armoured Car Company which served in the Western Desert 1940/41 and in Iraq and Syria in 1941.

Formidable, HMS – Illustrious Class Aircraft Carrier

Formidable served in the East Indies and with the Mediterranean Fleet during 1941. She took part in the Battle of CAPE MATAPAN and was badly damaged by air attack off CRETE. After completing repairs in the USA she joined the Eastern Fleet in 1942, and later served with Force H in 1943, the Home Fleet in 1944 and the Pacific Fleet in 1945.

Formosa, 1944

Formosa was ceded to Japan following the Sino-Japanese War of 1894–95. During the prelude to the American invasion of the PHILIPPINES, Japanese aircraft launched a series of heavy attacks against Admiral HALSEY's 3rd Fleet off Formosa, 13–16 October 1944. As a result, the carefully rebuilt Japanese naval air strength was crippled by the loss of 600 aircraft. The American loss amounted to 75 aircraft, two cruisers badly damaged and a number of other vessels hit. For the remainder of the year Japanese air bases on Formosa were attacked by carrier aircraft and raided by B-29 heavy bombers flying from airfields in China and India.

Forrestal, James V. (1892–1949)

American Under-Secretary of the Navy until 1944 and then Secretary of the Navy, Forrestal was a retiring man who shunned publicity but who nevertheless was a driving force in providing the US Navy with ships and equipment. As Under-Secretary he was responsible for procurement of ships, guns, aircraft and every other naval requirement, and his considerable success in this role ensured him the succession when Secretary Knox died in 1944. Not content with running the Navy from his office, Forrestal went to Britain in 1941, made two visits to the South Pacific and was present at the invasion of IWO JIMA, and visited the Mediterranean theatre in time to observe the American DRAGOON landings in southern France. Forrestal had a naval background, having been trained as a naval aviator in World War I, and spent some time in the office of the Chief of Naval Operations. He spent the years between the wars building up a career in banking and in the summer of 1940 became one of President ROOSEVELT's special advisers on national defence matters; it was from this post that, on Presidential recommendation, he was made Under-Secretary when that post was established by Congress later in the year.

Fortitude
Deception plan for OVERLORD.

Foul Point, Burma, 1943–45
See DONBAIK and ARAKAN.

Fox Armoured Car (Canada)
Similar to the HUMBER ARMOURED CAR Mark III but manufactured in Canada by General Motors. Armament consisted of .50-cal and .30-cal Browning machine guns mounted coaxially. The vehicle was powered by a General Motors 104bhp petrol engine. About 200 were built.

France, Belgium, Holland, 1940
General Maurice GAMELIN, the Allied Commander-in-Chief, believed that the expected German offensive in the West would consist of a

German parachute troops go into action in Holland, May 1940.

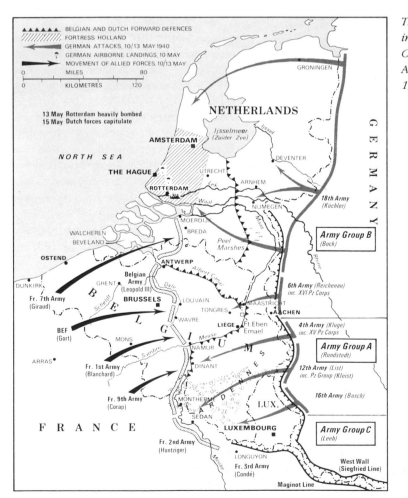

The German invasion of the Low Countries and the Allied reaction, May 1940.

mechanized version of the Schlieffen Plan of 1914, outflanking the MAGINOT LINE with an advance through neutral Holland and Belgium. In that event he planned to despatch the British Expeditionary Force (BEF) and the best French armies north to join the 11 Dutch and 23 Belgian divisions which would increase the Allied strength to the point at which ultimate victory was possible after the Germans had been halted along the line of the River DYLE. The initial German plans had indeed envisaged a limited advance into Belgium, but these were abandoned when HITLER accepted a more radical alternative strategy devised by von MANSTEIN. This involved an invasion of Holland and Belgium which was *intended* to draw the BEF and much of the French strength north. The bulk of the German armour would then break through the weakly held ARDENNES sector, cross the Meuse and cut a swathe across northern France to the Channel, the effect being to entrap those Allied forces in the north within a pocket; this phase of the operation was codenamed SICHELSCHNITT (Sickle Cut). The attack on the Low Countries would be delivered by von BOCK's Army Group B with two Panzer Corps under command; the *Sichelschnitt* blow would be delivered by von RUNDSTEDT's Army Group A, spearheaded by three Panzer Corps; in the south von LEEB's Army Group C would mount holding attacks against the Maginot Line and along the upper Rhine. On the eve of the offensive the German Army fielded 2439 tanks, the majority in the light class, plus a small reserve. The French, on the other hand, deployed about 3000 tanks, many of them better armed and armoured than the German machines, although most were dispersed along the front; the BEF possessed 210 light tanks and 100 infantry tanks. In the air the Luftwaffe possessed a decisive superiority and was able to put up 1268 fighters, 1120 level bombers, 350 dive-bombers and a large transport fleet, against which the French *Armée de l'Air* could muster only 700 inferior fighters and up to 175 bombers. The BEF's Air Component included 500 fighters and light bombers, but only the few Hurricane squadrons available could compete with the Germans on even terms.

On 10 May German paratroops and air landing formations seized strategic locations in Holland. A single Panzer division drove west from the frontier to relieve them, isolating the Dutch Army from French formations which were racing north to reinforce it. The Germans threatened to destroy every Dutch city unless Holland surrendered and to prove their point the Luftwaffe turned the centre of ROTTERDAM into an inferno. Holland capitulated on 15 May. The lynch-pin of the Belgian defence system, Fort EBEN EMAEL, was also captured by German airborne units on 10 May and von Bock's troops began streaming across the ALBERT CANAL. In accordance with Gamelin's intentions, the BEF and French armies wheeled north-east onto the Dyle line while the first major tank battle of the war took place in the GEMBLOUX GAP. Meanwhile, led by von KLEIST's Panzer Group, Army Group A had advanced through the Ardennes and, between 13 and 15 May, secured crossings of the Meuse at DINANT, Monthermé and Sedan with close and protracted support from the Luftwaffe. During these operations Corap's French 9th Army was shattered and HUNTZIGER's French 2nd Army was severely mauled. Breaking out of their bridgeheads, the Panzer Corps cut a 40-miles-wide swathe across northern France to the Channel between 16 and 21 May, being temporarily checked at the latter date by the British counter-attack at ARRAS. They then swung north into the rear of the Franco-British-Belgian forces in Belgium, which were already under constant pressure

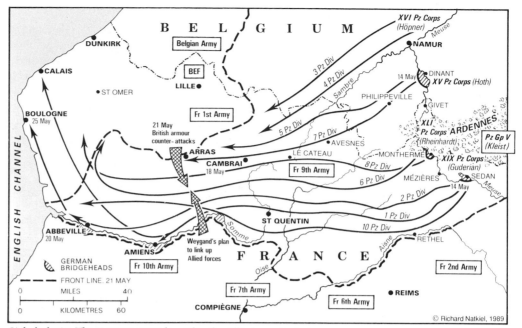

Sichelschnitt: The Panzer corridor splits the Allied armies in two.

from Army Group B. The position of the troops in the pocket was now impossible and the DUNKIRK evacuation commenced on 26 May. This continued until 3 June, complicated by King LEOPOLD's decision that Belgium would capitulate at midnight on 27 May.

General Maxime WEYGAND, who had replaced Gamelin on 20 May, deployed the remaining French armies along a line stretching from the Somme and the Aisne to the MAGINOT LINE. Having regrouped, the Germans renewed their attack on 5 June and, despite fierce resistance, broke through to the south. The French government moved to Bordeaux on 10 June; on the same day Italy declared war and invaded southern France. Paris, declared an open city, was entered by the Germans on 14 June. The French retreat continued, General Prételat's Army Group 2 being pinned back against the Maginot Line and forced to surrender on 22 June. Marshal PÉTAIN, who had assumed the Presidency on 16 June, requested an armistice and hostilities ended on 25 June.

The historic meeting of the French and German commanders in a railway carriage, in a clearing in the forest near Compeigne, 50 miles (80km) northeast of Paris.

The campaign, brilliantly conceived and ruthlessly executed, cost Germany 27,000 killed, 110,000 wounded and 18,000 missing. France suffered 90,000 dead, 200,000 wounded and 1,900,000 of her soldiers had been taken prisoner or were missing. Total British losses came to 68,000, Belgian 23,000 and Dutch 10,000. The Luftwaffe lost 1284 aircraft, the RAF 931 and the *Armée de l'Air* 560. The BEF lost all its tanks and artillery, the French all but a small proportion of theirs. At the end of the campaign German tank strength showed a reduction by 50%, but in part this was due to mechanical breakdowns. See *To Lose a Battle – France 1940* by Alistair Horne (Macmillan) and *A History of Blitzkrieg* by Bryan Perrett (Robert Hale).

Franco, Gen Francisco (1892–1975)

Franco came from a naval family and was intended for the Spanish Navy, but there was no vacancy at the Naval Cadet School and in 1907 he went to the Infantry Academy. After commissioning he was sent to Morocco in 1912 and his undoubted talent soon propelled him upwards. By 1916 he was a general and, wounded in the stomach, returned to command a garrison in Spain. He was appointed second-in-command of the Spanish Legion on its formation in 1920 and commanded it from 1923 to 1927, laying a firm foundation of discipline and efficiency. In 1934 Franco and Foreign Legion troops were called in by the government to suppress a miners' strike in Asturias, and in the following year he was made Chief of Staff. On the election of a leftist coalition government in February 1936, Franco was sent to a minor command in the Canaries, from whence he returned in July to lead the Republican forces in the Civil War, emerging as the dictator of Spain. During World War II he trod a skilful path of non-belligerence, if not strict neutrality, in spite of strong pressure to join the Axis. He met HITLER in October 1939 to discuss the possibility of a Spanish-German attack on Gibraltar, to be followed by the seizure of the Azores, the Canaries, Madeira and Cape Verde; but his price for co-operation was Morocco and other French African territory which Hitler was reluctant to offer for fear of offending Vichy. Thereafter as Britain's position appeared to improve, so Franco gradually grew cooler towards the Axis and he was able to secure the defence of Spain without upsetting either Germany or Italy to any significant degree.

Frangible Grenade

An American incendiary grenade consisting of a glass bottle filled with alcohol and gasoline and ignited by a tube of chromic anhydride attached to the bottle neck. These proved unsafe in transport and were abandoned in 1943. An ignition system based on a commercial blank cartridge was then adopted. Half a million were produced but they were rarely used.

Frank, Fort, Philippines, 1942

American coast-defence fort on Carabao Island in Manila Bay. The southernmost fort of the Manila Bay defences, it was armed with two 14-inch guns, two 3-inch guns and eight 12-inch MORTARS. All these guns duelled with Japanese artillery in 1942, and the fort surrendered with the other Manila Bay defences on 6 May 1942. It was retaken by US forces on 16 April 1945 with no opposition, the Japanese garrison having abandoned the fort four days previously.

Frank, Hans (1900–46)

Frank was a lawyer and one of the early members of the Nazi Party. In 1933 he was appointed Reichs Commissioner for Justice, and in 1939 Governor-General of the "Gouvernement-General", that portion of German-overrun Poland which had not been incorporated into the German Reich. A ruthless man, he instituted a brutal and repressive regime which had the declared aim of subju-

Dr Hans Frank.

gating the Poles and extracting as much as possible of the country's resources for the benefit of Germany. He was acquiescent in the slave labour and Jewish extermination programmes and did his best to exterminate the Polish intelligentsia. After attempting suicide several times as the Soviet Army approached, he eventually resigned in August 1944 during the WARSAW Uprising. Captured after the defeat of Germany, he was tried at NUREMBERG and hanged on 16 October 1946.

Frank, Karl Hermann (1898–1946)

Karl Frank was a Sudeten German and, with Henlein, leader of the Sudeten German Nazi Party. In 1939, after the annexation of Czechoslovakia, he became Secretary of State for the Reichs Protectorate of Bohemia and Moravia, acting as the deputy to HEYDRICH and later FRICK. Effectively the executive head of the Reichs Protectorate, he was responsible for ordering the destruction of the village of LIDICE, together with the massacre of its inhabitants, as a reprisal for the assassination of Heydrich. Captured at the end of the war, he was tried in Czechoslovakia and publicly hanged near Prague in May 1946.

Frantic

Codeword for continuous day and night bombing of targets in Germany from bases in the United Kingdom, Italy and the Soviet Union, 1944–45.

Fraser, Adm Sir Bruce (1888–1982)

Fraser was Controller of the Royal Navy for the early part of the war and then became Commander-in-Chief of the Home Fleet. In this capacity he directed the search for and sinking of the *Scharnhorst* in December 1943. In August 1944 he became Commander-in-Chief of the Eastern Fleet, in the Indian Ocean, and in November 1944 took command of the Pacific Fleet. On 2 September 1945 he signed the Japanese surrender in Tokyo Bay on behalf of the British government. After the war he became First Sea Lord and Chief of the Naval Staff from 1948 to 1951.

Fraser, Peter (1884–1950)

Fraser began his career in New Zealand politics as a dock labourer active in union affairs. By the outbreak of war he was a well-known and respected figure, and in 1940 succeeded to the office of Prime Minister after the death of Michael Savage. A strong leader, he was a staunch supporter of CHURCHILL's policies, but nevertheless insisted that New Zealand troops would only be employed with his approval. His Commander-in-Chief, General FREYBERG, always acted in accordance with Fraser's directives. In 1941 he attended several meetings of the British War Cabinet, to make New Zealand's position known, and in 1942 he visited President ROOSEVELT in Washington for the same purpose. In 1943 he became Minister for External Affairs in addition to being Prime Minister, and he was confirmed in office in the general election in September 1943.

Fredendall, Gen Lloyd

Fredendall commanded the Centre Task Force in Operation TORCH, charged with landing and taking ORAN. This was accomplished successfully, and he was then placed in command of US 2nd Corps in Tunisia. However, Fredendall's tactical grasp was poor, and he dispersed his troops too widely across a 100-mile sector from Fondouk to El Guettar. When attacked by von ARNIM on 14 February 1943 his troops were routed, and at the crucial point in the battle Fredendall was occupied in moving his headquarters and was out of touch with his troops. The resulting panic allowed von Arnim to take the KASSERINE PASS. Fredendall, whose overbearing manner towards his fellow-commanders and allies had gained him many enemies, was held responsible and dismissed. He returned to the USA to take up a training post and was never again employed on operations.

Fredericus

German elimination of the Izyum Salient, south-east of KHARKOV, May 1942.

Free French Forces

Title given to those French military and naval units which rallied to General DE GAULLE following the debacle of 1940, and which continued to fight with the Allies. Relations between the Free French and the rest of the French military establishment remained bitter even after the liberation of France in 1944. See BIR HACHEIM, DAKAR, MADAGASCAR, MERS-EL-KEBIR and SYRIA.

French Forces of the Interior (FFI)

General term for the main French resistance groups. By early 1944 their activities were being co-ordinated by a National Council which was in turn represented on DE GAULLE's National Committee of Liberation; General Pierre KOENIG was appointed the FFI's Commander-in-Chief on 2 June 1944. During the period immediately prior to D-DAY the FFI contributed to the Allied deception plan by not attacking targets in the NORMANDY and Brittany areas. Elsewhere in France, however, the FFI supported the Allied landings with a massive programme of interdiction operations which included harassing, sabotage, attacks on road and rail transport and disruption of the telephone network. Coupled with intense air activity, these operations virtually isolated the Normandy battlefield during the critical period. When the Allies broke out of their beach-heads, the FFI were responsible for securing bridges and other installations which were vital both to the advance and to the subsequent lines of communication. On 19/20 August the FFI rising in Paris expedited the German departure from the city.

French North Africa, 1940 and 1942

See ALGIERS; CASABLANCA; MERS-EL-KEBIR; MOROCCO; ORAN; TUNISIA.

Freya

Freya was the codename given to the standard German early-warning RADAR set manufactured by the Gema Company. Design began in 1936 and by 1939 over 100 sets were operational. It remained in service in increasing numbers throughout the war.

Freyberg, Gen Sir Bernard (1889–1963)

Freyberg was born in England but raised in New Zealand, and as a young man had fought with Pancho Villa in the Mexican Civil War. He then joined the British Army and fought at Gallipoli in 1915 and on the Western Front, where he won the Victoria Cross and three DSOs and was wounded nine times. He was a Major-General in 1939 and commanded the 2nd New Zealand Division. He took his troops to the Mediterranean theatre, where they rapidly acquired a reputation as tough and skilful soldiers. In 1941 his force was sent to GREECE, from which it was evacuated to CRETE. In the battle for Crete the New Zealanders were able to inflict such severe casualties on the German parachute troops that they were

Free French troops and Foreign Legionnaires at Bir Hacheim, June 1942.

never again used in the airborne role. Returning to LIBYA, the division took part in almost all the operations in the Western Desert up to the capitulation in TUNISIA. They then went to Italy as part of the 8th Army, but were later detached and placed under command of the US 5th Army. Their principal action in Italy was the Battle of CASSINO, at which Freyberg was the Corps Commander. Freyberg has frequently been identified as "the man who ordered the bombing of Cassino Monastery". This is incorrect and based on an account of General CLARK's memoirs in which he attempted to blame his lack of decision on others. Clark, afraid of the political consequences, actually passed the responsibility to ALEXANDER, who authorized the bombing on Freyberg's recommendation that his attack would probably not succeed without it. Moreover, Freyberg asked for fighter-bombers. The question of who was responsible for changing this request to a force of 135 heavy and 87 medium and light bombers has never been satisfactorily resolved.

Frick, Wilhelm (1877–1946)

Frick was Minister of the Interior in HITLER's government from 1933 to 1943, and was largely responsible for enacting various measures to ensure the firm control of the state by the Nazi Party. In 1943 he was appointed Reichs Protector of Bohemia and Moravia, though his Secretary of State FRANK wielded the power in the Protectorate. Arrested after the war, he was tried at NUREMBERG and hanged in October 1946.

Friedeburg, Adm Hans von (1895–1945)

Von Friedeburg was a relatively unknown German naval officer who succeeded Admiral Dönitz as Commander-in-Chief of the German Navy in April 1945. Dönitz then despatched Friedeburg to negotiate the surrender with the Allies at MONTGOMERY's headquarters at LÜNEBURG HEATH on 3 May 1945. After negotiation, it was Friedeburg who signed the surrender document which covered all German forces in northern Europe and Germany and which brought about the end of the war in Europe on 7 May.

Fritsch, Gen Werner von (1880–1939)

Von Fritsch had been commissioned into the artillery and served in World War I with distinction. By 1934 he was a general, with strictly

General Baron Werner von Fritsch.

military interests and nothing but contempt for politicians and the Nazi Party. He was appointed Commander-in-Chief of the Army in 1934, but his intransigent attitude, and uncompromising opposition to the introduction of ideology into service life, soon upset the Nazis and he was manoeuvred into retirement in 1938 by means of a trumped-up accusation of homosexuality. His departure removed the principal obstacle to HITLER's reorganization of the High Command. He retained honorary colonelcy of his old artillery regiment, and in 1939 accompanied them on the invasion of Poland, where he was killed on 22 September by a sniper outside Warsaw.

Fritz

Initial outline plan for the German invasion of the Soviet Union.

Fritz-X

Also known as FX-1000 or SD-1400, this was a German air-to-ground guided gliding bomb controlled by the observer in the parent aircraft who sent steering commands to the bomb by radio. It was basically a 3086lb (1400kg) armour-piercing bomb to which wings and a tail unit, complete with radio control system, had been added. Development began in 1939 and it went into service in mid-1943, scoring its greatest success on 9 September 1943, east of Sardinia, when the Italian battleship *Roma* was sunk after being hit by three of these bombs. Other designs, up to 5510lb (2500kg), were planned, but the idea was abandoned due to Allied radio countermeasures which upset the control system.

Frogmen

A name given to underwater warfare specialists because of their masks, flippers and wetsuits. Although normally associated with attacks on enemy shipping and sabotage, they also played a vital role in amphibious operations, including beach reconnaissance and demolishing submerged obstacles.

Fromm, Gen Friedrich (1888–1945)

Fromm was an officer of the General Staff and in 1939 became Chief of Army Equipment and Commander of the Replacement Training Army, his task being to administer that portion of the General Staff in Berlin, control all army units stationed in the Home Command, and supply the field armies with men and equipment. He undoubtedly performed this function well, but he had the misfortune to number Count von STAUFFENBERG among his staff, as a result of which he became embroiled in the JULY BOMB PLOT. As soon as the plot misfired, Fromm convened a court-martial and had the plotters shot, ostensibly to prove his loyalty, in fact to cover his complicity. It availed him nothing; he was arrested by the GESTAPO and hanged by them on 19 March 1945.

General Friedrich Fromm.

Front

The Soviet equivalent of a Western army group. The various Fronts took their titles from the sectors of the main front which they were holding or from major operational areas, for example West Front and Stalingrad Front. These titles changed as the war progressed; for example, on 20 October 1943 Voronezh, Steppe, South-West and South Fronts became respectively 1st, 2nd, 3rd and 4th Ukrainian Fronts. A Front consisted of several armies and its commander was responsible for securing the strategic objectives set by *Stavka*, the Soviet High Command.

Frühlingserwachen (Spring Awakening)

German counteroffensive in HUNGARY, March 1945.

Frühlingswind (Spring Wind)

German counteroffensive in central Tunisia, February 1943.

FTP Francs-Tireurs et Partisans. French resistance organization; part of the FFI.

Fubuki Class Destroyers (Jap)

Displacement 2090 tons; *dimensions* 388ft 6in×34ft (118.4×10.3m); mean draught 10ft 6in (3.18m); *machinery* 2-shaft geared turbines producing shp 50,000; *speed* 34 knots; *armament* 6×5in (3×2); 2×13mm; 9×24in torpedo tubes (3×3); *complement* 197; *number in class* 19, launched 1927–31.

Fuchida, Cdr Mitsuo (1902–76)

The experienced Japanese naval pilot selected to lead the attack on PEARL HARBOR on 7 December 1941. He was responsible for the co-ordination of the various elements of the attack and personally led the first wave. He was subsequently active in naval air operations throughout the war, missing the Battle of MIDWAY because of appendicitis.

Fuller

British naval and air watch on the German warships SCHARNHORST, GNEISENAU and PRINZ EUGEN in BREST harbour, 1941–42.

"Funnies", the (UK)

Generic name applied in British service to armoured assault engineer vehicles, particularly to those serving with 79th Armoured Division, i.e. ARKS, AVRES, CRABS, CROCODILES, LANDING VEHICLES TRACKED, etc.

FUP Forming-up Point (UK). The location at which troops or tanks assembled prior to beginning an attack.

Furious, HMS – Aircraft Carrier

Launched in 1916, *Furious* had been laid down as a battlecruiser but was converted into a hybrid aircraft carrier. On 2 August 1917 the first aircraft landing on a ship at sea was made on her decks by Commander E. H. Dunning in a Sopwith Pup. After further reconstruction she emerged as a flush deck carrier with an island superstructure. She was the only one of the Royal Navy's first generation of aircraft carriers to remain active throughout World War II, serving with the Home Fleet. She was scrapped between 1948 and 1954. *Displacement* 22,450 tons; *dimensions* 786ft 3in×90ft (239×27m); mean draught 24ft (7.3m); *machinery* 4-shaft geared turbines producing shp 90,000; *speed* 30.5 knots; *protection* main belt 3in; deck 3in; *armament* 12×4in AA (6×2); 24×2-pdr AA (3×8); *aircraft* 33; *complement* 748.

Furutaka Class Cruisers (Jap)

Displacement 9150 tons; *dimensions* 602ft×55ft 6in (183.4×16.7m); mean draught 18ft 6in (5.5m); *machinery* 4-shaft geared turbines producing shp 103,340; *speed* 33 knots; *protection* main belt 3in; deck 2in; turrets 5in; *armament* 6×7.9 (3×2); 4×4.7in AA (4×1); 8×25mm AA (4×2); 4×13mm AA; 8×24in torpedo tubes (2×4); *aircraft* 2; *complement* 625; *number in class* 2, launched 1925.

Fuso Class Battleships (Jap)

Both ships in this class, *Fuso* and *Yamashiro*, were sunk at LEYTE GULF. *Displacement* 34,700 tons; *dimensions* 698ft×108ft 6in (212× 32.9m); mean draught 31ft 9in (9.7m); *machinery* 4-shaft geared turbines producing shp 75,000; *speed* 24.75 knots; *protection* main belt 8–12in amidships, 4–5in fore and aft; turrets 8–12in; control tower 6–12in; deck 1.25–2in; *armament* 12×14in (6×2); 14×6in (14×1); 8×5in AA (4×2); 16×25mm AA; *aircraft* 3; *complement* 1396; *number in class* 2.

Futa Pass, Italy, 1944

Heavily fortified feature 20 miles (32km) north of FLORENCE through which Route 65 passed to BOLOGNA. Rather than launch a frontal assault, General Mark CLARK, commanding the US 5th Army, outflanked the defences by capturing the secondary IL GIOGIO PASS, some seven miles (11km) to the east, during the third week of September. The success of this operation compelled the defenders of the Futa Pass to abandon the positions.

FZG-76

Commonly called the V-1, the FZG-76 was the first operational guided missile, deployed by Germany against England in June 1944. It was a midwing monoplane propelled by a pulsating flow duct motor. Guidance was by a preset mechanism within the missile, and the whole machine was designed for ease and cheapness of manufacture. It was built principally of steel plate, though later versions used wooden wings. Launched from a fixed ramp about 164ft (50m) long, a piston was used to propel the missile into the air with sufficient speed to allow the duct motor to generate thrust. Speed in level flight was about 350mph (560kph) and it flew at about 3500ft (1070m) with a maximum range of about 130 miles (209km). The warhead contained 1874lb (850kg) of high explosive with three fuzes to ensure detonation. Development begun in June 1942 at PEENEMUNDE, the first successful flight took place in December 1942 and mass production began on 1 March 1944. In all, 9251 missiles were fired against England and 6551 against ANTWERP.

G

G-1 Personnel section of US military staff.

G-2 Intelligence section of US military staff.

G-3 Operations and Training section of US military staff.

G-4 Logistics and Supply section of US military staff.

G-5 Civil Affairs section of US military staff.

"G" and "H" Class Destroyers (UK)
Displacement 1335 tons; *dimensions* 323ft×32ft 3in (98.4×9.8m); mean draught 8ft 6in (2.6m); *machinery* 2-shaft geared turbines producing shp 34,000; *speed* 35.5 knots; *armament* 4×4.7in (4×1); 8×0.5in AA (2×4); 8×21in torpedo tubes; *complement* 145; *number in class* 18, launched 1935–36.

Gabbiano Class Corvettes (Italy)
Displacement 743 tons; *dimensions* 211ft 3in×28ft 6in (64.3×8.7m); mean draught 8ft 3in (2.5m); *machinery* 2-shaft diesel producing bhp 3500; 2 electric motors for silent approach hp 150; *speed* 18 knots; *armament* 1×3.9in; 7×20mm AA; 2×17.7in torpedo tubes. 10 depth charge throwers; *complement* 109; *number in class* 29, launched 1942–43. Following Italy's surrender several more uncompleted vessels of this class were seized by the Germans and taken into service.

Gabes, Tunisia, 1943
See EL HAMMA; MARETH LINE; TEBAGA GAP; WADI AKARIT.

Gafsa, Tunisia, 1943
In January a LONG RANGE DESERT GROUP patrol made the first contact between the British 8th Army and units of Major-General Lloyd FREDENDALL's US II Corps (Allied 1st Army) near Gafsa. The town was captured by ROMMEL's Afrika Korps Detachment on 16 February during the KASSERINE PASS operations, and recaptured by US II Corps (now commanded

by Major-General George S. PATTON) on 17 March. While 8th Army attacked the MARETH LINE, Patton maintained his advance towards the coast and succeeded in defeating a counter-attack by 10th Panzer Division near El Guettar. A permanent junction between 1st and 8th Armies was effected on 7 April, following the latter's successful attack on the WADI AKARIT defence line.

Galatos, Crete, 1941
A village and defensive position west of CANEA held by Commonwealth and Greek troops, 20–26 May.

Gale, Gen Sir Humphrey Middleton (1890–1971)
Gale joined the Artists' Rifles (TA) and attended Sandhurst in 1910, becoming an officer in the Royal Army Service Corps in 1911. During World War I he became a staff officer, gaining the MC. Between the wars he filled various posts in Britain and Egypt, instructed at Camberley and attended the Staff College. In 1939 he became DAQMG of III Corps in France, and for his work in the administration of the DUNKIRK evacuation was awarded the CBE. He then became Major-General Administration for Scotland and in 1941 for the Home Forces. In 1942 he was appointed as General EISENHOWER's administration commander for Operation TORCH, for which he received the US Legion of Merit. He then controlled the administrative side of the Sicily and Italy invasions, for which he was appointed KBE in August 1943.

In January 1944 he returned to Britain to take charge of the administration for Operation OVERLORD, becoming Adviser to the Supreme Commander, and he remained Eisenhower's right-hand man to the end of the war, receiving the US Distinguished Service Medal. Appointed European Director of the United Nations Relief and Rehabilitation Agency in September 1945, he retained this post until July 1947, retiring to go into business.

Gale, Gen Sir Richard (1896–)
Gale served with the British and Indian armies before 1939, and volunteered for parachute training. He raised and trained the 1st Parachute Brigade and by June 1944 was commanding the 6th Airborne Division. With only a small force, Gale captured and held the vital Orne bridges which were the key to the British expansion from the NORMANDY beachhead. In postwar years he commanded British troops in Germany and later became Chief of the General Staff.

Galland, Lt Gen Adolf (1912–)
The best-known of the Luftwaffe's fighter aces, Galland saw action in the Spanish Civil War and flew a ground-attack HS 123 with II Gruppe of Lehrgeschwader 2 in the Polish campaign. He then transferred to a fighter unit, Jagdgeschwader 27 (JG27), with whom he scored his first combat victories on 10 May 1940. Appointed commander of III Gruppe of JG26, Galland scored 38 more kills in the Battle of BRITAIN, ending the campaign of JG26 with the Oak Leaves added to the Knight's Cross he had received after his 17th combat victory. By June 1941 Galland had raised his victory total to 70 and became the first pilot to win the Swords to the Knight's Cross. After the death of Mölders in November 1941, Galland was promoted to general rank – at the age of 30 he was the youngest in the German armed services – in overall control of fighter operations in the West, the Balkans and Mediterranean and the Russian front. He ceased operational flying at the end of January 1942, with 94 victories and the award of Diamonds to the Knight's Cross. As head of the Luftwaffe's fighter arm Galland faced not only an increasingly powerful Allied air offensive but also bureaucratic infighting and the opposition of his superiors. He was relieved of his strategic duties at the end of 1944, but at HITLER's request he formed and led a jet fighter squadron, Jagdverband 44 (JG44), equipped with Me262s. Galland raised his score to 104 before a knee injury finally grounded him.

Galvanic

American assault on the GILBERT ISLANDS, 1943.

Gambut, Libya, 1941–42

An airfield between BARDIA and TOBRUK captured by 2nd New Zealand Division during Operation CRUSADER. The British 8th Army Headquarters was located near Gambut during the GAZALA battles.

Gamelin, Gen Maurice Gustave (1872–1958)

Gamelin graduated from St Cyr in 1893, was commissioned into the Algerian Tirailleurs, and by 1914 he was a colonel on General Joffre's staff. Promoted Major-General in 1915, he commanded a division and ended the war with an excellent record. Made a general in 1931, he became Chief of the French General Staff and, in accordance with the policies of the time, pinned his faith on the MAGINOT LINE and passive defence. He became Commander-in-Chief in 1938, but the German attack in 1940 revealed his deficiencies and he was replaced by General WEYGAND. Placed on trial in France for his defeat, he was able to excuse his actions and the trial was abandoned. He was interned in Germany until 1945.

Gammon Grenade

A British hand grenade invented by Captain Gammon of the Parachute Regiment. It consisted of an ALLWAYS FUZE attached to a cloth bag with an elastic hem. When required for use the bag was filled with plastic explosive and the grenade was then thrown. Its advantage was that the fuze and empty cloth bag took up little space in a man's pack, and the amount of explosive used could be adjusted to fit the task in view.

Garand Rifle

The standard service rifle of the US Army, introduced in 1936. Designed and developed by John Garand at Springfield Arsenal in the late 1920s, the rifle was a gas-operated semi-automatic of .30in (7.62mm) calibre, and was loaded by means of an eight-round clip. An excellent rifle, if somewhat heavy, the basic principle was perpetuated in the M14 rifle, in service from the middle 1950s until the 1980s.

Garigliano River, Italy, 1943–44

The Garigliano River covered the western sector of the GUSTAV LINE. On 30 December 1943 British units, including Commandos,

Coldstream and Scots Guards, executed a successful raid across the river, returning with prisoners and information regarding the defences. On 17/18 January 1944 General Mark CLARK's US 5th Army launched a major offensive on the Garigliano sector. This resulted in Lieutenant-General McCREERY's British X Corps securing crossings on the left with the 5th, 46th and 56th Divisions, but subsequent attacks by Major-General Geoffrey KEYES' US II Corps on the right were thrown back with serious loss. See CASSINO.

Gasmask

A protective face-mask intended to shield the wearer from the effects of poison gas. It generally consisted of a rubber face-piece with transparent eyepieces and a canister containing filters and chemicals which would remove or neutralize any war gas. The canister could be attached to the face-piece (German) or carried in a haversack and connected to the face-piece by flexible tube (UK, USA). Since poison gas was never used during the 1939–45 conflict, the gasmask became a superfluous piece of equipment, frequently thrown away by soldiers. In British service, known as a Respirator, Anti-gas.

Gas Warfare

All the combatants were prepared for gas warfare, but so general was the fear of retaliation in kind that it was never used. The most research in this field was carried out in Germany and resulted in the discovery of the nerve agents. Research in the UK and USA was on a smaller scale and was largely into matters of production and employment. Quantities of gas were held in the major theatres of war, but it is generally accepted that the UK and USA could have sustained gas warfare for no more than one month before stocks would have been exhausted, and their replacement would have been difficult since no mass-production facilities were built. Germany had much greater stocks and would have had little trouble in maintaining them if necessary.

Gato Class Submarines (USA)

Displacement 1525/2415 tons; *dimensions* 311ft 9in×27ft 3in (95×8.3m); *machinery* 2-shaft diesels producing shp 5400/2740; *speed* 20.25/10 knots; *armament* 1×5in; 1×40mm; 10×21in torpedo tubes (6 bow and 4 stern); *complement* 80; *number in class* 195, launched 1941–47.

Gauntlet

British commando raid on SPITZBERGEN, August 1941.

Gavutu Island, Solomon Islands, 1942

The islet of Gavutu measuring 300 by 500 yards (274 by 457m) off the south coast of

John Garand (left), inventor of the US Garand rifle, demonstrates the rifle to a private of the US Army.

Florida Island, was attacked 7 August by 1st Marine Raider Battalion during the US 1st Marine Division's landing on GUADALCANAL. Despite naval gunfire and air support, the Japanese garrison resisted desperately and was not overwhelmed until the following day.

Gazala, Libya, 1942

In May 1942 the battlefront in the Western Desert ran southwards from Gazala on the coast to BIR HACHEIM. Both sides were preparing to take the offensive but by the middle of the month it became apparent that it would be the Axis who struck the first blow. ROMMEL'S combined tank strength amounted to 560, including 50 PzKw IIIs, 223 up-armoured PzKw IIIs, 19 up-gunned PzKw IIIs, 40 PzKw IVs, 50 PzKw IIs and 228 Italian M13s. The

Deutsches Afrika Korps and the Italian XX Mechanized Corps assembled south-east of Rotonda Sagnali prior to commencing a drive which would take them round the southern end of the British positions and then northeast in the general direction of TOBRUK. Simultaneously, the Italian X and XXI Corps were to mount diversionary attacks against the northern sector of the British defences. The British 8th Army, commanded by Lieutenant-General Neil RITCHIE, contained two corps, XIII under GOTT and XXX under Norrie: XIII Corps consisted of 1st South African and 50th (Northumbrian) Divisions manning fortified boxes in the line and 2nd South African Division in Tobruk, and was supported by 1st and 32nd Army Tank Brigades with 110 MATILDAS and 166 VALENTINES; XXX Corps consisted of

the 1st and 7th Armoured Divisions plus a number of infantry brigades, including the 1st Free French Brigade occupying a box at Bir Hacheim. Excluding the two Army Tank Brigades, 8th Army could muster 167 GRANTS, 149 STUARTS and 257 CRUSADERS, plus a further 75 Grants and 70 Stuarts which would become available when 1st Armoured Brigade reached the front. The Grant was the most powerful tank available to either side and both British armoured divisions were able to produce six Grant squadrons apiece.

Rommel's offensive began during the night of 26/27 May, achieving tactical surprise and overrunning 3rd Indian Motor Brigade's recently established box five miles south-east of Bir Hacheim. Despite being caught off balance, the British rallied during the day and

Gazala, opening moves, 26–27 May 1942.

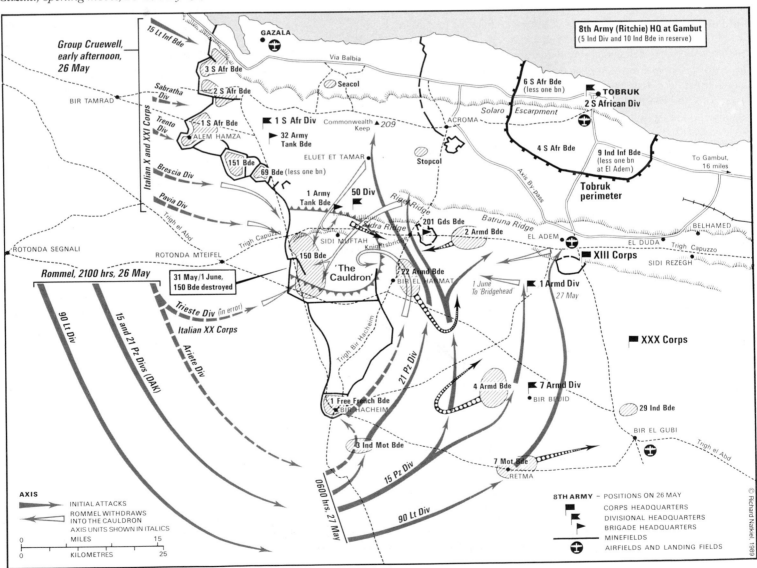

Gurkhas attack, rifle with bayonet in the left hand and khukri in the right, Western Desert, June 1942.

inflicted heavy losses on the Axis armour. By evening Rommel had been pushed back against the British minebelt and a box held by 150th Brigade. Starved of supplies, he considered asking Ritchie for terms but the position eased when the Italian *Trieste* Division opened a corridor through the minefields. An opportunity existed for the British to bring the war in Africa to an early conclusion, but this was lost as a result of discussion and delay at the highest levels. Rommel's position, known as The CAULDRON, remained unmolested while the Axis recovered their strength and on 1 June the 150th Brigade box was overwhelmed. Not until 5 June did Ritchie mount converging but unco-ordinated attacks against The Cauldron at Sidra Ridge and Aslagh Ridge. These were easily repulsed and the following day Rommel returned to the offensive, over-running most of 10th and part of 9th Indian

Infantry Brigades as well as eliminating the entire artillery of 5th Indian Division, Ritchie's artillery reserve. He next turned his attention to the box at Bir Hacheim, but during the night of 10/11 June the French garrison broke out and succeeded in reaching safety. Having removed this last obstacle across his rear, Rommel repeated the north-easterly thrust with which he had begun the battle. On 12 June Norrie's three armoured brigades counter-attacked but were defeated in detail with the loss of 90 tanks. The following day 15th and 21st Panzer Division attempted to isolate the KNIGHTSBRIDGE box, held by 201st Guards Brigade. The attempt was foiled by 2nd and 22nd Armoured Brigades and 32nd Army Tank Brigade, but by evening 8th Army had only 70 battleworthy tanks left and the Guards were withdrawn during the night. Ritchie now recognized that the battle was lost

and gave permission for the 1st South African and 50th Divisions to withdraw from the remaining fragment of the Gazala Line. The former retreated along the coast road but the latter, now only two brigades strong, broke out through the Italian formations opposite and drove round Bir Hacheim to reach the Egyptian frontier. Leaving 2nd South African Division, 201st Guards, 11th Indian Infantry and 32nd Army Tank Brigades to hold Tobruk, the rest of Ritchie's troops also withdrew into Egypt. Gazala was the worst defeat in 8th Army's history, and Rommel was able to crown his achievement by storming Tobruk on 20/21 June. See *And We Shall Shock Them* by David Fraser (Hodder and Stoughton), *Dilemmas of the Desert War* by Michael Carver (Batsford) and *Rommel's War in Africa* by Wolf Heckmann (Granada).

GB Guided Bombs

A series of guided bombs developed by the USAAF from 1941 onwards, they were numbered GB-1 to GB-15 and varied in construction and concept. Early models were winged with tail booms and flew on a pre-set course; later models had TV cameras to permit remote control by a bombardier in the parent aircraft. They were used on a few occasions against targets in Germany but were generally inaccurate and had little effect.

GCI Ground Controlled Interception (UK). An air defence system for directing a fighter aircraft to meet attacking bombers, using instructions from a ground controller derived from RADAR information.

Gearing Class Destroyers (USA)

Displacement 2425 tons; *dimensions* 390ft 6in × 40ft 9in (119 × 12.4m); mean draught 19ft (5.7m); *machinery* 2-shaft geared turbines producing shp 60,000; *speed* 35 knots; *arma-*

Gearing class destroyer.

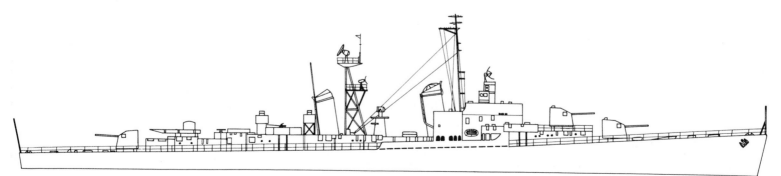

ment 6×5in (3×2); 12×40mm AA; 10×21in torpedo tubes; or 6×5in (3×2); 16×40mm AA; *complement* 350; *number in class* 98, launched 1944–46.

Gebirgsjäger

German mountain troops, mostly of Austrian or Bavarian origin, regarded as an élite. During World War II the German Army formed ten Mountain Divisions. Mountain troops served with distinction in NORWAY, GREECE, CRETE, FINLAND, THE CAUCASUS and ITALY.

Gee

A British navigational and blind-bombing aid, developed and placed in service in 1941. It consisted of a master and two slave transmitting stations on a base-line some 200 miles (320km) long, and a receiver in the aircraft. Signals were transmitted in sequence, and the time differences, applied to a special chart, gave the aircraft's position. Accuracy was quite good, but fell off with distance; results also depended upon the navigator's skill. First used in March 1942 for a raid on Lübeck, it was being effectively jammed by the Germans by August of that year and was eventually replaced by OBOE and H2S.

Gehlen, Gen Reinhard (1902–79)

Gehlen was a professional intelligence officer who in 1942 was given command of the Russian section of the "Fremdeheer Ost" (Foreign Armies, East) department of the OKH. He ran this with considerable efficiency until 1945 when he surrendered himself, his staff and all his archives to the US forces. He continued to operate a freelance intelligence agency for the West until his death.

Geiger, Maj Gen Roy (1885–1947)

A professional Marine, Geiger first saw action in the GUADALCANAL campaign in 1942. He was then recalled to become Director of Marine Aviation, but in November 1943 was given command of the I Marine Amphibious Corps in the Pacific. He led this force in the taking of BOUGAINVILLE, after which he was appointed to command III Marine Amphibious Corps for the assault on GUAM in July 1944 and for the invasion of OKINAWA in 1945. After General Buckner was killed on Okinawa, Geiger briefly assumed command of US 10th Army, becoming the only US Marine Corps officer to command a US Army in the field.

German mountain troops during the invasion of Crete.

Gela, Gulf of Sicily, 1943

Scene of the assault landing of Lieutenant-General George S. PATTON's US 7th Army on the southern coast, 10 July 1943. The landings were made by Lieutenant-General Omar BRADLEY's US II Corps with 45th Division on the right at Scoglitti, 1st Division in the centre, where Gela town was captured by a Ranger battalion, and 3rd Division plus a Combat Command of 2nd Armored Division on the left at Licata. The previous night Colonel James Gavin's 505th Regimental Combat Team of 82nd Airborne Division had been dropped inland from Gela with a view to capturing high ground dominating the town and other important features but were scattered over a wide area. On the other hand, aggressive actions by the paratroopers seriously delayed the approach of the Hermann Göring Panzer Division and when the latter did launch its counter-attack it was broken up by naval gunfire, as was that of the Italian *Livorno* Division.

Gelb, Fall (Case Yellow)

Original German plan for the invasion of France, Belgium and Holland; later modified by inclusion of SICHELSCHNITT.

Gembloux Gap, Belgium, 1940

Location of the first major tank battle of the war, fought by HÖPNER's XVI Panzer Corps (3rd and 4th Panzer Divisions) and PRIOUX's 1st Cavalry Corps (2nd and 3rd Divisions Légères Mécaniques) on 12–13 May while the latter successfully covered the deployment of Blanchard's French 1st Army along the DYLE Line. Each side lost over 100 tanks but the Germans were able to recover many of their casualties when the French, having fulfilled their mission, withdrew. In some German sources the battle is also referred to as Hannut or Namur.

Gembok

German anti-partisan operations in Greece, July 1944.

Gemmano, Italy, 1944

A mile-long (1.5km) 1500ft (457m) ridge south of the River Conca forming part of the GOTHIC LINE defences, held by the 100th Mountain Regiment, an Austrian unit consisting of four 600-strong rifle battalions and a reconnaissance battalion. Between 5 and 14 September the ridge was the scene of a series of bloody battles as it was attacked in succession by the 56th, 46th and 4th Indian Divisions of Lieutenant-General Sir Charles Keightley's British V Corps (8th Army). The 4th Indian Division's attack was made during the night of 14/15 September and was supported by no less than five field and two medium artillery regiments, one heavy battery, 16 4.2-inch MORTARS and the sustained fire of a medium machine gun platoon. The attack succeeded as advances elsewhere had made the ridge untenable and most of the Austrians had already withdrawn, having sustained the loss of 900 killed in defence of the feature.

Genoa, Italy, 1940–41 and 1944

Naval base to which the Italian battle fleet retired in the immediate aftermath of TARANTO. On 8 February 1941 the base was subjected to a heavy bombardment by the battleships and other warships of FORCE H. In 1944 the Allied deception plan succeeded in convincing the Germans that the objective of Operation *Anvil* was Genoa rather than the invasion of southern France.

George II, King of Greece (1884–1947)

George was a nephew of Kaiser Wilhelm II and became King of Greece in 1922. He was deposed in 1923 and remained in exile until 1933 when he was recalled after a plebiscite. When the Axis forces invaded Greece in 1941 he fled the country, settling briefly in Egypt and then making his way to London to set up a government-in-exile. After the war, and a further plebiscite, he returned to Greece.

George VI, King of England (1895–1952)

The second son of King George V, Albert Frederick Arthur George was not expected to succeed to the throne and did so only because of the abdication in 1936 of his elder brother Edward VIII. His shy and unassuming manner, long battle with a stammer, and exemplary conduct throughout the war years, won him the undivided affection of his people. During the war he visited the army in France, the fleet in various bases, and never failed to travel to the scene of particularly bad air raids as soon as possible after the event. Buckingham Palace, his London residence, was bombed on 13 September 1940, leading to a memorable exchange between His Majesty and a London householder who had been bombed out. Upon the King observing that his home had also been bombed, the householder is said to have replied, "Yes, Your Majesty, but I've only got the one."

In 1943 he visited the 1st and 8th Armies in North Africa and then travelled to MALTA, where he awarded the island the George Cross for its gallantry in resisting German and Italian attacks. He visited Allied forces in Britain prior to the invasion of Europe, and once the bridgehead had been established, he wasted no time in visiting units in NORMANDY. Later he went to Italy and Holland. Without doubt, his conduct during the war, coupled with that of Her Majesty Queen Elizabeth, did much to restore a respect for the monarchy which had been damaged by the Abdication.

Georges, Gen Joseph (1875–1951)

The French general who in May 1940 commanded the North-East Front, the key area in the battle for France. Under Georges were Billots's 1st Army Group, Prételat's 2nd Army Group, Besson's 3rd Army Group and, nominally, the British Expeditionary Force. After the defeat of France, in 1943 he escaped to Algeria where he joined the National Liberation Committee but played no significant part in later events.

Gerät 104

A 13.8in (35cm) calibre recoilless gun developed in Germany by Rheinmetall-Borsig for carriage by bomber aircraft and to be used in a diving attack against warships. The gun was slung beneath the aircraft fuselage and was hydraulically retracted during flight to reduce drag. It was lowered into position prior to beginning an attack, and the recoil of the weapon was controlled by allowing the 1400lb (635kg) steel cartridge case to be ejected rearwards as the 1400lb (635kg) shell was fired forwards. The weapon was seen as a method of attacking the British fleet in Scapa Flow. The gun was successfully fired, but development was stopped in September 1939 and the designers turned to other, more urgent, tasks.

Germany, Surrender of, 1945

In Italy, General von Veitinghoff signed an instrument of unconditional surrender at CASERTA on 29 April, effective from noon on 2 May, the Senior Allied representative present being General Sir William Morgan, Field-Marshal ALEXANDER's Chief of Staff. HITLER committed suicide on 30 April, appointing Grand Admiral Karl DÖNITZ as his successor. On 4 May a delegation led by Admiral von FRIEDEBURG, acting on Dönitz's behalf, formally surrendered all German forces in north-west Germany, Holland and Denmark at Field-Marshal MONTGOMERY's headquarters on LÜNEBURG HEATH, the surrender to be effective from 0800 on 5 May. In southern Germany, SS Colonel-General Paul Hausser's Army Group G surrendered to General Jacob DEVERS, commander of the US 6th Army Group on 6 May. Elsewhere, the German armies, crushed between the Allied advances from east and west, simply disintegrated.

Meanwhile, Admiral von Friedeburg and General Alfred JODL reached General EISENHOWER's headquarters at Rheims and on 7 May concluded the unconditional surrender of the Third Reich with Lieutenant-General Walter BEDELL SMITH, Eisenhower's Chief of Staff. The following day these proceedings were ratified in BERLIN by Friedeburg, Field-Marshal

HM Queen Elizabeth (now the Queen Mother) and Princess Elizabeth (now Queen Elizabeth II) visiting a mixed battery RA in 1944.

General Stumpff, Field-Marshal Keitel and Admiral Friedeburg ratify the Nazi surrender at Berlin, 9 May 1945.

Wilhelm KEITEL and Luftwaffe General Hans-Jurgen Stumpff in the presence of Marshal Georgi ZHUKOV, Air Marshal Sir Arthur TEDDER, Eisenhower's Deputy Supreme Commander, General Carl SPAATZ and General DE LATTRE DE TASSIGNY. In the western hemisphere, World War II officially ended at midnight on 8 May.

GESTAPO Geheimstaatspolizei (German Secret State Police). An internal German police force created in 1933 under GÖRING, then Minister-President of Prussia, to replace the existing political police. In 1934 it was commanded by HEYDRICH, under the general direction of HIMMLER, and gradually became less a judiciary body than a totally independent executive arm of the Nazi party. No appeal was permitted against its decisions and it had sweeping authority to deal with any act which it considered inimical to the interests of the State. In 1939 it was combined with the criminal police to form the *Sicherheitspolizei* (State Security Police or "Sipo") under the control of the RHSA (Reichsicherheitshauptamt – Reich Central Security Office or RHSA) and Heydrich was appointed to command the RHSA.

Ghormley, V Adm Robert L. (1883–1953)

After pre-war sea and staff service, Ghormley was sent to England in 1940 as US Naval Liaison officer, where he made a study of the Royal Navy's tactics and procedures. After America's entry into the war he was appointed as Commander South Pacific and took up his post in New Zealand in March 1942. His first task was to organize the taking of TULAGI and GUADALCANAL, and he objected to the lack of time for preparation. The resulting administrative problems proved his point, but made him few friends.

He was responsible for the decision which caused FLETCHER to withdraw naval cover from Guadalcanal at a critical juncture and which contributed to the loss of four ships in the Battle of SAVO ISLAND. The lack of confidence in his mission displayed by Ghormley led to his replacement by HALSEY in October 1942. Ghormley returned to take up a staff post in Washington and held no significant command thereafter.

GHQ   General Headquarters.

GI   General Issue (US).

A descriptive term for military equipment common to all corps and services; thus, "Bucket, GI". Also the collective nickname of the American soldier.

Giap, Gen Vo Nguyen (1910–75)

A Vietnamese, Giap was active in student revolutionary causes and was imprisoned by the French from 1928 to 1931. He then taught economics at Hanoi University until fleeing into the Communist-controlled area of China in 1939, thereafter serving with MAO TSE-TUNG until 1944. He then returned to Indo-China, leading guerrillas under HO CHI MINH against the Japanese occupation forces. This activity continued against the French reoccupation, Giap allying himself with China and the USSR to obtain aid.

Gibson, W Cdr Guy Penrose (1918–44)

Gibson was one of RAF BOMBER COMMAND'S outstanding pilots. He joined the RAF in 1936 and on the outbreak of war was flying HANDLEY-PAGE HAMPDEN bombers with No. 83 Squadron. He won a DFC in July 1940 before joining No. 29 Squadron in November 1940, flying Beaufighter night fighters, adding a Bar to his DFC in September 1941. After a short spell as Chief Flying Instructor at 51 OTU at Cranfield, he returned to operations as commander of No. 106 Squadron, flying the new four-engined AVRO LANCASTER bomber. He led No. 106 Squadron for a year, winning a DSO and Bar. In March 1943 he was asked by the commander of No. 5 Group, Bomber Command, Sir Ralph Cochrane, to form No. 617 Squadron for a raid on the Ruhr dams using the BOUNCING BOMB designed by Barnes WALLIS. The raid was mounted on 16/17 May, with Gibson dropping the first bomb on the Möhne dam and then directing the attack on the Eder dam. It was for his leadership in this operation that he was awarded the Victoria Cross. Thereafter Bomber Command tried hard to keep their hero away from active service. He accompanied CHURCHILL to the Quebec Conference in August 1943. In the USA on 13 October he was awarded the American Legion of Merit by "Hap" ARNOLD. In September 1944 the Air Officer Commander-in-Chief Bomber Command, Sir Arthur HARRIS, reluctantly granted Gibson the favour of a "last op", flying a Mosquito of No. 627 Squadron as the Master Bomber on a relatively unimportant raid on industrial and rail targets in Rheydt and München Gladbach. He died on this raid (19 September) when his Mosquito crashed in Holland. The precise circumstances of his death remain a mystery. At the time of his death Gibson had flown an overall total of 177 operational sorties, 76 of them as a bomber pilot and the remainder in fighters, an operational record matched by few, if any, RAF pilots in World War II.

Gideon Force

Formed in late 1940 under the command of the then Major Orde WINGATE to conduct guerrilla operations behind Italian lines in ETHIO-

PIA. Gideon Force never consisted of more than 70 British officers and NCOs, 800 Sudanese and 800 Ethiopian volunteers. It sometimes fought concentrated and sometimes in detachments, staging ambushes, capturing forts and harassing the withdrawal of the Italians, who were forced to deploy no less than seven brigades, plus locally recruited Ethiopian groups, in an attempt to contain it. The success of Gideon Force subsequently enabled Wingate to convince the authorities of the validity of his theories on Long Range Penetration and contributed to the formation of the CHINDITS.

Giffard, Gen Sir George (1886–1964)

Giffard had spent most of his early service in Africa and was regarded as an expert on African military matters. At the outbreak of war he was Military Secretary at the War Office and early in 1940 was appointed GOC Palestine, transferring from there to become GOC West Africa in June 1940. A great trainer, he built up the West African forces, and saw the Gold Coast Rifles and Nigeria Regiment acquit themselves well in the Eritrean campaign. In 1942 he was sent to India as GOC Eastern Army, where he became responsible for much of the organization and logistics for the BURMA campaign. In August 1943 he became Commander in Chief 11th Army Group and began planning the ARAKAN offensive for January 1944. Although he and SLIM worked well together, he found it almost impossible to work with MOUNTBATTEN and in spite of his excellent work during the battles of IMPHAL and KOHIMA, at the end of 1944 he was replaced by General Sir Oliver LEESE.

Gilbert Is., Central Pacific, 1941–43

Occupied by Japanese troops on 10 December 1941. In August 1943 Marine Raiders attacked MAKIN ATOLL destroying the radio station and killing a number of the garrison. As a result of this the Japanese strengthened their defences. Operation *Galvanic*, the recapture of the islands, commenced on 20 November 1943 with the landing of Major-General Julian C. Smith's US 2nd Marine Division on Betio Island in the TARAWA Atoll, which was secured after extremely heavy fighting. Simultaneously, Makin Atoll was captured by the US Army's 165th Infantry Regiment. Apamama Atoll, the last Japanese foothold in the Gilberts, was occupied by Marine units on 25 November.

Giman-Shi

A Japanese RADAR countermeasure similar to WINDOW or DUPPEL, it consisted of metallized paper strips 75cm (30in) long, half the wavelength of the American gunnery control radar sets used in the Pacific. It was first used in May 1943 to protect bombers attacking GUADALCANAL and was highly effective. This was the first combat use of this type of countermeasure.

Gin Drinkers' Line, Hong Kong, 1941

Defence line in the New Territories stretching from Gin Drinkers' Bay to Port Shelter, a distance of 11 miles (18km). The capture of the Shing Mun Redoubt by Colonel Teihichi Doi's 228th Regiment during the night of 9/10 December made the rest of the line untenable and the British were forced to withdraw to Hong Kong Island.

Giraud, Gen Henri (1879–1949)

A French officer who came to prominence first as an instructor at the Ecole de Guerre and, in 1936, as Governor of the Fortress of Metz. On 10 May 1940 he was commanding 7th Army, five days later replacing Corap as commander of 9th Army, bringing the remnants of 7th Army with him. He was taken prisoner on 19 May and imprisoned, along with General PRIOUX in Königstein castle. He escaped in 1942 and made his way to ALGIERS, where he succeeded Admiral DARLAN as civil and military commander in December. He became co-president, with General DE GAULLE, of the National Committee for Liberation in May 1943 and became Commander-in-Chief of the French Army, in which capacity he was able to liberate CORSICA in September 1943. In spite of efforts by ROOSEVELT and CHURCHILL to bring about some sort of agreement, De Gaulle refused to accept Giraud as supreme commander of the French forces and Giraud resigned his co-presidency in October, thereafter giving up political ambitions. In April 1944 pressure from the De Gaulle faction led to his resigning from the post of Commander-in-Chief French Forces in North Africa and he thereafter played no part in public affairs.

Gisela

German plan for the occupation of Spain.

American troops advance on Makin Island.

Gleiwitz (Gliwice), Poland, 1939

A town on the 1939 German-Polish border which held a German radio station. On 31 August 1939 the station was reported as having been attacked by a handful of Polish troops, all of whom had been shot dead. The bodies, in Polish uniform, were shown to the press, and the incident provided HITLER with the excuse he needed to attack Poland on the next day. In fact the bodies were those of German concentration camp inmates who had been dressed up and shot to provide the *causus belli*.

Glorious, HMS – Courageous Class Aircraft Carrier

Glorious served with the Mediterranean Fleet 1939–40 and then joined the Home Fleet. On 8 June 1940, escorted by the destroyers *Ardent* and *Acasta*, she was returning from Norway when she was intercepted and sunk by the battlecruisers SCHARNHORST and GNEISENAU. Her escorts were also sunk, but not before a torpedo from *Acasta* had badly damaged *Scharnhorst* and forced her to head for Trondheim, thereby missing a number of lightly escorted troop convoys.

Gloster Aircraft (UK)

Gloster Gladiator The last RAF biplane fighter, the Gladiator appeared in 1936 and over 700 were built. They saw wide service over Norway, France, Greece and North Africa early in the war, and a number of Sea Gladi-ators (the Fleet Air Arm variant) defended MALTA initially during the first Italian air attacks in 1940. *Span* 32.25ft (9.8m); *engine* 1 840hp radial; *armament* 4 machine guns; *speed* 250mph (402kph).

Gloster Meteor The Meteor was the first British jet fighter and the only Allied jet aircraft to see service during the war. Development, allied to the Whittle jet engine, had begun in early 1941, but it was not until July 1944 that production machines entered service. They proved invaluable in pursuing flying bombs, and later extended their activity to the continent in order to counter the German Me262 jet fighter, although in the event they never engaged German aircraft in combat. Originally a fighter, subsequent modification fitted it for reconnaissance, night fighting and training roles, though these came in postwar years. *Span* 43ft (13m); *engines* 2 2000lb (907kg) thrust Rolls-Royce Derwent turbojet; *armament* 4 20mm cannon; *speed* 410mph (660kph).

Glowworm, HMS – "G" Class Destroyer

On 8 April 1940 *Glowworm*, commanded by Lieutenant-Commander Gerard Roope, formed part of a force covering a minelaying operation off the Norwegian coast. She became detached from her companions while searching for a man lost overboard and encountered two German destroyers which she engaged and pursued. The enemy destroyers were screening the cruiser ADMIRAL HIPPER, which Roope unhesitatingly rammed after launching an unsuccessful torpedo attack, inflicting serious damage. *Glowworm* was herself crippled and then blown apart by the heavier ship's guns; 31 of her crew survived. Roope was awarded a posthumous Victoria Cross.

"Glubb's Girls"

Name given to the ARAB LEGION because of the long hair of its members.

Gneisenau, KMS – Scharnhorst Class Battlecruiser

Gneisenau's career ran parallel to that of her sister ship SCHARNHORST until she returned from Brest. However, on 26/27 February 1942 she was seriously damaged by RAF bombing at Kiel, and moved to Gdynia. There her 11-inch gun turrets were removed and transported to Norway for coast defence. She was to have been re-armed with 15-inch guns, but the project was abandoned in 1943 and her hulk sunk as a blockship in Gdynia harbour in March 1945.

Goat (UK)

See AVRE.

Goblet

Allied option during the planning of the invasion of southern Italy, involving amphibious assault by British V Corps near Crotone.

Gobuen, Italian Somaliland, 1941

A coastal town at the mouth of the Juba River captured by 1st South African Brigade Group on 14 February. The Italians retained the opposite bank of the river but a week later the South Africans secured a bridgehead seven miles (11km) upstream and held it for two days against counter-attacks. The Italians then withdrew from the area. See EAST AFRICAN CAMPAIGN.

GOC General Officer Commanding (UK).

Goebbels, Dr Josef (1897–1945)

Goebbels was Minister of Information and Propaganda in the Nazi Government. A graduate of Heidelberg University, Goebbels was an early follower of HITLER, joining the Nazi Party in 1924. Elected to the Reichstag, in 1933 he was appointed Minister for Public Enlightenment and Propaganda. Probably the most

HMS Glowworm, *seen from KMS* Admiral Hipper.

intelligent of the Nazi hierarchy, he was nevertheless totally committed to Hitler, and his skills as an administrator and an orator were of immense importance in promulgating Nazi ideology. He could also move decisively when events demanded, as was shown in July 1944 when Goebbels' reaction to the abortive bomb plot against Hitler was instrumental in saving the day and retaining Nazi domination at a critical moment. After STALINGRAD, Goebbels became an increasingly important figure in the total mobilization of the German war economy. On 24 August 1944 he was appointed Plenipotentiary for Total War with sweeping powers. Women up to the age of 50 were conscripted; all remotely fit men between the ages of 16 and 60 were drafted into the VOLKS-STURM; theatres and cinemas were closed. Goebbels' flair for propaganda never deserted him. In the closing stages of the war Goebbels created the myth of a last-ditch "National Redoubt" in Bavaria, which became a fixation of the Allied Supreme Commander EISENHOWER. A man of small stature, crippled by a childhood illness, Goebbels had a reputation for leading a quiet and dignified home life, often being held up as a model by Hitler. This did not prevent him from maintaining a succession of mistresses. As the Russians closed in on BERLIN he moved, with his family, into the Führerbunker and, after Hitler's suicide, poisoned his six children and then had himself and his wife shot by an SS officer.

Goebbels (left) and Göring at the Nazi Party Congress, Nuremberg.

Goliath self-propelled demolition charge, Warsaw 1944.

Gold Beach, Normandy, 1944

Located on the right flank of the British D-DAY landing sector. The leading brigades of 50th (Northumbrian) Division and No. 47 Commando began coming ashore at 0725 following a two-hour naval bombardment. Sea conditions were so severe that the DD amphibious tanks could not be launched and were landed directly from their LSTs, just ahead of the infantry. These were followed by special-purpose armoured teams from 79th Armoured Division which proved invaluable in reducing strongpoints at Arromanches, Le Hamel, La Rivière and elsewhere. By midnight the 50th Division's second-wave brigades were ashore and had advanced inland as far as the outskirts of Bayeux, which fell the following day. On the eastern flank contact had been established with the Canadians on JUNO Beach and on the west flank No. 47 Commando had advanced nine miles (14.5km) towards OMAHA Beach and was within sight of Port-en-Bessin. Approximately 25,000 men landed on Gold Beach during 6 June. The German 352nd Infantry Division, manning this sector of the coastal defences, offered determined resistance but by 7 June its strength had fallen to that of a battle group.

Goliath (Ger)

An un-manned miniature tank driven by a small petrol or electric motor and steered by trailing wires. The vehicle had a maximum speed of 12mph (19kph) and a range of 660 yards (609m). It carried a 200lb (90kg) explosive charge which was detonated by remote control when it reached the objective. The Goliath's tracks, however, were vulnerable to small arms fire and the device was a failure. It was employed on the Eastern Front and at ANZIO.

Gomorrah

Series of RAF raids on Hamburg, July 1943.

Gondar, Ethiopia, 1941

Town north of Lake Tana in an area consisting of almost impregnable positions located at the top of escarpments up to 10,000ft (3048m) in height, held by General Nasi with 40,000 troops, the last remaining Italian force in East Africa. The only all-weather road approached Gondar via the 4000ft (1219m) Wolchefit Pass, 70 miles (112km) to the north-east, which was held by a garrison of 5000; a good-weather track from DEBRA TABOR approached Gondar from the south-east, passing through Kulkaber, which also contained an Italian garrison. In June the demoralized defenders of Debra Tabor surrendered. In September the garrison of Wolchefit Pass, which had hitherto repulsed all attacks but was now on the verge of starvation, also surrendered. The 12th African Division, commanded by Major-General C. C. Fowkes, began converging on Gondar, the 25th East African Brigade from Wolchefit and the 26th East African Brigade from Debra Tabor. The 2500-strong Italian force at Kulkaber beat off an assault on 11 November but surrendered, after a hard fight, when it was attacked by both brigades on 21 November. The final assault on Gondar was delivered by 26th Brigade from the east and 25th Brigade from the south on 27 November. By afternoon both brigades and Ethiopian troops had taken mountain features overlooking the objective. A squadron of the Kenya Armoured Car Regiment penetrated the town, followed by an Ethiopian group. Shortly after, General Nasi requested terms and the following day the remaining 22,000 Italians laid down their arms.

Goodtime

Assault on Treasury Islands, SOLOMON ISLANDS, by 8th New Zealand Brigade Group, 27 October 1943.

Goodwood

British offensive east of CAEN, July 1944.

Göring, Hermann (1893–1946)

In World War I Göring had commanded von Richthofen's "Flying Circus" after the death of the great ace. In the Third Reich, he rose to become Reichsmarshal, Commander of the German Air Force, President of the Council of Defence for Reich and Chief Reichs Huntsman. He joined the Nazi party in 1922 and was one of the original Storm Troop commanders. After HITLER came to power in 1933, he was appointed Minister of the Interior for Prussia, organized the GESTAPO and set up the first concentration camps. In 1933 he was appointed Minister for Aviation, responsible for the Luftwaffe, and became its commander on its

Hermann Göring on his 41st birthday, Berlin, 1934.

official formation in 1935. He was later appointed to oversee the Four Year economic plan for harnessing the economy to war, which he did with considerable success, but was less effective after war broke out. The Luftwaffe failure in the Battle of BRITAIN made Operation SEELÖWE (the invasion of Britain) impossible, and this gave his many enemies the chance to intrigue against him. In 1942 he virtually retired to his country estate Karinhall, but remained faithful to Hitler until the end. In April 1945 he sent a message to Hitler in Berlin, assuring him of his loyalty and declaring his intention of taking over as Führer unless assured that Hitler was still alive and well. Hitler immediately assumed that Göring was attempting to supplant him. He had the Reichsmarshal placed under arrest and expelled him from the Nazi Party. However, by this time, these measures had little significance, and soon afterwards Göring was captured by the Americans. He was arraigned at NUREMBERG for war crimes, argued his case with considerable ability and force, but was nevertheless condemned to death. On the eve of his execution he committed suicide.

Gort, FM John (1886–1946)

Of Irish descent, Gort served in the Grenadier Guards during World War I, winning the Victoria Cross, the DSO and two Bars, the MC,

and nine Mentions in Despatches. He became Director of Military Training India in 1932, Commandant of the Staff College in 1936, and CIGS in the same year. Serving under the Secretary of State for War, Leslie Hore-Belisha, Gort acted as a "new broom" and made many changes in command during his tenure of this post, and in 1939 he went to France as Commander-in-Chief of the British Expeditionary Force. Significantly, up to that moment he had never commanded any unit larger than a brigade. When the German invasion took place in 1940, Gort handled his force with skill, doggedly accepting the off-hand treatment accorded him by his nominal superior GEORGES, and on 23 May took the unpleasant but correct decision to evacuate the British troops through DUNKIRK. Once back in the UK Gort became Inspector-General of Training, and in 1941 was appointed as Governor of Gibraltar and Commander-in-Chief, Malta. His steadfast approach and refusal to countenance defeat was an important factor in providing an example during a testing phase of the war.

Gotha Go 242/244

The Go 242 was a glider built in three versions; the 242A-1 was a cargo carrier, while the 242A-2 was for the carriage of airborne troops. Both these used skid-type undercarriage, whilst the third version, the 242B, had a tricycle-wheeled undercarriage and could be configured for either type of load. Later the design was modified by adding two engines, turning the 242B into the 244. The gliders were used in moderate numbers from 1942, principally in the cargo role, but the 244, after a short period of use in North Africa, was relegated to training roles. *Span* 80.3ft (24.5m); *engines* 2 750hp radial; *speed* 180mph (290kph).

Gothic Line, Italy, 1944

A heavily-fortified defensive line running from the Magra valley, some miles south of La Spezia on the west coast, through the Apuan mountains to a chain of strongpoints guarding the Apennine passes and thence to the Foglia valley to a point on the Adriatic between Pesaro and Cattolica, to which the German 10th and 14th Armies retired slowly following the fall of ROME. Work on the line had begun the previous year but had been accelerated in June. The line itself was approximately 10 miles (16km) deep and included every conceivable field fortification, including 2376 machine gun posts, 479 prepared positions for assault guns, anti-tank guns and mortars, and mile upon mile of anti-tank ditches and wire entanglements; wherever possible, defences were sited on ridges lying across the line of the Allied advance. By now both the British 8th and US 5th Armies were accustomed to the difficulties of fighting in the mountainous Italian terrain and had developed a tight interlock between arms which enabled them to secure objectives which were, of necessity, limited. ALEXANDER's plan was for 8th Army to break through on the right flank and unleash its armour into the Po valley while 5th Army maintained steady pressure further west. However, the Germans bitterly contested every feature, including the vital GEMMANO and Coriano Ridges, and even after these had fallen they retired so slowly that the arrival of the autumn rains rendered movement extremely difficult. The Allied offensive, which began on 30 August and ended on 28 October, succeeded in breaching the Gothic Line but exploitation proved impossible. Both sides sustained heavy casualties in the protracted fighting. See FUTA and IL GIOGIO PASSES. See also *The Gothic Line* by Douglas Orgill (Heinemann).

Gott, Gen William Henry Ewart (1897–1942)

Gott was a relatively unknown British officer who came to prominence as a corps commander in the Desert campaign in 1941. He was nicknamed "Strafer", not from any personality trait, since he was a mild-mannered man, but simply from the World War I German phrase "Gott Strafe England". In 1942 he was appointed to succeed RITCHIE as commander of 8th Army, but flying to his new headquarters, he was killed when the aircraft crashed. His place was taken by MONTGOMERY.

Govorov, Marshal Leonid (1897–1955)

Govorov was a career artillery officer in the Soviet Army who was appointed to command of the 5th Army outside MOSCOW in November 1941. In December his forces played a major role in the Red Army's counteroffensive. Govorov was then given command of the Leningrad Front, then under siege by the Germans. He conducted an active defence of the beleaguered city, opened up the supply route via Lake Ladoga, and organized the manufacture of weapons within Leningrad. On 18 January

1943 the Volkhor and Leningrad Fronts linked to form a corridor 5–7 miles (8–11km) wide south of Lake Ladoga, but it was not until January 1944 that the siege was finally broken by the simultaneous attack of three Soviet Fronts, led by 2nd Shock Army from the Oranienbaum bridgehead. Thereafter Govorov's Leningrad Front pursued the Germans across the Baltic states to East Prussia, and its commander was promoted Marshal.

Graf Zeppelin, KMS – Aircraft Carrier

Graf Zeppelin was still fitting out when the war began and although work continued fitfully the project was finally abandoned in 1943. The ship was scuttled at Stettin on 24 April 1945. *Displacement* 18,250 declared; 23,430 actual planned; *dimensions* 820×103ft

Grants on the move in the Western Desert.

(250×31.5m); mean draught 27ft (8.2m); *machinery* 4-shaft geared turbines producing shp 200,000; *speed* 33.5 knots; *protection* main belt 4in; deck 2in; *armament* 16×5.9in (8×2); 12×4.1in AA (6×2); 22×37mm AA (11×2); 28×20mm AA; *aircraft* 28 Ju 87D and 12 Me 109G (projected); *complement* 1760; *launched* 8 December 1938.

Granit

American operations in the Central Pacific, March 1944.

Grant – Medium Tank M3 Modified For British Service (USA)

Specification similar to LEE. The Grant, however, was ordered by the British Tank Commission with a larger cast turret to conform with the British practice of mounting the vehicle's radio in the turret, where it was operated by the loader. The effect of this was to reduce the Grant's crew to six as opposed to seven required for the Lee. The vehicle first saw action during the GAZALA/KNIGHTSBRIDGE battles of May/June 1942, where the ability of its sponson-mounted 75mm gun to fire armour piercing or high explosive ammunition gave 8th Army a definite qualitative advantage. It also took part in the Battles of ALAM HALFA and ALAMEIN and the pursuit of the Axis army to Tunisia, being gradually replaced by the SHERMAN. During the period when 8th Army's fortunes were at their lowest ebb the Grant was referred to as ELH (Egypt's Last Hope). Over 500 were purchased by the British Army and a number were supplied to the Australian Army as well. When the vehicle was withdrawn from first line service it was converted to other roles. These included command vehicle, two types of SCORPION flail tank, and CANAL DEFENCE LIGHT.

Graziani, Marshal Rodolfo (1882–1955)

Graziani joined the Italian Army in the 1890s and served in various North African posts, assuming command in Libya in 1927 where he gained a reputation for harshness and repressive control of the natives. In 1935 he became Governor of Italian Somaliland and in 1936 succeeded BADOGLIO as Viceroy of Ethiopia. In June 1940 he was given command of

Marshal Rodolfo Graziani.

the Italian Army in LIBYA and spent three months making careful preparations for an advance into Egypt which took place in September. British units fell back and he advanced to SIDI BARRANI, where he established a vast series of fortified outposts, the purpose of which has never been understood by any military analyst. On 9 December 1940 he was attacked by General O'Connor and overrun in four days, suffering a catastrophic defeat with the loss of 12,000 casualties, 38,000 prisoners and the entire equipment of five divisions. Further defeats followed as he was pursued by the British under WAVELL to a final halt at Benghazi. He then resigned his command and returned to Italy. He took no further part in operations. In 1943, after the Italian armistice, he took the Fascist side, surrendered to the US Army in 1945 and was handed back to the Italian government in 1946. After four years of house arrest he was sentenced in 1950 to 19 years' imprisonment, but by political intrigue managed to obtain his release after a few months. He thereafter took part in neo-Fascist political activity until his death.

Grease Gun

The nickname applied by US troops to their M3 submachine gun, since it was tubular and had the barrel extending from the centre of the tube, just like a simple lubricating grease gun. The M3 was developed in 1942 and was, like the British STEN gun, cheaply and easily manufactured. Chambered for the .45 Colt Auto Pistol cartridge, by changing the bolt and barrel it could be adjusted to fire the 9mm Parabellum cartridge, though this was rarely done. The first model used a hand crank to cock the bolt; the M3A1 had holes in the bolt into which the firer poked his finger to cock the weapon.

Greater East Asia Co-Prosperity Sphere, 1941–45

A Japanese propaganda term intended to convey to the inhabitants of occupied colonial territories that their association with Japan would result in long-term mutual benefit. In the event Japanese rule was harsher and economic exploitation more ruthless than that of the colonial powers.

Great Marianas Turkey Shoot

The name given to part of the air conflict during the naval Battle of the PHILIPPINE SEA, 20 June 1944. Japanese Admiral TOYODA planned

to trap the US 5th Fleet carrier force between Vice-Admiral OZAWA's carriers and land-based aircraft flying from Guam. The Japanese, with six carriers and 342 aircraft, were outnumbered by the US Fleet with 15 carriers and 956 aircraft, and were counting on the shore-based aircraft to tip the scale. Admiral MITSCHER beat the Japanese to the draw by flying off his aircraft to intercept the Japanese planes some 50 miles (80km) ahead of the US ships. The Japanese attack was in four waves, and only a few of the second wave got close to their targets, the remainder, over 300, being shot down. It was this enormous loss of aircraft which earned this battle its nickname.

Great Purge, the, 1937

Initiated by STALIN and his close supporters in the Communist Party of the Soviet Union, who felt themselves threatened by more progressive elements within the Army. On 9 June Marshal Mikhail TUKHACHEVSKY and his two principal supporters were relieved of their posts. On 11 June they were court-martialled, found guilty and shot at dawn the following day. During the months that followed the Army was mercilessly purged from top to bottom of any who were even suspected of the slightest disloyalty. The full extent of the slaughter will probably never be known, but estimates suggest that some 35,000 officers were murdered, disappeared without trace or sent to labour camps. During the Great Purge the Army lost three of its five marshals, 13 of its 15 army commanders, 57 out of 85 corps commanders, nine out of every ten divisional and brigade commanders and eight out of ten colonels. The effect of this reign of terror was to stifle initiative within the Army and as a direct result of this it performed badly during the 1939 occupation of Poland, in the RUSSO-FINNISH CAMPAIGN and against the Wehrmacht in 1941.

Grebbe Line, Holland, 1940

An interim defence line to be held by the Dutch Army in the event of German invasion, running south from the Ijsselmeer to the Nieder Rijn. The line was intended to impose delay while the Dutch withdrew into "Fortress Holland", which incorporated the core of the country and the cities of Amsterdam, ROTTERDAM and The Hague, pending the arrival of British and French assistance. The extensive German use of parachute and air-landing formations rendered the position untenable.

Greece, 1941–44

See AEGEAN THEATRE; ALIAKMON LINE; ATHENS; BALKAN CAMPAIGNS; CORINTH CANAL; CRETE; METAXAS LINE.

Greim, FM Ritter von (1892–1945)

In April 1945 von Greim was a Luftwaffe career officer, commanding Luftflotte 6, based in Munich. After HITLER's dismissal of GÖRING, von Greim was summoned to the Führerbunker in Berlin, where he was promoted Field-Marshal and made Commander-in-Chief of what remained of the Luftwaffe. On the night of 28/29 April, von Greim flew out of Berlin to DÖNITZ's headquarters at Plön. Their Arado 96 observation 'plane was the last German aircraft to leave Berlin. Greim had inherited a bankrupt command, and he committed suicide after his capture by US forces on 24 June 1945.

Grenade

American offensive between the Meuse and Rhine, February 1945.

Grese, Irma (d. 1945)

A female SS Auxiliary officer and assistant to Josef KRAMER, commandant of Bergen-BELSEN concentration camp. On her capture by British forces, she showed little or no remorse over the horrors surrounding her, and stories of how she set Alsatian dogs on to the inmates and made lampshades from tattooed human skin were current. At the NUREMBERG TRIALS, she was found guilty of murdering inmates and other crimes and was hanged, with Kramer, in November 1945.

Greyhound – Armoured Car M8 (USA)

Developed by the Ford Motor Company in 1942, the 6×6 rear-engined Greyhound entered service with the US Army the following year. The vehicle was fast and quiet but its vulnerability to mine damage made it unpopular with its crews, who reinforced the floor with sandbags. The Greyhound served in armoured cavalry reconnaissance squadrons and remained active with many armies long after the war. A turretless derivative armed with a single machine gun was known as the Car Armoured Utility M20. During World War II 8523 M8s were built, plus 3791 M20s. *Weight* 7.5 tons; *speed* 55mph (88kph); *armour* 25mm; *armament* 1 37mm gun; 1 .30-cal Browning machine gun; *engine* Hercules 6-cylinder 110hp petrol; *crew* 4.

Grief

German commando operations in the ARDENNES, December 1944.

Griswold, Maj Gen Oscar W. (1886–1954)

General Griswold commanded the US XV Corps in the taking of GUADALCANAL, NEW GEORGIA and the PHILIPPINES. In the first two campaigns Griswold's role was that of consolidation and support, which he performed competently, but in the Philippine invasion his Corps was in the forefront of the fighting in LUZON and Griswold was revealed as overcautious and with little tactical imagination. His Corps suffered excessive casualties and was relieved of front line duty in March 1945 to return to a consolidating role.

Groves, Gen Leslie (1896–1970)

Groves was an officer of the US Corps of Engineers who had spent most of his career carrying out civil engineering projects. In 1942 he was picked to direct the "Manhattan Engineer District", the cover name for the development of the ATOMIC BOMB. Groves became entirely responsible for the construction of facilities, procurement of raw materials and equipment, provision of accommodation and testing facilities for the eventual bomb. At its height the project employed some 125,000 people and had a budget in excess of $500 million per year. Groves ran it with great efficiency, ensuring good relations with labour, scientists and government and also maintaining the most strict secrecy of any wartime project.

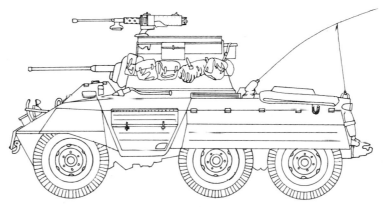

Greyhound light armoured car.

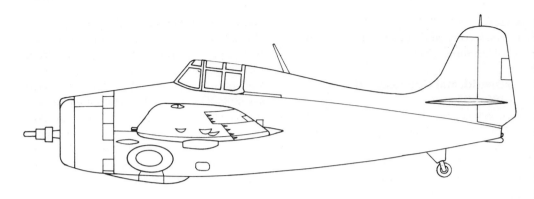

Grumman F4F-4 Wildcat fighter-bomber.

Grozny, Soviet Union, 1942–43
See CAUCASUS.

Grumman Aircraft (USA)
Grumman F4F Wildcat The Wildcat was the US Navy's standard fighter at the outbreak of war and, known as the Martlet, had been in service with the Royal Navy since 1940. They were widely used as carrier aircraft in the Atlantic, Pacific and Mediterranean theatres. *Span* 38ft (11.6m); *engine* 1 1200hp radial; *crew* 1; armament 4 .50 machine guns, 220lb (100kg) of bombs; *speed* 328mph (528kph).

Grumman F6F Hellcat The F6F was an improved development of the F4F Wildcat, and although heavier was more streamlined and had better performance. It went into production in mid-1942 and first saw action in the Pacific in September 1943. Numbers were also supplied to the Royal Navy. *Span* 43ft (13m); *engine* 1 2000hp radial; *crew* 1; armament 6 .50 machine guns, 2000lb (900kg) of bombs or 6 5in rockets; *speed* 375mph (603kph).

Grumman TBF/TBM Avenger The TBF was among the most successful torpedo-bombers of the war period and survived in service for many years afterwards. It was one of the first American aircraft to carry a power-operated turret and was also unusual in carrying a 22-inch torpedo internally. *Span* 54ft (16.5m); *engine* 1 1700hp radial; *crew* 3; *armament* 1 .50 and 2 .30 machine guns or 3 .50 and 1 .30 machine guns, 2000lb (900kg) of bombs or torpedoes; *speed* 270mph (434kph).

GS General Service (UK). The British equivalent of GI as a designation for common equipment; thus, "Bucket, GS".

GS General Staff (UK).

GSC General Service Corps (UK). Army corps established to provide a "home" for troops under training and awaiting selection to particular regiments, and also for officers and men on special duties.

GSO General Staff Officer (UK).

Guadalcanal, Land Campaign, 1942–43
Confirmation that the Japanese were constructing an airfield on Guadalcanal led to the landing of Major-General Alexander A. VANDEGRIFT's reinforced US 1st Marine Division on 7 August. The small Japanese garrison was quickly scattered and the airfield, subsequently known as HENDERSON FIELD, was completed, receiving its first aircraft on 20 August. The Japanese poured reinforcements into the island with a view to recapturing the airfield and commenced a naval and air offensive against the American beach-head. Patrol clashes escalated into a full scale assault on the sector of the Marine perimeter now known as Bloody Ridge, 12–14 September; American casualties were 143 killed and wounded but the Japanese were forced to fall back leaving 600 dead. Both sides continued to build up their strength, the Japanese forming 17th Army under Major-General Haruyoshi HYAKUTAKE. Further unco-ordinated assaults on the perimeter took place 23–25 October but were repulsed with the loss of

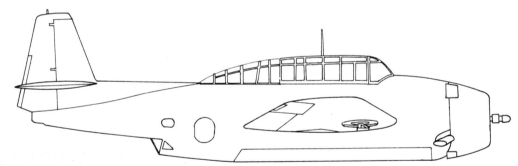

Grumman TBM-3 torpedo bomber.

Grumman TBF-1 Avenger torpedo bomber

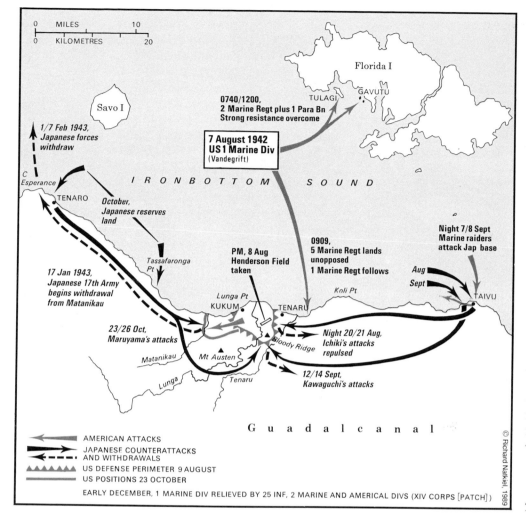

Map labels:
- MILES 0 10
- KILOMETRES 0 20
- Florida I
- Savo I
- TULAGI
- GAVUTU
- 0740/1200, 2 Marine Regt plus 1 Para Bn Strong resistance overcome
- 7 August 1942 US 1 Marine Div (Vandegrift)
- 1/7 Feb 1943, Japanese forces withdraw
- C Esperance
- TENARO
- I R O N B O T T O M   S O U N D
- October, Japanese reserves land
- Night 7/8 Sept Marine raiders attack Jap base
- 17 Jan 1943, Japanese 17th Army begins withdrawal from Matanikau
- Tassaronga Pt
- PM, 8 Aug Henderson Field taken
- 0909, 5 Marine Regt lands unopposed 1 Marine Regt follows
- Aug Sept
- TAIVU
- Lunga Pt KUKUM
- Koli Pt
- TENARU
- 23/26 Oct, Maruyama's attacks
- Bloody Ridge
- Night 20/21 Aug, Ichiki's attacks repulsed
- Matanikau
- Mt Austen
- Lunga
- Tenaru
- 12/14 Sept, Kawaguchi's attacks
- G u a d a l c a n a l
- © Richard Natkiel, 1989

Legend:
- AMERICAN ATTACKS
- JAPANESE COUNTERATTACKS AND WITHDRAWALS
- US DEFENSE PERIMETER 9 AUGUST
- US POSITIONS 23 OCTOBER
- EARLY DECEMBER, 1 MARINE DIV RELIEVED BY 25 INF, 2 MARINE AND AMERICAL DIVS (XIV CORPS [PATCH])

Guadalcanal, Naval Campaign, 1942

Commenced 7 August 1942 with the landing of American troops on Guadalcanal and TULAGI and ended with the Japanese evacuation of Guadalcanal on 7 February 1943. The aim of both sides was the reinforcement and supply of their ground troops, and the Japanese repeatedly strove to eliminate HENDERSON FIELD, the lynchpin of the American defence, by naval bombardment and air attack. The Japanese showed a marked superiority in night-fighting techniques and this, coupled with their formidable LONG LANCE torpedoes, enabled them to emerge the tactical victors in most engagements, although strategic success eluded them. Ultimately their failure to match the American build-up ashore made a Japanese defeat inevitable. Each side lost 24 warships, but for the Americans these losses were quickly made good by their huge ship-building programme, which the Japanese could not hope to equal. Further losses which Japan could not afford were over 600 experienced naval pilots and 300,000 tons of merchant shipping. See also SAVO ISLAND; EASTERN SOLOMONS; CAPE ESPERANCE; SANTA CRUZ; FIRST and SECOND GUADALCANAL; and TASSAFARONGA.

The six-month battle for Guadalcanal, 1942–43.

Japanese dead on the sand-bar of the Ilu River, Guadalcanal.

over 2000 killed. On 26 October Vandegrift went over to the offensive, pushing back the Japanese until Henderson Field was no longer within range of their artillery. The 1st Marine Division was relieved on 8 December and the XIV Corps, consisting of the 2nd Marine, Americal and 25th Divisions, was formed under Major-General Alexander M. PATCH. During January 1943 the Americans drove the starving, diseased Japanese steadily west towards Cape Esperance but were unable to prevent the evacuation of approximately 10,000 men in night naval operations 1–7 February. Total American casualties in the land campaign amounted to 1600 killed, 4200 wounded and over 12,000 incapacitated by disease. The Japanese lost 14,000 killed in action, 9000 dead from disease or starvation, an unknown number of wounded and 1000 captured. The Guadalcanal campaign provided the Allies with their first large-scale victory over the Japanese. See GUADALCANAL, NAVAL CAMPAIGN.

Guadalcanal, First Battle of, 1942

By early November 1942 Admiral YAMAMOTO was determined to strike a decisive blow which would end the American presence on Guadalcanal once and for all. His plan involved the destruction of HENDERSON FIELD by a bombardment force commanded by Vice-Admiral Hiroaki Abe and based on the battleships *Hiei* (Flag) and *Kirishima*, following which Rear-Admiral TANAKA would land 13,500 reinforcements to overwhelm the American defences. The battleships were escorted by the cruiser *Nagara* and 14 destroyers, which Abe deployed as advanced scouts, flank guards and close escort against attack by PT boats. The details of Yamamoto's plan, however, had been de-coded and Abe's approach was detected by American aircraft during 12 November. Thus, when his ships attempted to pass between Savo Island and the north coast of Guadalcanal that night they were intercepted by a squadron under Rear-Admiral Daniel Callaghan, consisting of the cruisers *San Francisco* (Flag), *Atlanta*, *Helena*, *Juneau* and *Portland* and the destroyers *Aaron Ward*, *Barton*, *Cushing*, *Fletcher*, *Laffey*, *Monssen*, *O'Bannon* and *Sterrett*, moving on an opposite course in line ahead with the cruisers in the centre. The Americans failed to take full advantage of their radar, and when contact was made at 0124, bad radio discipline and over-strict control prevented them from opening fire until the Japanese did so at 0150. Aboard *Hiei* and *Kirishima* the main armament had been loaded with high explosive shells for the anticipated bombardment and the delay enabled these to be replaced with armour-piercing ammunition. During a confused gun and torpedo battle lasting 24 minutes Cal-

US naval dive-bombers on Henderson Field, Guadalcanal.

laghan was killed and *San Francisco* was severely damaged; Rear-Admiral Scott, the victor of the Battle of CAPE ESPERANCE, was killed aboard *Atlanta*, which was so badly damaged that she later sank; *Portland* and *Juneau* were both crippled by LONG LANCE torpedoes, and the latter blew up the following morning when torpedoed again by the submarine *I-26*; and the destroyers *Barton*, *Cushing*, *Laffey* and *Monssen* were sunk. The Japanese lost the destroyers *Akatsuki* and *Yudachi* but most of the American response had been directed at *Hiei*, which was forced to limp out of action to the west of Savo Island, shattered by more than 50 hits and with fires raging. Simultaneously, *Kirishima* and the rest of the Japanese ships withdrew. *Hiei* sustained fur-

ther damage from air attack next day and was scuttled north of Savo Island at 1800, an act which resulted directly in Abe's dismissal.

A further consequence of the action was that Tanaka's reinforcement operation was postponed for 24 hours while a cruiser force under Vice-Admiral MIKAWA executed the mission Abe had been unable to complete. Arriving off Savo Island at midnight on 13/14 November, Mikawa despatched Rear-Admiral Nishimura with the cruisers *Suzuya*, *Maya*, *Tenryu* and six destroyers to bombard Henderson Field while he provided a covering screen with the cruisers *Chokai*, *Kinugasa*, *Isuzu* and two destroyers. No surface opposition was encountered and at 0205 Nishimura retired, having fired 1000 shells and wrecked

First Battle of Guadalcanal (left) and Second Battle of Guadalcanal.

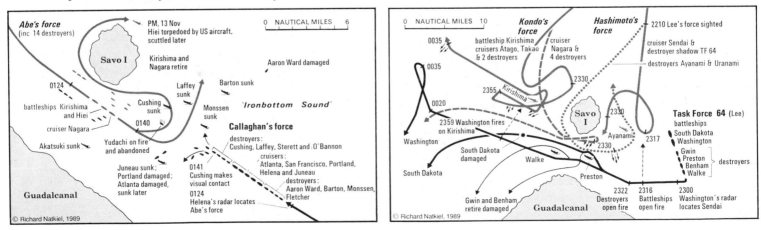

18 aircraft, but failing to put the airstrip out of action. With the coming of daylight American aircraft pursued Mikawa and Nishimura, sinking *Kinugasa* and damaging *Chokai*, *Isuzu* and the destroyer *Michishio*. Coastwatchers and radio interceptions kept the Americans informed of the progress of Tanaka's reinforcement group, consisting of eleven transports escorted by eleven destroyers. From 0830 onwards the convoy remained under constant air attack until at dusk the number of transports had been reduced to four. The scene was now set for the Second Battle of GUADALCANAL.

Guadalcanal, Second Battle of, 1942

Admiral YAMAMOTO, disappointed by the results of the First Battle of GUADALCANAL and its immediate aftermath, ordered Admiral Nobutaki KONDO to bombard HENDERSON FIELD during the night of 14/15 November 1942, while Rear-Admiral TANAKA completed his task of landing reinforcements on Guadalcanal. Kondo's force consisted of the battleship *Kirishima*, the cruisers *Atago* (Flag), *Takao*, *Nagara* and six destroyers, plus an advance screen under Rear-Admiral Shintaro Hashimoto containing the cruiser *Sendai* and three destroyers. Meanwhile Admiral HALSEY had sent forward a task force under Rear-Admiral Willis LEE to replace Callaghan's cruiser squadron. Lee's command contained the battleships *Washington* (Flag) and *South Dakota*, escorted by the destroyers *Walke*, *Benham*, *Preston* and *Gwin*. By 2200 the task force, in line ahead with the battleships at the rear, had rounded Savo Island and was steering south towards the coast of Guadalcanal. At 2252 Lee, warned by the submarine USS *Trout* of Kondo's approach, turned west hoping to cross the latter's T when he appeared from the north. Unknown to him, the Japanese screen had been in visual contact with his ships since 2210. At 2317 the American battleships sighted *Sendai* and opened fire, causing her to withdraw behind a smokescreen. However, two of Hashimoto's destroyers, joined by *Nagara* and the six destroyers from Kondo's main body, had passed to the west of Savo Island with the heavier ships following behind, and were thus in position to intercept Lee. At 2322 the action became general. During the next 13 minutes *Preston* was sunk by gunfire and LONG LANCE torpedoes struck *Walke* and *Benham*; the former sank at once and the latter was abandoned and sunk the following day. *Gwin*

was also seriously damaged. To compound the confusion *Sendai* and a destroyer attacked the American rear. At 2333 an electric power failure put *South Dakota*'s radar out of action and she lost contact with *Washington*. Kondo now joined the action with *Kirishima* and the rest of his cruisers. *South Dakota*, illuminated by their searchlights, was battered by a storm of 14-inch and 8-inch shells which shot away her masts and started fires in her upperworks. At this critical juncture *Washington*, which had worked her way clear of the mêlée, obtained a clear radar picture of *Kirishima* at 8400 yards (7680m) and for seven minutes hammered the enemy battleship with her main and secondary armaments, obtaining hits with nine 16-inch and 40 5-inch shells. *Kirishima*, with her steering gear wrecked, two of her turrets out of action and fires raging, staggered to the west of Savo Island where she was later scuttled. Kondo broke contact at 0025 and covered his retreat with a smoke screen, scuttling the badly damaged destroyer *Ayanami* as he withdrew. Tanaka ran his four transports aground at 0400 and then retired at speed with his destroyers, still with troops aboard, to avoid daylight air attack. Only 2000 men, 260 cases of ammunition and 1500 bags of rice were landed, a trivial return for so great an investment.

The two battles of Guadalcanal proved to be decisive. Yamamoto decided that no more heavy naval units or transports would be risked on bombardment or reinforcement missions. This, coupled with the fact that the Americans were able to continue their own build-up of men and supplies, meant that the defeat of the Japanese forces on Guadalcanal was simply a matter of time.

Guam, Marianas Islands, 1944

An island at the southern end of the group possessing a large natural anchorage and the potential for the development of air bases. The Japanese occupied Guam on 10 December 1941, overwhelming the small American garrison. On 21 July 1944 Major-General Allen H. Turnage's US 3rd Marine Division landed at Asan while Brigadier Lemuel C. Shepherd's 1st Provisional Marine Brigade, followed by Major-General Andrew D. Bruce's 77th Infantry Division, fought their way ashore further south at Agat. The Japanese garrison, commanded by Lieutenant-General Takeshi Takashina, launched a series of suicidal counter-attacks, but the Americans fought their way steadily northwards and by 10 August the entire island was in their hands. American losses were 1744 killed and 5970 wounded; 18,250 Japanese were killed and 1250 captured. Some Japanese took refuge in the island's interior and the last of these did not surrender until 1960. Airfield construction commenced as soon as the occupation was complete, the first B-29s landing in October. See also Battle of the PHILIPPINE SEA.

Marines moving forward with tank support, Guam, July 1944.

Gubbins, Gen Sir Colin McVean (1896–1976)

Gubbins was commissioned into the Royal Artillery and served during World War I, after which he went to Russia in 1919 with the Allied Intervention Force. He was an observer in Poland in 1939 and fought with the Polish Army, and in 1940, in a similar role, fought in NORWAY. This experience of irregular warfare served him well when he was appointed Director of Operations for the SOE in November 1940. In September 1943 he became the executive head of SOE. In both posts his acumen and military sense were of the greatest value in guiding the formation and employment of resistance groups throughout Europe.

Guderian, Gen Heinz (1888–1954)

Born in Chelmno (Kulm), he was commissioned into the infantry and served as a staff officer during World War I. In postwar years he became first a signals and then a motor transport specialist, and with this technical background began to interest himself in the tank and its employment. In 1937 he published an influential book, *Achtung Panzer!* In 1938 he became Chief of the Mobile Forces – embracing both armoured and motorized troops – and commanded armoured columns during the occupations of CZECHOSLOVAKIA and Austria. In 1939 he led XIX Panzer Corps into Poland, displaying his ability to move rapidly and boldly and learning several practical lessons. In 1940 he led

General Heinz Guderian in his armoured command vehicle: Enigma coding machine in the foreground.

the same Corps into France, cut through the French defences at Sedan, forced the crossing of the Meuse and justified all his pre-war arguments about armoured operations. When Germany invaded Russia in 1941, Guderian commanded 2nd Panzer Group, Army Group Centre. His advance was meteoric, but with the onset of winter and the stiffening of Soviet resistance, Guderian made a tactical withdrawal which led to his being dismissed by HITLER. He remained in retirement until March 1943, when he was appointed Inspector of Armoured Troops, responsible for production priorities as well as for military training and operations. By now he was suffering from ill health, and this, together with political jealousies and military obstruction from his opponents, meant that he could do little to salvage the war for Germany, although it is doubtful if any other German general could have done as much. In 1944, after the JULY BOMB PLOT against Hitler, he replaced ZEITZLER as Chief of Staff. Guderian never shrank from standing up to the Führer, and he was dismissed on 28 March 1945 after a blazing row with Hitler. Guderian was probably the best manipulator of armoured formations ever seen.

Guernsey, Channel Islands, 1940

Guernsey was occupied by German troops on 30 June 1940 and was raided by No. 11 Independent Company and H Troop No. 3 Commando on the night of 14/15 July. The raid, while bloodless, achieved nothing and was not repeated. The German garrison of the Channel Islands surrendered on 9 May 1945.

Guinea Pigs

A sardonic term applied to themselves by Royal Air Force personnel who were severely burned in combat and were given extensive plastic surgery under the guidance of Sir Archibald McINDOE, a brilliant surgeon.

Gumrak, Soviet Union, 1942–43

A railway junction and airfield west of STALINGRAD, for a while the headquarters of the trapped German 6th Army. The fall of Gumrak airfield on 21 January 1943 closed the German air supply route and accelerated von PAULUS' surrender. See *Stalingrad – The Turning Point* by Geoffrey Jukes (Macdonald).

Gun Motor Carriage M3 (USA)

An interim design for a tank destroyer, combining the M3 half-track and the M1897 A4

75mm gun on a pedestal mount, firing forward. The design was initiated in June 1941 and 2202 were produced of which all but 842 were subsequently reconverted to the armoured personnel carrier role. The vehicle saw active service during the Japanese invasion of the PHILIPPINES and later in North Africa until replaced by the GUN MOTOR CARRIAGE M10. Numbers were then supplied to the British Army which employed them in the heavy troops of armoured car regiments and divisional reconnaissance regiments.

Gun Motor Carriage M6 (USA)

A light tank destroyer based on the DODGE 4×4 Command and Reconnaissance Vehicle T214, the GMC M6 was armed with the 37mm anti-tank gun M3, mounted at the rear of the vehicle in the manner of British *portées*. The vehicle was intended as an expedient pending the production of larger tank destroyers but some did serve in North Africa. A total of 3117 were produced.

Gun Motor Carriage M10 (USA)

A tank destroyer based on the chassis of the SHERMAN M4A2 medium tank, the M10 possessed angled hull armour and was fitted with an open-topped turret, capable of all-round traverse, mounting a 3-inch high velocity gun. The design was standardised in June 1942 and to increase production capacity the Sherman M4A3 chassis was also employed, this version being known as the M10A1. An eventual total of 4993 M10s and 1413 M10A1s were built. A number of turretless M10A1s were later converted for use as the heavy artillery tractor M35. The M10 entered service during the closing stages of the war in North Africa and subsequently saw action in every major war zone in which American troops were employed, as well as being supplied to Allied armies. In British service the vehicle was known as the Wolverine; see also ACHILLES. *Weight* 29.4 tons; *speed* 30mph (48kph); *armour* 37mm; *armament* 1 3-inch gun M7; 1 .50-cal Browning machine gun; *engine* Twin GMS6/71 Diesels (M10); Ford GAA V8 petrol (M10A1); *crew* 5.

Gun Motor Carriage M12 (USA)

Based on the LEE M3 medium tank chassis with the engine moved forward to provide space for the mounting of the 155mm gun M1918-M1, a World War I weapon of French design. The vehicle had a speed of 24mph (39kph)

and was manned by a crew of six. One hundred were built, of which the majority served in the European theatre of operations. A weaponless version designated Cargo Carrier M30 acted as an ammunition tender, stowing 40 rounds. See also GUN MOTOR CARRIAGE M40.

Gun Motor Carriage M18 (USA)

Purpose-built as a light tracked tank destroyer with particular emphasis on speed and firepower, the M18 was armed with the same 76mm gun which was fitted to the later models of the SHERMAN medium tank. However, unlike the GUN MOTOR CARRIAGES M10 and M36, the vehicle employed a torsion bar suspension. The Buick Division of General Motors built a total of 2507 M18s between July 1943 and October 1944. A turretless version, known as the Armored Utility Vehicle M39, was employed as an armoured personnel carrier, as an ammunition carrier, and as a tractor for the towed anti-tank guns M1 and M6. M18s served in both the European and Pacific theatres of operation. The vehicle was popularly known as the Hellcat. *Weight* 18.25 tons; *speed* 50mph (80kph); *armour* 12mm; *armament* 1×76mm gun M1 series; 1×.50-cal Browning machine gun; *engine* Continental R-975 400hp air-cooled petrol; *crew* 5.

Gun Motor Carriage M19 (USA)

Based on the chassis of the CHAFFEE M24 light tank with the engine moved forward to provide space for a twin 40mm M2 anti-aircraft cannon mounting. The vehicle had a maximum speed of 35mph (56kph) and was manned by a crew of six. Over 900 were ordered in August 1944 but only 285 had been completed when hostilities ended. The GMC M19 remained active in American service for many years after the war.

Gun Motor Carriage M36 (USA)

Essentially an up-gunned GUN MOTOR CARRIAGE M10 or M10A1, designed early in 1943 in response to the appearance of the German TIGER and PANTHER tanks. The M36 was similar in general appearance and layout to the M10 but mounted a larger turret housing a 90mm gun M3, and maximum armour thickness was increased to 50mm. The design proved to be satisfactory for its purpose and 1722 were built, including 500 converted M10A1s.

Gun Motor Carriage M40 (USA)

Based on a widened SHERMAN M4A3 medium tank chassis with the engine moved forward to provide space for the mounting of the recently developed 155mm gun M1. Similar in

Gun motor carriage M18 "Hellcat" with 90mm gun firing pointblank on a Nazi pillbox, Brest 1944.

layout to the GUN MOTOR CARRIAGE M12, the vehicle had a maximum speed of 24mph (39kph) and was manned by a crew of six. The design was standardized in March 1945 and 311 had been built when the war ended. The vehicle first went into action during the American assault on COLOGNE. The GMC M40 was sometimes referred to unofficially as "Long Tom".

Gustav

A German 80cm railway gun devised by Krupp and intended to breach the MAGINOT LINE fortifications. The design was offered to the German Army in 1937 and accepted, but manufacture proved more complex than had been foreseen and the first gun, named after Gustav Krupp, was not delivered until early 1942. A second gun, named "Dora", was built later. Gustav was used in the siege of Sevastopol; Dora was sent to Leningrad but arrived too late and had to be withdrawn before it could fire. So far as is known, neither was ever used again. Components were found after the war, but not the complete equipments. Each gun weighed 1350 tonnes emplaced across two double-track railway lines, was 141ft (43m) long, and fired a 4.73 ton shell to 29.2 miles (47km) or a 7 ton shell to 23.6 miles (38km). These were the largest guns (but not the largest calibre) ever built.

Gustav Line, Italy, 1943–44

Defence line running from the mouth of the GARIGLIANO River through CASSINO and across the Apennines to a point south of ORTONA to which the German 10th Army retired following the break-out of the US 5th Army from the SALERNO beach-head and the advance of the British 8th Army from Reggio Calabria and Taranto. The Allied advance was delayed by bad weather and expert German demolitions. The stubborn defence of the Gustav Line throughout December and January led an Allied attempt to outflank it with an amphibious landing at ANZIO on 22 January, but this was contained by prompt German countermeasures. Heavy fighting continued until May, when Cassino, the lynch-pin of the German defences, was taken, enabling 5th Army to effect a junction with the Anzio beach-head and continue its advance on ROME. It is sometimes referred to as the Winter Line.

The biggest gun in the world – 1,328 tons of the 80cm Gustav railway gun, firing on Sevastopol in 1942.

Guy Armoured Car (UK)

Based on the Guy Quad 4×4 artillery tractor. Production commenced in 1939 and 101 were built. Two troops each of three cars served in France during the 1940 campaign, forming part of the unit known first as No 3 Air Mission then as GHQ Liaison Regiment or "Phantom". The remainder were retained in the United Kingdom for Home Defence, training or VIP escort duties. *Weight* 5.2 tons; *speed* 40mph (64kph); *armour* 15mm; *armament* 1 Vickers .5-cal machine gun and 1 Vickers .303-inch machine gun or 1 Besa 15mm machine gun and 1 Besa 7.92mm machine gun; *engine* Meadows 53bhp; *crew* 3.

Gymnast

Preliminary Allied plan for the invasion of French North Africa, November 1942. See also SUPER-GYMNAST.

H

H2S

A British aerial navigation aid consisting of a radar scanner and receiver fitted beneath an aircraft, transmitting a beam to the ground below. The system provided a clearly defined differential between water and land, and a discernible differentiation between open countryside and built-up areas. The Germans quickly developed an airborne receiver which homed on to the transmissions, so the device became unpopular.

"H" Class Destroyers (UK)

See "G" AND "H" CLASS DESTROYERS.

Haakon VII, King of Norway (1872–1957)

Haakon became Norway's king when that country gained its independence in 1905. When the Germans invaded and the QUISLING government was formed (9 April 1940), Haakon refused to negotiate, threatening to abdicate rather than violate the country's constitution, withdrawing from Oslo under German fire and setting up a resistance government in Trondheim. Refusing to accept the authority of the Quisling government, when the British withdrew their forces, Haakon and his ministers went with them. From London he made several important broadcasts condemning the German aggression; he actively encouraged the formation of a Free Norwegian army, navy and air force in Britain; and he supported the work of the resistance movement within Norway. In October 1944, free Norwegian forces acting upon Haakon's orders joined with the Russians in attacking German positions in northern Norway from Finland. He returned to his country in June 1945, to the acclamation of his people.

Habbaniyah, Iraq, 1941

A Royal Air Force base commanded by Air Vice-Marshal H. G. Smart, located on the Euphrates 55 miles (88km) west of Baghdad. During RASHID ALI's pro-German insurrection, the base was surrounded on 30 April by a division-sized force of regular Iraqi troops. The garrison consisted of 1000 airmen, 300 men of the King's Own Royal Regiment and 1200 Assyrian and Kurdish levies under the overall command of Colonel O. L. Roberts, supported by 18 RAF armoured cars and two ancient ornamental howitzers which had been brought into commission. The base contained 88 aircraft, but the majority of these were obsolete or training types. On 2 May the Iraqis bombarded the camp, which also contained some 9000 civilian refugees. When the RAF reacted by bombing and strafing the enemy positions, many of the Iraqis fled. Further British air strikes continued and on 5 May the ground troops also took the offensive, using their armoured cars to harry the Iraqis as they withdrew to FALLUJAH. The garrison was not threatened seriously again and was relieved by a flying column from Transjordan on 18 May.

Habbaniyah Artillery, the

Consisted of two World War I vintage howitzers used to ornament the camp gates at Habbaniyah and brought back into service when the Iraqi Army invested the base in May 1941. The presence of such heavy weapons was not suspected by the Iraqis and the moral effect contributed to their defeat. See IRAQ and HABBANIYAH.

Habforce

British expedition to IRAQ, May 1941.

Hadrian Glider (UK)

RAF name for the American WACO CG-4A glider.

Hafid Ridge, Libya, 1941

Feature south-west of Fort CAPUZZO successfully defended by elements of 15th Panzer Division during Operation BATTLEAXE, the abortive British attempt to relieve TOBRUK and secure the frontier defences in June.

Members of the Arab Legion inspect the wreckage of a bombed and burned-out column, Habbaniyah, June 1941.

Hagen Line, Soviet Union, 1943

An interim defence line across the base of the OREL salient to which the German 2nd Panzer and 9th Armies withdrew during·the Soviet counteroffensive which followed the failure of Operation ZITADELLE. See KURSK.

Ha-Go

Japanese counteroffensive in the ARAKAN, Burma, February 1944.

Hague, the, Holland, 1944–45

The location of German V-WEAPON sites from which missiles were launched against London, ANTWERP, Bruges and Liège until March 1945. The isolation of these sites from Germany was one of the objects of Operation MARKET GARDEN. In the harbour area of Antwerp over 300 V-weapons sank two large cargo ships and 58 smaller vessels as well as causing frequent damage to railways and other installations, but failed to interfere with the working of the port.

Haguro, IJN – Myoko Class Cruiser

Sunk by the British destroyers *Saumarez*, *Venus*, *Verulam* and *Virago* of the 26th Destroyer Flotilla, south-west of Penang on 16 May 1945.

Haile Selassie (1891–1976)

Emperor of Ethiopia, Haile Selassie had been driven from his country by the Italian invasion in 1936, being evacuated by a British warship. He remained in exile until 1940 when, with the entry of Italy into the war, Britain agreed to assist in restoring him to his throne. He went to Khartoum in Anglo-Egyptian Sudan, where he formed a Patriot Army with assistance from General Orde WINGATE, and on 20 January 1941 entered Ethiopian soil at the head of his army. While Haile Selassie's force pushed into Ethiopia, British forces advanced via Somaliland and Eritrea. On 6 April Addis Ababa fell to British troops, and on 5 May 1941, exactly five years after the Italians took the city, Haile Selassie returned. In subsequent years, in spite of political opposition from various British quarters, Haile Selassie managed to stabilize his government, achieved charter membership of the United Nations and was a signatory to the final peace treaties. Having successfully vanquished Fascism, however, he was to fall victim to Communism in his later years.

Halberd

MALTA relief convoy, September 1941.

Halcyon Class Minesweeping Sloops (UK)

Displacement 815–875 tons; *dimensions* 230–245ft×33ft 6in (69–73.5×10m); mean draught 6ft 9in–8ft (2.07–2.4m); *machinery* 2-shaft reciprocating engines with ihp 1770–2000 or geared turbines producing shp 1750; *speed* 16.5/17 knots; *armament* 1×4in; 1×4in AA or 2×4in AA (2×1); 4×0.5in AA (1×4); *complement* 80; *number in class* 21, launched 1933–39.

Halder, Gen Franz (1884–1971)

Halder is said to have been one of the premier intellects of the German General Staff, though his career shows little evidence of it. Born into a Bavarian military family, he rose to the rank of lieutenant-general by February 1938, when he was appointed Deputy Chief of Staff and Chief of Operations. Upon the resignation of BECK, the Chief of Staff, in September 1938 Halder succeeded to the post. It has been said that he accepted the post with a view to opposing HITLER, but although he appears to have argued often with the Führer, he rarely influenced events. He lacked the conviction to take decisive steps, though he talked of arresting Hitler before the Western offensive in 1940. He conducted the Polish campaign in 1939 with competence but opposed Hitler's plans for the invasion of the Low Countries and France, being of the opinion that the French Army was invincible. In the summer of 1940 he was ordered to prepare for the invasion of Russia. He played an important part in drawing up the plans for operation BAR-

BAROSSA, but he suppressed disagreeable facts which might have qualified the optimistic forecasts of a quick victory. In an effort to rectify Hitler's blunder in attacking LENINGRAD rather than MOSCOW in 1941, Halder went to the front and took command, but on 24 September 1942 he was dismissed after an argument with Hitler over the latter's policy of simultaneous advance on two fronts which led to disaster at STALINGRAD. He had tenuous connections with the July bomb plotters and was arrested on suspicion, being detained in Dachau. He survived to be liberated by US troops in May 1945 and to give evidence at the NUREMBERG TRIALS.

Hal Far, Malta, 1941–42

Airfield which served as a base for the defence of the island and strikes against Axis shipping routes to North Africa, kept operational by Herculean efforts despite, at times, being under continuous air attack.

Halfaya Pass, Egypt 1941–42

Located some miles east of SOLLUM and offering a means of ascending the escarpment from the coastal plain by motor road. The pass was secured by ROMMEL during his first desert offensive. During Operation BREVITY it was captured by 22nd Guards Brigade, with MATILDA support, on 15 May 1941 but was lost again on 27 May when Rommel counter-attacked with most of his armour, forcing the single infantry battalion and its supporting Matilda squadron to withdraw after a spirited defence. During Operation BATTLEAXE a further British attack on 15 June was defeated when a Matilda squadron was shot to pieces by German 88mm guns which had been

M3A2 halftrack.

integrated into the defences. The Halfaya area was by-passed during the CRUSADER fighting and its isolated Axis garrison surrendered on 17 January 1942.

Half-Tracks (Ger)

See SONDERKRAFTFAHRZEUG 250 and 251 SERIES.

Half-Tracks (USA)

Developed during the late 1930s as a result of a request from the cavalry for a scout vehicle and artillery tractor with good cross-country performance. The design was standardized as the Half-Track Armoured Car M2 in September 1940, as was a longer version, designated Half-Track Personnel Carrier M3, intended to carry an infantry squad. The vehicles were manufactured by the White, Autocar and Diamond T organizations, the first production models being delivered in May 1941. As demand soared after the United States entered the war, the International Harvester Company was brought into the programme and built the M9 and M5 versions (corresponding respectively to the M2 and M3) using its own 143hp engine. Standard versions of the half-track served as armoured personnel carriers, artillery prime movers and in many other roles throughout the army. The layout of the vehicles also rendered them suitable for weapons carriers and among the numerous conversions produced were the GUN MOTOR CARRIAGE M3 tank destroyer, the M4 and M21 81mm mortar carriers, the 75mm Howitzer Motor Carriage T30, which served in Tunisia and Italy, and the 105mm Howitzer Motor Carriage T19, which served in Tunisia as a stop-gap pending the arrival of the HOWITZER MOTOR CARRIAGE M7. There was also a series of Multiple Gun Motor Carriages designed for anti-aircraft defence. These included the M13 with twin .50-cal machine guns, the M15 with one 37mm cannon and twin .50-cal machine guns on a common mounting, and the M16 with quadruple .50-cal machine guns; when used against ground targets these weapon systems were known as "meat grinders". A total of 53,813 half-tracks of all types were produced during the war. They served in every theatre in which American troops were engaged and were also supplied to the United States' allies, including the Soviet Union. The half-track series saw further action during the Korean War and was extensively used by the Israeli Army for many years. See also *US Half-Tracks of World War II* by Steven Zaloga (Osprey).

Carrier Personnel Half-Track M3 or M3A1 *Weight* 9 tons; *speed* 45mph (72kph); *armour* 12.72mm; *armament* 1 .50-cal or 1 .30-cal Browning machine gun; *engine* White 160 AZ 147hp petrol; *crew* 3 plus 10 infantrymen.

Halifax, Earl of (1881–1959)

Lord Halifax was British Foreign Secretary from 1938 to 1940 and a supporter of Neville CHAMBERLAIN's appeasement policy. Chamberlain hoped that Halifax would succeed him as Prime Minister, but he stood down in favour of CHURCHILL, remaining a member of the War Cabinet until 1945. In December 1940 he left the Foreign Ministry and went to Washington as British Ambassador. To the surprise of many, who thought his aristocratic bearing would not impress the Americans, Halifax proved an excellent ambassador and gained the confidence of all classes in the USA, becoming a confidant of both President ROOSEVELT and Cordell HULL.

Halsey, Vice-Admiral William E. (1882–1959)

"Bull" Halsey was a flamboyant and skilled naval air tactician who played a significant part in the defeat of Japan. He arrived in the Pacific Theatre in April 1942 as Commander, Task Force 16, among which were the carriers *Hornet* and *Enterprise*, and almost immediately sailed to launch the DOOLITTLE RAID on Tokyo. Hospitalized during the time of the Battle of MIDWAY, he was appointed Commander of the South Pacific Area in October 1942 and this was followed by his involvement in the Battle of SANTA CRUZ ISLAND, in which the Japanese outmanoeuvred the US fleet and sank the carrier *Hornet*. In the following month he fought in the GUADALCANAL NAVAL CAMPAIGN which ended in an American victory but pointed up the deficiencies in night fighting which prevented the US Navy from making a clean sweep of the Japanese opposition. During 1943 his forces were involved in the taking of islands in the Russells and Trobriands, and BOUGAINVILLE. In June 1944 he took command of the US 3rd Fleet, a command which he alternated with Admiral SPRUANCE. In October 1944 he led the 3rd Fleet in the Battle of LEYTE GULF but fell for a Japanese ruse and led his fleet after a decoy, a situation which was only saved by the timely arrival of Admiral KINKAID and the 7th Fleet. While

Admiral William Halsey.

Kinkaid dealt with the Japanese battleship fleet, Halsey engaged their carrier fleet and destroyed the last vestiges of the enemy's naval air capability.

Hamburg

An expression used in some German reports of 1943–44, referring to the WINDOW anti-radar countermeasure used by Allied aircraft. It gained this name because its first operational use was in an air raid over Hamburg on 24 July 1943.

Hamilcar Glider (UK)

The General Aircraft Co. Hamilcar was the largest glider used by British airborne forces and was capable of carrying a Tetrarch light tank. Almost 400 were built and were used on various airborne operations. A powered version, fitted with two radial engines, was built in small numbers. *Span* 110ft (33.5m); *gliding speed* ca. 100mph (160kph).

Hammamet, Tunisia, 1943

Following the break-out of the Allied Army from the Tunisian mountains, it was essential that the Axis forces should be denied the chance of rallying in the Cape Bon peninsula. This was achieved by directing the British 6th Armoured Division south from Hammam Lif across the base of the peninsula to Hammamet, which was taken on 10 May.

Hammer

Also known as "Panzertodt", this was a German short-range anti-tank gun under development in 1945. It was a form of recoilless launcher firing a 105mm projectile; the propellant was wrapped around the tail boom of the projectile and, when exploded, the gases escaped to the rear, over a bulbous fin support, so shaped that the space between the support and the launcher tube became a venturi, developing the thrust required to launch the projectile. The bomb weighed 7lb (3kg) and had a range of about 1640ft (500m).

Handley, Tommy (1892–1949)

Tommy Handley was a popular English comedian who made his name with a radio comedy show called "It's That Man Again", generally abbreviated to "ITMA". Backed by extremely able scriptwriters and a well-chosen cast of character actors, Handley created an imaginary community of eccentrics which was adept at making the best of impossible wartime situations. It was one of the first British radio programmes to generate catchphrases, which became common currency among all walks of life in Britain. When he died in 1949 there was a national memorial service for him in St Paul's Cathedral.

Handley-Page Aircraft (UK)

Handley-Page Halifax The Halifax was the second of the four-engined heavy bombers designed in 1936–37, and entered service shortly after the SHORT STIRLING. Like the AVRO MANCHESTER–LANCASTER combination, it began as a twin-engined design but was converted on the drawing board to four engines in 1937. The Halifax began operations in March 1941 with No. 35 Squadron. Although capable of absorbing a huge amount of damage, the Halifax suffered a high casualty rate in the night skies over Germany. The design was modified and improved as the war progressed, but it was not until the beginning of 1944 that the Halifax could hope to hold its own

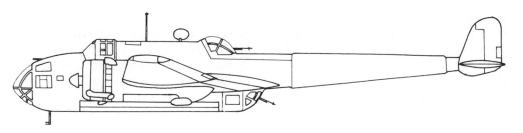

Handley-Page Hampden medium bomber.

against the fighter defences of the Reich. A total of 6176 were built by various companies. *Span* 104ft (31.7m); *engines* 4 1280hp in-line, or 4 1615hp radial; *armament* 9 machine guns, 13,000lb (5900kg) of bombs; *speed* 282mph (434kph).

Handley-Page Hampden This was the last monoplane bomber designed for the RAF before the war, known from its tall and thin body as the "Flying Suitcase". Production lasted from 1938 to 1942, and the Hampden was widely used in the early years of the war. When employed by day it was found vulnerable and was hastily given additional armament and armour. After being replaced as a bomber, numbers were used as stop-gap long-range torpedo bombers. *Span* 69ft (21m); *engines* 2 1000hp radial; *crew* 4; *armament* 4 machine guns, 4000lb (1800kg) of bombs; *speed* 255mph (410kph).

Handley-Page Harrow The Harrow, a high-wing monoplane, was designed in 1935 as a transport, but in 1936 it was decided to adapt it as a heavy bomber and it entered service in this role in 1937. By the outbreak of war it had been replaced by the HAMPDEN and returned to the transport role, though a few were used for mine-laying in 1940–41. *Span* 88.5ft (27m); *engines* 2 925hp radial; *speed* 200mph (322kph).

Handley-Page Hereford The Hereford was a HAMPDEN fitted with Napier Dagger H-type 24-cylinder engines instead of the Bristol Pegasus radial engines used on the Hampden. 100 were built but due to problems with the complicated engines they were never used operationally, most being re-engined and converted to Hampden specification.

Hanford, United States, 1943

Situated on the Columbia River in Washington State, Hanford was the location chosen for the construction of three nuclear reactors in 1943. These produced plutonium for use in the development of nuclear weapons.

Hankow, Central China, 1937–44

CHIANG KAI-SHEK made Hankow his temporary capital in December 1937, but the city fell to the Japanese after a five-month battle on 25 October 1938. It became an important Japanese command and supply centre which was raided by Major-General Claire CHENNAULT's 14th Air Force and Major-General Curtis LEMAY's 20th Bomber Command in December 1944. The raids were delivered from below the customary 30,000ft and employed a high proportion of incendiary bombs. The satisfactory results obtained led to the fire raids against cities in the Japanese homeland.

Harbin, Manchuria, 1945

The objective of converging thrusts by the 1st and 2nd Far East Fronts during the whirlwind Soviet campaign against the Japanese armies in MANCHURIA. On 18 August Russian airborne units secured Harbin airport and at 2300 the Japanese garrison commander ordered his 43,000 men to lay down their arms while negotiations for the general surrender of the Kwantung Army took place. The leading elements of the two Soviet Fronts reached Harbin on 20 August. See *World War II – Decisive Battles of the Soviet Army* by V. Larianov and others (Progress Publishers, Moscow).

Hardihood

Projected Allied military assistance to Turkey.

Harding, Gen Sir John (1896–   )

A career soldier, Harding first came to prominence as Chief of Staff to General O'CONNOR in North Africa when he was responsible for the planning which led to the victory at SIDI BARRANI in December 1940. He later became Chief of Staff to XIII Corps under General Godwin-Austen and early in 1942 was appointed Director of Military Training. At the time of the ALAMEIN offensive he was Deputy Chief of the General Staff. In January 1944 he became CoS to General ALEXANDER in Italy, and when Alexander became SAC Mediterranean in December 1944 Harding assumed command of XIII Corps.

Harfe

A German air-to-air weapon comprising a battery of 20mm recoilless gun barrels mounted behind the cockpit of a fighter aircraft and aimed upwards. The pilot was to dive beneath his target and fire the guns so that the projectiles struck the underside of the bomber. Several similar ideas were explored by the Germans, but this one appears to have had low priority and never entered service.

Harmon, Gen Millard F. (1888–1945)

A US Army aviator with considerable experience who in 1942 was given command of US military forces in the South Pacific. His command was responsible for the invasion of the SOLOMON ISLANDS and the GUADALCANAL campaign. In July 1944 he was appointed to command the US Army Air Forces in the whole of the Pacific Ocean region, with the primary role of organizing the bombing offensive against the Japanese home islands. In addition to supervising the operations, he also took a personal responsibility for logistics and supply, and proved to be one of the most versatile and effective of American commanders. He died in February 1945 when an aircraft in which he was flying on a routine tour of visits disappeared over the sea.

Harpoon

MALTA relief convoy, June 1942.

Harrier

Planned Allied attack on Trondheim, Norway, April 1940.

Harriman, Averill W. (1891–   )

Averill Harriman was a prominent American businessman chosen by ROOSEVELT to go to London in March 1941 to negotiate details of the Lend-Lease agreement. Completing this task, he was given diplomatic status and accompanied Lord BEAVERBROOK's mission to Moscow in September 1941 to organize American supplies of munitions to Russia. Returning to London, in 1942 he served on a number of Joint Allied Missions dealing with supplies, and in October 1943 was appointed US ambassador to Russia. Here he appears to have made a favourable impression on STALIN, but this did him little good in the long run. In

August 1944 he tried, and failed, to obtain Soviet permission for US aircraft to use Soviet airfields to supply the WARSAW Uprising. In spite of pleading the case of the Polish people, and attempting to ensure a leavening of non-Communists in the government established by the Russians in liberated Poland, he made no impression on STALIN or MOLOTOV and was left with the certain impression that Communist domination of Eastern Europe was inevitable. At the YALTA Conference he was largely responsible for organizing the terms upon which Russia joined the war against Japan and is generally conceded to have secured as good a deal as could have been expected from Molotov. He left Moscow in 1946 and returned to private life.

Harris, ACM Sir Arthur (1892–1985)

One of the great operational commanders of World War II, Harris remains a controversial figure, principally because of his tireless advocacy of AREA BOMBING. A keen disciple of TRENCHARD's philosophy of strategic bombing, he rose to command No. 4 Group (BOMBER COMMAND) in 1937. He served as Air Officer Commanding No. 5 Group in 1939–40 and was then appointed Deputy Chief of Air Staff at the Air Ministry. He led the RAF delegation in Washington before replacing Sir Richard PEIRSE as Air Officer Commanding-in-Chief Bomber Command in February 1942. Harris never abandoned the belief that the system-

atic destruction of the urban areas of Germany would, by itself, bring an end to the war. His flair for publicity, equalled only by MONTGOMERY's, was quickly demonstrated in the celebrated 1000-bomber raid on COLOGNE on 30/31 May 1942. The highwater mark of the area bombing campaign was reached in July–August 1943 when, in Operation GOMORRAH, Bomber Command flew a series of devastating raids against Hamburg. Harris resisted the implementation of the POINTBLANK directive of 10 June 1943, in which targets associated with German fighter production were made the top priority for the RAF and the USAAF in the autumn of 1943. He regarded these, and oil- and transportation-linked targets, as mere "panaceas". Instead he chose to test the theory of area bombing almost to destruction in the Battle of BERLIN. With great reluctance Harris committed Bomber Command to the Transportation Plan, the attacking of railway communications in France prior to OVERLORD, returning thereafter to devoting resources to attacks on German cities. This culminated in Operation THUNDERCLAP, the destruction of DRESDEN on 13/14 February, which, terrible though it was, was the logical conclusion to the policy Harris had been pursuing for three years, with the full approval of the British War Cabinet. After the war, Harris was the only senior British commander not to be given a peerage, and no campaign medal was struck for the men of Bomber Command.

Air Chief Marshal Harris and his staff.

Harry Hopkins – Light Tank Mark VIII (UK)

Improved version of the TETRARCH light tank with maximum armour thickness increased to 38mm. A total of 99 were built but never saw active service. The vehicle served as the basis for the ALECTO assault gun.

Hart, Adm Thomas C. (1877–1971)

Hart was a member of the Board of the US Navy from 1936 to 1939, after which he returned to active duty as Commander of the US Asiatic Fleet. After the Japanese attack on PEARL HARBOR all Allied warships in the Pacific were placed under his command. Having reached the age limit he retired in 1942, but in view of his considerable experience he returned to duty on the Navy Board until 1945.

Harvey

Codename for the British Flamethrower, Transportable No. 1 Mark 1; a crude wheelbarrow-type of machine of which 2000 were made in 1940 and issued to the Home Guard.

Harz Mountains, Germany, 1945

Following the destruction of the PEENEMUNDE complex in 1943, the V-WEAPON production facilities were moved to sites in the Harz Mountains. In the spring of 1945 HITLER reactivated his 11th and 12th Armies in the area of the Harz with personnel largely drawn from training establishments, hoping that these formations would be able to break through to the German forces trapped in the RUHR pocket. The plan was hopelessly unrealistic and 11th Army, 70,000-strong but short of heavy weapons, was itself encircled in the mountains by the US 9th Army from the north and the US 1st Army from the south. Relief attempts by 12th Army were quickly defeated and by 23 April the Harz Mountains had been cleared of German troops.

Hassell, Baron Ulrich von (1881–1944)

Hassell was a German diplomat who in February 1938 was Ambassador to Italy. When RIBBENTROP became Foreign Minister, Hassell was summarily dismissed due to his outspoken criticism of the Nazi regime. He took up a post as lecturer on economic affairs and, using this as a cover, became active in anti-Hitler circles. He pressed for a coup d'état and looked for active support from the Allies without success. He made little headway in trying to win the

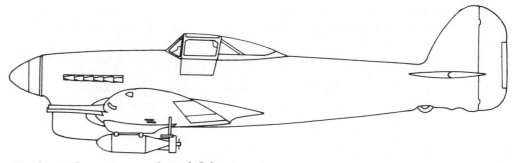

Hawker Typhoon 1B ground attack fighter.

Army to his point of view, and became involved with a monarchist group, by whom he was nominated as "shadow" Foreign Minister. After the 1944 JULY BOMB PLOT Hassell was arrested, tried and executed.

Hatsuharu Class Destroyers (Jap)

Displacement 1715 tons; *dimensions* 359ft 3in×32ft 9in (109.4×9.91m); *mean draught* 11ft 6in (3.5m); *machinery* 2-shaft geared turbines producing shp 42,000; *speed* 33.3 knots; *armament* 5×5in DP (2×2 and 1×1); 2×13mm; 6×24in torpedo tubes (2×3); *complement* 228; *number in class* 6, launched 1932–34.

Haw-Haw, Lord

See JOYCE, WILLIAM.

Hawker Aircraft (UK)

Hawker Hurricane The Hawker Hurricane was the RAF's first monoplane fighter and the first of its aircraft which could exceed 300mph (482kph). It equipped over 60 per cent of fighter squadrons during the Battle of BRITAIN

and was adapted to a number of roles including ground attack, light bomber and night fighter. Numbers were supplied to Russia, where it was highly regarded. It first flew in November 1935 and went into service in December 1937. During the war it went through a number of modifications, particularly improving armament, and it was also produced as the Sea Hurricane for catapult launching from armed merchant ships and for carrier use. *Span* 40ft (12.2m); *engine* 1 1030/1280hp in-line; *armament* 8 or 12 machine guns, or 4 20mm cannon, or 2 40mm cannon, up to 1000lb (450kg) of bombs, or 8 rocket launchers; *speed* 315/340mph (506/547kph).

Hawker Typhoon Originally conceived as a fighter, the Typhoon became the best ground-attack aircraft of the war, making its reputation over Normandy in 1944. The Typhoon first flew in 1940 but did not reach service until July 1941. Capable of carrying 2000lb (900kg) of bombs, it was most effective when fitted with eight rocket projectors and used as a tank-buster. *Span* 41.5ft (12.7m); *engine* 1 2200hp in-line; *armament* 4 20mm cannon,

RAF Hurricane fighters patrolling in France, 1939.

British 6-inch howitzers in training.

up to 2000lb (900kg) of bombs, 8 rocket launchers; *speed* 405mph (652kph).

Hawker Tempest This was proposed in 1941 as an improved Typhoon; several designs were drawn up, using various engines which were then being developed, but the main production version used the Napier Sabre engine and entered service in January 1944. It had more speed than the Typhoon and was particularly valuable in countering the flying bomb attacks in summer 1944. It also performed well with the 2nd TAF in Normandy as an air superiority fighter. *Span* 41ft (12.5m); *engine* 1 2420hp in-line; *armament* 4 20mm cannon, 2000lb (900kg) of bombs, or 8 rocket launchers (bombs and rockets were not generally carried by Tempests until after the conclusion of the war); *speed* 435mph (700kph).

HE High explosive.

HEAP High explosive, armour-piercing.

HEAT High explosive, anti-tank. An abbreviation which always implies the use of SHAPED CHARGE technology.

Heavy Artillery

Heavy artillery is the range of guns and howitzers above 150mm calibre which are generally employed under corps or army command to provide support in field operations or to carry out long-range bombardment of tactical targets. The heavy weapons used with field forces were generally of 150mm to 280mm calibre; long-range weapons and heavy bombardment howitzers ran from 150mm to 800mm calibre. The larger calibres were often railway-mounted. See RAILWAY ARTILLERY.

Britain: The heavy weapons of the British Army comprised 6in (152mm) guns, 8in (203mm), 9.2in (234mm) and 12in (305mm) howitzers. Many of these weapons were lost in the evacuation from France in 1940 and were subsequently emplaced by the Germans for anti-invasion defence. Their place in the field armies was taken by a 7.2in (183mm) howitzer and American 155mm, 203mm and 240mm guns and howitzers.

USA: American heavy artillery comprised 155mm and 203mm guns, 203mm and 240mm howitzers. A 914mm howitzer "Little David" was developed with the intention of using it to defeat Japanese defences on the mainland of Japan, but the war ended before it could be employed.

Germany: The German Army had an enormous variety of heavy artillery, from the 10cm K18 gun firing a 33lb (15kg) shell to 11.8 miles (19km) to the 60cm self-propelled howitzer "Karl" firing a 1.56 tonne shell to 7295yds (6675m) range. The most common weapons were the 17cm K18 gun, 139lb (63kg) shell, 32,350yds (29,600m) range, and the 21cm howitzer 18, 293lb (133kg) shell, 18,250yds (16,700m) range.

Russia: The Soviet army had a limited number of heavy calibres and concentrated production on a few of these. Their principal heavy weapons were the 152mm gun BR-2, 108lb (49kg) shell, range 29,480yds (26,975m); the 21cm gun M39/40, 297lb (135kg) shell, 33,224yds (30,400m); and the 305mm howitzer BR-18, 727lb (330kg) shell, range 17,923yds (16,4000m).

The Italian and Japanese armies held a small number of heavy pieces but they saw little use in the field. The Japanese deployed small numbers of 15cm guns in Singapore and the Philippines, but otherwise relied almost entirely upon field artillery.

Hedgehog

Used in conjunction with ASDIC, Hedgehog was a multi-barrel spigot mortar which threw a pattern of up to 24 contact-fuzed bombs ahead of a ship engaged in a submarine hunt. The system had the advantage of not interrupting the Asdic contact unless there was a hit, which was likely to force the submarine to the surface. See also SQUID.

Hedgerow

A shore bombardment weapon developed by the Royal Navy and based upon the HEDGEHOG anti-submarine mortar. It was a spigot mortar, with a hollow tail unit which fitted over a steel rod emplaced in a landing craft. A cartridge inside the tail was exploded, which blew the projectile off the spigot and into the air. The warhead contained high explosive and an impact fuze. It was used for bombarding the beaches prior to the D-DAY landings in NORMANDY.

Heinkel Aircraft (Ger)

Heinkel He111 Designed ostensibly as a civil airliner in 1935, the He111 almost immediately went into production as a medium bomber. It first saw combat in Spain in 1937, where its success against negligible opposition led the Luftwaffe to neglect the improvement of armour and defensive armament. Used extensively in raids over England in 1940 it suffered heavily and was relegated to employment in night bombing, mine-laying and torpedo-bombing roles. It also saw much service on the Eastern Front. *Span* 74ft

A Heinkel He111 was the first German aircraft to be shot down over Britain, crashing in the Firth of Forth on 16 October 1939.

(22.6m); *engines* 2 1340hp in-line; *crew* 5; *armament* 1 20mm cannon, 6 machine guns, 5500lb (2500kg) of bombs; *speed* 258mph (415kph).

Heinkel He115 The prototype of this torpedo-bomber-reconnaissance floatplane set up several world speed records in 1938. It was then ordered by the Norwegian and Swedish air forces, and by the Luftwaffe as a maritime reconnaissance machine. It was later employed for mine-laying and torpedo-bombing duties with success. *Span* 76ft (23.2m); *engines* 2 900hp radial; *crew* 4; *armament* 2 machine guns, 2200lb (1000kg) of bombs, torpedoes or mines; *speed* 203mph (327kph).

Heinkel He162 Salamander This machine is remarkable because it went from initial inception to first flight in less than three months. A jet fighter called into existence as a last-ditch effort on the part of the Luftwaffe, and popularly called the Volksjäger (People's Fighter), it was a wooden twin-tail machine with the jet engine perched on top of the fuselage. An enormous workforce was assembled and plans called for production of 4000, but no more than about 300 were built before the war ended; even this was a creditable performance. At least one unit became operational, but the shortage of fuel prevented it taking part in combat. *Span* 23.5ft (7.2m); *engine* 1 1760lb (800kg)/s.t. BMW turbo-jet; *armament* 2 20mm or 30mm cannon; *speed* 522mph (840kph).

Heinkel He177 This was designed in 1938 in response to a German request for a long-range heavy bomber. It proved to be the only heavy bomber to see service with the Luftwaffe. Due to changes in the design it was never a reliable machine and disliked by its crews. A notable innovation was the use of paired engines, two in a single nacelle driving a single propeller on each wing. It suffered from fires and inexplicable accidents, and was probably one of the most unsatisfactory aircraft ever introduced into unit service with any air force. Some were used to bomb England in 1944, others were employed in the Mediterranean and on the Eastern Front, but their effect in combat was negligible. *Span* 103ft (31.4m); *engines* 4 paired 2950hp in-line; *crew* 6; *armament* 2 20mm cannon, 6 machine guns, 13,225lb (6000kg) of bombs; *speed* 295mph (475kph).

Heinkel He219 Ubu Originally conceived as a high-altitude fighter, this became a successful night fighter, being put into production in mid-1943. Fast and formidable, it wrought havoc among RAF raids, but due to internal dissension among the German air authorities, it was built in insufficient numbers. *Span* 60.75ft (18.5m); *engines* 2 1900hp in-line; *crew* 2; *armament* 6 30mm and 2 20mm cannon; *speed* 416mph (669kph).

Heinrici, Col Gen Gotthard

Germany's leading expert on defensive battles in World War II, a field of operations in which he had ample opportunity to demonstrate his talent in 1944–45. In France, Heinrici commanded 1st Army's XII Corps, spearheading the assault on the MAGINOT LINE. In Operation BARBAROSSA he commanded XLIII Corps before being promoted to command 4th Army in May 1942. In the aftermath of KURSK, in the autumn of 1943, 4th Army held the Rogachev–Orsha line astride the highway from Moscow to Minsk. In May 1944 Heinrici assumed command of 1st Panzer Army together with 1st Hungarian Army on the Carpathian front, conducting a skilful retreat to Silesia early in 1945 after the German front had collapsed in the north. In March 1945 GUDERIAN persuaded HITLER to replace the incompetent Heinrich HIMMLER with Heinrici as commander of Army Group Vistula, facing the Russians' final push for BERLIN. At the end of the war Heinrici was captured by the Russians and imprisoned until 1955.

Heinsburg Salient, Germany, 1945

German bridgehead west of the RUHR River between Roermond and Geilenkirchen, eliminated by Lieutenant-General Neil RITCHIE's British XII Corps during Operation *Blackcock*, 16–26 January 1945. The German defence was assisted by the boggy ground and bad weather, but on 22 January the skies cleared and the British attack was reinforced with tactical air support.

Heinkel He162 Salamander jet fighter.

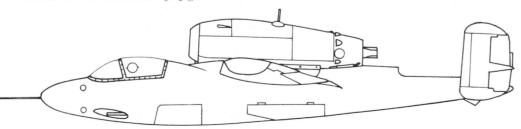

Hellcat – Tank Destroyer (USA)

See GUN MOTOR CARRIAGE M18.

Henderson Field, Guadalcanal, 1942–43

A captured Japanese airstrip south of Lunga Point completed by American engineers and named after Major Lofton Henderson, a Marine Pilot killed during the Battle of MIDWAY. The base became operational on 20 August 1942, the Marine, Navy and USAAF squadrons serving there being known collectively as Cactus Air Force (after the codename for the landings on Guadalcanal). To ease congestion a fighter airstrip, known as Fighter One, was constructed 2000 yards east of Henderson Field and parallel to it, becoming operational on 9 September. For both sides, possession of Henderson Field became the entire purpose of the Guadalcanal campaign. The Japanese army failed in its attempts to recapture the field, which was also subjected to regular air attack and naval bombardment; during the night of 13/14 October no less than 918 14-inch shells landed on or around the airstrips. Nevertheless, there were few periods when Henderson Field was not operational and Cactus Air Force, supported by B-17s flying from ESPIRITU SANTO, took a heavy toll of Japanese aircraft and shipping as well as supporting the operations of the American ground troops. By the middle of November the immediate danger to Henderson Field had passed, although the campaign itself continued until February 1943. See GUADALCANAL, LAND CAMPAIGN and GUADALCANAL, NAVAL CAMPAIGN.

Henschel Aircraft (Ger)

Henschel Hs123 Designed in 1934, this biplane ground-attack aircraft remained in service almost until the end of the war, even though obsolete by that time. Originally designed as a dive-bomber, it was modified for ground attack and the aircraft first saw action in Spain in 1937–8. Experience here convinced the Luftwaffe of the value of air support for ground troops, underlining their development of the air element of BLITZKRIEG. The Hs123 was used in Poland, France and the Balkans, and then on the Eastern Front, where it displayed a remarkable capacity to take punishment. *Span* 34.5ft (10.5m); *engine* 1 870hp radial; *armament* 2 machine guns or 20mm cannon, 440lb (200kg) of bombs; *speed* 214mph (344kph)

Henschel Hs126 This was a high-wing monoplane designed for artillery fire control and reconnaissance duties. It entered service in 1938 and was employed in its designated roles until about 1942, after which it was retired to training and glider-towing duties. *Span* 47.5ft (14.5m); *engine* 1 870hp radial; *crew* 2; *speed* 220mph (354kph).

Henschel Hs129 Designed in the light of lessons learned in Spain, the Hs129 was a purpose-built ground-attack machine. The first versions were underpowered, but after 1940 large numbers of French engines became available and its performance was thereby improved. Used with poor results in North Africa, it was much more effective on the Eastern Front. *Span* 44.5ft (13.6m); *engines* 2 750hp radial; *armament* varied – originally 4 machine guns, later 4 20mm cannon or 2 30mm cannon or even 37mm or 75mm guns; up to 550lb (250kg) of bombs; *speed* 253mph (407mph).

Herakles

Axis plan for the invasion of MALTA. Italian name *Esigenza*.

Heraklion, Crete, 1941

A port and airfield on the northern coast which formed the eastern objectives of the German airborne invasion. The 1st Parachute Rifle Regiment and one battalion of 2nd Parachute Rifle Regiment dropped during the afternoon of 20 May but their attacks were contained by Brigadier R. H. Chappel's reinforced British 14th Infantry Brigade and, having sustained serious loss, they were forced onto the defensive. When the decision to evacuate the island was taken, 14th Brigade was taken off by the Royal Navy at Heraklion, sustaining greater casualties during the voyage to Egypt than it had against the German paratroopers.

Herbstnebel (Autumn Fog)

Early codename for the German counter-offensive in the ARDENNES, December 1944, executed as WACHT AM RHEIN (Watch on the Rhine). Also applied to a German contingency plan for a withdrawal north of the Po, Italy, during the autumn of 1944.

Hermes, HMS – Aircraft Carrier

Hermes was the Royal Navy's first purpose-built aircraft carrier. In July 1940 her torpedo bombers seriously damaged the French battleship RICHELIEU at DAKAR. She subsequently joined the Eastern Fleet and was sunk by Japanese aircraft off Ceylon on 9 April 1942. *Displacement* 10,850 tons; *dimensions* 598ft×70ft 3in (182×21.4m); *mean draught* 26ft 7in (8.1m); *machinery* 3-shaft geared turbines producing shp 102,000; *speed* 26.2 knots (trials); *protection* main belt 3in; deck 1in; gunshields 1in; *armament* 6×5.5in (6×1); 3×4in AA (3×1); *aircraft* 15; *complement* 664; *launched* 1919.

Hertz, Fort, Northern Burma, 1943–44

Base for British-led Kachin guerrilla activity directed against Japanese troops in the MYITKYINA area.

Hess, Rudolf (1896–1987)

Hess befriended Hitler in the early 1920s and became one of the first supporters of the Nazi party, taking part in the abortive Munich putsch in November 1923. Hitler dedicated *Mein Kampf* to him. He was Deputy Führer until 1 September 1939, when he was succeeded by GÖRING. However, on 10 May 1941 he flew an Me 110 on a lone and unauthorized mission to Scotland. His aim was to make contact with the Duke of Hamilton, whom he had met before the war, and, using him as an intermediary, persuade the British Government to come to terms with Germany. He considered that Britain's defeat was inevitable and that a negotiated peace was the only

Rudolf Hess, imprisoned in Spandau.

solution. To his astonishment, he was treated simply as a prisoner-of-war and peace proposals were ignored. At the end of the war he was arraigned with the other surviving Nazi leaders at NUREMBERG and sentenced to life imprisonment in Spandau prison in Berlin, where he remained until committing suicide in 1987.

Hetzer (Troublemaker) – Tank Destroyer (Ger)

The Hetzer's angled superstructure occupied the whole of the obsolete PANZERKAMPFWAGEN 38(T) chassis on which it was based. The vehicle was armed with the 75mm L/48 Pak 39 offset to the right of the fighting compartment, on the roof of which was a machine gun that could be operated from within. The Hetzer weighed 16 tons, had a maximum speed of 23mph (37kph) and its frontal armour was 60mm thick. It was manned by a crew of four. 1577 were built during 1944 and a flame-thrower version was also produced. The vehicle served with the anti-tank battalions of infantry divisions but was unpopular with its crews because of its cramped and awkward interior layout. Hetzers continued to serve in the Swiss Army for some years after the war.

Hewitt, V Adm H. Kent (1887–1972)

Hewitt was an American Navy officer and an expert in amphibious operations. In 1942 he was placed in command of the landings which put General PATTON's 35,000 troops ashore on the beaches around CASABLANCA in Operation TORCH. In spite of forecasts of adverse weather from London and Washington, Hewitt backed his judgement and took the word of his fleet meteorologists that there would be a break in the weather. This duly happened and the landings were successful. In the following year he was given command of the US 8th Fleet operating in North African waters, after which he commanded the Western Naval Task Force which put US troops ashore on Sicily and Italy. He was then chosen to command the ANVIL landings in southern France in August 1944.

Heydrich, SS Gen Reinhardt (1904–42)

Heydrich began his career in the post-1918 German Navy, but was dismissed in 1931 after a scandal involving a young woman. This soured his views of the traditional armed forces and he joined the SS. Here he attracted

SS General Heydrich (left) and Karl Frank.

the attention of HIMMLER, who placed him in charge of building up and reorganizing the SD, the SS secret police. He was then given a similar role in smartening up the SS and eventually became Himmler's Deputy Commander. Placed in charge of the Reichs Main Security Office, he was responsible for arranging the incident at GLEIWITZ, on the Polish border, which gave HITLER his excuse for invading Poland on 1 September 1939. In 1941 he took charge of the operations of the EINSATZGRUPPEN (Action Groups), exterminating Jews throughout the Eastern territories. On 31 July 1941 GÖRING called upon Heydrich to submit a protocol for the "Final Solution to the Jewish Problem", which in turn led to the setting up of the extermination camps in Poland and the intensification of the operations of the Action Groups. As a reward for his work, Heydrich was appointed Reichs Protector of Bohemia and Moravia, making him the virtual ruler of Czechoslovakia. On 4 June 1942 he died of wounds sustained when his car was ambushed by a party of Czech resistance fighters. In retaliation the nearby village of LIDICE was surrounded by SS troops, the occupants murdered and the village destroyed.

HF Harassing fire. Artillery fire at irregular intervals against targets in the enemy's rear areas, such as supply points, railheads, road junctions, in the hope of catching them unexpectedly and so "harassing" them.

High-Low Pressure Gun

A weapon developed by the Rheinmetall-Borsig AG using an entirely new ballistic system, the gun was the 8cm Panzerabwehrwerfer 600, an infantry anti-tank gun firing a fin-stabilized SHAPED CHARGE bomb. This was attached to a very strong cartridge case which was closed by a heavy steel plate with holes. The plate abutted a step in the gun chamber, and, when the propellant inside the case was ignited, exploded at high pressure ($375lb/in^2$ ($1100kg/cm^2$)). The gas then leaked through the holes into the space behind the bomb; when the pressure in this space built up to $187lb/in^2$ ($550kg/cm^2$) the connection sheared and the bomb was fired from the barrel. This system kept the high pressure inside the cartridge case and chamber area, and subjected the barrel only to low pressure, enabling the weight of the gun to be reduced. About 260 guns were built late in 1944 to early 1945 and they were successful. The principle has been little used since 1945.

Himmelbett

German codename (literally "four-poster bed") for a radar-controlled night-fighter system introduced in the spring of 1942. The system was based on a chain of radar-guided fighter "boxes" established along the European coast from north Germany to Belgium and around Germany's principal cities. It employed one WURZBURG radar to track the target while another tracked the night fighter. Initially, ground control used the plots of the two aircraft to trap the target bomber in a searchlight cone, for the fighter to attack. After the night fighters had been equipped with LICHTENSTEIN airborne radar, fighter controllers were able to vector the fighters to within two miles of the target, at which point Lichtenstein took over. The system's principal limitation was that each "box" could handle only one interception at a time, although the development of overlapping zones made it possible to send three fighters into one zone, provided the outer portions of the other zones could be left unattended. BOMBER COMMAND countered Himmelbett by streaming its bombers through a single box at maximum speed and density. This severely limited the number of kills possible to about six per cent.

Himmler, Reichsführer-SS Heinrich (1900–45)

The son of a Bavarian schoolmaster, Himmler joined the Nazi party in its early days and in 1923 was present at the Munich putsch. In 1928 Himmler was running a small poultry farm near Munich when he was asked by HITLER to take over the SS from Erhard Heiden. From an original troop of some 200 men Himmler fashioned a disciplined force to rival the SA. With GÖRING, he planned the Blood Purge of 30 June 1934, in which Röhm and the other SA leaders were assassinated and the power of the SA broken. In 1938 he provided the perjured evidence which led to the dismissal of VON BLOMBERG and von Fritsch. He became the close confidant of Hitler and without doubt was second in power to the Führer himself. In addition to heading the SS, he controlled the WAFFEN SS, the Reich Security Head Office, much of the civil police, the Gestapo, and the Foreign Intelligence Service. An astute organizer and administrator, he was adept at plotting the downfall of his rivals, and eventually manoeuvred himself into the positions of Minister of the Interior (1943) and Commander-in-Chief of the Home Army (1944). A fanatical believer in the ideology of

Himmler at Dachau, 1936.

racial purity, he was responsible for the extermination campaign against the Jews and other "undesirables". Himmler was captured by the British Army on 23 May 1945, disguised as a private soldier. He was recognized by a British officer and forthwith committed suicide by biting on a poison capsule concealed in his mouth. To prevent his grave becoming a Nazi shrine, his body was secretly buried by two British NCOs, both of whom died many years later without revealing the location of the grave.

Hirohito, Emperor of Japan (1901–1989)

Emperor Hirohito ascended the throne in 1926, and in spite of his nominal position as head of state had little influence over affairs. He attended cabinet meetings, but by tradition took no part in debate, merely giving his assent to the decisions reached. A mild and ineffectual man, he was more interested in marine biology than in matters of state and left the day-to-day running of affairs to his politicians. He was, therefore, led by the nose by his militaristic cabinet in spite of his preference for diplomacy over outright war. As the tide of war turned against Japan from June 1942

Emperor Hirohito inspects his troops.

onwards, so Prime Minister TOJO tended to involve the Emperor more in daily affairs, calling upon the nation to make sacrifices in the Emperor's name. In 1945, with defeat becoming obvious, Hirohito began to exert some influence against the military clique, but before he could do very much the ATOMIC BOMBS were dropped and it became obvious that surrender was the only course. On 15 August 1945, the day after the surrender, he made a speech on the radio to announce the fact to the people of Japan; it was the first time in history that a Japanese emperor had spoken directly to his subjects. Before the start of the Tokyo war crimes trials (1946–48), General MACARTHUR decided that prosecuting Hirohito would be an unwise move, realizing that it would be easier to control a docile and fatalistic population. Hirohito was granted immunity from trial and, having renounced his divine status, became one of the principal instruments of postwar American rule in occupied Japan.

Hiroshima, 1945

Hiroshima, an industrial city and embarkation port, was selected by the US Air Force as their target for the first ATOMIC BOMB. As it was tactically important and had not been raided before, it would permit a clear demonstration of the power of the nuclear weapon. It was attacked by a single B-29 bomber *Enola Gay*, commanded by Colonel Paul TIBBETS, at 0915 on 6 August 1945. The bomb, dropped from

Hiroshima, August 1945.

an altitude of 31,000 feet (9455m), detonated at 800 feet (244m) above the selected target point. With a force equal to 29,000 tons of conventional explosive, it devastated about five square miles (13 square km) of the city and killed an estimated 70,000 people.

Hitler, Adolf (1889–1945)

Born in Austria, in World War I Hitler joined a Bavarian infantry regiment and served on the Western Front, reaching the rank of corporal and winning the Iron Cross (First Class). He bitterly opposed the German politicians who had signed the Treaty of Versailles in 1919, and the postwar unrest in Germany convinced him that his destiny was to reverse the defeat of 1918 and restore Germany as a world power. He joined an extreme right-wing Bavarian political party, the German Workers' Party, quickly assumed control and turned it into the National Socialist German Workers' Party, known as the "Nazis". On 8 November 1923 he attempted to seize control of Bavaria in the Munich "putsch", which was put down by the police and military in conditions bordering on farce. He was tried for treason in February 1924 and served a token sentence in Landsberg prison, where he wrote *Mein Kampf*, which formed the unchanging basis of his beliefs until his death. The experience of

the Munich "putsch" convinced Hitler that he should pursue a constitutional path to power. Party membership had reached 178,000 by 1929, when the German economy collapsed

Adolf Hitler.

in ruins. Hitler exploited the resulting political chaos, manoeuvring himself into power as German Chancellor on 30 January 1933. When President von Hindenburg died on 2 August 1934, Hitler immediately merged the office of President with that of Chancellor, announcing that henceforth he would be Head of State and Commander-in-Chief of the armed forces of the Reich (Reichswehr). On the same day he bound the Reichswehr to him with an oath of allegiance. He was now the dictator of Germany.

The impressive German economic recovery of the mid-1930s – achieved by a bold policy of deficit financing – underwrote rearmament, at first undertaken clandestinely and then announced to the world on 16 March 1935. Skilful propaganda concealed the underlying weakness of Germany's rapidly expanding armed forces, and their strength was continually overestimated abroad. War, or the threat of it, was the dynamic of Hitler's foreign policy in the 1930s. Chief among his political weapons was an intuitive feel for the weaknesses of other nations. Thus Hitler was able to play on the popular desire for peace in France and Britain, their governments' fear of a bloodletting even more terrible than that of World War I, and their inability to ally with the Soviet Union. In March 1936 Hitler reoccupied the demilitarized Rhineland, against the advice of his senior commanders. Britain and France failed to react, and Hitler embarked on an increasingly aggressive foreign policy. "Volunteers" and much material were sent to FRANCO's Nationalist forces in Spain for combat testing. On 30 July 1937 Hitler formally withdrew Germany's signature from those clauses in the Treaty of Versailles which denied her equality of rights and laid on her the responsibility for World War I. In March 1938 he annexed Austria, opening the way to Czechoslovakia. In September 1938 Hitler outmanoeuvred CHAMBERLAIN at Godesberg and MUNICH to seize control of the Sudetenland. In March 1939 he swallowed up the rest of Czechoslovakia. In the same month Memel, with its large German population, was annexed. Hitler then turned to the free port of DANZIG and the POLISH CORRIDOR to the Baltic, which stood between Germany and East Prussia. On 23 August he secured his eastern flank through a non-aggression pact with STALIN. Poland was invaded on 1 September 1939, and two days later Britain and France declared war on Germany. For over two years Hitler retained the initiative. By May 1941 he had occupied Norway and Denmark, crushed France and the Low Countries in a lightning campaign and bundled the British Expeditionary Force out of Europe. Yugoslavia and Greece had been overwhelmed with devastating speed, and Italy, Bulgaria, Romania and Hungary reduced to vassal status. The invasion of England (Operation SEELÖWE) had been indefinitely postponed after the Luftwaffe's failure in the Battle of BRITAIN, but the British were effectively isolated from Continental Europe and taking heavy losses in the Battle of the ATLANTIC. In June 1941 Hitler turned eastward against the Soviet Union. The central motives for Operation BARBAROSSA were the overthrow of Bolshevism and acquisition of *Lebensraum* (living space) in European Russia, the possession of which would ensure Germany's survival as a world power. By the winter of 1941 the Germans had destroyed more than 200 of the Red Army's divisions, but the initiative began to slip away from Hitler in December 1941, when the German army was halted outside MOSCOW. On 11 December 1941, four days after the Japanese attack on PEARL HARBOR, he declared war on the United States, a decision which ensured that the fate of Western Europe now lay in the hands of two extra-European

powers, the Soviet Union and the United States. From this point Hitler assumed personal control of operations, dismissing the Commander-in-Chief of the Army, von BRAUCHITSCH, on 19 December 1941. It was a role for which he was not well suited. Hitler was essentially a brilliant military amateur with an unshakeable belief in his own genius. His easy victories of 1939 and 1940 had bred a contempt for his generals, the majority of whom had urged caution, and a corresponding reluctance to heed their practical advice. Those who argued against the Führer too vehemently were dismissed, a process which inexorably weakened morale.

In 1942 Hitler resumed the offensive, but after the defeats at ALAMEIN and STALINGRAD he was forced on to the defensive. The last great German offensive on the Eastern Front, at KURSK, was broken by the Red Army in July 1943. Thereafter Hitler fought the war from the map, clinging stubbornly to a strategy of holding every inch of ground and leaving his generals little or no room for manoeuvre. In the West, he made his last gambler's throw in the ARDENNES, hoping to repeat the success of May–June 1940 but succeeding only in squandering his dwindling reserves of armour. As the Allied armies closed on Berlin, he retreated to the bunker in the grounds of the Reichs Chancellery, withdrawing into a fantasy world in which non-existent armies were moved across the map at the daily conferences. Remarkably, he maintained his hold on the German people to the end. Opposition at the higher levels of command, notably in the JULY BOMB PLOT of 1944, had been so inept, and his own organizations so strong, that he remained unchallenged. On 30 April 1945, with Russian troops only a few streets away, he committed suicide in the Berlin bunker, having named DÖNITZ as his successor.

Hitlerjugend

The Hitler Youth Organization. By the outbreak of war, virtually every young German male between the ages of ten and 18 was a member of the Hitlerjugend. It stressed the importance of patriotism in German national life and employed well-organized camps and rallies to inculcate boys with Nazi values and beliefs. From the Hitlerjugend young men graduated naturally into the mainstream of Party activity, including the WAFFEN SS; the 12th SS Panzer Division *Hitlerjugend* was recruited from recent graduates of the organization and

Hitler Youth Rally, 1935.

was noted for its fanatical and self-destructive style of fighting. The female equivalent of the Hitlerjugend was the BUND DEUTSCHER MÄDCHEN.

HIWI Hilfsfreiwillige (German – voluntary aid) A German military auxiliary organization formed from White Russian and Ukrainian prisoner-of-war volunteers; it carried out lines-of-communication duties, e.g. supply transportation, road-mending and minor pioneer work, behind the German Eastern Front and, to a lesser extent, within Germany.

HMAS His Majesty's Australian Ship.

HMG Heavy machine gun.

HMIS His Majesty's Indian Ship.

HMNZS His Majesty's New Zealand Ship.

Hobart, Gen Sir Percy Cleghorn Stanley (1885–1957)

Hobart joined the Bengal Sappers and Miners in 1906 and served with the Indian Corps in France from 1915, then fought the Turks in Mesopotamia until the end of the war. In 1931 he took up command of the 2nd Royal Tank Regiment where he pioneered the use of radio-telephony to command tanks in action.

In 1933 he was promoted to Inspector of the RTC and in the following year took command of 1st Tank Brigade. In this post he pressed for full mechanization of the army and for many innovations in tank policy and succeeded in making himself disliked in several parts of the War Office. In 1938 he was sent to Egypt to form a Mobile Division and, in spite of personality clashes with the GOC Egypt, was successful in setting up the force which later became 7th Armoured Division. In late 1939, however, Hobart was relieved of command, returned to England and, early in 1940, placed on the retired list. He was later recalled and given command of an armoured division, and in the summer of 1942 was appointed to command the 79th Armoured Division, a formation which was raised to operate a variety of specialized armoured vehicles ready for the invasion of Europe. Under Hobart's vigorous leadership special tanks were built and their crews trained, and without the 79th Armoured Division the British Army's task in Europe would undoubtedly have been much harder. Hobart retired in 1946.

Hochdruckpumpe

Also known as "Busy Lizzie", "The Millipede" and V-3, the Hochdruckpumpe was a 15cm smooth-bore multiple-chambered gun designed by Engineer Conders of the Rochling Company. Conders revived the idea of fitting a very long gun barrel with multiple side chambers carrying additional cartridges. The shell would be started up the bore by a normal cartridge and as it passed the ports leading to the side chambers the additional cartridges would be fired in turn, so producing more propelling gas and boosting the muzzle velocity to about 5000ft (1500m) per second, developing a maximum range of about 186 miles (300km). After experiments with a 20mm model, Conders managed to interest HITLER in the proposal and was given authority to continue development without informing the Army Weapons Office. A full-sized gun of 6in (150mm) calibre and 492ft (150m) barrel length was made and erected on the island of Misdroy, but trial firings showed the projectiles to be unstable and the gun prone to blowing up.

A site was under preparation at Mimoyecques, near Calais, to take a fifty-barrel installation aimed at the centre of London, but this was discovered by Allied air reconnaissance and bombed, and it was overrun by

President Ho Chi Minh speaks at the City Hall, Paris, July 1946.

the invasion before the gun could be perfected. The Army Weapons Office were eventually brought in to solve the problems and produced two short-barrelled working guns which, mounted on railway trucks, fired a few shots during the ARDENNES Offensive in 1944, after which they were destroyed in situ when the German Army retreated.

Ho Chi Minh (1890–1969)

Born in Annam as Nguyen Tat Tan, Ho Chi Minh espoused Socialism as a young man, but after visiting France in 1921–22 and Russia in 1923–26 became a militant Communist. After a period in Siam in the late 1920s, he spent some years with the Communist Army in China, where he organized the Viet Minh, an expatriate party of Vietnamese Communists. He was jailed by CHIANG KAI-SHEK in 1942, but on American insistence he was released in September 1943 and returned to Indo-China to organize guerrilla warfare against the Japanese. He was given arms and equipment by the US authorities in China, but instead of waging serious operations against the Japanese, he merely mounted a few raids and spent the rest of the war securing himself a base in the Tonkin area and preparing for the day when the Japanese departed. When this came, he immediately opened operations against the French, proclaiming the Republic of Vietnam in September 1945.

Hodges, Gen Courtney (1887–1966)

Courtney Hodges was an infantry officer, but on the outbreak of war became Chief of Military Intelligence, US Army until 1942. He then took brief command of the Replacement and Training organization, after which he took over X Army Corps late in 1942. In 1943 he was promoted Lieutenant-General and briefly commanded US 3rd Army, then training in Texas, before being appointed Deputy Commander of the 1st Army under General BRADLEY. In this post he organized the 1st Army's landings on UTAH and OMAHA beaches on D-DAY. In August 1944, when Bradley was given command of 12 Army Group, Hodges succeeded to the command of 1st Army. He was one of the most able of American commanders, though little publicized. By October 1944 1st Army had cleared Luxembourg and southern Belgium, breached the SIEGFRIED LINE and captured AACHEN, the first major German city to be taken by the Allies. The full weight of the German Ardennes winter offensive – the Battle of the BULGE – fell on his army, which held firm and eventually threw the Germans back. Hodges then advanced to seize the Ruhr Dams, cross the Rhine at REMAGEN and link up with US 9th Army to encircle the RUHR Pocket.

Hoess, Rudolf (1900–47)

Hoess was a member of the SS who at the outbreak of war was adjutant of SACHSENHAUSEN concentration camp. Early in 1940 he was appointed to command the newly-built concentration camp at AUSCHWITZ (Oswiecim) in Poland, scheduled to begin receiving prisoners in June 1940. A fanatical believer in obedience to orders and administrative efficiency, Hoess set to work at Auschwitz with a will. When ordered to begin the extermination of the camp's inmates, he set up four gas chambers and the necessary crematoria. Discovering that carbon monoxide, the recommended method of gassing, was "inefficient" he introduced the use of ZYKLON B, a cyanide derivative, stepping up the rate of executions to an estimated 6000 victims per day. Late in 1943, Hoess was appointed Chief Inspector of Concentration Camps and strove hard to introduce his brand of efficiency into other extermination camps. Arrested in 1945, he was placed on trial at NUREMBERG, where he seemed more concerned with defending himself against charges of inefficiency than with the deaths of the inmates of his camps.

Handed over to a Polish People's Court in 1947 he was sentenced to death and hanged at Auschwitz.

Holland, 1940–45

See ARNHEM; BEVELAND PENINSULA; BRESKENS POCKET; EINDHOVEN; FRANCE, BELGIUM, HOLLAND 1940; GREBBE LINE; THE HAGUE; HEINSBURG SALIENT; NIJMEGEN; ROTTERDAM; SCHELDT; WALCHEREN.

Hollandia, Dutch New Guinea (West Irian), 1944

Early in 1944 General MACARTHUR decided to bypass Lieutenant-General Hatazo ADACHI's Japanese 18th Army, deployed between Madang and Wewak, and strike directly at its base area in Hollandia, some 300 miles (482km) to the west. Following a prolonged bomber offensive, the US 24th and 41st Divisions landed at Hollandia on 22 April and, with carrier air support, advanced inland to capture the Japanese airfields and base facilities, all of which had been secured by 27 April. The Americans lost approximately 100 killed and 1000 wounded, the Japanese over 5000 killed. The operation achieved the strategic isolation of the Japanese 18th Army.

Home Guard (UK)

A voluntary para-military organization formed in 1940 for the purpose of home defence in the event of invasion. Members were civilians who worked at normal occupations but trained and carried out duties in their free time. Initially poorly armed with shotguns and pistols, by 1942 they were a well-armed force with automatic weapons and various forms of light mortar and artillery. The Home Guard was disbanded in December 1944.

Homma, Gen Masaharu (1888–1946)

Homma was the Japanese Army officer chosen to command the force which invaded the PHILIPPINES. He had spent the greater part of his career in intelligence and had little experience in the field. He was unwise enough to boast that he would conquer the Philippines in 45 days, but MacArthur's withdrawal to the BATAAN peninsula threw his strategy awry and the campaign dragged on. A harsh and ruthless commander, he was none the less summarily relieved of his command after reaching a stalemate in Bataan. He remained as a figurehead, although the campaign was henceforth controlled by General YAMASHITA. After the US

surrender in April 1942, the captives were force-marched 60 miles to a railhead, during which ill-treatment by the Japanese resulted in the deaths of about 16,000 US and Filipino troops. Homma then took charge of mopping-up operations in MINDANAO and other outlying parts of the Philippines, after which he was summoned to Japan and given an administrative post for the remainder of the war. The Americans, though, bore Homma in mind, and in September 1945 arrested him in Tokyo. He was tried for war crimes, notably the Bataan "Death March", and executed in Manila in 1946.

Honda, Lt Gen Masaki

Honda commanded the 33rd Japanese Army in BURMA and conducted an able fighting retirement following the collapse of the KOHIMA and IMPHAL offensives of 1944. Under orders to hold the Lashio–Mandalay line in January 1945, he dispersed his troops widely and was able to hold off US and Chinese forces which were attempting to open the Burma Road. Threatened by SLIM's 14th Army advancing to MEIKTILA, he took command of the defence of Meiktila and almost succeeded in cutting off the British troops who had broken through to the city. He missed the opportunity, however, and thereafter conducted a fighting retreat through southern Burma.

Honey (USA)

Name conferred by British crews on the American STUART Light Tank M3 because of its excellent handling qualities, reliability and ease of maintenance. Retained more or less officially throughout the war.

Hong Kong, China, 1941

At 0730 on 8 December the colony was attacked by Major-General Tadayoshi Sano's 20,000-strong 38th Division, which enjoyed total air superiority. The British garrison, consisting of six battalions commanded by Major-General C. M. Maltby, withdrew to the GIN DRINKERS' LINE, but when this was penetrated during the night of 9 December a further withdrawal from the mainland to Hong Kong island became necessary, this being completed on 13 December. On 18 December the Japanese crossed the Lei U Mun Strait and began pushing south across the island. Despite determined resistance, they succeeded in splitting the defences and on 25 December Maltby accepted the inevitable and surrendered. During the fighting 2113 British, Canadian and Indian servicemen were killed; the Japanese sustained approximately 3000 casualties. The Japanese celebrated their victory with an orgy of killing and rape which extended to the wounded and the civilian population.

Japanese troops enter Hong Kong, December 1941.

HMS Hood.

Hood, HMS – Battlecruiser

Served in the Home Fleet 1939–41, and was sunk by gunfire from the battleship BISMARCK south of Greenland on 24 May 1941. *Displacement* 41,200 tons; *dimensions* 860ft 6in × 105ft 3in (262×32m); mean draught 28ft 6in (8.6m); *machinery* 4-shaft geared turbines producing shp 144,000; *speed* 31 knots; *protection* main belt 12in; deck 3.75in; turrets 15in; *armament* 8×15in (4×2); 12×5.5in (12×1); 8×4in AA (4×2); 24×2-pdr AA (3×8); 20×0.5in AA (5×4); 4×21in torpedo tubes; *complement* 1420; *launched* 1918.

Hopkins, Harry (1890–1946)

An American statesman, Hopkins was a close friend and confidant of ROOSEVELT and had served a term as Secretary of Commerce. During the war he became Chairman of the Munitions Assignment Board, the Pacific War Council, the War Production Board and the War Resources Board. Although in poor health, he travelled extensively to supervise the Lend-Lease programme, visiting Russia and Britain and attending the CASABLANCA, Teheran and YALTA conferences. After the death of Roosevelt, President TRUMAN sent Hopkins to Moscow once more as his special envoy in a final attempt to reach agreement over the Polish question. His health then failed completely and he died soon after the war. Hopkins must be the only non-military man after whom a combat tank was named.

Höpner, Gen Erich (1886–1944)

A cavalry officer who became a skilled exponent of armoured warfare, Höpner was involved in a 1938 conspiracy against HITLER.

The intention was to arrest Hitler when he gave orders to attack Czechoslovakia, but the plot collapsed when the MUNICH Agreement gave him the country without military effort. Höpner then took part in the Polish and Low Countries campaigns, being promoted Colonel-General in July 1940. He commanded 4th Panzer Group in the invasion of Russia in 1941 and at the beginning of December was within sight of Moscow when his advance was halted by the Soviets. Under a ferocious counter-attack unleashed by ZHUKOV, Höpner was compelled to pull back, for which Hitler dismissed him, discharging him from the Army with ignominy. He then renewed his contacts with anti-Hitler plotters and was nominated to replace FROMM as Commander-in-Chief of the Home Army if the JULY BOMB PLOT succeeded. The plot failed, Höpner was among those arrested, and he was executed on 8 August 1944.

Hornet, USS – Yorktown and Essex Class Aircraft Carriers

Hornet (CV.8) launched the DOOLITTLE RAID against the Japanese mainland on 18 April 1942 and took part in the Battle of MIDWAY. She was sunk during the Battle of SANTA CRUZ, but her name was transferred to the ESSEX CLASS carrier *Kearsarge*, which was launched on 30 August 1943. The new *Hornet* (CV.12) saw active service at the MARIANAS, Palau and LEYTE GULF.

Hornum, Germany, 1940

A seaplane base on the island of Sylt raided by 30 Whitleys and 20 Hampdens of RAF BOMBER COMMAND on the night of 19 March in retaliation for a German raid on the base at Hatston in the Orkneys. This was the first bomber raid of the war to be mounted by the RAF against a German land target.

Horrocks, Lt Gen Sir Brian (1895–1985)

Horrocks served in the infantry during World War I and afterwards served with the North Russian Intervention Force. In the early part of World War II he commanded a battalion in 3rd Division under MONTGOMERY and had thus come to the latter's attention. As a result Montgomery sent for him in 1942 and gave him command of XIII Corps. In the subsequent battle of ALAM HALFA Horrocks held the German and Italian attacks without allowing his corps to suffer too much damage, which was precisely what Montgomery wanted. After the Second Battle of El ALAMEIN Horrocks was given command of X Corps in the advance to Tripoli, and Montgomery later transferred him to 1st Army where he handled the taking of Tunis on 7 May 1943. Just before the end of the Tunis campaign he was severely wounded in an air raid and was returned to England. Upon his recovery Montgomery immediately sent for him to command XXX Corps in NORMANDY. He retained this command to the end of the war, and counted among his more notable successes the advance towards ARNHEM and his conduct of the REICHSWALD battle in 1945. Horrocks, known throughout the British Army as "Jorrocks", was one of the best Corps commanders of the war, an excellent

General Horrocks in the ruined town of Rees, March 1945.

tactician who knew how to get the best out of his troops. In his retirement, Horrocks became Gentleman Usher of the Black Rod of the House of Commons.

Horsa Glider (UK)

The Airspeed Horsa was introduced in 1942 and was the first British glider to use tricycle undercarriage, the two side wheels of which were jettisoned after takeoff, leaving the nosewheel and a skid to support the landing. It could carry 30 men or approximately 3500kg (7700lb) of cargo. After landing, the rear fuselage could be removed to facilitate unloading, and there was also a side door. Over 6700 were built and most were used in combat, delivering airborne troops into battle. *Span* 88ft (26.8m); *gliding speed* 100mph (161kph).

Horse Draught (Ger)

In the German Army only the armoured and mechanized formations, about 20 per cent of the whole, had a nominal full establishment of motorized transport and towing vehicles. The remaining 80 per cent relied on the horse as a prime mover. During Operation BARBAROSSA, for example, there were approximately 750,000 horses hauling guns and supply wagons into Russia, half of which did not survive the first winter. Altogether, 2,500,000 served with the German Army on the Eastern Front, an average of 1000 dying each day. The most common cause of death was artillery fire or low-level strafing, but nearly one-fifth died from heart failure brought on by overwork, and the remainder were killed by disease or intense cold. Whenever possible, losses were made good from hardier Russian stock, often used in conjunction with the native *panje* (farm cart) or sledges in winter. Although conditions were less severe on other fronts, the effect of such reliance on horse draught tended to reduce the strategic mobility of the German Army as a whole and contribute to such disasters as the FALAISE pocket, where escape routes were blocked by tangled wreckage of horse-drawn transport and guns. The Soviet Army also relied heavily upon the horse and other armies used it to a lesser degree. Exceptions were the British and American armies, which were fully mechanized, although both used pack-mules in theatres of war unsuited to mechanical transport, such as Burma and certain sectors of the Italian front in winter.

Horthy, Adm Miklos (1868–1957)

A former officer in the Austro-Hungarian Navy, Horthy became Regent of Hungary in 1920 and ruled the country thereafter until 1944. Although sympathetic to HITLER's views, Horthy was reluctant to involve Hungary in a war with the Western nations, but in August 1941 nevertheless ordered the Hungarian forces to invade Yugoslavia in support of Hitler's aims, and the following month declared his alliance with Hitler in the campaign against Russia. In May 1943, however, he refused Hitler more reinforcements for the Russian front, and in 1944 went to Germany to request the return of Hungarian troops from Russia and the end of German use of Hungary as a supply base. When Hitler threatened to occupy Hungary, Horthy backed down. In June 1944 he was able to halt the deportation of Hungarian Jews for some time, though eventually the German will prevailed. When Romania surrendered to Russia in August 1944, Horthy attempted to remove Hungary from the war and submitted a tentative armistice agreement to Russia on 11 October 1944. He was later seized by German troops and deported to Austria, where he was released by American troops in May 1945.

Horton, Admiral Sir Max (1883–1951)

Horton was a career sailor who had specialized in submarines, and by 1937 he had risen to command the Reserve Fleet of the Royal Navy, a post which he held until 1939. On the outbreak of war he was made responsible for commanding the Northern Patrol, and in January 1940 was appointed Flag Offi-

cer, Submarines. In 1942 he was appointed Commander-in-Chief Western Approaches, with responsibility for the safety of convoys crossing the Atlantic. To this task he brought his immense knowledge of submarine warfare. His principal task was to outwit the German U-boats commanded by DÖNITZ. Taking over the job when the Allied sinkings in the Atlantic were at record levels, he soon began to reduce the U-boat fleets in both numbers and effectiveness by a variety of measures. He continued in this appointment until the end of the war.

Hosho, IJN – Aircraft Carrier

Hosho was the Imperial Japanese Navy's first aircraft carrier and was completed in 1922. She saw active service during Japan's war against China but was mostly used as a training ship in World War II. *Displacement* 7470 tons; *dimensions* 551ft 6in×59ft (168×17.9m); mean draught 20ft 9in (6.3m); *machinery* 2-shaft geared turbines producing shp 30,000; *speed* 25 knots; *armament* 4×5.5in (4×1); 8×25mm AA; *aircraft* 21; *complement* 550.

Hotchkiss H35 – Light Tank (Fr)

Designed for service with mechanized cavalry formations. Very similar in appearance to the RENAULT R35. *Weight* 11.4 tons; *speed* 17.5mph (28kph); *armour* 34mm; *armament* 1 37mm gun; 1 7.5mm Reibel machine gun; *engine* Hotchkiss six-cylinder 75hp petrol; *crew* 2.

Hotchkiss H39/40 – Light Tank (Fr)

An improved version of the HOTCHKISS H35 with a more powerful gun and engine, thicker armour and greater fuel capacity. Served with

Hotchkiss H-35.

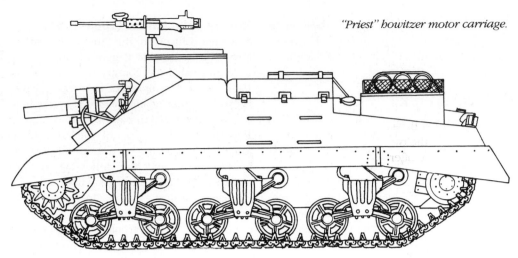

"Priest" howitzer motor carriage.

mechanized cavalry formations but was also used for infantry support. *Weight* 12 tons; *speed* 25mph (40kph); *armour* 45mm; *armament* 1 37mm gun; 1 7.5mm Reibel machine gun; *engine* Hotchkiss six-cylinder 120hp petrol; *crew* 2.

Hoth, Gen Hermann (1895–1971)

Hoth served as a German cavalry officer during World War I and remained in the Reichswehr after 1918, becoming an expert on armoured warfare. In June 1941 he commanded 3rd Panzer Army during the invasion of Russia and, working in conjunction with GUDERIAN, closed the BIALYSTOK pocket, capturing about 300,000 prisoners and an immense amount of equipment. In December his forces penetrated to within 12 miles (19km) of Moscow before being halted and then thrown back. He escaped the wholesale sackings which followed the Russian counter-offensive and was appointed to command 4th Panzer Army in the drive on STALINGRAD. Hoth led the last desperate attempt to relieve von PAULUS' trapped 6th Army, but was halted 30 miles short of his objective and then beaten back. At KURSK, Hoth led the 4th Panzer Army on the southern side of the salient, but failed to break through the Soviet defences. After the fall of KIEV in November 1943 he was removed by Hitler and retired from active service.

From the left: Colonel-General von Richthofen, General Kampf, Colonel-General Hoth in an observation post on the Eastern front.

Hotspur Glider (UK)

Designed as a troop-carrying glider, the Hotspur, built by the General Aircraft Co., was found to be too small for the task and was replaced by the HORSA. It was then put to use as a training glider for British airborne forces. *Span* 46ft (14m); *gliding speed* ca 75mph (120kph).

Houffalize, Belgium, 1945

A village and road junction where the US 1st and 3rd Armies, advancing respectively from north and south, met on 16 January while eliminating the German gains made during the Battle of the BULGE.

Howitzer Motor Carriage M7 (USA)

Based on the chassis of the LEE M3 medium tank, with a 105mm howitzer M1A2, M2 or M2A1 mounted in an open-topped superstructure. The pilot model was produced in late 1941 and the design was standardized in April 1942, some 3500 being built; later models were based on the SHERMAN M4A3 medium tank chassis and were designated M7B1. The M7 was manned by a crew of seven, stowed 69 rounds and had a maximum speed of 26mph (42kph). A distinguishing feature was the pulpit mounting for a .50-calibre Browning anti-aircraft machine gun situated to the right of the main armament. Although regarded as an expedient design, the vehicle gave excellent service in North Africa, Italy, Europe, Burma and the Pacific theatre of war. It first saw action during the Second Battle of ALAMEIN and was known in British service as the Priest. See also KANGAROO.

Howitzer Motor Carriage M8 (USA)

Based on the STUART M5 light tank chassis and armed with a 75mm pack howitzer housed in a purpose-built open-topped turret. 1778 were produced by Cadillac between September 1942 and January 1944, serving in the close support role with the Headquarters Company of medium tank battalions until replaced by the 105mm howitzer version of the SHERMAN. The M8 stowed 46 rounds and its mechanical performance was similar to that of the Stuart M5.

Hs 293

A German rocket-boosted gliding bomb, carrying a 1200lb (550kg) explosive warhead and propelled by a ten-second rocket thrust after launch. Development began in 1940 and production in 1941. It was first employed in August 1943 in the Bay of Biscay, when HMS *Bideford* was damaged by a near-miss. It was then used with some success against Allied shipping at Salerno, during the invasion of Sicily, and against shipping in the Dodecanese islands. The bomb was steered by radio commands from aircraft which dropped it, and radio countermeasures were soon devised to jam the control system, after which use of the bomb was abandoned.

The Italian Navy's "Human Torpedo".

Hubertus

German contingency plan for the defence of Moldavia and the Romanian oil-fields in the event of Russian attack, March 1941.

Huff-Duff

A British term derived from "HF-DF" for "High Frequency Direction Finding". This was a radio direction-finding system set up specifically to identify signals from, and thus locate the position of, German U-boats in the North Atlantic.

Hughes, Fort, Philippines, 1942

American coast-defence fort on Caballo Island, Manila Bay. It was close to the eastern side of the bay and, with Forts MILLS and DRUM, formed a barrier to prevent naval incursions. It was armed with two 14-inch guns, two 6-inch guns, two 3-inch guns and four 12-inch MORTARS. It was surrendered with the other Manila Bay defences on 6 May 1942. It was retaken by US forces in April 1945, after a difficult battle which was only resolved by pumping some 6000 gallons of gasoline-diesel oil mixture into the underground tunnels and igniting this with a phosphorus mortar bomb. Even after the ensuing conflagration several individual Japanese soldiers held out, and the commanding officer of the US 1/151 Infantry Regiment was shot by a sniper two weeks after the island had officially been declared secure.

Hukawng Valley, northern Burma, 1943–44

STILWELL's Chinese 38th Division began advancing southwards into the valley in October 1943 as part of the overall plan to reopen land communications between Burma and China, followed by the Chinese 22nd Division, meeting stiff resistance from Major-General Shinichi Tanaka's Japanese

18th Division. In February 1944 Stilwell's command was joined by the American long-range penetration group subsequently known as Merrill's Marauders, commanded by Brigadier-General Frank D. MERRILL, which outflanked the Japanese positions against which the Chinese formations were already maintaining pressure. In this way Tanaka's troops were defeated at Wawlumbum, 3–7 March, and again at Shaduzup, 28 March–1 April. Stilwell's successes in the Hukawng Valley enabled him to penetrate the MOGAUNG Valley and advance on MYITKYINA.

Hull, Cordell (1871–1955)

Hull was the US Secretary of State under ROOSEVELT from 1933 to 1944. A confirmed internationalist, he spent much of his time in the years 1937–41 locked in protracted and ultimately fruitless negotiations with the Japanese over the situation in the Far East. After the entry of the USA into the war, foreign affairs were largely taken out of his hands by Roosevelt, but Hull retained several areas of influence and was particularly active in reaching agreement with Vichy France, though this was negated by the rise of DE GAULLE. Although suffering from ill-health he was able to attend the Moscow Conference of Foreign Ministers in October 1943, and took an active part in the Dumbarton Oaks Conference at which the various proposals for the United Nations were discussed. His health finally forced his retirement in 1944.

"Human Torpedo"

Torpedo modified to carry a detachable explosive charge in place of the normal warhead, controlled by a crew of two who sat astride the casing in specially designed diving suits. Officially designated SLC (*Siluro a Lenta Corsa* – Slow Running Torpedo) by the Royal

Italian Navy, its nickname was *Maiale* or Pig. In British service a human torpedo was known as a Chariot. Driven by a 1.6hp electric motor, the craft had an operational radius of up to 15 miles (24km) at 2.5 knots and up to 4 miles (6.5km) at 4.5 knots and could dive to a maximum depth of 82 feet (25m). On arriving beneath the target vessel the crew detached the explosive charge and fixed it to the ship's bottom, then set a time fuze and attempted to escape aboard their craft. Three Italian human torpedoes penetrated Alexandria harbour on 19 December 1941 and damaged the battleships HMS *Queen Elizabeth* and HMS *Valiant* so severely that they were out of action for several months. On 3 January 1943 two British craft sank the newly-launched cruiser *Ulpio Traiano* and an 8500-ton transport at Palermo. On 21 June 1944 a joint British/Italian human torpedo attack on the naval base of La Spezia resulted in the sinking of the TRENTO Class cruiser *Bolzano*.

Humber Armoured Car (UK)

Introduced in 1941, the Humber was very similar in appearance to the GUY armoured car and saw extensive service throughout the Middle East. The Mark IV was employed in Italy, North-West Europe and Burma. The design was based on the chassis of the Karrier

Humber armoured car.

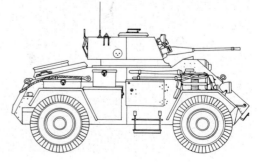

KT4 field artillery tractor and incorporated vision devices for rear-steering by the driver. See also FOX armoured car.

Weight	*Mark I* – 6.85 tons; *Marks II–IV* – 7.1 tons
Speed	45mph (72kph)
Armour	15mm
Armament	*Marks I–III* – 1 Besa 15mm machine gun; 1 Besa 7.92mm machine gun
	Mark IV – 1 37mm gun; 1 Besa 7.92mm machine gun
Engine	Rootes 95bhp petrol
Crew	*Marks I, II and IV* – 3
	Mark III – 4.

Humberette (UK)

Light reconnaissance car, similar to the BEAVERETTE but based on the Humber Super Snipe private car chassis. Armament consisted of a BOYS anti-tank rifle and a BREN light machine gun. Three marks of Humberette were produced, all being manned by a crew of three; their maximum speed was 45–50mph (72–80kph). Used only for Home Defence.

Hummel (Bumble Bee) (Ger)

A self-propelled 150mm howitzer, the Hummel employed a PANZERKAMPFWAGEN IV chassis incorporating the final drive of the PANZERKAMPFWAGEN III, the engine being located amidships so as to leave the rear of the vehicle clear for the gun mounting, which was protected by a fixed, open-topped superstructure of 10mm plate. Early models of the vehicle were fitted with a muzzle brake and had an angled driver's cab, but as the series progressed the former was dispensed with and the latter was extended across the front to include the radio operator's compartment. The Hummel weighed 23.5 tons, had a maximum speed of 25mph (40kph) and was manned by a crew of six. It entered service during 1943 and equipped the six-gun heavy battery of the Panzer division's artillery regiment; such an allocation was far from universal, as the total production run was only 666, and only the most favoured divisions would have received their full quota. The sFH 18 threw a 96-lb (43.5kg) shell 16,500 yards (15,097m). Only 18 rounds of ammunition could be stowed but immediate replenishment was available from a munitions carrier with the same layout but without a gun, several of which formed part of the battery establishment.

Hump, the, India–China, 1942–45

The name given to the eastern Himalayas over which passed the Allied air supply route from Assam to China. The route, which was 530 miles (852km) long and crossed mountains 12,000ft (3657m) high, was opened in April 1942 when the Japanese cut the BURMA ROAD and remained in use after the latter was reopened in 1945. The aircraft most commonly used on The Hump Route was the DOUGLAS DC-3 DAKOTA.

Hungary, 1938–45

In the interwar years, the object of Hungary's foreign policy was to recover the territories of which she had been deprived by the 1920 Treaty of Trianon, and for that reason she developed close links with Nazi Germany. In 1938 Slovakia was recovered as part of the MUNICH settlement. Hungarian troops occupied Czechoslovakian Ruthenia in March 1939, and in August 1940 Germany compelled Romania to cede northern Transylvania. In April 1941 Hungarian troops occupied the Banat in Yugoslavia following the Axis conquest of that country. In return the Hungarian Regent, Admiral Miklos HORTHY, sent a large contingent to fight alongside the German armies on the Eastern Front. By 1944 Horthy recognized that Germany would lose the war and would have concluded an armistice with the Allies had he not been deposed on 15 October and replaced by the pro-German puppet Szalasi. Hungary thus remained an ally of Germany to the end. While the Soviet armies overran their country, those

Hummel self-propelled howitzer in Russia.

Hungarian units that could retreated westwards and surrendered to the British or Americans. See BALATON, LAKE; and BUDAPEST.

Hunt Class Escort Destroyers (UK)

Type I *Displacement* 907 tons; *dimensions* 280×29ft (85×8.7m); mean draught 7ft 9in (2.3m); *machinery* 2-shaft geared turbines producing shp 19,000; *speed* 26 knots; *armament* 4×4in AA (2×2); 4/5×2-pdr AA (1×4 and 1×1); 2×20mm AA; *complement* 146; *number in class* 20, launched 1939–40.

Type II *Displacement* 1050 tons; *dimensions* 282ft 6in×31ft 6in (85.9×9.6m); mean draught 7ft 9in (2.38m); *machinery* 2-shaft geared turbines producing shp 19,000; *speed* 25 knots; *armament* 6×4in AA (3×2); 4×2-pdr AA (1×4); 2/3×20mm AA (2/3×1); *complement* 168; *number in class* 36, launched 1940–42.

Type III *Displacement* 1087 tons; *dimensions* 282ft 6in×31ft 6in (86.1×9.6m); mean draught 7ft 9in (2.36m); *machinery* 2-shaft geared turbines producing shp 19,000; *speed* 25 knots; *armament* 4×4in AA (2×2); 4×2-pdr AA (1×4); 2/3×20mm AA (2/3×1); 2×21in torpedo tubes (1×2); *complement* 168; *number in class* 28, launched 1941–43.

Type IV *Displacement* 1175 tons; *dimensions* 296ft×33ft 3in (90.2×10.1m); mean draught 8ft (2.4m); *machinery* 2-shaft geared turbines producing shp 19,000; *speed* 25 knots; *armament* 6×4in AA (3×2); 4×2-pdr AA (1×4); 2×40mm AA (2×1) and 4×20mm AA (2×2) or 8×20mm AA (4×2); 3×21in torpedo tubes (1×3); *complement* 170; *number in class* 2, launched 1942.

Hunt Class Minesweeping Sloops (UK)

Displacement 710 tons; *dimensions* 231ft×28ft 6in (70.4×8.68m); mean draught 7ft 6in (2.3m); *machinery* 2-shaft reciprocating engines with ihp 2200; *speed* 16 knots; *armament* 1×4in; 1×3in AA plus machine guns; *complement* 73; *number in class* 26, launched 1917–19.

Hunt's Gap, Tunisia, 1943

In February the communications centre of Beja was the objective of the northern thrust of the German *Ochsenkopf* counteroffensive and its loss would have caused a British withdrawal many miles to the west. The German battle group detailed to capture Beja, commanded by Colonel Rudolph Lang, was spearheaded by 74 tanks of which 14 were TIGERS, but its route wound through mountainous country to a natural defensive position known as Hunt's Gap, where the British 128th Brigade was digging in, supported by CHURCHILL tanks of the North Irish Horse and artillery. Early on 26 February Lang ran into the outpost of SIDI NSIR, which was not overrun until evening, and then at serious cost. This remarkable stand enabled the defences of Hunt's Gap to be consolidated so that when Lang finally attacked at noon on 28 February he ran on to a killing ground and was forced to withdraw after sustaining further serious loss from mines, Churchills, anti-tank guns, medium artillery and air attack. The southern thrust of the counteroffensive also failed.

Huntziger, Gen Charles, 1880–1941

Huntziger graduated from St Cyr in 1901 and joined the Marines. After fighting in pre-1914 colonial wars in Madagascar and Indo-China, he commanded a battalion in World War I, rising to the rank of Lieutenant-Colonel as Chief of Operations in Salonika under General Franchet D'Esperey. By 1938 he was a member of France's Supreme War Council, having commanded French forces in Syria. On the eve of the German invasion of the Low Countries on 10 May 1940 Huntziger commanded the French 2nd Army on the Meuse. To guard against an outflanking attack on the MAGINOT LINE, he had deployed his best divisions on the right and his weakest on the left immediately behind Sedan, where they linked hands with the equally unreliable troops of Corap's 9th Army. It was at Sedan that the crucial breakthrough was made by GUDERIAN's XIX Corps. Huntziger then pulled back to protect the Maginot Line, by now a complete irrelevance, and ended the war shut up in one of the forts at Verdun, from which he emerged to lead the French delegation which signed the Armistice in Marshal Foch's *wagon-lit* at Rhéthondes on 22 June. He was killed in a 'plane crash in 1941.

Huon Peninsula, New Guinea, 1943

Allied operations during September and October secured the peninsula and so paved the way for the invasion of NEW BRITAIN to the north. See FINSCHHAFEN; LAE; SALAMAUA; SATTELBERG RIDGE.

Hurricane

Allied assault on Biak, New Guinea, 1944.

Husky

Allied invasion of Sicily, July 1943.

Husseini, Amin el (1900–)

The Grand Mufti of Jerusalem, Husseini was an Arab political and religious leader who was sympathetic to the Nazi movement largely because of their attitude towards the Jews. In October 1939 he visited IRAQ to press for its neutrality, and sent envoys to Germany to seek recognition of Arab independence in return for Arab support. Receiving a favourable reply, in April 1941 he engineered the overthrow of Nur es-Said, the pro-Allied ruler of Iraq, and established a pro-Axis government under RASHID ALI. A month later British troops moved against Iraq, no German support was forthcoming, and the regime collapsed. The Mufti fled to Iran, then to Italy where he visited MUSSOLINI, and finally to Germany where he met HITLER in November 1941. He finally secured German recognition of Arab independence in April 1943, after which he worked for Germany in forming ethnic SS formations from Muslims in German-occupied territory. He left Germany in 1945, was placed under house arrest in France, but escaped to Cairo in 1946.

Hyakutake, Gen Haruyoshi (1888–1947)

One of the younger Japanese generals, in April 1942 he was appointed to command the 17th Army, with his HQ at RABAUL. In August he was given orders to effect the recapture of GUADALCANAL, where the US 1st Marine Division had landed on the 7th, and given responsibility for overseeing Japanese operations in NEW GUINEA. In spite of his best efforts, his forces failed to evict the Americans from Guadalcanal and he was barely able to escape himself with some 10,000 of his troops. Subsequently he was surprised by US landings at RENDOVA, and failed in a counteroffensive on BOUGAINVILLE. He was removed from command of 17th Army in April 1945 and given an administrative post.

Hydra

RAF attack on PEENEMUNDE V-WEAPON development site, 17 August 1943.

I

I 15 Class (Type B1) Submarines (Jap)

I 19 torpedoed and sank the carrier USS WASP south of GUADALCANAL on 15 September 1942. *Displacement* 2198 tons (2584/3654 tons normal); *dimensions* 356ft 6in×30ft 6in (108.5×9.29m); *machinery* 2-shaft diesel/ electric motors hp 12,400/2000; *speed* 23.5/8 knots; *armament* 1×5.5in; 2×25mm AA (1×2); 6×21in torpedo tubes (bow) and 17 torpedoes; *aircraft* 1; *complement* 100; *number in class* 20, launched 1939–42.

I 40 Class (Type B2) Submarines (Jap)

Displacement 2230 tons (2624/3700 tons normal); *dimensions* 356ft 6in×30ft 6in (109×9m); *machinery* 2-shaft diesel/electric motors hp 11,000/2000; *speed* 23.5/8 knots; *armament* 1×5.5in; 2×25mm AA (1×2); 6×21in torpedo tubes (bow) and 17 torpedoes; *aircraft* 1; *complement* 100; *number in class* 6, launched 1942–43.

I 168 Class (Type KD 6A) Submarines (Jap)

I 168 sank the carrier USS YORKTOWN and the destroyer USS *Hamman* at MIDWAY. *Displacement* 1400 tons (1785/2440 tons normal; *dimensions* 343ft 6in×27ft (104.69×8.2m); *machinery* 2-shaft diesel/electric motors hp 9000/1800; *speed* 23/8 knots; *armament* 1×3.9in; 1×13mm; 6×21in torpedo tubes (bow); 14 torpedoes; *complement* 70; *number in class* 6, launched 1933–35.

I 176 Class (Type KD7) Submarines (Jap)

Displacement 1630 tons (1833/2602 tons normal); *dimensions* 346×27ft (105×8.2m); *machinery* 2-shaft diesel/electric motors hp 8000/1800; *speed* 23/8 knots; *armament* 1×4.7in; 2×25mm AA (1×2); 6×21in torpedo tubes (bow) and 12 torpedoes; *complement* 80; *number in class* 10, launched 1943–44.

I 361 Class (Type DI) Submarines (Jap)

Designed to supply and reinforce isolated island garrisons in the Pacific, this class had a radius of action of 15,000 sea miles (24,140km) at 10 knots surfaced and 120 sea miles (193km) at 3 knots submerged, the latter being larger than any other Japanese submarine. At the end of 1944 the majority of the class were converted to carry five KAITEN midget submarines. *Displacement* 1440 tons (1779/2215 tons normal); *dimensions* 241ft×29ft 3in (73.4×8.9m); *machinery* 2-shaft diesel/electric motors hp 1850/1200; *speed* 13/6.5 knots; *armament* 1×5.5in; 2×25mm AA (1×2); *cargo* 82 tons; 110 men; 2 Daihatsu landing craft; *complement* 75; *number in class* 12, launched 1943–44.

I 400 Class (Type STo) Submarines (Jap)

At the time of building, the I 400 Class were the largest submarines in the world and were capable of catapult-launching up to three light reconnaissance bombers. Their radius of action was 30,000 sea miles (48,280km) at 14 knots surfaced and 60 sea miles (96.5km) at 3 knots submerged. *Displacement* 3530 tons (5223/6560 tons normal); *dimensions* 400ft 3in×39ft 4in (121.99×11.98m); *machinery* 2-shaft diesel/electric motors hp 7700/2400; *speed* 18.5/6.5 knots; *armament* 1×5.5in; 10×25mm AA (3×3 and 1×1); 8×21in torpedo tubes (bow) and 20 torpedoes; *air-*

Japanese submarines I 400, I 401, and I 14 moored alongside the tender Proteus, *in Tokyo Bay, 1945.*

craft 3; *complement* 100; *number in class* 3, plus one fitting out, all launched 1944.

"I" Class Destroyers (UK)
Displacement 1370 tons; *dimensions* 323ft×32ft 3in (98.4×9.82m); mean draught 8ft 6in (2.6m); *machinery* 2-shaft geared turbines producing shp 34,000; *speed* 36 knots; *armament* 4×4.7in (4×1); 8×0.5in AA (2×4); 10×21in torpedo tubes; *complement* 145; *number in class* 9, launched 1936–37.

IAR 80 (Romania)
This monoplane fighter was the only Romanian-designed combat aircraft of any note which appeared during the war. The IAR (Industria Aeronautic Romania) had obtained a licence to build the Polish PZL P-24, and in 1938 set about designing their own machine using the P-24 as the basis. The IAR 80 flew in 1938 and went into production in 1941. About 125 were built and were used on the Eastern Front until late 1942, when they were replaced by an improved model, the IAR 81, which could function as a fighter or fighter-bomber. They also saw considerable service on home defence against USAAF raids on the Romanian oilfields in 1944. Some remained in use by the Romanians into the early 1950s. *Span* 33ft (10m); *engine* 1 1025hp radial; *armament* 2 20mm cannons, 4 machine guns, 440lb (200kg) of bombs; *speed* 342mph (550kph).

Iceberg
American assault on OKINAWA and the RYUKU ISLANDS, April 1945.

Iceland, 1940–45
At the request of the Danish and Icelandic governments, the United States despatched the 1st Marine Brigade (Provisional) to relieve the British garrison on 7 July 1941. The development of naval and air bases in Iceland was a critical factor in winning the Battle of the ATLANTIC.

Ie Shima, Ryuku Islands, 1945
An island off the west coast of OKINAWA, captured by elements of the US III Amphibious Corps 16–20 April. Fighter strips were quickly constructed on the island and were operational during the final months of the war.

IFF
IFF means "Identification, Friend or Foe" and is the generic name for a radio/radar device in an aircraft which, when "interrogated" by a signal from a RADAR set, will respond, if the radar set is friendly, by returning a signal which modifies the appearance of the trace shown on the radar's cathode ray tube, positively identifying the trace as a friendly aircraft. It is the only way in which aircraft targets can be so identified on a radar screen. It is, however, also susceptible to being interrogated by a false signal of the correct frequency, which causes it to respond and thus announce the identity of the aircraft to an enemy. The Germans discovered this in 1944 and were using British bomber IFF sets to identify targets for their night fighters.

I-Go
Japanese air offensive against GUADALCANAL and NEW GUINEA, March 1943.

Il Giogo Pass, Italy, 1944
Heavily fortified route from FLORENCE to BOLOGNA via Firenzuola, seven miles (11km) east of the larger FUTA PASS. During the GOTHIC LINE battles General Mark CLARK directed the major effort of his US 5th Army against the Il Giogo Pass, which was taken by US II Corps (Lieutenant-General Geoffrey KEYES) after heavy fighting, 13–17 September. The American capture of Monte Altuzzo, the core of the German defence, was assisted by the attack of the 1st Infantry Division of Lieutenant-General Sidney Kirkman's British XIII Corps, which outflanked the feature to the east. The three divisions of US II Corps (34th, 85th and 91st) employed at Il Giogo Pass sustained the loss of over 500 killed and 2000 wounded.

Illustrious, HMS – Aircraft Carrier
Name ship of her class, *Illustrious* served with the Mediterranean Fleet 1940–41. On 11 November 1940 she launched the air attack which crippled the Italian battlefleet in TARANTO harbour, but was herself badly damaged by air attack on 10 January 1941. After completing repairs in the USA, she served with the Eastern Fleet 1942–43 and then with Force H. She returned to the Eastern Fleet in 1944 and joined the Pacific Fleet the following year.

Illustrious Class Aircraft Carriers (UK)
Group 1 Displacement 23,000 tons; *dimensions* 753ft 6in×95ft 9in (229×29m); mean draught 24ft (7.3m); *machinery* 3-shaft geared turbines producing shp 110,000; *speed* 31 knots; *protection* main belt 4.5in; hangar side 4.5in; deck 3in; *armament* 16×4.5in DP (8×2); 48×2-pdr AA (6×8); 8×20mm AA (8×1); *aircraft* 36; *complement* 1392; *number in class* 4, launched 1939–40.

Group 2 Displacement 26,000 tons; *dimensions* 766ft×95ft 9in (233.4×29m); mean draught 26ft (7.9m); *machinery* 4-shaft geared

HMS Illustrious.

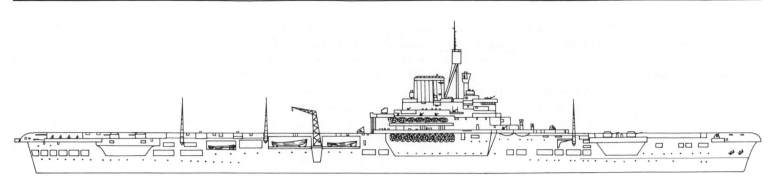

Illustrious class aircraft carrier.

turbines producing shp 148,000; *speed* 32 knots; *protection* main belt 4.5in; hangar side 1.5in; deck 3in; *armament* 16×4.5in AA (8×2), 48×2-pdr AA (6×8); 38×20mm AA (17×2 and 4×1); *aircraft* 72; *complement* 1785; *number in class* 2, launched 1942.

Ilmen, Lake, 1942
See DEMYANSK.

Ilyushin Aircraft (USSR)
Ilyushin Il-2 Stormovik Probably the most famous Soviet aircraft of the war, the Ilyushin

Stormovik was a formidable ground-attack and close ground-support machine. Well armed and armoured, the original single-seat version was found vulnerable to attack from behind and the cockpit was extended to make room for a rear-seat gunner. This aircraft also qualified as the most numerous of the war; over 35,000 were built in three factories. *Span* 48ft (14.6m); *engine* 1 1600hp in-line; *crew* 2; *armament* 2 20mm cannon, 3 machine guns, 8 rocket projectiles or 1300lb (600kg) of bombs; *speed* 257mph (413kph).

Ilyushin Il-4 The Il-4 was the standard Soviet medium bomber throughout the war years,

and it was also adapted for service as a torpedo-bomber in the Baltic. As a bomber it functioned equally well as a long-range machine for bombing strategic targets or as a close-support machine for ground attack, the role in which it was principally employed. Production ran from 1937 to 1944 and over 10,000 were built. *Span* 70ft (21.3m); *engines* 2 1100hp radial; *crew* 3 or 4; *armament* 3 machine guns, 2200lb (1000kg) of bombs internally stowed for long ranges, plus 3300lb (1500kg) of bombs or one torpedo externally for short range missions; *speed* 265mph (426kph).

Impact Plain and Impact Royal
Stages in British amphibious operations on Lake COMACCHIO, April 1945.

Imphal, Manipur, India, 1944
The strategic objective of Lieutenant-General Masakuzu KAWABE's U-GO offensive was to secure an impregnable defence line along the line of the Naga Hills, lying beyond the Imphal Plain, which would contain the British within India and prevent their resuming operations in Burma. For this enterprise, grandiloquently named the March on Delhi, he had available Lieutenant-General Renya MUTAGUCHI's 15th Army, consisting of Major-General Kotoku SATO's 31st Division, which was ordered to isolate the British IV Corps on the Imphal Plain by cutting the road behind it at KOHIMA; Major-General Yamauchi's 15th Division, which would attack IV Corps from the north and east; and Major-General Yanagida's 33rd Division, which would converge on the Plain from the south and west. Commanded by Lieutenant-General G. A. P. SCOONES, IV Corps initially consisted of Major-General D. T. COWAN's 17th Indian Division, operating well to the south in the Tiddim area; Major-General Roberts' 23rd Indian Division at Imphal; Major-General Gracey's 20th Indian Division

Ilyushin Il-2 Stormoviks, known as "flying tanks", on their way to bomb Berlin.

Ilyushin Il-2 Stormovik ground attack fighter.

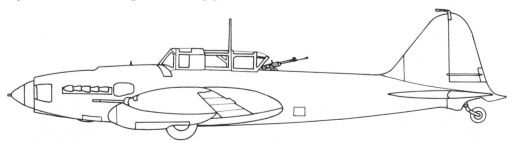

in the KABAW VALLEY to the east; and two regiments of 254 Indian Tank Brigade. General SLIM, commanding the British 14th Army, was aware of Kawabe's intentions and his plan was that Scoones should concentrate his corps on the Imphal Plain, where it could be supplied by air and the British armour could be used to best effect. Once the Japanese had exhausted themselves in attacks on defensive boxes, IV Corps would take the offensive.

Scoones' troops, reinforced by 5th Indian Division flown in from the ARAKAN, retired before the Japanese advance and on 29 March the Imphal Plain was isolated. On 10 April the Japanese almost succeeded in capturing the vital hill feature of Nunshigum, which overlooked the principal airstrips, but were driven off after vicious fighting. Thereafter, the battle took the form Slim had predicted, involving numerous hard-fought actions around the perimeter of the plain. The Japanese divisions, prevented by distance from co-ordinating their operations, began to exhaust their supplies while, further afield, CHINDIT operations tied down troops in protecting their lines of communications. The attrition imposed by the British air superiority and armour sapped the enemy's strength and further progress was impeded by serious quarrels between their generals. At the end of May Lieutenant-General Montagu STOPFORD's British XXXIII Corps broke through Sato's roadblock at Kohima and on 22 June effected a junction with IV Corps north of Imphal. The Japanese, starving and diseased, were already withdraw-

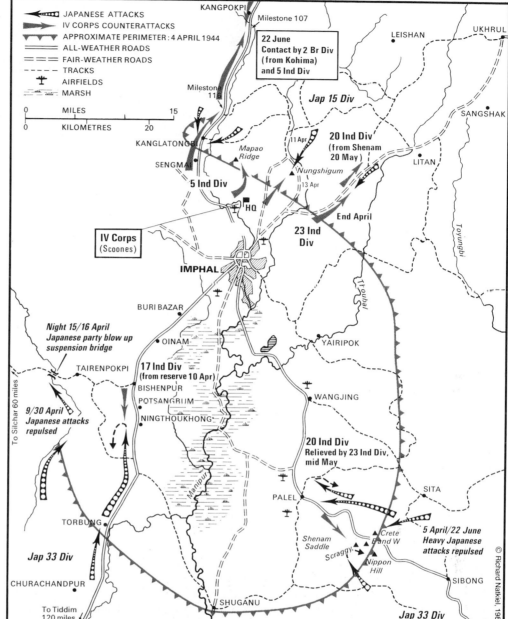

The Imphal plain, April 1944.

Mountbatten at Imphal, February 1944.

ing to the Chindwin, having lost some 53,000 men and all their heavy equipment. The decisive defeat of Mutaguchi's 15th Army was a major turning point in the war in Burma and led to bitter recriminations among the Japanese military establishment. See INDAW. See also *Tank Tracks to Rangoon* by Bryan Perrett (Robert Hale).

Improved Birmingham Class Cruisers (UK)

Displacement 9550 to 9800 tons; *dimensions* 605×65ft (184×19.8m); mean draught 17ft 3in (5.25m); *machinery* 4-shaft geared turbines producing shp 65,000; *speed* 30.5 knots;

protection main belt 3in; deck 1.5in; gun shields 2.5in; *armament* 5/7×7.5in (5/7×1); 4/5×4in AA (4/5×1); 8×2-pdr AA (2×4); 10×20mm AA (10×1); 6×21in torpedo tubes or (*Effingham* only) 9×6in (9×1); 8×4in AA (4×2); 8×2-pdr AA (2×4); 8×0.5in AA (2×4); 4×21in torpedo tubes; *aircraft* 1 (*Effingham* only); *complement* 712; *number in class* 4, launched 1918–21.

INA Indian National Army. A force formed of disaffected Indian troops under Japanese organization, intended to assist in the invasion and "liberation" of India. When put into action in Burma, most deserted back to the Allies, though a hard core were captured and court-martialled after the war.

Indaw, Burma, 1944

Situated on the MANDALAY–MYITKYINA railway with tracks leading west to IMPHAL and KOHIMA, it was essential that the Japanese retain possession of Indaw. Their efforts to defend the town against CHINDIT attacks not only contributed to the defeats sustained by their 18th Division in northern Burma but also prevented units from that formation being sent to reinforce the hard-pressed Imphal front. In December, Indaw was captured by the British 36th Division, operating under STILWELL's command, and a junction was effected with 19th Indian Division (IV Corps), thereby establishing a continuous Allied front in northern Burma.

Independence Class Light Carriers (USA)

Displacement 11,000 tons; *dimensions* 622ft 6in×71ft 6in (189×21m); mean draught 26ft (7.8m); *machinery* 4-shaft geared turbines producing shp 100,000; *speed* 31.5 knots; *armament* 26×40mm AA guns; *aircraft* 45; *complement* 1560; *number in class* 9, launched 1942–43.

India, 1939–45

The basic stability of the British Raj in India is underlined by the fact that in 1939 a subcontinent with a population of 350 million required a mere 250,000 troops – less than a quarter of them British – as contingency aid to the civil power, and that of these a large number were always stationed along the turbulent North-West Frontier. During World War II the Indian princes and a majority of the population supported the United Kingdom to the extent that over two million Indians volun-

Unrest in India after the arrest of Congress Leaders, 1942.

teered for the armed forces; the Indian Army was, in fact, the largest volunteeer army in the world, and served with distinction in North and East Africa, the Middle East, Italy and Burma. This is particularly significant when it is remembered that only the Gurkhas of Nepal and members of the martial races of northern India were eligible to serve in fighting regiments. However, the Indian National Congress Party, led by Mahatma Gandhi, did not support the British and the underlying political theme of Indian life remained independence and self-government. Gandhi was already aware that the United Kingdom was inclined to grant both and in March 1942 the Lord Privy Seal, Sir Stafford CRIPPS, confirmed the fact; only the means and the date remained to be decided. Some Congress leaders were in favour of accepting, but Gandhi was not. Conscious that the British had been defeated in Malaya, Burma and at sea, he demanded that they leave India immediately and so avoid provoking a Japanese attack. When the British declined, he called for a "non-violent" open rebellion. The Congress leaders were arrested on 9 August 1942 and, although no rising took place, carefully orchestrated mobs attacked the railway system and public buildings. It took 57 battalions, the majority of them Indian, some six weeks to restore order. The British defeats during the early years of the war against Japan

also affected some Indian prisoners of war who, deprived of the steadying influence exercised by their Viceroy's Commissioned Officers, were cynically manipulated by Congress politicians working with the Japanese. Some joined the so-called Indian National Army organized by Subhas Chandra BHOSE and fought against the British and their own countrymen. In the aftermath of the war and with independence on the horizon, the British wisely left the judgement of such men to the Indians themselves.

Indiana, USS – South Dakota Class Battleship

Served in the Pacific at the GILBERT ISLANDS, KWAJALEIN, the MARIANAS, Palau, IWO JIMA and OKINAWA.

Indianapolis Class Heavy Cruisers (USA)

Displacement 9950 tons; *dimensions* 610ft 3in×66ft 3in (186×20.19m); mean draught 17ft 3in (5.2m); *machinery* 4-shaft geared turbines producing shp 107,000; *speed* 32.5 knots; *armament* 9×8in (3×3); 8×5in AA (8×1); *aircraft* 3; *complement* 1150; *number in class* 2, launched 1931–32.

Indian Ocean, Operations in, 1942

See COLOMBO; DIEGO SUAREZ; MADAGASCAR.

Indian Wheeled Carriers (UK)

Developed in India from 1940 onwards to perform the same functions as the tracked UNIVERSAL CARRIER, viz reconnaissance, transport of heavy infantry weapons and artillery observation. The most common version was the Mark II, which was based on a 4×4 rear-engined chassis produced by the Ford Motor Company of Canada and shipped to India in kit form, the armoured bodies being constructed from locally made plate. Total production of the Mark II amounted to 4655 vehicles, which saw action in North Africa, the Middle East, Italy and Burma with Indian divisions. The Mark II was manned by a crew of three or four, was powered by a Ford 95bhp engine producing a maximum speed of 50mph (80kph), and was armed with a BOYS anti-tank rifle and a BREN light machine gun.

Indo-China, 1940–45

Following the fall of France the Japanese, anxious to isolate China from all external aid, brought pressure to bear on the Vichy French government and on 29 August 1940 the latter permitted Japanese troops to establish bases in northern Indo-China. On 24 July 1941 base facilities were also granted in the south. The response of the United States, the United Kingdom and the Dutch government in exile was to freeze Japanese assets, thus making war almost inevitable.

Despite talk of the joint Franco-Japanese defence of Indo-China, the Japanese were in effective occupation of the country and

Japanese troops enter Saigon, 1941.

established their principal headquarters in South-East Asia in Saigon. Without the use of Indo-China as a springboard, the Japanese invasions of Malaya and Burma would have been infinitely more difficult. By 1943 HO CHI MINH and his infant Viet Minh guerrilla organization were receiving supplies of Allied arms and were able to offer some resistance. In March 1945 all pretence of co-operation with the French vanished when the Japanese assumed complete control of the country. Those French garrisons which offered resistance were massacred; the Foreign Legion's 5th Regiment escaped by marching 500 miles through Thailand to China. At the POTSDAM Conference in July it was agreed that the British would disarm the Japanese in southern Indo-China while the Nationalist Chinese did the same in the north. On 18 August, three days after their capitulation, the Japanese transferred power to the Viet Minh. On 13 September Major-General Douglas Gracey, commanding the 20th Indian Division and supporting units, landed at Saigon to establish the Allied presence. French troops returned shortly after and clashes with the Viet Minh soon followed.

Indomitable, HMS – Illustrious Class Aircraft Carrier

Indomitable served with the Home Fleet in 1941 and briefly with the Eastern Fleet the following year. She then returned to the Home Fleet and FORCE H, being one of three aircraft carriers which provided air cover dur-

ing the passage of the vital PEDESTAL CONVOY to Malta in August 1942. She joined the Eastern Fleet in 1944 and the Pacific Fleet in 1945.

Infatuate

Allied operations involving the capture of WALCHEREN and the clearance of the SCHELDT estuary, October 1944.

Inonu, President Ismet (1884–1974)

Inonu was President of Turkey throughout the war and in spite of overtures from both Axis and Allied sides maintained a strict neutrality. The German occupation of Greece and their domination of the Balkans inclined Inonu neither to fall in with the Germans nor to oppose them. In December 1943 Inonu met ROOSEVELT and CHURCHILL in Cairo, but pointed out that the risk of having his country occupied by the Germans and subsequently "liberated" by the Russians was one he was not prepared to take.

Inshore Squadron

Force of Royal Navy lighters and landing craft which shipped supplies forward from Egypt to British troops operating in the Western Desert. While TOBRUK was besieged in 1941 the squadron made regular supply runs but sustained heavy loss from enemy air attack. Following the Second Battle of ALAMEIN the squadron formed an important element of the logistic support required to sustain the advance of the British 8th Army and contained 28 landing craft and 52 lighters, 12 of the latter being powered.

Intercept Services

A British term for radio listening posts which monitored every German (and later other enemy) radio transmission and recorded the contents, whether in code or clear speech. These intercepts were then sent for analysis and provided information of considerable value. The service was largely run by civilian radio amateurs who spent a certain amount of time every week listening to specified frequencies.

Iosef Stalin Series – Heavy Tanks (USSR)

Designed to replace the KLIMENTI VOROSHILOV (KV) heavy tank series which, by 1943, was clearly under-gunned. The running gear of the IS series was similar to that of the KV, although the hull overhung the wide tracks

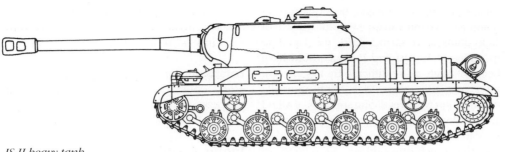

IS-II heavy tank.

and incorporated heavy castings. The early IS-Is were armed with an 85mm gun but this was considered inadequate for so heavy a tank and it was decided to take a major step forward by fitting a 122mm L/43 artillery weapon. This was fitted as standard to the IS-II and replaced the 85mm gun on those IS-Is which had already been completed. Initially, the 122mm gun retained its interrupted-screw breech pending development of the more convenient falling-block mechanism. The heavy ammunition was split for ease of handling, with the result that only three or four rounds per minute could be fired, and a further disadvantage was that only 28 rounds could be stowed. These limitations were, however, considered acceptable in view of the fact that the gun was capable of penetrating 185mm of armour at 1000 yards (915m). The IS-II began entering service with heavy tank regiments early in 1944. These operated under the control of army commanders. As more vehicles became available a heavy regiment was attached to each tank corps whenever possible, and in due course heavy tank brigades were formed, each of three IS-II regiments. The tank was considered to be a match for the PANTHER, and the TIGER was only able to penetrate it at under 1900 yards (1735m), at which range it was itself vulnerable to the 122mm gun. Some 3400 IS-IIs were built during the war, remaining in service with the Soviet and Warsaw Pact armies until well into the 1950s. The IS-III retained the 122mm gun but benefited from a more scientific armour layout, the principal features of which were a low, domed turret and well-angled hull armour. The prototype was completed in November 1944 and some 350 had been built when the war ended, although it remains doubtful whether these saw anything more than limited action. The IS-III subsequently replaced the IS-II on the production lines and remained in service with some armies until the late 1960s. *Weight IS-I* – 45 tons; *IS-II and*

IS-III – 46 tons; *speed IS-I and IS-II* – 20mph (32kph); *IS-III* – 23mph (37kph); *armour IS-I and IS-II* – 160mm; *IS-III* – 200mm; *armament* IS-I – 1 85mm gun; *IS-II and IS-III* – 1 122mm gun; 1 7.62mm machine gun mounted coaxially; *engine* V-12 diesel 520hp; *crew* 4.

Iowa, USS – Iowa Class Battleship

Carried President ROOSEVELT to the CASABLANCA CONFERENCE in 1943 and saw active service in the Pacific at KWAJALEIN, TRUK, HOLLANDIA, the MARIANAS, Palau, LEYTE GULF and OKINAWA. Recommissioned during the Korean War, *Iowa* was laid up in 1958 but was commissioned again in 1984, fitted with Tomahawk cruise missiles, Harpoon anti-ship missiles and 20mm Phalanx close-in weapon systems.

Iowa Class Battleships (USA)

See also USS IOWA, NEW JERSEY, MISSOURI and WISCONSIN. *Displacement* 45,000 tons; *dimensions* 887ft 3in × 108ft 3in (270 × 33m); mean draught 36ft (10.9m); *machinery* 4-shaft geared turbines producing shp 212,000; *speed* 33 knots; *protection* main belt 19in; turrets 18in; *armament* 9 × 16in (3 × 3); 20 × 5in DP (10 × 2); 80 × 40mm AA; *aircraft* 3; *complement* 2978; *number in class* 4, launched 1942–44.

IRA (Irish Republican Army)

A political movement which also organized terrorist attacks against Britain. The IRA had been active in Britain in 1939, planting bombs in Post Offices and carrying out other minor acts of terrorism, but in spite of encouragement from Germany operations against Britain were virtually suspended for the duration of the war.

Iran, 1941

Although the Shah strove to pursue a neutral path, it was clear by 1941 that Axis influence within the country was growing steadily. Further, such was the scale of the Wehrmacht's initial success when it invaded the Soviet

Union in June 1941, that the possibility existed of a German strike south into Iran to secure the vital oil-producing areas, thereby inflicting critical damage on the British and Soviet war efforts. The British and Soviet governments therefore decided to implement the 1907 Entente, which divided the country into respective spheres of influence. When the Shah refused to accede to a request that all German nationals be asked to leave the country, an invasion became inevitable. In the British sector this involved Major-General G. O. Harvey's 8th Indian Division, whose objectives included Abadan, Khorramshar and Ahwaz, while further north Major-General William SLIM's 10th Indian Division forced the Pai Tak Pass and advanced through Kermanshah to Hamadan, effecting a junction with Soviet troops which had advanced south from the Caspian through BANDAR PAHLEVI and BANDAR SHAH. The Allied invasion began on 25 August, and although there were pockets of Iranian resistance the Shah ordered his troops to cease fire on 28 August. Shortly afterwards, he abdicated in favour of his son. In addition to safeguarding the Allies' oil supplies, the occupation of Iran provided an additional benefit for the Allies in that over five million tons of war supplies were shipped to the Soviet Union through the Persian Gulf. See also IRAQ.

Iraq, 1941

On the termination of the British mandate in 1930, Iraq and the United Kingdom signed a treaty which permitted the latter to maintain air bases at Shaibah, near Basra, and HABBANIYAH, 55 miles (88km) west of Baghdad. In September 1939 the country was ruled by a regent in the name of the young King Feisal II, but on 1 April 1941 he was deposed by a military junta known as The Golden Square, led by a politician named RASHID ALI who was in the pay of Germany. The British responded by shipping reinforcements to Basra, including the 10th Indian Division. Rashid Ali therefore decided to attack the apparently weaker British garrison at Habbaniyah, but the Iraqi troops involved were repulsed on 2 May and driven back to FALLUJAH. Habbaniyah was relieved by a flying column from Transjordan which went on to capture Fallujah on 18 May and advanced on Baghdad itself. Meanwhile, British reinforcements had continued to arrive at Basra, despite hostile demonstrations. Lieutenant-General E. P. Quinan, com-

Iron Guard members in Bucharest.

commanded the North Russian Intervention Force in 1918–19. Having risen to the post of Inspector-General Overseas Forces, he was appointed Chief of the Imperial General Staff in 1939, replacing GORT who had not enjoyed a happy working relationship with the War Minister Hore-Belisha. On 20 May 1940, a week after the German breakthrough at Sedan, Ironside was despatched to France by CHURCHILL to tell Gort to attack south to link up with the French at Amiens, a potentially disastrous course of action which was skilfully deflected by Gort. Before the battle for France was over Ironside had been replaced as CIGS by DILL and assumed command of Home Forces. He was replaced by General BROOKE in July 1940 and retired.

Irrawaddy River, Burma, 1945

In the aftermath of the failed offensive at IMPHAL General Hoyotaro Kimura, commanding the Japanese Burma Area Army, was prepared to allow General SLIM's British 14th Army to penetrate central Burma where he believed that the latter would outrun its supplies and suffer a decisive defeat. He imagined that the main British offensive against MANDALAY would be delivered from the north,

Battle for Meiktila and Mandalay, February–March 1945.

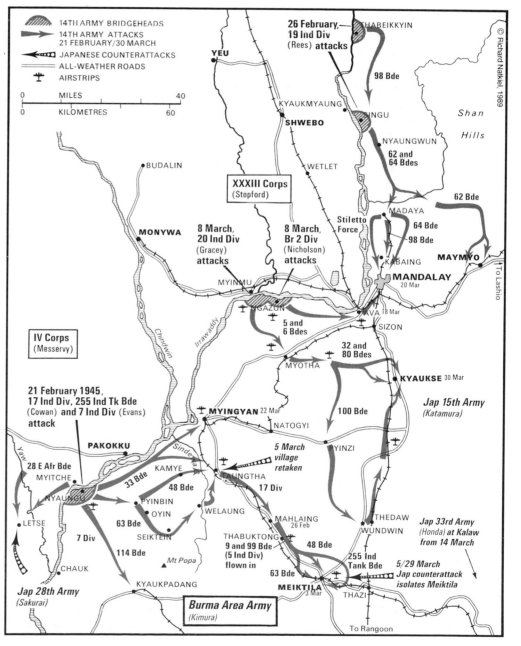

manding British troops in Iraq from 7 May, ordered them to converge on Baghdad from the south. Before the city could be assaulted, however, an armistice was concluded with the Iraqis on 31 May. The regent was reinstated and Rashid Ali and his supporters fled to Iran. The British then moved north to secure the Kirkuk and Mosul oilfields. While the despatch of British troops to Iraq was not regarded as a welcome development at the time, their presence was of considerable assistance during the subsequent campaigns in SYRIA and IRAN.

"Ironbottom Sound"

Name given to the stretch of water lying between Guadalcanal to the south and Savo and Florida Islands to the north, because of the number of ships sunk there during the naval campaign of GUADALCANAL. See also the Battles of SAVO ISLAND; CAPE ESPERANCE; First and Second GUADALCANAL; TASSAFARONGA.

Ironclad

Final Allied plan for the capture of DIEGO SUAREZ, Madagascar, September–November 1942.

Iron Guard

The Romanian equivalent of the German Nazi Party.

Ironside, FM Sir Edmund (1880–1959)

Ironside began his military career as an intelligence officer in the Boer War. After serving in various staff posts in France in 1914–18, he

Gurkhas and other troops crossing the Irawaddy, in the advance on Mandalay, 1945.

and in this context the Irrawaddy would serve as a moat against attacks from the west.

The three divisions of Lieutenant-General Sir Montagu STOPFORD's XXXIII Corps established bridgeheads across the Irrawaddy in January and February 1945. First across was 19th Indian Division, which crossed at Thabeikyin, 60 miles (96km) north of Mandalay, on 9 January. On 12 February 20th Indian Division obtained a secure hold at Allagappa, 40 miles (64km) downstream of the city. This was followed on 24 February by 2nd British Division, which established itself between 20th Division and Mandalay.

While Kimura's attention was focused on eliminating these bridgeheads, Lieutenant-General Frank MESSERVY's IV Corps was moving south through the Kabaw and Gangaw Valleys and on 14 February established a bridgehead at Pagan, downstream from the confluence of the Chindwin with the

Irrawaddy. This was steadily expanded until IV Corps broke out to capture MEIKTILA, the hub of Kimura's communications; starved of supplies, the Japanese divisions facing XXXIII Corps were compelled to embark on a retreat from which they never recovered.

The assault crossings of the Irrawaddy, in places over two miles (3.2km) wide with a minimum two-knot current, were remarkable achievements, made with simple infantry assault boats, followed by tanks and guns on rafts, and consolidated with bridging equipment which had sustained considerable damage in its long journey.

Isabella

Planned German occupation of the Atlantic coasts of Spain and Portugal, 1941.

Ise Class Battleships (Jap)

After the Battle of MIDWAY both members of

this class, *Ise* and *Iyuga*, were converted to hybrid battleship/aircraft carriers. This involved stripping out X and Y turrets and constructing a flight deck over the after part of the ship. 22 bomber seaplanes were carried, being launched by catapult and recovered by crane after they had landed alongside. Both vessels formed part of Admiral OZAWA's decoy force at the Battle of LEYTE GULF. In July 1945 they were sunk in their home ports by American air action. *Displacement* 36,000 tons; *dimensions* 708ft×111ft (215.7×33.8m); mean draught 30ft (9m); *machinery* 4-shaft geared turbines producing shp 80,000; *speed* 25.25 knots; *protection* main belt 8–12in amidships, 3–5in fore and aft; turrets 8–12in; control tower 6–12in; deck 1.25–2.5in; *armament* 12×14in (6×2); 16×5.5in (16×1) 8×5in AA (4×2); 20×25mm AA (10×2); *aircraft* 3; *complement* 1376; *number in class* 2.

Ismay, Gen Sir Hastings (1887–1965)

"Pug" Ismay was sent to Somaliland during World War I and thus saw no major action. Conscious of his lack of practical experience, he confined himself to staff appointments and rose through his undoubted ability as an administrator. In 1939 he was Head of the Secretariat of the Committee of Imperial Defence, which was the military side of the War Cabinet. When CHURCHILL took office and assumed the post of Minister of Defence, he appointed Ismay as his Chief-of-Staff. In this post he acted as the link between Churchill and the Chiefs-of-Staff Committee, frequently toning down the somewhat acerbic exchanges which passed between BROOKE and Churchill. He was also a tactful emissary between Churchill and the Americans, and attended most Allied conferences.

ISUM   Intelligence summary.

ISU-122 – Heavy Tank Destroyer (USSR)

Based on the IOSEF STALIN (IS) heavy tank chassis and armed with either a 122mm L/43 gun with a double-baffle muzzle brake or a 122mm L/45 gun with a small counter-weight on the muzzle, housed in an enclosed superstructure protected by 120mm frontal armour. Manned by a crew of five, the IS-122 served in heavy tank destroyer battalions which provided direct gunfire support during breakthrough battles. In service from early 1944.

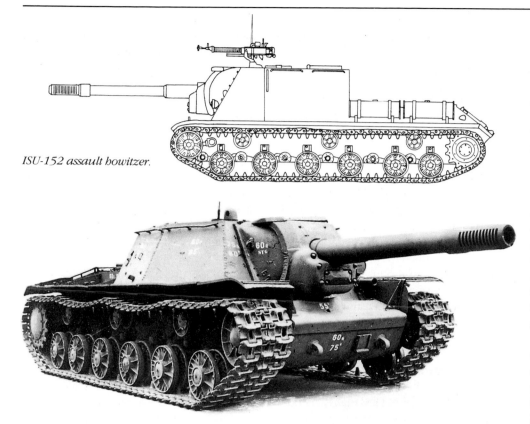

ISU-152 assault howitzer.

ISU-152 – Heavy Assault Howitzer (USSR)

Based on the IOSEF STALIN (IS) heavy tank chassis and armed with a 152mm L/29 howitzer with a prominent slotted muzzle brake, housed in an enclosed superstructure protected by 120mm frontal armour. Manned by a crew of five, the ISU-152 served in heavy assault gun units which provided direct gun-fire support during breakthrough battles. In service from early 1944.

Italian Campaign, 1943–45

The surrender of the Italian garrison on the island of PANTELLARIA on 11 June 1943 cleared the way for the invasion of SICILY by General Sir Harold ALEXANDER's 15th Army Group. On 9–10 July MONTGOMERY's British 8th Army and PATTON's US 7th Army obtained beach-heads on the south-eastern coast. After the Axis counter-attacks had been defeated, 8th Army advanced northwards towards the Mount Etna massif while 7th Army broke out to the west. The Americans, many of whom had family ties with the population, quickly cleared the western end of the island and then swung east along the northern coast towards Messina. The Axis began evacuating their troops on 3 August and on 17 August the conquest of Sicily was complete. The Italian dictator MUSSOLINI had been deposed on 24 July. His successor,

South African artillery battery advancing through the mountains of Southern Italy, summer 1944.

Marshal BADOGLIO, opened negotiations with the Allies and on 3 September Italy was secretly granted an armistice, to be effective 8 September. On 3 September 8th Army crossed the Straits of Messina and established itself in Calabria on the Italian mainland. When the terms of the armistice were published on 8 September the German troops in Italy, commanded by Field-Marshal Albert KESSELRING, reacted rapidly and disarmed their former allies. On 9 September a British division secured TARANTO and Lieutenant-General Mark CLARK's US 5th Army made an assault landing in the Gulf of SALERNO. The response of von VIETINGHOFF's German 10th Army to the latter was as prompt as it was violent and for several days the issue hung in the balance, but the approach of the British 8th Army from the south caused the Germans to withdraw.

The Italian terrain favoured the defence and the Allies' advance was halted by the GUSTAV LINE in November. Heavy fighting at CASSINO led to an Allied attempt to outflank the Gustav Line with an amphibious landing at ANZIO on 22 January 1944, but this was quickly contained. Cassino did not fall until May but the US 5th Army captured ROME on 4 June. The

German 10th and 14th Armies withdrew slowly to the prepared defences of the GOTHIC LINE. These were stormed in a series of attritional battles during the autumn but the onset of winter prevented the Allies achieving a clean breakthrough. Various command changes occurred during the winter. Vietinghoff took over from Kesselring and Clark relieved Alexander as army group commander. Command of 8th Army passed from General Sir Oliver LEESE, who had relieved Montgomery in January 1944, to General Sir Richard MCCREERY, while General Lucien TRUSCOTT assumed command of the US 5th Army for the final offensive. This succeeded in breaking through the German defences in April 1945 and a general pursuit ensued. On 29 April Vietinghoff agreed to the unconditional surrender of his troops.

Italian Somaliland, 1940–41

See EAST AFRICAN CAMPAIGN and SOMALILAND.

Iwabuchi, R Adm Sanji

In 1945 Iwabuchi commanded the Japanese naval forces in Manila. His command was independent of General YAMASHITA in the Philippines and when Yamashita ordered a withdrawal from Manila in the face of American attacks Iwabuchi determined to fight to the last man to hold the city. Dividing his 17,000-man force among the various areas of the city, Iwabuchi ordered that rather than retreat the city should be demolished building by building. This fanatical resistance caused immense difficulties for the attacking US forces, who had hoped to capture the city relatively undamaged. Artillery was brought up and although churches and hospitals largely escaped damage, almost every building suffered, any Japanese strongpoint being completely smashed. The battle raged for almost a month, at the end of which there were few surviving Japanese, very little left standing in Manila and an estimated 100,000 civilian dead. Iwabuchi was killed during the closing stages of the battle.

Iwo Jima, Bonin Islands, 1945

The airfields on this small island, only eight miles (20km) square and less than two-hours' flying time from Japan, made it an essential objective during the American advance towards the Japanese home islands. The island was heavily fortified with some 800 pillboxes, three miles of tunnels and extensive minefield and trench systems, and defended by 22,000 Japanese troops commanded by Major-General Todomichi KURIBYASHI. After a massive preliminary bombardment, the assault on Iwo Jima went in at 0900 on 19 February. The attacking force comprised two Marine divisions of Major-General Harry Schmidt's US V Amphibious Corps, 4th and 5th, with 3rd Marine Division initially held back as the corps reserve. Resistance was fanatical, but on 23 February the island's dominating physical feature, Mount Suribachi, was stormed. By 11 March the surviving Japanese had been confined to a pocket at the northern tip of the island, and organized resistance ended on 16 March. Casualties among Schmidt's men amounted to 6891 killed and 18,700 wounded. Only 212 of the Japanese garrison chose to surrender. Iwo Jima subsequently played an important role in the air offensive against Japan. Using its airfields, short-range fighters flew top-cover escort for bomber forces, and the airstrip also provided damaged bombers with an emergency stopping point.

Marines on Iwo Jima, February 1945.

J

"J" and "K" Class Destroyers (UK)

Displacement 1690 tons; *dimensions* 356ft 6in×35ft 9in (109×10.9m); *mean draught* 9ft (2.7m); *machinery* 2-shaft geared turbines producing shp 40,000; *speed* 36 knots; *armament* 6×4.7in (3×2); 4×2-pdr AA (1×4); 8×0.5in AA (2×4) guns; 10×21in (2×5) torpedo tubes; *complement* 183; *number in class* 16, launched 1938–39.

Jagdpanther (Hunting Panther) – Heavy Tank Destroyer (Ger)

The Jagdpanther, as its name implies, was based on the PANTHER tank chassis and was armed with an 88mm L/71 Pak 43/3 gun mounted in a well-angled enclosed superstructure. This weapon was capable of penetrating every Allied tank in service and the vehicle's 80mm front armour was laid back to provide the equivalent protection of 160mm; secondary armament was provided by a machine gun housed in the glacis. The Jagdpanther weighed 45 tons, had a maximum speed of 45mph (72kph) and was manned by a crew of five. It was regarded by many as the best tank destroyer design of the war, although the main armament's limited traverse was a disadvantage, as was the vehicle's height of almost nine feet, which made concealment difficult. The Jagdpanther entered service in

Jagdpanzer IV.

1944, replacing the NASHORN in the heavy tank destroyer battalions operating under the control of army commanders. It had been hoped that 150 of these impressive vehicles could be built each month, but bombing and material shortages combined to reduce the total production run to 382.

Jagdpanzer IV – Tank Destroyer (Ger)

The Jagdpanzer IV was based on the chassis of the PANZERKAMPFWAGEN IV and its layout followed that of the assault gun, with the fighting compartment forward. The superstructure consisted of well-angled armour plate, extended to the vehicle's rear, the overall configuration giving rise to the nickname of "Guderian's Duck". The first gun to be fitted was the 75mm L/48 Pak 39, later replaced by

the more powerful 75mm L/70 KwK 42, the main armament entering the vehicle through a "Pig's Head" mantlet, to the right of which a conical hatch concealed a machine gun. The Jagdpanzer IV was manned by a crew of four and its frontal armour was 80mm thick; it weighed 24 tons and had a maximum speed of 24mph (39kph). Side skirts were often fitted as a defence against shaped charge ammunition and a coating of ZIMMERIT was usually applied. It began entering service towards the end of 1943, replacing the MARDERS in the tank destroyer battalions of the Panzer divisions. Although an efficient design, only 1531 vehicles of this type had been completed when the war ended.

Jagdtiger (Hunting Tiger) – Heavy Tank Destroyer (Ger)

The most heavily armed AFV of the war, the Jagdtiger was based on the complicated TIGER B tank chassis and mounted a 128mm L/55 Pak 80 gun, housed in a fixed superstructure consisting of 250mm front, 80mm side and 40mm roof armour. The vehicle weighed over 70 tons and while it was capable of achieving a maximum speed of 23mph (37kph) its electro-mechanical transmission was subject to failure, attempts to tow by another Jagdtiger often resulting in a second breakdown. 38 rounds of main armament ammunition could be stowed, split for ease of handling by the loader, although this meant that the vehicle's rate of fire was slower than that of tank destroyers using fixed ammunition. A

Jagdpanther.

machine gun was housed in the glacis plate. 48 of these vehicles were built in 1944, serving with heavy tank destroyer battalions and Waffen SS armoured formations. Given the existence of efficient tank destroyer designs like the HETZER, JAGDPANTHER and JAGDPANZER IV, they represented a waste of resources. The Jagdtiger was manned by a crew of six.

Jägerfaust

Also known as SG-500, this was a German air-to-air weapon consisting of a thick-walled rifled steel tube, closed at one end and loaded with a propelling charge and a 50mm (2in) high explosive shell. This was loaded into a vertically-mounted tube fitted into the wing or body of an aircraft; the number of tubes varied – the MESSERSCHMITT Me 163 carried six, while the Me 240 was to have carried 30. The tubes were mounted at a slight angle to spread the shots. In use, the aircraft attacked its target from below and fired the Jägerfaust when beneath; the shell was fired upwards, and the steel tube was ejected downwards to give a recoilless effect. By March 1945, 12 Me 163 aircraft fitted with Jägerfaust were deployed at an airfield near Leipzig; some sources aver that Allied aircraft were shot down with this weapon, but this has never been confirmed.

Jalo, Libya, 1941–42

Oasis located 250 miles (402km) south of BENGHAZI and west of the Kalansho Sand Sea, containing a small fort, barracks and an airstrip. Jalo changed hands several times during the desert war and at one stage was used as a forward base by the LONG RANGE DESERT GROUP. In September 1942 it was held by an Italian garrison which succeeded in beating off a determined attack by the Sudan Defence Force. See *The Raiders – Desert Strike Force* by Arthur Swinson (Macdonald).

Japanese Aircraft Reporting Codes

When the war between the USA and Japan broke out in 1941 the US forces were confronted with many aircraft of which they had little knowledge, and this lack of information included the correct nomenclature. The US therefore adopted the practice of bestowing nicknames on all Japanese aircraft so as to identify them more readily. Even when the correct nomenclature became known, the nicknames were retained for their conciseness and convenience. Much the same practice is used with Soviet equipment today.

The following are the nicknames used: Alf – Kawanishi E7K2; Ann – Mitsubishi Ki-30; Babs – Mitsubishi Ki-15; Baka – Yokosuka MXY-7; Betty – Mitsubishi G4M; Buzzard – Nippon Ku-7; Cherry – Yokosuka H5Y1; Clara – Tachikawa Ki-70; Claude – Mitsubishi A5M; Cypress – Nippon Ki-8; Dave – Nakajima E8N; Dinah – Mitsubishi Ki-46; Emily – Kawanishi H8K; Frances – Yokosuka P1Y; Frank – Nakajima Ki-84; George – Kawanishi Shiden; Glen – Yokosuka E14Y1; Goose – Nippon Ku-8; Grace – Aichi B7A; Helen – Nakajima Ki-49; Hickory – Tachikawa Ki-54; Ida – Tachikawa Ki-36; Irving – Nakajima J1N; Jack – Mitsubishi J2M; Jake – Aichi E13A; Jill – Nakajima B6N; Judy – Yokosuka D4Y; Kate – Nakajima B5N; Lily – Kawasaki Ki-48; Liz – Nakajima G5N1; Lorna – Kyushu Q1W1; Mary – Kawasaki Ki-32; Mavis – Kawanishi H6K; Myrt – Nakajima C6N; Nate – Nakajima Ki-27; Nell – Mitsubishi G3M; Nick – Kawasaki Ki-45; Norm – Kawanishi E15K1; Oscar – Nakajima Ki-43; Patsy – Tachikawa Ki-74; Paul – Aichi E16A1; Peggy – Mitsubishi Ki-67; Pete – Mitsubishi F1M2; Pine – Mitsubishi K3M; Randy – Kawasaki Ki-102; Rex – Kawanishi N1K1; Rita – Nakajima G8N1; Rob – Kawasaki Ki-64; Rufe – Mitsubishi A6M2-N; Sally – Mitsubishi Ki-21; Sam – Mitsubishi A7M2; Slim – Kyushu E9W1; Sonia – Mitsubishi Ki-51; Spruce – Tachikawa Ki-9; Stella – Nippon Ki-76; Susie – Aichi D1A2-K; Tabby – Showa L2D2; Thalia – Kawasaki Ki-56; Theresa – Nippon Ki-49; Thora – Nakajima Ki-34; Tojo – Nakajima Ki-44; Tony – Kawasaki Ki-61; Topsy – Mitsubishi Ki-57; Val – Aichi D3A; Willow – Yokosuka K5Y; Zeke – Mitsubishi A6M.

Jassy–Kishinev, Romania/Soviet Union, 1944

The area in which the Soviet 2nd Ukrainian Front (MALINOVSKY) and 3rd Ukrainian Front (TOLBUKHIN) smashed through, respectively, the Romanian 4th and 3rd Armies on 20 August, executing a double envelopment which trapped part of the German 6th Army and other elements of Freissner's Army Group South Ukraine. The speed with which the Russians exploited their victory led directly to the defection of Romania and BULGARIA from the Axis cause. See also BUCHAREST.

Java Sea, Battle of the, 1942

On 27 February 1942 an Allied squadron commanded by Rear-Admiral Karel Doorman and consisting of the cruisers RNNS *De Ruyter* and *Java*, HMS *Exeter*, HMAS *Perth* and USS *Houston*, escorted by five American, three British and two Dutch destroyers, attempted to intercept the Japanese Eastern Invasion Force heading for Java. The 41 transports of this were protected by a close escort consisting of the cruiser *Naka* and six destroyers under Rear-Admiral Nishimura, plus a covering force composed of the cruisers *Nachi*, *Naguro* and *Jintsu* and twelve destroyers under Rear-Admiral Takeo TAKAGI. The action commenced at 1616 with a gunnery duel in which the only Allied ships capable of reaching the enemy were *Exeter* and *Houston*. At 1708 *Exeter* was hit in the boiler room and turned out of line, and at about the same time the Dutch destroyer *Kortenaer* was sunk by a LONG LANCE torpedo. At 1800 the destroyer HMS *Electra* was sunk by gunfire but in return *Perth* crippled the Japanese destroyer *Asugumo*. The range had now closed somewhat and when *Perth* scored again at 1830, hitting *Nagumo*, both sides broke contact. Doorman detached his remaining Dutch destroyer, *Witte de With*, to escort *Exeter* to Surabaya, followed by the American destroyers, which were critically short of fuel. He then attempted a further attack on the Japanese convoy but at 2125 the destroyer HMS *Jupiter* struck a mine and sank and at 2200 the last Allied destroyer, HMS *Encounter*, was detached to pick up *Kortenaer*'s survivors. At 2300 Doorman's cruisers encountered Takagi's screening force again and after a brief exchange of gunfire the latter launched a salvo of Long Lance torpedoes which sank *De Ruyter*, with Doorman aboard, and *Java*. *Perth* and *Houston* broke contact and the following night attempted to pass through the Sunda Strait. They ran straight into the equally heavily escorted Japanese Western Invasion Force and went down fighting after an epic battle in which they sank a minesweeper and a transport, damaged three destroyers and drove three transports ashore. *Exeter*, having completed temporary repairs, left Surabaya on 28 February escorted by *Encounter* and the American destroyer *Pope* but all three were sunk by Japanese warships and aircraft next day. Of Doorman's entire squadron only four American destroyers managed to reach the safety of Australian waters. The decisive nature of the battle enabled the Japanese to complete their conquest of the Dutch East Indies in half the time they had anticipated.

JCS Joint Chiefs of Staff.

Jebel Akhdar, Libya, 1941–42

Massif occupying the northern area of the BENGHAZI Bulge in central Cyrenaica.

Jeep (USA)

Officially designated the Truck Utility Quarter-ton, the Jeep was evolved as a result of a US Army specification for a "go anywhere" light vehicle issued in June 1940. The organizations most closely involved in its design were the Bantam Car Company of Butler, Pennsylvania, Willys-Overland of Toledo, Ohio, and the Ford Motor Company. Willys were awarded the contract in July 1941 but in view of heavy demands for the vehicle Ford were also brought in and together the two built 639,245 Jeeps before the war ended. The standard Jeep could seat four, weighed one-and-a-quarter tons, and was driven by a Willys 441 or 442 "Go Devil" four-cylinder petrol engine developing 60bhp. Its transmission included a three-speed synchromesh gearbox and two-speed transfer box giving six forward and two reverse gears, and the driver could engage two- or four-wheel drive depending on the going to be traversed. The Jeep served in every theatre of war and became a byword for mobility in terrain as diverse as frozen steppeland, mountains, desert and jungle, as well as being air-portable aboard the RAF's HORSA glider. It was supplied to all of America's allies, being used for every conceivable military purpose compatible with its size. Armed with Vickers K and Browning machine guns, it provided the Long Range Desert Group and the Special Air Service Regiment with an ideal raiding vehicle and, fitted with flanged steel wheels, it provided motive power on the railways of northern Burma. The original Jeep remained in service for many years after the war and the concept still survives.

Jervis Bay, HMS – Armed Merchant Cruiser

On 5 November 1940 a British convoy of 37 merchant ships, escorted by *Jervis Bay*, was intercepted in the North Atlantic by the German pocket-battleship ADMIRAL SCHEER. Captain E. S. F. Fegen, commanding *Jervis Bay*, ordered the convoy to scatter and, although hopelessly outgunned and outranged, engaged his heavily armoured opponent until his ship went down fighting. As a result of the *Jervis Bay*'s gallant self-sacrifice most of the convoy escaped and only five ships were lost. Fegen was awarded the Victoria Cross posthumously. See also SAN DEMETRIO.

Jeeps in Italy.

Jeschonnek, Col Gen Hans (1899–1943)

In March 1942 Jeschonnek was the youngest Colonel-General in the Wehrmacht. He was a dedicated National Socialist and unswervingly loyal to HITLER. However, he failed to gain the undivided respect of the Luftwaffe high command, many of whom were his seniors in age and rank, and was equally unsuccessful in establishing a satisfactory working relationship with GÖRING and MILCH. Jeschonnek displayed a limited grasp of the tactical and technical demands of the air war from 1942. He neglected the fighter defences of the Reich and underestimated the Allies' four-engined bombers. Moreover, his position was increasingly undermined by political in-fighting in the Luftwaffe. He was forced to endure a tongue-lashing from Hitler immediately after the US 8th Air Force's raids on SCHWEINFURT and Regensburg on 17 August 1943. Early next morning he received the news that RAF BOMBER COMMAND had made a heavy raid on PEENEMUNDE. On Jeschonnek's orders his night fighters had mistakenly assembled over Berlin, where they had been fired upon by their own anti-aircraft batteries. The demoralized Jeschonnek shot himself on the same day.

Jimma, Ethiopia, 1941

In June the Italian garrison commander, General Gazzera, anxious that the civilians for whom he was responsible would be protected from Ethiopian guerrilla groups when he withdrew, wrote to General CUNNINGHAM inviting him to take the town. He then retreated north with the bulk of his forces, leaving 15,000 men behind to maintain order while 22nd East African Brigade (11th African Division) hurried forward, entering Jimma unopposed on 21 June.

Jock Column

Small mobile column consisting of armoured cars, lorried infantry, anti-tank and field guns, named after the originator of the idea, Lieutenant-Colonel (later Brigadier) Jock CAMPBELL. During the early months of the war in North Africa the British used Jock Columns effectively against the numerically superior but less mobile Italians. It was, however, a mistake to continue using them after the better-equipped Germans arrived in Africa as they detracted from divisional artillery resources.

General Jodl speaking to Hitler in his headquarters.

Jodl, General Alfried (1890–1946)

Jodl served with the Bavarian artillery and the General Staff in World War I and remained in the Reichswehr after 1918. In 1938 he became head of the Operations Section of the OKW, and in August 1939 was appointed Chief of Staff to Field Marshal KEITEL. Since Keitel was primarily a political appointee, Jodl became the effective commander of German operations in all theatres except Russia. Jodl attended the twice-daily HITLER conferences, becoming the principal presenting officer, and was the instrument for turning Hitler's ideas into practical orders for the armies. He probably had more responsibility for German operations than anyone other than Hitler, and was regarded as the only reliable source of information on Hitler's thoughts and intentions. He was, however, a realist and by 1942 had concluded that the war was lost. Convinced that Germany's defeat in 1918 had been brought about by internal dissensions within the Reich, he strove to keep his true feelings in check. Thus loyalty to the Führer overrode direct objections to Hitler's conduct of operations, while Jodl's lack of experience in the field tended to make him underrate the practical effect of orders on troops in the field. Jodl was reluctant to listen to the views of field commanders, so that as well as sharing the credit for Germany's victories, he was also responsible in large measure for her defeats.

Jodl signed the German surrender at Rheims on 7 May 1945. He was tried at NUREMBERG for war crimes, principally his approval of the shooting of hostages and prisoners, was sentenced to death and hanged.

"Joe's Bridge", Belgium, 1944

A bridge over the Meuse–Escaut Canal near Neerpelt captured intact by 2nd Irish Guards (Guards Armoured Division) on 9 September, thus opening up an avenue of advance into Holland. Officially known as the De Groot Bridge, it was renamed in honour of the regiment's commanding officer, Lieutenant-Colonel "Joe" Vandaleur.

John C. Butler Class Destroyer Escorts (USA)

Displacement 1350 tons; *dimensions* 306ft×36ft 9in (91.8×10.8m); *machinery* 2-shaft geared turbines producing shp 12,000; *speed* 24 knots; *armament* 2×5in; 10×40mm AA; 3×21in torpedo tubes; *complement* 200; *number in class* 83, launched 1943–44.

Jones, Dr R. V. (1911–   )

A physicist, Dr Jones became involved in 1935 in research for the TIZARD Committee on Air Defence into the use of infra-red techniques for the detection of aircraft. From this he became involved in the early research on RADAR, and on the outbreak of war moved to the Air Ministry's Directorate of Scientific Research and finally to Air Intelligence, where he remained for the rest of the war. He was instrumental in detecting many German electronic warfare systems, notably the KNICKEBEIN and X-GERÄT beams which guided German bombers and the various stages in German radar deployment, and was also of vital importance in the countermeasures devised against the German V-WEAPONS.

Joubert de la Ferté, ACM Sir Philip B. (1897–1965)

Joubert de la Ferté was among the pioneers of aviation. He learned to fly before 1914, and served as a pilot throughout World War I with the Royal Flying Corps and latterly with the RAF. He served in a number of staff and line appointments between the wars and in 1941 was appointed Commander-in-Chief of COASTAL COMMAND, tasked with the protection of convoys and the destruction of German submarines and surface craft. Coastal Command discharged its duties with exemplary efficiency, though for much of the time it was starved of equipment as the result of the high priority given to BOMBER COMMAND. In 1943 Joubert de la Ferté was appointed Deputy Chief of Staff for Information and Civil Affairs in Lord Louis MOUNTBATTEN's South-East Asia Command.

Joyce, William (1906–40)

Joyce was born in New York to an Irish father and an English mother, but moved to England in 1921, attended London University and later became involved with Mosley's British Union of Fascists. Too extreme for Mosley, he was expelled, whereupon he founded his own party, the British National Socialist League. On the eve of the war he and his wife left for Germany, where he offered his services to the Nazis and became a broadcaster. His transmissions to England became legendary, and his pseudo-upper class accent led to his nickname of "Lord Haw-Haw". Although he was scarcely taken seriously in Britain, he nevertheless acquired a reputation for omniscience; stories abounded of how he had commented on the stopping of a church clock in some town, or some other minor occurrence which would never reach the national press. None of these stories were ever authenticated, and the records of his broadcasts do not bear them out, but he became notorious for his assumed network of informers. Captured by British troops near Flensburg in 1945, he was tried in London for high treason and sentenced to death. His defence was that he was an American citizen, but the fact that he possessed a British passport until the middle of 1940 was sufficient to condemn him. In truth, the British public wanted him hanged irrespective of any legal niceties, and he was.

JPS Joint Planning Staff.

Jubilee
British–Canadian raid on DIEPPE, August 1942.

Judgement
Fleet Air Arm attack on the Italian battlefleet at TARANTO, November 1940.

Juin, Marshal Alphonse (1888–1967)
Juin was a graduate of St Cyr and contemporary with DE GAULLE. In 1940 he commanded the 15th Motorized Brigade of the 1st French Army and was captured by the Germans in May. In June 1941, at the request of PÉTAIN, he was released and was offered the post of Minister of War in the Vichy government, but turned it down in favour of being Commander-in-Chief North Africa, succeeding WEYGAND. When the Allies invaded in November 1942, he joined them, subsequently leading French troops against ROMMEL in Tunisia and against KESSELRING in Italy and distinguishing himself in the Battle of the GARIGLIANO in 1944. He then became Chief of Staff of the French National Defence Committee and aided in the liberation of France. He was posthumously appointed a Marshal of France by De Gaulle.

July Bomb Plot, Germany, 1944
As the war continued a number of senior German officers and prominent civilians recognized that HITLER would bring nothing but ruin to Germany and that the only solution lay in his assassination and the removal of the Nazi administration. Among the principal conspirators were General Ludwig BECK, a former chief of Army General Staff who was to be Head of State on Hitler's death; Admiral Wilhelm CANARIS, Chief of the *Abwehr*; General Oster, Canaris' Deputy; Field-Marshal von WITZLEBEN, who was to be made Commander-in-Chief of the German Army if the coup succeeded; Colonel-General Olbricht, on the staff of the Replacement Army; Colonel-General von STÜLPNAGEL, the Military Governor of France; Major-General

Mussolini visits Hitler after the July Bomb Plot. Left to right: Göring, Himmler, Schaub, Loerzer, Hitler and Mussolini.

von TRESKOW, Chief of Staff to Army Group Centre; Colonel Count Claus von STAUFFENBERG; Dr Carl Gördeler, a former Mayor of Leipzig; Pastor Dietrich BONHOFFER; and Ulrich von Hassell, a former German Ambassador to Rome. Many senior officers, including von KLUGE, von MANSTEIN, ROMMEL and von RUNDSTEDT, were aware of the conspiracy and while they did not provide active support, neither did they betray it. The conspirators masked their activities under the codename of VALKYRIE, which was also the name of a contingency plan to be activated in the event of a rising by slave labour in Germany. They were aware that previous attempts on the Führer's life had failed because his excellent security precautions made him difficult to approach. Stauffenberg, however, was trusted by the Nazi Establishment and he was selected to place an explosive device in the briefing room at Hitler's headquarters near Rastenburg, East Prussia, during a conference held on 20 July. The bomb, contained in his briefcase, was deposited under the map table and Stauffenberg left the room, apparently to answer a telephone call but in reality to make good his escape. At 1242 the bomb exploded, killing General Korten, the Luftwaffe Chief of Staff, General Schmundt, Hitler's personal adjutant, and two others, but Hitler sustained

only minor injuries and at 1800 the news that he had survived an assassination attempt was broadcast. In Berlin and Paris the conspirators bungled their attempt to seize power and the coup collapsed.

Hitler's revenge was swift and terrible. The conspirators and those suspected of being sympathetic towards them were either permitted the privilege of committing suicide or were executed after sham trials. At least 250, including two field-marshals and 16 generals, are known to have met their end in this way, their death agonies being filmed for the entertainment of Hitler and his entourage. An estimated 10,000 were sent to concentration camps. See *The German Army 1933–1945* by Matthew Cooper (Macdonald and Jane's).

Junkers Aircraft (Ger)
Junkers Ju52/3m This classic aircraft first appeared in 1932, replacing the original Ju52 design. In trimotor form the Ju52 was first developed as a 15/18 seater airliner which was used throughout the world. In 1935 a bomber adaptation went into Luftwaffe service and a number saw combat in Spain. Subsequently the type became the standard troop and cargo transport for the German forces and saw service in every theatre. Highly resistant to damage, reliable, and with excellent short

German infantrymen leave a Ju52 transport after landing on Crete, May 1941.

proved very vulnerable, particularly as it came out of its dive. Thereafter it was used only where the Luftwaffe had air superiority or against shipping. The celebrated name, Stuka, was an abbreviation of the German *Sturzkampfflugzeug*, literally "diving warplane". Originally applicable to all dive-bombers, the contraction became the name for the Ju87. *Span* 45.25ft (13.8m); *engine* 1 1400hp in-line; *crew* 2; *armament* 4 machine guns, 1550lb (7000kg) of bombs; *speed* 255mph (410kph).

Junkers Ju88 The best all-round aircraft of the war was designed as a high-speed medium bomber with a dive-bombing capability. It entered service in 1939. Few other aircraft proved so suitable for modification and adaptation to other roles. It was developed constantly in the bombing role, being given more powerful engines, heavier armament and armour and a greater wingspan. It was employed as a dive-bomber, as a highly effec-

take-off and landing capabilities, "Iron Annie" or "Auntie Ju" earned the affection of soldiers and airmen alike until the war ended, and many stayed in service with other air forces until the late 1970s. *Span* 96ft (29.3m); *engines* 3 830hp radial; *crew* 2 or 3; *armament* 3 machine guns; *speed* 165mph (265kph).

Junkers Ju86 Originally conceived as a commercial airliner, the Ju86 then became a medium bomber. A number went to Spain in 1937 where they proved vulnerable to fighters, and various modifications, notably better engines, were made. Some were used to bomb Poland in 1939 but were subsequently withdrawn from bombing and used as trainers and transports. Versions with greater wingspan, more powerful engines, and pressurized cabins were developed for high-altitude reconnaissance, in which role they were very successful. *Span* 84ft (25.6m) (enlarged to 105ft (32m)); *engines* 2 1000hp in-line; *crew* 5; *armament* 3 machine guns, 2200lb (1000kg) of bombs; *speed* 260mph (418kph).

Junkers Ju87 One of the most famous of German aircraft, the Stuka dive-bomber formed the spearhead of the BLITZKRIEG, acting as the flying artillery arm of the mobile ground force. Attacking in a near-vertical dive, with siren screaming, the effect of the Stuka was as much psychological as real. However when confronted with fighter aircraft the Ju87

Junkers Ju87 dive bomber.

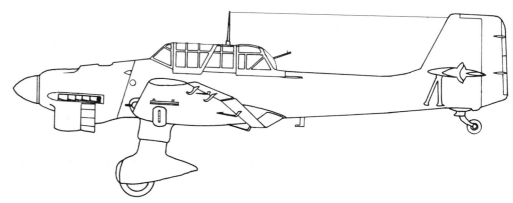

Junkers Ju87 "Stuka" dive bombers in flight.

Junkers Ju 88 at a forward Luftwaffe base near the River Don, Russia.

tive night fighter, on mine-laying, reconnaissance, torpedo-bombing, day fighting, ground-attack, photographic and training tasks, all of which it performed well. By 1945 almost 15,000 had been built. *Span* 66ft (20m); *engines* 2 1410hp in-line; *crew* 3; *armament* varied, up to 5 20mm cannon, 4 machine guns, up to 6600lb (3000kg) of bombs; *speed* 270mph (434kph).

Junkers Ju188 The Ju188 was an improved version of the JU88 which appeared in 1941. It was larger and more powerful and the crew were located so as to improve the defensive armament. Like the Ju88, it was modified into several variants, including night fighter, torpedo-bomber and reconnaissance. Over 1000 were built, and there were improved versions such as the Ju288, 388 and 488. *Span* 72ft (22m); *engines* 2 1776hp in-line; *crew* 4; *armament* 1 20mm cannon, 4 machine guns, 6600lb (3000kg) of bombs; *speed* 325mph (523kph).

Junkers Ju290 This was a militarized version of the pre-war Ju90 commercial transport developed in 1941. It was intended to replace the FOCKE-WULF FW 200 in the maritime recon-

naissance role, but it never fulfilled this role, although it saw limited service as a maritime bomber. Clearly underpowered for this task, it was relegated to transport and reconnaissance duties. *Span* 138ft (42m); *engines* 4 1600hp radial; *armament* 3 20mm cannon, 1 machine gun, bombs or glider-bombs up to 2200lb (1000kg); *speed* 280mph (450kph).

Juno Beach, Normandy, 1944

Located in the centre of the British D-DAY landing sector. Because of offshore reefs H-Hour had been set at 0735, when the rising tide would permit sufficient margin for the landing craft to pass over them. However, sea conditions were the worst encountered on any sector and the assault was delayed. This meant that the tide had risen to the point at which the beach obstacles were invisible, but in the event few landing craft were damaged during the run-in, although many were sunk or damaged when they attempted to return to their mother ships. The two leading brigades of 3rd Canadian Division landed ahead of their armour, meeting determined resistance from the enemy positions on the waterfront,

particularly at Bernières-sur-Mer. Some amphibious tanks were launched on the right flank of the assault but on the left they were landed direct from their LSTs. Their arrival, followed by 79th Armoured Division's specialist teams at 0830, eased the situation but as more troops landed the congestion produced a traffic jam which reduced the momentum of the Canadian advance inland. A handful of tanks almost reached CARPIQUET but were forced to retire due to lack of support. Nevertheless, by midnight the 9th Canadian Brigade was seven miles (11km) from the coast and on the western flank contact had been established with the British 50th Division at La Rivière. Some 21,500 troops and their equipment landed on Juno Beach during D-Day.

Junyo Class Aircraft Carriers (Jap)

The two ships of this class, *Junyo* and *Hiyo*, were originally laid down as commercial liners and converted to aircraft carriers in 1940–42. *Junyo* took part in the operations against the ALEUTIAN ISLANDS and fought at the Battle of SANTA CRUZ, where her aircraft played a significant part in sinking the carrier USS HORNET. With *Hiyo*, she subsequently formed the 2nd Carrier Division. During the Battle of the PHILIPPINE SEA *Hiyo* was struck by two air-launched torpedoes and, although she survived their impact, blew up and sank several hours later. *Junyo* was seriously damaged in the same engagement and was torpedoed shortly after repairs had been completed in December 1944. She returned to her base in Japan and took no further part in the war. *Displacement* 24,140 tons; *dimensions* 719ft 6in×87ft 9in (219×26m); mean draught 26ft 9in (8.15m); *machinery* 2-shaft geared turbines producing shp 56,250; *speed* 25.5 knots designed, 22.5 max in operations; *armament* 12×5in AA (6×2); 24×25mm AA (8×3); *aircraft* 53; *complement* 1224; *number in class* 2.

Jupiter

British capture of Hill 112, near CAEN, July 1944.

K

"K" Class Destroyers

See "J" AND "K" CLASS DESTROYERS.

Kabaw Valley, Manipur, India, 1944

The Kabaw Valley lies west of and parallel to the CHINDWIN. Used by part of the Japanese 15th Army during its approach march to IMPHAL and by the British 14th Army in the pursuit which followed the collapse of the Japanese U-GO offensive.

Kaga, IJN – Aircraft Carrier

Originally laid down as a battleship, *Kaga* was completed as a carrier in 1928 and modernized in 1935. With AKAGI she formed the First Carrier Division and took part in the attack on PEARL HARBOR as well as Admiral NAGUMO's subsequent operations in the East Indies, the South Pacific and the Indian Ocean. During the Battle of MIDWAY she was hit by four bombs which started uncontrollable fires and, after blazing for more than nine hours, she blew up and sank. *Displacement* 38,200 tons; *dimensions* 812ft 6in×106ft 9in (247.6×32.5m); mean draught 30ft (9.1m); *machinery* 4-shaft geared turbines producing shp 127,400; *speed* 28.5 knots; *protection* main belt 11in amidships, 9–11in fore and aft; *armament* 10×8in (10×1 in casemates); 16×5in; 30×25mm AA (11×2); *aircraft* 90; *complement* 2016.

Kagero Class Destroyers (Jap)

Displacement 2033 tons; *dimensions* 388ft 9in×35ft 6in (118.5×10.82m); mean draught 12ft 4in (3.75m); *machinery* 2-shaft geared turbines producing shp 52,000; *speed* 35.5 knots; *armament* 6×5in DP (3×2); 4×25mm AA; 2×13mm; 8×24in torpedo tubes (2×4); *complement* 240; *number in class* 18, launched 1938–41.

Kaikoban Class I Escorts (Jap)

Displacement 745 tons; *dimensions* 221ft 6in×27ft 6in (67.5×8.4m); mean draught 9ft 6in (2.9m); *machinery* 2-shaft geared diesels producing shp 1900; *speed* 16.5 knots; *arma-

ment* 2×4.7in DP (2×1); 6×25mm AA; 1×3in trench mortar; 120 depth charges; *complement* 136; *number in class* 56, launched 1944–45.

Kaikoban Class II Escorts (Jap)

Displacement 740 tons; *dimensions* 228ft×28ft 3in (69.4×8.6m); mean draught 11ft 9in (3.6m); *machinery* 1-shaft geared turbine producing shp 2500; *speed* 17.5 knots; *armament* 2×4.7in DP (2×1); 6×25mm AA; 1×3in trench mortar; 120 depth charges and 12 throwers; *complement* 160; *number in class* 68, launched 1944–45.

Kaiser, Henry J. (1882–1967)

After leaving school at the age of 11 Kaiser found his niche as a constructional engineer and in the 1930s was responsible for building the Boulder, Bonneville and Grand Coulee dams in the United States. In 1941 he was made responsible for many of the shipyards which were to build the LIBERTY SHIPS, standardized cargo vessels for supplying the

Allied requirements all over the world. Kaiser had never seen a shipyard, but set about organizing new methods of construction and fabrication and reduced the time for building a ship from 105 to 46 days. In postwar years he developed a revolutionary car but was less successful with this.

Kaiten Suicide Submarines (Jap)

These craft were based on the Type 93 torpedo, the intention being that they should be guided towards their target by their pilot, the warhead detonating on impact. Several types were built, the most numerous being the Kaiten 1, which were powered by a 550hp petrol and oxygen engine. At their maximum speed of 30 knots the craft had an operational radius of 25,100 yards (22,950m), rising proportionately to 85,300 yards (26,000m) at 12 knots. The Kaiten were conceived as a last line of defence against the Allied advance on the Japanese home islands, and this in itself demonstrated the bankrupt state of the Imperial Navy in 1945. See also SHINYO.

Japanese kaiten tested from the cruiser Kitakami, *February 1945.*

Kalinin Front: Soviet infantry close in on the wreckage of a crashed German aircraft.

retained at Hotin, since this offered good going and would allow his army to withdraw into Romania. Hübe, however, chose to break out to the west, although this route traversed broken country and involved crossing the rivers Sbrucz, Sereth and Strypa, his reasons being that it would seem unattractive to the Russians and provided the possibility of a junction with a relief force from the restored German line. The break-out began during the night of 27/28 March and for the next fortnight 1st Panzer Army slowly fought its way westwards. On 15 April its spearheads crossed the Strypa and the following day effected a junction with the relief force, consisting of the reinforced II SS Panzer Corps, near Buczacz. Hübe was awarded the Diamonds to his Knight's Cross but on 21 April was killed in an air crash on his way to receive the decoration.

Kaiyo, IJN – Aircraft Carrier

Originally the liner *Argentina Maru*, converted to a light aircraft carrier 1942–43. *Kaiyo* was used to ferry aircraft to isolated island garrisons and then for training. She was sunk by air attack in Beppu Bay on 10 August 1945. *Displacement* 13,600 tons; *dimensions* 545ft 4in×69ft (166×21m); mean draught 26ft 6in (8m); *machinery* 2-shaft geared turbines producing shp 52,000; *speed* 23.75 knots; *armament* 8×5in AA (4×2); 24×25mm AA (8×3); *aircraft* 24; *complement* 829.

Kalamata, Greece, 1941

A town on the south coast of the Peloponnesus. On 28 May the leading elements of 5th Panzer Division penetrated Kalamata, where some 7000 British troops, mainly from line-of-communication units, were awaiting evacuation. Many were captured but the remainder counter-attacked with such vigour that the German spearhead was itself surrounded and forced to surrender. However, the ferocity of the fighting ashore convinced the commander of the approaching Royal Navy squadron that he was not justified in hazarding his ships for so few men and he gave orders to turn away. Thus, at the end of the day, the roles of captor and captive were again reversed.

Kalewa, Burma, 1942–45

A town on the CHINDWIN through which the British withdrew from Burma in 1942. During the 14th Army's advance into Burma in 1944, Kalewa was captured by the 11th East African Division (XXXIII Corps) on 2 December and a

1150ft (350m) Bailey bridge – the longest in history – was constructed within a period of eight days.

Kalinin, Soviet Union, 1941

City on the main LENINGRAD highway 100 miles (160km) north-west of MOSCOW, captured by the German 9th Army on 14 October. Recaptured after heavy fighting by KONEV's Kalinin Front during the Soviet counteroffensive in December.

Kaltenbrunner, Dr Ernst (1902–46)

Kaltenbrunner was an early member of the Nazi party who by 1938 had risen to the head of the Austrian SS. In 1943 he replaced the assassinated HEYDRICH as head of the Reichs Main Security Office. Here he controlled the Gestapo, the SS, the extermination squads and the concentration camps. He continued to implement HITLER's policies of extermination of Jews, gypsies, prisoners-of-war, commissars and enemies of the state, showing not a shred of conscience. At the NUREMBERG trials he coolly refused to acknowledge his own signature on documents. He was sentenced to death and hanged in October 1946.

Kamenets-Podolsk, Soviet Union, 1944

Area in which the 1st and 2nd Ukrainian Fronts isolated Colonel-General Hans Hübe's 1st Panzer Army in a double envelopment on 25 March. The Russians anticipated that Hübe would attempt to break out to the south, using a bridgehead over the Dniester which he still

Kamikaze

Kamikaze is a Japanese word meaning "divine wind" and originally referred to a fortuitous wind which wrecked a Mongol fleet sailing to invade Japan in the 13th century. The term was appropriated in 1944 to describe a Special Force of suicide pilots who flew their aircraft into collision with US warships in an attempt to destroy them. Initially any type of military aircraft capable of carrying a bomb was employed, but late in the war a specially-designed piloted flying bomb known as Okha (but known to the US forces as Baka) was developed. The initial attacks did considerable damage to the wooden decks of US carriers, less so to the armoured steel decks of US warships and British carriers, but the full-scale employment of proximity fuzes on the warships' AA shells managed to shoot down most of these attacks before they reached their target. Between November 1944 and January 1945 about six major Allied ships were sunk or severely damaged by Kamikaze attacks, and the threat did not recede until Allied air attacks on the airfields in the Philippines destroyed their bases.

Kamikaze Class Destroyers (Jap)

Displacement 1270 tons; *dimensions* 377×30ft (114×9.14m); mean draught 10ft (3m); *machinery* 2-shaft geared turbines producing shp 38,500; *speed* 37.25 knots; *armament* 4×4.7in (4×1); 2×7.7mm; 6×21in torpedo tubes (3×2); *complement* 148; *number in class* 9, launched 1922–25.

Kammhuber, Gen Josef C.

Kammhuber was appointed in October 1940 to take command of all German night fighter operations. He redeployed most of the German searchlight and gun defences into a line stretching from Schleswig Holstein to Liège, which became known to the British as the Kammhuber Line. This was accompanied by radar early warning and tactical equipment which alerted the defences and then guided night fighters on to the British bombers. The system was reasonably successful until 1943, when the British began using electronic countermeasures against the radars. On 15 September 1943, after a period in which his night fighters had enjoyed little success, Kammhuber was relieved of his command.

Kampfpistole

German adaptation of their standard 25mm signal pistol to fire small grenades.

Kangaroo – Armoured Personnel Carriers (UK and Canada)

Developed at the suggestion of Lieutenant-General G. G. SIMONDS, the commander of II Canadian Corps, the first Kangaroos were used during the later stages of the 1944 campaign in NORMANDY, being known as "Unfrocked Priests" since they consisted of the HOWITZER MOTOR CARRIAGE M7 (Priest) with the main armament removed, so providing space for up to 12 infantrymen. Later, turretless SHERMAN and RAM medium tanks were

Kangaroo armoured personnel carrier.

employed in the Kangaroo role, a section of infantry riding in what had been the fighting compartment. By December 1944 the 79th Armoured Division possessed two APC regiments with a total of 300 Kangaroos. A third Kangaroo regiment served with the 8th Army during the final stages of the war in Italy.

Karelia, 1939–44

South-eastern province of Finland. The Karelian Isthmus, lying between the Gulf of Finland and Lake LADOGA, was the principal area of operations during the Winter War and again during the period in which Finland was allied to Germany, 1941–1944.

Karl – Super-Heavy Self-Propelled Howitzer (Ger)

Developed by Rheinmetall-Borsig in response to a 1936 German Army request for a heavy artillery weapon which could be used where railway guns could not. The weapon was a 600mm howitzer capable of firing a 4836-lb (2194-kg) concrete-piercing shell to a range of 4920 yards (4500m), or a 3472-lb (1575-kg) high explosive shell to 7300 yards (6675m). A tracked chassis with a torsion bar suspension was employed, carried on 11 wheels per side; the torsion bars could be turned by electrical gearing, thus retracting the wheels and permitting the hull to lie on the ground during firing. Recoil was controlled by a dual hydropneumatic system, part of which was contained within the hull. A

mechanical rammer assisted loading once the weapon had been returned to the horizontal. Six of these equipments were delivered between November 1940 and August 1941 but the Army was apparently disappointed with the range obtained and in May 1942 ordered six 540mm barrels which were to be interchangeable with the existing barrels. These were delivered in August 1943 and fired a 2756-lb (1250kg) shell to a range of 6.5 miles (10.45km). The equipment, which weighed 122 tons, possessed very limited mobility and was normally carried aboard specially designed road or rail transporters. In action it was supplied by munitions carriers based on the chassis of the PANZERKAMPFWAGEN IV; these were equipped with a 2.5 ton crane and carried three rounds of ammunition. The Karls, named after General Karl Becker, the artillery officer who instigated the project, were employed during siege operations on the Eastern Front, notably at SEVASTOPOL.

Karlsruhe, KMS – Köln Class Light Cruiser

Severely damaged by torpedoes from the submarine HMS *Truant* off the Norwegian coast on 10 April 1940, then abandoned and sunk by torpedoes from the German torpedo boat *Greif*.

Kasserine Pass, Tunisia, 1943

Early in February von ARNIM and ROMMEL, commanding 5th Panzer Army and the AFRIKA KORPS respectively, planned a spoiling attack which would temporarily eliminate the Allied 1st Army's offensive capacity and permit the Axis to consolidate their hold on Tunisia. On 14 February 5th Panzer Army struck, breaking through the forward positions of Major-General Lloyd R. FREDENDALL's US II Corps at Sidi Bou Zid, isolating one combat command of Major-General Orlando Ward's 1st Armored Division and savaging two more when they counter-attacked the following day. Simultaneously, the Afrika Korps burst through GAFSA and Thelepte and advanced to Kasserine, where it was joined by 10th Panzer Division before storming the pass. ALEXANDER quickly moved Anglo-American blocking forces into position on the Thala and Sbiba roads, where they halted further thrusts by the 10th and 21st Panzer Divisions while the rallied 1st Armored Division checked further progress by the Afrika Korps east of Tebessa. Some of the American units which took part in

8th Field Squadron, Royal Engineers, probing the Thale–Kasserine road for mines.

these battles had driven non-stop from Morocco to arrive in time. Having inflicted serious damage on II Corps, Rommel withdrew so skilfully during the night of 22 February that at first the Allies did not know he had gone. Fredendall's handling of the battle attracted sharp criticism and he was replaced by Major-General George S. PATTON.

Kater Gerät

German infra-red detector carried by frontline troops. Studies of British pre-war patents led the Germans to suspect that infra-red detection equipment would be used in night operations. The KaterGerät was like a small telescope; exposed to daylight for a short period, which stimulated the phosphor, it was then carried at night by patrols. On pointing the telescope at an infra-red source the phosphor would glow red. Issued early in the war, it fell into disuse since the British were not, at that time, using infra-red in that role.

Katori Class Cruisers (Jap)

Designed as light training cruisers, these vessels served as Flagships for most of the war but in 1944 *Kashii* and *Kashima* were converted to the anti-submarine role. *Displacement* 5890 tons; *dimensions* 425×52ft (130×15.8m); mean draught 18ft (5.5m); *machinery* 2-shaft geared turbines producing shp 8000; *speed* 18 knots; *armament* 4×5.5in (2×2); 2×5in AA; 4×25mm AA; 4×21in torpedo tubes; *aircraft* 1 (1 catapult); *number in class* 3, launched 1939–41.

Katyn Wood, Poland, 1943

In April 1943 German troops in occupied Russia discovered a mass grave at Katyn Wood, close to Smolensk, in which the bodies of some 4,500 Polish officers were buried. German propagandists made the most of the discovery, accusing the Russians of murdering the Poles and thus driving a wedge into the fragile Anglo-Polish–Russian alliance. Russia denied the charge vehemently; the Poles believed it implicitly; and the British attempted to keep the arguments muted for the sake of the common war effort. The Germans invited a commission of the International Red Cross to inspect the site, but the Red Cross declined to attend unless Soviet representatives were also there, a request the Soviets refused. A neutral commission was formed and examined the bodies, finding that all had their hands tied behind their backs and had been shot in the back of the neck. The Soviets reacted by severing relations with the Polish government-in-exile in London and set up their own puppet government in Moscow. Before the commission could complete its examination the advancing Red Army had occupied the area, which was again taken under Soviet control in September 1943. The question of guilt was evaded at the NUREMBERG trials, and no satisfactory explanation has ever been given, though there seems little doubt

Discovery of bodies of Polish officers, Katyn Wood, 1943.

that the Poles were executed by the Soviets in a deliberate programme to exterminate the Polish governing class. The fate of several thousand other Polish officers and officials who vanished at approximately the same time has never been determined.

Katyusha

Nickname given to a Soviet Army free-flight rocket, also known as "Kostikov's Artillery" after the designer. The equipment consisted of a heavy truck upon which a number of rails were mounted, each capable of elevation and carrying a fin-stabilized rocket. The rocket was 5.9ft (1.8m) long and 130mm in diameter, and weighed 92.5lb (42kg) complete with its 48.5lb (22kg) warhead. The maximum range was about 3 miles (5km) and launchers capable of firing up to 48 rockets in a volley were produced in large numbers.

Kawabe, Lt Gen Masakuzo (1886–)

Kawabe was a staff officer in the Kwangtung Army in the 1930s who rose to become Chief of the General Staff of the Japanese Army in China. Later appointed to command the Japanese Forces in BURMA, he planned the offensive against KOHIMA and IMPHAL in 1944. The offensive failed and Kawabe was recalled to Japan where he was moved sideways to command the Japanese Air Force during the closing period of the war.

Kawanishi Aircraft (Japan)

Kawanishi H6K (Mavis) This was a militarized version of a pre-war commercial flying boat and was employed on maritime surveillance tasks, as a transport and, occasionally, as a torpedo-bomber. It was replaced in 1943 by the H8K. *Span* 131ft (40m); *engines* 4 1070hp radial; *crew* 9; *armament* 20mm cannon and 4 machine guns, 3500lb (1600kg) of bombs; *speed* 210mph (338kph).

Kawanishi H8K (Emily) This went into production in 1941 to replace the H6K and was generally considered to be the most advanced flying boat in the world at that time. Like its forerunner it was used for maritime tasks, and had a useful range of 4000 miles (6435km). *Span* 124.5ft (38m); *engines* 4 1850hp radial; *crew* 10; *armament* 5 20mm cannon, 4 machine guns, 4400lb (2000kg) of bombs; *speed* 285mph (458kph).

Kawanishi N1K2J Shiden (George) Design of this naval fighter began in 1942, using an existing floatplane as the basis, but it did not enter service until early in 1944, when it rapidly acquired a reputation as possibly the best Japanese naval fighter of the war. *Span* 39.3ft (12m); *engine* 1 1990hp radial; *armament* 4 20mm cannon, 1100lb (500kg) of bombs; *speed* 370mph (595kph).

Kawanishi N1K1 (Rex) One of the last floatplane fighters to be developed anywhere, the "Mighty Wind" appeared late in 1942. It was so good that the decision was then taken to continue development and turn it into a carrier fighter, resulting in the SHIDEN. As a result of this decision less than 100 N1K1 were built. *Span* 39.25ft (12m); *engine* 1 1460hp radial; *armament* 2 20mm cannon, 2 machine guns; *speed* 300mph (483kph).

Kawasaki Aircraft (Jap)

Kawasaki Ki45 (Nick) This was the first Japanese twin-engined fighter; designed in 1937, it suffered a protracted development due to problems in finding a suitable engine, and production did not begin until 1941. Used all over the Pacific theatre, a small number were successfully converted into night fighters, and a few were used for suicide bombing attacks in NEW GUINEA. *Span* 49.5ft (15m); *engines* 2 1080hp radial; *crew* 2; *armament* 1 37mm cannon, 2 machine guns; *speed* 340mph (547kph).

Kawasaki Ki-48 (Lily) Developed as a four-man twin-engined bomber, the Ki-48 saw service all over the Far East but was not considered to be a great success, lacking speed and manoeuvrability and having a poor bomb-load. Over 2000 were built, including a number adapted as dive-bombers. *Span* 57.25ft (17.5m); *engines* 2 1130hp radial; *crew* 4; *armament* 4 machine guns, 770lb (360kg) of bombs; *speed* 315mph (507kph).

Kawasaki Ki-56 (Thalia) This was actually the American Lockheed Super Electra commercial airliner, a licence for which had been obtained before the war. Kawasaki built 56 in 1940–41, and the Tachikawa company built a further 688 before 1945. They were widely used as transports throughout the Far East. *Span* 64.5ft (19.7m); *engines* 2 990hp radial; *speed* 250mph (402kph).

Kawasaki Ki-61 (Tony) The only Japanese fighter to use an in-line engine, the Ki-61 was at first thought by the Allies to be a licensed-built Messerschmitt Bf 109. It went into production early in 1942 and the first models were armed with German Mauser cannons. Later versions used Japanese weapons and various modifications were tried in order to find a substitute engine, since the liquid-cooled copy of the Daimler-Benz proved slow to manufacture. Nevertheless, those which went into action were effective machines. *Span* 39.3ft (12m); *engine* 1 1175hp in-line; *armament* 2 20mm cannon, 2 machine guns, 1100lb (500kg) of bombs; *speed* 348mph (560kph).

Kawasaki Ki-100 One of the few Japanese aircraft not to be given a codename by the Allies, this was the best Army Air Force fighter of the war yet it was developed almost accidentally. There was a surplus of Ki-61 airframes and a shortage of engines, so the airframe was adapted to take a much larger Mitsubishi radial engine. It outperformed all other Japanese fighters and was one of the few capable of holding their own against American machines. After making the conversion, a further 100 were built, but American bombing raids stopped production thereafter. *Span* 39.3ft (12m); *engine* 1 1500hp radial; *armament* 2 20mm cannon, 2 machine guns; *speed* 367mph (590kph).

Kawasaki Ki-102 (Randy) This went into production in 1944 as an anti-shipping attack version of the Ki-45. Powerfully armed, it was then further developed as a high-altitude fighter, but few were built before the war ended. *Span* 50ft (15.25m); *engines* 2 1500hp radial; *crew* 2; *armament* 1 57mm gun, 2 20mm cannon, 1 machine gun; *speed* 360mph (579kph).

Keitel, FM Wilhelm (1882–1946)

Keitel was commissioned into the artillery and served on the German General Staff during World War I, rising to the rank of Colonel. In postwar years he became involved with the Nazi party and in 1935 was appointed by BLOMBERG as his chef de bureau in the War Ministry. When HITLER assumed the role of Commander-in-Chief in 1938, Keitel succeeded Blomberg as Chief of Oberkommando der Wehrmacht (OKW, High Command of the Armed Forces), though with a much lower status than his predecessor. Keitel was no more than a tirelessly efficient clerk, totally subservient to the Führer, and these were precisely the qualities which recommended him to Hitler. Keitel exerted no influence over operations; he was merely a functionary, carrying out his master's orders. Keitel was responsible for dictating the terms

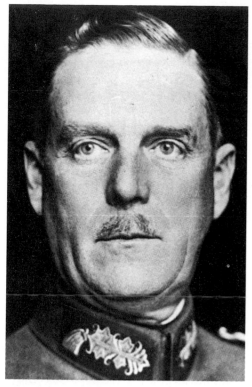

Field-Marshal Wilhelm Keitel.

of the French armistice in 1940, for signing orders relating to the execution of prisoners of war, and in 1944 was a member of the court which sentenced many officers to death for their complicity in the JULY BOMB PLOT. He was tried for war crimes by the NUREMBERG Tribunal and hanged on 16 October 1946.

Kelly, HMS – "K" Class Destroyer

Commanded by the then Captain Lord Louis MOUNTBATTEN, *Kelly* was leader of the 5th Destroyer Flotilla. She assisted in rescuing the survivors of the aircraft carrier COURAGEOUS and sank two enemy submarines during the first weeks of the war. After an active career in Home and Norwegian waters, during which she sustained serious damage on several occasions, she joined 5th Flotilla in the Mediterranean. During the German invasion of CRETE the 5th Flotilla bombarded enemy positions ashore and prevented seaborne reinforcements reaching the island. *Kelly* was sunk by air attack south of Crete on 23 May 1941.

Kennedy, Joseph (1888–1970)

Kennedy, father of US President John F. Kennedy, was the US Ambassador to Britain from 1937 to 1941 and a firm supporter of US isolationism. He had little political skill and a poor grasp of foreign affairs. Incapable of understanding CHAMBERLAIN's policy of appeasement, he was convinced that Britain could not survive against Germany and advised ROOSEVELT accordingly. In November 1940 he resigned his post and returned to the USA, where he became active in isolationist circles, arguing against US participation in the war and Lend-Lease to Britain.

Kenney, Maj Gen George C. (1889–)

Kenney was Commander-in-Chief of the US Far East Air Forces in the South-West Pacific Area – MACARTHUR's principal air officer. On his appointment he set about streamlining the organization of his command, separating the USAAF and Royal Australian Air Force elements and overhauling the administration, a task to which he brought great drive and energy. He was responsible for air support in the NEW GUINEA and SOLOMON ISLANDS campaigns, and oversaw pioneer work on aerial supply of ground troops in New Guinea. His forces were later to accompany MacArthur in the invasion of the PHILIPPINES where he is said to have been the first commander to use NAPALM bombs, against CORREGIDOR and Clark Field. He attended the Japanese surrender in Tokyo Bay with MacArthur in 1945.

Kenya, 1940–41

See EAST AFRICAN CAMPAIGN.

Kerch Peninsula, Crimea, Soviet Union, 1941–42

Between 26–30 December 1941 20,000 men of the Soviet 44th and 51st Armies landed on the peninsula with the object of relieving SEVASTOPOL, which was besieged by von MANSTEIN's German 11th Army. This force was expanded to become the Crimean Front under General D. T. Kozlov but its advance was halted and on 8 May 1942 Manstein, leaving five divisions to guard Sevastopol, launched a counteroffensive with heavy Luftwaffe support. The Russians were routed and although 86,000 men were evacuated from the peninsula the Crimean Front's losses amounted to 176,000 and all its equipment. In April 1944 General I. E. Petrov's Independent Coastal Army effected a successful landing on the peninsula in support of 4th Ukrainian Front's offensive on the Perekop Isthmus. See also CRIMEA.

Keren, Eritrea, 1941

The scene of a determined stand made by General Frusci's Italian army during the British invasion of Eritrea. The town of Keren could only be approached through a gorge in a mountain wall dominated by 11 peaks towering 2000ft (607m) above the pass, Cameron Ridge, Sanchil, Brig's Peak, Hog's Back, Saddle, Flat Top and Samanna being on

HMS Kelly *struggles home after sustaining serious damage in the North Sea.*

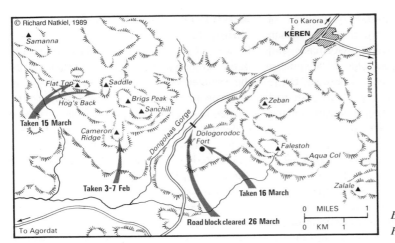

© Richard Natkiel, 1989

To Karora

KEREN

To Asmara

Samanna

Flat Top

Saddle

Hog's Back

Brigs Peak

Sanchill

Zeban

Taken 15 March

Cameron Ridge

Dologorodoc Fort

Falestoh

Aqua Col

Taken 3–7 Feb

Taken 16 March

Zalale

Road block cleared 26 March

To Agordat

0   MILES   1

0   KM   1

Battle of Keren, February–March 1941.

the left of the road and DOLOGORODOC, Falestoh, Zenab and Zalale on the right. The British troops under Major-General William Platt, consisting of the 4th and 5th Indian Divisions, opened their attacks on 3 February. Every feature was bitterly contested and the majority changed hands several times. When Dologorodoc finally fell on 15/16 March, the British engineers began clearing the road block in the gorge. On 26 March an attack spearheaded by a squadron of MATILDA tanks broke through the gorge and entered the town. The Italians withdrew with great skill, only the defenders of Sanchil being unable to extricate themselves. The eight-week battle cost the British 536 killed and 3229 wounded; the Italians lost more than 3000 killed. See also EAST AFRICAN CAMPAIGN.

Keru, Eritrea, 1941

A town between Kassala and AGORDAT where an Italian brigade fought a rearguard action during the British invasion of Eritrea from the Sudan. The Italians were outflanked by Major-General Noel Beresford-Peirse's 4th Indian Division and although many of them managed to fight their way out, the brigade commander and 900 of his men were captured. See EAST AFRICAN CAMPAIGN.

Kesselring, FM Albrecht (1885–1960)

One of the ablest commanders of World War II, Kesselring entered the Army in 1904, training as a balloon observer. During World War I he served as an adjutant on the General Staff, and in 1919 was promoted to the rank of Captain. He transferred to the infant German air force in 1933, and in 1936 was appointed Chief of Air Staff. He commanded Luftflotte 1 in the campaign in Poland, and Luftflotte 2 in the Battle of France and the Battle of BRITAIN.

After the Battle of Britain, Kesselring – now a Field-Marshal – took Luftflotte 2 to the Russian Front, from which it was transferred in December 1941 to Italy to take control of the increased air activity in the Mediterranean theatre. By January 1942, Kesselring had some 650 front-line aircraft at his disposal, of which 260 were in North Africa. He was made Commander-in-Chief South, with headquarters in Rome, and empowered to issue orders to German naval units in the area. He unsuccessfully urged an airborne invasion of MALTA,

Field-Marshal Albrecht Kesselring (left).

inflicted heavy losses on Allied shipping in the Mediterranean, and oversaw the evacuation of German troops from TUNISIA. When the Allies invaded Sicily and southern Italy in September 1943, Kesselring fought a brilliant defensive campaign, even managing to halt General ALEXANDER's forces south of the Po once they had broken through the GUSTAV LINE. In March 1945 he replaced RUNDSTEDT as Commander-in-Chief West, a month later receiving command of all remaining forces in the south. He surrendered at the beginning of May after hearing news of the Führer's death. In May 1947 he was sentenced to death for war crimes, but this was commuted to life imprisonment and he was released in October 1952.

Ketsu-Go

Japanese plan for the air defence of the homeland.

Keyes, Lt Col Geoffrey (1917–41)

Keyes was an officer in the Royal Scots Greys who volunteered for service with the COMMANDOS. During 1941 he served with General LAYCOCK's "Layforce" in the Mediterranean,

seeing action in CRETE and Syria. In November 1941 he led a raid on what was thought to be ROMMEL's headquarters near Appolonia in Tripolitania. Landed from a submarine, his group reached the house and killed a number of the occupants, but Keyes himself was killed and the party were scattered. It later transpired that intelligence had been faulty and that, although Rommel had once lived in the house, it was no longer in use as a headquarters. In spite of Keyes' undoubted bravery, the fact remains that most of his exploits were ill-conceived and of little military value.

Khabarovsk, Eastern Siberia, 1945

A town on the Trans-Siberian Railway, the base of the 2nd Far East Front (Purkayev) during the Soviet campaign in MANCHURIA, August–September 1945.

Khalkin Gol, Battle of, 1939

Battle fought between Japanese and Soviet troops on the borders of MANCHURIA in August 1939. The Japanese sought to extend their border by pushing across the Nomonhan River; what began as a minor raid rapidly escalated into a major incident, with air and armour being drawn into the battle. Eventually a Soviet armoured force under General ZHUKOV surrounded and virtually destroyed the Japanese 6th Army, which suffered several thousand casualties. This incident gave the Japanese a new respect for the Red Army and was instrumental in preventing them making any moves against Russia during the subsequent war.

Kharkov, Soviet Union, 1941–43

The third most important city of the Soviet Union, Kharkov fell to the German 6th Army (Army Group South) without a major engagement on 24 October 1941. In May 1942 STALIN directed TIMOSHENKO's South-West Front, which had amassed 640,000 men and 1200 tanks, to recapture the city by striking northwest from the Izyum salient, a bulge in the German lines 60 miles (96km) deep and the same across which had been produced during the Soviet counteroffensive in January. Timoshenko's offensive began on 12 May, but between 17 and 22 May Army Group von KLEIST and von PAULUS' 6th Army launched converging attacks into the salient which left the Russian spearhead trapped to the west. Over 250,000 prisoners were taken and every

Soviet armoured formation in the pocket was wiped out. On 16 February 1943 Kharkov was briefly recaptured when Golikov's Voronezh Front and VATUTIN's South-West Front swept across the Ukraine in the aftermath of the Soviet victory at STALINGRAD. Four days later von MANSTEIN's Army Group South counterattacked into the southern flank of both Fronts, inflicting heavy loss and forcing them to retire behind the Donets. On 15 March the city was once more in German hands. Kharkov was finally liberated by South-West Front, now commanded by MALINOVSKY, on 22 August 1943, following the failure of the German offensive against the KURSK salient. See *Knights of the Black Cross* by Bryan Perrett (Robert Hale).

KIA Killed in Action.

Kidney Ridge, Egypt, 1942

Scene of heavy fighting during the Second Battle of ALAMEIN, particularly on 27 October when the determined defence of Outpost Snipe, held by 2nd Battalion The Rifle Brigade and 239 Battery of 76th Anti-Tank Regiment, Royal Artillery, under the overall command of Lieutenant-Colonel Victor Turner, inflicted heavy damage on the Axis armour. See *Alamein* by C. E. Lucas Phillips (Heinemann).

Kiel, Germany, 1939–45

Naval base on the Baltic, connected to the North Sea by the Kiel Canal. Kiel was one of RAF BOMBER COMMAND's regular targets. During the 10 weeks to the end of May 1941, 900 sorties were flown against the base, temporarily reducing the production capacity of the three major shipbuilding yards by 25%, 60% and 100%. The intensity of the raids increased steadily until 15 September 1944 when 490 bombers inflicted catastrophic damage. During the last weeks of the war further air attacks succeeded in sinking the *Admiral Scheer* and 10 U-boats and damaging the *Admiral Hipper* and *Emden*. Following the German surrender, Kiel was occupied by the British 11th Armoured Division.

Kiev, Soviet Union, 1941–43

Following his defeat at the Battle of BRODY-DUBNO, Colonel-General Mikhail KIRPONOS withdrew his South-West Front towards Kiev, which STALIN insisted must be held at all costs. On 19 July 1941 HITLER began meddling with the internal workings of Operation BAR-

BAROSSA and, contrary to professional advice, ordered GUDERIAN's Panzer Group 2 to swing south and assist von RUNDSTEDT's Army Group South in its conquest of the Ukraine. On 16 September Guderian's spearhead, driving south from SMOLENSK, met that of von KLEIST's Panzer Group 1 moving north at a village named Lokhvitsa some 100 miles (160km) east of Kiev, effectively trapping most of South-West Front within a huge pocket. The Russians were slow to appreciate their danger and by the time they did Rundstedt had them held tight within an iron ring. Kirponos was killed leading one of several attempts to break out and when resistance finally collapsed on 26 September the pocket yielded no less than 665,000 prisoners, 900 tanks and 3719 guns. Great though the victory was, it had cost priceless time, the loss of which ensured that the strategic objective of MOSCOW could not be reached before the onset of the Russian winter, and in the overall context, therefore, it contributed to the failure of *Barbarossa*. Kiev remained under German occupation until liberated by VATUTIN's 1st Ukrainian Front on 6 November 1943. The ancient city was found to have been deliberately devastated and most of its art treasures had been sent to Germany.

Kikusui-1

Suicide mission of the Japanese battleship YAMATO.

Kilkis, HHMS – Battleship

Formerly the American pre-Dreadnought battleship *Idaho*, *Kilkis* was launched in 1908 and transferred to the Royal Hellenic Navy in 1914. She displaced 13,000 tons and retained her original main and secondary armament of four 12-inch and eight 8-inch guns, but her role latterly was that of an anti-aircraft training ship. She was sunk by Axis air attack in Salamis harbour on 23 April 1941.

Kimmel, Adm Husband E. (1882–1968)

Kimmel had the misfortune to be the Commander-in-Chief of the US Pacific Fleet at PEARL HARBOR on 7 December 1941. He was relieved of his duties ten days after the Japanese attack. Heavily criticized for his failure to take effective defensive measures, Kimmel maintained that the authorities in Washington had not warned him of the proximity of war and that he had carried out all the preventive measures which they had

Admiral King and General Marshall visit the USS Lexington, *July 1943.*

requested. The one positive action that he had taken – the despatch of his carriers on manoeuvres – proved crucial to the survival of the US Pacific Fleet as a fighting unit.

King II

American liberation of LUZON, PHILIPPINE ISLANDS, October 1944.

King, Adm Ernest J. (1878–1956)

King was Commander-in-Chief of the US Fleet at the time of America's entry into the war. In March 1942 he also became Chief of Naval Operations, a unique double appointment. He was a member of the Joint Chiefs of Staff and the Anglo-US Combined Chiefs of Staff throughout the war and was promoted to Fleet Admiral in 1944. King organized and directed the American forces in the Pacific Ocean with a single-minded drive and ability which made him numerous enemies. He was always reluctant to admit that Germany and the German war existed, and his devotion to acquiring the lion's share of any supplies for the Pacific often had repercussions in the European theatre. Nevertheless, even his opponents admitted that King's conduct of the campaigns in the east was masterly and his organization of the logistic aspects was unparalleled in history in its size and scope.

King, William MacKenzie (1874–1950)

MacKenzie King was Prime Minister of Canada from 1921 to 1930 and again from 1935 to 1948, serving also as foreign minister from 1935 to 1946. A shrewd politician, he adopted an isolationist stance before the war, but bowed to public opinion in 1939 and led Canada into war. Anxious to avoid conscription, he concentrated on building up naval and air forces before expanding the army and committing it to overseas service. He worked towards Canadian-American amity, leading the foundation of the Joint Defense Board, and hosted two major conferences at Quebec in 1943 and 1944. In 1942 he organized a successful plebiscite to introduce conscription, though he managed to avoid sending conscripted troops overseas until late in the war.

King George V Class Battleships (UK)

King George V served with the Home Fleet 1940–44, save for a period in 1943 when she joined FORCE H. She joined the Pacific Fleet in 1945. See also HMS DUKE OF YORK and PRINCE OF WALES. *Displacement* 36,830 tons; *dimensions* 745×103ft (227×31.3m); mean draught 27.9ft (8.37m); *machinery* 4-shaft geared turbines producing shp 110,000; *speed* 27.5 knots; *protection* main belt 15in; deck 6in; turrets 16in; *armament* 10×14in (2×4 and 1×2); 16×5.25in DP (8×2); 48×2-pdr AA (6×8); *aircraft* 4; *complement* 1612; *number in class* 5, launched 1939–40.

Kinkaid, V Adm Thomas C. (1888–1972)

Kinkaid spent the early part of his naval career in battleships, but then specialized as an ordnance engineer, attending the Geneva Disarmament Conference in 1933 as an American armaments expert. In 1942 he commanded Task Force 16, which included the carriers *Hornet* and *Enterprise*, during the Battle of the SANTA CRUZ ISLANDS. *Hornet* was lost and *Enterprise* severely damaged, but the Japanese sustained heavy aircraft losses. After the NAVAL CAMPAIGN OF GUADALCANAL in November 1942, Kinkaid was given command of Task Force 67, a cruiser squadron, where he concentrated on training his force for night fighting in order to disrupt Japanese transports attempting to resupply Guadalcanal at night. He was then

King George V class battleship.

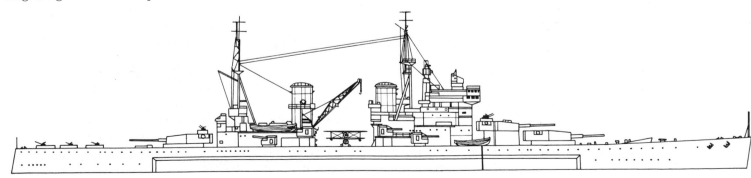

General Kenney and Vice-Admiral Kinkaid in the Philippines, June 1945.

moved to command the Northern Pacific Force in the operations to retake the ALEUTIAN ISLANDS, after which he took command of the 7th Fleet, a force of second-line warships and transports which carried the 6th US Army to LEYTE in October 1944. During the Battle of LEYTE GULF one of the fleet's Task Forces was attacked by Vice-Admiral KURITA's force, but by rapid deployment of aircraft from his escort carriers Kinkaid was able to stave off disaster until Kurita lost his nerve and withdrew.

Kippenberger, Gen Howard (1897–)

Kippenberger was a solicitor by profession but joined the New Zealand Territorial Army in peacetime and by 1939 was commanding the 20th NZ Infantry Battalion. He took the battalion to Egypt, where it trained for a year before going into action in Greece and CRETE, where Kippenberger commanded a composite Brigade. The survivors of Crete were evacuated to LIBYA and the battalion re-formed, after which he led it in action in the Western Desert with success until in December 1941 he was wounded and taken prisoner. He very quickly escaped from captivity and returned to the Allied lines to command 5th Infantry Brigade in the Desert and later in SYRIA. The New Zealanders particularly distinguished themselves during the CRUSADER

battles and at El ALAMEIN, after which Kippenberger, acting commander of the New Zealand Division, pursued the Germans across North Africa to Tunisia. After a period of furlough he returned to command 5th NZ Brigade in Italy, taking part in the battle of the SANGRO, after which he commanded the NZ Division at Monte CASSINO. On 2 March 1944 he was seriously injured by a mine, losing one foot in the explosion and having the other amputated shortly afterwards. Henceforth barred from active duty, he took charge of the repatriation of NZ prisoners after the war and then returned to New Zealand to edit the national war histories.

Kirponos, Col Gen Mikhail P. (1892–1941)

A survivor of the Stalin purge of the Red Army in 1937, Kirponos commanded the 70th Infantry Division against Finland in 1939–40 and captured Viborg after an audacious attack across the frozen Gulf of Finland. This brought him into the limelight and he was appointed commander of the Kiev Military District. When Germany invaded the Soviet Union in June 1941, Kirponos, aided by good defensive country (the Pripet Marshes) and by a hesitant von KLEIST and his 1st Panzer Group, delayed the German advance before being

driven back into KIEV and surrounded. In attempting to lead a break-out through the German lines, Kirponos was killed.

Kismayu, Italian Somaliland, 1941

A port close to the Kenyan border. It was anticipated that the garrison would put up a stiff fight but the Italian Commander-in-Chief, the Duke of Aosta, overestimated the strength of General CUNNINGHAM's advance from Kenya and ordered the evacuation of the town, which was entered by 12th African Division on 14 February. Ironically, Cunningham had considered withdrawing if Kismayu had not fallen by the tenth day of his offensive. See EAST AFRICAN CAMPAIGN.

Kleist, FM Ewald von (1881–1954)

Commissioned into an artillery regiment in 1902, von Kleist later transferred to a Hussar regiment. He served in the field and in staff posts during World War I and remained in the Army after 1918. He became commanding officer of 9th Infantry Regiment in 1931, commander of 2nd Cavalry Division in 1932 and, with the rank of Lieutenant-General, commander of VII Army Corps in 1935. He retired from the army in 1938 at the time of the FRITSCH-BLOMBERG "purge". Recalled at the outbreak of the war, Kleist was given command of XXII Army Corps in Poland and then

Field-Marshal Ewald von Kleist.

led Panzer Group Kleist in France in 1940. Von Kleist then commanded 1st Panzer Group in the Balkans and led 1st Panzer Army in Operation BARBAROSSA. Promoted Field-Marshal in November 1942, he took command of Army Group A, which fought in the long retreat from the Ukraine in 1943–44. He retired for a second time on 30 March 1944. In 1945 he was captured by the Red Army and remained a prisoner until his death.

Klimenti Voroshilov Series – Heavy Tanks (USSR)

Designed by the Kotin Bureau, the KV-1 entered service in 1940 and ran to three marks. The KV-1A was armed with a 76.2mm L/30.5 gun and was protected by 90mm frontal armour. The KV-1B was armed with the same gun but protection was increased by adding 30mm appliqué plates to the front and sides of the hull and turret. The KV-1C was armed with a more powerful 76.2mm L/41.5 gun and further plates were added, giving a maximum thickness of 130mm. The KV-2 entered service

in 1941 and although its main armament was housed in a high, slab-sided turret, the concept had more in common with that of an assault howitzer. By 1943 the KVs were clearly undergunned and, pending the introduction of the IOSEF STALIN SERIES, the KV-85 was introduced as an interim measure, armed with an 85mm L/53 gun housed in a cast turret. 508 KVs were in service when the Wehrmacht invaded Russia and in the short term these generated even greater concern than the T-34/76 since the German tank and anti-tank guns then in service were incapable of penetrating the heavy armour; often only a round sent through the thinner stern plating or an explosive charge placed beneath the turret overhang would suffice to disable them. About 10,500 KVs were built between 1940 and 1943. A number of captured KV-2s were to have taken part in the planned invasion of MALTA. See also SU-152. *Weight KV-1 – 43.5/48 tons; KV-2 – 52 tons; KV-85 – 46 tons; speed KV-1 – 22mph (35kph); KV-2 – 16mph (26kph); KV-85 – 27mph (43kph); armour KV-1 – 90/*

130mm; KV-2 – 110mm; KV-85 – 110mm; armament KV-1 – 1 76.2mm gun; 3 7.62mm machine guns; KV-2 – 1 152mm howitzer; 3 7.62mm machine guns; KV-85 – 1 85mm gun; 3 7.62mm machine guns; engine V-12 550hp diesel; crew KV-1 – 5; KV-2 – 6; KV-85 – 5.

Kluge, FM Gunther von (1882–1944)

A non-political soldier, von Kluge was one of the most capable German generals of the war, quick to seize the intiative and with the ability to make clear and accurate decisions. He commanded 4th Army in Poland and France with conspicuous success, and in July 1940 was promoted Field-Marshal. In operation BARBAROSSA he again commanded 4th Army as part of Army Group Centre, clashing with his subordinate GUDERIAN over the speed of the advance. After von BOCK was put on the shelf early in 1942, Kluge succeeded him as commander of Army Group Centre. He constructed a well-knit defence which withstood successive Soviet attacks during the next two years. Early in 1944 Kluge was injured in a plane crash. After his recovery he was sent to replace von RUNDSTEDT as Commander-in-Chief West in July 1944, with orders to throw the Allies back into the sea. However, with the Führer refusing to sanction a withdrawal and Kluge powerless to prevent the Allied breakout from the NORMANDY beach-head, 50,000 men were trapped in the Falaise Pocket. On 17 August, two days before the FALAISE GAP was closed, he was relieved of his command and replaced by MODEL. Although not involved in the JULY BOMB PLOT, he had, at times, discussed affairs with some of the plotters, and so committed suicide.

Knee Mortar

Erroneous term used for the Japanese Type 89 grenade discharger. This consisted of a short tube and a curved base-plate; it was the habit of the Japanese troops to carry the MORTAR strapped to the leg of the mortar-man, and from this it was known in Japanese texts as the "Leg Mortar". A mistranslation by Allied Intelligence turned this into "knee mortar", and since the curved baseplate just fitted the average man's thigh, it was assumed that it was fired from the leg of a kneeling man. Several Allied soldiers attempted this and suffered broken thighs as a result. The mortar was rifled and fired a 28oz (900g) high explosive shell to a range of 700yds (640m) or a 23oz (745g) hand grenade to about 500yds (457m).

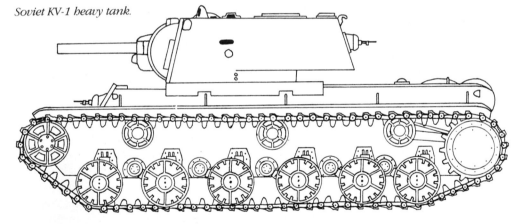

Soviet KV-1 heavy tank.

Knickebein

A German electronic blind-bombing system used to direct air raids against England in 1940. Two radio beams were directed from stations on the Continent and positioned to intersect over the targets; the aircraft would fly along one beam and release their bombs when they encountered the intersecting beam. It was susceptible to countermeasures and was only in use for a short time before being discovered and countered by "bending" the beams.

Knightsbridge, Libya, 1942

The name given to fortified box held by 201st Guards Brigade, 25 miles (40km) south-west of TOBRUK. See GAZALA.

Kobe, Japan, 1942 and 1945

Naval base and industrial city which was one of the targets attacked during the DOOLITTLE raid on Japan, 18 April 1942. In 1945 Kobe suffered severely during the American fire-bombing offensive against Japanese targets, 57 per cent of the city being burned out.

Koenig, Gen Marie Pierre (1898–1970)

In 1940 Koenig was a Captain in the French Army and fought in Norway during the Allied counterstroke to the German invasion. On the fall of France he escaped to England and joined DE GAULLE. He was then sent to French Equatorial Africa at the head of a small force and captured Libreville in November 1940. In 1941 he commanded the French Brigade in the Libyan Desert and in 1942 conducted a short but spirited defence of BIR HACHEIM before being evicted by ROMMEL. He was later appointed to EISENHOWER's staff as commander-designate of the French Forces of the Interior (FFI), and played a significant role in co-ordinating the work of the French resistance before the invasion in 1944. When this took place, Koenig assumed command of the FFI and after the surrender of Paris was appointed military governor of the city. From 1945 to 1949 he commanded French occupation troops in Germany.

Koga, Adm Mineichi (1885–1943)

Koga succeeded YAMAMOTO as Commander-in-Chief of the Japanese Combined Fleet in April 1943. He maintained his predecessor's policy of defending the Pacific islands, but suffered numerous defeats at American hands, notably in attempting to reinforce RABAUL in trying to stave off the US invasion of the Gilberts. Koga set up his headquarters in SINGAPORE, with the intention of concentrating the remainder of the Japanese fleet for a last-ditch naval battle with the US Navy, but before he could execute his plan (Operation Z), he was killed in an aircraft accident on 31 March 1944.

Kohima, Manipur, India, 1944

A hill town attacked by Major-General SATO's 31st Division on 5 April during the Japanese U-GO offensive, the effect being to isolate the British IV Corps at IMPHAL. The garrison consisted of 161 Indian Infantry Brigade with 4th Battalion The Queen's Own Royal West Kent Regiment in Kohima itself and 1/1st Punjabis and 4/7th Rajputs holding a defensive box at Jotsoma, two miles (3.2km) along the Dimapur road, the latter also being isolated on 7 April. The battle witnessed some of the most savage fighting of the war as repeated Japanese attacks were thrown back with heavy loss. Meanwhile, Lieutenant-General Montagu STOPFORD's XXXIII Corps had assembled at Manipur and begun advancing to the relief of Kohima and Imphal. On 14 April the 2nd British Division, spearheaded by Lee tanks, relieved the Jotsoma box and four days later broke through to the exhausted West Kents at Kohima. The Japanese were now thrown on the defensive, but they occupied excellent positions blocking further progress towards Imphal and defended these tenaciously until the end of May when, starving and diseased, the survivors began withdrawing towards the Chindwin, pursued by the 7th Indian Division. During the fighting Sato's logistic support failed completely and he initiated a bitter and insubordinate quarrel with his superior, Lieutenant-General Renya MUTAGUCHI, commanding the Japanese 15th Army, concerning this and the conduct of operations generally. Very few of his men succeeded in returning to Burma. XXXIII Corps continued its advance through Kohima and effected a junction with IV Corps on 22 June.

Koiso, Lt Gen Kuniaki (1880–1950)

A career soldier who was appointed Chief of Staff to the Kwangtung Army in MANCHURIA in 1932. A supporter of Ishiwara's East Asian League, he was involved in an abortive conspiracy to promote a military coup in Tokyo. In 1939–40 he served in the government as Minister of Colonial Development, where he advocated full military control of Japan's economy and military expansion in order to seize raw materials and resources throughout South-East Asia. From 1941 to 1944 he served as Governor-General of Korea, then returned to Tokyo to become Prime Minister after TOJO was forced out of office in July 1944. Here he was confronted with fighting a defensive war whilst attempting to extract favourable peace terms from the Allies. The task was too much for him and he resigned in March 1945, handing over his ministry to Admiral Suzuki. After the war he was arraigned as a war criminal and sentenced to life imprisonment.

Kokoda Trail, New Guinea

A track leading across the OWEN STANLEY MOUNTAINS in NEW GUINEA, scene of an advance southward from Buna by the Japanese in August 1942. They reached a position about 20 miles (32km) from Port Moresby before being brought to a halt by Australian troops, after which an Australian counterattack gradually drove them back up the trail to the north side of the mountain range. The climatic and terrain conditions were probably the worst in which any troops fought during the war.

Kokumbona, Guadalcanal, Solomon Islands, 1942–43

Japanese base area west of HENDERSON FIELD, captured 23 January 1943.

Köln Class Light Cruisers (Ger)

Köln took part in the Norwegian Campaign of 1940 and served in Norwegian waters 1942–43. She then joined the Training Squadron in the Baltic and in 1944 supported army operations with her gunfire. She was bombed and sunk at Wilhelmshaven on 30 April 1945. See also NORWAY, NAVAL CAMPAIGN, KARLSRUHE and KÖNIGSBERG. *Displacement* 6650 tons; *dimensions* 570×50ft (171×15m); mean draught 18ft (5.4m); *machinery* 2-shaft geared turbines producing shp 68,000 plus 2 diesels with bhp 1800 for cruising; *speed* 32 knots; *protection* main belt 3–4in; turrets 3in; *armament* 9×5.9in (3×3); 6×3.5in AA (3×2); 8×37mm AA (4×2); 12×21in torpedo tubes (4×3); *aircraft* 2; *complement* 820; *number in class* 3, launched 1927–37.

Kolombangara, Battle of, 1943

During the night of 12/13 July 1943 a Japanese naval squadron under Rear-Admiral Shunji Izaki attempted to reinforce the garrison of Kolombangara, Solomon Islands, using four destroyer transports escorted by the cruiser *Jintsu* and five more destroyers. The Americans were warned of Izaki's approach and deployed an interception force commanded by Rear-Admiral W. T. Ainsworth and consisting of the cruisers USS *Honolulu*, USS *St Louis* and HMNZS *Leander*, escorted by nine destroyers, off Kula Gulf. At 0112 the Allied cruisers opened fire, wrecking *Jintsu*, which sank at 0145. Izaki's destroyers responded with a salvo of LONG LANCE torpedoes, one of which crippled *Leander*. At 0205 the two forces clashed again and as a result of a second Long Lance torpedo strike *Honolulu* and *St Louis* were both hit in the bows and the destroyer USS *Gwin* was sunk. Having completed their mission, the Japanese withdrew.

Komandorski Islands, Battle of the, 1943

On 26 March 1943 Vice-Admiral Hosogaya was escorting a reinforcement convoy to ATTU ISLAND in the Aleutians with four cruisers and four destroyers when he was intercepted by an American squadron of two cruisers and four destroyers under Rear-Admiral Charles H. McMorris. In a long-range gunnery duel the American cruiser *Salt Lake City* was seriously damaged, as was the Japanese cruiser *Nachi*, but when Hosogaya closed in for the kill he was driven off when three of McMorris' destroyers launched a determined torpedo attack, and, fearing American air strikes from Dutch Harbour, he withdrew, and consequently was relieved of his command. After the battle the Japanese relied on submarines to supply their garrisons in the Aleutians.

Komet – Surface raider (Ger)

Also known as Ship 45 and Raider B. Sailed from Bergen on 9 July 1940. Joined ORION, operating in the Atlantic, Indian and Pacific Oceans, and shared in the destruction of seven ships. After the raiders separated, *Komet* sank a further three ships of 21,378 tons and returned to Hamburg on 30 November 1941. Her second cruise commenced on 7 October 1942, but on 14 October she was intercepted by British coastal forces off Cap de la Hague and blew up after being torpedoed by *MTB 236*. *Displacement* 3287 tons; *speed* 16 knots; *armament* 6×5.9in; 1×60mm; 2×37mm AA; 4×20mm AA; 6×21in torpedo tubes (2×2 and 2×1 submerged); equipped for minelaying; *aircraft* 2; *complement* 270.

Kondo, V Adm Nobutaki (1856–1953)

Kondo came to prominence as commander of the Southern Sea Force which sank the British Force Z, the battleship PRINCE OF WALES and the battle-cruiser REPULSE, off the Malayan coast on 10 December 1941. At the Battle of MIDWAY he was in command of the Main Support Force, his objective the capture of Midway Island, but after the destruction of Admiral NAGUMO's First Carrier Striking Force he withdrew without engaging the enemy. Kondo played an important part in the naval actions which took place in the Solomon Islands during the struggle for GUADALCANAL. On 23 August 1942 he was in tactical command of the combined fleet during the Battle of the EASTERN SOLOMONS, in which the Japanese carrier RYUJO was sunk by aircraft of Admiral FLETCHER's Task Force 61.

Konev, Marshal Ivan Stepanovitch (1897–1973)

Konev enlisted as a private in the Tsar's army, joining the Bolshevik Party and the Red Army in 1918. Given a commission, he survived the Stalin purges and in 1938 became commander of the Transbaikal Military District. In 1942 he was given command of a corps in the southern front and fought competently, but without attracting any attention, until January 1944 when, commanding the 2nd Ukrainian Front, he assisted ZHUKOV to encircle two German army corps near Korsun. He went on to capture Lvov, and reached the Vistula on 7 August 1944. After a pause to reorganize his supply lines, he advanced to the ODER–NEISSE LINE in February 1945 and on

Marshal Ivan Konev.

25 April leading elements of his corps met US troops of BRADLEY's 12th Army Group at Torgau on the river Elbe. Together with Zhukov, Konev took BERLIN on 2 May. From 1946–66 he held the post of Commander-in-Chief, Land Forces, then became Soviet Minister of Defence and Supreme Commander of the Warsaw Pact Forces. He was twice decorated Hero of the Soviet Union and received the Order of Lenin for his wartime services.

Kongo Class Battleships (Jap)

Displacement 31,720 tons; *dimensions* 728ft 6in×95ft 3in (222×29m); mean draught 32ft (9.7m); *machinery* 4-shaft geared turbines producing shp 136,000; *speed* 30.5 knots; *protection* main belt 8in amidships, 3in fore and aft; turrets 9in; control tower 10in; deck 2ft 9in; *armament* 8×14in (4×2); 14×6in (14×1); 8×5in AA (4×2); 20×25mm AA (10×2); *aircraft* 3; *complement* 1437; *number in class* 4.

Königsberg (Kaliningrad), East Prussia, 1945

STALIN announced his determination to incorporate Königsberg within the Soviet Union at the Tehran Conference in November 1943. The city, ringed by three lines of defence incorporating 15 major forts, was isolated by Bagramyan's 1st Baltic Front and CHERNYAKHOVSKY's 3rd Belorussian Front in February. Great care was taken in planning the assault on the fortress, overall command being exercised by Marshal Alexandr VASILEVSKY. On 6 April four Soviet armies (39th, 43rd, 50th and 11th Guards), supported by 5000 guns, 538 tanks and 2444 aircraft, opened their attack and steadily fought their way into the defences. The German garrison commander, General Otto Lasch, surrendered on 9 April. HITLER immediately sentenced him to death *in absentia* and had his family arrested. Some 42,000 German soldiers were killed and 92,000 captured; an estimated 25,000 German civilians also died during the fighting. See *The Road to Berlin* by John Erickson (Weidenfeld and Nicolson).

Königsberg, KMS – Köln Class Light Cruiser

Sunk at Bergen on 10 April 1940 by dive-bombing attack of Fleet Air Arm Skuas. The wreck was refloated in 1943 but capsized the following year and was finally abandoned.

Konoye, Prince Fumimaro (1891–1945)

Prince Konoye became Prime Minister of Japan in 1937. Considered a moderate, he adopted a policy of expansion but did not advocate extreme military action to achieve it. He was unable to prevent the outbreak of war with China in July 1937, and in January 1939 he resigned. Recalled as Prime Minister in 1940, he signed the Tripartite Axis Pact with Germany and Italy and attempted to reach a compromise with the USA over the China issue and Indo-China. He failed, not least because Japan's military leaders refused to countenance a withdrawal from China, and he resigned for a second time in October 1941, to be replaced by General TOJO. For much of the war Konoye was an adviser to the Emperor, and played a part in toppling Tojo and his cabinet in July 1944. In July 1945 he was appointed as a peace envoy to Moscow, but the mission was overtaken by events when ATOMIC BOMBS were dropped on Hiroshima and Nagasaki and the Soviet Union declared war on Japan on 8 August. Konoye served as Vice-President in the immediate Japanese postwar Cabinet, but when informed that he was to be arrested and tried as a war criminal he took poison.

Konstantin

See ACHSE.

Korea, 1945

Annexed by Japan in 1910. In August 1945 troops of the Soviet 1st Far East Front (Meretskov) overran the peninsula as far south as the 38th Parallel, this being the limit of the occupation zone previously agreed with the United States.

Koritsa, Greece, 1940

The scene of the defeat of the Italian 9th Army by Greek troops on 22 November. The Italians withdrew into ALBANIA.

Kormoran – Surface Raider (Ger)

Also known as Ship 41 and Raider G. Sailed on 3 December under Commander Theodor Detmers and operated in the Atlantic, Indian and Pacific Oceans, sinking or capturing 11 ships totalling 68,264 tons. On 19 November 1941 she encountered the cruiser HMAS SYD-NEY off the coast of Western Australia, and during the subsequent engagement she was set ablaze and abandoned. *Sydney* was also seriously damaged and was on fire when last sighted. It has been suggested that although Japan was not yet officially at war *Kormoran* may have had a secret rendezvous with a Japanese submarine, and that the latter may have intervened to finish off the Australian cruiser. *Displacement* 8736 tons; *speed* 18 knots; *armament* 6×5.9in; 4×37mm AA; 4×20mm AA; 4×21in torpedo tubes (2×2); equipped for minelaying; *aircraft* 2; *motor torpedo boat* 1; *complement* 400.

Korsun, Soviet Union, 1944

Soviet successes at Kirovgrad and ZHITOMIR left a German-held salient betwen the two which was isolated by the converging thrusts of 1st and 2nd Ukrainian Fronts on 6 February. The pocket thus formed contained the German XI and XLII Corps, commanded respectively by Lieutenant-Generals Stemmermann and Lieb, the 5th SS Panzer Division *Wiking* and the Belgian SS *Wallonien* Brigade, a total of 50,000 men known collectively as Group Stemmermann. After rejecting a surrender call on 9 February, Stemmermann decided to break out to the south-west while units of the 1st Panzer Army attempted to create an escape corridor from the outside. The break-out commenced during the night of 16/17 February, by which time the pocket had been compressed into an area measuring eight miles by five. Contact was established with 1st Panzer Army the following afternoon, but both German corps and the *Wiking* Division required complete re-equipment and were unfit for action for several months, while *Wallonien* had been virtually wiped out; Stemmermann was killed fighting among his rearguard. German accounts admit that the wounded had to be abandoned within the pocket but claim that 35,000 men took part in the break-out and 30,000 got through. Russian claims to have inflicted 55,000 casualties and taken 18,000 prisoners were clearly exaggerated but KONEV's reward for his part in the battle was to be made a Marshal of the Soviet Union. The pocket took its name from the village and airstrip in its centre, but is sometimes referred to as Cherkassy, which lies to the east.

Kos, Dodecanese Islands, 1943

On 14 September a British force consisting of the 1st Battalion Durham Light Infantry and a company of the 11th Battalion The Parachute Regiment occupied the island with the assistance of the 5000-strong Italian garrison. The Germans, however, enjoyed total air superiority and on 3 October a brigade group landed at various points, capturing the airfield. By the evening of 4 October the Germans controlled all the strategic areas and the British troops were ordered to disperse into the interior and fight a guerrilla war. Some managed to escape in caiques manned by the Special Boat Squadron, but 900 British and

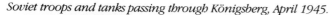

Soviet troops and tanks passing through Königsberg, April 1945.

3000 Italians were captured; 90 Italian officers were shot by the SS for fighting against their former allies. See also AEGEAN THEATRE.

Kota Bharu, Malaya, 1941

A town and airfield on the north-east coast held by the 8th Indian Brigade of 9th Indian Division (Major-General Barstow). At midnight on 7/8 December the 5300 men of the reinforced Japanese 56th Infantry Regiment, commanded by Major-General Hiroshi Takumi, began disembarking from their transports. Their landing was met with determined resistance and they sustained the loss of 320 killed and 538 wounded, while the RAF crippled one transport and severely damaged two more. By evening, however, the Japanese had established a firm beach-head and taken the airfield, forcing the 8th Indian Brigade to withdraw south of the Kelantan River.

Kozielsk, Poland, 1939–41

Kozielsk was a prisoner-of-war camp for Polish officers taken by the Soviet forces during their invasion of Poland in September 1939. It was located about 155 miles (250km) south-east of SMOLENSK. About 5000 officers were held there until April 1940, when the camp was gradually emptied. Of the 5000 prisoners, 190 were sent to a fresh camp and eventually released in 1941; the remainder were taken to KATYN WOOD and murdered.

Krakow, Poland, 1939–45

A city on the Vistula captured by Army Group South during the 1939 campaign, subsequently the headquarters of the Nazi Government-General which presided over the rump of Poland. Liberated by KONEV's 1st Ukrainian Front on 19 January 1945.

Kramer, Josef (1906–45)

Kramer was a member of the SS and a concentration camp commandant. His career began as a camp guard in 1934, and he was soon promoted to command the camp at Natzweiler, where he inaugurated the first gas chambers and personally gassed many of the inmates before moving on to command AUSCHWITZ in May 1944. In November 1944 he was appointed commandant of Bergen-BELSEN, a camp for invalids transferred from other camps in Germany. The camp was quite unable to handle the swelling number of inmates, which rose to about 40,000. When

spotted fever became epidemic, Kramer protested to Berlin but was told to continue operating the camp. When it was eventually overrun by elements of the British Army on 15 April 1945 deaths were occurring at the rate of several hundred a day and the camp was littered with some 13,000 corpses. Film of these scenes was the first indication to the general public in Britain and the USA that such camps existed, and it was in revulsion from these revelations that Kramer was dubbed the "Beast of Belsen" in the popular press. Placed on trial at NUREMBERG, it became apparent that although he had killed relatively few with his own hands, his subservience to orders and his indifference to suffering had caused thousands of deaths. He was found guilty of war crimes and hanged.

Kreipe, Gen Karl-Heinrich-Georg F.

Kreipe was a German officer who had been a divisional commander on the Leningrad and Kuban fronts and had been awarded the Knight's Cross for his victories. In 1943 he was promoted Major-General and given command of 22nd Panzer Grenadier Division, then acting as garrison troops in CRETE. In April 1944 his car was ambushed by a party of British and Cretan guerrillas and he was kidnapped. The force escaped to Egypt with Kreipe, who remained a prisoner for the remainder of the war. This was the only occasion on which British commandos or irregular forces succeeded in seizing a German general.

Kremenchug, Soviet Union, 1941 and 1943

The city on the DNIEPR where the German 17th Army established a bridgehead in September 1941. This served as a launching pad for the northward drive of von KLEIST's Panzer Group 1 which, together with a converse drive by GUDERIAN's Panzer Group 2, isolated the greater part of the Soviet South-West Front in the KIEV area. During the autumn battles of 1943 KONEV's Steppe Front (later known as 2nd Ukrainian Front) liberated the city and secured bridgeheads across the Dniepr, which HITLER had called Germany's Eastern Rampart.

Kremlin

German deception plan designed to focus Soviet attention on the MOSCOW sector prior to the activation of plan BLAU, 1942.

Kretschmer, Lt Cdr Otto (1912–   )

One of the foremost German submarine commanders in the early part of the war, in 1939 Kretschmer was commanding U-23, a small coastal U-boat. After nine successful patrols he was given command of U-99, an ocean-going boat, and began devastating Allied shipping in the North Atlantic. He received the Knight's Cross for sinking seven ships during a single patrol, and was later awarded the Oak Leaves. Estimates vary, but he is generally credited with sinking about 300,000 tons of Allied shipping during his 18-month active service. On 27 March 1941 the U-99, together with U-100, was trapped by two British destroyers. Kretschmer and his crew scuttled their boat and surrendered, spending the rest of the war as prisoners.

Krueger, Gen Walter (1881–1967)

Krueger was a self-effacing officer who had a high reputation in the American army as a competent trainer of troops in the early part of the war. In 1943 he was placed in command of the newly-activated 6th US Army in Australia, becoming part of MACARTHUR's command. Under his strict discipline and expert instruction, the 6th Army soon became a most competent force; it fought in NEW GUINEA, then in

General Walter Krueger.

236

NEW BRITAIN, the ADMIRALTIES, Biak, Noemfoor and Morotai. In October 1944 he invaded the PHILIPPINES, landing on LEYTE. In December his forces landed on MINDANAO, and in January 1945 they invaded LUZON. They then fought on to take Manila after a month of hard house-to-house fighting. Krueger was solicitous of his troops and was never inclined to stretch them beyond their capabilities. He was frequently harried by MacArthur, anxious for spectacular gains, but refused to be rushed and conducted his campaigns in a workmanlike and effective manner. His 6th Army was unusual in having fought through just about every type of terrain to be found in the Pacific theatres, from jungles and mountains to city streets.

Krummlauf

A curved barrel attachment which could be fitted to the German StuG 44 assault rifle to allow the weapon to be fired round corners. It was developed as a short-range defence weapon for tank crews, to enable them to shoot at infantry alongside their tank without having to expose themselves to fire. The curved barrel could be thrust through a port in the side of the tank and fire directed downwards and close to the vehicle. It was also found useful in street fighting. The bullets were turned through a 30-degree angle, but the range was short and the weapon inaccurate.

Krupp von Bohlen und Halbach, Alfried (1907–67)

Alfried Krupp von Bohlen was the fifth-generation Krupp of the famous armaments works family. In 1939 he was a deputy director in charge of the Mining and Armaments department. Although his father Gustav was nominally head of the firm, he was virtually senile and thus Alfried was, with a co-director Loesser, in total control of the Krupp empire. From 1939 to 1943 Krupp's principal concern was the exploitation of industrial plants in occupied territories, either by incorporating them into the administrative structure of the Krupp organization or by dismantling them and transporting the machinery, plant and workers to Germany. In 1942 he was responsible for the dismantling of much of the Soviet steel industry in the Ukraine, and after consultations with SPEER he agreed to use Soviet prisoners, civilian forced labour and concentration camp inmates in his workforce. Special workshops and factories were built in

German "Krummlauf" MP 44 machine carbine fitted with bent barrel and prism sight for shooting round corners.

or close to concentration camps, whilst other camps were sited near his factories. In 1943 the "Lex Krupp" law was passed, exempting the Krupp family from inheritance tax, whereupon Bertha Krupp von Bohlen, Alfried's mother, relinquished her inheritance and Alfried became the sole owner of the Krupp empire. Since 1934 the company had been furnishing a major part of the heavy armaments for the German forces, and the factories had a remarkable run of luck, escaping serious damage until March 1943, when Essen suffered its first major air attack. In 1944 Alfried was captured by US troops, and was arraigned as a war criminal, partly for his furnishing of armaments but more for his acquiescence in the harsh treatment of slave labour. He was sentenced to 12 years' imprisonment and the confiscation of his property, but within three years he had secured a pardon and was back at the Krupp industrial empire.

Kuchler, FM Georg Von (1881–1968)

Von Kuchler commanded the 3rd Army as part of Army Group North during the Polish campaign. In 1941 he commanded 18th Army of Army Group North in the invasion of Russia, and in January 1942 replaced von LEEB as commander of Army Group North. He retained this post until January 1944 when, after withdrawing one of his armies to avoid encirclement, he was dismissed by HITLER and placed on the reserve. Tried at NUREMBERG, he was sentenced to 20 years' imprisonment but was released in 1953.

Kufra, Libya, 1941–43

Oasis and fort in southern Cyrenaica at the eastern edge of the Rebiana Sand Sea, some 350 miles (563km) south of JALO. Kufra was captured from the Italians by General Philippe LECLERC's Free French troops on 1 March 1941 and became the forward base for LONG RANGE DESERT GROUP, SPECIAL AIR SERVICE and Sudan Defence Force operations.

Kugelblitz (Fireball) – Anti-Aircraft Tank (Ger)

Based on the chassis of the PANZERKAMPFWAGEN IV and powered by an improved performance version of the standard engine, the Kugelblitz was armed with twin 30mm cannon enclosed in a domed turret which required only 25 seconds for a complete traverse of 360 degrees. The vehicle was a notably efficient design and was capable of firing up to 900 rounds per minute, but only half a dozen or so had been completed by the end of the war.

Kula Gulf, Battle of, 1943

During the night of 5–6 July 1943 a Japanese naval squadron under Rear-Admiral Teruo Akiyami attempted to reinforce the garrison of Kolombangara, Solomon Islands, using seven destroyer transports escorted by the destroyers *Niizuki*, *Tanikaze* and *Suzukaze*. The Americans were warned of Akiyama's approach and deployed an interception force commanded by Rear-Admiral W. T. Ainsworth and consisting of the cruisers *Honolulu*, *Helena* and *St Louis*, escorted by four destroyers, across the mouth of Kula Gulf. At 0157 Ainsworth's ships opened fire, wrecking *Niizuki* and killing Akiyama, but *Tanikaze* and *Suzukaze* responded with a salvo of LONG LANCE torpedoes, three of which blew the bows off *Helena*, causing her to sink within minutes. Despite being harried by the Americans, the Japanese completed their reinforcement mission and escaped, abandoning the destroyer *Nagatsuki* when she ran aground.

Kuma Class Cruisers (Jap)

Displacement 5870 tons; *dimensions* 535ft×46ft 6in (163×14.2m); mean draught 15ft 9in (4.8m); *machinery* 4-shaft geared turbines producing shp 90,000; *speed* 31.75 knots; *protection* main belt 2in; deck 1.5–2in; *armament* 7×5.5in (7×1); 2×3in AA (2×1); 8×24in torpedo tubes (4×2); 80 mines; *aircraft* 1; *complement* 439; *number in class* 5, launched 1919–20.

Kummersdorf, Germany, 1939–45

An artillery range and weapons-proving ground used to test early rocket weapons during the 1930s.

Kunming, China, 1942–45

City in Yunnan Province which was the terminus of the BURMA ROAD and later of The HUMP air supply route from India to China. Kunming also served as a base for CHENNAULT'S American Volunteer Group, better known as "The Flying Tigers".

Kuribyashi, Gen Todomichi (1885–1945)

Kuribyashi was the Japanese commander on IWO JIMA, and constructed a formidable series of defensive works which were garrisoned by some 23,000 troops. The US Marine Corps forces which invaded the island on 19 February 1945 had a nightmarish task ahead of them, which was not made easier by Kuribyashi's exhortation to his soldiers that each must kill ten enemy before dying. Kuribyashi signalled "Goodbye" to his remaining garrison on 23 March and is presumed to have gone into the front line and been killed.

Kurita, V Adm Takeo

Kurita commanded the Close Support Force during the Battle of MIDWAY. In October 1944 he was commander of the First Striking Force in the Battle of LEYTE GULF, his objective being KINCAID's 7th US Fleet covering the American landings. On 23 October US submarines sighted Kurita's force, sinking two heavy cruisers; he sailed on into the Sibuyan Sea where on the next day aircraft from MITSCHER's Task Force 38 sank the battleship *Musashi*. In spite of these setbacks, Kurita passed undetected through the San Bernadino Strait, and on 25 August surprised Admiral Sprague's small carrier force, sinking three destroyers and an escort carrier. Convinced he was sailing into a trap, Kurita then abruptly withdrew without attacking the transports.

Kurland, Latvia, Soviet Union, 1944–45

Following the destruction of the German Army Group Centre during Operation BAGRATION, Army Group North was forced to withdraw under pressure from the Soviet Baltic Fronts until it was isolated on the Kurland Peninsula. Renamed Army Group Kurland in

German Panzers at Belgorod, Kursk 1943.

January 1945, HITLER refused to sanction the evacuation by sea of its 26 divisions on the grounds that it was tying down Soviet troops who would otherwise be available for the invasion of Germany, although he relented to the extent that the Navy later took off elements of two Panzer and four infantry divisions, 157,000 wounded and an estimated 1.5 million refugees. The army group finally surrendered to the Soviets in May 1945.

Kursk, Soviet Union, 1943

When the spring thaw halted the counteroffensive with which von MANSTEIN had recovered KHARKOV, a huge salient 100 miles (160km) across and 70 miles (112km) deep, centred on the city of Kursk, remained in the German line. HITLER felt that if the salient could be eliminated by the converging thrusts of Army Group South (Manstein) and Army Group North (von KLUGE) directed through its southern and northern flanks, the Soviet Army would be so weakened that it might be possible to negotiate some sort of peace with the Kremlin, based on the *status quo ante bellum*. The detailed planning of the operation, codenamed ZITADELLE, was undertaken by General ZEITZLER, the Chief of Army General Staff, but the idea received a mixed reception from senior German officers. Kluge was in favour but Manstein had serious reservations and MODEL, commander of 9th Army, was opposed, pointing out that the objective was so obvious that the Russians were not only fortifying the walls of the salient in depth but

had also concentrated their armour in suitable counter-attack zones. GUDERIAN, the Inspector-General of Armoured Troops, was also worried by the fact that the new Panther tank's teething troubles were far from over and that, whatever the outcome, losses were bound to be heavy at a time when reserves should be conserved to meet the anticipated Allied landing in France. Nevertheless, it was decided that *Zitadelle* would commence on 5

Kursk: The German plan, July 1943.

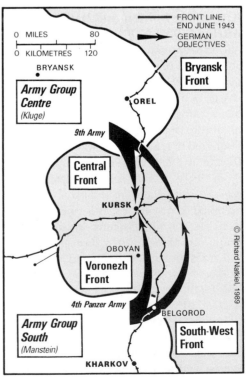

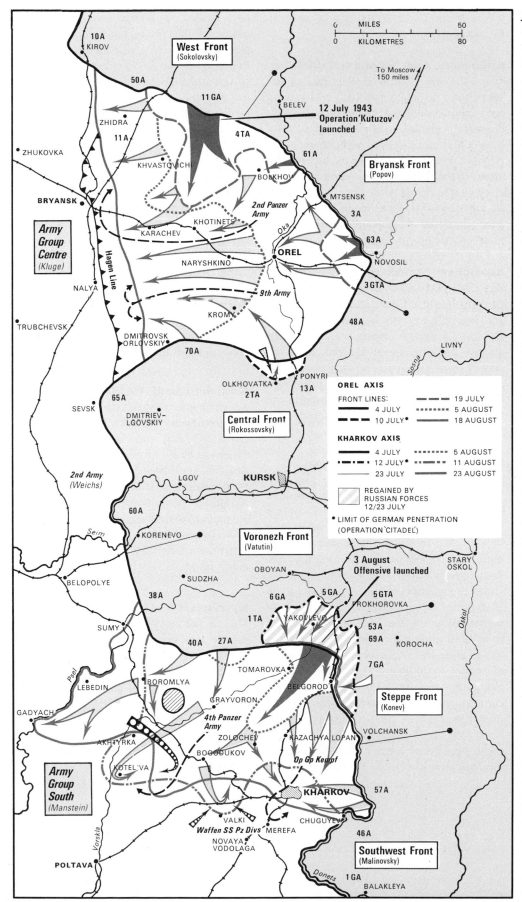

West Front
(Sokolovsky)

To Moscow
150 miles

10 A
KIROV

50 A

11 GA

BELEV

**12 July 1943
Operation'Kutuzov'
launched**

ZHIDRA

4 TA

61 A

Bryansk Front
(Popov)

11 A

ZHUKOVKA

KHVASTOVICH

BOLKHOV

MTSENSK

3 A

BRYANSK

*2nd Panzer
Army*

63 A

Army
Group
Centre
(Kluge)

KHOTINETS

NOVOSIL

KARACHEV

OREL

NARYSHKINO

NALYA

9th Army

3 GTA

TRUBCHEVSK

KROMY

48 A

LIVNY

DMITROVSK
ORLOVSKIY

70 A

OLKHOVATKA

PONYRI

OREL AXIS

FRONT LINES:

65 A

2 TA

13 A

4 JULY — — — 19 JULY
5 AUGUST

SEVSK

DMITRIEV-
LGOVSKIY

10 JULY — — — 18 AUGUST

Central Front
(Rokossovsky)

KHARKOV AXIS

4 JULY — — — 5 AUGUST

2nd Army
(Weichs)

LGOV

KURSK

12 JULY — — — 11 AUGUST

23 JULY — — — 23 AUGUST

60 A

REGAINED BY
RUSSIAN FORCES
12/23 JULY

KORENEVO

Seim

Voronezh Front
(Vatutin)

• LIMIT OF GERMAN PENETRATION
(OPERATION 'CITADEL')

BELOPOLYE

OBOYAN

SUDZHA

STARY
OSKOL

38 A

6 GA

5 GA

**3 August
Offensive launched**

5 GTA
PROKHOROVKA

SUMY

1 TA

YAKOVLEVO

53 A

40 A

27 A

69 A

KOROCHA

Psel

TOMAROVKA

7 GA

LEBEDIN

BOROMLYA

BELGOROD

GADYACH

GRAYVORON

*4th Panzer
Army*

VOLCHANSK

AKHTYRKA

ZOLOCHEV

KAZACHYA LOPAN

KOTEL'VA

BOGODUKOV

Op Gp Kempf

Army
Group
South
(Manstein)

KHARKOV

57 A

Vorskla

VALKI

CHUGUYEV

Waffen SS Pz Divs

MEREFA

46 A

NOVAYA
VODOLAGA

POLTAVA

Southwest Front
(Malinovsky)

Donets

1 GA

BALAKLEYA

*Kursk: The Soviet counter-offensive, July–
August 1943.*

July. Altogether, the Germans could deploy 2380 tanks and assault guns, 10,000 artillery weapons, 2500 aircraft and 900,000 men. The Soviets were kept fully informed of German intentions by the Lucy spy ring and prepared accordingly. The defences of the salient consisted of three fortified zones, 25 miles (40km) deep, covered by 20,000 guns of various types, over one-third of which were anti-tank weapons, and corseted by minefields laid to a density of 2500 anti-personnel mines and 2200 anti-tank mines per mile of front. Apart from their 2:1 advantage in artillery weapons, the Soviet strength was not greatly superior to that of their opponents and consisted of 3300 tanks and assault guns, 2650 aircraft and 1,337,000 men. These forces were deployed in three fronts, the northern half of the salient being held by ROKOSSOVSKY's Central Front and the southern half by VATUTIN's Voronezh Front, while in the immediate rear lay KONEV's Reserve or Steppe Front. The Soviet strategy was to absorb the German thrust before launching their own counteroffensive. From the outset, *Zitadelle* developed into a contest of attrition. The attack was launched in driving rain which turned the ground into a quagmire. In the north 9th Army advanced ten miles and was then fought to a standstill. A deeper penetration was made in the south, almost breaking through the echeloned Soviet defences. On 12 July the largest tank battle in history reached its climax on the southern sector when the 700 tanks of HOTH's 4th Panzer Army met the 850 tanks of ROTMISTROV's 5th Guards Tank Army in a gigantic but inconclusive mêlée near the village of Prokhorovka.

Events in other theatres now impinged on *Zitadelle*. On 10 July the Allies landed in SICILY and three days later Hitler told his senior commanders that the Eastern Front would have to be stripped of troops to form fresh armies in Italy. Simultaneously, the Soviets initiated a counteroffensive against the OREL salient – a mirror image of the Kursk salient and lying immediately to its north, using SOKOLOVSKY's West Front and POPOV's Bryansk Front. The 2nd Panzer Army was badly mauled and Manstein reluctantly transferred several Panzer divisions to Kluge so that his flank and rear could be protected against the Soviet onslaught. On 17 July Hitler terminated the

Zitadelle offensive. During the Kursk operations each side lost over 1500 tanks. For the Russians this was less serious, since they could recover many of their casualties from the battlefield, and their tank production capacity was far greater than Germany's. After the failure of *Zitadelle* the German Army never recovered the strategic initiative on the Eastern Front. See *Kursk – The Clash of Armour* by Geoffrey Jukes (Macdonald).

Kurt

This was a German attempt to duplicate the Barnes Wallis BOUNCING BOMB used by the British against the EDER and MÖHNE dams. Like the British bomb it was intended to roll or skip along the surface of water to its target, then sink and be detonated by an hydrostatic fuse. To give greater safety to the dropping aircraft a rocket propulsion unit was added, and since this caused the bomb to veer off course, gyroscopic stabilization was added. Development was stopped in November 1944 before the design was finalized.

Kurzzeitsperre

A German device intended to prevent low-level air attacks on gun batteries and airfields, consisting of a battery of projectors spaced some 98ft (30m) apart around the objective and capable of being electrically fired in groups. The projectile was a simple rocket which trailed a length of wire behind it in flight which was attached to the projector. When the rocket reached the end of its tether it burst and released a parachute, which drifted down at about 16ft (5m) per second. The wire was a flat ribbon of hard steel; when struck by an aircraft it would spin and saw its way through the average aircraft wing in less than a second. The height achieved was 3280ft (1000m) but it is doubtful if many systems were installed.

Kutuzov

Russian counteroffensive directed against OREL 12 July–18 August 1943, following the failure of the German ZITADELLE offensive in the KURSK salient.

Kuznetsov, Adm Nikolai G. (1902–74)

Kuznetsov was Commander-in-Chief of the Soviet Navy throughout the war and a member of the Stavka (High Command). He took no part in operations, but attended all planning conferences and was also present at the POTSDAM and YALTA Conferences. In 1945 elements of the fleet, under his command, gave assistance to Soviet Army forces in the invasion of Manchuria. After the war he appears to have fallen foul of Stalin and was reduced in rank before his retirement.

Kuznetsov, Gen Vassily (1894–1964)

Kuznetsov was a relatively young general officer who fought in the defence of KIEV in 1941 and was subsequently held responsible for the loss of the city, being a scapegoat for BUDENNY's shortcomings. He was given the command of 1st Guards Army at STALINGRAD, and subsequently became Deputy Commander of the South-West Front, fighting in the Donbass, Warsaw, East Pomeranian and BERLIN campaigns.

Kwai Railway, Thailand–Burma, 1942–45

In May 1942 the Japanese decided to build a railway from Bangkok to Moulmein, where it would join the Burmese railway system, the object being to shorten their lines of communication by eliminating the long sea passage to RANGOON round the Malayan peninsula. Using prisoners-of-war captured in Singapore, supplemented by an army of native labourers, the line was constructed from both ends with little more than hand tools and the occasional assistance of elephants. In addition to clearing the jungle along the route, it was necessary to excavate cuttings, build embankments and construct numerous bridges. The southern part of the route followed the Kwai valley but before this could be entered it was necessary to bridge the Mekhong River near Kanchanaburi. The first bridge, a timber structure, proved unequal to the task and was replaced by one of steel and concrete which was later bombed; the story of the bridge, somewhat altered, served as the basis for the film *The Bridge on the River Kwai* (1957). The first ARAKAN campaign and CHINDIT raids resulted in demands that construction be accelerated and the physical condition of the prisoners, already intolerable, degenerated even further. The Japanese engineers responsible for the line were capable and energetic, but the guards were the sweepings of the Japanese Army. When the railway was officially opened in November 1943, it had cost the lives of 13,000 Allied prisoners of war and 90,000 native labourers, an average of 400 for every one of its 250 miles (402km). These men died as a result of tropical diseases, exhaustion, accidents and brutal treatment. The line was rendered unworkable by Allied air attack and very few trains travelled its full length.

Kwajalein Atoll, Pacific, 1944

An atoll in the MARSHALL Islands, Kwajalein was captured by US 4th Marine and 7th Infantry Divisions, under the overall command of Major-General Holland M. SMITH's V Amphibious Corps, 1–4 February 1944. The 8000-strong garrison under Rear-Admiral Akiyama fought to the death. Kwajalein Island, 2.5 miles (3.8km) long, was taken by 32nd and 184th Infantry Regiments of 7th Infantry Division (Major-General Charles Corlett). See also NAMUR ISLAND and ROI ISLAND.

Kyushu Q1W1 (Lorna) (Jap)

This aircraft looked like a copy of the JUNKERS JU88 medium bomber; but less than 200 were built. It was employed as a maritime patrol aircraft and used on anti-submarine duties, some being equipped with early RADAR and other types of submarine detection apparatus. *Span* 52.5ft (16m); *engines* 2 610hp radial; *crew* 3; *armament* 1 20mm cannon, 2 machine guns, 1100lb (500kg) of bombs; *speed* 200mph (322kph).

L

"L" and "M" Class Destroyers (UK)

Displacement 1920 tons; *dimensions* 362ft 6in×36ft 9in (110.5×11.2m); mean draught 10ft (3m); *machinery* 2-shaft geared turbines producing shp 48,000; *speed* 36 knots; *armament* 6×4.7in DP (3×2); 4×2-pdr AA (1×4); 2×20mm AA (2×1); 8×0.5in AA (2×4) guns; 8×21in torpedo tubes (2×4); *complement* 221; *number in class* 16, launched 1939–42.

Laconia Order

An order to German U-boat commanders given by DÖNITZ on 12 September 1942. It arose from an incident in which *U-156* sank the ship *Laconia* in the Atlantic, just south of the equator. The ship was carrying Italian prisoners-of-war and the wives and children of Allied servicemen. The U-boat commander, Captain Hartenstein, surfaced to assist the survivors and radioed the Allied authorities to inform them of the sinking and the plight of the survivors. The U-boat was then seen and attacked by a US aircraft. Dönitz ordered that in future no such rescue attempt would be made by any U-boat. This "Laconia Order" formed one of the indictments against Dönitz at the NUREMBERG Trials.

Ladoga, Lake, Soviet Union, 1941–43

Large freshwater lake north-east of LENINGRAD. It formed a useful natural obstacle to invasion by the Germans and Finns in 1941 since it split their advance in two. Frozen, it formed a vital means of communication during the German siege in 1942–43.

L'Adroit Class Destroyers (Fr)

Very similar to the BOURRASQUE CLASS. Number in class 14, launched 1926–29. Of these, *L'Adroit* and *Le Foudroyant* were sunk during the DUNKIRK evacuation; *Boulonnais* and *Fougueux* were sunk off Casablanca on 8 November 1942, while resisting the Allied landings in North Africa, and *Brestois* and *Frondeur* were crippled in the same engagement. *La Palme*, *Le Mars* and *Le Bordelais* were scuttled at TOULON on 27 November 1942.

Lae, New Guinea, 1942–43

A minor seaport on the Huon Gulf, in north-east New Guinea. It was taken by a Japanese landing on 8 March 1942 and remained in Japanese hands until 15 September 1943, when an attack by the Australian 7th and 9th Divisions drove them out.

La Galissonnière Class Light Cruisers (Fr)

La Galissonière, *Jean de Vienne* and *Marseillaise* were scuttled at TOULON on 27 November 1942. *Montcalm* and *George Leygues* took part in the defence of DAKAR against British and Free French naval forces in September 1940, but joined the Allies in November 1943 and together with *Gloire*, the sixth member of the class, refitted in the United States. *Montcalm* and *George Leygues* bombarded shore installations on Omaha beach during the Allied invasion of NORMANDY and, with *Gloire*, supported the Allied landings in the south of France. *Displacement* 7600 tons; *dimensions* 587ft×57ft 3in (178.9×17.5m); mean draught 17ft 3in (5.2m); *machinery* 2-shaft geared turbines producing shp 81,000; *speed* 31 knots; *protection* main belt 4.7in; deck 2in; turrets 5.1in; *armament* 9×152mm (3×3); 8×90mm AA (4×2); 8×37mm (4×2); 12×13.2mm AA; 4×550mm torpedo tubes; *aircraft* 2 (1 catapult); *complement* 540; *number in class* 6, launched 1933–36.

Lameng, Burma, 1944

A small town close to the Salween River and astride the BURMA ROAD which was maintained as a Japanese garrison by the 33rd Army under General HONDA. They were driven out by the Chinese 11th Army in late September 1944.

Lamy, Fort, Chad

A fort manned by elements of the French Foreign Legion and Senegalese troops. After General LECLERC failed to take DAKAR in September 1940, he captured Gabon and then moved to Fort LAMY, where the garrison declared for DE GAULLE. Under Leclerc's command, the garrison left the fort and made their way to KUFRA Oasis, defeating the Italian garrison there, after which he associated his force with the British 8th Army.

Lanchester Armoured Car (UK)

A total of 39 vehicles of this type were built, based on prototypes delivered in 1927. A number saw action in MALAYA 1941–42 and those that survived were taken into Japanese service. In 1940 one was converted to a passenger carrying role for the transport of Cabinet Ministers and other VIPs. *Weight* 7.5 tons; *speed* 45mph (72kph); *armour* 9mm; *armament* 1 Vickers 0.5in machine gun; two Vickers 0.303in machine guns; *engine* Lanchester 88bhp petrol; *crew* 4.

Lanchester Submachine Gun

A copy of the German Bergmann MP28/II submachine gun manufactured in Britain in 1941 when weapons were urgently needed. Although intended for general use, it was overtaken by the cheaper STEN gun and was eventually made solely for the Royal Navy.

Landing Ships and Landing Craft

Designed specifically for amphibious warfare, namely the transport and landing of an invasion force and its equipment on a stretch of open enemy coastline. The Landing Ship Infantry (LSI) was equipped with landing craft for the last stage of the run in to the beach. The Landing Ship Tank (LST) was designed to beach and was fitted with opening bow doors, so tanks and other vehicles aboard could drive ashore across a lowered ramp. The Landing Ship Headquarters (LSH) was similar in design to the LSI and was fitted with communications equipment to co-ordinate activities until the invasion force could establish its own headquarters ashore. Landing Ships Fighter Direction (LSF) controlled the invasion force's forward air support, and Landing Ships Rocket (LSMR) could deliver a concentrated bombardment of thirty 5-inch rockets per minute. Various types of Landing Ship

Carrier (LSC) with their own landing craft were produced, but the difficulty in handling these led to the development of the Landing Ship Dock (LSD), essentially a self-propelled floating dock.

All landing craft were intended to beach and their size increased steadily throughout the war until the larger types, displacing over 500 tons, were capable of completing a passage on their own bottoms. Numerous versions were produced, including the Landing Craft Infantry (LCI), Landing Craft Personnel (LCP), Landing Craft Tank (LCT), Landing Craft Mechanized (LCM) capable of carrying wheeled vehicles or a tank, Landing Craft Flak (LCF) for anti-aircraft defence, Landing Craft Gun (LCG) for direct gunfire support, and Landing Craft Rocket (LCR). Some LCIs and LCMs were also modified to lay off-shore smoke screens, and other landing craft were adapted for casualty evacuation. Although landing craft were built in large numbers, there were never enough to go round and the allocation of these resources depended upon strategic priorities.

Landing Vehicles Tracked (USA)

Family of amphibious vehicles developed by the United States Marine Corps for its landing operations, based initially on the design of a tracked swamp rescue vehicle produced by the engineer Donald Roebling. The vehicles, officially designated Landing Vehicles Tracked (LVTs), were also variously known as Alligators, Buffaloes, Amphibious Tractors, Amtracs or Amtraks, and were propelled when afloat by curved grousers which formed part of each track link. The role of the LVTs was originally conceived as being that of ship-to-shore supply carriers, and in this capacity they were employed at GUADALCANAL in August 1942, Morocco in November 1942, the ALEUTIANS in May 1943 and BOUGAINVILLE in November 1943. However, at TARAWA in November 1943 they formed part of the assault force and although many were knocked out the remainder managed to land sufficient troops to win a bitterly contested victory. After Tarawa it was clear that LVTs would play a critical part in every subsequent opposed landing, and fortunately fresh designs were already in hand which resulted in up-armoured and up-gunned vehicles. Of these the most significant were the LVT(A)1, which mounted the turret and armament of the STUART light tank, the LVT(A)4, which mounted that of the HOWITZER MOTOR CARRIAGE M8, and the LVT4, with its engine housed forward, so permitting exit for troops and weapons by means of a hand operated ramp at the rear. The LVT(A)1 and LVT(A)4 were known as "amtanks" and their function was to provide direct fire support until conventional gun tanks could be got ashore. As use of LVTs became universal throughout the Pacific theatre of war, the US Army recognized their value and eventually formed seven amtank and 23 amtrac battalions, compared with the Marine Corps' respective three and eleven. In the spring of 1944 Marine divisions lost their organic amtrac battalions, which became corps troops. In North-West Europe the British 79th Armoured Division contained several LVT (Buffalo) regiments which took part in the clearance of the SCHELDT estuary and the crossing of the RHINE and ELBE rivers. In Italy British and American troops used LVTs, known locally as Fantails, to cross water obstacles during the final stages of the war. A total of 18,621 LVTs were built between 1941 and 1945, the most numerous type being the LVT4, of which 8351 were produced. See *Amtracs: US Amphibious Assault Vehicles*, by Steven Zaloga (Osprey).

Land Mines

Land mines – explosive charges buried in the ground in order to have ANTI-PERSONNEL or anti-vehicle effect – came to prominence during World War II, being extensively employed by all the combatants. They were first used in quantity in the Western Desert, as a barrier to prevent armour outflanking positions in the desert, and mines were buried by tens of thousands. The most famous of these were the German TELLERMINE, so-called from its platter-like shape and capable of stopping any tank, and the German S-MINE which, when fired, leapt from the ground to explode at waist-height. Detecting mines was at first a matter of probing the ground with prods, but the Polish Army devised an electronic detector which responded to the magnetic field disturbance due to the buried mass of metal. The response to this was to make mines of wood, glass, plastic and papier-mâché in an effort to outwit the detector. In many cases the setting of mines was done hurriedly and without proper records being kept, and even today there are areas of North Africa, Europe and Russia which are still dangerous on account of the presence of undetected mines.

Embarkation for D-Day.

Captain Hans Langsdorff of the Admiral Graf Spee, *in Montevideo.*

Langsdorff, Capt Hans (1890–1939)

Langsdorff commanded the German pocket-battleship ADMIRAL GRAF SPEE. An honourable man, he safeguarded the lives of the British merchant seamen whose ships he had sunk. When he was pursued into Montevideo after the Battle of the RIVER PLATE he recognized that escape was impossible and on HITLER's orders he scuttled his ship. He then took his own life.

La Panne, France, 1940

A coastal village north-east of DUNKIRK, from whose beach many British troops were evacuated in May 1940.

LVT in action at Lake Comacchio, Italy 1945.

Lashio, Burma, 1942

Town in north Burma, on the BURMA ROAD. Occupied after the British withdrawal in 1942, it was relinquished in the face of the advancing Chinese 1st New Army on 6 March 1945.

Latvia

An independent state since 1919, in 1939 Latvia was secretly designated by the Nazi–Soviet Pact as being in the "Soviet sphere of interest". On 5 October 1939 the Soviet Union negotiated a "mutual assistance pact" with Latvia. In April–May 1940, while world attention was focused on the German drive in Belgium and France, it overran the Baltic states, completing the occupation of Latvia on 18 June. On 21 July the new government requested transformation into a Soviet Republic; in August this request was granted, since when the country has been a Soviet colony. Soviet rule was briefly broken in 1941–44 when the country was occupied by the German Army as part of the Reichskommissariat Ostland.

Laval, Pierre (1883–1945)

Laval served as Marshal PÉTAIN's Deputy Head of State and as Foreign Minister of the VICHY French Government. His pro-German stance and willing co-operation with the occupation forces made him extremely unpopular with his fellow countrymen. His opinion that France should side with the Axis powers was not shared by Pétain, who dismissed him in December 1940, although, at German insistence, he was reinstated in April 1942. He was executed shortly after the war.

Lavochkin Aircraft (USSR)

Lavochkin LaGG-3 This single-seat fighter became operational in 1941. To overcome shortages of strategic metals, the airframe was of resin-bonded wood, making it rather heavier than a metal airframe but more easily built. The weight affected performance, requiring more powerful engines, but while over 6500 LaGG-3 were built, the aircraft was not particularly successful and losses were high. It was widely used as both fighter and ground-attack machine. *Span* 32ft (9.75m); *engine* 1 1100hp in-line; *armament* 1 20mm cannon, 3 machine guns, 485lb (220kg) of bombs or 6 rocket launchers; *speed* 345mph (555kph).

Lavochkin La-5 This was an improved LAGG-3 having a modified front fuselage to take a more powerful radial engine. It was first used during the siege of STALINGRAD and gradually replaced the LaGG-3 as a general fighter and ground-attack aircraft. The improvement was so marked that Lavochkin, the designer, was made a Hero of Socialist Labour. *Span* 32ft (9.75m); *engine* 1 1640hp radial; *armament* 2 20mm cannon, 330lb (150kg) of bombs; *speed* 400mph (644kph).

Lavochkin La-7 The La-7 was a further improvement of the LA-5 design, using metal wing spars to reduce the weight and improving the engine power. The outline was cleaned up and made smoother, and the firepower was improved. As a result it proved a

match for the German Bf 109 and Fw 190 fighters and achieved considerable success in air combat during the closing months of the war. Significantly, an La-7 was the only Soviet fighter to shoot down an Me 262 jet fighter. *Span* 32ft (9.75m); *engine* 1 1700hp radial; *armament* 3 20mm cannon, 330lb (200kg) of bombs; *speed* 423mph (681kph).

Laycock, Maj Gen Robert (1907–68)

Laycock, a former officer of the Royal Horse Guards, led a brigade-sized Commando group known as *Layforce* which was activated in Egypt during the spring of 1941. Layforce carried out raids throughout the Middle East and in May 1941 provided the rearguard in CRETE, incurring such heavy casualties that it had to be disbanded. During the night of 17/18 November 1941 Laycock was in overall command of the raid against the house at Beda Littoria in Cyrenaica which was believed, incorrectly, to be ROMMEL's headquarters. Only Laycock and one other soldier returned from this raid, reaching the British lines after a desert march lasting 41 days. "Lucky" Laycock was then posted back to the United Kingdom, where he commanded the Special Service Brigade, and subsequently led Commando operations in SICILY and at SALERNO. In the Autumn of 1943 he succeeded MOUNTBATTEN as Chief of Combined Operations and was closely involved in the planning of the Allied invasion of NORMANDY.

LCA Landing Craft Assault. Small landing craft, armoured and with quiet engines, capable of carrying about 35 fully-equipped infantry for an initial assault on an enemy-held beach.

LCI Landing Craft Infantry. Small craft capable of carrying 200–250 fully-equipped infantry soldiers. It could be beached in 29in (75cm) of water, and a ramp enabled the men to run ashore.

LCM Landing Craft Mechanized. Small landing craft designed to carry vehicles or cargo to an assault beach. It could normally carry one light tank or a number of "soft" supply vehicles.

LCP Landing Craft Personnel. Light craft about 40ft (12m) long and of wooden construction, used for ferrying troops or stores to a beach once the initial assault had succeeded.

LCT Landing Craft Tank. A small craft capable of carrying tanks to a beach. There were a number of different sizes, capable of carrying from three to eight tanks of various types.

LCT(R) Landing Craft Tank (Rocket). An LCT modified to carry a number of bombardment rockets for use against shore installations during the final phase of the assault.

LCVP Landing Craft, vehicle and personnel. A small craft capable of ferrying men and unarmoured vehicles to an assault beach.

LDV Local Defence Volunteers (UK). The name originally given, in May 1940, to the organization of part-time volunteers in Britain which was later renamed HOME GUARD.

Leahy, Adm William D. (1875–1959)

Leahy was appointed President ROOSEVELT's military representative in 1942 and was responsible for conveying the President's views to the Joint Chiefs of Staff, whose meetings he attended. During the last months of the war he also acted as military adviser to President TRUMAN.

Leander Class Cruisers (UK)

Displacement Group 1 6985–7270 tons, *Group 2* 6830–7105 tons; *dimensions Group 1* 554ft 6in × 55ft 3in (169 × 16.8m); mean draught 16ft (4.9m), *Group 2* 555ft × 56ft 9in (169 × 17m); mean draught 15ft 9in (4.8m); *machinery* 4-shaft geared turbines producing shp 72,000; *speed* 32.5 knots; *protection* main belt 4in; deck 2in; turrets 1in; *armament* 8 × 6in (4 × 2); 8 × 4in AA (4 × 2); 8 × 2-pdr AA (2 × 4, *Group 1* only); 12 × 0.5in AA (3 × 4); 8 × 21in torpedo tubes; *aircraft* 1; *complement* 550; *number in class Group 1* 5 launched 1931–34, *Group 2* 3 launched 1934.

Lebanon

Lebanon, separated from the Ottoman Empire in 1918, became a French mandate under the League of Nations. In 1940 the governor elected to serve the Vichy government. To forestall the possibility of a German Middle Eastern drive through Syria and Lebanon, the two countries were invaded by British, Commonwealth and Free French forces in June 1941. The campaign was short but vicious, ending on 11 July, after which Lebanon remained under Free French control for the remainder of the war.

Leberecht Maass Class Destroyers (Ger)

Displacement 2200 tons; *dimensions* 374 × 37ft (113.9 × 11.1m); mean draught 9ft 6in (2.9m); *machinery* 2-shaft geared turbines producing shp 70,000; *speed* 30 knots; *armament* 5 × 5in (5 × 1); 4 × 37mm AA (2 × 2); 6 × 20mm AA; 8 × 21in torpedo tubes (2 × 4); equipped for minelaying; *complement* 315; *number in class* 16, launched 1937–39.

Leclerc, Gen Philippe (1902–47)

Leclerc was the *nom de guerre* of Jacques Philippe de Hautecloque, a career soldier and scion of an aristocratic French family, who in May 1940 was serving as a captain with the French 4th Infantry Division. On 28 May he deserted to avoid surrender to the Germans and thereafter fell into enemy hands twice. He escaped on both occasions, the second time successfully, reaching England on 25 July via Spain and Portugal. He joined DE GAULLE and was appointed General Officer Commanding French Equatorial Africa and Military Governor of CHAD and Cameroun. It was at this point that he changed his name, to protect his family in France, and to disguise his aristocratic origins which he felt might be a source of prejudice against him. In December 1942 he led the Free French Forces (555 French and 2713 African troops) on an epic 1553 miles (2500km) dash across the Sahara to Libya, where they joined British 8th Army, then advancing west after its victory at EL ALAMEIN. In March 1943 his unit was equipped with a few tanks and anti-tank guns and, designated Force L, played an important part in the battle for the MARETH LINE. After the defeat of the Axis forces in North Africa, Leclerc blended the French component of Force L and French North African troops formerly loyal to Vichy into 2nd Armoured Division. In April 1944 they joined PATTON's 3rd Army in England and subsequently fought in NORMANDY. On 25 August Leclerc formally received the German surrender in Paris. He subsequently led 2nd Armoured Division in the fighting in Alsace, taking Strasbourg after a daring thrust on 21–25 November. Still mistrustful of the French military establishment after the disaster of 1940, he refused to join DE LATTRE DE TASSIGNY's French 1st Army and returned to Patton's 3rd Army for the advance across Germany. His division had the distinction of being the first Allied toops to reach Hitler's "Eagle's Nest" at BERCHTESGADEN. After

General Philippe Leclerc at the Liberation of Paris.

the war Leclerc served in Indo-China and French North Africa, where he was killed in an air crash on 28 November 1947.

Ledo Road, Burma, 1942–45

The Japanese hold on the BURMA ROAD stopped the overland supply of China in early 1942. In December 1942 General STILWELL decided to construct a road from Ledo, in upper Assam, across the Patkai Range into the Hukawng Valley, where he intended to link up with the old Burma Road and re-establish the supply line into China. An oil pipeline was to be built alongside the road, with the aim of pumping oil from Calcutta to Kunming. By the end of February 1943 the road had reached the Burma–India border but was halted by shortages of men and equipment and Japanese resistance. Work began again in October 1943, but it was not until the capture of MYITKYINA in August 1944 that the road could push forward and it was eventually completed to join the old Burma Road at Mongyu, just south of the Burma–China border on 27 January l945. When the first truck convoy arrived in Kunming on 4 February, CHIANG KAI-SHEK renamed the route the "Stilwell Road". So far as can be discovered, the oil pipeline was never built.

Lee, Adm Willis A.

Before the war Willis had been the US Navy's Director of Fleet Training. During the campaign in the SOLOMON ISLANDS he was given command of Task Force 64, flying his flag in the battleship *Washington* and sinking the Japanese battleship *Kirishima* during the night action known as the Second Battle of GUADALCANAL, 14/15 November 1942. He later commanded the American battleship group at the Battle of THE PHILIPPINE SEA and Task Force 34 during the Battle of LEYTE GULF.

Lee – Medium Tank M3 (USA)

By the summer of 1940 the success of the German Panzer divisions in France and the low countries had convinced American senior officers that their medium tanks should be armed with a 75mm gun which was a match for the PANZERKAMPFWAGEN III and IV. It would be some time before a medium tank mounting a 75mm gun in a fully traversing turret, the SHERMAN M4, would be ready for quantity production, and it was decided to produce an interim design based on an infantry tank, the

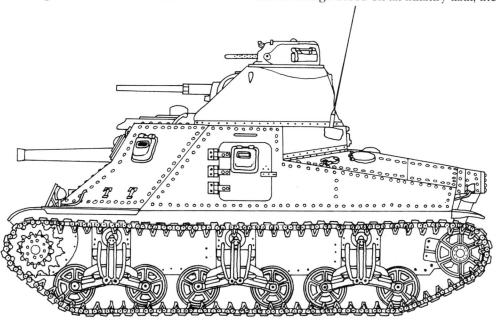

Lee medium tank M3.

Medium M2, construction of which was about to commence. This was achieved by using the wide hull of the latter to its best advantage, moving the 37mm turret to a position over what had been the left sponson and adding a commander's cupola, while the right sponson was enlarged to accommodate a 75mm gun with limited traverse. The British Tank Commission, arriving in America in June 1940, were able to make constructive suggestions during the design phase, based on experience in the field. Construction of the Medium Tank M3 commenced in August 1941 and continued until December 1942, a total of 6258 being produced. The Commission placed substantial orders for the tank, which became known as the Lee, and also for a variation of its own, which was called the GRANT: Lees equipped American medium tank battalions in North Africa until replaced by the Sherman, and a few were present with the British 8th Army during the Second Battle of ALAMEIN. The vehicle also equipped a number of British armoured regiments in Burma. The sponson mounting inhibited the use of hull-down fighting positions but this mattered little in the jungle, where it was actually an advantage to have the 75mm engaging ahead while the 37mm fired at targets on either side. *Weight* 29 tons; *speed* 26mph (42kph); *armour* 65mm; *armament* 1 75mm gun; 1 37mm gun; 3 .30 cal Browning machine guns; *engine* Wright radial 340hp petrol, or Chrysler 5-unit multibank 370hp petrol, or twin General Motors diesel producing 375hp; *crew* 7.

Leeb, FM Wilhelm Ritter von (1876–1956)

Leeb had retired from the German Army in 1938 but was recalled to command Army Group C on the Western Front. In May 1940 his army group, comprising 19 infantry divisions of moderate quality, mounted holding attacks against the MAGINOT LINE while Army Groups A and B executed the main German offensive in France and the Low Countries. During Operation BARBAROSSA he commanded Army Group North, which advanced through the Baltic States on LENINGRAD. In January 1942 he asked to be relieved of his command rather than carry out orders which ran contrary to his judgement. He was not employed again.

Lee-Enfield Rifles

The standard rifle of the British and Commonwealth forces took its name from the combination of the Lee bolt and magazine system and the Enfield pattern of barrel rifling. The first Lee-Enfield rifle was issued in 1895. A "Short" model, replacing the long infantry and short CARBINE models, appeared in 1903 and was later used during World War II. However, the majority of Lee-Enfield rifles in use during the war were the No. 4 rifles, a pattern designed for mass-production in the early 1930s. The Rifle No. 5, devised in 1944, was a short carbine type for use in jungle warfare. All Lee-Enfield rifles were of .303in (7.7mm) calibre and used a 10-shot magazine.

Leese, Lt Gen Sir Oliver (1894–1978)

Leese served with the British Expeditionary Force during the 1940 campaign in France and then as a divisional commander in the United Kingdom until he was appointed commander of the 8th Army's XXX Corps shortly before the Second Battle of ALAMEIN. He remained one of MONTGOMERY's most trusted and capable corps commanders, serving under him for the rest of the campaign in North Africa, in Sicily and in Italy, and succeeding him as commander of 8th Army on 30 December 1943. In November 1944 he was appointed Commander-in-Chief Allied Land Forces South-East Asia and held this post until succeeded by SLIM in 1945.

Le Havre, France, 1944

A major port on the English Channel. In 1944 it held a civil population of about 50,000 and a German garrison of 11,000. It was besieged by the British I Corps under General Crocker with two infantry divisions, two tank brigades, and a considerable element of specialized armour from 79th Armoured Division, including flamethrowers. In addition there were warships, a heavy concentration of artillery and assistance from the RAF dropping upwards of 4000 tons of bombs per day. The siege began on 2 September, the first assaults took place on 10 September, and at noon on the 11th the German garrison surrendered.

Leibstandarte

In 1933 HITLER formed a new personal bodyguard, the "Leibstandarte SS Adolf Hitler", under the command of Joseph "Sepp" DIETRICH. Originally comprising 120 men, the Leibstandarte swore an oath of bravery and loyalty to Hitler on 9 November 1933. The Leibstandarte served as a motorized infantry regiment during the 1939 campaign in Poland and the 1940 campaign in the West. It was expanded to become a motorized division in 1941 and saw further action during the Balkan campaign and the invasion of the Soviet Union. It took part in the occupation of Vichy

Paratroopers at Arnhem using the standard Lee-Enfield rifle.

France 1942 and was designated a Panzergrenadier division, returning to the Eastern Front in the spring of 1943. It served in Italy and then returned to the Eastern Front, being redesignated a Panzer division on 22 October. It refitted in Belgium May 1944 and fought in NORMANDY and the Battle of the BULGE. In 1945 the division fought its last battles in Hungary and Austria.

Leigh Light

An airborne searchlight, directed by RADAR before being illuminated, carried in an RAF Wellington bomber and used for detecting and illuminating submarines prior to attack. Developed by Wing-Commander H. de V. Leigh, it was first used in June 1942. By the end of the war 218 U-boats had been attacked by night, 27 sunk and 31 severely damaged. It was also used for attacks on surface shipping.

Leigh-Mallory, ACM Sir Trafford (1892–1944)

During the Battle of BRITAIN Leigh-Mallory commanded 12 Fighter Group, Fighter Command, and was responsible for the defence of the Midlands and much of East Anglia. He advocated a concentrated or "big wing" response to the Luftwaffe's attacks but the idea was opposed by DOWDING, the Head of Fighter Command, and by PARK, the commander of 11 Group, based in south-east England. When, in December 1940, Leigh-Mallory took over No. 11 Group, the threat of invasion had passed and, under the direction of DOUGLAS, he began to pursue an aggressive policy against the enemy across the Channel. In November 1942 he became Head of Fighter Command, and a year later was appointed commander of the Allied Expeditionary Air Force, which included the US 9th Air Force. Leigh-Mallory wanted to bring the British and American strategic bomber forces under his control, but neither HARRIS nor SPAATZ was prepared to tolerate this and they retained their independence. During the Allied invasion of NORMANDY his aircraft retained complete command of the air and his Transportation Plan, which destroyed the enemy's road and rail communications, ensured that the German armies on the invasion front were all but isolated during the critical period. In November 1944 he was nominated Commander-in-Chief South-East Asia Command, but died in an air crash on his way to take up the appointment.

Leipzig, KMS – Light Cruiser

Leipzig was seriously damaged in December 1939 by a torpedo from the submarine HMS *Salmon*. From 1941 onwards she served in the Baltic with the Training Squadron and later supported army operations with her gunfire. She was rammed and badly damaged by PRINZ EUGEN in a collision off Gdynia on 15 October 1944. In July 1946 she was sunk in the North Sea with a cargo of poison gas. *Displacement* 6710 tons; *dimensions* 580ft×53ft 6in (176.7×16.3m); *mean draught* 15ft 9in (4.8m); *machinery* 2-shaft geared turbines producing shp 66,000 plus 1-shaft diesel with bhp 12,400 for cruising; *speed* 32 knots; *protection* main belt 3–4in; turrets 2in; *armament* 9×5.9in (3×3); 8×3.5in AA (4×2); 8×37mm AA (4×2); 12×21in torpedo tubes (4×3); *aircraft* 2; *complement* 850; *launched* 1929.

LeMay, Gen Curtis (1906–)

A hard-driving career officer in the USAAF, dubbed "Iron Ass" by his men, LeMay commanded one of the first bombing groups, the 305th, to arrive in England with VIII Bomber Command in 1942. It was with 305th Group that LeMay devised many of the basic formation features and bombing tactics employed by 8th Air Force for the remainder of the war. In June 1943 he became commander of the relatively new 4th Bombardment Wing, which he led on the SCHWEINFURT–Regensburg mission of 17 August 1943. In July 1944 he was appointed commander of the 20th Bomber Command in the India–Burma–China theatre and executed long-range B-29 raids against targets in FORMOSA and western Japan. On 20 January 1945 he assumed command of 21st

Bomber Command, based in the MARIANAS, and commenced an air offensive against Japan's cities. To reduce his losses, he drastically modified his tactics, switching from high-level bombing to low-level night area bombing (at heights as low as 5000ft), employing incendiary bombs to destroy the highly combustible Japanese cities. On 9/10 March a force of 325 B-29s created a FIRESTORM which destroyed 16 square miles (25 square km) of TOKYO and killed approximately 84,000 people. Before the war was over similar raids reduced Osaka, KOBE, Nagoya and other Japanese cities to rubble. The final blow was delivered in August 1945 when B-29s under LeMay's overall command dropped ATOMIC BOMBS on HIROSHIMA and NAGASAKI.

Lemnitzer, Gen Lyman (1899–)

In October 1942 Lemnitzer was a member of General Mark CLARK's team of American officers who landed from a British submarine near ALGIERS to conduct clandestine negotiations with the authorities in French North Africa. During the campaign in SICILY he became ALEXANDER's Deputy Chief of Staff and held this appointment for the remainder of the war, latterly playing an important role in secret discussions culminating in the surrender of the German armies in Italy. He later became Supreme Allied Commander NATO.

Leningrad, Soviet Union, 1941–44

City on the Neva River, at the head of the Baltic. In Operation BARBAROSSA the German advance reached Leningrad on 1 September 1941. The army wanted to storm it, but HITLER ordered it to be besieged, to achieve a blood-

Battle of Leningrad, 1941.

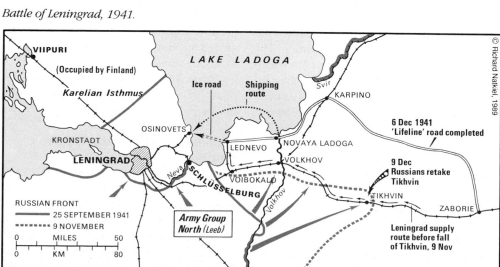

247

German infantry in a captured trench, Leningrad 1941.

less occupation. By 8 September all land communication had been cut off, limiting supply to air and river links, both under attack from German and Finnish forces. The city was constantly bombarded by air and artillery attacks. In October starvation began to take hold, and by November was causing about 300 deaths per day. Once Lake LADOGA froze, an overland supply via Tikhvin to the lake was established, but this was cut when Tikhvin was taken by the Germans on 9 November. Subsequently a second route was pioneered from Zaborie to Novaya Ladoga and thence across the lake to Leningrad, this taking effect from 6 December. Although this diminished the threat of starvation, 52,000 people died in December. Meanwhile, the inhabitants built defences, operated munitions factories and assisted the army in manning the defensive lines. The siege continued until 27 January 1944, when the German forces were finally driven beyond artillery range. During its 900 days it has been estimated that about one million inhabitants died of the privations imposed by the siege or were killed by German bombardment.

Lentaigne, Maj Gen Walter (1899–1955)

Lentaigne raised and trained the 111th Indian Infantry Brigade, which became part of WINGATE's Long Range Penetration Group, better known as the CHINDITS. On 24 March 1944 he took command of the Chindit opera-

tions in northern Burma when Wingate was killed in an air crash. He conducted the remainder of this difficult campaign with skill and determination, despite attracting criticism from STILWELL, who seemed unable to grasp that during the closing stages the Chindits were utterly exhausted and had been decimated by incessant combat and disease.

Leone Class Destroyers (Italy)

The three ships of this class formed part of the Royal Italian Navy's Red Sea destroyer flotilla, based on MASSAWA, ERITREA. *Leone* sank after striking an uncharted rock on 1 April 1941; *Pantera* and *Tigre* were scuttled two days later. See also SAURO CLASS. *Displacement* 2648 tons; *dimensions* 372×34ft (113.3×10.3m); *mean draught* 10ft (3m); *machinery* 2-shaft geared turbines producing shp 42,000; *speed* 34 knots; *armament* 8×4.7in; 2×40mm AA; 4×20mm AA; 4×21in torpedo tubes equipped for minelaying; *complement* 206; *number in class* 3, launched 1923–24.

Leopold III, King of the Belgians (1901–)

When Germany invaded Belgium on 10 May 1940, Leopold assumed command of his armed forces and formally requested Allied assistance, which was immediately forthcoming. However, after a fortnight's fighting it was clear that the war was going badly and on 28 May Leopold surrendered, contrary to the

wishes of his government, his senior officers and the majority of his people. His action rendered the position of the British and French troops in Belgium untenable and made the DUNKIRK evacuation an urgent necessity. During the German occupation he further alienated himself from his people by contracting an unpopular morganatic marriage. He was removed to Germany in 1944 and was not permitted to resume the throne after the war.

Letov S-328 (Czech)

This biplane reconnaissance-bomber was developed in the early 1930s and was widely sold to the Baltic states. The Czech Air Force purchased several batches in variant models, as night fighters and reconnaissance bombers. When the Germans took over in 1938, some 445 were in service, all of which were taken into German use. *Span* 45ft (13.7m); *engine* 1 635hp radial; *crew* 2; *armament* 4 machine guns, 660lb (300kg) of bombs; *speed* 175mph (282kph).

Lexington, USS – Saratoga and Essex Class Aircraft Carriers

Following the loss of the SARATOGA CLASS *Lexington* (CV.2) at the Battle of the CORAL SEA, her name was transferred to the ESSEX CLASS carrier *Cabot*, which was launched on 26 September 1942. The new *Lexington* (CV.16) saw action at the GILBERT ISLANDS, HOLLANDIA, the MARIANAS, Palau, LEYTE GULF and IWO JIMA. She was damaged by torpedo attack off KWAJALEIN on 4 December 1943 and again by Kamikaze aircraft off LUZON on 5 November 1944.

Leyte, Philippines, 1944

Leyte was invaded by the 6th US Army under General KRUEGER on 20 October 1944, the opening move of the recapture of the Philippines. The Battle of LEYTE GULF having shattered Japanese sea power and prevented reinforcement of the island, by a series of overland and amphibious operations the US 10th and 24th Corps ended Japanese resistance on 25 December.

Leyte Gulf, Battle of, 1944

When the American intention to invade LEYTE in the PHILIPPINE ISLANDS became clear on 17 October 1944, Admiral Soemu TOYODA, Commander-in-Chief of the Imperial Japanese Navy, decided to activate the "Sho" (Victory) Plan which had been prepared as a con-

Survivors leap from the sinking USS Lexington, *Battle of the Coral Sea.*

tingency for this event. This involved a decoy force under Vice-Admiral Jisaburo OZAWA which would approach Leyte from the north and lure Admiral William HALSEY's Third Fleet away from the invasion beach-head, the bait offered being Japan's four remaining aircraft carriers. While this was taking place a powerful Centre Force commanded by Vice-Admiral Takeo KURITA would pass through the San Bernardino Strait and a southern striking force, designated Force C, under the com-

mand of Vice-Admiral Shoji Nishimura, would negotiate the Surigao Strait, followed by a group under Vice-Admiral Kiyohide Shima. The central and southern arms of the attack would then converge on the invasion area and destroy Vice-Admiral Thomas KINKAID's Seventh Fleet, isolating the American troops ashore.

The plan was a desperate one, the major flaw being the lack of necessary air cover. Ozawa's carriers had only 116 aircraft aboard,

manned by half-trained pilots, and only doubtful support could be expected from land-based air units. Even so, Toyoda was willing to risk his fleet provided he could inflict equal damage on the numerically superior Americans. When the US Sixth Army began landing on Leyte on 20 October, the scene was set for the largest naval battle in history, involving 216 American, two Australian and 64 Japanese warships in a series of widely separated actions.

US 7th division march through a Leyte village en route to Burauen, November 1944.

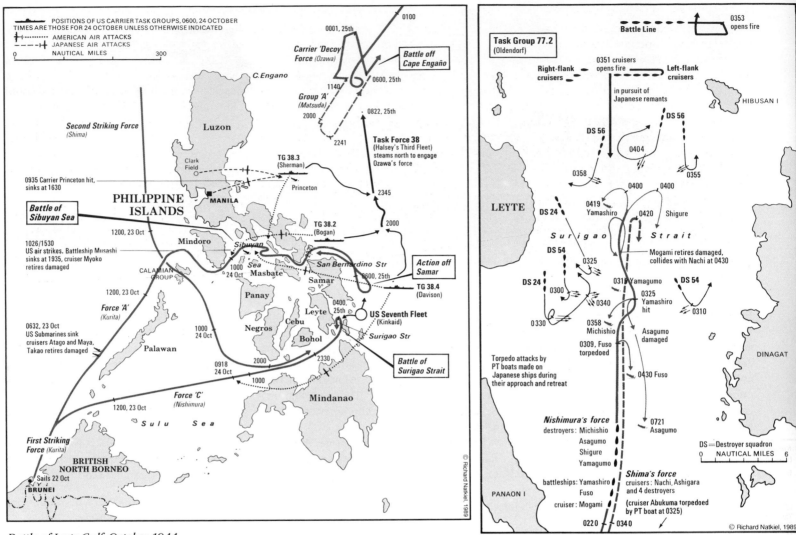

Battle of Leyte Gulf, October 1944.

Leyte Gulf: Battle of Surigao Strait.

Battle of the Sibuyan Sea, 23–24 October

Approaching from Brunei, Kurita's Centre Force, consisting of the battleships *Yamato*, *Musashi*, *Nagato*, *Kongo* and *Maruna*, 12 cruisers and 15 destroyers, was in trouble before it reached its operational area. In the Palawan Passage the submarine USS *Darter* sank Kurita's flagship, the cruiser *Atago*, causing him to transfer to *Yamato*. *Darter* also damaged the cruiser *Takao* so badly that she was forced to limp away to Singapore escorted by a destroyer. Simultaneously, the submarine USS *Dace* torpedoed and sank the cruiser *Maya*. In the Sibuyan Sea, Centre Force came under attack from the air, directed mainly at the battleships. *Musashi* was hit repeatedly by torpedoes and at 1935 on 24 October rolled over and sank. In return, land-based air strikes sank the light carrier *Princeton* and damaged the cruiser

Birmingham. During the evening Kurita reversed course and Halsey, believing that he was withdrawing, abandoned his watch over the San Bernardino Strait and set off in pursuit of Ozawa's decoy force, which had been detected that afternoon. After dark, however, Kurita reversed course again and entered the San Bernardino Strait. Thus far, Toyoda's plan was working, albeit at heavy cost.

Battle of Surigao Strait, 24–25 October

Warned of the approach of Nishimura's Force C, Kinkaid deployed Rear-Admiral J. B. Oldendorf's Bombardment and Fire Support Group, containing the battleships *Maryland*, *West Virginia*, *Mississippi*, *Tennessee*, *California* and *Pennsylvania*, eight cruisers and fifteen destroyers, to block the exit from Surigao Strait while seven more destroyers and PT boats patrolled ahead. Nishimura's force, consisting of the battleships *Yamashiro* and *Fuso*,

one cruiser and four destroyers, entered the Strait at 0300 on 25 October and were immediately assailed by destroyers and PT boats which sank *Fuso* and two destroyers and crippled a third. Unwisely persisting, Nishimura ran into the concentrated gunfire of Oldendorf's line, drawn up across his path. *Yamashiro* was wrecked, and later sunk by torpedoes, while the cruiser *Mogami* limped off with the surviving destroyer. Shima's group, consisting of three cruisers and four destroyers, arrived to find that Nishimura's force had been wiped out, and withdrew.

Action off Samar, 25 October

Kurita's Centre Force emerged from the San Bernardino Strait at 0035 and swung south. At 0645 it surprised Rear-Admiral Clifton Sprague's Escort Carrier Group 3, consisting of six escort carriers, three destroyers and four destroyer escorts, opening fire on the American ships at 0659. A chase followed in which the Japanese steadily closed the range. A counter-attack by Sprague's destroyers crippled the cruiser *Kumano* and the carrier's aircraft, joined later by others from the Seventh Fleet's Escort Carrier Groups 1 and 2, severely damaged a second cruiser, *Suzuya*, and sank two more, *Chokai* and *Chikuma*. Meanwhile, Kurita's gunfire had started to hit home, damaging four carriers, one of which, *Gambier Bay*, on fire and listing, began to fall behind. The destroyers *Johnston* and *Roberts* were sunk trying to protect her, and a third destroyer, *Dennis*, was seriously damaged. *Gambier Bay* was abandoned at 0850 and sank at 0907. Escort Carrier Group 3 now faced almost certain destruction, but at 0915 Kurita turned away to the north. His decision provoked serious criticism, but the vigour of the American response convinced him that he was dealing with a much larger force than was actually the case and so he feared that he might be entering a trap. He retired through the San Bernardino Strait, harried by a carrier

task group sent back by Halsey at Kinkaid's request. The ordeal of Sprague's crews was not yet ended, however, for land-based aircraft launched the first KAMIKAZE attacks of the war, sinking one escort carrier, *St Lô*, and damaging another, *Kalinin Bay*; two more carriers, *Suwannee* and *Santee*, were similarly damaged in Escort Carrier Group 1.

Battle off Cape Engaño, 25 October

Halsey was in contact with Ozawa's decoy force, consisting of the battleships *Hyuga* and *Ise*, the carriers *Zuikaku*, *Chitose*, *Chiyoda* and

Zuiho, three cruisers and eight destroyers, by 0240, and at dawn Vice-Admiral Marc MITS-CHER's Task Force 38, containing five fleet and five light carriers, launched the first of repeated air strikes. Ozawa had flown off the majority of his aircraft to land bases and could offer little defence. When he was mercifully able to disengage at the end of the day, the decoy force had been reduced to two battleships, two cruisers and five destroyers. Ozawa had performed his role brilliantly, but his sacrifice had been in vain.

Leyte Gulf: Battle of Cape Engaño.

Leyte Gulf: Action off Samar.

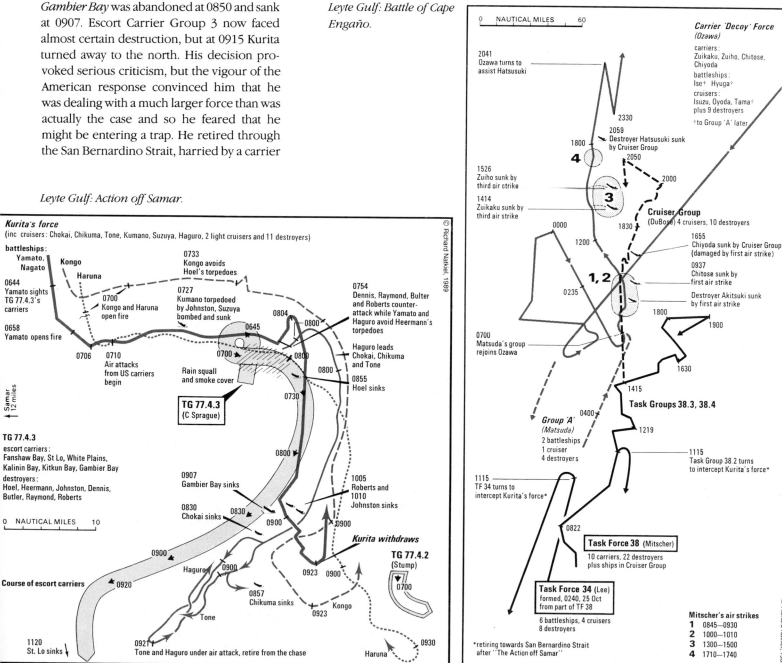

Landing craft off Leyte, 20 October 1944.

Leyte Gulf finished the Imperial Japanese Navy as a fighting force. Three battleships, four carriers, ten cruisers, eleven destroyers and one submarine had been sunk and the majority of the surviving warships were damaged. In addition, 500 aircraft were lost. Personnel casualties amounted to 10,500 seamen and aircrew. The Americans lost three light carriers, two destroyers, one destroyer escort and some 200 aircraft, plus 2800 killed and 1000 wounded.

Liberty Ships (USA)

Built in American yards as a mass-production answer to the heavy losses in merchantmen during the Battle of the ATLANTIC. They were of simple, standardized construction, displacing 10,500 tons deadweight and were driven by a single screw at a speed of 11 knots. 2770 were built in 1941–45, serving not only in the Atlantic and Mediterranean war zones but also with the US Navy's fleet trains in the Pacific. The majority were general cargo carriers but some were purpose-built tank and aircraft transports or repair and supply ships. Although usually considered an American concept, the basic design for these quickly-constructed general-purpose freighters had been produced by the Sunderland Shipping Company of Newcastle as early as 1879.

Libya, 1940–43

North African country. In 1940 Libya was an Italian colony. After Italy's entry into the war, it was attacked by British and Commonwealth troops under General O'CONNOR. The demand for forces in ERITREA and later GREECE prevented the British from completely occupying Libya, thus allowing General ROMMEL and the AFRIKA KORPS to gain a foothold, after which Libya became a battleground until 1943.

Lichtenstein

Lichtenstein was a German airborne interception RADAR for night fighter use. The first successful German equipment of this nature, it went into service in August 1943. Its presence could be recognized by the antenna placed on the nose of the aircraft.

Liddell Hart, Capt Basil (1895–1970)

Liddell Hart served as an infantryman in World War I and was severely gassed on the Somme. He subsequently wrote a number of infantry training pamphlets, including one which recommended what he termed the "expanding torrent" method of attack, which bore great similarity to that employed by Ludendorff's Storm Troop battalions in the German offensives of 1918. As a professional infantryman he remained firmly convinced that his own branch of service was the dominant factor on the battlefield until the events of 1918 and the writings of Major-General J. F. C. Fuller converted him to the belief that the tank was a battle-winner in its own right. In 1927 he was invalided out of the army and took up the pen as a career, his newspaper articles and books constantly commending the joint use of armour and air power to achieve strategic paralysis by deep penetration, simultaneously exhorting the benefits of the indirect as opposed to the direct approach to a strategic objective. His work was widely read abroad, especially in Germany, as was that of Fuller and MARTEL, and was one of several factors which shaped the technique of Blitzkrieg. He did not share the French view that the ARDENNES were tank-proof, and the events of May 1940 were to prove him correct. In 1937 he briefly served as an adviser to the War Minister Hore-Belisha, but he held no official appointment during World War II. After the war he interviewed many of the senior German commanders and incorporated their views into an analysis of German strategy, *The Other Side of the Hill*. He was knighted in 1966.

Lidice, Czechoslovakia, 1942

A village near Kladno, Bohemia, which was destroyed on 10 June 1942 as a reprisal for the assassination of HEYDRICH, then Reichs Protector of Bohemia–Moravia. All males over 16 years of age were shot; all females were transported to RAVENSBRUCK concentration camp; and all children were moved to a concentration camp at Gneisenau. There were few survivors at the end of the war.

Liège

German counterattack at MORTAIN, August 1944.

Lightfoot

Codename for the Second Battle of ALAMEIN, October 1942.

Light Gun

German terminology for recoilless artillery guns developed for use by airborne troops. These guns fired a conventional shell by means of a cartridge which discharged a proportion of its blast backwards through a venturi in the gun breech. This balanced the momentum of the forward-moving shell, thus making the gun stationary. The gun did not, therefore, require a heavy recoil control mechanism, nor a heavy and robust carriage. The first model, the LG 40, was a 75mm weapon which fired a 12.75lb (5.8kg) shell to a maximum range of 7432yds (6800m). This was used with success during the airborne invasion of Crete. Numerous later models, of 75mm and 105mm calibre, were developed but were used entirely as light infantry support weapons.

Lila

German plan for the seizure of the Vichy French Fleet, November 1942.

The ruins of Lidice, on the day after it was razed to the ground.

Lili Marleen or Lilli Marlene

The most popular song of the war, with words by Hans Leip and music by Norbert Schultze. The original version was sung by Lale Anderson and broadcast by the German-controlled Radio Belgrade from 18 August 1941 onwards for the benefit of German troops serving in North Africa. It became equally popular with British and Commonwealth troops and several English versions were recorded. The words, which were written during World War I, tell the story of a young soldier and the girlfriend whom he used to meet "underneath the lantern, by the barrack gate".

Limpet Mine

A type of explosive mine fitted with magnets for attachment to the bottom of ships. It was used by frogmen and covert sabotage teams.

Lion-Sur-Mer, France, 1944

A coastal village in NORMANDY which was the easternmost point of the Allied invasion on 6 June 1944. It was attacked by Canadian troops of the North Shore Regiment, supported by tanks of the Fort Garry Horse.

Liri River, Italy, 1944

An Italian river running south-east to join the GARIGLIANO south of CASSINO. It formed the right anchor of the German defensive line from the Cassino monastery confronting the British 8th Army in May 1944. After the fall of Cassino, the Liri Valley was the advance route of British and Canadian troops. The 1st Canadian Division took the brunt of the fighting between 16 and 23 May, by which time the valley was secured.

List, FM Wilhelm (1880–1971)

List commanded the German 14th Army during the 1939 campaign in POLAND and the 12th Army during the 1940 campaign in the West, following which he received his Field-Marshal's baton. In the spring of 1941 he was responsible for the southern wing of the invasion of GREECE and YUGOSLAVIA. During the 1942 offensive in the USSR he commanded Army Group A's advance into the Caucasus but was dismissed on 6 September for failing to comply with HITLER's directives. He was convicted of war crimes at NUREMBERG and served five years of a life sentence.

Lisunov L1-2 (USSR)

This aircraft was the American DOUGLAS DC-3 transport built, with modifications, under licence in Russia. The principal difference was the use of Russian engines but, with this exception, the modifications were largely to suit Russian manufacturing methods. *Span* 95ft (29m); *engines* 2 1000hp radial; *crew* 4; *speed* 225mph (362kph).

Lithuania

An independent country since 1919, Lithuania was deemed to be within the Soviet sphere of influence by the Nazi–Soviet Pact of 23 August 1939. On 15 June 1940 Soviet forces invaded Lithuania, including a border strip which had been reserved by Germany in the Pact. On 21 July, in common with the other Baltic States, the newly-installed puppet government requested incorporation as a Soviet Socialist Republic, which followed in August 1940. After the German invasion in 1941, Lithuania became part of the Reichskommissariat Ostland until recaptured by the Soviet advances in 1944. Since that time the country has been part of the Soviet Union.

Little Boy

Little Boy was the codename for the first ATOMIC BOMB, dropped on HIROSHIMA on 6 August 1945. Originally named "Thin Man", the bomb weighed about five tons and carried a core of 137lb (62kg) of Uranium 235.

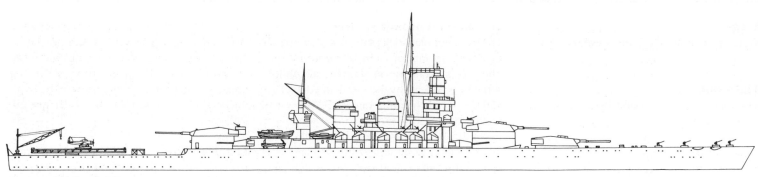

Littorio class battleship.

Littlejohn Adapter

A muzzle attachment used on British 2pr and US 37mm tank guns, it was a short extension of the barrel in which the calibre gradually decreased, so that the 40mm version had an exit calibre of about 32mm. Although they were in use from 1943 onwards, the 2pr and 37mm guns were by that time no longer significant weapons and little used in action, having been replaced by the 57mm 6-pounder guns.

Little Saturn

Soviet counteroffensive against German forces attempting to relieve STALINGRAD.

Littorio Class Battleships (Italy)

Littorio was sunk by British aircraft at TARANTO on 12 November 1940 and although raised and repaired was out of action for several months. *Vittorio Veneto* was damaged by air-launched torpedo on 28 March 1941, and was again torpedoed by the submarine HMS *Urge* in December that year, spending three months undergoing repair. She was further damaged by air attack in June 1943. *Roma* was sunk by a German radio-controlled glide bomb in September 1943 while on passage to surrender at Malta. *Displacement* 41,650 tons; *dimensions* 780×108ft (237.7×32.9m); mean draught 34ft 5in (10.5m); *machinery* 4-shaft geared turbines producing shp 128,000; *speed* 30 knots; *protection* main belt 2.4–13.6in; deck 6.4in; turrets 7.9–11in; *armament* 9×15in (3×3); 12×6in; 12×3.5in AA; 20×37mm AA; 28–32×20mm AA; *aircraft* 3; *complement* 1872; *number in class* 3, launched 1937–39.

Litvinov, Maxim M. (1876–1952)

Litvinov was Soviet Commissar for Foreign Affairs from 1930 to May 1939, when he was replaced by MOLOTOV. He had always favoured a policy of co-operation between the USSR and the West against the Fascist powers and this resulted in his being appointed Ambassador to the United States, a post which he held from 1941 to 1943.

Liuzzi Class Submarines (Italy)

On Italy's surrender *Reginaldo Guiliani* was interned by the Japanese at SINGAPORE and handed over to the German Navy in which she served as *UIT 23*; she was sunk in the Malacca Straits by HM submarine *Tally-ho* on 14 February 1944. *Displacement* 1031 tons (1166/1484 tons normal); *dimensions* 249ft 9in×23ft (76.1×7m); *machinery* 2-shaft diesel/electric motors hp 3500/1500; *speed* 18/8 knots; *armament* 1×3.9in; 3×13.2mm AA; 8×21in torpedo tubes and 12 torpedoes; *complement* 58; *number in class* 4, launched 1939–40.

Livens Projector

A specialized MORTAR developed during World War I, the projector was the invention of a Captain Livens. It consisted of a short barrel which was buried in the ground, canted towards the enemy at an angle of 45 degrees. It was then loaded with a guncotton propelling charge and a cylinder of liquid gas. Livens Projectors were emplaced by the hundred, in long lines behind the forward trench line, and fired en masse by electricity, so throwing a very large quantity of gas into the enemy trenches. Manufacture of Livens Projectors and gas cylinders was resumed in 1939 in Britain and they were held in reserve for most of the war, though they were never used.

LMG Light machine gun. Magazine fed, supported by a bipod and capable of being carried by one man.

LO Liaison Officer.

Loch/Bay Class Frigates (UK)

Displacement Loch Class 1435 tons; *Bay Class* 1580 tons; *dimensions* 307ft 3in×38ft 6in (93.6×11.7m); mean draught 9ft 9in (2.97m); *machinery* 2-shaft reciprocating engines with ihp 5500; *speed* 20 knots; *armament Loch Class* 1×4in; 4×2-pdr AA (1×4); 6×20mm AA (2×2 and 2×1); 2 Squid; *Bay Class* 4×4in AA (2×2); 4×40mm AA (2×2); 4×20mm AA (2×2); 1 Hedgehog; *complement Loch Class* 114; *Bay Class* 157; *number in class* 53, launched 1943–45.

Lockheed Aircraft (USA)

Lockheed A-28/29 Hudson This was the first American aircraft to see combat service during the war, since it had been purchased by the RAF in 1938 as a maritime patrol bomber

Lockheed Hudson GR.V patrol bomber.

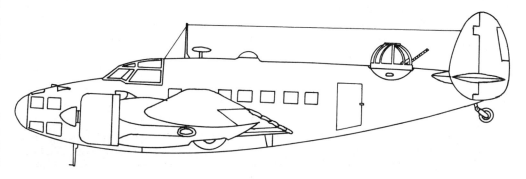

and reconnaissance machine. Over 2000 were used by the RAF, and the USAAF and Navy adopted them in smaller numbers. An A-28 Hudson shot down the first German aircraft to be destroyed by the RAF during the war, on 8 October 1939. *Span* 65.6ft (20m); *engines* 2 1200hp radial; *crew* 5; *armament* 5 to 7 machine guns, 1400lb (635kg) of bombs; *speed* 250mph (402kph).

Lockheed C-56 Lodestar Designed as a commercial airliner before the war, the Lodestar was requisitioned into US service in 1941, after which a slightly modified version was built for service use. A twin-engined, twin-tail monoplane, it was widely used by US and British forces as troop transport, ambulance and general cargo carrier. *Span* 65.5ft (20m); *engines* 2 1200hp radial; *crew* 4; *payload* 18 troops; *speed* 255mph (410kph).

Lockheed C-69 Constellation Design of this commercial airliner, destined for adoption by TWA, began in 1939 but upon America's entry into the war it was requisitioned for military use and became a troop transport. No more than 20 were built during the war, 19 of them as 65-scat C-69s and one as a 43-seat C 69C. *Span* 123ft (37.5m) *engines* 4 2200hp radial; *speed* 329mph (529kph).

Lockheed P-38 Lightning The P-38 was Lockheed's first venture into fighter aircraft and it was a highly advanced design for 1937, a twin tail-boom machine with turbo-charged Allison engines and the pilot in a small nacelle between the booms. In 1940 the RAF ordered 143 but, after testing the first three, rejected the balance of the order; the trouble lay in the US embargo on exporting the turbo-charged engine, without which the P-38 had a very poor performance at altitude. The USAAF began receiving the P-38 in 1941 and it became one of their more important wartime aircraft, its pilots claiming the destruction of more Japanese aircraft in the Pacific theatre than by any other type. It was also valuable as a long-range escort for bombers in Europe, and was used for photo-reconnaissance and as a fighter-bomber. *Span* 52ft (15.9m); *engines*, 2 1745hp in-line; *armament* 1 20mm cannon, 4 machine guns, 4000lb (1800kg) of bombs or 10 5in rocket launchers; *speed* 414mph (666kph).

Lockheed PV-1 Ventura This was a further development from the LODESTAR intended as a maritime patrol bomber, and was originally designed to meet an RAF demand for a successor to the HUDSON. First issues were made

The Lockheed P-38 "Lightning" long-range fighter.

to the RAF in mid-1942 as a light bomber, and it was adopted by the USAAF for coastal patrol and training duties. The principal production model was the US Navy PV-1, used mainly in the Pacific theatre. *Span* 65.5ft (20m); *engines* 2 2000hp radial; *crew* 4; *armament* 6 machine guns, 3500lb (1600kg) of bombs or depth charges, or 1 torpedo; *speed* 300mph (482kph).

Lockheed PV-2 Harpoon This was a development of the PV-1, with redesigned wings, a new tail, greater range and a larger bombload. It was adopted as a maritime patrol bomber by the US Navy and was highly successful. *Span* 75ft (22.9m); *engines* 2 2000hp radial; *armament* 10 machine guns 4000lb (1800kg) of bombs, or 1 torpedo; *speed* 280mph (450kph).

L of C Line of Communication (UK).

Lofoten Islands, Norway, 1941

A group of islands off the Norwegian coast, about 125 miles (200km) north of the Arctic Circle. An important source of fish and fish-oil for the German economy, it was the target of the first major British COMMANDO raid on 4 March 1941. About 300 British and 50 Norwegian troops landed with complete surprise, destroyed some 800,000 gallons of oil and 18 factories, took 250 prisoners, and returned

with 314 Norwegian volunteers. There were no British casualties. A second successful raid was carried out on 26/27 December 1941, more factories and shipping being destroyed.

Lomax, Gen Cyril Ernest Napier (1893–1973)

During World War I Lomax was decorated on several occasions and was Mentioned in Despatches no less than five times. After commanding an infantry brigade in the Middle East he was appointed GOC 26th Indian Division, which he led during the abortive ARAKAN campaign of 1943, the second Arakan campaign the following year, and the successful amphibious landings which resulted in the capture of RAMREE ISLAND and RANGOON in 1945.

Lombok Strait, Battle of, 1942

During the night of 19/20 February 1942 a Dutch/American squadron, under the command of Rear-Admiral Karel Doorman and consisting of the cruisers RNNS *De Ruyter*, *Java* and *Tromp* and one Dutch and six American destroyers, attempted to disrupt the Japanese landing on BALI. In a confused action one Japanese destroyer and a transport were damaged, but the Dutch destroyer *Piet Hein* was sunk, and *Tromp* had to withdraw to Australia for repairs. The invasion of Bali continued as planned. See also JAVA SEA.

Air raid damage in London.

Long Range Desert Group

Formed in July 1940 by Major Ralph Bagnold, a noted desert traveller of the interwar years, as a deep-penetration reconnaissance force capable of operating in the outer reaches of the Western Desert. The LRDG employed selective recruiting and was subdivided into patrols which normally operated in two halves, each of five or six vehicles. Its training included driving and recovery techniques in all sorts of terrain, desert navigation of the highest standard, long-range radio communications and survival. In March 1942 it reached its full establishment of 25 officers and 324 other ranks, manning 110 vehicles. Operating from oases far to the south of the main battle area, the LRDG carried out reconnaissance of specific objectives, intelligence-gathering missions which included surveillance of enemy traffic on the coast road, the insertion and extraction of agents and SPECIAL AIR SERVICE teams, and occasionally direct action such as harassing attacks, ambushes and minelaying. In March 1943 the Group was withdrawn to Cairo to re-equip for subsequent operations in Greece, Italy and Yugoslavia. It was disbanded in August 1945.

Long Range Penetration Group

Conceived by the future Major-General Orde WINGATE as a means of disrupting the enemy's rear areas and forcing him to divert first line troops for their defence. Wingate's own handling of GIDEON FORCE in Ethiopia vindicated the concept and was a factor which enabled him to obtain approval for the formation of the CHINDITS.

London, 1940–45

The capital city of Great Britain was the target of major air raids by the German Luftwaffe which commenced on 7 September 1940, turned to night bombing in early October, and continued until 13 November; on 14 November COVENTRY was raided, and thereafter the targets were spread throughout Britain. London continued to receive sporadic raids throughout 1941–43, then became the target for the V-1 and V-2 missiles in 1944–45. See BLITZ.

Long Island Class Escort Carriers (USA)

Displacement 11,300 tons; *dimensions* 492ft×69ft 6in (150×21.2m); mean draught 25ft 9in (7.8m); *machinery* 1-shaft diesel motors producing shp 8500; *speed* 18 knots; *armament* 1×5in; 2×3in; *aircraft* 21; *complement* 950; *number in class* 2, completed 1941–42.

Long Lance – Torpedo (Jap)

The Type 93 24-inch torpedo was fitted with a warhead twice the size of its Allied counterparts and was propelled by oxygen-enriched fuel to a range of 44,000 yards (40,200m) at 36 knots or half that distance at 50 knots. Its range, accuracy and destructive power gave the Japanese an immense advantage during the Battle of the JAVA SEA and the fighting off GUADALCANAL. Although its development was marred by a series of fatal accidents, Long Lance proved to be one of the most effective weapon systems of the war.

Longstop Hill, Tunisia, 1942–43

A commanding feature in the Medjerda Valley, North Africa, which in German hands blocked the British advance from Medjez to Tunis and the American advance towards Mateur. Longstop Hill was captured in December 1942 by the Coldstream Guards, but was almost immediately retaken by the Germans, in whose hands it remained until taken by the Argyll and Sutherland Highlanders on Good Friday 1943.

Long Tom

A nickname applied to many sorts of artillery pieces over the years, but in World War II it was used particularly to describe the American 155mm Gun M1 which fired a 95lb (43kg) shell to a range of 14 miles (23km).

Lorient, France, 1944–45

Seaport and naval base in Brittany which became a major submarine base under German occupation. The US 4th and 6th Armored Divisions attacked in August 1944, but the German XXV Corps under General Fahrmbacher withdrew into Lorient and mounted a determined defence. Since the port was not essential to Allied supply, and the U-boats there could be neutralized by coastal blockade, the Allies were content to leave the port besieged, and it did not surrender until the general German capitulation on 8 May 1945.

Lorraine – Battleship (Fr)

Launched in 1913, *Lorraine* originally formed part of the BRETAGNE CLASS but was extensively rebuilt 1934–35, her midships turret being replaced by an aircraft catapult. When France surrendered in June 1940 she was at ALEXANDRIA with several other French ships. The French commander, Admiral Godfroy, reached an agreement with Admiral CUNNINGHAM by which the ships were disarmed but remained under French control, and in May 1943 the squadron joined the Allies. *Lorraine* took part in the liberation of TOULON and in April 1945 bombarded German positions which were still holding out at the mouth of the Gironde. *Displacement* 23,549 tons; *dimensions* 544ft×88ft 6in (165.8×26.9m); mean draught 30ft (9m); *machinery* 4-shaft geared turbines producing shp 43,000; *speed* 21.5 knots; *protection* main belt 10in; deck 1.5in; turrets 13in; *armament* 8×340mm (4×2); 14×138mm (14×1); 8×100mm AA (4×2); 8×37mm AA; 12×13.2mm AA; *aircraft* 2; *complement* 1190.

Lorraine – Tracked Carrier (Fr)

Lightly armoured, fully tracked supply and personnel carrier introduced in 1938. After the fall of France the German Army made extensive use of captured chassis as self-propelled artillery mountings. These included 150mm and 105mm howitzers and a MARDER tank destroyer armed with a 75mm PAK 40/1 anti-tank gun.

Los Alamos, United States

American experimental establishment in New Mexico, principal laboratory of the "Manhattan Engineer District" in which the first ATOMIC BOMB was perfected, using Uranium U235 for the nuclear reaction.

Los Angeles, Battle of, 1942

An erroneous US Army Air Corps engagement in the vicinity of Los Angeles in February 1942, when misinterpreted RADAR information led to the deployment of fighter aircraft which then proceeded to chase each other and add more confusion to the radar picture. Fortunately no damage was done. This fiasco was very similar to the Battle of BARKING CREEK, an ordeal which every wartime air force had to go through before its warning and control system was perfected.

LRDG   LONG RANGE DESERT GROUP.

LSA   Landing Ship Assault.

LSD   Landing Ship Dock.

LSH   Landing Ship Headquarters. A ship capable of being beached, containing communications and other facilities for command. It could serve as a floating headquarters or administrative unit until facilities could be set up on shore.

LSI   Landing Ship Infantry. A ship of between 3000 and 10,000 tons displacement, which was designed to carry infantry and tranship them into LCI prior to the assault. Not intended to be beached, but could, after the initial assault, ferry troops close in to the target.

LSL   Landing Ship Logistic.

LST   Landing Ship Tank. The largest landing ship capable of grounding on the beach and then recovering itself. Designed to carry from 40 to 70 tanks, the vessel had bow doors and ramps which allowed the vehicles to drive straight off the vessel and on to the beach. There were three types of LST varying in displacement from about 1100 to 3100 tons.

Lübeck, Germany, 1942

Seaport on the Baltic and the target of one of the first major incendiary raids flown by RAF BOMBER COMMAND. A medieval town with many wooden buildings, Lübeck was highly combustible. Essentially, Lübeck, and its civilian population, were attacked because they were vulnerable; the city was not an important military target. The raid was mounted on 28 March 1942 by 234 bombers, which delivered several thousand incendiary bombs and 3000 tons of high-explosive bombs. Lübeck was severely damaged, but military production was back to normal within a week.

Lublin, Poland, 1944

A Polish city, south-east of Warsaw. It became the seat of the "Lublin Committee" or "Lublin Government", the Polish Committee for National Liberation, on 25 July 1944 immediately after the Soviet liberation of the city. This committee – the nucleus of the Polish Communist government of 1944–45 – created the Polish People's Army, which combined the Polish Army formed in the USSR in 1943 and the People's Army, a clandestine Communist force created in Poland in 1942.

Lucas, Maj Gen John P. (1890–1949)

Lucas took over the US VI Corps at a difficult moment during the SALERNO operations and led it capably during the American 5th Army's break-out and advance to the GUSTAV LINE. He was then selected by General CLARK to command Operation SHINGLE, the Allied landing at ANZIO to outflank the Gustav Line and render the German position at Monte CASSINO untenable. Clark's choice was influenced by Lucas' thorough approach to the problems with which he had been confronted, but when VI Corps, which had been reinforced with British formations, landed at Anzio on 22 January 1944 Lucas was tired, depressed, pessimistic and indecisive. He could have taken the ALBAN HILLS, which dominated the enemy's main supply route, but seems to have been unduly influenced by Clark's warning not to "stick his neck out". This, coupled with the rapid German response to the landing, meant that Anzio beach-head was quickly contained and its defenders soon became involved in desperate fighting to maintain their positions. Both Clark and ALEXANDER soon lost confidence in Lucas and on 22 February he was replaced by Major-General Lucien K. TRUSCOTT, Jr, the commander of the US 3rd Division.

Luchs (Lynx) – Light Tank (Ger)

A reconnaissance version of the PANZERKAMPFWAGEN II employing a distinctive suspension consisting of five large interleaved bogie units per side, carried on torsion bars. Development began in 1938, much emphasis being placed on the installation of medium and short wave radio equipment and this, together with the need for an additional operator, resulted in an impossibly crowded interior. The vehicle began entering service in 1943. Of the 131 built, the last 31 were armed with a 50mm L/60 gun which was overlarge for the space available. The Luchs served exclusively in armoured reconnaissance battalions. Plans for a more heavily armoured version mounting a 50mm gun and coaxial machine gun were shelved although the turret was later fitted to the PUMA armoured car. Had the vehicle been built, it would have been known as the Leopard. *Weight* 11.8 tons; *speed* 37.5mph (60kph); *armour* 30mm; *armament* 1 20mm cannon plus 1 7.92mm machine gun; or 1 50mm gun; *engine* Maybach HL 66P 180hp petrol; *crew* 4.

Ludendorff Bridge, Germany, 1945

A major bridge over the Rhine at REMAGEN. It was a rail bridge, but the track had been planked over to allow road transport to supply the German 15th Army in 1945. The speed of the American advance, coupled with German errors, allowed the bridge to fall into the hands of the US 9th Armored Division on 7 March 1945. An abortive attempt to demolish the bridge, previous bombing attacks, and heavy American traffic as the US 12th Army Group drove as much armour as possible across it, brought about its collapse on 17 March.

Lumberjack

American drive to the Rhine following GRENADE, March 1945.

Lumsden, Lt Gen Herbert (1897–1945)

Lumsden, a cavalryman, was one of very few serving officers to have ridden as a gentleman jockey in the gruelling Grand National steeplechase. During the 1940 campaign in France he commanded the 12th Lancers, an armoured car regiment which distinguished itself in the retreat to DUNKIRK. A notably strict disciplinarian out of the line, in action he led by example and encouragement but tended to be dogmatic in his views and was not on good terms with his fellow-generals. In 1942 he commanded the 1st Armoured Division at GAZALA–KNIGHTSBRIDGE, where he was wounded, and at the First Battle of ALAMEIN, where he was wounded again. At the Second Battle of ALAMEIN he commanded X Corps, which contained the greatest proportion of the 8th Army's armour and was detailed to exploit the victory. The pursuit of ROMMEL's

army, however, was delayed by fuel shortages and heavy going caused by torrential rain and, following disagreements with MONTGOMERY, Lumsden was replaced by HORROCKS.

Lüneburg Heath, 1945

Area of Germany south-east of Hamburg, open moorland and scrub, where the German surrender in the West took place on 8 May 1945.

Lustre

Movement of British troops from Egypt to Greece, March 1941.

Luth, Capt. Wolfgang

Second highest-scoring German submarine commander of World War II. Luth commanded four submarines during his operational career, the Type IIB *U-9*, the TYPE IID *U-138*, the Type IXA *U-43* and the Type IXD2 *U-181*. In 14 patrols he sank 43 ships totalling 225,712 tons, and one submarine.

Lütjens, Adm Günther

Lütjens' first appointment during World War II was as Commander Scout Forces. He led several sorties into the North Sea and pro-

KMS Lützow.

vided the covering force for the German invasion of NORWAY, after which he became Fleet Commander, controlling the operations of surface warships and commerce raiders, including the cruise undertaken by the SCHARNHORST and GNEISENAU early in 1941. He was then directed by Grand Admiral RAEDER to lead RHEINÜBUNG (Operation Rhine), a major sortie by German surface units against British shipping in the Atlantic. This involved two groups, the BISMARCK and PRINZ EUGEN from the Baltic, and *Scharnhorst* and *Gneisenau* from BREST, which would rendezvous at sea, with logistic support provided by seven tankers and supply ships. However, the Brest group was undergoing repairs and Lütjens was overruled when he suggested delaying departure until these had been completed. Flying his flag aboard *Bismarck*, he sailed from Gdynia on 18 May 1941, but five days later his force was sighted and shadowed by the cruiser Suffolk. On 24 May he was engaged by the HOOD and PRINCE OF WALES, sinking the former but inexplicably permitting the latter to break contact. He ignored the advice of his flag captain, Lindemann, that the group should return to Germany after its undoubted victory, although he did detach *Prinz Eugen* in the

hope that she would draw off the pursuit. On 25 May the shadowing warships lost contact with *Bismarck* but Lütjens, who had decided to make for Brest, failed to keep radio silence and his transmissions were monitored, giving his approximate position. On 26 May the battleship was sighted by an RAF flying boat and during the next 24 hours she was hunted down and finally sunk by units of the Home Fleet and FORCE H. Lütjens did not survive.

Lüttwitz, Lt Gen Freiherr Heinrich von

Lüttwitz commanded the 20th Panzer Division (1943) and then the 2nd Panzer Division (1943–44) on the Eastern Front. In 1944 he took over XLVII Panzer Corps, which he led in NORMANDY, being wounded as his troops fought their way out of the FALAISE pocket. During the ARDENNES counteroffensive in December he failed to capture BASTOGNE and was forced to divert much of his corps' strength to its siege. In February 1945 he opposed the British and Canadian advance on the REICHSWALD sector of the Western Front. XLVII Panzer Corps was later trapped in the RUHR pocket and forced to surrender.

Lutz, Gen Oswald

Lutz was closely involved in the development of the German Panzerwaffe, both before and after HITLER'S repudiation of the Treaty of Versailles in 1935. He served as Inspector of Transport Troops, then as Inspector of Mechanized Troops from June 1934, and became Head of Armoured Troops Command in September 1935. For much of this period GUDERIAN served as his Chief of Staff and together the two worked on the development of AFVs and their associated weapon systems, the internal establishment of armoured formations and the tactics which they were to employ. In 1937 Lutz was appointed commander of XVI Corps, containing three Panzer divisions, and was thus the first officer to lead an armoured formation of this size. He was succeeded by GUDERIAN in February 1938.

Lützow, KMS – Deutschland Class Pocket Battleship

Formerly *Deutschland*, renamed February 1940. She served in the Non-Intervention Patrol during the Spanish Civil War and cruised in the Atlantic August–November 1939, sinking two ships of 6902 tons. *Lützow* took part in the Norwegian Campaign and subsequently served in Norwegian waters, taking part with ADMIRAL HIPPER in the Battle of the BARENTS SEA on 31 December 1942. She then formed part of the Training Squadron in the Baltic and in 1944 supported army operations with her gunfire. On 16 April 1945 she was badly damaged by bombs at Swinemunde and was scuttled the following month.

Luzon, Philippines, 1941 and 1945

The principal island of the Philippines. It was attacked by the Japanese 14th Army under General HOMMA on 10 December 1941. General MACARTHUR was outmanoeuvred and forced to withdraw his forces to the Bataan Peninsula on 23 December; these surrendered on 9 April 1942, and with the fall of CORREGIDOR on 6 May the Japanese occupation was complete. The US 6th Army under General KRUEGER invaded Luzon on 9 January 1945 in what became the largest land battle of the Pacific War. General YAMASHITA had some 350,000 troops and put up a strong resistance, finally retiring into the mountainous area in the north-east of the island where, with about 50,000 troops, he continued fighting until the end of the war, surrendering on 15 August 1945. The Luzon campaign claimed about 8000 American and 90,000 Japanese dead.

Lvov, Soviet Union

An old Polish city, now in the USSR, Lvov (or Lemberg) fell into Soviet hands as a result of their partitioning of Poland with Germany in 1939. It was occupied by the Germans in 1941 and remained under German control until taken by the advancing Red Army on 27 July 1944. It is now in the Ukrainian SSR.

LVT Landing vehicle tracked.

LVT(A) Landing vehicle tracked, armoured.

Lynn, Vera (1917–)

Gave her first public performance in 1924. She subsequently broadcast with Joe Loss, joined Charlie Kunz in 1935 and sang with the Ambrose Orchestra from 1937 to 1940, after which she went solo. She was voted the United Kingdom's most popular singer in a 1939 *Daily Express* competition. From 1941 to 1947 she had her own radio show, entitled "Sincerely Yours", and in 1944 she sang to troops in Burma. Most of her songs were sentimental and had obvious appeal to men serving away from home, earning her the nickname of "The Forces' Sweetheart".

Lys River, Belgium, 1940

A river, running north-east across Belgium, which became the main line of defence behind which the British and Belgian armies took up position in May 1940. The line was breached by German thrusts on 24 and 25 May, after which Belgian resistance collapsed and the British troops were outflanked and forced to retire.

US troops in Manila, February 1945.

M

M11/39 – Medium Tank (Italy)

Obsolete and unreliable design which entered service in 1939, the vehicle's principle defect being that its main armament was housed in the hull and its secondary armament in the turret. Two battalions were sent to Libya in 1940 but did not survive the first British offensive. 24 were also shipped to East Africa, taking part in the occupation of British Somaliland, but these were lost when the Italian army in Abyssinia was defeated in 1941. *Weight* 10.8 tons; *speed* 21mph (34kph); *armour* 30mm; *armament* 1 37mm L/40 gun; 2 8mm Breda machine guns; *engine* Fiat-SPA 8T 43hp diesel; *crew* 3.

M11/39 medium tank.

M13/40 Series – Medium Tanks (Italy)

Introduced in 1940 and served throughout the campaign in North Africa, with the exception of the first few months, as well as taking part in the 1941 invasion of Greece and Yugoslavia. An improved model, designated M14/41, was fitted with a 125hp diesel engine and began reaching the Western Desert in the autumn of 1942. The final version of the tank, the M15/42, was armed with a 47mm L/40 gun and driven by a 170hp petrol engine; only 82 vehicles of this type had been built when, in March 1943, it was decided that all medium tank chassis production should be turned over to the manufacture of SEMOVENTI assault guns. The M13/40 was the principal weapon of the Italian armoured divisions but losses were heavy because of its mechanical unreliability and the fact that, after 1940, the basis of its armour was inadequate. In the aftermath of BEDA FOMM sufficient were captured intact to re-equip a British armoured regiment. *M13/40 Weight* 13.5 tons; *speed* 19mph (30kph); *armour* 40mm; *armament* 1 47mm L/32 gun; 3 8mm Breda machine guns; *engine* Fiat-SPA 8T 105hp diesel; *crew* 4.

M13/40 medium tanks in North Africa.

"M" Class Destroyers

See "L" AND "M" CLASS DESTROYERS.

MAAF Mediterranean Allied Air Force.

Maaloy Island, Norway, 1941

A small Norwegian island, adjacent to VAAGSO, which was the site of a powerful German gun battery. The battery posed a threat to the British Commando raid on Vaagso on 27 December 1941 and was neutralized by a naval bombardment followed by a Commando assault, which cleared the way for the major part of the operation against Vaagso.

MAC Mediterranean Air Command (US).

MacArthur, Gen Douglas (1880–1964)

MacArthur served in Mexico and in France during World War I, being decorated for gallantry on several occasions. On his return to the US he was appointed Superintendent of West Point. In 1922 he was given command of the Manila District in the Philippine Islands for three years, before returning home for a period of staff duties, after which he served as President of the American Olympic Committee. A second tour in the Philippines followed and in 1930 he was appointed the US Army's Chief of Staff with the rank of full general. In July 1932 he received the distasteful order to disperse a large gathering of unemployed veterans which threatened the maintenance of law and order in Washington, and performed this difficult task with the minimum use of force. Under his direction the Army also administered the employment creation scheme initiated by President ROOSEVELT under the title of the Civilian Conservation Corps. In 1935 he became the principal military adviser to the Philippine government and in July 1941 was recalled to the active list and instructed to prepare the Philippine armed forces for war. During the next five months he achieved an eight-fold expansion in Filipino strength, although the vast majority of the men were untrained and poorly armed. When the Japanese invaded the islands in December 1941 most Filipinos deserted and MacArthur, recognizing that in the absence of adequate naval and air support the campaign could have only one ending, withdrew his troops into the BATAAN Peninsula. On 11 March 1942 he left the Philippines at ROOSEVELT's insistence, vowing that he would return, and was appointed Commander-in-Chief Allied Forces in the South-West Pacific. He maintained the Allied strategy of recapturing NEW GUINEA and the SOLOMON ISLANDS, the latter commenced by Admiral NIMITZ at GUADALCANAL, and initiated the policy of island-hopping which bypassed tens of thousands of

trained Japanese troops in isolated garrisons and left them without hope of support or relief. In September 1944 the Joint Chiefs of Staff agreed to his demand for the Recapture of the Philippines and he went ashore with the invasion force on 9 January 1945, thereby keeping the promise he had made almost three years earlier. Following further operations in the DUTCH EAST INDIES he crowned his achievements in World War II when, on 2 September 1945, he received the Japanese surrender aboard NIMITZ's flagship USS *Missouri* in Tokyo Bay. The historian Liddell Hart believed that MacArthur's "strong personality, strategic grasp, tactical skill, operative ability and vision put him in a class above Allied commanders in any theatre".

Macassar Strait, Battle of, 1942

During the night of 23/24 January 1942 four American destroyers under Rear-Admiral Glassford attacked the Japanese invasion force anchored off Balikpapan, Borneo, sinking three transports and a small escort vessel. The Americans withdrew without loss.

McAuliffe, Brig Gen Anthony

Commander of the American troops besieged in BASTOGNE during the Battle of the BULGE. On 22 December 1944 two German officers arrived at his headquarters under a flag of

truce and told him that unless he accepted an honourable surrender his command would be annihilated by the fire of an artillery corps and six anti-aircraft battalions. McAuliffe, who had served in the artillery before transferring to the paratroops, regarded the threat as absurd and gave vent to his celebrated retort of "Nuts!"

Macchi Aircraft (Italy)

Macchi C200 Saetta Developed from a series of record-breaking seaplanes, the C200 was a sound airframe hampered by an insufficiently powerful engine. It was manoeuvrable and effective within its limits and had the best record of all the early Italian fighters in combat. Used extensively in the Mediterranean theatre, it also performed well against the early Russian fighters on the Eastern Front. *Span* 34.75ft (10.6m); *engine* 840hp radial; *armament* 2 12.7mm machine guns, 700lb (320kg) of bombs; *speed* 312mph (502kph).

Macchi C202 Folgore This was virtually the C200 modified by the addition of a German Daimler-Benz in-line engine, built under licence in Italy. This substantial increase in power, together with the better streamlining, turned the C200 into an excellent fighter, but the transformation was too late to have much effect on events. *Span* 34.75ft (10.6m); *engine* 1 1200hp in-line; *armament* 2 12.7mm guns; *speed* 370mph (595kph).

Macchi C205V Veltro This was a further progression from the C200/202 series, by adopting an even more powerful Daimler-Benz engine and improving the armament. It did not enter service until 1943 and thus very few were seen in combat. *Span* 34.75ft (10.6m); *engine* 1 1475hp in-line; *armament* 2 20mm cannon, 2 machine guns, 700lb (320kg) of bombs; *speed* 400mph (644kph).

McClusky, Lt Cdr Clarence W.

Commander of the USS *Enterprise*'s dive bomber strike force at the Battle of MIDWAY. Although the Japanese carrier group had unexpectedly changed course, McClusky persisted in his search and was eventually led to his target by an enemy destroyer rejoining the main body of its fleet. McClusky's attack achieved complete surprise and inflicted fatal damage on the carriers *Akagi* and *Soryu*.

McCreery, Gen Sir R. (1898–1967)

McCreery served with the British Expeditionary Force during the 1940 campaign in France.

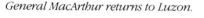
General MacArthur returns to Luzon.

In May 1941 he was posted to North Africa as Chief of Staff to AUCHINLECK, with whom he got on so badly that the appointment was soon terminated. In August 1942 he was appointed Chief of Staff to ALEXANDER and was largely responsible for the detailed planning of the Second Battle of ALAMEIN. He subsequently commanded the British X Corps at SALERNO and Monte CASSINO. In November 1944 he was appointed commander of the 8th Army, which he led during its final offensive the following spring.

McIndoe, Archibald (1900–60)

Working with pilots who had been badly burned during the Battle of BRITAIN, Archibald McIndoe developed advanced techniques of plastic surgery with which serious physical damage and disfigurements could be repaired. He was also concerned for his patients' mental welfare and was responsible for the abolition of the 90-day rule under which badly injured men were compulsorily invalided out of the service after that period had elapsed.

Mackensen, Col Gen Eberhard von (1889–   )

The son of the famous Field-Marshal, von Mackensen was commissioned into Hussar Regiment 1 in 1910. He held a number of staff appointments throughout World War I and during his subsequent career with the Reichsheer. On 1 September 1939 he was appointed Chief of Staff to 14th Army, transferring to 12th Army on 1 November 1939 in the same capacity. He was given command of III Panzer Corps on 15 January 1941 and of 1st Panzer Army on 21 November 1942. On 5 November 1943 he was posted to Italy where he commanded 14th Army until he retired on 5 June 1944. The rapid reaction of the troops under his command was largely responsible for containing the Allied landing at ANZIO. He was sentenced to death for war crimes but this was commuted to a term of imprisonment from which he was released in 1952.

Maclean, Brig Fitzroy (1911–   )

Maclean parachuted into Yugoslavia in September 1943 as head of the British Military Mission, his principal task being to report on the activities of TITO'S PARTISANS. Two months later he arrived back in London and advised the government that TITO should be given additional support and supplies of arms. He then returned to Yugoslavia and took part in the fighting against the German occupation forces, remaining the British government's representative until March 1945. His experiences were later recorded in his book *Eastern Approaches*.

Macmillan, Rt Hon Maurice Harold (1894–1984)

Harold Macmillan served with the Grenadier Guards throughout World War I, being wounded three times. During World War II he served as Parliamentary Secretary, Ministry of Supply, from 1940 until 1942, and then briefly as Parliamentary Under-Secretary of State for the Colonies before taking up the post of Minister Resident at Allied Headquarters in North-West Africa, which he held from 1942 until 1945, earning the confidence of EISENHOWER and DE GAULLE. He attended the CASABLANCA CONFERENCE in January 1943 and took part in the negotiations leading to the Italian armistice. In November 1943, while still retaining his post as Minister Resident, he was appointed British High Commissioner for Italy and influenced the outcome of the Yugoslav and Greek settlements. In 1945 he was appointed Secretary for Air. His subsequent offices included Minister of Housing and Local Government 1951–54; Minister of Defence October 1954–April 1955; Secretary of State for Foreign Affairs April–December 1955; Chancellor of the Exchequer December 1955–January 1957; and Prime Minister and First Lord of the Treasury January 1957–October 1963.

Maczek, Lt Gen Stanislaw (1892–   )

In September 1939 Maczek commanded Poland's only viable mechanized formation, the 10th Cavalry Brigade, with which he was able to impose checks on the advance of the German XXII Panzer Corps on the KRAKOW and Karpaty Armies' sectors of the front. When the campaign ended the Brigade crossed the frontier into Hungary and from there its men made their way as individuals to France, where Maczek reformed it to fight with the French Army during the 1940 campaign in the West. Its personnel were evacuated to Britain, enabling Maczek to reform the Brigade yet again. On 26 February 1942 he was appointed commander of the 1st Polish Armoured Division, which he led with distinction in NORMANDY and North-West Europe. In May 1945 he was promoted to the command of I Polish Corps.

Madagascar, Indian Ocean, 1941–42

A French colony, Madagascar remained under Vichy control and was, for a time, regarded by the Germans as a possible place of resettlement for European Jews. After the Tokyo–Vichy Treaty of July 1941, it appeared likely that it would be used by the Japanese as a naval base to threaten the Indian Ocean, and on 5 May 1942 British and South African troops landed. They were reinforced in September, and resistance, never very strong, was formally ended by the governor of the island on 6 November.

Maestrale Class Destroyers (Italy)

Displacement 2243 tons; *dimensions* 350ft×33ft 3in (106.7×10m); mean draught 10ft 9in (3.2m); *machinery* 2-shaft geared turbines producing shp 44,000; *speed* 38 knots; *armament* 4×4.7in; 6–8×20mm AA; 2×13.2mm AA; 6×21in torpedo tubes; 4 depth charge throwers; equipped for minelaying; *complement* 191; *number in class* 4, all launched 1934.

Maginot Line

A French system of fortification, built between 1929 and 1940, and intended to provide a fixed defensive line on the Franco-German border behind which manoeuvre armies could form and deploy. It consisted of numbers of fortress complexes running from the Swiss border near Belfort, north along the Rhine valley, around Metz, to the Belgian

The principal portion of the Maginot Line; in lesser strength the line continued to the Mediterranean coast.

border near Longwy, a distance of about 385 miles (620km). It was not continued westward to the North Sea because of the politically sensitive position of Belgium; fortifying the Belgian frontier would have given the appearance of abandoning Belgium to her fate or, at best, forcing her into neutrality. Moreover the projected course of the line would have run through the mining and industrial areas of northern France, raising enormous engineering and financial problems.

The Maginot Line was bypassed by the main thrust of the German invasion of 1940, which drove through the ARDENNES and Sedan, thus outflanking the line. It was named after André Maginot, Minister of War 1929–32, who authorized the original construction.

Magnet
Arrival of American troops in Northern Ireland, February 1942.

Magnetic Mines
These differed from the normal contact mine in that their explosion was triggered by the magnetic field of a ship passing over them. They were difficult to sweep and had been used briefly by the Royal Navy in 1918. The German Navy took up the idea in the interwar years and in the autumn of 1939 began laying them. Within weeks they had claimed 27 victims and all but paralysed shipping in the Thames estuary and along the east coast of England. However, on 23 November one was recovered intact and its secrets were revealed. The immediate answer was to fit merchant ships sailing in home waters with a degaussing girdle which contained the field within the critical level of 50 milligauss, enabling them to proceed safely. In January 1940 VICKERS WELLINGTON bombers were fitted with 48-feet (14.6m) diameter dural hoops which emitted a field capable of detonating these mines harmlessly. This very successful conversion was known as the DW1.

Magnetron
The short form for "resonant cavity magnetron", the generator of oscillation in centimetric RADAR transmitters. In the wartime equipments it took the form of a heavy copper disc with a central hole, from which a number of circular cavities opened. A central pole acted as the cathode, and when an electric field is applied between this and the anode –

the surrounding disc – a radio-frequency field is generated. This can be extracted by means of a coupling to one of the cavities, and in this way the required centimetric signal, at high power, is produced. The cavity magnetron was developed at Birmingham by Boot and others in 1940 and was the key to the future development of radar.

Mahan Class Destroyers (USA)
Displacement 1500 tons; *dimensions* 341ft 6in×35ft 6in (104×10.8m); mean draught 10ft (3m); *machinery* 2-shaft geared turbines producing shp 49,000; *speed* 36.5 knots; *armament* 5×5in (5×1); 12×21in torpedo tubes (3×4); *complement* 172; *number in class* 18, launched 1935–36.

Maidanek, Poland, 1940–44
A German camp close to Lublin, established late in 1940. Originally a labour camp, in early 1942 it was converted into an extermination centre and was functioning by the middle of the year. Although less well known than Auschwitz, it came close in its extermination record, some 1,380,000 Jews being killed there before the camp closed early in 1944.

Mailed Fist
Planned recapture of SINGAPORE, 1945.

Maisky, Ivan (1884–1975)
Maisky was Soviet ambassador in London from 1932 until 1943 and was a popular and respected figure in diplomatic circles. Follow-

ing the fall of France he informed STALIN of the United Kingdom's determination to continue the war and was also able to provide advance warnings of HITLER's intended invasion of the Soviet Union, although these were disregarded. He established relations with various governments-in-exile in London and was instrumental in persuading HOPKINS to visit Moscow and negotiate a Lend-Lease agreement between the USA and the USSR. He relayed Stalin's repeated demands that the Allies should open a Second Front but privately understood that these were premature. Upon his recall to Moscow he was appointed Deputy Commissar of Foreign Affairs and participated in the YALTA and POTSDAM CONFERENCES. In 1945 he acted as Chairman Allied Reparations Commission.

Makin Atoll, Pacific, 1943
A small atoll north of the GILBERT Islands, Makin was held by a Japanese garrison of about 800 men. It was attacked by US Army and Marine forces on 20 November 1943 and taken for the loss of only 66 US troops. This landing formed part of Operation GALVANIC, the principal part of which was the taking of TARAWA atoll.

Malaya, 1941–42
A British colony in South-East Asia, Malaya produced 38 per cent of the world's rubber and 58 per cent of its tin. At the southern tip was the naval base of SINGAPORE, heavily defended against sea attack, but the land

The Japanese surrender in Malaya, 1945.

defences were negligible throughout the peninsula. British commanders had asked for improvements, but little was given to them. On 8 December 1941 the Japanese 25th Army (three divisions) landed at Singora and Patani, in Thailand, and Khota Baru in northern Malaya, and advanced rapidly southwards. British commanders had foreseen the possible use of Singora and were about to mount an invasion to forestall such a landing. As a result, the Japanese moves caught this force off balance, leading to confusion and retreats. Japan had command of the air and sea, allowing them to mount several minor seaborne invasions on the west coast, so as to harry and cut off retreating British troops. British command was inept, which led to a loss of confidence and morale among the troops, and the speed and pressure of the Japanese attack drove through to Singapore, some 350 miles (563km), in 58 days. After a short period of consolidation the assault on Singapore was mounted, and British resistance came to an end on 15 February 1942. British and Commonwealth casualties amounted to 9000 killed and wounded and 130,000 taken prisoner; Japanese casualties amounted to 3000 killed and 6000 wounded.

Maleme, Crete, 1941

This small coastal town's airfield was one of the principal German objectives in their airborne invasion of CRETE in 1941. The German plan was to use the airfield to fly in transport aircraft carrying 5000 mountain infantry troops. On 20 May a mixed German force of glider and parachute troops landed around the airfield, where they met a fierce reception from New Zealand troops; over two-thirds of the parachute troops died on their drop zone. The survivors held on, and early the following morning, due to a mistaken withdrawal by a New Zealand battalion commander, they were able to capture Hill 107, giving them command over Maleme airfield. Reinforced shortly afterwards by another 550 parachute troops, the German force was able to overrun the airfield and hold it so that transport aircraft could land, albeit under Allied fire. This proved to be the crucial point of the battle for Crete, since these reinforcements were able to secure the Maleme area and the supply of more troops and stores was assured.

Malenkov, Georgiy (1902–)

When Germany invaded the Soviet Union, Malenkov was appointed to the newly constituted Committee for the Defence of the State (GKO), the other members of which were STALIN, MOLOTOV, VOROSHILOV and BERIA. His principal responsibility was the equipment of the Soviet Army and Air Force, his most remarkable achievement being the wholesale evacuation to the east of the Urals of the means of industial production and the establishment of new armaments factories in areas beyond the reach of the Luftwaffe's bombers. From 1941–43 he also served as Political Commissar on several fronts, and for the remainder of the war acted as Chairman of the Committee for the Restoration of the Economy, dealing with countries recently liberated from German occupation. After the war Malenkov was appointed Deputy Chairman of the Council of Ministers and assumed power briefly on Stalin's death, only to be ousted by Khrushchev.

Malik, Jacob A.

Malik was the Soviet Ambassador to Japan. In June 1945 he was approached by a group of Japanese leaders known collectively as the Supreme Council for the Direction of the War. Shaken by the collapse of Nazi Germany, the Japanese proposed most favourable terms for a non-aggression treaty with the Soviet Union, hoping thereby to forestall Russian involvement in the war in the Far East. Malik, however, recognizing that the Japanese were negotiating from a position of weakness, played for time and instead of cabling his government despatched a courier on the long journey to Moscow, from whence a reply could not be expected for several weeks. The negotiations collapsed when Malik declined further meetings on the grounds of illness.

Malinovsky, Marshal Rodion (1898–1951)

Appointed commander of the Russian South-West Front in December 1941 and a year later frustrated German attempts to relieve von PAULUS' 6th Army at STALINGRAD. He then commanded the 3rd Ukrainian Front, and completed the liberation of the Donbass and the western Ukraine. In 1944 he transferred to the 2nd Ukrainian Front and was responsible for the Axis debacle in ROMANIA. He next led his troops into HUNGARY capturing BUDAPEST in February 1945, and liberated Slovakia. In August 1945 he took part in the Soviet rout of the Japanese in MANCHURIA.

Malinta Tunnel, Corregidor, 1942

A tunnel complex driven under Malinta Hill on the island of CORREGIDOR. The main tunnel was 1400ft (426m) long and 30ft (9m) wide, and there were 25 lateral tunnels, each about 400ft (122m) long, at right-angles to the main tunnel. Another set of lateral tunnels on the north side housed a hospital, and a further set on the south housed a Quartermaster Corps store. When Corregidor came under attack, the tunnel became the home for General MACARTHUR's headquarters and for several thousand soldiers who had been bombed out of their barracks.

Malmédy, Belgium, 1944

During the Battle of the BULGE, on 17 December 1944, a battle group of the SS Panzer LEIBSTANDARTE Adolf Hitler captured 125 men of a US field artillery observation battery in the town of Malmédy and, some two hours later, murdered them by machine-gun fire. Some lost consciousness, or feigned death, but, in all, 86 US soldiers died. The commander, Colonel Joachim Peiper, and 42 other officers were condemned to death for this and other crimes after the war, but political intrigue in the USA resulted in the sentences being commuted to varying terms of imprisonment.

Malta, 1941–43

An island in the Mediterranean, a British Crown Colony, about 50 miles (80km) from Sicily. Control of Malta meant control of the Mediterranean, and at VALETTA was a major British naval base, little-used until 1943 because of the proximity of many Axis airfields. Heavily defended by coast artillery, and with three squadrons of fighter aircraft, two of light bombers and one of torpedo bombers, the island also held a civil population of about 280,000 and was supplied by regular convoys from Gibraltar. It was heavily attacked from the air throughout 1941–42, and the convoys en route to the island were also attacked. Attempts were made by the Italian Navy to attack Valetta with "human torpedos" and light craft, but these were beaten off by coast guns. RAF operations from Malta were a vital part of the defeat of Axis forces in North Africa, on account of both attacks against Axis land forces and attacks against supply convoys attempting to reinforce ROMMEL's Afrika Korps. In August 1942 KING GEORGE VI awarded the George Cross to the island in recognition of the heroism of the civil population in the face of attacks, the only time this medal was ever awarded collectively.

"Man Who Never Was", the

In the weeks leading up to Operation TORCH, the Allied invasion of French North Africa, it was considered essential that the true destination of the shipping assembling at Gibraltar should be concealed from Axis agents in Spain. The decision was taken that a body should be allowed to wash ashore on the Spanish coast with plans for a projected invasion of Greece in its possession. With some difficulty a body of the right age and physical condition was found and given the identity of a fictitious Major William Martin, Royal Marines. As well as documents, Martin was provided with a photograph and letters from his girlfriend and a bank statement. The ruse was completely successful and is described in Ewen Montagu's book *The Man Who Never Was*.

Manchuria

Effectively a Japanese colony since 1930,

The population of Harbin meets Soviet troops, 1945.

Manchuria formed an industrial base for Japan but otherwise played no part in the war until invaded by Soviet forces on 8 August 1945. Soviet forces had been stripped from their Far Eastern borders to assist on the Eastern Front, but after the tide of battle had turned, STALIN began building up his forces on the Manchurian border once more. After the fall

An Italian air raid on Malta, 1940.

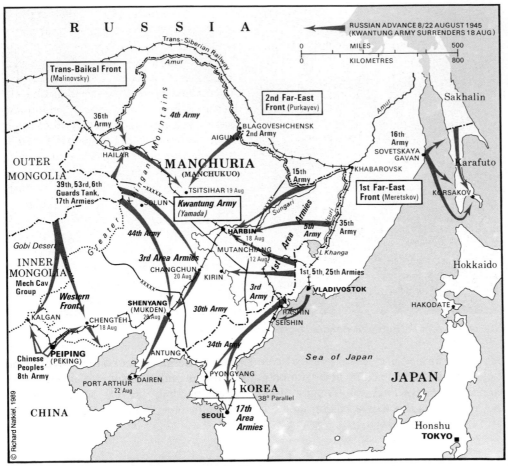

The Soviet invasion of Manchuria, August 1945.

of Germany, four Soviet armies were rapidly transferred to Siberia and Mongolia, and Manchuria was invaded from four directions. Five armies attacked from the Vladivostok area, two from the northern border between Blagoveschensk and Khabarovsk, one from the north-west, Chital, area, and four from Outer Mongolia. About 1.5 million men and 5500 tanks ensured a rapid advance, assisted by air supply, and the country was completely occupied within two weeks.

Mandalay, Burma, 1942 and 1945

The second largest city in Burma, Mandalay fell to the Japanese on 1 May 1942 during the British retreat. It was retaken by the British 14th Army on 20 March 1945 after a siege of a month.

Mandrel

An electronic jamming device used by the RAF against the German "Freya" early warning radar sets. Effective when first used in 1942, but operators soon learnt to cope with the jamming.

Manhattan Project

Codename for the development of the ATOMIC BOMB.

Manila, Philippines, 1942 and 1945

The capital of the PHILIPPINE Islands, Manila was abandoned by MACARTHUR as being indefensible, and declared an open city. It was occupied by Japanese forces on 2 January 1942. Troops of the 1st US Cavalry Division reached the outskirts on 3 February 1945 and the city was secured on 28 February.

Manna

Air drop of food to starving Dutch civilians, April 1945.

Manna

British landings in Greece, October 1944.

Mannerheim, Marshal Carl Gustav von (1867–1951)

Mannerheim served in the Imperial Russian Army but after the Revolution returned to his native Finland to command her forces in the

successful war of independence against Soviet Russia, acting as Regent for seven months in 1918–19. During the Winter War of 1939–40 he was recalled to conduct the defence of his country. He performed this task to such good effect that although the Finns were forced to accede to Russian demands they preserved their autonomy. In 1941 Finland joined Germany in her attack on the Soviet Union, hoping to recover the territory lost the previous year. However, by 1944 it was clear that the war was lost and it was largely due to the diplomatic skills of Mannerheim, now President, that Finland was able to withdraw from the conflict on reasonable terms. See also FINLAND.

Mannerheim Line

Named after von Mannerheim, Field-Marshal of the Finnish Army, this was a defensive line of blockhouses and field fortifications built across the Karelian Isthmus for about 80 miles (129km), to defend Finland's south-eastern border. In October 1939 the Russians invaded Finland, following Finnish refusals to cede part of their territory to Russia, and the Mannerheim Line effectively halted the Russian advance. A Russian attack in the north caused troops to be removed from the Mannerheim Line, after which a sudden renewal of their advance allowed the Russians to break through the line towards Viipuri (now Vyborg, USSR). The Finns sued for peace and had to cede the whole of the Karelian Isthmus.

Mannheim

A German anti-aircraft fire control RADAR. Development began in the spring of 1940, but it was then suspended since it was a defensive weapon. Later revived, it entered service late in 1943 and about 400 were eventually in use, principally around the more important target areas to replace WURZBURG sets.

Manstein, FM Erich von (1887–1973)

Manstein is widely deemed to have possessed the finest strategic mind of any senior commander in World War II. Commissioned into the 3rd Regiment of Foot Guards in 1906, he served on both the Eastern and Western Fronts and in Serbia during World War I, being severely wounded in November 1914. In 1916 he served as a staff captain with General von Gallwitz during the worst fighting at Verdun. He held a number of regimen-

The Mannerheim Line: Finns dragging an anti-tank gun behind a barricade.

tal and staff posts in the post-war Reichsheer and in 1936 was appointed deputy to General BECK, the Chief of General Staff. During this period he advocated the development of the assault gun as a means of providing direct gunfire support for infantry operations and came to be regarded as the father of the prestigious *Sturmartillerie* (Assault Artillery). He served as von RUNDSTEDT's Chief of Staff when the latter commanded Army Group

Von Manstein at the Donetz Basin, 1943.

South during the 1939 campaign in Poland, and again when he was appointed commander of Army Group A on the Western Front. With Rundstedt's approval he developed the SICHELSCHNITT (Sickle Cut) plan which was ultimately adopted by HITLER as the most important element of the 1940 campaign in the West and resulted in a complete German victory. However, in pressing the merits of *Sichelschnitt* Manstein had made himself unpopular with OKH and was posted away from Army Group A to command XXXVIII Infantry Corps, with which he fought in France. In March 1941 he was appointed commander of LVI Panzer Corps, which was employed on Army Group North's sector during Operation BARBAROSSA. In September 1941 he was given command of the 11th Army and with this conquered the CRIMEA, being promoted Field-Marshal on the fall of SEVASTOPOL. In August 1942 he was given the task of capturing LENINGRAD and although he destroyed a Soviet army in the area of LAKE LADOGA he was unable to complete this mission before being appointed commander of Army Group Don with orders to break through to the trapped 6th Army in STALINGRAD. Despite some initial success his resources were insufficient and the relief attempt had to be abandoned in the face of heavy counter-attacks. None the less, when the Soviets attempted to exploit their victory in February 1943 Manstein (now command-

ing Army Group South) severely mauled their South-West and Voronezh Fronts and recaptured KHARKOV. In July 1943 he took part in Operation ZITADELLE (Citadel), the last major German offensive in the East, and when this was curtailed he conducted the difficult withdrawal of Army Group South behind the DNIEPR, constantly hindered by Hitler's interference in the conduct of operations. In March 1944, following a series of disagreements with Hitler, Manstein was dismissed and took no further part in the war. The loss of his services was a very serious blow to Germany, there being general agreement in professional circles that, given a free hand, he was the only commander capable of restoring stability to the Eastern Front. He was aware of the plot to assassinate Hitler but declined to participate.

Manteuffel, Gen Baron Hasso Eccard von (1897–)

Manteuffel was involved with the development of Germany's armoured forces at an early stage and at one period served as an instructor at the Panzer Troops Training School. During the first years of World War II he commanded several mechanized infantry units. In February 1943 he was appointed commander of a scratch division in Tunisia but left North Africa before the Axis surrender. He commanded 7th Panzer Division from 1 August 1943 until 1 February 1944 when he became commander of the crack Panzer Division *Grossdeutschland*. On 12 September 1944 he was appointed commander of the 5th Panzer Army, which he led throughout the winter offensive in the ARDENNES. On 10 March 1945 he assumed command of the 3rd Panzer Army and held this appointment until the end of the war. A former hussar and sometime gentleman jockey, Manteuffel was one of Germany's best Panzer leaders, noted for his quick thinking and tenacity.

Manus, Pacific, 1944

The largest of the Admiralty Islands, Manus was assaulted by the US 7th and 8th Cavalry Regiments on 15 March 1944. Although held by only about 250 Japanese, the US forces had a hard battle before finally securing the island on 26 March.

Mao Tse-Tung (1893–1976)

Chairman of the Chinese Communist Party from 1931 to his death. In 1937 Mao formed an alliance with CHIANG KAI-SHEK to fight the

Mao Tse Tung (centre) confers with Colonel Barratt of the US Army Observer section.

Japanese invaders but this foundered in 1940 and most of his subsequent effort during World War II was directed against Chiang's forces, his operations being based on Yenan in the province of Shensi. After the defeat of Japan, Mao led his own troops to victory in the ensuing civil war. He was adept in the techniques of revolutionary guerrilla warfare, particularly in a rural environment, and his methods have since been widely copied.

Maquis

French resistance movement which came into being in April 1943 as a result of demands for an additional 400,000 men to work in German industry. Many thousands of those likely to be affected left their homes and formed groups in the mountains, loosely controlled by the National Council of the Resistance. By May 1944 some 35,000 Maquisards had acquired arms but of these only one-quarter had sufficient ammunition for more than one day's serious fighting. However, between D-DAY and the end of August 1944 over 6500 tons of supplies were dropped to the Maquis and other resistance movements. By weakening German control of central and southern France, the Maquisards greatly assisted the Allied landings and advance northwards.

Marabu

German experimental proximity fuse.

Maraventano, Col

Commander of an Italian force of brigade strength which held the mountain fortress of Addis Derra, Ethiopia, until May 1941, when shortage of food compelled it to withdraw. Part of GIDEON FORCE, commanded by the then Major Orde WINGATE, succeeded in blocking its escape route with the aid of local tribesmen. After three days' inconclusive fighting Wingate resorted to bluff, telling Maraventano that he had been ordered elsewhere and that unless the Italians gave up they would be left to the mercy of the large number of Ethiopians who had converged on the area. Knowing that this would ultimately mean the massacre of his 8100 men, Maraventano surrendered his command to a force less than one quarter its size.

Marcello Class Submarines (Italy)

Displacement 962 tons (1063/1317 tons normal); *dimensions* 239ft 6in×23ft 6in (71.7× 7.65m); *machinery* 2-shaft diesel/electric motors hp 3600/1100; *speed* 17.5/8 knots; *armament* 2×3.9in; 4×13.2mm AA; 8×21in torpedo tubes and 16 torpedoes; *complement* 58; *number in class* 9, launched 1937–38.

Marcks, Maj Gen Erich

On 29 July 1940 Marcks, then serving as the 18th Army's Chief of Staff, was given the task of preparing outline plans for a German invasion of the USSR. These were submitted to OKH on 5 August and envisaged two major thrusts into the heart of the Soviet Union, one directed at MOSCOW and the other at KIEV, the left flank of the invasion being covered by a subsidiary drive on LENINGRAD. Marcks saw the campaign evolving in two distinct phases, the first of which would involve the destruction of the Soviet armies as close to the frontier as possible and be followed immediately by the capture of Moscow, which he emphasized constituted "the economic, political and spiritual centre of the USSR (whose) capture would destroy the co-ordination of the Russian state". The ultimate limit of the German advance was set at the line ROSTOV–Gorki–ARCHANGEL. Marcks correctly appreciated the general weakness of the Soviet Army but underestimated its powers of recovery and the effects of distance and the Russian terrain on mechanized operations. However, many of his ideas corresponded with HITLER's and, in a modified form, his plan provided the basis for Operation BARBAROSSA.

Marconi Class Submarines (Italy)

Luigi Torelli was converted to a transport submarine in 1943. On Italy's surrender she was interned by the Japanese at SINGAPORE and handed over to the German Navy, in which she served as *UIT 25*. On Germany's surrender she passed again into Japanese hands and was re-numbered *I 504*. *Displacement* 1036 tons (1190/1489 tons normal); *dimensions* 251ft×22ft 3in (76.5×6.8m); *machinery* 2-shaft diesel/electric motors hp 3600/1500; *speed* 18/8 knots; *armament* 1×3.9in; 4×13.2mm AA; 8×21in torpedo tubes and 12 torpedoes; *number in class* 6, launched 1939–40.

Marda Pass, Ethiopia, 1941

A narrow defile containing the only road between Jijiga and Harar, the Marda Pass was an obvious danger to any advance between the two towns. Held by a strong Italian force, it formed a block to the British and South African troops advancing from Jijiga in March 1941. On 27 March it was subjected to a heavy bombardment by South African artillery and then assaulted by the 23rd Nigerian Brigade. By nightfall a small Nigerian group had reached the summit of the ridge and during the night they were reinforced, ready for a dawn attack, but the Italian defenders fell back in the darkness and the Allied force was able to continue its advance.

Marder (Marten) – Tank Destroyers

Name given to the majority of German first generation tank destroyers, developed urgently as a result of early encounters with the MATILDA, KLIMENTI VOROSHILOV and T-34/76 tanks. The Marders all followed the same basic pattern, consisting of an anti-tank gun mounted on the chassis of an obsolete or foreign tank, the fighting compartment being protected by a fixed, open-topped superstructure of armour plate. The Marder II entered service in 1942. Two versions were produced, the first of which employed the chassis of the PZKW II Models A, B, C and F in conjunction with 75mm L/46 Pak 40/2 anti-tank gun; the second employed the chassis of the PzKw II Models D and E and was armed with a captured Russian Model 36 76.2mm anti-tank gun re-chambered to take the German 75mm round. The Russian gun was also used on the early models of the Marder III, which entered service in 1942 and was based on the chassis of the Czech-built PZKW 38(T). Later models mounted the German 75mm L/46 Pak 40/3 anti-tank gun, some having their fighting compartment forward and others aft. Perversely, the Marder I did not appear until 1943; this conversion was armed with the 75mm Pak 40/1 anti-tank gun mounted on the LORRAINE tracked carrier or the chassis of French HOTCHKISS or FCM tanks. The Marder I was regarded as second-line equipment and was employed mainly in occupied countries on training or anti-inva-sion duties. Marders II and III, however, gave excellent service with the anti-tank units of first-line armoured and infantry divisions until replaced by the JAGDPANZER IV and HETZER purpose-built tank destroyers. A total of 716 Marder II and 1577 Marder III conversions were made. *Crew* four; *speed* 25mph (40kph).

Mareth Line

Defended line of field fortifications in North Africa, running from the shores of the Gulf of Gabes close to Mareth, inland to the foot of the Matmata Hills, a distance of about 30 miles (48km). It was firmly based on the Wadi Zigzaou, a dried river bed which made a formidable obstacle. ROMMEL fell back to this line in March 1943, and frontal assaults by MONTGOMERY and the British 8th Army ran into difficulties. Montgomery had despatched the New Zealand Corps across the southern end of the Matmata Hills in a flanking movement which met with some success, and when his frontal attack faltered he switched 1st Armoured Division to the New Zealand Corps front, thus outflanking the German positions. A hasty defence at El Hamma by 21st Panzer Division held the outflanking force and gave the German troops in the Mareth Line the chance to escape the trap.

Margarethe

German occupation of Hungary, 1944.

Marder 75mm tank destroyers, based on PzKw 38(t) chassis.

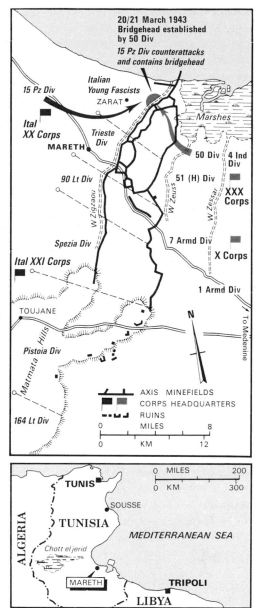

The initial attack on the Mareth Line; 50 Division managed to establish a bridgehead and get some 40 tanks across the Wadi Zigzaou, but a counter-attack by XV Panzer Division sealed this off, leading Montgomery to change the axis of his attack to the Tebaga Gap.

Marianas, Pacific, 1944

A group of islands, north of the Carolines, in which the principal islands were GUAM, SAIPAN and TINIAN. The Marianas were an important objective, since with airfields established there the US could raid mainland Japan using their new B-29 bombers. The campaign to capture the Marianas began with the invasion of Saipan on 15 June 1944 and ended with the securing of Guam on 10 August.

Market Garden

Anglo-American 1st Airborne Army and British 2nd Army offensive to cross the Meuse, Waal and Neder–Rijn rivers, September 1944. See ARNHEM.

Marmon-Herrington Armoured Cars (South Africa)

Designed and built in South Africa using chassis imported from the United States and Canada, armament supplied by the United Kingdom and locally manufactured hulls. They served with British as well as South African armoured car units in the Western Desert and were also employed in ETHIOPIA and MADAGASCAR. Some were sent to MALAYA and the Netherlands East Indies where they were ultimately taken into service by the Japanese. In North Africa turretless versions were armed with captured heavy automatic weapons or light anti-tank guns to improve their firepower. The Mark IV, which entered service in 1943, was an entirely different concept which dispensed with a chassis and had its engines mounted at the rear; this version was armed with a 2-pdr gun and a .30 cal Browning machine gun. *Weight* 6 tons; *speed* 50mph (80kph); *armour* 12mm; *armament* 1 Boys anti-tank rifle; 1 Bren light machine gun; *engine* Ford 95hp petrol; *crew* 3 or 4.

Marsden

British Flamethrower, Portable, No. 1. A heavy and cumbersome back-pack type of which 1500 were made but few issued.

Marshall, Gen George Catlett (1880–1959)

Marshall was appointed Chief of Staff of the US Army shortly before the outbreak of World War II. An able administrator, he believed that the USA would sooner or later become involved in the conflict and it was due to his foresight, sound planning and selection of key personnel that the Army was able to expand as rapidly as it did when the time came. As a result of his reorganization the Army was divided into Ground Forces, Air Forces and Service Forces. After PEARL HARBOR he was appointed Chairman of the new Joint Chiefs of Staff Committee which had been established to advise the President on the conduct of the war. He supported the basic Anglo-American strategy that the defeat of Germany took priority over that of Japan, despite opposition from senior US Navy officers. He maintained a

A Japanese bunker blows up on Namur Island, February 1944.

close relationship with ROOSEVELT and accompanied him to most of the more important inter-Allied conferences of the war. Although Marshall was considered as a potential commander of the American armies in Europe, the President believed that the national interest would be better served if he remained as Chief of Staff in Washington and he continued to hold this post until the war ended. In the postwar period he was appointed Secretary of State and was the architect of

General George Marshall, Chief of Staff, US Army.

the Marshall Plan which restored the economic viability of Europe.

Marshall Islands, Pacific, 1944

The principal islands were Kwajalein, Eniwetok and Majuro; the island of Bikini did not achieve fame until after the war when it was used as a test area for nuclear bombs. The group was attacked in Operation Flintlock on 30 January 1944, Majuro being the first objective. Kwajalein followed, and Eniwetok, the most difficult objective, was secured by 23rd February. The Marshalls were the first pre-war Japanese possessions to be captured by Allied forces.

Martel, Lt Gen Sir Giffard le Q. (1889–1958)

Martel served on the staff of the Tank Corps during World War I and in November 1916 produced the first important paper on the employment of armour, entitled *A Tank Army*. During the 1920s his particular interest lay in TKS TANKETTES and throughout the interwar years he continued to develop his theories, publishing his book *In The Wake Of The Tank* in 1931. While attending the Soviet Army's 1936 manoeuvres with Major-General WAVELL he was so impressed by the performance of the Russian BT SERIES Christie-type tanks that a Christie M-1931 hull was purchased on his recommendation. From this the A13 CRUISER TANK MARK III was produced, initiating a line of development which continued until 1944. However, in common with the rest of the Tank Pioneers, the majority of his ideas went unheeded. In 1940 he commanded the 50th (Northumbrian) Division and with this executed the counter-attack at ARRAS led by 1st Army Tank Brigade, which was one of a number of important factors contributing to the success of the DUNKIRK evacuation. In December 1940 he was appointed Commander Royal Armoured Corps and held this post until it was abolished two years later, restructuring the armoured divisions to produce a more satisfactory balance between their tank and infantry elements.

Martin Aircaft (USA)

Martin A-30 Baltimore This was built to an RAF requirement for a development of the MARYLAND with more capacious fuselage and increased power; 1575 were built, the five variants differing mainly in armaments. The design was given the American nomenclature of A-30 to facilitate supply via Lend-Lease, although it was never adopted by the US services. Used widely in the North African and Mediterranean theatre, numbers were passed on to the co-belligerent Italian air force in 1944 and saw service in the Balkans. *Span* 61.3ft (18.7m); *engines* 2 1700hp radial; *crew* 4; *armament* 12 machine guns, 2000lb (900kg) of bombs; *speed* 320mph (515kph).

Martin B-26 Marauder Designed to a USAAF request of 1939, the B-26 was advanced for its day and acquired an early reputation for being difficult and dangerous to fly. Once the pilots learned how to handle it, the Marauder had the lowest loss-rate of any American bomber. Widely used in the Pacific from 1942 onwards, it entered service in Europe in 1943, and numbers were also used by the RAF and the South African air force. *Span* 71ft (21.6m); *engines* 2 2000hp radial; *crew* 5 to 7; *armament* 12 machine guns, up to 5500lb (2500kg) of bombs; *speed* 310mph (499kph).

Martin PBM Mariner This flying boat was ordered by the US Navy in 1937 as a patrol bomber and transport, and, with subsequent modification, remained in production until 1947. A small number were adopted by RAF COASTAL COMMAND for coast patrol duties. *Span* 118ft (36m); *engines* 2 1700hp radial; *armament* varied, but generally 6 machine guns, 4000lb (1800kg) of bombs or torpedoes;

speed 198mph (316kph).

Martin Maryland Designed to meet a US Army demand for an attack bomber, the Maryland was turned down by US forces but bought by the French in 1939. About 75 reached France, performed well, and some survivors flew to Britain and were assimilated into the RAF together with the balance of the French contract. The remaining French machines went to the Vichy air force and were active in the Mediterranean and Syria. The RAF bought a further 150 machines and used them to good effect in North Africa, while a small number were used by the Royal Navy as maritime reconnaissance aircraft. *Span* 61.3ft (18.7m); *engines* 2 1200hp radial; *crew* 3; *armament* 6 machine guns, 2000lb (900kg), of bombs; *speed* 305mph (491kph).

Maryland Class Battleships (USA)

The three members of this class (*Maryland, Colorado* and WEST VIRGINIA) provided fire support for numerous amphibious operations during the war in the Pacific. *Displacement* 31,500 tons; *dimensions* 624×108ft (190×32.9m); *mean draught* 30ft (9.1m); *machinery* 4-shaft turbo-electric drive producing shp 31,000; *speed* 21 knots; *protection* main belt 16in; turrets 18in; *armament* 8×16in (4×2); 10×5in (10×1); 8×5in AA (8×1); *aircraft* 3; *complement* 2100; *number in class* 3, launched 1920–21.

MAS Boats – Torpedo and Anti-Submarine Craft (Italy)

MAS stood for *Motoscafo Armato SVAN*, as the SVAN yard in Venice had also built torpedo craft of this type during World War I. The more numerous classes displaced 21/26 tons, were 55–60 feet (16.7–18m) in length and powered by 2000hp Isotta Fraschini engines giving a maximum speed of 42 knots. Armament consisted of one 13.2mm machine gun, two 17.7-inch torpedoes and six depth charges. In June 1940 Italy could deploy over 100 of these craft in the Mediterranean and Red Seas against the Royal Navy's nine elderly motor torpedo boats. The MAS boats were particularly active against the MALTA convoys, scoring a number of successes, and on 26 July 1941 launched a major attack on Malta itself. Of the 144 MAS boats which saw active service, 50 were destroyed and 20 were scuttled; a further 41 were captured by the Germans when Italy surrendered and of these 24 were destroyed. See MOTOSILURANTI.

Masaryk, Jan (1896–1948)

Masaryk was the son of Thomas Masaryk, the Czechoslovakian patriot who had played a leading role in obtaining his country's independence. At the time of the MUNICH Agreement and the partition of Czechoslovakia, he was serving as Ambassador to the Court of St James. He later became Foreign Minister of President Edouard BENES' government-in-exile in London, for which he secured recognition as well as the repudiation of the Munich Agreement. He made daily radio broadcasts to his countrymen through the medium of the BBC and carried out speaking tours of the United Kingdom and the United States in furtherance of his country's cause. He also established good relations with the USSR which resulted in the formation of Czech units within the Soviet Army. He died in Prague as a result of a fall from a window, the circumstances of which remain unexplained.

Massachusetts, USS – South Dakota Class Battleship

After supporting the North African landings, *Massachusetts* transferred to the Pacific, where she was in action at the GILBERT ISLANDS, KWAJALEIN, TRUK, HOLLANDIA, Palau, LEYTE GULF, IWO JIMA and OKINAWA.

Massawa, Eritrea, 1941

Italian naval base on the Red Sea. Commanded by Admiral Bonetti, it was attacked by the 7th and 10th Indian Infantry Brigades and the Free French Brigade on 8 April 1941. Assisted by air support, they broke through the perimeter in several places and by late afternoon Bonetti surrendered with 9600 men and 127 guns. This ended the Eritrean campaign.

Masson, Brig

Masson, an anti-Nazi, was head of the Swiss secret service and principal contact of the Lucy spy ring, sanctioning the release of information emanating within OKW both to the Western Allies and to the Soviet Union. By 1943 German counter-intelligence knew that he was somehow involved in the disastrous series of leaks and asked him to reveal the identity of the traitors. This he was unable to do as they were known only to Lucy himself, Rudolf RÖSSLER.

Masterdom

Allied occupation of French Indo-China, 1945.

Mastiff
Supply of emergency medical aid to Allied prisoners held in Japanese camps, 1945.

Matador
British plan for the defence of northern Malaya, December 1941.

Matilda I – AII Infantry Tank Mark I (UK)
Only 139 of these tanks were built, production commencing in 1937. They formed the principal equipment of the British Expeditionary Force's 1st Army Tank Brigade, which spearheaded the counter-attack at ARRAS on 21 May 1940, cutting ROMMEL's 7th Panzer Division in two for a period. During this engagement their armour proved impervious to the German 37mm anti-tank gun. Their odd appearance led to them being named Matilda after a cartoon duck of the period, the name being inherited by the vehicle's larger and more famous successor, the Infantry Tank Mark II (A12), which became known as the MATILDA II. *Weight* 11 tons; *speed* 8mph (13kph); *armour* 60mm; *armament* 1 .303in Vickers machine gun or 1 .50in Vickers machine gun; *engine* Ford V8 70hp petrol; *crew* 2.

Matilda II – A12 Infantry Tank Mark II (UK)
Developed as a larger, gun-armed version of the MATILDA I, the vehicle entered production in 1939 and by association became popularly known as Matilda II, although the II was dropped when construction of the smaller tank was discontinued after the DUNKIRK evacuation. Sixteen were present with 1st Army Tank Brigade at the ARRAS counter-attack on 21 May 1940. During the early battles in the Western Desert the Italians lacked a weapon which was capable of penetrating the Matilda's armour and for a while the tank was hailed as "Queen of the Battlefield". However, this immunity ended with the arrival of the Afrika Korps' 88mm dual-purpose guns, and although the Matilda took part in every major desert battle until mid-1942 the basic design could not be up-gunned and after large numbers were lost during the GAZALA/KNIGHTSBRIDGE battle it ceased to be used as a gun tank in this theatre of war, its last action in this role taking place during the early stages of the First Battle of ALAMEIN. In smaller numbers, Matildas were also employed in

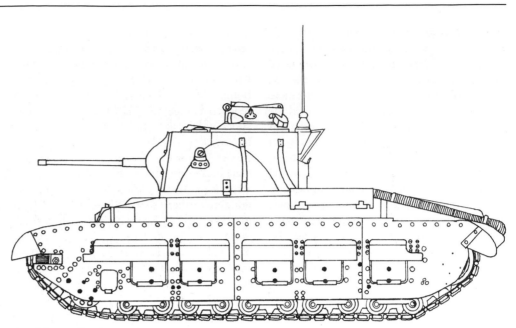

Matilda II infantry tank.

ERITREA, CRETE and MALTA, and some were sent to the Soviet Union. In Australian hands, the vehicle continued to serve as a gun tank in the Far East, where the anti-tank capability of the Japanese was substantially less than that of the Germans, and saw further action in BORNEO, BOUGAINVILLE and NEW GUINEA. Several special purpose vehicles were based on the Matilda, including a CANAL DEFENCE LIGHT, a SCORPION flail, a few of which took part in the Second Battle of ALAMEIN, and an Australian flame-thrower with a range of 100 yards, known as the Frog. Altogether, 2987 Matildas were built under the parentage of the Vulcan Foundry of Warrington; production ceased in August 1943. *Weight* 26.5 tons; *speed* 15mph (24kph); *armour* 78mm; *armament* 1 2-pdr gun or 1 3-in howitzer on close support models; 1 Vickers .303-in machine gun (Mark I) replaced by 1 Besa 7.92mm on subsequent Marks; *engines Marks I and II* – 2 AEC 87hp diesel; *Marks III–V* – 2 Leyland 95hp diesel; *crew* 4.

Matildas of 4th Royal Tank Regiment.

Matmata Hills, Tunisia, 1943

A range of hills, inland of the Gulf of Gabes, which acted as the inland flank of the MARETH LINE. When confronted by this defensive line, MONTGOMERY sent the New Zealand Corps over the hills to reconnoitre the German flanks, then reinforced the corps by an armoured division and thus outflanked the Mareth Line.

Matsu Class Destroyers (Jap)

Laid down as a result of the heavy losses incurred by the Imperial Japanese Navy during the fighting around the SOLOMON ISLANDS in 1943. The overall emphasis was on simplicity of design and construction. *Displacement* 1289 tons; *dimensions* 328ft×30ft 6in (99.9×9.3m); mean draught 11ft (3.3m); *machinery* 2-shaft geared turbines producing shp 19,000; *speed* 27.75 knots; *armament* 3×5in (1×2 and 1×1); 24×25mm AA (4×3 and 12×1); 4×24in torpedo tubes (1×4); 60 depth charges; *number in class* 33, launched 1944–45.

Matsuoka, Yosuke (1880–1946)

As Japanese delegate to the League of Nations, Matsuoka had led the walk-out which followed censure of his country's invasion of MANCHURIA. He served as Foreign Minister from September 1940 until July 1941, concluding a Tripartite Pact with Germany and Italy shortly after assuming office. In April 1941 he signed a neutrality pact with the Soviet Union, but this proved unpopular at home and led to his downfall. He was tried and executed by the Allies in 1946 for the part he had played in leading Japan into the war. It was Matsuoka who conceived the propaganda term GREATER EAST ASIA CO-PROSPERITY SPHERE.

Maultier Panzerwerfer (Ger)

Lightly armoured version of the Opel Maultier standard truck chassis, converted to half-track by means of a Carden-Loyd type suspension at the rear. The vehicle was armed with a Nebelwerfer rocket launcher with a pair of quintuple tubes. In service with German rocket launcher battalions from 1944 and used to bring down heavy concentrations of fire.

Maungdaw, 1942–44

A small seaport on the Burma coast, northwest of AKYAB. It formed the left end of the Maungdaw–Buthidaung defensive line,

German infantry using Mauser Kar98 rifle and MG15 machine gun.

manned by the Japanese against the British ARAKAN offensives of September 1942–May 1943 and December 1943–April 1944.

Maus (Mouse)

German Army Group A's offensive in the Caucasus, 1942.

Maus (Mouse) – Super-Heavy Tank (Ger)

Commissioned by HITLER in June 1942, the Maus reflected the Führer's growing obsession with bizarre weapon systems. The vehicle was designed by Professor Ferdinand Porsche and, because of the obvious bridge limitations posed by its weight and size, provision was made for deep fording. Two prototypes were available for testing in 1944, plus one of the slightly smaller E.100, but further development was halted by the deteriorating industrial situation. The Maus was an interesting exercise in design, although it had virtually no tactical value and was therefore a waste of resources. *Weight* 188 tons; *speed* 12.5mph (20kph); *armour* 240mm; *armament* 1 150mm L/38 gun mounted co-axially with a 75mm L/36.5 gun, 2 machine guns; *engine* 1200hp diesel; *crew* 6.

Mauser

One of the foremost German small arms manufacturers, the Mauser company was founded in the 1870s to manufacture rifles for the German Army and went on to become one of the world's principal exporters of small arms. It provided the German Army's standard rifle, the 7.92mm Model 1898, in various forms until 1945 and was also responsible for the manufacture of pistols, machine guns and aircraft cannon, including designs originating with other companies. In 1945 the works were dismantled by the French, the machinery removed to France and much of the plant blown up. The company was later reconstituted and returned to the arms business, though much of its present-day production is of sporting weapons.

Mauthausen, Austria

A German concentration camp near Linz. Though not an extermination camp, an estimated 185,000 inmates died there.

Maxim Gun

Developed in 1884, the Maxim was the first completely automatic machine gun, relying upon the power generated by the firing of the cartridge to provide the mechanical operation

Soviet soldier carrying some 60kg of Maxim gun and wheeled mounting.

which loaded and fired the next round. The original design had been simplified and was adopted by several countries in different forms; the most important of these was the British VICKERS machine gun, widely used by British and Commonwealth forces in 1939–45. However the original Maxim design was still used by the Soviet Army in great numbers and formed their principal heavy machine gun strength until the 1950s.

Maydon, Lt S. L. C. RN

Third highest-scoring British submarine commander of World War II. Maydon was skipper of the "U" CLASS submarine *Umbra* which formed part of the 10th Submarine Flotilla based on MALTA. Between 17 January 1942 and 11 January 1943 he sank or damaged 16 vessels totalling 69,922 tons, his most notable victim being the cruiser *Trento*, which was sunk in the Ionian Sea on 15 June 1942. Later in the war Maydon commanded the "T" CLASS submarine *Tradewind* in the Far East.

Mayu Peninsula, Burma, 1943

A peninsula in the ARAKAN region, the MAUNG-DAW–Buthidaung line closing the inland end and the port of DONBAIK situated at the tip. The peninsula was attacked by British and Indian forces in the Arakan offensives, and, having broken the Maungdaw–Buthidaung line in early March 1943, was occupied almost as far as Donbaik. On 29 March, due to setbacks in the IMPHAL region, the need for reinforcements there caused the British attacks in the peninsula to be terminated and the force withdrawn.

Mechanized Infantry Formations

Although the British and American armies formed temporary mechanized infantry groupings for specific operations, both the German and Soviet armies established permanent higher formations for this branch of service. The German Panzergrenadier Division of 1944 consisted of two Panzergrenadier regiments, each of three battalions; a tank (or assault gun) battalion; a reconnaissance battalion; a motorized artillery battalion; a tank destroyer battalion; an anti-aircraft battalion; an engineer battalion; and divisional service units. It was rare for more than one of the division's six Panzergrenadier battalions to be equipped with armoured personnel carriers; the remainder rode in unarmoured half-tracks or lorries.

The contemporary Soviet Mechanized Corps consisted of three mechanized brigades, each containing three motor rifle battalions and one tank regiment (35 tanks); a tank brigade with 65 tanks; a light self-propelled artillery regiment (SU-76); a medium self-propelled artillery regiment (SU-85); a medium mortar regiment; a heavy mortar battalion; an anti-aircraft regiment; a motorcycle reconnaissance battalion; a signals battalion; an engineer battalion; and corps service units. Soviet mechanized infantry lacked armoured personnel carriers and even lorries were often in short supply, so their casualties tended to be heavy.

Mechili, Cyrenaica, 1941

A small town south of Derna, Mechili was the location of one of the first tank battles in the Western Desert on 24 January 1941, when the British 7th Armoured Division destroyed eight Italian medium tanks and captured one, for the loss of one cruiser and six light tanks.

Mechlin, Belgium, 1939

A Belgian village near the German border, close to which a German light aircraft force-landed in November 1939. When Belgian gendarmes arrived on the scene, a German liaison officer passenger in the aircraft was attempting to burn documents which, when seized, proved to be German plans for the invasion of France and the Low Countries. When the contents were passed to the British and French governments it was assumed to be a ruse, but, in fact, the documents were genuine and the loss led to the postponement of the German plans.

Medenine, Tunisia, 1943

A small town, south of the MARETH LINE, which was on the British line of advance in January 1943. After being taken, it was used as a resting point while supplies were brought up, and ROMMEL decided to attack here in order to disrupt Montgomery's preparations. From cipher intercepts the British got wind of the proposed attack and were able to reinforce Medenine in time. Rommel attacked on 6 March 1943 with his troops spread out; a fierce artillery barrage decimated his infantry, leaving his tanks exposed to anti-tank fire. Over 50 German tanks were destroyed and the assault foundered before it was within rifle range of the British lines. Rommel finally withdrew, relinquished his command and returned to Germany.

Medjerda, Tunisia, 1943

A river valley running north-east towards Tunis and forming a natural route for Allied attack in the final phase of the Tunisian campaign. A night attack by 4th Indian Division on 6 May 1943, under General Sir Francis Tuker, broke through the German defensive lines, after which the route to Tunis lay open. The German commander, General von ARNIM, surrendered on 12 May, bringing the campaign to an end.

Meiktila, Burma

Road and rail centre and location of the Japanese HQ controlling the administration of Central BURMA, Meiktila was vigorously defended by a force of about 4000 Japanese troops under Major-General Kasuya. The British advance to Mandalay in 1945 had first to neutralize Meiktila, and it was attacked by the 17th Indian Division and 255th Indian Tank Brigade under General COWAN. The attack began on 28 February from three directions and bitter house-to-house fighting ensued before the town was taken on 3 March. It was then necessary to hold the town against Japanese counter-attacks in order to paralyse the railway system and prevent Japanese reinforcements reaching MANDALAY.

Mellenthin, Maj Gen F. W. von (1904–)

After holding a number of staff appointments during the Polish, French and Balkan campaigns of 1939–41, Mellenthin was appointed Third General Staff Officer to Panzer Group Afrika on 1 June 1941, then Deputy First General Staff Officer on 3 April

1942. After a period of hospitalization he was posted to the Eastern Front on 1 November 1942 as Chief of Staff, XLVIII Panzer Corps, then served as Chief of Staff, 4th Panzer Army from 15 August 1944 until 14 September 1944. He then moved to the Western Front as Chief of Staff, Army Group G, a post he held until 30 November 1944. Between 1 January and 28 February 1945 he was attached to 9th Panzer Division and was then appointed Chief of Staff, 5th Panzer Army, in which capacity he was still serving when the war ended. His book *Panzer Battles* is a classic reference work on the armoured warfare of the period.

Memel, Lithuania, 1939–45

A Baltic seaport, originally in East Prussia and part of Lithuania after World War I. It was "ceded" by Lithuania to Germany on 23 March 1939, the last peaceful German conquest. In October 1944 Soviet forces reached the Baltic around Memel and besieged the town, which was defended by the German 28th Army Corps. Memel's defenders withdrew by sea on 22 January 1945 and it was subsequently occupied by the Soviets.

Menace

Anglo-Free French attempt to capture DAKAR, September 1940.

Mengele, Dr Josef (1911–1984)

Known as "The Blond Angel of Auschwitz", Josef Mengele was senior doctor at AUSCHWITZ concentration camp, where he was responsible for conducting countless experimental operations on prisoners. These were as notable for their sadistic barbarity as they were for their lack of scientific justification. After the war he was able to escape to South America where he managed to stay one step ahead of his pursuers until he died in comparative poverty in 1984.

Menzies, Robert (1894–1978)

Robert Menzies was Prime Minister of Australia from April 1939 until August 1941. Although leading a minority government, he was able to announce Australia's entry into the war on 3 September 1939 and quickly despatched three divisions to the Middle Eastern theatre of war. In August 1940 his United Australia Party formed a coalition government with the Country Party, but he resigned in 1941, and was succeeded by a Labour administration under CURTIN.

Merchant Aircraft Carriers

These ships were bulk grain carriers or tankers of approximately 8000–9250 tons gross fitted with a flight deck and a small island bridge. Nineteen of these conversions were made, six of which belonged to the Empire MacAlpine Class and nine to the Rapana Class. The former had a maximum speed of 12.5 knots, the latter 13 knots and the remainder 11 knots. The Empire MacAlpine Class were armed with one 4-inch gun, two 40mm and four 20mm anti-aircraft guns and the remainder with one 4-inch gun and eight 20mm anti-aircraft guns. Four aircraft were carried, parked permanently on the flight deck in the case of the tanker conversions, although the shorter grain-carrying Empire MacAlpine Class were fitted with a lift and hangar. The merchant aircraft carriers continued to perform their mercantile function as well as supplying air cover for the convoys with which they sailed. With the exception of the air crew and their maintenance team, they were manned by the merchant service and flew the Red Ensign. They provided an interim stage between the CAM SHIP and the escort carrier until greater numbers of the latter became available. The idea was revived during the Falklands War of 1982.

Meretskov, Marshal Kirill (1897–   )

Meretskov commanded an army during the Winter War against Finland and succeeded in breaking through the MANNERHEIM LINE. When Germany invaded the Soviet Union he was serving as Chief of General Staff but was superseded by ZHUKOV. He commanded the Volkhov Front during the siege of LENINGRAD and was ultimately successful in breaking the enemy's blockade of the city. In February 1944 he was given command of the Karelian Front with the responsibility of driving the Germans out of Finland. His last appointment in World War II was as commander of the 1st Far Eastern Front, which he took up in August 1945.

Merkur (Mercury)

German airborne invasion of CRETE, May 1941.

Merrill, Brig Gen Frank (1903–55)

Merrill joined the US Army as a private soldier at the age of 18 and passed the West Point Entrance Examination no less than six times before the authorities were willing to overlook his shortsightedness and accept him as an officer candidate. He was commissioned in 1929 and nine years later served as Assistant Military Attaché in Tokyo, where he familiarized himself with the Japanese language and military methods. He was in RANGOON when Japan entered the war and served with STILWELL's Chinese army during the retreat from Burma. On 4 January 1944 he assumed command of the 5307th Composite Unit (Provisional), an American long-range penetration group which had been formed for operations against the Japanese rear areas, taking WINGATE's CHINDITS as its model. The group was committed to action the following month and soon became known as MERRILL's MARAUDERS, a nickname conferred by James Shepley, the *Time/Life* war correspondent. It distinguished itself in the HUKAWNG VALLEY (Northern Burma) and at MYITKYINA, although Merrill was himself hospitalized for part of this period. He later became Deputy US Commander in the Burma–India theatre and then Chief of Staff to the US 10th Army in the Pacific.

Merrill's Marauders

See MERRILL.

Mersa Brega, Libya, 1941

A small coastal town on the Gulf of Sirte. In February 1941 it was one of the most advanced posts of the British Army and was defended by the Support Group of 2nd British Armoured Division (one infantry battalion with one regiment of field guns and one of anti-tank guns). Some three miles to the rear were the tanks of 3rd Armoured Brigade, whose role was to counter-attack any enemy penetration of the Support Group. On 24 March 1941 General ROMMEL drove the British outposts from EL AGHEILA and advanced on Mersa Brega on 31 March. The 5th German Light Division attacked the Support Group who, after a spirited defence, called for assistance from 3rd Armoured Brigade. Major-General Gambier-Parry refused, claiming that there was insufficient daylight left for the tanks to attack. This decision, coinciding with a fresh attack by the Germans, led to the Support Group being overcome, and Rommel forthwith began his advance into CYRENAICA.

Mers-el-Kebir, British Bombardment of, 1940

Following the fall of France in June 1940 the British government was anxious that the French battle fleet, the more important units

Bombardment of French Fleet, Mers-el-Kebir 1940.

of which were lying in the naval base at Mers-el-Kebir, Algeria, should not fall into German hands. On 3 July 1940 a force commanded by Vice-Admiral SOMERVILLE, consisting of two battleships, a battlecruiser, an aircraft carrier, two cruisers and eleven destroyers, arrived off Mers-el-Kebir and presented the French with the alternatives of continuing the war against the Axis powers; sailing with reduced crews to a British port; sailing under escort to a port in the French West Indies or the USA and there being disarmed; or, in the last resort, being destroyed in harbour by gunfire and air attack. Admiral Gensoul, the French commander, rejected the ultimatum and at 1656, with extreme reluctance, the British opened fire, sinking the battleship BRETAGNE and seriously damaging the battleships DUNKERQUE and *Provence* as well as the destroyer *Mogador*. The battleship *Strasbourg* and several destroyers escaped to TOULON. The French sustained over 1000 casualties and the operation only achieved its purpose with an inevitable legacy of bitterness.

Merville, France, 1944

A village in Normandy lying east of Ouistreham and just outside the boundary of the invasion beaches. It contained a battery of German 15cm guns in concrete emplacements, well defended by wire, mines and light weapons, which threatened the left flank of the Allied seaborne attack on 6 June 1944. Heavy air attacks had made no impression on the battery, and it was assaulted by an airborne attack in the early hours of 6 June by troops of the 6th British Airborne Division. In spite of the drop being scattered, due to poor visibility, the attack was successful and by 0500 the battery had been put out of action.

Messe, Marshal Giovanni (1883–   )

Messe commanded the Italian Expeditionary Force in Russia until January 1943, when he was posted to TUNISIA as commander of the Italian 1st Army, consisting of those formations which had fought in the desert under ROMMEL, less the *Deutsches Afrika Korps*. In fact Messe's command remained purely nominal as the Germans retained effective control of 1st Army through his German Chief of Staff, Major-General Fritz Bayerlein. He was promoted Marshal the day before the Axis general surrender in North Africa.

Messerschmitt Aircraft (Ger)

Messerschmitt Bf109 Designed in 1935, the Bf109 set up a world speed record of 379mph in 1937, by which time it had also appeared in combat in Spain. In 1939 the Bf109E went into production to become the principal fighter of the Luftwaffe until 1941. Heavy losses against the RAF in 1940–41 led to the development of the F model as a "defensive" fighter, and then to the G model which was widely used in Russia. It was this ability to improve on a sound basic design which made the Messerschmitt one of the great combat aircraft of all time; it was built in greater numbers than any other German aircraft. *Span* 32.6ft (9.9m); *engine* (Bf109G) 1 1900hp in-line; *armament* (G model) 1 30mm cannon, 2 machine guns; *speed* 428mph (689kph).

Messerschmitt Bf110 This was the Messerschmitt contribution to the 1930s vogue for twin-engined fighters. Delays in developing adequately powerful engines meant that it did not appear in Spain and saw its first combat in Poland in 1939. As a day escort fighter it was a signal failure, the weight of guns, armour, two

The Messerschmidt Bf109, principal German protagonist in the Battle of Britain.

engines and extra fuel fatally restricting its manoeuvrability; it suffered heavy losses in the Battle of BRITAIN. However as a defensive night fighter against bomber attacks, particularly when RADAR-equipped, it performed well. It was also widely used as a ground-attack fighter-bomber and, with reduced armament, as a photo-reconnaissance machine. It remained in production until February 1945. *Span* 53.3ft (16.25m); *engines* 2 1475hp in-line; *crew* 3; *armament,* typically, 2 30mm cannon, 2 20mm cannon, 2 machine guns, 2200lb (1000kg) of bombs; *speed* 340mph (547kph).

Messerschmitt Me163 Komet A unique ultra-short-range defensive fighter, the Me163 was designed very simply to get up among the bombers, shoot something down, and then return within ten minutes. Even the undercarriage was jettisoned on takeoff, the aircraft landing on skids. Power came from a liquid-fuel rocket motor which gave it phenomenal speed and climbing ability, but its failing was a tendency to explode like a bomb if the pilot landed it too hard, due to the mixing of hypergolic fuel residues. *Span* 30.5ft (9.3m); *engine* 1 3750lb (1700kg) s.t. Walter rocket; *armament* 2 30mm cannon; *speed* 596mph (959kph).

Messerschmitt Me210/410 The Me210 set out to improve on the ME110 as a twin-engined fighter-bomber, but it turned out to be a failure, beset by instability problems, landing gear failures, and a high accident rate; it was withdrawn from production after only 350 had been made. Extensively redesigned, and with new engines, it reappeared in late 1942 as the Me410, which went into service early in 1943. This was a better machine, but still a disappointment. Almost 2000 were built and it was used on the Eastern Front in ground-attack and fighter-bomber roles in night attacks on Southern England, and as a bomber-destroyer on home defence, while a few were also employed on photo-reconnaissance. *Span* 53.5ft (16.3m); *engines* 2 1720hp in-line; *crew* 2; *armament* 4 20mm cannon, 4 machine guns, up to 2200lb (1000kg) of bombs; *speed* 385mph (619kph).

Messerschmitt Me262 Schwalbe Turbojet engines were under development in Germany before the war but it was not until 1942 that engines of sufficient power allowed the development of an operational jet aircraft. The Me262 had been designed much earlier, around engines of lesser power, but even with increased power the Luftwaffe were reluctant to consider it as a practical aircraft. Production deliveries of a fighter version began in May 1944; on Hitler's orders all initial aircraft were completed as fighter-bombers, and not until late 1944 was the fighter version given priority. Production was then too late to be effective, although the aircraft took a heavy toll of USAAF bombers during early 1945. *Span* 41ft (12.5m); *engines* 2 1980lb (869kg) s.t. turbojets; *armament* 4 30mm cannons; *speed* 540mph (869kph).

Messerschmitt Me321/323 Gigant One of the largest aircraft of the war, the Me321 was a transport glider which went into service in 1941. Capable of carrying 100 fully-equipped troops, plus a crew of up to seven, or 21,500lb (9750kg) of cargo, the principal difficulty was finding aircraft sufficiently powerful to tow it, the eventual solution being groups of three Me110s with the assistance of rockets for takeoff. Later in 1942 a powered version was developed, and this was used extensively as a heavy transport machine. *Span* 181ft (55m); *engines* 6 990hp radial; *speed* 136mph (219kph).

Messervy, Gen Sir Frank (1893–1974) A cavalryman, Messervy was commissioned into the Indian Army in 1914 and during World War I served in France, Palestine and the Middle East. His first major appointments in World War II were as commander of Gazelle Force in the Sudan and ERITREA, 1940–41, and later of the 9th Indian Infantry Brigade at KEREN. He then commanded the 4th Indian Division in the Western Desert, 1941–42, before assuming command of the 7th Armoured Division. His handling of the latter during the Battle of GAZALA was the subject of some criticism, and at one stage both he and his Chief of Staff were captured when the division's headquarters was overrun, but later escaped. After Gazala he was appointed Deputy Chief of General Staff at GHQ Middle East Forces and then commanded the 43rd Indian Armoured Division, 1942–43, until taking up the post of senior armoured adviser at GHQ India in 1943. His next field appointment was as commander of the 7th Indian Division, which he led with distinction in the ARAKAN and at KOHIMA in 1944. He was then appointed commander of IV Corps, with which he executed the dramatic seizure of the Japanese communications centre of Meiktila and the subsequent dashing advance through Tamu to RANGOON in 1945. He was appointed Commander-in-Chief of the Pakistan Army in 1947 and retired the following year.

Metaxas, Gen Joannis (1871–1941) From 1936 until his death Metaxas was virtual dictator of GREECE. Although suspected of being pro-Axis in his sympathies, he reacted strongly to the Italian invasion of his country in October 1940 and mobilized his resources to such good effect that the invaders were pushed back into ALBANIA.

Metaxas Line, 1941 A fortified Greek defensive position about 100 miles (160km) long, running along part of the Greek-Bulgarian border from the Beles Mountains near Dojran to the mouth of the River Nestos; there were also a number of isolated fortresses to the east, in Thrace. A second line, behind the first, ran from the Beles Mountains along the Stroumon River to the sea. The line was eventually breached by German frontal attack, but it was also outflanked by German advances through YUGOSLAVIA.

Metox A German RADAR receiver fitted to U-boats to detect the radar emissions from British anti-submarine patrol aircraft. It was a simple receiver which gave audible warning when the radar was about 30 miles (48km) away, a distance about twice that at which the radar could detect the submarine, thus the U-boat had plenty of time to dive and disappear before being spotted. Tuned to the 30cm band, it was eventually outwitted by the adoption of 10cm band search radar.

Metz, France, 1940 and 1944 A border city which lies on the natural invasion path between France and Germany and has thus been fortified since the Middle Ages. In the Franco-Prussian War (1870) Metz was lost to the Germans, who modernized the fortifications. After World War I it was restored to France, and the fortifications were again modernized. Captured again by Germany in 1940, the defences were overhauled, but they were not called upon until the US 3rd Army, under General PATTON, attacked in late 1944. The forts stopped Patton in his tracks and, in spite of several attacks, little impression was made until the major part of the Allied advance had bypassed Metz and cut it off, condemning the garrisons to starvation. Metz eventually fell to US troops in November 1944.

Meyer, SS Maj Gen Kurt

An ardent Nazi, Meyer is best remembered as commander of the 12th SS Panzer Division *Hitlerjugend* during the 1944 campaign in NORMANDY. Under his leadership the division was noted for its ferocious and self-destructive style of fighting which more than once blunted Allied offensives. Only a handful of its survivors were able to fight their way clear of the carnage of the FALAISE pocket. Meyer, often referred to by his nickname of "Panzer", was captured during the retreat across France.

MG 34

German standard infantry machine gun, developed in 1934 and entered service in 1936. Used with a bipod as the squad weapon, it could also be used on a tripod as a sustained-fire support machine gun and introduced the General Purpose Machine Gun concept. Of high quality, it was difficult to manufacture at the speed necessary in wartime and was superseded by the MG 42 in 1943, although it continued in service until the war ended. The calibre was 7.92mm and the rate of fire about 850 rounds per minute.

MG 42

A German infantry machine gun which, like the MG 34, could be used either as the squad weapon or as the company support weapon. Designed for mass-production and thus more quickly manufactured than the MG 34, it had an extremely high rate of fire of 1200 rounds per minute. Over 750,000 were made by the end of the war, and in the 1950s it was re-adopted by the Bundeswehr and is still in use both by them and by other armies.

Mi2H Miles in two hours (UK). The measure of the speed of marching columns, based on a two-hour period so as to include a ten-minute rest break.

MIA Missing in Action.

Michael, King of Romania (reigned 1940–47)

Michael assumed the throne on the abdication of his father Carol in 1940, but his accession coincided with the coup in which Prime Minister ANTONESCU seized power. On 23 August 1944 the King staged a coup of his own which removed Antonescu from office, the first act of the new government being to declare war on Germany. Michael abdicated in 1947, finding his role incompatible with a Communist state.

Michel – Surface Raider (Ger)

Also known as Ship 28 and Raider H. Sailed 13 March 1942 under Lieutenant-Commander von Ruckteschell and operated in the Atlantic, Indian and Pacific Oceans, sinking 14 ships totalling 94,362 tons. Arrived Kobe, Japan, 2 March 1943 and refitted. Commenced second cruise 21 May 1943 under Captain Gumprich, former commander of THOR, and sank three ships of 27,632 tons before being torpedoed and sunk by the submarine USS *Tarpon* off Yokohama on 17 October 1943. *Displacement* 4740 tons; *speed* 16 knots; *armament* 6×5.9in; 3×37mm AA; 2×20mm AA; 4×21in torpedo tubes; *aircraft* 2; *motor torpedo boat* 1; *complement* 400.

Middleton, Maj Gen Troy H. (1889–1976)

During 1943 Middleton commanded the US 45th Division in SICILY, at the SALERNO landing and in the subsequent advances to the GUSTAV LINE. He was then appointed commander of the US VIII Corps, which he led for the remainder of the war. This formation served in NORMANDY, was responsible for the capture of BREST and bore the brunt of the German offensive directed through the ARDENNES in December 1944, where Middleton's deployment of his reserves, notably at ST VITH and on the routes leading into BASTOGNE, did much to contain the enemy's advance. In 1945 VIII Corps took part in the RHINE Crossing and the final advance across Germany.

Midget Submarines (Ger)

Type XXVIIA Hecht was an 11.75-ton two-man miniature submarine powered by a single shaft 13-shp electric motor which gave a maximum submerged speed of 6 knots. It was armed with a single mine housed inboard or one 21-inch torpedo carried outboard and had an operational radius of 38 miles (61km) at 4 knots, or 69 miles (111km) at 4 knots if additional batteries were carried in the mine chamber. Used for training.

Type XXVIIB Seehund was a 15-ton two-man miniature submarine with two 21-inch torpedoes carried externally beneath the hull. It was driven by a single-shaft diesel/electric motor set with bhp 60/25, giving maximum surfaced/submerged speeds of 7.75/6 knots. It

German midget submarine.

had operational radii of 300 miles (480km) at 7 knots/63 miles (100km) at 3 knots, but when additional saddle fuel tanks were fitted the surface radius expanded to 500 miles (800km).

Type Heger was a one-man development of the HUMAN TORPEDO. The carrier was a torpedo casing on which a cockpit and controls covered by a perspex dome had been substituted for the warhead, the craft being driven by a 12 shp electric motor at a maximum speed of 30 knots, a live torpedo slung below. At 3 knots these craft had an operational radius of 30 miles (48km). As the driver lacked an organic air supply the Type Heger could only operate on the surface but this defect was remedied on the Type Marder.

Type Biber was a 6.25-ton one-man midget submarine armed with two 21-inch torpedoes, slung from launching rails on either side of the hull. The boat was powered by a single-shaft petrol/electric motor set with bhp 32/13, giving maximum surfaced/submerged speed of 6.5/5.25 knots. It had an operational radius of 130 miles (209km) at 6 knots surfaced, or 10 miles (16km) at 5 knots submerged.

Type Molch was a 10.75-ton one-man midget submarine armed with two 21-inch torpedoes. It was driven by a single-shaft 13 shp electric motor and had maximum speeds of 4.5 knots surfaced and 5 knots submerged with respective operational radii of 50 miles (80km) at 4 knots and 40 miles (64km) at 5 knots. All types were built in large numbers, the intention being that they would be used *en masse* against invasion shipping, the smaller craft being transported to their launching sites by road or rail. However, during the Allied invasion of NORMANDY intense air activity effectively severed all communications with the combat zone and the naval defensive screens proved capable of defeating those craft which were launched. The results obtained were disappointing and did not justify so large a diversion of resources.

Midget Submarines (Italy)

Twelve CB (Coastal Type B) class submarines were delivered to the Royal Italian Navy in 1941–43. Powered by a single shaft diesel/electric motor set with respective hp of 80/50, their surface/submerged speed was 7.5/6.5 knots. They were manned by a crew of four, and carried two 17.7-inch torpedoes in exterior tubes, or two mines. Six served in the

Black Sea against the Soviet Union. Of these, one was sunk in Yalta harbour by Russian aircraft on 13 June 1942; the remainder were transferred to the Royal Romanian Navy when Italy surrendered, and scuttled in August 1944 following the advance of the Soviet Army into the Balkans. A further craft was captured by the Germans in September 1943, as were 10 uncompleted hulls, all being transferred to the Italian Fascist Republic.

Midget Submarines (Jap)

Type A. Built 1938–42. Crewed by two men, it could be launched from seaplane tenders and other warships. It was powered by a 600-hp single shaft electric motor which gave a maximum submerged speed of 19 knots. Submerged displacement 46 tons. Type A midget submarines took part in the attacks on PEARL HARBOR and Sydney, and severely damaged the battleship HMS *Ramillies* at DIEGO SUAREZ. Types B and C. Laid down 1942–44. With a crew of three, they provided a better operational radius than Type A, as the design incorporated a battery-charging diesel generator. Submerged displacement 49.33 tons. Type D, built 1944–45, was a larger craft powered by a single shaft diesel electric motor with respective hp of 150/500, producing a surface/submerged speed of 8/16 knots,

and was manned by a crew of five. Submerged displacement 59.33 tons. It took part in the defence of the PHILIPPINES and OKINAWA and was occasionally used as a suicide craft. Like Types B and C, it was transported aboard an LST prior to launching. All four types carried two 18-inch torpedoes in superimposed tubes.

Midway, Battle of, 1942

A complex naval and air battle which took place in the vicinity of Midway island, in the Pacific Ocean, in June 1942. At the time the US Navy had only two operational aircraft carriers in the Pacific, whilst the Japanese had four. Admiral YAMAMOTO therefore devised a complex plan to divert the US fleet to the north by landings in the ALEUTIANS, allowing the Japanese to attack Midway and land troops there. Their plans were, however, known to Admiral NIMITZ, the US commander, since the Japanese code had been broken. Moreover, unknown to the Japanese a third US carrier had been repaired and was serviceable. The US fleet was therefore able to surprise the Japanese by appearing closer to Midway than expected. Both forces launched aircraft, and in the ensuing battle one Japanese carrier was sunk and two so badly damaged that they had to be abandoned. A Japanese strike from the

Battle of Midway, 1942.

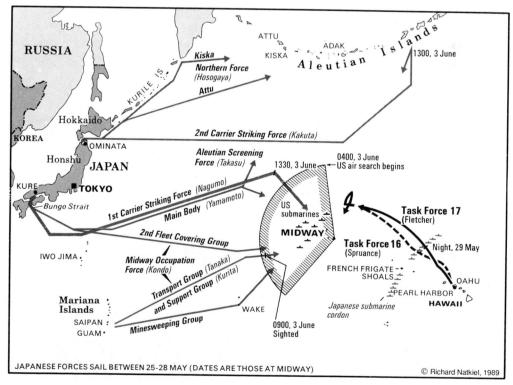

Douglas Dauntless A24 dive bomber, over the wreck of the Japanese cruiser Mikuma, *Battle of Midway, June 1942.*

remaining carrier was successful in sinking the USS *Yorktown*, but later in the day US aircraft from the *Lexington* attacked the remaining Japanese carrier and damaged it so severely that it had to be scuttled. With neither aircraft nor carriers remaining, the Japanese force was now virtually powerless and the Midway operation had to be abandoned. The Battle of Midway was among the most decisive of the war, since in one blow it removed Japanese naval air superiority; the easy run of victories was at an end, and from then on Japan fought on the defensive.

Midway Class Aircraft Carriers (USA)

The largest aircraft carriers of their day and the first American carriers to be provided with armoured flight decks. Commissioned just too late to see active service. *Displacement* 45,000 tons; *dimensions* 986×113ft (300.5× 34.4m); mean draught 32ft 9in (9.98m); *machinery* 4-shaft geared turbines producing shp 212,000; *speed* 33 knots; *armament* 18×5in AA (18×1); 84×40mm AA (21×4); *aircraft* 137; *complement* 4085; *number in class* 3, launched 1945–46.

Mihailović, Gen Draza (1893–1946)

When Germany invaded Yugoslavia in April 1941 Mihailović, until then head of the Yugoslav Army's Operations Bureau, established a resistance movement known as the Četniks. In January 1942 this led to his being appointed Commander-in-Chief and War Minister by the government-in-exile,

which failed to appreciate the devious game he was playing. A royalist and a dedicated anti-Communist, Mihailović found it impossible to co-operate with TITO's partisans, but instead of attacking the common enemy he preferred to stand aloof in the hope that Tito's forces would be wiped out. When Tito showed every sign of surviving, his policy changed to one of active collaboration with the Germans. By late 1942 the Allies were aware of the situation and shifted their support to Tito, who was emerging as the national leader in the struggle against the invaders, and in May 1944 Mihailović was dismissed by his government. He was tried for treason and executed in 1946.

Mikawa, V Adm Gunichi

Mikawa commanded the Japanese naval group at the Battle of SAVO ISLAND, in which he inflicted heavy casualties on the American covering force and returned to his base without loss. However, in the mistaken belief that the Americans had carriers in the area, he did not extend his attack to include their undefended but vitally important supply ships. See also SOLOMON ISLANDS and GUADALCANAL.

Mikolajczyk, Stanislaw (1901–67)

In 1941 Mikolajczyk was appointed Deputy Prime Minister and Minister of the Interior in the Polish government-in-exile in London, his special responsibility being liaison with the Resistance movement in Poland. He became Prime Minister after the death of SIKORSKI but

lacked the latter's appeal and resigned in November 1944 because of the failure of the Allies to support the WARSAW Rising. He was one of the few Polish politicians to return after the war, but never held high office again.

Mikoyan and Gurevich MiG-1/3 (USSR)

The first MiG fighter, the MiG-1 flew in 1940 and was just entering service when Germany launched Operation BARBAROSSA in June 1941. It was soon replaced on the production line by the MiG-3, a direct development with better engine and other improvements; several thousand are said to have been built. Essentially a high-altitude bomber-interceptor, it was no match for the Luftwaffe fighters and by 1942 had been relegated to reconnaissance and rear area defence roles. *Span* 33.75ft (10.3m); *engine* 1 1350hp in-line; *armament* 5 machine guns, 6 rocket launchers or 440lb (200kg) of bombs; *speed* 398mph (640kph).

Mikura Class Escorts (Jap)

Displacement 940 tons; *dimensions* 256ft 3in×29ft 9in (78.1×9m); mean draught 10ft (3m); *machinery* 2-shaft geared diesels producing shp 4200; *speed* 19.5 knots; *armament* 3×4.7in (1×2 and 1×1); 4×25mm AA (2×2); 1×3in mortar; 120 depth charges; *number in class* 8, launched 1943–44.

Milch, FM Erhard (1892–1972)

Milch joined the Army in 1910 and by 1918 had risen to the rank of captain. Although not an airman, he commanded a fighter Gruppe for the last five weeks of World War I. In 1926 he was appointed chairman of Lufthansa, which he used as a cover for the training of personnel and the development of equipment with which a German air force could be established when the moment arrived. In September 1933 he was made GÖRING's deputy in the newly formed Air Ministry (RLM) with the rank of colonel of the Army. In 1936 Milch was appointed General der Flieger in the new Luftwaffe, a promotion which caused considerable resentment among Germany's senior air officers. In July 1941 he assumed overall responsibility for aircraft production after the failure of UDET. He was also one of the 12 Field-Marshals created by HITLER to celebrate the victory in the West. He was imprisoned as a war criminal but released on parole in 1955.

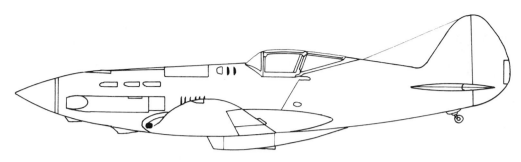

Mikoyan MiG-3 fighter.

Miles Aircraft (UK)

Miles Magister The first monoplane training aircraft to be adopted by the RAF, and it remained in use throughout the war. *Span* 34ft (10.4m); *engine* 1 130hp in-line; *speed* 132mph (212kph).

Miles Master An advanced monoplane trainer, the Master was placed in service in 1939 and over 3000 were built. Early models used a Rolls-Royce in-line engine, but subsequent versions used a radial engine. *Span* 39ft (12m); *engine* 1 870hp radial; *speed* 243mph (391kph).

Miles Messenger This was built at the request of the Army as an artillery air observation machine, and was a low-wing monoplane with a large "greenhouse" canopy to afford excellent visibility, and an unusual triple-fin tail. Although serviceable in the role required, relatively few were built, the Taylorcraft "Auster" being cheaper and quicker to manufacture. *Span* 36ft (11m); *engine* 1 140hp in-line; *speed* 115mph (185kph).

Millenium

RAF 1000-bomber raid on Cologne, 30 May 1942.

Mills, Fort, Philippines, 1942 and 1945

American coast-defence fort which occupied the island of CORREGIDOR in Manila Bay. It was armed with 12 12-inch MORTARS, 8 12-inch guns, two 10-inch guns, five 6-inch guns, 10 3-inch guns and 18 3-inch anti-aircraft guns, to which a number of 155mm field guns were added in 1941. One of the most powerful forts in the world, it was besieged by the Japanese after the fall of the BATAAN peninsula in 1942. After several weeks of severe aerial and artillery bombardment, it was assaulted by Japanese infantry on the night of 5/6 May 1942. American defence was inept and the fort was surrendered on the following day. It was recaptured by a US combined seaborne and airborne attack on 16 February 1945, the battle for the island taking several days. Over 6000 Japanese dead were counted, and an unknown number were entombed in the Fort's tunnels. The Fort is now a Philippine National War Memorial.

Mills Bomb

A British hand grenade invented by a Mr Mills of Birmingham in 1915, it consisted of a cast-iron body filled with explosive, and a central tube containing a spring-driven plunger, an ignition cap, a short length of safety fuze, and a detonator. The plunger was held away from the cap by an external safety lever which was locked in place by a split pin and ring. The thrower held the grenade so that the lever was pressed against the grenade body and removed the pin; he then threw it, releasing the lever. The plunger spring threw the lever off and allowed the plunger to go down and fire the cap; this lit the fuze which burned for four seconds and fired the detonator, exploding the grenade. The original model entered British service as the Grenade Hand No. 5. It was improved into the Grenade 36M, and this remained in British service after 1918 to become the standard British hand grenade during World War II. It remained in service until the late 1960s.

Milne Bay, New Guinea, 1942

A small bay at the eastern tip of Papua New Guinea, this was the scene of a Japanese landing on 26 August 1942. Japanese intelligence considered the area to be lightly held; in fact the bay was defended by two Australian infantry brigades backed up by two squadrons of fighter aircraft. The Australian troops put up a strong defence, the aircraft attacked Japanese shipping, and the Japanese attack made little headway, suffering heavy casualties. On 6 September the Japanese force withdrew under cover of a naval bombardment and the attack was not renewed. Milne Bay was the first occasion on which a Japanese force was defeated by Western troops.

Mincemeat

Allied deception plan for the invasion of SICILY, 1943.

Mindanao

Principal southern island of the Philippines, occupied by the Japanese 35th Army in 1945. It was attacked in March 1945 by troops of the US 8th Army under General EICHELBERGER, and fighting continued until the end of the war.

Japanese soldiers killed in a banzai attack near Maramos, Mindanao.

Mineclearing

The simplest and most common form of mineclearing was by hand, lifting mines which had been detected either by prodding with a metal rod or bayonet, or by simple man-pack electronic detectors, although the latter often failed to reveal mines with non-metallic cases. The process was slow and dangerous and since well-laid minefields were always covered by defensive fire the clearing parties required infantry protection. As the war progressed, various means of mechanical mineclearing were devised. These included flail tanks such as the SCOPRION and CRAB, which exploded mines in their path with rotating chains; mine rollers, which were pushed ahead of a tank, detonating mines by their weight; and mine ploughs, which were also pushed ahead of a tank, lifting and turning mines to one side, where they could be rendered inactive. Explosive methods of clearing mines were also used, the explosion itself serving to detonate the mines in the vicinity. These included the Bangalore Torpedo; the Snake, which consisted of lengths of explosive-filled 3-inch pipe which were joined together, pushed into the minefield and detonated; and the Conger, consisting of 300 yards (275m) of 2-inch hosepipe fired by rocket across a minefield, the hose then being pumped full of liquid explosive and detonated. In an emergency, artillery and direct gunfire could be used to create a minefield gap, although the method was risky. For obvious reasons, most mineclearing operations took place at night, with special provision having to be made for direction keeping. Gaps were taped and separate lanes designated for tanks, which could tear up the ground and render it unusable by wheeled vehicles.

Minekaze Class Destroyers (Jap)

Displacement 1215 tons; *dimensions* 336ft 6in×29ft (102.5×8.8m); *mean draught* 10ft (3m); *machinery* 2-shaft geared turbines producing shp 38,500; *speed* 39 knots; *armament* 4×4.7in (4×1); 2×7.7mm; 6×21in torpedo tubes (3×2); *complement* 148; *number in class* 13, launched 1919–22.

Mine Shell

Type of high explosive projectile developed in Germany for use in aircraft cannon. By 1942 experience showed that the existing types of 20mm cannon shell, with small explosive

The Japanese surrender aboard USS Missouri.

capacity, were becoming ineffective against armoured and heavier aircraft. A 30mm cannon was developed, and – to obtain the maximum destructive effect – alongside it, the mine shell. This shell was of drawn, rather than cast, steel, with a very thin wall and consequently an extremely high capacity for explosive. It relied almost entirely upon blast for its effect, rather than fragmentation. It proved highly successful, and in postwar years, adopted by other designers, has become the standard aircraft cannon projectile.

Minotaur Class Cruisers (UK)

Modified Fiji design; the earlier Minotaur class. Later vessels of this class, *Blake, Tiger, Lion,* were completed after the war with a different armament. *Displacement* 8800–8885 tons; *dimensions* 555ft 6in×63ft (170× 19.2m); mean draught 17ft 3in (5.2m); *machinery* 4-shaft geared turbines producing shp 72,500; *speed* 32.5 knots; *protection* main belt 3.25in; deck 2in; turrets 2in; *armament* 9×6in (3×3); 10×4in AA (5×2); 16×2-pdr AA (4×4); 6×40mm AA (8×1); 6×21in torpedo tubes (2×3); *complement* 960–1000; *number in class* 2, launched 1943.

Minsk, Soviet Union

The provincial capital of the Minsk district, about 275 miles (442km) north-east of WARSAW. Minsk was the objective of the 2nd and

3rd Panzer Groups in Operation BARBAROSSA in June 1941, their intention being to make sweeps from the areas of Wilno and Slonim to cut off a large number of Soviet troops. Although their advance was slower than expected, the manoeuvre took place substantially as planned, the two groups meeting and taking Minsk on 9 July. Although a large number of Soviet troops managed to evade capture, about 15 Soviet divisions were destroyed in the "Minsk Pocket".

Missouri, USS – Iowa Class Battleship

Saw active service in the Pacific at IWO JIMA and OKINAWA and was used for the formal Japanese surrender ceremony in Tokyo Bay on 2 September 1945. Laid up in 1954 but presently in process of recommissioning.

Mistel

A composite of a JUNKERS JU-88 bomber filled with a 3.5-tonne high explosive shaped charge in place of the usual crew space and controls, hooked beneath an Me-109 or Fw190 fighter aircraft. The fighter pilot controlled the entire assembly and flew it off the ground as a double-deck aircraft. Developed in 1943, it was proposed as a method of attacking capital ships, the bomber being released into a shallow dive. The fighter then turned back, while the bomber, controlled by an automatic pilot, carried on its course to hit the target. Mistel went into service but was only used against bridges on the Eastern Front and the Rhine and to achieve some pointless hits on block-ships in the MULBERRY HARBOUR off Normandy.

Mitscher, V Adm Marc A. (1887–1947)

Mitscher was one of the US Navy's pioneer aviators, having learned to fly in 1915 while serving aboard the battleship *North Carolina*, which carried an aircraft. His singleminded dedication to naval aviation was rewarded when in 1941 he was given command of the carrier *Hornet*, from which the DOOLITTLE bombing raid on TOKYO was launched on 18 April 1942, and which took part in the Battle of MIDWAY. On 1 April 1943 he was appointed Air Commander of GUADALCANAL with the responsibility of co-ordinating the operation of the US Army, Navy, Marine Corps and Allied air arms. In January 1944 he assumed command of Task Force 58 (later redesignated Task Force 38), a huge concentration of carriers with its own organic supply and support which enabled it to remain operational for long periods. This provided air cover for the invasions of the MARSHALL ISLANDS and HOLLANDIA and in June moved to the MARIANAS. It played a critical part in the Battle of the PHILIPPINE SEA and in August and September executed raids on the BONIN ISLANDS, Palau, MINDANAO and FORMOSA. It took part in the Battle of LEYTE GULF in October and in 1945 provided air support for the IWO JIMA and OKINAWA campaigns. Mitscher's Task Force was a decisive strategic weapon against which the Japanese were unable to offer an effective defence.

Mitsubishi Aircraft (Jap)

Mitsubishi A5M (Claude) The principal Japanese naval fighter during the Sino-Japanese war, the A5M was the Navy's first monoplane, and the first all-metal stressed-skin military aircraft to be built in Japan. About 1000 were built and it was a well-liked and effective machine. *Span* 35.5ft (11m); *engine* 1 710hp radial; *armament* 2 machine guns, 110lb (50kg) of bombs; *speed* 273mph (439kph).

Mitsubishi A6M (Zero/Zeke) The most famous of Japanese warplanes, the "Zero-Sen" was developed to replace the A5M (above). It first flew in 1939 and by the time of PEARL HARBOR had been blooded in 16 months of active combat over China. It was the first naval carrier fighter which could outperform land-based fighters and as such came as an

unpleasant shock to the Allies. As a naval fighter it could operate at a range of up to 1500 miles (2410km). It appeared in a number of variants, each improving the performance, and over 10,000 were built of which some 300 were the A6M2-N "Rufe" floatplane version. *Span* 36ft (11m); *engine* 1 1130hp radial; *armament* 2 20mm cannon, 2 7.7mm machine guns, 660lb (300kg) of bombs; *speed* 351mph (565kph).

Mitsubishi F1M (Pete) Designed as a ship-board reconnaissance floatplane for use from Japanese warships, the F1M biplane eventually performed admirably as a bomber, patrol, submarine attacker, convoy escort and air-sea rescue machine. A smooth and sleek design, it could also perform well as a fighter and was seen in most of the Pacific campaigns. *Span* 36ft (11m); *engine* 1 875hp radial; *crew* 2; *armament* 3 machine guns, 265lb (120kg) of bombs; *speed* 230mph (370kph).

Mitsubishi G3M (Nell) Japan's standard naval medium and torpedo-bomber at the outbreak of war, the G3M continued in service until 1945 in spite of being officially super-seded by more modern designs. Used orig-inally in its designed role, it was responsible with the G4M for the sinking of *Prince of Wales* and *Repulse* in December 1941, but in the latter stages of the war it was principally employed as a transport. *Span* 82ft (25m); *engines* 2 1000hp radial; *crew* 7; *armament* 1 20mm cannon, 2 machine guns, 2200lb (1000kg) of bombs; *speed* 238mph (383kph).

Mitsubishi G4M (Betty) Designed to meet a Japanese Navy specification which demanded long range and a heavy bomb load, the G4M was consequently built with an eye to weight-saving, and economies were made in protec-tion and strength. Initially the Betty carried no armour or self-sealing tanks, and was dubbed the "one-shot lighter" by American pilots. Although one of Japan's principal bombers, it

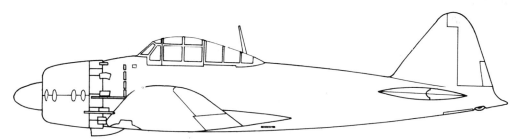

The Mitsubishi A6M "Zero" or "Zeke" fighter.

was highly vulnerable in combat and never popular with its crews. As well as normal bombing missions, it was also employed as a torpedo-bomber. In the later stages of the war a large number of G4Ms were equipped to carry the Okha piloted suicide bomb. *Span* 81.6ft (25m); *engines* 2 1850hp radial; *crew* 7; *armament* 4 20mm cannons, 1 machine gun, 2200lb (1000kg) of bombs; *speed* 270mph (434kph).

Mitsubishi J2M (Jack) A land-based interceptor for the Japanese Navy, the J2M was a sleek monoplane built for speed and climbing ability but with poor manoeuvrability. Subsequently redesigned several times, the last form (the J2M5) proved an effective fighter against high-flying American bombers. *Span* 35.5ft (10.8m); *engine* 1820hp radial; *armament* 2 20mm cannon, 2 machine guns; *speed* 371mph (597kph).

Mitsubishi Ki-21 (Sally) This was the standard Japanese Army heavy bomber throughout the war. Entering service early in 1938 it was used in China; experience there led to modifications and heavier armament. It subsequently saw service all over the Pacific throughout the war years. *Span* 72.75ft (22m); *engines* 2 1490hp radial; *crew* 7; *armament* 6 machine guns, 2200lb (1000kg) of bombs; *speed* 295mph (475kph).

Mitsubishi Ki-30 (Ann) Ordered by the Japanese Army in its modernization plan of 1935, this was a single-engined monoplane light bomber. It was used extensively in China, but after brief employment during the invasion of the PHILIPPINES it was withdrawn from service and employed in training roles thereafter. *Span* 47.75ft (14.6m); *engine* 1 950hp radial; *crew* 2; *armament* 3 machine guns, 660lb (300kg) of bombs; *speed* 265mph (426kph).

Mitsubishi Ki-46 (Dinah) Designed as a strategic reconnaissance aircraft, the Ki-46 is generally conceded to be the most aerodynamically perfect aircraft of World War II. It had sufficient performance in speed and altitude to outrun most Allied fighters and, converted by the addition of heavy nose armament, became an effective fighter and ground-attack machine. *Span* 48ft (14.6m); *engines* 2 1050hp radial; *crew* 2; *armament* (reconnaissance) 1 machine gun; (fighter) 1 37mm cannon, 2 20mm cannon; *speed* 390mph (627kph).

Mitsubishi Ki-67 (Peggy) Probably the best all-round aircraft produced in Japan, the Peggy was designed as a heavy bomber but proved agile enough to serve also as an escort fighter, though this application was not pursued since the bomber version had a higher priority. Production did not begin until 1944 but over 700 were built before the war ended. Towards the end of the war a number were converted into three-seat suicide bombers. *Span* 73.75ft (22.5m); *engines* 2 2000hp radial; *crew* 6 to 8; *armament* 1 20mm cannon, 4 machine guns, 1750lb (800kg) of bombs; *speed* 334mph (537kph).

Miyazaki, Maj Gen

During the Battle of KOHIMA Miyazaki led a detachment of the Japanese 31st Division, distinguishing himself as commander of the divisional rearguard during the ensuing retreat from India. He was then appointed commander of the 54th Division in the ARAKAN. Despite the general collapse of the Japanese BURMA AREA ARMY he managed to preserve his formation until it was finally destroyed during the abortive attempt by HONDA's 33rd Army to break out into Lower Burma.

MMG Medium machine gun. A machine gun, usually water-cooled, fed from a belt and supported on a tripod, not capable of being carried by one man. It was used for long-range and continuous fire.

MO Medical officer.

Mo

Japanese plan for attack on PORT MORESBY, 1942.

Moaning Minnie

The name given by Allied troops to the projectile fired by the German *Nebelwerfer* 21cm rocket-launcher, on account of the noise made as it flew through the air.

Möbelwagen (Furniture Van) – Anti-Aircraft Tank (Ger)

Based on the PANZERKAMPFWAGEN IV chassis with the turret replaced by an anti-aircraft mounting protected by four hinged rectangular flaps which were lowered when the vehicle was in action. The first examples, armed with quadruple 20mm machine guns, began entering service in the autumn of 1943. An alternative mounting carried a single 37mm cannon. A total of 211 Möbelwagen were built.

Model, FM Walter (1891–1945)

The son of an impoverished music teacher, Model served as the 16th Army's Chief of Staff during the 1940 campaign in France. He was given command of the 3rd Panzer Division on 13 November 1940 and led this during the early stages of BARBAROSSA until appointed commander of XLI Panzer Corps. He then commanded both 2nd Panzer Army and 9th Army, which he led during Operation ZITADELLE and its aftermath. As HITLER lost confidence in the older generation of senior commanders Model's star continued to rise and between October 1943 and August 1944 he was the Führer's favourite troubleshooter, commanding in succession Army Groups North, South and Centre, restoring the stability of the Eastern Front.

On 17 August he was appointed Commander-in-Chief West following the death of von KLUGE but was unable to prevent the debacle in NORMANDY. On 5 September he was replaced by von RUNDSTEDT but retained command of Army Group B and was responsible for the defeat of the British airborne landing at ARNHEM as well as mounting the great German counteroffensive through the ARDENNES in December 1944. In the spring of 1945 his army group was trapped in the RUHR pocket and, true to his stated belief that no German Field-Marshal should allow himself to be taken alive, shot himself on 21 April. Model was a capable and energetic commander but tended to interfere in the internal dispositions of subordinate formations.

Modified Black Swan Class Escort Sloops (UK)

See also BLACK SWAN CLASS. *Displacement* 1350 tons; *dimensions* 299ft 6in×38ft 6in (91.3×11.5m); mean draught 8ft 9in (2.66m); *machinery* 2-shaft geared turbines producing shp 4300; *speed* 20 knots; *armament* 6×4in AA (3×2); 12×20mm AA (6×2); *complement* 192–219; *number in class* 29, launched 1942–46.

Modified Flower Class Corvettes (UK)

See also FLOWER CLASS. *Displacement* 980 tons; *dimensions* 208ft 3in×33ft 3in (63.4×10.1m); mean draught 11ft (3.3m); *machinery* 1-shaft reciprocating engine with ihp 2880; *speed* 16 knots; *armament* 1×4in; 1×2-pdr AA; 6×20mm AA (6×1); 1 Hedgehog; *complement* 109; *number in class* 52, launched 1942–44.

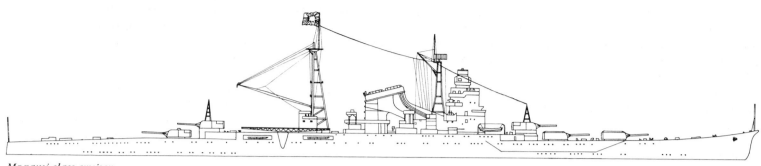

Mogami class cruiser.

Mogadishu, Italian Somaliland, 1941

A seaport and capital of Italian Somaliland, on the Indian Ocean. Allied troops advancing from Kenya defeated an Italian force at Gelib, after which Italian command disintegrated and General Godwin-Austen decided to go straight for Mogadishu, abandoning his previous plans. The 23rd Nigerian Brigade entered the town on 25 February 1941 to find 350,000 gallons (1,325,000l) of petrol and 80,000 gallons (302,800l) of aviation spirit, plus considerable quantities of valuable stores. The harbour was virtually undamaged.

Mogami Class Cruisers (Jap)

Displacement 12,400 tons; *dimensions* 646ft 6in×66ft 4in (197×20.2m); mean draught 19ft 4in (5.9m); *machinery* 4-shaft geared turbines producing shp 152,000; *speed* 34.75 knots; *protection* main belt 3.9in; deck 1.5in; turrets 1in; *armament* 10×8 (5×2); 8×5in DP (4×2); 8×25mm AA (4×2); 4×13mm AA; 12×24in torpedo tubes (4×3); *aircraft* 3; *complement* 850; *number in class* 4, launched 1934–36.

Mogaung

A small Burmese town west of MYITKYINA. It was held by the Japanese in some strength and formed a block covering the routes between Kamiang and Myitkyina and the exit from Railway Valley. By taking Mogaung the Japanese at Kamiang would be cut off from their supplies and Myitkyina isolated, to be attacked at leisure. Mogaung was attacked on 6 June 1944 by the CHINDIT 77th Brigade. Because of its difficult location, between two rivers, and its strong garrison, the battle for Mogaung lasted 16 days. General STILWELL's headquarters then announced that it had been captured by the Chinese, at which Colonel Calvert signalled to Stilwell, "The Chinese having taken Mogaung, 77 Brigade is proceeding to take Umbrage."

Möhne Dam, Germany, 1943

Dam blocking the valley of the Möhne River in Germany. Together with a dam on the Sorpe River, the Möhne dam supplied 70 per cent of the industrial water supply for the Ruhr as well as domestic water for about five million people. The dams, together with another in the EDER Valley which regulated the level of the River Weser, were attacked by RAF bombers on the night of 16/17 May 1943. The Möhne and Eder dams were breached and the Sorpe damaged, causing about 1500 deaths and severe flooding but doing little damage to the industrial output of the Ruhr complex. See also GIBSON and WALLIS.

Molotov, Vlachislav (1890–1986)

Molotov held the post of Soviet Commissar for Foreign Affairs from 3 May 1939 until 1952. In

Russian Commisar Molotov signs a 10-year non-aggression pact with Germany, watched by von Ribbentrop (left of Molotov) and Stalin August 1939.

August 1939 he negotiated a Non-Aggression Pact with Germany which included provision for the partition of Poland. On 13 April 1941 he achieved a considerable diplomatic coup by concluding a further Non-Aggression Pact with the Japanese Foreign Minister MATSUOKA. After the German invasion of the USSR he served on the Committee for the Defence of the State, assuming many of STALIN's responsibilities, and constantly urged the Western Allies to open a Second Front in Europe and increase the level of their aid to the Soviet Union. In June 1943 he was involved in secret peace negotiations with RIBBENTROP, but these failed on the question of postwar boundaries. Molotov attended all the major Allied conferences and in June 1945 was the Soviet Union's first delegate to the United Nations.

Molotov Breadbasket

The name given by the Finns in 1940 to a Soviet aerial bomb which consisted of a framework carrying a large number of small incendiary bombs. On release from the aircraft as a single unit, the frame opened and scattered the incendiaries around the target.

Molotov Cocktail

A term loosely applied to any incendiary grenade made up from a glass bottle full of petrol and ignited by some simple device such as a burning rag tied around the neck. Such grenades were first seen during the Spanish Civil War; they were then used by the Finns against Soviet tanks during the 1940 Winter War, and it is believed that the "Molotov" connection dates from this time, having been applied by a newspaper correspondent in emulation of the MOLOTOV BREADBASKET term already in use.

Momi Class Destroyers (Jap)

Displacement 770 tons; *dimensions* 275×26ft (83.8×7.9m); mean draught 8ft (2.4m);

machinery 2 direct drive turbines producing shp 21,500; *speed* 36 knots; *armament* 3×4.7in (3×1); 2×7.7mm; 4×4 21in torpedo tubes (2×2); *complement* 110; *number in class* 3, launched 1918–22.

Monica

RADAR tail-warning device fitted to RAF bombers. Countered by the German airborne Flensburg detector.

Monitors – Shallow-Draught Bombardment Vessels (UK)

Only two of this once-numerous type of warship, HMS *Erebus* and *Terror*, remained operational on the outbreak of war. Launched in 1916, they displaced 7200 tons, drew 11 feet (3.3m) and were powered by two-shaft reciprocating engines which gave a maximum speed of 12 knots. Their main armament consisted of two 15-inch guns, plus eight 4-inch guns and two 3-inch anti-aircraft guns. Two further monitors, HMS *Roberts* and *Abercrombie*, were launched respectively in 1941 and 1942. They displaced 7970 tons, drew 11 feet (3.3m) and were powered by two-shaft geared turbines with shp 4800, giving a maximum speed of 12 knots. They were armed with two 15-inch guns in turrets stripped from two hulked monitors, HMS *Marshal Soult* and *Marshal Ney*. As *Terror* had sunk as a result of damage inflicted by Italian aircraft off Derna on 22 February 1941, their anti-aircraft armament was augmented to eight 4-inch, sixteen 2-pdr and sixteen 20mm guns. The older ships had a complement of 315, the newer 350. *Erebus* and *Roberts* formed part of the Bombardment Force during the Allied invasion of NORMANDY. Because of their wide beam, monitors were referred to as "Flat Irons".

Monter, Col (1896–1960)

Monter was the wartime codename of Colonel Antoni Chrusciel. During the 1939 campaign in Poland he commanded the 82nd Infantry Regiment and, after escaping from captivity, made his way to Warsaw where he joined the POLISH HOME ARMY, commanding the Warsaw District from 1940 until the WARSAW Rising of August–September 1944. During the Rising Warsaw District was redesignated Warsaw Army Corps and *Monter* was confirmed as its commander. Taken prisoner when the Rising was crushed, he later reached the United Kingdom and was appointed Deputy Chief of General Staff of the Polish Forces in the West.

Montgomery, FM Sir Bernard Law (1887–1976)

Montgomery was commissioned into the Royal Warwickshire Regiment in 1908. In 1914 he took part in the retreat from Mons; he fought at the Battle of Le Cateau; and was seriously wounded at the First Battle of Ypres, being awarded the Distinguished Service Order while still a subaltern. He returned to duty in February 1915 as a brigade major and served on the staff on the Western Front for the remainder of the war, latterly as Chief of Staff of the 47th (London) Division. Between 1926 and 1928 he instructed at the Staff College at Camberley and in 1931 produced the official manual *Infantry Training*. He commanded the 1st Battalion Royal Warwickshire Regiment 1931–34 and then spent three years as senior British Service Instructor at the Staff College in Quetta before returning home to command first the 9th Infantry Brigade and then the 8th Division. In 1939–40 he commanded the 3rd Division in France and Belgium and in the final stages of this campaign II Corps during the retreat to DUNKIRK. He then commanded V Corps, XII Corps and the important South-Eastern Command before being selected by CHURCHILL in July 1942 to replace AUCHINLECK as commander of the BRITISH 8TH ARMY in Egypt. He immediately set about eliminating the unorthodoxy which had troubled the army's operations for the previous 12 months and infused it with a new confidence in itself and its commander. This, coupled with the arrival of plentiful modern equipment and the poor Axis supply line, enabled him to inflict a decisive defeat on ROMMEL at the Second Battle of ALAMEIN and pursue him across Africa. After the landings of the Anglo-American 1st Army in French North Africa he became subject to EISENHOWER'S command and together the two armies eliminated the Axis forces in TUNISIA. During the invasion of SICILY he commanded on the British sector and when Italy was invaded he led 8th Army to the line of the SANGRO RIVER. In January 1944 he was recalled to plan the invasion of Europe, in which he was to command the Allied ground forces under Eisenhower's direction as Supreme Commander. It was at Montgomery's insistence that the D-DAY LANDINGS were made with five divisions instead of three as originally intended. His strategy in NORMANDY was entirely successful but his plan to seize a bridgehead across the Rhine by means of Operation MARKET GARDEN attracted unfavourable criticism after the gallant failure at ARNHEM. In September 1944 he surrendered control of the Allied ground forces to Eisenhower but retained command of the British 21st ARMY GROUP until the war ended. During the German ARDENNES offens-

General Bernard Montgomery issues cigarettes to troops north of Syracuse.

ive of December 1944 Eisenhower appointed him commander of the Anglo-American troops containing the northern shoulder of the enemy penetration. His last major achievement of the war was the RHINE crossing in March 1945 and on 4 May 1945 he received the surrender of all German forces in northern Europe on Lüneburg Heath. Montgomery's abilities were seen at their best in a set-piece battle, and as the first British general to defeat a German army in the field he naturally attracted hero-worship. Against this, his fastidious manner, lack of tact and an egocentricity amounting to arrogance were qualities which many, and particularly his American colleagues, found difficult to accept. In 1946 he was made Viscount Montgomery of Alamein. His postwar appointments included Chief of the Imperial General Staff (1948–51) and Deputy Supreme Allied Commander in Europe (1951–58).

Mont Pinçon, France, 1944

A small hill in Normandy, some 365 metres high, which appeared to dominate the area of the "Bocage" south of Caen. It was a formidable obstacle and was finally captured on 6 August 1944 as the culmination of Operation BLUECOAT.

Monty's Foxhounds

Unofficial title conferred by the soldiers of the 51st Highland Division on the 40th Royal Tank Regiment, which formed the divisional advance guard during the long advance from ALAMEIN to Tripoli.

Morane-Saulnier MS 406 (Fr)

Castigated by its pilots as "too slow to catch Germans and too weakly armed to shoot them down", the MS 406 was also inadequately protected and, all in all, gave little chance to its pilots. It equipped 19 French units in 1939 but had very little effect on the course of events. *Span* 34.75ft (10.6m); *engine* 1 860hp in-line; *armament* 1 20mm cannon, 2 machine guns; *speed* 300mph (483kph).

Morgan, Gen Sir Frederick (1894–1967)

In January 1943 Morgan was appointed Chief of Staff to an as-yet undesignated Supreme Allied Commander and ordered to produce plans for the invasion of Europe. His plan for Operation OVERLORD, as the NORMANDY land-

ings were codenamed, was accepted in July 1943, and for the next year Morgan and his staff were engaged in working out the details of this enormous undertaking. Morgan considered that the resources initially allocated were inadequate for the task, but this situation was remedied when EISENHOWER was appointed Supreme Allied Commander.

Morgenluft (Morning Air)

AFRIKA KORPS counteroffensive directed against GAFSA, February 1943.

Morgenthau, Henry (1891–1967)

Morgenthau was ROOSEVELT's Secretary of the Treasury from 1934 until 1945 and responsible for placing the American economy on a war footing. Prior to the United States' entry into the war he organized economic sanctions against the Axis powers and froze Japanese assets in America, as well as operating the Lend-Lease programme. At the September 1944 Quebec Conference he submitted a plan under which postwar Germany would be stripped of her industry and converted to an agricultural economy. This provided the Germans with a propaganda gift, and GOEBBELS was able to make much of the fact that Morgenthau was a Jew and that his plan provided ample warning of what would happen in the event of the Third Reich being defeated. Although CHURCHILL at first subscribed to the scheme, he withdrew his support under pressure from his advisers and the Morgenthau plan was eventually abandoned by Roosevelt.

Morrison, Herbert (1888–1965)

As a leading member of the Labour Opposition in the House of Commons Morrison initiated the motion of "No Confidence" which resulted in the fall of the CHAMBERLAIN administration on 8 May 1940. He then served in CHURCHILL's Cabinet throughout the war, his first appointment being Minister of Supply. In October 1940 he was given the dual roles of Home Secretary and Minister of Home Security, organizing the HOME GUARD, Civil Defence, the National Fire Service and a national system of fire watching. His responsibilities included censorship, the internment of aliens and the detention of potential enemies of the State. Like his predecessor as Home Secretary, Sir John ANDERSON, he had a family air-raid shelter named after him. The Morrison shelter was a box-like steel contrap-

tion, with sides of wire mesh, which could be erected indoors. Over 500,000 had been distributed by November 1941.

Morshead, Lt Gen Sir Leslie (1889–1959)

Morshead commanded the 9th Australian Division during the siege of TOBRUK, at the Second Battle of ALAMEIN and in NEW GUINEA. In 1944 he was appointed General Officer Commanding New Guinea Force and commander of the Australian 2nd Army. His final campaign of the war was the re-conquest of BORNEO.

Mortain, France, 1944

A town in NORMANDY which became the focal point of von KLUGE's abortive counteroffensive against US forces on 6 August 1944. Ordered by HITLER, this manoeuvre involved plundering the tank reserves on the rest of the Normandy front for a drive against Mortain and thence to the sea at Avranches, with the aim of cutting off much of the US force from its supply base. The attack was broken up by Allied air superiority and the stubborn American defence of Hill 317, which commanded the German attack route. General BRADLEY had foreseen the possibility of such an attack, and was later warned by an ULTRA decrypt, though this was only a few hours before the attack began and did not give him time to make any fresh dispositions. In the event the German assault was held and turned back, and by 14 August was over. However, it helped to place the German forces in position to be annihilated in the FALAISE pocket.

Mortar

A short-barrelled, usually smooth-bored, bomb-throwing weapon used by infantry for bombardment. It fires at angles greater than 45 degrees, throwing its bomb high into the air to drop steeply on to the target, so overcoming minor field defences. Since the bomb is almost vertical when it strikes the ground, the subsequent fragmentation spreads in all directions, and mortars were thus particularly feared by most soldiers during the war.

Mortars can be classed as light, medium or heavy. Light mortars are of 50–60mm calibre and fire a small bomb to a range of about 1093yds (1000m). They are usually carried by the infantry platoon and used for covering fire or to deliver smoke to conceal movement. Medium mortars are of 80–90mm calibre and are the infantry company support weapon,

Soviet 120mm mortars, Northern Caucasus, September 1942.

firing a bomb of about 7.7lb (3.5kg) to a range of about 2732yds (2500m). Heavy mortars are of 100–120mm calibre, fire a bomb of about 22–26lb (10–12kg) and have a range of 3–3.75m (5–6km).

The British army used a 2in (50mm) platoon mortar, a 3in (76mm) company mortar, and occasionally a 4.2in (107mm) mortar which was usually under artillery control. The US Army used 60mm and 81mm mortars for infantry and also had a 4.2in (107mm) rifled mortar used by Chemical Warfare Companies as a heavy infantry support weapon. The German Army used 50mm, 81mm and 120mm weapons manned by infantry, while the Soviet army also used the same range of calibres. Towards the end of the war the British Army perfected a method of using surplus anti-aircraft RADAR sets to detect the mortar bomb in flight and deduce its trajectory, from which it was possible to calculate the approximate position of the mortar and subject it to counter fire from artillery.

Morton, Cdr D. W., USN

Third highest-scoring American submarine commander of World War II. In June 1940 Morton was appointed to the old submarine *R-5*, then refitting, and commanded her until April 1942. He joined the GATO CLASS submarine *Wahoo* in November 1942 and assumed command on 31 December 1942; his executive officer until July 1943 was the then Lieutenant-Commander Richard H. O'KANE. Morton made six patrols and was credited with sinking 17 ships totalling 100,500 tons.

Wahoo was sunk with all hands by Japanese aircraft in La Perouse Strait on 12 October 1943.

Mortrep

Mortaring report (UK). A report submitted by troops after being attacked by mortars, giving details of the type of MORTAR and direction of the fire, for use by counter-mortar artillery.

Moscow, Soviet Union, 1941

The capital city of the USSR, Moscow was threatened by the German advance in 1941.

Elements of 17th Panzer Division reached Kashira, 19 miles (30km) from Moscow, on 25 November where the combination of severe weather and Russian resistance halted them. Reinforcements flowed into Moscow from the East, and under the command of General ZHUKOV the Soviets reorganized and forced the Germans back.

Motor-Cycle Troops (Ger)

While every army made use of motor-cycles for such duties as traffic control and delivery of written orders, only the German Army made extensive use of motor-cycle troops in combat. Each Panzer division initially contained a motor-cycle battalion within its mechanized infantry brigade and each armoured reconnaissance battalion possessed an organic motor-cycle squadron, equipped with 750cc BMW or Zundapp sidecar combinations. Armed with light machine guns and mortars, motor-cycle units possessed impressive firepower and speed but their mobility suffered in heavy going and they were terribly vulnerable.

By the end of the first winter on the Eastern Front the motor-cycle battalions had suffered severe casualties and they were disbanded, the survivors joining the armoured reconnaissance battalions which, for a while, contained three motor-cycle machine gun squadrons. These, too, were gradually run down as more SdKfz 250 Series half-tracks became available and finally disappeared altogether.

Soviet troops pile captured Nazi standards at the foot of Lenin's memorial, June 1945.

Motor Torpedo Boats and Motor Gun Boats

Although Coastal Motor Boats had distinguished themselves during World War I and its immediate aftermath, the Royal Navy neglected its coastal forces during the interwar years and it was not until 1935 that the first orders for Motor Torpedo Boats (MTBs) were placed. In 1939 the Navy possessed only 24 MTBs and Motor Anti-Submarine Boats (MA/SBs) but the need to dominate the coastal waters of the Narrow Seas, the English Channel and then the Mediterranean led to a major construction programme. The typical MTB displaced about 40 tons, was driven by three-shaft petrol engines with bhp 3600, had a speed of 40 knots and was armed with two 21-inch torpedo tubes, one 20mm cannon, two 0.5-inch heavy machine guns and four 0.303-inch machine guns. However, the German S-BOATS and R-BOATS proved to be formidable opponents and it was clear that the MTBs required heavier armament. This led to the development of the Motor Gun Boat (MGB), the first of which were simply up-gunned MA/SBs. The purpose-built MGB was very similar to the MTB but typical armament might consist of one 2-pdr gun, two 20mm cannon and four 0.303-inch machine guns. In action the MTB and the MGB complemented each other and as the war progressed larger composite designs were produced, of which the Fairmile Type "D" Boats are best remembered. These displaced 90–105 tons, were driven by four-shaft Packard petrol engines with bhp 5000 and had a speed of 27.5–31 knots, the later versions being armed with two 21-inch torpedo tubes, two 6-pdr guns, two 20mm cannon, four 0.5-inch heavy machine guns and four 0.303-inch machine guns. The majority of MTBs and MGBs had an average complement of 12, but this rose to 30 in the case of the composite Fairmile "D" Type.

Over 1600 MTBs, MGBs and composite designs were built during the war and by 1945 they were serving not only in home waters and the Mediterranean but also along the Arakan coast of Burma, in the East Indies and in the South West Pacific with the Royal Australian and Royal New Zealand Navies. Losses amounted to 223 craft of all types. Enemy vessels sunk included one cruiser, one surface raider, five small destroyers, one submarine, 63 S-Boats, R-Boats and Italian MAS BOATS, and about 140 merchantmen.

Motosiluranti – Motor Torpedo Boats (Italy)

Developed as a result of the MAS BOATS' inability to operate in heavy seas. They displaced 63/66 tons, were 90 feet (27.4m) long and were powered by three Isotta-Fraschini engines with total hp 3450, giving a maximum speed of 34 knots. Armament consisted of two or four 20mm heavy machine guns, two 21-inch torpedo tubes and 12–20 depth charges; the second of the two 18-strong groups to be built was additionally armed with two 17.7-inch torpedo tubes. Delivery commenced April 1942.

Moulin, Jean (1899–1943)

Moulin, formerly prefect of Chartres, was responsible from 1940 onwards for uniting those resistance movements in France which were loyal to DE GAULLE and in May 1943 established the National Council of the Resistance. However, in the following month he was captured by the Germans and tortured to death.

Mountbatten, V Adm Lord Louis (1900–79)

Mountbatten entered the Royal Navy in 1913 and saw active service during World War I. During the interwar years he specialized in communications and in 1939 was appointed commander of the 5th Destroyer Flotilla, which he led in HMS KELLY. In 1940 his flotilla took part in the evacuation of Allied troops from NORWAY and in 1941 was posted to the Mediterranean, where *Kelly* was sunk by German dive bombers off CRETE on 23 May. After a period in command of HMS ILLUSTRIOUS, Mountbatten was appointed Adviser on Combined Operations in October 1941. In March 1942 he became Chief of Combined Operations with a seat on the British Chiefs of Staff Committee, working on the ST NAZAIRE and DIEPPE raids as well as Operation TORCH, the Allied landings in French North Africa, and the preliminary plans for an Allied invasion of the European mainland. He was present at the CASABLANCA CONFERENCE in January 1943 and at the Quebec Conference the following July and in October was appointed Supreme Allied Commander South-East Asia Command (SEAC). In view of the limited resources available his strategy was to concentrate on the reconquest of BURMA by means of a land campaign, his obvious ability, clear understanding of the problems involved and charis-

Earl Mountbatten of Burma, Admiral of the Fleet.

matic personality doing much to restore the troops' morale in this theatre of war. The campaign itself, conducted by General William SLIM, began with the defeat of the Japanese offensive aimed at IMPHAL and KOHIMA in March 1944 and was successfully concluded a year later. In September 1945 Mountbatten accepted the surrender of the 750,000 Japanese troops present in his command area at a formal parade held in SINGAPORE. Created Viscount Mountbatten of Burma in 1946 and Earl the following year, he served as the last Viceroy of India from March until August 1947 and then as Governor General of India until June 1948. He then resumed his naval career, his appointments being commander of the Mediterranean Fleet's 1st Cruiser Squadron 1948–49; Fourth Sea Lord 1950–52; Commander-in-Chief Mediterranean 1952–54 and concurrently Commander-in-Chief Allied Forces Mediterranean 1953–54; First Sea Lord 1955–59, being promoted Admiral of the Fleet in 1956; Chief of the United Kingdom Defence Staff and Chairman of the Chiefs of Staff Committee 1959–65. A highly respected and popular figure, he continued to play a full and active part in public life until murdered by Irish terrorists in 1979.

Möwe

A German remote-controlled anti-aircraft rocket designed for use by small ships against low-flying aircraft. Development began in May 1944, the objective being a cheap and simple device. Guided by optical tracking and radio link, the missile weighed 220lb (100kg) at launch, was propelled by a two-stage solid fuel rocket, carried a 26lb (12kg) warhead with proximity fuze, and had an effective range of about 1.25 miles (2km). Although it appears to have reached an advanced stage of development, work was abandoned in late 1944.

MP 38/MP 40

A German standard submachine gun, popularly but wrongly known as the *Schmeisser*. Developed by Ermawerke in 1937, it went into service as the Maschinen Pistole 38 and was the first submachine gun to be entirely made of metal and plastic, without the traditional wooden butt. Whilst an excellent weapon, it was designed for traditional manufacturing methods and was thus slow and expensive to produce. It was therefore redesigned for mass-production, and the resulting weapon was known as the MP 40. Apart from manufacturing expedients, the differences between the two are very small, and the visual difference is confined to longitudinal grooves in the receiver of the MP 38.

M-Stoff

Methyl alcohol used in German rocket fuels.

MT Mechanical transport (UK).

MTB Motor Torpedo Boat.

MTGAS Motor transport gasoline (US).

MTM – Explosive Motor Boats (Italy)

MTM stood for *Motoscafi da Turismo Modificati* (Modified Tourist Motor Boats). They displaced 1.5 tons, were 17 feet (5.2m) long and were powered by an 80hp Alfa Romeo petrol engine which gave a maximum speed of 34 knots; a 660-lb explosive charge was stowed in the bows. The driver abandoned the craft after directing it towards the target vessel. The MTMs' most notable victim was the cruiser HMS YORK, which was immobilized in Suda Bay, Crete, and had to be abandoned after additional bomb damage.

MTO Mechanical Transport Officer (UK).

MTOUSA Mediterranean Theater of Operations, US Army.

Mukden, China, 1931

The "Mukden Incident", one of many incidents which, collectively, led to World War II, took place on 18 September 1931, when Japanese units attacked the barracks of the Chinese 7th Army at Peitaying, outside Mukden. This action was in response to alleged Chinese "sabotage" of the South Manchurian Railway, and, as a result, the Japanese Kwangtung Army gradually occupied all MANCHURIA, extended their activities to China, and fomented political feeling which was to lead to Japan's further involvement in war. A major manufacturing town, railway junction and arsenal, Mukden was valuable to the Japanese through the war period. It was eventually captured by the Soviet Army on 20 August 1945.

Mulberry Harbours

It was appreciated as early as 1942 that when the Western Allies returned to the continent of Europe they could not rely upon capturing a harbour in working order. During the planning of OVERLORD, therefore, it was decided that two artificial harbours would be constructed off the NORMANDY beach-head, one on the British sector at Arromanches and the other on the American sector at St Laurent, the prefabricated components of these being towed across the Channel from the United Kingdom. Codenamed Mulberries, the harbours consisted of off-shore and flanking breakwaters constructed with large ferro-concrete caissons which were towed into position and sunk, supplemented by blockships. Within each area so protected were three floating piers, connected to the shore by floating roadways. The project absorbed two million tons of steel and concrete. Over 200 caissons, some the size of five-storey buildings, required every tug in the United Kingdom, plus others requisitioned in America, to tow them into position. In addition, no less than 70 blockships were employed. Unfortunately, between 18 and 22 June 1944, both harbours were seriously damaged by the worst gale recorded for 40 years, that at St Laurent so badly that it was never used. The effect of this was to delay the Allied build-up within the beach-head at a critical time when German reinforcement divisions were reaching the front. Eventually the Americans were able to land more across open beaches than could be handled by the repaired British harbour at Arromanches and this led to criticism of the Mulberry concept. On balance, most authorities conclude that it was worthwhile, if only for the sheltered waters provided by the breakwaters and the comparative ease with which the British were able to land difficult loads.

A section of the prefabricated "Mulberry Harbour" under tow across the Channel, October 1944.

Munich 1938: The rights of Czechoslovakia are signed away.

in January 1941, after a 1500-mile (2400-km) drive across featureless desert. The attack was a complete success, the fort being set on fire by MORTAR bombs and the three aircraft burned in their hangar.

Mussolini, Benito (1883–1945)

Mussolini served as a junior NCO in the Bersaglieri during World War I. In 1922, after the seizure of power by his Fascist Party, he adopted the title of *Il Duce* (Leader) and ruled Italy as a dictator. His burning ambition was to restore Rome's ancient prestige and he thirsted after military glory, expanding the armed forces to a point which neither Italy's economy nor her industrial capacity could sustain. In 1935 he secured an easy victory over backward ETHIOPIA and the following year sent a large contingent to fight for FRANCO in the Spanish Civil War. He declared war against the Western Allies on 10 June 1940, when a German victory in FRANCE was beyond doubt. However, in a fit of pique at not being consulted regarding the German occupation of ROMANIA, he announced that he would "occupy" GREECE, launching an invasion from ALBANIA on 28 October. This ended disastrously, while in North Africa his army was virtually destroyed by a much smaller British force and in East Africa Italy's colonies were lost altogether. From this point onwards Italy became the junior partner in the Axis alliance,

Munda, Solomon Islands, 1943

A Japanese airfield on NEW GEORGIA island in the SOLOMONS. On 2 July 1943 two US infantry regiments landed on beaches nearby, followed by a Marine Corps landing north of Munda on 5 July. The subsequent advance was slow and bitterly contested, US troops suffering many casualties. The airfield was finally secured on 5 August and within ten days Allied aircraft were operating from it.

Munich, Germany, 1938–45

The scene of the meeting on 29 September 1938 between HITLER and representatives of France, Italy and Britain, when the fate of CZECHOSLOVAKIA was decided. On 8 November 1940 Hitler was addressing a political gathering there when the city was bombed by British aircraft, in retaliation for which, allegedly, the German Air Force raided COVENTRY on 14 November. The last strategic bombing attacks conducted by the RAF, on 25 April 1945, included Munich, and on 30 May 1945 the city was occupied by American troops.

Murmansk, Soviet Union

An ice-free Soviet seaport on the Barents Sea which served as the winter terminal for Allied supply convoys. In summer the ships could reach Archangel, which, being further south, had shorter rail links. The railway from Archangel went to LENINGRAD and was thus cut when the Germans besieged that city, but at

that time Archangel was in use and it was possible to realign the railway to form a rail link from Murmansk to Moscow before the ice closed in.

Murzuq, Libya, 1941

An oasis in south-west Libya, garrisoned by the Italian Army and with a small airstrip. It was attacked by the LONG RANGE DESERT GROUP

Mussolini lies dead in the public square of Milan with his mistress Clara Petacci.

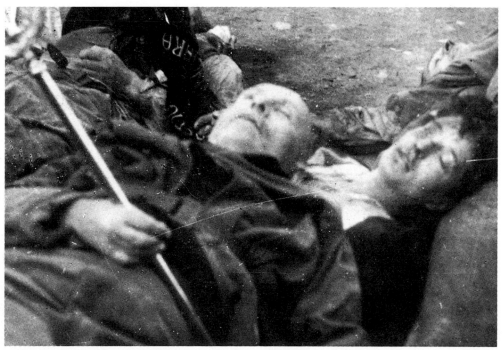

relying more and more on German support as one catastrophe followed another. The Italian Expeditionary Force in Russia was almost wiped out at STALINGRAD and a large part of the army was lost during the Tunisian debacle of May 1943. With the Allies on the point of launching an invasion of the Italian mainland, the Fascist Grand Council deposed Mussolini on 24 July 1943. He was imprisoned in a mountain hotel on the Gran Sasso but was rescued on 12 September by German commandos under the command of Otto SKORZENY. He attempted to form a government of the "Italian Social Republic" in German-occupied northern Italy but his importance had by now declined to that of a mere puppet. Both he and his mistress, Clara Petacci, were captured by Italian partisans in April 1945 and summarily executed.

Mutaguchi, Lt Gen Renya (1888–1966)

Variously described as splenetic, hot-tempered and ambitious, Mutaguchi commanded the 18th Division during the Japanese conquest of MALAYA in 1942. His division was then transferred to BURMA where he succeeded Lieutenant-General SHORJIRO IIDA as commander of 15th Army. Mutaguchi asked the impossible from his troops and although 15th Army's achievements during the 1944 U-GO offensive directed against IMPHAL and

KOHIMA were little short of astonishing, his unreasonable demands largely contributed to its virtual destruction. He was denounced by Major-General Kotoku SATO, who commanded the 31st Division at KOHIMA, in such terms that a court martial would have ensued had it not been considered contrary to the public interest in the aftermath of the disaster. Both men were dismissed to administrative posts but Mutaguchi took the feud to the grave with him, mourners at his funeral being handed a pamphlet arraigning Sato as the cause of his defeat.

Mutsuki Class Destroyers (Jap)

Displacement 1313 tons; *dimensions* 336×30ft (102.4×9m); mean draught 9ft 9in (2.97m); *machinery* 2-shaft geared turbines producing shp 38,500; *speed* 37 knots; *armament* 4×4.7in (4×1); 2×7.7mm; 6×24in torpedo tubes (2×3); *complement* 150; *number in class* 12, launched 1925–27.

Myitkyina, Burma, 1944

A town in northern Burma, close to the Yunnan border, Myitkyina became the objective of an advance by General STILWELL and the Chinese Army in India in their 1944 invasion of northern Burma. This operation was to coincide with a British advance through ARAKAN and Tiddim and operations in north

central Burma by the CHINDITS under General WINGATE. Stilwell's force was later augmented by MERRILL'S MARAUDERS, the only US ground element in the force. The advance was far more difficult and slow than had been anticipated but the Marauders, with elements of the Chinese 30th Division, took Myitkyina airfield in a surprise attack on 17 May 1944. The town was then besieged by Allied forces, though the investment was never complete and the Japanese were able to reinforce it and defend it with great skill. They finally withdrew on 3 August and the town fell into Allied hands.

Myoko Class Cruisers (Jap)

Displacement 13,380 tons; *dimensions* 661ft 9in×68ft (201×20.73m); mean draught 20ft 9in (6.32m); *machinery* 4-shaft geared turbines producing shp 130,250; *speed* 33.6 knots; *protection* main belt 4in; turrets 3in; deck 2.5–5in; *armament* 10×8in (5×2); 8×5in AA (4×2); 8×25mm AA (4×2); 4×13mm AA (2×2); 16×24in torpedo tubes (4×4); *aircraft* 3 (2 catapults); *complement* 773; *number in class* 4, launched 1927–28.

Myrol

German liquid explosive consisting of a solution of methyl nitrate in methanol, used as a constituent in various service explosives.

Myoko class cruiser.

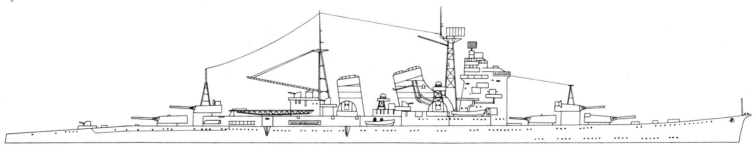

N

"N" Class Destroyers (UK)

Displacement 1690 tons; *dimensions* 356ft 6in×35ft 9in (108.6×10.9m); mean draught 9ft (2.7m); *machinery* 2-shaft geared turbines producing shp 40,000; *speed* 36 knots; *armament* 6×4.7in (3×2); 4×2-pdr AA (1×4); 2×20mm AA (8×1); 8×0.5in AA (2×4) guns; 10×21in (2×5) torpedo tubes; *complement* 183; *number in class* 8, launched 1940–41.

NAAF North African Air Force (UK).

NAAFI Navy, Army and Air Force Institutes (UK). Canteen and welfare service for British forces not in a theatre of operations.

Nachtigall Gruppe (Nightingale Group)

Special operations battalion containing three Ukrainian companies and one BRANDENBURG company, formed to carry out subversive tasks behind Soviet lines in the Ukraine during the early stages of Operation BARBAROSSA. The unit performed its mission efficiently but Ukrainian goodwill towards the German Army was quickly extinguished by the barbarities of the SS EINSATZGRUPPEN.

Nacht und Nebel ("Night and Fog") Decree

An order issued by HITLER on 7 December 1941, whereby inhabitants of the Occupied territories who were considered to be "endangering German security" but who were not to be immediately executed were to vanish into the "night and fog" of the unknown. No information was to be given to their families or relations as to their destination or eventual fate. It has never been determined how many people were the victims of this order.

Nadzab, New Guinea, 1943

A small town in the Markham Valley, inland from Lae, in north-west New Guinea. As part of operations against Lae, on 5 September 1943 troops of the US 503rd Paratroop Regi-ment, supported by Australian artillery, were dropped into Nadzab and occupied the area, enabling the 7th Australian Division to be flown in and then move against Lae. This was one of the few airborne operations in the Pacific theatre.

Nagara Class Cruisers (Jap)

Displacement 5170 tons; *dimensions* 535ft×46ft 6in (163×14.1m); mean draught 15ft 9in (4.8m); *machinery* 4-shaft geared turbines producing shp 90,000; *speed* 36 knots; *protection* main belt 2in; deck 1.5–2in; *armament* 7×5.5in (7×1); 2×3in AA (2×1); 8×24in torpedo tubes (4×2); *aircraft* 1; *complement* 438; *number in class* 6, launched 1921–23.

Nagasaki

Nagasaki was the second target attacked by the US Air Force using an ATOMIC BOMB. The attack took place on 9 August 1945, three days after the dropping of the first bomb on HIROSHIMA and was intended to reinforce the demonstration of Allied power and encourage the Japanese to surrender. In fact the target for the

Nagasaki under atomic bomb attack, August 1945.

second bomb was originally Kokura, but this was obscured by thick cloud and the aircraft commander elected to bomb his secondary target, Nagasaki, through cloud by the use of RADAR. Due to the surrounding hills, the devastation was less in area than that which took place at Hiroshima and the death toll about 35,000.

Nagato Class Battleships (Jap)

Displacement 39,130 tons; *dimensions* 738ft×113ft 6in (224.9×34.6m); mean draught 31ft (9.5m); *machinery* 4-shaft geared turbines producing shp 82,300; *speed* 25 knots; *protection* main belt 12–13in amidships, 4–8in fore and aft; turrets 14in; control tower 12in; deck 3.5in; *armament* 8×16in (4×2); 18×5.5in (18×1); 8×5in AA (4×2); 20×25mm AA (10×2); *aircraft* 3; *complement* 1368; *number in class* 2.

Nagumo, Vice-Admiral Chuichi (1886–1944)

The choice of Nagumo as commander of the Imperial Japanese Navy's élite Fast Carrier Striking Force was a curious one, since his background was that of a cruiser officer and torpedo specialist. Moreover, he was cautious by nature and uneasy in the appointment because of his lack of aviation experience. He carried out the attack on PEARL HARBOR on 7 December 1941 and although his carriers delivered two successful strikes he decided, contrary to the advice of his air commander, not to mount a third, which would probably have destroyed the vast oil stocks on Oahu, estimated at 4.5 million barrels, most of it stored above ground. The loss of its fuel reserves and port facilities at Pearl Harbor would have forced the US Pacific Fleet to withdraw its base to San Diego, from which it would have been impossible to launch the counteroffensive which led to the Battles of CORAL SEA and MIDWAY. In April 1942 he entered the Indian Ocean, where his aircraft attacked British naval bases in CEYLON and sank several warships of the Royal Navy's Eastern Fleet.

Vice-Admiral Chuichi Nagumo.

However, his task force suffered a devastating blow at the Battle of Midway when, through a combination of faulty intelligence and ill luck, all four Japanese carriers present were lost. His carriers also took part in the inconclusive Battle of the EASTERN SOLOMONS and the Battle of the SANTA CRUZ ISLANDS, but despite the fact that the latter was a Japanese victory the heavy loss of aircraft further eroded the Imperial Navy's rapidly declining number of experienced carrier pilots. Nagumo was relieved of his command and posted to the MARIANAS, where he organized the defence of SAIPAN. He committed suicide on 6 July 1944 when it was apparent that the American landing would succeed.

Nakajima Aircraft (Jap)

Nakajima B5N (Kate) Introduced in 1937 this carrier-based bomber boasted many modern features, including mechanically folding wings, retractable landing gear and integral fuel tanks. After initial success in China it became the principal naval bomber, 103 of them being used at PEARL HARBOR as high-level bombers and another 40 as torpedo-bombers. By the end of 1942, B5Ns had been wholly or partially responsible for the sinking of the US aircraft carriers YORKTOWN, LEXINGTON, WASP and HORNET. The B5N remained in front-line service well into 1944, and served in second-line service until the end of the war. *Span* 51ft (15.5m); *engine* 1 970hp radial; *crew* 3; *armament* 4 machine guns, 1750lb (800kg) of bombs; *speed* 235mph (378kph).

Nakajima B6N (Jill) Designed as a replacement for the B5N, the B6N entered service in 1944 and rapidly became the principal Japanese torpedo-bomber, with over 1200 built. It also performed reconnaissance tasks and featured as one of the earliest "Kamikaze" aircraft. *Span* 49ft (15m); *engine* 1 1850hp radial; *crew* 3; *armament* 2 machine guns, 1 torpedo or 1300lb (600kg) of bombs; *speed* 300mph (483kph).

Nakajima C6N (Myrt) The first Japanese aircraft specifically designed for carrier-borne reconnaissance duties, the C6N did not appear until late in 1944, but it was then adapted to torpedo-bombing and night fighter roles. *Span* 41ft (12.5m); *engine* 1 1990hp radial; *crew* 3; *armament* (reconnaissance) 1 machine gun, (fighter) 2 20mm cannon; *speed* 380mph (611kph).

Nakajima E8N1 (Dave) A biplane floatplane, the E8N1 was elderly by 1941 but nevertheless served as one of the Japanese Navy's principal scouts, being catapult-launched from warships. It was widely used until the early months of 1943, by which time it was pathetically vulnerable. *Span* 33ft (10m); *engine* 1 580hp radial; *crew* 2; *armament* 2 machine guns, 120lb (60kg) of bombs; *speed* 185mph (298kph).

Nakajima J1N (Irving) Designed originally as a twin-engined long range naval escort fighter, development of the J1N was slow due to technical problems, but it went into production in 1942 in the photo-reconnaissance role. It was then modified by adding oblique-firing cannons and became perhaps the best Japanese night fighter. *Span* 55.6ft (17m); *engines* 2 1130hp radial; *crew* 2; *armament* 4 20mm cannon; *speed* 315mph (509kph).

Nakajima Ki-27 (Nate) The Japanese Army's first low-wing monoplane fighter, this became the most numerous of all Japanese wartime aircraft. Fast and highly manoeuvrable, it performed well in China and particularly against the Russians in the 1939 border incidents. It remained in first-line service until the early part of 1943. *Span* 37ft (11.3m); *engine* 1 710hp radial; *armament* 2 machine guns; *speed* 285mph (458kph).

Nakajima Ki-43 (Oscar) The Japanese Army's principal wartime fighter, a small number having entered service before PEARL HARBOR. It was improved through a series of variants as the war progressed, and over 5800 were built. *Span* 35.5ft (10.8m); *engine* 1 1130hp radial; *armament* 2 12.7mm machine guns or 20mm cannon, 500kg of bombs; *speed* 320mph (515kph).

Nakajima Ki-44 (Tojo) Most Japanese fighters strove for high manoeuvrability, but

A Nakajima bomber takes off from a Japanese aircraft carrier.

the Ki-44 aimed for speed and climb rate. Initially it was unpopular with pilots, but its ability to chase Allied high-altitude bombers gradually came to be appreciated. *Span* 31ft (9.5m); *engine* 1 1520hp radial; *armament* 2 machine guns, 2 40mm or 20mm cannon; *speed* 375mph (603kph).

Nakajima Ki-49 (Helen) The first Japanese Army bomber to carry 20mm cannon, the Ki-49 entered service in 1941. However, it suffered from poor range and inadequate bomb-load in trying to achieve higher speed with heavier armament. By 1944 it had been withdrawn from bombing duties and relegated to a training and anti-submarine role. A few appeared as "Kamikaze" machines. *Span* 66.6ft (20.3m); *engines* 2 2500hp radial; *crew* 8; *armament* 1 20mm cannon and 5 machine guns, 2200lb (1000kg) of bombs; *speed* 305mph (490kph).

Nakajima Ki-84 (Frank) A Japanese Army fighter, the Ki-84 gave considerable trouble during development and did not enter service until late 1943. It proved fast and manoeuvrable, and in China was a formidable threat to the US 14th Air Force. Its record in other parts of the Pacific was less impressive, due to mechanical problems. *Span* 37ft (11.3m); *engine* 1 1900hp radial; *armament* 2 20mm or 30mm cannon, 2 machine guns; *speed* 388mph (624kph).

Namsos, Norway, 1940

A small seaport 100 miles (160km) north of Trondheim. The 146th British Infantry Brigade were landed there on 16/17 April 1940 to link up with local Norwegian troops with the intention of advancing on Trondheim. They were quickly outflanked by German troops landed from destroyers, and forced to march over rough country to escape. More German attacks together with air bombardment soon rendered the British plans unworkable, and the surviving troops were withdrawn through Namsos, by sea, on 2 September.

Namur Island

Part of the KWAJALEIN Atoll in the Central Pacific, Namur and its neighbouring island Roi were attacked by US Marines on 1 February 1944. Roi was a relatively easy operation, but Namur was covered in jungle and thickly sown with pillboxes and defended posts. Tanks were put ashore and with their aid the Marines secured the island in two days. Namur was the scene of a remarkable

accident: a Marine demolitions team threw a satchel charge into a blockhouse which, it turned out, was a torpedo warhead store. The subsequent explosion killed 20 Marines and wounded another 100.

Nankin, SS – Cargo/passenger Liner

Australian cargo/passenger liner intercepted by the German surface raider THOR on 10 May 1942 and captured after a running fight. The *Nankin* was on passage from Fremantle to Colombo and although her confidential books were thrown overboard before she surrendered, her mail sacks contained a number of top secret documents, the presence of which was not suspected by her master. These proved beyond any reasonable doubt that American Naval Intelligence had broken the Japanese JN25 Fleet cipher and was aware of the Imperial Navy's movements. This information was not communicated by the Germans to the Japanese until 29 August and therefore did not affect the outcome of the Battle of MIDWAY. However, the Japanese immediately imposed a signals blackout and partly as a result of this the US Navy sustained serious losses during the naval battles off GUADALCANAL. Further penetration of the Japanese naval signals network was not achieved until the middle of 1943.

Napalm

American incendiary material, the name being derived from naphtha and palmitic acid, two constituents of the thickening mixture which was mixed with gasolene to produce the incendiary agent. It was used principally in aerial bombs, though it was also tried in artillery and mortar projectiles.

Naples, Italy, 1943

A major seaport and city on the western coast of Italy. Naples was the immediate objective of the Allied invasion force which landed at SALERNO on 9 September 1943. Three weeks later, on 1 October, Naples was entered by troops of British X Corps. The city was then taken over by the US 82nd Airborne Division while the British advanced to the Volturno River. Allied bombing and German demolitions had rendered the industrial area and port unusable, and the harbour was choked with wrecked shipping. Nevertheless, within three days it was possible to dock at least one ship and within two weeks 3500 tons of supplies were being unloaded daily.

Narew River, Poland, 1939

A river in northern Poland. It gave its name to the "Narew Group" of the Polish Army, positioned on a rough line along the river from Ostrolecka to the Lithuanian border, with the role of stopping German incursions from East Prussia. In September 1939 it was outflanked as German 3rd Army's thrust from East Prussia drove through the gap between the Narew Group and its western neighbour, the Modlin Army.

Narvik, Norway, 1940

German forces were landed by sea in this northern town and port on 9 April 1940 and prepared their defences. British forces landed close to Narvik on 15 April but were ill-equipped for operations in snow, while the British commander Major-General Mackesy considered his base inadequate. He was reinforced by French *Chasseurs Alpins*, under General Bethouart, a demi-brigade of the French Foreign Legion, and a brigade of Polish *Chasseurs du Nord*, as well as some artillery and tanks, but was still unable to make an impression on the German defenders in Narvik. Mackesy was replaced by Bethouart, and on 13 May an attack supported by six tanks broke through a German blocking position to make contact with Norwegian forces who had come down from the mountains. After manoeuvring around Narvik the town was finally captured on 28 May. Unfortunately, the end of operations in other parts of Norway had freed ample German forces to come to Narvik's aid, particularly with air attacks. Additionally, the events in the Low Countries and France were now uppermost in the Allies' minds, and on 31 May the evacuation of Allied troops from Narvik began.

Narvik, First Battle of, 1940

At noon on 9 April 1940 the Admiralty ordered Captain B. A. W. Warburton-Lee's 2nd Destroyer Flotilla, consisting of HMS *Hardy* (Leader), *Hotspur*, *Havock*, *Hunter* and *Hostile*, to penetrate Ofot Fjord and destroy the German invasion transports and escorting destroyers lying off Narvik. Warburton-Lee's ships entered the fjord at dawn the following day, sinking two destroyers, *Wilhelm Heidkamp* and *Anton Schmidt*, and six transports, as well as damaging three more destroyers. However, while Warburton-Lee had estimated that six enemy destroyers were

Wrecked German shipping in Narvik harbour, April 1940.

fjord where *Georg Thiele* was driven ashore after she had damaged *Cossack* with a torpedo strike. The three remaining destroyers of the German flotilla, *Bernd von Arnim*, *Hans Lüdemann* and *Wolfgang Zenker*, were found abandoned at the head of the fjord, one having been scuttled as a result of damage received in the battle on 10 April. Having wrecked these, Whitworth's force withdrew, picking up *Hardy*'s surviving crew from a Norwegian vessel at the mouth of Ofot Fjord. Together, the two Battles of Narvik reduced the German Navy's effective destroyer strength by half.

Nashorn (Rhinoceros) – Heavy Tank Destroyer (Ger)

Based on the chassis of the PANZERKAMPFWAGEN IV, the Nashorn was the largest of the first generation of German tank destroyers and was armed with an 88mm L/71 Pak 43/1 gun mounted in an open-topped fighting compartment. Introduced in 1943, the vehicle served in 30-strong heavy tank destroyer battalions which operated under the control of army commanders. The Nashorn was manned by a crew of five and had a maximum speed of 26mph (42kph). A total of 473 were built, being replaced in due course by the JAGDPANTHER.

NATOUSA North African Theater of Operations, US Army.

Natter

Natter was a piloted, rocket-propelled interceptor fighter for the defence of vulnerable targets against heavy bomber formations. Developed by Bachem AG of Germany in August 1944 it was given the full support of the SS and by November unmanned flight tests had begun. It resembled a small single engined aircraft but was propelled by a liquid fuel rocket, and was launched vertically. In February 1945 the SS demanded faster progress and ordered manned flights to begin. The piloted Natter was duly launched, but the canopy flew off and the pilot, Oberleutnant Lothar Siebert, fell from the cockpit and was killed. Unmanned flight tests continued, and 30 Natter were constructed, but the war ended before the project made much more progress.

Naval Losses, Allied Warships operating under British Control
French Navy and Free French Naval Force Battleship 1 (expended as breakwater

---

present, the actual number was ten, and five of them launched a counter-attack from side fjords, sinking *Hunter*, driving *Hardy* ashore, and damaging *Hotspur*. The Germans also sustained damage and did not press their attack. As the British withdrew down Ofot Fjord they engaged the transport *Rauenfels*, carrying the bulk of the invasion force's ammunition, which blew up and sank. Warburton-Lee, mortally wounded, was awarded a posthumous Victoria Cross.

Narvik, Second Battle of, 1940

At 0030 on 13 April 1940 a British naval squadron commanded by Vice-Admiral W. J. Whitworth, consisting of the battleship *Warspite* (Flag) and the destroyers *Bedouin*, *Cossack*, *Eskimo*, *Punjabi*, *Hero*, *Icarus*, *Kimberley*, *Forester* and *Foxhound*, entered Ofot Fjord to complete the destruction of German shipping begun during the First Battle of NARVIK. The *Warspite*'s floatplane warned that an enemy destroyer, *Erich Koellner*, was lying in ambush; this was torpedoed and left a blazing wreck. The floatplane also spotted and sank the submarine *U-64*. Six German destroyers now emerged to fight a fast-moving battle in which three, *Dieter von Roeder*, *Hermann Künne* and *Erich Giese*, were sunk. The survivors were pursued into Rombaks-

the NORMANDY landings); *destroyers* 2; *submarines* 5.
Polish Navy *Destroyer* 1; *submarine* 1.
Royal Hellenic Navy *Destroyer* 1; *submarines* 4.
Royal Italian Navy *Submarine* 1.
Royal Netherlands Navy *Cruiser* 1 (expended as breakwater during the NORMANDY landings); *destroyer* 1; *submarines* 2.

Naval Losses, American

Battleships 2; *aircraft carriers* 11 (inc. 6 escort carriers); *cruisers* 10; *destroyers* 70+10 constructive total loss; *destroyer escorts* 11+1 constructive total loss; *submarines* 52.

Naval Losses, British and Commonwealth Navies

Battleships 3; *battlecruisers* 2; *aircraft carriers* 5; *escort carriers* 3; *CAM Ships* 2; *cruisers* 32; *destroyers* 149; *submarines* 77; *sloops* 13; *frigates* 11; *corvettes* 38; *monitor* 1; *armed merchant cruisers* 15. These figures include British ships on loan to and manned by Allied navies, including the Royal Norwegian Navy, the Free French Naval Force and the Polish and Soviet Navies.

Naval Losses, French

Battleships 4; *seaplane carrier* 1; *heavy cruisers* 4; *light cruisers* 6; *destroyers* 58; *submarines* 58; *escorts* 32. These figures include losses sustained by the French Navy and the Free French Naval Force (FNFL) as a result of Axis, British or American action, as well as accidents and scuttlings to avoid capture. See also DAKAR, MERS-EL-KEBIR and TOULON.

Naval Losses, German

Battleships 2; *pocket battleships* 3; *pre-Dreadnought battleships* 2; *battlecruisers* 2; *aircraft carrier* 1; *heavy cruisers* 4; *light cruisers* 6; *destroyers* 43; *commerce raiders* 14. Lost as a result of enemy action, accident, scuttled or captured in 1945. See also SUBMARINES, GERMAN.

Naval Losses, Italian

Battleships 2, including 1 constructive total loss; *cruisers* 12; *destroyers* 41; *destroyer escorts* 6; *corvettes* 3; *torpedo boats (small destroyers)* 34; *submarines* 83. These losses occurred from 10 June 1940 to 9 September 1943, when the armistice between Italy and the Western Allies came into effect. Many additional vessels were then scuttled to prevent their falling into German hands.

Others, however, including vessels fitting out or on the slipway, were commandeered and taken into service by the German Navy; of these, some were lost in action but the majority were scuttled at the end of the war. Further losses were incurred by the Royal Italian Navy when it commenced hostilities against Germany and by 1945 it had been reduced to a fraction of its former strength.

Naval Losses, Japanese

Battleships 11; *aircraft carriers* 26; *cruisers* 41; *destroyers* 134; *submarines (excluding midget submarines and kaiten)* 129; *escorts* 80.

Navigatori Class Destroyers (Italy)

Displacement 2580 tons; *dimensions* 353ft 6in×33ft 6in (107.7×10.2m); mean draught 11ft (3.3m); *machinery* 2-shaft geared turbines producing shp 50,000; *speed* 38 knots; *armament* 6×4.7in; 3×37mm AA; 8–10×20mm AA; 4–6×21in torpedo tubes; 2 depth charge throwers; equipped for minelaying; *complement* 225; *number in class* 12, launched 1928-30.

Naxos

German night-fighter radar, introduced in early 1944, which could home in on H2S transmissions from British aircraft. This forced BOMBER COMMAND to order that H2S sets should be switched on at short intervals over enemy territory.

Naxos-U

A German RADAR receiver fitted to U-boats in order to detect radar emissions from Allied anti-submarine patrol aircraft. The U-boats had first used the METOX receiver for this task, but this was rendered obsolete by the British adoption of the 10cm wavelength. After the German discovery of the use of radars of this wavelength, the Naxos-U receiver was designed and adopted in October 1943. A variant, for use by night fighters against the radars carried in bombers attacking Germany, was adopted in January 1944.

NCWTF Naval Commander, Western Task Force (US).

Nebeltruppen ("Smoke Troops")

German troops operating heavy MORTARS and rocket launchers known as *Nebelwerfers* ("smoke throwers"). These weapons, and their operating units, were originally intended for duties in connection with smokescreens and gas warfare, but the latter was never implemented and the weapons gradually became more useful firing high-explosive projectiles. Nevertheless, the units retained their special title.

Nehring, Gen Walther (1892–)

Nehring was given command of 5th Panzer Regiment in 1937 and appointed Chief of Staff to XIX Motorized Corps on 1 July 1939. On 1

German 15cm Nebelwerfer.

June 1940 he became Chief of Staff to Panzer Group GUDERIAN and on 26 October was appointed commander of the 18th Panzer Division. He then commanded the Afrika Korps from 9 March until 31 August 1942, being seriously wounded at the Battle of ALAM HALFA. Following the Anglo-American landings in French North Africa in November that year he commanded an *ad hoc* formation designated XC Corps and was responsible for thwarting an Allied attempt to seize Tunis by coup de main. In February 1943 he returned to the Eastern Front as commander of XXIV Panzer Corps and from 21 April to 1 May 1944 assumed temporary command of 4th Panzer Army. He was appointed commander of 1st Panzer Army on 20 March 1945.

Nehru, Pandit Shri Jawaharlal (1889–1964)

After Mahatma Gandhi, Pandit Nehru was the most prominent leader of the All-India Congress Party which, on 8 August 1942, passed a resolution threatening a nationwide campaign of civil disobedience and non-violent disruption unless the British immediately withdrew from India. Nehru, along with other Congress leaders, was placed in detention for a period, their arrest provoking widespread rioting in eastern India. This was brought under control but seriously delayed the build-up of forces facing the Japanese on the Assam–Burma frontier. In the postwar negotiations leading to the independence of the Indian subcontinent, it was Nehru's irreconcilable differences with Muhammed Ali Jinnah, the leader of the Muslim League, which led to the formation of the separate state of Pakistan.

NEI Netherlands East Indies.

Nelson Class Battleships (UK)

Nelson served with the Home Fleet 1939–43, with FORCE H during 1943, and again with the Home Fleet 1943–44. After refitting in the USA she was transferred to the East Indies in 1945. Her sister ship *Rodney* served with the Home Fleet throughout the war save for a period with Force H in 1943. *Displacement* 33,950 tons; *dimensions* 710×106ft (216.5×32.3m); mean draught 28ft 3in (8.6m); *machinery* 2-shaft geared turbines producing shp 45,000; *speed* 23 knots; *protection* main belt 14in; deck 6.25in; turrets 16in; *armament* 9×16in (3×3); 12×6in (6×2); 6×4.7in AA (6×1); 16×2-pdr AA (2×8); 16×0.5in AA; 2×24.5in torpedo tubes; *aircraft Nelson* 1, *Rodney* 2; *complement* 1361; *number in class* 2, both launched 1925.

Neptune

The naval plan of campaign for OVERLORD, June 1944, and the subsequent support of the ground forces in Normandy.

Nerve Gas

The nerve gases TABUN, SARIN and SOMAN were developed in Germany between 1936 and 1942 as a result of pre-war study of organic phosphorus weed-killers. These gases have their effect on the human body by attacking the central nervous system, and in 1944–45 it is unlikely that any antidote would have been discovered in time had the gases been used. However, similar research for agricultural purposes had been carried out in Britain, and, together with other fields of study, British censors had asked scientific journals not to publish papers on organic phosphate research; this absence was noted in Germany and taken to indicate that the British were developing similar war gases. Since no effective antidote was then known, this was enough to prevent any possibility of German use. About half a million artillery shells and over 100,000 aircraft bombs charged with Tabun were found in dumps throughout Germany after the war.

Neubaufahrzeuge (NbFz) – Experimental Heavy Tanks (Ger)

Produced in 1936 under the concealed purpose name of "New Construction Vehicles", the NbFz were similar to the British Independent design of 1926 in that they mounted auxiliary machine gun turrets fore and aft of the main turret. Two versions existed, one with a 75mm gun and the other with a 105mm howitzer, known respectively for a while as the Panzerkampfwagen V and VI. As the heavy tank lay outside the Panzerwaffe's operational philosophy very few were built although these saw limited active service during the 1940 campaign in NORWAY. *Weight* 35 tons; *speed* 22mph (35kph); *armour* 70mm; *armament* 1 75mm gun or 1 105mm howitzer; 1 37mm gun; 5 7.92mm machine guns; *engine* Maybach 360hp petrol; *crew* 6.

Nevada Class Battleships (USA)

Oklahoma capsized as a result of damage sustained in the attack on PEARL HARBOR and, although raised in 1944, was not repaired. Her sister ship, the USS *Nevada*, was also seriously damaged at Pearl Harbor but was repaired and recommissioned in December 1942. She was present at the capture of Attu, and the landings in NORMANDY and the South of France in 1944, before being transferred to the Pacific where she saw further action at IWO JIMA and OKINAWA, where she was damaged by Kamikaze aircraft 26 March 1945. *Displacement* 29,000 tons; *dimensions* 583×108ft (177.7×32.9m); mean draught 27ft 6in (8.38m); *machinery* 2-shaft geared turbines (*Oklahoma* reciprocating) producing shp 26,500; *speed* 20.5 knots; *protection* main belt 13.5in; turrets 18in; *armament* 10×14in (2×3 and 2×2); 12×5in (12×1); 12×5in AA; *aircraft* 3 (2 catapults); *complement* 1301; *number in class* 2, both launched 1914 and rebuilt 1927–29.

Nelson class battleship.

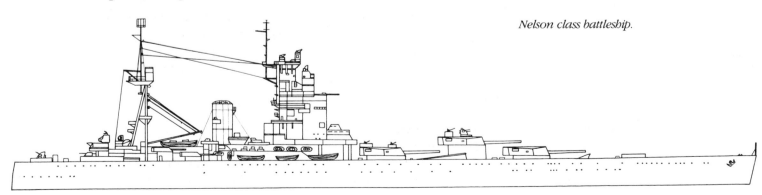

New Britain, Pacific, 1941–44

The principal island of the Bismarck Archipelago, New Britain lies to the north-east of NEW GUINEA. The Japanese took the island in their general southward advance in 1941–42 and established a major airbase at RABAUL, on the eastern tip, together with another at Kavieng, on New Ireland Island across the St George's Channel. Rabaul had five airfields, the best harbour in the area and a garrison of about 100,000 troops, a combination which posed a threat in several directions. The original Allied plan was to assault Rabaul directly, but it was later realized that it could easily be neutralized by seizing the western half of New Britain and establishing airfields there with which to dominate the area. Elements of the 1st and 7th US Marine Divisions were landed at Cape Gloucester, at the western end of the island, on 26 December 1943, secured about one-third of the island and established air bases. Manus Island, in the Admiralties, was taken in February 1944 and in March the islands of the St Matthias Group were taken. This effectively isolated Rabaul from any contact with Japan for the remainder of the war.

New Georgia, Pacific, 1943

One of the principal islands of the SOLOMONS Group, New Georgia was occupied by the Japanese in their southward advance of 1941–42. A major airbase was built at Munda, on the south coast, and a subsidiary airfield at Seqi, to the east. When Admiral HALSEY's drive through the Solomons began, the New Georgia airfields were subjected to heavy attacks from both air and naval forces. Landings were made on the eastern tip of the island on 21 June 1943; these were followed by landings on the south coast, close to Munda, on 2 July and on the west coast, to take Munda by a pincer movement, on 5 July. Fighting was hampered by tropical rain which turned the area into a swamp, and fierce Japanese resistance. Munda was taken on 5 August but resistance in the island did not end until 25 August.

New Guinea, Pacific, 1942–45

One of the largest islands in the world, New Guinea was divided between Dutch and Australian administrations. Much of it was unexplored and difficult of access. In July 1942 Japanese army elements landed on the north coast, at Buna and Gona, and advanced into the OWEN STANLEY MOUNTAINS with the intention of taking PORT MORESBY. They were

Australian-manned General Stuart tanks bust Japanese pill-boxes in the first assault on Buna, July 1942.

held up by Australian and American forces and eventually fell back to positions on the northern coast. A Japanese landing in Milne Bay, on the south-eastern tip of the island, was decisively beaten off by Australian troops, the first time that Western forces had defeated the Japanese. The major Japanese strongpoints were gradually reduced by the end of 1943. The remaining minor forces were contained by Allied troops, and the island was not completely cleared until May 1945.

New Jersey, USS – Iowa Class Battleship

Saw active service in the Pacific at KWAJALEIN, TRUK, the MARIANAS, LEYTE GULF, IWO JIMA and OKINAWA. Recommissioned during the Korean War, *New Jersey* was laid up in 1957 but was reactivated in the Vietnam War. She was again recommissioned in 1983, provided US Marine Corps with fire support and bombarded hostile positions overlooking Beirut.

New Mexico Class Battleships (USA)

The three members of this class (*New Mexico, Mississippi* and *Idaho*) all served in the Atlantic throughout 1941. After PEARL HARBOR they were transferred to the Pacific where they provided fire support for numerous amphibious operations. *Displacement* 33,400 tons; *dimensions* 624ft×106ft 3in (190.1×32.4m); mean draught 29ft 6in (8.9m); *machinery* 4-shaft geared turbines producing shp 40,000; *speed* 21 knots; *protec-* tion main belt 14in; turrets 18in; *armament* 12×14in (4×3); 12×5in (12×1); 12×5in AA; *aircraft* 3; *complement* 1930; *number in class* 3, all launched 1917 and rebuilt 1930–34.

New Orleans Class Heavy Cruisers (USA)

Displacement 9375–9975 tons; *dimensions* 588ft×61ft 9in (179×18.8m); mean draught 19ft 6in (5.9m); *machinery* 4-shaft geared turbines producing shp 107,000; *speed* 32.75 knots; *armament* 9×8in (3×3); 8×5in AA (8×1); 2×3-pdr (3×1); 8×12.7mm (8×1); *aircraft* 4 (2 catapults); *complement* 1200; *number in class* 7, launched 1933–36.

Newton Mortar

A simple but large MORTAR which threw a drum of flamethrower fluid to a range between 300 and 500 yards (275 and 450m). An anti-invasion device, development of which was later abandoned.

New York, USS – New York Class Battleship

New York served in the Atlantic during 1941 and supported the landings in North Africa the following year. She was subsequently transferred to the Pacific and saw further active service at IWO JIMA and OKINAWA. See NEW YORK CLASS BATTLESHIPS.

New York Class Battleships (USA)

Texas served in the Atlantic during 1941. She

covered the landings in North Africa (1942), NORMANDY (1944) and southern France (1944) before transferring to the Pacific, where she fought at IWO JIMA and OKINAWA. On de-commissioning in 1948 she was preserved in Texas. See NEW YORK. *Displacement* 27,000 tons; *dimensions* 573×106ft (174.6×32.4m); mean draught 26ft (7.9m); *machinery* 2-shaft reciprocating producing shp 28,100; *speed* 21 knots; *protection* main belt 12in; turrets 14in; *armament* 10×14in (5×2); 16×5in (16×1); 8×3in AA (8×1); *aircraft* 3 (1 catapult); *complement* 1530; *number in class* 2, both launched 1912 and rebuilt 1925–27.

New Zealand, 1939–45

A British Dominion since 1901, New Zealand entered the war on 3 September 1939. Troops were sent to Egypt to train, and were employed in LIBYA, TUNISIA, GREECE and Italy. A total of two infantry divisions and an armoured brigade were employed in the Middle East. More troops were raised by conscription, and these were employed with US forces in the Pacific against the Japanese.

Ngakyedauk Pass, Burma, 1943

A pass in the Mayu Range of mountains in the ARAKAN district. It was discovered late in 1943 when it became imperative to find a way across the mountains in order to supply the 7th Indian Division advancing from Goppe Bazaar via Taung Bazaar to attack Buthidaung. All supplies were being sent over the Goppe Pass, which was little better than a track. The Ngakyedauk Pass was reconnoitred and engineers eventually built a road capable of taking three-ton trucks and tanks. A supply base was set up at Sinzweya, and the supplies for the second Arakan campaign were secured.

Nibeiwa, 1940

One of a ring of fortified positions defending SIDI BARRANI and held in 1940 by elements of the Italian Army. Nibeiwa consisted of four defended camps garrisoned by approximately one division. The entire Nibeiwa complex was taken by 4th Indian Division on 9 December 1940 within two hours in the opening moves of General WAVELL's campaign.

Nijmegen, Holland, 1944

Nijmegen is a small Dutch town on the Waal river, with two bridges spanning the river. In September 1944 it became a vital objective in

The wreckage of an American glider on the Nijmegen operation.

Operation MARKET GARDEN, the airborne assault on ARNHEM. The aim was to seize bridges at Grave, Nijmegen and Arnhem, opening a direct route for the British 2nd Army to outflank the SIEGFRIED LINE and drive straight into northern Germany. The Nijmegen and Grave bridges were assigned to the US 82nd Airborne Division under General Gavin. His parachute drop was successful, the forces assigned to Grave landing astride the bridge and securing it within an hour. But at Nijmegen, German forces counter-attacked and overran the area intended as a landing zone for gliders bringing in reinforcements. The Germans were driven back and the gliders, fortunately delayed two hours by fog, were able to land infantry reinforcements and artillery. More fog prevented further reinforcements from leaving England on the following day, and Gavin's force was placed under heavy pressure by German counter-attacks. He was joined by elements of the British Guards Armoured Division which had come through Grave, and in two days of heavy fighting the two forces secured the two bridges. The route was now open for British XXX Corps, under General HORROCKS, to advance towards Arnhem. But the delay had been fatal. The British paratroops at Arnhem were exhausted and there were still powerful German forces between Nijmegen and Arnhem.

Nimitz, Adm Chester W. (1885–1966)

Nimitz graduated from the US Naval Academy at Annapolis in 1905 and by 1917 was Chief of Staff to the commander of the US Atlantic submarine force. In 1939 Nimitz was made Chief of the Bureau of Navigation. In the aftermath of PEARL HARBOR he was appointed Commander-in-Chief of the American Pacific Fleet and held this post until the end of the war. The weakness of the Fleet in the months after Pearl Harbor was in large measure offset by the breaking of the Japanese Navy's signal code some months earlier, and this contributed greatly to the Nimitz' victory at MIDWAY. Nimitz was given responsibility for the Central Pacific and launched the invasion of GUADALCANAL, his subsequent strategy of an "island-hopping" approach to Japan being broadly similar to MACARTHUR's in the South-West Pacific. In this way MAKIN, TARAWA, the MARSHALL ISLANDS, and the MARIANAS were all captured between November 1943 and July 1944. Nimitz and MacArthur then combined to mount the invasion of the PHILIPPINES, which was followed by the capture of IWO JIMA and OKINAWA. The final Japanese surrender took place aboard Nimitz' flagship USS *Missouri* on 2 September 1945. At the end of 1945 Nimitz succeeded Admiral KING as Chief of Naval Operations, remaining on the US Joint Chiefs of Staff Committee until November 1947. He was one of the outstanding naval strategists of the war. Among the many honours he received after the war was the naming after him of the US Navy's nuclear-powered aircraft carrier, USS *Nimitz*.

Nipolit

A solid high explosive, based on nitro-cellulose smokeless powder with the addition of a high explosive such as TNT or Hexogen. Developed in an endeavour to economize in nitric acid, it had the virtue of being mechanically strong, so that devices such as grenades and mines could be fabricated from solid Nipolit without requiring an exterior metal casing. By using quantities of old gun propellant which was no longer ballistically suitable, it was possible to manufacture 1000 tons of Nipolit for every 430 tons of nitric acid used, whereas an equal amount of TNT would have required 1100 tons of acid. A number of Nipolit grenades and mines were in use by the end of the war but the idea has not been pursued since.

Nisei

American citizens of Japanese descent, of whom the majority lived on the west coast of the USA. In 1941–42, with the threat of possible Japanese attacks on that coast, numbers of Nisei were arrested and interned. The conditions were bad, and there was much illegal expropriation of their property. Numbers of young Nisei men enlisted in the US Army and were of considerable value in Europe and the Pacific theatres of war, several performing acts of extreme heroism. As a result, the restrictions on the Nisei in the USA were gradually relaxed, though many never received compensation for their losses.

Nishina, Yoshio

Nishina was a Japanese nuclear physicist who, in 1937, built his country's first cyclotron. In February 1944 he suggested to Prime Minister TOJO that a bomb should be developed employing the principle of nuclear fission, but neither funds nor facilities were available for such a project. He was part of the investigation team which visited HIROSHIMA following the dropping of the American ATOMIC BOMB on 6 August 1945.

NKVD Narodnyy Kommissariat Vnutrennikh Del (Russian – Peoples' Commissariat for Domestic Affairs). The Soviet secret service created in July 1934 to succeed the GPU (State Political Administration) and control all espionage and counter-intelligence activities. Headed by Lavrenty BERIA. In addition to its internal security duties, the NKVD controlled its own frontier troops and was responsible for the reliability of the armed services, the crushing of separatist movements and the supervision of forced labour. It played a major part in the GREAT PURGE and the mass-murder of Polish officers captured when the Soviet Union invaded eastern Poland in 1939. The NKVD also ran prisoner-of-war camps and was made responsible for restoring the loyalty of those regions which had been occupied by the Wehrmacht; the latter task involved the immediate dispersion of those PARTISAN groups which welcomed the return of Soviet rule and the extermination of those that did not. Like the GESTAPO, the NKVD employed terror to impose its will.

Noah's Ark

Allied plan to interdict German withdrawal from Greece and the Balkan Peninsula, 1944.

Noball

Allied air operations against German V-weapons, 1944.

Noble, Adm Sir Percy (1880–1955)

Noble was appointed Commander-in-Chief Western Approaches in February 1941 and held this appointment until November 1942. A firm believer in thorough training, he set up anti-submarine warfare schools at Dunoon and Campbeltown and a sea-training establishment for newly commissioned escort vessels at Tobermory. He also enhanced the efficiency of escorts by forming them into permanent groups and later established support groups which would join a threatened convoy and hunt detected U-boats to their destruction, leaving the escort groups free to continue with their designated task. These measures laid the foundations for ultimate victory in the Battle of the ATLANTIC. Noble was succeeded by Admiral Sir Max HORTON.

Noguès, Gen M

Noguès was the French Army's Commander-in-Chief in North Africa at the time of the Anglo-American landings in November 1942. Exhorted by PÉTAIN to resist, he was at first inclined to temporize, although some of his units engaged Allied troops as they came ashore. He finally decided to throw in his lot

Admiral Chester Nimitz congratulates his men after a raid on Makin Island.

with Admiral DARLAN, the Commander-in-Chief French Armed Forces, and obeyed the latter's call to cease fighting. He was subsequently made commander of the Western Sector of the North African theatre of war and confirmed in his appointment as French Resident General in Morocco.

Nomura, Adm Kochisaburo (1877–1964)

Nomura was appointed Japanese Ambassador to Washington in 1941 and was involved in negotiations with American Secretary of State Cordell HULL on the question of Japan's military, political and economic position in the Far East when the attack on PEARL HARBOR took place on 7 December. He handed Japan's formal declaration of war to Hull some 80 minutes after hostilities had commenced.

Noorduyn C-64 Norseman

A high-wing cabin monoplane, the Norseman was designed in 1935 as a commercial machine for use in Northern Canada. In 1942 the USAAF ordered several for light transport and communications duties, and it was also used by the RCAF for training radio operators and navigators. *Span* 51.5ft (15.7m); *engine* 1 600hp radial; *crew* 2 plus 8 passengers; *speed* 165mph (265kph).

Nordlicht (Northern Light)

German plan to capture LENINGRAD and effect a junction with the Finnish Army on the northern sector of the Eastern Front, 1942.

Normandy, 1944

A department of France which forms the southern coastline of the English Channel, Normandy was the area selected for the Allied invasion of Europe on 6 June 1944. The coast from Varreville in the west to Ouistreham in the east was the area chosen for the landing beaches. The broad Allied strategy was for the British forces on the eastern side to take CAEN and strike towards Paris, while the US forces on the western side were to turn and head for CHERBOURG, then swing inland and also head for Paris. Caen proved a more difficult target than had been anticipated and did not fall immediately. The commander of the Allied ground forces, MONTGOMERY, therefore changed his strategy and fought a series of limited attacks intended to draw much of the German defensive strength on to his sectors, thus reducing the forces facing the Americans.

This enabled the American forces to break through to Cherbourg and also released PATTON and his US 3rd Army to strike across the rear of the German area, towards Paris, enveloping large numbers of German troops in the FALAISE POCKET. Perhaps the most difficult aspect of the Normandy campaign for the Allies was the "Bocage" country south-west of Caen, a district of small fields, narrow lanes and high hedgerow grown on earth banks, which restricted movement, gave ample opportunities for ambush, and was extremely difficult terrain in which to operate tanks.

North American Aircraft (USA)
North American AT-6 Texan/Harvard

This was designed in the late 1930s as a low-cost trainer which would simulate a modern fighter, and it eventually became the universal training aircraft for almost every Allied air force, continuing in use well into the 1960s. A low-wing monoplane, it was used for flying, navigational, gunnery, camera, bombing and blind flying training duties. It had (at that time) the remarkable feature that the propeller tips moved at more than the speed of sound, so producing an unforgettable rasping noise which was instantly identifiable. It was manufactured in Australia as the Wirraway. *Span* 42ft (12.8m); *engine* 1 600hp radial; *crew* 2; *speed* 205mph (330kph).

North American B-25 Mitchell Often called the best medium attack-bomber of the war, the Mitchell achieved fame as the bomber used in the DOOLITTLE RAID on Tokyo in April 1942. Entering service in 1940, it went through numerous modifications, improving power, armament and bomb-load, and was also configured as a ground-attack machine and as a torpedo-bomber. One model even mounted a 75m field gun in the nose, effective in dealing with submarines or ground targets. *Span* 67ft (20.4m); *engines* 2 1850hp radial; *crew* 4 to 6; *armament* up to 13 .50 machine

German Panzers advancing, Normandy 1944.

North American B-25 Mitchell bomber of 2nd TAF attacking Caen.

guns and 4400lb (2000kg) of bombs; *speed* 275mph (442kph).

North American P-51 Mustang Designed in 1940 to meet an RAF specification, the P-51 was not, at that time, given much attention by the USAAF. The original version, powered by an Allison engine, offered a poor altitude performance, though its excellent low-level speed made it an effective tactical reconnaissance machine. When fitted with the Rolls-Royce Merlin engine, it became the outstanding long-range fighter of the war, capable of escorting heavy bombers across Germany to Berlin and beyond. *Span* 37ft (11.25m); *engine* 1 1490hp in-line; *armament* 6 .50 machine guns; *speed* 437mph (703kph).

Northampton Class Heavy Cruisers (USA)

Displacement 9050 tons; *dimensions* 600ft 3in × 66ft 3in (183 × 20.5m); mean draught 16ft 6in (4.9m); *machinery* 4-shaft geared turbines producing shp 107,000; *speed* 32.5 knots; *armament* 9 × 8in (3 × 3); 8 × 5in AA (8 × 1); *aircraft* 3 (2 catapults); *complement* 1100; *number in class* 6, launched 1929–30.

North Cape, Battle of the, 1943

During the evening of 25 December 1943 the battlecruiser *Scharnhorst*, escorted by five destroyers and with Rear-Admiral Erich Bey aboard, left Alten Fjord in northern Norway to intercept the Murmansk-bound Convoy JW-55B. The convoy had a close escort of fourteen destroyers, which was followed by the battleship *Duke of York*, the cruiser *Jamaica* and four destroyers under the command of Admiral Sir Bruce FRASER. Also present in the Barents Sea were the cruisers *Sheffield*, *Belfast* and *Norfolk* under Rear-Admiral Robert

BURNETT, screening Convoy RA-55A during its return from Russia. At 0700 on 26 December Bey despatched his destroyers to scout for JW-55B in deteriorating weather conditions. An hour later *Scharnhorst* was detected by *Belfast*'s radar and at 0929 Burnett's cruisers opened fire on the battlecruiser at a range of 6.5 miles (10.5km). *Scharnhorst* was hit several times, and Bey turned away, ordering his destroyers to rejoin him. At 1158 he resumed the search for JW-55B and again dispersed his destroyers, but at 1205 was again picked up by Burnett's radar. The cruisers opened fire again at 1221 and a 20-minute gunnery duel followed in which *Norfolk* was twice hit by 11-inch shells. Bey then turned away once more and steamed southeast, shadowed by Burnett. The sweep by the German destroyers proved abortive and at 1418 they were ordered to return to base, leaving *Scharnhorst* on her own. A signal from Luftwaffe Group Lofoten warned Bey of the approach of Fraser's group but omitted the critically important fact that this contained a battleship. At 1617 *Scharnhorst* appeared on Fraser's radar, and at 1650, after *Belfast* had illuminated the target with starshell, *Duke of York* and *Jamaica* opened fire. In the ensuing fight, *Duke of York* was hit twice, while *Scharnhorst* was beaten into wreckage by the impact of thirteen 14-inch shells. The British destroyers then closed in to cripple the battlecruiser with torpedo strikes. At 1901 *Duke of York* and *Jamaica* began administering the *coup de grâce* at a range of five miles (8km) and at 1945, ablaze and riven by internal explosions, *Scharnhorst* heeled over and sank. Only 36 of the 1839 men aboard her were picked up; Bey, whose problem throughout the operations had been lack of adequate information, was not among them.

North Carolina Class Battleships (USA)

North Carolina was transferred from the

North Carolina class battleship.

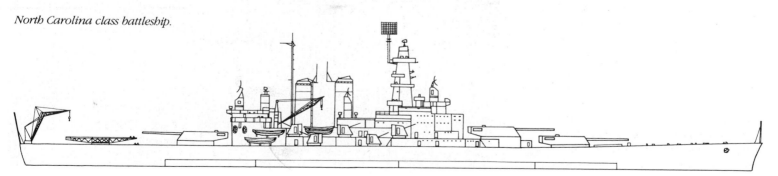

Atlantic to the Pacific in the aftermath of PEARL HARBOR. She supported the GUADALCANAL landings and was torpedoed by the Japanese submarine *I-15* during the Battle of the EASTERN SOLOMONS. After repairs she saw further action at the GILBERT ISLANDS, KWAJALEIN, TRUK, SAIPAN, THE PHILIPPINE SEA, and IWO JIMA. See also USS WASHINGTON. *Displacement* 35,000 tons; *dimensions* 729ft×108ft 3in (222×33m); mean draught 26ft 9in (7.9m); *machinery* 4-shaft geared turbines producing shp 121,000; *speed* 28 knots; *protection* main belt 16in; turrets 18in; *armament* 9×16in (3×3); 20×5in DP (10×2); 16×1.1in AA (4×4); *aircraft* 3; *complement* 2339; *number in class* 2, launched 1940.

Northover Projector

A simple gun issued to the British Home Guard in 1942. It was a smooth-bored weapon of 2.5 inch calibre, designed to shoot either a standard hand grenade, a rifle grenade, or a glass bottle filled with incendiary material, to a range of about 100–150yds (90–135m).

Northrop P61 Black Widow

The first aircraft specifically designed as a night fighter, incorporating RADAR into the initial design. Work began early in 1941 after the USAAF had been informed of the RAF successes with the first radar-carrying night fighters over Britain. A twin-boom machine, the central nacelle carried the radar in the nose, surrounded by weapons, and the pilot, radar operator and gunner. Entering service in May 1944, it proved successful in both the European and Pacific theatres, not least because of its massive fuel capacity and superb agility for its size. *Span* 66ft (20m); *engines* 2 2000hp radial; *crew* 3; *armament* 4 20mm cannon, 4 .50 machine guns; *speed* 415mph (668kph).

Norway, 1940–45

In 1940 Norway was neutral; German ships traded there, principally collecting Swedish iron ore from the port of NARVIK. With the intention of cutting off this source of supply, the British contemplated mining the coastal waters and even occupying Narvik, but while this was being debated HITLER forestalled the move by invading Denmark and Norway. Without a declaration of war, German air and naval forces attacked on 9 April 1940, troops being landed by sea at the ports of Kristiansand, Stavanger, Bergen, Trondheim and Narvik. There was resistance in Oslo, where the cruiser BLÜCHER was sunk and the battleship LÜTZOW damaged by shore batteries at OSKARSBORG before paratroops captured the city. Continued resistance was fatally undermined by an active "fifth column" led by Vidkun QUISLING, a Nazi sympathizer. Subsequently the Allies could only improvise. British and French troops were hastily assembled and sent to Narvik, Andalsnes and Namsos, but they were ill-equipped to fight in snow, badly led and had little or no air support. Faced with numerically superior forces trained in winter warfare and with overpowering air support, the Allies could do little and the last of their troops were evacuated on 10 June. The invasion of the Low Countries and France was a significant factor in the decision to withdraw troops from Norway. King HAAKON escaped from Oslo under fire, and set up his government in Trondheim, but when the Quisling government was established by the Germans the King and his ministers accompanied the British forces and set up a Free Norwegian government in LONDON. After the withdrawal, Britain maintained clandestine contacts in Norway and there was a more or less regular movement of small craft between the two countries. Many Norwegians escaped to join the British, notably some who were to form the nucleus of the COMMANDOS. Within Norway there was a significant Resistance movement. These forces, and the constant threat of Commando raids on the coastline, together with the possibility of invasion, obliged the Germans to station a large number of troops in Norway throughout the war. On 7 May 1945 the Resistance forces seized most of the country's strategic points without resistance from the Germans, who surrendered on the following day. On 9 May Allied airborne advance parties landed on the principal air bases, and on 10 May the British 1st Airborne Division entered Oslo together with Norwegian paratroops.

Norway, Naval Campaign, 1940

On 8/9 April 1940 the German Navy employed one pocket battleship, two battlecruisers, 6 cruisers and 14 destroyers to make five widely separated landings on the Norwegian coast, backed by airborne drops. During the course of this operation the cruiser ADMIRAL HIPPER sank the British destroyer GLOW-WORM. The Norwegian and British reaction was prompt and fierce. On 9 April one German cruiser, BLÜCHER, was sunk by shore-launched torpedoes while approaching Oslo, and another, KARLSRUHE, was torpedoed and sunk by the submarine *Truant* south of Kristian-

A German tank entering a railway tunnel in Norway, July 1940.

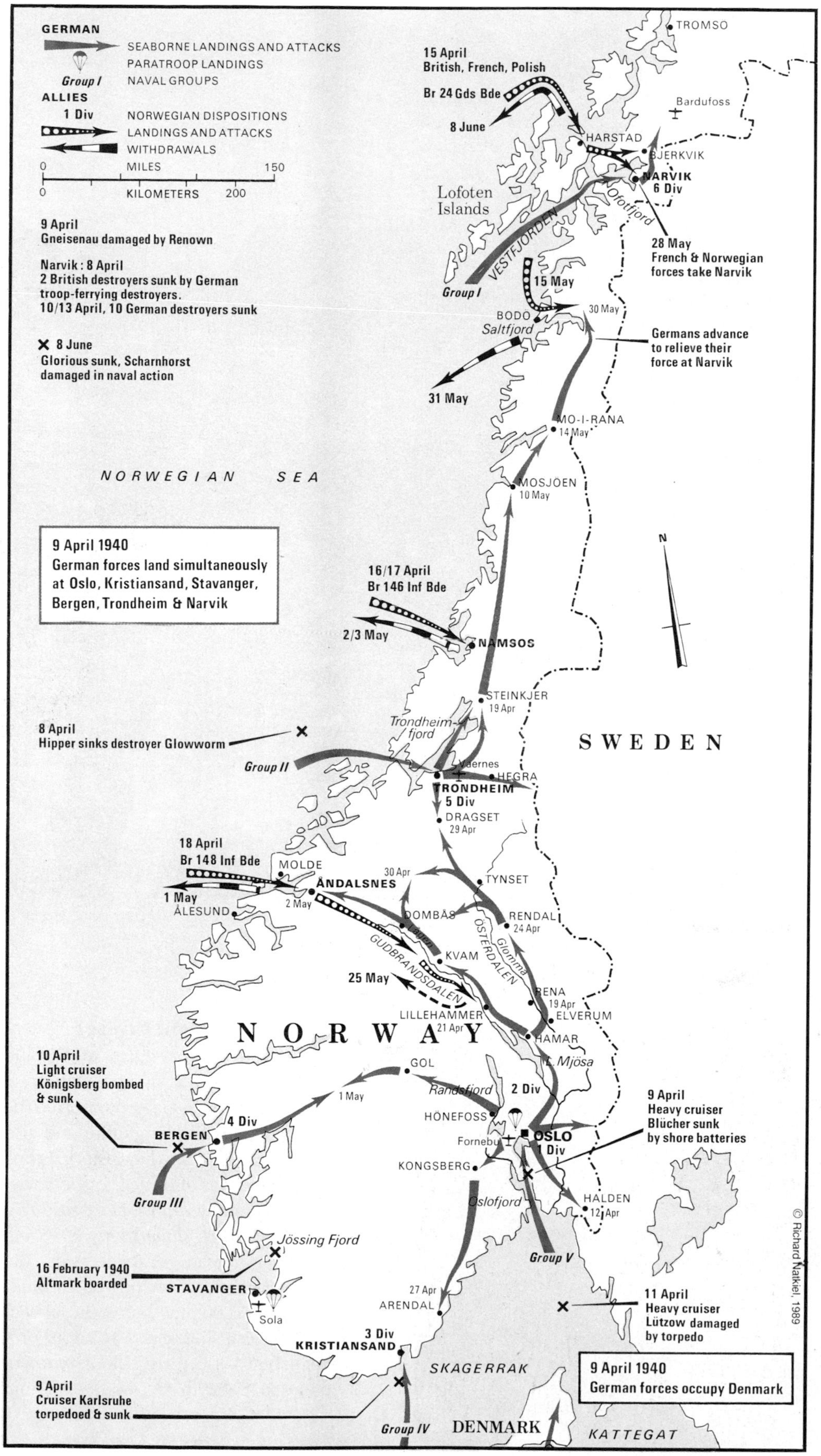
GERMAN
SEABORNE LANDINGS AND ATTACKS
PARATROOP LANDINGS
Group I
NAVAL GROUPS
ALLIES
1 Div
NORWEGIAN DISPOSITIONS
LANDINGS AND ATTACKS
WITHDRAWALS
0
MILES
150
0
KILOMETERS
200
9 April
Gneisenau damaged by Renown
Narvik: 8 April
2 British destroyers sunk by German troop-ferrying destroyers.
10/13 April, 10 German destroyers sunk
8 June
Glorious sunk, Scharnhorst damaged in naval action
NORWEGIAN SEA
9 April 1940
German forces land simultaneously at Oslo, Kristiansand, Stavanger, Bergen, Trondheim & Narvik
8 April
Hipper sinks destroyer Glowworm
Group II
18 April
Br 148 Inf Bde
1 May
ÅLESUND
MOLDE
ÅNDALSNES
2 May
30 Apr
NORWAY
10 April
Light cruiser Königsberg bombed & sunk
BERGEN
4 Div
Group III
Jössing Fjord
16 February 1940
Altmark boarded
STAVANGER
Sola
3 Div
KRISTIANSAND
9 April
Cruiser Karlsruhe torpedoed & sunk
Group IV
SKAGERRAK
DENMARK
KATTEGAT
9 April 1940
German forces occupy Denmark
TROMSO
15 April
British, French, Polish
Br 24 Gds Bde
8 June
Bardufoss
HARSTAD
BJERKVIK
NARVIK
6 Div
Lofoten Islands
VESTFJORDEN
Ofotfjord
28 May
French & Norwegian forces take Narvik
Group I
15 May
BODO
Saltfjord
30 May
Germans advance to relieve their force at Narvik
31 May
MO-I-RANA
14 May
MOSJOEN
10 May
N
16/17 April
Br 146 Inf Bde
2/3 May
NAMSOS
STEINKJER
19 Apr
Trondheim-fjord
Vaernes
HEGRA
TRONDHEIM
5 Div
DRAGSET
29 Apr
SWEDEN
TYNSET
DOMBÅS
RENDAL
24 Apr
Lagen
GUDBRANDSDALEN
ØSTERDALEN
Glomma
KVAM
25 May
HAMAR
ELVERUM
19 Apr
LILLEHAMMER
21 Apr
L. Mjösa
GOL
1 May
Randsfjord
2 Div
HÖNEFOSS
Fornebu
OSLO
1 Div
9 April
Heavy cruiser Blücher sunk by shore batteries
KONGSBERG
Oslofjord
HALDEN
12 Apr
Group V
27 Apr
ARENDAL
11 April
Heavy cruiser Lützow damaged by torpedo
© Richard Natkiel, 1989

The invasion of Norway, April–June 1940.

sand, while in a clash between battlecruisers GNEISENAU was damaged by *Renown*. On 10 April the cruiser KÖNIGSBERG was sunk by air attack at Bergen and the following day the pocket battleship LÜTZOW, already hit by coastal artillery, sustained further damage from a torpedo fired by the submarine *Spearfish*. Ten German and two British destroyers were lost during the First and Second Battles of NARVIK. Nevertheless, despite the destruction of so high a proportion of its surface fleet, the German Navy achieved its object of putting ashore an invasion force which, in the weeks to come, fought a successful campaign against Norwegian, British and French troops under skies dominated by the Luftwaffe.

The second phase of the naval campaign involved the evacuation of the Allied troops in May and June. This was accomplished despite the loss of several British and French ships to air attack. On 8 June the aircraft carrier GLORIOUS and her two escorting destroyers were sunk by SCHARNHORST, but not before one of the latter had damaged the battlecruiser with a torpedo, forcing her to put into Trondheim, escorted by her sister ship *Gneisenau*. On 23 June, while the two battlecruisers were heading back to Germany, *Gneisenau* was seriously damaged by a torpedo from the submarine *Clyde*.

Novikov, Col Gen Aleksandr (1900–1976)
Novikov served as Chief of Staff (Air) on the Karelian Front during the Soviet Union's Winter War against Finland. In 1942 he was appointed Commander-in-Chief of the Soviet Air Force, which he reconstructed after its virtual destruction by the Luftwaffe. He was responsible for air operations during the critical battles of STALINGRAD, KURSK, BELORUSSIA, and KÖNIGSBERG. In 1945 he moved to MANCHURIA, where he directed air operations against the Japanese. The following year he quarrelled with STALIN and was imprisoned.

NSDAP Nationalsozialistiche Deutsche Arbeiterpartei (German – National Socialist German Workers' Party). The formal name of the ruling German political party, more commonly abbreviated to Nazi.

NSKK Nationalsozialistische Kraftfahr-korps (German – Nazi Drivers' Corps). A Nazi Party organization which provided initial driving training for recruits prior to enlistment and also provided an auxiliary transportation corps for the German services.

Nuremberg, Germany

A city in southern Germany, Nuremberg was the spiritual home of the Nazi Party. The original "German Socialist Party" had been founded there by STREICHER in 1921, and in 1923 HITLER was a prominent speaker at a major right-wing rally in Nuremberg which saw the birth of the *Deutscher Kampfbund*. The city became the venue for the annual Nazi Party Rally and many of Hitler's more important speeches were made there. During the war work continued on massive public buildings which were to confirm the city as the home of the Party. Nuremberg was bombed frequently by Allied aircraft, and on 30/31 March 1944 the RAF mounted a particularly disastrous raid in which 95 out of 795 aircraft failed to return and 71 were severely damaged, a casualty rate which had the effect of reducing the number of long-range raids until suitable fighter cover could be achieved. The city was captured by troops of the US 3rd Army on 20 April 1945. Resistance had been extremely fierce and the city was severely damaged by air attacks and artillery fire. After the war it was selected as the venue for the International Tribunal on War Crimes, where the major Nazi Party and military leaders were tried.

March of the SS and the SA through Nuremberg, 1934.

Nuremberg trials, 1945. From left; Göring, Hess, von Ribbentrop, Keitel. Behind: Dönitz and Raeder.

Nürnberg, KMS – Light Cruiser

Nürnberg served in Norwegian waters and then formed part of the Training Squadron in the Baltic. During 1944–45 she supported the army's operations with her gunfire and also evacuated refugees from the Eastern Front. After the war she was allocated to the Soviet Navy and renamed *Admiral Makarov*. *Displacement* 6980 tons; *dimensions* 603×54ft (183.7×16.4m); mean draught 14ft 6in (4.41m); *machinery* 2-shaft geared turbines producing shp 66,000 plus 1-shaft diesel with bhp 12,400 for cruising; *speed* 32 knots; *protection* main belt 3–4in; turrets 2in; *armament* 9×5.9in (3×3); 8×3.5in AA (4×2); 8×37mm AA (4×2); 12×21in torpedo tubes (4×3); *aircraft* 2; *complement* 896; *launched* 1934.

O

"O" Class Submarines (UK)

Group 1 *Displacement* 1350–1850 tons; *dimensions* 286×28ft (87.1×8.5m); *machinery* 2-shaft diesel/electric motors producing bhp 3000/1350; *speed* 15.5/9 knots; *armament* 1×4in; 2 machine guns; 8×21in torpedo tubes (6 bow and 2 stern); *complement* 54; *number in class* 3, launched 1926.

Group 2 *Displacement* 1475–2030 tons; *dimensions* 283ft 6ins×29ft 9ins (86.2×9m); *machinery* 2-shaft diesel/electric motors producing bhp 4400/1320; *speed* 17.5/9 knots; *armament* as Group 1; *complement* 54; *number in class* 6, launched 1928–29.

"O" and "P" Class Destroyers (UK)

Displacement 1540 tons; *dimensions* 345×35ft (105×10.5m); *mean draught* 9ft (2.7m); *machinery* 2-shaft geared turbines producing shp 40,000; *speed* 36.75 knots; *armament* 4×4.7in (4×1); 4×2-pdr AA (1×4); 8×20mm AA (4×2) guns; 8×21in (2×4) torpedo tubes; *complement* 175; *number in class* 16, launched 1941–42.

Oak Ridge, Tennessee, USA

Locality in which the principal uranium separation plant for the production of material for the ATOMIC BOMB was built.

OB   Ordnance Board (UK).

Ob   Oberbefehlshaber (German – Commander-in-Chief).

Oboe

British radio blind bombing system used from 1942 onwards. It depended upon the aircraft flying on an arc at a constant range from a radio beam from a station in Britain which passed over the target. A signal conveyed by a second, intersecting radio beam cut the arc at the correct point of bomb release when the aircraft was over the target. Oboe was the most effective system used during the war and was so accurate that it cast doubt upon parts of the geodetic survey of Europe.

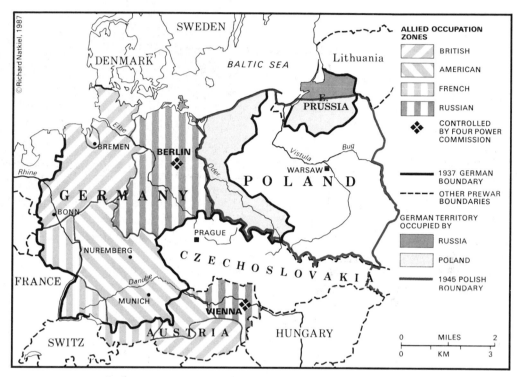

Four power control of Germany.

OC   Ordnance Committee (US).

Occupied Zones

Areas of influence within Germany and Austria in which the varied Allied armies held military control from the time of their occupation until civilian control was resumed. The cities of BERLIN and Vienna were divided between the Russian, American and British armies, whilst Germany itself was divided into Russian, British, American and French zones. Broadly, the Russian Zone covered what is today East Germany; the US Zone Bavaria and the Palatinate; the French Zone part of the Saar and Rhineland, and the British Zone central and northern Germany. Although the zones no longer exist, the location of British and US troops in Germany stays very much the same as the Occupation Zones.

Ochsenkopf (Oxhead)

German counteroffensive in northern Tunisia, February 1943.

O'Connor, Gen Sir Richard Nugent (1889–1981)

At the age of 20 O'Connor was commissioned from Sandhurst into the 2nd Battalion Cameronians (Scottish Rifles). He fought on the Western and Italian Fronts in World War I, winning two DSOs, an MC and an Italian Silver Medal for Valour. In 1936 he went to the Middle East to command a brigade during the Arab Revolt before becoming military governor of Jerusalem. In June 1940 O'Connor was appointed commander of the WESTERN DESERT FORCE in Egypt, and in December inflicted a serious defeat on the Italians at SIDI BARRANI during Operation COMPASS. Exploiting this success, he went on to capture BARDIA and TOBRUK and in February 1942 destroyed the Italian 10th Army at BEDA FOMM, Cyrenaica. The subsequent lull enabled the Germans to send reinforcements to assist the Italians in Libya. O'Connor had returned to Egypt when ROMMEL launched a counteroffensive, and he was taken prisoner on 6 April while conducting a forward reconnaissance. After over two years in an Italian prisoner-of-war camp he escaped (at the fourth attempt) in December 1943, reaching the Allied lines in the confusion of the Italian surrender. In the following year he commanded VIII Corps during the campaign in NORMANDY. O'Connor was one of the very few British commanders who, in the early years of the war, had the flair to exploit the flexibility and mobility of armour. But for his untimely capture, he would have proved a worthy opponent of Rommel in the ensuing desert campaign.

OCTU   Officer Cadet Training Unit (UK).

Oder-Neisse Line

The boundary between the eastern and western German provinces which later became the German-Polish frontier line. Set up by the POTSDAM Conference in 1945, it was named after the two rivers followed by the boundary.

Odessa, Soviet Union, 1941 and 1944

A seaport on the Black Sea, Odessa was the objective of German troops supported by the 4th Romanian Army in Operation BARBAROSSA. Odessa was reached on 5 August, but the defences were too strong and the city was placed under siege, which lasted 73 days before the Russian forces surrendered. Even before the city was captured, it was incorporated, along with its hinterland, into Romania, under the title *Transdniestria*. It was recaptured by Soviet troops on 10 April 1944.

Odette

See SANSOM.

Oerlikon Gun

An automatic gun of 20mm calibre developed in the 1920s by the Oerlikon-Buhrle Machine Tool Company of Zürich and sold widely throughout the world. It was employed both as an aircraft weapon and as an anti-aircraft defence and was fundamentally a very large machine gun. Used by the German forces from the mid-1930s, it was adopted by British and American forces during the war and manufactured in both countries under licence.

Ofenrohr (Stovepipe)

German nickname for the 88mm rocket launcher.

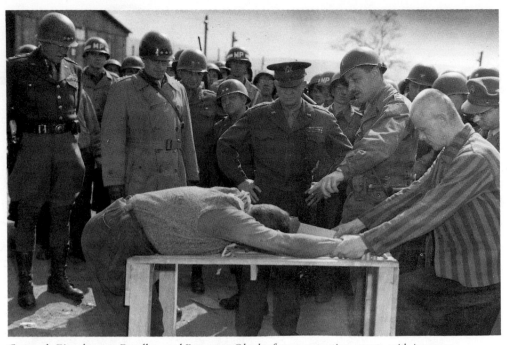

Generals Eisenhower, Bradley and Patton at Ohrdruf concentration camp, with inmates demonstrating how they had been flogged.

OFLAG   Offizierenlager (German – Prisoner-of-War camp for officer prisoners).

OFP   Ordnance Field Park (UK).

Ohrdruf, Germany

A minor concentration camp a few miles from Gotha, Ohrdruf was liberated on 4 April 1945 by troops of General PATTON's US 3rd Army. This was the first concentration camp to be seen by American troops. Patton was reputedly physically sick at the sight, and the Burgomeister of Ohrdruf and his wife, after being marched round the camp by infuriated American troops, returned home and committed suicide.

O'Kane, Cdr R. H., USN

Highest-scoring American submarine commander of World War II. O'Kane served aboard the USS ARGONAUT from June 1938 until April 1942, then joined the GATO CLASS submarine USS *Wahoo*, in which he served as executive officer under Commander Dudley W. MORTON until July 1943. In October 1943 he assumed command of the Gato Class submarine USS *Tang*, with which he made five patrols, being credited with sinking 31 ships totalling 227,800 tons. On 25 October 1944 he fired his two remaining torpedoes at a crippled freighter, but one of these ran wild, circled and struck *Tang*, sinking her. O'Kane

was picked up by the Japanese and imprisoned first on Formosa and then near Tokyo. His naval career continued until 1957, when he retired at the rank of Rear-Admiral.

Oke

The first flame-throwing CHURCHILL tank, armed with the RONSON projector. Three took part in the DIEPPE raid but all were lost.

OKH   Oberkommando des Heeres (German – Army High Command).

Okinawa, Pacific, 1945

A Japanese island, midway between Formosa and Japan and about 360 miles (580km) off the Chinese coast. Okinawa is 67 miles (107km) long and averages about 8 miles (12km) wide. It was selected as a US objective since it would afford useful airbases for attacking the Japanese mainland and would also enable the US Navy to cut sea communications with Japanese outposts in South China. It was attacked on 1 April 1945 by the US 10th Army under General Simon B. Buckner, comprising the US II Amphibious Corps and US XXIV Corps, a total of about 170,000 troops. Preliminary bombardment by air and naval forces began on 25 March. The island was defended by the Japanese 32nd Army under General Ushijima, with some 77,000 first-line troops and about 20,000 service and rear echelon troops. The terrain of the island was mountainous and Ushijima had supervised the building of a formidable network of strongpoints and cave defences. A fleet of some 2,000 Japanese aircraft was also available for support. The initial US landings were virtually unopposed, the Japanese strategy being to concentrate the defence inland, out of the range of US naval gunfire support and in more difficult terrain. By the end of the first day some 60,000 US troops were ashore and a nine-mile beach-head was secured. Advances were then made inland but it was not until 4 April that serious opposition was encountered. By 13 April, 6th Marine Division had cleared the north of the island, but the main Japanese defences were located in the south, and on 9 April HODGES' IV Corps ran into the strongly defended Shuri Line. On 3–4 May the Japanese launched a suicidal counter-attack, but it was not until the end of the month that Buckner broke the line. The island

US operations against Okinawa, 1945.

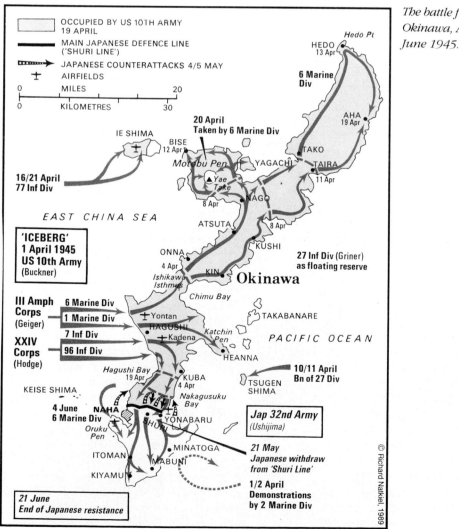

The battle for Okinawa, April–June 1945.

was finally secured on 21 June; on the following day Ushijima and his staff committed suicide. Only about 7,400 Japanese were taken prisoner; taking into account naval and air losses, it is probable that Japanese dead totalled 110,000. US losses were 12,513 dead and 36,600 wounded, the highest toll of any Pacific campaign. Among the dead was General Buckner, who was killed in the closing days of the campaign.

OKL Oberkommando der Luftwaffe (German – Air Force High Command).

OKM Oberkommando der Kriegsmarine (German – Naval High Command).

OKW Oberkommando der Wehrmacht (German – Armed Forces High Command).

Old "R", "S", "V", "W", Shakespeare and Scott Class Obsolete Destroyers (UK)

Launched 1917–20, eighty of these World War I destroyers were still serving in 1939. It was appreciated that they were no longer equal to first line destroyer duties and a few were converted to minelayers but the majority of the remainder became escort destroyers, short-range escorts or long-range escorts, their armament being modified to improve

309

their anti-aircraft and anti-submarine capability. A typical armament of a long-range escort consisted of two 4-inch, one 3-inch AA, two 2-pdr AA, two 20mm AA guns, one HEDGEHOG and, in some cases, three 21-inch torpedo tubes which were used to project 1-ton depth charges. These classes displaced 905–1530 tons, with a complement of 90–183. The unaltered ships, escort destroyers and short-range escorts retained their high speed of 34–36.5 knots but the long-range escorts, having had their forward boiler and its uptake removed to provide extra bunkerage space for extended endurance, had a maximum speed of 24.5 knots. A few were relegated to training duties 1944–45. See also TOWN CLASS.

Olive

British 8th Army offensive against the GOTHIC LINE, Italy, autumn 1944.

Olympic

American plan for the invasion of Kyushu, Japan, 1945.

Omaha Beach, Normandy, 1944

Landing beach in the area of Colleville, Vierville and Pointe de la Percée, on which the US V Corps came ashore on 6 June 1944. Omaha was somewhat exposed, and rough surf and a heavy sea took a high toll of invasion craft, particularly swimming tanks, most of which were launched too far from the beach. Naval gunfire support lifted too quickly, and the troops who eventually landed came under heavy fire, the area having recently been reinforced by fresh German troops of the 352nd Infantry Division. The initial setback went unrecognized on the command ships and back-up waves of troops and equipment kept flowing in, reducing the beach to a disorganized shambles of burning vehicles and wounded men. Only about 100 of the scheduled 24,500 tons of equipment landed in a condition fit to use. Nevertheless, by sheer force of will, good leadership and extreme examples of personal bravery, the US troops broke through the German defensive line and by mid-afternoon on 6 June elements of the US force were advancing off the beach-head.

Omaha Class Light Cruisers (USA)

Displacement 7050 tons; *dimensions* 555ft 6in×55ft 6in (169.3×16.84m); mean draught 13ft 6in (4.08m); *machinery* 4-shaft geared turbines producing shp 90,000; *speed* 34 knots; *armament* 10×6in (2×2 and 6×1); 8×3in; (2×3) 2×3-pdr; 8×12.7mm; 6×21in torpedo tubes; *aircraft* 2 (2 catapults); *complement* 458; *number in class* 10, launched 1920–24.

Onion (UK)

Demolition device. See CARROT and AVRE.

Onishi, V Adm Takajiro (1891–1945)

In 1941, while serving under YAMAMOTO as Chief of Staff to the 11th Air Fleet, Onishi carried out a feasibility study for the Japanese attack on PEARL HARBOR and later led a destructive raid on bases in the PHILIPPINES, eliminating American air power in the Far East. Appointed commander of the 5th Base Air Force on LUZON in October 1944, he set up a Special Attack Group with pilots willing to sacrifice their lives, and the early successes achieved by this unit inspired the KAMIKAZE movement. Onishi himself committed suicide following Japan's surrender.

Oosterbeek, Holland, 1944

A small village to the west of ARNHEM into which the remnants of the British and Polish airborne troops concentrated after being driven out of Arnhem, and from which some were able to escape across the Neder Rijn river.

OP Observation Post.

ORA Organisation de Résistance de l'Armée. French resistance organization forming part of the FFI.

Oradour-sur-Glane, France, 1944

A village in the Département Haute Vienne. In June 1944, as a reprisal for a raid on German troops by French Resistance forces, the village was surrounded by troops of the SS Division *Das Reich*, the entire population herded into the church, and the church set alight. Those attempting to escape were shot.

American assault troops, Omaha beach, June 1944.

Oran, France, 1940

A seaport and French naval base in Algeria, on the Gulf of Oran. In 1940 a major part of the French fleet was docked there, a cause for concern to the British government, who feared that the Germans would commandeer the French warships and put them to use, despite the various treaty agreements between Germany and France. In consequence, Admiral SOMERVILLE was ordered to take Naval Force H and offer the French Admiral at Oran the choice of three alternatives: to join the British and fight on, to sail with reduced crews to a British-designated port, or scuttle the French fleet where it lay. Should none of these be accepted, Somerville was to sink the French fleet. The French admiral refused all the options and accordingly Somerville opened fire and severely damaged a number of the major French warships. Having mined the entrance to the harbour, he then broke off the action. A number of minor French warships escaped to Toulon.

Orange

American pre-war contingency plan for a drive through the Central Pacific.

ORBAT

Order of Battle. Organization of a military force for combat, detailing the various units, equipment, etc.

Ordzhonikidze, Soviet Union, 1942

A town in the Caucasus region, north of the Caucasus mountains and about 250 miles (400km) north-west of Baku. In August 1942 it became the most easterly point in Russian territory reached by the Germans, but by December the town had been retaken by the Red Army.

Orel, Soviet Union, 1943

A city, 175 miles (280km) north-west of Voronezh. It formed the focal point of the Orel salient, a German intrusion into Soviet territory north of the KURSK salient. The salient was eliminated and Orel recaptured in a counter-attack mounted by the Soviet army in the wake of the Kursk battle, July 1943.

Oriani Class Destroyers (Italy)

Displacement 2290 tons; *dimensions* 350ft×33ft 3in (107×10.1m); mean draught 11ft 3in (3.4m); *machinery* 2-shaft geared turbines producing shp 48,000; *speed* 39 knots; *armament* 4×4.7in; 2×37mm AA; 8–

12×20mm AA; 6×21in torpedo tubes; 2–4 depth charge throwers; equipped for minelaying; *complement* 207; *number in class* 4, all launched 1936.

Orion – Surface Raider (Ger)

Also known as Ship 36 and Raider A. Sailed on 6 April 1940 and operated in the Atlantic, Indian and Pacific Oceans, sinking or capturing 9½ ships (7 shared with KOMET) totalling 80,279 tons. Returned to Bordeaux on 23 August 1941. Became a gunnery training ship and was bombed and sunk at Swinemunde on 4 May 1945. *Displacement* 7021 tons; *speed* 14 knots; *armament* 6×5.9in; 1×3in; 4×37mm AA; 4×20mm AA; 6×21in torpedo tubes; equipped for minelaying; *aircraft* 2; *complement* 377.

Orsa Class Destroyer Escorts (Italy)

Displacement 1699 tons; *dimensions* 292ft 9in×31ft (89×9.4m); mean draught 9ft 6in (2.88m); *machinery* 2-shaft geared turbines producing shp 16,000; *speed* 28 knots; *armament* 2×3.9in; 11×20mm AA; 6 depth charge throwers; equipped for minelaying; *complement* 169; *number in class* 4, all launched 1937.

Ortona, Italy, 1943

A small seaport on the Adriatic coast. Retreating before the advance of British V Corps in December 1943, German Panzergrenadiers and parachute troops prepared the town for defence by building strongpoints, demolishing buildings and booby-trapping houses. Assaulted by two Canadian infantry battalions, the capture of the town required a week of savage fighting. It was the first major street-fighting battle fought by the Allies and many lessons were learned.

Oskarsborg, Norway, 1940

A coast defence fortress in OSLO fjord. It put up a spirited defence during the German invasion of Norway in April 1940, sinking the German cruiser *Blucher* and damaging several other ships as they attempted to land troops. The fortress was eventually taken by German airborne troops flown into Oslo.

Oslo, Norway

The capital of Norway, Oslo was captured by a combined force of German paratroops dropped on the airport and infantry concealed in merchant ships which ran past the

OSKARSBORG defences on 9 April 1940. It remained under German control until the end of the war in Europe.

OSS (Office of Strategic Services)

American agency established in 1942 to gather intelligence and support resistance movements in Axis-occupied countries. Friction sometimes arose between the OSS and its British counterpart, the SOE, particularly over dealings with the Vichy French authorities in North Africa. This was largely eliminated when EISENHOWER brought the two organizations together under a Special Forces Headquarters which formed part of the Operations Division of the Supreme Headquarters Allied Expeditionary Force (SHAEF).

Ostwind (East Wind) – Anti-Aircraft Tank (Ger)

Introduced in March 1944, the Ostwind was very similar to the WIRBELWIND but was armed with a single 37mm cannon with an output of 160 rounds per minute. Only 40 were built.

OTS Officer Training School (US).

Otter – Armoured Personnel Carrier (Canada)

Officially designated "Car 4×4 Light Reconnaissance, Canadian GM Mark I", the Otter was built in Canada by General Motors using many of the same components as the FOX armoured car. Armament consisted of a single machine gun. The vehicle was used by Canadian troops in Italy and North-West Europe and a number were supplied to the British Army and the RAF Regiment. A total of 1761 were produced.

Otto

Alternative codename for FRITZ.

Overcast

Transfer of German scientists to the United States for work in research laboratories, 1945.

Overlord

Allied invasion of NORMANDY, June 1944.

OVRA Organizzazione di Vigilanza e Repressione dell'Antifascismo. Secret political police charged with the suppression of anti-Fascist elements and counter-intelligence duties.

Owen Gun

An Australian submachine gun designed by Corporal Evelyn Owen of the Australian Army. It was a conventional blowback weapon, but had the novel feature of the magazine being mounted above the gun. Extremely reliable, it was held in high regard, particularly in jungle conditions, and remained the standard Australian weapon until the 1960s.

Owen Stanley Mountains, New Guinea

A range of mountains separating the north and south coasts of New Guinea. It was crossed by the KOKODA TRAIL, down which the Japanese attacked from Buna and up which the Australian and US forces counter-attacked.

OWI Office of War Information (US).

Oyodo, IJN – Improved Agano Class Cruiser

Designed as an attack-group Flagship, *Oyodo* was capable of catapult-launching six reconnaissance bombers housed in a hangar which replaced the after gun position, but in practice she never carried more than two scoutplanes. She was fitted with more powerful engines giving a maximum speed of 36 knots. The thickness of the deck armour was increased to 2 inches (5cm) and that of the forward turrets, each mounting three 6.1-inch guns, to 2.75 inches (7cm). Launched in April 1942, *Oyodo* was sunk by air attack in Kure harbour on 28 July 1945.

Ozawa, V Adm Jisaburo (1896–1966)

Ozawa was regarded as one of the Imperial Japanese Navy's finest strategists. He had served as an instructor at the Naval Academy in 1935 and then commanded a cruiser and a battleship before being appointed Chief of Staff to the Combined Fleet 1937–38. He believed that carriers should be used aggressively and in large numbers but it was not until November 1942 that the Third Fleet (later renamed the Mobile Fleet) came under his command, following NAGUMO's dismissal. He commanded at the Battle of the PHILIPPINE SEA where his sound tactics were offset by superior American aircraft, the accumulated experience of his opponents and his own shortage of adequately trained pilots. These factors resulted in such heavy loss of aircraft and ships that the naval balance in the Pacific swung irreversibly against Japan. At the Battle of LEYTE GULF he came closest of any Japanese commander to inflicting a reverse on the Americans but success finally eluded him. In

Vice-Admiral Jisaburo Ozawa, IJN.

November 1944 Ozawa was appointed Vice-Chief of the Naval General Staff. In May 1945 he took control of the entire Combined Fleet, after the fall of OKINAWA. By now, however, he faced a hopeless task.

P

"P" Class Destroyers

See "O" AND "P" CLASS DESTROYERS.

"P" Class Submarines (USA)

Displacement 1310/1960 tons; *dimensions* 310×25ft (94×7.5m); *machinery* 2-shaft diesels producing shp 4300/2085; *speed* 19/8 knots; *armament* 1×3in or 1×4in; 6×21in torpedo tubes (4 bow and 2 stern); *complement* 55; *number in class* 10, launched 1935–37.

"P" and "R" Class Submarines (UK)

Displacement 1475/2040 tons; *dimensions* 290ft×29ft 9in (88×9m); *machinery* 2-shaft diesel/electric motors producing bhp 4400/1320; *speed* 17.5/9 knots; *armament* 1×4in; 2 machine guns; 8×21in torpedo tubes (6 bow and 2 stern); *complement* 53; *number in class* 10, launched 1929–30.

Pacific Theatres

The Pacific Ocean was an American strategic responsibility and was designated the Pacific Ocean Area, under the general command of Admiral Chester W. NIMITZ, Commander-in-Chief, Pacific Ocean Area. The area was then subdivided into theatres: *South-East Pacific Theatre*: The area west of the Panama Canal and South America, to the line of 110° West. *South Pacific Area*: The area below the equator and west of 110°W, to 160°W, but excluding the Solomon Islands. *South-West Pacific Area*: The area below the equator between 160°W and 110°E, including Australia. The east and west boundaries were bent at their northern ends so that the west longitudinal line passed between the New Hebrides and the Solomon Islands to include the latter, and the east line passed between Java and Sumatra, to include the latter. *Central Pacific Area*: the remaining area of the Pacific Ocean north of the equator.

Panhard Model 178 Armoured Car (Fr)

Rear-engined 4×4 armoured car which entered service with the French Army in 1935. After the fall of France a number were used by the Wehrmacht, which designated the vehicle P.204 (f). *Weight* 6.7 tons; *speed* 50mph (80kph); *armour* 20mm; *armament* 1 25mm cannon; 1 7.5mm machine gun; *engine* Panhard 105hp petrol; *crew* 4.

Panhard Model 201 Armoured Car (Fr)

Advanced design for an 8-wheeled armoured car. By 1940 one prototype had been constructed but after the defeat of the French Army this was shipped to North Africa, where it was lost in the Sahara. The drawings, too, were destroyed, although after the war the design ideas were revived and incorporated in the well-known Panhard EBR Model 212 armoured car.

Pantellaria, Italy, 1943

A small Mediterranean island some 60 miles (96km) south of Sicily, belonging to Italy. Occupied by a mixed German-Italian garrison, principally manning anti-aircraft guns, it was taken under attack by the Allies in mid-1943 as a preparatory step to the invasion of Sicily. For about one month, Allied aircraft flew over 5000 sorties and dropped over 6000 tons of bombs on the island, which is only 32 square miles (82 square km) in area. On 11 June a seaborne assault by the British 1st Division took the island with very little opposition.

Panther

German anti-partisan sweep, Yugoslavia, spring 1944.

Panther (Panzerkampfwagen V) – Medium Tank (Ger)

Developed with great urgency by Maschinenfabrik Augsburg-Nurnburg in response to the threat posed by the Soviet T-34/76, the Panther entered production in November 1942. The most notable features of the design were its 75mm L/70 gun, sloped glacis, wide tracks and interleaved suspension. Unfortunately, the penalty paid for rushing the vehicle through its development and trials was mechanical unreliability. Much of the trouble occurred in the transmission and steering linkages, where parts intended for use in a lighter vehicle were intolerant of the stresses imposed by a combination of increased weight and power, but the engine itself also had a tendency to overheat and petrol fires were common. In March 1943 GUDERIAN informed HITLER that the Panther was far from ready for active service but the Führer insisted that it should take part in the July offensive at KURSK, the result being that many were lost to causes other than enemy action. Subsequent modifications

Panzerkampfwagen V Panther.

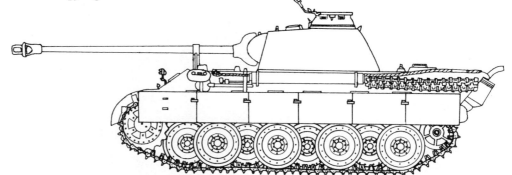

Panther Model D2 near Monte Cassino.

removed many of the tank's teething troubles and the Panther quickly acquired a formidable reputation, equipping one of each Panzer regiment's two battalions. Three major versions were produced, first Model D, then Model A and finally Model G; these incorporated successive detailed improvements without altering the vehicle's basic characteristics. Altogether, 5508 Panthers were built, of which 3740 were Model Gs. The vehicle's most notable derivative was the JAGD-PANTHER heavy tank destroyer, but command, artillery observation post and recovery versions were also produced. In Italy Panther turrets on ground mounting were integrated into the ADOLF HITLER and GOTHIC LINES. *Weight* 43–45.5 tons; *speed* 34mph (55kph); *armour* 120mm; *armament* 1 75mm L/70 gun; 2 7.92mm machine guns; *engine* Maybach HL230 P30 700hp petrol; *crew* 5.

Panzerbuchse

The general term for all German anti-tank rifles and also applied to the 28mm TAPER-BORE anti-tank gun. The PzB 38 was a 7.92mm manually-operated single shot weapon, capable of piercing 30mm of armour at 328ft (100m) range. The PzB 39 had a similar performance but was of somewhat simpler and cheaper design. The PzB 41 was a 20mm semi-automatic weapon based on a Swiss design,

and this designation was also used for the 28mm taper-bore gun.

Panzerfaust

A German recoilless anti-tank weapon capable of being fired by one man. It consisted of a short steel tube containing a propelling charge and with the tail stem of a SHAPED-CHARGE bomb inserted into the mouth of the tube. The bomb had a warhead of about 120mm diameter, while the diameter of the launcher tube was about 35mm. The weapon

Panzerfaust 30, Ukraine 1943/44.

was tucked underneath the arm, aim taken across the top of the bomb, and a trigger pressed; this fired the charge and the bomb was blown forward whilst the gas expelled from the rear end of the tube countered the recoil. The first model, the PzF 30, appeared in 1942 and had a range of about 115ft (35m). Later models, with better propulsion and more effective warheads, could reach to 500ft (150m) range. All were effective against any wartime tank, provided the firer selected the side or rear at which to shoot; they were marginal against frontal armour.

Panzerjäger – Tank Hunters (Ger)

General term denoting troops performing the anti-tank role, whether equipped with tracked or wheeled tank destroyers, towed anti-tank guns or hand-held weapons, reflecting the German Army's positive psychological approach. In more recent years the term has been used specifically to denote mechanized tank destroyer units and their equipment. See ELEFANT, HETZER, JAGDPANTHER, JAGDPANZER IV, JAGDTIGER, MARDER, NASHORN.

Panzerkampfwagen I – Light Tank (Ger)

Ordered as a light training vehicle in 1932. The first prototypes were delivered in December 1933 and production began in July 1934. The Model A was found to be underpowered and was replaced by the longer and more powerful Model B, respective construction figures being 300 and 1500. An infantry support version with 80mm armour and an interleaved suspension began entering service in June 1940 but only 30 were built. The PzKw I saw active service with the Nationalists and the Kondor Legion during the Spanish Civil War, some being fitted with a 20mm cannon in an attempt to improve its meagre firepower. The vehicle also took part in the campaigns in Poland, France and the Low Countries, Norway, the Balkans, North Africa and the invasion of Soviet Russia. By the end of 1941 its day was long past and it was withdrawn from first-line service, although turretless versions powered by wood gas were used for driver training for some years after. Derivatives included a small command tank with a fixed superstructure, a tank destroyer mounting a 47mm L/43.4 Czech anti-tank gun, a self-propelled mounting for the Type 33 150mm Heavy Infantry Gun, and an explosive charge layer. *Model B Weight* 5.8

tons; *speed* 25mph (40kph); *armour* 13mm; *armament* 2 7.92mm machine guns; *engine* Maybach NL38 TR 100hp petrol; *crew* 2.

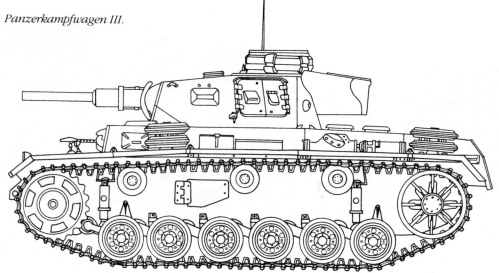

Panzerkampfwagen III.

Panzerkampfwagen II – Light Tank (Ger)

Ordered in July 1934 as a stopgap during the development of the PANZERKAMPFWAGEN III and IV and designed by Maschinenfabrik Augsburg-Nurnburg with a layout similar to that of the PANZERKAMPFWAGEN I. In 1938 Daimler-Benz were contracted to produce a fast version of the tank with which to equip the Light Divisions. This was achieved by replacing the standard leaf-spring suspension with a torsion bar system mounting large road-wheels, enabling a maximum speed of 34mph (55kph) to be maintained on roads. These vehicles, designated Models D and E, performed less satisfactorily across country and subsequent Marks reverted to the original suspension. During the preparations for the cancelled invasion of the United Kingdom an amphibious version, known as *Schwimmpanzer II*, was developed, using a kit of flotation tanks attached to the return rollers and powered when afloat by a propeller driven by an extension shaft from the engine. Further developments included a reconnaissance vehicle, the LUCHS, which entered service in small numbers in 1943, and a flamethrower conversion known as *Flammpanzer II* or Flamingo, 95 of which were built using Model D and E chassis, the flame gun having a range of approximately 40 yards. The PzKw II served during the campaigns in Poland, Norway, France and the Low Countries, the Balkans,

Panzerkampfwagen II.

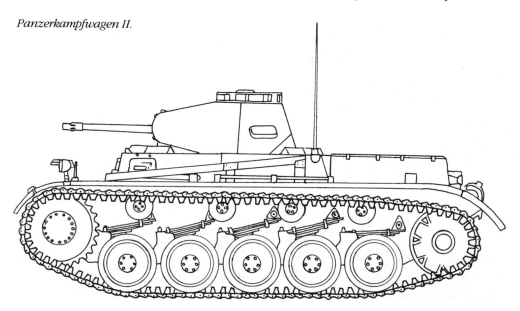

North Africa and the invasion of Soviet Russia but by the beginning of 1942 it was obvious that its usefulness as a gun tank was at an end and large numbers of chassis were turned over for conversion to other uses. These included a self-propelled carriage for the Type 33 150mm Heavy Infantry Gun, the WESPE self-propelled 105mm howitzer and the MARDER II tank destroyer. Nearly 2000 PzKw IIs of various types were built and production did not finally cease until the beginning of 1944. *Model F Weight* 9.35 tons; *speed* 25mph (40kph); *armour* 30mm; *armament* 1 20mm cannon; 1 7.92mm machine gun; *engine* Maybach HL62 140hp petrol; *crew* 3.

Panzerkampfwagen III – Medium Tank (Ger)

Intended as the German Army's main battle tank and developed under the supervision of

Daimler-Benz from 1935 onwards. Senior tank officers wished the vehicle to be armed with a 50mm gun but accepted the 37mm, which was in quantity production, with the proviso that the turret ring be made wide enough to accommodate the 50mm if the need arose. The first models were built in small numbers only with inadequate coil or leaf spring suspensions and it was not until the torsion bar system was introduced with the Model E in 1939 that the suspension was standardized. Following encounters with heavily armoured British and French tanks during the 1940 campaign in the West, HITLER gave instructions that the tank should be armed with the 50mm L/60 gun. Partly because of supply difficulties, the less powerful 50mm L/42 gun was fitted, the result being that the PzKw III fared badly in its initial engagements with the Soviet KLIMENTI VOROSHILOV and T-34/76. Hitler was furious that his orders had been ignored and the L/60 weapon was fitted as standard to the later Model Js and subsequent Marks, while earlier models which had been returned to Germany for refit were also up-gunned. Simultaneously, the tank was regularly up-armoured both by increasing the thickness of integral armour to 50mm and the use of *appliqué* plates. These processes considerably increased the vehicle's weight, this problem being solved by fitting wider tracks from Model H onwards, so maintaining an acceptable ground pressure. The PzKw III was the mainstay of the Panzerwaffe during the first half of the war, although there were never enough to go round. By 1942, however, the design had reached the limit of its potential and the final version, the Model N, was a close support vehicle armed with a 75mm L/24 howitzer which served in the fire support role in Panzergrenadier divisions and TIGER tank battalions. Between 1939 and 1943, when production ceased, over 5500 PzKw IIIs were built. A submerged wading version was produced for the aborted invasion of the United Kingdom and later used at the crossing of the River Bug during Operation BARBAROSSA. Other derivatives included command, artillery observation post and recovery vehicles, a self-propelled carriage for the Type 33 150mm Heavy Infantry Gun, a flamethrower with a range of 60 yards, and a tracked supply carrier. See also STURMGESCHUTZE.

Model F Weight 20 tons; *speed* 25mph (40kph); *armour* 30mm; *armament* 1 37mm gun or 1 50mm L/42 gun; 2 7.92mm machine guns; *engine* Maybach HL120 TRM 300hp petrol; *crew* 5.

Upgunned PzKw IVs parade through Toulouse, 1942.

Panzerkampfwagen IV – Medium Tank (Ger)

Developed by the Krupp organization in response to a 1934 specification issued by the German Army for a close support tank armed with a 75mm L/24 howitzer with which to equip the heavy companies of tank battalions. The vehicle entered production in 1936 but comparatively few had been built by the time war broke out. The Model A was protected by 14.5mm armour, increased to 30mm on Models B, C and D, but experience gained during the 1939 campaign in Poland revealed that this was inadequate and the Model E saw the addition of 30mm *appliqué* plate. The Model F, introduced in 1941, had 50mm integral armour, supplemented by 30mm *appliqué* plate in the Model G of 1942, and standardized as 80mm integral armour with

Panzerkampfwagen IV.

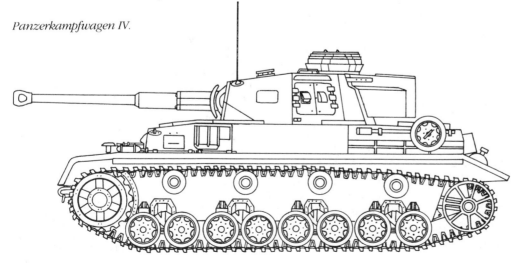

the introduction of the Model H the following year. Meanwhile, early encounters with the Soviet KLIMENTI VOROSHILOV and T-34/76 had caused serious concern and as the PzKw IV's turret ring was large enough to accommodate a high velocity gun of the same calibre as the howitzer, it was decided that the vehicle would gradually take over the role of main battle tank from the PANZERKAMPFWAGEN III, pending the arrival of the PANTHER. The 75mm L/43 gun was fitted to the Model F2, followed by the more powerful 75mm L/48 gun to the later Model Gs and subsequent Marks, the latter weapon also being fitted to older models when they were returned to Germany for refit. The effect of this continuous increase

in weight was to overload the leaf-spring suspension, somewhat reducing mobility. In its final form the vehicle was fitted with side skirts and a turret girdle of spaced armour as a defence against shaped charge ammunition. During the last years of the war the PzKw IV equipped one of the Panzer regiment's two tank battalions, and the Panther the other. Over 8000 were built between 1939 and 1944. A submerged wading version was produced for the aborted invasion of the United Kingdom and later used at the crossing of the River Bug during Operation BARBAROSSA. Other derivatives included command, artillery observation post and recovery versions; a version of the STURMGESCHUTZ; the BRUMMBÄR heavy assault gun; the NASHORN and PANZERJÄGER IV tank destroyers; the HUMMEL 150mm self-propelled howitzer; the MÖBELWAGEN, WIRBELWIND, ÖSTWIND and KUGELBLITZ anti-aircraft tanks; a munitions carrier; and a series of experimental weapon carriers. *Model H Weight* 25 tons; *speed* 26mph (42kph); *armour* 80mm; *armament* 1 75mm L/48 gun; 2 7.92mm machine guns; *engine* Maybach HL120 TRM 300hp petrol; *crew* 5.

Panzerkampfwagen 35(t) – Light Tank (Czech)

Produced jointly by Československa Kolben Danek and Skoda in 1935 under the designation of LTvz.35 and taken into German

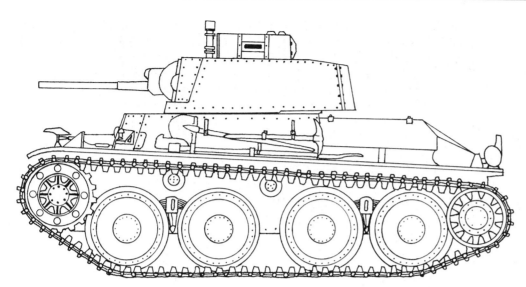

Panzerkampfwagen 38(t).

service as the PzKw 35(t) when Czechoslovakia was occupied. The vehicle's 37mm gun enabled it to be substituted for the PANZERKAMPFWAGEN III during the campaigns in Poland and France and the invasion of Soviet Russia. Its career with the German Army ended during the winter of 1941/42 but it continued to serve with Romanian and Slovak formations on the Eastern Front until the STALINGRAD campaign. The layout of the PzKw 35(t) rendered it unsuitable for conversion to other roles but turretless versions were used as recovery vehicles and mortar carriers. *Weight* 10.5 tons; *speed* 22mph (35kph); *armour* 25mm; *armament* 1 37mm gun; 2 7.92mm machine guns; *engine* Skoda T/11 120hp petrol; *crew* 3.

Panzerkampfwagen 38(t) – Medium Tank (Czech)

Produced jointly by Českomoravska Kolben Danek and Skoda in response to a Czech Army General Staff specification of 1937, the vehicle was designated TNHP and taken into German service as the PzKw 38(t) when Czechoslovakia was occupied. The tank offered a number of improvements upon its immediate predecessor, the PANZERKAMPFWAGEN 35(T), including a more convenient layout, better suspension and a superior performance 37mm gun. It served as an efficient substitute for the PANZERKAMPFWAGEN III in several Panzer divisions during the campaigns in Poland, France, the Balkans and the invasion of Soviet Russia, as well as equipping the armoured formations of the Bulgarian, Hungarian and Slovak armies. A total of 1414 PzKw 38(t)s

were built but by the end of 1941 the 37mm main armament was clearly inadequate for German requirements and as the design could not absorb up-gunning large numbers of chassis were turned over to other uses. These included the MARDER III series of tank destroyers; the HETZER tank destroyer and a flamethrowing derivative known as *Flammpanzer 38(t)* which was used in the 1944 ARDENNES offensive; an anti-aircraft tank armed with a single 20mm cannon; a reconnaissance tank in which the original turret was replaced by that of the SONDERKRAFTFAHRZEUG 222 armoured car; a recovery vehicle and a smoke

generator. *Weight* 9.7 tons; *speed* 26mph (42kph); *armour* 25mm; *armament* 1 37mm gun; 2 7.92mm machine guns; *engine* Praga EPA 125hp petrol; *crew* 4.

Panzerschreck

A German anti-tank rocket launcher copied from the American BAZOOKA and firing an 8.8cm shaped-charge rocket to a range of about 500ft (150m). Also known as *Ofenrohr* (stove-pipe) to German troops because of the cloud of smoke emitted on firing.

Papagos, Gen Alexander (1883–1955)

Papagos was Commander-in-Chief of the Greek Army when the Italians invaded GREECE from ALBANIA on 28 October 1940, and was responsible for driving them back across the frontier. When in the following spring German troops turned his flank, Papagos recognized that defeat was inevitable but chivalrously volunteered to continue fighting until the British contingent in Greece could be re-embarked. He survived imprisonment in DACHAU concentration camp and resumed his position as Commander in-Chief in 1945, leading the campaign against left-wing insurgents in northern Greece.

Paris, 1940 and 1944

The capital city of France, it was declared an open city on 11 June 1940 and was entered by the German Army on 14 June. It was liberated

The liberation of Paris, August 1944.

on 25 August 1944 by the French 4th Armoured Division under General LECLERC. On the previous day HITLER had ordered that Paris was to be held at all costs, to keep east-west communications open. The German commander in Paris, General von Choltitz ignored these orders and surrendered the city.

Park, AM Sir Keith (1892–1975)

Park, a New Zealander, was appointed Air Officer Commanding (AOC) 11 Group, Fighter Command, in 1939 and in June 1940 achieved a local air superiority which prevented the attempt by the Luftwaffe's bombers to halt the DUNKIRK evacuation. During the Battle of BRITAIN he pursued a policy of forward defence which steadily eroded the German strength. In the autumn of 1941 he was appointed AOC at GHQ Middle East in Egypt and on 15 July 1942 was made AOC MALTA, from which he launched an aggressive campaign against Axis shipping and air routes to North Africa. He was responsible for providing air support for the Allied landings in French North Africa (November 1942), Sicily (July 1943) and Italy (September 1943) and in January 1944 was appointed Supreme Commander (Air) in the Middle East. In February 1945 he became Air Commander-in-Chief South-East Asia Command, co-ordinating Allied air support during the offensive which culminated in the destruction of the Japanese BURMA AREA ARMY and the capture of RANGOON.

Partisans

A general term for irregular groups which preyed upon the German rear areas, particularly in the Balkans and on the Eastern Front, requiring the diversion of substantial bodies of troops for defence of lines of communication. In addition to receiving arms and equipment from the Allies by air, groups also employed captured weapons. Partisan activity could provoke savage reprisals against the local civilian population, amongst whom it was not universally popular. The most effective and best organized partisan movement of the war was that commanded by TITO in Yugoslavia. Tito's partisans controlled large areas of the countryside, were strong enough to defeat their pro-German opponents, fight pitched battles against the Wehrmacht, and follow up the latter's withdrawal from the Balkans. Partisan groups were also active in Greece, CRETE and northern Italy.

The greatest number of partisan groups was to be found in the Soviet Union. Some of these groups were controlled by and remained loyal to the Soviet Army, but others were little better than armed gangs who terrorized the villages in their area. Others, again, were opposed to the return of Soviet rule and provided active assistance for the Germans. One such group, the *Ukrainska Povstanska Armia* (Ukrainian National Army), is believed to have been responsible for the killing of General Nikolay VATUTIN on 29 February 1944. When the Wehrmacht withdrew from Russia the Soviet policy was to disarm even loyal groups and disperse their members to regular army units; those groups which attempted to fight it out with army and NKVD troops were ruthlessly exterminated. The scale of partisan activity in the Soviet Union is indicated by the fact that in 1942 the Wehrmacht deployed 25 special security divisions on anti-partisan operations, plus 30 regiments and more than 100 battalions of police.

Pas de Calais, France, 1944

The hinterland behind Calais and Boulogne, where the English Channel is at its most narrow. The Pas de Calais was the logical place to launch the invasion of Europe, but its suitability as an eventual invasion point was dismissed by the Allies in favour of the NORMANDY beaches. However, the possibility of Allied landings in the Pas de Calais was fostered by various ruses, to keep the German eyes firmly fixed on the area and induce them to divert troops for its defence. Even as the invasion landed in Normandy, a range of deception measures was deployed to persuade the German Army that the Normandy venture was a feint and that the main attack was against the Pas de Calais. This was so successful that a major proportion of the German reserve was kept out of Normandy until it was too late for them to defeat the landings.

British-trained partisans, Yugoslavia.

General Alexander Patch.

Patch, Gen Alexander McCarrell (1889–1945)

Patch served in New Caledonia early in 1942 and on 9 December was appointed commander of the US XIV Corps on GUADALCANAL, bringing the land campaign there to a successful conclusion. In March 1944 he was appointed commander of the US 7th Army, which landed in the south of France on 15 August and advanced up the Rhone Valley to Alsace. Patch's army crossed the RHINE on 26 March 1945 and then advanced rapidly across southern Germany, receiving the surrender of Army Group G on 5 May.

Pathfinder Force

Pathfinder Force was a special force of skilled RAF bomber crews set up in August 1942. Their task was to fly to targets, identify them, and mark them with coloured flares that would guide the body of the bombing force to their allotted targets. They were provided with the best navigational aids, thus relieving the average bomber crews of much of the responsibility for navigating their way to a distant target in darkness. Their establishment was resisted by ACM HARRIS, of BOMBER COMMAND, since he felt that it reflected on the morale and skill of the average crew, but he was overruled. At the time of the formation of Pathfinder Force the average bombing accuracy of the RAF was poor, and only by adopting this system was it improved.

Patton, Gen George S., Jr (1885–1945)

Patton was one of very few American senior officers to have served in tanks during World War I, being badly wounded in the Meuse–Argonne offensive. He was an aggressive advocate of the tank as a decisive weapon throughout the interwar years. In 1940 he was rewarded with the appointment as divisional Commander of the 2nd Armored Division. Frequently tactless, he was extrovert to the point of exhibitionism. But it was his energy, drive and unwavering belief in speed, movement and the indirect approach which placed him in the leading ranks of American commanders. One of his favourite adages was, "Catch the enemy by the nose, then kick him in the pants." During the Allied landings in French North Africa he commanded the Western Task Force which came ashore at CASABLANCA and in March 1943 assumed command of the US II Corps, restoring its discipline and morale after the reverse it had sustained the previous month at KASSERINE PASS. He was then appointed commander of the US 7TH ARMY for the invasion of SICILY in July 1943, during which his dashing advance did much to bring the campaign to a speedy conclusion. At this point his career came close

Lieutenant-General George S. Patton, US 3rd Army.

to being terminated when, during a visit to a military hospital, he struck a soldier suffering from combat fatigue. The penalty amounted to a loss of seniority which prevented him reaching the highest levels of command but it was decided to re-employ him as the commander of the US 3RD ARMY during the Allied invasion of Europe and he retained this post for the remainder of the war. In July 1944 his army led the breakout from NORMANDY, conducting a rapid advance across France and over the Meuse until, by the end of August, its fuel supplies were exhausted. Patton complained that EISENHOWER favoured MONTGOMERY over fuel supplies, commenting that if he had possessed sufficient fuel he could have entered Germany and perhaps ended the war that year, although the latter is highly improbable. The 3rd Army then became involved in bitter attritional fighting on the German frontier, punctuated in December by the Battle of the BULGE, in which Patton quickly redeployed his troops to drive north through the southern flank of the German penetration and relieve BASTOGNE. In March 1945 he conducted a brilliant crossing of the RHINE and followed this with a further high speed advance which had penetrated deep into Czechoslovakia when the war ended. Patton was killed in a traffic accident in December 1945.

Paul, Prince Regent of Yugoslavia (1893–1976)

Paul served as Regent to King PETER II from the latter's accession in 1934 until 27 March 1941. He believed, correctly, that YUGOSLAVIA was in no condition to fight a war and signed a secret pact with the Axis powers on 25 March 1941, despite being warned that such an apparent capitulation to German threats would be greatly resented by the armed services and the general public. Two days later his period of Regency was ended by a bloodless *coup* staged by General SIMOVIĆ and he went into exile.

Paulus, FM Friedrich von (1890–1957)

Paulus served as Chief of Staff to the German 6th Army during the 1939 campaign in Poland and the 1940 campaign in the West. He was then selected by HALDER as his Deputy Chief of General Staff, with the rank of Lieutenant-General, and was responsible for the detailed planning of Operation BARBAROSSA, the German invasion of the Soviet Union. In January 1942 he was promoted full general and

Field-Marshal Friedrich von Paulus, taken prisoner with his staff.

appointed commander of 6th Army, which he led to STALINGRAD during the German summer offensive. In November his army, together with part of 4th Panzer Army, was isolated by the Soviet double envelopment codenamed Operation URANUS. A relief attempt was mounted by von MANSTEIN's Army Group Don and by 18 December this had reached a point only 35 miles (56km) from the trapped army's perimeter. Paulus declined to execute the previously agreed plan that he should break out towards the relief force, choosing to place a literal interpretation on HITLER's order that he should remain in his existing positions. The moment soon passed and the incident fully justified the nickname of *Cunctator* (Procrastinator) by which Paulus was already known among his peers. On 30 January 1943 Hitler promoted him Field-Marshal, in the hope that this would stiffen his resolve, but his troops were starving and on 2 February he

surrendered, provoking criticism that he should not have allowed himself to be taken alive. By mid-1944 he clearly recognized that Germany had lost the war and, following the JULY BOMB PLOT and the execution of many of his friends, he made broadcasts urging German troops to give up. He gave evidence for the prosecution at the NUREMBERG trials and made his postwar home in Dresden, in the Soviet zone of Germany.

Pavlov, Col Gen Dmitri (d. 1941)

Pavlov served with the Russian contingent during the Spanish Civil War, advising STALIN on his return home that the correct role for tanks was infantry support, the consequence being that the large armoured formations raised by TUKHACHEVSKY were broken up. However, the Soviet armour did not distinguish itself in the Winter War and the clear example set by the German Panzer formations

in Poland and the West meant that this radical decision had to be reversed. Thus, when the Germans invaded the USSR in June 1941, the Soviet armoured corps was in a state of internal flux and lacked a clear operational doctrine. Pavlov, hitherto regarded by Stalin as his tank expert, was then commanding West Front and, following the disastrous reverses sustained by his command during the early days of the campaign, was arrested and shot for incompetence.

PCNL Polish Committee of National Liberation.

PD Point detonating (US). A type of artillery fuze.

PDE Projectile Development Establishment (UK). A cover name for the organization developing rockets and missiles.

Pearl Harbor

The US Naval base on the island of Oahu, Hawaii. On 7 December 1941 a US Squadron of 94 warships and auxiliaries were at anchor in Pearl Harbor, among them eight battleships on "Battleship Row", two lines of vessels separated from each other by no more than about 100ft (30m). At 0755 the first of a Japanese force of 360 aircraft burst through the overcast to deliver a surprise attack. The first wave was directed against airfields, destroying or disabling most of the US air strength on the ground. This was followed by attacks by torpedo and dive bombers directed against the warships. The eight battleships, three cruisers and a large number of other ships were either sunk or immobilized, and by 0945 almost the whole of the US Pacific Fleet was incapable of action. The only relief was that the US aircraft carriers had been despatched on a routine training cruise and thus escaped the attack, so that they were saved to form the nucleus of the rebuilt US fleet. The Japanese force had been brought to some 200 miles (320km) from the islands by a carrier fleet, supported by submarine tenders and five small special-purpose MIDGET SUB-MARINES. Japanese losses amounted to about 30 aircraft and the five submarines, which had attempted to enter the harbour but were detected and sunk. The attack did not seriously damage the land defences, nor did it destroy oil reserves, power stations or dock workshops, so that repairs to the damaged

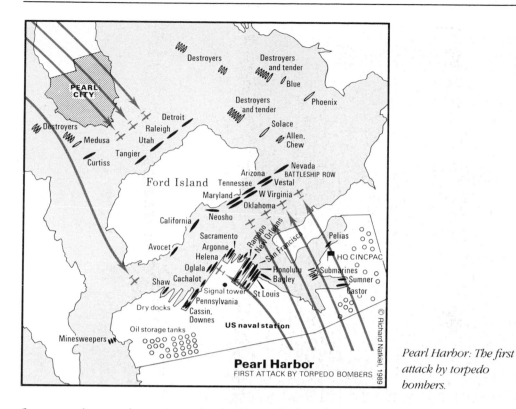

Pearl Harbor: The first attack by torpedo bombers.

Pearl Harbor
FIRST ATTACK BY TORPEDO BOMBERS

fleet were begun almost immediately. The attack, without formal declaration of war, unified the American population behind President ROOSEVELT with a determination to "Remember Pearl Harbor".

Pedestal Convoy, 1942

By August 1942 the situation on MALTA had become so critical that it was decided to run a convoy of 14 fast merchantmen from Gibraltar to the island. The codename for the operation was *Pedestal*, and the convoy was to be escorted by the battleships *Nelson* and *Rodney*, the carriers *Victorious*, *Indomitable* and *Eagle*, three cruisers, four anti-aircraft cruisers and 24 destroyers, under the overall command of Vice-Admiral E. N. Syfret. The heavy ships would turn back on reaching the Sicilian Narrows and thereafter the convoy would have the protection of three cruisers, one anti-aircraft cruiser and twelve destroyers. Recognizing its importance, the Axis made every effort to destroy it, using 784 aircraft flying from bases in Sardinia and Sicily, 21 submarines already at sea and squadrons of S-boats deployed off the Tunisian coast, as well as a freshly laid minefield. The convoy picked up its escort in the Straits of Gibraltar on 10 August and proceeded eastwards. At noon on the 11th the carrier *Eagle* was torpedoed and sunk by *U-73* and later the same day the convoy sustained the first of many air attacks. On the 12th the freighter *Deucalion* sank after sustaining bomb and torpedo damage, but during the afternoon the destroyer *Ithuriel* rammed and sank the Italian submarine *Cobalto*. By evening the convoy was within range of the Sicilian airfields, and *Indomitable* was damaged and the destroyer *Foresight* sunk. Off Skorki Bank a spread of torpedoes fired by the submarine *Axum* at 1955 inflicted fatal damage on the anti-aircraft cruiser *Cairo*, damaged the cruiser *Nigeria* so seriously that she turned back to Gibraltar, and blew a large hole in the side of the tanker *Ohio*. Shortly later the freighter *Empire Hope* was set ablaze by bombs and had to be abandoned. Simultaneously a torpedo spread from the submarine *Alagi* damaged the cruiser *Kenya* and the freighter *Brisbane Star*, and sank the freighter *Clan Ferguson*. Darkness brought several hours' relief but from 0100 until dawn on the 13th the convoy was savaged by the high-speed attacks of S- and MAS boats. In these attacks the cruiser *Manchester* was so badly damaged that she had to be scuttled and four more freighters, *Almeria Lykes*, *Wairangi*, *Glenorchy* and *Santa Elisa* were sunk, while another, *Rochester Castle*, was damaged but able to continue. According to the original Axis plan the convoy and its escort were to have been wiped out at this juncture by a force of six cruisers and 11 destroyers, provided the Italian ships could be given air cover. This was denied because of inter-service rivalry and the squadron returned to its bases; on the way the

The sinking of the battleships USS California *(centre) and USS* Oklahoma *(right), Pearl Harbor 1941.*

HMS Indomitable *emerges from a curtain of near misses during an attack on the Pedestal Convoy, 1942.*

cruisers *Bolzano* and *Attendolo* were severely damaged by torpedoes from the submarine *Unbroken* at 0800 on the 13th, neither taking any further part in the war. At about the same time air attacks on the convoy were resumed and the freighter *Waimara* blew up. During the next four hours another freighter, *Dorset*, was sunk, and *Ohio* and *Rochester Castle* both sustained further damage. That afternoon three of the convoy's survivors, *Port Chalmers*, *Rochester Castle* and *Melbourne Star*, reached Malta; *Ohio*, barely afloat, came in next day after a triumph of seamanship which earned her master, Captain D. W. Mason, the George Cross. Despite the heavy losses involved, Operation *Pedestal* restored Malta's ability to resist and the island's defensive and offensive capacity improved steadily thereafter.

Peenemunde, 1943

German rocket research establishment set up on the island of Usedom in the Baltic in 1936. Development of the A-4 (V-2) ROCKET was carried out at Peenemunde, and later work on the FZG-76 (V-1 missile) was also moved there. The installation was attacked on the night of 17/18 August 1943 by 597 aircraft of RAF BOMBER COMMAND, the only occasion in the war when the whole weight of Bomber Command

was thrown into a precision raid on such a small target. Among the 735 dead were Professor Thiel, a propulsion specialist, and Herr Walther, the plant's chief engineer. The V-2 programme was set back by at least two months.

Peenemunde Arrow Shell

A dart-like projectile fired from special smooth-bore versions of standard German artillery guns. Developed in the Aerodynamic Research Laboratory at PEENEMUNDE, the shell had a thin body with full-calibre fins at the tail

Ruins at Liedburg near Karlshagen showing Peenemunde buildings after the first heavy air raid, August 1943.

and a discarding belt around the waist which took the propellant gas thrust. Fired from the 31cm smoothbored version of the 28cm K5 railway gun, it could achieve a range of 99 miles (160km). The principle was also used in developing a high-altitude shell for the 105mm anti-aircraft gun, though this did not reach service due to a shortage of the special steel required. A few rounds of the 31cm PPG (Peenemunde Pfeil-Geschosse) were fired against US troops near Bonn at a range of about 68 miles (110km).

Peirse, AM Sir Richard (1892–1970)

Peirse was Deputy Chief of Air Staff in 1939 and became Vice-Chief the following year. He held the post of Air Officer Commanding-in-Chief BOMBER COMMAND from 1940 until January 1942. Peirse was made a convenient scapegoat for Bomber Command's failures in the first two years of the war, when it lacked the resources to wage a strategic bombing offensive against Germany. He was succeeded by Air Marshal Arthur HARRIS. Peirse was then made AOC-in-India, where he built up the RAF's strength and laid the groundwork for the Assam–China airlift. In November 1943 he was appointed Allied Air Commander South East Asia Command and established the efficient system of air support and supply for the offensive which was to culminate in the re-occupation of Burma. He retired in November 1944. See also BURMA and THE HUMP.

Pennsylvania Class Battleships (USA)

Pennsylvania was damaged during the attack on PEARL HARBOR, but was repaired and saw active service in the ALEUTIANS, the GILBERT ISLANDS, KWAJALEIN, ENIWETOK, SAIPAN, GUAM, Palau, LEYTE, SURIGAO STRAIT and Lingayen. See also USS ARIZONA. *Displacement* 33,100 tons; *dimensions* 608ft×106ft 3in (185.3×32.4m); mean draught 29ft 6in (8.9m); *machinery* 4-shaft geared turbines producing shp 33,375; *speed* 21 knots; *protection* main belt 14in; turrets 18in; *armament* 12×14in (4×3); 12×5in (12×1); 12×5in AA; *aircraft* 3; *complement* 2290; *number in class* 2, both launched 1915 and rebuilt 1928–31.

Pensacola Class Heavy Cruisers (USA)

Displacement 9100 tons; *dimensions* 585ft 9in×65ft 3in (178.5×19.8m); mean draught 16ft 3in (4.95m); *machinery* 4-shaft geared turbines producing shp 107,000; *speed* 32.5 knots; *armament* 10×8in (2×3 and 2×2);

8×5in (8×1); *aircraft* 2; *complement* 1200; *number in class* 2, both launched 1929.

Percival, Lt Gen Arthur (1887–1966)

Percival was appointed General Officer Commanding MALAYA in July 1941. When the Japanese invaded on 8 December, many of the troops at his disposal were poorly trained and badly led and he was forced to conduct the ensuing campaign without adequate naval or air support. Outfought on the mainland, Percival ordered a withdrawal to SINGAPORE island on 27 January 1942. The Japanese crossed the Strait of Johore on 8 February and, although ordered by CHURCHILL to fight to the last man, he felt compelled to surrender unconditionally to General YAMASHITA on 15 February.

It was Percival's great misfortune to preside over the most catastrophic defeat in British military history, although many of the factors which contributed to the debacle lay beyond his control. He was imprisoned in Manchuria but was present aboard the USS *Missouri* to witness the final Japanese surrender in Tokyo Bay on 2 September 1945.

Perla Class Submarines (Italy)

Displacement 626 tons (700–860 tons normal); *dimensions* 197ft 6in×21ft (60.1×6.3m); *machinery* 2-shaft diesel/electric motors hp 1400/800; *speed* 14/8 knots; *armament* 1×3ft 9in; 2–4×13.2mm AA; 6×21in

torpedo tubes and 12 torpedoes; *complement* 45; *number in class* 10, all launched 1936.

Persecution

Allied assault on Aitape, New Guinea.

Pershing – Heavy Tank M26 (USA)

Conceived as a counter to the TIGER and PANTHER, the Pershing was developed through a series of experimental designs culminating in the T-26E3, the criteria set being a gun capable of penetrating the German tanks, low silhouette, heavy armour and overall battlefield mobility. The programme provoked disagreement between the Ordnance Department, the Armored Force and Army Ground Forces on technical as well as tactical grounds but in December 1944 the US Army's General Staff gave orders that the 20 available T-26E3s should be sent to Europe, where the enemy's counteroffensive in the ARDENNES was in progress. The tanks acquitted themselves well and in March 1945 the design was standardized as Heavy Tank M26 General Pershing. Wartime production amounted to 1436, of which 310 were shipped to Europe, although comparatively few saw action. A further 12 were sent to Okinawa but arrived too late to take part in the fighting. The Pershing was subsequently re-classified as a medium tank and in a re-designed form gave excellent service in the Korean War as the M46 Patton. *Weight* 41.7 tons; *speed* 30mph (48kph); *armour*

US Pershing tanks passing the burning town hall in Magdeburg.

102mm; *armament* 1 90mm gun; 2 .30-cal machine guns; 1 .50-cal machine gun; *engine* Ford GAF V-8 500hp petrol; *crew* 5.

Perth, HMAS – Leander Class Cruiser

Perth served with the Mediterranean Fleet in 1941, taking part in the Battle of CAPE MATAPAN and the fighting off CRETE, during which she sustained bomb damage. She then returned to Australia and took part in the Battle of the JAVA SEA, in the aftermath of which she was sunk by Japanese surface units during a hard fight against odds in the Sunda Strait.

Pétain, Marshal Henri Philippe Omer (1856–1951)

In World War I Pétain's defence of Verdun made him a national hero. He assumed the Presidency on 16 June 1940 and on 22 June offered the Germans an armistice, convinced that it was contrary to France's best interests to continue fighting and that the United Kingdom was also close to defeat. He established his government at VICHY in the unoccupied zone and pursued a policy of collaboration with the Germans, although in December 1940 he dismissed his Deputy, Pierre LAVAL, who wanted France to side with the Axis powers in the war. The Germans insisted on Laval's reinstatement, which was delayed until April 1942, and in November that year occupied the Vichy-controlled area of France following the Allied landings in French North Africa, reducing the status of Pétain's government to that of a puppet.

In August 1944 Pétain was taken to Germany but the following April he decided to return to France, where he was tried for treason and sentenced to death, although under pressure from DE GAULLE this was commuted to life imprisonment.

Peter II, King of Yugoslavia (1923–70)

Peter came to the throne in 1934 following the assassination of King Alexander, ruling through his Regent, Prince PAUL, until the latter was ousted by General SIMOVIĆ's coup in March 1941. When the Germans invaded in the following month, Peter and his government escaped to London, where they remained for the duration of the war. The King made a serious error of judgement in backing MIHAILOVIĆ and his Četniks, and although he reached an accommodation with TITO in November 1944, his influence had by then declined sharply. He never returned to

Soviet Petlyakov Pe-2 attack bombers.

YUGOSLAVIA and on 29 November 1945 Tito declared the country a republic.

Petlyakov Aircraft (USSR)

Petlyakov Pe-2 This outstanding combat aircraft entered service in 1940 and was frequently upgraded throughout the war. It was designed as a high-altitude fighter but was eventually employed as a bomber, interceptor fighter, reconnaissance machine and trainer at various times. Its principal employment was as a ground-attack aircraft and dive-bomber. *Span* 56.25ft (17m); *engines* 2 1600hp in-line; *crew* 2; *armament* 5 machine guns, 2200lb (1000kg) of bombs; *speed* 335mph (539kph).

Petlyakov Pe-8 The principal Russian heavy bomber, although strategic bombing played only a minor role in Soviet air planning. It appeared in 1940 with in-line engines, then changed to radials, and one version used diesel engines. Used principally against German and Balkan targets, numbers were also adapted as transporters. It remained in production until 1944, but relatively few were built as the Russians found the performance of their twin-engined bombers satisfactory. An unusual feature was the mounting of a single hand-held 127mm machine-gun in an open position in each of the inboard engine nacelles. *Span* 131.25ft (40m); *engines* 4 1630hp radial; *crew* 11; *armament* 2 20mm cannon, 4 machine guns, 8800lb (4000kg) of bombs; *speed* 275mph (442kph).

Petsamo, Finland, 1939–44

A part of northern Finland which was lost to Russia in the aftermath of the 1939–40 Winter War. In 1944 it was recaptured by German troops operating as Finland's allies against Russia. It was finally retaken by the Soviet 14th Army on 7 October 1944 and the German garrison, principally the 20th Mountain Army, withdrew into Norway.

Phantom

The codename for the British GHQ Liaison Regiment, Royal Armoured Corps. The regiment served in NORMANDY and North-West Europe where its role was to gather information on activity in the forward areas and beyond and report directly by radio to GHQ 21st Army Group rather through the more usual tiers of command. In similar fashion it immediately advised local formation commanders of the latest intelligence estimates prepared by GHQ. Despite its title, the regiment's personnel were recruited throughout the Army and included a large contingent drawn from the Royal Corps of Signals, the qualities required being similar to those demanded by the SPECIAL AIR SERVICE with special emphasis on above-average intelligence. One squadron was detached for service with the SAS Brigade and during Operation MARKET GARDEN the regimental teams with the various airborne divisions reported directly to HQ 1st Allied Airborne Army. The regiment took particular pride in its communications skills.

Philippine Islands, 1941–45

Although a US possession, by 1939 the Philippine Islands were largely self-governed, with General MACARTHUR as their defence chief. The islands were invaded by the Japanese on 8 December 1941. The combined US and Filipino forces were unable to stem the advancing Japanese and retreated into the BATAAN peninsula, where they held out until April 1942, and finally to CORREGIDOR, which surrendered on 6 May. Until 1944 the Japanese used the airfields and port facilities in the Philippines to aid their operations, but had little impact upon the civil population who did not rally to their cause. On 20 October 1944 US troops returned, led by MacArthur, landing on LEYTE Island. Japanese resistance on Leyte was over by the end of December 1944. KRUEGER's 6th Army then moved north to Luzon, liberating MANILA, the capital of the Philippines on 3/4 March 1945, after a desperate street-by-street battle. The fortress of CORREGIDOR had been cleared by the end of February and FORT DRUM, guarding Manila Bay, fell on 13 April. The bulk of US 6th Army then turned its attention to the mountain strongholds of YAMASHITA's Japanese 14th Army, which laid down its arms on 15 August. Nearly 200,000 Japanese were killed in the fight for Luzon; American dead were approximately 8000. Meanwhile, EICHELBERGER's US 8th Army had conducted a series of amphibious island-hopping operations to isolate and mop up the remaining elements of the Japanese 35th Army, concentrated on Mindanao in the southern Philippines. The islands were given their independence on 4 July 1946.

Philippine Sea, Battle of, 1944

With the gradual movement of the American forces across the Pacific and closer to Japan, the Japanese Navy had drawn up various plans for bringing the US Fleets into decisive battle, and when the Americans landed on SAIPAN on 15 June 1944, Admiral TOYODA felt that the time had come and issued orders to concentrate the Japanese fleet in the Philippine Sea. The Japanese movements were seen by US patrol submarines and reported to Admiral SPRUANCE at Saipan. He considered

Invasion of Cebu Island, Philippines, by 3rd Battalion, 132nd Infantry, Americal Division, March 1945.

Curtiss SB2C Helldiver bombers during the Great Marianas Turkey Shoot, July 1944.

sailing westwards to attack the Japanese, but felt that doing so would uncover Saipan and Tinian and risk being outflanked, so he decided to let the enemy come to him. Spruance's Task Force 58 consisted of four groups (TG58-1,-2,-3 and -4) totalling 15 aircraft carriers, with some 896 aircraft, each group supported by battleships, cruisers and destroyers. The Japanese fleet was in three groups (A, B and C) with six carriers and about 430 aircraft, but Admiral OZAWA, commanding the fleet, was also hoping for considerable support from land-based aircraft on GUAM, having no firm information on conditions on that island since the American attack.

The action began at 0455 hrs on 19 June 1944 when 16 seaplanes were catapulted from Japanese Force C to search for the Americans. Most were shot down by US standing patrols, some failed to find any target, but one sighted TG58-4 and reported it. This gave Ozawa some firm information at last, and he despatched his first strike force at 0845, a total of 244 aircraft, and immediately things began to go wrong. An American submarine, the USS *Albacore* struck the carrier TAIHO with a torpedo whilst it was actually launching aircraft; the damage was not lethal, but was poorly controlled and was to have fatal results in due course. Next came a slight contretemps when one Japanese squadron flew across a Japanese ship of another Group and was forth-

with attacked by anti-aircraft gunfire, resulting in two aircraft being shot down and eight having to return to their carrier for repair.

The action which followed has been called "THE GREAT MARIANAS TURKEY SHOOT" because of the execution done by American pilots. By this time the shortage of trained Japanese pilots was acute. US fighters were patrolling over the fleet and over Guam, and as land-based Japanese aircraft flew in to reinforce Guam, they were mostly destroyed. Then radar gave warning of the approach of the Japanese carrier aircraft, and the US carriers immediately launched every fighter they possessed, to be fought, landed, refuelled and re-flown throughout the day. The Japanese attacks were met some 50 miles (80km) out from the US fleet; of the first wave, none survived to threaten the US carriers. Of the second wave, about 20 survived the fighters to be decimated by fleet gunfire, and no more than a handful were able to attack, doing very little damage. But the survivors managed to regain their carriers and deliver glowing reports of American aircraft in flames and American carriers sunk.

Now more disaster befell the Japanese; another US submarine, the *Cavalla*, had spotted the Japanese fleet on the previous day, reported it, and had then followed in the hope of catching it. At 1220 Ozawa turned his fleet into wind to launch more aircraft and *Cavalla*

put three torpedoes into the carrier SHOKAKU, which exploded and sank some three hours later. At almost the same time as this attack took place, the *Taiho* succumbed to its earlier torpedo hit; this had ruptured the aircraft fuelling system and the ship had filled with petrol fumes, which were now ignited by a chance spark and set her ablaze from end to end; she finally capsized and sank.

The last Japanese aircraft strikes were now launched, with orders to make for the southern US carrier group, attack, and then fly on to land at Guam to refuel and re-arm, Ozawa still being under the impression that Guam was operating normally. The aircraft were misdirected, less than half managed to find targets, against which they made ineffective attacks and were mostly shot down. The remainder flew on to Guam to find the Japanese airfield a mass of craters and ruins and covered by American fighters which promptly shot most of them down. About 18 carrier planes managed to land, but they were ineffective from then on. At the end of the day Ozawa had about 100 serviceable aircraft on his carriers. American losses had been 29 aircraft. However, Ozawa was under the impression that many of his missing aircraft had landed on Guam and that there were also ample reinforcing aircraft there. He had also believed the stories told by his pilots of vast American losses.

Overnight the two fleets had veered apart, but on the following day Ozawa first turned west to make a refuelling rendezvous, and then postponed this and turned eastward once more to find the US fleet and resume battle. The delay had allowed the American fleet to get within flying range and at 1600 on 20 June a scout from the *Enterprise* detected the Japanese force. According to the book, it was now too late to fly off a US strike, since it would be dark when they returned and the US pilots were not trained in making night carrier landings. Nevertheless, Admiral MITSCHER decided to risk all for a final blow and flew off 77 dive-bombers, 54 torpedo-bombers and an escort of 85 fighters. The Japanese fighter screen was brushed aside and in 20 minutes three Japanese carriers were damaged, one sinking; one battleship and one cruiser were severely damaged, and only 35 Japanese aircraft remained. The six Japanese fleet tankers had also been found and set on fire, and Ozawa had no choice but to turn tail and run for Okinawa with what was left of his fleet.

The returning American aircraft arrived over their carriers in darkness, and, disregarding risk from possible submarines, the carriers employed every form of illumination they could to aid the landings. But no less than 80 aircraft crashed on landing or plunged into the sea as their fuel ran out, though almost all the crews were saved. Only 16 pilots and 33 aircraft were lost during the entire action.

So ended the last of the great carrier battles, a decisive victory for the American forces. Although a number of Japanese carriers remained afloat, they had few aircraft and fewer pilots, and at that stage of the war little chance of replacing either. The Japanese Navy was a spent force.

Phoenix, USS – Brooklyn Class Light Cruiser

A veteran of PEARL HARBOR, *Phoenix* also saw active service at HOLLANDIA, LEYTE, Mindoro, Lingayen and BORNEO. Sold to Argentina as *17 de Octubre* in 1951 and renamed *General Belgrano* in 1956, she was torpedoed and sunk by the submarine HMS *Conqueror* during the Falklands War on 2 May 1982.

Piaggio P108B (I)

Italy's principal heavy bomber, the P108 entered service in 1942. An unusual feature was the provision of remote-controlled 12.7mm machine guns in the outer engine nacelles. No more than 163 were built, but they served in the Mediterranean area, making several raids on Malta and Gibraltar, and on Tunisia. *Span* 105ft (32m); *engine* 4 1500hp radial; *crew* 7; *armament* 8 machine guns, 7700lb (3500kg) of bombs; *speed* 270mph (434kph).

PIAT

An abbreviation for Projector, Infantry, Anti-tank, a British weapon which discharged a small anti-tank bomb to a range of about 120yds (110m). The weapon was a "spigot discharger", using a heavy steel rod propelled by a spring as its operating mode. The bomb had a hollow tail shaft containing a propelling cartridge and a shaped-charge warhead. The bomb was laid in a trough at the front of the PIAT; on pulling the trigger the steel spigot was released and flew forward, into the tail of the bomb, to fire the cartridge. The explosion launched the bomb and also re-cocked the spigot ready for the next shot.

Piecemaker

A British 13.5inch RAILWAY GUN, one of three (the others were Scene-shifter and Gladiator) operating in the vicinity of Dover in 1940–44 to defend the coastline and also to shell German positions on the French coast. They were originally manned by Royal Marine Artillery, one of whose gunners was killed on 10 December 1940 when a German 28cm shell fell close to Piecemaker and damaged its running gear. In November 1943 they were handed over to the Royal Artillery and formed into a Superheavy Railway Regiment, intended for use on the continent, but Allied air superiority rendered them superfluous and they were never shipped from England.

Pinguin – Surface Raider (Ger)

Also known as Ship 33 and Raider F. Sailed 22 June 1940 and operated in the Atlantic, Indian

Piat in action, Germany 1945.

and Pacific Oceans, sinking or capturing 28 ships of 136,551 tons, including three factory ships and 11 whale catchers of the Norwegian Whaling Fleet in the Antarctic on 14–15 January 1941. Sunk by the cruiser HMS *Cornwall* off the Seychelles on 8 May 1941. *Displacement* 7766 tons; *speed* 16 knots; *armament* 6×5.9in; 1×3in; 2×37mm AA; 2×20mm AA; 4×21in torpedo tubes; equipped for mine-laying; *aircraft* 2; *complement* 470.

Piper L4 Grasshopper (USA)

A high-wing cabin monoplane, the Grasshopper was widely used by the US Army as a liaison and observation plane, and for laying telephone cable at high speed in the wake of advancing troops, delivering mail and rations and dropping smoke bombs to guide air strikes. *Span* 35.25ft (10.75m); *engine* 1 65hp in-line; *speed* 90mph (145kph).

Plastic Armour

A type of armour developed by the Royal Navy for protecting the upperworks of merchant ships against machine-gun bullets and bomb fragments. Due to the critical shortage of armour plate steel, Plastic Armour, made from a bitumen composition containing granite chippings, was cast in blocks and attached around ships' bridges and pilot houses, providing adequate protection against casual air attacks.

Platoon

Tactical and administrative sub-unit of a COMPANY. The infantry platoon consisted of platoon headquarters and three rifle sections. The tank platoon contained three or more tanks, but in British and Commonwealth armies this was referred to as a troop.

Ploesti, Romania, 1943–44

City some 35 miles (56km) north of Bucharest and centre of the Romanian oil industry. Under German domination, it was a vital centre for the supply of fuel for the German Army and so an important target for air attack. Its location, far from any Allied airfields, left it inviolate for a long time, but on 1 August 1943 it was struck by a strong force of US Liberator bombers. A force of 177 bombers made the attack, of which 50 were lost, principally due to the long flight over a strongly defended area. Attacks from Italy became possible in April 1944. The area was captured by the Russians on 30 August 1944, finally cutting off the supply of fuel to the Germans.

Plum

American codename for the PHILIPPINE ISLANDS.

Plunder

Crossing of the RHINE by MONTGOMERY's 21st Army Group, March 1945.

Pluto

The supply of petrol from England to the Continent by means of submarine pipeline following OVERLORD. Acronym for Pipeline Under The Ocean.

Pointblank

Directive issued to RAF BOMBER COMMAND and US 8th Air Force to focus attacks on German fighter production targets, 10 June 1943.

POL Petrol, Oil and Lubricants (UK). Generic term to cover fuel requirements when planning.

9th Air Force bombers swooping over Ploesti, August 1943.

Poland

Poland came into existence as an independent nation in 1919, fighting for survival against Russia, Lithuania and Czechoslovakia in its early years. Due to a long history of occupation, the Poles had great difficulty in forming a stable government, and in 1919 Marshal Pilsudski marched on Warsaw and replaced the faltering democratic government with his own form of dictatorship. The Versailles Treaty sowed the seeds of war in establishing the POLISH CORRIDOR, and this, coupled with the Polish inability to temporize with neighbours, was to prove fatal.

HITLER, appreciating the anti-Soviet attitude of the Poles, signed the Polish-German Treaty in 1934. This allowed him to deal with the Rhineland, Austria and Czechoslovakia, after which he turned back to Poland to demand access across the Polish Corridor and the return of the old German port of DANZIG. When this was refused, Hitler allied himself with Russia, and Britain and France assured Poland of aid if war broke out.

Poland was invaded by Hitler on 1 September 1939, the first demonstration of the BLITZKRIEG tactic, and the main body of Polish forces surrendered after 36 days of fighting, though the Fortress of Modlin and other outposts held out until 7 October. The Polish defensive strategy was finally undermined on 17 September when, in accordance with a secret agreement in the German-Soviet Pact, Soviet troops advanced across Poland's eastern border to occupy the country to the line of the Narva, Bug and San rivers. (See POLAND, INVASION OF.) Within the German half of Poland some territory was incorporated directly into the Reich, whilst the remainder became the "General Government" of Occupied Poland. Conditions here were repressive, but the principal victims were the Jews, and Poland was selected as the site for the extermination camps of the FINAL SOLUTION.

Eastern Poland was entirely absorbed into the USSR and has remained there ever since. Conditions here deteriorated rapidly; the Ukrainian minority rose against the Poles, and all Poles of any social standing were carried off to labour camps in Siberia. Polish troops who surrendered to the Soviet army were either imprisoned or murdered. This area subsequently became a battleground during the German invasion of Russia and again as the Soviet forces drove the Germans back in

Poles are shown how to operate a Piat gun, one of the weapons supplied from the air by the British during the 1944 Rebellion.

1944. Abortive risings in WARSAW in 1943 and 1944 merely added to the damage. A Polish government-in-exile was formed under General SIKORSKI in Paris on 30 September 1939; it was subsequently located in Angers and then moved to London in 1940. With the German invasion of Russia the Soviet attitude towards the Poles changed; those prisoners who had survived were released to fight against Germany, and an alternative, Communist, government-in-exile was formed in Moscow and later installed in LUBLIN. Subsequently, the London government was spurned by the Soviets after the KATYN WOOD incident. At the cessation of hostilities, therefore, Poland had two governments, one backed by the Western Allies and the other manipulated by the Soviets. A provisional Government of National Unity was formed in June 1945, and in July recognition of the London government was withdrawn by the Western Allies.

Poland, Invasion of

Poland was invaded on 1 September 1939 by a German force approximating to 58 divisions, including seven armoured, four light armoured and four motorized infantry divisions. This force included about 2800 tanks and armoured vehicles and was supported by some 2000 aircraft, including 900 bombers and 230 dive-bombers. In defence, Poland had 32 infantry brigades, 11 cavalry brigades and two mechanized brigades. In accordance with the treaties signed with Britain and France, the Poles expected to have to hold the German onslaught for about 14 days while the British and French mobilized and attacked Germany in the west. In the event, this never happened and the Poles survived 36 days before being overwhelmed.

The German plan used two Army Groups, the southern under General von RUNDSTEDT and the northern under General von BOCK. Their basic tactic was that of encirclement; the northern group, moving from both sides of the POLISH CORRIDOR, aimed two assaults, one towards WARSAW and one towards Brest-Litovsk, while the southern group, moving from southern Germany, also aimed two assaults towards the same objectives. The "inner encirclement" would remove a high proportion of the Polish defences, while the "outer encirclement" would take care of the rest. Initial air strikes against Polish airfields neutralized most of the Polish air force and gave the Luftwaffe air superiority for the entire campaign. The Poles fought back valiantly, but by 6 September the "inner encirclement" was completed and tens of thousands of Poles were cut off. On 9 September a Polish counter-attack from the area of Torun and Lodz posed a threat to the Germans advancing towards Warsaw, but rapid redeployment of the German forces resulted in the Battle of the Bzura in which over 100,000 Poles were taken prisoner. The "outer encirclement" was completed on 17 September when the two Army Groups met to the east of Brest-Litovsk, and on the same day Soviet troops invaded across the eastern Polish border. The Polish government fled to Romania, and on 27 September Warsaw fell to the Germans. The fortress of Modlin and other small outposts continued resistance until 7 October. Large numbers of Polish troops managed to escape over the Romanian border and eventually made their way to France, to form a Polish Army in exile.

Polikarpov Aircraft (USSR)

Polikarpov I-15 The I-15 biplane fighter entered Soviet service in 1933 and in 1935 a modified machine held the World Altitude Record at 47,818ft (14,574m). Large numbers were built and they saw service in the Spanish Civil War, China and the Russo-Finnish War. By the time of the German invasion they were obsolescent, but a number of the late production I-153 model with retractable undercarriage were employed during the early period of the war, mainly as fighter-bombers. *Span* 30ft (9.1m); *engine* 1 1000hp radial; *armament* 4 machine guns, 220lb (100kg) of bombs; *speed* 267mph (430kph).

Polikarpov I-16 This was contemporary with the I-15 but was a more modern design, a single-engined low-wing monoplane. It saw combat in Spain, China and Finland, and it continued in first-line service until 1943. Powered by the same 1000hp engine, it reached 326mph (525kph) and was armed with two 20mm ShVAK cannon and two ShKAS machine guns. It could also carry a small bomb load and was armed with rockets towards the end of its service. *Span* 29.5ft (9m).

Polikarpov Po-2 A basic two-seat biplane trainer which became a maid of all work, used for training, dropping agents in enemy territory, towing gliders and night bombing. With a 110hp engine it could barely reach 95mph (153kph) when fully loaded, and like most of the "stick and string" aircraft of its era was highly resistant to damage. Its armament varied according to its role but rarely exceeded three machine guns.

Polish Corridor

Part of Poland which extended north to the Baltic, separating East Prussia from Germany proper. One of the points of contention between Germany and Poland was a German demand to be permitted to build an autobahn and double-track railway from Germany to East Prussia across the Corridor, this communication zone to be granted extra-territorial rights, a proposal which the Poles refused to consider.

Polish Home Army

Formed as a clandestine army at the end of September 1939 by General Michal Karaszewicz-Tokrzewski, who was arrested after only a few months. His successor, General Stephan Rowecki, commanded the Army from 1940 until his arrest in 1943, when he was succeeded by General Tadeusz BOR KOMOROWSKI. After the WARSAW rising, August–October 1944, the Army was commanded by General Leopold Okulicki. In 1945 the Soviets, wishing to rid themselves of the pre-war Polish establishment, arrested Okulicki on trumped-up charges, staged a show trial and sentenced him to a term of imprisonment which he did not survive. The Army was

responsible to the Polish government-in-exile in London and had its headquarters in Warsaw, dividing the country into military regions, districts and sub-districts. It was commanded by regular army officers and its recruits consisted of former soldiers and civilian volunteers of both sexes. Its maximum strength fluctuated between 350,000 and 600,000. It was armed with stocks of weapons which had been hidden in 1939, supplemented with captured German equipment, and was eventually able to produce its own arms. Later in the war supplies from the West were air-dropped. Its functions included sabotage and intelligence gathering, and although it provided ample warning that HITLER intended invading the Soviet Union, this was ignored. In 1944 some of its units materially assisted the advance of the Soviet Army, particularly at VILNA, but after they had served their purpose the Russians disbanded them and interned their leaders. The Soviet attitude to the Warsaw rising was based on self-interested cynicism; no matter who emerged the victor, the continued existence of a Polish army loyal to the government-in-exile was not acceptable to the Kremlin.

Polish Tanks

On the outbreak of war the approximate tank strength of the Polish Army was 450 TKS tankettes; 125 7 TP light tanks; 50 RENAULT R35S; 55

RENAULT FT-17S; 35 locally-built Vickers six-ton tanks; and 90 armoured cars. After 1939 Polish troops in exile used the equipment of the army with which they were fighting, i.e. French, British or Soviet.

Popov, Gen Markian M. (1902–   )

When Germany invaded the Soviet Union in June 1941, Popov was Commander of the Leningrad Military District, designated the Northern Front later in the year. He was reprimanded for his lack of energy and reduced to the level of army commander. In the autumn of 1942 he was appointed Deputy to YEREMENKO, then commanding the Stalingrad Front. After the German surrender at STALINGRAD in February 1943, Popov led a Front Mobile Group during the advance on KHARKOV. This consisted of four tank corps, two independent tank brigades, three rifle divisions and ski troops and, although a formidable force, outran its supplies and was routed when von MANSTEIN counter-attacked in May 1943. Popov then became commander of the Bryansk Front, launching the Soviet counteroffensive into the OREL salient when the German offensive directed at KURSK failed in July 1943. In 1944 he was given command of the 2nd Baltic Front, but the stubborn German defence on this sector halted his advance on Ostrov in February 1944, earning him his dismissal and another reprimand from the Committee for the Defence of the State. He was replaced by YEREMENKO.

Porpoise Class Minelaying Submarines (UK)

Displacement 1520/2157 tons; *dimensions* 289ft×25ft 6in (88×7.77m); *machinery* 2-shaft diesel/electric motors producing bhp 3300/1630; *speed* 15/8.75 knots; *armament* 1×4in; 2 machine guns; 6×21in torpedo tubes (bow); 50 mines; *complement* 59; *number in class* 6, launched 1932–38.

Portal, ACM Sir Charles (1893–1971)

Portal was Chief of Air Staff from 4 October 1940 until 1945, establishing a constructive working relationship with CHURCHILL and the Americans. He was an early advocate of AREA BOMBING, and at the CASABLANCA CONFERENCE reached agreement with the Americans on the form of the Combined Bomber Offensive to be pursued by BOMBER COMMAND and the USAAF. The objectives were to be "the progressive destruction and dislocation of the German

General Sikorski's Secret Army, Poland 1944.

Rhodesian anti-tank battery in action against German tanks.

military, industrial system, and the undermining of the morale of the German people to a point where their capacity for armed resistance is fatally weakened". By September 1944 Portal was in full agreement with SPAATZ, Commander-in-Chief of the US Strategic Air Forces in Europe, that the combined air offensive should concentrate on targets associated with the German oil industry. However, Portal signally failed to persuade the wilful Commander-in-Chief of Bomber Command, HARRIS, to join the Americans wholeheartedly in the oil campaign. Harris virtually chose to ignore his superior, and such was his prestige and authority that Portal shrank from relieving him of his command at this stage in the war. Had priority been given to the oil campaign, rather than the continued pounding of Germany's cities, the war would almost certainly have been shortened.

Portcullis

MALTA relief convoy, December 1942.

Portée

The practice of carrying light guns into action on the back of motor vehicles from which they were removed when required to fire. This was adopted by the British Army in the Western Desert in 1940/41 in order to move anti-tank guns more rapidly than they could be safely towed. It was soon discovered that it was possible to fire these guns without removing them from the carrying vehicle and this practice superseded the earlier definition.

Porter Class Destroyers (USA)

Displacement 1850 tons; *dimensions* 381ft 3in×37ft (116.2×11.1m); mean draught 10ft 6in (3.2m); *machinery* 2-shaft geared turbines producing shp 50,000; *speed* 37 knots; *armament* 8×5in (4×2); 8×21in torpedo tubes (2×4); *complement* 290; *number in class* 8, launched 1935–36.

Port Moresby, New Guinea

A seaport and small town on the south coast of New Guinea, control of which would have enabled the Japanese to isolate Australia. It was the objective of a Japanese campaign in mid-1942, being first bombed on 5 May. The Battle of the CORAL SEA destroyed Japanese hopes of direct invasion, and their next move was to land a force on the northern coast of New Guinea and attempt to advance on Port Moresby across the OWEN STANLEY MOUNTAINS by way of the KOKODA TRAIL. They were held by Australian and American troops and withdrew, after which Port Moresby was no longer in danger.

Portugal

Portugal, under the rule of Antonio Salazar, who combined the offices of Prime and Foreign Minister, remained neutral throughout the war, largely for economic reasons, Salazar considering the country too poor to provide any worthwhile force and likely to be bankrupted by intervention. As a result Portugal played a valuable role as the forum in which combatants could meet for secret and informal conferences, was a hive of espionage

activity, and acted as a staging point for air transport for both sides. It also became the terminus of various escape and resistance organizations moving escaping prisoners of war and refugees out of German-occupied Europe. Citing a 14th-century treaty, CHURCHILL persuaded Salazar, in October 1943, to permit the Allies to use the Azores as a base for aircraft, which gave them total coverage of the Atlantic with significant results in the war against the U-boats. Thus from 1943 Portugal was a co-belligerent in fact, if not in name, and was rewarded by founder membership of the United Nations.

Potez Aircraft (Fr)

Potez 54 A French bomber and reconnaissance aircraft, the Potez 54 was a high-wing monoplane with twin engines on short wing stubs at the bottom of the fuselage. With two 690hp or 780hp in-line engines, it carried a bomb-load of 2200lb (1000kg) and had a top speed of 150mph (240kph). Entering service in 1935, some 220 were built. Early models had a twin tail unit, but most production versions had a large single fin. A civil variant, the Potez 62 was used by Air France and a modification of this, known as the Potez 620, was used as a troop-carrier by the French Army.

Potez 63 The Potez 63 was a twin-engined low-wing monoplane aircraft which functioned as fighter, attack aircraft, light bomber, dive-bomber and reconnaissance machine. As a fighter it entered French service in 1937, and just under 300 were built. With two 640hp radial engines it attained a top speed of 277mph (445kph) and was armed with two 20mm cannon and eight machine guns. A further 115 were built as attack bombers, 61 as observation machines and 717 as reconnaissance aircraft. Numbers were also exported to Greece, Romania and Switzerland. Several of the French machines were taken into use by the Luftwaffe for communications duties.

Potsdam

Now almost a suburb of Berlin, Potsdam was about 12 miles (20km) to the south-west and was the state residence of the Kaisers, imperial capital of the Second Reich and a military garrison town. Its state buildings were the site of a conference between Allied heads of state on 17 July–2 August 1945. STALIN attended, as did President TRUMAN, and CHURCHILL brought ATTLEE with him; both returned to England to hear the election results on 26 July, after which Churchill remained at home and Attlee returned to the conference as Prime Minister. Beyond celebrating victory, the most significant result was the Potsdam Declaration of 26 July, a broadcast to Japan repeating the demand for unconditional surrender. Truman and Churchill had also informed Stalin of a "new and powerful weapon" for use against Japan, though without specifying its nature; it is probable that Stalin had been fully informed of the atomic bomb by his espionage organization.

Pound, Adm of the Fleet Sir Dudley (1877–1943)

Pound commanded the battleship *Colossus* at Jutland in 1916. He was Commander-in-Chief Mediterranean, 1936–39, and was then appointed First Sea Lord and Chief of Naval Staff. Until March 1942 he chaired the British Chiefs of Staff Committee, when BROOKE took over the function. Pound was also a member of the Anglo-US Combined Chiefs of Staff Committee. Pound was the only member of the COS responsible both for the operational control of his own service and for its direction in battle. He was a glutton for hard work, and during this period was suffering from a brain tumour. Inevitably, this impaired his judgement, notably when he ordered the scattering of CONVOY PQ-17. He died on 21 October 1943, three weeks after resigning, and was succeeded by CUNNINGHAM.

PoW Prisoner-of-War (UK).

PPI Plan Position Indicator. A type of display used with RADAR in which a circular cathode ray tube displays a map of the surrounding area.

PPR Polish Workers' Party.

PR Photographic Reconnaissance. A survey using aerial photography.

Prasca, Gen Visconti

In October 1940 Prasca was Commander-in-Chief of the Italian forces in ALBANIA. He was responsible for planning MUSSOLINI's invasion of GREECE, expressing confidence that it would achieve its object before the Greek Army was fully mobilized. When the Italians were routed by the Greek counteroffensive, Mus-

solini blamed the failure on Prasca's unfounded optimism, although he was the real author of his own misfortune.

Prételat, Gen G.

In May 1940 Prételat commanded the French 2nd Army Group, the three armies of which held the MAGINOT LINE from the Swiss frontier to Longuyon. Most of the Army Group was trapped in its positions when the Germans overran central France in June. In September 1939 Prételat had commanded the so-called "Saar Offensive" in which nine divisions had advanced five miles (8km) to the outposts of the German SIEGFRIED LINE before withdrawing after the capitulation of POLAND. It was France's first and last offensive operation of the war.

PRF Pulse Repetition Frequency. The frequency with which a RADAR set emits a measuring pulse, several thousands of times per second.

Prien, Lt Cdr Günther (1908–41)

During his career as commander of the German submarine *U-47* Prien sank 28 ships, a total of 160,000 tons. On 14 October 1939 he penetrated the British Home Fleet anchorage of Scapa Flow and torpedoed the battleship HMS ROYAL OAK, which sank with heavy loss of life. On 7 March 1941 *U-47* was herself sunk by the British corvettes *Arbutus* and *Camellia* and the destroyer *Wolverine*. Prien went down with his submarine. Such was his popularity that the news of his death was concealed from the German public for a further two months.

Priest 105mm Self-Propelled Howitzer

See HOWITZER MOTOR CARRIAGE M7.

Prince of Wales, HMS – King George V Class Battleship

On 24 May 1941, while serving with the Home Fleet, *Prince of Wales* sustained damage when, in company with the battlecruiser HMS HOOD, she engaged the German battleship BISMARCK and cruiser PRINZ EUGEN in the Denmark Strait. In return she damaged the *Bismarck*, causing a critical loss of fuel, but was forced to disengage following the loss of the *Hood*. In August she took CHURCHILL to Newfoundland for his meeting with ROOSEVELT. She was then sent to Singapore with the battlecruiser HMS REPULSE, forming

the major units of Force Z. She was sunk by Japanese aircraft off the east coast of Malaya on 10 December 1941.

Princeton, USS – Independence and Essex Class Aircraft Carriers

Princeton (CVL.23) was launched on 18 October 1942 and saw active service at BOUGAINVILLE, the GILBERT ISLANDS, KWAJALEIN, ENIWETOK, HOLLANDIA, the MARIANAS and Palau. She was sunk after an air attack east of LUZON during the Battle of LEYTE GULF on 24 October 1944. Her name, however, was transferred to the ESSEX CLASS carrier *Valley Forge* (CV.37), which was launched on 8 July 1945.

Prinz Eugen, KMS – Admiral Hipper Class Heavy Cruiser

Prinz Eugen accompanied the battleship BISMARCK during her foray into the Atlantic and took part in the engagement against HMS HOOD and PRINCE OF WALES on 24 May 1941. Following this she was detached by Admiral LÜTJENS and reached Brest on 1 June. On 12 February 1942 she broke out in company with SCHARNHORST and GNEISENAU and succeeded in reaching home water. She then formed part of the Training Squadron in the Baltic and in 1944 supported the army's operations with gunfire. Allocated to the USA after the war, *Prinz Eugen* was used in the Bikini Atoll atomic bomb tests and was finally sunk at Kwajalein on 15 November 1947.

Prioux, Gen R.

During the 1940 campaign in the West Prioux commanded the French Army's élite Cavalry Corps, which on 13 May fought the first major tank battle of the war against HÖPNER's XVI Panzer Corps in the GEMBLOUX GAP, enabling Blanchard's 1st French Army to consolidate its positions on the DYLE. The losses incurred in this action, and the subsequent dispersion of his strength, seriously reduced Prioux's capacity to act but on 21 May some of his units took part in the ARRAS counter-attack. He assumed command of the 1st Army when Blanchard took over the 1st Army Group following BILLOTTE's death in a traffic accident. After his command post was overrun on 27 May he was interned in Königstein Castle.

Pripet Marshes, Poland-Soviet Union

A large area of swampland lying along the Pripet river, roughly between Brest-Litovsk and Pinsk. In 1939 it was wild and sparsely populated, and thus became a haven for Polish resistance forces in 1940–41. In June 1941 it served to split the German fronts in the opening phase of Operation BARBAROSSA. Thereafter it provided an almost impregnable refuge for Soviet partisans operating behind the German lines.

Prisoners-of-War, Treatment of

The basic rights of prisoners to humane treatment, the limitations imposed on their interrogation and the nature of the duties on which they could or could not be employed were defined by the Geneva Convention of 1929, to which the majority of combatant nations were signatories, the most notable exceptions being the Soviet Union and Japan. The Western Allies abided by the terms of the Convention with regard to Axis prisoners and, in general, the Germans and Italians treated their Western prisoners correctly. The Nazi authorities felt they were under no obligation towards their Soviet captives, thousands of whom were massacred by the SS EINSATZGRUP-PEN while many more perished as a result of overwork, starvation and brutal treatment in slave labour camps. The Germans also

regarded PARTISANS and *francs-tireurs* as being outside the law and frequently executed any who fell into their hands, often after torturing them. The protection of the Geneva Convention was also refused to members of the SPECIAL AIR SERVICE brigade. The Soviets also felt little obligation towards their prisoners and were guilty of the mass murder of Polish officers at KATYN WOOD. Of those Germans captured on the Eastern Front only a small percentage survived the climate, the hard labour, the harsh conditions of their confinement, and the attentions of the NKVD; those who returned home did so many years after the war had ended. The concept of surrender was deeply abhorrent to the Japanese, the majority of whom preferred suicide to submission. As a result comparatively few Japanese were captured, although the numbers rose towards the end of the war. Conversely, the Japanese regarded Allied prisoners as being dishonoured men who had forfeited any right to respect. This attitude was reflected in the treatment of captives, which varied between sadistic cruelty and callous indifference, particularly in the matters of rations and medical treatment, and as a result

of this thousands died or emerged with their health permanently broken. Prisoners were employed by the Japanese on such hard-labour projects as the KWAI RAILWAY and coal mining in the home islands. The majority of Japanese guards were unemployable in any other capacity.

Prome, Burma, 1945

A town on the Irrawaddy River, at the end of a railway line from RANGOON. It was captured by the 20th Indian Division on 2 May 1945, during the advance on Rangoon, a key manoeuvre which prevented any Japanese troops escaping from the ARAKAN area and reinforcing Rangoon.

Proximity Fuze

A fuze designed to function by detecting the presence of the target without having to make contact with it. The first such fuze was the British "Pistol No 710" introduced in 1941 for use with 3inch anti-aircraft rockets, which relied upon photo-electric circuitry, detecting the shadow of an aircraft and detonating the rocket warhead. A shell fuze which would detect the reflections from ground RADAR sets

American prisoners en route to POW camps, Tunisia, March 1945.

was proposed in 1940 but found unworkable. The next idea was to build a small radio transmitter and receiver into a fuze so that it would emit radio signals and detect their reflection from the target, triggering the explosive when within lethal distance. Since no facilities for research or manufacture were available in Britain, the plans were sent to the USA with the Tizard Mission in 1940 and the development was undertaken by the US Navy. A workable radio proximity fuze was in use by the middle of 1943 with the US Navy in the Pacific, and designs suitable for field anti-aircraft guns were ready in time for use against the V-1 flying bomb attack on Britain in 1944. In December 1944 proximity fuzes were used in the Ardennes against ground troops for the first time. Proximity fuzes were also developed for use in aerial bombs so as to obtain a controlled height of burst. The Germans developed a number of proximity fuzes for use with guided missiles, relying upon radio, acoustic, photo-electric and electrostatic principles, but none went past the research stage.

PT (Patrol-Torpedo) Boats (USA)

Displacing 34 to 38 tons, these craft were powered by 3-shaft petrol engines producing 4050 shp and had a maximum speed of 40 knots. They were armed with four 18- or 21-inch torpedo tubes, plus one 40mm and/or two 20mm guns. They also carried 0.50-inch heavy machine guns. Their complement varied between 12 and 17 depending upon type. Their early exploits included the evacuation of General MACARTHUR from the PHILIPPINES and a series of fierce engagements with Japanese destroyers during the GUADALCANAL campaign, one of them involving *PT-109*, commanded by the then Lieutenant John F. Kennedy, later President of the United States.

Patrol-torpedo (PT) boats.

PT Boat squadrons took part in all subsequent South Pacific coastal operations as well as the liberation of the Philippines. For over a year they were the only American naval craft in the Mediterranean and four squadrons were transferred from the Pacific to take part in the Allied invasion of NORMANDY.

Ptolmais, Greece, 1941

A town in northern Greece which lay on the route of the main German advance in 1941. With a dyke, a river and two ridges of hills, the town presented a natural obstacle, and it was selected as a British rearguard position on 13 April 1941 to hold up the German advance and allow other troops to retire to regroup. It was held by the 4th Hussars with light tanks, a squadron of 3rd Royal Tank Regiment with cruiser tanks, two troops of 2-pdr anti-tank guns of the Northumberland Hussars, two Greek infantry companies and a regiment of Royal Horse Artillery armed with 25-pdr guns. This scratch force inflicted severe casualties on the German 9th Panzer division but by 15 April was reduced to half its strength and had to abandon the position and fall back.

Pugilist

British 8th Army attack on the MARETH LINE, Tunisia, March 1943.

Puma

Planned British occupation of the Canary Islands, 1941.

Puma Armoured Car (Ger)

See SONDERKRAFTFAHRZEUG 234 SERIES.

Punishment

German invasion of YUGOSLAVIA, April 1941.

Puppchen

A German wheeled 88mm rocket launcher which resembled a small artillery gun. Using a closed breech, it fired a fin-stabilised shaped charge anti-tank projectile. A small number were completed and put into service late in 1944.

Purple Code

The American name for a Japanese diplomatic cipher system generated by the Alphabetical Typewriter 97, a machine similar to the German ENIGMA. The cipher was broken on 25 September 1940 and thereafter the Americans were able to read all Japanese diplomatic messages. Deciphering machines were built and a number were supplied to the British early in 1941.

Pu Yi, Henry, Emperor of Manchukuo (1906–67)

Pu Yi was the great nephew of Tzu Hsi, the Dowager Empress of China, and came to the Manchu throne while still a boy in 1908. He abdicated following the revolution of 1911, but on 18 February 1932 the Japanese made him Emperor of their puppet state of Manchukuo (Manchuria). He possessed neither power nor any interest in politics and for these reasons survived World War II and the Chinese Civil War. He was subsequently employed in industry and often stated that he enjoyed more freedom as a factory worker than he had ever done as Emperor.

PW Prisoner-of-War (US).

PWE Political Warfare Executive (UK). British organization responsible for propaganda and clandestine operations in occupied Europe.

PWS 26 (Poland)

A two-seat biplane used principally as a trainer and for liaison flights, although a few were used operationally as reconnaissance light bombers. 243 were built, of which almost all were destroyed during the German invasion. Powered by a 220hp radial engine it achieved a speed of 135mph (217kph) and was armed with a single machine gun.

PX Post Exchange (US). American forces canteen and welfare service.

Pyle, Ernest (1900–45)

An American war correspondent famous for his graphic despatches on the German bombing offensive against LONDON. He later covered the campaigns in North Africa, SICILY, Italy and FRANCE, as well as the assault landings on IWO JIMA and OKINAWA, being killed in the forward combat area on 18 April 1945. He concentrated on the experiences of the ordinary citizen and soldier at war, his vivid first-hand accounts winning him the Pulitzer Prize and many other awards.

PZL Aircraft (Poland)

PZL P-11 A single-seat monoplane fighter aircraft powered by a 500hp engine, the P-11 entered Polish service in 1933 and was soon followed by the P11c variant with redesigned fuselage and a 645hp engine giving it a top speed of 242mph (389kph). It was designed to carry four machine guns, though frequently only two were fitted. By 1937 200 were in service, but by 1939 they were obsolescent. Despite this they put up a hard fight and were able to claim 128 German aircraft shot down. *Span* 35ft (10.7m).

PZL P-23B Karas A three-seat reconnaissance bomber which entered service in 1936 and was the principal tactical attack aircraft of the Polish air force. Powered by a 580hp engine and with a span of 45.5ft (13.9m), it could reach a speed of 198mph (318kph) and carried a 1550lb (700kg) bomb-load; it was armed with three machine guns. Many were destroyed on the ground in September 1939, or shot down during costly attacks on German columns, but a few were able to escape to Romania where they were taken into use by the Romanian air force.

PZL P-24 This was the most modern of the PZL fighters and was exported or built under licence in Romania, Bulgaria, Turkey and Greece but not produced for the Polish air force. Those in Greek hands served well against the Italian and German attacks in 1941. It was a gull-winged monoplane with a 970hp radial engine. *Span* 35ft (10.7m); *armament* 2 20mm cannon and 2 machine guns or 4 machine guns; *speed* 267mph (430kph).

PZL P-37B Los The P-37 was a sleek, modern twin-engined mid-wing monoplane bomber with twin tail assembly. Over sixty were ordered for the Polish air force and entered service late in 1938. With a wingspan of 58.5ft (17.9m), it could carry 5700lb (2580kg) of bombs, was armed with three machine guns, and using two 925hp engines could reach a speed of 273mph (439kph). About fifty managed to escape to Romania where they served with the Romanian air force and were later used against the Soviets.

Q

"Q" and "R" Class Destroyers (UK)

Displacement 1705 tons; *dimensions* 358ft 9in×35ft 9in (109.3×10.9m); mean draught 9ft 6in (2.88m); *machinery* 2-shaft geared turbines producing shp 40,000; *speed* 36.75 knots; *armament* 4×4.7in (4×1); 4×2-pdr AA (1×3); 8×20mm AA (4×2) guns; 8×21in (2×4) torpedo tubes; *complement* 175; *number in class* 16, launched 1941–42.

QAIMNS

Queen Alexandra's Imperial Military Nursing Service (UK).

QARANC

Queen Alexandra's Royal Army Nursing Corps (UK).

QMG

Quartermaster-General.

Quad (UK)

Name given to the Morris 4×4 Artillery Tractor, which was the standard towing vehicle for the 25-pdr gun-howitzer and its limber, and also transported the gun crew. The Quad had the appearance of being lightly armoured, but was not. For a while, ROMMEL used a captured Quad as a mobile command post.

Queen

US 12th Army Group operation between the Ruhr and Wurm rivers.

Queen Elizabeth Class Battleships (UK)

Displacement 30,600 to 32,700 tons; *dimensions* 643ft 3in×104ft (196.2×31.6m); mean draught 32ft 9in (10m); *machinery* 4-shaft geared turbines producing shp 75,000 to 80,000; *speed* 24 knots; *protection* main belt 13in; deck 5.5in; turrets 13in; *armament* 8×15in (4×2); 12×6in plus 8×4in AA or 20×4.5in DP; 16/32×2-pdr AA; 2/4×21in torpedo tubes; *aircraft* 1; *complement* 1124; *number in class* 5, launched 1913–15 and subsequently modernized.

Quezon, Manuel (1878–1944)

Quezon, a staunch ally of the United States, was President of the Commonwealth of the PHILIPPINE ISLANDS from 1935 until 1944. Following the Japanese invasion in December 1941, he accepted MACARTHUR'S advice and moved from the mainland to the island

Queen Elizabeth class battleship HMS Barham.

fortress of CORREGIDOR, from whence he was evacuated to Australia in March 1942. He then travelled to the United States, where he restated Filipino resolve to go on fighting. A victim of tuberculosis, he died on 1 August 1944, only months before the American return to the Philippines.

Quisling, Vidkun (1887–1945)

Quisling was leader of the Norwegian Nazi Party, the *Nasjonal Samling*, and was appointed head of the puppet government formed after the German invasion of April 1940. The majority of his fellow-countrymen declined to work with him and in September he was dismissed. In February 1942 he was installed as Minister President but was little more than a figurehead. After the war he was tried for treason and executed on 24 November 1945. His name has become an international synonym for traitor.

Queen Elizabeth class battleship.

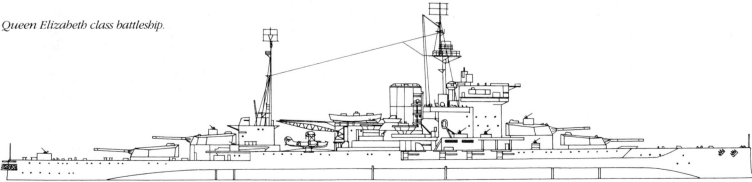

R

Bombing of Rabaul harbour.

"R" Class Submarine

See "P" AND "R" CLASS SUBMARINES.

RAAF Royal Australian Air Force.

Rabaul, New Britain, 1943–45

Town on the north-east tip of the Pacific island of New Britain, which became the major Japanese base in the area. The US forces under MACARTHUR and HALSEY planned to isolate Rabaul, outflank it and approach the Philippines from the south. The western tip, CAPE GLOUCESTER, was invaded by elements of the 1st and 7th US Marine Divisions on 26 December 1943, and they were later reinforced by 5th Marine Division in March 1944. This force pushed slowly eastward, compressing the Japanese into the eastern end of the island. Meanwhile in February and March 1944, the nearby Admiralty and St Mathias Islands were taken by US forces, isolating Rabaul and its sub-base Kavieng on New Ireland Island. With advanced US air bases established in the Admiralties and St Mathias, and with a firm ground force in place, Rabaul and Kavieng were successfully neutralized and were allowed to remain so until the war ended.

Radar

Radar is an acronym for "Radio Direction and Ranging" and was coined by the Americans in about 1942. Before this the system was known variously as "RDF" (Britain), "DT" (Germany), or "Derax" (USA). The principle upon which radar works is that of sending out a pulse of radio energy which strikes its target; some of the energy is reflected back and can be detected. Since the speed of the pulse is known, measurement of the time between sending and receiving gives an accurate measurement of the target range. This principle appears to have been discovered and developed independently in Britain, the USA, France and Germany in the middle 1930s. Britain, who required it for air defence, made the greatest progress; German development was principally aimed at providing accurate gunfire control for warships, France treated it principally as a navigational aid for ships, and the USA saw its advantages as a warning device but treated it with a low priority. At the outbreak of war in 1939 only Britain had a practical defensive radar system in being, and was well ahead in the development of airborne radar for fighters, radar target detection for bombers, radar counter-measures, and radar control of gunfire. Germany also developed a warning system, but this suffered from the ruling that only offensive weapon designs were to be pursued. American radar development benefitted from the British invention of the CAVITY MAGNETRON.

Radieschen

A radio homing device intended to be fitted to the German FRITZ-X bomb so as to attack Allied Loran transmitting radio stations which provided guidance for bombers over Germany. The device picked up the radio signal and then homed along it to strike the transmitter. The project was abandoned late in 1944 because of the unlikelihood of the parent aircraft getting close enough to the transmitter without being shot down. The principle was then applied to the Bv 246 glide bomb, but the war ended before it could be perfected.

Raeder, Gr Adm Erich (1876–1960)

Raeder joined the Imperial German Navy in 1894 and during World War I served under

Admiral Erich Raeder with Commander Otto Kretschner, his top U-boat commander.

337

Admiral Hipper. He became Chief of Naval Staff in 1928, and in 1935 was appointed Commander-in-Chief of the German Navy. He presided over an expanding warship construction programme, and evaded the provisions of the Versailles Treaty by authorizing the building of "pocket battleships", which squeezed the armament of a battleship within the size of a heavy cruiser. Raeder planned the naval strategy for the invasion of NORWAY. A sound strategist, he was sceptical about the German Army's plans for the invasion of England (Operation SEELÖWE), an undertaking which his own staff's careful study of logistics had revealed as being beyond the capacity of his fleet. Access to bases on the French Atlantic seaboard gave Raeder the chance to launch a successful U-boat campaign against Britain. Raeder's last surface ship success occurred when SCHARNHORST, GNEISENAU and PRINZ EUGEN made their "Channel Dash" in February 1942, a severe embarrassment to the British but little more than a hollow victory. With the Allied ARCTIC CONVOYS now reaching the USSR, HITLER ordered Raeder to employ his surface units to attack them. Operating from Norwegian waters, the triple threat of the TIRPITZ, U-boats and aircraft brought about the destruction of CONVOY PQ-17 in July 1942, but this was followed in December by a humiliating reverse in the Battle of the BARENTS SEA. Raeder resigned after an enraged Hitler threatened to remove the guns from the Navy's heavy warships for use on land. He took up an honorary inspectorate but took no further part in German naval strategy. At NUREMBERG Raeder was given a life sentence, but he was released in 1955.

RAF Royal Air Force.

Railroad Corridor

The name given to the narrow valley in BURMA between Pinbaw and Indaw, through which ran the railway from MYITKYINA to MANDALAY and RANGOON and a fair-weather road, both vital supply lines for the Japanese. The area was attacked by the first CHINDIT force, but was not finally cleared until August 1944 when the British 36th Division attacked down the valley, leaving Pinbaw on 27 August and taking Indaw on 10 December.

Railway Guns

A railway gun is a heavy artillery weapon mounted on a special carriage so that it can be moved on standard railway tracks; development of this type of weapon began in the American Civil War but did not become common until World War I, when it was seen as the only practical method of moving very heavy weapons. The railway gun is primarily the weapon of the continental power with several borders to be guarded and thus with a requirement to move heavy guns rapidly from one area to another. After World War I the use of railway guns as mobile coast defence weapons became common, since it allowed a reserve to be maintained centrally and then despatched rapidly to wherever danger threatened. At the start of World War II all the major armies had railway artillery; the British sent some to France where it was lost at the DUNKIRK evacuation, and what remained was employed in the southeast of England to protect possible landing areas from invasion. Two 13.5-inch guns were used for cross-Channel bombardment of German positions in France. The US Army had a number of railway guns, and built a few more, but they were all deployed as coast defence guns in various parts of the USA. France had numerous guns, but these saw little use in 1940 and most were captured by the Germans who used them, together with their own weapons, principally on the Eastern Front. Some German railway guns were highly specialized long-range weapons and were deployed on the Pas de Calais for the attack of convoys in the Channel and for bombarding south-east England. Rus-sia had numbers of railway guns but little is known of their deployment, and in view of the few working railway lines on the Russian side and the relatively rapid movements once the Soviet Army took the offensive, it is not believed that they contributed much to the war.

Ram – Medium Tank (Canada)

Due to pressure on the British armaments industry in the aftermath of the DUNKIRK evacuation the Canadian government decided that it would build its own medium tank, using components of the American LEE, a hull and turret to suit Canadian requirements, and British main armament, responsibility for the project being given to the Montreal Locomotive Works. A prototype was completed in June 1941 and the first 50 vehicles, designated Ram Mark I, were produced with a 2-pdr gun as main armament. The Ram Mark II, armed with a 6-pdr gun, entered production in January 1942 and 1094 were built. The Ram did not see active service as a gun tank, most being used for training in Canada and the United Kingdom. However, 84 were converted as artillery observation posts in 1943, and the hull was used both as a KANGAROO APC and as the basis of the SEXTON self-propelled 25-pdr gun-howitzer. *Weight* 28 tons; *speed* 25mph (40kph); *armour* 87mm; *armament* 1 2-pdr gun or 1 6-pdr gun; 2 .30-cal Browning machine guns; *engine* Continental R-975 400hp petrol; *crew* 5.

German 28cm K5(E) long range railway gun on its firing turntable.

General Ramcke goes into captivity, following his surrender at Brest.

Ramcke, Maj Gen Hermann

One of Germany's most prominent paratroop leaders, Ramcke fought in CRETE and commanded the 2nd Parachute Brigade at the Second Battle of ALAMEIN. Although left without transport at the end of the latter, he contrived his formation's escape by ambushing a British column. He later commanded the 2nd Parachute Division which stubbornly defended BREST until forced to surrender in September 1944.

Ramree Island, 1945

A large island off the coast of BURMA which protected the sea approach to the ARAKAN peninsula. It was assaulted on 21 January 1945 by the British 71st Brigade, with heavy naval gunfire support, since it was thought that the Japanese had powerful beach defences concealed in caves. The initial defences were therefore easily overcome and the advance inland met little difficulty until it arrived at the town of Ramree, where the Japanese garrison put up a stiff opposition. Reinforcements were provided by 4th Brigade and an armoured regiment, and the town was taken after two days of fighting, after which the Allied troops began clearing the smaller islands between Ramree and the mainland. Once the island

had been secured it was turned into an all-weather air base from which the attack on RANGOON could be supported.

Ramsay, Adm Sir Bertram Home (1883–1945)

In May 1940 Ramsay was the Flag Officer Dover, responsible for planning and executing Operation DYNAMO, the evacuation of almost 340,000 British and Allied troops from DUNKIRK. An expert in amphibious warfare, he served as Deputy Naval Commander Expeditionary Force during the Anglo-American landings in Algeria in November 1942 and then planned the July 1943 Allied landings in SICILY. In 1944 he was appointed Naval Commander-in-Chief for Operation OVERLORD, the Allied invasion of NORMANDY, which remains the largest amphibious undertaking in history. The last operation in which he was involved was the clearance of the islands at the mouth of the SCHELDT in October and November 1944. He was killed when the aircraft in which he was travelling to meet MONTGOMERY in Brussels crashed on 2 January 1945.

Ramsden, Lt Gen W. H. C. (1888–1969)

Ramsden commanded the 50th (Northumbrian) Division at the Battle of GAZALA. During

the closing stages of the battle the division was in danger of being encircled but successfully broke out through the Italian troops to the west and then swung south round BIR HACHEIM to rejoin the main body of the 8th Army in its retreat into Egypt. During the First Battle of ALAMEIN, Ramsden was appointed commander of XXX Corps, which he also commanded during the Battle of ALAM HALFA.

Ranger, USS – Aircraft Carrier

Ranger was the first American aircraft carrier to be laid down as such. She served in the Atlantic 1941–44 and provided air cover for the Allied landings in North Africa. During the last year of the war she reverted to the training role. *Displacement* 14,500 tons; *dimensions* 769×80ft (234×24.5m); mean draught 19ft 9in (6m); *machinery* 2-shaft geared turbines producing shp 53,500; *speed* 29.5 knots; *armament* 8×5in (8×1); 24×40mm AA; 46×20mm AA; *aircraft* 86; *complement* 2000; *launched* 25 February 1933.

Rangers

US Army units intended to perform the same function as the British COMMANDOS. The Ranger battalion contained six companies, each consisting of three officers and 64 men, companies being subdivided into two platoons each of two assault sections and a mortar section. The 1st Ranger Battalion completed its training at the Commando Training Centre at Achnacarry, Scotland, in 1942, and four more battalions were subsequently raised. Rangers served with distinction during the Allied landings in French North Africa, SICILY, SALERNO, ANZIO, and two Ranger battalions took part in the D-DAY landings on the NORMANDY coast, one landing on OMAHA Beach and the other capturing the coastal battery at Pointe du Hoe, some way to the west. Unfortunately, some senior American commanders failed to grasp the specialist nature of the Rangers' role and tended to employ them as conventional if élite infantry units; this contributed to the loss of the 1st and 3rd Ranger Battalions at Anzio, following a gallant fight against odds.

Rangoon, Burma, 1942–45

The capital city of Burma, located on the Gulf of Martaban, and a major seaport and terminus of the country's railway lines. It was occupied by the Japanese on 8 March 1942 and became their principal entrepôt and base.

In 1944–45 it was the prime objective of the Allied offensive. By the end of March 1945 combined Chinese and British manoeuvres had recaptured northern Burma, MEIKTILA, MANDALAY and the ARAKAN, and General SLIM ordered an immediate advance on Rangoon before the monsoon season made progress impossible. The 20th Indian Division advanced down the IRRAWADDY to take PROME, while the 5th and 17th Indian Divisions moved down the railway line through Toungoo to Pegu. Although these two forces moved quickly they were overtaken by the monsoon. Rangoon was taken by the 26th Indian Division, which was brought round from the Arakan by sea and made a landing south of Rangoon on 2 May, the day after the rains began. It occupied Rangoon on the following day, which brought organized Japanese resistance to an end, with the exception of isolated pockets which were rendered impotent by the monsoon.

Rankin

Study developed by the British in 1943 to deal with the steps to be taken in the event of a sudden German collapse or capitulation either before or after the proposed invasion of north-west Europe. In its Rankin C form it also set out the boundaries of the postwar division of Germany between the Allies.

RAP   Regimental Aid Post (UK). A medical facility close to the front line.

Rapido River, Italy, 1944

A river running south-west through CASSINO to join the Garigliano River. It became a major German defensive feature in the GUSTAV LINE and was assaulted by the US 36th Division on 20 January 1944. The attack was a failure, and became known as the "Battle of Bloody River", the total US casualties being some 1000 killed and 600 wounded. On 24 January the US 34th Division made a fresh attack north of Cassino, where the river was shallower but wider, due to destruction of a dam by the Germans and consequent flooding. It took two days to establish a small force on the far side of the river, but once this was achieved it was rapidly reinforced with armour and the Rapido was no longer an obstacle.

Rashid Ali, el-Gaylani

Despite his obvious pro-Axis sympathies, Rashid Ali promised his country's continued support for the United Kingdom when he seized power in IRAQ on 1 April 1941. None the less, he continued to intrigue with HITLER and obtained a promise of military assistance delivered through VICHY-controlled SYRIA. When the British, who were fully aware of his unreliability, began to reinforce their garrison in Iraq, he mounted an abortive attack against their base at HABBANIYAH on 29 April. His revolt was quickly crushed by a combination of air power and mobile columns and on 30 May he fled to IRAN.

Rastenburg, East Prussia

Now known as Ketrzyn, Poland, this was Hitler's headquarters, codenamed WOLFS-SCHANZE, during most of the Russian campaign. It was here that the assassination attempt of the JULY BOMB PLOT took place.

Ratweek

Allied air offensive against German communications in the Balkans, September 1944.

Ravensbruck, Germany

A CONCENTRATION CAMP in Mecklenburg, established in 1934 and used entirely for the imprisonment of female political prisoners. Medical experiments on gas gangrene were carried out here on Polish women, and it was also the place of execution for Allied female agents.

Rawalpindi, HMS – Armed Merchant Cruiser

During the afternoon of 23 November 1939 the 16,697-ton former P & O liner, commanded by Captain Kennedy and armed with eight 6-inch guns, was intercepted by the battlecruisers SCHARNHORST and GNEISENAU between the Faroe Islands and Iceland. While *Scharnhorst* closed in, signalling the British vessel to stop, Kennedy played for time by using his signal lamp, simultaneously transmitting his own position and details of the enemy ship, which he believed to be the *Deutschland* (*Lützow*). When, at 1703, *Scharnhorst* opened fire, it was immediately returned. A brief, unequal but fierce battle ensued in which *Gneisenau* joined at 1711, but by 1715 *Rawalpindi* had been reduced to a burning wreck and the German ships ceased firing. The battlecruisers stopped to pick up survivors but made off when the cruiser HMS *Newcastle* appeared, drawn by *Rawalpindi's* sighting report. Admiral Marschall, the German commander, was subjected to serious criticism for not making a second kill, and although he had sound if cautious reasons for not hazarding his ships in a night action with the possibility of the British Home Fleet in the offing, neither the German surface fleet nor the Berlin Admiralty viewed the affair with anything like satisfaction.

R-Boats

The official designation of these craft was *Raumboote* (Clearance Boats), but in addition to coastal minesweeping they were employed for minelaying, as convoy escorts and for the rescue of air crew. Several classes were built, displacing 110–175 tons. They were powered by 2- or 3-shaft diesel engines with bhp 1836/3825 and had a maximum speed of 19–24 knots. The most common armament was one 37mm AA and three (later six) 20mm AA guns, plus mines or depth charges. Their normal complement was 34–38.

A German R-boat captured by coastal forces in the Channel.

RCT Regimental Combat Team (US).

RDF Radio Direction Finding (UK). Early acronym for RADAR.

Rebecca

A RADAR homing and distance-measuring device used by British airborne troops in conjunction with the Eureka beacon. The latter was placed in the target area or drop zone either by agents or an advance party parachuted in; the main force then used the Rebecca device which triggered a response from Eureka and thus guided the force to their landing point.

Rechlin, Germany

An air base, in Mecklenburg, west of Neustrelitz. It was primarily an experimental station where new aircraft designs were tested and evaluated. In 1944–45 it became virtually an operational station, as experimental aircraft were now being tested by flying them in combat against Allied bombers.

Reckless

Allied assault on Hollandia, April 1944.

Recoilless Guns

A type of gun in which the recoil induced by the ejection of the projectile through the barrel is balanced by the ejection rearwards of body of similar momentum. In the first practical RCL gun this was achieved by simultaneous ejection of two equal weights, the projectile forward and a countershot of lead shot and grease to the rear, both moving at the same velocity. It can be shown that the countershot can be half the weight if it moves at twice the velocity, or any other combination which produces the same momentum, and the ultimate step is to eject a body of gas at very high velocity. This is done by utilizing the major part of the propellant gas and directing it to the rear through a venturi to increase the velocity. The advantage of the RCL gun is the absence of stress on the mounting and the absence of a heavy and complex recoil braking system, so permitting a very light weight artillery piece. The disadvantage is the large amount of propellant required and the limited range due to the use of propellant gas to produce the countershot effect.

The first RCL guns employed during the war were of German design, 75mm calibre weapons used by airborne troops in CRETE.

Development then began in Britain and the USA, and the US Army had two types, of 57mm and 75mm calibre, in service in small numbers in the Pacific theatre shortly before the war's end. British development was close to completion but was stopped in 1945 and shelved for further research into basic principles.

Red Ball Route

The US Army Services of Supply's solution to the logistical problems which followed the NORMANDY break-out in August 1944. The Atlantic ports and channel ports beyond Normandy were still in German hands and the railway system had been wrecked by Allied bombing. A route from the Normandy beaches to the front – at this time in northern France and Belgium – was designated "Red Ball Up" and appropriated solely for the use of supply trucks. A similar return route, designated "Red Ball Down", was used by empty trucks. No other traffic was allowed on these routes, and military police patrolled the route. In many respects a grossly inefficient system – the trucks themselves probably consumed as much fuel as they delivered – it nevertheless kept the Allied armies supplied with their basic requirements of fuel, rations and ammunition until the French railways were put in running order and sufficient ports brought into use.

Red Devil Grenade

The name given by Allied troops to various Italian hand grenades of the OTO-35 and similar patterns. These were painted red and had an ALLWAYS impact fuze which frequently failed to work on impact but which all too often worked subsequently when disturbed. They were responsible for a number of accidents in the Western Desert, from which they earned their name.

Regenbogen (Rainbow)

German plan for attack by heavy surface units on Convoy JW-51B resulting in the Battle of the BARENTS SEA, December 1942.

Regenbogen (Rainbow)

Scuttling of German submarines at the end of the war.

Reggiane Aircraft (Italy)

Reggiane Re 2000 Falco I This design was based on the REPUBLIC SEVERSKY P-35 fighter

and although built in Italy was almost entirely used elsewhere, notably in Sweden and Hungary; in the latter air force they saw service on the Eastern Front in support of the German forces. A low-wing monoplane with elliptical wing planform. *Span* 36ft (11m); *engine* 1 986hp radial; *armament* 2 12.7mm machine guns; *speed* 329mph (529kph).

Reggiane Re 2001 Falco II Developed from the Re 2000 from which it differed mainly in being fitted with a licence-built Daimler-Benz in-line engine of 1175hp, the Falco II was produced for the Regia Aeronautica and saw considerable service over Malta and Tunisia in 1942. A few served as night fighters in mainland Italy. *Span* 36ft (11m); *armament* 2 12.7mm and 2 7.7mm machine guns; *speed* 337mph (542kph).

Reggiane Re 2002 Ariete Derived from the Re 2000 and 2001, the Ariete was a fighter-bomber which entered service in 1943, seeing service during the invasion of Sicily and southern Italy. It was later used by the Italian Co-Belligerent air force against targets in German-occupied Yugoslavia and by Luftwaffe anti-partisan units in France. *Span* 36ft (11m); *engine* 1 1175hp radial; *armament* 2 12.7mm and 2 7.7mm machine guns and 1433lb (650kg) of bombs; *speed* 329mph (529kph).

Reggiane Re 2005 Sagittario Further developed from the Re 2001 with a more powerful in-line engine of 1475hp, the Sagittario was one of the best Italian fighters of the war. Too late for full-scale production, it equipped a single unit during the invasion of Sicily. *Span* 36ft (11m); *armament* 1 engine-mounted 20mm cannon, 2 20mm cannon and 2 12.7mm machine guns in the wings, 1390lb (630kg) of bombs; *speed* 390mph (627kph).

Regiment

A tactical and administrative unit consisting of regimental headquarters and up to three battalions, plus service units. In British and Commonwealth armies, however, common usage has resulted in battalion-sized units being regularly referred to as regiments; furthermore, a carefully fostered *esprit de corps* and a consequent reluctance to abandon unit identity has produced a system of numbering which is initially extremely confusing. Thus, while 1st/6th Ghurka Rifles is easily intelligible as the 1st Battalion 6th Gurkha Rifles, the Australian 2nd/23rd stands for the second raising of the 23rd Australian Infantry Battalion, i.e. for service in World War II. The situation is further complicated by amalgamated regiments such as the 17th/21st Lancers, formed from the old 17th and 21st Lancers in 1922 when the strength of the cavalry was reduced. On balance, the British and Commonwealth brigade had a strength comparable to that of a regiment in other armies.

Reichenau, FM Walther von (1884–1942)

A dedicated Nazi, Reichenau commanded 10th Army during the 1939 campaign in Poland and 6th Army in Belgium and France in 1940. He remained in command of 6th Army during the invasion of the Soviet Union and played a major part in the KIEV encirclement. In December 1941 he was appointed commander of Army Group South but suffered a fatal heart attack shortly afterwards.

Reichswald, Battle of, 1945

The Reichswald was an enormous German state forest stretching east and west of Cleve, and bordered north and south by floodwaters of the Rhine and Maas rivers, released deliberately by the German Army. As part of the general advance on the RHINE the area was attacked in Operation VERITABLE by the 1st

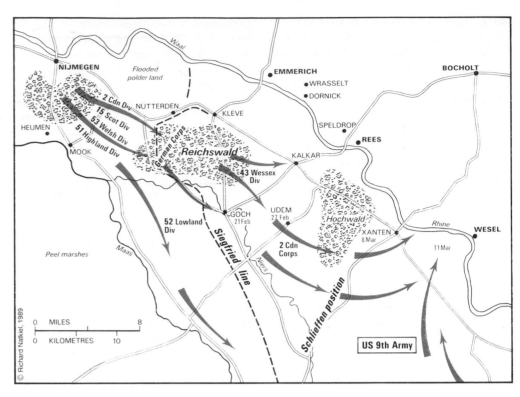

The battle for the Reichswald and the Rhine, February–March 1945.

British advance through Reichswald forest, February 1945.

Canadian Army on 8 February 1945. Veritable was preceded by an artillery barrage which was probably the largest Allied concentration of gun power ever employed during the war.

Over 6000 tons of shells were fired during the first day of the attack and, in spite of fighting in difficult terrain, the first phase of the operation was successful and all Allied objectives were taken on schedule. After that, bad weather and stiffening German resistance slowed progress and it was not until 21 February that the final objective was reached and the Reichswald cleared.

Reindeer

Arctic element of BARBAROSSA designed to secure nickel deposits in northern Finland.

Reinhard Line, Italy

A defensive line, also called the "Bernhard Line". It ran from Castel di Sangri south to Venafron, round the front of Monte Rotundo and Monte Cesima to link up with the GUSTAV LINE close to Monte Camino.

Reinhardt, Col Gen Georg-Hans

Reinhardt, who had formerly led the 4th Panzer Division, commanded XLI Panzer Corps during the 1940 campaign in the West. On 5 October 1941 he relieved HOTH as commander of Panzer Group 3 (later 3rd Panzer Army) and held this appointment until 16 August 1944. He was then given command of Army Group Centre and in January 1945 moved to Army Group North. He was dismissed by HITLER, after only two days in command, for demanding that EAST PRUSSIA be abandoned to avoid the encirclement of his troops. He was sentenced to 15 years' imprisonment at NUREMBERG but served only seven.

Reising Submachine Gun

An American submachine gun developed shortly before the war and placed in production in 1941. Most were supplied to the US Marine Corps, though numbers also went to Russia and other allies. Of .45in calibre, it had some unusual mechanical features and was found to be unreliable in combat due to a weak magazine and a mechanism susceptible to jamming from dust and dirt. Those not thrown away were withdrawn from service use and used to arm factory guards and police forces in the USA, in which role they were satisfactory.

Remagen Bridge, 1945

Remagen is a town on the RHINE, and on 7 March 1945 the US 9th Armored Division discovered that the LUDENDORFF BRIDGE there was still standing. Together with the 78th Division, they secured a valuable crossing point and bridgehead. The bridge later collapsed due to damage by bombing and to the excessive burden placed upon it by convoys of tanks.

Renault FT-17 – Light Tank (Fr)

Designed in 1916, the FT-17 first went into action in May the following year. Although hopelessly obsolete, a number took part in the 1940 campaign in France and also saw action briefly during the Allied landings in French North Africa in November 1942. *Weight* 6.7 tons; *speed* 6mph (10kph); *armour* 22mm; *armament* 1 37mm gun or 18mm machine gun; *engine* Renault 40hp petrol; *crew* 2.

Renault R35 – Infantry Tank (Fr)

Designed as a replacement for the RENAULT FT-17 in 1933. Some 2000 were built, equipping 23 infantry support battalions during the 1940 campaign in France, and a number were taken into German service as artillery tractors. The vehicle later fought against Allied troops in Syria, briefly opposed the November 1942 landings in French North Africa, and was then used by the French Army in Tunisia. A later version, the R40, benefited from an improved suspension and a more powerful 37mm gun. *Weight* 9.8 tons; *speed* 12.5mph (20kph); *armour* 40mm; *armament* 1 37mm gun; 1 7.5mm machine gun; *engine* Renault 83hp petrol; *crew* 2.

Rendova, Pacific, 1943

A Pacific island in the New Georgia group, Rendova was lightly garrisoned by the Japanese. It was attacked on 30 June 1943 by a specially-trained "Barracuda" scouting force of the US 172nd Infantry Regiment. Unfortunately the US Navy put them ashore in the wrong place, and by the time they had found their way back to their objective the main landing force had arrived and secured most of the island.

Rendulic, Col Gen Dr Lothar

Rendulic was an Austrian Nazi who became one of HITLER's favourites during the closing stages of the war. He commanded XXXV Corps on the Eastern Front in 1942–43, proving himself to be a capable defensive general. He then commanded the 2nd Panzer

1st US Army men and equipment pour across the Remagen Bridge, March 1945.

Army in the Balkans from 15 August 1943 until 24 June 1944, being transferred to FINLAND to conduct the withdrawal of 20th Army. In 1945 he commanded, in rapid succession, Army Group Courland, Army Group North and Army Group South. Under Rendulic's command, troops who failed to hold their ground were punished with extreme severity, but towards the end even he realized that Germany's defeat was inevitable.

Reno III and Reno V
American plans for the liberation of the PHILIPPINES.

Republic Aircraft (USA)
Republic (Seversky) P-35 One of the first two modern fighter monoplanes to see service in the US, the P-35 was obsolescent in 1939, and had been replaced in USAAF units by 1942. However, quantities of an improved version built for Sweden were taken over by the Americans in 1940 and saw service in the Philippines at the outbreak of hostilities as the P-35A. Totally outclassed, they did not last long. *Span* 36ft (11m); *engine* 1050hp radial; *armament* 2 .50in and 2 .30in machine guns and 350lb (160kg) bombs; *speed* 310mph (499kph).

Republic P-43 Lancer First delivered to the USAAF in 1940, relatively few of the P-43 were built, although it was a relatively effective aircraft. Used as a fighter and reconnaissance machine, most were supplied to the Chinese air force although a few were employed by the Australian air force for use as photo-reconnaissance aircraft. *Span* 36ft (11m); *engine* 1 1200hp radial; *armament* 4 .50in machine guns; *speed* 350mph (563kph).

Republic P-47 Thunderbolt While the P-43 was entering production, study of reports from Europe indicated the need for greater power and firepower, and the design was reworked to produce the P-47 "Thunderbolt".

There were protracted development problems, due to the fitting of an enormous engine and propeller, but it went into production in 1942 and was first used in 1943 as a long-range escort fighter, a role which was enhanced by the use of additional fuel tanks. The powerful armament gave it a valuable ground-attack capability, in which role it saw extensive use in both Europe and the Pacific. *Span* 40.75ft (12.43m); *engine* 1 2800hp radial; *armament* 8 .50in machine guns, plus up to 2500lb (1135kg) of rockets or bombs; *speed* 428mph (689kph).

Repulse Class Battlecruisers (UK)
Repulse served in the Home Fleet 1939–41 and was then transferred to the Eastern Fleet. She was sunk by Japanese aircraft off the east coast of MALAYA on 10 December 1941. *Displacement* 32,000 tons; *dimensions* 794ft 3in × 102ft 9in (238.2 × 30.6m); *mean draught* 26ft 9in (8.07m); *machinery* 4-shaft geared turbines

HMS Repulse, *sunk off Malaya, 1941.*

producing shp 112,000/120,000; *speed* 29 knots; *protection* main belt 9in; deck 4in; turrets 11in; *armament* 6 × 15in (3 × 2); 20 × 4.5in DP (*Renown*)/12 × 4in and 8 × 4in AA (*Repulse*); 24 × 2-pdr AA (*Renown*)/16 × 2-pdr AA (*Repulse*); 8 × 21in torpedo tubes *Repulse* only; *aircraft* 4; *complement* 1181; *number in class* 2, both launched 1916.

Retimo, Crete, 1941
A small town on the north coast of CRETE, Retimo was the objective for one of the secondary waves of German paratroops in the invasion of the island on 21 May 1941. The 3rd Battalion of Parachute Regiment 2 captured the town but were prevented by their small numbers from exploiting this success. Nevertheless, they held on to their position until they were relieved on 29 May by Kampfgruppe Krakau, a ground force which had been landed by sea and marched overland.

Repulse class battlecruiser.

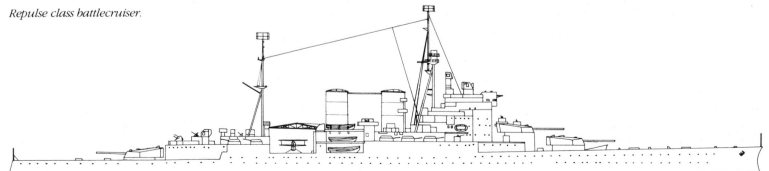

Rheintochter 1 air defence missile on launcher.

explosive charge on striking the target. The increase in range with the K5 gun was from 38 miles (62km) with conventional shell to 54 miles (86km) with rocket assistance. The price paid was a reduction in accuracy. Rocket shells were also developed for the 10.5cm and 12.8cm anti-aircraft guns but the designs had not been perfected when the war ended.

Rheinbote

Also known as RhZ-61/9, this was a German long range surface-to-surface missile, developed to carry 88lb (40kg) of explosive to a range of 99 miles (160km). Design began in 1942, and the final model was a four-stage rocket using solid propellant. Length overall was 37ft (11.4m), weight at launch 3780lb (1715kg), maximum range 137 miles (220km). Some 220 were built and most were fired against Antwerp early in 1945.

Rheintochter

A German ground-to-air missile developed by Rheinmetall-Borsig from 1942 onwards. Launched by means of rocket boost motors, it was sustained in flight by a solid-fuel rocket and was guided by radio command. The warhead contained 330lb (150kg) of high explosive and was fitted with a "Kranich" acoustic proximity fuze. Development continued throughout the war and by 1 January 1945 some 82 missiles had been fired, of which only four failed. In early 1944 the German Air Ministry changed the specification, demanding greater range, and the weapon was redesigned as "Rheintochter 3", using either solid or liquid fuel motors and with an over-riding firing control which allowed the operator to detonate the warhead whenever he wished. Development was stopped in February 1945, by which time six of the improved model had been fired but the radio control system had not been perfected.

Rheinübung (Exercise Rhine)

German plan for operations by the battleship BISMARCK and other heavy naval units in the North Atlantic, May 1941

Rhine, 1945

The principal river of Germany, forming its southern border for much of its length, and the principal obstacle to the Allied advance into Germany from the west. The first crossing was made as a byproduct of Operation MARKET GARDEN and gave 1st Canadian Army a

Retribution

Allied naval operations off the coast of Tunisia designed to prevent the evacuation of the Axis armies from North Africa, May 1943.

Reuben James, USS – "Flush-Deck" Class Destroyer

Torpedoed and sunk by *U-562* on 31 October 1941 while escorting a convoy 600 miles (965km) south-west of Iceland, although the United States and Germany were still technically not at war. The first American warship to be sunk during World War II.

Reynaud, Paul (1878–1966)

Reynaud succeeded DALADIER as Prime Minister of France on 21 March 1940. Following the German breakthrough on the Meuse in May he dismissed GAMELIN, the Allied commander of land forces, replacing him with WEYGAND. As France's defeat became inevitable, Reynaud proposed moving the government, the fleet and the air force to North Africa and continuing the fight from there, but there was little enthusiasm for the idea and on 16 June he resigned. He was arrested by the VICHY authorities on 6 September but when tried by them in 1942 for the national humiliation during his period in office he was able to defeat his political opponents and reveal them as the real traitors. He was deported to Germany in 1943 and released in 1945.

Reza Shah Pahlevi, Shah of Persia

Having worked his way up through the ranks of the Persian Army to become Commander-in-Chief, Reza seized power in 1921 and, after serving as Prime Minister, was elected Shah in 1925. A patriot who sought to modernize his country, he also wished to preserve strict neutrality, but in 1941 found himself unable to accede to an Allied demand that all German nationals should be expelled from Iran. In August British and Russian troops crossed the frontier and, after his army had put up token resistance, the Shah ordered it to cease fighting. His position within Iran had now become impossible and the following month he abdicated in favour of his son, Crown Prince Mohammed Reza.

RFSS

Reichsführer, Schutzstaffel (SS) (German – Head of ss).

R-Granate

To extract the maximum range from artillery, the development of rocket-assisted shells was begun in Germany in the early 1930s. The first to reach service, early in 1942, were for the 15cm and 10.5cm howitzers, but these were more in the nature of extended troop trials. Later a more reliable version was developed for the 28cm K5(E) railway gun. This divided the shell in two halves, the forward half holding the solid fuel rocket motor and the rear half the shell's bursting charge. The blast pipe for the motor passed through the centre of the bursting charge compartment. A time fuze ignited the rocket motor during the upward part of the trajectory, so that the upward leg was thus extended and the range increased. Impact fuzes within the shell detonated the

Troops of US 3rd Army cross the Rhine at Oberwesel, March 1945.

precarious bridgehead at Nijmegen on the Dutch border, which they later exploited in Operation VERITABLE. Troops of PATTON's US 3rd Army crossed at Oppenheim, near Mainz, on 21 March 1945. The major crossings, however, were carefully planned to take place in the north so as to open a direct route into the RUHR, the only remaining German source of industrial power. The British 2nd and US 9th Armies launched their attacks on the 23 March, the British crossing at Wesel and the Americans in the Rheinberg area. Both assaults were accompanied by heavy artillery and air bombardment, parachute assaults to secure bridgeheads and COMMANDO and RANGER preliminary attacks.

"Rhubarbs"

RAF fighter sweeps over occupied France, 1941.

Ribbentrop, Joachim von (1893–1946)

Ribbentrop, a former champagne salesman noted for his vain, frivolous and loquacious manner, became Nazi Germany's Foreign Minister in 1938. On 22 May 1939 he concluded the Pact of Steel with Italian Foreign Minister COUNT CIANO and on 23 August was signatory to a Non-Aggression Pact between Germany and the Soviet Union. Although warned by his Ambassador in London that the British attitude towards Germany was hardening, he failed to convince HITLER that an attack on Poland would almost certainly lead to war with the United Kingdom. In 1943 he conducted secret negotiations with MOLOTOV in the hope of ending the war with the USSR but these foundered on the question of postwar

frontiers. He was captured by the Allies in 1945 and tried at NUREMBERG, being executed the following year.

Richard

Planned German intervention in the event of a Republican victory in the Spanish Civil War, 1939.

Richelieu Class Battleships (Fr)

Richelieu was damaged by torpedo aircraft from HMS HERMES at DAKAR on 8 July 1940 but took part in the defence of the base against British and Free French forces in September 1940. In 1943 she joined the Allies and was refitted in the United States. She then formed part of the British Home Fleet, covering the ARCTIC CONVOYS, and in March 1944 departed

for the first of two attachments to the British Eastern Fleet, during which she bombarded Japanese shore installations at Sabang and in the Nicobar Islands. *Jean Bart* escaped to Casablanca when France surrendered in June 1940, but lacking much of her main armament. In November 1942 she resisted the Allied landings in North Africa but was damaged by torpedo aircraft and finally crippled by the gunfire of the battleship USS MASSACHUSETTS. *Displacement* 35,000 tons; *dimensions* 813ft 6in × 108ft 6in (247.9 × 33m); mean draught 29ft 6in (8.7m); *machinery* 4-shaft geared turbines producing shp 150,000; *speed* 30 knots; *protection* main belt 15.75in; deck 6.70in; turrets 17in; *armament* 8 × 380mm (2 × 4); 9 × 152mm DP (3 × 3); 12 × 100mm AA (6 × 2); 16 × 37mm AA (8 × 2); 28 × 13.2mm AA; *aircraft* 3; *complement* 1670; *number in class* 2, launched 1939–40.

Richthofen, FM Wolfram von (1895–1945)

A cousin of the famous "Red Baron", Richthofen also served as a fighter pilot in World War I, scoring eight kills. He was involved in the early development of the Luftwaffe and commanded the air arm of the German Condor Legion during the Spanish Civil War. An expert in close tactical ground support, his Fliegerkorps 8, which included the majority of the Luftwaffe's dive bomber units, smashed opposition in the path of the advancing armoured spearheads in POLAND, BELGIUM and FRANCE, but was severely mauled during the Battle of BRITAIN. Under his command Flie-

Von Ribbentrop (left) and the German delegation to London, 1936.

gerkorps 8 also provided close support during the 1941 campaign in the BALKANS, the airborne invasion of CRETE, during which it inflicted serious loss on the British Mediterranean Fleet, and the invasion of the Soviet Union. In 1943 Richthofen was appointed commander of the Luftflotte 4 raising special tank destroyer squadrons, although in the aftermath of the STALINGRAD disaster he became increasingly disillusioned with the German High Command's conduct of the war, commenting to von MANSTEIN that his position could be compared to that of "an attendant in a lunatic asylum". In mid-1943 he was transferred to the Mediterranean theatre of war as commander of Luftflotte 2 but the Luftwaffe was now in steady decline and unable to influence events.

Ridgway, Maj Gen Matthew Bunker (1895–   )

Ridgway commanded the US 82nd Airborne Division during its operations in SICILY, Italy and NORMANDY. He was then appointed commander of the XVIII Airborne Corps which took part in Operation MARKET GARDEN, the Battle of the BULGE, the breaking of the SIEGFRIED LINE and the subsequent advance across Germany. During the Korean War Ridgway commanded the US 8th Army before succeeding MACARTHUR as Commander-in-Chief United Nations Command. In May 1952 he succeeded EISENHOWER as NATO Supreme Allied Commander Europe (SACEUR); he was US Army Chief of Staff, 1953–55.

Ring

Soviet plan for the elimination of German formations trapped in the STALINGRAD pocket, 1942–43.

Rising

Signal for Polish insurrection, 1944.

Ritchie, Lt Gen Neil Methuen (1897–1983)

Ritchie commanded the 51st (Highland) Division 1940–41 before being posted to the Middle East as Deputy Chief of Staff to General AUCHINLECK. He was appointed commander of the 8th Army during Operation CRUSADER, which he brought to a successful conclusion, relieving TOBRUK and forcing ROMMEL to evacuate CYRENAICA. However, much of the ground gained was lost again in January 1942, and although Ritchie managed to stabilize the situation, he was decisively defeated during the Battle of GAZALA in May–June 1942 and compelled to withdraw into Egypt. On 25 June Auchinleck assumed personal command of 8th Army. Ritchie returned home to command the 52nd (Lowland) Division and in 1944 was appointed commander of XII Corps, which he led successfully throughout the campaign in NORMANDY and North-West Europe.

River Class Frigates (UK)

Displacement 1370 tons; *dimensions* 301ft 3in × 36ft 6in (91.8 × 11.1m); mean draught 9ft (2.7m); *machinery* 2-shaft reciprocating engines with ihp 5500; *speed* 20 knots; *armament* 2 × 4in; 10 × 20mm AA (10 × 1); 1 Hedgehog; *complement* 140; *number in class* 140, launched 1942–44.

River Plate, Battle of the, 1939

Early on 13 December 1939 Commodore Henry Harwood's cruiser squadron, consisting of HMS AJAX, HMNZS ACHILLES and HMS EXETER, caught up with the German pocket-battleship ADMIRAL GRAF SPEE, commanded by Captain Hans LANGSDORFF, off the mouth of the River Plate. Although his ships were outranged and seriously under-gunned in relation to the German vessel, Harwood promptly launched a converging attack on his formidable opponent. For his part, Langsdorff made a serious tactical error in accepting battle at the range dictated by the British but first concentrated his fire on *Exeter*, inflicting serious damage, then silenced half of *Ajax*'s guns and damaged *Achilles*. None the less, Harwood's ships continued to press their attack and although *Graf Spee*'s damage was largely superficial and her casualties light, Langsdorff broke off the engagement and made for Montevideo, Uruguay, with the British in pursuit. Harwood stood off the neutral port with *Ajax* and *Achilles* while *Exeter* limped to the Falkland Islands, later being replaced by the cruiser *Cumberland*. As a result of intense diplomatic activity the Uruguayan government refused to permit *Graf Spee* to remain in harbour for more than 72 hours and HITLER, rather than risk an outright defeat at the hands of heavier British units converging on the Plate, ordered Langsdorff to scuttle his ship, this task being completed on 17 December. Three days later Langsdorff took his own life.

Rjukan

Norwegian electricity power station, also known as Vemork, about 100 miles (160km) west of Oslo. It was one of the few places capable of producing "heavy water" which at

Battle of the River Plate, 1939.

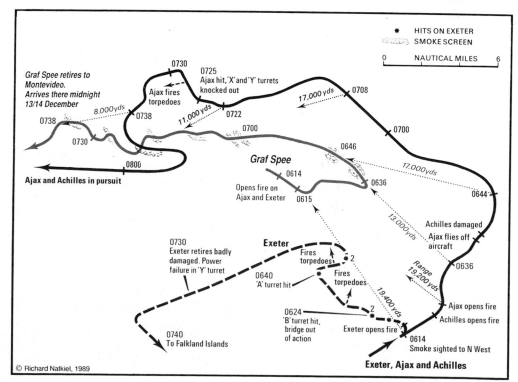

© Richard Natkiel, 1989

that time was a vital material for experiments in the development of atomic munitions. On 28 February 1943 nine SOE saboteurs destroyed the plant in a daring operation. It was back in production after five months of repair work, and on 16 November 1943 US heavy bombers again destroyed the hydro-electric plant but failed to damage the heavy water production unit, which had been given additional protection. In January 1944 SOE discovered that the major part of the heavy water stock was to be shipped to Germany, and a sabotage attack by SOE sank the ferry and its cargo in Lake Tinnsjoe. This operation effectively put an end to the German atomic munitions programme.

RM Royal Marines.

RN Royal Navy.

RO 35 Class (Type K6) Submarines (Jap)

Displacement 960 tons (1115/1447 tons normal); *dimensions* 264×23ft (80.4×7m); *machinery* 2-shaft diesel/electric motors hp 4200/1200; *speed* 19.75/8 knots; *armament* 1×3in; 2×25mm AA (1×2); 4×21in torpedo tubes (bow) and 10 torpedoes; *complement* 80; *number in class* 18, launched 1942–44.

RO 100 Class (Type KS) Submarines (Jap)

Displacement 525 tons (601/782 tons normal); *dimensions* 199ft 9in×20ft (60.88×6m); *machinery* 2-shaft diesel/electric motors hp 1100/760; *speed* 14/8 knots; *armament* 1×3in; 4×21in torpedo tubes (bow) and 5 torpedoes; *complement* 75; *number in class* 18, launched 1942–43.

Rochling Shells

Named after their inventor, these were German concrete-piercing projectiles of extraordinary length, stabilized by fins. They were between 12 and 20 times their calibre and were principally manufactured for the 21cm howitzer. Tested against Fort Neufchatel near Liège, a test shell penetrated 118ft (36m) of concrete, a layer of broken stone, the wall of an underground store-room, through the room's stone floor and finally detonated several feet below. A stockpile of shells was assembled but a Führer directive of January 1943 forbade their use except under his specific direction, in order that the secret should not be compromised. As a result, they were very rarely used.

ROF Royal Ordnance Factory (UK).

Roi Island, Pacific, 1944

One of the principal islands of the KWAJALEIN ATOLL in the Pacific Ocean, Roi was assaulted by the 23rd and 24th Regiments US Marine Corps on 1 February 1944. There was relatively little resistance and the island was secured within the day.

Rokossovksy, Marshal Konstantin (1896–1968)

Rokossovsky saw active service with the Soviet contingent during the Spanish Civil War and although he was arrested during the GREAT PURGE he was later reinstated. His first major achievements were as commander of 16th Army during the defence of MOSCOW, November–December 1941. In 1942 he was appointed commander of Don Front which, in November, formed the northern arm of the great pincer movement which isolated the German 6th Army in STALINGRAD. At the decisive Battle of KURSK in July 1943 he commanded the Central Front, first holding the German attack and then going over to the offensive, his advance taking him to the River DNIEPR and the PRIPET MARSHES. During the 1944 Soviet offensive which all but destroyed the German Army Group Centre he commanded the 1st Belorussian Front, the advance of which almost brought it to WARSAW. Within the city the POLISH HOME ARMY rose against the Germans but was ruthlessly crushed when Rokossovsky denied the insurgents his assistance; according to Soviet historians his resources were exhausted and the rising was premature. In January 1945, now commanding 2nd Belorussian Front, he took Warsaw and advanced across Poland to capture DANZIG, encircling the German formations holding EAST PRUSSIA. His leading elements made contact with British units at Wismar on 5 May. His postwar appointments included Commander-in-Chief of the Armed Forces in Poland, interpreted as a snub from a still mistrustful STALIN.

Rolls-Royce Armoured Cars (UK)

On the outbreak of war the British Army still had in service 52 1920 Pattern and 24 1924 Pattern Rolls-Royce armoured cars. The majority were used for training in the United Kingdom but in Egypt the 11th Hussars were equipped with modernized cars mounting an open-topped turret armed with a BOYS anti-tank rifle and a BREN light machine gun, and these were used operationally during the early months of the war in the Western Desert. See also FORDSON ARMOURED CARS. *Weight* 3.8 tons (1920); 4.15 tons (1924); *speed* 45mph (72kph); *armour* 9mm; *armament* 1 Vickers .303-in machine gun; *engine* Rolls-Royce 40–50hp petrol; *crew* 3.

Romania

Romania, situated between Germany and Russia, was in a difficult position in 1939. Pressure exerted on Romania by HITLER and STALIN, led to the cession of Bessarabia and northern Bukhovina to the Soviet Union, which was followed by an order to cede northern Transylvania to Hungary. This caused enormous civil unrest and General ANTONESCU seized the opportunity to dethrone King Carol and replace him with Carol's son MICHAEL, after which Antonescu established a dictatorship which leaned toward Nazi Germany. This did little to appease Hitler whose demand was the cession of southern Dobruja to Bulgaria. In October 1940 Antonescu allowed the country to be occupied by 12 divisions of the German Army, and in June 1941 the Romanian army aided the Germans in the attack on Russia under the orders of Hitler to "regain" Bessarabia. The badly equipped and poorly trained Romanian army suffered huge losses on the Eastern Front. Within Romania resistance movements sprang up, carrying out many acts of sabotage against the occupying German forces and against various strategic installations such as the PLOESTI oil refineries. On 23 August 1944 Romanian guerrillas staged an armed rebellion in Bucharest and took over the city, arrested Antonescu and overthrew his government. King Michael formed a new government and negotiated an armistice with the Allies, declaring war on Germany. By the end of August most of the German forces had fled the country and on 30 August Soviet troops occupied Bucharest without encountering resistance. The country then entered the Soviet political sphere, and has remained there ever since.

Rome, 1944

The capital city of Italy, Rome was the principal objective before General Mark CLARK and the US 5th Army, his intention being to

Rome: US prisoners captured at Anzio, February 1944.

line was far from secure he then decided to pursue the 8th Army into Egypt, imposing a further reverse on it at Mersa Matruh, but his further progress was halted by AUCHINLECK at the First Battle of ALAMEIN in July. The following month his attempt to revive the offensive was defeated by MONTGOMERY at ALAM HALFA. Critically short of fuel, his capacity for manoeuvre was now severely restricted and he sustained a decisive defeat during the Second Battle of ALAMEIN. He conducted a well-ordered retreat to TUNISIA where, in February 1943, he inflicted a sharp reverse on the US II Corps at KASSERINE PASS. Turning about, he then attacked the 8th Army at MEDENINE on 6 March but was repulsed by a model defence. After this engagement he left Africa to demand the evacuation of his men but was sent on sick leave. He was made responsible for the defence of northern Italy and then moved to France as commander of Army Group B, doing much to strengthen the coastal defences prior to the Allied invasion of June 1944. His belief that the Allies should be defeated at the water's edge was not shared by other German commanders and the result was an unfortunate compromise. He was severely injured on 17 July when his car was strafed by a British fighter and while recovering came under suspicion of being implicated in the JULY BOMB PLOT against Hitler. Offered the choice of poison or a show trial with attendant threats against his family, he opted

liberate it with US troops before any other Allied army could reach it. On 3 June 1944 HITLER authorized KESSELRING to withdraw and declare Rome an open city, to avoid the unnecessary destruction of the first Axis capital city to fall. Troops of the US 5th Army entered the city on 4 June.

Rommel, FM Erwin (1891–1944)

Rommel served as an infantryman during World War I, being awarded the *Pour le Mérite* for his brilliant exploitation during the Battle of Caporetto, where he demonstrated the dashing style of forward leadership which was to be the hallmark of his subsequent operations. His textbook *Infanterie Greift An* (*The Infantry Attacks*), now regarded as a classic, attracted HITLER's favourable attention and earned him command of the Führer Escort Battalion. During the 1940 campaign in the West he commanded the 7th Panzer Division, the successful progress of which was marred only by the ARRAS counter-attack on 21 May. In February 1941 he was appointed commander of the German troops sent to support the Italian army in Libya. However, he had no intention of playing a secondary role and exceeded this strictly limited brief, quickly recovering the whole of CYRENAICA with the exception of TOBRUK in the process. Although defeated and forced to withdraw by Operation CRUSADER (November–December 1941)

he counter-attacked with a small force in January 1942 and recovered much of the lost ground. In May–June he inflicted a major defeat on the BRITISH 8TH ARMY during the Battle of GAZALA-KNIGHTSBRIDGE, despite initial reverses which brought him close to disaster. This was followed immediately by the capture of Tobruk, for which he was rewarded with his Field-Marshal's baton. Although his supply

From the left: von Mellenthin, an aide, Rommel and Nehring, North Africa 1942.

for the former. It was publicly announced that he had died from his wounds and he was accorded a state funeral.

Romulus

British offensive in the ARAKAN, Burma, December 1944.

Ronson Flamethrower (Canada)

Developed in 1941 by R. P. Fraser of the Lagonda company in conjunction with the Royal Canadian Engineers. The Ronson equipment consisted of a flame projector mounted in the gunner's compartment of a UNIVERSAL CARRIER, fed by a pipe from pressurized tanks mounted on the rear of the vehicle. It had a range of 40 yards (36m), which the War Office considered inadequate. 500 Ronson sets were produced, but the significance of the equipment was that it led to improved designs, notably the WASP.

Roosevelt, Franklin Delano (1882–1945)

Roosevelt was elected President in 1932 and devoted most of his energy to reviving the American economy after the Great Depression. Although aware of the strength of isolationist feeling within the country, he also knew that it was not in the United States' interest that Great Britain should be defeated by the Axis powers and by means of the Lend-Lease Act of March 1941 ensured her supply of weapons and war materials. He was on excellent terms with CHURCHILL and, after the Japanese attack on PEARL HARBOR brought America into the war, agreed with him that the destruction of Nazi Germany was the Allies' foremost priority. He declared the United States to be the arsenal of democracy and that she would support any enemy of the Axis, including the Soviet Union. Although crippled by polio, he willingly shouldered the immense burden of leading the American war effort, attending the Inter-Allied Conferences at CASABLANCA in January 1943, Quebec in August, CAIRO in November, Teheran in December, Quebec in September 1944 and YALTA in February 1945. On a day-to-day basis, while agreeing with Churchill on war aims, he frequently disagreed with him on the means by which these were to be achieved and, in particular, left him in no doubt that he wished to see an end to colonialism in the postwar world. A generous and sincere man, he attributed these qualities to others, seeking to allay Soviet suspicion of the West by fair dealing, an attitude which Churchill justly felt the devious STALIN would interpret as weakness and turn to his own advantage. He died on 12 April 1945.

Rosenberg, Alfred (1893–1940)

Although of ethnic German descent, Rosenberg was born in Russia. After the Revolution he emigrated to Germany, joining the infant Nazi Party, which he led briefly during HITLER's period of imprisonment following the failure of the Munich Putsch in November 1923. He was editor of the Party's newspaper, the *Völkischer Beobachter*, which he used as an organ for his violently anti-Semitic and anti-Bolshevik views as well as his theories on racial superiority. Hitler appointed him Minister for the Occupied Eastern Territories in 1941 but in practice he wielded little power. None the less, as one who had been a major force in forming the Nazi philosophy and who had connived at its barbarities, he was tried and executed at NUREMBERG.

Rösselsprung (Knight's Move)

German attack on Tito's Headquarters at Kvar, 25 May 1944.

Nazi leader Alfred Rosenberg speaking at a Handel memorial concert in Halle.

Rösselsprung (Knight's Move)

German plan for attack by heavy surface units on Allied Arctic convoys, notably CONVOY PQ-17, July 1942.

Rössler, Rudolf (1897–1958)

Rössler, a publisher by profession and an anti-Nazi liberal by inclination, left Germany for

Roosevelt and Churchill confer at Casablanca, 1943.

Switzerland in 1933 and re-established his business there. While serving in the German Army during World War I he had made a number of friends who were now equally opposed to HITLER's regime and prepared to betray their country if it would ensure its downfall. By 1939 many of these men occupied senior positions in the Wehrmacht, eight holding apointments within the German High Command (OKW), while two were Luftwaffe generals. These contacts supplied Rössler with advance warning of German intentions and, with the connivance of Swiss Military Intelligence, this information was passed to the Allies. In this way they were advised of Hitler's projected invasion of NORWAY and DENMARK and given accurate details of GELB, FALL (CASE YELLOW), the German plan for the 1940 campaign in the West, but failed to act. Rössler also gave the Soviet authorities ample warning of Operation BARBAROSSA, although this did not influence events. However, he was now being taken seriously and he was recruited by the director of Soviet intelligence in Switzerland, Alexander Radolfi, under the codename "Lucy". Thereafter, every major decision taken at OKW was promptly relayed to Moscow, the result being that in 1942 the German offensive failed to inflict serious damage on the Soviet Army and ended in the disaster of STALINGRAD. He was unable to give details of the successful German counteroffensive in February 1943, since this was planned at MANSTEIN's own headquarters, but later revealed the entire plan for Operation ZITADELLE, the offensive against the KURSK salient, his most notable coup. As a result of the massive preparations which the Russians made to meet the attack, the Wehrmacht's capacity for further offensive operations on the Eastern Front was destroyed. Until 1944, when the Swiss finally moved against it, the "Lucy Ring" remained one of the Soviet Union's most important hidden assets of the war. The Germans became aware of this yawning breach in their security in August 1941 and by June 1942 had traced it to Switzerland but, despite immense pressure exerted on the Swiss, failed to unmask Rössler. The master spy never revealed the identity of any of his high-ranking contacts, taking the secret to the grave with him in 1958.

Rostov, Soviet Union

Also known as Rostov-on-Don, a city in southern Russia close to the Sea of Azov and a

Fighting in the outskirts of Rostov, 1942.

major rail junction. In the autumn of 1941 it was strongly defended by the Soviet 9th Army and attacked by the German 1st Panzer Army under RUNDSTEDT. After a severe battle the city was taken on 21 November 1941, but the Soviets were able to mount a counter-attack, crossing the frozen River Don to form two small bridgeheads. At the same time other Soviet forces outflanked the city and brought pressure on to the German supply lines. As these were already stretched to the limit, the Germans wisely abandoned the city on 29 November and fell back to the Mius River, abandoning Taganrog, another brief gain. Rundstedt did not advise HITLER of his withdrawal until it was well in train. Hitler ordered him to cancel the orders and stand firm, whereupon Rundstedt resigned. Rostov was the first severe defeat suffered by the Germans, and Rundstedt's virtual dismissal an additional setback.

Rot, Fall (Plan Red)

German codename for the second phase of the Battle of France, June 1940.

ROTC Reserve Officers Training Corps (US).

Rotmistrov, Marshal Pavel (1901–   )

In December 1942 Rotmistrov's VII Tank Corps played an important role in halting MANSTEIN's attempted relief of the German 6th Army, besieged in STALINGRAD. He was promoted commander of the 5th Guards Tank Army which, during the KURSK operations of July 1943, engaged the SS Panzer Corps at Prokhorovka in the largest tank battle in history, blunting the German offensive. During the Red Army's advance across Russia, Rotmistrov's army fought with KONEV's 2nd Ukrainian Front, taking part in the liberation of KHARKOV and Kirovgrad. Now regarded as the élite of the Soviet armoured formations, STALIN only permitted it to be committed with his personal approval and it next saw action with CHERNYAKHOVSKY's 3rd Belorussian Front during the autumn 1944 drive through the Baltic states. Rotmistrov, who had proved himself to be the Soviet Army's most capable tank general, was promoted Marshal of Armoured Troops and appointed Deputy Commander of Armoured Forces.

Rotterdam

The German codename for the British H2S centimetric RADAR set used in bombers, so-called because the first example to fall into German hands came from a British bomber which crashed near Rotterdam in January 1943. This acquisition disclosed to the Germans that Britain had developed the cavity magnetron and, from that, the use of centimetric wavelengths. It resulted in a HITLER conference on radar, the abandonment of work on longer wavelengths and a redirection of effort into centimetric research.

Rotterdam, 1940

The capital city of the Netherlands, Rotterdam was subjected to a heavy German bombing raid on 14 May 1940. A German surrender demand of the previous day was still under consideration when the attack was delivered, and its ferocity was sufficient to persuade the Dutch to surrender rather than see other towns similarly destroyed. Almost 1000 people were killed and 78,000 made homeless in the raid.

Roundhammer

Early codename for OVERLORD.

Roundup

Allied plan for the invasion of continental Europe, 1942.

Royal Marine

British operations in Norway, 1940.

Royal Oak, HMS – Royal Sovereign Class Battleship

Torpedoed and sunk with heavy loss of life on 14 October 1939 when *U-47*, commanded by the then Lieutenant Günther PRIEN, penetrated the Home Fleet's anchorage at Scapa Flow.

Royal Sovereign Class Battleships (UK)

Displacement 29,150 tons; *dimensions* 620ft 6in×102ft 6in (189.2×31.2m); mean draught 28ft 6in (8.7m); *machinery* 4-shaft turbines producing shp 40,000; *speed* 22 knots; *protection* main belt 13in; deck 5.5in; turrets 13in; *armament* 8×15in (4×2); 12×6in (12×1); 8×4in AA (4×2); 16×2-pdr AA (2×8); 8×5in (2×4); 2/4×21in torpedo tubes; *aircraft* 1; *complement* 1146; *number in class* 5, launched 1914–16 with subsequent addition of AA armament.

RSAF   Royal Small Arms Factory (UK).

Rotterdam reduced to rubble by German bombing, 1940.

R/T   Radio Telephony (UK). An abbreviation implying the use of voice transmission as opposed to W/T which used morse code.

Rudderow Class Destroyer Escorts (USA)

Number in class 22, launched 1943–44. *Displacement* 1450 tons; *armament* 2×5in; 10×40mm AA; 3×21in torpedo tubes; *complement* 200. Other details as for BUCKLEY CLASS.

Ruhr, Germany, 1945

An industrial area, encompassing Dusseldorf, Dortmund, Wuppertal, Essen and the surrounding area, and taking its name from the River Ruhr. Its ready access to coal and iron, and excellent transportation network, made the Ruhr the centre of German heavy industry and home of many of the heavy munitions industries. Its factories and cities were prime objectives for Allied bombing attacks, though

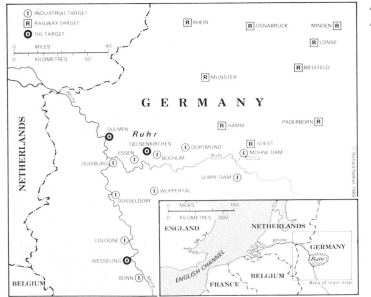

Bombing targets in the Ruhr.

the industrial haze and the strength of the German air defences made the area a difficult target. The military and economic importance of the area lay behind MONTGOMERY's conviction that the entire thrust of the Allied invasion should be directed against the Ruhr, but the idea was rejected by EISENHOWER in favour of a broad-front advance. The area was encircled and isolated by the US 1st and 9th Armies, which met at Lippstadt on 1 April 1945. The Allied armies then moved into the Ruhr and all resistance ceased on 18 April.

Ruhr Dams, Germany, 1945

A group of seven dams controlling the waters of the Ruhr River. Attempts to bomb them by the RAF had failed, and in early 1945 the German Army controlled their outlets so that the Ruhr and Maas rivers overflowed and formed serious obstacles for the 1st Canadian and 9th US Armies. As a preliminary to assaulting the RHINE, therefore, it was necessary to secure these dams and cut off the flow, so reducing the floodwater and allowing those two armies more room in which to operate. The attack on the dams was conducted by the 1st US Army, late in January 1945. The terrain was difficult and the weather bad, and the Germans put up a strong resistance. Although US troops captured the last of the dams on 10 February, they discovered that the outflow valves had been wrecked and that the flow of water could not be stopped. As a result, some parts of the advance to the Rhine had to be delayed until the dams emptied themselves and the floodwater level had fallen.

Ruler Class Escort Carriers (UK)

Displacement 11,420 tons; *dimensions* 492ft 3in×69ft 6in (150×21.18m); mean draught 25ft 6in (7.8m); *machinery* 1-shaft geared turbines producing shp 9350; *speed* 17 knots; *armament* 2×4in AA (2×1); 16×40mm AA (8×2); 20×20mm AA (20×1); *aircraft* 24; *complement* 646; *number in class* 26, launched 1942–43.

Rundstedt, FM Gerd von (1875–1953)

When HITLER came to power in 1933, Rundstedt was commanding 1st Army Group in Berlin, a post he held for six years. He retired in 1938, the year of the BLOMBERG–FRITSCH purge, but was recalled to service in 1939 at the age of 64. Rundstedt commanded Army Group A during the 1939 campaign in Poland and again during the 1940 campaign in the

Hitler with von Rundstedt (right) in his headquarters, April 1942.

West, his armoured spearheads breaking the French front on the Meuse and driving across France to the coast. On 24 June he persuaded HITLER that the contracting DUNKIRK pocket was no longer relevant and that the Panzer divisions should be redeployed against the surviving French armies, a decision that was militarily sound but which permitted the

evacuation of some 340,000 Allied troops. Promoted Field-Marshal, he commanded Army Group South in Operation BARBAROSSA, tendering his resignation in November 1941 rather than comply with Hitler's order that there should be no withdrawals. He returned to favour in 1942, being appointed Commander-in-Chief West, where he was responsible for the construction of the ATLANTIC WALL and the defence of "Fortress Europe". When the Allies landed in NORMANDY, Rundstedt was caught off balance, with his strongest forces concentrated in the Pas de Calais region and his Panzers well to the rear. His every decision had to be approved by Hitler and he was unable to fight the campaign as he wished. Recognizing the German position as being hopeless, he bluntly advised KEITEL that there was no alternative but to make peace, and was promptly dismissed. He was recalled in September 1944 but there was little he could do to halt the Allied advance. Although sometimes credited with planning the German counteroffensive in the ARDENNES, better known as the Battle of the BULGE, Rundstedt merely followed orders and was scornful of the entire concept, which originated with Hitler. He retired in March 1945 and was captured by US forces a month later. Respected by friend and foe alike for his astute professionalism, he remained above politics and higher strategy, and was one of the few senior Wehrmacht commanders to whom no taint of war crimes was ever attached.

Rupertforce

Allied expedition to NARVIK, Norway, April 1940.

Russo-Finnish Campaign, 1939–40

In a secret clause of the Nazi-Soviet Pact of 23 August 1939, Finland was placed within the Soviet sphere of influence. In October, Russia demanded a mutual assistance treaty with Finland and the ceding of parts of KARELIA to provide a cordon sanitaire around LENINGRAD. The Finns, anxious to remain neutral, refused both requests. The Soviets therefore fabricated a border incident as a pretext to launch attacks on several points on 30 November 1939. In the following "Winter War", 15 Finnish divisions, fighting in forests which they knew well, were able to inflict heavy losses on

45 Soviet divisions and prevent their further advance. In February 1940 the Allied War Council decided to send a 50,000-man expeditionary force, but before anything could be done the Soviets threw in more forces against weak areas of the Finnish front and the Finns were forced to sue for peace. A treaty was signed on 15 March 1940 under which the Finns ceded the Karelian Isthmus, the city of Viborg and other territories.

Ruweisat Ridge, North Africa, 1942

A low ridge of hills which were a principal feature of the EL ALAMEIN position, held by Commonwealth forces under General AUCHINLECK in 1942. The British 18th Independent Brigade, 22nd Armoured Brigade and 1st Armoured Division held positions on this ridge in July 1942 from which they were able to beat off ROMMEL's attack in the First Battle of ALAMEIN, thus denying him his only chance of breaking through into Egypt.

RV Rendezvous.

Rybalko, Col Gen Pavel (1894–1948)

During the Soviet offensive of January 1943, Rybalko's 3rd Tank Army all but destroyed the Hungarian 2nd Army south of Voronezh but was itself severely mauled by von MANSTEIN's counteroffensive the following month. When the Soviets returned to the offensive after the Battle of the KURSK salient, Rybalko's command again incurred serious losses when repeatedly committed against heavily fortified positions at STALIN's specific order, its efforts being recognized by the award of the honorific title Guards. During October–November the 3rd Guards Tank Army took part in the encirclement and liberation of KIEV and in December was involved in the tank battles on the ZHITOMIR sector. In July 1944 it captured LVOV and during the VISTULA–Oder offensive of January–February 1945 took KRAKOW. In April Rybalko's army took part in the siege of BERLIN,

capturing ZOSSEN, where OKW and OKH headquarters were located. Following rapid redeployment it drove south against DRESDEN and Prague, which it entered on 9 May.

Ryder, Maj Gen Charles W.

During the Anglo-American landings in French North Africa in November 1942, Ryder commanded the Eastern Task Force, which went ashore at ALGIERS. He then led the US 34th Division for the remainder of the campaign in North Africa and during the opening stages of the campaign in Italy. Under his command the 34th Division fought at Sbiba, FONDOUK, SALERNO, the crossing of the VOLTURNO and Monte CASSINO.

Ryujo, IJN – Aircraft Carrier

Completed in 1933, *Ryujo* was a small carrier designed to circumvent the provisions of the Washington Naval Treaty. She supported the Japanese invasion of the PHILIPPINES and took part in operations against the ALEUTIAN ISLANDS. She was then deployed to support the GUADALCANAL garrison and on 24 August 1942 was sunk by aircraft from the USS ENTERPRISE and SARATOGA during the Battle of the EASTERN SOLOMONS. *Displacement* 10,600 tons; *dimensions* 590ft 6in×68ft 3in (180×20.8m); mean draught 23ft 6in (7.16m); *machinery* 2-shaft geared turbines producing shp 66,269; *speed* 29 knots; *armament* 8×5in AA (4×2); 4×25mm AA; 24×13mm AA; *aircraft* 48; *complement* 900.

Ryukyu Islands, Pacific, 1944

A group of islands which stretch south-west from Japan, forming an approximate boundary between the Pacific Ocean and the China Sea. The principal island is OKINAWA. Operations by US forces against the Ryukyu group began in October 1944 with carrier-borne air strikes and naval bombardment, and the various islands were invaded by land forces in April 1945.

S

S-1

Allied codename for the ATOMIC BOMB.

"S" Class Submarines (UK)

Group 1 *Displacement* 670/960 tons; *dimensions* 208ft 9in×24ft (63.6×7.4m); *machinery* 2-shaft diesel/electric motors producing bhp 1550/1300; *speed* 13.75/10 knots; *armament* 1×3in; 1 machine gun; 6×21in torpedo tubes (all bow); *complement* 38; *number in class* 12, launched 1932–37.

Group 2 *Displacement* 715/990 tons; *dimensions* 217ft×23ft 9in (66.1×7.23m); *machinery* 2-shaft diesel/electric motors producing bhp 1900/1300; *speed* 14.75/9 knots; *armament* earlier boats 1×3in; 3 machine guns; 7×21in torpedo tubes (6 bow and 1 stern); later boats 1×4in; 1×20mm AA; 6×21in torpedo tubes (all bow); *complement* 44; *number in class* 50, launched 1941–45.

"S" Class (New) Submarines (USA)

Displacement 1435/2210–1460/2350 tons; *dimensions* 308ft×26ft 3in–310ft 6in×27ft 3in (93.8×8m)–(94.6×8.3m); *machinery* 2-shaft diesels producing shp 5500/3300; *speed* 21/9 knots; *armament* 1×4in; 8×21in torpedo tubes (4 bow and 4 stern); *complement* 70; *number in class* 16, launched 1937–39.

"S" Class (Old) Submarines (USA)

Launched 1918–24, 38 members of this class were still serving in December 1941. The majority were employed on training duties but in 1941–42 six were transferred to the Royal Navy and re-numbered HMS *P-551–P-556*; *P-551* became the Polish submarine *Jastrzab*. *Displacement* 850/1090 tons; *dimensions* 219ft 3in×20ft 6in (66.8×6.2m); *machinery* 2-shaft diesels producing shp 1200/1500; *speed* 14.5/11 knots; *armament* 1×4in; 4×21in torpedo tubes (bow); *complement* 42.

"S" and "T" Class Destroyers (UK)

Displacement 1710 tons; *dimension* 362ft 9in×35ft 9in (110.5×10.9m); *mean draught* 10ft (3m); *machinery* 2-shaft geared turbines producing shp 40,000; *speed* 36.75 knots; *armament* 4×4.7in (4×1); 2×40mm AA (1×2); 8×20mm AA (4×2) or 12×20mm AA (6×2) guns; 8×21in (2×4) torpedo tubes; *complement* 180; *number in class* 16, launched 1942–43.

SA

Abbreviation for the Nazi Party's Sturmabteilungen (Assault Battalions), the members of which were known as Storm Troopers or Brownshirts (from their uniform). Although the SA were political thugs, many recruits were disillusioned ex-servicemen and former members of the Freikorps, and during the Party's street-brawling days their organization and discipline enabled them to defeat their less regimented enemies of the Iron Front, which included Communist and Socialist private armies. Once the Nazis were legally elected to power in January 1933, however, the SA had served its purpose. Its strength had risen to 400,000 and it had begun to regard itself as the rival of the Army, towards which it maintained a hostile and highly provocative attitude. HITLER was also aware that the SA could unseat him, and decided to break its power. On the night of 30 June, subsequently known as The Night of the Long Knives, the SA's leadership throughout Germany was murdered by Hitler's own bodyguard, the ss (Schutzstaffeln) and the security service, the SD (Sicherheitsdienst). In the Reichstag, Hitler claimed that the killings had been necessary to protect the integrity of the Army and preserve it as the non-political instrument of the nation, although the victims had also included anyone against whom he bore a grudge, including two generals. The ageing President Hindenburg, now failing visibly, did not perhaps fully understand the implications and sent Hitler a congratulatory telegram. The Army, as Hitler had intended, viewed the dismemberment of the SA as an act of good faith and somewhat modified its attitude towards him.

SA Brownshirts, c.1933.

SAA Small Arms Ammunition.

SAAF South African Air Force.

SACEUR Supreme Allied Commander, Europe.

Sachsenhausen, Germany

A concentration camp north of Berlin, close to the Oranienburg camp, which it gradually replaced. The regime was as strict as in any other camp, but it was not specifically an extermination camp and was principally used to imprison "high-profile" political and religious prisoners such as the former Chancellor of Austria Dr Kurt von Schussnig and the dissident clergyman Pastor Niemoller.

SACMED Supreme Allied Commander, Mediterranean.

Sagan, Germany, 1944

Now Zagan, Poland. A small town near the 1939 German–Polish border, close to which a prisoner-of-war camp (Stalag Luft III) was set up for air force officers. On 24 March 1944, 76 RAF officers made a mass escape; three managed to reach England but the rest were recaptured and 50 were shot by the GESTAPO on orders from HITLER.

St Lô

A small French town about 12 miles (20km) inland from OMAHA BEACH. It was the inland objective of General BRADLEY's US 1st Army, and after the US VII Corps had broken out towards CHERBOURG, Bradley attacked through the *bocage* country. St Lô was strongly defended by 2nd SS Panzer Division and there was heavy fighting before St Lô was captured on 18 July 1944.

St Malo, France, 1944

A seaport on the north coast of Brittany. It became notable for the fanatical defence organized by the German Army under General Andreas von Aulock, who evicted all civilians in the face of American attack and then proceeded to more or less demolish the town. His forces held several strongly fortified points and in spite of intense American bombardment by heavy artillery and aircraft it took almost two weeks of hard fighting before Aulock and the remains of his garrison surrendered. The town was devastated and the port facilities quite unusable.

British dead after the raid on St Nazaire, March 1942.

St Nazaire, France, 1942

A seaport on the Bay of Biscay, used by the German Navy as a base and submarine depot. In March 1942 British Commandos mounted a raid to destroy St Nazaire's sea-lock gates and thus deny the dock facilities to the battleship TIRPITZ, then in Norway. On the morning of 28 March some 260 men in the ex-US destroyer *Campbeltown*, which was packed with explosives, accompanied by 18 small coastal assault craft, rammed the lock. The subsequent action cost 16 of the small ships and 170 commandos killed or captured, but the *Campbeltown* blew up and wrecked the lock gate, denying the Germans the use of the facilities for most of the war.

St Vith, Belgium, 1944

A small town close to the German border, St Vith was in the path of the German advance during the Battle of the BULGE in December 1944. It was fiercely defended by troops of the US VIII Corps and in particular the US 7th Armored Division under Major-General Hasbrouck. This resistance upset the German plans and caused them to divert some of their forces to take the town. The 7th Armored Division retired on 22 December, but the delay imposed by their stand had seriously affected the German timetable and on 25 December the German forces were driven back.

Saipan, Pacific, 1944

One of the principal islands of the MARIANAS group, about 1300 miles (2100km) south-west of Japan. Its capture would provide the Americans with a forward base for air assaults on Japan and severance of communication lines. The operation was originally planned for

The first marines to reach Saipan beach in the invasion of the Marianas, June 1944.

November 1944, but the swiftness of the American advance brought the assault forward to 15 June; this proved fortuitous since the Japanese were still in the process of constructing fortifications when the US forces landed. The island was defended by about 32,000 Japanese troops under General Saito and Admiral NAGUMO, but the defensive plan was badly co-ordinated, if fiercely executed. The assault was carried out by US 2nd and 4th Marine Divisions under General Holland M. SMITH, supported by 1st Provisional Marine Brigade and 27th Infantry Division. Two small beach-heads on the south-west of the island were achieved on the first day. On 17 June, 27th Infantry Division, with armour and artillery, was landed, taking Istey airfield and enabling REPUBLIC P-47 THUNDERBOLTS to fly in. Thereafter the battle became a bitter struggle for every foot of ground before the island was finally declared secure on 19 July, though pockets of resistance continued to hold out until the war ended a year later. The island's civilian population chose to commit mass suicide rather than be taken prisoner by the Americans. Several hundred people threw themselves over the 1000ft (300m) Suicide Cliff into the sea, or blew themselves up with grenades. The island's garrison of 32,000 perished almost to the last man; US casualties were 2521 dead and almost 9000 wounded.

Sakurai, Lt Gen Seizo

Sakurai commanded the Japanese 33rd Division during the invasion of Burma. Although his troops captured RANGOON, he was unable to prevent the withdrawal of British forces in the area. He later commanded the 28th Army covering the ARAKAN, YENANGYAUNG and the IRRAWADDY Delta. In 1944 his HA-GO offensive in the Arakan was defeated and his troops were forced to retire following their failure at the Battle of the ADMIN BOX. When the British offensive of 1945 broke the Japanese armies in Central Burma, he was already under pressure from amphibious operations mounted by the British XV Corps along the Arakan coast and withdrew the remnants of his army into the Pegu Yomas, from whence he attempted to break out across the SITTANG, an operation which only 6000 of his 18,000 men survived.

Salamaua, Pacific, 1942–43

A seaport and major settlement in north-east New Guinea, on the Huon Gulf. It had been occupied by a Japanese force in August 1942,

and was the jumping-off point for the push up the KOKODA TRAIL in their attempt to take PORT MORESBY. When this operation was withdrawn, Salamaua became a major Japanese base. It was attacked in January 1943 by the 17th Australian Brigade who were flown in to Wau, some 25 miles (40km) away. The Japanese held up the Australian advance as they waited for reinforcements. But the reinforcement convoy was destroyed at sea, and Australian attacks in other parts of the area began to close in on the Japanese flanks. Salamaua eventually fell to the Australians on 11 September 1943.

Salerno, Italy, 1943

A seaport in the Gulf of Salerno, about 40 miles (64km) south-east of NAPLES. It was assaulted by the US 5th Army under General Mark CLARK and the British X Corps under General MCCREERY on 8/9 September 1943, the intention being to land there and turn to attack Naples. En route the invasion force was informed of the Italian surrender, and thus anticipated little or no resistance. However, they met strong opposition from German forces under General VIETINGHOFF, principally the 16th Panzer Division and 29th Panzergrenadier Division. At one point US staff officers seriously considered withdrawing from the beach-heads. But with Montgomery's British 8th Army approaching from the south, and with the US forces gradually gaining the upper hand, Vietinghoff decided to break off the battle and withdrew north to the GUSTAV LINE. The battle for Salerno is considered to have ended on 19 September.

Salo Republic

A notional Italian state founded by MUSSOLINI around Lake Garda in September 1943, after he had been rescued from imprisonment by SKORZENY. He set up a reign of terror, executed several political enemies and activated a number of Italian Army units to assist the Germans. The Republic collapsed when Mussolini fled in April 1945.

Samar, Action off   See LEYTE GULF, Battle of.

Sanananda, Pacific, 1942–43

A small seaport on the northern shore of New Guinea, Sanananda was captured by the Japanese in July 1942 and became their supply base for their advance across the OWEN STANLEY MOUNTAINS by the KOKODA TRAIL. Repelled by combined Australian and US forces, the Japanese fell back on Sanananda, Buna and Gona in November 1942, where they were reinforced by sea. Strong defensive lines had been set up around the area and the Japanese, with a strength of about 5000, were able to keep the counter-attack at bay, since the Allied troops had suffered severe casualties from combat and disease. Allied air superiority prevented further Japanese reinforcement, and fresh US and Australian troops were moved into the area for a flanking attack which captured first Buna, then Gona, and finally Sanananda on 22 January 1943.

Sanchill, Battle of, 1941

Sanchill was a small peak some 2300ft (700m) high which flanked the road leading into

The first German prisoners taken by the invading forces, Salerno 1943.

KEREN, ERITREA. Strongly defended by Italian troops under General Carnimeo, it was attacked on 3 February 1941 by 11th Indian Infantry Brigade. The peak was taken, but the Indians were driven off by a determined counter-attack in which the Italians displayed a degree of determination seldom seen elsewhere in the East African campaign. After dealing with other strongpoints in the area, 11th Indian Brigade resumed the attack on Sanchill on 15 March, with strong artillery support. They took the hill, but were again driven off by an Italian counter-attack. Another attack on 16 March failed, but by this time other strongpoints had been defeated and the Allied force was able to squeeze through the gap and drive for Keren, ignoring the flanking fire from Sanchill. Keren was evacuated by the Italians, and British armour entered on 27 March. The gallant defenders of Sanchill were thus abandoned and obliged to surrender.

San Demetrio – Tanker (UK)

The *San Demetrio*, with 12,000 tons of aviation fuel aboard, formed part of the convoy which was saved by the sacrifice of the armed merchant cruiser HMS JERVIS BAY from the German pocket-battleship ADMIRAL SCHEER on 5 November 1940. After shellfire had set the *San Demetrio* ablaze and smashed her bridge, killing everyone on it, the survivors took to a boat. The following afternoon they sighted the ship and next morning they decided to board her, preferring to take their chance with the fires rather than spend another night in the boat. They managed to start the engines and extinguish the fires and, despite the lack of steering, compass or charts, courageously succeeded in bringing their ship into Glasgow.

Sangamon Class Escort Carriers (USA)

See also COMMENCEMENT BAY CLASS. *Displacement* 11,400 tons; *dimensions* 553×75ft (166×22.5m); mean draught 30ft 6in (9.2m); *machinery* 2-shaft geared turbines producing shp 13,500; *speed* 18 knots; *armament* 2×5in; 28×40mm AA; *aircraft* 34; *complement* 1100; *number in class* 4, completed 1942.

San Giorgio – Heavy Cruiser (Italy)

Launched 1908 and rebuilt 1937–38. Scuttled in TOBRUK harbour 22 January 1941. *Displacement* 11,700 tons; *dimensions* 430×69ft (131×21m); mean draught 22ft 6in (6.8m); *machinery* 2-shaft triple expansion producing shp 18,000; *speed* 16 knots; *protection* main belt 8in; deck 2in; turrets 8in; *armament* 4×10in; 8×7.5in; 10×3.9in AA; 6×37mm AA; 12×20mm AA; 14×13.2mm AA.

Sangro River, Italy, 1943

A river rising in the Apennine mountains and flowing roughly north to the Adriatic near ORTONA. In late 1943 it formed a natural barrier to the advance of the British 8th Army. German forces under General Herr retreated across the river in November and into prepared defensive positions in advance of the GUSTAV LINE. The British 78th Division arrived at the river on 8 November to find it swollen by heavy rain and flooding. The combination of natural obstacle and foul weather led MONTGOMERY to pause for some time before attempting a crossing in force, though small parties were able to cross and establish bridgeheads for forward patrolling. A major crossing was made on 20 November by 36th Brigade, and by 22 November five battalions of 78th Division were across and held a bridgehead sufficiently large to permit bridge building to begin. By 27 November 100 tanks were across and action against the German defensive line could commence, the British objective being the town of Ortona which was taken on 27 December after extremely hard fighting.

Sansom, Odette (1912–)

Odette Sansom was born in France but married a British subject and was living in the United Kingdom when war broke out. She was recruited by the SPECIAL OPERATIONS EXECUTIVE in 1942 and trained as a radio operator. She arrived in France that November and worked with Peter Churchill, being based at Annecy. Their cell, however, had been penetrated and she was arrested in April 1943, tortured and ultimately imprisoned in RAVENSBRUCK concentration camp, insisting the while that Churchill was her husband and that he was not an agent. She survived because the camp commandant believed that she might be related to the British Prime Minister.

Santa Cruz, Battle of, 24/26 October 1942

As the battle of GUADALCANAL continued, a Japanese fleet under Vice-Admiral KONDO was loitering north of the SOLOMON ISLANDS waiting for the Japanese capture of Henderson Field, when naval aircraft would fly in and support ground operations. On 24 October the US Task Force 16, with the carrier ENTERPRISE, joined Task Force 17, carrier HORNET, under orders from Admiral HALSEY to sweep around the Santa Cruz Islands to intercept any Japanese attempt at reinforcing Guadalcanal. On the morning of 26 October dive-bombers from *Enterprise* set out to attack the Japanese fleet, discovered by a flying-boat patrol. At more or less the same time Japanese reconnaisance aircraft had found the US fleet and a force of 65 aircraft left the three Japanese carriers. Almost immediately two US scout bombers arrived and severely damaged the carrier *Zuiho*. They reported back the position of the Japanese fleet and a series of strikes were launched from *Hornet* and *Enterprise*. These met the Japanese attack coming in the opposite direction, heavily escorted by fighters which did severe damage to the US squadrons. The *Enterprise* sailed into a rain squall which concealed it, and the main weight of the Japanese attack fell on *Hornet* which was struck by two torpedoes and six bombs, plus two suicide dives by damaged Japanese aircraft. A second wave concentrated on *Enterprise*, her rain cover having lifted, damaging her flight deck and forward lift but not affecting her sailing powers so that she was able to avoid torpedo attacks. At virtually the same time the US squadrons found the Japanese fleet and attacked, doing severe damage to the carriers *Zuiho* and *Shokaku*. After a further Japanese attack which did no serious damage, the US fleet withdrew, leaving *Hornet* ablaze but floating, to be subsequently sunk by the Japanese. Tactically the battle went to the Japanese, since they had two carriers damaged but repairable, while the US fleet had lost one carrier and had the other damaged, which meant that there was no fully operational US carrier in the Pacific.

Saratoga, USS – Saratoga Class Aircraft Carrier

Saratoga was damaged by submarine torpedo attack off Hawaii on 11 January 1942 but was repaired in time to provide air cover for the GUADALCANAL landings later that year. She was again damaged by submarine torpedo at the Battle of the EASTERN SOLOMONS. After repairs she saw further action at BOUGAINVILLE, the GILBERT ISLANDS, KWAJALEIN and ENIWETOK. She served with the British Eastern Fleet during 1944 and on 21 February 1945 was severely

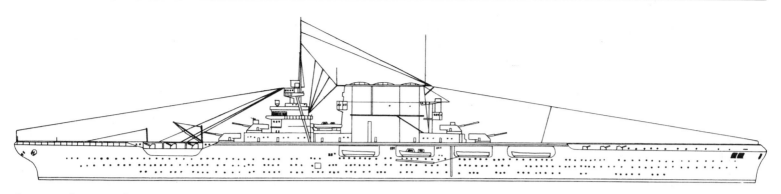

Saratoga class aircraft carrier.

damaged by Kamikaze air attack off IWO JIMA. She was finally expended as a target during the 1946 Bikini atomic bomb tests.

Saratoga Class Aircraft Carriers (USA)

Originally laid down as battlecruisers. *Displacement* 33,000 tons; *dimensions* 888ft×105ft 6in (270.6×32.1m); *mean draught* 24ft 3in (7.29m); *machinery* 4-shaft turbo-electric drive producing shp 180,000; *speed* 34 knots; *armament* 8×8in (4×2); 12×5in AA (12×1); *aircraft* 90; *complement* 3300; *number in class* 2, both launched 1925.

Sarin

One of the German nerve gases, Sarin was properly known as isopropyl methyl phos-

phoro-fluoride. Discovered in 1938, it was developed by the same research team which had perfected Tabun, the first nerve gas. Sarin was found to be exceedingly difficult to manufacture and only a pilot plant existed when the war ended.

SAS   SPECIAL AIR SERVICE (UK).

Sato, Lt Gen Kotoku

During the Japanese U-GO offensive Sato commanded the 31st Division at KOHIMA. He was unable to capture the vital ground and his troops were steadily pushed back from their early gains. He blamed MUTAGUCHI, the commander of the 15th Army, for not supplying his troops with food and ammunition, initi-

ating a bitter public feud. Contrary to his orders, he withdrew from Kohima to avoid the piecemeal destruction of his division and was unjustly blamed by many for the failure of the so-called "March on Delhi". After U-Go, Sato held only administrative posts.

Sattelberg Ridge, New Guinea, 1943

A ridge at the end of the Finisterre Range, northern New Guinea, giving command over Sattelberg and Finschhafen. It was occupied by the Japanese and had to be cleared by Australian troops in the campaign to secure the Huon Peninsula. The operation was launched in November 1943 by the 26th Australian Brigade supported by MATILDA tanks which were soon left behind due to the vertical nature of the terrain. The latter part of the battle, for the ultimate heights, was a hand-to-hand affair, but the Australian 2/48th Infantry Battalion took the ridge on 26 November.

Saturn

Soviet offensive following URANUS, mounted by South-West Front and part of Voronezh Front, aimed at Millerovo and ROSTOV, November–December 1942.

Sauckel, Fritz (1894–1946)

As Plenipotentiary General for the Allocation of Labour between 1942 and 1944 Sauckel was responsible for supplying German industry with labour recruited voluntarily or by force in the occupied territories. It is estimated that he was responsible for the deportation of over five million people, many of whom died. At the NUREMBERG TRIALS he was convicted of crimes against humanity and executed.

Sauro Class Destroyers (Italy)

The four ships of this class formed part of the Royal Italian Navy's Red Sea destroyer flotilla, based on MASSAWA, ERITREA. *Francesco Nullo*

Fires aboard USS Saratoga, *following a kamikaze attack off Iwo Jima, February 1945.*

was sunk by the destroyer HMS *Kimberley* on 21 October 1940; *Nazario Sauro* and *Daniele Manin* were sunk by air attack on 3 April 1941 and *Cesare Battisti* was scuttled the same day. See also LEONE CLASS. *Displacement* 1600 tons; *dimensions* 296×30ft (90.2×9m); mean draught 9ft 6in (2.88m); *machinery* 2-shaft geared turbines producing shp 36,000; *speed* 35 knots; *armament* 4×4.7in; 2×40mm AA; 2×13.2mm AA; 6×21in torpedo tubes; equipped for minelaying; *complement* 156; *number in class* 4, launched 1925–26.

Savo Island, Battle of, 1942

During the night of 8/9 August 1942 Vice-Admiral MIKAWA, commanding a cruiser squadron consisting of *Chokai, Aoba, Kako, Kinugasa, Furutaka, Tenryu, Yubari* and the destroyer *Yunagi*, attempted to destroy the American transports unloading off GUADALCANAL. These were protected by a screening force commanded by Rear-Admiral V. Crutchley, RN, deployed in two groups covering the probable approaches north and south of Savo Island. The Northern Group consisted of the cruisers USS *Vincennes, Quincy* and *Astoria* and the destroyers USS *Helm* and *Wilson*; the Southern Group contained the cruisers HMAS *Australia* (Flag) and *Canberra*, the USS *Chicago*, and the destroyers USS *Patterson* and *Bagley*; in

advance of the two groups were two picket destroyers, the USS *Ralph Talbot* and *Blue*. The Japanese were by far the more experienced in night fighting and, despite the fact that Crutchley's scouts were equipped with radar, achieved complete tactical surprise. Furthermore, throughout the subsequent engagement the Allied conduct of the battle was marred by poor communications. This was compounded by the earlier departure of Crutchley in *Australia* to attend a commanders' conference, without informing his senior captain that he was now in overall command of the screen. Thus when the Japanese struck the Southern Group, the result was confusion, from which the Allies never recovered. *Canberra* was wrecked by a storm of gunfire, and was abandoned and sunk the following morning. *Chicago* was also damaged by gunfire and was struck by a LONG LANCE torpedo but remained afloat. At 0146 Mikawa swung north to engage the equally unprepared Northern Group, sinking the *Vincennes* and *Quincy*, and damaging the *Astoria* so badly that she sank next day. By 0240 the Japanese had the American transport fleet at their mercy but instead of destroying it Mikawa ordered a withdrawal, worried by the possibility of a daylight air strike against his ships. This proved to be one of the most critical decisions of the Guadalcanal

campaign and one which earned the private censure of Admiral YAMAMOTO, although in public Mikawa was congratulated on his success. Japanese damage and casualties during the engagement were well within acceptable levels, but while the withdrawal was in progress *Kako* was torpedoed and sunk by the submarine USS *S-44*. Savo Island was, none the less, a serious tactical defeat for the Allies, but one which ultimately resulted in greatly improved communications and damage control procedures.

Savoia-Marchetti Aircraft (Italy)

Savoia-Marchetti SM79 Sparviero The Sparviero was an ungainly tri-motor monoplane which, nevertheless, was a robust and efficient aircraft which was successfully used in bombing, torpedo-bombing and reconnaissance tasks throughout the war; it had first been used in the Spanish Civil War. A twin-engined export version, the SM79B, saw service with the Iraqi and Romanian air forces: it was built under licence in Romania, where its radial engines were replaced by German in-lines. This version saw action on the Russian front. *Span* 69.5ft (21.2m); *engines* 3 1000hp radial, or (Romania) 2 1220hp in-line; *crew* 5; *armament* 5 machine guns, 2645lb (1200kg) of bombs or torpedoes; *speed* 270mph (434kph).

Savoia-Marchetti SM81 Pipistrello Another tri-motor, the Pipistrello was the Italian equivalent of the JUNKERS 52, a heavy bomber-transport which, in its early days, had seen service (in Spain and Ethiopia) as a bomber. It remained in service as a bomber early in the war, mainly operating by night. *Span* 78.75ft (24m); *engines* 3 560hp radial; *crew* 6; *armament* 5 machine guns; *speed* 195mph (314kph).

Savoia-Marchetti SM82 Canguro A heavy tri-motor transport aircraft, the Canguro could carry up to 40 fully-equipped troops or heavy loads of supplies and even stripped-down aircraft in its commodious hull. A small number were also employed as heavy night bombers early in the war. *Span* 97.5ft (29.75m); *engines* 3 850hp radial; *crew* 5; *armament* (as bomber) 1 12.7mm and 3 7.7mm machine guns, 8800lb (4000kg) bombs; *speed* 200mph (322kph).

Savoia-Marchetti SM84 Developed from the SM79, the SM84 was a cleaner aircraft specifically designed for torpedo-bombing. Still a tri-motor, but with a twin fin and rudder

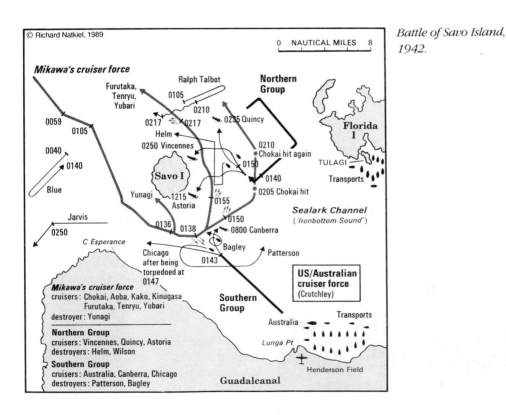

Battle of Savo Island, 1942.

tailplane, it saw service in its designed role and as the standard bomber against convoys in the Mediterranean, over Malta and Tunisia from late 1941 and 1943. However it was never to be as successful as its predecessor. *Span* 69.5ft (21.2m); *engines* 3 1000hp radials; *armament* 6 12.7mm machine guns, 4400lb (1995kg) of torpedoes or bombs; *speed* 266mph (428kph).

S-boats

The official designation of these craft was *Schnellboote* (Fast Boats), although they are generally referred to in British records as E-boats. Several classes were built, most displacing 100–105 tons. They were powered by 3-shaft diesel engines with bhp 6000/7500 and had a maximum speed of 39/42 knots. Armament varied but for most of the war consisted of two 20mm AA guns and two 21-inch torpedo tubes, or one 40mm AA, one 20mm AA and two 21-inch torpedo tubes; from 1944 onwards the gun armament of the larger craft consisted of either one 40mm AA and three 20mm AA, or one 37mm and five 20mm AA. The larger types could also carry six or eight mines in place of re-load torpedoes. The S-boats had a complement of 21/23.

SCAEF Supreme Commander, Allied Expeditionary Force.

Schacht, Dr Hjalmar (1877–1970)

Schacht was a brilliant economist who cured Germany's economic ills during the 1920s. He acted as HITLER's economic adviser during the latter's rise to power, believing that he would restore stability within Germany. In turn this attracted the support of many respectable elements within German society which would otherwise have regarded the Nazis with suspicion. He was appointed President of the Reichsbank in 1933 and Economic Minister two years later, but resigned this post in 1937

KMS Scharnhorst, *with KMS* Gneisenau *in background.*

as he believed that rearmament was absorbing too great a share of the national wealth, an opinion which also cost him his position at the Reichsbank in 1939. Although he placed the German economy on a sound war footing, Schacht did not believe that it was capable of supporting a prolonged conflict. When he retired from the public affairs of the Third Reich in 1943 the Nazis suspected, correctly, that he had long since become disillusioned with Hitler and, in the aftermath of the JULY BOMB PLOT in 1944, he was imprisoned. He was tried by the Allies at NUREMBERG but was acquitted and resumed his career as a highly respected figure in the field of international finance.

Scharnhorst Class Battlecruisers (Ger)

During her first Atlantic cruise *Scharnhorst* sank the armed merchant cruiser HMS RAWALPINDI to the south-east of Iceland on 23 November 1939. She then took part in the

Norwegian Campaign of 1940, sinking the aircraft carrier HMS GLORIOUS and the destroyers HMS *Acaster* and *Ardent*. In 1941, in company with her sister ship GNEISENAU, she sank 22 ships totalling 115,622 tons in the Atlantic, returning to Brest, where she was subjected to bombing by the RAF. On 12 February 1942, together with *Gneisenau* and the heavy cruiser PRINZ EUGEN, she broke out of Brest and succeeded in reaching home waters, sustaining mine and other damage en route. In company with the battleship TIRPITZ she bombarded shore installations on SPITZBERGEN on 6 September 1943. During the Battle of NORTH CAPE (26 December 1943) she was wrecked by gunfire from the battleship HMS DUKE OF YORK and finally sunk by destroyer-launched torpedoes. See also NORWAY, NAVAL CAMPAIGN and GNEISENAU. *Displacement* 31,850 tons; *dimensions* 771ft×98ft 6in (235×30m); *mean draught* 24ft (7.3m); *machinery* 3-shaft geared turbines producing

Scharnhorst class battlecruiser.

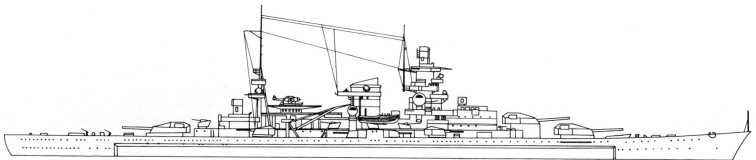

shp 160,000; *speed* 32 knots; *protection* main belt 12–13in; deck 6in; turrets 12in; *armament* 9×11in (3×3); 12×5.9in (6×2); 14×4.1in (7×2); 16×37mm AA (8×2); 10 (later 38)×20mm AA; 6×21in torpedo tubes; *aircraft* 4 (1 catapult); *complement* 1840; *number in class* 2, both launched 1936.

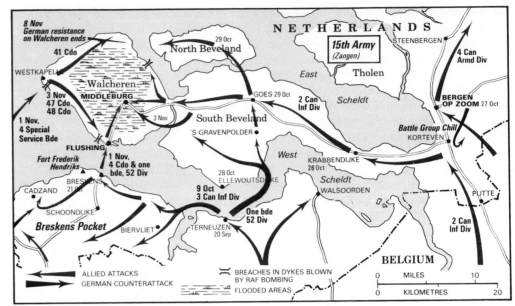

The clearing of the Scheldt Estuary, ending in a two-pronged assault on Walcheren Island.

Scheldt Estuary, 1944

The estuary of the River Scheldt runs from close to ANTWERP to Flushing, and in 1944 was severely flooded by the German demolition of the dykes. MONTGOMERY had directed his attack towards Antwerp, but was eager to turn east to threaten the Ruhr. He left the clearance of the Scheldt estuary, upon which the utility of Antwerp as a supply port depended, to the Canadian 1st Army under General CRERAR. Montgomery later admitted that this was a mistake and that he should have devoted more forces to the task of clearing the estuary. The Germans realized the importance of Antwerp to the Allied forces and had decided to defend the Scheldt vigorously. The Canadians were therefore faced with the task of forcing crossings of a wide river, full of obstacles, against determined troops in excellent defensive positions.

Schellenberg, SS Gen Walther (1911–52)

Schellenberg graduated from the University of Bonn with a degree in law and was already familiar with several languages when he joined the SD (Security Service) in 1934. In 1938, under the direction of HEYDRICH, he formed the first EINSATZGRUPPEN (Special Employment Groups) with SD, SS and Gestapo personnel, for use at HIMMLER's discretion. The following year he was responsible for the kidnapping of three British agents from neutral Holland by an SS unit. He enjoyed intelligence work and produced excellent results, although he failed to break the Lucy spy ring. In 1944, following the fall of Admiral CANARIS and the dismemberment of the ABWEHR, Schellenberg was appointed Head of the Combined Secret Services. He was latterly involved in Himmler's abortive attempt to conclude an armistice with the Western Allies. He escaped to Sweden at the end of the war, where he surrendered himself to SHAEF. Schellenberg compiled an exhaustive diary of the events of the last months of the war. In 1949 he was sentenced to six years' imprisonment.

Schepke, Lt Cdr Joachim

Schepke was one of Germany's leading U-boat aces, sinking 39 ships (a total of 159,130 tons). He preferred to attack at night and on the surface, when his conning tower was difficult to spot and the escorts' ASDIC equipment was unable to function to full advantage. This often enabled him to penetrate within the convoy, where he would sink several ships before slipping away. However, this was an extremely risky tactic, and while attacking Convoy HX 112 on the night of 16 March 1941 his *U-100* was rammed and sunk by the destroyer HMS *Vanoc*. Schepke was killed and only seven of his crew survived.

Schirach, Baldur von (1907–74)

Schirach was leader of the Hitler Youth Movement until August 1940. He was then appointed Gauleiter and Defence Commissioner of Vienna and held this appointment until the war ended. He was responsible for mass deportations, including that of the Jewish population of Vienna. After the war he was sentenced to 20 years' imprisonment by the Allies.

Schlabrendorff, Dr Fabian von

Schlabrendorff, a lawyer by profession, was violently opposed to HITLER and in 1939 advised CHURCHILL, who had still to come to power, that a resistance movement was evolving in Germany. In March 1943, while serving as a lieutenant on the staff of General Hinning von TRESKOW in KLUGE's Army Group Centre,

he managed to plant a bomb, which failed to explode, aboard the aircraft in which the Führer was travelling. He was arrested after the JULY BOMB PLOT of 1944 and savagely tortured by the Gestapo.

Schmetterling

Also known as Hs 117 and Hs 297, this was a German anti-aircraft missile. Originally developed in 1941 it was refused by the Luftwaffe since it was a defensive weapon, and it was then forgotten until 1943 when the Henschel

Baldur von Schirach, leader of the Hitler Youth.

firm received a development contract with an in-service date of February 1945. It consisted of a streamlined missile with tail fins and wings, with two rocket boost take-off units attached. The sustainer motor was a liquid-fuel rocket, and the warhead contained about 44lb (20kg) of high explosive. The missile was to be radio controlled and it had an effective range of about ten miles (16km), with a ceiling of 39,000ft (12,000m) and an alleged accuracy of 20ft (6m) radius. Though some 60 experimental firings were made, the weapon was nowhere near production when the war ended.

Schmundt, Gen Rudolf (1896–1944)

Schmundt, an artilleryman, was still a major when he was appointed HITLER's military adjutant in 1938, and held this post until he was killed by the bomb intended for the Führer in July 1944. Described as a decent man, he was none the less completely under Hitler's spell and encouraged his belief that he possessed a rare military genius. In 1942 Hitler wished to tighten his grip on the German officer corps still further and appointed Schmundt Head of the important Army Personnel Office. Schmundt's major achievement lay in drawing Hitler's attention to MANSTEIN's brilliant plan for the 1940 campaign in the West, and he was probably responsible for persuading the Führer to recall GUDERIAN to active duty in February 1943.

Schniewind, Adm Otto

Throughout his career Schniewind believed that the battleship was the key to power at sea. He began the war as Chief of Naval Staff and on 29 July 1940 issued a memorandum stating that Operation SEELÖWE, the planned invasion of England, could not be mounted that year and that in any event its outcome could not be predicted. In March 1942 he was appointed Flag Officer Navy Group North, a post he held jointly with that of Fleet Commander. He won a notable victory in July, when CONVOY PQ-17 was scattered by the threat of a sortie by his heavy surface units, losing the majority of its ships to attacks by U-boats and the Luftwaffe. However, following the fiasco of the Battle of the BARENTS SEA in December, and the loss of the SCHARNHORST at the Battle of NORTH CAPE a year later, HITLER lost all confidence in the Navy's surface units, the subsequent activities of which were largely confined to the Baltic.

Schnorkel Submarine Breathing Tube

Essentially an air tube leading from a submarine to the surface, enabling the boat to run submerged on its diesel engines. The upper end of the tube was fitted with a valve which closed automatically when water entered. Invented shortly before World War II by Commander I. Wichers of the Royal Netherlands Navy and fitted to several Dutch submarines. It was adopted by the German U-boat arm in 1942–43, when the use of RADAR by Allied aircraft and escorts had resulted in the detection and destruction of many surfaced boats, even during the hours of darkness. The schnorkel's major disadvantages were that, like a periscope, it left a tell-tale plume of spray, and in heavy seas the frequent closing of the waterproof valve often reduced the available air in the boat to dangerously low levels, causing extreme discomfort. Conversely, the schnorkel permitted a greater degree of concealment, particularly when leaving or returning to base in heavily patrolled areas, although continuous submerged running reduced the tempo at which submarine operations could be conducted. Also known colloquially as a "Snort".

Schofield Wheel-cum-Track – Experimental Light Tank (NZ)

Due to pressure on the British armaments industry following the DUNKIRK evacuation, the New Zealand government was forced to consider building tanks of its own. With the

Admiral Schniewind, with Captains Topp and Brinckmann.

exception of the Bob Semple tank, the only vehicle to reach the prototype stage was designed by E. J. Schofield of General Motors (Wellington). This employed the chassis, wheels and other components of the GMC six-cwt truck, together with the tracks and suspension units of the UNIVERSAL CARRIER, the idea being to combine high road speed on wheels with good cross-country performance on tracks. The vehicle was armed with a 2-pdr gun and coaxial 7.92mm Besa machine gun, protected by 10mm armour and manned by a crew of three. Powered by a Chevrolet 29.5hp petrol engine, its maximum speed was 45.6mph (73kph) on wheels and 25.7mph (41kph) on tracks. The design was not developed beyond the prototype.

Schörner, FM Ferdinand (1892–1973)

Schörner commanded the 6th Mountain Division in northern Norway where, in late 1941, it took part in the advance on MURMANSK. He then commanded XIX Mountain Corps in Finland. In 1943 he was given command of XL Panzer Corps, which he led ably during the fighting on the DNIEPR. In February 1944 he was made Chief of the National Socialist Leadership Corps, but the following month was appointed commander of Army Group South Ukraine. In July he became commander of Army Group North and in January 1945 commander of Army Group Centre. An ardent Nazi, he was careless of his men's lives and in the last year of the war his philosophy of holding ground at any price earned HITLER's admiration and gratitude. On 29 April 1945, the day before the Führer committed suicide, he was named the Army's last Commander-in-Chief. He was sentenced to 25 years' imprisonment by the Russians but was released after serving nine.

Schrage Musik ("Jazz Musik")

A pair of fixed upward-firing cannon mounted behind the cockpit of twin-engined German night fighters. The mounting was introduced in August 1943 and proved extremely effective. The night-fighter pilot had only to manoeuvre beneath the bomber, where he remained invisible, and fire a short, lethal burst into one of its engines.

Schulenberg, Count Werner von der

Schulenberg was German ambassador to Moscow and in 1939 laid the groundwork for the Non-Aggression Pact with STALIN. He tried to persuade HITLER against attacking the Soviet Union, believing that Stalin was willing to make concessions, and suggested the creation of a quasi-independent Ukraine as a buffer state. He was one of the conspirators in the JULY BOMB PLOT against the Führer in 1944.

Schwartz, Fall (Plan Black)

German plan for the establishment of a strong defence line in Italy, August 1943.

Schweinfurt, Germany, 1943

A city in Bavaria, 28 miles (45km) north-east of Wurzberg. During the war it was a centre of the German ball-bearing industry, and as such was considered a valuable economic target for bombing. On 17 August 1943, together with Regensburg, another ball-bearing centre, it was the target for a daylight raid by the US Air Force. Of the 230 bombers which attacked Schweinfurt, 36 (15.5%) failed to return, a casualty figure the USAF were unwilling to sustain. A second daylight raid took place on 14 October 1943, when 291 BOEING FLYING FORTRESSES were accompanied by fighters as far as AACHEN, after which the fighters had to turn back and the unescorted bombers were at the mercy of the German defences. Of this force 60 were lost, and 138 damaged, an attrition rate which caused the USAF to hold back on long-range raiding until a suitable long-range escort fighter was available to protect the bombers.

Schweppenburg, Lt Gen Freiherr Leo Geyr von

Schweppenburg served as German military attaché in London in 1936. He led the 3rd Panzer Division during the campaign in Poland and commanded the XXIV and XL Panzer Corps on the Eastern Front. At the end of 1943 he was appointed commander of Panzer Group West, which he led during the first weeks of the NORMANDY campaign, being seriously wounded on 9 June 1944. He returned to his command later in the month but was dismissed by HITLER in July and was not employed again.

Scobie, Gen Ronald (1893–1969)

In October 1941 Scobie's 6th Division (redesignated 70th Division) arrived by sea at TOBRUK, replacing the besieged Australian garrison. The following month his troops broke out to meet the advancing 8TH ARMY during Operation CRUSADER. In 1942 he was appointed garrison commander of MALTA and in 1943 became Chief of Staff Middle East Command. He was appointed GOC Greece in the autumn of 1944, a task made the more difficult by the civil war which continued until January 1945, when a temporary halt was brought to the activities of the Communist forces.

Scoones, General Sir Geoffrey Allen Percival (1893–1975)

Scoones commanded the British IV Corps on the India–Burma frontier from 1942 until 1944. In February 1944, having received warning of the impending Japanese HA-GO offensive, he decided to withdraw his divisions to the IMPHAL plain and fight the decisive battle there with the full benefit of air support and supply. He also accepted the advice of his brother, Brigadier Reginald Scoones, that the country was suitable for armoured operations, and the bulk of the latter's 254th Indian Tank Brigade was brought forward. These factors, coupled with some of the bitterest fighting of the entire war, resulted in a humiliating defeat for the Japanese. In June, IV Corps went over to the offensive, driving the enemy across the CHINDWIN and into Central Burma. Scoones was appointed GOC Central India Command on 7 December 1944 and knighted a week later.

Scorpion – Mineclearing Flail Tank (UK)

The MATILDA Scorpion was a normal gun tank fitted with a Ford or Bedford engine on the right of the hull. This drove a chain flail ahead of the vehicle, exploding mines in its path. Twelve of these vehicles were used in night

Bombs from US AAF Flying Fortresses fall on Schweinfurt, 1943. The aiming point (AP) is marked in the middle of the map.

attacks during the Second Battle of ALAMEIN, two rear-facing red lights being mounted on antennae to indicate their position to following troops. The GRANT Scorpion, developed in Tunisia, followed the same layout, an improved version having a second Bedford engine mounted on the left of the hull. In both cases the 75mm main armament had to be stripped out of its sponson to provide clearance for the chains. A few Grant Scorpions took part in the campaign in Sicily. SHERMAN Scorpions, which retained their main armament and used two Dodge engines to drive the flail, served in Italy. A VALENTINE version of the Scorpion, equipped with two Ford flail engines, was produced in the UK and used for training in 1943 and 1944. The Scorpion was replaced by the Sherman CRAB as these became available.

SD Sicherheitsdienst (German – Security Force). The security element of the SS, controlled by HIMMLER.

Seabees

The nickname for the US Navy's construction battalions (CBs) formed to build airfields and base facilities on captured islands during the American advance across the Pacific. The Seabees were also trained to fight as infantrymen, but their primary responsibility was construction. The first Seabee units to see active service were employed at HENDERSON FIELD on GUADALCANAL.

SEAC South-East Asia Command.

Sealion/Seatrain

Allied contingency plan for the evacuation of the SALERNO beach-head, September 1943.

Section

Tactical sub-unit of an infantry PLATOON normally commanded by a Corporal and consisting of a seven-man rifle group and a three-man light machine gun group.

Seeckt, Col Gen Hans von (1866–1936)

Seeckt, a former Guards officer, was Commander-in-Chief of the 100,000-strong army which the Allies permitted Germany to retain after the Treaty of Versailles. By means of selective recruiting, he produced an army of potential leaders so that when the time for expansion came under HITLER it proceeded smoothly. Seeckt was dismissed from his post

in 1926 following an uncharacteristic lapse which betrayed his sympathy for the now-defunct monarchy, but served with the military mission to China until 1935.

Seelöwe (Sea Lion)

Projected German invasion of the United Kingdom, 1940.

Self-Propelled Artillery

See BISHOP, GUN MOTOR CARRIAGE, HUMMEL, HOWITZER MOTOR CARRIAGE, PRIEST, SEXTON, WESPE.

Semoventi – Assault Guns (Italy)

Copy of the German STURMGESCHUTZ based on the M13/40 and subsequent medium tank chassis with the main armament in a ball mounting at the front of a low superstructure. The Semovente da 75/18 entered service in 1941 and equipped artillery assault groups consisting of two four-gun batteries, later increased to three six-gun batteries. The design proved so successful that in March 1943 all medium tank chassis production was diverted to Semoventi. After the conclusion of the armistice between Italy and the Allies manufacture continued and large numbers were used by the German Army in Italy as well as by Fascist troops fighting for MUSSOLINI's newly created republic. In 1943 the design was up-armoured to 50mm and later models were up-gunned with 75mm L/34 or L/46 dual purpose guns, or a 105mm L/25 howitzer. Somewhat outside the mainstream of development was the Semovente da 50/53 su Scafo M41, which employed an open mounting for its 30mm L/53 anti-aircraft/anti-tank gun on the rear of a cut-down medium tank chassis; several of these vehicles saw active service in Tunisia. A medium tank chassis was also used as a self-

propelled carriage for the Model 1935 149mm howitzer. The post-war Italian Army was equipped with Semoventi 75/18 for several years. *Semovente da 75/18 su Scafo M40 Weight* 13 tons; *speed* 20.5mph (33kph); *armour* 30mm; *armament* 1 75mm L/18 howitzer; *engine* Fiat-SPA 15T 125hp diesel; *crew* 3.

Sendai Class Cruisers (Jap)

Displacement 5195 tons; *dimensions* 534ft×46ft 6in (162.7×14m); *mean draught* 16ft (4.8m); *machinery* 4-shaft geared turbines producing shp 90,000; *speed* 35.25 knots; *protection* main belt 2in; *armament* 7×5.5in (7×1); 2×3in AA; 8×24in torpedo tubes (4×2); *aircraft* 1; *complement* 450; *number in class* 3, launched 1923–25.

Senger und Etterlin, General Fridolin von

A cavalryman, Senger was appointed commander of the 17th Panzer Division in 1942 and led it during the abortive attempt to relieve STALINGRAD. In 1943 he conducted the skilful retreat and evacuation of the German forces in SICILY and withdrew the isolated garrisons of CORSICA and Sardinia to the Italian mainland. He commanded XIV Panzer Corps during the campaign in Italy and was responsible for the stubborn defence of the Monte CASSINO sector of the GUSTAV LINE. As the campaign drew to its close in 1945, he deliberately avoided fighting in the historic city centre of BOLOGNA, thereby preserving its priceless art treasures.

Senger–Riegel Line

The German name for a defensive line in Italy, known commonly to the Allies as the "ADOLF HITLER LINE".

Semovente da 75/18 assault gun.

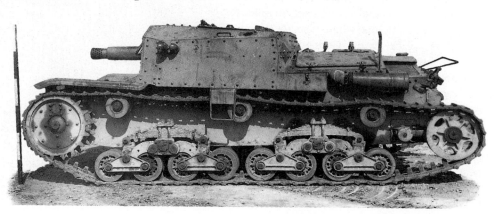

Senio River, Italy, 1944–45

One of many Italian rivers flowing into the Adriatic and presenting a natural barrier to the progress of the British 8th Army, the Senio joined the River Reno north of Ravenna and formed the obstacle in front of which the Germans set up defensive positions during the winter of 1944–45. General Herr, commanding the German 10th Army, decided (against the instructions of OKW) to hold the Senio lightly and concentrate his main defences further back, along the river Santerno, out of Allied artillery range. The Senio position was attacked on 9 April 1945 by a tremendous artillery bombardment, accompanied by air strikes on the Santerno line, and by 12 April the New Zealand and 8th Indian divisions had crossed both rivers and broken the German defences.

Sentinel – Cruiser Tank (Australia)

Due to pressure on the British armaments industry in the aftermath of the DUNKIRK evacuation, the Australian government decided in June 1940 that it would build its own cruiser tank. This employed a cast one-piece hull and a Hotchkiss-type suspension with horizontal volute springing. By 1943, however, GRANTS, LEES, MATILDAS and STUARTS were becoming available and in July the Sentinel project was cancelled. Simultaneously, experimental prototypes had been produced armed with a 25- or 17-pdr gun in place of the 2-pdr. The Sentinel was used solely for training and was not withdrawn until 1956. *Weight* 28 tons; *speed* 30mph (48kph); *armour* 65mm; *armament* 1 2-pdr gun; 2 Vickers .303-cal machine guns; *engines* 3 Cadillac V-8 petrol, each 117hp; *crew* 5.

Seraph, HMS – "S" Class Submarine

On 22 October 1942 *Seraph*, commanded by Lieutenant J. Jewell, landed Major-General Mark CLARK and his staff at Cherchel, 50 miles (80km) west of Algiers, where a secret meeting took place with General GIRAUD's representatives in North Africa. The result was a doubtful understanding that French forces in North Africa would offer only token resistance to an Anglo-American landing. The Allied delegates were then taken off by the submarine, but not without difficulty. On 6 November *Seraph* picked up Giraud himself near Toulon and then transferred him to a flying boat in which he completed his journey to Gibraltar on the eve of the TORCH landings.

Serov, Gen Ivan (1905–)

Serov served as Soviet Commissar for Internal Affairs and in 1941 was appointed Deputy Commissar for State Security under the infamous BERIA, Head of the NKVD. He was responsible for the mass deportation of several million people and also executed many whom he considered undesirable, the majority of his victims coming from the Ukraine or the Baltic States. In 1945 he was appointed Deputy Supreme Commander of Soviet Forces in Germany.

Servia Pass, Greece, 1941

One of three routes through the Mount Olympus massif, which in April 1941 lay in the path of the advancing German 12th Army, the Servia pass was held by a combined Australian–New Zealand force. Occupying an excellent position and supported by artillery, they formed an impenetrable block and the Germans, after several attempts which led to severe losses, abandoned their attempt to force the pass. By this time they had penetrated the other routes and were able to outflank the Servia position, and the Anzac force withdrew in good order on 17 April.

Sevastopol, Soviet Union, 1942

A city on the Black Sea and one of the country's major seaports. In Operation BARBAROSSA, Sevastopol was originally

The progress of the siege of Sevastopol.

approached in November 1941 as the general German advance swept into and past the Crimea. But with the greater prizes of MOSCOW and LENINGRAD in view, it was decided simply to isolate the city by a five-division blockade until a more convenient time. That time arrived in May 1942 when the city was besieged by the 11th German Army, under MANSTEIN, with a strength of ten infantry divisions and 120 batteries of artillery, including the monster 600mm "Thor" howitzers and 800mm "GUSTAV" railway gun. The German Navy also mounted a sea blockade. The Soviet defenders numbered about 106,000 men with

German and Romanian troops besiege and take Sevastopol, 1942.

some 700 guns and MORTARS. On 2 June 1942 the German artillery began a five-day bombardment, accompanied by air strikes, and on 7 June the infantry assault began. Fighting was extremely bitter, much of it hand-to-hand, and the Germans took heavy casualties, requiring reinforcements to be sent from other formations. On 18 June German forces had broken through to the sea at North Bay and on the 23rd the Soviet command ordered its forces to fall back to the city and the southern part of the area. The defenders were now feeling the effects of the siege in a shortage of ammunition and other supplies, even though these were being brought in at great risk by Soviet submarines, and on 30 June the Germans succeeded in breaking into the city. This led the Soviet command to authorize complete withdrawal, and many of the Soviet troops were evacuated by small boats between 30 June and 3 July, when the German occupation of the city and surrounding area was complete.

Sexton – Self-Propelled 25-pdr Gun (UK and Canada)

A combination of the Canadian RAM medium tank chassis and the British 25-pdr gun-howitzer, with layout similar to that of the American HOWITZER MOTOR CARRIAGE M7. Production of the Sexton commenced at the Montreal Locomotive Works early in 1943 and a total of 2150 were built. As the vehicle became available it replaced the M7 in British and Canadian service in which it remained active for many years after the war. The Sexton stowed 87 rounds of high explosive or smoke, plus 18 rounds of armour piercing ammunition.

Sexton self-propelled 25-pdr.

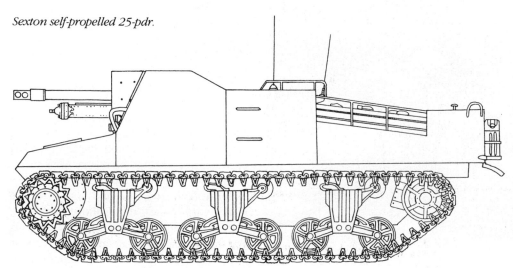

Seyss-Inquart, Artur von (1892–1946)

Seyss-Inquart was an Austrian Nazi who came to power in 1938, first as his country's Minister of the Interior and then as Chancellor following the German occupation. In October 1939 he was appointed Governor General of those areas of Poland which had not been absorbed into Germany or the Soviet Union. In May 1940 he became Reich Commissioner of the Netherlands with almost absolute power, being responsible only to HITLER for his actions. During his period in office he imposed fines and confiscations, inflicted reprisals, deported 117,000 Jews and compelled five million Dutch citizens to work for Germany. He was captured in 1945 and executed for his crimes the following year.

SHAEF Supreme Headquarters, Allied Expeditionary Force.

Shaped Charge Munitions

The shaped charge (also called Hollow Charge, Neumann Effect, Monroe Effect, Hohlladung) is a method of using high explosive to penetrate hard targets, particularly armour or reinforced concrete. It relies upon a charge of explosive which has the face hollowed out in a cone or hemisphere and lined with metal or glass. On detonation, the shape of the hollow causes the blast waves to converge on the axis of the hollow and advance at high speed in the form of a jet of finely-divided liner material and high temperature gas. The momentum of this jet is sufficient to penetrate armour or any other obstacle. The shaped charge was used in grenades, artillery projectiles and static demolition charges, but was eventually found

to be best when delivered by a fin-stabilized device such as a rocket. It was the only method of defeating armour capable of being used with a light weapon and was thus invaluable for infantry.

The shaped charge effect was originally discovered by Monroe in the USA in the 1880s; it remained a scientific curiosity until the 1914–18 war when it was investigated as a possible weapon. Neumann, in Germany, was responsible for discovering the importance of the liner in the 1920s. It was perfected by two Swiss experimenters, Matthias and Mohaupt, in 1938. Their announcement caused research to be undertaken in Britain and Germany – resulting in the introduction of weapons early in 1941.

Shaposhnikov, Marshal Boris (1882–1945)

During the early part of the war Shaposhnikov served at various periods as Deputy People's Commissar for Defence, Chief of General Staff and as Head of Stavka, his role depending on the degree to which STALIN found his advice acceptable. He counselled against the forward deployment of the Soviet Army on the western frontier, where it was vulnerable to the German BLITZKRIEG technique, and his judgement was vindicated by the disasters of 1941. He assisted in planning the counteroffensive at MOSCOW in the winter of 1941, but believed that the Soviet Army should remain on the strategic defensive until it had recovered from its terrible losses. In 1942 he opposed Stalin's ill-fated KHARKOV counteroffensive, which he considered to be premature, and was again proved correct. In June 1943 he was appointed Commandant of the Voroshilov Military Academy and held this post until his death.

SHELREP Shelling report (UK). Report submitted by troops after being shelled, giving details of the type of gun and direction of fire, for use by the counter-bombardment artillery.

Sherman – Medium Tank M4 Series (USA)

Designed as the successor to the stop-gap Medium Tank M3 LEE, retaining the latter's proven chassis, engine, transmission and lower hull but mounting the 75mm main armament in a cast turret with all-round traverse, thereby eliminating the 37mm gun and reducing the crew to five. The various design features were incorporated in a trials vehicle, the T6, which inherited the Lee's sponson doors; these were dispensed with when the design was standardized as the Medium Tank M4 on 5 September 1941. By the time the Lima Locomotive Works produced the pilot model in February 1942 the United States was at war and mass production commenced the following month. Altogether, ten major manufacturers were involved in the construction programme, including the American Locomotive Company, Baldwin Locomotive Works, Chrysler Detroit Tank Arsenal, Federal Machine and Welder Company, Fisher Grand Blanc Arsenal, Ford Motor Company, Lima Locomotive Works, Pacific Car and Foundry Company, Pressed Steel Car Company and Pullman Standard Manufacturing Company. When production ceased in June 1945 no less than 49,234 had been built, a figure which exceeded the combined tank output of the United Kingdom and Germany. The Canadians also built 188 M4A1s, which they called the Grizzly I. The principal dif-

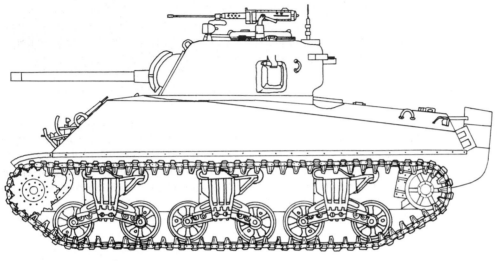

Sherman medium tank M4.

Upgunned Sherman M4A1 with 76mm gun.

ference between the various Marks lay in their power units, but the M4A1 was easily identified by its cast as opposed to welded hull; the US Ordnance Department's designation M4A5 is misleading in that it refers to the broadly similar Canadian RAM medium tank. Combat experience revealed that the Sherman was undergunned in comparison with the TIGER and PANTHER and later models of the M4A1, M4A2 and M4A3 were armed with a 76mm gun in a re-designed turret, adding the suffix (76) to their designation. This provided some improvement in armour-piercing capability but performance fell below that of the British FIREFLY conversion, which was armed with a 17-pdr gun. Close support versions of the M4 and M4A3, armed with a 105mm howitzer, were produced in 1944, adding (105) to their designation. The steady increase in the tank's weight led to the development of wider tracks used in conjunction with a horizontal volute spring suspension (HVSS) which replaced the vertical volute springs on some Marks from mid-1944. Active service also revealed that fire spread very rapidly throughout the vehicle if it was penetrated and in an attempt to contain this wet stowage was adopted for the ammunition, which was re-housed in water protected racks beneath the turret floor; models thus equipped, including the M4A1(76), M4A2(76), M4A3 and M4A3(76), added W to their designation. The last version of the tank to enter service was the M4A3E2, of which 254 were built. This was designed as an assault tank with 150mm armour and weighed 42 tons.

In British service the following designations were used to distinguish between the various Models: *Sherman I* – M4; *Sherman II* – M4A1; *Sherman III* – M4A2; *Sherman IV* – M4A3; *Sherman V* – M4A4. Where applicable, these were qualified by the suffixes: A – 76mm gun; B – 105mm howitzer; C – 17-pdr gun; Y – HVSS. The Sherman first saw action with the British 8th Army during the Second Battle of ALAMEIN and subsequently served in every major theatre of war. As well as providing the backbone of the US Armored Force it was supplied to the majority of America's allies, including the Soviet Union. Its better known derivates included the DD DUPLEX-DRIVE swimming tank, the CRAB flail tank, GUN MOTOR CARRIAGES M10, M12, M36 and M40, HOWITZER MOTOR CARRIAGE M7, the Calliope and Whiz Bang multi-barrel rocket launcher systems and the SKINK anti-aircraft tank, and its chassis was also used for scores of experimental projects. Service since 1945 has included the Korean War, the Arab/Israeli Wars and the Indo/Pakistani Wars, and in some armies the Sherman remains active to this day, albeit in a much altered form. See *M4 Sherman* by George Forty (Blandford). *Weight* 30.2–33.6 tons; *speed* 24–29mph (38–47kph); *armour* 75–105mm; *armament* 1 75mm gun; 2 .30-cal Browning machine guns; *engine(s)* 1 Wright Continental R-975 petrol radial 353hp (M4 and M4A1); 2 General Motors 6-71 diesel, each 187.5hp (M4A2); 1 Ford GAA V-8 petrol 500hp (M4A3); 5 Chrysler WC Multibank petrol, total 370hp (M4A4); 1 Caterpillar RD-1820 diesel radial 450hp (M4A6); *crew* 5.

Shigemitsu, Mamoru (1881–1957)
Shigemitsu served as Japanese ambassador to the USSR 1936–38, to the Court of St James, 1938–41, and to Vichy France, 1942–43. He became Foreign Minister in 1943 and held this appointment until April 1945, when he was replaced by TOGO. Although he wished to substitute a policy of conciliation for that of military occupation of conquered territories, the Allies sentenced him to several years' imprisonment for war crimes in 1945.

Shimikaze, IJN – Destroyer
Shimikaze, launched in 1942 and commissioned in May 1943, was an experimental high-speed destroyer fitted with newly designed engines capable of working at 400°C with a pressure of 571lbs per square inch. *Shimikaze* was sunk by air attack 55 miles (88km) north-east of Cebu on 11 November 1944. Although 16 more vessels of this type were ordered, all were cancelled. *Displacement* 2567 tons; *dimensions* 415ft×36ft 9in (126.5×11.2m); mean draught 13ft 6in (4m); *machinery* 2-shaft geared turbines producing shp 75,000; *speed* 39.75 knots; *armament* 6×5in DP (3×2); 4×25mm AA (2×2); 15×24in torpedo tubes (3×5); 2 depth charge throwers and 18 depth charges.

Shinano, IJN – Aircraft Carrier
Shinano was laid down as a YAMATO Class battleship in May 1940 and completed as an aircraft carrier in November 1944. She was to have been a base ship for repairing aircraft from other carriers, and supplying them with munitions and fuel. She was, however, sunk by the submarine USS *Archerfish* on 29 November 1944 while on passage to complete fitting out. *Displacement* 64,800 tons; *dimen-*

Japanese Shinyo (suicide boat) being tested by US forces.

sions 872ft 8in×119ft 3in (266×36.3m); mean draught 33ft 9in (10.3m); *machinery* 4-shaft geared turbines producing shp 150,000; *speed* 27 knots; *protection* main belt 8in; magazine 7in; flight deck 4in; *armament* 16×5in DP (8×2); 145×25mm AA (35×3 and 40×1); 12×28 120mm rocket launchers; *aircraft* 47; *complement* 2400.

Shingle
Allied landing at ANZIO, January 1944.

Shinyo, IJN – Aircraft Carrier
Converted as a light carrier from the former German liner *Scharnhorst* 1942–43. *Shinyo* was sunk in the South Yellow Sea on 17 November 1944 by the submarine USS *Spadefish*. *Displacement* 17,500 tons; *dimensions* 650ft 6in×84ft 9in (198×25.8m); mean draught 25ft 6in (7.7m); *machinery* 2-shaft geared turbines producing shp 26,000; *speed* 22 knots; *armament* 8×5in DP; 42×25mm AA (10×3 and 12×1); *aircraft* 33; *complement* 948.

Shinyo – Explosive Motor Boats (Jap)
Together with the KAITEN suicide submarines, these craft were the naval equivalent of the air force KAMIKAZE. The majority were wooden hulled and powered by one or two engines, giving a speed of 25/30 knots. The bows were packed with 4400lbs (2000 kg) of TNT designed to explode on impact with the enemy vessel, towards which the craft was steered by its pilot. Approximately 6000 were built but their results were disappointing.

Shiratsuyu Class Destroyers (Jap)
Displacement 1580 tons; *dimensions* 335ft 6in×32ft 6in (102.2×9.9m); mean draught 11ft 6in (3.5m); *machinery* 2-shaft geared turbines producing shp 42,000; *speed* 34 knots; *armament* 5×5in DP (2×2 and 1×1); 4×25mm AA; 2×13mm; 8×24in torpedo tubes (2×4); *complement* 180; *number in class* 10, launched 1935–37.

Shock Troops
Pre-war propaganda term implying troops and formations specifically trained and equipped to break through the enemy's front. Although the term suggests an élite, this is a misleading valuation as on the Eastern Front both the German and Soviet armies often spearheaded their most difficult assaults with penal battalions which were driven forward at gunpoint until they were destroyed. Nevertheless, the term is also frequently applied to WAFFEN SS and Soviet Guards formations, and indeed to any troops of high fighting value, and the Russians employed several Shock Armies which were suitably reinforced for specific tasks.

Sho-Go (Operation Victory)
Japanese naval plan for the defence of the PHILIPPINES, resulting in the Battle of LEYTE GULF, October 1944.

Shoho Class Aircraft Carriers (Jap)
Both vessels in this class, *Shoho* and *Zuiho*, were based on the hulls of submarine tenders and entered service at the end of 1940. *Shoho*

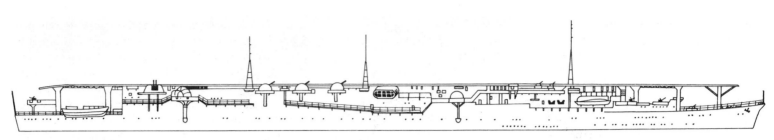

Shoho class aircraft carrier.

was sunk by air attack at the Battle of the CORAL SEA. *Zuiho* was damaged at the Battle of SANTA CRUZ but was present at the Battle of the PHILIPPINE SEA where her aircraft scored a hit on the battleship USS *South Dakota*. She was herself sunk by air attack during the Battle of LEYTE GULF. *Displacement* 11,262 tons; *dimensions* 712×59ft (217×18m); mean draught 21ft 9in (6.6m); *machinery* 2-shaft geared turbines producing shp 52,000; *speed* 28 knots; *armament* 8×5in AA (4×2); 15×25mm AA (5×3); *aircraft* 30; *complement* 785; *number in class* 2.

Shokaku Class Aircraft Carriers (Jap)

Shokaku and her sister ship *Zuikaku* entered service in 1941 and formed the 5th Carrier Division. This had a supporting role during the attack on PEARL HARBOR and took part in subsequent carrier operations in the East Indies and the Indian Ocean. *Shokaku* was damaged at the Battle of the CORAL SEA and the division returned to Japan to make good its loss in air-crews, so missing the Battle of MIDWAY. *Shokaku* was torpedoed and sunk by the submarine USS *Cavella* during the Battle of the PHILIPPINE SEA. *Zuikaku*, serving with the 3rd Carrier Division, was sunk by air attack during the Battle of LEYTE GULF. *Displacement* 25,675 tons; *dimensions* 844ft 9in×85ft 4in (257.5×26m); mean draught 29ft (8.9m); *machinery* 4-shaft geared turbines producing shp 160,000; *speed* 34 knots; *armament* 16×5in DP (8×2); 42–96×25mm AA (12×3); 6×28 120mm rocket launchers (1944 – *Zuikaku*); *aircraft* 72; *complement* 1660.

Short Aircraft (UK)

Short Stirling The first RAF four-engined bomber to enter service, in late 1940. The Stirling was an ungainly-looking aircraft, but it was extremely agile, due to its low aspect ratio wing and powerful elevators, and despite its limited ceiling, about 18,000ft (5490m), it was popular with its crews. It was able to sustain massive damage and still keep flying. Although it had a substantial bomb capacity, the bomb bays were so designed that it could not carry any individual bomb larger than 2000lb (907kg) weight. It was phased out of the bombing offensive in late 1943, ending the war as a minelayer, carrier for electronic countermeasures, glider tug and a transport. *Span* 99ft (30.2m); *engines* 4 1650hp radial; *crew* 8; *armament* 10 machine guns, 18,000lb (8165kg) of bombs; *speed* 270mph (434kph).

Short Sunderland This was derived from the pre-war Imperial Airways "Empire" commercial flying boat, and retained quite a luxurious specification with two decks, galley, wardroom, sleeping quarters and other refinements. Used mainly for maritime surveillance, it had a range of almost 3000 miles (4827km), allowing it to patrol far into the Atlantic Ocean. Its armament earned it the nickname of "Flying Porcupine", for in spite of its appearance it had a formidable record of shooting down enemy aircraft. It was also highly successful as a submarine hunter and destroyer. *Span* 112.75ft (34.4m); *engines* 4 1200hp radial; *crew* 13; *armament* 14 machine guns, 2200lb (1000kg) of bombs or depth charges; *speed* 215mph (346kph).

Shrapnel

British plan to occupy the Cape Verde Islands if Spain entered the war and Gibraltar was besieged, 1940.

Shumushu Class Escorts (Jap)

Displacement 860 tons; *dimensions* 255ft×32ft 6in (77.7×9.8m); mean draught 10ft (3m); *machinery* 2-shaft geared diesels

An RAF Sunderland flying boat, unarmed, used in the long distance transport role.

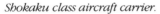

Shokaku class aircraft carrier.

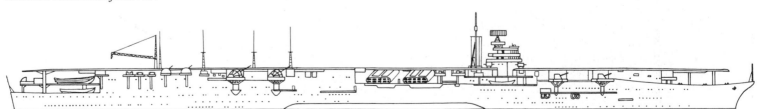

producing shp 4200; *speed* 19.5 knots; *armament* 3×4.7in (3×1); 4×25mm AA (2×2); 12 depth charges; *number in class* 4, launched 1939–40.

Sibuyan Sea, Battle of the

See LEYTE GULF, Battle of

Sichelschnitt (Sickle-Cut)

Modification of GELB, FALL, involving a drive across France from the ARDENNES to the sea, May 1940.

Sicily, Mediterranean Sea, 1943

The Mediterranean island off the "toe" of Italy. It was invaded by the US 7th Army, under General PATTON, and the British 8th Army, under General MONTGOMERY, on 10 July 1943. The US forces landed on the southern coast between Licata and Scoglitti and advanced north-west to take Palermo on 22 July, then swung east to clear the island in the direction of Italy. The British force landed on the south-eastern tip, between Pozzallo and Avola and advanced up the eastern half of the island towards Messina. Airborne forces were used in the initial assault but with scant success due to poor navigation, many of the gliders crashing into the sea and paratroops landing in the wrong place. The campaign was hard fought, since the island was strongly defended by good German formations (15th Panzergrenadier and "Hermann Göring" Divisions) who took advantage of the difficult terrain. Messina was entered by Patton on 17 August 1943, though in fact the outskirts of the town were by then in the hands of British troops. By then over 100,000 German and Italian troops had escaped to the mainland.

The British landing in Sicily, July 1943.

Sickle

Build-up of the US 8th Air Force in the United Kingdom.

Sidi Barrani, Egypt, 1940

A village on the Mediterranean coast, close to the Libyan border. In September 1940 Marshal GRAZIANI advanced towards Egypt from his base in Tripolitania, reached Sidi Barrani and there constructed a fortified position, garrisoned by five divisions supported by artillery and armour. Once installed, Graziani was reluctant to move, and on 8 December the British Western Desert Force (4th Indian and 7th Armoured divisions plus an independent force of approximately two-battalion strength – a total of 30,000 men) under the command of General O'CONNOR attacked the outlying defences. They were rapidly subdued, 7th Armoured Division made a flanking swing to cut the escape road from Sidi Barrani while the rest of the force advanced on the village, and on 10 December the battle was over. The Italians lost 38,000 prisoners, 237 guns and 73 tanks; total Allied casualties were 624.

Sidi Nsir, Battle of, 1943

The northern thrust of the German OCH-SENKOPF offensive was aimed at the communication centre of Béja, being spearheaded by an armoured battle-group of 74 tanks, including 14 Tigers, under the command of Colonel Rudolph Lang. Lang's route took him through mountainous country in which he could not deploy effectively and on 26 February 1943 his advance was checked by the British outpost at Sidi Nsir, held by the 5th Battalion The Hampshire Regiment and two troops of 155 Battery Royal Artillery. Under constant attack, the outpost put up the most determined resistance throughout the day, disabling 40 tanks before being overrun during the evening. Only 120 Hampshires and nine artillerymen succeeded in reaching their own lines after dark but the defence enabled a co-ordinated defence to be prepared at HUNT'S GAP, and against this Lang's continued advance was finally halted.

Sidi Rezegh, Cyrenaica, 1941

A village south-east of TOBRUK which in 1941 held an Italian airfield and small garrison. It was the objective of the British 7th Armoured Division in Operation CRUSADER and was taken on 19 November. The British force then defended the position, in preparation for the relief of Tobruk, and was reinforced by the Support Group and a brigade of South African infantry. Seeing the threat, ROMMEL ordered 15th and 21st Panzer Divisions to attack Sidi Rezegh. On 21 November 7th Armoured Division was to attack northward while the Tobruk garrison simultaneously attempted to break out; but the former were themselves attacked by the Panzers from the south, drawing its main force southwards and leaving the Tobruk garrison to its own devices. Meanwhile 4th and 22nd British Armoured Brigades were advancing against the Panzers from the south. As a result, the ensuing battle was extremely confused and tank losses on both sides were considerable. Rommel now considered that the threat to Tobruk had been contained and withdrew most of his remaining tanks for an assault on the Egyptian border, hoping to find it relatively undefended. On 24 November he made his "dash to the wire", to relieve the Halfaya garrison, but was frustrated by the recovery of British XXX Corps and the threat posed by the New Zealand Division advancing on Tobruk.

Siebel Si 204 (Ger)

Developed in 1940 as a potential light transport, the design was changed after only a few had been built to this specification and the Si 204 became the Luftwaffe's principal aircrew trainer, capable of carrying five students in addition to its operating crew. In order to concentrate German aircraft production on more urgently needed types, manufacture of the Si 204 was carried out in various Czech and French factories under German supervision. *Span* 69.75ft (21.25m); *engines* 2 575hp in-line; *crew* 2; *speed* 220mph (354kph).

Siegfried

Advance by German Army Group B on STALIN-GRAD, 1942.

Siegfried Line

A German fortified defensive line running along the Dutch and French borders approximately from München-Gladbach to the Swiss border near Freiburg. It was originally conceived by the German Army as a series of earth redoubts facing the MAGINOT LINE, the object being merely to slow and disrupt any advance rather than offer a solid resistance. When HITLER became Commander-in-Chief in 1938, he issued orders for a far more grandiose scheme of permanent fortifications, and this was featured prominently in contemporary propaganda as a counter to the French line. In fact very little was done, and the films and press pictures were actually of Czech defences on the east German border, taken over by the Germans in 1938. Work on the Siegfried Line continued in desultory fashion, the principal features being a deep belt of concrete "Dragon's Teeth" tank obstacles covered by pillboxes. Behind this a second line of artillery positions was intended but very few were built, and work was virtually suspended from 1940 to 1944. With the prospect, and then fact, of an Allied invasion, work was resumed, but the Line never became a formidable obstacle. Nevertheless, its propaganda had been successful and it loomed large in Allied planning fears.

Sikorski, Gen Wladyslaw (1881–1943)

Sikorski was not offered a command in the Polish Army when war broke out and was in Paris when POLAND was overrun. He became

39th Infantry regiment of 3rd US Armored Division crossing the Siegfried Line, 18 February 1945.

General Wladyslaw Sikorski greeted by Dr Litauer, President of the Foreign Press Association, Allied Conference, London 1942.

Prime Minister of the Polish government-in-exile and Commander-in-Chief of the Free Polish Forces, which numbered 100,000 by the spring of 1940. After the fall of France, Sikorski and his troops moved to the United Kingdom. Following the German invasion of Russia in 1941, he concluded an alliance with MAISKY, the Soviet ambassador in London, repudiating the partition of Poland, re-establishing her pre-war frontiers and sanctioning the creation of an army from Polish prisoners in Russian hands. However, the fact that so many of the latter had disappeared without trace progressively soured relations between the Polish government and the Kremlin, and it was only at CHURCHILL's insistence that a serious rift between the Allies was avoided in 1943 when Sikorski produced evidence pointing to the Soviet massacre of 5000 Polish officers at KATYN WOOD. When Sikorski died in a plane crash at Gibraltar on 4 July 1943, the Polish government lost the only leader with sufficient prestige to negotiate with STALIN and its influence slowly declined.

Sikorsky R-4 (USA)

The R-4 was the first helicopter in the world to enter series production. Igor Sikorsky had a long history of aircraft design, and had worked on a helicopter for many years before

flying his VS-300 in the USA in 1939. From this he developed the R-4, which was employed by both the US Army and Navy on observation and rescue work from 1944 onwards. *Rotor diameter* 38ft (11.6m); *engine* 1 200hp radial; *speed* 82mph (132kph).

Silberfuchs (Silver Fox)

Element of BARBAROSSA involving a German attack on MURMANSK, 1941.

Simonds, Lt Gen Guy (1903–74)

Simonds commanded the 1st Canadian Division during the campaign in SICILY and the 5th Canadian Armoured Division in Italy. In January 1944 he was appointed commander of II Canadian Corps, which he led throughout the campaign in NORMANDY and North-West EUROPE. A tactical innovator, he employed "UNFROCKED PRIESTS" as armoured personnel carriers for his infantry during the night phase of Operation TOTALIZE (8 August 1944), the flanks of the advance being simultaneously covered by heavy precision bombing.

Simović, Gen Dusăn (1882–)

Simović, a Serbian nationalist, became the Yugoslav Army's Chief of General Staff in 1939 and Chief of the Air Force Staff the following year. When HITLER demanded passage through

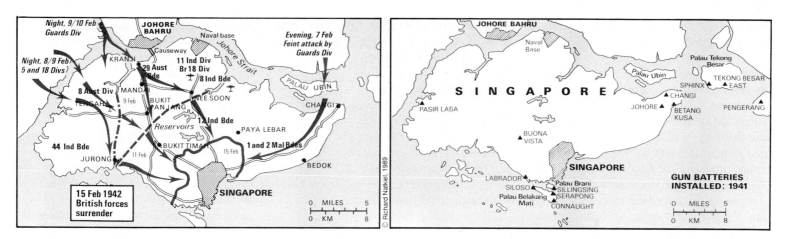

Left: The Japanese assault on Singapore island. Right: The coast gun batteries of Singapore fortress: though primarily sited to defend against sea attack, they could, and did, fire landwards.

Yugoslavia in February 1941, Simović urged the Regent, PRINCE PAUL, to resist German pressure. However, Paul concluded a secret treaty with the Nazis on 25 March. Two days later the Army deposed Paul and Simović was appointed to lead King PETER II's government. When the Germans invaded on 6 April, Simović fled to Greece and thence to London, where he served as Prime Minister of the government-in-exile until he resigned in 1942.

Simpson, Lt Gen William H.

Simpson, popularly known as "Big Bill", was a tolerant and understanding commander who had been at West Point with PATTON, with whom he remained on good terms. His US 9th Army captured BREST on 18 September 1944 and then moved into the line on the Western Front between the US 1st and British 2nd Armies. During the December 1944 German counteroffensive in the ARDENNES his army, in common with all American troops north of the enemy penetration, was placed under MONTGOMERY's control, and Simpson took over part of the US 1st Army's sector as well as contributing some of his own formations to deal with the emergency. On 23 February 1945, his 9th Army mounted Operation GRENADE, which took it across the Ruhr River and to the left bank of the RHINE. It effected a crossing of the Rhine between Düsseldorf and Duisburg in March and by 11 April had reached the ELBE near Magdeburg.

Sims Class Destroyers (USA)

Displacement 1570 tons; *dimensions* 348×36ft (106×10.9m); mean draught 10ft (3m); *machinery* 2-shaft geared turbines pro-

ducing shp 49,000; *speed* 38 knots; *armament* 5×5in (5×1); 4×1.1in AA; 12×21in torpedo tubes (3×4); *complement* 250; *number in class* 12, launched 1938–39.

Singapore, 1942

An island off the southern tip of MALAYA and British naval base. The base was strongly fortified in the 1930s against possible Japanese naval attack, but in 1941 the Japanese landed troops in Malaya and marched south to take the base from the rear. The defences were inadequate and the base fell to the Japanese on 15 February 1942 with the loss of 138,000 British and Australian troops, the greatest military defeat in British history.

Singora, Thailand, 1941

A seaport on the Isthmus of Kra and a short distance from the Malayan border. Japanese troops landed here on 8 December 1941 to begin their advance into MALAYA which culminated in the fall of SINGAPORE. Somewhat confusingly, "Singora" was also the Japanese name for Singapore, used in some of their reports.

Sinyavino

Soviet attempt to raise the siege of LENINGRAD, August–September 1942.

Sirena Class Submarines (Italy)

Displacement 623 tons (701/860 tons normal); *dimensions* 197ft 6in×21ft (60.1×6.4m); *machinery* 2-shaft diesel/electric motors hp 1200/800; *speed* 15/8 knots; *armament* 1×3.9in; 2–4×13.2mm AA; 6×21in torpedo tubes and 12 torpedoes; *complement* 45; *number in class* 12, all launched 1933.

The Japanese march into Singapore, 1942.

Sirte, First Battle of

During 17 December 1941 Rear-Admiral Philip VIAN, with four cruisers and 12 destroyers, was escorting the transport *Breconshire* from Alexandria to Malta and, after beating off German and Italian air attacks all afternoon, had reached a point off the Gulf of Sirte. Several reports during the day indicated that a major Italian force was approaching from the north. This consisted of four battleships, five cruisers and 21 destroyers which Admiral Iachino was using to escort a convoy from Taranto to Tripoli and Benghazi. At 1742 Vian had the enemy's masts in sight and, detaching two destroyers to escort *Brecon-*

shire and her vital cargo of fuel oil, he turned towards the Italians and launched a simulated attack into the teeth of accurate gunfire, hoping that the use of smoke and the onset of darkness would conceal his real strength. This succeeded, assisted by faulty intelligence which led Iachino to believe that *Breconshire* was actually a battleship. Both sides disengaged without loss and delivered their charges safely. However, during the night of 18/19 December, Force K from Malta, searching for the Tripoli portion of the Italian convoy, ran into a minefield 17 miles (27km) off Tripoli; one cruiser, *Neptune*, and one destroyer, *Kandahar*, were sunk and two cruisers, *Aurora* and *Penelope*, were seriously damaged.

Sirte, Second Battle of, 1942

On 20 March 1942 Rear-Admiral Philip VIAN, with four cruisers and 11 destroyers, was detailed to escort a convoy of four merchantmen, including the Special Supply Ship *Breconshire*, from Alexandria to Malta. The convoy was detected by German aircraft and Admiral Iachino, with one battleship, three cruisers and four destroyers, left Taranto to intercept it.

During the 22nd the convoy came under attack from German and Italian aircraft, and at 1427 Iachino's ships were in sight. Vian ordered the convoy and its close escort to turn away to the south-west and, knowing that the Italians were reluctant to attack through a smoke screen and were ill-equipped for night fighting, launched a series of counter-attacks which held Iachino at bay until dusk. During these attacks the cruiser *Cleopatra* and the destroyers *Havock* and *Kingston* sustained damage from the enemy's gunfire but at 1845, concerned by the onset of darkness and steadily rising seas, Iachino broke off the action. Two Italian destroyers foundered in the subsequent gale and the cruiser *Bande Nere* was damaged by heavy weather; she was torpedoed and sunk by the submarine *Urge* on 1 April on passage to the dockyard. Meanwhile, the convoy continued on its way to Malta, under air attack the while. Two ships reached harbour safely but a third was sunk, and *Breconshire*, the survivor of so many Malta convoys, sustained serious damage and finally sank on the 27th. So great were the efforts of the Axis air forces that of the 26,000 tons of cargo which left Egypt only 5000 tons were landed.

SITREP

Situation Report (UK). Daily summary of events submitted by military formations to higher headquarters.

Sittang, Burma, 1942

A town on the river of the same name, northwest of RANGOON. The river was the major natural obstacle to the Japanese advance in 1942 and the town a natural objective since it had the only bridge for miles. The bridge was strongly defended but was eventually blown in the face of the Japanese on 23 February.

Skink – Anti-Aircraft Tank (Canada)

Based on the hull and chassis of the Grizzly I medium tank (the Canadian-built version of the SHERMAN M4A1), the Skink was armed with four 20mm Polsten cannon mounted in a specially adapted turret. Production commenced early in 1944, but as a result of Allied air superiority over European battlefields the project was cancelled after only a handful had been completed.

Skorzeny, Lt Col Otto (1908–75)

Skorzeny commanded the German commando unit which rescued MUSSOLINI from the Gran Sasso in September 1943. In October 1944 he thwarted Admiral HORTHY's planned repudiation of Hungary's alliance with Germany by forcing the Regent to abdicate after kidnapping his son. During the German counteroffensive in the ARDENNES in December 1944 he caused serious confusion behind the American lines with teams of English-speaking German soldiers wearing American uniforms. Skorzeny was tried at NUREMBERG and acquitted.

Skyline Drive

The American nickname for the road running from Luxembourg north to Hosingen and ST VITH. It was on a ridge line, frequently shelled by the German artillery, and was used by supply columns to the US 9th Army.

Slapstick

British landing at TARANTO, southern Italy, 9 September 1943.

Sledgehammer

Allied plan to invade northern France, 1942.

Slessor, AM Sir John (1897–1979)

During the early war years Slessor held a number of staff appointments before assuming command of BOMBER COMMAND's No. 5 Group. In 1942 he became Assistant Chief of Air Staff (Policy) and in February 1943 was appointed head of COASTAL COMMAND. This involved close co-operation with the Royal Navy and American air and naval forces during the critical phase of the Battle of the ATLANTIC and resulted in heavy U-boat losses. In January 1944 Slessor was appointed commander of the RAF units in the Mediterranean, and simultaneously Deputy Commander-in-Chief of Allied Air Forces in this theatre of war, being closely involved in Operation ANVIL, the invasion of southern France, in August 1944.

Slim, Gen Sir William Joseph (1891–1970)

During World War I Slim served at Gallipoli, in France and in Mesopotamia, being wounded twice. In 1941 he commanded the 10th Infantry Brigade in the Sudan and ERITREA, where he was again wounded. He was then given command of the 10th Indian Division, which he led in a series of successful operations in IRAQ, SYRIA and IRAN later that year. On 19 March 1942 he took over I Burma Corps and conducted its long and difficult

Lieutenant-General William Slim, March 1945.

retreat from RANGOON to the Burma–India frontier. He then commanded XV Indian Corps and in 1943 was selected to lead the newly formed 14th Army. In the spring of 1944 he defeated the Japanese U-GO offensive at IMPHAL and KOHIMA. Slim promptly followed up his success, driving the enemy back across the CHINDWIN. His strategy in 1945 involved nothing less than the destruction of the Japanese armies in Burma. In January XXXIII Corps commenced operations aimed at the capture of MANDALAY, concentrating Japanese attention on that sector. Meanwhile, IV Corps moved in secret down the KABAW and Gangaw valleys, secured a crossing of the IRRAWADDY on 13 February and captured the vital communications centre of MEIKTILA on 4 March. This the Japanese themselves regard as the master stroke of the entire campaign in Burma since it led directly to the disintegration of the front they had established further north. Mandalay fell on 21 March. Both of Slim's corps then conducted a lightning advance on Rangoon, assisted by a series of amphibious operations executed by XV Corps in the ARAKAN and at Rangoon itself, which was captured on 2 May. This effectively concluded the campaign, and shortly after Slim was appointed Commander-in-Chief Allied Land Forces South East Asia. He ranks among the greatest of British commanders and was remarkable as much for the manner in which he restored his men's morale, winning their trust and respect, as for his use of deep penetration groups such as WINGATE's CHINDITS and MERRILL's MARAUDERS and the sustained use of air support and supply both in attack and defence. He was subsequently promoted Field-Marshal and held the posts of Chief of the Imperial General Staff 1948–52 and Governor-General of Australia 1953–60. He was created a Viscount in 1960.

Slot, The, Solomon Islands

An American naval nickname for the sheltered strip of water inside the SOLOMON ISLANDS group, and principally the area south of Choiseul Island.

SMG Submachine gun. Light automatic weapon using pistol ammunition.

Smigly-Rydz, Marshal Edward (1886–1943)

Having been designated by Marshal Pilsudski as his successor, Smigly-Rydz was the virtual ruler of POLAND in 1939 as well as Inspector-General of the country's armed forces. It was at his suggestion that the remnants of the Polish armies withdrew to the south-eastern corner of the country in the hope that British and French pressure on the Western Front would compel the Wehrmacht to abandon its offensive. The plan collapsed when the Soviet Union invaded eastern Poland and Smigly-Rydz fled to Romania, where he was interned. He was later criticized by the Polish Government-in-Exile for his conduct of the campaign. He is reported to have been killed by the Germans in 1943.

S-mine

A German anti-personnel mine (Schrapnel-Mine) which was in the form of a small MORTAR. Buried beneath the ground, when subjected to foot pressure it discharged a shrapnel bomb up into the air alongside the victim, where it burst at about 4.5ft (1.5m) height. Similar mines were developed by the British and American armies, and the class were generally known as BOUNCING BETTIES.

Smith, Gen Holland M. (1882–1967)

A US Marine Corps officer, Smith's ruthless drive and the fiery style of command earned him the nickname of "Howlin' Mad". He was largely responsible for developing the techniques of amphibious warfare employed in the Pacific, including the co-ordination of land, sea and air effort to secure the desired objective. He commanded V Amphibious Corps, which he led during the landings in the ALEUTIAN ISLANDS, at TARAWA, MAKIN, KWAJALEIN, ENIWETOK, SAIPAN and TINIAN. He was appointed Commanding General Fleet Marine Force Pacific in August 1944 and directed further amphibious assaults on GUAM and IWO JIMA. Although his operations sometimes resulted in heavy casualties, these stemmed from the suicidal nature of the Japanese defence rather than from any inherent fault in their planning and execution.

Smolensk, Soviet Union, 1941 and 1943

City 250 miles (400km) west of MOSCOW and important rail junction. In Operation BARBAROSSA it was one of the objectives of the German Army Group Centre, driving on Moscow, but General GUDERIAN's advance was halted on orders from HITLER to allow elements of Army Group North to swing round and complete an encirclement which trapped some 310,000 Soviet troops, 3200 tanks and 3200 guns. While tactically sound, this was a major strategic error, as it delayed the attack on Moscow and gave the Russians time to organize their defences. In 1943 Smolensk was the objective of a Russian attack by the 31st Army under YEREMENKO and the 5th Army under SOKOLOVSKY, part of a larger assault along the centre of the battle line. Smolensk was finally liberated by Soviet troops on 25 September 1943.

Soviet troops parade with PPSh-41 submachine guns.

The Russians burn Smolensk as the Germans approach, August 1941.

Smuts, FM Jan Christiaan (1870–1950)

A South African, Smuts served against the British as a local commander in the Boer War in 1901–2. After the war he played a major part in the establishment of the Union of South Africa. He commanded British troops in British East Africa in 1916, was the South African representative in the Imperial War Cabinet, 1917–18, and attended the Paris Peace Conference. In 1939 he was elected Prime Minister of the South African Union for the second time. Smuts was in favour of South African involvement in the war and directed the country's war effort, providing staunch support for CHURCHILL throughout the conflict. In 1945 he attended the San Francisco Conference at which the UN Charter was formulated, and was the only national leader to attend the peace conferences ending both world wars.

Snake

See MINECLEARING.

Sobibor, Poland, 1942–43

A German extermination camp established in March 1942 and located on the edge of the PRIPET MARSHES, north-west of LÜBLIN. About 250,000 Jews were killed here before the camp was closed in late 1943 after a rebellion by the prisoners, led by a Soviet prisoner-of-war.

SOE SPECIAL OPERATIONS EXECUTIVE (UK).

Sokolovksy, Marshal Vasiliy (1897–1968)

Sokolovsky served as West Front's Chief of Staff from 1941 until 1943 when he became its commander, leading it during the general Soviet counteroffensive which followed the German defeat at KURSK and liberating SMOLENSK on 25 September 1943. He was censured for his subsequent slow advance and in 1944 was transferred to 1st Ukrainian Front as KONEV's Chief of Staff. In 1945 he was posted to ZHUKOV's 1st Belorussian Front as Deputy Front Commander for the assault on BERLIN. It was Sokolovsky who verified HITLER's death by means of a comparison of the charred body with the Führer's dental records. After the war he was appointed Commander-in-Chief of the Soviet forces in Germany.

Soldati Class Destroyers (Italy)

Displacement Group 1 2290–2459 tons, *Group 2* 2450–2550 tons; *dimensions* 350ft×33ft 3in (106.7×10.1m); mean draught 11ft 9in (3.5m); *machinery* 2-shaft geared turbines producing shp 48,000 (*Group 1*) and shp 50,000 (*Group 2*); *speed* 39 knots; *armament Group 1* 4×4.7in; 1×37mm AA; 8–12 20mm AA; 6×21in torpedo tubes; 2–4 depth charge throwers, equipped for minelaying; *Group 2* 5×4.7in; 8–10×20mm AA; 6×21in torpedo tubes; 2–4 depth charge throwers; equipped for minelaying; *complement* 220; *number in class Group 1* – 12, launched 1937–38, *Group 2* – 5, launched 1941–42.

Sollum, North Africa, 1940–42

A town on the border of Egypt and CYRENAICA. It was held by a small British garrison in 1940, which retired in the face of the Italian advance under Marshal GRAZIANI which reached SIDI BARRANI. It was recaptured by the British on 17 December and subsequently changed hands a number of times as the battle ebbed and flowed across the coast in 1941–42.

Solomon Islands, Pacific, 1942–43

A group of islands east of NEW GUINEA, the principal ones being BOUGAINVILLE, Choiseul, NEW GEORGIA, Santa Isabel and GUADALCANAL. Most of the islands were occupied by the Japanese in their advance southwards in 1941–42. Their liberation by Allied forces began with the assault on Guadalcanal on 7 August 1942. This was followed by the establishment of airfields and bases there and on the Russell Islands (February 1943). On 21 June the Solomons campaign opened with the assault on New Georgia and the capture of Munda airfield on 5 August. This was followed by the taking of the Treasury Islands (27 October), Choiseul (28 October) and finally Bougainville (1 November).

Somaliland, East Africa, 1940

There were three Somalilands in 1940: French, a small area opposite Aden; British, a larger area on the south side of the Gulf of Aden, stretching almost to the Horn of Africa; and Italian, running from the Horn of Africa south, on the Indian Ocean, to the border of Kenya. (British and Italian Somaliland are now the Somali Republic, French Somaliland

The Italian attack on British Somaliland, August 1940.

Unit of the British Somaliland Camel Corps, Abyssinia.

is now Djibouti.) In August 1940 a strong Italian force invaded British Somaliland from Ethiopia. The British garrison consisted of four infantry battalions and four 3.7-inch mountain howitzers, reinforced by an additional battalion from Aden. The Italian force numbered 26 infantry battalions, four field gun batteries, tanks and armoured cars. In spite of spirited resistance, the British force was gradually driven back and was finally evacuated by sea on 18 August. The presence of Italian forces in Somaliland posed a threat to Kenya. To forestall any Italian move, African and South African troops, supported by the South African Air Force, invaded Italian Somaliland in February 1941. Italian resistance crumbled in the face of a determined and rapid advance, and a limited manoeuvre to remove the risk of Italian attack became a campaign to occupy the entire country and use it as a base for operations against the Italian forces in Ethiopia. Within two months of the start of the operation, the Italians had been driven from Italian Somaliland, and British troops from Aden reoccupied British Somaliland without opposition.

Soman

Soman was the third of the German nerve gases, being chemically known as pinacolyl methyl phosphoro-fluoridate. Discovered in 1944, it was never taken beyond the laboratory stage.

Somers Class Destroyers (USA)

Displacement 1850 tons; *dimensions* 391×37ft (119.1×11.2m); mean draught 10ft 3in (3.1m); *machinery* 2-shaft geared turbines producing shp 52,000; *speed* 37.5 knots; *armament* 8×5in (4×2); 12×21in torpedo tubes (3×4); *complement* 270; *number in class* 5, launched 1937–38.

Somerville, Adm Sir James (1882–1949)

Somerville assumed command of the Royal Navy's FORCE H, based on Gibraltar, on 28 June 1940. His first task was the distasteful one of neutralizing the French naval units at MERS-EL-

Somua S-35 medium tank.

KEBIR and ORAN. When the French rejected his ultimatum on 3 July, he was forced to open fire, inflicting heavy damage and loss of life. Thereafter much of his attention was absorbed in escorting convoys to MALTA in the face of Italian naval and air opposition. On 9 February 1941 his ships bombarded the enemy naval base of GENOA. In May he escorted the vital TIGER convoy, carrying tanks for the British army in Egypt, as far as the Narrows, where the Mediterranean Fleet took over responsibility for its safety during the rest of its successful passage to ALEXANDRIA. Later that month Force H played a critical role in hunting down the BISMARCK. In 1942 Somerville became Commander-in-Chief of the Eastern Fleet, based on CEYLON, until 1944, when he was appointed head of the British naval delegation in Washington.

Somua S35 – Medium Tank (Fr)

Designed as the medium tank of cavalry formations, the Somua S35 entered service in 1935 and by the outbreak of war some 500 had been built. In 1940 a modified version, the S40, was produced, driven by a 220hp diesel engine. The majority of S35s served in the *Divisions Légères Mécaniques* and acquitted themselves well in local engagements. The vehicle saw further limited action during the 1942/43 campaign in Tunisia. *Weight* 20 tons; *speed* 29mph (47kph); *armour* 40mm; *armament* 1 47mm gun; 1 7.5mm machine gun; *engine* Somua V-8 190hp petrol; *crew* 3.

Sonar

A "manufactured" word to indicate the sound equivalent of RADAR, Sonar was developed by

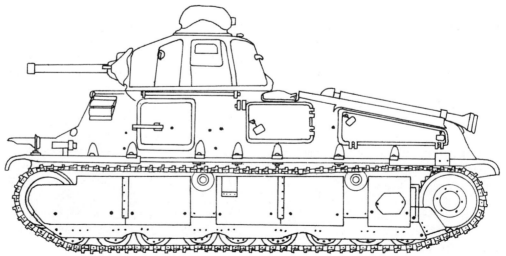

the US Navy and was their equivalent of the British ASDIC, a system of detecting underwater targets by the sending and receiving of sound impulses through the water.

Sonderkraftfahrzeug 13 Scout Car (Ger)

Open-topped scout car based on an Adler 4×2-wheel drive commercial chassis and known as "The Bathtub". The vehicle entered service with the cavalry in 1933 but its cross-country performance was found to be inadequate and by the start of the war it had been relegated to the heavy squadron of the infantry divisions' reconnaissance battalions. The Polish campaign confirmed its unsuitability for first line use and it was subsequently employed on internal security duties in occupied countries. A radio-equipped version, the SdKfz 14, was fitted with a frame aerial and carried an extra crew member. *Weight* 2.25 tons; *speed* 31mph (50kph); *armour* 8mm; *armament* 1 7.92mm machine gun; *engine* Adler 60hp petrol; *crew* 2.

Sonderkraftfahrzeug 221 Series Light Armoured Cars (Ger)

Designed as a replacement for the SDKFZ 13 and entered service in 1937. An improved version, the SdKfz 222, was produced the following year. This had a larger turret mounting a 20mm cannon and a coaxial 7.92mm machine gun, although some cars were armed with a 28mm anti-tank rifle. The SdKfz 223 was a radio-equipped version and retained the smaller turret but could be distinguished by its frame aerial. Two turretless command versions, the SdKfz 260 and 261, were based on the hull of the SdKfz 221, employing respect-

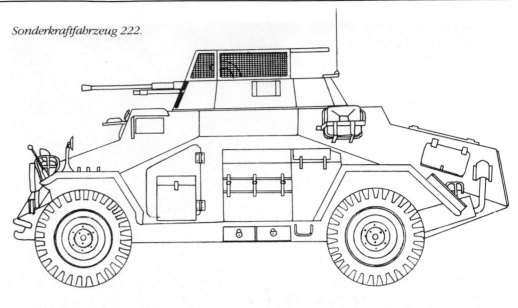

Sonderkraftfahrzeug 222.

ively rod and frame aerials. Production of the SdKfz 221 Series was discontinued in 1942 but many vehicles remained in service until the end of the war.

SdKfz 221 Weight 4 tons; *speed* 46mph (74kph); *armour* 14.5mm; *armament* 1 7.92mm machine gun or 1 28mm anti-tank rifle; *engine* Horch 75hp petrol; *crew* 2.

Sonderkraftfahrzeug 231 (Six-Wheel) Series Heavy Armoured Cars (Ger)

Interim design based on the Daimler G3 6×4-wheel drive commercial chassis, incorporating rear-steering and driver's controls, introduced in 1933. Radio and command versions, respectively the SdKfz 232 (six-wheel) and SdKfz 263 (six-wheel), were also developed; these employed frame aerials and in the latter case the turret was fixed, its armament consisting of a single 7.92mm machine gun. After

the fall of France in 1940 the SdKfz 231 (six-wheel) Series was withdrawn from first line service and relegated to internal security duties in occupied countries.

SdKfz 231 (6-wheel) Weight 5 tons; *speed* 37mph (59kph); *armour* 14.5mm; *armament* 1 20mm cannon; 1 7.92mm machine gun; *engine* Daimler 68hp or Magirus 70hp or Bussing 65hp, petrol; *crew* 4.

Sonderkraftfahrzeug 231 (Eight Wheel) Series Heavy Armoured Cars (Ger)

The German Army's requirement for a heavy armoured car during the 1930s called for a rear-engined, eight-wheeled vehicle with front and rear driving positions and drive and steering on all wheels. Experience gained with an experimental design known as the *Achtradwagen* and the defects revealed in the operational performance of the interim SDKFZ 231 (SIX-WHEEL) were taken into account during the vehicle's development by Deutsche Werk of Kiel and the SdKfz 231 (eight-wheel) began entering service with armoured reconnaissance battalions in 1938, demonstrating a cross-country mobility comparable to that of a tracked chassis. Also developed were radio and command versions designated respectively SdKfz 232 (eight-wheel) and SdKfz 263 (eight-wheel), the latter with a fixed superstructure in place of a turret. These employed the same frame aerials as the six-wheeler designs. Last in the series was the SdKfz 233, which entered service in 1941 and was armed with a 75mm L/24 howitzer in a limited traverse mounting at the front of an

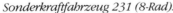

Sonderkraftfahrzeug 231 (8-Rad).

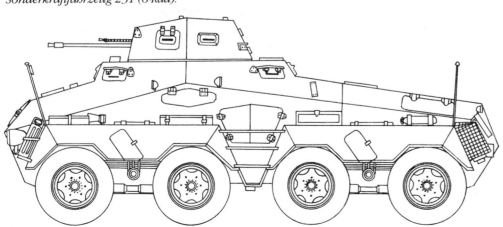

open-topped fighting compartment. Production of the SdKfz 231 (eight-wheel) Series was discontinued in 1942 but many remained in service until the end of the war.

SdKfz 231 (8-wheel) Weight 8.5 tons; *speed* 53mph (85kph); *armour* 14.5mm; *armament* 1 20mm cannon; 1 7.92mm machine gun; *engine* Bussing 155hp (later 180hp) petrol; *crew* 4.

Sonderkraftfahrzeug 234 Series Heavy Armoured Cars (Ger)

Developed by the Bussing organization from August 1940 onwards, the SdKfz 234 Series employed a hull which closely resembled that of the SDKFZ 231 (EIGHT-WHEEL) Series but was of monocoque construction and therefore dispensed with the need for a separate chassis. Increased fuel capacity gave an operational radius almost twice that of the earlier eight-wheeler armoured cars and the use of larger diameter tyres produced an outstanding cross-country performance. Although intended for service in hot climates, the SdKfz 234/1 was not standardized until July 1943, some two months after the war in North Africa had ended. Complaints by German armoured car crews that their vehicles were undergunned led to the development of the SdKfz 234/2, otherwise known as the Puma, which was armed with a 50mm L/60 gun with muzzle brake mounted in a cramped but workable enclosed turret with all-round traverse. Also produced were a close support car (SdKfz 234/3) armed with a 75mm L/24 howitzer, and a tank destroyer (SdKfz 234/4) armed with a 75mm Pak 40 anti-tank gun, these weapons being housed in an open-topped fighting compartment on limited traverse mountings. About 2300 SdKfz 234 Series armoured cars were built.

SdKfz 234/1 Weight 10.33 tons; *speed* 53mph (85kph); *armour* 30mm; *armament* 1 20mm cannon; 1 7.92mm machine gun; *engine* Tatra air-cooled V-12 220hp diesel; *crew* 4.

Sonderkraftfahrzeug 250 Series Light Armoured Half-Tracks (Ger)

Developed by the Demag organization from 1940 onwards as a smaller version of the SDKFZ 251 Series of armoured half-tracks. The SdKfz 250 Series was widely employed but its most notable users were the armoured reconnaissance battalions, in which it replaced the SDKFZ 221 Series light armoured cars, which were unable to cope with the heavy going on

Sonderkraftfahrzeug 250 half-track.

the Eastern Front, and also provided a safer means of bringing the battalions' organic motor rifle troops into action; another feature which made it suitable for the reconnaissance role was its height of only 5.5ft (1.68m), enabling it to take advantage of even limited cover. The series was built in 12 variants, as follows:

250/1 – Light armoured personnel carrier
250/2 – Telephone cable layer
250/3 – Radio vehicle
250/4 – Air support communications vehicle
250/5 – Artillery observation post vehicle
250/6 – Ammunition and supply carrier
250/7 – 80mm mortar carrier
250/8 – Close support vehicle armed with 75mm L/24 howitzer
250/9 – Armoured reconnaissance vehicle, fitted with the turret and armament of the SdKfz 222 light armoured car
250/10 – Tank destroyer, armed with 37mm anti-tank gun
250/11 – Tank destroyer, armed with 28mm anti-tank rifle
250/12 – Artillery survey section vehicle

See also *German Armoured Cars and Reconnaissance Half-Tracks* by Bryan Perrett (Osprey).

SdKfz 250/1 Weight 5.7 tons; *speed* 37mph (59kph); *armour* 12mm; *engine* Maybach 100hp petrol; *crew* 6.

Sonderkraftfahrzeug 251 Series Armoured Half-Tracks (Ger)

Based on a chassis developed by Hanomag from the SdKfz 11 half-tracked artillery tractor and fitted with a well-angled armoured superstructure designed by Bussing, the series began entering service in the spring of 1939 and became the most numerous of all German armoured vehicles, over 15,000 being built during the war. They served with the mechanized infantry units of Panzer and motorized divisions, these being designated Panzergrenadier in June 1942 and March 1943 respectively, as well as in many other roles, and although they were underpowered and difficult to handle they were capable of performing the tasks for which they had been designed. The supply of SdKfz 251 half-tracks never came close to approaching demand and at best amounted to approximately 10 per cent of requirements. A number of minor modifications were made to the basic design during its production history and 22 variants were produced, as follows:

251/1 – Armoured personnel carrier
251/2 – 80mm mortar carrier
251/3 – Radio vehicle
251/4 – Ammunition carrier
251/5 – Assault engineer vehicle
251/6 – Command vehicle
251/7 – Engineer stores vehicle

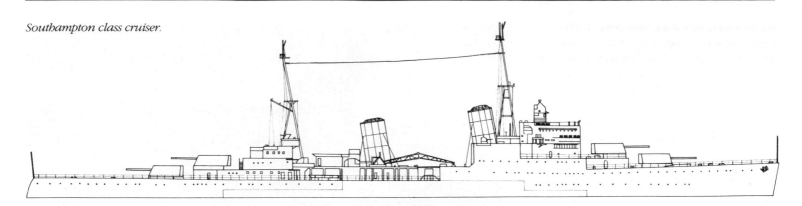

Southampton class cruiser.

251/8 – Armoured ambulance
251/9 – Close support vehicle armed with 75mm L/24 howitzer
251/10 – Tank destroyer armed with 37mm anti-tank gun
251/11 – Telephone cable layer
251/12 – Artillery survey section vehicle
251/13 – Artillery sound recording vehicle
251/14 – Artillery sound ranging vehicle
251/15 – Artillery flash spotting vehicle
251/16 – Flamethrower
251/17 – Anti-aircraft vehicle armed with one 20mm cannon
251/18 – Artillery observation post vehicle
251/19 – Telephone exchange vehicle
251/20 – Infra-red searchlight vehicle
251/21 – Anti-aircraft vehicle armed with triple 15mm or 20mm cannon
251/22 – Tank destroyer armed with 75mm Pak 40 anti-tank gun.

After the war a modified version of the SdKfz 251/1 served with the Czech Army under the designation OT-810. See also *The SdKfz 251 Half-Track* by Bruce Culver (Osprey) and *SdKfz 251 In Action* by Charles Kliment (Squadron/Signal). *SdKfz 251/1 Weight* 8.5 tons; *speed* 31mph (50kph); *armour* 12mm; *engine* Maybach HL42 100hp petrol; *crew* 12.

Sonnenblume (Sunflower)

German contingency plan to send military assistance to the Italians in Libya, January 1941.

SOP   Standard Operating Procedure (US).

Sorge, Richard (1895–1944)

Sorge, a German journalist based in Japan, was a Soviet agent who had been active in the Far East since 1929. He set up a network of agents within Japan, including high-ranking civil servants and diplomats, and was privy to many international secrets. In 1941 he provided advance warning of the German invasion of the USSR, although this was ignored. He then confirmed that Japan had no plans to acquire Soviet territory in the Far East, enabling STALIN to employ Siberian formations in the MOSCOW counteroffensive. Shortly after this Sorge was arrested by Japanese counter-intelligence and was hanged three years later.

Sorpe Dam, Germany, 1943

One of the RUHR dams attacked by No. 617 Squadron RAF on 16/17 May 1943. In the opinion of experts, the breaching of this dam would have brought about a critical water shortage in the Ruhr, but it was of earthen construction and the special "bouncing bomb" used on the raid, developed for attacking concrete dams, was relatively ineffective. Only two of No. 617 Squadron's Lancaster bombers reached this target, dropping their bombs directly on to the dam but causing little damage.

Soryu Class Aircraft Carriers (Jap)

Soryu and her sister ship *Hiryu* formed the Imperial Japanese Navy's 2nd Carrier Division and took part in the attack on PEARL HARBOR and subsequent operations in the East Indies, South Pacific and Indian Ocean. At the Battle of MIDWAY *Soryu* was hit by dive-bombers from the USS YORKTOWN and set ablaze, sinking after a series of internal explosions; *Hiryu*'s aircraft, after launching a strike at Midway island, scored several hits on the *Yorktown*, but *Hiryu* herself was hit by a counter-strike from the USS ENTERPRISE and became a floating inferno which sank 18 hours later. *Displacement* 15,900 tons; *dimensions* 746ft 6in×70ft (227.5×21m); mean draught 25ft (7.62m); *machinery* 4-shaft geared turbines producing shp 153,000; *speed* 34.5 knots; *armament* 12×5in DP (6×2); 28×25mm AA (14×2); *aircraft* 73; *complement* 1101; *number in class* 2.

Sosabowski, Maj Gen Stanislaw (1892–1967)

A former professor at the Polish War Academy, Sosabowski commanded the 1st Polish Parachute Brigade during Operation MARKET GARDEN and was one of very few senior officers who had grave and fully justified misgivings regarding the strategic and tactical concept of seizing the road bridge at ARNHEM. His brigade was to have dropped at the southern end of the bridge but was held in reserve. When the situation at Arnhem deteriorated, it was dropped at Driel, on the south bank of the Neder Rhine, on 22 September 1944; the leading elements of the British XXX Corps broke through to it that night. Possession of the south bank of the river enabled some 2000 survivors of the British 1st Airborne Division to be evacuated on the night of 25 September.

Sound Ranging

A system of detecting enemy artillery by the sound of its discharge. A number of microphones are placed at measured distances across the front and connected by wire or radio to a recording device. As the sound wave from the enemy gun sweeps across this line of microphones, each will detect the sound at a different time. When this time difference is graphically plotted, it is possible to determine the location of the gun by lines from each pair of microphones in the line. Similarly, it is possible to bombard the enemy position by plotting the sound of the bursting shells and adjusting the fire until the sound pattern of the shell matches that of the target gun. Sound ranging was extensively used by all armies during the war and is still an effective method of target location.

Southampton Class Cruisers (UK)

Displacement Group 1 9100 tons; *Group 2* 9400 tons; *Group 3* 10,000 tons; *dimensions Group 1* 591ft 6in×61ft 9in (180.2×18.8m); mean draught 17ft (5.2m); *Group 2* 591ft 6in×62ft 3in (180.2×18.9m); mean draught 17ft 6in (5.33m); *Group 3* 613ft 6in×63ft 3in (186.9×19.3m); mean draught 17ft 3in (5.3m); *machinery* 4-shaft geared turbines producing shp 75,000 *Group 1*, 82,500 *Group 2*, 80,000 *Group 3*; *speed Group 1* 32 knots; *Group 2* 32.5 knots; *Group 3* 32 knots; *protection Groups 1 and 2* main belt 4in; deck 2in; turrets 2in; *Group 3* main belt 4.5in; deck 2in; turrets 2.5in; *armament Groups 1 and 2* 12×6in (4×3); 8×4in AA (4×2); 8×2-pdr AA (2×4); 8×0.5in AA (2×4); 6×21in torpedo tubes; *Group 3* 12×6in (4×3); 12×4in AA (4×2); 16×2-pdr AA (2×8); 8×0.5in AA (2×4); 6×21in torpedo tubes; *aircraft* 3; *complement Groups 1 and 2* 700; *Group 3* 850; *number in class Group 1* 5, launched 1936; *Group 2* 3, launched 1937; *Group 3* 2, launched 1938.

South Dakota Class Battleships (USA)

South Dakota was damaged at the Battle of SANTA CRUZ and again at the Second Battle of GUADALCANAL. After completing her repairs in the USA, she served with the British Home Fleet in 1943 before returning to the Pacific, where she saw further action at the GILBERT ISLANDS, KWAJALEIN, TRUK, HOLLANDIA, SAIPAN, the Battles of the PHILIPPINE SEA and LEYTE GULF, IWO JIMA and OKINAWA. See also USS ALABAMA, INDIANA and MASSACHUSETTS. *Displacement* 35,000 tons; *dimensions* 680ft×108ft 3in (185.3×33m); mean draught 29ft 9in (9.07m); *machinery* 4-shaft geared turbines producing shp 130,000; *speed* 28 knots; *protection* main belt 18in; turrets 18in; *armament* 9×16in (3×3); 20×5in DP (10×2); 48×40mm AA; 35×20mm AA; *aircraft* 3; *complement* 2354; *number in class* 4, launched 1941–42.

The battleship Parizhskaya Kommuna *during the defence of Sevastopol.*

Soviet Navy

Immediately prior to the German invasion of the USSR in June 1941, the Soviet Navy consisted of 3 old battleships, 10 cruisers, 60 destroyers and 180 submarines with a further 3 battleships, 12 cruisers, 45 destroyers and 90 submarines under construction. This superficially impressive force was divided between the Baltic, Black Sea, Northern and Pacific Fleets which were incapable of supporting each other, as the bulk of the Soviet naval strength was concentrated in the land-locked Baltic and Black Seas. The standard of efficiency and training was also low; the 1917 Revolutions had deprived the Navy of the services of all but a few of the former Tsarist officers who would normally be holding flag rank. Also, STALIN's purges during the interwar years, embracing not only naval officers but also ship designers, had stifled both initiative and technical progress. So rapid was the German advance that one naval base after another had to be abandoned in both the

Baltic and Black Seas. The Baltic Fleet was bottled up in Kronstadt, where on 23 September 1941 the *Marat* became the first battleship to be sunk by dive-bombers; during the same attack the battleship *Oktobrescaya Revolutsia*, the cruiser *Kirov* and many other vessels were also severely damaged. In December 1941 the Black Sea Fleet took part in an amphibious counter-offensive on the KERCH PENINSULA in the CRIMEA, but this ended disastrously, and when SEVASTOPOL fell in July 1942 the fleet had lost its major naval base as well as many ships. With the Navy's strength so seriously reduced its role in both the Black Sea and Baltic was limited to supplying gunfire support for local land operations, and many of its crews were brought ashore to fight as infantry. The Northern Fleet provided a small number of escorts for the ARCTIC CONVOYS during the last stage of their passage but following the virtual destruction of CONVOY PQ-17, CHURCHILL made it clear to Stalin that he did not regard this contribution as adequate, and the latter

South Dakota class battleship.

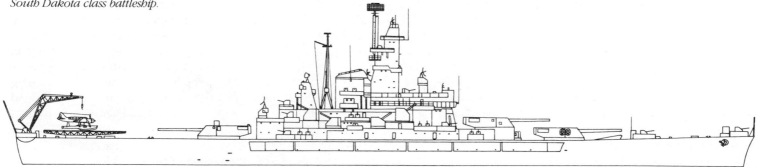

responded by increasing available air cover. The Soviet Navy did, however, manage to retain possession of Lake LADOGA, across which supplies were ferried to the besieged city of LENINGRAD, and in 1945 its Pacific Fleet successfully executed a number of amphibious operations against Japanese-held islands off the Manchurian coast. Because the majority of construction yards were destroyed during the fighting, the Navy was unable to replace its warship losses, but to some extent these were made good by the transfer of Allied warships, notably the battleship HMS *Royal Sovereign*, renamed *Archangelsk*. This also provided the Russians with their first ASDIC and naval radar systems. On the conclusion of hostilities the Soviet Navy also acquired a number of former Axis warships.

Soviet Tank Army, 1944–45

Two TANK CORPS; mechanized corps, at discretion; light artillery brigade consisting of two 76mm artillery regiments and one 100mm artillery regiment; light self-propelled artillery brigade consisting of three light self-propelled artillery battalions (SU-76), a machine gun battalion and an anti-aircraft machine gun company; a heavy mortar regiment (MRLs); anti-aircraft division consisting of four anti-aircraft regiments; motorized engineer brigade consisting of two motorized engineer battalions and one pontoon-bridging battalion; motor-cycle reconnaissance regiment; signals regiment; aviation communications regiment; supply and service units.

Soviet Tank Corps, 1944–45

Three tank brigades, each of 65 tanks; motor rifle regiment; light self-propelled artillery regiment (SU-76); medium self-propelled artillery regiment (SU-85/SU-122); heavy self-propelled artillery regiment (SU-152) in some corps; light artillery regiment; anti-aircraft regiment; heavy mortar battalion (MRLs); motorcycle reconnaissance battalion; engineer battalion; signals battalion; aviation company; supply and service units.

Spaatz, Gen Carl (1891–1974)

Spaatz was present in the United Kingdom during the Battle of BRITAIN as an official USAAF observer. He returned in 1942 as commander of the US 8th Air Force and initiated its daylight precision bombing offensive against targets on the Continent. In February 1943 he

moved to North Africa to co-ordinate American air activity in that theatre of war, commanding the North-West Africa Air Force during the campaigns in TUNISIA and SICILY. In January 1944 he was appointed Commanding General of the Strategic Air Forces in Europe and was responsible for the air offensive which preceded the Allied landings in NORMANDY. His next targets were Germany's synthetic fuel plants and internal transportation systems, which he left all but completely wrecked. In July 1945 he took command of the Strategic Air Forces in the Pacific, bombing cities on the Japanese mainland; aircraft under his command dropped the ATOMIC BOMBS on HIROSHIMA and NAGASAKI. After the war Spaatz was the US Air Force's Chief of Staff in 1947–48.

Special Air Service

Formed in Egypt in July 1941 by the then Captain David STIRLING under the title of L Detachment of the Special Air Services Brigade, a higher formation which did not as yet exist. Stirling believed that a small group of highly trained and motivated men could, in appropriate circumstances, achieve better results than a much larger force, and his

SAS patrol, Western Desert, January 1943.

particular targets were German and Italian airfields in North Africa. Although his first operation was a failure, he obtained the co-operation of the LONG RANGE DESERT GROUP and before the desert war ended the SAS had destroyed approximately 400 Axis aircraft on the ground, plus uncounted tons of aviation fuel, bombs, ammunition and other stores. Following ROMMEL's invasion of Egypt the SAS acquired heavily armed jeeps with which it raided the Axis lines of communication. By October 1942, L Detachment had expanded to the point at which it became 1st Special Air Service Regiment, and a 2nd SAS Regiment was raised for service with the Allied 1st Army in Tunisia.

When the war in Africa ended, the 1st SAS was briefly redesignated the Special Raiding Squadron (SRS) and was employed on commando-type raids in Sicily and Italy; the 2nd SAS also fought in Italy. In January 1944 the Special Air Service Brigade became a fact, consisting of 1st SAS (SRS), 2nd SAS, 3rd SAS (French), 4th SAS (French), 5th SAS (Belgian) and F Squadron PHANTOM (the GHQ Liaison Regiment). In the months following the D-DAY landings in France SAS teams, inserted by air with their jeeps and equipment into the German rear areas, co-ordinated Resistance activity and carried out numerous acts of sabotage, disruption of communications and attacks on enemy transport, all of which contributed to the difficulties of German reinforcements attempting to reach the battle zone. When the war reached Germany itself, the tasks of the SAS included deep reconnaissance and, latterly, the capture of war criminals. 1st and 2nd SAS were disbanded when hostilities ended; 3rd and 4th SAS went to the French Army and 5th SAS to the Belgian Army. See SPECIAL BOAT SQUADRON. See also *The SAS* by Philip Warner (Wm Kimber).

Special Boat Squadron

Formed in the spring of 1943 in Palestine from the Special Boat Sections of the 1st SPECIAL AIR SERVICE, under the command of Lieutenant-Colonel the Earl Jellicoe. The SBS carried out extensive raids and intelligence gathering in the Aegean and the Adriatic for the remainder of the war. The unit was disbanded in 1945.

Special Operations Executive

A British agency established in July 1940 to gather intelligence, carry out sabotage and support resistance movements in Axis-occupied countries, over 11,000 agents being employed on these tasks. Unfortunately, a number of foreign refugees recruited during the early stages were deliberate enemy plants or potential double agents, and in this way the Germans were able to infiltrate a number of SOE networks. This fatally undermined operations in Holland, where for almost three years the Germans manipulated radio communications to suit themselves, feeding false information, capturing agents and intercepting arms supplies destined for Dutch resistance groups. Some aspects of the agency's operations aroused unresolved controversy, and the relationship between the SOE and other British and Allied intelligence agencies was frequently acrimonious. Nevertheless, SOE scored numerous successes, particularly in 1944. See also OSS.

Speer, Albert (1905–81)

Speer was trained as an architect and his outstanding organizational abilities first attracted HITLER's attention when the Nazi Party buildings in Nuremberg were being planned. In 1942 he was appointed Armaments Minister following the death of TODT. His policy of rationalization, including the employment of experienced industrialists rather than military bureaucrats to control the manufacture of armaments, resulted in a steady rise in production until September 1944. Central to Speer's success was his drive to exploit the considerable slack capacity in the economy and his policy of dispersal, which ensured that only a fraction of German industrial capacity was located in the 58 towns attacked in strength by the USAAF and BOMBER COMMAND. As a result the index of German arms production rose from 100 in January 1942 to 322 in July 1944. Thereafter output continued until the end of the war, although Speer's efforts were increasingly thwarted by the destruction of Germany's transportation systems and synthetic oil plants. As the war drew to a close Speer spent much of his time frustrating Hitler's orders to destroy German industry in the face of the advancing Allies. In February 1945 he toyed with the idea of killing Hitler by introducing poison gas into the ventilation system of the Chancellery Bunker. The plan came to nothing, and on 24 April 1945 Speer took his leave of the Führer, making a full confession of the steps he had taken to prevent the implementation of Hitler's scorched earth directives. He was allowed to go free and in Hitler's Last Testament was replaced by his deputy Saur. At the NUREMBERG trials Speer's use of slave labour in industry led to his being sentenced to 20 years' imprisonment. His book *Inside the Third Reich* provides a remarkable picture of the manner in which Hitler's Germany conducted its affairs.

Sperrle, FM Hugo (1885–1953)

Sperrle had been a fighter pilot in World War I and commanded the Kondor Legion during the Spanish Civil War. In January 1939 he was appointed commander of Luftflotte 3, which he led during the 1939 campaign in Poland, the 1940 campaign in the West and the Battle of BRITAIN. Luftflotte 3 remained in France but had been so run down by the time the Allies invaded NORMANDY in June 1944 that he was unable to offer much more than token resistance. On 23 August 1944 Sperrle was removed from his command and replaced by General Delosch.

Spica Class Torpedo Boats (Italy)

Despite their official designation, the Spica Class were really small destroyers, as were several smaller classes of torpedo boat dating from World War I and the 1920s. They were used as escorts and several survivors of the Spica Class were rebuilt as fast corvettes during the early 1950s. *Displacement* 1055 tons; *dimensions* 281ft 3in×27ft (85.7×8.2m); mean draught 8ft 9in (2.7m); *machinery* 2-shaft geared turbines producing shp 19,000; *speed* 34 knots; *armament* 3×3.9in; 6–10×20mm AA; 2–4×13.2mm AA; 4×17.7in torpedo tubes; 2–4 depth charge throwers; equipped for minelaying; *complement* 119; *number in class* 30, launched 1935–38.

Spitzbergen, 1941

A group of islands some 380 miles (600km) north of Norway. Mountainous and barren, with many glaciers, it nevertheless has a high concentration of minerals, notably good quality coal. In July 1941 an agreement was reached between Britain, Norway and the Soviet Union to take steps to keep the coal out of German hands. As it was impossible to maintain a garrison on the islands, the decision was taken to demolish the mines. (The mines were worked by a Soviet company and some 2000 Soviet citizens resided there.) Accordingly a raid was made by Canadian troops on 25 August 1941. No opposition was encountered, the civil population was evacuated – the Soviets to Russia and the Norwegians to Britain – and the mines were destroyed. The stockpile of 540,000 tons of coal and 275,000 gallons of fuel oil were set on fire, and essential machinery removed. Spitzbergen remained virtually uninhabited for the remainder of the war.

SPOBS Special Observer Group (US).

Spring

Canadian holding operation in NORMANDY, timed to coincide with COBRA, July 1944.

Spruance, VAdm Raymond A. (1886–1969)

Spruance was commissioned into the US Navy in 1906. After service in World War I he became head of the Electrical Division at the Bureau of Engineering, later teaching at the Naval War College and serving a tour of duty with Naval Intelligence. By 1939 he had reached the rank of Rear-Admiral, commanding the 10th Naval District, and in 1941 took over 5 Cruiser Division, based at PEARL HARBOR. Spruance commanded Task Force 16 at MIDWAY. After the disabling of the carrier *York-*

town, flagship of Vice-Admiral Fletcher, Spruance took over control of the battle. Although he was inexperienced in carrier warfare, he clinched a decisive victory in which all four of the carriers deployed by the Japanese were sunk. He then served as Chief of Staff to Admiral NIMITZ until August 1943, when he was appointed commander of the 5th (Central Pacific) Fleet, which he led at TARAWA, KWAJALEIN, TRUK, the Battle of the PHILIPPINE SEA, OKINAWA and IWO JIMA. The US Navy was now operating thousands of miles from its base at Pearl Harbor, but Spruance proved himself a master of the logistical intricacies of this long-range warfare. He introduced the circular formation for carrier groups, enabling them to operate with maximum efficiency in action, and also the fleet train supply system, which permitted task groups to remain at sea for long periods. During the last phase of the war Spruance was closely involved in planning the projected invasion of the Japanese mainland, against which his carriers were already launching strikes. He succeeded Nimitz as Commander-in-Chief of the US Pacific Fleet.

Squeeze Bore Guns

Guns in which the calibre is reduced during the shot's travel along the bore; not to be confused with TAPER BORE GUNS in which the calibre reduces steadily from chamber to muzzle, the squeeze bore gun uses a short tapering section placed either part-way down the bore or at the muzzle, the remainder of the gun barrel being parallel-bored. The German firm of Krupp developed a 75mm anti-tank gun which squeezed its special shot down to 55mm by an adapter half-way along the barrel. As with the taper bore gun this increased the muzzle velocity and thus enhanced the penetrating ability. The 7.5cm PAK 41 fired a 5.7lb (2.59kg) shot at 3691ft/sec (1125m/sec) to pierce 209mm of armour at 1640ft (500m) range. A conventional gun of the same calibre fired a 15lb (6.8kg) steel shell at 2600ft/sec (792m/sec) to pierce 132mm of armour at the same range. As with the taper bore guns, shortage of tungsten, necessary for the special shot, stopped production in 1942 and very few guns were put into service. In Britain a muzzle adapter for the 40mm 2-pounder tank gun was developed by Janacek. This gave a substantial increase in performance, but by the time it had been perfected the gun was obsolete.

Squid

Used in conjunction with ASDIC, Squid was a three-barrel MORTAR system which threw bombs ahead of a ship engaged in a submarine hunt. The bombs dropped at different speeds and exploded at different depths so as to enclose the widest possible area, the combined concussion waves damaging or destroying the submarine's hull. Although the explosions broke the Asdic contact, a near miss was often enough to drive the target to the surface, where it could be destroyed by gunfire. See also HEDGEHOG.

SS

Abbreviation for Schutzstaffeln (Protection Squads). The SS originated as Hitler's personal bodyguard during the Nazi Party's early days. From these small and seedy beginnings the organisation evolved into the most powerful arm of the Nazi administration, under the personal control of Heinrich HIMMLER. The SS consisted of two principal branches. The Allgemein (General) SS staffed the CONCENTRATION CAMPS, supervised deportations, formed EINSATZGRUPPEN, and imposed the Nazi diktat throughout occupied Europe, generally in the

Pre-war German SS troops.

most ruthless manner imaginable. The WAFFEN (ARMED) SS, on the other hand, provided military formations which were dedicated to the Führer and the Party and fought alongside the German Army.

Stagg, Group Capt J. M.

Stagg was Chief Meteorological Officer at Supreme Headquarters Allied Expeditionary Force and was responsible for advising EISENHOWER on anticipated weather conditions in the English Channel, a vital consideration since it affected the choice of date upon which the Allies launched their invasion of NORMANDY. Although the first days of June 1944 were notable for their poor conditions, Stagg and his team accurately predicted that a fair-weather window would open on 6 June and last for several days. Eisenhower therefore decided that D-DAY was to be 6 June, although this was not finally confirmed until 0430 the previous day.

Stalin, Iosef (1879–1953)

Iosef Vissarionovich Dzugashvili was the son of a Tiflis cobbler and in his youth was briefly a candidate for the priesthood. He changed his name to Stalin, meaning "Man of Steel", when he became involved in Bolshevik revolutionary politics in 1903. The city of Tsaritsyn was renamed STALINGRAD in honour of his somewhat exaggerated part in its defence during the Russian Civil War. He was imprisoned from 1913 to 1917 and freed at the start of the Revolution, becoming a close associate of Lenin. He was a member of the Revolutionary Military Council, 1921–23. Between 1925 and 1928, Stalin was engaged in a bitter leadership struggle, from which he emerged as virtual dictator of the Soviet Union. The majority of his former Bolshevik comrades and many thousands of Russians were ruthlessly liquidated. His purge of the Army in 1937 involved the slaughter of thousands of officers, including the brilliant Marshal TUKHACHEVSKY, leaving the Soviet Army so thoroughly cowed that it performed badly during the forcible annexation of eastern Poland in 1939 and the subsequent Winter War with Finland. There is no doubt that Stalin was fully aware of HITLER's intention to invade the Soviet Union in 1941, but he took no steps to counter the threat. When the blow fell he relied at first upon commanders who had fought successfully in the Civil War, including BUDENNY, TIMOSHENKO and

VOROSHILOV, but they were unable to cope with the enemy's BLITZKRIEG technique and the situation only began to stabilize under ZHUKOV's control. However, he did succeed in rallying the country against the invaders and ensured that the war effort could be maintained by moving the means of armaments production east of the Urals. He continued to direct the war personally as Commander-in-Chief, Commissar for Defence and Chairman of the Council of People's Commissars, but unlike Hitler was prepared to accept professional advice from his senior officers, although he dealt harshly with local commanders who failed to achieve their objectives and was careful to subdue military heroes who might otherwise have become rivals. He constantly threatened his Western Allies that he would make a separate peace with Hitler unless they opened a second front in Europe, and came close to doing so in 1943. At the YALTA Conference of February 1945 he reached agreement with CHURCHILL on postwar spheres of influence, and although he kept his promise not to intervene in Greece, he quickly turned the remaining countries of Eastern Europe into Soviet satellites. Under Stalin's leadership the USSR emerged from World War II as one of the world's superpowers, but such is the memory of the terrible and total sway he held over the Russian people that the history of the Soviet Union since 1953 can be seen largely in terms of the dynamic of "de-Stalinization".

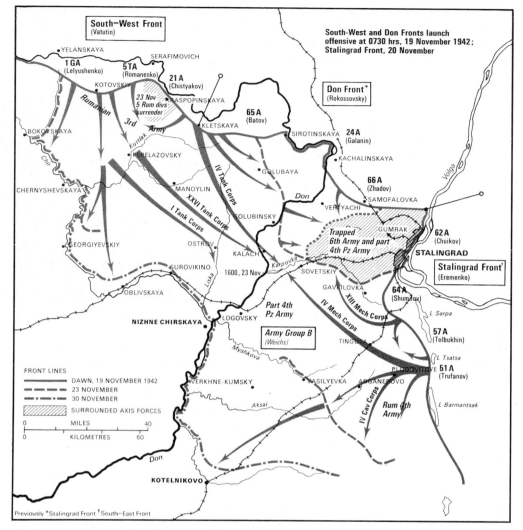

The Soviet counter-attack which trapped the German 6th Army at Stalingrad.

Stalingrad

A city on the River Volga, Stalingrad was a major industrial centre and the objective of German Army Group B in the 1942 campaign to take the CAUCASUS. In the face of this advance the Russians reinforced Stalingrad with troops from the Moscow reserve and placed General CHUIKOV in command. General VON PAULUS attempted to assault the city with elements of the German 6th Army as they arrived, but they were fed into battle piecemeal and were successfully beaten off by the Russians. By 10 August the full strength of the 6th Army was in place, backed by artillery, but waited for reinforcements from HOTH's 4th Panzer Army who were moving up from the south. On 19 August the first major German attack was launched. The initial German advance through the outskirts was relatively easy, but once the troops entered the built-up area the advance became a house-to-house fight, a

tactic at which the Soviets had the advantages. The battle continued throughout the next two months with neither side gaining a significant advantage. Meanwhile, the Russians were preparing a counter-attack force of over one million men, 13,500 guns and 894 tanks under Marshal ZHUKOV. On 19 November they began their assault around the flanks of the German armies. By 23 November they had closed the trap, and then concentrated their efforts on beating off German attempts to relieve von Paulus. With this done, in January 1943 they began the systematic destruction of the German forces held inside the ring, and on 31 January 1943 Paulus surrendered. German losses amounted to about 1.5 million men, 3500 tanks and assault guns, 12,000 guns and mortars, 75,000 vehicles and 3000 aircraft.

Stalin Line

The German name for a line of Russian per-

Zhukov's troops retake Stalingrad, 1943.

manent fortifications on the 1939 Russo-Polish frontier in the north-east corner of Poland, close to Lithuania. Its function was to block any advance towards Leningrad. Soviet troops withdrew to the Line during the opening phase of Operation BARBAROSSA, but it had not been maintained after the westward shift of the Russo-Polish border in 1939 and was rapidly outflanked by the German 6th Army in early July.

Stamina

Air-supply of British garrisons at IMPHAL and KOHIMA, 1944.

Stangl, Franz (1908–1971)

Stangl was commandant of the TREBLINKA concentration camp and was responsible for the murder of 700,000 of its inmates. After the war he managed to escape to South America.

Starfish

British deception plan designed to draw German bombers away from their targets by lighting dummy fires, etc.

Stark, Adm Harold (1880–1972)

Stark became the US Navy's Commander of Naval Operations in 1939 and was closely involved in the naval expansion programme which was undertaken in the period immediately prior to America's entry into the war. During this period he also took part in secret talks with his British counterparts on the security of American shipping in the Atlantic. As relations between the United States and Japan deteriorated, he placed the Navy on a war footing, enabling it to react with greater speed than the Japanese had anticipated in the aftermath of PEARL HARBOR, although he was criticized for failing to give Admiral KIMMEL adequate warning of the attack itself. He believed that the defeat of Germany should be the Allies' first priority and in March 1942 was appointed Commander of US Naval Forces in the European theatre of war, a post which despite its title was largely diplomatic and involved liaison at the highest level, particularly in the months preceding Operation OVERLORD.

Starobielsk, Soviet Union, 1939–40

A small town in the eastern part of the Ukraine, south-east of KHARKOV. A prison camp for about 4000 regular and reserve Polish officers was established here by the Soviets in 1939, in the grounds of a former monastery. In April 1940 the prisoners were removed. A small number were sent to a new camp at Pavlischev Bor and eventually, in 1941, were liberated. The remainder were never seen again. It is believed that they were taken north, put in barges and towed out into the White Sea, where the barges were scuttled.

Starvation

Mining of Japanese waters by the US Navy, March 1945.

Stauffenberg, Col Count Claus von (1907–44)

Von Stauffenberg was a General Staff officer who served with distinction in Poland, France and North Africa. He was severely wounded by a low-level strafing attack in April 1943, losing his right eye, right arm and part of his left hand. On his release from hospital he was given a post on the staff of Reserve Army Headquarters, where he joined the conspiracy against HITLER. Among his duties was attendance at briefings at the Führer's headquarters at RASTENBURG. Since the nature of his injuries apparently placed him above suspicion, his briefcase was never examined by the guards. He decided to use this combination of circumstances to plant a bomb, and did so on 20 July 1944. Unfortunately, another officer moved the briefcase when he left the room and Hitler survived the blast. Believing the Führer to be dead, von Stauffenberg returned to Berlin, only to find his fellow conspirators HÖPNER and BECK a prey to indecision. They were overpowered that night and von Stauffenberg was immediately shot in the courtyard of the War Ministry.

Steinbock (Ibex)

German bombing attacks on the United Kingdom, spring 1944.

Steiner, SS Gen Felix

Steiner commanded the SS Regiment *Germania* during the 1940 campaign in France and then led the 5th SS Panzer Grenadier Division *Wiking* on the Eastern Front until 1943. In 1944 he was appointed commander of III SS Corps. When the Russians encircled BERLIN in April 1945, the remnants of Steiner's command, consisting of approximately six battalions drawn from the 4th SS Panzer Grenadier Division *Polizei*, 25th Panzer Grenadier Division, 5th Jäger Division and 3rd Navy Division, were located at Eberswalde, some 25 miles north of the city. HITLER, by now completely divorced from reality, elevated the status of this tiny force to that of an army and ordered it to relieve the capital, isolating the Soviet spearheads as it did so, promising Steiner that he would "pay with his head" in the event of failure. Steiner, lacking artillery and armour, had no intention of becoming involved in this insane plan and made only the most token effort. Those of his men who could then made their way west and surrendered to the British and Americans. To the end, signals from Hitler poured from his bunker, demanding details of Steiner's progress. Latterly they received no answer.

Sten Gun

British 9mm calibre submachine gun, developed in 1940 by *S*hepherd and *T*urpin at the Royal Small Arms Factory, *En*field, from which combination the name was constructed. Of extremely simple design, it was cheaply made (£3 each) and as well as arming British troops it was widely distributed to resistance fighters on the Continent. A silenced version was also developed for use by Commandos and raiding parties. The Sten was produced in four different models in Britain and Canada, and an estimated 3.25 million were manufactured.

The British Sten Mark IIs with integral silencer, used by clandestine forces.

Stettinius, Edward (1900–49)

An American industrialist who advised ROOSEVELT on matters relating to industry and the war economy. In May 1940 he joined the National Defense Advisory Commission and in January 1941 was appointed Director of the Office of Production Management. He became Under-Secretary of State in 1943 and in November 1944 succeeded Cordell HULL as Secretary of State. He was the United States' first delegate to the United Nations.

Stier – Surface Raider (Ger)

Also known as Ship 23 and Raider J. Sailed 12 May 1942 and operated in the Atlantic, sinking four ships of 29,406 tons. However, her last victim, the American freighter *Stephen Hopkins*, fought back so effectively with her single 4-inch gun that *Stier* was herself set ablaze and sank, 27 September 1942. *Displacement* 4778 tons; *speed* 14 knots; *armament* 6×5.9in; 2×37mm AA; 4×20mm AA; 2×21in torpedo tubes (submerged); *aircraft* 2; *complement* 324.

Stilwell, Gen Joseph (1893–1946)

Nicknamed "Vinegar Joe" for his acerbic manner, Stilwell served as American military attaché at the Peking embassy between 1932 and 1939 and two years later was appointed commander of the American forces in the India–Burma–China theatre of war, with the additional responsibility of raising the efficiency of CHIANG KAI-SHEK's army. He became Chiang's Chief of Staff in March 1942 but was under no illusions about the Nationalist leader's policy of diverting military aid into his fight against the Chinese Communists rather than the Japanese, referring to Chiang contemptuously as "The Peanut". He led the Chinese 5th and 6th Armies during the 1942 campaign in Burma, conducting a difficult withdrawal to India. A convinced Anglophobe, he was sharply critical of British motives and effort. However, after his appointment as Deputy Supreme Allied Commander South-East Asia Command under MOUNTBATTEN in October 1943, he became more co-operative. In November 1943 he commenced offensive operations in northern Burma with the object of re-opening land communications with China. He succeeded in capturing MOGAUNG on 26 June 1944 but was held up by stubborn Japanese resistance at MYITKYINA, which did not fall until 3 August. In October the success of the Japanese Ichi-Go

General Joseph Stilwell and staff during the retreat from Burma.

offensive in China led to a request from the American Joint Chiefs of Staff that Chiang appoint Stilwell commander of all the Chinese armies. Chiang declined and insisted that he be recalled. Stilwell later succeeded Buckner as commander of the US 10th Army on OKINAWA.

Stimson, Henry L. (1867–1950)

Stimson was brought into ROOSEVELT's Cabinet as Secretary for War in July 1940 and held this appointment throughout World War II. He was an opponent of American isolationism and one of his first acts was the introduction of conscription. He supported the Lend-Lease programme and was responsible for arming American merchant vessels against attacks by Axis naval units. When the United States entered the war, he was in favour of the "Germany first" policy and, although anxious to open a Second Front in Europe at the earliest opportunity, he later concurred with CHURCHILL's view that it would be premature to launch a major invasion before 1944. He was also responsible for military scientific research, including the development of nuclear devices, and advocated the use of the ATOMIC BOMB against Japan.

Stinson Aircraft (USA)

Stinson AT-19 Reliant The Reliant was a pre-war commercial cabin monoplane, adopted into US service as a general transport and navigation trainer. It was also employed by the Royal Navy under its civilian name of Reliant. *Span* 42ft (12.8m); *engine* 1 280hp radial; *speed* 135mph (217kph).

Stinson L-5 Sentinel This was the militarized version of the pre-war Voyager cabin monoplane, adopted by the US Army as a general light transport, ambulance, liaison and photography machine. The RAF also took large numbers, calling them the Sentinel, and they were used principally in Burma in transport and artillery observation roles. *Span* 34ft (10.4m); *engine* 1 175hp in-line; *speed* 118mph (190kph).

Stirling, Col Archibald David (1915–)

After serving with the Scots Guards, Stirling transferred to No. 3 (Brigade of Guards) Commando and was posted with this unit to the Middle East. Here he conceived the idea of using deep penetration raiding parties to destroy enemy aircraft on their home airfields and was permitted to form a unit for this purpose. This evolved into the SPECIAL AIR SERVICE (SAS) Regiment. Stirling's concept, which involved close co-operation with the LONG RANGE DESERT GROUP, was fully justified by the spectacular results achieved by his teams. He was captured in Tunisia in 1943 and, after repeated attempts to escape, was confined in COLDITZ castle for the remainder of the war.

Stoneage

MALTA relief convoy, November 1942.

Stooge

A British radio-guided air defence weapon, developed from 1944 as a counter against KAMIKAZE attacks on warships. Resembling a small aircraft, it carried a 220lb (100kg) explosive warhead and was launched by three

3in (76mm) solid-fuel rocket motors. It was sustained in flight by four 5in (127mm) motors which gave it a speed of about 500mph (800kph). The first development models flew in February 1945 but development was not completed before the war ended and was subsequently abandoned.

Stopford, Gen Sir Montagu George North (1892–1971)

Stopford commanded the 17th Infantry Brigade during the 1940 campaign in France and Belgium. He was GOC 56th (London) Division in 1941 and became Commandant of the Staff College the following year. He was appointed commander of XXXIII Corps in November 1943 and with it relieved KOHIMA and IMPHAL in 1944. His corps took part in the advance into central Burma, taking MANDALAY on 25 March 1945, and then continued towards RANGOON along the valley of IRRAWADDY, capturing the important oilfield of YENANGYAUNG on the way. As the campaign in Burma drew to its close, he was appointed commander of the 12th Army.

Strachwitz von Gross-Zauche und Camminetz, Col Count Hyazinth

Strachwitz belonged to an old Silesian military family and as a young man had seen active service during World War I and then with the *Freikorps*. During World War II he became the Panzerwaffe's most successful battle group commander, being responsible for the destruction of several hundred Soviet tanks and other vehicles. He was awarded the Knight's Cross on 28 August 1941, Oakleaves on 13 November 1942, both while serving with I/Panzer Regiment 2; Swords on 28 March 1943 while commanding Panzer Regiment *Grossdeutschland*; and Diamonds on 15 April 1944 while commanding a battle group on Army Group North's sector. He was wounded no less than 14 times but survived the war to become a prisoner of the Americans.

Strangle

Allied bombing offensive in Italy aimed at the disruption of German communications, commencing March 1944.

Strategic Bombing

Air attacks intended to affect the overall course of a war by interrupting the enemy's manufacture of armaments, destroying raw materials, disrupting transportation, reducing civilian morale and provoking similar long-term disruptions. Its roots lie in theories propounded in the 1920s and 1930s by General Douhet, Colonel Billy Mitchell, Air Marshal TRENCHARD and others who were convinced that air bombing could be a decisive factor in future wars, and could even win wars without the need for ground or naval forces. These theories were tested over Germany and Japan by the British and US Air Forces during the course of the war, but, in spite of enormous efforts in material and manpower, strategic bombing failed to have the desired effect. Experience was to show that strategic bombing was effective only when directed against specific types of target – for example, oil production, ball-bearing production, and railway junctions – and for most of the war the means of achieving this degree of application was lacking.

Streicher, Julius (1885–1946)

After World War I Streicher formed a small anti-Semitic party in Nuremberg but soon merged his interests with those of HITLER playing a part in the Munich putsch of November 1923. In 1925 he founded *Die Stürmer*, a violently anti-Semitic journal which he continued to edit until 1943. In 1935 he staged the Nuremberg rallies and the same year was appointed Gauleiter of Franconia. He was notably corrupt and in 1940 was found guilty of misappropriating confiscated Jewish property and was removed from public life. At the NUREMBERG trials he was convicted of crimes against humanity and hanged. To the bitter end he took pleasure in his self-conferred title of "Jew-Baiter".

Stuart – Light Tank M3 and M5 Series (USA)

Developed from a series of experimental light tanks and combat cars produced during the 1930s, culminating in the M2A4, an improved version of which was standardized as the Light Tank M3 in July 1940. M3 production commenced at American Car and Foundry in March 1941 and ended in August 1942. The M3A1 was built between April 1942 and February 1943, incorporating several modifications which included the removal of the cupola and the fitting of two turret hatches, the installation of power traverse and the provision of a turret basket. The M3A3, built between December 1942 and August 1943, incorporated radically re-designed frontal armour and extra fuel tanks. In the meantime, a shortage of Continental engines had given rise to a suggestion from Cadillac that two of their standard V-8 engines working in tandem could supply the required output, and that this arrangement could be used in conjunction with their Hydromatic automatic transmission. Tests confirmed that the concept was viable and the new design was standardized as the Light Tank M5 in February 1943, using the M3A1 turret. In December 1943 the M3A3

Reichsparteitag 1937. On the left of Hitler: Lutze and Himmler; on the right: Hess, Frank, Schaub and Bormann with Streicher behind them.

Stuart light tank M3A1.

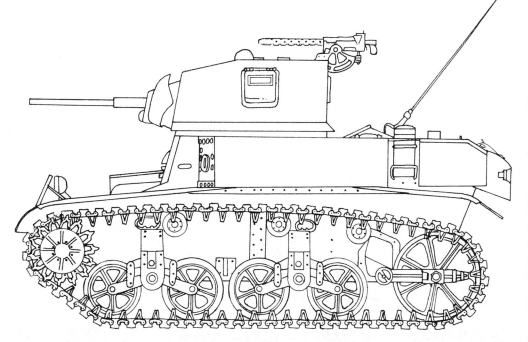

turret became available and this was fitted to the M5 chassis to produce the M5A1. The M5 Series was built by Cadillac and Massey-Harris with later participation by American Car and Foundry. Production ceased in June 1944. The total number of Stuarts built was 22,743 (M3 – 5811 including 1285 diesel; M3A1 – 4621 including 211 diesel; M3A3 – 3427; M5 – 2074; M5A1 – 6810). The vehicle first saw action in November 1941 with the British 8th Army, its 37mm gun making it an acceptable substitute for the British 2-pdr Cruiser tanks. During this period its ease of handling and mechanical reliability earned it the nickname of Honey,

although the limited fuel capacity of the early models gave cause for concern. Initially the M3 was armed with two additional machine guns in fixed sponson mountings but these contributed little and were soon stripped out. In British service the series was known by the following designations: M3 (petrol) – *Stuart I*; M3 (diesel) – *Stuart II*; M3A1 (petrol) – *Stuart III*; M3A1 (diesel) – *Stuart IV*; M3A3 – *Stuart V*; M5 and M5A1 – *Stuart VI*. The Stuart series was also supplied to the Australian, Chinese, French and Soviet armies and to TITO's Yugoslav partisans, serving in every major theatre of war. The layout of the vehicle did

not lend itself to conversion to other uses but the eight-ton air-portable Locust Light Tank M22, armed with a 37mm gun, employed a modified M3 chassis and a number accompanied the British 6th Airlanding Brigade during the RHINE crossing on 24 March 1945. In addition, the M5 chassis provided the basis of the HOWITZER MOTOR CARRIAGE M8. Flame-throwing Stuarts known as Satans, their 37mm gun replaced by the RONSON system, were used by the US Marine Corps in the Pacific. Turretless Stuarts were employed by the British and American armies as command and reconnaissance vehicles, KANGAROOS and armoured ambulances. The Stuart remained active in many armies long after the war had ended. See also *The Stuart Light Tank Series* by Bryan Perrett (Osprey). *Weight* 12.3 tons (M3); 15 tons (M5); *speed* 36mph (58kph) (M3); 40mph (64kph) (M5); *armour* 43mm; *armament* 1 37mm gun; 3 .30 cal Browning machine guns; *engine(s)* 1 Continental radial air-cooled 250hp petrol or 1 Guiberson radial air-cooled 220hp diesel (M3 Series); 2 Cadillac V-8 petrol, each 121hp (M5 Series); *crew* 4.

Student, Col Gen Kurt (1890–)

Student served as a pilot during World War I, and remained in the much-reduced German Army after the war. He transferred to the Luftwaffe on its formation in 1934 and was chosen by GÖRING to train an experimental parachute infantry force, which was later expanded to form the 7th Air Division, and to examine the use of gliders as a vehicle for use by air-landing troops. In 1940 Student's paratroops proved their worth in Scandinavia, Holland and Belgium. In Belgium the supposedly impregnable fortress of EBEN EMAEL was captured by glider-borne forces which landed on the fort itself. Equally important was the seizure of the bridges across the Maas estuary in Holland, and the establishment of units on the airfields at Rotterdam and Waalhaven. Student was wounded, ironically by a stray German bullet, during the fighting in Rotterdam and played no further part in the campaign in the West. In 1941 he directed the successful airborne invasion of CRETE by XI Air Corps. However, the operation resulted in such heavy casualties that HITLER forbade further large-scale parachute operations. Student planned a similar invasion of MALTA in 1942, but this was cancelled. Thereafter, although the number of parachute divisions continued to rise, they fought as élite infantry units.

Colonel-General Student observing artillery fire.

Student commanded the 1st Parachute Army in Holland and Germany 1944–45 and on 29 April succeeded HEINRICI as commander of Army Group Vistula, which had all but ceased to exist.

Stülpnagel, Gen Karl-Heinrich von (1886–1944)

In 1939 Stülpnagel was appointed Quartermaster General and then Deputy Chief of General Staff. During Operation BAR-BAROSSA he commanded the 17th Army in Army Group South and played a prominent part in the encirclement of Soviet forces within the KIEV pocket. In 1942 he became Military Governor of occupied France. His real significance, however, was as an active opponent of HITLER and the Nazi regime. In 1939 he planned a coup which had to be abandoned for lack of support, but despite this failure he continued recruiting support-ers for his cause among high-ranking officers. In May 1944 he planned to conclude an armis-tice with the Western Allies, but RUNDSTEDT, then Commander-in-Chief West, declined to participate. In July he received a promise of support from KLUGE, who had succeeded Rundstedt, but this was conditional upon the Führer's death. When Hitler survived STAUF-FENBERG's bomb Stülpnagel had already com-promised himself by arresting the SS, Gestapo

and Nazi hierarchy in Paris, and Kluge offered him no assistance. He failed in a suicide attempt and was tried with his fellow con-spirators and hanged.

Sturmgeschutze – Assault Guns (Ger)

Conceived in 1935 as a means of providing infantry with armoured support, the Sturm-geschutz was based on the chassis of the PANZERKAMPFWAGEN III and armed with a 75mm L/24 howitzer housed in a low, fixed superstructure with overhead cover. The prototype Sturmgeschutz III (StuG III) was tested in 1937 but the first four batteries did not see active service until the 1940 campaign in the West. Thereafter, the number of assault gun units rose steadily and they served in every major campaign in which German troops were involved, although they did not reach North Africa in any numbers until the fighting in Tunisia. Following encounters with the KLIMENTI VOROSHILOV and T-34/76 Soviet tanks, the StuG III Model F of 1942 was up-gunned first with a 75mm L/43 gun and then with a 75mm L/48 gun, as well as being up-armoured by the addition of 30mm *appliqué* plates. This gave the vehicle an impressive anti-tank capability, although its primary purpose remained infantry support and L/24 howitzer models were retained until the appearance of the Sturmhaubitze 42 (Assault Howitzer 42) in 1943. This was based on the StuG III Model G and armed with a 105mm L/28.3 howitzer. A total of 10,528 assault guns on the PzKw III chassis, including 1114 Sturmhaubitze 42, were built during the war, the majority by Alkett of Berlin. In addi-tion, 632 75mm L/48 StuG IVs were produced, using the chassis of the PANZERKAMPFWAGEN IV Model G. In their final form assault guns were fitted with side skirts as a defence against shaped charge ammunition and received a

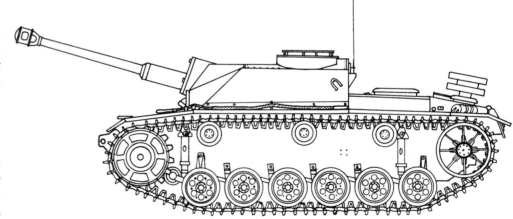

Sturmgeschutz III.

Infantry aboard a Sturmgeschutz III on the Eastern Front.

coating of ZIMMERIT. The Sturmgeschutze were manned by the specially raised Sturmartillerie (Assault Artillery), which became an élite branch of service, and were formed into battalions (later designated brigades) which were at the disposal of divisional and higher commanders. Latterly, with the German Army engaged in mainly defensive battles, their function became that of tank destroyers. During the final stages of the war many Panzer divisions were issued with assault guns to supplement their dwindling tank strength. See also BRUMMBÄR and STURMTIGER. *Stug III Model B Weight* 22 tons; *speed* 25mph (40kph); *armour* 50mm; *armament* 1×75mm L/24 howitzer; *engine* Maybach HL120 TRM 300hp petrol; *crew* 4.

Sturmgewehr

Literally "assault rifle" – the name applied (reputedly by HITLER) to a German automatic rifle originally known as the Maschinen Pistole 43 and then as the Sturmgewehr 44. The German Army had attempted several designs of automatic rifle, and after experience on the Russian Front the MP 43 was devised. It was constructed around a new short 7.62mm cartridge, on the premise that since the infantryman rarely shot at ranges greater than 330yds (300m), a low-powered cartridge would suffice and would permit a lightweight automatic rifle to be constructed. The weapon was gas operated and largely made from steel pressings, but it was nevertheless a reliable and effective weapon. The concept of the assault rifle was widely copied in postwar years and is now the standard infantry weapon of most of the world's armies.

Sturmtiger (Assault Tiger) – Heavy Assault Gun (Ger)

Based on the chassis of the TIGER E and protected by 150mm armour, the 68-ton Sturmtiger was designed to demolish large buildings and concrete fortifications. It was armed with a 380mm anti-submarine rocket launcher which fired a 761lb (345kg) spin-stabilized projectile up to 6000 yards (5490m), although normally would have been used at much closer range. The projectiles were of two types, one standard high explosive and the other a SHAPED CHARGE for use against concrete. By the time the vehicle appeared in 1944 the German Army was largely engaged in defensive battles and it had little practical application. Only a few were built.

A British general inspecting captured weapons, and holding a Sturmgewehr 44 assault rifle.

Stutthof, Poland

A German concentration camp, a few miles east of DANZIG. It was also used as an extermination camp for Jews, about 67,500 of whom were killed here.

SU-76 – Self-Propelled 76.2mm Gun (USSR)

Entered service in 1942 and consisted of a 76.2mm anti-tank gun with double-baffle muzzle brake mounted in a fixed open-topped fighting compartment at the rear of an extended T-70 light tank chassis. Originally designed as a tank destroyer, it was relegated to infantry support after more heavily

SU-100 tank destroyer.

armoured German tanks began reaching the front. Although obsolete by the end of World War II, it was encountered by United Nations forces in Korea.

SU-85 and SU-100 – Tank Destroyers (USSR)

Based on the chassis of the T-34 medium tank series with the gun mounted forward in an enclosed superstructure of angled 45mm plate. The SU-85 was introduced in 1943 and was armed with the DS-S-85 85mm gun. However, as heavier German tanks were being met in increasing numbers and the T-34/85 was itself about to enter service it was

decided that the vehicle should be up-gunned with the D-10-S 100mm gun and the result, designated SU-100, was introduced in 1944. The SU-100 enjoyed a long postwar career with the Soviet Union's allies and client states and is still active in some armies today; its 100mm gun armed the Soviet Army's T-54 medium tank series.

SU-122 Assault Howitzer (USSR)

Based on the T-34/76 medium tank chassis and armed with a short 122mm howitzer, layout being similar to that of the SU-85 and SU 100 tank destroyers. The SU-122 was introduced in 1942 and used for direct gunfire support.

SU-152 – Assault Howitzer (USSR)

Designed by the Kotin Bureau and said to have reached the prototype stage after only 25 days, following the capture of a TIGER E on the LENINGRAD sector in January 1943. The vehicle was based on the KLIMENTI VOROSHILOV chassis and armed with an ML-20 152mm L/29 gun howitzer mounted forward in a heavily armoured enclosed superstructure. Production commenced in March 1943 and at KURSK the SU-152 proved capable of defeating both the Tiger and the ELEFANT, earning itself the nickname of Animal Killer. The vehicle served in heavy assault gun regiments which were at the disposal of senior commanders.

Submarines, American

The pre-war "P", NEW "S" and "T" CLASSES of submarine evolved into the GATO CLASS, which became the United States Navy's standard submarine and was built in large numbers. These classes possessed all-electric drive in which the diesel engines were coupled to the generators rather than to the propeller shafts. Another feature of American submarines was their wide operational radius which made them particularly suitable for the Pacific theatre of war in which they were principally employed. Although their early operations were marred by faulty torpedoes which failed to explode, they virtually eliminated the Japanese merchant marine, sinking over 1100 vessels of 4,700,000 tons plus numerous warships. For their part, the Japanese seriously neglected anti-submarine warfare and only began to produce escort vessels during the last years of the war, but by then American and Allied submarines, supported by air activity, had obtained a stranglehold on Japanese seaborne communications. American sub-

marines also rescued downed carrier pilots from the sea, supported guerrilla activity in the PHILIPPINES and carried out detailed reconnaissance of enemy positions.

Submarines, British

British submarine warfare policy during World War II was that of the *guerre de course*, involving the sinking of enemy warships and merchantmen, maintaining the blockade on enemy-held coasts and severing the enemy's sea-borne supply lines. In northern waters British submarine attacks on German merchant vessels were governed by the terms of international law during the early months of the war, but when it became clear that the Germans were themselves committed to unrestricted submarine warfare these limitations were suspended in 1940. By May 1945 the German Merchant Marine had ceased to exist, British submarines having accounted for approximately 25% (318,000 tons) of the shipping sunk, in addition to numerous successes against warship targets. It was in the Mediterranean, however, that the activities of the British submarine service were of greatest significance. Here, between June 1940 and the end of 1944, the 1st, 8th and 10th Flotillas, based respectively at Alexandria, Gibraltar and Malta, sank 286 merchantmen and transports of over one million tons, plus four cruisers, 17 destroyers, 16 Italian and five German submarines as well as damaging many more warships, and the dislocation caused to the supply line of the Axis armies in North Africa was a major factor in their ultimate defeat. Conversely, in 1942, the PORPOISE CLASS minelaying submarines were for a while the only vessels capable of maintaining communications with MALTA. None the less, the success of British submarines in the Mediterranean was purchased at the high price of 45 boats lost. In the Pacific the submarine war against Japan was dominated by the larger American boats with their long endurance, but from 1944 onwards British flotillas based on Trincomalee began operating in the Indian Ocean and East Indies and, in company with Dutch submarines, sank over 97,000 tons of Japanese shipping. Several "A" Class submarines, designed specifically for operations in the Pacific, were launched during the last stages of the war but none were completed in time to see active service. In addition to their normal duties, British submarines were used in clandestine operations,

including transporting agents and raiding parties. See "O", "P AND R", "S", "T", "U", "V", PORPOISE and THAMES CLASSES; also "X" CRAFT.

Submarines, German

When war broke out in September 1939 the German Navy possessed 57 U-boats; by May 1945 total production had reached 1170. At first boats were built on conventional lines but from 1943 onwards dispersed pre-fabrication was common, with the various completed sections being finally welded together on the slipway. After the German victories of 1940 the U-boats were able to operate not only from their home ports but also from bases established in France and Norway, giving them easy access to the Atlantic. Good communications enabled patrol lines and attack groups, frequently referred to as "wolfpacks", to be deployed efficiently, and special types were developed to replenish operational boats with fuel oil, torpedoes and supplies. Like their World War I forbears, the U-boats came close to defeating the UK by severing its vital sea-borne communications, as well as making an important contribution to the sea war in the Mediterranean. Their fortunes began to decline with the development of more sophisticated anti-submarine warfare weapons and techniques, particularly after Allied air cover was extended over the entire North Atlantic, and the loss of their French bases in the latter half of 1944 seriously curtailed their operational deployment. However, the morale of the German submarine service remained high and aggressive patrolling was maintained until the German surrender. A plan known as Operation *Regenbogen* (Rainbow) had been devised for this eventuality, involving the wholesale scuttling of the entire U-boat fleet, but the executive codeword was not given for political reasons; despite this, many captains acted on their own initiative and scuttled their boats in the Baltic or the North Sea. Others surrendered in compliance with the terms of the cease-fire, and the majority of their boats were sunk in the Atlantic 1945–46 by the Royal Navy during Operation *Deadlight*.

In total, the U-boats sank 2603 merchant vessels of 13,500,000 tons, plus 175 Allied warships. Over 30,000 British merchant seamen alone were killed and the full extent of the personnel casualties inflicted will never be accurately known. All of this was achieved at a terrible cost. 630 U-boats were lost on

U-boat Type VII in the Baltic.

operations, 81 were destroyed in home waters or at base because of enemy action, and a further 42 were sunk accidentally. 215 were lost while evacuating the French bases or scuttled during Operation *Regenbogen*. 38 were so seriously damaged as to be constructive total losses, or were paid off because of obsolescence. 11 were captured or forced to seek internment in neutral ports because of damage sustained. The remaining 153 surrendered at the end of the war. Of the 41,000 men who served in the U-boat arm during the war, 28,000 were killed and 5000 were taken prisoner, yet the service never lacked volunteers. See also ATLANTIC, BATTLE OF THE, DÖNITZ, ADMIRAL KARL, MIDGET SUBMARINES, GERMAN, SCHNORKEL, U-BOATS TYPES IID, VIID, IXC, XB, XIV, XXI and XXIII, and WALTER TURBINE.

Submarines, Italian

The Royal Italian Navy possessed approximately 100 operational submarines when it entered the war, including a small flotilla based at MASSAWA in the Red Sea. Although the vast majority of Italian submarine operations naturally took place within the Mediterranean, some of the larger craft served in the Atlantic and as far afield as the Indian and Pacific Oceans, and a flotilla of coastal submarines was sent to the Black Sea in support of Axis operations against the Soviet Union. As well as engaging in normal patrol activity, Italian submarines frequently carried supplies for the Axis armies in North Africa; the R Class transport submarines, with a cargo capa-

city of 610 tons, were designed for this purpose but the only two to be completed were sunk within a month. In general, the Italian submarine service sustained far higher losses than were justified by the modest return of Allied shipping sunk. See also ACCIAIO, ADUA, ARCHIMEDE, ARGONAUTA, BRIN, CAGNI, FLUTTO, LIUZZI, MARCELLO, MARCONI, PERLA and SIRENA CLASSES; MIDGET SUBMARINES and "HUMAN TORPEDO".

Submarines, Japanese

The Japanese preferred to use their submarines within the context of normal fleet operations. This proved to be a fundamental error as attacks on heavily escorted warships resulted in crippling losses for little return, whereas attacks on Allied troop transport convoys would have yielded greater benefit at lower cost. After the heavy loss of destroyers around the SOLOMON ISLANDS in 1943, a large proportion of the submarine building programme was diverted to transport and supply submarines by means of which contact could be maintained with isolated island garrisons throughout the Pacific. During the final phase of the war many of the surviving fleet submarines were adapted to carry KAITEN underwater suicide craft. The majority of the older classes of submarine had short production runs but representative details of the more important modern classes can be found under I 5, I 40, I 168, I 176, I 361, I 400, RO 35, RO 100, MIDGET SUBMARINES and KAITEN suicide submarines.

Substance

MALTA relief convoy, July 1941.

Sugiyama, FM Hajime (1880–1945)

Sugiyama, a fervent advocate of Japanese territorial expansion, became a member of the Supreme War Council in 1935. He then served as War Minister from 1937 to 1938, when he was appointed Chief of the General Staff, holding this post until February 1944. He cooperated closely with Admiral Nagano, the Imperial Navy's Chief of Staff, in preparing the timetable for the attack on PEARL HARBOR and the invasion of Western possessions throughout the Far East. During the last year of the war he served again as War Minister in Prime Minister KOISO's government. He committed suicide on 12 September 1945.

Sukhoi Su-2 (USSR)

Pavel Sukhoi was a member of Tupolev's design team and developed the ANT-1 light bomber in 1937; the design was gradually improved and refined until in 1940 it was approved for service as the BB-1, the title changing to Su-2 when the Soviets adopted the practice of naming their machines after the designer rather than after their function. A low-wing monoplane with a turret for the gunner, similar in concept to the FAIREY BATTLE and many others of its day, it suffered the same blind spot below and to the rear which made it easy prey for German fighters in 1941. *Span* 47ft (14.3m); *engine* 1 1520hp radial; *crew* 2; *armament* 5 machine guns, 1300lb (600kg) of bombs; *speed* 285mph (458kph).

Sultan, Gen Daniel (1885–1947)

Sultan served as Deputy Commander of American troops in the India–Burma–China theatre of war from April 1942 until November 1944, when he succeeded STILWELL as Commander following the latter's recall. He continued the Allied offensive in northern Burma and in January 1945 re-opened the BURMA ROAD, thereby restoring land communications with China.

Sumatra, Pacific, 1942

One of the principal islands of the Dutch East Indies, Sumatra was attacked by Japanese paratroop forces on 16 February 1942. This was followed by landings on Java, where the American–British–Dutch–Australian command headquarters was located. The problem of attempting to stem several Japanese thrusts in the area with the limited troops available was insoluble, and Japanese naval strength effectively prevented troop movements or evacuations (see the Battle of the JAVA SEA). The Dutch East Indies government surrendered on 8 March 1942.

Sumida M-2593 Armoured Car (Jap)

A design which was obsolete long before it entered service in 1933 but which had some interest in that it incorporated flanged steel rims which could be fitted to the wheels for railway use. *Weight* 7.5 tons; *speed* 36mph (58kph); *armour* 13mm; *armament* Up to 6 6.5mm machine guns; *engine* 100hp petrol.

Sun Li-jen, Lt Gen

The American-educated commander of the Chinese 38th Division, which fought with great distinction during the 1942 campaign in Burma. In April, at ALEXANDER's request, STILWELL despatched the 38th Division to the relief of the 1st Burma Division, which had been cut off by the Japanese north of YENANGYAUNG. This brought Sun under SLIM's immediate command and the 2nd Royal Tank Regiment, plus supporting artillery, were temporarily attached to his division for the relief operation, which was completely successful. This is believed to be the only occasion in history when British troops fought under the direct control of a Chinese general. After this operation Sun conducted the withdrawal of his division to IMPHAL with such skill that it remained a fighting force. He later commanded the Chinese New 1st Army during Stilwell's offensive in northern Burma.

Sunrise

Secret Allied negotiations with senior WAFFEN ss officers in Italy, 1945.

Supercharge

British 8th Army's final breakthrough during the Second Battle of ALAMEIN.

Super-Gymnast

Preliminary Allied plan for the invasion of French North Africa.

Supermarine Aircraft (UK)

Supermarine Sea Otter The last biplane to see service with the RAF, the Sea Otter was little more than an updated version of the WALRUS, with the engine pulling instead of pushing. Aerodynamically improved, and

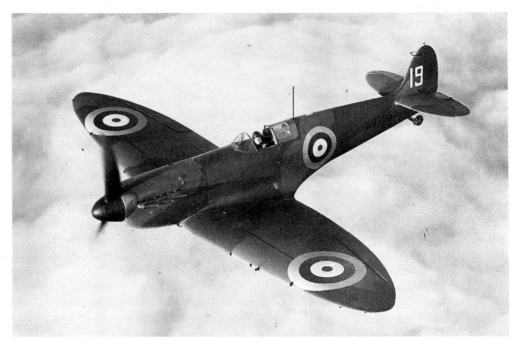

Spitfire Mark I in level flight.

with more power, it went into service in 1944 and was used on air-sea rescue tasks in European and Far Eastern areas for the remainder of the war and for several years afterwards. *Span* 46ft (14m); *engine* 1 855hp radial; *crew* 4; *speed* 150mph (241kph).

Supermarine Seafire The Seafire, as the name suggests, was the SPITFIRE modified for use from aircraft carriers. Entering service late in 1941, over 2000 were built during the war in various versions, and production continued in postwar years. The first models were little more than slightly-modified Spitfires, but the Mark III and subsequent models had folding wings and other modifications for naval work. *Span* 36.6ft (11.15m); *engine* 1 1470hp in-line; *armament* 2 20mm cannon, 4 machine guns, 550lb (250kg) of bombs; *speed* 352mph (566kph).

Supermarine Spitfire The first Spitfire flew in June 1936 and entered service in August 1938, to become the only British operational type to remain in full-scale production throughout the war. At the outbreak of war there were nine squadrons with FIGHTER COMMAND, all retained for home defence and seeing little action prior to the DUNKIRK evacuation. Of higher performance than the then more numerous HAWKER HURRICANE, 19 squadrons were available to play a major part in the Battle of BRITAIN.

Slightly faster and more manoeuvrable than its main adversary the MESSERSCHMITT BF 109E,

the Spitfire I was outdived and outclimbed by the latter. Progressive development continued throughout the war, the much more numerous cannon-armed Mark V of 1941 undertaking the bulk of cross-Channel offensives for the next two years. Later versions of the Mark V could carry underwing bombs, but all Spitfire fighters suffered from short range, having been designed primarily for defensive interception. Many Tactical Air Force units were equipped with Spitfire IX in 1944 for the Normandy invasion, and these were later supplemented by the Mark XVI using an American engine. Later versions of both these aircraft replaced the four .303 machine guns with two .50 guns, and as opposition in the air decreased, so the Spitfire undertook more fighter-bomber duties.

In all there were 21 different Marks of the Spitfire, and production totalled 20,334 aircraft; in addition there were eight Marks of the Seafire, the naval equivalent, with total production of 2556. *Mark IX Wingspan* 32.55ft (9.92m); *power* 1660hp Rolls-Royce Merlin, supercharged; *top speed* 408mph (657kph); *service ceiling* 45,000ft (13,716m); *range* 434 miles (700km). *Armament* was originally 8×.303 machine guns but varied in later models with various numbers of .303 and .50in guns and 20mm cannon.

Supermarine Walrus An ungainly biplane, using a single pusher engine mounted in a nacelle above the fuselage, the Walrus amphibian operated from land fields, was catapulted from warships and served as a fleet spotter, transport, convoy patrol and anti-submarine attack machine. Its slow speed belied its manoeuvrability, and fighters found it a difficult target. Walrus was to remain in use in the Far East until the early 1950s. *Span* 46ft (14m); *engine* 1 775hp radial; *crew* 4; *armament* 2 machine guns; *speed* 135mph (217kph).

Surcouf – Submarine (Fr)

Designed as a submarine cruiser, *Surcouf* displaced more than any other submersible of her day. When France surrendered in June 1940 she escaped from Brest to the UK, where she was later handed over to the Free French Naval Force. She patrolled in the North Atlantic and took part in the Gaullist capture of the islands of St Pierre and Miquelon. On 18 February 1942 she was in collision with the American freighter *Thomson Lykes* and later sank. *Displacement* 3304/4218 tons; *dimensions* 361ft×29ft 6in (110×9m); *machinery* 2-shaft diesel/electric motors producing shp 7600/3400; *speed* 18/8.5 knots; *operational radius* 10,000 miles (16,000km) at 10 knots/70 miles (110km) at 4.5 knots; *armament* 2×203mm (1×2); 2×37mm AA; 6×550mm torpedo tubes; 4×400mm torpedo tubes; *aircraft* 1; *complement* 118.

Suribachi, Mount, 1945

A mountain forming the south-west tip of the island of IWO JIMA. On 23 February 1945 it was taken by men of 28th Marines, who raised the Stars and Stripes on the peak after days of bitter fighting. A photograph of the flag raising became one of the classic war pictures of all time and provided the theme of the Iwo Jima memorial in Washington DC.

Surigao Strait, Battle of

See LEYTE GULF, Battle of

Suzuki, Adm Kantaro (1867–1948)

Although he was a member of the Japanese Supreme War Council, Suzuki was a venerated elder statesman with strong inclinations towards moderation. He was appointed President of the Privy Council in August 1944 and in April 1945 became Prime Minister on the fall of KOISO's government. Although he was convinced that Japan had lost the war, his peace overtures were ill-directed and ambiguous in their expression if not their intent.

On 14 August he took the unprecedented step of asking the Emperor HIROHITO to decide whether the war should continue or not and resigned immediately after the Japanese surrender.

Suzuki, Lt Gen Sosaku

Suzuki served as Chief of Staff to YAMASHITA during the campaign in MALAYA. In 1944 he commanded the 35th Army, which was responsible for the defence of the central and southern PHILIPPINES. When the Americans landed on LEYTE in October, he personally conducted the vigorous resistance of its garrison, and fighting continued until the end of December. In March 1945 he managed to reach CEBU with his staff, but was killed by an air strike the following month while trying to cross to MINDANAO.

Sweden

Sweden declared its neutrality in September 1939 and remained neutral throughout the war. Several thousand Swedes fought for Finland as volunteers during the "Winter War" of 1939–40, and the country continued to sell iron ore to Germany and ball-bearings to Britain. Until 1943 Germany insisted on rights of passage for troops en route to NORWAY. Thereafter, following strong protests from Britain and the USSR, this facility was withheld. The country also provided refuge for thousands of Jews, escaped prisoners-of-war and refugees from the Baltic states.

Switzerland

The Swiss, acutely conscious of their vulnerable geographical position in relation to the Axis states, declared their neutrality in March 1938. On 28 August 1939 they alerted their frontier troops, elected General Guisan as Commander-in-Chief and mobilized 450,000 men. Under Guisan the "national redoubt" was activated and existing fortifications brought up to modern standards. Their need to continue external trade obliged the Swiss to allow German and Italian military supply trains to pass through their country, but the passage of troop trains was forbidden. Like Portugal, Switzerland provided an arena in which espionage flourished and agents of opposing powers could meet, although its location increased the difficulties of access. Switzerland became a haven for about half a million refugees, though it refused asylum to Jews in 1942–43.

Sword Beach, France, 1944

The left-flank beach of the Allied invasion of NORMANDY on 6 June 1944, extending from Lyon-sur-Mer to Ouistreham. It was assaulted by the British 8th Brigade and 41st Royal Marine Commando, after which 185th Brigade, 9th Brigade, 22nd Armoured and 3rd Infantry Divisions landed there.

Sydney, HMAS – Leander Class Cruiser

Sydney served with the Mediterranean Fleet during 1940, crippling the Italian cruiser BARTOLOMEO COLLEONI and sinking an Italian destroyer. She returned home the following February and on 19 November 1941 encountered and sank the German commerce raider KORMORAN off the coast of Western Australia. *Sydney* was badly damaged and, on fire amidships, was last seen limping towards the horizon in the gathering dusk. No trace of the cruiser or her crew has ever been found, but there exists a strong possibility that she was finally torpedoed and sunk by a technically neutral Japanese submarine.

Syria

Syria became independent in 1920, but the French took de facto control of the country and obtained a mandate from the League of Nations in 1922. In June 1940 the French High Commissioner announced support for the Vichy Government, and in 1941 the country became a refuelling stop for German military aircraft en route to IRAQ. To forestall a possible German occupation, British and Free French forces under General Maitland WILSON and General Catroux invaded and conquered the country after five weeks of fighting. The Free French resumed control of the country, but elections in 1943 returned a Nationalist majority. In 1945 Syria was invited to send a delegation to the founding conference of the United Nations.

Szabo, Violette (1918–45)

Violette Szabo was of Anglo-French parentage. When her husband was killed on active service, she volunteered for the French Section of the SPECIAL OPERATIONS EXECUTIVE. In 1944 she carried out several missions in France but was captured while covering the escape of a MAQUIS leader. After being brutally interrogated she was sent to Germany and executed on 26 January 1945. Her story was told in the film *Carve Her Name With Pride*.

T

T1 Class Torpedo Boats (Small Destroyers) (Ger)

Displacement 839–844 tons; *dimensions* 267×28ft (81.4×8.5m); mean draught 7ft (2.1m); *machinery* 2-shaft geared turbines producing shp 31,000; *speed* 35.5 knots; *armament* 1×4.1in; 8×20mm AA (4×2); 6×21in torpedo tubes (2×3); equipped for minelaying; *complement* 119; *number in class* 12, launched 1939–40.

T-4 Programme

A euthanasia programme set up by HITLER in 1939 for the extermination of the insane, mentally deficient and crippled, named after its administrative office in Tiergartenstrasse 4, Berlin. Largely run by the SS, candidates were selected from hospitals, sent to an "observation centre" for certification, then sent to one of six euthanasia centres to be killed. It was in these centres that the techniques for mass killing by ZYKLON-B cyanide gas were perfected and between 80 and 100,000 were killed before the programme ended. During the latter part of the operation, Jewish and non-Aryan prisoners from concentration camps, certified as too ill to work, were also sent to these centres. The gas equipment and much of the personnel were later used to outfit the extermination camps in Poland.

T13 Class Torpedo Boats (Small Destroyers) (Ger)

Displacement 853 tons; *dimensions* 267×28ft (81.3×8.5m); mean draught 7ft (2.1m); *machinery* 2-shaft geared turbines producing shp 31,000; *speed* 35.5 knots; *armament* 1×4.1in; 1×37mm AA; 7×20mm AA (2×2 and 3×1); 6×21in torpedo tubes (2×3); equipped for minelaying; *complement* 190; *number in class* 9, launched 1941–42.

T22 Class Torpedo Boats (Small Destroyers) (Ger)

Displacement 1294 tons; *dimensions* 315×31ft (96×9.4m); mean draught 9ft (2.7m); *machinery* 2-shaft geared turbines

producing shp 32,000; *speed* 33.5 knots; *armament* 4×4.1in (4×1); 4×37mm AA (2×2); 9×20mm AA (1×4 and 5×1); 6×21in torpedo tubes (2×3); *complement* 198; *number in class* 15, launched 1942–44.

T-26 – Light Tank (USSR)

A Soviet copy of the Vickers Six Ton light tank. The Model A, which appeared in 1931, had two small machine gun turrets. The Model B had a single turret armed with a 45mm gun and a coaxial machine gun; the Model C was similar but better armoured. The T-26 served in the Spanish Civil War, in Manchuria, Finland and the 1939 Soviet invasion of Poland. Large numbers were lost during the German invasion of the Soviet Union but several units equipped with the vehicle took part in the Anglo-Soviet occupation of Iran in 1941. The T-26 remained active as late as 1942. *Weight* 8.5 tons (Model A); 9.4 tons (Model B); 10.3 tons (Model C); *speed* 22mph (35kph) (Model A); 17.4mph (28kph) (Model B); 17mph (27kph) (Model C); *armour* 15mm (Models A and B); 25mm (Model C); *armament* 2 7.62mm machine guns (Model A); 1 45mm gun and 1 7.62mm machine gun (Models B and C); *engine* GAZ T-26 91hp petrol; *crew* 3.

T-28 – Medium Tank (USSR)

Introduced in 1933. Layout was similar to the British Independent, with two machine gun sub-turrets forward of the main turret. In 1935 an improved version appeared with a 76.2mm L/26 main armament. The T-28 served in the Soviet invasion of Poland in 1939 and in the Winter War with Finland, as a result of which it was up-armoured. Very few survived the German invasion of the Soviet Union in 1941. *Weight* 29 tons; *speed* 23mph (37kph); *armour* 30mm; *armament* 1 76.2mm L/16.5 gun; 3 7.62mm machine guns; *engine* Liberty M-17 500hp petrol; *crew* 6.

T-34/76 – Medium Tank (USSR)

Evolved by Mikhail Koshkin's design team at the Kharkov Locomotive Works as a replacement for the BT SERIES, incorporating features from several experimental tanks including the A-20, A-30 and T-32. Koshkin's final blueprint provided an excellent balance between mobility, protection and firepower and is widely regarded as being the foundation of modern tank design. The vehicle employed the CHRISTIE SUSPENSION in conjunction with wide tracks which enabled it to remain mobile in mud or snow. The hull overhung

T-34 in Berlin, April 1945.

the tracks and had sloped sides, the 45mm glacis plate being laid back at an angle of 60 degrees, thus giving the same ballistic protection as a 90mm vertical plate. The prototype T-34/76 was completed in January 1940 and mass production commenced in June of that year. The Model 41 of 1941 was armed with a more powerful 76.2mm L/41.2 gun, as was the Model 42, which also incorporated a number of less important modifications; the Germans referred to both models as the T-34/76B. The Model 43 (T-34/76C) employed a hexagonal turret with two roof hatches and, later, a commander's cupola. This version entered service late in 1942 and remained in production until the spring of 1945. An improved model with 110mm frontal armour is often referred to as the T-43.

The impact of the T-34/76 during the battles of 1941 was such that at one point senior German officers seriously considered copying the design and putting it into production, but national pride and the technical difficulties involved in manufacturing aluminium components of the diesel engine prevented this. Instead, the German Army was forced to embark on a hasty programme of up-gunning existing tanks and assault guns, accelerating the introduction of the TIGER E, initiating the design of the PANTHER and producing a fleet of MARDER tank destroyers on obsolete tank chassis. See also T-34/85. *Model 40 (German designation T-34/76A) Weight* 26.3 tons; *speed* 31mph (50kph); *armour* 45mm; *armament* 1 76.2mm L/30.5 gun; 2 7.62 machine gun; *engine* V-2-34 500hp diesel; *crew* 4.

T-34/85 – Medium Tank (USSR)

By 1943 the T-34/76 had lost something of its qualitative edge and the Soviet Army was faced with greatly improved German tank designs. It was apparent that the T-34 series now required a more powerful main armament and that the 76.2mm versions had reached the limit of their development potential. During the summer of 1943 it was decided that the vehicle would be up-gunned with the same 85mm weapon which armed the KLIMENTI VOROSHILOV-85 and the SU-85. This required the design of a larger three-man turret, although the basic T-34 hull and chassis were retained. The T-34/85 entered service in the spring of 1944, equipping independent tank brigades, and, like the T-34/76, was supplied to the Soviet Union's Eastern European allies.

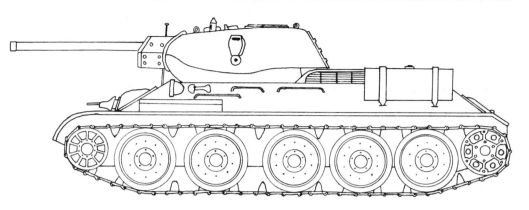

T-34/76 medium tank.

Wartime production of the T-34 series came close to that of the SHERMAN and, if post-war production is added, exceeded it by a wide margin. The T-34/85 saw further active service in the Korean War, the Arab/Israeli Wars and numerous other conflicts. It served in the Warsaw Pact armies until the 1950s and was supplied to the Soviet Union's clients around the world. See *The T-34 Tank* by Steven J. Zaloga and James Grandsen (Osprey). *Weight* 32 tons; *speed* 31mph (50kph); *armour* 60mm; *armament* 1 85mm L/53 gun; 2 7.62mm machine guns; *engine* V-2-34 500hp diesel; *crew* 5.

T-35 – Heavy Tank (USSR)

Designed as a breakthrough tank and entered service in 1935. The vehicle possessed no less than five turrets – a centrally mounted main turret housing the 76.2mm, two 45mm turrets and two machine gun sub-turrets, one of each mounted fore and aft. An improved version appeared in 1938 but production was halted the following year. Only 61 T-35s were built, serving in two independent heavy battalions. The vehicle was difficult to command, had serious steering problems and was prone to breakdown. The majority were lost during the battles of 1941. *T-35A Weight* 45 tons; *speed* 18mph (29kph); *armour* 30mm; *armament* 1 76.2mm L/10 gun; 2 45mm L/46 guns; 4 7.62mm machine guns; *engine* Liberty M-17 500hp petrol; *crew* 9.

T-37, T-38 and T-40 – Amphibious Light Tanks (USSR)

The T-37 entered service in 1933, the T-38 in 1936 and the T-40 in 1940. They incorporated built-in buoyancy tanks in their design and when afloat were steered by rudder and driven by a screw which could produce a

T-37 amphibious light tank.

speed of four knots in calm water. The T-37 and T-38 were based on an adapted Vickers Carden-Loyd suspension but the T-40 employed a torsion bar system. Later versions of the T-40 were built without an amphibious capability. These vehicles served in the reconnaissance units of cavalry and armoured formations but their light armour was a handicap and few survived the battles of 1941. *Weight* 3 tons (T-37); 4 tons (T-38); 6 tons (T-40); *speed* 40mph (64kph) (T-37 and T-38); 28mph (45kph) (T-40); *armour* 10mm (T-37 and T-38); 13mm (T-40); *armament* 1 medium or heavy machine gun; *engine* GAZ 65hp petrol (T-37); GAZ 50hp petrol (T-38); GAZ 85hp petrol (T-40); *crew* 2.

T-60 and T-70 – Light Tanks (USSR)

After an interim design, the T-50, had proved unsatisfactory, the T-60 replaced the T-40 in armoured reconnaissance units in November 1941. Unfortunately, the T-60 proved to be under-gunned, under-armoured and under-powered for current requirements and was rapidly redesigned with a 45mm gun, thicker armour and two engines, using a lengthened and strengthened chassis. In this form the vehicle entered service in 1942 as the T-70. A later version of the T-70 with 50mm armour and a two-man turret was designated T-80. *Weight* 5.8 tons (T-60); 9.2 tons (T-70); *speed* 28mph (45kph); *armour* 20mm (T-60); 45mm (T-70); *armament* 1 20mm cannon and 1 7.62mm machine gun (T-60); 1 45mm L/46 gun and 1 7.62mm machine gun (T-70); *engine(s)* 1 GAZ 85hp petrol (T-60); 2 GAZ 70hp petrol (T-70); *crew* 2.

T-100 – Heavy Tank (USSR)

Prototype produced in 1938, based like the T-35 on the obsolete breakthrough concept. The 76.2mm gun was housed in an upper central turret on a tall plinth with the 45mm gun in a lower turret forward of this. A very similar design produced about the same time was the SMK (Sergei Mironovitch Kirov). The vehicles were subjected to operational trials during the Winter War with Finland, with disappointing results. The T-100 chassis was used as the basis for a 130mm self-propelled gun, the SU-100Y, and the experience gained with the SMK was employed in the design of the KLIMENTI VOROSHILOV heavy tank series. *Weight* 58 tons; *armour* 60mm; *armament* 1 76.2mm gun; 1 45mm gun; 3 7.62mm machine guns; *engine* 500hp petrol; *crew* 7.

"T" Class Submarines (UK)

Displacement 1090/1575 tons; *dimensions* 275ft×26ft 6in (83.8×8.07m); *machinery* 2-shaft diesel/electric motors producing bhp 2500/1450; *speed* 15.25/9 knots; *armament Group 1* 1×4in; 3 machine guns; 10/11×21in torpedo tubes (8 bow of which 2 external and 2/3 stern external); *Group 2* 1×4in; 1×20mm AA; 3 machine guns; 11×21in torpedo tubes (8 bow of which 2 external and 3 stern external); *complement Group 1* 59; *Group 2* 65; *number in class Group 1* 22, launched 1937–41; *Group 2* 31, launched 1942–45.

"T" Class Submarines (USA)

Displacement 1475/2370 tons; *dimensions* 307ft 3in×27ft 3in (93.6×8.3m); *machinery* 2-shaft diesels producing shp 5400/2740; *speed* 20/8.5 knots; *armament* 1×5in; 1×40mm; 10×21in torpedo tubes (6 bow and 4 stern); *complement* 85; *number in class* 12, launched 1939–41.

Tabby

The British codename for infra-red driving equipment used by tanks and other vehicles in limited quantities. It consisted of infra-red headlights and special driving goggles.

Tabun

Tabun was the original German nerve gas, discovered in about 1936 by Dr Gebhard Schrader in the course of investigations into organic phosphorus compounds for weed-killing; its chemical name is ethyl-dimethylamido-phosphorcyanidate. After great difficulty it was placed in production in 1942, a special factory being built near Dyhernfurth on the River Oder. Production of 1000 tons per month was planned, and it is believed that total production, which ended when the factory was captured by Soviet forces early in 1945, was about 15,000 tons. The factory, and its stock, was later removed to Soviet Russia.

Tachikawa Ki54 (Hickory) (Japan)

This twin-engined monoplane was introduced into Japanese service in 1940 and served as an advanced trainer for bomber crews. Towards the end of the war several were adapted as fast transports, and some were loaded with explosives and expended on suicide missions. *Span* 58ft (17.7m); *engines* 2 450hp *radial*; *crew* 5; *speed* 228mph (367kph).

TacR Tactical reconnaissance (UK). Aerial reconnaissance specifically over the battlefield.

TAF Tactical Air Force (UK).

Taifun (Typhoon)

German drive on MOSCOW, October 1941.

Taifun

Taifun was a German liquid-fuel free-flight anti-aircraft rocket, development of which began at PEENEMUNDE late in 1944. Production began in January 1945, and 600 had been made when the war ended, though very few were fired operationally. When fired it weighed about 46lb (21kg), had a 1.1lb (500g) explosive warhead and had an operational ceiling of about 9 miles (14km).

Taiho, IJN – Aircraft Carrier

Taiho was laid down in July 1941 and completed in March 1944. She served as Admiral OZAWA's flagship at the Battle of the PHILIPPINE SEA, during which she was torpedoed by the submarine USS *Albacore*. Although she survived this, she was blown apart a few hours later in an explosion of accumulated fuel vapour. *Displacement* 29,300 tons; *dimensions* 854ft 8in×90ft 9in (260.5×27.7m); *mean draught* 31ft 5in (9.6m); *machinery* 4-shaft geared turbines producing shp 160,000; *speed* 33.3 knots; *protection* flight deck 3.75in; magazine 6in; engine room 2in; *armament* 12×3.9in AA (6×2); 51×25mm AA (17×3); *aircraft* 60–63; *complement* 1751.

Taiyo Class Aircraft Carriers (Jap)

Originally laid down as commercial liners and converted to aircraft carriers 1941–42. Their lack of catapults and arrestor gear made them unsuitable for employment with the fleet, so they were used for training and the delivery of aircraft to isolated island garrisons. The three members of the class, *Taiyo*, *Chuyo* and *Unyo*, were sunk respectively by the American submarines *Rasher* (18 August 1944), *Sailfish* (4 December 1943) and *Barb* (16 September 1944). *Displacement* 17,830 tons; *dimensions* 591ft 6in×73ft 9in (180×22.5m); *mean draught* 26ft 3in (8m); *machinery* 2-shaft geared turbines producing shp 25,200; *speed* 21 knots; *armament* 8×4.7in AA; 8×25mm AA; *aircraft* 27; *complement* 850; *number in class* 3.

Takagi, V Adm Takeo

Takagi commanded the Japanese naval forces at the Battle of the JAVA SEA, 27 February 1942, which eliminated the British, American and Dutch naval presence in the East Indies. Takagi commanded a fleet carrier squadron consisting of the *Shokaku* and *Zuikaku* during the drawn Battle of the CORAL SEA. *Shokaku* sustained serious damage, but Takagi's aircraft so crippled the American carrier *Lexington* that she had to be abandoned and sunk.

Takao Class Cruisers (Jap)

Takao was severely damaged in Singapore harbour by the British midget submarines XE-1 and XE-3 on 31 July 1945, and was out of action for the remainder of the war. *Displacement* 13,160 tons; *dimensions* 663ft 9in×68ft (202.3×20.7m); mean draught 21ft 4in (6.5m); *machinery* 4-shaft geared turbines producing shp 133,100; *speed* 34.25 knots; *protection* main belt 3–4in; deck and turrets 3in; magazine 5in; *armament* 10×8in (5×2); 8×5in AA (4×2); 8×25mm AA; 4×13mm AA; 16×24in torpedo tubes (4×4); *aircraft* 3; *complement* 773; *number in class* 4, launched 1930–31.

Talon

Assault by British XV Corps on AKYAB ISLAND, January 1945.

Tanahashi, Col

Tanahashi was the energetic battle group commander of the Japanese 55th Division who played a prominent role in defeating the 1943 British offensive in the ARAKAN. When the British mounted a fresh offensive the following year, Tanahashi commanded a similar battle group and attempted to repeat his success by operating against their rear. He captured the NGAKYEDAUK PASS but failed to subdue the ADMIN BOX. His command, starving and decimated by casualties, was itself forced to withdraw.

Tanaka, Gen Nobuo

Tanaka assumed command of the Japanese 33rd Division during the closing stages of the Battle of IMPHAL. He was noted for his drive and ruthlessness, ordering his officers to execute with their swords any soldier who displayed less than suicidal enthusiasm. However, he was unable to secure his objectives and was eventually compelled to conduct a fighting withdrawal through Tiddim to

the IRRAWADDY. In 1945 he was appointed Chief of Staff to General Kimura, the commander of the BURMA AREA ARMY, presiding over the conference which, due to the arrival of a corrupt signal, fatally underestimated the nature of the British IV Corps' threat to MEIKTILA, the loss of which made the position of Japanese divisions further north untenable.

Tanaka, R Adm Raizo

"Tenacious" Tanaka earned the reputation of being the Imperial Japanese Navy's most redoubtable destroyer flotilla commander. He was present at the Battle of the JAVA SEA and escorted the Transport Group during the Battle of MIDWAY but is best remembered as commander of the Reinforcement Force, better known as the "TOKYO EXPRESS", which, in the face of superior American opposition, made regular resupply and reinforcement runs to GUADALCANAL under cover of darkness. The night-fighting skills of Tanaka's crews enabled them to inflict sharp losses on their opponents, but the Reinforcement Force was never able to deliver sufficient men and material to influence the outcome of the campaign. As the Americans gained experience, Tanaka's losses began to mount and on 12 December 1942 his own destroyer, the *Teruzuki*, was torpedoed and sunk by *PT-45*. Tanaka survived but was relieved of his command shortly after when he protested that continuance of the Solomons campaign represented a squandering of resources which Japan could ill afford.

Tank Destroyers

Armoured fighting vehicles designed specifically for the destruction of the enemy's tanks. See also ACHILLES, ARCHER, ELEFANT, GUN MOTOR CARRIAGES M3, M6, M10, M18, M36, HETZER, ISU-122, JAGDPANTHER, JADPANZER IV, JAGDTIGER, MARDER, NASHORN, PANZERJÄGER, STURMGESCHUTZE, SU-85 AND SU-100.

Tank Transporters

Articulated vehicles consisting of a tractor unit and multi-wheel flat-bed trailer with loading ramps used to transport tanks into the forward area, thereby saving the latter track mileage and mechanical wear before they were committed to action. The longest forward lift of the war took place after the Second Battle of ALAMEIN, when several armoured regiments were transported from Egypt across Cyrenaica into Tripolitania. An alternative use was the

Rear-Admiral Raizo Tanaka, IJN.

backloading of battle-damaged tanks to workshops, many transporters being equipped with a winch to haul vehicle casualties aboard. The principal tank transporter users were the British, American and German armies.

Tanne (Fir)

German plan to seize the Åland Islands and the Finnish island of Suusaari, September 1944.

Taper Bore Guns

Guns in which the calibre reduces from the chamber to the muzzle and which fire a special projectile with deformable "skirts" which will reduce in diameter during the travel down the bore. Due to the reducing area of the shot, the unit pressure and the velocity are increased. First patented by K. Puff in 1903 but incapable of realization at that time, the idea was revived by a German engineer called Gerlich in the late 1920s. He designed and produced a number of sporting rifles with taper bores and tried to interest various military authorities without success. He was then retained by the Rheinmetall company in Germany and assisted in developing two taper-bore anti-tank guns: the 28/20mm schwere PANZERBUCHSE 41 and the 42/29mm Panzerjägerkanone 41. Both were highly successful, the latter firing a shot at 4150ft per second (1265m/sec) which was capable of penetrating 87mm of armour at

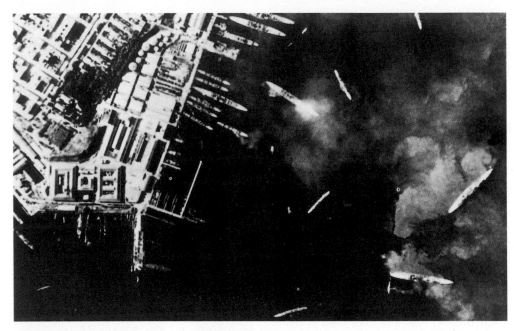

Oil leaks from crippled Italian warships after the Fleet Air Arm's attack on Taranto Harbour.

550yds (500m) range. The special projectiles used tungsten carbide cores and, due to the critical shortage of tungsten in Germany, production of ammunition and weapons ceased in 1942. See also SQUEEZE BORE GUNS.

Taranto, Italy, 1940

A naval base in southern Italy. On 11 November 1940 the British Mediterranean fleet, under Admiral CUNNINGHAM, escorted the aircraft carrier HMS *Illustrious* to a position 170 miles (270km) from Taranto from where 21 Swordfish aircraft, in two waves, were launched. Of the first wave of 12, six carried bombs and six torpedoes, and two of the bombers carried flares. Arriving over Taranto the flares were dropped, and by their light diversionary attacks on shipping in the harbour were made by the bombers while the torpedo-carriers attacked various warships. The first wave then returned to the carrier, and the second wave of 9 aircraft took off to make a similar attack. Only two aircraft were lost; three Italian battleships had been hit, two of which were under repair for several months, and the third never came back into service. The Italian fleet withdrew from Taranto to bases on the west coast, where it was less vulnerable but further from the scene of action. This operation radically altered the balance of naval power in the Mediterranean.

Tarawa, Pacific, 1943

An atoll in the GILBERT Archipelago, Tarawa consists of several islands in a roughly triangular shape, of which the most important is Betio. Betio was assaulted on 20 November 1943 by 2nd US Marine Division, under General Julian C. Smith, supported by the 27th US Army Division under General Ralph C. Smith, overall command of the operation being in the hands of General Holland M. Smith, a chain of command which is confusing for historians.

This was the first landing to use amphibious tractors tactically – for landing the assault – rather than simply for resupply, due to the coral reefs surrounding the island and the lack of hydrographical information. The island was strongly defended and the initial landings were held up on the beaches by obstacles and strong firepower which had not been destroyed by poorly co-ordinated air attacks and naval bombardment before the landings. Supporting waves of assaulting Marines in landing craft ran aground on the reefs and had to wade ashore, suffering severe casualties in the process. A handful of tanks were able to get ashore and these helped to get the assault moving. The island was secured on 23 November, after three days of bitter fighting. Of the original Japanese garrison of over 4800 men, only 146 prisoners were taken. The US Marines suffered over 1000 killed and 2100 wounded, and since this was the first battle in the Pacific theatre to produce such a large number of casualties in such a short time, the effect on public opinion in the USA was traumatic.

Tassafaronga, Battle of, 1942

On 30 November 1942 Rear-Admiral TANAKA, with eight destroyers under command, left

Aftermath of the amphibious landings on Tarawa Island 1943.

Buin to drop supplies to the Japanese troops on GUADALCANAL by means of buoyant drums which would float ashore. His progress was reported by Coastwatchers and that night a newly assembled American squadron under Rear-Admiral Carleton Wright was cruising off Tassafaronga, the Japanese landing area. The squadron, consisting of the cruisers *Minneapolis* (Flag), *New Orleans*, *Pensacola*, *Honolulu* and *Northampton* and the destroyers *Fletcher, Perkins, Maury, Drayton, Lamson* and *Lardner*, obtained radar contact at 2306, revealing Tanaka's ships approaching on an opposite and parallel course. The American plan had been based on opening the engagement with a mass torpedo strike but last minute alterations in course rendered this difficult and the initial advantage was largely wasted when Wright withheld permission to commence firing until 2320. The torpedoes had only just been launched when Wright gave the order to engage with gunfire, thereby warning Tanaka of the danger and revealing the presence of his own ships. *Takanami* was reduced to a sinking wreck but the remainder of the Japanese destroyers reversed course by divisions, launching their LONG LANCE torpedoes as they did so. These began to strike at 2327, blowing the bows off *Minneapolis* and *New Orleans* and blasting great holes in the hulls of *Pensacola* and *Northampton*. Having dropped their drums the Japanese then withdrew at speed and by midnight the action was over. Good damage control drill saved the majority of the stricken cruisers, which limped to Tulagi, but *Northampton* sank at 0304.

The battle demonstrated that the Japanese still possessed a clear superiority in night-fighting techniques, but their success came too late for ashore their troops could no longer avoid defeat. Of the 1500 drums dropped, only 300 reached their intended destination. Tassafaronga was the last major naval battle of the Guadalcanal campaign but Tanaka continued with his supply missions until, during the night of 11/12 December, his *Teruzuki* was sunk by PT boats and he was himself wounded.

Taylor, Maj Gen Maxwell D.

Commander of the US 101st Airborne Division during the Allied invasion of NORMANDY, Operation MARKET GARDEN and the Battle of the BULGE. In the 1960s Taylor became an advocate of the use of airmobility in Vietnam.

Tazoe, Lt Gen

Commander of the Japanese 5th Air Division in BURMA, 1944, Tazoe was one of few Japanese officers who perceived the Allied potential for air supply. He recognized that the CHINDITS could be supported in this manner for months at a time and advised General KAWABE, commander of the BURMA AREA ARMY, to cancel the projected U-GO offensive against IMPHAL and KOHIMA because of the threat they posed to the Japanese rear areas. Although his views received limited support from the staff of the 3rd Air Army, based in Singapore, Kawabe chose to ignore them. Ironically, Tazoe was himself criticized for failing to supply SATO's division at Kohima by air, although he lacked the means to do this.

TBS Talk between ships (US). Short-range radio system used for ship-to-ship communication at sea.

TCV Troop-carrying Vehicle (UK). Specifically, a 3-ton Austin truck provided with bench seats sufficient to carry an infantry platoon.

Tebaga Gap, Tunisia, 1943

A valley between the north end of the Matmata Hills and the Djebel Tebaga hills in eastern TUNISIA. The space between the Matmata Hills and the Mediterranean was occupied by the German positions of the MARETH LINE, and in an endeavour to outflank this General MONTGOMERY sent the New Zealand Corps up the west of the Matmata Hills to turn east through the Tebaga Gap to cut the German escape route. The Germans got wind of this and inserted 21st Panzer and 164th Light Divisions into the Gap, where they succeeded in holding the New Zealanders. Since the Mareth Line showed no signs of yielding, Montgomery now sent the 1st Armoured Division on the heels of the New Zealanders, and with strong artillery support they eventually burst through the Gap on 26 March 1943. However, the German divisions had managed to hold them long enough to allow most of the Mareth Line forces to escape to a fresh position on the WADI AKARIT.

Tedder, ACM Sir Arthur W. (1890–1967)

Tedder took over the Western Desert Air Force in 1941, giving priority to improving his command's technical infrastructure and perfecting close support techniques in co-operation with the ground troops. Despite fierce opposition from the Axis air forces, the WDAF obtained air superiority during Operation CRUSADER and held it thereafter. Following the

Allied air leaders in Libya. Left to right: Air-Marshal Tedder, Brigadier General Strickland and Air Vice-Marshal Cunningham.

CASABLANCA CONFERENCE in January 1943 Tedder was appointed Commander-in-Chief of Mediterranean Air Command, directly under EISENHOWER. After the victory in North Africa he was responsible for co-ordinating land and air operations during the invasions of SICILY and Italy. In 1944 he served under Eisenhower again as Deputy Supreme Commander of the Allied Expeditionary Force during Operation OVERLORD and was responsible for integrating the Allied tactical and strategic air offensives against the enemy's communications, effectively isolating the NORMANDY battlefield from the rest of France. After the Normandy campaign had been brought to a satisfactory conclusion, he co-ordinated the effort of the tactical air forces and arranged intervention by the strategic air forces to aid ground forces. On 8 May 1945 Tedder ratified the instrument of German surrender on Eisenhower's behalf in Berlin. In September 1945 he was appointed Marshal of the RAF, and on 1 January 1946 was promoted Chief of Air Staff and created First Baron Tedder.

Tellermine

A German ANTI-TANK MINE, widely used in all theatres of war and probably the most common German anti-tank mine. A circular metal device, the T-Mine 35 was 13in (332mm) in diameter and 4in (100mm) high, it contained 11.3lb (5.16kg) of explosive and carried a pressure-operated fuze in the centre of the top cover. There were also detonator sockets in the bottom and side into which booby-trap devices could be fitted to deter attempts to remove the mine. This model was replaced by the T-Mine 42 of similar size and shape but with different fuze assembly, the fuze being concealed within the mine and protected by a cover plate. A pressure of about 550lb (250kg) was necessary to fire the mine. Finally came the T-Mine Pilz 43 with a larger cover plate designed to give a larger sensitive area over which the mine could be triggered.

Tenaru, Battle of, 1942

An action during the taking of GUADALCANAL, named for the Tenaru River, three miles (5km) to the east. The Ilu River flanked the initial US beachhead on Guadalcanal, around HENDERSON FIELD airstrip. A Japanese reserve force under Colonel Ichiki had been landed at Taivu on 18 August 1942 and force-marched along the coast to take the US landing in the flank. Ichiki believed the US force to be small

and ill-trained, and threw his troops across the Ilu in a bayonet charge which was immediately cut down by firepower from carefully-sited Marine positions. General VANDEGRIFT, commanding the US force, anticipating a reinforced attack from this quarter, despatched a reserve Marine battalion across the river above Ichiki's position, surrounding the Japanese force. Although mauled by artillery and tank attacks supporting the Marines, the Japanese force refused to surrender and had to be killed one by one. Even survivors and wounded attempted to kill Marines by grenade attacks. The battle was a relatively minor engagement, but it was a clear lesson to the US Marines, who were now under no illusions about the fanatical Japanese belief in "total resistance".

Tench Class Submarines (USA)

Improved GATO CLASS. *Displacement* 1570/2415 tons; *dimensions* 311ft 9in×27ft 3in (95×8.3m); *machinery* 2-shaft diesels producing shp 5400/2740; *speed* 20.25/10 knots; *armament* 1×5in; 1×40mm; 10×21in torpedo tubes (6 bow and 4 stern); *complement* 85; *number in class* 31, launched 1944–46.

Ten-Go (Operation Heaven)

Japanese plan for the air defence of the homeland, March 1945.

Tench class submarine on patrol in the Pacific.

Tennessee, USS – Tennessee Class Battleship

Damaged during the attack on PEARL HARBOR, *Tennessee* was repaired and took part in numerous actions throughout the Pacific war, including the GILBERT ISLANDS, KWAJALEIN, ENIWETOK, SAIPAN, GUAM, Palau, LEYTE, SURIGAO STRAIT, IWO JIMA and OKINAWA.

Tennessee Class Battleships (USA)

USS *Tennessee* and USS *California* were based on a modified New Mexico design. *Displacement* 32,300 tons; *dimensions* 624×108ft (190×32.9m); mean draught 30ft 6in (9.3m); *machinery* 4-shaft turbo-electric drive producing shp 30,000; *speed* 21 knots; *protection* main belt 14in; turrets 18in; *armament* 12×14in (4×3); 12×5in (12×1); 8×5in AA (8×1); 16×5in DP, 40×40mm quad (*California* 56×40mm quad), 48–52×20mm after conversion; *aircraft* 3; *complement* 2200; *number in class* 2, launched 1919.

Tenryu Class Cruisers (Jap)

Displacement 3230 tons; *dimensions* 468ft×40ft 6in (142.6×12.3m); mean draught 13ft (3.9m); *machinery* 3-shaft geared turbines producing shp 51,000; *speed* 33 knots; *protection* main belt 1.5–2in; *armament* 4×5.5in (4×1); 1×3in AA; 2×13mm AA; 6×21in torpedo tubes (2×3); *complement* 332; *number in class* 2, launched 1918.

Terauchi, FM Count Hisaichi (1879–1945)

Terauchi was appointed Commander-in-Chief of the Japanese Southern Army on 6 November 1941 and held this post until the end of the war, conducting operations from his headquarters in Saigon. He accomplished the task of seizing all American, British and Dutch possessions in his operational zone well ahead of schedule, although his success stemmed as much from Allied unpreparedness as from Japanese efficiency, and eventually controlled an area stretching from the PHILIPPINES to BURMA. In 1944 he was considered as a possible replacement for Prime Minister TOJO. He was, however, no strategist and stubbornly wasted his assets by repeatedly reinforcing inevitable defeats, notably at LEYTE in 1944. He has been described as the most brutal Japanese commander of the war, willingly sacrificing his men's lives to little purpose, and was totally indifferent to the fate of his prisoners. He severely censured those of his subordinates whom he considered to be too indulgent, including HOMMA, who had ordered the infamous Death March from BATAAN. Terauchi was responsible for building the equally infamous Burma Railway, which cost the lives of 17,000 prisoners-of-war and a large number of his own troops. He suffered a stroke in September 1945.

Ter Poorten, Gen Hein (1887–1948)

Ter Poorten was Commander-in-Chief of the land forces in the DUTCH EAST INDIES when the Japanese invaded in January 1942. Lacking air support and adequate artillery, he resisted until April 1942, having destroyed the local oilfields to prevent their use by the enemy.

Territorial Army

A British auxiliary and reserve military force. The Territorial Army (TA) was so-called because it was organized by counties and was affiliated to the various county infantry and cavalry regiments. It was an entirely voluntary force, the men being unpaid except during their annual training period spent with the Regular Army. For the remainder of the year training was carried out in evenings and at weekends, the officers and men being in civilian employment. In the 1930s, with the mechanization of cavalry, many Territorial cavalry units were reorganized into air defence artillery to man guns in their own area. Territorial soldiers also manned coast defence guns in most of the forts around Britain. The Territorial Army also functioned as a reserve, and on the outbreak of war all TA units were immediately embodied into the standing army. Several units were sent to France and fought there in 1940; much of the air defence of Britain was undertaken by TA batteries. Eventually all TA units saw active service, although as the war progressed their ranks were augmented by conscripted soldiers.

Tetrarch – Light Tank Mark VII (UK)

Developed by Vickers in 1937 using a novel steering system in which the road wheels could be turned, so curving the track. A total of 177 were produced between 1940 and 1942, a number being supplied to the Soviet Army. A half-squadron took part in the invasion of MADAGASCAR in May 1942 and several were air-landed in HAMILCAR gliders with 6th Airborne Division in NORMANDY on the eve of D-Day. A few Tetrarchs were converted to the close support role with a 3-inch howitzer and some standard models were fitted with the LITTLE-JOHN ADAPTER. The Tetrarch was also used in DD amphibious tank trials. *Weight* 7.5 tons; *speed* 40mph (64kph); *armour* 16mm; *armament* 1 2-pdr gun; 1 7.92mm Besa machine gun; *engine* Meadows 165hp petrol; *crew* 3.

TEWT Tactical Exercise without Troops (UK). Form of training in which trainees walk the terrain and deploy imaginary forces.

TF Task Force (US).

Thames Class Submarines (UK)

The last fleet submarines built for the Royal Navy. *Displacement* 1859/2723 tons; *dimensions* 345ft × 28ft 3in (105.1 × 8.6m); *machinery* 2-shaft diesel/electric motors producing bhp 10,000/2500; *speed* 22.25/10 knots; *armament* 1 × 4in; 2 machine guns; 8 × 21in torpedo tubes (6 bow and 2 stern); *complement* 61; *number in class* 3, launched 1932–34.

Theresienstadt (Teresin), Czechoslovakia

A fortified town of the Austro-Hungarian Empire, its minor outlying fort was taken over by the Germans in 1940 as a prison and later adapted as a concentration camp. It was primarily used for politically important Jewish and other detainees. Whilst maintaining a very strict regime, it was kept in relatively good order as a "show" camp for display to international humanitarian bodies as an example of the concentration camp system and to repudiate accusations of cruel and inhuman conditions for prisoners. Nevertheless, several thousand prisoners died there during the course of the occupation.

Thermos Bomb

The nickname given to the British Grenade, Hand, No 73, since it was approximately the size and shape of a Thermos flask. It consisted of a cylindrical body filled with Nobel's 808 high explosive, with an ALLWAYS fuze at the top. It was exceptionally powerful and was intended solely for use against tanks; the approved method of use was to remove the cap from the fuze, hold the grenade along the forearm, and throw it under the track of the approaching tank. The blast was sufficient to cut the track of almost any tank of the period (1940–42).

Theseus

German plan for the recapture of eastern CYRENAICA, May 1942.

Thoma, Gen Wilhelm Ritter von

Thoma commanded the German Kondor Legion's tank unit during the Spanish Civil War and Panzer Regiment 3 (2nd Panzer Division) during the 1939 campaign in POLAND. In March 1940 he was posted to the office of the Head of Mobile Troops at Army Headquarters. Later that year he was sent on a fact-finding mission to Libya to examine the possibility of German troops being employed in North Africa, but at this period the Italians made it clear that such assistance was not required. He commanded first the 6th and then the 20th Panzer Divisions during the invasion of the Soviet Union. In May 1942 he became head of Mobile Troops, and on 17 September was appointed commander of the Deutsches Afrika Korps. He was captured on 4 November 1942 during the closing stages of the Second Battle of ALAMEIN. Thoma was one of the ablest and most perceptive of Germany's Panzer leaders; during the course of his career he was wounded no fewer than 17 times.

Thor – German Surface Raider

Also known as Ship 10 and Raider E. Sailed on 6 June 1940 under Captain Otto Kähler and cruised in the Atlantic, sinking or capturing 12 ships totalling 96,547 tons and fighting three duels with British armed merchant cruisers: HMS *Alcantara* on 28 July 1940, in which both ships sustained damage; HMS *Carnarvon Castle* on 5 December 1940, the British vessel sustaining damage and being forced to break off the action; and HMS *Voltaire*, which was sunk on 4 April 1941. Returned to Hamburg on 30 April 1941.

During her second cruise, which commenced on 30 November 1941, *Thor* was commanded by Captain Günther Gumprich and operated in the Atlantic, Indian and Pacific Oceans, sinking or capturing 10 ships totalling 56,037 tons. She reached Yokohama on 10 October 1942, but on 30 November 1941 was destroyed by the explosion of a nearby burning tanker. *Displacement* 3862 tons; *speed* 18 knots; *armament* 6×5.9in; 2×37mm AA; 2×20mm AA; 4×21in torpedo tubes; equipped for minelaying; *aircraft* 2; *complement* 345.

Thousand-Bomber Raid, 1942

Although a number of Allied air raids employed 1000 bombers, this name is given to the raid against Cologne on the night of 30/31 May 1942, and two follow-up raids on Essen (1 June) and Bremen (25 June). All three raids were codenamed MILLENIUM. Millenium was the brainchild of BOMBER COMMAND's new Commander-in-Chief Air Marshal HARRIS, and its principal aim was the revival of the Command's flagging fortunes with a massive raid calculated to inflict severe damage and boost British morale. Harris accumulated 1046 aircraft for the raid, drafting in machines from operational training and conversion units, and crews from every RAF Command, and these took off from 52 bases in Britain. Of these, 898 attacked Cologne, dropping 1455 tons of bombs, of which two-thirds were incendiaries which started over 1200 fires. According to German records, 486 people were killed, 5027 injured, 59,100 made homeless, and over 18,440 buildings completely destroyed. Bomber Command lost only 40 aircraft in the operation, a remarkable figure considering the inexperience of many of the crews involved. The subsequent raids on Essen and Bremen were not successful, and at the end of June Harris broke up his "1000 Force" to avoid serious damage to the training and logistics of Bomber Command. Nevertheless, he had secured a significant propaganda coup.

Thunderclap

Allied bombing offensive aimed at breaking German civilian morale, executed against DRESDEN, February 1945.

Thursday

Second CHINDIT operation, Burma, 1944.

Tibbets, Col Paul (1915–   )

Tibbets distinguished himself while leading BOEING B-17 Flying Fortress bombing missions over Europe and was then posted back to the United States to advise on modifications to the new B-29 Super Fortress. In September 1944 he was detailed to train Crew 15, the men who were to drop the atomic bombs on Japan. On 6 August 1945 he piloted the B-29 *Enola Gay* on its mission to HIROSHIMA, releasing the sixton "Little Boy" nuclear device from a height of 31,600 feet.

Tidal Wave

Allied air attacks on Ploesti oilfields, Romania, August 1943.

Tiger

Rehearsal for assault phase of OVERLORD, 1944.

Tiger B – Heavy Tank (Ger)

Larger, better protected and up-gunned version of the TIGER E concept developed under competitive tender during 1942/43, the con-

tract being awarded to the Henschel organization. The Tiger B's armour was not only thicker but was also more scientifically arranged, using angled planes. The first 50 were fitted with a round-fronted turret designed by Porsche, but the front of the standard Henschel turret was flat. The vehicle began leaving the production lines in February 1944, a total of 484 being built before the war ended. It served alongside the Tiger E in heavy tank battalions which were usually at the disposal of Panzer corps commanders. The Tiger B was the heaviest tank to enter general service during World War II and was also known variously as the Tiger II, King Tiger and Royal Tiger. Its chassis formed the basis of the JAGDTIGER tank destroyer. See also *The Tiger Tanks* by Bryan Perrett (Osprey). *Weight* 68.7 tons; *speed* 23.5mph (38kph); *armour* 150mm; *armament* 1 88mm L/71 gun; 2 7.92mm machine guns; *engine* Maybach HL230 P30 700hp petrol; *crew* 5.

Tiger Convoy, 1941

In May 1941 it was decided to reinforce the British forces in Egypt by a fast convoy through the Mediterranean rather than round the Cape, thereby saving three weeks. The codename for the operation was *Tiger*. The convoy passed through the Straits of Gibraltar on 6 May, escorted by FORCE H to a point south of Malta where the Mediterranean Fleet took

PzKw VI Tiger B on the Western Front.

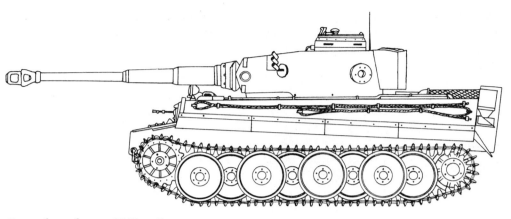

Panzerkampfwagen VI Tiger E.

over. The convoy was attacked several times by German and Italian aircraft which were intercepted by the carriers' Fulmars. One merchantman was sunk by a mine off the Tunisian coast but the remaining five reached Alexandria safely on 12 May, delivering 238 tanks and 43 Hurricanes.

Tiger E – Heavy Tank (Ger)
Consolidation of a series of competitive designs which had their roots in a pre-war requirement for a breakthrough tank, updated to incorporate heavier armour and an 88mm main armament, the contract being awarded to the Henschel organization in April 1942. The Tiger E employed an interleaved torsion bar suspension in conjunction with wide tracks, the latter having to be replaced with a narrower set when the vehicle was in transit by rail. The armour was badly arranged but its thickness rendered the tank almost invulnerable at the time it was introduced, while the 88mm gun could defeat any enemy AFV in service. The Tiger E had a premature baptism of fire on the LENINGRAD sector in August 1942 and continued to serve on the Eastern Front for the duration of the war, as well as in Tunisia, Sicily, Italy, France and North-West Europe, equipping heavy tank battalions which were usually at the disposal of Panzer corps commanders. It earned itself a formidable reputation and won most of its battles although it failed to influence the outcome of a single campaign. Its major defects were its weight and bulk, which inhibited its use in certain tactical situations, its limited operational radius, and the fact that it was complicated and costly to build. Production lasted for two years, ending in August 1944 after 1350 had been built. Derivatives included command and recovery versions

and the STURMTIGER. The vehicle is sometimes referred to as Tiger I. See also TIGER B. *Weight* 55 tons; *speed* 23mph (37kph); *armour* 100mm; *armament* 1 88mm L/56 gun; 2 7.92mm machine guns; *engine* Maybach HL230 V-12 700hp petrol; *crew* 5.

Tikhvin, Soviet Union, 1941
A railway station and small town on the MOSCOW–LENINGRAD railway line, close to Leningrad. In the first stages of the siege of Leningrad, supplies were able to enter the city along this railway, but a sudden advance by the German army captured Tikhvin on 9 November 1941 and thus closed the supply route. Thereafter supplies could be brought only as far as Zaborie, a station some 200 miles (320km) from Leningrad. In order to open up a supply route, a road was built from Zaborie to Novaya Ladoga, on the shores of Lake LADOGA, through forest which had never been penetrated. The road, over 200 miles (320km) long, was built in 27 days at a cost of thousands of lives, deaths principally from starvation and German artillery fire.

Timor, Pacific, 1942
An island in the Timor Sea, north of Australia, with about 90,000 inhabitants. Divided between Dutch and Portuguese control, it was invaded and captured by Japanese forces in February 1942 and remained in their hands until the war ended.

Timoshenko, Marshal Semyon K. (1895–1970)
Timoshenko had served with STALIN during the Russian Civil War and belonged to the small group of senior officers whom the Soviet dictator was prepared to trust. He commanded the Karelian sector during the Winter

War against Finland and in May 1940 succeeded VOROSHILOV as Commissar of Defence. When Germany invaded the Soviet Union in 1941, Timoshenko replaced the discredited PAVLOV as commander of West Front but was unable to impose more than limited delays and lost a large proportion of his command in the SMOLENSK pocket. He was transferred to South-West Front and in May 1942 mounted a major but premature counteroffensive aimed at KHARKOV. This failed disastrously and was followed immediately by the German offensive which broke through to STALINGRAD and the CAUCASUS. Timoshenko was moved to the less active North-West Front for a while but thereafter was employed in strategic planning and as a Stavka co-ordinator.

Tinian, Battle of, Pacific, 1944
One of the two major islands in the MARIANAS group, Tinian was a difficult target since it was largely cliff-bound, with beaches only at Tinian Town, Asiga Bay and on the north-western tip. The US attacked on 24 July 1944 by making a feint attack against Tinian Town, whilst making the genuine landings in the north-west, on beaches no more than 50 yards (45m) wide, against light resistance. Over 15,000 US Marines were put ashore and by nightfall held a firm beach-head some 1.5 miles (2.5km) wide. Marine casualties were low (15 killed and 225 wounded), and Tinian was generally held to be the best conceived and executed amphibious assault of the entire war. The Japanese reacted swiftly, throwing in an attack during the night, but it was beaten off with severe Japanese losses. After severe fighting, Japanese resistance formally ended on 1 August, though isolated pockets kept fighting for some days. Tinian subsequently became a major US airfield.

Tirpitz, KMS – Bismarck Class Battleship
Launched on 1 April 1939, *Tirpitz* sailed from Wilhelmshaven on 16 January 1942. She remained in northern Norwegian waters, becoming known as the Lone Queen of the North, and posing a continual threat to the ARCTIC CONVOYS. She contributed to the disastrous scattering of CONVOY PQ 17, as well as tying down many units of the British Home Fleet which were badly needed elsewhere. On 6 September 1943, accompanied by SCHARNHORST and escorted by 10 destroyers, she bombarded shore installations on

KMS Tirpitz, *camouflaged, in one of her Norwegian lairs.*

serious casualties and was temporarily forced to abandon territory and retire into the mountains, but none the less remained a coherent force. Tito's position improved steadily after Fitzroy MACLEAN's mission and he became the largest recipient of Allied aid. When Italy withdrew from the war in 1943, he captured a huge quantity of arms and was able to extend his hold on large areas of the country. He was eventually able to muster an army of 250,000 men and obtained recognition from the Yugoslav government-in-exile, which abandoned Mihailović in May 1944. He liberated BELGRADE in October 1944 and took part in a coalition government under a regency until the monarchy was abolished following a Communist victory in the first election. As President of postwar Yugoslavia, Tito proved himself to be as able a statesman as he had been a soldier, administering a Communist regime which lay outside the Soviet Union's control but which simultaneously was able to preserve friendly relations with the West.

SPITZBERGEN, but this was her only active operation of the war. She was damaged by "x" CRAFT MIDGET SUBMARINES *X5*, *X6* and *X7* in Kaafjord on 23 September, and was further damaged by a carrier air strike on 3 April 1944. On 22 August a second carrier air strike found her concealed beneath a smoke screen, but she was damaged again when the operation was repeated two days later. After sustaining further damage from RAF Lancasters on 15 September, she was moved to Tromso. In a final attack on 12 November the Lancasters employed 12,000-lb bombs and *Tirpitz* finally capsized and sank.

Tiso, Monsignor Joseph (1887–1946)

With HITLER's support, Tiso succeeded in establishing an independent Slovak state in 1938 and, despite strenuous objections from the Czech government, this was recognized by the United Kingdom, France and the Soviet Union. In August 1944 Tiso was removed from power by a partisan uprising which preceded the occupation of Slovakia by the Soviet Army. He was hanged in December 1946.

Tito, Marshal (1892–1980)

Tito was the *nom de guerre* adopted by the Yugoslav communist leader Josip Broz. He had seen active service during the Russian and Spanish Civil Wars and quickly organized a resistance movement based on Serbia following the German invasion of his country in

1941. By the autumn of that year his forces were in possession of several towns but soon came into conflict with General MIHAILOVIĆ and his rival royalist resistance movement, which he defeated. His disciplined and well-organized partisans succeeded in tying down many Axis formations which were badly needed in other theatres of war. Altogether, seven major Axis offensives were mounted against Tito's army, which often sustained

Tito gives orders during the battle for the liberation of Bosnia, June 1942.

Tizard, Sir Henry (1885–1959)

A distinguished British scientist, Tizard pioneered the military application of radar and was responsible for the establishment of secret radar stations on the coast before the outbreak of war. He was Chairman of the Air Ministry's Committee for the Scientific Survey of Air Defence but resigned from this and several other posts in June 1940 because of fundamental differences with Lord CHERWELL, the scientific adviser to CHURCHILL's government. However, his services remained at the government's disposal throughout the war, and he led a group of prominent scientists to the USA to initiate a programme of co-operation for military services. Although, like Cherwell, he was initially sceptical about the feasibility of harnessing nuclear fission in a weapon system, he played a leading role in initiating Anglo-American co-operation in this field. In June 1941 he joined the Air Council as representative of the Ministry of Aircraft Production.

Tk/A Tank Attack (gun). Australian version of A/TK, chosen to symbolize a more aggressive attitude towards enemy armour.

TKS – Tankette (Poland)

Based on the Carden-Loyd suspension. The TKS served in the Polish Army's armoured reconnaissance squadrons, approximately

The British wait to enter Tobruk, January 1941.

450 being available on the outbreak of war. *Weight* 2.65 tons; *speed* 24mph (38kph); *armour* 10mm; *armament* 1 7.92mm machine gun; *engine* Fiat 42hp petrol; *crew* 2.

Tobruk, North Africa, 1941–42

One of the best harbours in the Mediterranean, Tobruk is a town on the coast of Libya which formed a most useful supply point for the armies operating in that area. It was originally captured from the Italians on 22 January 1941 by General WAVELL's forces. The attack by General ROMMEL in April 1941 carried the German forces past Tobruk, to the Egyptian border, but Tobruk was held by the 7th Australian Division, denying its facilities to Rommel and threatening his flank. Rommel attempted three attacks in April but without success. Subsequent British actions kept Rommel too occupied to deal with Tobruk, and in November 1941 the British mounted Operation CRUSADER in an attempt to bring Rommel's armour to battle and relieve Tobruk. This succeeded, after some confusion, and Rommel fell back to the area of Benghazi. A fresh German attack swept forward again and Rommel besieged Tobruk once more on 18 June 1942, by which time it was held by British, Indian and South African troops. On 20 June he attacked and within three hours had breached the defences and reached the harbour; on the following day the garrison surrendered and Rommel took 33,000 prisoners. It remained in German hands until it was taken for the last time during General MONTGOMERY's advance after Second ALAMEIN.

Todt, Dr Fritz (1891–1942)

A qualified engineer, Todt joined the Nazi Party in 1922 and was a founder member of the Nazi League of German Technicians. In 1933 HITLER rewarded his loyalty by appointing him Inspector General of Road Construction and under his direction the Autobahn network took shape. By May 1938 it was becoming apparent that the Army's fortress engineers would not complete the construction of the SIEGFRIED LINE on schedule and the Organisation Todt (OT) was formed to finish the work which, under Todt's personal supervision, it was able to do in 18 months. In February 1940, Todt received the additional appointment of Reichsminister for Arms and Munitions, a post which, despite its title, related solely to the Army, as the Navy and the Luftwaffe had their own procurement bureaux. In December 1941, OT was made responsible for the technical direction of the ATLANTIC WALL project in co-operation with the Commander-in-Chief West. For this and other undertakings OT at first offered inducements to foreign workers but later relied heavily on forced and slave labour. In February 1942 Todt, seriously alarmed by the rate at which equipment was being destroyed on the Eastern Front, counselled Hitler to end the war with the Soviet Union. He was killed when his aircraft crashed in suspicious circumstances while he was returning from this meeting. He was replaced by SPEER.

TOE   Table of Organization and Equipment (US). The formal organization and equipment

scales covering any US military formation or unit, detailing the number and qualification of all soldiers, number and type of all weapons, vehicles and other equipment.

Toenails

American landings on NEW GEORGIA, SOLOMON ISLANDS, June–July 1943.

TOET   Tests of Elementary Training (UK). Series of graduated tests of recruits.

Togo, Shigenori (1882–1950)

Togo was Japan's Foreign Minister at the beginning of the war. Although he was personally opposed to the use of force as a means of solving his country's problems, he was overruled by the military clique which dominated Japanese politics. He resigned shortly after the declaration of war and lived in retirement until he was recalled in April 1945 to serve again as Foreign Minister, accepting the post only on condition that he was permitted to seek an honourable peace which guaranteed the Emperor's status, thereby incurring the dangerous hostility of those who wished to fight on to the bitter end. He was in favour of accepting the POTSDAM Declaration and had serious and justifiable reservations about the opening of negotiations through the Soviet Union. He resigned in August 1945 following the decision to surrender.

TOGs – Heavy Tanks (UK)

Designed in 1939/40 in response to a General Staff request for a heavy tank proof against modern anti-tank guns and field artillery at 100 yards, capable of operating in conditions similar to the Western Front in World War I. The design committee under Sir Albert Stern included many members who had been involved in World War I tank development and production and was known as The Old Gang (TOG). The prototype TOG I was completed in October 1940 and resembled the French CHAR B, being armed with a 75mm howitzer in the bow and surmounted by a MATILDA turret. The TOG II prototype, weighing 80 tons, appeared in March 1941 and in its final form was armed with a 17-pdr gun and coaxial machine gun in a turret. Driven by a Paxman-Ricardo 600hp diesel engine with electric transmission, the TOGs had a top speed of 8.5mph (13.5kph); their maximum armour thickness was 75mm. No further development took place as the CHURCHILL had been accepted as the Army's heavy infantry tank.

Tojo, Gen Hideki (1884–1948)

Tojo was appointed Chief of Staff of the Japanese Kwantung Army in MANCHURIA in 1937 and the following year received the Emperor's permission to hold military and political posts simultaneously. He served as Vice-Minister and then as Minister of War and in 1940 was prominent in negotiating the Tripartite Pact with Germany and Italy. On 17 October 1941 he became Prime Minister, personally retaining the posts of War Minister and Army Chief of Staff, which gave him virtual autocratic power. Tojo, however, was not an absolute dictator in the manner of HITLER, MUSSOLINI and STALIN. Rather, he represented the Army's belief that to win its war in CHINA it required resources which were denied by the Western powers and that these could be obtained by a short victorious war involving occupation of the latter's colonial possessions. The Army's view, with which Tojo fully concurred, was that such a war would present the West with a *fait accompli* and place Japan in a position of unassailable strength in any subsequent peace negotiations. Tojo immediately implemented this policy, preserving the fiction of negotiating with the United States until the attack on PEARL HARBOR. One of his first steps was the occupation of French Indo-China, which was achieved with the assistance of German pressure on the Vichy government. However, as Japan's fortunes declined, Tojo's position became increasingly difficult and to deflect some of the criticism levelled at him he transferred the Ministry of War to General Yoshijiro UMEZU. After the fall of the MARIANAS, his situation became untenable and he resigned on 18 July 1944, being replaced by Lieutenant-General Kuniaki KOISO. When Japan surrendered, Tojo made an abortive suicide attempt. He subsequently suffered numerous indignities at the hands of his American captors, including an Army dentist drilling "Remember Pearl Harbor" on his teeth. He stood trial and was hanged as a war criminal in 1948.

Tokyo

The capital city of Japan, Tokyo was raided by a small American force led by Colonel DOOLIT-TLE on 18 April 1942, when 24 B-25 Mitchell bombers were flown off the carrier *Hornet*.

General Hideki Tojo, Japanese Prime Minister.

The plan had been to launch 450 miles (725km) from Japan, but a sighting by a Japanese fishing boat jeopardized the plan and the aircraft were launched 825 miles (1330km) out. They reached Tokyo and also bombed Kobe, Yokohama and Nagoya. The force then flew on to China, but their premature take-off meant that several aircraft crash-landed in the sea. Tokyo was next a target on 24 November 1944 when 111 B-29 bombers attacked an aircraft engine factory. The bombing was inaccurate, and the large amount of fuel required to fly from the bases in the MARIANAS severely reduced the bomb-load. The alternative was to fire-bomb Tokyo, since incendiary bombs were small and many thousands could be carried for the weight of a few high-explosive bombs. The first of these fire-raids was mounted 9/10 March 1944, when 279 B-29s arrived over the target, led by special pathfinder crews who marked a central aiming point. In a raid which lasted two hours, the centre of Tokyo was devastated. It has been estimated that over 100,000 people were killed by fire – more than were killed by the ATOMIC BOMB in HIROSHIMA and NAGASAKI.

Tokyo Express

Nickname given to the Japanese resupply and reinforcement convoys which were sailed nightly down "THE SLOT" in the attempts to

Bomb damage after Boeing B-29 incendiary attack, Tokyo 1944.

support the Japanese garrison on GUADALCANAL after the American invasion in August 1942. The attempts were made by ships under command of Rear-Admiral Raizo "Tenacious" TANAKA, the crews of which became adept at night operations. Casualties and increasing American opposition made the operation ineffective, since it was never able to deliver enough men or supplies to influence the battle, and the Express made its last runs in December 1942.

Tokyo Rose (b. 1916)

The name conferred on Mrs Iva Ikuko Toguri d'Aquino, an American citizen of Japanese parentage who made propaganda broadcasts for the Japanese Broadcasting Company, the purpose of which was to contrast Japan's victories with Allied defeats and lower the morale of American troops serving in the Pacific war zone. In 1948 she was fined and imprisoned for treason but continued to reside in the United States after her release, denying any connection with Tokyo Rose. Iva d'Aquino was pardoned in 1977.

Tolbukhin, Marshal Fedor Ivanovich (1894–1949)

Tolbukhin began the war as Chief of Staff of the Transcaucasus Military District and was responsible for organizing the Soviet occupation of northern IRAN in the autumn of 1941. He then planned the landing of two armies, the 51st and 54th, on the KERCH PENINSULA in the CRIMEA, where MANSTEIN's 11th German Army was besieging SEVASTOPOL. This venture ended disastrously, and on 10 March 1942 Tolbukhin was relieved of his post. Having satisfied the Chief of General Staff that he had not been guilty of negligence, he was appointed commander of the 57th Army in July 1942 and led this during the withdrawal to STALINGRAD and the subsequent counteroffensive. He then commanded the 68th Army on North-West Front before transferring to command South Front in March 1943. In July his attack against the Mius River line was repulsed, but a second attempt in August succeeded and broke through to the DONBASS industrial region. In April 1944 the 4th Ukrainian Front, as South Front had been renamed, liberated the Crimea, taking 67,000 German and Romanian prisoners. The following month Tolbukhin transferred to the 3rd Ukrainian Front, which he commanded for the remainder of the war. He established a close working relationship with MALINOVSKY, the commander of the neighbouring 2nd Ukrainian Front, and in a series of joint operations they encircled five German corps at JASSY-KISHINEV and forced Romania to change sides. Tolbukhin then advanced to BELGRADE, assisting in its liberation by TITO's partisans, before turning north to meet Malinovsky for a series of operations which resulted in the fall of BUDAPEST, the defeat of the March 1945 German counteroffensive in HUNGARY, and the capture of Vienna. Tolbukhin was noted as much for his sound planning and attention to detail as he was for his consideration to his subordinates and his determination to avoid excessive losses whenever possible.

Tomkinson, Lt Cdr E. P., RN

Second highest-scoring British submarine commander of World War II. Tomkinson was appointed commander of the "U" CLASS submarine *Urge* while she was fitting out. In April 1941 she sailed from England for the Mediterranean, sinking the 10,500-ton tanker *Franco Martelli* on passage. In the Mediterranean *Urge* joined the 10th Submarine Flotilla at MALTA and during the next eleven months sank or damaged a further ten vessels, totalling 116,290 tons. *Urge* sailed from Malta for Alexandria on 27 April 1942 but never arrived. It seems probable that she was sunk by air attack on 29 April while engaged in gun action against the motor vessel *San Giusto* off Ras el Hilal.

Tommy-gun

A familar nickname for the .45in calibre Thomson submachine gun, used by the US, British and Commonwealth armies. The weapon was developed in the early 1920s by Colonel John T. Thomson, USA (Ret'd) and achieved an unsavoury reputation during the Prohibition gangster years. It was adopted by the US Marines in 1928 in small numbers. In 1939 quantities were ordered by the British and French armies, though few reached the French before 1940. It was then mass-produced throughout the war. Although heavy, it was extremely reliable and was the favoured submachine gun of Commando, Ranger and Airborne troops.

Tone Class Cruisers (Jap)

Displacement 11,215 tons; *dimensions* 661ft 6in×63ft 6in (198.5×19m); mean draught 21ft 4in (6.35m); *machinery* 4-shaft geared turbines producing shp 152,200; *speed* 35 knots; *armament* 8×8in (4×2); 8×5in DP (4×2); 12×25mm AA (6×2); 4×13mm AA; 12×24in torpedo tubes; *aircraft* 5; *complement* 850; *number in class* 2, launched 1937–38.

Tonka

German liquid rocket fuel consisting of aniline, monoethyaniline, gasoline and naphtha used with nitric acid to propel the X-4 missile.

Topp, Cdr Erich

Third highest-scoring German submarine commander of World War II. While commanding the Type IIC *U-57* and the TYPE VIIC *U-552* U-BOATS he completed 13 patrols during which he sank 34 ships totalling 193,684 tons, plus one destroyer.

Torch

Allied invasion of French North Africa, November 1942.

Torgau, Germany, 1945

A small German town on the River Elbe, north-east of Leipzig. It was here, on 25 April 1945, that the US 1st Army met the Soviet 5th Guards Army, in the first contact of the Western and Eastern Fronts.

Tortoise – A39 Heavy Assault Tank (UK)

Design commenced in 1942, based on similar requirements to those which initiated the TOG. Although the vehicle was designated a tank, its fixed superstructure and the limited traverse of the main armament had more in common with the layout of an assault gun. The 32-pdr was the largest weapon fitted to any British AFV during World War II. Six prototypes were constructed by the Nuffield organization, although these were not completed until 1947. *Weight* 78 tons; *speed* 12mph (19kph); *armour* 225mm; *armament* 1 32-pdr gun; 3 7.92mm machine guns; *engine* Rolls-Royce Meteor 600hp petrol; *crew* 7.

TOT Time on Target. Type of artillery fire whereby guns at varying places open fire at varying times so that all shells arrive at the designated moment.

Totalize

First Canadian Army's offensive towards FALAISE, Phase I, 8–11 August 1944.

Self-destruction of the French fleet, Toulon harbour, 1942.

Toulon, 1942

Following the success of the Allied landings in North Africa, HITLER gave orders that Vichy France was to be occupied. This operation, codenamed *Anton*, was executed on 11 November 1942 and, on Marshal PÉTAIN's order, no resistance was offered. On 19 November Hitler decided to seize the French fleet in Toulon, contrary to the provisions of the armistice of June 1940. Toulon contained some 60 vessels, including the battleships *Dunkerque*, *Strasbourg* and *Provence*. Admiral DARLAN signalled the fleet to proceed to DAKAR, but the order was ignored by its commander, Admiral de Laborde, a staunch supporter of Pétain. Meanwhile, the German plan to capture the fleet intact, Operation *Lila*, was subjected to delays and it was not until 0520 on 27 November that Hausser's II Panzer Corps (7, 10 and 2 SS Panzer Divisions) commenced its attack on the dockyard. German progress was slow, however, and the French ships responded immediately to de Laborde's signal to scuttle. With the exception of five submarines which escaped, the entire fleet was sunk or set ablaze, so fulfilling the French pledge that it would not fall into German hands. Casualties on both sides were light.

Tovey, Adm Sir John (1895–1971)

Tovey commanded the British Home Fleet, based at Scapa Flow, from 1940 to 1943. After the threat of a German invasion of the United Kingdom had faded, Tovey's primary responsibilities were the protection of the Atlantic and Arctic convoys. In May 1941 he directed the hunt for and destruction of the battleship BISMARCK, which the Home Fleet accomplished in co-operation with SOMERVILLE's Force H from Gibraltar.

Town Class Destroyers (UK)

Name given to the fifty "FLUSH-DECK" destroyers transferred by the US Navy to the Royal Navy in 1940. To improve their seaworthiness as well as their anti-aircraft and anti-submarine capabilities their original armament of four 4-inch, one 3-inch AA, three 0.5-in AA guns and twelve 21-inch torpedo tubes was extensively altered, typical converted armaments being three 4-inch, one 3-inch AA, three 0.5-in AA guns, six 21-inch torpedo tubes and depth charges or one 4-inch, one 3-inch AA, four 20mm AA guns, three 21-inch torpedo tubes, one HEDGEHOG and depth charges. The Town Class displaced 1020–1190 tons, had a speed of 35 knots and were manned by a complement of 146. The most famous member of the class was HMS CAMPBELTOWN, which was expended during the raid on ST NAZAIRE on 28 March 1942.

Toyoda, Adm Soemu (1885–1957)

Toyoda commanded the Yokasuka Naval Base before being appointed Commander-in-Chief of the Japanese Combined Fleet following the death of Admiral KOGA in March 1943. His entire strategy hinged upon luring the United States' Central Pacific Fleet into a decisive battle. In June 1944 this resulted in the Battle of the PHILIPPINE SEA, which resulted in the virtual destruction of Japanese naval air power. Toyoda, however, still clung firmly to the belief that one climactic naval battle would restore Japan's fortunes and mounted the complex series of operations which, in October 1944, culminated in the Battle of LEYTE GULF. Poor co-ordination, inflexibility and lack of adequate air power contributed to heavy losses which effectively crippled the Imperial Japanese Navy. In April 1945 Toyoda despatched the giant battleship YAMATO on her suicide mission to OKINAWA, but she was attacked and sunk on passage. Together with UMEZU and ANAMI, Toyoda refused to face reality and was flatly opposed to Japan's inevitable surrender.

7 TP – Light Tank (Poland)

Based on the Vickers Six-Ton light tank design. Early models had twin turrets each mounting a single machine gun; later models had one turret armed with a 37mm gun and coaxial machine gun. On the outbreak of war 125 7 TPs were in service, equipping two light tank battalions. *Weight* 9.4 tons; *speed* 20mph (32kph); *armour* 17mm; *armament* 2 7.92mm machine guns or 1 37mm gun and 1 7.92mm machine gun; *engine* VBLD-6 110hp diesel; *crew* 3.

Tractable

First Canadian Army's offensive towards FALAISE, Phase II, 14–16 August 1944.

Tradewind

Assault on Morotai, PHILIPPINE ISLANDS, 1944.

Treblinka, Poland, 1940–43

A German extermination camp located some 50 miles (80km) north-west of WARSAW. It was originally established in late 1940 as a labour

SS troops round up Warsaw Jews for despatch to Treblinka.

camp for political detainees, but in the summer of 1941 was converted into an extermination facility by the installation of gassing devices of various types. By July 1942 it was fully operational and was receiving transports from the Warsaw ghetto. In all, some 800,000 Jews were executed here before a revolt and mass escape by prisoners, accompanied by the killing of several SS guards, took place in April 1943. After severe reprisals, the camp was closed down in November 1943.

Trenchard, AM Sir Hugh Montague (1873–1956)

Trenchard transferred from the Army to the Royal Flying Corps in 1912 and was appointed its commander in August 1915. He became Chief of Air Staff in January 1918, but resigned in April, shortly after the formation of the Royal Air Force, following a quarrel with the Air Secretary, Lord Rothermere. In June 1918 he was appointed commander of the Independent Air Force, charged with the bombing of strategic targets in Germany, a task for which Trenchard lacked the resources and of which he was deeply sceptical. In February 1919 he returned as Chief of Air Staff, remaining in this post until 1929. He was responsible for the establishment and growth of the Air Ministry and the preservation of the Royal Air Force as an independent service. He also ensured that the RAF maintained a high public profile at minimum cost with his successful policy of "air-policing" British territories overseas where the maintenance of a large garrison was uneconomical. Trenchard was a powerful advocate of the offensive use of air power, particularly the strategic bomber. As early as 1923 he argued that "the nation that can stand being bombed the longest will win in the end". Among his loyal disciples was the future Air Officer Commanding-in-Chief BOMBER COMMAND, Arthur

HARRIS. Significantly, Trenchard pointed out that air power was of greater importance to the defence of SINGAPORE than fixed fortifications, and events were to prove him tragically correct. Following his retirement from the RAF he served as Commissioner of the Metropolitan Police 1931–35 and as Chairman of the United Africa Company 1936–53.

Trento Class Heavy Cruisers (Italy)

Displacement 13,540 tons; *dimensions* 636ft 3in×67ft 9in (193.9×20.6m); mean draught 19ft 3in (5.9m); *machinery* 4-shaft geared turbines producing shp 150,000; *speed* 34 knots; *protection* main belt 3in; deck 2in; turrets 4in; *armament* 8×8in; 16×3.9in AA; 8×37mm AA; 8×13.2mm AA; 8×21in torpedo tubes; *aircraft* 3; *complement* 788; *number in class* 3, launched 1926–32.

Treskow, Maj Gen Henning von (1901–1944)

In March 1943, while serving as KLUGE's Chief of Staff, Treskow assisted SCHLABRENDORFF in placing a bomb aboard HITLER's aircraft during one of the Führer's visits to the Eastern Front. Unfortunately, the device failed to explode. He then played a leading role in the 1944 JULY BOMB PLOT. When he heard that it had failed, Treskow committed suicide by walking towards the Russian lines and allowing himself to be shot down.

Tribal Class Destroyers (UK)

Displacement RN vessels 1870 tons; *RAN* and *RCN* vessels 1927 tons; *dimensions* 377ft 6in×36ft 6in (115×11.1m); mean draught 9ft (2.7m); *machinery* 2-shaft geared turbines producing shp 44,000; *speed* 36 knots; *armament RN* vessels 8×4.7in (4×2); 4×2-pdr AA (1×4); 8×0.5in AA (2×4); 4×21in torpedo tubes (1×4); *RAN* and *RCN* vessels 6×4.7in (3×2); 2×4in AA (1×2); 4×2-pdr AA (1×4);

8×0.5in AA (2×4); 4×21in torpedo tubes; *complement RN* vessels 190; *RAN* vessels 250; *RCN* vessels 240; *number in class* 27, launched 1937–46.

Trinity

Codename for the test of the first ATOMIC BOMB.

Tripolitania

The western portion of the Italian colony of Libya, the capital of which was Tripoli. It formed the base for German and Italian operations in North Africa and was not entered by Allied forces until the major Axis retreat after the Second Battle of ALAMEIN.

Trojanisches Pferd (Trojan Horse)

Covert operations by German groups to secure vital bridges in the Low Countries, May 1940.

Truk, Pacific, 1944 and 1945

An island in the Carolines group. Originally a German possession, it was mandated to the Japanese in 1920 and was then turned into a powerful naval and air base. It was regularly bombarded by US naval and air forces in 1944–45. It was abandoned by the Japanese as a major naval base in February 1944, but continued as an air base. As the US advances in the Pacific gradually moved out of range, and as attacks grew stronger, Truk's usefulness declined. It was never directly attacked by land force, merely left in isolation until the war ended.

Truman, Harry S. (1884–1972)

When the United States entered the war, Truman was serving as a Senator for Missouri. He was appointed Chairman of a Senate Special Committee set up to investigate misappropriation of funds allocated to the National

Tribal class destroyer.

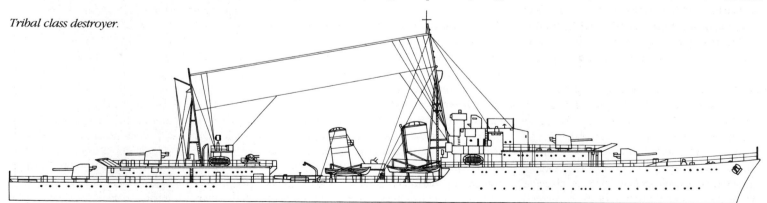

Defense Program and was able to save the American taxpayer vast sums without provoking an undesirable national scandal. In 1944 he became Vice-President, and on ROOSEVELT's death on 12 April 1945 succeeded to the Presidency. In July 1945 he attended the POTSDAM CONFERENCE with ATTLEE and STALIN. While returning from the conference he announced his decision to drop an atomic bomb on HIROSHIMA in order to expedite the end of the war in the Far East. Truman's Presidency continued for a further seven years and included the Korean War.

Truscott, Gen Lucien K. Jr (1895–1965)

Truscott commanded EISENHOWER's Forward Headquarters at Constantine during the campaign in North Africa. He was then appointed commander of the US 3rd Infantry Division, which he led in SICILY, at SALERNO, during the advance to the GUSTAV LINE and at ANZIO where, on 22 February 1944, he succeeded General John P. LUCAS as commander of US VI Corps and later led the breakout towards ROME. In August 1944 VI Corps formed part of General Alexander PATCH's US

Major-General Lucien K. Truscott.

7th Army and took part in Operation ANVIL-DRAGOON, the Allied invasion of southern France, making a spectacular advance up the Rhône Valley. In April 1945, Truscott returned to Italy to command the US 5th Army during the final phase of the fighting in that theatre.

TSO   Technical Staff Officer (UK).

T-Stoff

German rocket fuel consisting of concentrated hydrogen peroxide.

Tube Alloys (UK)

Research and development of the ATOMIC BOMB.

Tukhachevsky, Marshal Mikhail N.

Tukhachevsky, a former Tsarist officer, became one of the most successful Bolshevik commanders during the Russian Civil War but was defeated at the Battle of Warsaw during the Russo-Polish War of 1920. He was greatly influenced by the writings of Fuller and LIDDELL HART and in the mid-1930s began forming mechanized corps with which his own version of their strategic theories could be implemented. In 1937, however, he became the most notable victim of STALIN's Great Purge. He was summarily court-martialled and shot, his ideas were officially discredited and the corps were broken up, their component units being assigned tactical roles. The poor performance of the Soviet armour in Poland in 1939 and during the subsequent RUSSO-FINNISH CAMPAIGN led to this decision being reversed. However, when Germany invaded the USSR in June 1941, the Soviet armoured corps was still demoralized by the effects of the Great Purge, its higher formations were untrained, and many of its unwieldy formations were unfit to take the field. The process of rebuilding the armoured corps was long and painful but the Soviet victories in 1944–45 fully vindicated Tukhachevsky.

Tulagi, Pacific, 1942

A small island in the Florida Islands, part of the SOLOMONS group, separated from GUADALCANAL by IRONBOTTOM SOUND. It was captured by the Japanese in May 1942, for use as a seaplane base to cover the projected invasion of PORT MORESBY and future south-western expansion. It was assaulted on 8 August 1942 by Colonel Edson's 1st Marine Raiders, who met fanatical resistance and had a very difficult fight before

the island was taken. The Marines felt somewhat bitter about this battle, since they had had little time to prepare for it, which gave rise to these ironic lines.

They sent for the Army to capture Tulagi
But Douglas MacArthur said "NO"
He gave as his reason
"It isn't the season
And besides, there is no USO."

Tummar West, North Africa, 1941

Italian fortified post protecting SIDI BARRANI. It was captured by 5th Indian Infantry Brigade during General WAVELL's advance in December 1941.

Tunisia, 1942

A French colony in North Africa in 1939–45, Tunisia was invaded by US and British forces in November 1942 as part of Operation TORCH. British Airborne troops were dropped ahead of the British 1st Army, but the ground troops did not join up in time and the Germans were therefore able to set up a powerful defensive line and hold off the Allied advance. It had been hoped to make a quick thrust through Tunisia to join up with the British 8th Army advancing from EL ALAMEIN, but the rapid build-up of German reinforcements flown in from SICILY prevented this, and the campaign became a very hard slog. Tunis itself was not taken until 7 May 1943.

Tupolev Aircraft (USSR)

Tupolev ANT-6 A ponderous and angular four-engined monoplane with fixed undercarriage, the ANT-6 was designed as a heavy bomber in 1930. Although obsolete by 1941, many were still available and were pressed into service as bombers, though most were retired from this role and converted into transports, capable of carrying 30 fully equipped parachutists or considerable cargo. *Span* 133ft (40.56m); *engines* 4 830hp in-line; *crew* 7; *armament* 6 machine guns, 6600lb (3000kg) of bombs; *speed* 155mph (249kph).
Tupolev SB-2 An advanced design for its day, and with extremely clean lines, the SB-2 entered squadron service with the Soviet air force in early 1936 and saw its first combat in Spain, where it outran contemporary fighters. It served in Manchuria against the Japanese in 1939, and in Finland in the Winter War, finishing its service as a night bomber against Germany in 1943. A twin-engined low-wing monoplane, it underwent periodic improve-

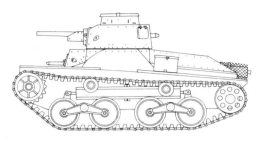

ments during its life. *Span* 66.6ft (20.3m); *engines* 2 750hp in-line; *crew* 3; *armament* 4 machine guns, 1100lb (500kg) of bombs; *speed* 280mph (450kph).

Tupolev Tu-2 The Tu-2 went into limited service in 1942; such was the basic soundness of its design, it stayed in service until 1961. A twin-engined low-wing monoplane, it proved extremely robust and reliable. Basically a light attack bomber, in postwar years it appeared in night fighter and close-support variants. *Span* 62ft (19m); *engines* 2 1850hp radial; *crew* 4; *armament* 2 20mm cannon and 3 machine guns, 6600lb (3000kg) of bombs; *speed* 342mph (550kph).

Turbine Class Destroyers (Italy)

Displacement 1700 tons; *dimensions* 304×30ft (92.6×9m); mean draught 10ft (3m); *machinery* 2-shaft geared turbines producing shp 40,000; *speed* 36 knots; *armament* 4×4.7in; 2×40mm AA; 4×13.2mm AA; 6×21in torpedo tubes; equipped for minclaying; *complement* 179; *number in class* 8, launched 1927–28.

Turner, Adm Richmond Kelly (1885–1961)

Turner, an amphibious warfare specialist, was appointed Commander South Pacific Amphibious Force in July 1942. His first major operation was the landing of troops on GUADALCANAL on 7 August 1942, which was safely accomplished despite the serious Allied naval reverse at the Battle of SAVO ISLAND. In July 1943 he directed the American landings

on NEW GEORGIA and in November those on the GILBERT ISLANDS. He transferred to the Central Pacific Area in 1944 and was responsible for the landings on the MARSHALL ISLANDS, ENIWETOK and the MARIANAS. In February and April 1945 he delivered the assault landings which culminated, respectively, in the capture of IWO JIMA and OKINAWA.

Twining, Gen Nathan F. (1897–)

Twining commanded the US 13th Air Force in the Pacific during 1943. The following year he was posted to Italy as commander of the US 15th Air Force which was engaged in the strategic bombing of targets in Germany and Central Europe. In 1945 he took over the US 20th Air Force, based on the MARIANAS, whence his B-29s carried out strategic bombing of the Japanese homeland.

Type 89 – Medium Tank (Jap)

Introduced in 1929, the Type 89 saw active service in China and Manchuria and, despite its obvious obsolescence, was also employed during the early years of World War II. The Type 89B, introduced in 1934, had an improved turret and was driven by a Mitsubishi 120hp air-cooled diesel engine. *Type 89A Weight* 9.8 tons; *speed* 17mph (27kph); *armour* 17mm; *armament* 1 57mm gun; 2 6.5mm machine guns; *engine* Daimler 100hp petrol; *crew* 4.

Type 94 – Tankette (Jap)

Based on the Carden-Loyd suspension. A redesigned version known as the Type 97

Type 95 light tank.

Tankette was armed with a 37mm gun or 7.7mm machine gun and driven by an Ikega 65hp air-cooled diesel engine. *Weight* 3.4 tons; *speed* 25mph (40kph); *armour* 12mm; *armament* 1 6.5mm or 7.7mm machine gun; *engine* 35hp air-cooled petrol; *crew* 2.

Type 95 – Light Tank (Jap)

Served in every theatre in which Japanese troops were engaged, about 1300 being built. An amphibious version, fitted with detachable pontoons and driven by two propellers, was used in small numbers in the MARSHALLS and the MARIANAS. A few type 95s remained active in Chinese service after the war. *Weight* 7.5 tons; *speed* 28mph (45kph); *armour* 12mm; *armament* 1 37mm gun; 2 7.7mm machine guns; *engine* Mitsubishi NVD 6120 120hp air-cooled diesel; *crew* 3.

Type 97 – Medium Tank (Jap)

Began entering service in 1937 and formed the backbone of Japanese tank regiments. In 1939, however, clashes with Soviet armour on the Manchurian border confirmed that Japan was falling behind the West in tank design and it was decided to re-arm the Type 97 with a 47mm L/48 high velocity gun housed in a larger turret; this version began reaching regiments in 1942. Perhaps as many as 2000 Type 97s were built but they were no match for the American, and later Soviet, tanks to which they were opposed. A number remained in service with the Chinese Army after the war. The Type 97 chassis was also used to produce three self-propelled mountings which appeared in 1942; these were the Ho-Ni I tank destroyer armed with a 75mm gun, the Ho-Ni II with a 105mm howitzer and the Ho-Ro with a 150mm howitzer, the weapons being protected by open gunshields. None were produced in significant numbers. *Weight* 15 tons; *speed* 24mph (39kph); *armour* 25mm; *armament* 1 57mm gun; 2 7.7mm machine guns; *engine* Mitsubishi 170hp air-cooled diesel; *crew* 4.

Tupolev SB-2 bombing up before setting out on a night raid.

U

"U" Class Submarines (UK)

Group 1 *Displacement* 540/730 tons; *dimensions* 191ft 6in×16ft (58.3×4.9m); *machinery* 2-shaft diesel/electric motors producing bhp 615/825; *speed* 11.25/9 knots; *armament* 1×3in; 3 machine guns; 4 or 6×21in torpedo tubes (all bow – 2 external in 6-tube boats); *complement* 31; *number in class* 15, launched 1937–41.

Group 2 *Displacement* 545/740 tons; *dimensions* 196ft 9in×16ft (59.9×49m); *armament* 1×3in; 3 machine guns; 4×21in torpedo tubes (all bow); *number in class* 34, launched 1940–43; *other specifications as Group 1*.

"U" and "V" Class Destroyers (UK)

Displacement 1710 tons; *dimensions* 362ft 9in×35ft 9in (110.5×10.89m); *mean draught* 10ft (3m); *machinery* 2-shaft geared turbines producing shp 40,000; *speed* 36.75 knots; *armament* 4×4.7in (4×1); 2×40mm AA (1×2); 8×20mm AA (4×2) or 12×20mm AA (6×2) guns; 8×21in (2×4) torpedo tubes; *complement* 180; *number in class* 16, launched 1942–43.

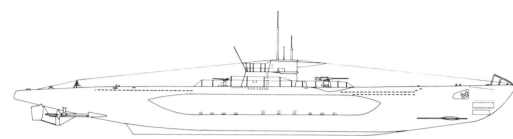

U-boat, type VIIB.

U-boat under air attack.

U-boats, Type IID – Submarines (Ger)

Coastal boats developed from Types IIA, IIB and IIC (respectively 8, 18 and 8 built) with greatly increased operational radius. Latterly confined to training duties. 18 built. *Displacement* 314/364 tons; *dimensions* 144×16ft (43.9×4.9m); *machinery* 2-shaft diesel electric motors producing bhp 700/410; *speed* 13.75/7.25 knots; *radius* 3500 miles (5630km) at 12 knots/56 miles (90km) at 4 knots; *armament* 4×20mm AA (2×2); 3×21in torpedo tubes (bow); six torpedoes or eight mines; *complement* 25.

U-boats, Type VIIC – Submarines (Ger)

Evolved from the Type VIIA (10 built) and the Type VIIB (24 built), the Type VIIC had a greater operational radius than the former and could carry two more torpedoes than the latter, as well as possessing an increased AA armament. The Type VIIC provided the backbone of the German submarine service and over 600 were built. As the war progressed a SCHNORKEL was fitted and the 3.5-inch gun was removed while the AA armament was progressively increased. Further developments included the Type VIIC 41/42 (62 built) which had a strengthened pressure hull for deeper diving; the Type VIID (6 built) with an improved minelaying capacity; and the Type VIIF (4 built), which carried 25 torpedoes as cargo for the replenishment of operational boats at sea. *Displacement* 769/871 tons; *dimensions* 220ft 3in×20ft 3in (67.1×6.17m); *machinery* 2-shaft diesel/electric motors producing bhp 2800/750; *speed* 17/7.5 knots; *radius* 6500 miles (10,460km) at 12 knots/80 miles (129km) at 4 knots; *armament* 1×3.5in; 1×37mm AA; 2×20mm AA (2×1); 5×21in torpedo tubes (4 bow and 1 stern); 14 torpedoes or 14 mines; *complement* 44.

U-boats, Type IXC – Submarines (Ger)

Evolved from the Type IXA (8 built) and Type IXB (14 built), with greater operational radius. 96 Type IXC boats were built, plus 48 Type IXC 40 boats, which were generally similar but possessed an operational radius of 11,400 miles (18,340km). As the war progres-

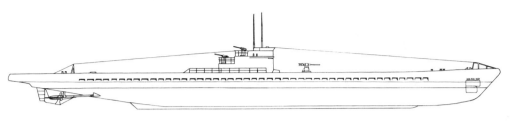

U-boat, type IXC.

sed a SCHNORKEL was fitted and the 4.1-inch gun was removed while the AA armament was progressively increased. A further development was the Type IXD1 submarine tanker (2 built), which was armed with light AA weapons but lacked torpedo tubes. The last of the Type IX series was the Type IXD2 (29 built), which was fitted with more powerful motors producing bhp 5400/1100, giving a higher surface speed of 19.25 knots. The Type IXD2 was somewhat larger than Types IXC and IXC 40, carried 24 torpedoes or six torpedoes and 32 mines, and had a surfaced operational radius of 23,700 miles (38,140km) at 12 knots. *Displacement* 1120/1232 tons; *dimensions* 252ft×22ft 3in (76.8×6.78m); *machinery* 2-shaft diesel/electric motors producing bhp 4400/1000; *speed* 18.25/7.25 knots; *radius* 11,000 miles (17,700km) at 12 knots/63 miles (101km) at 4 knots; *armament* 1×4.1in; 1×37mm AA; 1×20m AA; 6×21in torpedo tubes (4 bow and 2 stern); 22 torpedoes; *complement* 48.

U-boats, Type XB – Submarines (Ger)

Designed initially as minelayers with mines housed in 30 shafts, these boats were also used as supply carriers. As the war progressed a SCHNORKEL was fitted and the 4.1-inch gun removed, while the AA armament was augmented. Of the eight built only three survived the war, two surrendering while the third, *U-219*, served briefly in the Imperial Japanese Navy as *I-505*. *Displacement* 1763/2177 tons; *dimensions* 294ft 9in×30ft (89.8×9m); *machinery* 2-shaft diesel/electric motors producing bhp 4200/1100; *speed* 16.5/7 knots; *armament* 1×4.1in; 1×37mm AA; 1×20mm AA; 2×21in torpedo tubes (stern); 15 torpedoes and 66 mines; *complement* 52.

U-boats, Type XIV – Submarines (Ger)

Submarine tankers known as "milch cows", capable of carrying 423 tons of fuel oil and four torpedoes for the replenishment of operational boats at sea; lacked torpedo tubes.

10 built. *Displacement* 1688/1932 tons; *dimensions* 220ft×30ft 6in (67×9.2m); *machinery* 2-shaft diesel/electric motors producing bhp 2800/750; *speed* 14.5/6.75 knots; *radius* 9300 miles (14,960km) at 12 knots/53 miles (85km) at 4 knots; *armament* 2×37mm AA (2×1); 1×20mm AA; *complement* 53.

U-boats, Type XXI – Submarines (Ger)

128 built, fitted with SCHNORKEL as standard. *Displacement* 1612/1819 tons; *dimensions* 251ft×21ft 9in (76.5×6.6m); *machinery* 2-shaft diesel/electric motors producing bhp 4000/5000; silent creeping electric motors producing shp 226; *speed* 15.5/16 knots; silent creeping 5 knots; *radius* 11,150 miles (17,940km) at 12 knots/285 miles (460km) at 6 knots; *armament* 4×30mm AA (2×2) or 4×20mm AA (2×2); 6×21in torpedo tubes (bow); 23 torpedoes or 12 torpedoes and 12 mines; *complement* 57.

U-boats, Type XXIII – Submarines (Ger)

Coastal boats, fitted with SCHNORKEL as standard; 52 built. *Displacement* 232/256 tons; *dimensions* 112ft×21ft 9in (34.1×6.62m); *machinery* 2-shaft diesel/electric motors producing bhp 580/600; silent creeping electric motors producing shp 35; *speed* 9.75/12.5 knots; silent creeping 2 knots; *radius* 1350 miles (2170km) at 9.75 knots/175 miles (280km) at 4 knots; *armament* 2×21in torpedo tubes; 2 torpedoes; *complement* 14.

U-boat, type XXI.

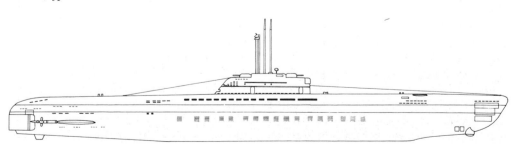

Udet, Lt Gen Ernst (1896–1941)

A World War I German fighter ace, and dashing postwar stunt flier and movie-maker, Udet was appointed Director of the Technical Bureau at the Air Ministry in June 1936, a position of great responsibility for which he possessed neither the training nor the temperament. In February 1939 he became the Luftwaffe's Inspector-General, responsible for equipping the air force. The aircraft he produced were more suited to tactical use in a short war than a prolonged strategic offensive and his lack of foresight left the Luftwaffe without an adequate second generation of aircraft once the early campaigns had been won. When it became clear during Operation BARBAROSSA that aircraft production could not keep pace with losses on the Eastern Front, Udet came under increasing criticism. Convinced that he was the victim of a conspiracy, and unable to control the chaotic bureaucracy he had allowed to grow up around him, he took his own life on 17 October 1941. He became a convenient scapegoat for the Luftwaffe's failings.

U-Go

Japanese offensive aimed at the capture of IMPHAL and KOHIMA, Burma 1944.

Ukraine

The Ukraine is an indeterminate region of southern Russia and pre-1939 Poland. Ukrainians historically claim all the area between the Caspian Sea and the old boundaries of pre-1914 Russian Poland and Romania. They have a long history of belligerence against Poland and the rest of Russia, and the history of the region between 1918 and 1929 is one of rebellion and counter-rebellion. Often described as the granary of Russia, the Ukraine was the objective of the German Army Group South in Operation BARBAROSSA. The area was almost completely overrun, the

Germans reaching STALINGRAD, Elista and Ord-zhonikidze by November 1942. The Red Army began to clear the area in August 1943, and by February 1944 almost the entire Ukraine was back in Soviet hands.

Ukuru Class Escorts (Jap)

Displacement 940 tons; *dimensions* 256ft×29ft 9in (78×9.06m); mean draught 10ft (3m); *machinery* 2-shaft geared diesels producing shp 4200; *speed* 19.5 knots; *armament* 3×4.7in DP (1×2 and 1×1); 6×25mm AA (2×3); 1×3in trench mortar; 120 depth charges; *number in class* 33, launched 1944–45.

Ultor, HMS – "U" Class Submarine (UK)

Commanded by Lieutenant G. E. Hunt, *Ultor* was noted for the accuracy of her torpedo attacks, which resulted in 50 per cent hits. During her fifteenth patrol, executed off the south coast of France in June 1944, this figure rose to 56 per cent when nine out of sixteen torpedoes fired reached their targets. In total, *Ultor* sank 29 vessels totalling 47,500 tons, including two destroyers, and so ranked ninth in the Royal Navy's list of submarine sinkings during World War II.

Ultra

A British codename indicating the security grading attached to information on German movements and intentions acquired by intercepting the ENIGMA coded signal traffic.

Uman, Soviet Union, 1941–44

A Russian town in the central Ukraine area, some 170 miles (273km) south of KIEV. In July 1941, I Panzer Group and 17th German Army completed a pincer movement which surrounded Uman, trapping the Soviet 6th and 12th Armies and elements of the 18th Army, a total of 15 infantry and five armoured divisions. Some Soviet troops managed to fight their way out, but resistance ended on 8 August and the Germans took 100,000 prisoners, 317 tanks and 1100 guns. Uman was retaken by the advancing Soviet armies on 10 March 1944.

Umberto, Prince Regent of Italy (b. 1904)

Umberto received the powers of Regent from his father, KING VICTOR EMMANUEL III, when ROME was liberated in June 1944. The monarchy's

Loyd carrier towing anti-tank gun.

position had been prejudiced by its former association with the Fascist regime and Umberto did all that he could to restore its standing, including serving in the line with Italian troops against their former German allies. This proved to be of no avail and Italy became a republic in 1946.

Umezu, Gen Yoshijiro (1880–1949)

Umezu was a veteran of the fighting in MANCHURIA and CHINA, where he served from 1931 to 1940. He was appointed Army Chief of Staff when TOJO fell from power in July 1944. Initially opposed to Japan's surrender, he eventually recognized the impossibility of her position and resisted pressure from the Army to continue fighting. Although unwilling to attend the surrender ceremony aboard the USS *Missouri* on 2 September 1945, he did so as the Army's representative on the personal command of the Emperor.

Unfrocked Priest (UK)

See KANGAROO.

Unicorn, HMS – Aircraft Carrier

Launched in 1941, *Unicorn* was designed as an aircraft maintenance carrier but was also employed as an operational unit. She served with the Home and Mediterranean Fleets 1943–44, the Eastern Fleet 1944 and the Pacific Fleet 1945. *Displacement* 14,750 tons; *dimensions* 640×90ft (195×27.4m); mean draught 19ft (5.8m); *machinery* 2-shaft geared turbines producing shp 40,000; *speed* 24 knots; *armament* 8×4in DP (4×2); 12×2-pdr AA (3×4); 12×20mm AA (2×2 and 8×1); *aircraft* 35; *complement* 1000.

Universal Carriers

Often referred to generally as Bren Carriers, this family of light armoured vehicles employed a Horstmann type suspension and evolved from the Vickers machine gun carrier series of the middle 1930s. About 35,000 were built in the United Kingdom, 29,000 in Canada, 5600 in Australia and over 500 in New Zealand. Their most common use was to transport the infantry battalions' heavy weapons but they were widely employed in other roles including reconnaissance, artillery observation post, anti-tank gun tractor, mortar carrier, flamethrower and assault engineering. The Windsor Carrier, 5000 of which were built in Canada and 14,000 in the USA, was somewhat larger and was powered by a Ford 95/100hp petrol engine. The Loyd Carrier was again similar to the Universal Carrier but was unarmoured. It was used as a tractor for anti-tank guns and 4.2-inch mortars, as a battery charger and slave starter for tanks, and as a field telephone cable layer. About 26,000 were built. The Universal and related carriers served in every theatre of war in which British and Commonwealth troops were engaged. *Carrier Universal No. 2 Mark II Weight* 3.95 tons; *speed* 32mph (51kph); *armour* 12mm; *armament* 1 Boys Anti-Tank Rifle; 1 Bren Light Machine Gun; *engine* Ford 85hp petrol; *crew* 4/5.

Unryu Class Aircraft Carriers (Jap)

The three completed ships in this class were *Unryu*, *Amagi* and *Katsuragi*, launched respectively on 29 September 1943, 15 October 1943 and 19 January 1944. *Unryu* was sunk in the East China Sea by the submarine USS *Redfish* on 19 December 1944; *Amagi* was sunk by air attack in Kobe dockyard on 24 July 1945. *Displacement* 17,150 tons; *dimensions* 741ft 6in×72ft (222.3×21.6m); mean draught 25ft 9in (7.7m); *machinery* 4-shaft geared turbines producing shp 104,000/152,000; *speed* 32/34 knots; *protection* main belt 1–5.9in; flight deck 2.17in; *armament* 12×5in AA (6×2); 51×25mm AA (17×3); *aircraft* 64; *complement* 1450; *number in class* 6, including 3 launched but uncompleted when the war ended.

Uranus

Soviet counteroffensive at STALINGRAD, November 1942.

Urquhart, Maj Gen Robert Elliott (1901–)

Urquhart served as GSO 1 of the 51st Highland Division in North Africa, 1942–43, and took part in the campaign in Sicily and the landings in Italy. He then returned home to become Brigadier-General Staff XIII Corps. In 1944 he was appointed commander of the 1st Airborne Division, which he led at ARNHEM. His postwar appointments included GOC Malaya 1950–52.

U/S   Unserviceable (UK).

USAAF   US Army Air Force.

USAFBI   US Armed Force, British Isles. Became ETOUSA in June 1942.

USMC   US Marine Corps.

USN   US Navy.

USO   United Services Organisation. American welfare and entertainment service.

USS   US Ship.

USTAF   US Tactical Air Force.

Utah Beach, 1944

The extreme right flank beach of the Allied invasion of NORMANDY on 6 June 1944. Utah was centred on the village of La Madeleine and was assaulted by the US VII Corps under General COLLINS, the initial landings being carried out by the US 4th Infantry Division. The landings took place at 0630 against negligible opposition and by 1200 the leading elements were clear of the beaches and advancing inland to link up with airborne troops which had landed in the area of Vierville.

UXB   Unexploded bomb (UK).

US soldiers landing at Utah beach, Normandy 1944.

V

V-1, V-2, V-3
See V-Weapons.

"V" Class Destroyers (UK)
See "U" and "V" Class Destroyers.

"V" Class Submarines (UK)
Displacement 545/740 tons; *dimensions* 206×16ft (62.7×4.9m); *machinery* 2-shaft diesel/electric motors producing bhp 800/760; *speed* 13/9 knots; *armament* 1×3in; 3 machine guns; 4×21in torpedo tubes (all bow); *complement* 37; *number in class* 22, launched 1943–44.

Valentine 6-pdr Mark IX.

Vaagso Island, 1941
Island off the Norwegian coast about 100 miles north of Bergen. Knowing Hitler to be obsessed with the need to garrison Norway strongly, a view not held by the OKW, British Combined Operations under Lord Louis MOUNTBATTEN decided to raid Vaagso, do what damage was possible, and so keep alive the threat of invasion and draw German troops into Norway. On 12 December 1941 a British force raided the port of South Vaagso, supported by naval gunfire against coast batteries on neighbouring islands and air attacks on local airfields. German resistance was fierce and British casualties severe, but the principal targets were destroyed and the raiding party was successfully withdrawn. As a result of this raid the German strength in Norway was considerably increased, and by 1944 stood at over 350,000 troops.

Valediction
Early name for VERITABLE.

Valentine – Infantry Tank Mark III (UK)
A private venture on the part of Vickers-Armstrong Ltd, utilizing many components of the cruiser tanks A9 and A10. The design was submitted to the War Office shortly before St Valentine's Day 1938 and so acquired the name by which the tank was subsequently

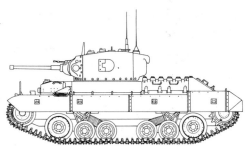

Valentine III infantry tank.

known. The first models appeared in May 1940 and when production ceased in 1944 over 8000 had been built, accounting for a quarter of British tank output. The Valentines Mark VI and VII were manufactured in Canada by the Canadian Pacific Railway Company and most of these, together with 1300 British-built models, were sent to the Soviet Union, where many were re-armed with Russian 76.2mm guns. Much of the tank's development history was concerned with the need to up-gun the basic design and increase the turret crew to a more efficient three, but the solutions to these problems were not mutually compatible; on the other hand, the Valentine was a by-word for mechanical reliability. The tank first saw action during Operation CRUSADER and served throughout the North African campaign in both the 8th and 1st Armies. At Second ALAMEIN the 200 Valentines of 23rd Armoured Brigade

provided continuous support for British and Commonwealth infantry divisions throughout the battle. The first 6-pdr Marks began reaching regiments just as the 8th Army entered Tunisia. When the war returned to North-West Europe some of the later models served in anti-tank regiments. Valentines were also employed in the invasion of MADAGASCAR in 1942, by the 3rd New Zealand Division in the Pacific theatre of war, and to a limited extent on the ARAKAN front in Burma. Derivatives included the ARCHER tank destroyer and the BISHOP self-propelled 25-pdr gun howitzer, a 30-foot (9.15m) scissors bridgelayer with a 30-ton capacity which gave valuable service in Italy and Burma, a DD (DUPLEX-DRIVE) amphibious version used for training, and experimental mineclearing vehicles and flamethrowers. See also *The Valentine in North Africa* by Bryan Perrett (Ian Allan).

Weight	16 tons (*Marks I–VII*); 17 tons (*Marks VIII–XI*)
Speed	15mph (24kph)
Armour	65mm
Armament	1 2-pdr gun; 1 7.92mm Besa machine gun (*Marks I–V*); 1 2-pdr gun; 1 .30-cal Browning machine gun (*Marks VI and VII*); 1 6-pdr gun (*Marks VIII and IX*); 1 6-pdr; 1 7.92mm Besa machine gun (*Mark X*); 1 75mm gun;

1 7.92mm Besa machine gun (*Mark XI*)

Engine AEC 135hp petrol (*Mark I*); AEC 131hp diesel (*Marks II, III and VIII*); GMC 138hp diesel (*Marks IV–VII and IX–XI*)

Crew 3 (*Marks I, II, IV and VI–XI*); 4 (*Marks III and V*).

Valetta, Malta, 1941

The capital of Malta, situated on a promontory on the north-east coast of the island, with commodious harbours on each side. Long the principal British Mediterranean naval base, the harbour was extensively fortified against both naval and overland attack. Frequently bombed by Italian and German forces, on the night 25/26 July 1941 the harbour was attacked by Italian torpedo-boats and "human torpedoes". Their objective was the submarine anchorage and a British convoy which was believed to be in Grand Harbour. The force was carried to a point about 14 miles (22km) to sea and then launched, with an air raid timed to coincide with the assault covering the engine noises. However, an approaching craft was seen by a coast defence gun sentry and searchlights were exposed, picking up the raiders just as the breakwater bridge was struck by a human torpedo and demolished. Six-pounder guns in Fort St Elmo opened fire immediately and within two minutes the attack was routed, three of the attackers being sunk and two disabled. The remainder turned away and were pursued by heavy gunfire. As dawn broke RAF HAWKER HURRICANE fighters flew out and attacked the

retreating survivors. This was notable as the only major coast defence action fought by the British Army throughout the war.

Valiant – A38 Infantry Tank (UK)

Conceived as a heavy version of the VALENTINE. By the time the prototypes had been produced, however, the CHURCHILL was already established as the standard British infantry tank and the project was dropped. *Weight* 27 tons; *speed* 12mph (19kph); *armour* 114mm; *armament* 1 6-pdr or 1 75mm gun; 1 7.92mm Besa machine gun; *engine* GMC 210hp diesel; *crew* 4.

Valkyrie

German contingency plan for action to be taken in the event of a revolt by slave labour in Germany, the codename being used as a cover by senior Army officers for their plot to assassinate HITLER and seize control from the Nazis, 1943–44.

Vandegrift, Lt Gen Alexander A. (1887–1972)

Vandegrift commanded the US 1st Marine Division which landed on GUADALCANAL on 7 August 1942. Despite intense Japanese pressure by land, sea and air, the Marines held their positions and successfully resisted all attempts by the enemy to recapture the airstrip known as HENDERSON FIELD. By November Vandegrift had inflicted heavy casualties on his opponents and was able to undertake limited offensive operations, but when his division was relieved the following month one-third of its men were no longer fit for

active duty. He was then appointed commander of I Marine Amphibious Corps, which he led during the landings on BOUGAINVILLE in November 1943. In 1944 he returned home to become Commandant of the US Marine Corps.

Vanguard, HMS – Battleship

Vanguard was the last British battleship to be built. She was completed too late to see active service and was scrapped in 1960. Her design incorporated many lessons learned throughout the war, including the most effective anti-aircraft armament installed to that date, capable of engaging up to 16 separate aerial targets at once. *Displacement* 42,500 tons; *dimensions* 814ft 3in×107ft 6in (248×32.7m); mean draught 28ft (8.5m); *machinery* 4-shaft geared turbines producing shp 130,000; *speed* 29.5 knots; *protection* main belt 14in; deck 6in; turrets 13in; *armament* 8×15in (4×2); 16×5.25in DP (8×2); 71×40mm AA (10×6, 1×4 and 7×1); *complement* 1600; *launched* 30 November 1944.

Varsity

Allied airborne operations east of the Rhine mounted concurrently with PLUNDER, March 1945.

Vasilevsky, Marshal Alexandr M. (1895–1977)

Vasilevsky served as Deputy Chief of Operations Control 1941–42 and was then appointed Chief of General Staff, a position which he held for most of the war. Together with ZHUKOV and VORONOV, he planned Operation URANUS, the Soviet counteroffensive which in November 1942 trapped the German 6th Army in STALINGRAD. He was responsible for the fortification of the KURSK salient, against which the Wehrmacht expended its offensive capacity in July 1943, and played a major part in planning the subsequent Soviet counteroffensive which liberated large areas of Russia. In 1944 he co-ordinated the advance of 2nd and 3rd Belorussian Fronts across Poland and in March 1945 assumed personal command of 3rd Belorussian Front when its commander, CHERNYAKHOVSKY, was killed, completing the conquest of East Prussia. After the defeat of Germany, Vasilevsky was appointed Commander-in-Chief of the Soviet armies in the Far East, overwhelming the Japanese defenders of Manchuria in a well-planned and vigorously conducted offensive.

HMS Warspite *in Grand Harbour, Valetta, Malta.*

General Nikolay Vatutin, Kursk 1943.

Vatutin, Gen Nikolay A. (1901–44)

After serving in the Operations Branch of Stavka, Vatutin was appointed commander of South-West Front in 1942. In November that year his Front took part in the encirclement of von PAULUS' 6th Army in STALINGRAD. When Paulus surrendered in February 1943, Vatutin attempted a deep penetration of the German rear areas, but his command was severely mauled by MANSTEIN's brilliant counterstroke into his flank. In July 1943 he commanded Voronezh Front and was responsible for the successful defence of the southern half of the KURSK salient during Operation ZITADELLE. His subsequent counteroffensive resulted in the capture of KHARKOV on 22 August and the liberation of much of the Ukraine. On 6 November Vatutin's command, renamed 1st Ukrainian Front, captured KIEV. He maintained pressure on the Germans throughout the winter but on 29 February 1944 he was ambushed by anti-Soviet partisans near Rovno and was fatally wounded.

VB Bombs

The VB (Vertical Bomb) series were guided missiles without wings, dropped from US bombers; they were standard 1000lb (454kg) bombs with the addition of guidance devices to the fins to permit some degree of steering to their target, guided by the bomb-aimer of the aircraft. The VB-1 was called AZON (for *AZ*imuth *ON*ly) and could only be guided in azimuth, i.e. steered to one side or another as it fell. Control was by radio, and a skilled bomb-aimer could guide five bombs at once. They were used successfully against locks on

the Danube and on a railway viaduct in Italy, and against bridges in Burma. The VB-3 was RAZON (*RA*nge and *AZ*imuth) which permitted control of the vertical trajectory as well as steering; this was developed too late for use in the war, as were several later designs which eventually saw service in the Korean War.

VCP Vehicle collecting point.

Vella Gulf, Battle of, 1943

During the night of 5/6 August 1943 a squadron of six American destroyers under the command of Commander F. Moosbrugger ambushed four Japanese destroyers attempting to reinforce the garrison of Kolombangara, Solomon Islands, sinking three of them with torpedoes and gunfire in Vella Gulf. Over 1500 Japanese soldiers were drowned. The Americans sustained no loss.

Vella Lavella, Battle of, 1943

During the night of 6/7 October 1943 a force of nine Japanese destroyers under Rear-Admiral Ijuin was covering the withdrawal of troops from Vella Lavella, Solomon Islands, when it encountered six American destroyers under Captain F. R. Walker. One Japanese and two American destroyers were sunk during the engagement. Ijuin retreated after the withdrawal had been completed.

Velvet

Plan to base British and American air force squadrons in the Caucasus, late 1942, but not implemented.

Venezia

Axis movement around the southern flank of the British defence line based on GAZALA, May 1942.

Venlo, 1939

A town on the German-Dutch border. In November 1939 two British officers of Military Intelligence, Payne-Best and Stevens, were decoyed across the border by German SS men masquerading as Allied sympathizers. Under torture, they gave information which jeopardized British intelligence work in Western Europe.

Vercors, France, 1944

A plateau in the French departments of Isère and Drôme, roughly south-west of Grenoble. A wild and mountainous region, it became a

gathering-place for resistance forces, and in June 1944, after the Allied invasion, some 3500 irregular French partisans gathered there with the intention of harassing the German forces in the area. The Germans discovered this, and sent a strong force of airborne and SS troops to clear the area. Although the French attempted resistance they suffered severe losses and were forced to disperse.

Veritable

British-Canadian offensive between the Maas and the Rhine, February 1945.

Very Pistol

A single-shot pistol of one-inch (26mm) calibre used for firing flares and pyrotechnic signals by all armies. The name comes from Lieutenant Very, US Navy, who invented the pistol and ammunition in the 1880s and is now loosely used for any pyrotechnic pistol.

Vian, Adm Sir Philip (1894–1968)

In February 1940, while commanding the 4th Destroyer Flotilla off the Norwegian coast, Vian received direct instructions from CHURCHILL to seize the German naval auxiliary ALTMARK, which had sought refuge in Jösenfjord. The *Altmark* had been the ADMIRAL GRAF SPEE's support ship and when she was boarded by the destroyer COSSACK this resulted in the release of 299 British merchant seamen who had been captured during the raider's cruise. In May 1940 he played a prominent role in the evacuation of NAMSOS and a year later his flotilla took part in the hunt for the BISMARCK, making torpedo attacks on the battleship during the night of 26/27 May and scoring a number of hits. In August he escorted the successful commando raid on SPITZBERGEN. He then moved to the Mediterranean, where he escorted convoys between ALEXANDRIA and MALTA. Here he fought the First and Second Battles of SIRTE, and on both occasions foiled a much superior Italian force by his aggressive defence. In July 1943 he commanded a covering force during the invasion of SICILY and in September a Carrier Air Support Force during the SALERNO landings. In June 1944 he served as Naval Commander of the Eastern Task Force during the Allied invasion of NORMANDY and later that year was posted to the Far East as commander of the Pacific Fleet's carrier squadron which in 1945 took part in the operations resulting in the capture of OKINAWA.

Vichy, France, 1940

A town and health resort some 75 miles (120km) north-west of Lyons. The government formed by Marshal PÉTAIN moved here on 29 June 1940 and controlled the two-fifths of France unoccupied by German forces and the French colonies. The collaborationist French State was thereafter generally known as the "Vichy Government".

Vickers Aircraft (UK)

Vickers Valentia This elderly twin-engined biplane, which gave every appearance of its 1934 origin, was employed as a troop transport, principally in the Mediterranean area in peace-time, and several survived in this role until 1943. *Span* 87.3ft (26.6m); *engines* 2 650hp radial; *speed* 130mph (209kph).

Vickers Vildebeeste This open-cockpit biplane torpedo-bomber went into service with the RAF in 1933, and at the outbreak of war it was still their only coastal defence torpedo-bomber in service. Those remaining were active in defence of Malaya early in 1942, but were wiped out. A general-purpose reconnaissance bombing and liaison version, the Vincent, served in East Africa against the Italians in 1940–41. *Span* 49ft (15m); *engine* 1 660hp radial; *crew* 3; *armament* 2 machine guns, 1000lb (450kg) of bombs or 1 18 inch torpedo; *speed* 142mph (228kph).

Vickers Warwick Designed to replace the WELLINGTON, it did not get into production until 1942, by which time it was outdated as a bomber. It was converted to carry an air-droppable lifeboat and was used on air-sea rescue service, after which numbers were converted to transports. *Span* 96.75ft (29.5m); *engines* 2 1850hp radial; *crew* 6; *armament* 8 machine guns; *speed* 225mph (362kph).

Vickers Wellington This twin-engined medium bomber was an outstanding machine, capable of absorbing phenomenal amounts of damage and still returning with its crew. Universally known as the "Wimpey" (after the Popeye cartoon character, J. Wellington Wimpey) it used a revolutionary form of "geodetic" construction invented by Barnes WALLIS, designer for Vickers, which gave it immense strength. The first machines went into service in 1938 and the first air raid against Germany was carried out by Wellingtons against Wilhelmshaven on 4 September 1939. After suffering crippling losses in daylight raids in December 1939, the Wellington was assigned to night bombing and

Vickers Wellington IIs returning from a raid.

remained the principal RAF bomber until the arrival of the four-engined types in 1942. In addition to bombing, the Wellington was converted for minelaying, magnetic mine detection and torpedo-bombing roles, as anti-submarine patrol aircraft, and as transports. Total production exceeded 11,600. *Span* 86ft (26.2m); *engines* 2 1585hp radial; *crew* 6; *armament* 6 machine guns, 6600lb (3000kg) of bombs; *speed* 255mph (410kph).

Vickers Wellesley This privately-developed monoplane pioneered the geodetic construction system, and was one of the longest wingspan single engined aircraft ever built. With a remarkable long-range ability (two flew non-stop from Egypt to Australia in 1938) it was adopted as a long-range light bomber by the RAF in 1937, and was used extensively in the East African theatre of war until late 1941. *Span* 74.5ft (22.7m); *engine* 1 925hp radial; *crew* 2; *armament* 2–4 machine guns, 2000lb (900kg) of bombs; *speed* 228mph (367kph).

Vickers Light Tanks (UK)

Based on the Horstmann coil spring suspension. The series began entering service in 1929 and production continued until 1940. Some were supplied to the Government of India and to China but most were retained for training. A number of Marks IIA and III took part in the opening stages of the war in North Africa as well as equipping a South African

Vickers light tank.

battalion during the campaign in Abyssinia. The Mark VIB served in France with the BEF, in North Africa until 1941, and took part in several engagements during the occupation of IRAN. The Mark VIC, in which the Vickers weapons were replaced by 7.92mm and 15mm Besa machine guns, also served in France. By the end of 1940 it was apparent that the series lacked the firepower and protection necessary on a modern battlefield although it remained in service in the United Kingdom until 1942.

Weight	4.25 tons (*Mark IIA*); 4.5 tons (*Mark III*); 5.2 tons (Mark VIB)
Speed	30mph (48kph) (*Marks IIA and III*); 35mph (56kph) (*Mark VIB*)
Armour	10mm (*Mark IIA*); 12mm (*Mark III*); 14mm (*Mark VIB*)
Armament	1 .303-in machine gun (*Mark IIA*); 1 .303-in machine gun or 1 .50-in machine gun (*Mark III*); 1 .303-in machine gun and 1 .50-in machine gun (*Mark VIB*)
Engine	Rolls-Royce 66hp petrol (*Marks IIA and III*); Meadows 88hp petrol (*Mark VIB*)
Crew	2 (*Marks IIA and III*); 3 (*Mark VIB*).

Vickers Machine Gun

The standard medium machine gun of the British and Commonwealth armies, the Vickers, designed in 1912, was an improved Maxim water-cooled, recoil-operated, belt-fed weapon. With a rate of fire of about 600 rounds per minute, it was extremely reliable and capable of continuous fire for extremely long periods.

The British Vickers .303 medium machine gun with steam condenser to recycle cool water during sustained fire.

HMS Victorious.

Victor Emmanuel III, King of Italy (1869–1947)

Under MUSSOLINI's Fascist regime Victor Emmanuel's position was little more than that of a figurehead, and although the King was opposed to Italian involvement in the war his opinion was disregarded. After the Axis defeat in North Africa he became involved in a plot to unseat Mussolini. When the Fascist Grand Council forced the dictator to resign on 25 July 1943, the King ordered his arrest and appointed Marshal Pietro BADOGLIO as Prime Minister. The new administration quickly opened peace negotiations with the Allies and on 1 September 1943 Victor Emmanuel ratified the terms of Italy's surrender. Following the German occupation of northern Italy, the King fled to Brindisi and in June 1944, hoping to preserve his throne, granted his son UMBERTO the powers of Regent. The monarchy, however, had been seriously compromised by its long association with Fascism, and in May 1946 Victor Emmanuel responded to public opinion and abdicated.

Victorious, HMS – Illustrious Class Aircraft Carrier

Served in the Home Fleet 1941–43. In May 1941 she took part in the hunt for the German battleship BISMARCK and in August 1942 provided part of the air cover for the vital PEDESTAL CONVOY to Malta. She was sent to the Pacific in the spring of 1943 in response to the US Navy's request for a British carrier to make good its own losses, but by the time she had become integrated the emergency had passed and she was returned, joining the Eastern Fleet in 1944 and the Pacific Fleet the following year.

Vietinghoff, Col Gen Heinrich von

Vietinghoff commanded the German 10th Army in Italy from 1943 to 1945, earning a reputation as a sound defensive strategist. In September 1943 he recognized that his attempt to drive the Allies into the sea at SALERNO had failed and retreated to the GUSTAV LINE. When Monte CASSINO fell he executed a skilful withdrawal north of ROME and throughout the autumn of 1944 his army conducted a tenacious defence of the eastern sector of the GOTHIC LINE. In February 1945 he briefly commanded Army Group Courland but returned to Italy the following month where he succeeded KESSELRING as commander of Army Group C (Army Group South-West). He wished to meet the Allied spring offensive with a defence based on manoeuvre but was inhibited by HITLER's insistence on holding ground for its own sake. Once his front had been broken, Vietinghoff had no alternative but to conclude a surrender, which he did on 2 May 1945.

Vigorous MALTA relief convoy, June 1942.

Viipuri, Finland, 1939

A Finnish town in 1939, it is now the Soviet Vyborg. In 1939 the Soviet Union demanded a portion of Finland on the Karelian Isthmus, including Viipuri, to extend their cordon sanitaire around LENINGRAD. The Finns refused and the result was the RUSSO-FINNISH CAMPAIGN or "Winter War". In spite of initial Finnish successes, the greater weight of Soviet forces prevailed and the Finns lost the disputed territory, which has remained part of the USSR ever since.

Vilna, Baltic, 1939–44

The capital of LITHUANIA in 1939, Vilna was absorbed into the Soviet Union in 1940 with the rest of the Baltic States. It was captured by the German Army on 24 June 1941 during the initial stages of Operation BARBAROSSA and remained in German hands until retaken by Soviet forces on 13 July 1944.

Visayan Islands, Pacific, 1941–45

The general term for the central group of Philippine Islands, between Luzon and Mindanao, i.e. Panay, Samar, Negros, Cebu and LEYTE, the water between them being known as the Visayan Sea. During the Japanese invasion in 1941 this area was the responsibility of the "Visayan–Mindanao Force" – three infantry divisions under General Sharp. This force was effectively abandoned when MACARTHUR retreated into BATAAN, and was easily mopped up by the Japanese. In the US clearance of the Philippines in 1945 this area was the responsibility of the US 8th Army, under General EICHELBERGER; the principal Japanese opposition was on Cebu Island, the others being cleared with less fighting.

Vishinsky, Andrey (1885–1955)

Vishinsky was a dedicated Stalinist who acted as public prosecutor during the treason trials of the 1930's. He served as MOLOTOV's Deputy Minister for Foreign Affairs from 1940 to 1949. He was the Soviet representative on the Allied Mediterranean Commission and attended the YALTA Conference in 1945. During the WARSAW uprising he acted as STALIN's spokesman, denying the use of Soviet air bases to the Western Allies, thereby preventing them from assisting the POLISH HOME ARMY in its tragic struggle. In February 1945 he bullied King MICHAEL of Romania into replacing his coalition government with a Communist regime.

Visol

German rocket fuel based on vinylethylether used in the Wasserfall missile.

Vistula River

A river of central Europe, almost all of which is in Poland. It rises in the Carpathian mountains and flows north to enter the Baltic at DANZIG (Gdansk). It forms a natural obstacle to east–west movement, and in July 1944 the German Army organized the "Vistula Line" to attempt to hold the Soviet advance. In the hopes of weakening the German line in the WARSAW area and accelerating the Soviet arrival in the city, the resistance forces within Warsaw rose in rebellion. The Soviets, apparently happy to see their future political enemies destroyed, rested on the Vistula and thus allowed the Germans to suppress the rising.

Vitebsk, Soviet Union, 1941 and 1944

A city on the OREL–Riga railway line, northwest of SMOLENSK. In the opening phase of Operation BARBAROSSA it was captured by III Panzer Group on 9 July 1941, together with some 290,000 Soviet prisoners, 2500 tanks and 1500 guns. In 1943 it became the objective of a Soviet encirclement, and by 31 December was isolated from the rest of the German forces. It was left in a state of siege until June 1944, when the Russian summer offensive opened with a drive to eliminate the "Vitebsk pocket". The city fell to the Soviet Army on 26 June 1944, 80,000 German troops being taken prisoner.

Vlasov, Lt Gen Andrey (1900–46)

Vlasov served as a Soviet military adviser to CHIANG KAI-SHEK, 1938–39. During Operation BARBAROSSA he commanded the IV Mechanized Corps and managed to fight his way out of the KIEV pocket. He was then appointed commander of the 20th Army, which he led during the defence of MOSCOW. Sent to the CRIMEA in command of the Second Shock Army, he was captured near SEVASTOPOL in May 1942. Intelligent, capable and ambitious, Vlasov had already attracted the unfavourable attention of BERIA, Head of the NKVD, and his loyalty to STALIN had become suspect. For his part he maintained that he had deliberately been left to his fate, and he soon began to make anti-Stalinist propaganda broadcasts on behalf of the Germans. In November 1944 he was permitted to form a Russian Liberation Army, sometimes referred

General Andrey Vlasov with a recruit at the ROA training base near Berlin.

to as the VLASOV ARMY. Vlasov was captured by the Soviets in May 1945 and executed for treason the following year.

Vlasov Army

Raised in Germany during the autumn of 1944 by General Andrey VLASOV to fight against the Soviets. The army, which was recruited from Russian prisoners-of-war and forced labour, eventually numbered 50,000 and consisted of two divisions. It was posted to the Czechoslovakian sector of the Eastern Front in April 1945 but proved unreliable. By now it was clear that Germany had lost the war and in May, Vlasov, hoping to redeem himself with his former Soviet masters, sent his 1st Division to assist the rising staged by the Czech Resistance in Prague. The latter, however, refused to accept his help on the orders of the government-in-exile in London. Most of the 2nd Division fell into Soviet hands shortly afterwards and although the 1st Division managed to surrender to the Americans it too was turned over to the Soviet Army. Vlasov and his senior officers are known to have been hanged and it is probable that most of his men were also executed.

Vlone, Albania, 1941

Vlone (now called Vlore) was a seaport on the Adriatic. In 1941 it became the objective of a Greek attack against the Italian Army in an endeavour either to destroy the Italians or force them to evacuate through the port, so that the Greek strength could then be turned against the (then) possible threat of German intervention from the direction of Macedonia. Aided by RAF bombing, the Greek forces made a two-pronged advance against Vlone in January 1941 with considerable initial success, but deteriorating weather conditions, together with the arrival of Italian reinforcements intended for their spring offensive, caused the operation to be abandoned.

Volksgewehr

A semi-automatic rifle developed in Germany in 1944–45, intended for the arming of the Volkssturm local defence organization. Designed by Gustloff-Werke of Suhl, it used a gas-delayed blowback system of operation and fired the short 7.92mm M43 cartridge. Few were made, since the development was barely completed before the war ended.

Volkssturm

The German equivalent of the British HOME GUARD, established on 25 September 1944 under the direct control of the Nazi Party. All males between the ages of 16 and 60 who were not in the armed services but capable of bearing arms were liable for service in the Volkssturm. Although organized and trained on military lines, the political nature of its leadership and the general shortage of arms severely limited its military effectiveness. At the end of January 1945 HITLER ordered that, whenever it was possible, Volkssturm units were to be combined with regular troops into mixed battle groups under a unified command.

Volturno River, Italy

Rising in the Apennine mountains, the Volturno winds its way to the sea north of NAPLES. On its final 30-mile (50-km) stretch to the sea it runs due east. It was the first major river obstacle encountered by the Allies as they advanced northwards from Naples in October 1943. General CLARK ordered the British X Corps to make the crossing close to the sea, but here the river was over 100 yards (91m) wide, fast-flowing, edged with mud and well strewn with mines. A crossing was made with great difficulty and a bridge thrown across, but it led to muddy terrain unsuitable for tanks. Clark then ordered the US 3rd Division to make a crossing higher up, where

the going was easier and the terrain more suitable for armour. This was quickly achieved, but delays in concentrating the necessary forces on the far side of the river allowed the German defenders to retire in good order and prepare a new defensive line.

Von Roeder Class Destroyers (Ger)

Displacement 2400 tons; *dimensions* 384ft×38ft 6in (115.2×11.4m); mean draught 9ft 6in (2.88m); *machinery* 2-shaft geared turbines producing shp 70,000; *speed* 38 knots; *armament* 5×5in (5×1); 6×37mm AA (2×2 and 2×1); 12×20m AA (5×2 and 2×1); 8×21in torpedo tubes (2×4); equipped for minelaying; *complement* 313; *number in class* 6, launched 1938–39.

Voronov, Marshal Nikolai N. (1899–1968)

Voronov was the Soviet Army's leading artillery expert and was a member of Stavka throughout the war. During the Winter War against Finland he breached the MANNERHEIM LINE with the fire of his guns and in 1941 controlled the artillery on the LENINGRAD sector. Together with ZHUKOV and VASILEVSKY he planned Operation URANUS, the encirclement of the German 6th Army at STALINGRAD in November 1942, which involved the concentrated fire of 13,500 guns and mortars. He was also responsible for the mass deployment of artillery and anti-aircraft weapons within the KURSK salient in 1943. Under Voronov's direction Soviet operations during the last two years of the war continued to enjoy the benefit of massive artillery preparation. In January 1945, for example, the 1st Belorussian and 1st Ukrainian Fronts together deployed a total of over 32,000 guns and mortars for their

offensive on the Lower Vistula, the majority grouped in artillery divisions and the whole controlled by an artillery general.

Voroshilov, Marshal Klimenti E. (1881–1969)

Voroshilov was an old Civil War comrade of STALIN. In 1934 he was appointed Commissar for Defence and was responsible for re-equipping the Soviet Army. By 1940, however, his influence had begun to wane and in May he was replaced by TIMOSHENKO and given the less demanding post of Deputy Chairman of the Defence Committee. When Germany invaded the Soviet Union he joined the five-man Committee for the Defence of the State. He was also given command of the North-West Front, but was unable to halt the German advance on LENINGRAD and was replaced by ZHUKOV. None the less, as a member of the Bolshevik Old Guard whose loyalty was beyond question he was not disgraced, although for the remainder of the war he held only staff and high-level liaison appointments. He attended the Teheran Conference in November 1943 and in 1945 accepted the Hungarian surrender on behalf of the Allies.

Vought Aircraft (USA)

Vought 4FU Corsair This inverted gull-wing monoplane was the first US combat aircraft to exceed 400mph (644kph). Although designed as a carrier-based fighter, the Corsair was initially rejected by the US Navy, since its big nose restricted visibility and its undercarriage tended to cause the aircraft to bounce on touchdown. It first saw combat with the US Marine Corps in the SOLOMON ISLANDS in February 1943, where it rapidly established its superiority over its Japanese opponents. In

Vought F4-U Corsair, an outstanding naval fighter aircraft.

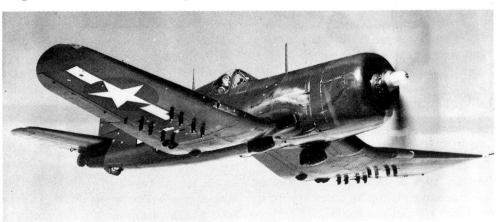

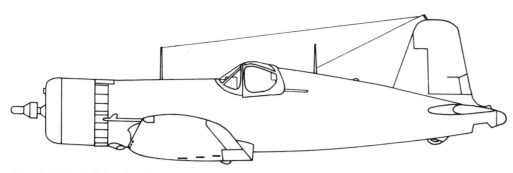

Vought F4U-1A fighter bomber.

early 1944 the US Navy began operating the Corsair as a carrier-based night fighter, but it was not until January 1945 that carrier-based Corsairs flew by day. The immensely powerful Corsair accounted for 2140 enemy aircraft with a kill ratio of 11:1. It was also a formidable dive-bomber, being first used in this role by the Marines in March 1944. It remained in production until December 1952. *Span* 41ft (12.5m); *engine* 1 2450hp radial; *armament* 4 20mm cannon or 6 .50 machine guns, 2000lb (900kg) of bombs or 8 rockets; *speed* 425–446mph (684–718kph) depending on model.

Vought OS2U This reconnaissance and light dive-bombing aircraft was produced in both floatplane and wheeled versions, and was the US Navy's first catapult-launched monoplane. Entering service in 1940, it was employed also on coastal patrols and air-sea rescue work, principally in the Pacific. A number were used by the Royal Navy as the Kingfisher. *Span* 36ft (11m); *engine* 1 450hp radial; *crew* 2; *armament* 3 machine guns, 220lb (100kg) of bombs; *speed* 170mph (273kph).

Vought SB2U Vindicator This was Vought's first monoplane and went into US Navy service in 1937 for service as naval scouts and dive-bombers, shortly afterwards being adopted by the US Marine Corps. In 1938 the French government ordered a number, most of which were either destroyed or captured by the Germans in 1940. The last fifty to be

built went to the Royal Navy in 1941 as trainers, where they were known as the Chesapeake. US Marine Corps Vindicators saw brief, and courageous, action in the Battle of MIDWAY. *Span* 42ft (12.8m); *engine* 1 750hp radial; *crew* 3; *armament* 3 machine guns, 550lb (250kg) of bombs; *speed* 243mph (391kph).

VP Vulnerable point (UK). Any location which was an especially attractive target for attack, either directly or from the air. VP status warranted special guarding and air defence measures.

Vulcan

Final Allied offensive in TUNISIA, April–May 1943.

Vultee Aircraft (USA)

Vultee A-35 Vengeance Designed in 1940 to meet a British specification, the Vengeance was a two-seat dive-bomber, but by the time it entered service was already considered of outdated concept. Most of them were eventually put to use in the Far East where local air superiority allowed them to function in the dive-bombing role in Burma with the RAF and New Guinea with the RAAF. The type was also adopted by the USAAF, but was employed only as an operational trainer and on miscellaneous support duties. *Span* 48ft (14.65m);

engine 1 1600hp radial; *crew* 2; *armament* 6 .50in machine guns, 2000lb (900kg) of bombs; *speed* 275mph (442kph).

Vultee BT-13 Valiant Entering service in 1940 this monoplane became the standard American primary training aircraft throughout the war, over 11,000 being built. *Span* 42ft (12.8m); *engine* 1 450hp radial; *speed* 156mph (251kph).

Vultee BT-13 Valiant Entering service in 1940 this monoplane became the standard American primary training aircraft throughout the war, over 11,000 being built. *Span* 42ft (12.8m); *engine* 1 450hp radial; *speed* 156mph (251kph).

Vultee-Stinson L-1 Vigilant Designed and first built by the Stinson Aircraft Company, who were taken over by Consolidated Vultee, (15.55m); *engine* 1 295hp radial; *speed* 122mph (196kph).

V-Weapons

Group name for three weapons developed in Germany, and called "Vergeltungswaffen" (vengeance weapons) by Hitler. The V-1 was the FZG-76 flying bomb; the V-2 was the A-4 guided rocket; and the V-3 was the HOCH-DRUCKPUMPE multiple-chambered gun.

Vyazma–Bryansk, Battle of, 1941

Vyazma is a town on the rail line between SMOLENSK and MOSCOW; the town of Bryansk lies about 140 miles (275km) due south. In 1941 the Red Army occupied a line of defensive positions between the two known as the Vyazma–Bryansk Defence Line. This was breached with relative ease by IV Panzer Group during the second phase of the advance on Moscow in September–October 1941. The subsequent encirclement of pockets close to both towns led to the capture of 633,000 Russian prisoners, 1240 tanks and 5200 guns, plus huge quantities of other equipment.

W

"W" and "Z" Class Destroyers (UK)

Displacement 1710 tons; *dimensions* 362ft 9in×35ft 9in (110.5×10.9m); mean draught 10ft (3m); *machinery* 2-shaft geared turbines producing shp 40,000; *speed* 36.75 knots; *armament* 4×4.7in ("W" Class) or 4.5in DP ("Z" Class) (4×1); 2×40mm AA (1×2) and 8×20mm (4×2) AA or 4×40mm AA (1×2 and 2×1); 4×20mm AA (2×2) or 6×40mm AA (1×2 and 4×1) guns; 8×21in (2×4) torpedo tubes; *complement* 186; *number in class* 16, launched 1943–44.

WAAC Women's Auxiliary Army Corps (US).

WAAF Women's Auxiliary Air Force (UK).

Wacht am Rhein (Watch on the Rhine)

German counteroffensive in the ARDENNES, December 1944.

Wachtel, Col Max

Wachtel was commander of the German 155th Flakregiment, which was formed to launch the V-1 "Flying Bomb" offensive against the United Kingdom from sites on the French and Belgian coasts. The first V-1 was launched on 13 June 1944 and by early July Wachtel's crews were launching an average of 120 missiles per day despite an Allied bombing offensive directed specifically against their sites.

Waco Aircraft (USA)

Waco CG-4A glider The only US glider to see combat service, this was produced by several factories and over 12,000 were built in two

years. The entire nose could be hinged upwards for loading wheeled vehicles or weapons, and it could carry 15 fully-equipped troops or 3750lb (1700kg) of cargo. It was first used in the invasion of SICILY and later for the NORMANDY landings. *Span* 83.6ft (25.5m); *gliding speed* 65mph (105kph).

Waco CG-13A glider This was simply a scaled-up version of the CG-4A, capable of carrying up to 40 troops or five tonnes of equipment. Relatively few were built, and they were only used for training. *Span* 85.5ft (26m); *gliding speed* 95mph (153kph).

Wadi Akarit, Tunisia, 1943

A dry river bed running inland from the Mediterranean coast about 15 miles (24km) north of Gabes. It was selected as a defensive position by ROMMEL after he had been manoeuvred out of the MARETH LINE in March 1943. Rommel's line diverged from the Wadi to take in the hills of the Djebel Roumana, ending in a tangle of hills around the Djebel Tebaga, and was strengthened by anti-tank ditches and minefields. The position was attacked on the night of 6/7 April 1943 by the British 50th and 51st and 4th Indian divisions with massive artillery support, and a five-mile (8km) gap was punched through the German position. A "Corps of Exploitation" consisting of two armoured divisions and an infantry division with attached armoured brigade, formed for this eventuality, was now fed through this gap but on encountering sporadic German anti-tank fire in the vicinity of the forward British infantry position, came to a dead halt. No satisfactory explanation of

this failure to advance has ever been discovered, but it allowed the German forces to escape deeper into Tunisia and set up another checking position.

Waffen SS

The Waffen (Armed) SS was the militarized arm of HIMMLER's SS. Its first militarized unit, the LEIBSTANDARTE SS Adolf Hitler, a guard company of 120 men, was formed in March 1933. By late 1944 the Waffen SS order of battle numbered 38 divisions, some 600,000 men. Himmler saw it as the natural historical successor to the Order of Teutonic Knights, combining what he believed to be traditional German and Aryan virtues in a brotherhood which was fiercely loyal to the Nazi Party. The Waffen SS contributed motorized infantry formations to the 1939 campaign in Poland and the 1940 campaign in the West, and thereafter grew rapidly. By June 1941 it contained 150,000 men disposed among five divisions, one infantry and four motorized infantry. Many of its recruits were former SA thugs or concentration camp guards, but others were genuine if misguided idealists and some transferred from the Army in the hope of enhanced promotion prospects; initially, the highest physical standards were demanded but this requirement was relaxed as the war progressed. When the supply of pure German recruits dwindled, Himmler began recruiting SS formations from Scandinavian and Dutch volunteers, but in due course abandoned his pure Nordic ideals and enlisted anyone willing to serve. This resulted in the formation of Yugoslav Muslim, Ukrainian, Latvian, Estonian, Albanian Muslim, Hungarian, Belgian, Italian and French SS Divisions; two Russian divisions were also formed but these were transferred to the VLASOV ARMY in 1944. The majority of non-German Waffen SS divisions were formed in 1944–45 and rarely exceeded battle groups in regimental strength. By the end of 1944 the Waffen SS had set up its own higher military organization. Individual divisions had formed corps, and

WACO CG-13A gliders, capable of carrying four tons of cargo.

Waffen SS troops near Demjansk, Eastern Front.

some of these had also been formed into 6th Panzer Army, which fought in the ARDENNES offensive and in Operation FRÜHLING-SERWACHEN in March 1945.

WAFS Women's Auxiliary Ferry Squadron (US).

Wainwright, Lt Gen Jonathan (1883–1953)

Wainwright graduated from West Point in 1906. He saw active service against Filipino insurgents in 1909–10 and served as a staff officer with the American Expeditionary Force in France during World War I. He was posted to the PHILIPPINES again in 1940 and the following year MACARTHUR appointed him commander of the North Luzon Force, consisting of four infantry divisions, a cavalry regiment and supporting artillery. When the Japanese invaded in December 1941, Wainwright retreated into the BATAAN PENINSULA where, despite the enemy's total air superiority, he held out until April 1942. He then retired to the island fortress of CORREGIDOR, which was subjected to continuous bombardment for the next month. On 5 May the Japanese landed on Corregidor. Wainwright failed to dislodge them, bowed to the inevitable and agreed to a general surrender. He took part in the subsequent BATAAN Death March and was then transported to Manchuria where he remained a prisoner for the rest of the war. He was present aboard the USS *Missouri* to witness the final Japanese surrender on 2 September 1945.

Wakatake Class Destroyers (Jap)

Displacement 820 tons; *dimensions* 275ft × 26ft 6in (83.8 × 8.07m); mean draught 8ft 3in (2.5m); *machinery* 2-shaft geared turbines producing shp 21,500; *speed* 35.5 knots; *armament* 3 × 4.7in (3 × 1); 2 × 7.7mm; 4 × 21in torpedo tubes (2 × 2); *complement* 110; *number in class* 6, launched 1922–23.

Wake Island, Defence of, 1941

In December 1941 the tiny atoll of Wake, lying 2000 miles (3220km) west of the Hawaiian Islands, was held by 525 US Marines under the overall command of Commander W. S. Cunningham. The garrison's twelve-strong Grumman Wildcat squadron was commanded by Major Paul A. Putnam and the ground troops by Major James P. S. Devereux. Wake Island was the objective of a Japanese task force based at KWAJALEIN and commanded by Rear-Admiral Kajioka. On 8 December the first Japanese air attack destroyed seven of the Wildcats, but thereafter the four remaining airworthy American aircraft and the anti-aircraft defence began to inflict a rising toll on the attackers. Kajioka's task force, consisting of two light cruisers, four destroyers and four transports, arrived off Wake on 11 December and subjected the island to a blanket bombardment before closing in for the assault. Devereux withheld the fire of his 5-inch batteries until the enemy ships were well within range, with devastating results. Kajioka's flagship, the cruiser *Yubari*, was hit several times on the waterline and was forced to turn away, trailing steam and smoke. The destroyer

Hyate was hit amidships and was torn apart by an internal explosion – the first Japanese warship to be destroyed in World War II. After a transport had been set ablaze and hits scored on his remaining ships, Kajioka aborted his mission and withdrew, pursued by the four Wildcats, one of which landed a bomb on the stern of the destroyer *Kisargi*, which disintegrated when her depth charges exploded. The epic defence of Wake Island provided a much-needed boost for American morale in the aftermath of PEARL HARBOR. In particular, a message from Cunningham requesting supplies and reinforcements was fortuitously corrupted in transmission to "send more ... Japs ..." and in this form caught the public imagination as symbolic of the garrison's determination to resist. The Japanese, however, were not prepared to risk a second failure and when Kajioka attacked again on 23 December he did so with additional cruisers and destroyers, plus the support of two fleet carriers, while two old destroyers were rammed onto the beach with the main landing force, regardless of cost. The American defences were swamped and Cunningham was at last forced to surrender; ironically a relief force which included the carrier SARATOGA had reached a point less than 500 miles (800km) distant. The defence of Wake Island cost Japan two modern warships, 21 aircraft and 1175 casualties, including 820 killed; 120 Americans were killed.

Walcheren, 1944

Island in the SCHELDT ESTUARY, approximately rectangular and about 12 miles by 9 (19 × 14km). Most of it is below sea level, but around three sides are sand dunes up to 100ft (30m) high, connecting with an area in the eastern corner where a causeway from South Beveland reaches the island. The Germans had built powerful coast defence batteries in concrete emplacements, covering the approaches to the Scheldt, and the coast was strongly sown with wire and mines and protected by machine gun posts. In order to isolate the gun positions and immobilize the German defensive forces, the RAF bombed the area of Westkapelle, on the eastern tip, breached the dunes and allowed the sea to flood the island. The RAF also dropped about 9000 tons (9,150 tonnes) of bombs on the German batteries and flew some 250 fighter-bomber sorties, though without doing much damage. A landing was then made by British

Commando forces, securing a beach-head at Flushing into which a second wave of British infantry and mountain artillery was landed. A further landing, with heavy naval gunfire support, was then made by more Commandos at Westkapelle, followed by tanks and amphibious Buffaloes and the 4th Special Service Brigade. After a six-day struggle against ferocious defence and natural obstacles, the island was secured on 8 November 1944.

Walker, Capt Frederick John, RN (1896–1944)

Walker served throughout World War I in small ships. During the interwar years he specialized in anti-submarine warfare. In January 1940 he was appointed Staff Officer Operations to Admiral RAMSAY at Dover and was mentioned in despatches for his part in organizing the DUNKIRK EVACUATION. In October 1941 he took command of the sloop HMS *Stork* as Senior Officer of the 36th Escort Group, which he trained in the anti-submarine tactics which he had devised, based on close co-operation between escorts and relentless pursuit to destruction once a contact had been obtained. Walker's methods began to produce results at once, for when a nine-strong U-boat wolf-pack attacked Convoy HG-76 that December, sinking the escort carrier HMS AUDACITY, one escort and two merchantmen, his group accounted for no less than five of the enemy submarines. His success led to his promotion to Captain, and in mid-1942 he became commander of the Western Approaches escort base at Liverpool. He was appointed Senior Officer of the 2nd Support Group on its formation in April 1943, personally commanding the sloop HMS *Starling*, and created a formidable hunter-killer unit which, in two years, destroyed 23 enemy submarines, including six between 31 January and 19 February 1944. Walker died in June 1944 from a stroke brought on by overwork; he was accorded a public funeral at Liverpool Cathedral.

Walkie-Talkie

American term coined to describe portable radio transmitter-receiver equipment.

Wallbuster Shell

A projectile developed in Britain by Commander Sir Dennistoun Burney for use in recoilless guns. It consisted of a thin-walled body, a

Royal Marine commandos land on beach-head, Scheldt Estuary, November 1944.

plastic explosive filling and a base fuze. On striking a hard target the body split open and the explosive was plastered on to the target surface, after which it was detonated by the fuze. The effect was to drive a shock wave into the target which detached large pieces of material from the inner surface. Originally devised to attack fortifications, it was later adapted as a method of attacking tanks.

Wallis, Sir Barnes

Wallis served in the Royal Naval Air Service during World War I before returning to the Vickers organization, in which he was employed as a designer. An aeronautical engineer, he designed the R100 airship in the 1920s and invented the geodetic fuselage employed on the VICKERS WELLESLEY and WELLINGTON bombers. He also developed the BOUNCING BOMB, which destroyed the MÖHNE, EDER and SORPE DAMS on 16 May 1943, and the "Grand Slam" and "Tall Boy" bombs, the last being used to sink the TIRPITZ on 12 November 1944.

Walter Turbine – Submarine Propulsion Unit (Ger)

Developed by Professor Helmuth Walter in response to the urgent need for submerged U-boats to outpace Allied escorts and take rapid evasive action. The system employed hydrogen peroxide rather than air for combustion and was expected to produce submerged speeds of 25 knots. One prototype submarine was built and later broken up, and none of the Walter-equipped Type XVII coastal or Type XVIII ocean-going boats had reached operational status when the war ended. The Walter system caused high fuel

consumption, but pioneered the concept of the continuously submerged patrol.

Walther P38

The standard service pistol of the German armed forces. The Pistole '38, named after its date of formal adoption, was of 9mm calibre and had an unusual double-action trigger mechanism which allowed it to be carried safely with a round in the chamber and fired by simply pulling the trigger; other automatic pistols of the time required the pistol to be manually cocked before it was possible to fire.

Wanklyn, Lt Cdr M. D., RN

Highest-scoring British submarine commander of World War II. In August 1940 Wanklyn was appointed commander of the "U" CLASS submarine *Upholder* while she was fitting out. In December 1940 she left England for the Mediterranean, joining the 10th Submarine Flotilla at MALTA on 12 January 1941. Altogether *Upholder* made 21 patrols during which she sank or damaged 23 vessels totalling 133,940 tons, including the cruiser *Garibaldi*, the destroyer *Libeccio* and the submarines *Almiraglio Bon* and *Tricheco*. Wanklyn was awarded the Victoria Cross for a difficult attack on the heavily escorted 18,000-ton liner *Conte Rosso* on 24 May 1941; the liner, which was transporting troops to North Africa, was struck by two torpedoes and sank with the loss of 2300 lives. The fate of *Upholder* remains uncertain but the most probable cause of her loss with all hands was a depth charge attack delivered by the Italian destroyer escort *Pegaso* to the north-east of Tripoli on 14 April 1942, during which she sustained damage which prevented her from surfacing.

Warlimont, Gen Walter (1894–   )

Warlimont saw active service in World War I and with the German contingent in the Spanish Civil War. In September 1939 he was appointed Deputy Chief of Operations Staff at OKW and held this post until September 1944, when he was sent on sick leave because of injuries sustained in the JULY BOMB PLOT against HITLER. His book *Inside Hitler's Headquarters 1939–45* provides interesting insights into the conduct of the war at the highest level.

Warsaw, 1943–44

The capital city of POLAND and the scene of two notable uprisings, the first between 19 April and 16 May 1943 by the Jews of the Warsaw Ghetto. This had been established in the autumn of 1940, encompassing an area some 2.5 square miles (6.5 square km) east of the VISTULA River, sealed off by a wall and barbed wire. Some 433,000 Jews were incarcerated in the ghetto, and in July 1942 shipments to the gas chambers of TREBLINKA began. On 19 April 1943 the SS were sent into the ghetto with orders to clear out the remaining inhabitants and destroy the buildings. They were met with small-arms fire and grenade attacks and were engaged in a running battle with small detachments of armed Jews. The Jews knew that resistance was futile, but chose to die in battle with the SS rather than to submit quietly to the gas chambers. Resistance finally ended on 16 May when the main synagogue was blown up. Some Jews managed to escape by the sewers and joined the Polish underground. Some 56,000 had been killed or "resettled" during the operation, about 7000 killed in combat, another 7–8000 sent to Treblinka, and an estimated 5–6000 were buried under the rubble. The ghetto was almost completely destroyed. In August 1944 the Germans began withdrawing from Warsaw, threatened by the approach of the Soviet Army. On 21 July HITLER ordered General GUDERIAN to take command of the Eastern Front, and under his reorganization German troops moved back into Warsaw to establish a defensive line along the Vistula. Under General BOR KOMOROWSKI the POLISH HOME ARMY, with authorization from the Polish Government-in-Exile in London, rose in rebellion with the aim of engaging the German troops and making entry easier for the Soviet Army. For some time Soviet radio stations had been making Polish language broadcasts calling for an uprising. About 48,000 men and women of the Home Army answered the call and street fighting began on 1 August 1944. On the following day the Russian attacks against the Vistula stopped and no Russian aircraft appeared over Warsaw. Freed of pressure from the Soviet Army, the Germans were able to concentrate on suppressing the rebellion, but bitter fighting continued until October. In spite of appeals for aid, Russia provided no assistance, and although British and US aircraft were willing to make an overflight to drop arms and supplies, they were denied landing facilities in Russian territory. Some supplies were flown in by British aircraft operating from Italy, but of the 186 flights made, only 83 were successful and 33 aircraft were lost. Britain threatened to stop the Arctic Convoy supply route unless the Soviets aided Warsaw, and on 10 September the overflight of Western aircraft was agreed. Home Army detachments from outside Warsaw which attempted to go to the aid of their companions in the city were surrounded and disarmed by Soviet troops. Eventually, Bor Komorowski realized that further fighting was hopeless, and he surrendered to the Germans on 2 October.

Warspite, HMS – Queen Elizabeth Class Battleship

A veteran of Jutland, *Warspite* served with the Home Fleet 1939–40 and took part in the Second Battle of NARVIK. She then served as Admiral CUNNINGHAM's flagship in the Mediterranean, and during the ACTION OFF CALABRIA on 9 July 1940 she scored a hit on the Italian battleship *Giulio Cesare* at the unprecedented range of 26,000 yards (23,775m). She fought at the Battle of CAPE MATAPAN and was damaged by air attack during the evacuation of CRETE. After being repaired in the United States she joined the Eastern Fleet in 1942 but returned to the Mediterranean the following year. Lying off SALERNO, she broke up German counter-attacks on the beach-head with her gunfire, but was very seriously damaged by a glide bomb. Patched up, she formed part of the bombardment force during the Allied landings in NORMANDY. She sustained mine damage shortly later, but took part in the bombardment of the German garrisons of BREST, LE HAVRE and WALCHEREN.

Washington, USS – North Carolina Class Battleship

Served with the British Home Fleet for a period in 1942 before being transferred to the Pacific. She sank the Japanese KONGO CLASS battleship *Kirishima* during the Second Battle of GUADALCANAL and saw further action at the GILBERT ISLANDS, KWAJALEIN, SAIPAN, the MARIANAS, Palau, SURIGAO STRAIT, IWO JIMA and OKINAWA.

WASP Women's Air Force Service Pilot (US).

Trade in old clothes goes on in the ghetto, Warsaw.

Wasp Flamethrower

Designed by R. P. Fraser of the Lagonda organization and successfully tested in July 1942. The equipment was mounted on a UNIVERSAL CARRIER with the flame projector in the gunner's compartment. Wasp Carriers were issued on the scale of six per infantry battalion and were used operationally in North-West Europe and Italy from August 1944 onwards. A concentration of 127 Wasps played a major part in the crossing of the SENIO in April 1945.

Wasp, USS – Aircraft Carrier

Wasp (CV.7) served in the Atlantic during 1941 and in the spring of 1942 ferried fighter reinforcements to the beleaguered island of MALTA, earning the personal commendation of Winston CHURCHILL. She was then transferred to the Pacific but was torpedoed and sunk by the Japanese submarine *I-19* south of GUADALCANAL on 15 September 1942. Her name, however, was subsequently conferred on the ESSEX CLASS carrier *Oriskany*, which was launched on 17 August 1943. The new *Wasp* (CV.18) saw active service off NEW GUINEA, the MARIANAS, PALAU, LEYTE and IWO JIMA. *Displacement* 14,700 tons; *dimensions* 741ft 3in × 80ft 9in (226 × 25m); mean draught 20ft (6m); *machinery* 2-shaft geared turbines producing shp 75,000; *speed* 29.5 knots; *armament* 8 × 5in (8 × 1); *aircraft* 84; *complement* 1800; *launched* 1939.

Wasseresel

(Water Donkey.) A dummy U-boat conning tower packed with explosive and mounted on a float. This could be placed in the water by a U-boat and then towed by the boat on a long line in order to distract hunters from the real boat and tempt them to ram the dummy and so blow themselves up. It was highly unpopular with U-boat captains, since towing such a mass made their boats difficult to manoeuvre. There is no record of any Allied warship being taken in by the device.

Wasserfall

A radio-controlled supersonic guided anti-aircraft missile, basically a smaller version of the A-4 rocket. It was intended to destroy aircraft at altitudes up to 65,000ft (20,000m), at speeds up to 550mph (900kph) and at ranges up to 50 miles (80km) from launch point. It was proposed to deploy over 200 batteries to defend Germany, with a production rate of 5000 per month. Work began at PEENEMUNDE in 1942, and the first successful firing took place in February 1944. Development was stopped in February 1945, though some work took place afterwards and some development missiles may have been fired against Allied aircraft, though there is no confirmation of this. Wasserfall weighed 7800lbs (3540kg) at launch, was about 26ft (7.92m) long and carried a warhead of 675lbs (305kg) of explosive.

Watchtower

American landings on SANTA CRUZ ISLANDS, TULAGI and GUADALCANAL, August 1942.

Watson-Watt, Sir Robert (1892–1974)

Watson-Watt pioneered the use of RADAR and by 1936 had convinced the Air Ministry of its military value with the result that when war broke out in 1939 a chain of radar stations had already been built along the British coast. As the war progressed, he continued to develop fresh applications for radar, notably in the field of anti-aircraft gunnery, night-fighter interception, U-boat detection, navigation and mutual recognition.

Wau, New Guinea, 1943

Village about 30 miles (48km) inland from Salamaua, close to an airfield. In August 1943 the Japanese based in Salamaua decided to move against Wau in order to control the "Bulldog Track", a fair-weather track into the interior. Australian forces under General BLAMEY were flown from MILNE BAY and landed at Wau in late January 1943 in time to put up a defence. Air superiority over the Japanese was neutralized by bad weather, and Japanese infantry managed to get within 50 yards (45m) of the airstrip on 29 January, but on that day the weather cleared and 57 Australian aircraft were able to land, in spite of Japanese fire, providing enough reinforcements to drive off the Japanese attack and force them to retreat towards Salamaua.

Wavell, FM Sir Archibald (1883–1950)

As a subaltern Wavell fought with the Black Watch in the Boer War. After a further period of active service on the North-West Frontier of India he went to France in 1914 and was present at the First and Second Battles of Ypres, losing his left eye at the latter. In 1916 he was appointed Military Attaché to the Grand Duke Nicholas, the commander of the Russian armies in the Caucasus. For the remainder of World War I he served in Palestine under Allenby, whom he greatly admired. His first book, *The Palestine Campaign*, appeared in 1928. After commanding an infantry brigade he was promoted Major-General in 1933 and wrote Volume 2 of *Field Service Regulations* before being appointed commander of the 2nd Infantry Division in 1935. After attending the Soviet Army manoeuvres in 1936 he became GOC Palestine and Transjordan the following year. He was promoted Lieutenant-General in 1938 and appointed GOC Southern Command. His book *Generals and Generalship* was published in 1939 and, significantly, became a favourite of ROMMEL's. The same year he was appointed GOC Middle East with the rank of General, responsible for a vast area stretching from the Syrian frontier to Somaliland. When the Italians invaded Egypt in 1940, Wavell and O'CONNOR, his field commander in the Western Desert, inflicted a serious defeat on them at SIDI BARRANI in December, stormed BARDIA and TOBRUK in January 1941, and destroyed the remains of the Italian army at BEDA FOMM the following month. Wavell next eliminated the Italian presence in East Africa and was then induced by CHURCHILL, with whom he was on poor terms, to divert most of his resources to Greece. The failure there was followed by the loss of CRETE and Rommel's first offensive in North Africa, which recaptured Cyrenaica and placed Tobruk under siege. Wavell mounted two abortive counter-offensives to relieve the embattled fortress,

General Archibald Wavell (right).

but when the second of these failed in June he was relieved by Churchill and posted to India as Commander-in-Chief. Following Japan's entry into the war in December, Wavell was concurrently appointed Allied Supreme Commander American-British-Dutch-Australian Command (ABDA), but was unable to halt the Japanese advance with the limited resources available and resigned in February 1942. In December he initiated a limited counteroffensive in the ARAKAN and was promoted Field-Marshal the following month. However, by March 1943 Japanese counter-attacks had eliminated all the gains which had been made. After this reverse Churchill lost confidence in his abilities as a military commander and in June appointed him Viceroy of India. Wavell was a popular commander who was both liked and respected by his men. The reasons for his defeats more often than not lay beyond his control, and his victory against odds over the Italians in 1940–41 not only restored British self-confidence in the aftermath of DUNKIRK, but also convinced FRANCO that Spain's interests would be best served by maintaining strict neutrality.

WAVES Women Accepted for Volunteer Emergency Service (US). Female component of US Navy.

WD War Department.

Weary Willy

A codeneme used by US Army Air Force to describe "war-weary" bombers which were stripped of most of their equipment, packed with high explosive, fitted with rudimentary automatic pilots, and then flown off by a crew who set a course for some target and then parachuted out before the aircraft left British airspace. It was hoped that the aircraft would fly to the target when a timing device would put it into a dive, thereby turning it into an enormous bomb. A number were flown off but the practice ceased after accidents in which the aircraft exploded in flight, in at least one case before the crew had jumped clear.

Weasel (UK)

Tracked amphibious cargo carrier used by British and Canadian troops during operations in North-West Europe 1944/45. The Weasel weighed 2.5 tons, had a crew of two and its maximum speed was 33mph (53kph) on land and 2.5mph (4kph) afloat.

The "Welbike" folding motor-cycle used by British paratroops.

Wedemeyer, Gen Albert (1897–   )

Wedemeyer held US Army General Staff appointments from 1941 until October 1943 when he became MOUNTBATTEN's Deputy Chief of Staff at South East Asia Command (SEAC) Headquarters. In October 1944, following STILWELL's recall, he was appointed Chief of Staff to CHIANG KAI-SHEK.

Wehrwolf, Ukraine, 1942–43

The codename for HITLER's field headquarters in the Russian Ukraine. It was set up in July 1942 in a wood about 5 miles (8km) north of Vinnitsa, east of the Vinnitsa–Zhitomir road. It was abandoned on 13 March 1943.

Weichs, FM Freiherr Maximilian von (1881–1954)

Weichs commanded the 1st Panzer Division on its formation in 1935. He later commanded the 2nd Army in France, the Balkans and Russia. He was briefly in command of Army Group South during January 1942 before returning to 2nd Army, and in July 1942 was appointed commander of Army Group B in place of BOCK, whose rate of advance HITLER considered unsatisfactory. In the aftermath of STALINGRAD, Weichs spent a period on the senior commanders' reserve but in August 1943 he was appointed Commander-in-Chief South-East, conducting the withdrawal of Army Group F from the southern Balkans in 1944. Dismissed by Hitler in March 1945.

Weiss, Fall (Plan White)

German invasion of POLAND, September 1939.

Welbike

A folding motorcycle developed by the SOE workshops in Welwyn, England, and adopted by the British Parachute Regiment. It had a 98cc petrol engine and small wheels, and the handlebars and seat pillar folded down on to the machine to make a load 4ft 2in (1.29m) long and 15in (38cm) wide weighing 31kg which could be fitted into the standard air-drop container. The wheels were too small and the power insufficient for cross-country use but it was effective enough on tracks and roads.

Welrod

A silenced .22 calibre automatic pistol developed by the British SOE organization for use by clandestine resistance units in Europe. The name was derived from the location of the designing office at Welwyn Garden City in Hertfordshire.

Werewolves

The name given to the planned Nazi resistance movement when the Allies overran Germany in 1945. With the exception of a few isolated incidents involving diehard fanatics, the movement had little public support and quickly collapsed when known Nazi supporters were rounded up.

Wesel, Germany, 1945

A German town on the east bank of the river RHINE. It was selected by MONTGOMERY as the focus of 21st Army Group's Rhine crossing because of the surrounding network of roads which fanned out into Germany and thus offered ample routes for his armies. On the night of 23 March 1945 the British 1st Commando Brigade crossed the river in small boats some three miles (5km) from Wesel, waiting until 201 RAF bombers raided the town, then moved in to deal with the defenders. The defenders were very active and it was not until late on the 24th that Wesel could be considered secure. Meanwhile other units, under heavy artillery barrages, had crossed the river above and below Wesel, and on the morning of 24 March 21,600 airborne troops were dropped or glider-landed northwest of Wesel and soon linked up with the forces which had crossed the river.

Weserübung (Exercise Weser)

German invasion of Norway and Denmark, April 1940.

Wespe

A German "Identification Friend or Foe" (IFF) equipment to be fitted into aircraft. When interrogated by a ground air defence RADAR, Wespe would automatically transmit a signal which modified the image seen on the radar's cathode ray tube so as to positively identify that "blip" as being a friendly machine.

Wespe (Wasp) – Self-Propelled 105mm Howitzer (Ger)

Based on the PANZERKAMPFWAGEN II chassis with a 105mm L/28 howitzer mounted in an open-topped fighting compartment at the rear of the vehicle. The Wespe entered service with the light batteries of the Panzer division's artillery regiment in 1942, weaponless versions serving as supplementary ammunition carriers. The vehicle was built by the Famo organization until 1944, when the plant was overrun by the Soviet Army after 683 had been produced. Similar conversions were based on captured French chassis.

Western Desert Force

Collective title of British and Commonwealth formations which fought against the Italians in the Western Desert, June–December 1940. On 1 January 1941 Western Desert Force was redesignated XIII Corps.

Westland Aircraft (UK)

Westland Lysander Perhaps the most readily identifiable aircraft of the war, the high-wing Lysander, with its fixed undercarriage, was designed as an army co-operation machine, for liaison and artillery spotting duties. First delivered in 1938, few, in fact, ever worked with the Army since their role had already been overtaken by events. Instead the RAF found several other roles for these aircraft. They were used as bombers, supply droppers, air/sea rescue aircraft, and particularly for delivering and collecting clandestine agents to and from occupied Europe. *Span* 50ft (15.25m); *engine* 1 890hp radial; *crew* 2; *armament* 4 machine guns, 500lb (225kg) of bombs; *speed* 229mph (368kph).

Westland Whirlwind Designed as a twin-engined escort fighter, the Whirlwind was a failure largely because it was designed around the Rolls-Royce Peregrine engine, which gave a great deal of trouble and consequently never achieved large production. Another problem was its high landing speed, which prevented its use on grass airstrips. Entering service in 1940 it served with moderate success as an escort fighter, with better results as a ground attack machine. Built only in small numbers, few were left in 1943 when it was replaced in service by other types. *Span* 45ft (13.7m); *engines* 2 885hp in-line; *armament* 4 20mm cannons, 1000lb (450kg) of bombs; *speed* 360mph (579kph).

West Virginia, USS – Maryland Class Battleship

Torpedoed and sunk during the attack on PEARL HARBOR, *West Virginia* was raised and repaired, taking part in the actions of LEYTE, SURIGAO STRAIT, Lingayen, IWO JIMA and OKINAWA.

Weygand, General Maxime (1867–1965)

Weygand served as Chief of Staff to Marshal Foch during World War I. He rose to be Commander-in-Chief of the French Army before retiring in 1935. He was recalled from retirement in August 1939 and appointed commander of French forces in Syria and Lebanon. In May 1940 he was summoned urgently to France and, aged 73, succeeded GAMELIN as Supreme Allied Commander. In his long career he had never commanded troops in action, and was unable to halt the German drive to the sea. He managed to construct a new front south of the Somme with the surviv-ing French armies, but when the enemy broke through this in June he urged PÉTAIN to seek an armistice and his advice was accepted. After a brief interlude as Minister of National Defence in Pétain's government, he was appointed Commander-in-Chief of the French forces in North Africa, but in November 1941 was relieved of this post at German insistence because of his anti-Nazi stance. He was arrested during the German occupation of Vichy France the following year and was imprisoned in Germany for the remainder of the war. The taint of 1940 led to his being needlessly tried for treason in 1948, but he was acquitted.

White City, Burma, 1944

The name given to a fortified base used by the CHINDIT force, under General Orde WINGATE, in their second operation. White City was at Henu, in the Railway Valley north of INDAW and close to the Indaw–MYITKYINA railway line, and took its name from the festoons of parachutes hanging from the neighbourhood trees after several resupply drops. After flying in to the Broadway landing strip, the 77th Brigade, under Brigadier Calvert, marched to White City and occupied it on 16 March 1944, driving off Japanese troops in the area after severe fighting. The stronghold was used as a base for ambushes and actions against the railway, was attacked several times by Japanese forces, and, after an airstrip had been made, was evacuated by air on the night of 9 May 1944.

White Scout Car (USA)

4×4-wheel drive design developed by the White Motor Company in 1939. Over 20,000 were built during World War II, being employed in a wide variety of roles including reconnaissance, command car, artillery observation post, mortar carrier, anti-tank gun tractor and light armoured personnel carrier. The vehicle served in every theatre in which American troops were engaged and was also supplied to America's allies, including the Soviet Union. *Scout Car M3A1 Weight* 4.1–4.9 tons; *speed* 56mph (90kph); *armour* 13mm; *armament* 1 .30-cal or 1 .50-cal Browning machine gun; *engine* White-Hercules 110hp petrol; *crew* Up to 8.

Whittle, Group Capt Frank (1907–)

Whittle graduated from the Royal Air Force College at Cranwell in 1928, and after service with a squadron and as a flying instructor attended the RAF School of Aeronautical Engineering at Henlow, 1932–34. For the next two years he attended Cambridge University, obtaining a Mechanical Science Tripos with First Class Honours. He was then placed on the Special Duty List, serving with Power Jets Ltd, 1937–46, where he was responsible for developing the British gas turbine jet engine. In May 1941 the GLOSTER METEOR, fitted with Whittle's engine, was flown for the first time. The Meteor (originally named the Thunderbolt) was the first jet aircraft to enter service with the RAF and was first engaged against the V-1 "Flying Bombs" in 1944. Whittle retired from the RAF as an Air Commodore in 1948 and was knighted for his services, which also earned him numerous honours and awards from the international scientific community.

WIA Wounded in Action.

Wichita, USS – Heavy Cruiser

BROOKLYN CLASS light cruiser but with 9×8in (3×3) main armament and 8×5in DP (8×1) secondary armament. Four of the latter were housed in enclosed mountings.

Widder – Surface Raider (Ger)

Also known as Ship 21 and Raider D. Sailed on 5 May 1940 and operated in the Atlantic, sinking 10 ships totalling 58,645 tons. She returned to Brest on 31 October 1940 and subsequently served as a floating workshop in Norwegian waters. *Displacement* 7851 tons; *speed* 14 knots; *armament* 6×5.9in; 4×37mm AA; 2×20mm AA; 4×21in torpedo tubes; equipped for minelaying; *aircraft* 2; *complement* 363.

Wietersheim, Gen Gustav von

Wietersheim commanded the XIV Motorized (later Panzer) Corps with distinction in Poland, France and the Soviet Union. Although initially successful during the 1942 drive on STALINGRAD, the massed fire of the Soviet artillery there caused heavy loss to his Panzer formations and he was dismissed by PAULUS for suggesting that they should be withdrawn and replaced with infantry divisions. He ended the war as a private soldier in the *Volkssturm*.

Wilder's Gap, Tunisia, 1943

A pass over the southern ridge of the MATMATA HILLS, across which in March 1943 MONTGOMERY sent the New Zealand Corps in a movement to outflank the German defences of the MARETH LINE. The move was successful, but the German defences resisted, so he followed this by sending the 1st Armoured Division across the same route to force the TEBAGA GAP.

Wilde Sau (Wild Sow)

Luftwaffe freelance visual night fighter system, operated over a FLAK-free zone and assisted by flares and searchlights, in which a single-engined fighter was directed into the bomber stream by a ground controller's running commentary; July 1943–spring 1944.

Wilhelmina, Queen of the Netherlands (1880–1962)

In May 1940, rather than remain in Holland under German occupation, Wilhelmina and her government chose voluntary exile in the United Kingdom. She remained active in the affairs of government and broadcast regularly to her people throughout the war, retaining their respect and affection. She returned to Holland in 1945.

Wilson, FM Sir Henry Maitland (1881–1964)

When war broke out in the Middle East in 1940, Wilson commanded the British troops in Egypt. After WAVELL had defeated GRAZIANI's army he was made responsible for the defence of Cyrenaica but in March 1941 was appointed commander of the British and Commonwealth corps which was despatched to GREECE, the retreat and evacuation of which he conducted with considerable skill. In June and July 1941 he led the successful invasion of Vichy-controlled SYRIA, and was then appointed commander of the 9th Army with responsibility for the security of IRAQ, IRAN and their oilfields. In 1943 he succeeded ALEXANDER as Commander-in-Chief Middle East and in January 1944 was appointed Supreme Allied Commander Mediterranean Theatre of War. He became Head of the British Joint Staff Mission to Washington in November 1944 and in that capacity attended the YALTA and POTSDAM CONFERENCES. Heavily built and of hearty manner, Wilson was known as "Jumbo", but was noted for his judgement and sound military common sense.

Winant, John (1889–1947)

Winant replaced the isolationist Joseph KENNEDY as the United States' Ambassador to the Court of St James in November 1941 and held this post until the end of the war. He was a popular ambassador who worked tirelessly to promote good Anglo-American relations, notably by generous use of the Lend-Lease agreement, and was instrumental in arranging Eleanor Roosevelt's visit to the United Kingdom in 1942. Winant also became the American representative to the European Advisory Commission which, *inter alia*, discussed the future of postwar Germany. He attended the CASABLANCA and Teheran Conferences and was the United States' representative at the first meeting of the United Nations.

Window

British codename for strips of metallized paper which were dropped from aircraft to form half-wave reflectors for enemy RADAR signals. This caused the German radar set displays to become obscured by spurious reflections, through which the genuine signals from aircraft could not be easily distinguished. Although the principle was suggested in 1937 by Dr R. V. Jones, the idea was not investigated until late in 1941. Proved successful, the idea was withheld for a long time, for fear that the Germans would retaliate against British radar in similar manner. The first use of Window was not until 23 July 1943. See also DUPPEL for the similar German development.

Wingate, Maj Gen Orde (1903–44)

Wingate was a specialist in guerrilla warfare. In 1936, while serving in Palestine, he formed Special Night Squads which inflicted serious

Signalling the aircraft to land at a Chindit base. Major-General Orde Wingate in topee, left.

"Winnie", a 14-inch gun manned by Royal Marines at Dover and used to bombard German convoys in the Channel and coastal batteries in France.

casualties on Arab insurgents. During the 1940–41 campaign in Ethiopia he commanded a mobile group, known as GIDEON FORCE, which successfully raised the local tribes against the Italians and captured many of the latter's forts. He then held a staff appointment in the United Kingdom until he was summoned to India by WAVELL in 1942 and given the chance to develop his ideas on Long Range Penetration Groups which were to operate behind the Japanese lines in Burma. The groups were of brigade size and Wingate named them CHINDITS after the stone lions, known as *Chinthé*, which guarded Burmese temples. The first Chindit operation involved the 77th Brigade and was mounted in February 1943. Losses in men and equipment were heavy but the experience gained led to the expansion of the Chindits so that their second operation, mounted in February 1944, involved no less than six brigades. Wingate was killed in an air crash on 24 March 1944. An irregular by inclination, he was a controversial figure and a difficult subordinate but was none the less capable of generating great enthusiasm for his ideas and his exploits caught the public imagination. Significantly, when the Special Air Service Regiment was reformed for the postwar Malayan Emergency it adopted many of Wingate's methods.

Winnie and Pooh

Two 14-inch (355mm) guns situated near Dover which could fire across the English Channel against targets in France. Manned by Royal Marine Artillery, the first was installed in August 1940 and, following an inspection by Winston CHURCHILL, was nicknamed "Winnie". The second gun was installed in February 1941 and was given the name "Pooh", after the bear in A. A. Milne's *Winnie the Pooh* stories for children. Both guns were frequently used to silence German batteries, and they last fired in September 1944 in support of Canadian troops who attacked the German batteries on the ground. They were dismantled as soon as the war ended.

Wintergewitter (Winter Storm)

German attempt to relieve formations trapped within the STALINGRAD pocket, December 1942.

Winter War

See RUSSO-FINNISH CAMPAIGN.

Wirbelwind (Whirlwind) – Anti-Aircraft Tank (Ger)

Based on the chassis of the PANZERKAMPFWAGEN IV and armed with a 20mm quadruple mounting housed in an open-topped fully rotating turret with 16mm armour. The maximum rate of fire was 1800 rounds per minute. 150 Wirbelwinds were produced, serving with the anti-aircraft platoons of tank battalions from December 1943.

Wisconsin, USS – Iowa Class Battleship

Saw active service in the Pacific at LEYTE, IWO JIMA and OKINAWA. Reactivated during the Korean War, *Wisconsin* was laid up in 1958 but has now recommissioned.

Wittmann, SS Lt Michael (1914–44)

Wittmann was a German Tiger tank ace credited with 119 kills on the Eastern Front. On 13 June 1944, while commanding the 2nd Company of SS Heavy Tank Battalion 101, Wittmann almost singlehandedly halted the advance of the British 7th Armoured Division at Villers-Bocage in NORMANDY. He was killed on 8 August 1944 during an engagement with a troop of British Shermans.

Witzig, Maj Rudolf

Witzig commanded the German parachute engineer company which formed part of the force that stormed the strategically important Belgian Fort EBEN EMAEL on 10 May 1940. Witzig's glider broke its tow and did not reach its objective but the company was so thoroughly trained that the assault went without a hitch. In November 1942 Witzig commanded a parachute engineer battalion which, having been reinforced with armour, played an important part in the defeat of the Anglo-American 1st Army's attempt to seize Tunis and BIZERTA by coup de main.

Witzleben, FM Erwin von (1881–1944)

Witzleben commanded the German 1st Army during the 1940 campaign in France. In May 1941 he was appointed Commander-in-Chief West but retired because of ill health the following year. A longstanding opponent of HITLER's, he was deeply involved in the JULY BOMB PLOT in 1944 and would have been appointed Commander-in-Chief had it succeeded. In the aftermath of the plot he was tried by a People's Court and hanged in August 1944.

Wolff, SS Gen Karl (1900–)

Wolff served as HIMMLER's liaison officer at HITLER's headquarters until September 1943, when he was appointed Military Governor of Northern Italy. In this capacity he assisted the recently rescued MUSSOLINI to establish a Fascist republic and organized the training of Italian troops for use in anti-partisan operations. By the spring of 1945, however, the end of the war was clearly in sight and in March he opened secret negotiations with Allen DULLES for the surrender of the German armies in Italy. When the military situation deteriorated VIETINGHOFF, the commander of Army Group C, agreed that a general surrender was the only course of action and this was concluded on 2 May.

Wolfsschanze, Rastenburg

Literally "Wolf's Lair", this was the codename allocated to HITLER's command headquarters in East Prussia. It was in the Gorlitz forest, a few miles east of RASTENBURG (now Ketrzyn, Poland) in the Masurian Lake district (Maszowze). It was the scene of the JULY BOMB PLOT when von STAUFFENBERG attempted to assassinate Hitler. It was abandoned on 20 November 1944, and many of the buildings demolished; but sufficient remains for it to be a tourist attraction today.

Wolfsschlucht

Literally "Wolf's Glen", this was the codename given to HITLER's command headquarters used in the summer of 1940 to oversee the campaign in France and the Low Countries. The Belgian village of Bruly-de-Pesche, 15 miles (25km) north-west of Charleville, was evacuated of its inhabitants and taken over, and the various buildings appropriated to different tasks. A special bunker was constructed in the woods outside the village. It was at this HQ that the famous photographs of the "Hitler Jig" were taken, in which the Führer appeared to dance with joy at the news of France's request for an armistice. Hitler left this HQ on 28 June 1940 and shortly afterwards the village was returned to its original owners.

Woolton, Lord Frederick James (1883–1964)

Frederick James Marquis had a wide experience of high-level business and commercial management and in 1937 sat on a government commission which had been formed to look into all aspects of Civil Defence. He believed that where the national interest was involved questions of supply were best dealt with by businessmen rather than professional politicians, who were subject to too many sectarian interests. He was created an Earl in 1939 and in the same year made Director-General of the Ministry of Supply, his particular responsibility being the clothing of the rapidly expanding armed services. In April 1940 he transferred to the Ministry of Food where he organized strict but fair rationing and arranged for the issue of recipes containing unrationed ingredients with which families could supplement their diet, the best remembered of these dishes being Woolton Pie. From 1943 to 1945 he was head of the Ministry of Reconstruction. Woolton was one of the most popular figures of CHURCHILL's administration and his measures reflected the national mood.

WOSB War Office Selection Board (UK). An examination board which tested potential officer candidates physically and psychologically before deciding whether they were acceptable for officer training.

WP White phosphorus.

WPD War Plans Division (US).

WRNS Women's Royal Naval Service (UK).

WSA War Shipping Administration (US).

W/T Wireless Telegraphy (UK). Radio transmission by morse code, as opposed to R/T.

WTF Western Task Force.

WTSFF Weapons Technical Staff Field Force (UK). Group of technicians who operated in all theatres of war and made technical reports on all enemy equipment captured.

Wurzburg

A German early warning and fire control RADAR set; one of the original German designs, it was put under development by the Telefunken Company in 1936. The first model went into service in April 1940, and several improved models were developed and produced throughout the war. *Wurzburg-Riese* was a version with an extra-large antenna, used for ground control of interceptor aircraft.

WVS Women's Voluntary Service (UK). Civilian women's service which provided welfare facilities for the armed forces and the civil population when bombed or otherwise affected by the war.

Left to right: Frank, Himmler, Wolff and Heydrich.

X

X-4

A German wire-guided air-to-air missile, development of which began in June 1943. The first successful flight was in late 1944 and production began shortly afterwards, though the 1000 or so built were never completed due to an air raid on the engine manufactory. The project was therefore abandoned in February 1945. The missile was about 6.5ft (1980mm) long with a wingspan of 29in (737mm) and weighed 132lbs (60kg). Range was about 3000yds (2745m) and propulsion was by liquid-fuel rocket. The warhead carried 48.5lb (22kg) of explosive.

"X" Craft – Midget Submarines (UK)

These craft, the first six of which were delivered to the Royal Navy in January 1943, were designed to attack enemy ships in defended harbours by dropping two time-fuzed charges, each containing two tons of high explosive, beneath the hull of the target vessel. The design incorporated a flooding chamber through which a diver could leave to secure the charges and limpet devices to the enemy ship and then re-enter the submarine. Notable successes were the immobilization of TIRPITZ in September 1943 and the crippling of the TAKAO in July 1945.

"X" Class Displacement 27/30 tons; *dimensions* 51ft 3in×5ft 9in (15.6×1.75m); *machinery* 1-shaft diesel/electric motor producing bhp 42/30; *speed* 6.5/5.5 knots; *complement* 4.

"XE" Class Displacement 30/34 tons; dimensions 53ft×5ft 9in (16.1×1.75m); *machinery* 1-shaft diesel/electric motor producing bhp 42/30; *speed* 6.5/6 knots; *complement* 4–5.

X-Gerät

A German blind-bombing system used in attacks on England in 1940–41. The system used a director beam emitted by a ground station on the Continent and directed at a target in England. Three other, finer, beams were directed from other ground stations so as to intercept the director beam. The first crossed about 31 miles (50km) before the target to give advance warning; the second crossed 12.5 miles (20km) before the target, and the third 3 miles (5km) before the target.

The distance between the two final beams gave an accurate indication of the aircraft speed and their signals were fed to a mechanical computer by the bomb-aimer. This device then calculated the optimum bomb release point from the final cross-beam.

"X" Craft 25 under way.

Y

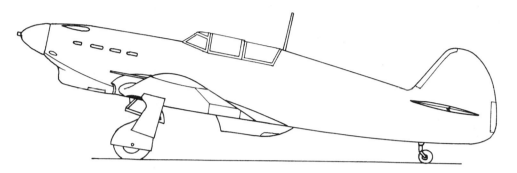

Yakovlev Yak-1 fighter-bomber.

Yakovlev Aircraft (USSR)

Yakovlev Yak-1 First of a long line of Yakovlev designs, the Yak-1 was entering service at the time of the German attack in June 1941; further deliveries were delayed by the need to move the factory over 1000 miles (1610km) eastwards to escape the German invasion. The design was later improved by lowering the rear fuselage line and installing a new cockpit canopy to give all-round vision, and this version became the Yak-7. Adopted as the principal Soviet fighter, over 37,000 of all Yak types, plus training versions, were built. *Span* 32.75ft (10m); *engine* 1 1260hp in-line; *armament* 1 20mm cannon, 2 machine guns, 6 rockets; *speed* 373mph (600kph).

Yakovlev Yak-3 This was an improved YAK-1, the changes being in lightening and streamlining the basic monoplane design. Entering service in the middle of 1943 it soon achieved a dangerous reputation among German pilots and was one of the top-scoring fighters on the Eastern Front. *Span* 30ft (9.15m); *engine* 1 1260hp in-line; *armament* 1 20mm cannon, 2 machine guns; *speed* 447mph (719kph).

Yakovlev Yak-9 The most numerous of the Yak fighters it first saw combat over STALINGRAD in 1942. It was an evolved version of the Yak-7 and was employed as a fighter, ground-attack machine, bomber and long-range escort fighter at various times. It was used to equip the Free French Normandie-Niemen squadron and also the Free Polish squadrons in Soviet service. An improved version, the 9U, with stressed-skin construction and a more powerful engine, was some 60mph (96kph) faster than its current German opponents. *Span* 32.75ft (10m); *engine* 1 1260hp in-line; *armament* 1 20mm cannon, 2 machine guns, 440lb (200kg) of bombs; *speed* 435mph (700kph).

Yalta, Soviet Union, 1945

A Russian city in the Crimea, 30 miles (48km) east of SEVASTOPOL. Though overrun by the Germans during their advance in the Crimea, it played no important part in the battle. It subsequently became famous as the meeting place of STALIN, CHURCHILL and ROOSEVELT on 4–11 February 1945. Roosevelt's principal aim was to bring Russia into the Far Eastern War, in which he succeeded. Stalin promised to enter the Far Eastern War within three months of the end of the war in Europe and recognized CHIANG KAI-SHEK. He also agreed to Roosevelt's plan for the United Nations and to Churchill's proposal that France should have her own zone of occupation in Germany. Churchill's aim was to limit Soviet influence in postwar Europe, and he attempted to enlist Roosevelt's help in this endeavour, with limited success. Churchill and Roosevelt agreed to the Soviet retention of the territories Stalin had taken from POLAND in 1939. Poland was to be compensated in the West at Germany's expense.

Yamamoto, Adm Isoroku (1884–1943)

An influential advocate of naval aviation, Yamamoto was appointed Vice-Minister of the Navy in 1936 and Chief of the Aviation Department of the Navy in 1938. He became Commander-in-Chief of the Combined Fleet in 1939. He believed that Japan would be

Churchill (left) and Roosevelt (centre) at the Yalta conference. Behind Churchill, Anthony Eden, with Molotov on the right.

437

defeated in a protracted war with the United States although he recognized that in the short term there were advantages to be gained if the US Navy could be eliminated from the contest by a pre-emptive strike. He therefore began planning the attack on PEARL HARBOR early in 1940, but failed to share in the general enthusiasm engendered by the strike itself, which was delivered on 7 December 1941, the future implications of the act causing him to caution his countrymen against "mindless rejoicing". The American carriers had been absent from Pearl Harbor during the attack and when these struck back with the DOOLITTLE RAID on Tokyo and at the Battle of the CORAL SEA, Yamamoto set in motion the complicated strategy intended to destroy the remains of the US Pacific Fleet, but which actually resulted in the destruction of the major part of his own carrier force at the Battle of MIDWAY on 4 June 1942. Though profoundly shocked by this he continued to direct the naval strategy of the SOLOMONS campaign and in early 1943 planned a naval air offensive codenamed I-GO, which was intended to halt the Allied advances. He decided to make a morale-raising series of visits to air bases in the Western Solomons, but the signals relating to his movements were intercepted and he was killed when his aircraft was shot down on 18 April 1943 by American fighters flying from GUADALCANAL. Yamamoto's prestige in Japan was immense and his death was a severe blow to national morale.

Yamashita, Lt Gen Tomoyuki (1885–1946)

As Inspector General of the Japanese Army Air Force Yamashita visited Germany in 1940 and formed the opinion that Japan should not become involved in a war with the West until her land and air forces had undergone an extensive programme of modernization. In 1941 he was appointed commander of the 25th Army, which had been detailed for the conquest of MALAYA and SINGAPORE. Yamashita's

invasion commenced on 8 December 1941 and in a campaign notable for its speed and drive he pushed the British forces steadily southwards until on 31 January 1942 they were compelled to retire to Singapore Island. On 8 February the Japanese crossed the Straits of Johore and established themselves firmly. They had, however, outrun their supplies of ammunition when Yamashita bluffed the dispirited British commander, General PERCIVAL, into accepting an unconditional surrender. At home, Yamashita's prestige soared and he was named "The Tiger of Malaya", but he had incurred the enmity of Prime Minister TOJO, who saw him as a potential rival and posted him into obscurity as commander of the 1st Army Group in Manchuria. Following Tojo's fall in July 1944 Yamashita was appointed commander of the 14th Area Army and given the responsibility of defending the PHILIPPINES. He conducted a skilful holding action on Luzon, eschewing fruitless suicide tactics, and surrendered after the Japanese capitulation in September 1945. He was tried for war crimes and executed in 1946.

Yamato Class Battleships (Jap)

Yamato and her sister ship *Musashi* were designed to outgun any battleship afloat, but by the time they entered service in 1940 the aircraft carrier was becoming the capital ship of the world's navies. *Yamato* was present at the Battles of MIDWAY, THE PHILIPPINE SEA and LEYTE GULF. On 7 April 1945 she was sunk by

carrier aircraft of TF 58 some 50 miles (80km) south-west of Kyushu while engaged in a suicidal mission against the American forces invading OKINAWA. Her anti-aircraft armament had been greatly enhanced throughout the war, and at the time of her sinking consisted of 24×5in (12×2), 146×25mm (40×3 and 26×1); in addition, her main armament could fire specially developed *shanshiki-dan* ammunition against low-flying aircraft, the effect being similar to that of a gigantic shotgun. *Musashi*, whose anti-aircraft armament was also considerably enhanced, was present at the battles of the Philippine Sea and Leyte Gulf, and was sunk at the latter on 24 October 1944. *Displacement* 64,170 tons; *dimensions* 863ft×127ft 9in (263×38.9m); mean draught 35ft 6in (10.4m); *machinery* 4-shaft geared turbines producing shp 150,000; *speed* 27 knots; *protection* main belt 16in; turrets 20–25.5in; deck 7.75in; *armament* 9×18.1in (3×3); 12×6.1in (4×3); 12×5in AA (6×2); 24×25mm AA (8×3); 4×13mm (2×2); *aircraft* 6 (2 catapults); *complement* 2500; *number in class* 2.

Yap, Pacific

A Japanese island in the north of the Caroline Islands. Used as a naval and air base, it was occasionally raided by US aircraft, but its remoteness from the operations in the South and South-west Pacific meant that it posed no direct threat and it was therefore left in isolation.

IJN Yamato under way.

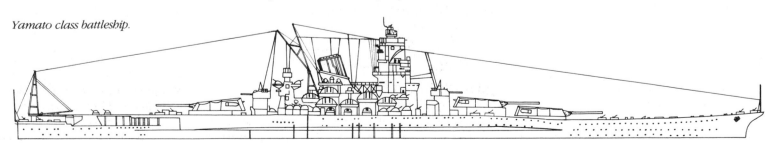

Yamato class battleship.

Yenangyaung, Burma, 1942 and 1945

Town about 250 miles (400km) north of RANGOON and a centre of oil production. It was abandoned by the British on 5 April 1942, the oil installations being destroyed. The Japanese later repaired the facilities and put them into operation again, after which they were frequently bombed by Allied aircraft. Yenangyaung was retaken by the British 33rd Brigade on 25 April 1945, when the oil installations were once again destroyed, this time by the retreating Japanese.

Yeo-Thomas, Wing Cdr Forest Frederick (1902–64)

Before the war Yeo-Thomas had been a director of the Paris fashion house of Molyneux. He joined the Special Operations Executive (SOE) in 1942 and carried out three missions to France, co-ordinating the activities of the Resistance and improving its internal security. Known in the field by the codenames of "Shelly" and "The White Rabbit", he was in constant danger of arrest and once escaped capture by riding in a hearse, hidden under a pile of flowers. He was betrayed in the spring of 1944 and was brutally tortured by the Gestapo before being sent to BUCHENWALD concentration camp. There he assumed the identity of a French officer who had recently died of typhus. He escaped but was recaptured and sent to a prisoner-of-war camp. He escaped again and reached the Allied lines in April 1945.

Yeremenko, Marshal Andrey I. (1892–1970)

Yeremenko was one of several senior Soviet officers who, in the aftermath of the German Blitzkrieg victories in Poland and France, recognized that a serious mistake had been made in discrediting the late Marshal TUKHACHEVSKY's theories on mechanized warfare. He led the VI Cavalry Corps during the Soviet occupation of the Baltic States in June 1940 and then formed the III Mechanized Corps before being posted to the Far East as commander of the 1st Red Banner Army. He was recalled to Moscow on the eve of the German Invasion of the Soviet Union and given command of the newly formed Bryansk Front, but was severely wounded and evacuated on 13 October 1941. In August 1942 he was appointed commander of the Stalingrad Front, which he led during the encirclement of the German 6th Army that November and

Marshal Andrey Yeremenko.

the subsequent general advance. He transferred to the Kalinin Front (later redesignated 1st Baltic Front) in 1943, taking part in the autumn battles which resulted in the capture of SMOLENSK. In April 1944 he commanded the Independent Coastal Army which, together with TOLBUKHIN's 4th Ukrainian Front, liberated the CRIMEA. His next appointment was commander of the 2nd Baltic Front, which he took over in July 1944, capturing Dvinsk and occupying most of LATVIA. He transferred to the 4th Ukrainian Front in March 1945, over-running CZECHOSLOVAKIA and destroying the remnants of the German Army Group Centre.

Y-Gerät

A German blind-bombing system used in attacks on England in 1940–41. It consisted of a radio beam emitted from a ground station in France or Germany, along which the bomber flew. The radio beam signal was received by a special radio in the bomber and retransmitted at a slightly different frequency, to be picked up by the beam station. From this it was possible to deduce the range of the aircraft and inform it when to bomb a specified target. The system was very susceptible to counter-measures and did not remain in use for long.

Yokosuka Aircraft (Japan)

Yokosuka D4Y (Judy) This was designed for the Japanese Navy as a dive-bomber for carrier use, and was intended to be as fast as con-

temporary fighters. For this reason it was given an in-line engine, uncommon in Japanese service, and a design prone to defects. After a short period in carrier service it was used from land strips in the Pacific islands with some success, but the engine problem proved intractable. Most were rebuilt with radial engines and some were adapted as night fighers. *Span* 37.75ft (11.5m); *engine* 1 1200hp in-line or 1 1560hp radial; *armament* 3 machine guns, 685lb (310kg) of bombs, 2 20mm cannon as night fighter; *speed* (in-line) 339mph (545kph); (radial) 360mph (579kph).

Yokosuka E14Y1 (Glen) This unusual machine was designed as a spotter aircraft to be carried by submarines. A floatplane, it was launched over the side and then took off from the water. Light and small, both necessitated by its storage in the submarine, its performance was limited but adequate for its role. *Span* 36ft (11m); *engine* 1 360hp radial; *crew* 2; *armament* 1 machine gun; *speed* 105mph (169kph).

Yokosuka P1Y (Frances) Primarily designed as a medium bomber, this sleek monoplane found employment as a torpedo-bomber, night fighter and reconnaissance machine as well as in its designated role. Fast, manoeuvrable, and with a long range, its impact on the war in the Pacific was limited by the shortage of skilled pilots and fuel which overtook the Japanese Navy in the later stages of the war. *Span* 65.5ft (20m); *engines* 2 1820hp radial; *crew* 3; *armament* 1 20mm cannon, 1 machine gun, 1100lb (500kg) of bombs or 1 torpedo; *speed* 345mph (555kph).

Yokosuka MXY-7 (Baka) The most remarkable aircraft ever built as far as tactical function is concerned, the MXY-7 was designed solely as a suicide attack aircraft for the "Kamikaze" programme. Cheap, built of wood, loaded with 2645lb (1200kg) of high explosive, and fitted with a rocket motor, the machine was carried to within 50 miles (80km) of its objective by a converted "Betty" bomber, then released to glide towards its target. When close to the target the pilot commended his soul to his ancestors, fired the rocket, and nosed over into a steep power dive to impact. A later version was propelled by a jet motor, but few of these were built. *Span* 16.5ft (5m); *engine* 3 588lb (267kg) static thrust rockets; *terminal speed* ca. 570mph (917kph).

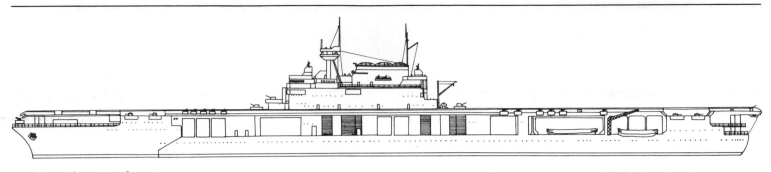

Yorktown class aircraft carrier.

York Class Cruisers (UK)

York was disabled by an Italian Explosive Motor Boat in Suda Bay, Crete, on 26 March 1941 and was later abandoned when she sustained further damage from air attack. See also EXETER. *Displacement* 8390 tons; *dimensions* 575ft×58ft (175.2×17.7m); mean draught 17ft (5.2m); *machinery* 4-shaft geared turbines producing shp 80,000; *speed* 32 knots; *protection* main belt 3in; deck 2in; turrets 2in; DCT 3in; *armament* 6×8in (3×2); 4×4in AA (4×1); 2×2 pdr AA (2×1); 6×21in (2×3) torpedo tubes; *aircraft* 1–2; *complement* 600; *number in class* 2, launched 1928–29.

Yorktown Class Aircraft Carriers (USA)

Displacement 19,900 tons; *dimensions* 809ft 6in×83ft 3in (246.7×25.3m); mean draught 21ft 9in (6.63m); *machinery* 4-shaft geared turbines producing shp 120,000; *speed* 34 knots; *armament* 8×5in (8×1); *aircraft* 100; *complement* 2200; *number in class* 3, launched 1936–40.

Yorktown, USS – Yorktown and Essex Class Aircraft Carriers

Yorktown (CV.5) was damaged at the Battle of the CORAL SEA but was repaired in time to participate in MIDWAY, where she had to be abandoned after air attack, her hulk being torpedoed and sunk by the Japanese submarine I 168 the following day. Her name was then transferred to the ESSEX CLASS carrier BON HOMME RICHARD, which was launched on 21 January l943. The new *Yorktown* (CV.10) saw action at the GILBERT ISLANDS, KWAJALEIN, TRUK, HOLLANDIA, the MARIANAS and IWO JIMA.

Yubari, IJN – Light Cruiser

Launched 1923. Sunk by the submarine USS *Bluegill* off the Caroline Islands 27 April 1944. *Displacement* 2890 tons; *dimensions* 463×40ft (141.1×12m); mean draught 11ft 9in (3.58m); *machinery* 3-shaft geared turbines producing shp 57,900; *speed* 35.5 knots; *protection* main belt 2in; *armament* 6×5.5in (2×2 and 2×1); 1×3in AA; 2×13mm AA; 4×24in torpedo tubes (2×2); 34 mines; *complement* 328.

Yugoslavia

Yugoslavia was invaded by the German Army on 6 April 1941. An artificial country, composed of several different nationalities, even more political parties, economically undeveloped and with negligible military forces, Yugoslavia was highly vulnerable to concerted attack, and within 11 days was completely occupied by a mixture of German, Italian, Hungarian and Bulgarian forces. King PETER and his government fled to London and the country was partitioned. The central portion of the country, consisting of Croatia and Bosnia-Herzegovina, became the new "state of Croatia" under the German puppet Pavelich. Macedonia and neighbouring parts were integrated into Albania. Other parts went to Bulgaria, Hungary, Germany and Italy. Various nationalist elements now began settling old scores, the Serbs getting the worst of it from several different factions. Two resistance movements sprang up, one led by the Communist Party under TITO and the other, the more right-wing "Četniks", led by Draza MIHAILOVIĆ. When in June 1941 the Germans reduced their garrisons due to the demands of the Eastern Front, both these groups seized their opportunity and began harassing the occupying forces. Tito's forces liberated large areas of Montenegro, and parts of Serbia and Bosnia, and by the end of the year he had over 80,000 men under his command. The Četniks had the backing of the British SOE, but it soon became clear that Mihailović was more interested in paying off old scores than in liberating his country, a policy which in late 1941 culminated in an abortive attack on one of Tito's strongholds. Subsequently the Četniks openly sought collaboration with the Germans, and Allied support was switched to Tito.

Yugumo Class Destroyers (Jap)

Displacement 2077 tons; *dimensions* 391×35ft (119.1×10.7m); mean draught 12ft (3.6m); *machinery* 2-shaft geared turbines producing shp 52,000; *speed* 35.5 knots; *armament* 6×5in DP (3×2); 4×25mm AA (2×2); 8×24in torpedo tubes (2×4); 4 depth charge throwers and 36 depth charges; *complement* 228; *number in class* 20, launched 1941–44.

USS Yorktown, *seen from USS* Wasp, *December 1941.*

Z

Z23 Class Destroyers (Ger)

Displacement 2600 tons; *dimensions* 390×30ft (118.8×9m); mean draught 10ft (3m); *machinery* 2-shaft geared turbines producing shp 70,000; *speed* 38.5 knots; *armament* 4×5.9in (4×1); 4×37mm AA (2×2); 14×20mm AA (6×2 and 2×1); 8×21in torpedo tubes (2×4); equipped for minelaying; *complement* 321; *number in class* 12, launched 1940–42.

Z35 Class Destroyers (Ger)

Both vessels in this class, *Z35* and *Z36*, were mined and sunk in the Gulf of Finland on 12 December 1944. *Displacement* 2527 tons; *dimensions* 390×40ft (118.8×12m); mean draught 10ft (3m); *machinery* 2-shaft geared turbines producing shp 70,000; *speed* 38 knots; *armament* 5×5in (5×1); 4×37mm AA (2×2); 6×20mm AA (1×4 and 2×1); 8×21in torpedo tubes (2×4); equipped for minelaying; *complement* 321; *number in class* 2, both launched 1943.

Z37 Class Destroyers (Ger)

Displacement 2603 tons; *dimensions* 390×40ft (118.8×12m); mean draught 10ft (3m); *machinery* 2-shaft geared turbines producing shp 70,000; *speed* 38 knots; *armament* 5×5.9in (3×1 and 1×2); 4×37mm AA (2×2); 14×20mm AA (7×2); 8×21in torpedo tubes; equipped for minelaying; *complement* 321; *number in class* 3, all launched 1942.

Zara class cruiser.

Z Batteries

British anti-aircraft rocket batteries. They consisted of numbers of multiple launchers, such that salvoes of 128 rockets were fired to form a barrage in the sky. Their effect was more upon morale than physical deterrence. Their defect was that, after firing, 128 rocket motors fell from the sky, and they were therefore carefully positioned so that these spent motors fell into the sea or on to open country where no damage could occur.

Zahme Sau (Tame Sow)

German night fighter direction system operating independently of HIMMELBETT.

Zamboanga, Philippines

Town at the western tip of MINDANAO Island. It was invaded on 10 March 1945 by the US 41st Division, part of General EICHELBERGER's US 8th Army, to commence the recapture of Mindanao.

Zara Class Heavy Cruisers (Italy)

Three members of this class, *Zara*, *Pola* and *Fiume*, were sunk by gunfire during the Battle of CAPE MATAPAN. *Displacement* 14,600 tons; *dimensions* 648ft 3in×67ft 6in (197.5× 20.5m); mean draught 19ft 3in (5.86m); *machinery* 2-shaft geared turbines producing shp 122,000; *protection* main belt 5.9in; deck 2.75in; turrets 5.9in; *armament* 8×8in; 16×3.9in AA; 8×37mm AA; 8×13.2mm AA; *aircraft* 2; *complement* 830; *number in class* 4, launched 1930–31.

The cruiser Zara, *later sunk during the Battle of Cape Matapan.*

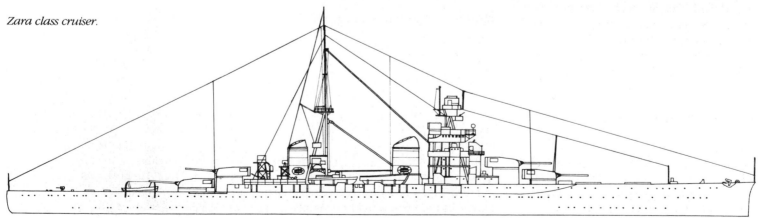

Zeitzler, Gen Kurt (1895–1963)

Zeitzler served as a staff officer during the Polish and French campaigns, where his brilliant handling of mechanized logistics led to his appointment as Chief of Staff to KLEIST's 1st Panzer Army, with which he served during Operation BARBAROSSA. He then served as Chief of Staff to the Commander-in-Chief West. HITLER regarded Zeitzler with particular favour, and in September 1942 he replaced HALDER as Chief of General Staff. He supported PAULUS' request that the trapped 6th Army should be permitted to break out of STALINGRAD, but Hitler refused to consider the idea. Shaken by the subsequent disaster, Hitler was prepared to accept his advice for a while and in the aftermath of MANSTEIN's successful counterstroke in February 1943 he planned Operation ZITADELLE, the major offensive directed against the KURSK salient. However, when this was launched in July 1943 the opportunities present earlier in the year had gone. The result was a severe defeat which so weakened the Wehrmacht's capacity that the strategic initiative on the Eastern Front passed irrevocably to the Russians. The succession of defeats which ensued eroded the once satisfactory relationship which had existed between Hitler and Zeitzler to the point where the latter was on the verge of a nervous breakdown. In July 1944, after the collapse of the armies on the Upper Dniepr, he was replaced by GUDERIAN. To emphasize his disgrace Hitler forbade him to wear his uniform.

Zeppelin

German plan to assassinate STALIN, July 1944.

Zervas, Gen Napoleon

Zervas was leader of the Greek EDES resistance movement during the Axis occupation of Greece. He was strongly opposed to the rival Communist ELAS group, the position of which was strengthened by the acquisition of Italian arms following Italy's surrender in 1943. Fighting broke out between the two groups that autumn. Zervas attended a meeting called by General WILSON at Caserta during which a temporary truce was agreed and this was followed in October 1944 by Operation MANNA, the British landing in Greece which coincided with the German withdrawal. The civil war continued, ending in the defeat of ELAS after CHURCHILL had received STALIN's assurance that Greece would remain a British sphere of influence.

Marshal Georgi Zhukov with soldiers on the Khalkin-Gol, 1939.

Zhitomir, Soviet Union

A town in the northern Ukraine, west of KIEV, Zhitomir was taken by the German Army Group South in July 1941 during the initial phase of Operation BARBAROSSA. It remained in German hands until the autumn offensive of 1943, when the Soviet advances after the KURSK battle took Kiev and forward elements "bounced" the Germans out of Zhitomir early in November. On 14 November the German XXXXVIII Panzer Corps mounted a strong counter-attack and regained the town on the 18th. The gain was shortlived, as a strong Soviet counter-attack recaptured the town for the last time on 31 December.

Zhukov, Marshal Georgi K. (1896–1974)

In August 1939 Zhukov was responsible for inflicting a serious defeat on the Japanese at KHALKIN-GOL, Mongolia, at a time when the Soviet Army's morale and prestige were at a low ebb. At the important High Command war games, held in January 1941 with a view to modernizing the Army's theories on mechanized war, Zhukov's "Western Force" decisively defeated PAVLOV's "Eastern Force" in a surprisingly prophetic projection of some aspects of the German BARBAROSSA plan. This led directly to his appointment as Chief of General Staff. Such was STALIN's respect for Zhukov that throughout the Great Patriotic War the dictator relied upon him to resolve the most difficult military situations. Although he was unable to halt the German advance at SMOLENSK in August 1941, he prevented the enemy from capturing LENINGRAD, having taken over responsibility for the defence of the city from VOROSHILOV. He was next ordered to co-ordinate the defence of MOSCOW, where he launched a successful counteroffensive with fresh Siberian troops in December. Following this he was appointed Deputy Commissar for Defence. In 1942 he co-ordinated the defence of STALINGRAD and, together with VASILEVSKY and VORONOV, planned Operation URANUS which, in November, resulted in the encirclement of the German 6th Army. The following year he was responsible for the strategic direction of the defence of the KURSK salient and the ensuing Soviet counteroffensive controlling the advance of the various Fronts across the UKRAINE. After VATUTIN's death in the spring of 1944 he assumed personal command of the 1st Ukrainian Front. He next planned Operation BAGRATION which, in June 1944, resulted in the virtual destruction of the German Army

Group Centre. During the final stages of the war he commanded the 1st Belorussian Front with which he advanced through eastern Germany to capture BERLIN, where he accepted the German surrender on 8 May 1945. Zhukov showed equal flair as a member of *Stavka* and Deputy Supreme Commander. Although by Soviet standards Zhukov was economical in the expenditure of the forces under his command, he brought a ruthlessness to the battlefield which would have been unacceptable to his Western counterparts. He was Deputy Minister of Defence of the USSR, 1953–55, and Minister of Defence, 1955–57.

Zimmerit (Ger)

A paste coating applied to German AFVs during the last years of the war as a defence against magnetic charges. The paste dried to an extremely hard finish which could not be chipped away by hand.

Zipper

Planned reconquest of MALAYA, 1945.

Zitadelle (Citadel)

German offensive aimed at eliminating the KURSK salient, July 1943.

Zog, King of Albania (1895–1961)

Zog ruled his backward country as a feudal autocrat and was forced to put down several liberal-inspired risings during the 1930s. On 7 April 1939 MUSSOLINI declared that his kingdom had become an Italian protectorate and, after a naval bombardment, the country was occupied with minimal resistance. Zog went into exile and played no further part in Albania's history.

Zossen, Germany

A small German town 20 miles (32km) south of BERLIN. It was the war location of German Army HQ, which moved there in August 1939, and was also the principal radio station for communication with German naval and military outposts.

Zyklon-B

A cyanide compound developed for fumigation purposes in the 1920s. It consisted of hydrogen cyanide stabilized with oxalic acid, in crystalline form, which exuded hydrogen cyanide gas when liberated from its container. It was first used against human victims in the T-4 euthanasia programme in 1939. Inmates were ordered to "shower", and once inside Zyklon-B was introduced through vents. The HCN gas killed the victims in a few minutes. The system was later extended to the extermination camps in Poland – including AUSCHWITZ, TREBLINKA, Belzec and SOBIBOR – and was responsible for several million deaths. The inventor, Dr Brune Tesch, was executed for his role in providing the gas for the camps.

A Panzer attack has been beaten off by the Russians, Operation Zitadelle, *1943.*

BIBLIOGRAPHY

The premier references to the conduct of the war are, of course, the various Official Histories produced by the participants. These form, as it were, the first level of enquiry. Those seeking more detailed, and perhaps more personalised, accounts of the many different aspects of the war and of the various campaigns, must go to the 'second level', commercially-published books. The number of books on World War II is legion; this list merely indicates some of the more useful and readable books on various aspects, and from which it will be possible to obtain further references to more detailed works.

Baker, Alan, *Merrill's Marauders*. London: Pan/Ballantine, 1972.

Barbarski, Krzysztof, *Polish Armour 1939–45*. London: Osprey, 1982.

Barnett, Corelli, *The Desert Generals*. London: William Kimber, 1960.

Bekker, Caius, *Hitler's Naval War*. London: Macdonald & Jane's, 1974.

Belchem, Major-General David, *Victory in Normandy*. London: Chatto & Windus, 1981.

Belfield, Eversley and Essame, H., *The Battle for Normandy*. London: Batsford, 1965; Pan, 1983.

Bidwell, Shelford, *The Chindit War*. London: Hodder & Stoughton, 1979.

Blumenson, Martin, *Sicily – Whose Victory?* London: Macdonald, 1968.

Brown, David, Shores, Christopher and Macksey, Kenneth, *The Guinness History of Air Warfare*, London: Guinness Superlatives, 1976.

Calvert, Michael, *Chindits – Long Range Penetration*. London: Pan/Ballantine, 1974.

Calvert, Michael, *Slim*. London: Pan/Ballantine, 1973.

Calvocoressi, Peter, *Top Secret Ultra*. London: Cassell, 1980.

Cannon, M. Hamlin, *Leyte – The Return to the Philippines*, US Government Printing Office, 1954.

Carell, Paul, *Hitler moves East, 1941–43*. Boston: Little, Brown & Co., 1964.

Carell, Paul, *Invasion – They're Coming!* London: Bantam, 1964.

Carver, Michael, *Dilemmas of the Desert War*. London: Batsford, 1986.

Carver, Michael, *El Alamein*. London: Batsford, 1964.

Carver, Michael, *Tobruk*. London: Batsford, 1961.

Chamberlain, Peter and Ellis, Chris, *British and American Tanks of World War II*. London: Arms & Armour Press, 1969.

Chuikov, V. I., *The Beginning of the Road*. London: MacGibbon & Kee, 1963.

Chuikov, V. I., *The End of the Third Reich*. London: MacGibbon & Kee, 1967.

Condon, Richard W., *The Winter War – Russia Against Finland*. London: Pan/Ballantine, 1972.

Cooper, Bryan, *The Battle of the Torpedo Boats*. London: Macdonald, 1970.

Cooper, Matthew, *The German Army 1933–1945*. London: Macdonald & Jane's, 1978.

Costello, John, *The Pacific War*. London: Collins, 1981.

Crow, Duncan, ed., *Armoured Fighting Vehicles of the World*:
  Vol. 2: British AFVs 1919–1940. Windsor: Profile Publications, 1970.
  Vol. 3: British & Commonwealth AFVs 1940–46. Windsor: Profile Publications, 1971.
  Vol. 4: American AFVs of World War II. Windsor: Profile Publications, 1972.
  Vol. 5: German AFVs of World War II. Windsor: Profile Publications, 1973.

Dawidowicz, Lucy S., *The War against the Jews*. London: Weidenfeld and Nicolson, 1975.

Deacon, Richard, *A History of the British Secret Service*. London: Frederick Muller, 1969.

D'Este, Carlo, *Decision in Normandy*. London: Collins, 1983.

Dornberger, Walter, *V-2*. London: Hurst & Blackett, 1954.

Downing, David, *The Devil's Virtuosos – German Generals At War, 1940/45*. London: New English Library, 1977.

Eisenbach, Artur, *Operation Reinhard; the Mass Extermination of the Jewish Population in Poland*. Poznan, 1962.

Ellis, Major L. F., *Victory in the West*. London: H.M.S.O., 1968.

Elstob, Peter, *Bastogne – The Road Block*. London: Macdonald, 1968.

Elstob, Peter, *Battle of the Reichswald*. London: Macdonald, 1970.

Erickson, John, *The Road to Berlin*. London: Weidenfeld & Nicolson, 1983.

Erickson, John, *The Road to Stalingrad*. London: Weidenfeld & Nicolson, 1975.

Falk, Stanley L., *Liberation of the Philippines*. London: Macdonald, 1971.

Frank, Benis M., *Okinawa – Touchstone to Victory*. London: Macdonald, 1970.

Fraser, David, *And We Shall Shock Them – The British Army in the Second World War*. London: Hodder & Stoughton, 1983.

Frere-Cook, Lieutenant-Commander Gervis and Macksey, Kenneth, *The Guinness History of Sea Warfare*. London: Guinness Superlatives, 1975.

Fugate, Bryan I., *Operation Barbarossa*. London: Presidio, 1984.

Goutard, Adolphe, *The Battle of France, 1940*. London: Frederick Muller, 1958.

Graham, Dominick, *Cassino*. London: Pan/Ballantine, 1972.

Graham, Dominick and Bidwell, Shelford, *Tug of War: The Battle for Italy 1943–45*. London: Hodder & Stoughton, 1986.

Grove, Eric, *World War II Tanks – The Axis Powers*. London: Orbis, 1975.

Guderian, General Heinz, *Panzer Leader*. London: Michael Joseph, 1970.

Gunston, Bill, *The Illustrated Encyclopedia of Combat Aircraft of World War II*. London: Salamander, 1978.

Hampshire, A. Cecil, *Lilliput Fleet*. London: William Kimber, 1957.

Hastings, Max, *Bomber Command*. London: Michael Joseph, 1979.

Hastings, Max, *Overlord*. London: Michael Joseph, 1984.

Hayashi, Saburo and Coox, Alvin D., *Kōgun: The Japanese Army in the Pacific War*. Quantico: The Marine Corps Association, 1959.

Heckmann, Wolf, *Rommel's War in Africa*. London: Granada, 1981.

Hibbert, Christopher, *Anzio – The Bid For Rome*. London: Macdonald, 1970.

Hibbert, Christopher, *Mussolini*. London: Pan/Ballantine, 1973.

Hickey, Michael. *Out of the sky; a History of Airborne Warfare*. London: Mills & Boon, 1979.

Hogg, Ian V., *Barrage – The Guns in Action*. London: Macdonald, 1971.

Hogg, Ian V., *British & American Artillery of World War II*. London: Arms & Armour Press, 1978.

Hogg, Ian V., *German Artillery of World War II*. London: Arms & Armour Press, 1975.

Hogg, Ian V., *The Guns 1939–45*. London: Macdonald, 1970.

Hogg, Ian V. and Weeks, John, *Military Small Arms of the 20th Century*. London: Arms & Armour Press, 1985.

Holmes, Richard, *Bir Hacheim – Desert Citadel*. London: Pan/Ballantine, 1972.

Horne, Alistair, *To Lose a Battle – France 1940*. London: Macmillan, 1969.

Horton, D. C., *New Georgia – Pattern for Victory*. London: Pan/Ballantine, 1972.

Hough, Richard, *The Longest Battle – The War at Sea 1939–45*. London: Weidenfeld & Nicolson, 1986.

Humble, Richard, *Hitler's High Seas Fleet*. London: Pan/Ballantine, 1972.

Humble, Richard, *Japanese High Seas Fleet*. London: Pan/Ballantine, 1974.

International Military Tribunal: *Trial of the Major War Criminals . . .* Official Text. 42 vols. Nuremberg: Blue Series, 1947–49.

Jacobsen, Hans-Adolf and Rohwer J., eds, *Decisive Battles of World War II: The German View*. London: Andre Deutsch, 1965.

Jones, R. V., *Most Secret War*. London: Hamish Hamilton, 1978.

Jukes, Geoffrey, *Kursk – The Clash of Armour*. London: Macdonald, 1969.

Jukes, Geoffrey, *Stalingrad – The Turning Point*. London: Macdonald, 1968.

Keegan, John, *Waffen SS*. London: Macdonald, 1970.

Kemp, Lieutenant Commander Peter K., *H. M. Submarines*. London: Herbert Jenkins, 1952.

Kent, Graeme, *Guadalcanal – Island Ordeal*. London: Pan/Ballantine, 1972.

Kesselring, Albert, *Memoirs*. London: William Kimber, 1953.

Larionov, V. and others, *Decisive Battles of the Soviet Army*. Moscow: Progress Publishers, 1984.

Leach, Barry, *German Strategy against Russia*. Oxford: Oxford University Press, 1973.

Lewin, Ronald, *Slim*. London: Leo Cooper, 1976.

Lucas, James, *War on the Eastern Front*. London: Jane's, 1979.

Lucas, James and Barker, James, *The Killing Ground – The Battle of the Falaise Gap August 1944*. London: Batsford, 1978.

Lucas Phillips, C. E., *Alamein*. London: Heinemann, 1962.

Lund, Paul and Ludlam, Harry, *The War of the Landing Craft*. Slough: Foulsham, 1976.

MacDonald, Charles B., *The Battle of the Bulge*. London: Weidenfeld & Nicolson, 1984.

Macintyre, Donald, *Aircraft Carrier*. London: Macdonald, 1968.

Macintyre, Donald, *The Battle for the Mediterranean*. London: Batsford, 1964.

Macintyre, Donald, *Fighting Under The Sea*. London: Evans Brothers, 1965.

Macintyre, Donald, *Leyte Gulf*. London: Macdonald, 1970.

Macintyre, Donald, *Narvik*. London: Evans Brothers, 1959.

McKee, Alexander, *Caen – Anvil of Victory*. London: Souvenir Press, 1964.

Macksey, Kenneth, *Guderian: Panzer General*. London: Macdonald & Jane's, 1975.

Macksey, Kenneth, *Afrika Korps*. London: Macdonald, 1968.

Macksey, Kenneth, *Beda Fomm – The Classic Victory*. London: Pan/Ballantine, 1972.

Macksey, Kenneth, *Crucible of Power – The Fight for Tunisia*. London: Hutchinson, 1969.

Mains, Lieutenant-Colonel Tony, *Retreat From Burma*. Slough: Foulsham, 1973.

Majdalany, Fred, *Cassino; Portrait of a Battle*. London: Longmans, Green & Co., 1957.

Manchester, W., *American Caesar: Douglas MacArthur 1880–1964*. London: Hutchinson, 1979.

Manstein, Field Marshal Erich von, *Lost Victories*. London: Methuen, 1958.

Mason, David, *Breakout – Drive to the Seine*. London: Macdonald, 1969.

Mason, David, *Raid on St Nazaire*, London: Macdonald, 1970.

Mason, David, *Salerno – Foothold in Europe*. London: Pan/Ballantine, 1972.

Mason, David, *U-Boat – The Secret Menace*. London: Macdonald, 1968.

Masters, J., *The Road Past Mandalay*. London: Michael Joseph, 1961.

Mayer, Sydney L. Jr., *MacArthur*. London: Pan/Ballantine, 1973.

Mayo, Lida, *Bloody Buna*. Newton Abbot: David & Charles, 1975.

Mellenthin, Major-General F. W. von, *Panzer Battles*. London: Cassell, 1955.

Messenger, Charles, *The Art of Blitzkrieg*. London: Ian Allan, 1976.

Messenger, Charles, *The Unknown Alamein*. London: Ian Allan, 1982.

Miller, John Jr., *Guadalcanal – The First Offensive*. Washington: US Government Printing Office, 1949.

Millot, Bernard, *The Battle of the Coral Sea*, London: Ian Allan, 1974.

Mitcham, Samuel W., *Hitler's Legions – German Army Order of Battle World War II*. London: Leo Cooper, 1985.

Munson, Kenneth, *Aircraft of World War II*. London: Ian Allan, 1962.

Nuremberg Military Tribunals: *Trial of War Criminals . . .*; 15 vols., Washington DC: Green Series, 1949–53.

Patton, George S. Jr., *War as I Knew It*. Boston: Houghton, Mifflin, 1947.

Orgill, Douglas, *The Gothic Line*. London: Heinemann, 1967.

Orgill, Douglas, *T34 – Russian Armour*. London: Macdonald, 1971.

Perrett, Bryan, *A History of Blitzkrieg*. London: Robert Hale, 1983.

Perrett, Bryan, *Allied Tank Destroyers*. London: Osprey, 1979.

Perrett, Bryan, *Desert Warfare*. London: Patrick Stephens, 1988.

Perrett, Bryan, *Jungle Warfare*. London: Patrick Stephens, 1989.

Perrett, Bryan, *Knights of the Black Cross – Hitler's Panzerwaffe and Its Leaders*. London: Robert Hale, 1986.

Perrett, Bryan, *Sturmartillerie and Panzerjager*. London: Osprey, 1979.

Perrett, Bryan, *Tank Tracks to Rangoon – The Story of British Armour in Burma*. London: Robert Hale, 1978.

Perrett, Bryan, *Through Mud and Blood – Infantry/Tank Operations in World War II*. London: Robert Hale, 1975.

Perrett, Bryan, *Wavell's Offensive*. London: Ian Allan, 1979.

Pitt, Barrie, ed., *History of the Second World War*. London: Purnell.

Playfair, Major-General I. S. O. and others, *The Mediterranean and Middle East*. London: H.M.S.O., 1966.

Polish Cultural Foundation, *The Crime of Katyn*. London: 1965.

Pope, Dudley, *The Battle of the River Plate*. London: William Kimber, 1956.

Pope, Dudley, *73 North – The Battle of the Barents Sea*. London: Weidenfeld & Nicolson, 1958.

Price, Alfred, *Instruments of Darkness; The History of Electronic Warfare*. London: Macdonald & Jane's, 1977.

Reitlinger, Gerald, *The Final Solution*, 2nd ed. New York: 1975.

Roberts, Major-General G. P. B., *From the Desert to the Baltic*. London: William Kimber, 1987.

Roetter, Charles, *Psychological Warfare*. London: Batsford, 1974.

Roland, Paul M., *Imperial Japanese Tanks 1918–1945*. Bellona, 1975.

Rooney, D. D., *Stilwell*. London: Pan/Ballantine, 1973.

Rutherford, Ward, *Fall of the Philippines*. London: Macdonald, 1972.

Rutherford, Ward, *Kasserine – Baptism of Fire*. London: Macdonald, 1971.

Ryan, Cornelius, *A Bridge Too Far*. London: Hamish Hamilton, 1974.

Ryan, Cornelius, *The Last Battle*. London: Collins, 1966.

Ste Croix, Philip de, ed., *Airborne Operations*. London: Salamander, 1978.

Salisbury, Harrison Evans, *Marshal Zhukov's Greatest Battles*. London: Macdonald, 1969.

Schultz, Duane, *Wake Island*. Magnum, 1979.

Seaton, Albert, *The German Army 1933–45*. London: Weidenfeld & Nicolson, 1982.

Senger und Etterlin, F. M. von, *German Tanks of World War II*. London: Arms & Armour Press, 1969.

Shaw, Henry I., Jr., *Tarawa – A Legend is Born*. London: Macdonald, 1969.

Shirer, William L., *The Rise & Fall of the Third Reich*. London: Secker & Warburg, 1959. Reprinted by Book Club Associates, 1985.

Slim, Viscount, *Defeat into Victory*. London: Cassell, 1956.

Smith, Peter C., *Convoy PQ18 – Arctic Victory*. London: William Kimber, 1975.

Smith, Peter C. and Walker, Edwin, *The Battles of the Malta Striking Forces*. London: Ian Allan, 1974.

Speidel, Hans, *Invasion 1944: Rommel and the Normandy Campaign*. Chicago: Henry Regnery, 1950.

Stewart, Adrian, *Guadalcanal – World War II's Fiercest Naval Campaign*.

London: William Kimber, 1985.

Stewart, Adrian, *The Underrated Enemy – Britain's War With Japan December 1941–May 1942*. London: William Kimber, 1987.

Strawson, John, *Hitler As Military Commander*. London: Batsford, 1971.

Swinson, Arthur, *Mountbatten*. London: Pan/Ballantine, 1973.

Swinson, Arthur, *The Raiders – Desert Strike Force*. London: Macdonald, 1969.

Trevor-Roper, H. R., *Hitler's War Directives 1939–1945*. London: Sidgwick & Jackson, 1964.

Tuchman, B., *Sand against the Wind: Stilwell and the American Experience in China*. London: Macmillan, 1971.

Turner, John Frayn, *D-Day – Invasion '44*. London: Harrap, 1959.

Tute, Warren, *The Deadly Stroke – The Destruction of the French Atlantic Fleet by the Royal Navy, July 1940*. London: Collins, 1973.

Urquhart, Robert, *Arnhem*. London: Cassell, 1958.

Vader, John, *New Guinea – The Tide is Stemmed*. London: Pan/Ballantine, 1972.

Warner, Philip, *Auchinleck*. London: Buchan & Enright, 1981.

Warner, Philip, *The Japanese Army of World War II*. London: Osprey, 1973.

Warner, Philip, *The SAS*. London: William Kimber, 1971.

Werth, Alexander, *Russia at War 1941–45*. London: Barrie & Rockliff, 1964.

White, B. T., *British Tanks and Fighting Vehicles 1914–1945*. London: Ian Allan, 1970.

Whiting, Charles, *Battle of the Ruhr Pocket*. London: Pan/Ballantine, 1972.

Whiting, Charles, *Bloody Aachen*. London: Leo Cooper, 1976.

Whiting, Charles, *Death of a Division*. London: Leo Cooper, 1979.

Whiting, Charles, *Finale at Flensburg*. London: Leo Cooper, 1973.

Whiting, Charles, *First Blood – The Battle of Kasserine Pass*. London: Leo Cooper, 1984.

Whiting, Charles, *Hunters From The Sky*. London: Leo Cooper, 1975.

Whiting, Charles, *Operation Northwind*. London: Leo Cooper, 1986.

Whiting, Charles, *Patton*. London: Pan/Ballantine, 1973.

Williams, John, *France – Summer 1940*. London: Macdonald, 1970.

Wilmot, Chester, *The Struggle for Europe*. London: Collins, 1952.

Winterbotham, F. W., *The Ultra Secret*. London: Weidenfeld & Nicolson, 1974.

Winton, John, *Sink the Haguro!* London: Seeley, 1979.

Winton, John, *The Death of the Scharnhorst*. Chichester: Antony Bird, 1983.

Wood, Tony and Gunston, Bill, *Hitler's Luftwaffe*. London: Salamander, 1977.

Wykes, Alan, *Himmler*. London: Pan/Ballantine, 1973.

Wykes, Alan, *Hitler*. London: Pan/Ballantine, 1973.

Wykes, Alan, *The Siege of Leningrad*. London: Macdonald, 1969.

Young, Peter, *Commando*. London: Pan/Ballatine, 1974.

Zaloga, Steven, *Amtracs – US Amphibious Assault Vehicles*. London: Osprey, 1987.

Ziemke, Earl F., *Battle for Berlin*. London: Macdonald, 1969.

WARSHIP SPECIFICATIONS

In the case of vessels or classes constructed pre-war, the details given are those applicable when their respective navies entered World War II. For vessels and classes built during the war years the basic specification has been given. It should, however, be remembered that variations did exist within classes as completed and that retrospective modifications to vessels of the same class were carried out at different times. In addition, both anti-aircraft and anti-submarine warfare weapons were considerably augmented as the war progressed.

Displacement: Standard unless otherwise stated. For submarines, the surfaced displacement is followed by the submerged displacement.

Dimensions: Overall length and maximum beam; mean draught at standard displacement.

Machinery: Number of propeller shafts, type of power unit and output given in shp (shaft horsepower), bhp (brake horsepower) or ihp (intended horsepower), as appropriate. For submarines, the diesel engine output is given first, followed by that of the electric motors.

Speed: At standard displacement and mean draught. For submarines, the surfaced speed is followed by the submerged speed.

Protection: Maximum armour thicknesses only unless otherwise stated.

Armament: Details of guns, torpedo tubes and other weapons where applicable, giving type of mounting. Thus the notation 12×6in (4×3); 8×4in AA (4×2); 6×21in torpedo tubes (2×3) signifies an armament of twelve 6-inch guns in four triple mountings, eight 4-inch anti-aircraft guns in four twin mountings and six 21-inch torpedo tubes in two triple mountings. AA = anti-aircraft; DP = dual purpose, i.e. that can be used against surface or air targets.

Complement: Approximate war figures, excluding air crew in aircraft carriers.

For further details consult the relevant editions of Jane's *Fighting Ships*; *French Warships of World War II* by J. Labayle Couhat; *German Warships of World War II* by J. C. Taylor; *Italian Warships of World War II* by A. Fraccaroli; *Japanese Warships of World War II* by A. J. Watts; *US Warships of World War II* by P. H. Silverstone; and *Warships of World War II* by H. T. Lenton and J. J. Colledge.

DATES

We have endeavoured to trace the dates of all the listed personalities; inevitably some are unknown, and these have been left blank.